THE LIFE OF

Emily Dickinson

EMILY DICKINSON
From the daguerreotype taken at Mount Holyoke, December 1847 or early 1848

THE LIFE OF
EMILY
DICKINSON

Richard B. Sewall

Harvard University Press

CAMBRIDGE, MASSACHUSETTS

This Harvard University Press paperback is published
by arrangement with Farrar, Straus and Giroux.

First Harvard University Press paperback edition, 1994

Library of Congress Cataloging-in-Publication Data
Sewall, Richard Benson.
   The Life of Emily Dickinson.
   Bibliography: p.
   1. Dickinson, Emily, 1830–1886—Biography.
I. Title
PS1541.Z5S42   811'.4[B]   74–8764
ISBN 0-674-53080-2

To Til
with love

Contents

CONTENTS

VOLUME TWO

Illustrations

ILLUSTRATIONS

x]

Illustrations

Illustrations

Preface

G REAT POETS, like great dramatists, need great audiences. This is not to
say that an audience, to be great, must be learned, or sophisticated,
or heroic. The Athenians who went to the plays were average folk, and
the Elizabethan groundlings were hardly noted for their high culture. Yet
they were great audiences, attuned, receptive, expectant, bringing to the
dramatic encounter shared traditions, fears and hopes, memories, passions,
and mysteries. They were willing to submit them all to the artist's master
humanity, as he unfolded essential truth before their eyes—to their amusement, or horror, or exaltation. They seem to have relished seeing the basic
issues laid bare and to have shared with the artist (however vaguely) a
sense of the ultimate issue, survival: what held the community together or
tore it apart, what sustained the human psyche or worked for its destruction. We like to think they went away from the plays wiser, stronger,
more humane.

My aim in this book is to help the reader into just such an experience
with the poems and letters of Emily Dickinson. She, too, understood
survival and its demands. She explored its limits with as probing an eye as
any dramatist. She knew what horror was, and exaltation, and the power of
humor. Only, her vision—dispersed and fragmented among the hundreds
of short, tense lyrics that make up her canon—comes to us with none of
the massive wholeness of the plays. It is not surprising that Sophocles and
Shakespeare should be closer to us, have clearer shape in our minds, than
our near-contemporary, the elusive poet of Amherst. With them, we
know where we are—roughly, that is, and with the help of generations of
scholarly and critical inquiry. With Emily Dickinson, the long process of
assimilation has, relatively speaking, just begun. She is not yet *ours,* and
she will not be until her hopes and fears and mysteries become as plain
to us as Antigone's or Hamlet's are, and with much the same claim on us.

In my efforts toward this end, I have learned a number of things about
the process. First, to work one's way, however partially, into the world of
Emily Dickinson, the inner world and the outer, takes time, patience, care,
and the sacrifice of many prejudices. The discerning reader can trace my
path as vista after vista opened up. If the path seems long and the bypaths
many, let me record my regret that it isn't longer and the bypaths so few.
Henry James remarked that "the art of the biographer—a devilish art!—
is somehow practically *thinning*. It simplifies even while seeking to enrich."

I hate the thought of having *thinned* Emily Dickinson. Even now, when I run through the poems and the letters again, I am appalled at what I left out: deft formulations that cut to the quick; revealing insights that, had I done them full justice, might even now qualify a generalization or a judgment; the seeming casual verse, or the chance remark in a letter that, apparently telling little, just might be telling all. As to the bypaths, there is no end. She is inexhaustible.

That I have come even this far is due in large part to those who opened the way. I think first of George Frisbie Whicher's pioneer biography in 1938 and of the work in the 1950s and 1960s by Thomas H. Johnson, Theodora Ward, Jay Leyda, and Millicent Todd Bingham which established the texts and expanded the area of relevant fact. No progress was possible until what they did was done. I have learned much, impossible to document completely, from the scholars and critics who, in the second wave of Dickinson studies, found new facts or (and here I learned to learn even as I disagreed) pressed old ones for what they would yield in theory or hypothesis. The dialectic has been kept alive and my understanding deepened by the work of Charles Anderson, Jack Capps, John Cody, Ralph Franklin, Albert Gelpi, David Higgins, Ruth Miller, Rebecca Patterson, David Porter, William Robert Sherwood. I have learned from scholars whose major manuscripts, unpublished as I write, will present, in still a third wave, new syntheses and open up new dimensions of the poetry: Joanne Diehl, Roland Hagenbüchle, Inder Nath Kher, Robert Lambert, Jr., Robert Weisbuch. From many of these, of both generations, I have benefited in conversation and conference; as they scan my chapters, they will hear echoes. To that indispensable group, those who typed, checked, indexed, read and criticized, my debt will be entirely clear—and infinite: Shirley Menn, Edith White, Helene Fineman, Wayland Schmidt, Leonard Conversi, Rosaline Schwartz, and Patricia Sierra. Gladys MacKenzie, Ruth Gay, and Polly Longsworth assisted my work with the Todd-Bingham Family Papers at Yale, and Carolyn Jakeman with the Dickinson Papers at Harvard. I have benefited throughout from the generous cooperation of Robert Giroux and the meticulous editing of Carmen Gomezplata.

It was in 1946, or shortly thereafter, that Mrs. Bingham first breathed to me the possibility of this work. Ten years later she gave me the first full view of its possible dimensions; and shortly after that her papers, indispensable to the project, came to Yale. She wanted, she said, "the whole story" of her mother's involvement told—but told in the setting of the larger story of Emily Dickinson. She tied no strings and asked for no prior commitments. She was unequivocal, and her aim was clear: through new documentation and the new insights it provided, to bring Emily Dickinson and her poetry closer to readers everywhere.

Finally, my deepest gratitude to Jay Leyda—scholar, critic, poet—who has been with this all the way.

Bethany, Connecticut   R. B. S.
May 19, 1974

Acknowledgments

I AM GRATEFUL FOR PERMISSION to quote manuscript materials, and materials under copyright, drawn from the following sources:

The Todd-Bingham Family Papers (herein called "Todd-Bingham Archive"), Yale University Library

The Dickinson Papers, The Houghton Library of the Harvard College Library

The Jones Library, Amherst, Mass.

The Amherst College Library

The University of Virginia Library

THE POEMS OF EMILY DICKINSON, *ed. Thomas H. Johnson, Cambridge, Mass.: The Belknap Press of Harvard University Press, copyright 1951, 1955 by The President and Fellows of Harvard College, reprinted by permission of the publishers and the Trustees of Amherst College. For poems originally published in* The Single Hound, *copyright 1914, 1942 by Martha Dickinson Bianchi; for poems originally published in* Further Poems, *copyright 1929, © 1957 by Mary L. Hampson; for poems originally published in* Unpublished Poems, *copyright 1935, © 1963 by Mary L. Hampson, reprinted by permission of Little, Brown and Company. For poems originally published in* Bolts of Melody, *edited by Mabel Loomis Todd and Millicent Todd Bingham, copyright 1945 by the Trustees of Amherst College, © renewed 1973 by Richard B. Sewall, reprinted by permission of Harper & Row, Publishers, Inc.*

THE LETTERS OF EMILY DICKINSON, *eds. Thomas H. Johnson and Theodora Ward, Cambridge, Mass.: The Belknap Press of Harvard University Press, copyright 1914, 1924, 1932 by Martha Dickinson Bianchi; copyright © 1958 by the President and Fellows of Harvard College, reprinted by permission of the publishers and the Trustees of Amherst College*

THE LYMAN LETTERS: NEW LIGHT ON EMILY DICKINSON AND HER FAMILY, *by Richard B. Sewall, Amherst, Mass.: The University of Massachusetts Press, copyright © 1965 by The Massachusetts Review, Inc.*

EMILY DICKINSON'S HOME, *by Millicent Todd Bingham, New York, Harper and Brothers, 1955*

THE YEARS AND HOURS OF EMILY DICKINSON, *by Jay Leyda, New Haven, Conn.: The Yale University Press, 1960*

The following abbreviations are used throughout:

P *The Poems of Emily Dickinson,* ed. Thomas H. Johnson. Cambridge, Mass.: The Belknap Press of Harvard University Press, 1955.

L *The Letters of Emily Dickinson,* ed. Thomas H. Johnson and Theodora Ward. Cambridge, Mass.: The Belknap Press of Harvard University Press, 1958.

YH *The Years and Hours of Emily Dickinson,* by Jay Leyda. New Haven, Conn.: Yale University Press, 1960.

LL *The Lyman Letters: New Light on Emily Dickinson and Her Family,* by Richard B. Sewall. Amherst, Mass.: University of Massachusetts Press, 1965.

AB *Ancestors' Brocades,* by Millicent Todd Bingham. New York and London: Harper & Brothers, 1945.

Home *Emily Dickinson's Home,* by Millicent Todd Bingham. New York: Harper & Brothers, 1955.

Quotations follow the original spelling, punctuation, and capitalization. The use of *sic* is reduced to a minimum.

Unless otherwise indicated:

Places mentioned, except for cities like New York, Philadelphia, etc., are in Massachusetts.

Ellipses are mine.

Dating of the poems and letters of Emily Dickinson follows the Harvard editions cited above.

The Harvard numbering of the poems is followed throughout. See also Index of First Lines.

Chronology

1775	*October 9*	Samuel Fowler Dickinson, grandfather, born ("gentle and sensitive, and with more than ordinary mental gifts")
1803	*January 1*	Edward Dickinson, father, born
1804	*July 3*	Emily Norcross, mother, born
1813		Samuel Fowler Dickinson builds the Homestead, or "Mansion," on Main Street ("said to have been the first brick house in Amherst")
1814		Amherst Academy founded
1821		Amherst College founded
1828	*May 6*	Edward Dickinson and Emily Norcross married
1829	*April 16*	William Austin Dickinson, brother, born
1830	*April 3*	Father buys half of Homestead from S. F. Dickinson
	October 15	Helen Fiske Hunt Jackson ("H.H.") born ("she is quite inclined to question the authority of everything")
	December 10	EMILY ELIZABETH DICKINSON born
	December 19	Susan Huntington Gilbert born
1833	*February 28*	Lavinia Norcross Dickinson, sister, born
	March	Grandfather Dickinson sells his half of the Homestead to General David Mack and moves to Cincinnati, Ohio
	early May ?– *June 10 ?*	Emily in Monson with Aunt Lavinia Norcross ("she is a very good child & but little trouble")
1835	*August 4*	Father appointed treasurer of Amherst College ("he never . . . lost a dollar")
	September 7	Emily begins four years at "Primary School"
1838	*January*	Father's first term in Massachusetts General Court begins
	April 22	Samuel Fowler Dickinson dies in Hudson, Ohio, "disillusioned, neglected, and forgotten"
1840	*April*	Edward Dickinson sells his half of Homestead to General Mack and moves his family to house on North Pleasant St.

September 7	Emily and Lavinia begin their first year at Amherst Academy ("you know I am always in love with my teachers")
1842 *April*	Austin at Williston Seminary; Emily's first extant letter (to Austin: "there was always such a Hurrah wherever you was")
1844 *April 29*	Death of Sophia Holland, age fifteen ("then it seemed to me I should die too . . .")
May	Emily visits Aunt Lavinia in Boston
June 4	Emily visits Uncle William Dickinson in Worcester
June	Friendship with Abiah Root begins ("you were always dignified")
December	Religious revival in Amherst ("I attended none of the meetings")
1845 *February*	Abiah Root leaves Amherst; first exchange of letters with Emily
April 15	Edward Hitchcock inaugurated president of Amherst College ("a large, noble looking man")
1846 *spring*	Religious revival in Amherst ("the small circle who met for prayer missed me from their number")
May 5	Joel Norcross, grandfather, dies
August 25	Emily to Boston for health (to mid-September)
August	Austin enters Amherst College
November 12	Father chairman at Amherst Cattle Show
1847 *August 4*	Frances Lavinia (Fanny) Norcross, cousin, born
August 10	Emily finishes seventh year at Academy
August ?	Abiah Root visits Amherst ("what delightful times we had")
September 28	Olivia M. Coleman dies, age twenty
September 30	Emily enters Mount Holyoke
October 16	Austin, Vinnie, and Abby Wood visit Emily at Mount Holyoke ("I watched you until you were out of sight Saturday evening")
October 21	To Austin: "Has the Mexican war terminated yet & how? Are we beat? Do you know of any nation about to besiege South Hadley?" [Treaty of Guadalupe-Hidalgo, Feb. 2, 1848]
November 3	Parents visit Emily at Mount Holyoke ("I danced & clapped my hands. . . . They wanted to surprise me")
November 24–29	Emily home for Thanksgiving ("never did Amherst look more lovely to me")

December ?	Emily sits for daguerreotype at Mount Holyoke
1848 *January*	To Abiah: "I am now studying 'Silliman's Chemistry' & Cutter's Physiology, in both of which I am much interested"
January 21– *February 7*	Winter vacation ("my visit at home was happy, very happy, to me")
March 25– *May 11*	Spring vacation; Emily home ill ("Father is quite a hand to give medicine, especially if it is not desirable")
May 11– *August*	Last session at Mount Holyoke ("Father has decided not to send me to Holyoke another year")
May 14	Jacob Holt dies, age twenty-six
August 3	Abiah Root attends Commencement at Mount Holyoke ("what had sealed your lips toward me?")
October 29	Emily to Abiah: "If you dont want to be my friend any longer . . ."
December 19	Emily Brontë dies ("gigantic Emily Brontë")
1849 *March 5*	Mary Lyon dies ("we may become almost what we will")
May	Longfellow's *Kavanagh* published (Austin brings it home)
August	Ben Newton leaves Amherst
October 9	Emily, Vinnie, and party climb Mt. Holyoke
December 5	Vinnie begins winter term at Ipswich ("they are not *Amherst girls,* yet some are pretty & fine scholars")
December	Austin finishes Hume's *History* amid "general uproar"; Emily returns *Jane Eyre* to Elbridge Bowdoin
1850 *January*	Ben Newton sends Emerson's *Poems* (publ. 1847) to Emily
late February	Amherst College *Indicator* publishes Emily's "Magnum bonum" valentine (first mention of Emily's dog Carlo)
March 4	Emily sends valentine ("Awake ye muses") to Elbridge Bowdoin
March–August	Religious revival in Amherst ("I am standing alone in rebellion")
May 5 ?	Mother ill, Emily (as nurse) declines invitation to ride in the woods ("I told him I could not go")
spring ?	Susan-Austin courtship begins
August 8	Austin graduates from Amherst
August 11	Father and Susan Gilbert admitted to First Church by profession of faith

August 14	Father attends semicentennial celebration at Yale
September	Austin begins teaching at Sunderland
September 20	Richard Henry Dana begins Shakespeare lectures in Amherst
October 14	Emily and Vinnie plan to attend the lecture on *Hamlet*
October 30	Dickinsons attend First Annual Amherst Cattle Show
November 3	Vinnie admitted to First Church by profession of faith
November 26	Eclectic Society orations ("This night is long to be remembered. New things have happened")
November 30	Leonard Humphrey dies, age twenty-seven ("my master has gone to rest")
December 31	Emily to Abiah Root: "I love to buffet the sea. . . . I love the danger!"
	Published this year: Ik Marvel, *Reveries of a Bachelor;* Hawthorne, *The Scarlet Letter*
1851 *January 1*	Vinnie begins diary
March	Joseph Lyman leaves for the South (Vinnie: "Joseph has gone, two years is a long time!")
June 4	Ben Newton marries
June 7	Austin begins teaching in Boston
July 3	Jenny Lind's recital in Northampton ("Father sat all the evening looking *mad,* and *silly*")
July 26	Serious fire in Amherst ("three cheers for Edward Dickinson, and three more for the Insurance Company!")
August 14	Commencement; honorary degree to J. G. Holland
September 6–22	Emily and Vinnie in Boston ("we were rich in disdain for Bostonians and Boston")
September	Susan takes up teaching post in Baltimore
September 18	Emily and Vinnie consult Dr. Wesselhoeft, homeopathic physician, in Boston
September 29	Father rings church bell for aurora borealis
	Published this year: *Moby-Dick*
1852 *February 20*	*Springfield Republican* publishes Emily's "Sic transit" valentine
June	Father at Whig Convention in Baltimore; calls on Susan
July 26	Austin home from Boston, through with teaching
December 17	Father elected Representative to Congress from Tenth Massachusetts District
1853 *March 9*	Austin enters Harvard Law School

March 23	Susan visits him in Boston (Revere House Hotel); engagement decided on
March 24	Ben Newton dies, age thirty-two ("The first of my own friends. Pace")
March 27	"Brother Pegasus" letter to Austin: "I've been in the habit *myself* of writing some few things . . ."
May 9	Amherst–Belchertown Railroad opens
June 9	"New London Day" on railroad: Father "like some old Roman General, upon a Triumph Day"
July 28 ?	Mother and Father at Yale reunion
August 11	Amherst Commencement; Austin receives M.A.
early September	Emily and Vinnie visit Hollands in Springfield
October 7	Father invited to Springfield Horse Show
November 3	Judge Otis Phillips Lord at Whig rally, Northampton
December 5	Father at 33rd Congress
December 8	Judge Lord elected Speaker of Massachusetts Legislature
1854 *March 31*	Death of Charlotte Brontë
April	Family in Washington; Emily, Susan, and John Graves in Homestead
July 19	Rev. E. S. Dwight installed as pastor of First Church; Austin graduates from Harvard Law School
September 19–20	Emily and Vinnie's second visit to Hollands
late September ?	Emily to Susan Gilbert: "Sue – you can go or stay –"
December	Austin in Chicago with Susan
1855 *early February ?*	Emily and Vinnie to Washington
early March	Emily and Vinnie visit Mount Vernon (". . . we reached the tomb of General George Washington . . . that marble story")
March 4 ?	Emily and Vinnie to Philadelphia, visiting Eliza Coleman; may have heard Rev. Charles Wadsworth preach
April	Father buys back the Homestead from General Mack
August 8	Emerson addresses Social Union at Amherst Commencement
September 28	Father appointed delegate to Whig Convention at Worcester
October 2	Judge Lord addresses the Convention
October 29	Father accepts Whig nomination for Congress; defeated Nov. 6

October 31	Father and Austin form law partnership
mid-November	Family moves to Homestead ("I cannot tell you how we moved. I had rather not remember . . . and still I cannot help laughing at my own catastrophe")
November 23	Abby Wood and Daniel Bliss marry; move to Beirut, Syria, to found mission school (later, American University)
November	Mother's long illness begins
	Published this year: *Leaves of Grass* ("I never read his Book – but was told that he was disgraceful")
1856 *January 6*	Austin joins First Church by profession of faith
July 1	Austin and Susan Gilbert married in Geneva, N.Y.; settle in the Evergreens
September	Mother in Northampton Spa for water cure
October 17	Emily's bread wins second prize at Agricultural Fair
October	Norcross cousins visit (ED to Louise: ". . . you and I in the dining-room decided to be distinguished")
1857 *August 28*	Emily on Cattle Show committee (rye and Indian bread)
October 20	Martha Gilbert and J. W. Smith marry and settle in Geneva, N.Y.
December 11	Wendell Phillips lectures in Amherst on "Lost Arts"
December 16	Emerson lectures on "The Beautiful in Rural Life" and is entertained at Evergreens ("as if he had come from where dreams are born")
1858 *spring ?*	First (?) Master letter: "You asked me what my flowers said . . ."
October	The Newman cousins (Clara and Anna) arrive at Evergreens as wards of Edward Dickinson; Austin has typhoid fever
1859 *January 4 ?*	First (?) letter to Louise Norcross: "You are one of the ones from whom I do not run away!"
mid-January ?	Catherine Scott Turner (Kate) visits Susan (Kate to Sue: ". . . those happy visits . . . those celestial evenings . . . *Emily – Austin* – the music – the rampant fun – the inextinguishable laughter . . .")
early February	Vinnie to Boston to be with ailing Aunt Lavinia Norcross
February 18	Chapman and Ware episode at Evergreens; Emily and Kate as "culprit mice"
March ?	Father escorts Emily home near midnight from "revel" at Evergreens

May	Judge Lord appointed to Massachusetts Superior Court
May 27	Father mentioned as candidate for governor
August 10	Emily meets Charles Wadsworth's friend, J. D. Clark (at the Dickinson Commencement Tea?)
	Published this year: Darwin's *Origin of Species* ("we thought Darwin had thrown 'the Redeemer' away")
1860 *mid-March ?*	Charles Wadsworth calls on Emily (" 'Why did you not tell me you were coming, so I could have it to hope for,' I said")
April 17	Aunt Lavinia Norcross dies
June 9	Judge and Mrs. Lord visit Amherst, call at Homestead
August 12	Major and Helen Fiske Hunt call at Homestead (Dickinson Commencement Tea?)
September 2	Rev. E. S. Dwight preaches farewell sermon
September 18	Father declines nomination for lieutenant governor
October	Emily and Vinnie visit Eliza Coleman in Middletown
1861 *January ?*	Second (?) Master letter: "If you saw a bullet hit a Bird . . ."
May 4, 11	*Springfield Republican* prints ED's poem "I taste a liquor never brewed," under title "The May-Wine"
June 6	Eliza Coleman and J. L. Dudley married in Monson
June 19	Austin and Susan's first child, Edward (Ned) Dickinson, born
June 29	Elizabeth Barrett Browning dies (ED to Bowles in Europe: ". . . if you touch her Grave, put one hand on the Head, for me – her unmentioned Mourner –")
December ?	Exchange with Susan on the poem "Safe in their Alabaster Chambers"
1862 *early 1862*	Third (?) Master letter: "Oh, did I offend it –"
March 1	*Republican* prints "Safe in their Alabaster Chambers"
March 14	Frazar Stearns killed in action
April	Thomas Wentworth Higginson's "Letter to a Young Contributor" appears in *Atlantic Monthly*
April 15	First letter (and four poems) to Higginson: "Are you too deeply occupied to say if my Verse is alive?"
April 25	Second letter (and three poems) to Higginson: "Thank you for the surgery –"
May 1	Charles Wadsworth and family sail for San Francisco
May 6	Death of Thoreau
June 7	Third letter to Higginson: ". . . will you be my Preceptor . . ."
July 9	Judge Lord delivers Amherst Commencement address

mid-July	Fourth letter (and four poems) to Higginson: "My Business is Circumference"
late July ?	To Hollands: *"My* business is to love"
August	Fifth letter (and two poems) to Higginson: "All men say 'What' to me . . ."
November 16	Bowles returns from Europe
December 4	Higginson made colonel of Negro regiment
1863 *January 17*	Loring Norcross, uncle, dies; ED to the cousins: "Let Emily sing for you . . ."
March ?	Bowles to Austin: ". . . to the Queen Recluse my especial sympathy –"
July 9	Father awarded LL.D. at Amherst Commencement
October 1	Major E. B. Hunt killed in Brooklyn
1864 *February 27*	Professor Edward Hitchcock dies
March 12	In New York, *Round Table* prints ED's poem "Some keep the Sabbath going to church"
March 30	*Republican* prints ED's poem "Blazing in gold, and quenching in purple"
late April	Emily to Boston for eye treatment (seven months); stays with Norcrosses in Cambridgeport ("Loo and Fanny take sweet care of me . . .")
May 13	Austin drafted, pays $500 for substitute
May 19	Death of Hawthorne
November 28	Emily returns from Cambridgeport
1865 *April 1 ?*	Emily again to Boston for eye treatment
October 17	Emerson lectures in Amherst on "Social Aims"
1866 *January 27*	ED's dog Carlo dies
February 10	"H.H." and Higginsons meet at Newport
February 14, 17	*Republican* prints ED's poem "A narrow fellow in the grass" (". . . it was robbed of me")
April 27	Samuel Bowles named Amherst trustee
July 11–12	Hollands visit Amherst for Commencement
October 10	Elisabeth Dickinson (aunt) and Augustus Currier, of Worcester, married (". . . the only male relative on the female side")
November 29	Austin and Susan's second child, Martha, born
1868 *May 25*	Holland family off for two years in Europe
September 23	Father dedicates new church
1869 *May 11*	Emily refuses Higginson's invitation to Boston ("I do not cross my Father's ground to any House or Town")

June 11	General and Mrs. George B. McClellan guests at Homestead
1870 *August 16*	Higginson visits Amherst; first meeting with Emily (TWH to his wife: "I never was with any one who drained my nerve power so much")
October	First number of *Scribner's* issued, J. G. Holland, editor
early December?	*Verses,* by "H.H.," published in Boston
1871 *June 3*	Eliza Coleman Dudley dies in Milwaukee, age thirty-nine
1871–72	Published this year: George Eliot's *Middlemarch* ("what do I think of glory –")
1872 *January 27*	Joseph B. Lyman dies in Richmond Hill, Long Island, New York
July 10	Father resigns as treasurer of the college
mid-October	Emily Fowler Ford's *My Recreations* published in New York
1873 *May 1*	Father: "I hereby give myself to God"
May?	Rev. Jenkins pronounces Emily theologically "sound"; Vinnie visits Hollands
July 9	Amherst Commencement: Bowles, Maria Whitney, Judge Lord attend
August?	Abby Bliss, back from Beirut, visits Emily
November 5	Father elected again to the General Court
December 1	Austin elected treasurer of the college
December 3	Higginson lectures in Amherst and calls on Emily (Mary Higginson to her husband: "Oh why do the insane so cling to you?")
1874 *June 16*	Father dies in Boston ("His Heart was pure and terrible . . .")
1875 *June 15*	Mother stricken with paralysis (". . . when she asks me the name of her sickness – I deceive for the first time")
August 1	Austin and Susan's third child, Thomas Gilbert (Gib) Dickinson, born
October 22	"H.H." and W. S. Jackson married at Wolfeboro, N.H.
December	Judge Lord elevated to Supreme Court of Massachusetts
1876 *March 20*	From "H.H.": "You are a great poet – and it is a wrong . . . that you will not sing aloud"
August 20	"H.H." invites Emily to participate in Roberts Brothers' No Name Series

	October	Judge and Mrs. Lord visit "a few days"
	October–	Austin ill with malaria
	November	
	December 26	Susan gives Emily *Of the Imitation of Christ* by Thomas à Kempis ("Emily with love")
1877	*June 28*	Bowles visits Emily ("Come down at once")
	September 2	Mary Higginson dies
	October	Bowles ill
	December 10	Mrs. Lord dies
1878	*January 16*	Samuel Bowles dies ("David's route was simple – 'I shall go to him' ")
	January 19	Austin and Vinnie attend Bowles's funeral
	April 29	"H.H." again asks permission to publish Emily's poems
	late June	Mother breaks hip
	July 25–31,	"Saxe Holm" inquiry in *Republican*
	August 3	
	September 10	*A Masque of Poets* announced for No Name Series
	October 24	"H.H." and husband visit Emily
	November 20	*A Masque of Poets* prints ED's poem "Success is counted sweetest"
	December 10	"Success" attributed to Emerson
1879	*mid-January ?*	Emily receives *A Masque of Poets* from Thomas Niles of Roberts Brothers
	March 19	Emerson lectures again in Amherst
	July 3–4	Amherst's worst fire (Vinnie to Emily: "It is only the fourth of July")
1880	*March*	Austin ill with malaria
	early August ?	Wadsworth visits unexpectedly ("I am liable at any time to die")
	August 23–30	Austin's diary: "Judge Lord & Troupe arrived at Amherst House"
	September 23	Austin's diary: "Ev'ng Judge Lord in & his nieces"
	September 26	Austin's diary: "Judge Lord and the Farleys to tea and evening"
	mid-November	Emily asks Higginson's advice about "Hymns for a Charity"
	December 24	George Eliot dies ("the look of the words as they lay in the print I shall never forget")
	December 25	Judge Lord gives Emily *Complete Concordance to Shakspere;* Susan gives Emily ("whom not seeing I still love") Disraeli's *Endymion*

1881	*March 15*	Judge Lord ill
	April 4	Another fire in Phoenix Row
	April 17	Judge Lord, recovered, guest at Evergreens
	July 2	President Garfield shot; dies September 19 ("when I look in the Morning Paper to see how the President is . . .")
	August 31	Professor and Mrs. David Peck Todd arrive in Amherst
	October 12	Dr. Holland dies ("Heaven is but a little way to one who gave it, here")
1882	*April 1*	Charles Wadsworth dies ("my closest earthly friend died in April –")
	April 16	Judge Lord visits ED
	April 24	Thomas Niles urges Emily to publish
	April 27	Emerson dies
	May 1	Judge Lord critically ill: "I ran to his [Tom's] Blue Jacket . . ."
	July 15	Emily does not receive Emily Fowler Ford ("Eheu! Emily Dickinson! . . .")
	September 10	Mabel Todd sings for Emily
	September 11	Mabel and Austin: "Rubicon"
	September– October	Mabel and Emily: Indian pipes–"Humming Bird" exchange
	November 10	David Todd leaves for California to observe transit of Venus
	November 14	Mother dies ("the dear Mother that could not walk, has *flown*")
1883	*January*	Mabel-Susan confrontation (". . . the old cordial, frank relations I am afraid can never be resumed")
	August 8–9	Dickinson family reunion in College Hall, 1,000 to 1,500 expected
	September 8	Austin's diary: "The Lords arrived this noon"
	October 5	Gilbert (nephew) dies, age eight ("No crescent was this Creature – He traveled from the Full – Such soar, but never set –")
	October 7	Austin has attack of malaria
	October 12	Vinnie ill
	December 7	Matthew Arnold lectures in Amherst
1884	*March 13*	Judge Lord dies ("I work to drive the awe away, yet awe impels the work")
	June 14	Emily has first attack of final illness ("revenge of the nerves")

September 5	"H.H." offers to be Emily's "literary legatee & executor"
1885 *late March*	To "H.H.": "Pity me . . . I have finished Ramona"
August 12	Helen Hunt Jackson dies
November	George S. Merriam's *The Life and Times of Samuel Bowles* published
1886 *January 12*	Mabel Todd's diary: "Emily Dickinson taken very ill in the afternoon"
early spring	Emily's last (?) letter to the Hollands: "I hope the little heart is well. . . . Emily and Vinnie give the love greater every hour"
spring	To Higginson: "I have been very ill . . . bereft of Book and Thought"
March 18	Austin's diary: "Evening sat an hour with Emily . . ."
March 24	Austin's diary: ". . . sat with Emily a while"
April 15	Emily to Charles H. Clark: "The velocity of the ill . . . is like that of the snail"
early May	Last (?) letter to the Norcrosses: "Little Cousins, Called back. Emily."
May 13	Emily loses consciousness
May 15	Austin's diary: "The day was awful She ceased to breathe that terrible breathing just before the whistles sounded for six"
May 19	Emily's funeral; Higginson reads Emily Brontë's "Last Lines" ("No coward soul . . .")
1890 *November 12*	*Poems* by Emily Dickinson, eds. Mabel Loomis Todd and T. W. Higginson (Roberts Brothers, Boston). Eleven editions by the end of 1892
1891 *November 9*	*Poems* by Emily Dickinson, second series, eds. T. W. Higginson and Mabel Loomis Todd (Roberts Brothers, Boston). Fifth edition, 1893
1894 *November 21*	*Letters of Emily Dickinson*, 2 vols., ed. Mabel Loomis Todd
1895 *August 16*	Austin dies (Vinnie: "There is no landscape since Austin died")
1896 *September 1*	*Poems* by Emily Dickinson, third series, ed. Mabel

		Loomis Todd (Roberts Brothers, Boston). Second edition, 1896
	November 16	Vinnie files suit against Todds (decided in her favor, April 1898)
1899	*August 31*	Vinnie dies
1913	*May 12*	Susan dies (Mabel: "Poor old Susan died last night")
1914		*The Single Hound,* ed. Martha Dickinson Bianchi
1924		*The Life and Letters of Emily Dickinson,* ed. Martha Dickinson Bianchi
		The Complete Poems of Emily Dickinson, eds. Martha Dickinson Bianchi and Alfred Leete Hampson
1929		*Further Poems of Emily Dickinson,* ed. Martha Dickinson Bianchi
1931		*Letters of Emily Dickinson,* ed. Mabel Loomis Todd
1932		*Emily Dickinson Face to Face: Unpublished Letters with Notes and Reminiscences,* Martha Dickinson Bianchi
	October 14	Mabel Todd dies
1935		*Unpublished Poems of Emily Dickinson,* eds. Martha Dickinson Bianchi and Alfred Leete Hampson
1937		*Poems by Emily Dickinson,* eds. Martha Dickinson Bianchi and Alfred Leete Hampson
1945		*Bolts of Melody: New Poems of Emily Dickinson,* eds. Mabel Loomis Todd and Millicent Todd Bingham
1951		*Emily Dickinson's Letters to Dr. and Mrs. Josiah Gilbert Holland,* ed. Theodora Van Wagenen Ward
1955		*The Poems of Emily Dickinson,* 3 vols., "Including variant readings critically compared with all known manuscripts," ed. Thomas H. Johnson
1958		*The Letters of Emily Dickinson,* 3 vols., eds. Thomas H. Johnson and Theodora Ward

THE LIFE OF

Emily Dickinson

VOLUME ONE

1

The Problem of the Biographer

Almost nothing to do with Emily Dickinson is simple and clear-cut. The reasons why this should be so are many and basic, and it is the delicate business of the biographer to explore and assess them all. Delicate, because, for one thing, she herself was almost no help. Seemingly with willful cunning and surely with an artist's skill, she avoided direct answers to the major questions that anyone interested in her as poet or person might have been moved to ask. With success seldom approached by one destined ultimately for literary fame, she kept her private life *private*. It is not that she said nothing about herself at any time; she said a great deal in nearly eighteen hundred poems and over a thousand letters. But it is as if she lived out the advice she gave in her famous lines: "Tell all the Truth but tell it slant – / Success in Circuit lies." She avoided specifics, dodged direct confrontations, reserved commitments. She told the truth, or an approximation of it, so metaphorically that nearly a hundred years after her death and after much painstaking research, scholars still grope for certainties.

It is virtually impossible to distinguish what was willful in her secretiveness from whatever there was in it which Emily Dickinson herself did not understand. Was it deliberate planning, or compulsive forces in her nature, that led to her withdrawal from society (almost complete by her late thirties) with never a reason that satisfied anybody?—anybody, that is, except those who knew her best, her immediate family, and they were inclined more to accept her choices than to ponder her motives. How much of her behavior was forced on her by circumstances? How much was arranged by herself because it suited certain purposes of her own or simply because she liked it that way?[1]

1. Emily Dickinson has in the last several decades been the subject of a number of suggestive psychoanalytic studies, some of them startling to those accustomed to conventional methods of literary biography or critical interpretation. To the literary

At the outset, and knowing well how qualified it will have to be, I should like to emphasize the degree to which her way of life represented a conscious choice. I think we should at least walk into the mystery standing up. More than is true of almost any other poet in the tradition, her life, like the major vehicle of her poetry, was metaphoric; and as she grew older, it became more and more deliberately so. From girlhood on, she enjoyed that way of conveying truth, whether by word or action. In a lively valentine to an Amherst student when she was twenty, she wrote, "I am Judith the heroine of the Apocrypha, and you the orator of Ephesus. That's what they call a metaphor in our country. Don't be afraid of it, sir, it won't bite." Superficially, this led to not a little archness, posing, keeping the world at bay. She enjoyed riddles, apparently enjoyed being one, and was keenly aware of the dullness of the easy riddle: "The Riddle we can guess / We speedily despise –"

On a higher level, the "riddle" became metaphoric of cosmic questions that, though they haunted Emily Dickinson throughout her life, provided her very reason for being and for writing poetry.[2] "In a Life that stopped guessing," she wrote her sister-in-law, "you and I should not feel at home." But she grew up in a community and in an atmosphere in which the cosmic questions (at least officially) were all answered; "guessing"

---

and psychoanalytical biographer alike, however, a persuasive interpretation of her life must rest on the establishment of a common ground of fact. To this end, the present study seeks to broaden the factual context against which any theoretical interpretation might be measured. As new materials are found—lost letters, fresh contemporary testimony—some of the current psychoanalytical theories may find convincing factual basis; but as yet, in my opinion, they have not. Given what we know and do not know, it seems wise at this point to keep the possibilities open.

Much psychoanalytic interpretation of Emily Dickinson has, in justifiable reaction to brighter early biographies, stressed the darker side of the poet's life as seen through some of the agonized poems, the troubled letters, and the strange behavior of her later years. I have based my view on what seems to have been the figure most real to those closest to Emily Dickinson, and of most communicative value (to the rest of us) through hundreds of letters of wit and discernment and through hundreds of poems giving assurance not only of artistic mastery but of mastery and full acceptance of self. Those who wish to follow the development of the varying theories about the sources of Emily Dickinson's inner tensions (parental inadequacy, suppressed homosexuality, frustrated love) should consult Rebecca Patterson, *The Riddle of Emily Dickinson* (1951) and "Emily Dickinson's 'Double' Tim: Masculine Identification," *American Imago* XXVIII (Winter, 1971), 330–62; Anna Mary Wells, "Was Emily Dickinson Psychotic?" *American Imago* XIX (Winter, 1962), 309–21; Clark Griffith, *The Long Shadow: Emily Dickinson's Tragic Poetry* (1964); and especially John Cody, *After Great Pain: The Inner Life of Emily Dickinson* (1971). On this last, see below, Chapter 5, note 2.

2. In *Emily Dickinson and Riddle* (1969), Dolores Dyer Lucas relates ED's poetry to the ancient tradition of the riddle and shows how important a literary device it was for her "in a generation which did not permit her, without the ambiguity of the riddle to 'tell all the truth.' . . . she early learned that 'success in circuit lies' " (p. 138).

was out of order. A sentence in one of her letters to her spinster cousins would have sounded strange to orthodox Amherst ears (and perhaps to her cousins, had it not been buried in a whimsical context): "It is true that the unknown is the largest need of the intellect, though for it, no one thinks to thank God."

Thus, I think it can be said that Emily Dickinson's manner of life and her way of telling about her life were symptomatic of her sense of the mystery of things. Central to this mystery (certainly central to the biographer) was the mystery of herself. At nineteen, she wrote to a friend, "[I] pause, and ponder, and ponder, and pause, and do work without knowing why." I think she came to realize remarkably soon who she was and what she was intended for; but it was a mystery that, for the outside world, she would not profane by explication. "All men say 'What' to me," she wrote when she was thirty-one, "but I thought it a fashion – " and a fashion she dismissed. Twice, in reference to her way of life, she used the word "embarrass" in a revealing way. First, when she gave her reasons for " 'shunning Men and Women' ": "they talk of Hallowed things, aloud – and embarrass my Dog – "; and second, when for the third time she refused an invitation to mingle with the Boston literati: "My life has been too simple and stern to embarrass any." But this does not explain much, and one is thrown back on some such remark as Emerson's strikingly similar statement about Thoreau: "He had many reserves, an unwillingness to exhibit to profane eyes what was still sacred in his own, and knew well how to throw a poetic veil over his experience." Emily Dickinson at age twenty-two wrote to a friend (in her preferred spelling): "I find I need more vail."

That the prying eye of the biographer has long been baffled is a matter of early record. The two notes about "embarrassment" were sent (the first when she was thirty-one, the second when she was thirty-eight) to the courtly man of letters, Thomas Wentworth Higginson, who, trying his best to fit her into the mold of his conventions, gave up in dismay. "I have the greatest desire to see you," he replied, "always feeling that perhaps if I could once take you by the hand I might be something to you; but till then you only enshroud yourself in this fiery mist & I cannot reach you, but only rejoice in the rare sparkles of light." His insight into the degree of willfulness in her pose was true. The mist enshrouding her was partly of her own making, and one is reminded of the spies who tried in vain to pluck out the heart of Hamlet's mystery. Higginson was scarcely more successful. When he finally visited Amherst and "held her by the hand," at least figuratively, he found that it did not help much. "I never was with any one who drained my nerve power so much. Without touching her," he wrote his wife, "she drew from me. I am glad not to live near her." And twenty years later, in the *Atlantic Monthly,* he admitted his failure:

She was much too enigmatical a being for me to solve in an hour's interview, and an instinct told me that the slightest attempt at direct cross-examination would make her withdraw into her shell; I could only sit still and watch, as one does in the woods; I must name my bird without a gun, as recommended by Emerson.

His impression of her, he went on to say, was of an "excess of tension" and of "an abnormal life." He later called her, variously, "my eccentric poetess," "my partially cracked poetess at Amherst." His wife asked him, three years after his first visit, "Oh why do the insane so cling to you?"

Emily Dickinson had her own formulation for those who would thus dismiss her:

> Much Madness is divinest Sense –
> To a discerning Eye –
> Much Sense – the starkest Madness –
> 'Tis the Majority
> In this, as All, prevail –
> Assent – and you are sane –
> Demur – you're straightway dangerous –
> And handled with a Chain –   (#435, about 1862)

Clearly, Higginson and his wife were of the Majority, and just as clearly Emily Dickinson's defenses were up, both to Higginson and to the world he represented. She told him (mostly) the truth, but she told it so slant that he went away mystified. The trouble is, since he was one of the few men of letters who paid any attention to her as poet, and the only one to leave on record an extended contemporary account of his impressions of her, his mystification has blurred the biographical picture ever since. Later research has cleared up much of it, but its effect in polarizing attitudes toward her still lingers.

Another and more serious effect of Higginson's mystification may be seen (it has often been so argued) in Emily Dickinson's failure to publish. He was as much mystified by her poetry as he was by her person, and as a literary adviser he failed her completely. He thought her poems formless and " 'spasmodic' " (at least this was the word she put in his mouth) and urged her not to publish them. Whether his advice was decisive or one of many causes is one of those delicate questions still to be answered definitively. Only seven of her poems found their way into print during her lifetime, all of them anonymous, most of them altered by others, and one of them, she later complained, was "robbed of me."[3] The great bulk of her poems was found in her room after her death. They were in a bewildering state. Some were in final form; there were many semifinal drafts, with variant readings undecided upon; there were hundreds of scraps and jottings; and there were almost no dates.

3. The seven are listed in *P* III, 1207. Each one has its own publication story. The "robbed" one ("The Snake," #986) was probably sent by ED's sister-in-law, Susan Dickinson, to their mutual friend, Samuel Bowles, who published it in the *Springfield Republican*, February 14, 1866.

The problem that this situation posed for the biographer (let alone the editor and critic) was enormous,[4] since Emily Dickinson's life, in a sense almost unique among poets, *was* her work. She left no hints as to the occasion or setting of any of the poems. Only a very few (twenty-four) had titles—and this in an age when it was the fashion to give titles to poems. Apparently Emily Dickinson had no notion that anyone at any future time would be curious about her poetic intention or development, or if she did, it was a curiosity she chose not to gratify. Fortunately, her handwriting, which varied greatly over the years and even from year to year, provided a chronological clue;[5] some poems could be dated approximately by internal evidence; and there were many she sent in letters either that she dated herself or that could be dated fairly accurately. All this evidence the editors of the first complete, scholarly edition of the poems (1955, sixty-nine years after her death) used in establishing at least a tentative chronological arrangement. But the date of almost every poem was prefaced by a qualifying "about," and subsequent research has shown how necessary that qualification was. Then, it was not until three years later (1958), that an edition of her letters brought together all the correspondence known to exist and added many new letters to the canon. Before this editing, the situation of the letters had been almost as bad as that of the poems. For scarcely more than a decade have students of her life been in a position to view the materials in approximate completeness.

As usual when such a vacuum exists, and especially with such an enigmatic figure as Emily Dickinson, whose tense and passionate writing is so at variance with her outwardly quiet and retired life, myth and legend rush in to fill it. The fictionists have written plays and stories on the flimsiest of evidence; biographers have indulged in the privileges of the novelist; the cultists and the gossips have always been with us; and most recently the methods of psychoanalysis have raised further possibilities. The difficulty for the biographer coming in the wake of all this is the impossibility of saying an absolute "no" to all but the wildest speculation—and even the wildest may have a grain of truth in it. Higginson, were he here today, would still have the right to be puzzled.

The three foci of legend—Lover, Father, Withdrawal—are closely

4. The difficulties were first described in detail by Millicent Todd Bingham, *Ancestors' Brocades: The Literary Debut of Emily Dickinson* (1945), and most recently by Ralph W. Franklin, *The Editing of Emily Dickinson: A Reconsideration* (1967).

5. Millicent Todd Bingham, in her introduction to *Bolts of Melody: New Poems of Emily Dickinson* (1945), was, again, the first to describe in detail the intricacies involved in deciphering the often difficult handwriting. Ten years later, the Introduction of the 1955 edition of the poems contained an invaluable section on "Characteristics of the Handwriting," indicating the criteria used in establishing the chronology adopted in that edition. All these editorial problems might have been cleared up, of course, had ED ever seen her poems through the press. As has often been pointed out, we are dealing with a poet's workshop—a life's work left for posterity to put in order and much of it defying the precision of modern editorship.

related, the first two serving to explain the third. Not that New England (or Amherst) had any reason to be surprised at eccentric and retiring spinsters. But Emily Dickinson was the Squire's daughter, known in her youth for her brilliance, her wit, even (to a small group) her literary talent. Something must have happened that could explain to concerned outsiders a withdrawal that by her late thirties was almost complete: "I do not cross my Father's ground to any House or Town," she wrote in refusing Higginson's invitation to come to Boston in 1869. In her later years, she conducted interviews (with the few friends permitted in the house) from the top of the stairs and behind half-closed doors. When the first thin volumes of her poems began to appear in the early 1890s (she died in 1886), the many poems of anguished passion and renunciation stirred rumors that had been circulating even before her death of a blighted romance that had cut her life in two. Then of course came the question: Who was the man? There have been many nominations (including both sexes) but as yet no firm, universally accepted choice.[6]

There is a legend that she renounced her lover at her father's command. Then, sensing her father's distrust, she committed herself to the narrow limits of his house and grounds, in order never to give him any further cause for suspicion. The story (again, it may contain an essential truth) has given rise to much speculation about Edward Dickinson's character and the nature of the home over which he presided. He has been variously described as a severe, latter-day Puritan, a power-minded tyrant, a Mr. Barrett of Wimpole Street; and Emily Dickinson's home depicted as a gloomy prison. Her fear and awe of him (it is said) dominated her life.[7] No doubt at times both these feelings entered into her attitude toward him; but, as with the hypothesis that it was one Love and one Lover for whom she renounced a so-called normal life and career, it is impossible in the light of what we now know to accept any such simple interpretation. Similarly, it is necessary to reassess her attitude toward her

6. My hope in this biography is, at the very least, to put this question, until recently overshadowing all others, into proper perspective. For now, let me warn the reader in the strongest terms against such a passage as the following from Martha Dickinson Bianchi (ED's niece), *The Life and Letters of Emily Dickinson* (1924), pp. 46–47:

It was on a visit to this same Eliza [Coleman], in Philadelphia, that Emily met the fate [the Reverend Charles Wadsworth] she had instinctively shunned. . . .
Certainly in that first witchery of an undreamed Southern springtime Emily was overtaken – doomed once and forever by her own heart. It was instantaneous, overwhelming, impossible. There is no doubt that two predestined souls were kept apart only by her high sense of duty, and the necessity for preserving love untarnished by the inevitable destruction of another woman's life.

As with so much in this mistitled book, this passage has little evidence to support it and much to call it in question. But its high romantic style and lofty sentiments have created an impression hard to dislodge. It must be seen in the light of the long and anguished story that will be the subject of later chapters.

7. This is Clark Griffith's thesis in *The Long Shadow*. But see below, Chapter 5, note 2, for John Cody's theory (in *After Great Pain*) about ED's mother.

home and the nature of its other inmates (besides her father)—her mother, her younger sister Lavinia, and especially her older brother Austin, perhaps the one human being who knew her and understood her best.[8]

Finally, was her withdrawal as complete as has been thought? Was its effect (as is often assumed) to detach her completely from the busy and expanding world of New England and from the great national events of her lifetime? Many accounts of her, especially the early ones, were so engrossed with her little world as to dissociate her entirely from the greater one. One would think that she saw no further than her own garden and had no thought but for her own private joys and sorrows. To allay such notions, the biographer must turn, among other things, to her friends, of whom she had a wide, varied, and distinguished circle. "My friends are my 'estate,'" she said, and she kept in touch with them—and with their doings in lands far and near—in thousands of letters (only a fraction of which survive)[9] to the end of her life. Although she boasted of seeing "New Englandly," there was nothing provincial in her interests. In recent years her friendships, sustained mostly by correspondence, have been the object of increasing study, but neither separately nor together have they yet yielded their whole truth.[10] (That among their number are several for whom the most detailed and vigorous claims have been made

8. Millicent Todd Bingham, *Emily Dickinson's Home* (1955), presented a wealth of new material concerning Edward Dickinson and his family. It is the unique source for many family letters and documents, the basis for a new estimate of her forebears, her surroundings, and her remarkable family. To see ED in solitary brilliance amidst mediocrity is to miss an important truth of her life. In *The Years and Hours of Emily Dickinson* (1960), Jay Leyda reduced to an almost daily chronology the existing materials concerning her life and the life of contemporary Amherst and added much of his own gleaning from journals, diaries, and local records of all sorts. Both these books, displacing legend and fancy with solid facts—the realities of daily existence— did much toward establishing a convincing continuity between ED's private life and the world she lived in. The present study draws heavily on both books; but even at its conclusion the reader should be aware of areas still incompletely explored—more convinced than ever, perhaps, that a "definitive" biography is an academic illusion.

9. See Appendix V ("A Note on the Missing Correspondences").

10. The decades of the 1950s and the 1960s saw many contributions in this area. The nature and depth of ED's friendship with Dr. and Mrs. Josiah Holland were unknown until the publication in 1951, by Theodora Ward, of sixty-four new letters from ED to Mrs. Holland. Mrs. Ward examined this relationship fully in *The Capsule of the Mind: Chapters in the Life of Emily Dickinson* (1961), where she also considers ED's relationships with Higginson and Samuel Bowles. Also in 1951, Rebecca Patterson's *The Riddle of Emily Dickinson* explored her friendship with Mrs. Kate Scott Anthon—a vigorous and significant one but hardly in itself the solution to the "riddle." Thomas H. Johnson's *Emily Dickinson: An Interpretive Biography* (1955), besides stressing the (at most) problematic relationship with Wadsworth, was the first to discuss in detail Higginson's importance in her literary career, as well as Helen Hunt Jackson's, another heretofore almost neglected figure. The discovery of the Lyman Archive (R. B. Sewall, *The Lyman Letters: New Light on Emily Dickinson and Her Family,* 1965) added another important name to the list of the friends of her youth and early maturity.

for the status and even the sex of the Lover makes the present undertaking all the more delicate—and precarious.)

Another way to allay the myth of her provincialism is to look more sharply, in both her letters and her poems, for her opinions on things temporal and concrete. She once wrote a friend, "So I conclude that space & time are things of the body & have little or nothing to do with our selves. My Country is Truth." Space and time may not have been her ultimate realities; but her reach for generalities, for essential truth, began with a very sharp perception of specifics. She was not reared in a household of lawyers and treasurers for nothing (both her father and her brother held long tenures as treasurers of Amherst College). Her animadversions upon a host of worldly matters, from the Civil War to the Stock Exchange, show acute understanding, however tersely or obliquely expressed. She was never discursive on these matters; sometimes she packed a whole complex of observation and insight into a single metaphor in a poem. But neither poem nor metaphor would have come into being had it not been for the original observation, sharp and shrewd.

A review of her cultural world, her schooling, her world of books, ideas, literary affinities, shows also a range and depth until recently denied her. Emily Dickinson did not dwell as far as many have thought from the main line of English and American literature. Again, she did not live in a college town for nothing. There were libraries, reading clubs, a good bookstore. She read widely and retentively throughout her lifetime; her letters stress again and again how necessary books were to her; and the more we know about her cultural resources, the less we are inclined to patronize them. Current research is making steady progress in all these matters, and its results must play a large part in any new synthesis.[11]

Jay Leyda, whose work has contributed much to this end, posed in 1955 the essential problem and stated the essential aim:

> Is it really possible that we can be shut away from the full work or real personality of so vital a poet? Can *any* false structure, no matter how buttressed by "family tradition" and scholarly authority, by poetical tributes and

---

11. The chapter, "Books and Reading," in George F. Whicher's pioneer biography *This Was a Poet* (1938) was the first treatment of the subject in any detail and is still a convenient summary. Subsequent studies have established more firmly many relationships and continuities; e.g., Judith Banzer, " 'Compound Manner': Emily Dickinson and the Metaphysical Poets," *American Literature* XXXII (1961), 417–33; Rebecca Patterson, "Elizabeth Browning and Emily Dickinson," *The Educational Leader* XX (1956), 21–48, and "Emily Dickinson's Debt to Günderode," *The Midwest Quarterly* VIII (1967), 331–54. Jack L. Capps, *Emily Dickinson's Reading* (1966), was the first full-length study; but it, too, is only a beginning. Two years later, Ruth Miller, *The Poetry of Emily Dickinson* (1968), added to it significantly, especially in her Appendix III, which lists the books found in the Dickinson library (now mostly in the Houghton Library at Harvard) and reprints relevant passages from them. John Evangelist Walsh, *The Hidden Life of Emily Dickinson* (1971), with its "whisper" of plagiarism (p. 108), argues mistakenly, I think, for her excessive dependence on books, old and new.

The daguerreotype, curls and ruff added, as it appeared in 1924
A stage in the developing Myth

Signatures, in ink, on back of envelope addressed,
in pencil, "Austin." Handwriting mid- to late 1870s

pilgrimages, by novels, plays, even two operas and a dance, forever obscure the real person who wrote those real poems? . . .

The worthiest aim for all Dickinson scholarship of the future is to make it easier for her poetry to speak directly and freshly to every reader.

His final words—"No pattern, please"—were a terse warning to the biographer. How to detach the real person from the stereotypes that have been imposed on her? How to bring her back alive? The word "pattern" is disturbing in all that it suggests of the preconceived, the rigid, the formulated. No human life, certainly not Emily Dickinson's, can be so reduced. But there is another sense in which the word may be legitimate. To question the old clichés—the Broken Heart, the Tyrant Father, the Recluse—is not to say that her life reveals no shape at all. Keats said of Byron that he "cuts a figure—but he is not figurative." Emily Dickinson cut no figure at all, but in a deeper sense her life was figurative, metaphoric.

As I have suggested, she was quite conscious of that deeper sense. The task of the biographer is to disclose what it was for the sake of which she *did* make certain renunciations. Emily Dickinson asked no favors from the world and granted it none. The truth seems to be that, like Thoreau, she had certain private affairs to transact that were more important to her. Thus the biographer must mediate between her and the world to which she refused so much, fill out the hints she dropped, be discursive where she was elliptical; give her a lineage, a background and foreground; a believable family, home, and friends; an education, culture, and (above all) a vocation. This must be done, I am convinced, *in the large,* in the richest possible profusion of detail. Only the "realest" context will suit the purpose for this perennially "unreal" figure. Goethe has been quoted in this connection with pertinent wisdom: "Nothing in nature is isolated; nothing is without reference to something else; nothing achieves meaning apart from that which neighbors it."

A word about plan and method. My approach to the problem is divided into two parts. Volume I concerns background. It involves, first, a look at what seems to me relevant in the culture of the Puritan New England Emily Dickinson was born into; as much about the Dickinson line as is salvageable from scanty records; and a sense of the Connecticut Valley and the town of Amherst, Massachusetts, where she was born. Then, when definable Dickinson traits begin to assert themselves, I have paused to deal in some detail with personality and personal history. I am aware that much remains still to be done. These Dickinsons were formidable people, especially the Dickinson men—Samuel Fowler, Emily's grandfather; Edward, her father; and William Austin, her brother. Each deserves, and I hope some day will receive, a full-length study. As for Emily's mother, if the word "formidable" hardly applies, the problem she presents to the biographer of the poet has a depth and complexity of its own.

Especially in the accounts of Emily's parents, of her brother Austin and his wife, and of her sister Lavinia, it should be noted that the chronological sequence of biography will be violated at every turn. Before taking Emily out into the world on her own (Volume II starts with the day of her birth), I shall take the members of the family, individually, through their lives and Emily with them. I shall try to show them as the world saw them, as Emily saw them, and as they saw Emily. This seems to me the truest way of presenting a figure upon whose biography no narrative structure can be imposed that is not to a degree arbitrary or fictitious. It is true that Emily Dickinson's life had a beginning, a middle, and an end. In Volume II we shall see her as she goes to school and college; as she makes her few, early sojourns abroad (to Washington and Boston); as she makes her early and futile gestures toward publishing her poems; as she confronts certain external, datable facts like the war and the deaths in her family; as she agonizes through her one documented (and late) love affair; and as she arrives at her final summing up in her last years. But the beginning, middle, and end are not articulated by any dramatic external events; her life can be divided only very roughly into periods. She can be known as a person not through what she *did* (excluding for the moment her poems and letters as forms of doing) so much as through her relationships with people, events, books, ideas—but mostly, being an intensely personal person, with people. Like Jamesian "reflectors," each relationship gives back a phase, or facet, of her character, her personality, and her literary purpose.

Volume I shows her in relationship with the people closest to her, her family. What we are after here is essence; and the essence is to be found not in actions but in character. Genevieve Taggard's insight was right:

> What has been called mystery is character; and character is the key to this extraordinary story—Dickinson family character and Emily's . . . under the pressure, the light and shade, of the moral climate of Amherst.[12]

This statement has particular bearing on the substance of the first volume.

The section "War between the Houses" (with its voluminous Appendix), on Austin Dickinson's marriage and his relations with Mrs. Mabel Loomis Todd, needs a word of explanation. Its size is dictated, simply, by its importance. Not only is it essential in the unfolding of Austin's character and of a situation that Emily lived with for thirty years, but it is the occasion for a fresh review of Emily's relations with Susan Gilbert Dickinson, Austin's wife, a relationship of crucial importance in Emily's life. Although ultimate clarity may still be far off, certain new

---

12. *The Life and Mind of Emily Dickinson* (1930), p. xii. It is worth noting that the family was to be the main focus of a biography of Emily Dickinson once projected by Amy Lowell. Millicent Todd Bingham (*Ancestors' Brocades*, p. 111) writes: "Miss Lowell had intended, as she told my mother, to write a life of Emily Dickinson in which analysis of her relationship to the members of her family would be the central theme."

materials, or materials at last made fully available, have shed light in many a dark corner: Austin and Mabel Todd's thirteen-year correspondence; Austin's diary; Mabel's diary and journal; and the materials represented in Appendix II.

The chapter on the Dickinson rhetoric (focusing on a theme suggested in the preceding chapters) shows the bearings of a family trait on Emily Dickinson's habits of expression and offers some suggestions, as we approach the narrative of her life, about a perennial problem: the Dickinson hyperbole. This is seen to lead to, and illuminate, the most basic problem of all: how *are* we to define the structure of this extraordinary life? In this final chapter of Volume I, I venture a prefigurement (in little) of this structure, thus pointing to the main concern of Volume II. To readers in haste to have her born and on the way, I can say only this: the more one knows about background, foreground, center, what's "above" and what's "below," the more real the poems become and the more awesome Emily Dickinson's achievement is seen to be.

Forebears and Family

2

The New England Dickinsons

and the Puritan Heritage

G ENIUS IS ULTIMATELY UNACCOUNTABLE, and none more so than Emily
Dickinson's. One is reminded of the perennial question about Shakespeare: How did the humbly born, locally educated boy from Stratford
write those plays? Even her niece, Martha Dickinson Bianchi, the most
family-proud of biographers, found "nothing in the parentage or direct
heredity of Emily Dickinson" to explain it. The Dickinson genealogy
begins in this country with Nathaniel Dickinson, who came over with the
Great Migration led by John Winthrop in 1630—not to be confused
with the expedition of the more radical Separatists, who landed at Plymouth in 1620—and settled in Wethersfield, Connecticut. It was a sturdy
stock, but its competence in worldly affairs, from founding and governing
townships to fighting Indians and (later) the British, was unrelieved by
any notable touch of the graces, at least until Emily's paternal grandfather;
his daughter, Emily's versifying Aunt Elisabeth; and a lively Aunt Lavinia
on her mother's side. The records show no Connecticut Valley Anne Brad-
streets, or preachers famous for eloquence, or teachers with literary inclinations. The Dickinsons were men of affairs, and the affairs of the early
generations were highly practical: farming, homesteading, problems of
town and church. There was no time (or they made none) for poetry.

In 1659, because of a church split in Wethersfield, Nathaniel Dickinson
led his family, with fifty-eight other men and their families, on another
homesteading venture to establish the new plantation of Hadley, just east
of Northampton in Massachusetts. He was a man of distinction in the
community: the first recorder, an assessor, a town magistrate, and (initiat-

ing a Dickinson tradition still vigorous in Emily's generation) one of the first trustees of the Hopkins Grammar School of Hadley.[1] It is recorded that his grandson, Ebenezer Dickinson, fought with the Indians at Deerfield after the Massacre of 1704.[2] In 1745 Ebenezer's son, Nathan, with his son, Nathan Jr., made the move northeast from Hadley to the district that in 1759 was to become Amherst. Here the Dickinsons prospered as farmers, the tax rolls showing both father and (later) son near the top of the assessment list. Here, in 1775, Nathan Jr.'s son, Emily Dickinson's grandfather, Samuel Fowler Dickinson, was born. And here, in 1825, only five years before Emily's birth, Nathan Jr. died at the age of ninety.

This brief, and chilly, summary of six generations of human beings who hoped and feared and bled and died does scant justice to the humanity and the heroism of the founders of such a line. Actually, the Dickinsons could well be listed among "Americans of Royal Descent"—a title given to another famous Amherst family, the Boltwoods (whose name occurs frequently in the Dickinson annals), by a memorialist in 1905:

> It is a high honor to be able to trace one's line to the kings and queens who peacefully invaded New England, and, braving all odds, founded dynasties on the bleak sands of Cape Cod, amid the jagged rocks and tangled swamps of the Bay, or on the broad alluvial fields of the Connecticut Valley.

It was not until the generation of Emily's grandfather, Samuel Fowler Dickinson, that the Dickinson line, as far as the records show, produced qualities that foreshadow in any specific way Emily Dickinson's peculiar nature and, above all, her vocation as poet. Samuel Fowler left the "alluvial fields" for others to cultivate, and following his older brother Timothy, went on to higher education and became something of a man of

---

1. The fullest account of Nathaniel Dickinson is in Frederick Dickinson, *To the Descendants of Thomas Dickinson* (1897), pp. 13–18. Among other distinctions, he was one of the few who were privy to the secret hiding place (in the vicinity of Hadley) of the regicide generals Goffe and Whalley.

2. In "a list of names of those that fought In the Dearfield Medow on the last of Febewarey, 1703–4," the following Dickinsons (Dickesons) are recorded (George Sheldon, *A History of Deerfield, Massachusetts*, I, 1895, 298):

Eben'r Dickeson
Nathaniell Dickeson
Samuell Dickeson

The annals of western Massachusetts fairly bristle with Dickinsons from the earliest years on. The patriarch Nathaniel had nine sons and two daughters (all his sons fought in King Philip's war). Families of nine or ten children were the rule. By the 1880s, a family historian records that the Dickinsons in the Amherst-Hadley area "threatened to choke out all other forms of vegetation." The Dickinsons are the largest family chronicled in E. W. Carpenter and C. F. Morehouse, *The History of the Town of Amherst, Massachusetts*, 1896, Chapter III, "Founders of Amherst Families." The *Boston Journal*, in its account of a Dickinson family reunion in Amherst on August 8, 1883, said that, even in the early years, "we may well doubt whether the Dickinsons belonged to Amherst or Amherst to the Dickinsons."

letters. Up to that time, the Dickinson heritage shows many of those massive traits of character we associate with New England and Puritanism, but little else.

A word about those "massive traits" before turning to their specific manifestations in the Dickinson forebears about whom there is detailed information. In an introductory note to his *The American Puritans,* Perry Miller wrote: "Without some understanding of Puritanism . . . there is no understanding of America," and (had it been within his purpose) he might have added that this is especially true, among its poets, of Emily Dickinson. Her relation to the Puritan tradition is the theme of a notable essay by Allen Tate. If, he argued, Hawthorne reconstituted in American fiction "the puritan drama of the soul" after Emerson had all but extinguished it, Emily Dickinson, with something of Emerson in her but more of Hawthorne, reconstituted it in her poetry. But she did so with sturdy independence, in itself one of the tradition's most massive traits.

One must not be misled by the fact that with her the drama was quite different in nature from the soul-torturings, the battles with sin and the Devil, recorded in Puritan literature. Indeed, her whole career may be regarded as a sustained, if muted, rebellion against this very inheritance. "I do not respect 'doctrines,' " she said at one point, and especially (she made clear) the Puritan doctrine of innate sin. Among her several rejections of this doctrine, perhaps the sharpest was a remark on a typical Amherst sermon: "While the Clergyman tells Father and Vinnie that 'this Corruptible shall put on Incorruption' – it has already done so and they go defrauded."

Emily Dickinson's sense of the past, certainly her New England past, could hardly be called vivid. She showed no interest in family lore as such. She left only one reference to her famous grandfather, Samuel Fowler, and that had more to do with her father than with him.[3] Nowhere in her surviving poems or letters did she cite any Dickinson accomplishment in the past. When in a letter of 1871 she used the phrase "Ancestors' Brocades" it was for an irrelevant metaphorical purpose: like Truth, they "stand alone." Yet she was very conscious of being an Amherst girl, and the line in her poem about seeing "New Englandly" is generally regarded as referring to herself. She knew what the massive Puritan traits were, saw them in her family and in herself, respected them, but was critical of them throughout her life. Speaking in large terms, Tate contended that Emily Dickinson came at the ideal time for a poet: when a once firm and mighty tradition was losing its vitality and opening for the poet new freedoms, some exalting, some terrifying. This is true; and it is the source of much of the anguish, as well as the ecstasy, in many of her poems. In the smaller, more intimate sphere, she saw the effects of the decaying

3. In a letter of about 1883 to her Aunt Catherine (Sweetser): "I have found and give it in love, but reluctant to entrust anything so sacred to my Father as my Grandfather's Bible to a public Messenger, will wait till Mr. Howard comes" (*L* III, 779).

tradition in, especially, the near-tragic lives of her father and brother and in the restricted life of the town—in the pettiness, the hypocrisy, and the narrow moral view that were the sad legacy of the tradition in many New England communities and a major reason, certainly, for her own alienation and withdrawal. Behind all the pages that follow, her New England, Puritan inheritance will be a sustained assumption. She could no more escape it, for better or for worse, than she could escape breathing the air of her native Amherst.

But what precisely was New England in Emily Dickinson's inheritance, and what Puritan? To start with the first, many of the qualities of these early generations in the northeastern part of the country are common to all folk who wrench their living from a grudging soil, in a climate of vivid extremes, and in pioneering conditions. They must be industrious or perish. The survival values, besides hard work, are practicality, shrewdness, stamina. "They were not easily discouraged" is still the definitive tribute to the early New Englanders. Living in tiny communities, often in widely separated farms, they became independent because they had to be. Existing close to the soil, with crops to raise and stock to keep alive, they were in daily contact with life and death, the creative and destructive forces of nature; and hence they were realists. Although life in mid-nineteenth-century Amherst was well beyond the primitive stage, the following passage is a good reminder of aspects of Amherst life in Emily Dickinson's time that would still seem crude to us:

> . . . the community was made up of self-sustaining homes in which the inhabitants were highly organized social units. At that time, Amherst's village green was still a rough pasture with birch trees and a frog pond, and the houses around it and along the few roads that led away from it were modified farms, provided with horses, cows, and chickens, vegetable gardens and orchards. Water was drawn by hand or by means of a pump from a well near the house. Many families owned their own woodlots, where the fuel was cut to supply their stoves and open hearths. No street lights brightened the paths along the unpaved roads. At night each house became a little island, where indoors the family gathered around an oil lamp after dark, and went to bed by the light of a tallow candle. . . .[4]

The forces of nature controlled much of the life in her own home and that of the village. Cold, heat, floods, and drought all had an immediate effect on everyday living.

4. In his essay, "Heating, Lighting, Plumbing, and Human Relations," *Landscape* (July 1971), Albert Eide Parr elaborates on the possible effect of such arrangements on family relationships "during the era of candles and kerosene." Because of fire hazard and the chore of tending wicks, cleaning sooty chimneys, and filling empty reservoirs, the number of lamps actually lit at any one time was kept to a minimum. The family's activities probably centered in one or two rooms and mostly in the living room, for reading, study, or conversation. This evening gathering "had a very strong effect upon the attitudes and personalities developed by the young members of the family during their formative years." Since reasonable quiet was essential to the family gathering, discipline among the children was more or less self-imposed:

This placed the parents in the favorable position of benevolent referees, rather than

The New England Dickinsons and the Puritan Heritage

New Englanders were understandably frugal with everything, until frugality became a virtue which in later, more prosperous generations was cherished for its own sake, quite apart from need. Emily Dickinson wrote her poems, thriftily, on odds and ends of paper, on the back of recipes, invitations, shopping lists, clippings, while her father drove the finest horse in town. Although doubtless there were garrulous New Englanders —there certainly are—the habit of thrift extended to speech. They hated to waste words, a quality which became perhaps Emily Dickinson's most obvious New Englandism. Or they hoarded their words unless it was their bounden duty to do otherwise, as when their theologians wrote their mighty books, or their pastors worshipped God for hours on end in the pulpit, or their prominent men, like Emily's father, were called upon to address their fellows on state occasions. (The irony of Thomas Wentworth Higginson's description of Edward Dickinson as "thin dry & speechless" lay in the fact that Edward Dickinson was one of the most famous orators in Hampshire County.) And, like all people close to the soil, and by education overqualified for the often backbreaking work their livelihoods demanded, they developed a humor that was pithy and ironic.

All these qualities were true of the Dickinsons at least down to, and to a large extent including, Emily's generation. We see them, once she had set the bearings of her career, in her intensity of purpose, in her extraordinary capacity for work, in her often caustic wit and clipped phrasing. The extent to which she, and her brother Austin and sister Lavinia, departed from some of the more restrictive of them will also be one of our themes.

The specifically Puritan qualities in Emily Dickinson's heritage are more difficult to isolate and define. The genus Puritan subsumes many species, and the Dickinson species was a mixture of many paradoxical qualities. The religious motive that, at least in part, impelled the first Dickinson to New England does not recur overtly in Emily's direct line until Samuel Fowler Dickinson's generation, and even he gave up his

---

principal adversaries, on most minor issues of discipline and consideration for others. The ephemeral animosities of daily life were more likely to develop between siblings than between generations. Could it be pure accident that the generation gap does not seem to have been invented until after the invention of the electric light? Quiet, without complete silence, was naturally a condition particularly strongly insisted upon around the evening lamp, since you could close or turn your eyes, but not your ears.

With the coming of electricity and central heating, "bedchambers became studies and playrooms . . . and the family dispersed itself and its activities throughout the house at all hours . . . Parents became the principal ogres and disciplinarians of the household, and because they saw less of the brood under their command they had less opportunity to time and to design their parental intervention in filial affairs to best advantage."

To what extent such sociological generalization illuminates Dickinson family relationships is problematic. It is useful to keep in mind, at any rate, in attempting to picture Emily Dickinson in her contemporary surroundings and to judge their effect on her. It may tend to mitigate the harsh view of her isolation in her own family and of the stringency of the family discipline.

early inclination toward the ministry for a vigorous lay career. It was the work of *this* world that occupied the early Dickinsons, their otherworldly concerns manifesting themselves outwardly in community participation in the usual affairs of church and school. At least there is no record of an apostate Dickinson; Emily herself was the first avowed "pagan" (a term she applied to herself several times and not, it seems, entirely in jest). In the course of the generations, when Puritanism reached Emily as a part of her family tradition, it was a checkered affair, much Dickinsonized. What she got of the real thing, "pure" Puritanism, came from her reading, from the Amherst pulpit, from the hymns and prayers. It was her distinction that she perceived its central meaning in spite of the cloud of accretions that obscured it in mid-nineteenth-century America.

The major characteristics of this pristine Puritanism have achieved a near-mythical status in our consciousness, and we need pause only over those that seem most pertinent to Emily Dickinson and her poetry. In her intercourse with the world and with herself, they often appeared in action; and, as always, what posterity abstracts into concepts and doctrines must be qualified when it takes on the inevitable ambiguities of experience. Or, as Tate describes the peculiar tension she achieved between abstraction and sensation, the Puritan ideals ceased to be abstractions, so thoroughly fused did they become with her character and sensibility: "She did not reason about the world she saw; she merely saw it." That is, here as everywhere, she proceeded inductively, experimentally, putting all she encountered to the test of her own sensibility. An epigram in mid-career summed up her lifelong way:

> Experiment escorts us last –
> His pungent company
> Will not allow an Axiom
> An Opportunity   (*#1770, about 1870*)

What occurs to us first, perhaps, among the "axioms" that are distinctively Puritan are the virtues of simplicity, austerity, hard work, and denial of the flesh. These were ever-present disciplines in her life. Although her father saw to it that his family lived in a fashion far short of hardship, he might have served as a model for Perry Miller's note on the "Protestant ethic":

Man is put into this world, not to spend his life in profitless singing of hymns or in unfruitful monastic contemplation, but to do what the world requires, according to its terms. He must raise children, he must work at his calling. No activity is outside the holy purpose of the overarching covenant. Yet the Christian works not for the gain that may (or may not) result from his labor, but for the glory of God. . . . It was a razor's edge, and the true Puritan was required to walk it. No wonder that some Puritans fell off to one side, becoming visionary idealists, while some fell to the other side, becoming hypocrites.

The New England Dickinsons and the Puritan Heritage

Emily Dickinson had a sharp eye for both idealists and hypocrites in pious, busy Amherst and caught occasional glimpses of her father teetering on the razor's edge. If she rejoiced in life, in the "ecstasy in living" (as she put it) in ways he would not have understood, the main outlines of her life were, like his, austere—"too simple and stern to embarrass any." But the sternness and simplicity had little to do with theological sanctions. Her experience taught her that these ways were best for her. Certainly she seems never to have undertaken them penitentially. "'Consider the Lilies,'" she wrote a friend two years before she died, was "the only Commandment I ever obeyed."

Another phase of Puritan living and thinking that could be considered axiomatic became, after testing, a part of Emily Dickinson's way—if, again, for reasons of her own. To the true Puritan, denial and renunciation had meaning only as they made for the greater glory of God and the salvation of the soul. The Puritan lived in constant, fearful awareness of his soul, maintained continual vigilance, and took his spiritual measurements daily, even hourly. "Almost every Puritan kept a diary," wrote Perry Miller, "not so much because he was infatuated with himself but because he needed a strict account of God's dealings with him, so that at any moment, and above all at the moment of death, he could review the long transaction." Here, too, as with denial and renunciation, Emily Dickinson's need for a strict account may not have been entirely theological, but the fierce introspection and the diary keeping of the Puritans surely had a bearing on her mental habits. Her poems, some of which are couched in these very terms, were her way of keeping the long transaction in constant review. Miller's description of the Puritan's inner turmoil is strikingly close to what puzzles readers of Emily Dickinson's poems today, their extraordinary shifts and changes of mood, tone, and even belief: the Puritan "lives inwardly a life of incessant fluctuation, ecstatically elated this day, depressed into despair the next." It required clinical skill to narrate, in diary, journal, or autobiography, "these surgings and sinkings, all the time striving to keep the line of the story clear." Similarly, Emily Dickinson's poems often have that same breathless sense that all may be over at any moment, that the instant of reckoning may be at hand.

Further, the Puritan drama of the soul had its dialogue, where in diaries or, as in Anne Bradstreet's and Edward Taylor's formal verse or prose, the Soul addressed its God, or the Soul addressed the Self, or the Flesh addressed the Spirit. The Puritans talked a great deal to themselves—a way of thinking, of attacking one's inner problems, that Emily Dickinson was born to. If her communication with her God or her Soul is a good deal more informal, even chatty, than a true Puritan would have thought seemly, she never permanently lost hold of these spiritual realities, whatever the vicissitudes of her faith. She lived and moved, however restlessly, in the dimension prepared for her by the New England Puritans.

To this general statement must be added one important particular: the peculiar quality of Connecticut Valley Puritanism. In the Great Revival in Northampton in 1740, Jonathan Edwards had given the drama of the soul a flaming immediacy for the people who came under the influence of his preaching. Always, as Miller noted, central to Puritan theology was the vision, the moment of inner light, the Augustinian revelation as opposed to the years of dialectical effort of Thomistic theology. The effort of Edwards was the continuation of the work of his grandfather, the great Solomon Stoddard, who in the "remote frontier fortress of Northampton" flailed away at the liberal tendencies he saw menacing the true faith. Stoddard had "made explicit that deep-seated reliance on the self which was from the beginning a hidden but irresistible thrust of the Puritan theology." It was this "spirit of sublime self-reliance" that Edwards preached as he reasserted in 1740 the primitive passion to the thousands who participated in the Revival.

The revival spirit, calling for deep individual soul-searching, confession of sin, and repentance, was very much alive in Emily Dickinson's time and caused her anguish. No fewer than eight revivals swept Amherst, college and town, during her formative years, roughly between 1840 and 1862. She could never see herself as a sinner in the hands of an angry God. She could never testify, as so many of her pious friends did, to that direct visitation of the Spirit which was essential to membership in the church. If she never became a "christian" (more often than not, she spelled the word with a small "c"), if her unique calling took her far from the ways of orthodoxy, it still was the Puritan in her that made her feel that the burden of proof was on her, and that the burden was a mighty one.[5] In

---

5. How continuously this sense of the burden was brought home to the community, especially to the young people, can be seen in this passage from Professor Edward Hitchcock's *Reminiscences of Amherst College* (1863), p. 162:

Up to the present time, (July, 1863), the College has enjoyed marked seasons of special religious interest in the following years, viz.: 1823, 1827, 1828, 1834, 1835, 1839, 1842, 1846, 1850, 1853, 1855, 1857, 1858, and 1862. Besides these . . . prominent revivals, many other seasons of special interest have existed in the institution, which, though not dignified by the name of revivals, have yet been of unspeakable importance in raising the standard of practical piety. . . .

Theodora Ward, *Capsule of the Mind*, pp. 15–18, emphasizes the pressure these revivals put upon the young people, especially the recalcitrants. She quotes a little book, *Revival Conversations* (1844) by Dr. Heman Humphrey, Hitchcock's predecessor as president of the college. A troubled young man has come to his pastor for spiritual guidance.

Inquirer O, you misunderstand me. I have not got so far. I have told you already that I am not even awakened yet, and how can I repent? I am somewhat troubled, to be sure, or I should not be here. But my feelings are all indefinite.

Pastor Do you think your not having *got so far* is any valid excuse for not repenting, and giving your heart to God? The question is not, how far you have

the constant test of her own sublime self-reliance her only weapon was the moment of perception, or vision, that imparted to her such a different and unique message:

On a Columnar Self –
How ample to rely
In Tumult – or Extremity –
How good the Certainty

That Lever cannot pry –
And Wedge cannot divide
Conviction – That Granitic Base –
Though None be on our Side –

Suffice Us – for a Crowd –
Ourself – and Rectitude –
And that Assembly – not far off
From furthest Spirit – God –   (*#789, about 1863*)

Over, behind, and through it all, of course, were the Puritan conceptions of Divine immanence, providential history, the Whole Duty of Man; the sense of being Chosen, or Elected; the idea of Redemption. All these were at work, I think, in her complicated consciousness, if not as theological convictions, at least as fixed points in her spiritual navigation—sometimes vividly seen, more often suffused in fog or mist, sometimes lost in the blackness of night. She herself often used the metaphor of the voyage. "The shore is safer," she wrote, when she was twenty, to a pious young friend, "but I love to buffet the sea . . . I love the danger!"

---

advanced, but how far you *ought* to have advanced, – not how you feel, but how you *ought* to feel.

Inquirer I do not feel anything. I have no sense of my sins, and how can I have? I wish I could feel as others do, but it is impossible.

Pastor My dear young friend, do stop and think what you are saying. You do not feel! You have no sense of sinfulness! Astonishing! A sinner against a holy God, and under condemnation, and liable every moment to drop into a burning hopeless eternity – and yet cannot feel, cannot be alarmed, cannot "flee from the wrath to come." O, how stupid you must be!

What troubled the young "Inquirer" comes uncannily close to ED's often expressed spiritual worries, most dramatic at age nineteen: "I am standing alone in rebellion . . ." (*L* I, 94; to Jane Humphrey, April 3, 1850). In 1859, Humphrey reprinted *Revival Conversations* (of which the selection above is a tiny fragment) in a book entitled *Revival Sketches and Manual,* published in New York by the American Tract Society. (The last line quoted above reads, incidentally, "O, how dead you must be!", p. 427.) Evangelical clichés abound. A question by the Pastor (p. 473 in the 1859 volume) may have provided Emily with a phrase she used in a letter to Abiah Root (*L* I, 60; January 17, 1848): *"Pastor . . . Whereas you was once blind, do you now see? The true question is, Are you in the ark of safety?"*

[25

The question of immortality—she called it "the Flood subject"—is seldom far distant from her poems and letters, even in their lighter moods. "The final direction of her poetry," writes Charles Anderson, "and the pressures that created it, can only be described as religious, using that word in its 'dimension of depth' "—the dimension, that is, of the ever-questing mind, not so much (in her case) rejecting the orthodoxies as pressing them for an assurance that continually eluded her. Although perhaps the most religious person in town, she had stopped going to church by the time she was thirty.

She was prepared to accept the loneliness of such a course, a loneliness endemic in the New England Puritan way and intensified by her own peculiar defections. A near-contemporary, Samuel G. Ward, the early Transcendentalist and writer for the *Dial,* sensed the Dickinson situation perceptively, even to Emily's relations with her family, in a letter to Higginson shortly after Higginson and Mabel Loomis Todd had brought out the first edition of *Poems:*

MY DEAR MR. HIGGINSON,

I am, with all the world, intensely interested in Emily Dickinson. No wonder six editions have been sold, every copy, I should think to a New Englander. She may become world famous, or she may never get out of New England. She is the quintessence of that element we all have who are of the Puritan descent *pur sang.* We came to this country to think our own thoughts with nobody to hinder. Ascetics of course, & this our Thebaid. We conversed with our own souls till we lost the art of communicating with other people. The typical family grew up strangers to each other, as in this case. It was *awfully* high, but awfully lonesome. Such prodigies of shyness do not exist elsewhere. We get it from the English, but the English were not alone in a corner of the world for a hundred & fifty years with no outside interest.

The following chapters will both confirm and qualify Mr. Ward's analysis. Higginson sent the letter to Mrs. Todd, calling it "the most remarkable criticism yet made on E.D."

All this grappling with the tradition she was born in, her debts and non-debts to her New England tradition and to Puritanism, will become more apparent when we follow Emily Dickinson in her lifelong struggle with her own attitudes and style. Confronting that tradition squarely, she appropriated its components selectively and shrewdly, revered it, but never capitulated to it. To quote Tate once more: "Unlike her contemporaries, she never succumbed to her ideas, to easy solutions, to her private desires. [In her poetry] there is no thought as such at all; nor is there feeling; there is that unique focus of experience which is at once neither and both." Her Columnar Self was founded solidly on the tradition, but its construction was her own work.

It is the tradition, however, that bears especially on this first part of our study, for the Dickinsons were pure stock, without even a wife in seven generations from outside New England. And the tensions inherent in

The New England Dickinsons and the Puritan Heritage

New England Puritanism, especially in the period of its decline, contributed directly to the "Vesuvius at Home" in which Emily Dickinson lived and wrote. It may be true that nothing in her parentage or ancestry explains her genius, but the closer we look into them, the more we understand what went into that unique focus of experience where the "thought" of tradition is fused with the "feeling" of the individual to produce something new. Nothing is more applicable to Emily Dickinson than a fine remark of Erik Erikson's about those "who trust their origins" but have the "courage to emerge from them."

3

Samuel Fowler Dickinson

S AMUEL FOWLER DICKINSON (1775–1838), the youngest son and seventh
of the eight children of Nathan and Esther (Fowler) Dickinson, is
the first of Emily Dickinson's forebears and the only one among the
grandparents on either side of the family about whom there is enough on
record to warrant examination. There is in fact a great deal, and to follow
it through in some detail is not only to learn much about the culture Emily
Dickinson was nurtured in—the town and the college—but to understand
better many of the tensions she had to live with in the Dickinson household and to cope with in her own person. Samuel Fowler's career, save for
its sad ending, was a model of the late-Puritan, New England way. Here
were all the elements: piety, work, singleness of purpose. It is essential
Amherst and essential Dickinson.

In 1896, Carpenter and Morehouse's fine old *History of Amherst* gave
the standard view of Samuel Fowler Dickinson:

> A descendant in direct line from Nathaniel Dickinson, who was among the
> original settlers of Hadley, he was the embodiment of those qualities and
> virtues that gave to New England strength and character from the earliest
> times.

One of the surest proofs that Emily was aware of these qualities in her
grandfather is that her brother Austin was. Seven years before the *History,* in 1889, Austin had paid him much the same tribute in an address
prepared for a celebration at the First Church in Amherst, the Dickinson
church.[1] Both tributes left out the sad ending, the shadow of which hung
over the family for years. In his all but fanatical work in the founding of

---

1. For Austin's tribute, see below, p. 41, and see Chapter 6 for a full account of
the address.

Amherst College, Dickinson ruined his health and his fortune, sold the Homestead,[2] and left Amherst when Emily was two.

His career started auspiciously. One of his daughters, probably Emily's Aunt Elisabeth, the family scribe, wrote of his early years:

> He was trained by the same maternal hand as his brother [Timothy], and with like results of character and piety. Gentle and sensitive, and with more than ordinary mental gifts, he was one of the best beloved in his home by brothers and sisters, and was encouraged by his parents to follow his taste for study. After instruction by Judge Strong of Amherst, he entered Dartmouth College at sixteen, and maintaining high rank as a scholar, graduated . . . with the second honor, of Latin salutatorian.

He entered Dartmouth in 1791, six years after his brother Timothy had graduated. By the time he got there, the college, established some twenty years earlier for the education and conversion of Indians, offered a sound "classical curriculum" to all students, many of whom came from Massachusetts and Connecticut. Many of his thirty-one classmates went on to notable careers, especially in teaching and in law—not so many, be it noted, in the ministry. Though sufficiently pious, education at Dartmouth seems to have been less theologically strict than at some of its sister institutions like Yale and less evangelical than what Samuel Fowler later helped create at Amherst. At least, in 1772, a parent, sending his son to Dartmouth, wrote President Eleazar Wheelock: "The Education at Yale is not Liberal: they are too Contracted in their Principles and do not Encourage a Free Enquiry."[3]

Significant of this difference may have been Dickinson's Salutatory Address at the 1795 Commencement, still preserved in manuscript in the Dartmouth archives. There was little piety in it and much about this world and its affairs; its full title read: *De administrationis civilis et morum natura; atque momento eorum mutuae relationis,* or, "Nature of Civil government & manners; their mutual relation & influence in society." Only two years after his graduation, when he must have been a marked young man in his community, he turned the address into a sturdily patriotic oration for the Fourth of July festivities in nearby Belchertown. Here the title became *The Connection of Civil Government*

---

2. In her writings on ED, Martha Dickinson Bianchi regularly refers to the "Mansion." In *Home* it is the Homestead. In the deed of sale in 1833, it is called The Homestead. When Edward Dickinson repurchased the property in 1855, he was congratulated in the *Hampshire and Franklin Express* for bringing "The Old Homestead" back into the family. I have adopted this designation throughout. (See *Home,* pp. 9, 390, 523.)

3. Although, as Leon Burr Richardson, *History of Dartmouth College* (1932), I, 120, reminds the reader, Wheelock's purpose was still predominantly evangelical, the curriculum Samuel Fowler studied sounds "liberal" enough: the "learned languages" for three years; speaking and writing, mathematics, geography and logic; and (senior year) English and Latin composition, metaphysics and the "elements of natural and physical law." This was the same curriculum that faced Daniel Webster when he entered Dartmouth two years after Samuel Fowler graduated.

with Manners and Taste. It was published soon after in pamphlet form, in Northampton, its author announced on the title page as "Samuel F. Dickinson, A.B. Student at Law, Amherst."

The oration is more than a curiosity. Here at least are Learning and Letters (and apparently for the first time) among Emily Dickinson's hard-driving, workaday forebears. It is full of the cant of patriotism, but it has verve and sweep, from the opening sentence, "Everything, which respects the happiness of human society, is interesting," to the closing wish that all the world might enjoy America's freedom: "Then shall the morning stars, again, sing together, and all the sons of men shout for joy." In between, it traces the painful history of civil government from prehistoric savagery to the present state of moral order and refinement. Almost everything turns up that one would expect, and in predictable terms, the winnowings from a bright undergraduate's learning. We hear about the "profusion and luxury" of Babylon and Persia, the "dissipation" of Turkish despotism, the "jealous cruelties of the Venetian aristocrat," the "constant fidelity of a republican Swiss." We are taken through the fall of Rome, the Dark Ages, the rise of the Italian cities, and improvements in the arts and sciences. There is nothing about Sin and Redemption, little about God and His beneficence, and much about "the progress of reason and taste," about "the fitness of things" as ordained by Nature, about "rational inquiry," and how "science and a knowledge of things enlarge the mind."

A few passages from the oration show the enormous distance between Fowler's gift and Emily's; but it will be noted that his language is under control, sometimes by the same rhetorical devices that Emily herself was to use. There is a good sense of rhythm, construction, and cadence. Often the pose is crude and the rhetoric obvious:

> Were it needful, we might say, the virtues of American citizens would be strangers, in the gaudy realms of eastern monarchs, or in the dominions of European kings. Were it needful, we might say, the vices of those countries would be vagabonds in this free and independent commonwealth. But, modesty forbids.

An effusion on the delights of nature, couched in terms that might have come right out of the Enlightenment, has a more subtle balance:

> In the temperate climes, in which we live, nature seems to have combined her powers, to aggrandize the intellectual world, and to complete the circle of rational enjoyment. Here she has planted her garden, adorned with the richest fruits, and the finest flowers, which can either improve the taste, or please the fancy, of intelligent beings. And here she has prepared a *banquet for reason.*

This is refreshingly un-Puritan, but one looks in vain for a sense either of the peculiar beauty of the hilly New Hampshire setting where the speech originated, or of Fowler's own lovely Connecticut Valley. It remained for his granddaughter to get her eye on the object; but here, two generations back, was something of the same response to the beauty of this world that (as she put it) "holds – so – ."

A final burst of eloquence, this time in praise of General George Washington, then in his declining years, shows how near Fowler was, not only to the Enlightenment, but to the Revolution (there had been a score of Dickinsons among the Minutemen) :

> I should do violence to original virtue, and to my own feelings, should I pass, in silence, the man, who has been our shield in war, our council in peace, George Washington, the illustrious patron of his country. The calm serenities of a pure unclouded mind shall *still* attend him, through the shadowy vale of declining age. The plaudits of an admiring world shall remain, a diadem to his memory, in the crown of hoary justice. The choir of guardian seraphs, who have protected him, through the perils of life, shall pitch their tents, in calm repose, around his venerable head, and softly tune their harps, to breathe his praise.

Again, here is no praise of a Divine Providence for sending the great man at the time of his country's need; and "the choir of guardian seraphs" have about as much theological significance as Emily's seraphs who swung their snowy hats "To see the little Tippler / Leaning against the – Sun – " There is not a fresh image in the passage, and its patriotic clichés are in the same vein as the clichés of the Revivalist preachers which were to fill Emily's letters when she was about Fowler's age. But the passage is well composed, and the last sentence, with its dying fall, has a rhythm perfectly suited to the declining state of the old general. Millicent Todd Bingham was the first to call attention to the interest "these stirring words – a kind of apotheosis of the living Washington – " might have for those "who search among the forebears of Emily Dickinson for intimations of genius." Unfortunately, we cannot be sure that Emily ever read the address.

In general, the slant of the oration is closer to Tom Paine than might have been considered seemly from a Connecticut Valley boy and closer to belles-lettres than might conventionally be expected from a boy descended from generations of farmers.[4] This is to say, of course, that the indepen-

---

4. Such latitude of thought gave considerable anxiety to the orthodox of the next generation. In 1859 Heman Humphrey's *Revival Sketches and Manual* included a brief history of revivals in New England (and abroad) from the earliest times. Commenting on the spirit of the period of the Revolution, Humphrey wrote (p. 99):

> The minds of the people were too much agitated and engrossed by conflicting political interests, to have much room for more than the ordinary routine of religious observances. . . . Zion languished. . . .
>
> In the mean time . . . *French Infidelity,* which our allies brought over with them, was sowed broadcast among our own officers and soldiers. Aided by Paine's "Age of Reason," Voltaire's assaults upon Christianity, Volney's Ruins, and other blasphemous publications, it spread rapidly, especially among the upper classes. . . . Instead of the Scriptures, French philosophy claimed to be the rule of faith

dence of thought and the cultural level of these so-called farmers should not be underestimated. If Samuel Fowler's lineage says nothing explicit about the origins of his tastes and abilities, and if it is condescending to call him the first literary Dickinson, at least it can be said with confidence that his descendants shared liberally in his qualities. His son Edward, Emily's father and the orator, wrote verses in his youth, read widely, and assembled a library of considerable diversity. Edward's sister Elisabeth was not only the chronicler but the bard of her generation. She once sent her young nephew Austin a rhymed letter of fifty stanzas on his toothache, and she wrote a long verse history of the family for a Dickinson reunion in 1883. In the next generation, Emily's brother and sister were lively readers, enjoyed discussing what they read, and prided themselves on the style of their letters and their talk, often peppery and unconventional. They both at one time or another wrote verses. All this hardly accounts for Emily's gifts; but it makes her seem less isolated, less alone in a household usually regarded as insensitive to literary matters. It may explain, too, why the members of her family took for granted the occasional verses they knew she wrote (they seem to have had no idea how many). Such occupation was to be expected in all genteel families, especially among the daughters.[5] We can look back at Samuel Fowler's oration simply as one discernible landmark, the beginning of Dickinson literaria.

It is not surprising to learn that, during the year after his graduation, Fowler tried his hand at teaching (in New Salem, Massachusetts), perhaps to inspire his pupils in the cultivation of this same Reason he exalted in the oration. (Fifty-five years later, his grandson, Austin, was to experiment with teaching as a profession—and with the same results: they

---

and life, and ignoring all the "rights of God," was to usher in the glorious millennium of the "rights of man."

Seen in this light, Fowler's emendation, "and all the sons of *men* shout for joy," is significant. It took some time to restore a climate favorable to religious revivals. Humphrey was in the forefront of the movement. By Emily Dickinson's youth it was in full swing.

It is worth noting that Fowler's brother Timothy entered the ministry after graduating from Dartmouth and became pastor of the Congregational Church in Holliston, Massachusetts. In 1800 he preached an ordination sermon for the Reverend Drury Fairbank in Plymouth, New Hampshire. Printed that year in Concord, New Hampshire, the sermon is as rigidly orthodox as any Connecticut Valley conservative could wish. Compare Fowler's tone and attitude with this: "God's people are a peculiar people, by entering into covenant with the Lord, by joining themselves to the Church of Christ, and by separating themselves from sinners . . ." (Timothy Dickinson, *Sermon . . . ,* Concord, 1800, p. 6).

5. In an unpublished study, "Emily Dickinson and the Practice of Poetry," Miriam Baker shows how widespread this practice was—and not only among daughters. Especially during the early decades of the century, the writing of verses for every occasion, or none, became almost a cultural status symbol; certainly it was the fashion. Many of the products spilled over into the journals and magazines. Edward Dickinson's, Austin's, and Lavinia's attempts will be discussed in the appropriate chapters.

each lasted a year.) It *is* surprising, in view of the sentiments in the oration, to learn that sometime during the year, and following an illness, Fowler was converted to Christianity and decided to be a minister. His calling was short-lived, however, and by 1797 we find him reading law in Amherst under the tutelage of Judge Simeon Strong, the leading barrister in the county. The law turned out to be his true vocation, and he very soon established himself as a leading citizen, a pillar of the church, and a distinguished lawyer.[6] He married Lucretia Gunn of Montague (some ten miles due north of Amherst) in 1802, had nine children, of whom Edward was the eldest, and in 1813 built an imposing house on Main Street, the first brick house in town, the Homestead, where Emily was born.

It was the founding of Amherst College during the next few years that was the triumph of Fowler's life, and also his tragedy. The challenge was extraordinary, and it brought out all his fine qualities, the "strength and character" that Carpenter and Morehouse praised. This was the heroic side of his involvement; the tragic lay in what can only be called an element of fanaticism, which, not so clear in the early stages of planning and discussion when he was at his best, is certainly apparent later, when all the resources of the town seemed for a time inadequate to achieve the purpose and he threw himself recklessly into the cause. It was here that Fowler (now "Squire Fowler") gave almost all he had, and gave too much. His practice—and his health—failed, he was near bankruptcy, and eventually he left town to take a job in the Midwest, where he died "disillusioned, neglected, and forgotten."

It is important, and worth a digression, to understand the nature of the new college for which Fowler Dickinson sacrificed himself. It both reflected and shaped the character of the community into which, nine years after the official opening of the college, Emily Dickinson was born. Not only was her grandfather a founder and member of the first Board of Trustees, but her father and then her brother were treasurers of the college for a span of sixty years, beginning when she was five. Its affairs and its people were daily in her consciousness. In her adult life, she could in turn be interested, inspired, repelled, or bored by the college and its people; but she was well aware of the distinction it brought to the town. It gave her something to match her spirit with, and sharpen her wits on, throughout her life.

From the beginning of the century, sentiment had been growing in the Connecticut Valley for an institution of higher learning somewhere in the vicinity of Amherst. Dartmouth, Williams, and Yale were too far away

6. His daughter Elisabeth testifies to his success in all these undertakings. "Accepting an invitation to become principal of the Academy at New Salem, he taught one year with marked success. . . ." At twenty-one he was elected deacon of the First Church and "for forty years 'filled the office well.'" As a lawyer, "his success was so great that it is said 'he *did* more business than *all* the lawyers in Hampshire County'" (*Reunion of the Dickinson Family at Amherst, Mass., 1883* [1884], p. 172).

for the indigent youth of the district, and Harvard too liberal in its theology for the pious. Various sites had been considered—Northampton, Hatfield, Hadley—and various proposals made. One of them was the addition of a professorship to the staff of Amherst Academy, in whose founding, in 1814, Fowler had also been deeply involved. It was he who insisted that such a step was inadequate, that only a separate collegiate institution would fill the need. In support of his conviction, he subscribed $600[7] and was one of the signers of a $15,000 bond.

The purpose of the new institution was clear and unequivocal: its "original object" was "civilizing and evangelizing the world by the classical education of indigent young men of piety and talents." And, it should be added, piety as the founders conceived it. Liberal Harvard was the enemy. When the Amherst leaders applied to the Massachusetts General Court for a charter for the college,[8] the Harvard Unitarians opposed it as "a priest factory,"[9] a sectarian tool. But the opposition merely strengthened the founding zeal, which grew into a flaming cause. The charter was eventually granted, and Amherst became a stronghold of orthodoxy, to remain so during Emily Dickinson's youth and early maturity; that is, until it could no longer hold out against the advancing secularism of the age, the unsettling influences of the Civil War, and the theological liberalism that inevitably spread from Boston and Cambridge.

It would be wrong, however, to represent the college as some sort of monolithic ogre or black theological cloud on Emily's bright young horizon. At least she never spoke of it in those terms. She saw it through the eyes of the faculty children with whom she was intimate, the students and young tutors who came to call, the graduates who read law in her father's office, and, above all, her father and (later) her brother, the treasurers, who were concerned mainly with its worldly affairs. She knew it through its public ceremonies and lectures, its Commencements, its receptions (some of which were held in her own house), its library,

7. This is the figure given in Carpenter and Morehouse, p. 159. He is said to have subscribed $1,005 for the founding of Amherst Academy (H. F. West, "Forgotten Dartmouth Men: A Founder of Dartmouth College—Samuel F. Dickinson, 1795," *Dartmouth Alumni Magazine* XXVII, February 1935, p. 62).

8. One of those leaders was Fowler Dickinson. A letter from home to Edward at Yale catches him in the act:

Father left in the yellow gig for the Bay Road this morning. He has gone to Boston by coach to see about getting a charter for something they propose to call Amherst College. He looked so fine in his white beaver and new great coat.

This passage is reproduced in Professor West's "Forgotten Dartmouth Men," p. 62. Professor West attributes the letter to Fowler's "sister Lucretia," in error either for his wife or for his daughter, both named Lucretia.

9. Thomas Le Duc, *Piety and Intellect at Amherst College 1865–1912* (1946), p. 5. In Chapter I ("A College for Training Parsons") Le Duc gives a lively account of the founding of the college, stressing the involvement of the whole community in "a genuine folk movement, vigorous and creative" (p. 2). The hostility of the Cambridge Unitarians and the determination of the Connecticut Valley people to resist the heretical influences from the East are main themes.

Lucretia Gunn Dickinson and Samuel Fowler Dickinson,
from silhouettes by William King, about 1828

"The birthplace of Samuel Fowler Dickinson Esq. Amherst Mass."
Charcoal drawing, date and artist unknown

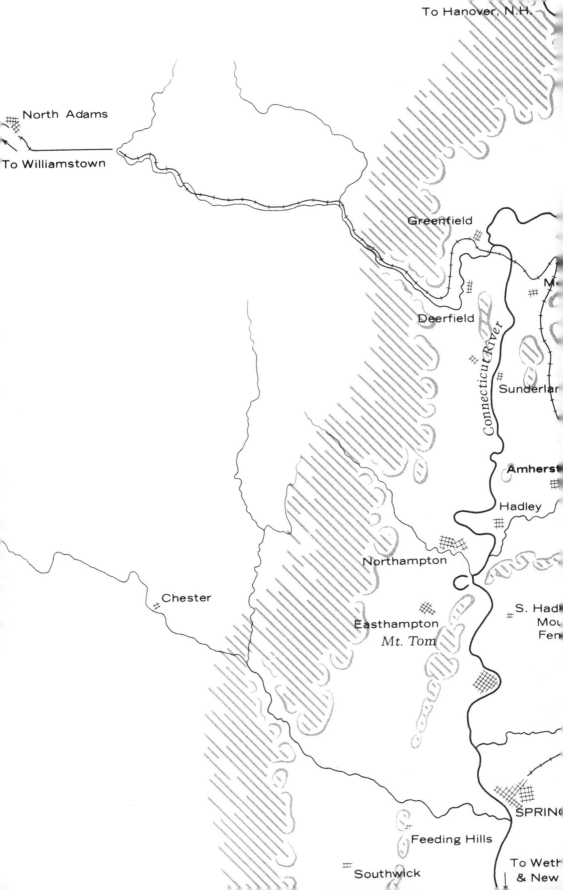

To Hanover, N.H.

North Adams

To Williamstown

Greenfield

Deerfield

Connecticut River

Sunderlar

M.

Amherst

Hadley

Northampton

S. Had
Mou
Fen

Chester

Easthampton
Mt. Tom

SPRING

Feeding Hills

Southwick

To Weth
& New

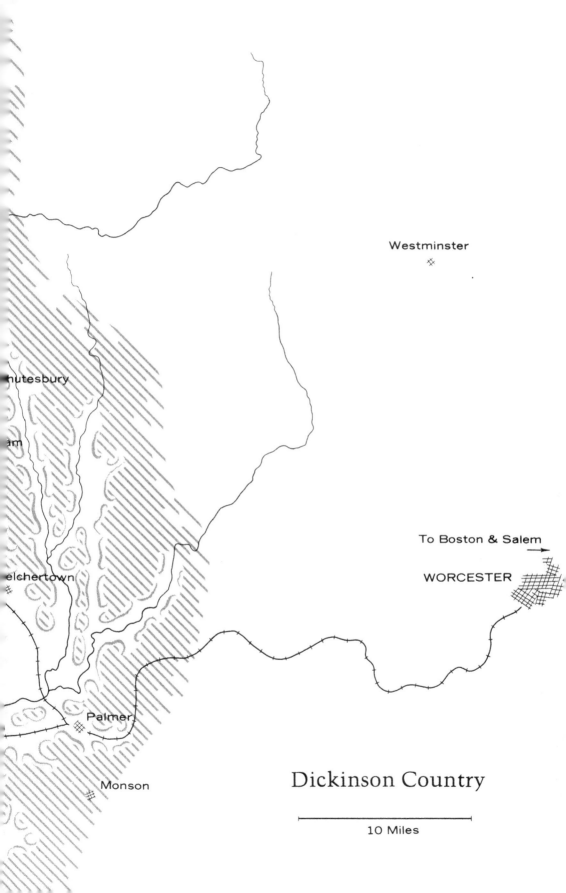

Westminster

To Boston & Salem

WORCESTER

hutesbury

am

elchertown

Palmer

Monson

Dickinson Country

10 Miles

The Dickinson Homestead, built by Samuel Fowler Dickinson, 1814
Lithograph by John Bachelder, 1858

Amherst College in 1848. Woods Cabinet and the College Observatory,
in center; built in 1847 at cost of $9,000

observatory, and "Cabinets" that housed the scientific and natural history displays. The atmosphere was not so theological as to overwhelm her. She surely benefited from the influence of Edward Hitchcock, who opened the eyes of a whole generation to the natural wonders of the Connecticut Valley and in the study of the natural sciences put Amherst far ahead of neighboring Williams, for instance, where Mark Hopkins was still resisting the geologists twenty years later. All this could go on, paradoxically, along with the periodic Revivals that upset Emily so and almost always had their start in the college—with Hitchcock himself, the pious scientist, in the forefront.

There was much of the revival spirit, certainly, in the founding of the college. Historians speak often of the crusading spirit of the founders. Rufus Graves, with Squire Fowler one of the two most prominent, was thought by his neighbors to be "beside himself." Fowler himself had apparently come a long way from the intellectual young Fourth of July orator, full of Reason and Nature and Scientific Inquiry. Hitchcock, who knew him well, later described him as "one of the most industrious and persevering men that I ever saw. . . . a man of very decided religious principles, and when once satisfied that he was in the path of duty, his face was as a flint, and he reminded one of the early Puritans." The cause to which he quite literally gave his life was a holy one, "urged by the command of our divine Saviour to preach the gospel to every creature."

There is a certain discrepancy in the early accounts of Squire Fowler's activities in the crusade, revealing a paradox in his character true of subsequent Dickinsons. On the one hand, he is the practical, judicious one, the "head" that guided Colonel Graves's impulsive "hand." As Hitchcock wrote: "Col. Graves was ardent and impulsive, and thought to be visionary, so that it needed the cooler and more practical judgment of Mr. Dickinson to prevent extravagance in opinion and give confidence to the public." Again, when the question of the location of the new college was being debated at a convention of delegates from thirty-seven Massachusetts towns, it was Dickinson's speech that won the day for Amherst. Tyler, the Amherst historian, called it "one of the most powerful and telling speeches which were made on this occasion." On the other hand, once the project was launched, his ardor was not only impractical but, for himself, ruinous. Tyler's *History,* which, published in 1873, was certainly available to Emily, describes her grandfather's sacrificial efforts. No modern summary covers the whole episode so movingly (the passage begins with a quotation from one of the participants) :

"A few will still remember how a few ministers came together often for prayer and consultation as to how the object could be accomplished. Nearly a whole week sometimes, would be thus spent. When it was decided to go forward and there were funds enough collected to begin the foundations of the first building, and the corner-stone was laid, the effort was only begun. As the work proceeded and they had used up all their available means, then he [Mr. Dickinson] would pledge his private property to the bank to obtain money that the work might go on. And when there was no money to pay for the teams to draw the brick or men to drive them, his own horses were sent for days and weeks till in one season two or three of them fell by the wayside. Sometimes his own laborers were sent to drive his horses, and in an emergency he went himself, rather than that the work should cease." At the same time, he boarded more or less of the workmen, and sometimes paid their wages out of his own pocket, while his wife and daughters toiled to board them. With all the zeal and efforts of numerous friends and benefactors, the work would often have stopped, had he not pledged his property till the money could be raised. His own means at last began to fail. His business which was so large as to require all his time and care, suffered from his devotion to the public. He became embarrassed and at length actually poor. And in his poverty he had the additional grief of feeling that his services were forgotten, like the poor wise man in the proverb who "by his wisdom delivered the city, yet no man remembered that same poor man."

Apparently the failure came on gradually and was more than merely financial. Local records show curious ups and downs in Squire Fowler's last years in Amherst. Only five years before he sold the Homestead and left town, he was elected Representative from Amherst to the Massachusetts General Court; and that same year (1828) he was "a prominent candidate" for the vacant office of Representative to Congress. He was not elected; but the *Hampshire Gazette* in a later tribute (November 7, 1838) said of his candidacy: "His native talents, his legal knowledge, his business habits, and his long experience in both branches of our State Legislature, would on the floor of Congress, have done honor to the district and the Commonwealth." And yet, also in 1828, there appeared in the *New-England Inquirer* (June 26) a curious proposal—curious, that is, for a man with a large and demanding law practice (if such it was), an active political life, and a consuming interest in the struggling young college:

> The subscriber proposes to open, at Amherst in the County of Hampshire, Massachusetts, a School for Instruction in the science and practice of the Law. . . . This Prospectus is issued *with extreme diffidence;* in as much as it promises only the efforts of *an humble individual* . . . Samuel F. Dickinson, Counsellor in the Supreme Judicial Court.

Diffidence and humility were hardly Dickinson traits—the italics are in the original—and do not square with the descriptions we have of Squire Fowler, the leader in community affairs.[10] A few weeks later (July 17), a sympathetic editorial in the *Inquirer* said perhaps more than it meant to say about the project and its initiator:

---

10. Professor West (*Dartmouth Alumni Magazine,* p. 62) quotes an unidentified source describing him at the time as

a tall, thin man, plain in his dress and appearance, of prodigious bodily and mental activity and energy, a famous walker, a ferocious worker, a born leader, a man of ideas and principles, of rare public spirit, strong religious faith and zeal, whose whole life was one of self-denial and self-sacrifice in the public service for education and religion, for the glory of God and the good of his fellow men.

We heartily wish [Samuel F. Dickinson] success in his undertaking. Mr. Dickinson has for some years been so unfortunately harrassed with cares and anxieties, that his attention has been considerably diverted from the business of his profession.

And in August the *Inquirer* again welcomed the project as a sign that Mr. Dickinson was about to return to his profession. Another heartening sign was a speech he gave before the Hampshire, Hampden and Franklin Agricultural Society in 1831, published that year in Northampton. He talked about education, his favorite theme, and even (an aspect not irrelevant to our purpose) about female education, of which he was very much in favor:

A good husbandman will also *educate well his daughters*. I distinguish the education of daughters from that of sons; because, Nature has designed them to occupy places, in family, and in society, altogether dissimilar.

Daughters should be *well instructed,* in the useful sciences; comprising a *good* English education: including a thorough knowledge of our own language, geography, history, mathematics and natural philosophy. The female mind, so sensitive, so susceptible of improvement, should not be neglected. . . . God hath designed nothing in vain.

Apparently, this was his swan song. Nothing permanent came of the law-school idea, and we hear no more of him as a public figure. By 1832 the college was in such serious financial straits that he saw the major work of his life threatened.

Shortly after this, and perhaps because of it, the low point of Fowler's career in Amherst was reached: the selling of the Homestead in March 1833. Next month, he left Amherst to take what must have seemed like an inferior position at Lane Theological Seminary in Cincinnati—the direction of the manual labor required of the students as part of the school's curriculum. (The job may have come to him through his Amherst associations with the Reverend Lyman Beecher, who had become Lane's first president in 1832.) His spirits steadily declined in the Western setting. Neither he nor his family adjusted well to the new environment. After three years he left Lane to become treasurer and supervisor of buildings in Western Reserve College in Hudson, Ohio, then referred to as in "the remote Ohio wilderness." Here his decline was rapid and complete. "His experience," writes a modern historian of Western Reserve, "was insufficient for the position and his health was poor. He died in the second year of service leaving his accounts in a sorry mess."

One is tempted to differ from this explanation of his failure. His experience was surely more than adequate. What he had suffered, apparently, was a general breakdown, the result of a gradual decline that had begun years earlier when he had overreached himself in his efforts for the college. Leaving Amherst had seemed like an exile. In May 1835 his daughter Catherine wrote from Cincinnati to her brother Edward in Amherst that their father's "spirits are completely broken down & probably will never rise again." The family letters following his death speak repeatedly of his last years as ones of "constant trouble," "gloomy apprehensions for the future," "anxiety & care & disappointment." Catherine wrote in April 1838 (a few days after he died) that "it seems as if his depression of spirits caused his sickness which terminated his life." This is hardly the same man whom President Hitchcock recalled as "one of the most industrious and persevering men that I ever saw," the man with the face of flint.[11]

The striking difference between Squire Fowler the Amherst leader and the miserable failure in the Midwest raises questions: Was his breakdown an isolated phenomenon or an aspect of the Dickinson heritage relevant to the next two generations? It is tempting to see in this experience—the intense dedication, the overreaching, the sense of exile, the collapse—a pattern that makes more understandable what seem on the surface to be the strange ways of the Dickinsons with whom we are directly concerned (Emily's, of course, being the "strangest" of all). We may well pause to examine a few of the clues embedded in this bit of family history.

To take one of the more obvious matters first, a problem around which much legend has accumulated and of especial relevance to Emily as recluse. If nothing else, Squire Fowler's sojourn in the West revealed a trait that became more extreme with each generation: home-centeredness. No Dickinson, at least in this branch of the family, flourished outside beloved Amherst. They did not transplant easily. They avoided travel whenever possible and were miserable when it was unavoidable. When daughter Catherine returned in 1835 from two years with her parents in Ohio, she wrote to them about her feelings in seeing Amherst again— "Everything looks beautifully here"—and included two sentences that might have been written by Emily herself: "I never saw any place half so beautiful as our own home. . . . I feel perfectly indifferent about going anywhere or seeing anybody." Once, to be sure, in the vigor of his young manhood, Emily's father Edward wrote his new wife from faraway New York that "I like travelling," and urged her on another occasion to see all

---

11. Nor does it sound like the man described in the memorial by his "loving daughter" (*Reunion,* p. 174):

He allowed himself but four hours of sleep, studying and reading till midnight, and rising at four o'clock he often walked to Pelham or some other town before breakfast. Going to court at Northampton, he would catch up his green bag and walk the whole seven miles. *"I cannot wait to ride,"* he would say to those who suggested that many horses in his stable would be idle, and outwalked the stage, with its four-in-hand, to Northampton. Bread, cheese and coffee, apples and old cider before breakfast were almost his sole diet. No man could outwork him, mentally or physically. He was ill but once in many years, till his last sickness of one week.

. . . I never saw him laugh but once, yet he was always cheerful and genial; always had the right word in the right place for every one, and could make himself agreeable to all classes of men, showing his appreciation of every effort.

the sights of the city (this time Boston) when she came. But from New York he added, "but *home* has charms for me, which I do not find abroad"; and the gist of his later letters from Boston or New York or Washington (he seldom got farther) is his longing for home. Also, there was a moment, at the time of his marriage, when Emily's brother Austin considered moving to Chicago, and another, only a few years before his death, when he thought of taking a job and starting a new life in Omaha. But the centripetal force was too strong. He never made the move and seldom traveled except on business. He took only one extended tour for pleasure (to the Midwest and South), with predictable results—he hated it.

This family peculiarity is all the more significant when viewed in the perspective of the times. One of mid-century America's greatest enthusiasms, it must be remembered, was the movement west and south. Even Amherst was on the move. "The world is full of people travelling *everywhere*," Emily wrote Austin in 1851. Lyman Beecher's move to Lane Seminary may have had something of the missionary motive in it, and (it has been suggested by those who would take the sting out of it) so might Squire Fowler's. Only a few years later Horace Greeley was to invite all young Americans to "go West and grow up with the country." Amherst men were investing in land in Michigan and Maine. In the other direction, European travel was becoming increasingly easy and fashionable. The Dickinsons, especially in Emily's generation, had many friends who traveled: Samuel Bowles of Springfield; Joseph Lyman, who left New England in 1850 to start his career in New Orleans, of which he wrote detailed accounts to the Dickinsons; Kate Scott Anthon, a frequent visitor in Austin's home and Emily's friend, who spent some eight of the years between 1864 and 1884 in prolonged travel in Europe and Great Britain; the cosmopolitan Thomas Wentworth Higginson; and others. Emily's girlhood friend, Abby Wood, married Daniel Bliss, a missionary, and moved to Beirut. Emily was very conscious of her friends in distant places, but her interest in travel remained utterly vicarious. In this she was true to family type.

Seen against this background, Emily's home-centeredness takes on less the aspect of some deep neurotic fear or psychological compulsion than of a family tendency carried to an extreme. Many times she was explicit on the subject. In 1851, when she went to Boston with sister Vinnie, they came back (she wrote Austin) "rich in disdain for Bostonians and Boston, and a coffer fuller of *scorn, pity, commisseration,* a miser hardly had." On her infrequent sojourns away from home, a recurrent theme of her letters is the superiority of Amherst to wherever she was. In Washington in 1855, she found that "all is jostle, here – scramble and confusion." Cambridge in 1864 was a "Wilderness," a "Jail"; she longed "to see the Grass, and hear the Wind blow the wide way in the Orchard." In 1870 Higginson asked her if she ever felt the need of something more than Amherst could offer her: "I never thought of conceiving that I could ever have the slightest approach to such a want in all future time," she answered. "I don't care for roving," she told him later; and again: "I do not go away, but the Grounds are ample – almost travel – ." Thoreau might have suggested some of this to her, he who traveled much in Concord—only, she went him one step farther: "To shut our eyes is Travel. The Seasons understand this." Here, too, may have been some of Emerson's self-reliance— and the Emerson who, home from a grueling trip to Europe, sighed with relief: "Back to myself." But mostly (although it is far from explaining her almost complete seclusion in the later years) in this most characteristic of family traits she was a Dickinson of the Dickinsons.

Another Dickinson tendency that certainly increased with the generations was the nervous instability (or whatever name medical science might give it) apparent in the nature of Squire Fowler's decline and collapse. He was the first complicated Dickinson—at least, the first whose complexities are a matter of record. Hitchcock's image of the face of flint missed some somber truth. Behind the bold front that both the succeeding male Dickinsons in Emily's family presented to the world were disquieting realities. Emily understood them well. She worried about her father's sad and lonely life. She worried about Austin, the most troubled of all, full of doubts, sensitivities, emotional conflicts, and (later) frustrations and wrecked hopes. Life was not easy for any of the Dickinsons, except perhaps Lavinia, though even she had a love affair that ended sadly, a temperament that was never placid, and eccentricities that in the end became extreme. How much of all this is foreshadowed in Squire Fowler's collapse no one can say, but there is something prophetic in the temperament that knew such extremes of enthusiasm and depression and that demonstrated for all to come that there was a Dickinson breaking point.

Compared with the rest of her family, Emily was one of the best composed of all, perhaps because she understood the problem better than any of them and through the discipline of her writing brought it under tolerable control. Nevertheless, the shifts in mood and tone in her poems, from despair to ecstasy, from a sense of the mastery of life to complete helplessness; the strange defenses that she eventually threw up to guard her privacy—the "fiery mist," as Higginson put it, with which she enshrouded herself; the behavior that even the most charitable could hardly call normal—all these signified, surely, an inner life that (to put it in the mildest terms) gave her a great deal of trouble. In this, too, she was very much a Dickinson.

The question is: How much did Emily know or think about her grandfather? (He died when she was seven.) The reference to the patriarchal Bible may tell much or little. There seems to have been a general reticence in the family about him, perhaps in itself a symptom. There are several bits of evidence. A dream that she recounted in a letter to Austin when she was sixteen may indicate how close to the family Squire Fowler's failure still was during her girlhood. She dreamed that her father had failed and that "our rye field . . . was mortgaged to Seth Nims" (the local postmaster and a political opponent of her father's). There is just a touch of panic in the passage; she seems to have wanted reassurance from Austin that all was well. The Dickinson family had once known failure and might know it again. Perhaps a hint of her grandfather's sacrificial career may be seen in her poems about noble failure and martyrdom, the saints of the earth who gave all for a cause.[12] But, to repeat, the surest evidence that Emily knew something about her grandfather is that Austin did. His 1889 memorial has the warmth of a family tradition:

> Samuel Fowler Dickinson; familiarly called Esq. Fowler; who stood in the forefront in the Amherst of his generation; a fine scholar; a lawyer of distinction and wide practice; a man of rare public spirit, the highest moral purpose, unflagging zeal; the leader in every local enterprise; holding many offices of trust, a dozen years and more a member of the Massachusetts Legislature, in both houses; of the most earnest and active religious faith and life, a deacon at twenty and for forty years thereafter, one of the leading founders of the college, sacrificing for it his property, time and professional opportunities, in the idea of getting the Gospel sooner to the ends of the earth.

Finally, of course, the work of Squire Fowler's hands was constantly around Emily from infancy on. *"Si monumentum requiris,"* wrote his "loving daughter" in her memorial, *"circumspice."* There was not only Amherst College but the house she was born in and (except for her years in the house on Pleasant Street, from 1840 to 1855) lived in all her life. Perhaps it was the sadness of his decline and the embarrassment of his financial failure that explained the family reticence, and hers.

This reticence, as I have suggested, seems to have been symptomatic. In Emily's family it extended to all things personal, certainly to the relations between parents and children. Indeed, it may have been at the heart of the family problem, which in turn may have been at the heart of the latter-day Puritan problem, when human nature, failing to meet the rigorous demands of the pristine discipline, began to hide its inadequacies behind smooth surfaces. Hence the much-maligned hypocrisy, the double lives, that have become almost synonymous with the tradition in its decline. In their eulogies of Samuel Fowler, neither his daughter Elisabeth nor Austin told the whole sad truth. Austin's father seems never to have talked freely with his children, and Austin in his maturity led one of the most grueling of double lives, all for the sake of appearances. No Dickinson, after Fowler, succeeded in bringing public and private life harmoniously together. Emily gave up the effort, developed a reticence of her own,

12. Such poems, for instance, as "Through the strait pass of suffering – / The Martyrs – even – trod" (#792, about 1863); "Each Life Converges to some Centre" (#680, about 1863); the theme of Moses denied Canaan (#597, about 1862, and #1201, about 1871) or the dying soldier in "Success is counted sweetest" (#67, about 1859), victory denied.

and resigned from public life. She dealt with the problem directly and without compromise.

In the light of such an analysis, there is something ironic about the following episode. The *Amherst Record* for August 30, 1871, recorded what a correspondent described as a "Beautiful Incident":

> In my walks about this beautiful town on the morning of the late Jubilee of Amherst College, I was attracted to the Cemetery. There I observed a Family gathering about the grave of the Hon. S. F. Dickinson. . . . All the daughters from their city homes with their husbands and children, and our friend Hon. E. Dickinson, were there. They came loaded with flowers.

This touching scene shows, among other things, the extent to which Squire Fowler, once a source of embarrassment to his children, was now revered by them. Speaking of the Squire's idealism that "outran his capacity to earn money," Jay Leyda says that it made him "a nobler figure to history than to those who lived beside him."[13] Yet here they were at his grave, thirty-three years after his death—with Edward, who had had to pay his debts and redeem the name of the family law practice, chief among the mourners. Perhaps there was a hint of expiation in this last gathering; there had been a general feeling in the family, following his death, that they had treated him shabbily in his declining years and had allowed him to die homeless. At any rate, here they were, with flowers.[14]

13. Apparently his difficulty lay not so much in earning money as in keeping it. He was overly generous—and not only to the college. His daughter writes:

> His large-heartedness and desire to help those in need sometimes overtaxed his judgment, and his name was often endorsed on notes to a large amount, which he was obliged to furnish the money for, while several men thus helped lived in affluence on his bounty, without recognizing the source.

She cites one final example of his civic-mindedness, a cause later to be espoused by his grandson Austin to the greater good of Amherst for generations to come: "His public spirit was shown in planting trees by the highway. When asked what benefit this would be to him, he would reply, 'Somebody will be benefited if not I'" (*Reunion*, pp. 172–74).

14. An even greater tribute came twelve years later at the Dickinson family reunion in Amherst in August 1883. Some five hundred persons attended, representing branches of the family from all over the country. This was the occasion of Elisabeth's verse history—in fifty-seven quatrains, with an introduction of forty-six lines in tetrameter couplets. It was printed in full in the Boston and Worcester papers. Samuel Fowler is the first Dickinson singled out for individual attention. After thirty-two stanzas in general praise of Dickinson qualities and achievements, he carries the poem for a full sixteen. A few samples will suffice:

> Of *Samuel Fowler*, Nathan's son,
> A townsman here, in Amherst born;
> We speak, of such as we've been told,
> And hope the venture not too bold.
>
> From Father, and from Mother, too,
> The love of knowledge straight he drew;

The only other comment about the scene is in the form of a question not hard to answer: Where was Emily?

So, youthful wish was gratified,
As with a College class he vied.

Old "Dartmouth" gave him his degree,
And second in his class was he;
To teaching, after, then he turned,
But for the *Law* his spirit yearned. . . .

Then follows the account of the founding of Amherst College and his sacrificial efforts:

His time, his infl'ence, and his prayers,
Despite his many worldly cares,
And all his gen'rous wealth, he gave
This College enterprise to save.

He sleeps, beneath the churchyard green,
Which from this place is plainly seen;
The words upon his marble plain –
"A man though dead, shall live again."

The only other Dickinson in Emily's branch of the family to be immortalized by Elisabeth's muse is *"Edward,* Samuel's eldest son, / An *honest Lawyer,* like his sire":

The College gave him, it appears,
Of College money – guardian care:
And not one cent in forty years,
But had its record full and fair.

Emily's letters of the period say nothing about the family reunion.

4

Edward Dickinson

Tradition has it that Emily Dickinson's home was dominated by her father. Of recent years the picture has been getting darker as scholars have been opening up possibilities in the drama of the family that all but villainize Edward Dickinson and make him accountable for much of what is generally thought of as the tragedy of his daughter's life. It is from such studies—based, to be sure, on much in the record that gives them plausibility—that Edward emerges as a Mr. Barrett of Wimpole Street and Emily as the imposed-upon daughter, frustrated and forlorn. Edward had his dark side and was something of a mystery to his closest friends—even, at times, to Emily herself. No one close to him could escape completely the influence of his powerful personality. The possibilities must remain open. But the probabilities, taking the evidence all in all, are not so melodramatic. Like Melville's Ahab, he "had his humanities."[1]

Edward Dickinson (1803–1874) was, first of all, an ambitious and hardworking man and, from his early thirties, a public figure. From the evidence especially of his early letters, those written before his marriage in 1828, he seems to have started out, at least, less the dour Puritan of tradition than a typical success-oriented, work-oriented citizen of expansionist America and, in his emphasis on Reason, or what he called "rational happiness," and on the amelioration of the species through good works and the improvement of social institutions, a child of the Enlightenment not unlike his father in *his* younger days.

From what survives of his early correspondence—a few letters from his college classmates but mostly about seventy courtship letters to Emily

---

1. Clark Griffith, *The Long Shadow,* and John Cody, *After Great Pain,* dwell, often persuasively, on the dark side of Edward Dickinson's nature and its effect on Emily. We will never, of course, know the whole truth. Any estimate of the father-daughter relationship must be speculative. My own feeling is that she held a safe lead most of the way—until he died.

Edward Dickinson, dated variously 1853, 1860, 1874

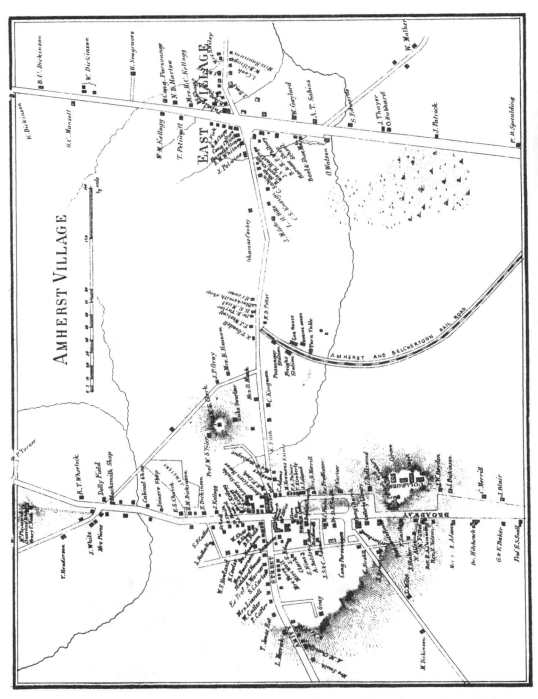

From "A Topographical Map of Hampshire County, Massachusetts," 1856. The Homestead, just to left of center, was owned by Deacon Mack when the map was drawn. The Edward Dickinsons were on North Pleasant Street, upper left

Norcross in Monson—the outlines of his character emerge sharp and clear, both as he quite frankly analyzes himself for Emily's benefit and from what can be inferred, at least, from the descriptions of his classmates. After schooling in Amherst Academy (which was to become a nursery of Dickinsons) and a year in Amherst College, he entered the class of 1823 at Yale. He seems to have been something of a figure. "To my Friend the Great Dickinson," begins a letter from a certain A. Thompson, Jr., written on June 24, 1820. The letters from his Yale friends—Osmyn Baker, George Ashmun, Talcott Bates—are breezy, cheerful, full of young ambition and high-flown rhetoric. "The Great Dickinson" becomes "Dick" and apparently a cherished member of a lively group. A letter from Baker (December 21, 1821), written perhaps during Edward's first Christmas vacation from Yale when he had to work off some academic requirements, sets the tone:

> How pass the heavy hours at the "Hill of Science?" Have you become reconciled to your situation or do you still savour [?] of better days? Does imagination travel back to Yale and dwell upon the scenes of friendship and good cheer which many a fireside within her walls, exhibit these long, cold evenings, and where many of your old friends tell stories of sophomore year and talk of Dick?

If many years later Higginson saw Edward Dickinson as "thin dry & speechless," he was anything but that to his friends at Yale.[2] But he had

2. Aside from such glimpses as this from Baker, the letters tell little about Edward's life at Yale, but we know that it resulted in a lifelong loyalty. (He attended his thirtieth reunion with his wife. *YH* I, 280; July 28 ?, 1853.) We can get a notion of its sources in some verses Edward contributed to a classbook, senior year. Apparently it was a custom to pass around among the seniors during the spring, when sentiment was running high, blank books, or albums, with a page reserved for each senior to record a thought or a bit of verse, his own or a quotation. Three such exist for the class of 1823. While most of his classmates quoted Burns or Shakespeare or Thomson, Edward Dickinson inscribed what appear to be his own compositions, even though each one is surrounded by quotation marks. Each is written in Edward's hand, dated, and signed.

> "With long farewell we leave the classic grove,
> Where science and the tuneful sisters rove,
> Abroad we wander, anxious to explore
> Antiquities of nations, now no more,
> To penetrate each distant realm unknown,
> And range excursive o'er the untravelled zone."

Yale College	Edward Dickinson
March 1st, 1823	Amherst, Mass.

> "One fatal remembrance – one sorrow that throws,
> Its bleak shade alike o'er our joys and our woes,
> To which life nothing darker nor brighter can bring,
> For which joy hath no balm – and affliction no sting."

Yale College	Edward Dickinson
March 21, 1823	Amherst, Mass.

moods. "Don't let your natural liveliness and universal good nature," wrote Baker about Edward's trouble with a certain tutor at Yale, "[receive] a tinge of sourness & discontent which will remain." The year after graduation, the moods deepened. Ashmun put his finger on at least one of the reasons in a lighthearted letter of December 23, 1823. He wrote enviously of the achievements of their classmates—two were already married, one had shot a man in a duel near New York, another had addressed a celebration at Plymouth Rock:

> Dick can't we do something to signalize ourselves – I hate to be left so much in the rear. I wish you would take the subject into consideration & when you write again permit me to profit by your ideas on it.

Four months later, Baker, answering a gloomy letter from Edward, took the matter seriously. Edward was lonely, unhappy, and depressed over the meager opportunities in little Amherst:

> I know well enough what a blackness of darkness that is which envelopes a young man in your situation. . . . "Act well your part," says Pope. . . . I don't see why you have not reason to go on your way rejoicing. Man is great only by comparison – and therefore I think it perfectly clear that you will not find it difficult to become and that shortly the greatest lawyer in A———t and that step being attained you will have nothing to do but step up another.

Talcott Bates echoed the refrain—perhaps as much a commonplace in the correspondence of young Americans of the era as sentimental effusion was in the letters of young ladies. But clearly in this instance Bates confirms a major insight into a fact of Edward's nature: ambition.

> "When time who steals our years away,
> Shall steal our pleasures, too,
> The memory of the past will stay,
> And half our joys renew.
>
> Then talk no more of future gloom,
> Our joys shall always last,
> And Hope shall brighten days to come
> And Memory gild the past." Farewell!
>
> Yale College   Edward Dickinson
> April 27, 1823   Amherst, Mass.

These may be cullings from the fugitive verse of the day; but the first has something of the genuine academic atmosphere and a young man's relish for it. Incidentally, Bingham, *Home,* p. 488, is mistaken in saying that Edward "was graduated as valedictorian of the class." The Order of Exercises for the 1823 Commencement reads: "Oration, 'On moral feeling,' with the Valedictory Address: By George Jones, *York, Pa.*" L III, 937, also thrusts this honor upon him by having him graduated "at the head of his class."

I suppose [he wrote] that you are applying yourself to your studies most intensely and that the "welkin" ere long will resound with your praise. Well, be it so.

> "The fault, dear Brutus, is not in our stars,
> But in *ourselves,* if we are underlings."

Edward did not intend to be an underling. His letters to Emily Norcross, which begin on February 8, 1826, shortly after he had met her in Monson, make that clear. "My life," he wrote in the very letter in which he proposed marriage, "must be a life of business, of labor and application to the study of my profession." He talked about the profession of the Law in terms of the most enlightened humanism, as it may "enlarge & liberate & ennoble the mind," pry into "the causes of things – the origin and reasons for the changes which have taken place in Laws, manners, & customs," and lead the practitioner to "familiarity with the human character – acquaintance with science & literature. . . ." Although later, as the expenses of a growing family mounted, he complained bitterly of financial restrictions, he was no mere fortune hunter. Always he held up to Emily Norcross his high ideal for them both, a life in which their own happiness would be sanctioned only by their promoting "as far as in our power, the melioration of the condition of all about us."

He was an idealist like his father but better fitted for the battle of life, a metaphor he himself once used to describe for Miss Norcross's edification his thrill of victory in winning the acquittal of an Amherst student charged with drunkenness and burglary. He rejoiced "in having assisted in rescuing a young man of promise from the inevitable destruction which must have followed a conviction"; but what pleased him even more was the satisfaction of the full and successful use of his powers:

Let me be obliged to accomplish some important and difficult task, and I enjoy myself.

> "Man was made for action
> Action's his sphere, & for that sphere designed
> Eternal pleasures open on his mind."

An active life is my delight – I like the battle of business – tho' [and here he gives a design for living several times reiterated in subsequent letters] the retirement of study is also pleasant – but could I choose for myself I would confine myself to study one third of the time – spend a reasonable portion *in the bosom of my family* – and the residue in the most arduous and responsible duties of professional life.

(The italics are his.) Two months before the wedding, he came out even more emphatically:

Let us prepare for a life of rational happiness. I do not expect, neither do I desire a life of *pleasure,* as some call it – I anticipate pleasure from engaging with my whole soul in my business . . . and with my dearest friend. . . . May we be happy, useful & successful.

[47

At the very least, he seems never to have foreseen the presence of a poet in the family.

The lines of his character and of his proposed way of life come out not only clear but hard. We ask where in such a scheme a poet could possibly fit. But other phases of his character and interests appear in the letters and are somewhat more reassuring. He was deeply interested in education, especially for females. "Females, also," he wrote, as if discovering a great truth, "have a sphere of action, which, tho' different entirely in its kind from that of the other sex, is no less important." He lectured Emily Norcross on the subject many times and propounded his theories with the urgency of a reformer. He was deeply interested in Emily's cultural activities in Monson and sent her books (*The Spectator* in twelve volumes; Jane Porter's *Thaddeus of Warsaw;* a "new novel," *Hope Leslie,* by Catharine Maria Sedgwick, "which I presume you will find interesting – as the characters are drawn in a striking light, and innocence and villainy strongly contrasted"). He wrote her rhapsodically in the heat of many young enthusiasms. In a stirring letter on the Greek struggle for independence, then (the mid-1820s) at its height, he lingered over the ancient glories when Greece was "the dwelling place of beauty & elegance – & the abode of the 'gods & goddesses' – ":

> & in short the very name of Greece fills the mind with the idea of all that is beautiful & elegant – with all that can charm & please & animate – and the imagination delights to revel amid her shady bowers, her groves & caves & grottoes – to wander amid the classic retreats – to view the place where Homer sang – where Plato taught – & the eloquence of Demosthenes charmed & persuaded & convinced & delighted.

A year later (December 19, 1827) he was thrilled by the news of the success of the Powers in establishing the new Greece: "Let all the nations shout 'Hallilujah,'" he exclaimed, and assured Emily that, rather than be a slave, he would fight even against hopeless odds, kill as many of his oppressors as he could, then *"plant a dagger in my own breast."* The deaths of the ex-Presidents Adams and Jefferson on the same day (July 4, 1826) stirred him to similar rhapsodies on the glorious examples of these men, their valor, eloquence, devotion to liberty. Throughout, the letters are punctuated by lyric passages on the beauties of nature—spring in the Connecticut Valley; summer evenings in Amherst ("It is very late. . . . The evenings are now beautiful, and the brilliant moonlight ought not to pass unenjoyed"); and the fury of winter storms, when "the wind whistles and the trees crash." What little there is of religion comes in only in the latter months of the correspondence. Perhaps it was so much taken for granted that it needed no stressing. The piety seems sincere—and conventional: "and let our prayers ascend for each other, morning & evening, that we may individually experience that change which we believe must take place, before we can be rec'd into the abodes of the pure spirits who dwell in the presence of the Eternal!"

One further enthusiasm cannot pass unnoticed, if only for the high irony it contains for us, who a century and a half later can only wonder how a man of such convictions could have been blind to their living embodiment in his own daughter. In a letter of August 3, 1826, he wrote:

I passed Tuesday evening, of this week, in company with Miss Sedgwick, the Authoress of "Redwood" & "New England Tale", at a party at Judge Lyman's. She had an interesting countenance – an appearance of much thought, & rather masculine features. And I feel happy at having an opportunity of seeing a female who had done so much to give our works of taste so pure and delicate a character – and a conscious pride that women of our own country & our own state, too, are emulating not only the females but the men of England & France & Germany & Italy in works of literature – & we are warranted in presuming that, if they had opportunities equal to their talents, they would not be inferior to our own sex in improving the sciences.

To this unexceptionable statement he tied only one moral string:

Tho' I should be sorry to see another Mme. de Stael – especially if any one wished to make a partner of her for life. Different qualities are more desirable in a female who enters into domestic relations – and you have already had my opinions on that subject –

But the problem of another de Staël in his own family was surely not his. His failure was not so much one of conviction as of perception; or his own business and ambition came first. As his daughter Emily was to say later, "Father [is] too busy with his Briefs – to notice what we do." One is moved to remark only that, had Edward Dickinson noticed what his daughter was up to, had he nurtured her as his darling genius or tried to impose his will on her creativity, he might have spoiled her or destroyed her. As it was, she survived—and wrote. Perhaps it was just as well that he was too busy.

Whenever the subject of marriage comes up in the courtship letters, Edward is preeminently the man of reason and forethought. He urged Emily Norcross to view "the subject, as I always have, in a candid and rational light, and as one which ought to be treated with the most perfect plainness and frankness." He urged her to take her time (which she did, somewhat to his annoyance) in answering his proposal, to inquire into his character and prospects, to consult "Judge Howe, Mr. Mills . . . or almost any clergyman in the neighboring towns." Their life together must be one of "industry, frugality, application." The $20,000 failure of a law firm in Waterbury, Connecticut, is "a warning [he wrote] to all young men to be prudent and industrious." "Preserve your health," he urged her several times (although Emily's health seems at that time to have been excellent), and once delivered a little lecture on the whole duty of woman:

Continue in the path of innocence and virtue and fidelity – continue to cultivate those graces which are the charm of your sex and let that sincere desire for that pure and unsullied reputation which are the pride of both sexes incite us to avoid the appearance of evil – and let our conduct be marked by that correctness which shall insure our happiness and may an approving conscience be our reward.

One of the steps in his rational approach to marriage (although it came a little late, only two months before the wedding) was a frank assessment of what he called their "dispositions." In previous letters his personal talk concerned mostly his work and ambitions; here he becomes introspective—he wants Emily to be clear about his virtues and defects, and about her own:

> I will plainly tell you what I think of my own disposition, and what I think of yours. I am naturally quick & ardent in my feelings, easily excited, tho' not so easily provoked – decided in my opinions – determined in accomplishing whatever I undertake – hard to be persuaded that I am wrong when I have once formed my opinion upon reflection – sometimes unyielding and obstinate – rather particular – like to have everything in the right place & done at the right time – have a little personal irritability in my constitution – am rather high-spirited, at times – tho generally moderate – like to have things go pretty smoothly, have business enough to keep me occupied. And now I come to you. I think you are resolute – decided – rather particular – want to see everything go on well – & see everybody happy. I think your disposition to be good – that you are kind – benevolent – patient in trouble – able to endure sickness – that you will deprive yourself of comfort & repose to render a friend more comfortable – and I think, too, that your feelings are somewhat easily excited, & that your vivacity might, in case of emergency, approach to spirit – Is this a correct picture? Of the many good qualities which I think you to possess, it may not be proper here to speak. I do not flatter, My Dear, when I say that I find in you just what I have long wished to find a lady to possess.

His analysis of his "dearest friend" will concern us later. She must have been pleased. As to himself, the "quick & ardent" feelings may come as a surprise. Actually, they should not, even though in later years Edward gave a very different impression to the world. His daughters were to report certain mild domestic explosions; but he was eminently the man of conviction, not feeling. As for the rest of his self-analysis, it was all too prophetic. At twenty-five he set his course, and he never deviated. Again, we cannot help looking to the future with foreboding. It was just as well that at a certain point his daughter Emily geared her life, not to happiness, but to a purpose and meaning of her own.

Only a few times in the letters does he talk tenderly, as on those moonlit nights and, in gentler mood than usual, when he contemplates coming home "after the business of the day is finished" to share confidences with "my friend" (twice he called them "secrets"). His rhetoric is always formal and restrained—the very opposite of the youthful letters of the next Dickinson generation—and we can only hope that Emily Norcross saw in it depths of feeling not apparent to us. Here is a typical valediction:

> And now, My Dear Emily, I must leave you, let me join with you in the wish that we could press the parting hand, & give the parting ———s, but while that is denied, let me hope that ere long we shall enjoy each other's society constantly, & experience the true happiness which kindred spirits (are not ours such?) are fitted to produce.

Actually, there is more feeling in later letters when he scolds her for refusing his many invitations to visit Amherst; for her failure to write—to his daily letters she answers but once a month; and finally when he all but loses patience over their delayed wedding plans: "I have already waited a year longer than I ever intended to wait." But he respected her deliberateness, insisting again and again that her happiness came first. He threw himself enthusiastically into the work of preparing their first home. He wanted to have everything right. He arranged for the carpenters, the painters, the cleaners, and oversaw every detail—always, be it said, asking for Emily's opinion on colors and arrangements. He may not have been a passionate lover, but he was persistent, considerate, and always practical. He wrote her a special note to say that the new stove drew beautifully.

This is the young man, who, after deciding against several opportunities to practice elsewhere, hung out his shingle in Amherst on September 27, 1826, started business that very afternoon, and went straight for the top, as Osmyn Baker predicted. The thrill of success often enlivens the early letters, and his marriage on May 6, 1828, provided further purpose and drive. Although he never said as much, either in the early letters or later, a part of that purpose may have been the restoration of the family name after his father's collapse. Edward was the eldest son and the only one of the children who stayed in Amherst.[3] At any rate, he soon estab-

---

3. After Squire Fowler's failure and the breakup of the family in 1833, the children scattered widely. William, the next eldest son, had left for Boston several years earlier. In 1829 he settled in Worcester, Massachusetts, where he became a successful industrialist and later insurance executive and director of companies. He died in 1887. Samuel Fowler, Jr., went to New York and then entered business in Savannah, Georgia. Timothy also went south; he died in Griffin, Georgia, in 1852. Frederick stayed with his brother Edward's family until he graduated from Amherst College in 1837, when he went west to join his parents in Ohio. Lucretia, the eldest daughter, married Asa Bullard (Amherst '28) and settled in Cambridge, Massachusetts. Mary married Mark Haskell Newman (Bowdoin '25) in 1828. They lived in New York City, where Newman founded a publishing house. Catherine married Joseph A. Sweetser in 1835, who had moved to New York City from Amherst in 1833. Elisabeth, the youngest child, lived variously in Amherst and Worcester, where she kept house for her brother William when his wife died in 1851. In 1866 she married Augustus N. Currier of Worcester. Together, these aunts and uncles presented ED with thirty-two cousins. Except for Edward, William was the most successful of Fowler's sons, kept on close terms with Edward, and with him bore the brunt of their father's failure. Of the daughters, Elisabeth, the family bard, was the most striking—"a large, tall

lished himself firmly and successfully in the areas of his father's main concern.

It is well first to follow, if only in outline, his long career of service to the town, the college, and the state. His career shows no such dramatic rise and fall as his father's. The year his father left for the Midwest, he became Moderator of the Town Meeting, a post to which he was elected, off and on, for the next sixteen years. In 1835 he undertook the work for the college his father had had to abandon and served it as treasurer for thirty-seven years. No accounts of *his,* it should be said, were ever "in a mess." Tyler reports:

> The best financier in the Corporation has publicly announced, as the result of careful examination for many successive years, that, as Treasurer of Amherst College, he has never lost a dollar. And one of the sharpest and shrewdest of the Board of Overseers declares that after the most prolonged and patient scrutiny of his books and accounts, only a single error of less than a hundred dollars could be detected, and that error was *against* himself.

He was zealous in good causes, even fanatically so. His passion for bringing the railroad to Amherst became almost as much of a cause with him as the college had been to his father. But he was better balanced and kept his family, his fortune, and his position in Amherst intact. Tyler, speaking from firsthand observation, wrote of his "unbending firmness of purpose and his great freedom and boldness of speech under excitement." Of all the brothers, Edward was most like his father, and here is perhaps the surest link between Squire Fowler's intellectual, literary turn and Emily's. At any rate, there can be no doubt that these qualities of firmness and dedication, and his power as a speaker, brought Edward Dickinson to a position of prominence, especially when his achievements in state and national politics are added to all he did for the town and college of Amherst, unapproached by any Dickinson and hardly equalled by any Amherst figure of his generation.

Edward's first major recognition outside Amherst came when he was elected Representative to the General Court of Massachusetts in 1838. He was twice elected State Senator (1842 and 1843), became president of the newly formed Henry Clay Club in Amherst in 1844, and in the mid-1840s was a member of the Governor's executive council and major in the militia. In 1852 he was delegate to the National Whig Convention in Baltimore and (the peak of his political career) was elected later that year to the Congress of the United States as Representative from the Tenth Massachusetts District. In 1854 he was admitted to practice before the Supreme Court. He was considered as a possible candidate for governor of

---

woman, rather distinguished in appearance"—and determined: "the only male relative," as ED described her, "on the female side." Many days after one of her visits, ED wrote, "its flavor of court-martial still sets my spirit tingling" (*L* II, 561; to Mrs. Holland, August 1876). (*Home,* pp. 486–87 and passim, is the best single source of information on the relatives.)

Massachusetts in 1859 and was offered the opportunity to run for lieu-tenant governor in 1861, which he refused. He received an LL.D. from Amherst College in 1863 (much, so it is recorded, to his surprise); and in 1873 (the year before he died) he was for the second time elected to the General Court of Massachusetts.

On the local scene, he became a commanding figure, not only as the leading lawyer in Amherst, a pillar of the church and a trusted town father, but as the close and valued associate of three presidents of Amherst College. He was the man of the hour on many occasions requiring more than sober judgment and learned counsel. Of a bad fire in the village in July 1851, which threatened a whole street, Emily wrote to Austin (with a touch of her usual satire at her father's expense):

> Father and Mr. Frink took charge of the fire, or rather of the *water,* since fire *usually* takes care of *itself.* The men all worked like heroes, and after the fire was out Father gave commands to have them march to Howe's [Hotel] where an entertainment was provided for them – after the whole was over, they gave "three cheers for Edward Dickinson, and three more for the In-surance Company"!

Of similar nature is the famous anecdote of his ringing the church bell to summon the town to witness an unusually fine display of northern lights. He was an inveterate speaker on patriotic holidays, at dedications and the laying of cornerstones. His speeches were variously described as "bold," "eloquent," "spirited."[4] For all his alleged austerity and dourness, he and

4. These are comments from the local scene. For samples of Edward Dickinson's oratory as a Congressman, see *Home,* Appendix IV, where his arguments against the civilian management of the national armories, a matter which concerned the House of Representatives during the session of 1854, are printed in full. He was one of the two members of the committee on the problem who dissented from the majority report. His hour-long speech was described as "blunt, stubborn, and forthright" (*Home,* p. 532). He was moved at one point to a flight of oratory (p. 544) that re-calls the heroics of the youthful Samuel Fowler Dickinson's Fourth of July oration.

It is said, too, that the military system discourages enterprise, paralyzes inven-tive genius, is an insult to the mechanics of the country, and weakens their attach-ment to our republican institutions. Sir, the mechanics of this country are above the need of any eulogium from me – their reputation for skill is world-wide; and if I believed the charge to be true, I should be found among the foremost in my efforts to put an end to a system which produces such results. Not believing the charge to be true, the obvious answer to it is, that while our mechanics, as a body, are superior to those of any other country in intelligence, skill, and mental power, and while the instances are numerous of those who have made the most brilliant discoveries, and signalized themselves by the highest scientific and literary at-tainments, and been conscious that no circumstances could control or diminish the power of the "Divinity that stirs within them" – while we are proud, as American citizens, of the honor they have earned for us as a nation, and while they are ac-quiring wealth and power by the force of their own talents, they need not the feeble aid which we can render them in placing them in responsible positions – they need not our praise to make them conscious of their own deserts. They are entitled to receive, and will ever receive from every intelligent man, the respect due

his wife were acknowledged social leaders in Amherst, not only for their famous Commencement receptions but for the stream of visitors, many of them famous or near-famous, who enjoyed their hospitality. He had many warm friends of high degree who came often to Amherst to see him—Judge Lord of Salem, Samuel Bowles of Springfield, the Hollands of Springfield and New York. On June 17, 1869, the *Amherst Record* printed the following item:

> Gen. and Mrs. Geo. B. McClellan were in town last Friday. . . . Among those who received calls from the distinguished personages were Profs. Warner and Crowell, Mrs. Jones, and Hon. Edward Dickinson.

(It is interesting to note, however, that as early as 1857 the social center of gravity had begun to shift. When Emerson and Wendell Phillips visited Amherst that year, they stayed with Susan and Austin Dickinson, who had been married and had moved next door into the Evergreens only the year before. As Sue triumphantly wrote many years later, "both were our royal guests.")

There was hardly a civic project in Amherst, from the founding of Massachusetts Agricultural College to the establishment of the local water works, in which Edward Dickinson was not a central figure. He not only brought the railroad to Amherst but became president of it—the Amherst & Belchertown Rail Road. He helped bring the telegraph to Amherst. He was a life director of the Home Mission Society and in 1859 was appointed by Governor Banks trustee of the lunatic hospital in Northampton. He led the pallbearers at President Hitchcock's funeral; he had a locomotive named for him; and during his own funeral the shops in Amherst were closed and all business was suspended in his honor.

Even this partial list of Edward's accomplishments shows how deserved his public image was. But, like most images, it has hardened into a cliché. Higginson's peremptory summing up is typical. Indeed, Emily's father seems to have attracted stereotyping—including the image of the ogre father—about as readily as Emily herself, suggesting a quality of these Dickinsons, from Edward on down and most certainly including her brother and sister, that stimulated legends. Another description by

---

to them for their mental and moral qualities, and for their manly virtues; and will ever look above all distinctions of class or caste, and render to every man according to his desert, and cordially adopt the noble sentiment of the poet:

> "Honor and shame from no condition rise;
> Act well your part, there all the honor lies"
> [Pope, *An Essay on Man*, IV, 193]

(Pope's "Act well your part" stuck with him since Osmyn Baker's letter.) Two years earlier (July 26, 1852), Dickinson's speech at a Whig meeting in Northampton to ratify the nomination of General Scott was received (so the *Springfield Republican* reported the next day) with "great applause." The speech was "sensible, strong, practical and effective" (*YH* I, 254).

Tyler shows the legendary Mr. Dickinson as he stood in the community, the embodiment of all those public virtues his daughter found a little tedious.

> At the age of threescore years and ten Mr. Dickinson still stands erect, perpendicular, with his senses of seeing and hearing unimpaired, with his natural force and fire chastened and subdued but scarcely abated, one of the firmest pillars of society, education, order, morality and every good cause in our community.

There is a touch of the legendary, too, in an account of Edward Dickinson in the *Boston Journal* (later reprinted in the *Springfield Republican*) eight months before he died. Here he was said to recall the patriarchs of the Connecticut Valley—the Hopkinses, the Stoddards, the Hookers of ancient fame:

> He is a man of sterling personal character and integrity, always manifesting the keenest interest in public affairs, especially in town affairs. He is a type of the men once known as the "River Gods."

"Although slow and conservative," the article concluded, "[he] will prove a valuable man in the [Massachusetts] House," to which, on November 10, 1873, he was elected on an independent ticket. When he died in harness the following spring—arguing in the House for more appropriations for the Massachusetts Central Railroad—he went out of public life as he came in, a model citizen, respected by all.

His inner life was another matter. For all his worldly success, his many good works, and his brilliant family, he was a lonely and somber man. The exclusiveness of his early ambitions took its toll. Two very different observers saw him as "remote." He had his humanities; but he shared another quality with Melville's Ahab; he lacked "the low, enjoying power"; or, as his daughter Emily put it (in a remark that will need some qualification), ". . . he never played, and the straightest engine has its leaning hour." Emily, it seems, saw him more clearly than did any of his intimates, but in a moment of bafflement even she said, "I am not very well acquainted with father," a view that many others shared most of the time. Once, at the height of his career, Emily said how happy she was for him in Washington "among men who sympathize with him, and know what he really is," but it may be doubted that they understood him any better in Washington than they did in Amherst. A public eulogy after his death—by Samuel Bowles in the *Republican*—even suggested that he had failed to "understand himself."

We come, in him, to another stage in the increasingly complicated inner life of the Dickinsons. As to its origins, we can only speculate: excessive ambition thwarted in the small town of Amherst; a tendency toward melancholy like his father's; or a too stern devotion to duty. Or it may have been a sense, only partly understood and never expressed (as Emily could express it), of the inadequacy of an ethic which had come to stress the public virtues of respectability and achievement at the expense of the private requirements of friendship and parenthood—warmth and play and easy availability. Emily understood this paradox of public success and private failure, and her understanding illuminates and warms her mixed, sometimes caustic, remarks on him during the long years of their life together. But, in essence, her understanding seems to have grown steadily in depth and humanity.

Although Emily was proud of her father, the public image of him was not a matter of importance to her. He might march perpendicular at the forefront of town affairs or be the last of the River Gods to the State of Massachusetts; but what struck her, in her youth, was the slightly comic aspect of it all. Early in 1852 when the decision (mostly her father's work) was made to construct the Amherst & Belchertown Rail Road, there was general rejoicing in the community. Emily's comment to Austin about their father was a nice combination of detachment, love, and humor: "Father is really *sober* from excessive satisfaction, and bears his honors with a most becoming air." And in June of 1853, on the day of his greatest local triumph—the celebration of the road's completion—she described him as "marching around the town with New London at his heels like some old Roman General, upon a Triumph Day." It is good to be reminded that the tone of these remarks is typical of some ninety percent of her recorded comments on him, a tone that does not noticeably change until after his death. In 1851 in a letter to Austin, she described his going forth on an errand with "his pantaloons tucked in his boots. . . . I don't think 'neglige' quite becoming to so mighty a man." "Father steps like Cromwell when he gets the kindlings," she wrote her Norcross cousins in 1870. He makes "the Barn sound like the Bible." During the real-estate boom in Amherst in the early 1850s, "Father [she wrote Austin] looks very grand, and carries his hands in his pockets in case he should meet a *Northampton man*." Indeed, about this time Emily (age twenty) confided to Austin that "we young ones . . . think he is rather crazy."

It was not that Emily failed to take her father seriously; she took him very seriously indeed, if more acutely after she lost him than during his life. But by the time she was twenty she recognized the profound differences between them and began to carve out for herself a separate domain in which she could live her own life intact—a domain from which she could emerge to give her father the kindnesses and attentions that naturally flowed from her fondness for him but to which she could repair whenever she chose. Her comment in a letter to Austin in 1851 marks the beginning, or near it, of this conscious effort to establish her own world within the world of the family. Lamenting Austin's absence, she writes:

When I know of anything funny, I am just as apt to cry, far *more* so than to *laugh*, for I know who *loves jokes best*, and who is not here to enjoy them. We don't *have* many jokes tho' *now*, it is pretty much all sobriety, and we do not have much poetry, father having made up his mind that its pretty much all *real life*. Fathers real life and *mine* sometimes come into collision, but as yet, escape unhurt!

Edward Dickinson's household has been described as a dictatorship, a prison, a "world of parental tyrannies" where "a little girl [Emily] suffered silently and stubbornly." Such a view needs qualifying, at least as it applies to the children's formative years. There may have been minor eruptions, but the real "Vesuvius at Home" came later. Like all sensitive, individualistic children, Emily must have had moments of feeling trapped and rebellious and at times, perhaps, ignored. She could complain about father and his "Briefs," but in the next sentence comes her acknowledgment that "He buys me many Books – but begs me not to read them – because he fears they joggle the Mind." There is ample evidence that, by the standards of his day—long before the era of permissiveness and child-oriented households—he was a good father. For better or worse, children demanded less then, and expected less. A passage from one of Emily's early letters to Austin has been used as evidence of Edward's absolute authority in the household:

> We're rejoiced that you're coming home – the first thing we said to father, when he got out of the stage, was to ask if you were coming. I was sure you would all the while, for father said "of course you would," he should "consent to no other arrangement," and as you say, Austin, what father *says*, "he means."

Millicent Todd Bingham took the episode quite seriously (although she may be partly right about Edward's authority in the family):

> No one openly opposed his decisions, least of all his family. He knew what was right and what was wrong and that was the end of it. As his daughter Emily remarked, "What Father says he means."

But Emily's concluding remark seems, in context, quite clearly the focus of a little family joke at father's expense, as if saying to Austin, "You and I know how he carries on."

Even against what I take to be Edward's mild authoritarianism, the children developed adequate defenses. One of them surely was humor, especially between Emily and Austin. They enjoyed making fun of him. The question is: Was it always behind his back? They clearly saw through the lawyer's manner and were not in the least awed by it. Emily recounted to Austin a minor domestic crisis of a few months back (June 8, 1851), involving a head-on collision between her father's "real life" and hers. The episode, like the one just cited, has been regarded as another example of parental tyranny. But note how blithely she tells it:

> Tutor Howland [sister Vinnie's suitor of the moment] was here *as usual*, during the afternoon – after tea I went to see Sue – had a nice little visit with her – then went to see Emily Fowler, and arrived home at 9 – found Father in great agitation at my protracted stay – and mother and Vinnie in tears, for fear that he would kill me.

[57

She gives an equally bland account of another episode of the next year, when her friend Martha Gilbert (several years her senior) was visiting:

> Mat came home from meeting with us last Sunday, was here Saturday afternoon when father came, and at her special request, was secreted by me in the *entry*, until he was fairly in the house, when she escaped, *unharmed*.

The episode is sandwiched into a happy letter, with no comment.[5]

The household seems to have been less a dictatorship than a confederation of independent states. It was certainly not a prison. Vinnie is reported as saying that they all lived "like friendly and absolute monarchs, each in his own domain." Higginson in 1870 described the household as one "where each member runs his or her own selves"; and Emily said later, perhaps with oblique reference to household management, "We have no statutes here, but each does as it will, which is the sweetest jurisprudence."

It is important to note that Edward himself encouraged this independence. Although the town of Amherst presented excellent educational facilities, he sent each of the children away to school—Austin to Williston Seminary in Easthampton, Lavinia to Ipswich Female Seminary, Emily to Mount Holyoke (in this case, of course, Amherst did not offer the equivalent). They each had a chance, that is, to see life on their own and to shape their destinies, should they have so chosen, apart from parental influences. That they all came back to center their lives in Amherst and in their home may have been due less to any authoritarian pressure by Edward than to their own peculiar natures. They had an excellent home, and they knew it.

To Joseph Lyman, the country cousin and Austin's schoolboy friend at Williston who visited him for some months in the 1840s in the house on North Pleasant Street, the Dickinson household was sheer delight; he called it "that charming second home of mine in Amherst," and a dozen years later he was still retailing its delights in his letters to his fiancée. A letter to Lyman from Austin, written during an Amherst vacation (Austin graduated in 1850), gives a sense of how well the young people functioned, for all the alleged repressiveness of the Dickinson home. To be sure, the atmosphere is perhaps more than usually relaxed: mother and father—"the ancient people"—are off on a trip to Monson:

> Now you have got enough of momentary description [the books, the crackling fire], to go a little fa[r]ther back, I go[t] up at 5: o.clock, fed the horse, then eat my breakfast. At 6: o.clock, I led the horse, attached to the buggy[,] to the front steps, and in the space of two or three minutes, perceived two mysterious forms emerging from the front door, apparently a male and female, which, upon raising my lantern, proved to be those of my father and mother, who immediately seated themselves in the wagon and drove off to

5. Mrs. Bingham (*Home*, p. 289) takes this as an example of Martha's timidity in contrast to her sister Susan's cool self-possession. But Martha was no child (she was nearing her mid-twenties) and she may have determined, for any one of a number of reasons, to avoid a meeting with Edward Dickinson that afternoon.

Monson, bidding us "good morning", as they went, expecting to return to-morrow – . . . . [Vinnie being away] Emily and I are left, lord and lady of the "mansion", "with none to molest or make us afraid". We are anticipating a fine time in the absence of the ancient people. Wish you were here to help us laugh – I think there is a chance for our having some company tonight.

Emily spoke often and fully on this subject. Her love of home was intense and her loyalty complete. During her first months at Mount Holyoke, her letters (although she loved her studies, her teachers, and her friends) are filled with longings for home—my "very dear home," "my *own* DEAR HOME"—and on her first return the very sight of Amherst filled her with ecstasy:

We rode swiftly along & soon the Colleges & the spire of our venerable Meeting House, rose to my delighted vision. Never did Amherst look more lovely to me & gratitude rose in my heart to God, for granting me such a safe return.

South Hadley, it should be noted, is all of ten miles from Amherst.

Once out of Mount Holyoke and well settled in her home (a spell of ill health had something to do with her leaving college after three terms), she did all she could to lure back the wandering Austin, who was then teaching school in Boston. "Come home," she said in a dozen different ways—come back "to freedom and the sunshine here at home. . . . Duty is black and brown – home is bright and shining." She even felt slightly guilty in loving her home so much, with Austin away and miserable in Boston. "I am so sorry for you," she wrote. "I do wish it was *me,* that you might be well and happy, for I have no profession, and have such a snug, warm home that I had as lief suffer some, a great deal rather than not, that by doing so, you were exempted from it." A few months later she confessed to her friend Jane Humphrey, "I'm afraid I'm growing *selfish* in my dear home, but I do love it so, and when some pleasant friend invites me to pass a week with her, I look at my father and mother and Vinnie, and all my friends, and I say no – no, cant leave them, what if they die when I'm gone." In her finer flights, her rhetoric becomes more exalted: "Home is the definition of God." "Home is a holy thing – nothing of doubt or distrust can enter it's blessed portals. . . . here seems indeed to be a bit of Eden." And many years later she wrote to a friend about the "Infinite power of Home."

The legend of the dismal home and the tyrannical father comes from the later years. Its source may be traced mainly to Lavinia in her embittered state, when she unbosomed herself to two late entrants upon the Dickinson scene, Mrs. Mabel Loomis Todd and Miss Mary Lee Hall. Although Vinnie's reminiscences are unquestionably part of the record and must remain so, they must be read in the context of her character and situation. They slip too neatly into stereotypes of the times (and of Edward Dickinson) that must be seen in connection not only with what Emily herself said about her home, her father, and her early social doings but with the prevailingly cheerful tone of Vinnie's own contemporary letters and diary, with several of Austin's comments, and with the warm recollections of such visitors as the Newman cousins (Edward's wards),[6] and Joseph Lyman. Mrs. Todd describes a conversation with Vinnie in the summer of 1893:

> Went to Vinnie's to tea, and had an interesting talk with her & Austin on the peculiarities of their bringing up. It must have been a stiff, Puritanical and trying home. Some of Vinnie's stories were appalling – of the way they were watched and guarded for fear some young man might wish to marry one of them. It made me indignant.

Such stories lost nothing in the telling, nor did they lose anything in the retelling. Vinnie had the Dickinson sense of the dramatic and the family gift for rhetoric; and there were many reasons why Mabel Todd, at that

6. Clara and Anna Newman, daughters of Edward's sister Mary, who became his wards when they were orphaned in 1852, lived next door in the Evergreens with Austin and Sue Dickinson for several years, beginning in 1858. Clara later recorded her impressions of the Dickinsons (both families) in a document entitled "My Personal Acquaintance with Emily Dickinson" (see Appendix II, 3). The two Newman girls, then in their teens, much preferred the Homestead. They took their troubles to Edward and to Emily, and were in and out of the house continually. They "never wavered in their love and loyalty to their Uncle Edward," writes Mrs. Clara Newman Pearl (Clara's niece), who says in her comments on her Aunt Clara's document:

> In my childhood recollections he [Edward Dickinson] is far from the stern, unapproachable person which he is represented in some of the recent biographies of Emily Dickinson. It only needed Edward Dickinson's "Very pleasantly impressed," in his most dignified manner, after my father had been presented to him at a cousin's home in Cambridge, to make my mother feel that she had chosen her husband wisely. Another anecdote of Edward Dickinson. When the circus came to town the young people wanted to go, but circuses were much frowned upon in those days. They were not quite respectable. My mother was appointed a committee of one to interview Uncle Edward. His advice, "Go and make it respectable," is still quoted in our family.

The following passage from the document itself recounts a revealing episode:

> [Edward Dickinson] was a grand type of a class now extinct – An Old-School-Gentleman-Whig! His bearing was almost stern in its dignity and nobility, but his nature was as beautiful, and sympathetic, and tender as a mother's. . . . As a child I feared him, until I found him out when trouble and difficulty came, and my Guardian became my strong, and tender, and lovingly-revered Friend. To show you a little glimpse of him – As I left the door of his son's house [the Evergreens] after my wedding [October 14, 1869], he turned to my husband with this remark, "If she makes you as little trouble as she has me, you will be much happier than most men." Not fulsome flattery, surely, but coming from this man, and crowned, as it was, with the beautiful and rare smile we all felt it a success to win, it was a benediction on my new life.

Perhaps Edward Dickinson was more successful with his nieces than with his own children. But the rare smile that Anna remembered is something of a benediction on the Homestead, too. Emily worried about him because he did not smile enough. But had the household been entirely without the spirit Anna here records, Emily's delight in her home, expressed again and again, would hardly be credible.

time, was especially impressed with the pathos of the Dickinson story. She later reported other gleanings from Vinnie's conversation, all pointing in the same direction, all open to question, and some simply contrary to fact. She summarized her impressions of Vinnie's talk as follows:

> The father was terrific. If he had married a different woman, he wouldn't have been such an overbearing man. He kept the girls down in a little valley in his mind. . . .
> He did not like to have students come to see the girls. . . .
> [Emily] was repressed, and had nothing to do with young men. Vinnie was pert and flirted if she wanted to. The father and mother would not let young men come [to the house] for fear they would marry. They [Mr. Dickinson and Austin] were men that could manage the world if they wanted to, and wouldn't have any foreigners in their family. They didn't want a strange young man in the family. Austin always admired his father very much, but he'd bang you if anything went wrong. The father never knew fine intellectual women. He needed to know about them.

Of a piece with this is the story, coming from Lavinia, of Edward Dickinson's refusal to let Emily receive the attentions of a young suitor—a refusal that (according to Vinnie) resulted in her lifelong withdrawal.[7] Miss Hall reported that "Miss Vinnie told me many times that she and Emily *feared* their father as long as he lived, and loved him after his death." Another story, again from Miss Hall, would seem to clinch the matter. Bending over his father's coffin, Austin kissed him on the forehead and is reported to have said, "There, father, I never dared do that while you were living."

In spite of such testimony, I cannot look upon the Dickinson household as fear-ridden. The children may have been reluctant to interrupt or impose upon their hard-working father; but this may have been more from disciplined respect than from fear. Austin's remark at his father's coffin may simply be another example of the almost pathological undemonstrativeness of this late-Puritan, New England family. An early letter of Austin's to Sue speaks of the lack of tenderness in his life: "I have never *before* received *any* – from any *body* – I never *would*." Emily's attitude toward her father, even as we have seen it so far, was compounded of many elements incompatible with fear. It developed early into an amused tolerance, a touch of condescension arising from an entirely justified sense of intellectual superiority, a tender devotion that made her delight in serving him in many ways (baking his bread, mending his

---

7. The suitor was George Gould, Amherst '50, and a close friend of Austin's. The story comes to us circuitously: from Lavinia, who told it to Mrs. Aurelia Davis (an Amherst neighbor), who told it to Mary Lee Hall, who told it to Genevieve Taggard, who made Gould the lost lover in her biography of ED. (See *YH* I, 177–78, entry of August 1850; and *YH* I, l, where Leyda urges that the dramatic details of the story be read "with some skepticism." Vinnie later made it clear that she thought Emily's withdrawal was due more to basic inclination and the family situation than to any such personal disaster.)

slippers, playing music for him), and later on into a deep, pervasive pity for his lonely and austere life. It was a complex and delicate relationship, changing and maturing with the years. Vinnie's, Miss Hall's, and Mrs. Todd's versions seem, in the light of all we know, oversimplified and static.

Not that life in the Dickinson household was one long idyl of prolonged though muted harmony. The place bristled with personalities, and there were frequent clashes. "Vesuvius at Home," even in a whimsical, lighthearted sense, was an apt metaphor; Vinnie used a similar one when, early in July 1853, she warned Austin against bringing home too many guests over Commencement: "You know home has not *altered* in your absence & sometimes the *fire kindles suddenly!*" This may refer to her father's temper, or it may mean simply that at Commencement time, when (as Vinnie wrote) "every thing is always so confused," the household was inclined to be on edge. Edward was not in fact notorious for his temper; he kept his "quick & ardent" feelings under control. Perhaps a remark of Emily's to Austin a few months earlier throws some light. It shows how Dickinson wills could clash—but against a background of mutual respect and affection. Speaking of Austin's letters home, she described them as

very funny indeed. . . . Father takes great delight in your remarks to him— puts on his spectacles and reads them o'er and o'er as if it was a blessing to have an only son. . . .

I do think it's so funny – you and father do nothing but 'fisticuff' all the while you're at home, and the minute you are separated, you become such devoted friends; but this is a checkered life.

I believe at this moment, Austin, that there's no body living for whom father has such respect as for you, and yet your conduct together is quite peculiar indeed.

Emily was clearly more adroit than her brother in managing their father, perhaps because she understood better than Austin that he needed managing. Her letters speak often of the little compromises she daily made—like joining in family prayers every morning while he addressed "an Eclipse" and she thought her own thoughts. When their ideas of real life collided, she contrived ways of stating her position that would avoid any serious rupture. There is an anecdote about a chipped plate. Mrs. Bingham used it to illustrate Edward's "standard of good workmanship," his insistence that everyone in the household live up to the same standard he set himself. But it also shows Emily as a master strategist, replying to his imperiousness with a humor and dispatch he could not have missed:

One day, sitting down at the dinner table, he inquired whether a certain nicked plate must always be placed before him. Emily took the hint. She carried the plate to the garden and pulverized it on a stone, "just to remind" her, she said, not to give it to her father again.

And "just to remind" him, I suggest, that two could play at the game of temperament as well as one.

There is record of only one real blowup between father and daughter, with tempers up and voices raised. Vinnie recounted it in a letter to Austin—but with enough whimsey to make one wonder how serious she was, and with no hint of how the situation was resolved:

> Oh! dear! Father is killing the horse. I wish you'd come quick if you want to see him alive. He is whipping him because he didn't look quite *"umble"* enough this morning. Oh! Austin, it makes me so angry to see that 'noble creature' so abused. Emilie is screaming to the top of her voice. She's so vexed about it.

Aside from the reassuring revelation that Emily could scream, it is not clear (again) precisely what this means about the father-daughter relationship. It may suggest that Emily, for all her usual tone of tolerant understanding, could match him, temper for temper.

Edward was never famous for gentleness, at least among his children. Vinnie said, "Father was the only one to say 'damn.' Someone in every family ought to say damn of course." He was "quite a hand to give medicine," said Emily, "especially if it is not desirable to the patient." When she returned from her eye treatments in Boston in 1864, she said that Father was "as gentle as he knows how."

There is something very touching about this and many similar remarks by Emily about her father. For all the humor and gentle satire with which she usually spoke of him, what in the end impressed her most was the pathos of his life, its austerity, its rigor, and its loneliness, even in the family. As the years went on, she saw the gap widen between him and his children. Although Edward as a young father had been protective and solicitous about his family's welfare, his early letters, peppered with do's and don'ts, were more admonitory and didactic than affectionate. He was devoted to his family and dependent upon them; but he seems to have been quite without the ability to say so. Even Vinnie, not so quick as Emily in these matters, sensed his remoteness. When she was twenty, she wrote Austin:

> Father was *thoughtful* enough to spend last evening with us *socially* & as he seemed rather dull, I endeavoured to entertain him by reading spicey passages from Fern leaves, where upon he brightened up sufficiently to correct me as I went along. . . . Father has seemed quite pensive & exhibited much of the martyr spirit since you went away. . . . I think Father is perfectly home sick with out you. What will he do when *we* are *all* gone?

As his family slipped away from him, whether geographically, intellectually, or emotionally, Edward showed his disappointment, or grief, not in words whose effect might have been restorative, but in what seems to have been a general moroseness and anxiety, the pensiveness that Vinnie noted. Emily refused invitations because father was "in the habit of me";

she felt he would miss her, would want something in her absence. Once she reminded Austin that "this is a lonely house, when we are not all here." Eventually, of course, they all stayed in Amherst—Emily and Lavinia in the Homestead; Austin, with his wife, next door—partly, perhaps, out of loyalty to this lonely, hard-working, melancholic, and dedicated man.

On one hand, Emily could poke fun at her father's Puritan streak, as when she described his reading "the letters of suspected gentlemen . . . [in] our family library . . . with a mixture of fun and perseverence, which is quite diabolical"; or, a different slant, perusing (with Mother, in the sitting room) "such papers only, as they are well assured have nothing carnal in them"; or leading family prayers with his "militant Accent"; or (perhaps her best vignette of him) sitting out, in Puritan impatience, Jenny Lind's recital in Northampton:

> Father [she wrote Austin] sat all the evening looking *mad,* and *silly,* and yet so much amused you would have *died* a laughing – when the performers bowed, he said "Good evening Sir" – and when they retired, "very well – that will do," it was'nt *sarcasm* exactly, nor it was'nt *disdain,* it was infinitely funnier than either of those virtues, as if old Abraham had come to see the show, and thought it was all very well, but a little excess of *Monkey!*

But she penetrated beneath the comic to the lonely figure who lacked the "low, enjoying power." And this for Emily, who was geared to "ecstasy" (a favorite word with her and apparently unknown to her father) as few human beings have ever been, was the saddest of losses. "He never played." Like old Abraham at the show, he kept his distance.[8]

8. Again we must qualify this generally dour picture. He could, on occasion, "play." Here he was, at least, at Jenny's concert, however skeptical he seems to have been of the whole performance. And there is other evidence. He took his wife and children on walks and rides. In August 1837 he and his wife ascended Mt. Holyoke (YH I, 34). In Boston, in 1838, he "attended a concert at the Odeon, last evening, of the Boston Academy of Music, and was delighted with it" (YH I, 49; April 5). Next year he went to the theater but (it must be admitted) "would not be hired to go again" (YH I, 52; January 13). In Amherst he did his share, with his wife, of calling and receiving calls. He apparently was something of a mimic and could take off important people. He chortled over Austin's letters home. The Dickinson teas were annual features of Commencement Week, and he went to his Yale reunion. Perhaps the one luxury he allowed himself was fine horses, an interest that (probably through Samuel Bowles) was known outside of Amherst. On October 11, 1853, the *Springfield Republican* printed the following letter, dated October 7, 1853:

GENTLEMEN, –
Your letter, inviting me to attend the "grand Agricultural Banquet during the progress of the National Horse Exhibition at Springfield on the 19th inst." has been received, and should have received an immediate answer. . . . I was much pleased with the first published suggestion of the project; and have watched, with the liveliest interest, the readiness with which the people, in all parts of the country, have seized upon it, to show their regard for the noblest of all irrational animals.
The occasion cannot fail to afford a fitting opportunity for the dissemination of

Thomas Wentworth Higginson, whose first impression of Emily's father was so far from the whole truth, in another remark came much closer. "Her father [he wrote] was not severe I should think but remote." Perhaps the distance between the two generations was no greater than in most families; but in spite of Emily's insistence on the solidarity of the family—"We are having a pleasant summer [she wrote Austin in July 1851] – without one of the five it is yet a *lonely* one"—communication never seems to have been good. The story of her father's trying to teach her to tell time, how she was too frightened to learn and too afraid to tell him or anyone else for years afterward, may indicate a real failure on Mr. Dickinson's part, although I cannot regard it as the traumatic experience of Emily's childhood that shut her off from her father forever.[9] Her humor about him may have been in part protective, according to her own theory of mirth as "the Mail of Anguish." Certainly she practiced minor evasions. She spoke of reading books he didn't approve of; of hesitating to read in his presence the "poetic" parts of Austin's letters to her; of the "kitchen meetings," when she and Austin (and Vinnie?) could talk freely.

I dont love to read your letters all out loud to father – it would be like opening the kitchen door when we get home from meeting Sunday, and are sitting down by the stove saying just what we're a mind to, and having father hear. I don't know why it is, but it gives me a dreadful feeling.

Things went better when "the ancient people" were away.

The most poignant expression we have of Emily's sense of her father's remoteness comes in a letter to Joseph Lyman, written probably in the

---

useful information, and the cultivation of those kindly and generous feelings which make all the participants happier and better; while it produces a liberality and nationality of views, and stimulates a laudable emulation in all to excel.

. . . I am sure it must be a glorious affair; and leave indelible "horse tracks" in the valley of the Connecticut, to mark an "epoch" in the "natural history" of the race, for a continent.

My love of fine horses, would, of itself, be sufficient to attract me to the exhibition; but the expectation of meeting and exchanging congratulations with gentlemen of the highest standing and character, from different sections of the country, all interested in promoting its welfare, will render it, in the highest degree, pleasant and profitable to be there. . . .

Yours very truly
EDWARD DICKINSON

The letter should be read, surely, in conjunction with Vinnie's story of his beating the horse. And finally, there is a legend that Edward, sitting for his picture, was asked by the town photographer to "smile, a little," please: "To which the Squire thundered back, 'I *yam* smiling.' " (See *AB*, p. 232.)

9. See Clark Griffith, *The Long Shadow*, pp. 278 ff., who finds "no reason to disbelieve this remarkable story." For the origin of the story (Higginson's gleanings from ED's conversation as he passed them on to his wife), see *L* II, 475. I find it hard to believe for many reasons, among them ED's careful scientific training in Amherst Academy. Either she willfully exaggerated to Higginson, or his reporting was faulty.

mid-1860s. It is also another example of what Emily complained of when she said, "All men say 'What' to me"—including, we now see, her father. It gives her mature sense of the pathos of his life:

> My father seems to me often the oldest and the oddest sort of a foreigner. Sometimes I say something and he stares in a curious sort of bewilderment though I speak a thought quite as old as his daughter. . . .
> Father says in fugitive moments when he forgets the barrister & lapses into the man, says that his life has been passed in a wilderness or on an island – of late he says on an island. And so it is, for in the morning I hear his voice and methinks it comes from afar & has a sea tone & there is a hum of hoarseness about [it] & a suggestion of remoteness as far as the isle of Juan Fernandez.

Apparently Edward Dickinson did "lapse into the man" occasionally and speak his heart. But here he is, a foreigner in his own family, bewildered by his daughter and as far from her as "the isle of Juan Fernandez." The picture is of a piece with what others said: the perpendicular stance, the failure of his fellows to understand him thoroughly, Higginson's impression of his remoteness.

It coincides, too, with another comment on him, this one having to do with another kind of isolation, or apartness, with which Emily was herself familiar. The story is recorded by Emily's supposed suitor, George Gould, who in September 1877 entered in his notebook the following description of Edward's religious conversion, which had taken place during the Revival in Amherst in 1850:

> While Hon. E. D. of Amherst was converted – who had been long under conviction – His pastor said to him in his study – "You want to come to Christ as a *lawyer* – but you must come to him as a *poor sinner* – get down on your knees & let me pray for you, & then pray for yourself."

It was not easy for Dickinsons to get down on their knees and pray before others—or to be demonstrative even before God. Although Edward had supported the church and attended its services for years, he was forty-seven before this episode occurred. It seems typical of the man as he faced the world. Emily, too, held out; she "paused and pondered and pondered and paused," and resisted the efforts of her friends to get her to accept Christ. "I am standing alone in rebellion," she said in 1850, the year of the Revival that led Edward into the church. The doctrine of the "poor sinner" was congenial to neither father nor daughter. Here surely was an element of Dickinson pride, a sense of self-sufficiency, of being able to get along without the spiritual support that others found necessary—"the ark of safety," Emily called it when she was seventeen. With Edward, if we are to believe Gould's anecdote, it seems to have been a stubborn unwillingness to humble himself completely. It was said of him that he thought himself imperishable; others might sicken and die but not he. Lawyer that he was, he left no will. He could have "managed the world" if he'd wanted to, said Mrs. Todd (who never saw him). Emily, with her intense love of nature and infinite pride in human capacities (not necessarily Dickinson capacities), sublimated this stubbornness and touch of imperiousness into her own personal theology, in which the World and Man and God were all but coordinate. This opened up relationships unknown, apparently, to her father. He was left with his public duties and dedications, while she at least—when things were going well—could be chatty with the Deity, her "Old Neighbor – God – " and, with the poets, make a summer that "lasts a Solid Year –." It is tempting to speculate how much of her attitude she derived from her father—and transformed.

Edward Dickinson died in Boston on June 16, 1874. That morning, "a cruelly hot day," he had felt faint while giving a speech before the General Court and was forced to stop. He repaired to his hotel, summoned a doctor, and died after (and perhaps because of) a dose of morphine. Though his fatigue had been noted, nothing like this sudden end had been expected. The House was adjourned and a Resolution (later published in the legislative *Journal*) was immediately prepared. The news appeared in papers across the state and was the occasion of much obituary comment. Here the note of perplexity comes in, the same that made Emily wonder about how "well acquainted" she was with her father. The *Amherst Record* for June 17 predicted that Edward Dickinson would be "even more respected and honored" when "his character is more fully understood." Samuel Bowles, writing in the *Springfield Republican* for that same day, turned the matter inward:

He was, indeed, a New England Chevalier Bayard, without fear and without reproach. He was a Puritan out of time for kinship and appreciation, but exactly in time for example and warning. His failing was he did not understand himself; consequently his misfortune was that others did not understand him. . . . he possessed and exhibited that rarest and yet most needed of all qualities in these days of cowardly conformity and base complaisance, *the courage of his convictions.* This was the essence of his life – this is his noblest bequest to his community and his state.

The second Sunday after the funeral, Reverend Jonathan L. Jenkins, strong friend of the Dickinsons and much cherished by Emily, preached a sermon on Edward Dickinson. Here, too, the stress was on his failure to be understood and on the gentleness he never successfully communicated. Jenkins compared him to the prophet Samuel:

It is a condition of human life that men are not known by contemporaries. . . . Here influences that warp and distort judgements are many and strong. Here occasions for conflict, for misunderstandings, for alienations are so frequent that perfect concord is impossible. . . .
It is said that in the apparition in which [Samuel] was evoked after death, there was something terrific, and yet this man whom a whole village feared, in whose appearance there was that which terrified, was gentle in na-

ture, and no more gentle in nature, than our friend and father whom we mourn to-day. . . . Aye there was yet a finer fibre in the gentleness which was in him, but which he so carefully, and may I say, so unwisely, concealed. Had he the Puritan notion that sentiment betrayed weakness, or was it his training in that elder school whose primal precept was repression . . . ?[10]

10. The sermon, in holograph among the Dickinson Papers, Houghton Library, Harvard, combines conventional funeral rhetoric with intimate personal insights. We can only speculate on how precisely Jenkins meant this description of Samuel to apply to Edward Dickinson:

> Not since Moses who died four hundred years before, had there been in Israel so great a man as Samuel. In troublesome times he preserved order, administered justice. He consolidated the nation, founded schools, faithfully served the state for thirty years in high offices.
>
> His external appearance was rough, he repelled men, inspired fear. He lived in extreme simplicity, his whole career was so just that learned Grotius gave him the name of the Jewish Aristides.
>
> Although such, his countrymen grew weary of him, preferred in his place the brilliant, fickle, incompetent Saul, practically forced him into retirement before, as Matthew Henry says, he was super-annuated.
>
> At last he died, and then from neglect and rejection, he passed at once to most generous appreciation and homage.

It is hard to understand Jenkins' emphasis on Samuel's rejection. Edward may have been losing touch with the town, but not, it would seem, to that extent. The rest of the sermon is a fine tribute to his character and to his influence, "intrinsically so beautiful," on Amherst. Jenkins commended him for having dedicated his life to one place:

> Not all men who are born in a place, and stay in it, love it. The fact of being born in it, often seems to create a dislike of it, an unwillingness to serve it. It has been said Amherst was Mr Dickinson's passion. I believe it was. . . . His right hand would sooner forget its cunning, than he forget Amherst.

Jenkins touched perceptively on other qualities, his gentleness, his taciturnity, his religion. The theme of the misunderstood man recurs several times.

> His was a deep-seated gentleness, working in and sweetening the secret fountains, not a gentleness that expended itself in pleasant speeches and manners assumed for effect, but a gentleness that felt others' pains and losses, and excited efforts for relief. . . . was it a native delicacy of soul that kept covered the choice bright feelings that too often like rare perfumes are ruined by exposure? . . .
>
> He had no great faith in ceremonies, in formulas of doctrine. He was free in his speech about religion, most unconventional in his practices. His religion was however most excellent and genuine. . . .
>
> Our friend and father was a silent man. If any must judge his religion this must be taken into account. . . . At one time he read much upon the subject of religion, read theological works, was always an attendant upon Sabbath worship, and a most generous supporter of the Parish. . . .
>
> I have had from the Rev Mr Colton an account so far as they were known to him of the steps by which Mr. Dickinson was led to a Christian profession [on the 11th of August 1850]. . . . The man who instinctively avoided all mention of himself would be pained at any publicity given to what he experiences at such a crisis. And I who loved him with something of a son's partial affection, could not by any possibility do it, and yet my love is so strong that since he suffered himself so often to be misjudged I would at any sacrifice have him known as he was, not as he seemed, by all christian men and women. Years after his connec-

The effect of her father's death on Emily was devastating. She remained in her room during the funeral and apparently did not attend the memorial service, if we can judge from a neighbor's letter to a friend: "Memorial service at our church today, lots of laurel & other white flowers. I think Austin & Wife, Vinnie & her mother were all at church. . . ." Emily was shocked to find how shocked she was: "I cannot recall myself [she wrote to her Norcross cousins]. I thought I was strongly built, but this stronger has undermined me. . . . Though it is many nights, my mind never comes home."

Emily now saw her father's life in a wholly new perspective. She seems not to have realized what she had in him until too late. The playfulness and the whimsey disappear entirely from her remarks about him. A letter she wrote Higginson during the month following her father's death touches the tragic, a tone from which she never departed. It begins with a description of one of the very few moments on record of complete rapport between Emily and her father:

> The last Afternoon that my Father lived, though with no premonition – I preferred to be with him, and invented an absence for Mother, Vinnie being asleep. He seemed peculiarly pleased as I oftenest stayed with myself, and remarked as the Afternoon withdrew, he "would like it to not end."
>
> His pleasure almost embarrassed me and my Brother coming – I suggested they walk. Next morning I woke him for the train [to Boston] – and saw him no more.

And then (in her next sentence) the new vision of this strange and remote man: "His Heart was pure and terrible and I think no other like it exists."

This is the figure that haunted her for a long time. Two years later she told her Norcross cousins: "I dream about father every night, always a different dream, and forget what I am doing daytimes, wondering where he is." Three years after his death she avoided a family reunion because "accustomed to all [the relatives] through Father, they remind me too deeply of him for Peace."

Her father grew and grew in her imagination. He is no longer "Cromwell with the kindlings" but a figure around whom revolve the great questions that had harassed her for years, now brought intensely home. Every death among her relatives and friends (and there had been many) had come as a peculiar shock to her; she adjusted slowly; but this was the first in her immediate family and the first of the "mighty" deaths that wracked her so in the decade of the 1870s and in the early 1880s. A

---

tion with the church while a member of Congress he wrote to Mr Colton from Washington these words, "I am even while I write, melted to tears at the remembrance of what we saw and felt at the working of God's spirit among us in 1850." In the same letter he wrote "I hope that I may never cease to have your prayers that I may illustrate the principles of Christianity in my life."

quatrain of the late period could apply to any of the deaths, certainly to her father's:

> Lives he in any other world
> My faith cannot reply
> Before it was imperative
> Twas all distinct to me –   (#*1557, about 1882*)

If the matter of faith—"wondering where he is"—became suddenly imperative, his death (or any death) forced a readjustment of her sense of time:

> The vastest earthly Day
> Is chastened small
> By one heroic Face
> Behind a Pall –[11]   (#*1328, about 1874*)

Perhaps (she reasoned in another poem), if we understood time—which is to say eternity—we would not be so shocked at its sudden intrusion:

> The Infinite a sudden Guest
> Has been assumed to be –
> But how can that stupendous come
> Which never went away?   (#*1309, about 1874*)

Several of her tiny epitaphs—the form her thoughts about her father seemed inevitably to take—point to personal qualities she had grumbled about during his lifetime. The sense of duty that had kept him from his children now becomes a mark of triumph over fate:

> To his simplicity
> To die – was little Fate –
> If Duty live – contented
> But her Confederate.   (#*1352, about 1876*)

"Old Abraham" at the show, keeping his skeptical distance from the entertainers, now becomes a figure of awe and glory:

> Gathered into the Earth,
> And out of story –
> Gathered to that strange Fame –
> That lonesome Glory
> That hath no omen here – but Awe – (#*1370, about 1876*)

11. In the light of the elegiac quatrain sent to Higginson ("Lay this Laurel on the One") and discussed below, ED's variants—"chastened" for "shrunken" in line 2 and "heroic" for "Defaulting" in line 3—seem applicable to her father.

The stiffness that amused her in his "Roman General" bearing now has the dignity of a tall cedar:

> To break so vast a Heart
> Required a Blow as vast –
> No Zephyr felled this Cedar straight –
> 'Twas undeserved Blast –   (*#1312, about 1874*)

If she chafed under his discipline around the house or smiled at his sometimes highhanded way in village affairs, now he is the departed king of subjects who love him all the more:

> From his slim Palace in the Dust
> He relegates the Realm,
> More loyal for the exody
> That has befallen him.   (*#1300, about 1874*)

Two poems explicitly about her father (the above can only be assumed to be) sum up her view of him most poignantly. Both were sent to Higginson, one about two years after Edward's death, the other near the third anniversary of it. In the first, a comment she had made about a poem sent earlier to Higginson on immortality suggested her father:

> When I think of my Father's lonely Life and his lonelier Death, there is this redress –

> Take all away –
> The only thing worth larceny
> Is left – the Immortality –   [*#1365*]

From what she wrote to Lyman, it is clear that, for all her joking, she had been keenly aware of her father's remoteness and what it meant in sadness to him as well as for the family. The poem at least shows her faith as by now more "certain."

The second poem to Higginson is a remarkable distillation of the thought and feeling, attitude and appraisal, that her ultimate view of her father became. The occasion needs some comment. Three years before, she had been much moved by Higginson's poem "Decoration," which had appeared in *Scribner's Monthly* for June 1874, the month her father died. Its seven lilting stanzas—in tribute to an unsung hero in a lonely and uncared-for grave—is in the standard Memorial Day tradition. Emily thanked Higginson for his "beautiful Hymn": "was it not prophetic? It has assisted that Pause of Space which I call 'Father' –." Then in 1877, she sent Higginson her own version, of which he later said, when he was editing the poems with Mabel Loomis Todd, "She wrote it after re-reading my 'Decoration.' It is the condensed essence of that & so far finer."

Emily's redaction is a model of a poetic procedure she followed many times. In Higginson's poem the speaker has gone to decorate the graves of the fallen heroes:

> Mid the flower-wreath'd tombs I stand
> Bearing lilies in my hand.
> Comrades! in what soldier-grave
> Sleeps the bravest of the brave?

Not, it seems, where his comrades think, in a grave surrounded by mourning friends and wreathed with flowers—"Garlands veil it; ask not mine." The speaker then turns to "one low grave," untended and unnoticed, where the true hero lies:

> One low grave, yon tree beneath,
> Bears no roses, wears no wreath;
> Yet no heart more high and warm
> Ever dared the battle-storm,
>
> Never gleamed a prouder eye
> In the front of victory,
> Never foot had firmer tread
> On the field where hope lay dead,
>
> Than are hid within this tomb,
> Where the untended grasses bloom;
> And no stone, with feign'd distress,
> Mocks the sacred loneliness.
>
> Youth and beauty, dauntless will,
> Dreams that life could ne'er fulfill,
> Here lie buried; here in peace
> Wrongs and woes have found release.
>
> Turning from my comrades' eyes,
> Kneeling where a woman lies,
> I strew lilies on the grave
> Of the bravest of the brave.

There was much here to suggest her father to her: his lonely death, especially; the world's failure to recognize his true virtues and to understand him; the peace after a life of dedication and self-sacrifice. Three years after his death, she may have felt that she was the last and lonely mourner, like the woman in Higginson's poem. So she changed the lilies to laurel and put it where it would redeem the world's failure:

72]

Lay this Laurel on the One
Too intrinsic for Renown –
Laurel – vail your deathless tree –
Him you chasten, that is He![12]   (#*1393*)

This lonely and angular man will continue to move in and out of these pages. When we take up Emily's life from the beginning, he will appear as the young husband and father, worried about his family, chafing under financial limitations and looking to the mid-century land boom for his fortune. His concern about his children's education and his own worldliness will come out in some revealing letters to his wife and one to all three children. I have chosen to leave these matters to later chapters, when they become of more immediate concern to Emily's early years. That he figured less and less in her life as she set out on her own lonely path is part of the pathos of their relationship. Her remark about her father's being too busy to notice his children is, like many of her remarks on her parents, a little quick and cruel. I think he noticed more than her remark implies. But there can be little doubt that at an early stage he began to lose touch. Such letters as we have from him to Austin are businesslike and terse. Emily could have helped him more than she did, a delinquency she realized only after he died. Such a failure, on both sides, is usually attributed to New England reticence or reserve. It is characteristic that, as she described her last day with him, she recalled her own "embarrassment" at his pleasure in her company and extricated herself by suggesting that he and Austin take a walk. To this extent, the failure of the relationship can be attributed less to his heartlessness or a willful desire to control than to the inhibiting effect of a tradition that put duty and diligence over love. "*My* business," Emily concluded as in her early thirties she faced the world on her own, "is to love." The emphasis is hers.

12. The explanatory note in *Poems* gives an account of the episode, the full text of Higginson's poem, and the existing MS. redactions of ED's poem. As the editor points out, the poem may well have been of eight lines, whether of two stanzas or one "it is impossible to know." The first four lines slip into Higginson's military rhetoric ("triumphed," "Victor"). The last four are more appropriate to her father:

> Lay this Laurel on the one
> Triumphed and remained unknown –
> Laurel – fell your futile Tree –
> Such a Victor could not be –
> Lay this Laurel on the one
> Too intrinsic for Renown –
> Laurel – vail your deathless Tree –
> Him you chasten – that is he –

5

Emily Norcross Dickinson

THERE IS A LEGEND that, on the day Emily Dickinson was born, Mrs. Dickinson, against her husband's express wishes, had her bedroom papered. If true, it is one of her few willful, assertive acts on record—one of the reasons, surely, she obtrudes so little into the annals of her family, at least compared with "Father," who appears on almost every page.[1] In character and temperament, Emily was a Dickinson; it has been said that all she inherited from her mother was her first name. Emily herself did much to establish this notion of her mother's nonentity in two remarks to Higginson, one in conversation in 1870 and the other in a letter in 1874. Both are often quoted: "I never had a mother. I suppose a mother is one to whom you hurry when you are troubled." "I always ran Home to Awe when a child, if anything befell me. He was an awful Mother, but I liked him better than none."

Both of these remarks require looking into. They must be seen in the

---

1. The source of the legend (it is probably little more than that but may contain a grain of truth) is a letter from Mary Adèle Allen (whose *Around a Village Green*, 1939, contains much Amherst lore) to Orton Clark, February 14, 1944: "[Lafayette Stebbins] was a painter and paper hanger in Amherst. . . . [his daughter] says that at the time Emily Dickinson was expected that Mrs. Dickinson wanted to have her bedroom painted but the Hon. Edward Dickinson would not allow her to have it done – nevertheless she went secretly to the paper hanger and asked him to come and paper her bedroom. This he did, while Emily was being born" (*YH* I, 16). To give Mrs. Dickinson her due, another instance of her willfulness, if it can be called that, should be recorded. Lavinia wrote Austin on March 23, 1853: "Father is so outraged towards parson Cooke [a temporary supply in the First Church] that he would not let Emilie or me go to church all day last Sunday. Mother would go part of the day though he preferred she should not" (*Home,* p. 268). It should be said, also, that the young lady of Edward's courtship letters seems much more spirited and assertive than the self-effacing figure of later years.

context of Emily's situation at the time and of the heightened, aphoristic rhetoric she habitually used with Higginson. It was her brother Austin's opinion that she "posed" in her letters to Higginson, as she certainly did in her conversations with him. She was turning forty in 1870 and was in the summing-up mood—only a few years earlier she had summed up her father, though more gently, to Joseph Lyman. The Dickinson family was nothing if not critical, of each other as well as everybody else. They had moods and, especially the younger generation, enjoyed hyperbole. Even her usually buoyant friend Samuel Bowles recognized this in Emily. In 1863 he wrote Austin: "I have been in a savage, turbulent state for some time – indulging in a sort of disgust at everything & everybody – I guess a good deal as Emily feels." It may have been that Emily was firmly convinced that her mother had been no mother at all and that she bore her a lifelong grudge. But the main outlines of the relationship as seen over the years tend to put in question her acerbic remarks to Higginson. At any rate, of first importance is what she made of the relationship. And even if we accept the notion that her mother's failure placed her under severe handicaps, it makes of her life with her mother even more of a triumph of self-discipline, humor, patience, and (however belated) love.[2]

2. Mrs. Dickinson's dark role in Emily Dickinson's life is the theme of Dr. John Cody's *After Great Pain.* Millicent Todd Bingham noted a potentially destructive trait in Mrs. Dickinson's character, her "tremulous fear of death" (*Home,* p. 4). Dr. Cody pressed this clue much further. He sees Mrs. Dickinson as a lifelong hypochondriac who must have communicated her fears to her children; an abjectly dependent wife; a fussily compulsive housekeeper; a failure as a mother, especially of her most sensitive child, Emily, whose "voracious love-hunger" (p. 101) was never satisfied. Emily interpreted this failure (so the theory goes) as a "cruel rejection" (p. 2) and grew up in repressed bitterness toward her mother; resented being female; tried to be unlike her mother by defying her father; rebelled against religious submission; read voraciously; and sublimated her "love needs" in her writing. Hence the persistent themes of death, anxiety, suffering in the poems and letters; the withdrawal, self-immolation, and exorbitant concern for every member of her family that became characteristic of her mode of life. All these are interpreted as symptoms of repressed guilt at her deep sense of hostility and alienation, at her unconscious wish to have all her friends and relatives dead, all of whom failed her in one way or another. And the principal failure was her mother's.

In such a diagnosis, everything becomes symptomatic, even (or perhaps especially) the poems, and all is woven into a seamless web. Motives are deduced from scanty evidence—widely scattered poems and remarks in letters that can be read in contradictory ways. To open up the possibility of the truth of other readings is not to deny the possibility that Dr. Cody's hypothesis may also contain an element of truth. He likens it to the "plaster bone" (p. 2) used by archaeologists in reconstructing the fossil skeleton. But the bone is still plaster; ". . . there exists no record," Dr. Cody admits, "of any concrete instance in which Mrs. Dickinson took such an attitude toward her daughter" (p. 2). But if it is permissible to question Dr. Cody's diagnosis, one must insist with him that the old sentimental view—of Emily's lovely, harmonious home and her own normal "blossoming"—is gone forever. Nor is it to slip into any biographical conspiracy to stress the positive side of her relations with her mother. As Dr. Cody himself says, "If I appear to be concentrating on the gloomy side of Emily Dickinson's childhood it is because the brighter side is overstressed by most biographers" (p. 83).

Emily Norcross Dickinson (1804–1882) was born in Monson, Massachusetts (about twenty miles south of Amherst), the daughter of Joel and Betsy Fay Norcross. Like the Dickinsons until Squire Fowler's generation, the Norcrosses were farmers.[3] They also read books and believed in education. Daughter Emily was the third child among her six brothers and two sisters. A baby brother died when she was seven, and her sister Lavinia was born the next year. Her girlhood seems to have been undistinguished,[4] but at least her family thought enough of her to send her to boarding school in New Haven, where she wrote to Lavinia the one letter we have from her girlhood, dated "New Haven July 1823." The letter is sweet and sisterly, full of affection and misspellings. She says she is happy, in good health, and longs for her *"dear dear* home." There is of course no mention of Edward, then in his senior year at Yale.

Whatever she may have become as wife of an exacting husband, Emily Norcross was no nonentity when Edward started courting her three years later in Monson. As he said again and again in the courtship letters, she embodied all the qualities of his ideal woman—"amiable disposition," "modest and unassuming manners," "thorough knowledge of every aspect of domestic economy," "good taste – cultivated & improved by a moderate acquaintance with a few of the most select works of taste" and by association with "refined society." Years later, her daughter Emily was to speak condescendingly of her "unobtrusive faculties," hardly up to the Amherst intellectual level. But one of Edward's letters shows Emily Norcross busy in local cultural programs equal to Amherst at its liveliest. Here is Edward, himself a bit condescending, speaking from the intellectual heights of his college town but obviously impressed by Monson's resources:

> I suppose you are now wading in the snow to or from some meeting and you have something to lead you from home every evening! – I would like to examine you on the subjects to which your attention is so much called, of late – perhaps I could judge of your proficiency and I might possibly give you some useful hints as to the best course to be pursued in making so many studies profitable, at the same time. Let us examine a little – singing school – Chemical Lectures, historical Lectures – Bible Class – Concerts – Missionary, Charitable, & Female Bible Associations – Cent [?] and Tract Society – and

3. Joel Norcross was one of the most substantial farmers in Monson. He kept in close touch with his married daughter in Amherst and at one point advised his son-in-law about building a new house. Relations seem to have been cordial. Emily made only one reference to him (he died when she was sixteen; his wife died the year before Emily was born): "We expect Grandpa Norcross . . . up here this week –" (*L* I, 5; to Austin, May 1, 1842). Her Norcross uncles, aunts, and cousins were another matter; to some of them Emily became devoted.

4. Unless a little yellow certificate, "treasured among the daughter's most cherished papers," be considered a mark of distinction (Martha Dickinson Bianchi, *The Life and Letters of Emily Dickinson,* p. 10):

> Miss Emily Norcross, for punctual attendance, close application, good acquirements, and discreet behavior merits the approbation of her preceptress.

Edward and Emily Norcross Dickinson,
from portraits by O. A. Bullard, 1840

Fishing Party. Water color by Emily Norcross, 1827

others of a name and description which do not now occur to me. Let me say in a word, My Dear Emily, that while I think that all these combined will not produce so much solid good as a much less number, with more time to reflect upon them will produce, still I would have you act your pleasure entirely, in regard to your attendance upon any or all of them – only preserve your health.

Two days later, when he warned her again about taking too many courses, he was confident that "your good sense will guide you right." As to belles-lettres, he himself saw that she was well supplied with the latest novels and with such cultural staples as the *Spectator,* in twelve volumes.

His assurance that she should "act her pleasure" about the evening events is one of many such remarks in his letters, both before the marriage and after.[5] He may have meant exactly the opposite of what he said, of course, but at least he gave her a nominally free rein. And in several ways during the courtship she asserted her independence. She answered his letters at her leisure. She braved his annoyance by refusing his many insistences that she come to Amherst to visit ("invitations without number," as he put it). She disregarded his impatience about the date of the wedding. He finally gave up: "I find that my arguments are without much weight, and I shall not press them against so decided an expression of your will in relation to it." As the date drew near, she was clear about the disposal of her things, which were soon to be sent from Monson by oxcart: "All I wish of you is to lay them in your part of the house and let them rest untill I come." And she was very clear about the arrangements for the ceremony itself, which he had left entirely to her: "I think it best that we stand up alone as I do not wish for company."

Apparently at one point during the courtship, *she* lectured him. In spite of the lofty tone of his response, he seems to have been both impressed and pleased by her show of spirit.

> I was much pleased with the *moral* part [of her letter] and shall endeavor to profit by the good advice which you gave in a few words . . . – I am happy to receive useful hints from any quarter but they come with a peculiar force from you – and will doubtless have a salutary effect – tho' I must confess I was rather amused at the decision of character . . . the air of *authority* & *independence* which you assumed – and I am sure that I have nothing

5. At least in the early years of the marriage, Mrs. Dickinson made frequent trips to see her family in Monson and her brother Joel in Boston. In July 1836 she visited in Springfield. A letter from Edward written (September 11, 1835) during one of her visits to Boston, again insists that she act her pleasure and includes a heart-warming domestic moment:

> Your letter was rec'd last evening, & Loring's this evening – and found us all well – and gave us much pleasure to hear that you were enjoying yourself so well in Boston – that you had concluded not to go to Portland – As to this, I would have you do exactly as you please – I want you to spend as much time & go as far as you desire to now you have got started – tho' I should not object to your coming home as soon as you wish to – . . . Austin enquired very anxiously when he awoke in the night, & found me in bed with him, & I told him I had rec'd a letter

to fear from the exercise of a freedom & frank avowal of sentiment which the fact that "we are not strangers" induced you to speak.

Edward may have been condescending, but he was no antifeminist, at least in principle. He was not only a strenuous advocate of female education, but he knew who set the tone in any household: "A woman, you know [he wrote Emily], gives a character to her house & family, if possible, more than her husband, and when she is what she should be, amiable, virtuous, prudent & intelligent & benevolent, she can hardly fail to draw blessings on herself and on her household."

Edward, as here, seldom resisted the temptation to itemize the qualities of the perfect wife, as if he thought Emily needed constant reminding. At least he included himself in similar reminders, which multiplied as the wedding approached. He outlined the qualities of the perfect married couple.

> May we be virtuous, intelligent, industrious and by the exercise of every virtue, & the cultivation of every excellence, be esteemed & respected & beloved by all – We must determine to do our duty to each other, & to all our friends, and let others do as they may.

Obviously these two young people looked upon marriage less as romantic fulfillment than as a contractual agreement to fulfill together certain social and religious aims and obligations. Tenderness was almost always subordinate to a loftier purpose, whether immediate or eternal. Sometimes Edward seems too tired or preoccupied. "My Dear," he wrote three weeks before the wedding, "my heart is with you, and you are constantly in mind – I can only give you the parting hand, this morning, & leave the expression of a more ardent attachment till another time." There is a wisp of sentiment, and perhaps trepidation, in one of Emily's remarks three days later: "I have many friends call upon me as they say to make their farewell visit. How do you suppose this sounds in my ear. But my dear it is to go and live with you." And Edward, just a week before the ceremony: "The time is short, My Dear, and we shall probably soon have occasion to enter upon the serious duties of life – Are we prepared? But I am too tired to 'moralize.'"

If all this sounds ominous to modern ears, it was pure New England— or at least pure Amherst and pure Dickinson—and seems to have been taken quite for granted by Emily Norcross. She grew into an eminently conventional woman and was probably so as a girl. (It was her spirited sister Lavinia who was the unconventional one, marrying her cousin against family opposition and, we are told, for love.) She apparently fitted without friction into the traditional pattern of dominant husband and sweet submissive wife, with both recognizing a still higher authority, Duty—to each other, their children, their community, and God. Just how dominant Edward became and whether his wife's submissiveness became

---

from his mother, whether *she said anything about* losing her luggage! We all want to see you. . . .

so abject as to degrade her in the eyes of the children (especially Emily's) are questions that must still, I think, remain open. There is little to indicate that the Dickinson domestic situation, at least in its beginnings, was anything but conventional, which is the way the new bride, apparently, liked it.

When, finally, she came to Amherst as Edward's bride, they settled in half of the Widow Jemima Montague's house, painstakingly prepared by Edward. The first year apparently went smoothly, Edward's business growing steadily and Emily adjusting to her new life, "situated pleasently," as her sister Lavinia described her, and only a touch homesick. There was a question of taking in a student boarder, partly for economy, partly as a protection for Emily during Edward's absences. From Court in Northampton, Edward wrote:

> The Hon. Mr. Bliss of Springfield has spoken to me to-day, about boarding his son. . . . You know my opinion respecting it, and I leave it entirely with you to manage as you think best. The work, you know, comes upon you, and it is wholly immaterial with me, what you conclude. . . .

The first child, William Austin, was born on April 16, 1829. (Sister Lavinia's comment during the pregnancy: "It is enough to make any-one discouraged to see what all the married folks are coming to.") A year later, Edward bought from his father one half of the brick Homestead on Main Street, a sign of his growing prosperity as it was of his father's decline. It was here that Emily Elizabeth was born in December, with or without benefit of paper hanger. The following June, Mrs. Dickinson wrote one of her infrequent letters to her husband, then in Boston on business. So far, the auspices were bright.

> I have retired to my chamber for a little space to converse with you, with my little companion on the bed asleep. I have as yet had the pleasure of heareing from you every day which has given me much support. . . . Little Austin often speaks of you. When the bell rings he thinks you are comeing and opens the door to welcome you. Sister Lavinia has not come yet, but I look for her evry day. . . . I must leave you my deare to resume my usual employment which you may well suppose.

The auspices may have been bright, but there is still the problem of Emily Norcross Dickinson as "nonentity" and her influence on her daughter Emily's character and career. Here again there is the baffling fact of Dickinson reticence, in the face of which one must proceed largely by inference. Emily, for instance, spoke once of her mother's "grieved life," but she was never precise about causes and only occasionally about symptoms, notably on matters of the ill health that plagued Mrs. Dickinson periodically from the early 1850s on. Much has been made of Mrs. Dickinson's tendency toward hypochondria, her "tremulous fear of death" (Mrs. Bingham's phrase), and the degree to which she communicated these fears to her children. The cause here is thought to be the early deaths in her immediate family—the baby brother, and two brothers in their twenties, one of them, and her mother, dying the year Austin was born. Surely these events were saddening, but the Norcross losses were not exceptional among the large families of the day. Edward recognized his wife's tendency to worry, especially when the children were young, and he did a good deal of worrying himself. In view of the precarious state of medicine at that time, their anxiety is hardly surprising. But nothing in the Dickinson annals suggests Mrs. Dickinson as the source of such anxieties in any of her children. If the recurrent theme of death in Emily's poems and letters was neurotic in origin, at least there was nothing tremulous about it, and what occupied her as mature artist and thinker was death as an existential phenomenon and as the central religious mystery, to be probed and pondered with the objectivity, almost, of the clinician and the philosopher. Whatever damaging effect, if any, her mother's nervous disabilities had on Emily can only be guessed at. Vinnie seems to have escaped entirely. Austin, even in his maturity, was shocked and stunned by deaths in his immediate circle, but there is no evidence that his fear of death was a constant neurotic disability.

It is well, however, to look for a moment into what *is* known about Mrs. Dickinson's ill health, which after a point was a more or less constant source of worry to the family and was of undoubted importance, good and bad, in Emily's life. It is known that her recovery from Lavinia's birth was much longer than it should have been; and the fact that she had no more children is notable in view of the large families (nine children in each) from which she and her husband came. There are indications that Emily began to worry about her in the mid-1850s. Then, and later when she suffered a stroke in 1875, the sisters spent a good deal of time nursing her and taking care of the house when she was incapacitated. For the last four years of her life she required constant attention.[6]

6. Here is a brief survey of Mrs. Dickinson's illnesses, in so far as they can be traced in the annals:

The trouble following Lavinia's birth in 1834 lasted, apparently, for some months. Mrs. Dickinson seems to have been in good health for the next dozen years or so. "We are sick hardly ever at home," ED wrote Abiah Root on May 7, 1850, reporting her dismay at a sudden illness of her mother's. On the seventeenth, she wrote, "Mother is still an invalid tho' a partially restored one. . . . [In her absence from the kitchen] I am yet the Queen of the court" (*L* I, 97, 99). On May 10, 1852, she wrote Austin that "[Mother] was attacked Friday, with a difficulty in her face, similar to the one you have, and with which you suffer so much once or twice in a year. . . . Vinnie and I have had to work pretty hard on account of her sickness" (*L* I, 204). Edward added a note: "Mother has been severely afflicted with the Neuralgia arising from her front tooth . . . it was lanced . . . & she is now relieved" (*YH* I, 248). In January 1856, ED wrote Mrs. Holland that "Mother has been an invalid since we came *home*, and Vinnie and I 'regulated,' and Vinnie and I 'got settled,' and still we keep our father's house, and mother lies upon the lounge, or sits in her easy chair. I don't know what her sickness is . . . (*L* II, 324). In September 1856, a letter from Jane Hitchcock to a friend outside Amherst speaks of "Mrs. D's health" as "poor": "she is at the

Certainly one of the influences that kept Emily at home and contributed to her secluded life was her mother's health and the extra work it entailed. Vinnie once called it the decisive one. Perhaps it was simple physical inadequacy that kept Mrs. Dickinson from the vigorous fulfillment of all her motherly duties. Emily spoke once of her weariness. Perhaps it was this kind of inadequacy, among others, that she had in mind in those two remarks to Higginson. But it is at least worth noting that we have no bitter complaints from either daughter—a hint of fatigue now and then, and preoccupation, but no resentment. A note of Emily's to the Norcross cousins in 1880 is typical:

I have only a moment, exiles, but you shall have the largest half. Mother's dear little wants so engross the time, – to read to her, to fan her, to tell her health will come tomorrow, to explain to her *why* the grasshopper is a burden, because he is not so new a grasshopper as he was, – this is so ensuing, I hardly have said "Good-morning, mother," when I hear myself saying "Mother, good-night."

Apparently, the tedious duties, undertaken with discipline and imagination, became even pleasant. Emily enjoyed at least something of what she called, when her mother was helpless, "a holier demand." After her mother's death she wrote a friend:

Only the night before she died, she was happy and hungry and ate a little Supper I made her with such enthusiasm, I laughed with delight, and told her she was as hungry as Dick.

One need not be a sentimentalist to see in Emily's ultimate feeling for both her mother and father a tenderness and humane understanding that redeem, if they do not contradict, her earlier posturings.

The picture brightens a bit, too, as we look beyond the family. Mrs. Dickinson was not quite the nonentity in the community she has been pictured. One commentator, more generous than most, has given an appealing account of her function both within the family and outside:

The habit that grew up among the Dickinson children of lampooning their neighbors may have had its origin in the characterizations formed by their father's keen and critical mind. Through their mother they were more directly connected with the joys and the calamities in the families of Amherst, rich and poor.

---

water-cure in N. Hampton" (*YH* I, 344). Her illness "was a condition that lasted for several years and caused the family much anxiety" (*L* II, 324 n.). Leyda (*YH* I, lxxvii) thinks her "nervous illness at that time" (*ca.* January 1858) may have prompted ED to write the Reverend Charles Wadsworth of Philadelphia for advice. ED wrote Mrs. Haven that summer: "Mother is much as usual. I know not what to hope of her" (*L* II, 337). But on July 12, 1863, a neighbor wrote a friend: "Mrs. Edward Dickinson sent [Dr. Stearns, president of the college] a most elegant Boquet . . . she . . . admires him, & is now quite herself" (*YH* II, 81). Nothing of importance is recorded from then until the stroke she suffered on June 15, 1875, from which she never fully recovered. It was from this time on that she required ED's and Lavinia's constant care, made all the more difficult when she broke her hip in June 1878.

Emily once caught her in a characteristic project: "Mother drives with Tim [the stableman] to carry pears to settlers." We hear of her sending apples to Samuel Bowles and a bouquet to President Stearns of the college. She seems to have been much more chatty and sociable than the mousy figure of tradition, loving her friends and her calls—Emily called them "rambles." We hear of her going to parties at "Prof. Warner's" and "Prof. Haven's." She loved gossip. Once, when her mother was sick, Emily wrote a friend: "Mother pines for you, and says you were 'so social.' Mother misses power to ramble to her Neighbors – and the stale inflation of the minor News." As to what her friends thought of her, the records are meager. The words "fluttering," "anxious," "timid," "meek" come mostly from those who knew her in her later years. Those who knew her at her best speak of her as "pleasant" and "sweet," though "plaintive." Edward, who was always conscious of family status, seems never to have wavered in his loyalty to her.[7]

Though hardly a leader, Mrs. Dickinson was active in the community in many ways that must have made Edward proud of her. In one of his courtship letters, he wrote enthusiastically from Northampton about the Cattle Show then on display:

> There are a great variety of fine specimens of domestic industry & skill which it would be creditable to any lady to imitate – and I consider it as an honor to any female to have her name publicly announced as having obtained a premium for her excellence in any branch of domestic economy.

The Amherst Cattle Show was no less an event, and Mrs. Dickinson contributed to it annually. She served on committees and won premiums for

7. Martha Dickinson Bianchi described her grandmother as the "fluttering little mother, always timorous, always anxious" (*Life and Letters*, p. 10). Martha was only sixteen when Mrs. Dickinson died, and hence knew only her invalid days. Mabel Loomis Todd, who hardly knew her at all, dismissed her as "a meek little thing" (*AB*, 232). Her immediate contemporaries, though sometimes agreeing, seem to have sensed other qualities. A caller in the early days found her "as usual full of plaintive talk" (*YH* I, 81, September 15, 1843), but another described her as "very pleasant" (*YH* I, 282, August 31, 1853). As for Edward, his letters home from his business trips during their early married years have been considered condescending, but I see no reason why remarks like the following cannot be taken at face value. After ten years of married life he could say of her letters: "I find you always have something to say, & it is very easy for you to say it" (*YH* I, 40, January 9, 1838). On his trips, he continually longs to be back home. (Cody, pp. 69, 87, sees him as protesting too much and as secretly wishing to be rid of his family.) As he became more and more involved in public affairs and as responsibilities mounted, he may have become increasingly aloof from her as he did from the children. Her ill health was obviously a burden. But his early respect and affection for her never seem to have diminished. When she died, she was among the "great losses" Mrs. Boltwood described to Mrs. Ford: ". . . Mr. & Mrs. Sweetser & now dear Mrs Edward Dickinson . . ." (*YH* II, 385, November 25, 1882). The opinion of those who knew her best in the later years seems to have been close to Emily's: she "achieved in sweetness what she lost in strength" (*L* III, 771, spring 1883).

her cooking and produce. She was the hostess, however anxious and fluttery, at the famous Dickinson receptions at Commencement time, a sign at least of some social talent. She joined the First Church, whether from tremulous fear or positive commitment we do not know, nineteen years before her husband, and was active in its work.

Her few ventures into the intellectual life of the college, it seems clear, were of mixed success. One lecture was said to have "interested" her, but she was apparently swamped by another on Adam Smith; it was this latter that she confessed (as Emily phrased it to Austin) to be "too high for her unobtrusive faculties." "My Mother," Emily later told Higginson, "does not care for thought." But that she was incapable of thought, or intellectually illiterate, is another matter. Her cultural activities in Monson before her marriage gave her at least a start on higher education. There are signs that she pursued it, however intermittently. Her brother William gave her three volumes of Cowper's poems for a wedding present; and in 1855 Edward's colleague in the General Court, Charles Sumner, the famous orator who had spoken at the Amherst Commencement in 1847 and had probably been entertained at the Dickinsons', sent her a copy of Lydia Child's biography of the Quaker, Isaac T. Hopper, just off the press. Emily gives us a glimpse of her reading "uncarnal" books in the family circle, and once spoke of her "reading a little" during her later years of illness. What little we have of her correspondence shows her as no ardent letter writer and a rather graceless one at that. She usually protested that she was too busy for letters, a tendency that started early and became a family joke. In 1836 her sister-in-law, Lucretia, writing to Edward, asked that she at least "write her *name*" in Edward's next letter, "so as not [to] forget how to write." Years later, when the family was well established, Emily wrote Austin, "Mother was much amused at the feebleness of your hopes of hearing from her – She got so far last week once, as to take a pen and paper and carry them into the kitchen." Once she sent him a lock of her hair in a letter of Emily's, who transmitted her message: "to put you in mind of your affectionate mother." This epistolary reticence is, of course, one of the reasons we know so little about her. Such a gap may have profound implications about her inadequacies; but one simple explanation may be that she enjoyed other ways of expressing herself, like sending flowers, or fruit, or locks of hair. Like her daughter Vinnie, she was a doer. Her literary deficiency, especially when Austin was away, gave Emily her chance. Emily's letters to him are sisterly and motherly at once, a function Mrs. Dickinson once used as an excuse for not writing herself.

One wonders how often Mrs. Dickinson joined in the family humor that Emily spoke of often and happily. It is reassuring to hear that she could be "much amused" by Austin's complaint about her not writing him; and Emily, once describing a family scene in which her "rheumatic sire" behaved badly toward some visitors, found her mother and Vinnie in the kitchen "making most desperate efforts to control themselves," presumably their mirth. In a family that enjoyed quoting one another, her voice is heard less than most and much less than her husband's. Sometimes she is quoted straight. Vinnie wrote Austin that "Mother had a nice time in Boston & told fine stories of your fame among Bostonians," and once, when he had not written for some time, "Mother says it seems as though you had been struck out of existance." When Mrs. Dickinson came home from the funeral of her brother-in-law, Loring Norcross, Emily wrote her cousins: "Mother tells how gently he looked on all who looked at him – how he held his bouquet sweet, as he were a guest in a friend's parlor and must still do honor. The meek, mild gentleman who thought no harm, but peace toward all"—a good description, probably, of Mrs. Dickinson herself; and if the simile of the first sentence is her own and not her daughter's, we must revise our notion of Mrs. Dickinson's lack of imagination. Apparently she was good at funerals. When Mrs. Hitchcock died, Emily wrote the Norcrosses:

> Jennie Hitchcock's mother was buried yesterday, so there is one orphan more, and her father is very sick besides. My father and mother went to the service, and mother said while the minister prayed, a hen with her chickens came up, and tried to fly into the window. I suppose the dead lady used to feed them, and they wanted to bid her good-by.

(The final thought, however, was probably Emily's.) Mostly, when Emily quoted her mother, it was to poke fun at her motherly anxieties—about Austin's clothes when he was in Boston teaching school; his safety ("and mother – oh she thought the bears in the wood had devoured you, or if you were not eaten up, you were such a monster of thoughtlessness and neglect!" for not writing); or the fierceness of his discipline in school: "Mother feels quite troubled about those little boys – fears you will kill one sometime when you are punishing him – for *her sake* be careful!" Sometimes she seems to be making fun of her mother's commonplace thought or language, as when Mrs. Dickinson hoped her grandson Ned "would be a very good Boy." "Not very dood," Emily has him say; and adds: "Obtuse ambition of Grandmamas!" Twice Emily quoted her mother condescendingly. Austin had sent her a bonnet: "Mother wants me to thank you for all your pains and trouble, and says you 'are very kind to do so much for your mother.'" And again about one of Mrs. Dickinson's simple pleasures: "The horse is doing nicely, he travels 'like a bird,' to use a favorite phrase of your delighted mother's."

A family scene in the spring of 1851, described for Austin's benefit, puts both mother and father under the same gentle fire and brings up the whole problem of Emily's humor toward her parents, and, indeed, her use of humor in general. Was her mirth protective—the "Mail of Anguish," her way of concealing bitter resentment or fear? Or was it carefree, unambiguous, lighthearted? How much of it was the exercise of wit, in this instance, on slightly vulnerable subjects?

Mother is warming her feet, which she assures me confidently are "just as cold as ice.["] I tell her I fear there is danger of icification, or ossification – I dont know certainly which! Father is reading the Bible – I take it for *consolation,* judging from outward things. He and mother take great delight in dwelling upon your character, and reviewing your many virtues, and Father's prayers for you at our morning devotions are enough to break one's heart – it is really very touching; surely "our blessings brighten" the farther off they fly! Mother wipes her eyes with the end of her linen apron, and consoles herself by thinking of several future places "where congregations ne'er break up," and Austins have no end!

Whatever the verdict on Emily's humor—what was going on subconsciously must remain a mystery—its part in her achievement, both personal and artistic, was powerful. It seldom left her for long. Through it she could maintain, or regain, her poise. What her moods were like when she was not writing we have no way of knowing; but her wits—and her wit—seldom failed her when she put pen to paper. She could even pun in her remark to Higginson about coming home to "Awe": "He was an awful Mother, but I liked him better than none."

The remarks got tenderer as time went on. A letter to the Norcrosses in the early spring of 1870 says that "Mother went rambling, and came in with a burdock on her shawl, so we know that the snow has perished from the earth. Noah would have liked mother." A little of the old bite, perhaps, came in a remark to Mrs. Holland three years later, thanking her for kindnesses to Vinnie (this was a year before her father's death and two before her mother's stroke): "She [Vinnie] has no Father and Mother but me and I have no Parents but her." The remark is an isolated one, and there is no bill of complaints. If Mrs. Holland was shocked, there is no record of it; apparently Emily felt she would make the proper discount. When Dr. Holland showed signs of failing strength in 1881, Emily described to Mrs. Holland, with unconcealed surprise and delight, one of her mother's finest moments:

I ask Mother "what message" she sends – She says, "Tell them I wish I could take them both in my Arms and carry them –"
I never before have heard her speak so – those were the very words –

And later that year, when Dr. Holland died, Emily reported her mother's earlier comment on Edward Dickinson's death: "I loved him so." Emily added: "Had he a tenderer eulogy?"

In the history of the Dickinson complexities—that is, the tendency, from Samuel Fowler on down, toward introversion and a highly developed inner life—Mrs. Dickinson hardly figures at all. There is no indication that she was admitted to the secret discontents of her husband, or her troubled son, or her two independent daughters. She seems to have had little idea of what Emily was up to. She found her, as one contemporary said, "a mystery and a constant surprise"—and sometimes a shock. Emily recorded one such incident in a letter to Mrs. Holland in July 1880:

Austin and I were talking the other Night about the Extension of Consciousness, after Death and Mother told Vinnie, afterward, she thought it was "very improper."

She forgets that we are past "Correction in Righteousness –"

I dont know what she would think if she knew that Austin told me confidentially "there was no such person as Elijah."

Indeed, it is hard to imagine what she would have thought had she known a fraction of the rebellious notions that crowded Emily's mind. Except for this attempt (certainly a futile one), there is no record that she ever interfered with Emily's inner life. But perhaps in this very way she contributed to it most. Whether intentionally or out of sheer bewilderment, she made herself dispensable. Emily had enough to contend with in her father; a prying or domineering mother would have made life intolerable.

Mrs. Dickinson seems to have been important in Emily's life both for what she did and for what she was. On the practical side, there is ample evidence that, as far as her strength permitted, she was a loving and attentive mother and did all she could to anticipate and meet the wants of her family. "Mother makes nicer pies with reference to your coming," Emily wrote Austin, then teaching in Boston. She had certain positive interests and skills that Emily shared. The herbarium that Emily kept as a girl must have owed something to the encouragement and guidance of her mother,[8] who loved flowers and kept a fine garden. One of Emily's abiding concerns, horticulture, may have had this simple, obvious source. Emily described her once, when the family was away, as never busier " – what with fruit, and plants, and chickens, and sympathizing friends."

In another practical way, Mrs. Dickinson contributed to her daughter's life. When Emily came home in the fall of 1864 from the months in Boston, where she had gone for treatments for her eyes, she was incapacitated for anything but housework. "Mother and Margaret [O'Brien] are so kind," she wrote her cousin.

They say I am a "help." Partly because it is true, I suppose, and the rest applause. . . . For the first few weeks I did nothing but comfort my plants. . . . I chop the chicken centres when we have roast fowl. . . . Then I make the yellow to the pies, and bang the spice for cake, and knit the soles to the stockings I knit the bodies to last June.

8. Now in the Dickinson Room of the Houghton Library, Harvard, the herbarium shows a fine sense of composition, as well as a concern for precise Latin nomenclature which she probably did *not* get from her mother. (Botany was one of her important studies at school.) Nor did her mother help her much in the matter of clothes; "for you may not remember," Emily wrote Joseph Lyman, "that our amiable mother never taught us tayloring and I am amused to remember those clothes, or rather those apologies made up from dry goods with which she covered us in nursery times . . ." (LL, p. 70). For samples of ED's herbarium, see the endpapers of this volume.

That she could do the work was due to her mother's training. Emily enjoyed cooking and was good at it. We have some of her recipes,[9] and Higginson reported that her father would eat no bread except that baked by her.

It is in this regard that the one bit of unqualified praise of Mrs. Dickinson has come down to us. Among the glowing memories of Joseph Lyman, that schoolboy visitor in the Dickinson home during the 1840s, none glowed more brightly than that of Mrs. Dickinson's cooking: "Vinnie's mother was a rare and delicate cook in such matters as crullers and custards and she taught the girls all those housewifely accomplishments." (Lyman was a sharp observer and saw enough, incidentally, to reverse the stock notion of the role of the two sisters in the household: "Em is an excellent housekeeper – Vinnie is sometimes afraid of soiling her little fat hands but can do very well when she chooses.") Later on, Lyman became something of an authority on domestic affairs, even to the point of writing a book on the subject, *The Philosophy of Housekeeping,* which had considerable currency in the late 1860s. It is clear from the many references in his early letters that he learned the first principles from his observations of Mrs. Dickinson's household.

Besides the domestic skills (although she hated the cleaning and

---

9. Here, for instance, are her recipes for gingerbread and black cake.

GINGERBREAD
    1 Quart Flour,
    ½ Cup Butter,
    ½ Cup Cream,
    1 Table Spoon Ginger,
    1 Tea Spoon Soda,
    1 Salt
Make up with Molasses –   (*L* II, 493)

BLACK CAKE –
    2 pounds Flour –
    2 Sugar –
    2 Butter –
    19 Eggs –
    5 pounds Raisins –
    1½ Currants –
    1½ Citron –
    ½ pint Brandy –
    ½ – Molasses –
    2 Nutmegs –
    5 teaspoons
        Cloves – Mace – Cinnamon –
    2 teaspoons Soda –
Beat Butter and Sugar together –
Add Eggs without beating – and beat the mixture again –
Bake 2½ or three hours, in Cake pans, or 5 to 6 hours in
    Milk pan, if full –   (*L* III, 783–84)

dusting, which she called "a prickly art"[10]), Emily learned from her what was perhaps more valuable than anything a brilliant mother could have given her: some lessons in simple, devoted humanity, important for a precocious girl not disinclined to the Dickinson snobbery and the satiric Dickinson wit. She may have condescended to her mother's unobtrusive faculties, but she could hardly doubt her tender heart or love. Here is the scene as Emily described it at her first homecoming from Mount Holyoke.

> Soon the carriage stopped in front of our own house & all were at the door to welcome the returned one, from Mother with tears in her eyes down to Pussy who tried to look as gracious as was becoming her dignity.

When Austin, on a similar occasion a few years later, failed to show up, she scolded him on her mother's account:

> Mother got a great dinner yesterday, thinking in her kind heart that you would be so hungry after your *long ride,* and the table was set for you, and nobody moved your chair, but there it stood at the table, until dinner was all done, a melancholy emblem of the blasted hopes of the world. And we had new custard pie, too, which is a rarity in days when hens dont lay, but mother knew you loved it, and when noon really got here, and you really did not come, then a big piece was saved in case you should come at night.

A deeper tenderness and a fuller understanding came when Emily had outgrown her youthful condescension. A late reminiscence sums up what she learned from her mother:

> Two things I have lost with Childhood – the rapture of losing my shoe in the Mud and going Home barefoot, wading for Cardinal flowers and the mothers reproof which was more for my sake than her weary own for she frowned with a smile [–] now Mother and Cardinal flower are parts of a closed world –

When Mrs. Dickinson died on November 14, 1882, after the long illness that demanded so much of her daughters, Emily's letters contain no sigh of relief, only shock and loss and an enlarged sense of what her mother was and what she meant to her. "I hoped to write you before," she wrote the Norcross cousins in Monson a few days after the event, "but mother's dying almost stunned my spirit. . . . She was scarcely the aunt you knew. The great mission of pain had been ratified – cultivated to tenderness by persistent sorrow, so that a larger mother died than had she died before." A few weeks later, she was still trying to rally her forces: "Blow has followed blow, till the wondering terror of the Mind clutches what is left, helpless of an accent." The metaphor and cadence of one of

---

10. *L* III, 827 (to the Norcrosses, early August 1884). This is in line with her earlier remark, "God keep me from what they call *households* . . ." *L* I, 99 (to Abiah Root, May 17, 1850). She liked the creative part—"making things"—but routine maintenance bored her. Nor did she ever show Vinnie's tendency to take charge.

her early poems came back to her: "Her dying feels to me like many kinds of Cold – at times electric, at times benumbing – then a trackless waste" (recall the last lines of "After great pain": "As Freezing persons, recollect the Snow – / First – Chill – then Stupor – then the letting go –"). Then came a summing up quite different from the aphoristic sentences to Higginson and Mrs. Holland:

> We were never intimate Mother and Children while she was our Mother – but Mines in the same Ground meet by tunneling and when she became our Child, the Affection came – When we were children and she journeyed, she always brought us something. Now, would she bring us but herself, what an only Gift – Memory is a strange Bell – Jubilee, and Knell.

There is reason enough, even here, for Emily's notion of her mother's "grieved life." Life for these late-Puritan parents was real and earnest, and it would seem especially so for Mrs. Dickinson, with an overworked husband and with children she had difficulty understanding. As in many New England homes, the parents did not cultivate intimacy with their children. Emily's admission of the belated affection is a striking one; we can guess that often in such households the affection did not come at all. It came, too, with Vinnie, who (in a letter to Mrs. Todd) composed her mother's tenderest eulogy:

> The days are beautiful but so sorrowful without my sweet Mother. I'm so glad you saw her dear face & *she* heard your bird voice. She was so fond of every bird & flower & so full of pity for every grief. Keep fast hold of your parents, for the world will always be strange & homesick without their affection.

Or, as Emily later wrote a friend who had lost her mother: "To have *had* a Mother – how mighty!"

Oddly enough, although it is seldom seen this way, the greatest tribute that Emily paid her mother lay perhaps in the fact that she never wanted to leave the home that Mrs. Dickinson helped create. There were many and more complicated reasons for her staying at home, but the fact that she stayed suggests strongly that she felt freest at home—free to live the kind of life and do the kind of work that suited her. Although Mrs. Dickinson may not have nurtured her daughter's genius with wise talk and literary encouragement, she was a central figure in establishing the milieu in which her genius came into its own. That Emily never wanted to leave it can, I suppose, be regarded as an unfortunate eccentricity or as a symptom of profound psychic fear. The undeniable facts are that she stayed home, wrote her poetry and letters, and learned to love her mother.

Though the love came late, there was nothing mawkish about it. Emily found a poem (probably more than one) in her mother as she had in her father—something awesome and fathomless in the life and death even of this fluttery, timid woman whom latterly she had to care for like a child. Some months after Mrs. Dickinson died, she wrote:

All is faint indeed without our vanished mother, who achieved in sweetness what she lost in strength, though grief of wonder at her fate made the winter short, and each night I reach finds my lungs more breathless, seeking what it means.

> To the bright east she flies
> Brothers of Paradise
> Remit her home,
> Without a change of wings,
> Or Love's convenient things,
> Enticed to come.
>
> Fashioning what she is,
> Fathoming what she was,
> We deem we dream –
> And that dissolves the days
> Through which existence strays
> Homeless at home. [#*1573*]

But again we will let Vinnie have the last word: "Father believed," she said in her later years, "and mother loved."

6

William Austin Dickinson

THE DEEPER WE GET into Dickinson complexities, the more grueling they become. And none are more so than those surrounding Emily's brother, Austin (1829-1895)—his character, his career, his establishment next door with his wife, Susan, and all that this tangled relationship meant to Emily, for better and for worse. Austin's story is the most harrowing and, in its innumerable relevancies to Emily, the most immediate to our purpose. Of all the family, he was closest to Emily in temperament, taste, sense of self and of the world. He had something of the philosopher and the poet in him, without the talent for either. From early manhood, he was a soul in trouble. His letters reveal, in groping but sometimes impressive prose, many of the inner problems and anxieties Emily worked out in her poems. The two of them had the same sense of humor and often talked as if they were the only Dickinsons who counted. Their sister Lavinia was indispensable, but in another way. It was Austin and Emily against the world, a relationship of infinite importance to both. What that "world" was, especially that aspect of it which pressed in on them both, daily, in the Dickinson enclave on Main Street, must be explored fully.

It has been said of Mrs. Dickinson that "she served chiefly as a carrier of Dickinson traits." In this humble function she served Austin as well as Emily, so at the outset it is proper to consider him in the light of the line we have traced from his grandfather. By the time he came to maturity, the family name and fortune were fully restored, to the point of acknowledged leadership in the town and some prominence in the state. The Dickinsons had acquired an aura of superiority in Amherst, even a snobbishness that some townsfolk found hard to forgive. There is a legend that they preempted the sidewalk in front of the two mansions—that lesser citizens gave way when members of the family walked abroad. Austin had a brusque and blunt way that made enemies in a fashion not recorded of his father. It was said he looked down on almost everyone—except his sister Emily. As treasurer of the college for twenty-two years, he (like his father before him) instructed Amherst presidents in their duties; as the saying went, "Presidents come and go but Dickinsons go on forever."

Nevertheless, Austin also had warmer friends, perhaps, than any recorded of his father. Henry Hills, a local businessman whom Austin helped in difficulty, wrote his wife, "Austin is the same royal friend in adversity as in prosperity and I declare life is worth something to have such a friend." Mabel Loomis Todd records Austin's fondness for taking Amherst ladies to drive—and "proud" they were to be asked. But like his father he had a sharp tongue. Once, Leander Skinner, postmaster and prominent citizen, complained bitterly of Austin, who had chided him on the station platform for leaving for vacation while others were working. Skinner wrote his wife: "Then Dickinson blated out in his rough way loud enough to be heard half a mile. . . . It seemed to me quite uncalled for in this bitter sort of way and so much in public." Earlier Skinner had spoken of Austin's "enemies," who, blaming him for increased expenses in the church that year, had kept him from being elected to the Parish Committee. "This," wrote Skinner, "is a little hard on Austin, should consider it so if it was me."

Austin was a more colorful and assertive figure than his father, with a temperament that pointed toward the future rather than the past—that is, away from the latter-day Puritanism that seems to have been at the core of his father's lonely and rigorous life. He developed tastes and a style that his father would not have understood. His flamboyant dress is a part of Amherst history: he "had about him a picturesque quality, as he appeared in his light-colored driving coat, his yellow wide-brimmed planter's hat, and his orange-wood cane."[1] As a youth he was described as tall and straight, "with a head of unruly reddish hair."[2] He had a deep love of nature and carried on a tradition started by his grandfather (but, as far as we know, neglected by his father) for beautifying Amherst with trees and shrubs. He often combed the countryside for the right specimen for a special purpose and was the leader in a movement from which the town

1. Claude M. Fuess, *Amherst: The Story of a New England College* (1935), p. 185. At least Fuess's description is part of Amherst legend. He calls him "high-strung, lavish, born to lead." Millicent Todd Bingham quotes Miss Vryling Buffum, friend of Vinnie's and principal of a girls' school in Amherst, as saying that Austin "used to preside over town meetings in lavender trousers and a Prince Albert coat" (record of conversation of November 2, 1934; Todd-Bingham Archive, Yale).

2. *Home*, p. 5. Mrs. Bingham (p. 293 n.) scouts the rumor that Austin in his later years wore a *green* wig. (Stanley King, *A History of the Endowment of Amherst College*, 1950, p. 104): "Following an attack of fever [malaria] after his visit to the Philadelphia Centennial in 1876, he wore a wig – a reddish wig." She continues: "As a child . . . I do remember wondering why his hair was so long. And I vividly recall the coppery glint of it and the shining highlights." King, like Fuess, makes much of Austin's unorthodox qualities: "he permitted himself more personal eccentricities than is usual with a college treasurer" (p. 104).

William Austin Dickinson, about 1890

North Pleasant Street. The Dickinson house was on the right, about a block down

Main Street. The Dickinson houses (the Homestead and the Evergreens) are on the left, the First Congregational Church (the Dickinsons' church) on the right

still benefits. He was passionately fond of art. His wife once described him as he returned from a trip to New York "in a feverish excitement over pictures – utterly worn out with his passion – The real fact of the matter is his desire and half plan for three of the Dusseldorf collection – He is fascinated with the longing, and I advise him to get them." On July 5, 1884, he noted in his diary, "bought a water color of some one at the door this P M for $20.00"—an extravagance his father would not have dreamed of.[3]

Austin was more sociable than his father, read widely, and was fond of giving advice (especially to his lady friends) on what to read. In his early years he was known among his friends as a budding Transcendentalist; at least, this is the implication of the long verse letter sent him in 1850 by his Aunt Elisabeth.[4] His letters show a conscious attention to the epistolary

3. Barton L. St. Armand, currently engaged in a study of Austin's art collection, finds his preference to have been for foreign genre scenes of the French and German schools.
4. The letter (dated "winter 1850"), now in the Dickinson archive in the Frost Library, Amherst College, is the fifty rhyming stanzas already referred to. *YH* I, 184, prints only the two and a half having to do with Austin's facial ailment and Emily's owing Aunt Elisabeth a letter. The stanzas about Austin's Transcendental tendencies are:

> Transcendentalism tis said,
> By one who's well and ably read,
> Is moonshine, shavings, dust, and fog
> And does some noble footsteps dog.
>
> Forgive me, if I tell you, "dear,"
> *Your* feet are dogged by it, I fear,
> And do you ask – "pray, tell me why"?
> Ah yes! I'll tell you by and by.

Whether Emily's footsteps were similarly dogged is a question. Perhaps so, in her youth. At any rate, Emily seems to have been more on Elisabeth's side when she chided Austin for being her "romantic Brother" (*L* I, 115, June 22, 1851). The racy stanza in her valentine of 1852 (*P* #3) shows no particular respect for Transcendentalism:

> I climb the "Hill of Science,"
> I "view the landscape o'er;"
> Such transcendental prospect,
> I ne'er beheld before!

But whatever his intellectual leanings, Austin's advice about this time to Susan Gilbert on what to read was conservative. "For myself," he writes, "I take most pleasure in looking over *old* books, what little time I have for reading – books that I have read before – piled on my shelf & scattered over my table are Bachelor's Reveries – Dana's Prose & Poems – The Bible – 'Grantley Manor,' 'Shirley' Pollok's Course of Time – Coleridge's Table Talk – Kent's Commentaries – &c &c &c and Mosses from an old Manse – I have been reading your Adam & Eve article & like it – I cant the moment think of anything among the things you havent read that will interest you more than Irving's 'Life of Columbus' " (*YH* I, 218, October 11 ?, 1851). Since all three of the young people exchanged literary gossip during these years, most likely this same kind of advice went to Emily. A year and a half later, he tells Susan in great detail

art in an age that made much of it. Emily found them "much funnier – much funnier" than *Punch,* and praised their *"descriptive* merits." Her father called them, so she told Austin, "altogether before Shakespeare."[5] He was deeply stirred by the theater at its best.[6] One of his enthusiasms

---

why he advised against her reading Georgiana Fullerton's *Lady Bird:* it is "unhealthy," "disease laden," "full of only wretchedness & misery. . . . a story of deeper suffering than many ever know – that it's best *any should* know till they are obliged to . . ." (*YH* I, 275). But Sue had read it anyway.

5. *L* I, 233, 113, 122. A letter from Austin to Joseph Lyman written when they both were in college (Austin in Amherst, Lyman at Yale) shows how these young people cultivated the art of letter writing. This, of course, was a conscious and lifelong concern also of ED's, to the extent, as Robert Lambert, Jr., shows in his forthcoming study, "The Prose of a Poet: A Critical Study of Emily Dickinson's Letters," that many of her letters can be compared with her poems as organic, coherent works of art. Austin's letter begins (*LL,* pp. 11–13):

> FRIEND JO.
> Pardon me for not having before answered your letter. The reasons have been various. In the first place, when studying constantly, as we must in term time, I feel but little in the mood of writing to anyone, and, consequently, am extremely dillatory, and even impolite about writing or answering letters, during term. – Secondly, (in order, not importance) in answer to your production, I hardly knew whether you expected me to criticize your essay on letter writing, to enter into an argument with you on the subjects of Epistles, or, strictly to follow the rules, so nicely and perspicuously laid down. I have, however, concluded, after much consideration and reflection, influenced somewhat by not being able to find your letter, just at present, to (this time) write what I please, in my own way. Before I write you again, I shall look up your letter, (which I believe is in my college room, and we are not allowed access to them in vacation) and receiving an answer to this, shall carefully compare the two, to see how well your practice accords with your theory. I will (by the way) mention here that, I liked you[r] idears on the subject, very well; and think that to be well followed, *your,* as well as all *other* rules on the subject should be speedily forgotten – for in attempting to follow rules for being easy, a person will be almost sure to be stiff – Dont you think so? – Well, Jo – whether you do, or not, – to dispense with your letter for the present, perhaps I cannot do better, as I feel rather dull, and egotism is allowable in letters, than to tell you just where and how I am at the present moment – then, something, of myself, family, and affairs in Amherst, generally –

There follows one of the nicest descriptions we have of life in the Dickinson household, with the fire crackling in the stove, the kitchen table littered with books (the list begins with "Webster's big Dictionary"), Emily going on a mysterious errand, and preparations being made for festivities in the absence of "the ancient people" (Father and Mother) who have gone to Monson to see the relatives. Austin is at his best, easy and relaxed. His letters were cherished by all the family, especially Father. That Austin valued Emily's letters and expected much of them is clear both from the fact that he preserved them carefully (while destroying his wife Susan's) and from such a comment as this from Emily: "John Emerson just went away from here – he has been spending the evening, and I'm so tired now, that I write just as it happens, so you must'nt expect any style" (*L* I, 296, early June 1854).

6. His diary for April 11, 1883, notes the following: "Evng went to the Museum [Boston] to hear Salvini and Clara Morris as Othello and Desdemona, a revelation to me of human power" (*YH* II, 396). The diary contains many other references to plays and musical events, especially during his trips to Boston (e.g., "Faust at the Globe," November 9, 1880; Sarah Bernhardt in *Camille,* December 13, 1880, and in *Frou Frou*

came down from father to son: he kept fine horses and was very proud of them.

In such ways, more than any Dickinson before him, Austin cut a figure. The style of life in the Evergreens, once he and his wife were well established, outshone anything the Homestead had known. His service to the community, the church, and the college was in the good Dickinson tradition, but unlike his grandfather and father he never became involved in politics outside Amherst. Respected like them, he was more of an eccentric than either, less inclined to restrain his moods and inclinations. He was disturbed early by religious doubts and cosmic anxieties that they either never knew or never expressed. His youth was much stormier than theirs appear to have been. And later, under heavy domestic pressures, he chafed sadly against the confining life and ethos of Amherst.

Emily appears most frequently in his early years, since all her letters to him cover that span. His youthful problems, as he broods over them in the scraps of correspondence that survive from that period, provide insights into much that may have been troubling her. But what for her became the stuff of poetry meant frustration, sadness, and tragedy for him. His development from exuberant if puzzled youth, toward melancholy and introversion, and finally to the harrowing complexities of his later relationships, is a continuous revelation of what Emily called "that Campaign inscrutable / Of the Interior."

Emily's first letter to Austin, the first of hers we have to anybody, was written when she was eleven. This was long before the clouds began to gather. He was away at school, and she missed him:

> As Father was going to Northampton and thought of coming over to see you [at Williston Seminary in nearby Easthampton] I thought I would improve the opportunity and write you a few lines – We miss you very much indeed you cannot think how odd it seems without you there was always such a Hurrah wherever you was.

Nearly ten years later she wrote in the same vein, though more moderately: "I long so to see you Austin, and hear your happy voice, it will do

---

the next evening; "Took half an hour of Oscar Wilde standing," January 31, 1882; "Went to see Black Crook," May 1, 1882; "Went to hear and see Mrs. [Lily] Langtry [at New York] in evening," November 21, 1882, etc.). At least once (and probably many more times) he shared his enthusiasm with Emily, who commented on his experience at *Othello:* "Austin heard Salvini before his Idol died, and the size of that manifestation even the Grave has not foreclosed –" (*L* III, 811; to Mrs. Holland, early 1884). A note suggests that Austin had seen Salvini in *Othello* in the winter of 1873-74, before the death of Salvini's wife, "his Idol." Some months later, autumn 1884, Emily wrote to Maria Whitney: "Austin brought me the picture of Salvini when he was last in Boston" (*L* III, 847). Henry James also heard Salvini (in 1883) and commented much as Austin did on this "revelation . . . of human power": ". . . the depth, the nobleness, the consistency, the passion, the visible, audible beauty of [his performance] are beyond praise" (*Notes on Acting and the Scenic Drama,* Rutgers University Press, 1948, p. 171).

us all more good than any other medicine." Again and again, she begged him to come home and bring the fun that, apparently, he alone could provide. Their Aunt Elisabeth, the poet, and only six years older than Austin, shared Emily's enthusiasm (and rhetoric): "We are very lonesome without you – one reason as Emily says, is 'because you always make such a hurra.'" Emily spoke repeatedly of the "uproar," "the famous stir" that his presence brought to the house—so quiet, she said, in his absence, with "nobody to laugh with – talk with, nobody down in the morning to make the fun for me!"

In a household in which it was pretty much all "real life," Austin's presence was tonic. Emily relished the release of spirit he could provide, his wits to match her own against, the joy of life which only he could share on something approaching her level. When he was away, she missed not only the fun but their long talks "upon the *kitchen stone hearth,* when the just are fast asleep." They developed a little language, a rapport which, though desperately exclusive, had survival value. Austin's side of the dialogue must be inferred from Emily's many and long letters to him.

Only two letters from him to her have survived, and one is a draft. (All of Emily's correspondence was destroyed by Lavinia after Emily's death, by Emily's direction.) Mrs. Bingham recounts all that is known about the drafted note, which was found in a little package among Austin's things. There were several drafts of it, the shortest addressed to "Dear Sister Emily." Evidently he had worked hard on this effusion, an elaborate fantasy on their youth in the Homestead. The allegory is far from clear, but the reference to early rising and "vigorous children" has obvious bearing on Father and domestic discipline. It is worth reproducing in full as an example of the play of wit Emily and Austin enjoyed together, the only two in the household who shared the taste or skill for it. (That Emily excelled in the same vein we know from the harum-scarum verse valentines that now grace the opening pages of her collected poems and from a certain glorious fantasy—a dream allegory—sent to her Uncle Joel Norcross when she was nineteen.) It begins with a nice genre piece on the Dickinson domestic scene.

From half past ten oclock of last evening until eleven of the same, your fathers house was the scene of great commotion. About the time first mentioned, as mother Lavinia & myself were seated around a bright blazing fire in the sitting room, each one attentive to his or her own peculiar duties, we were all of a sudden aroused by *loud shouts,* & huzza's followed by peals of laughter, and various strange sounds which seemed the effect of unbounded Joy. Quite startled by such a tumult at that time of night, in the quiet little village of Amherst, we all immediately rushed to the window, and from thence, I to the door from the outside of which I beheld a thing, from a hole in whose head, the noise seemed to proceed, dressed in man's attire and running at the top of its speed, in a moment it stoped short, turned sumerset, then rising up it leaped and danced, and shouted and gestured and performed the strangest evolutions, and oddest pranks imaginable. As the image drew near me I perceived that it was a man, who in his hand held an open letter which he seemed to be trying to read and at the sentiments and expressions of which he seemed to be almost transported out of himself. He was so intent on his letter that he evidently took no notice of any body or thing although a great number of people, both male and female, of all ages, ranks, and conditions, attracted by the disturbance had collected together and completely lined the street on both sides for a considerable distance, as he came nearer I distinctly heard him read these words, "I told her you were not afraid of her being too strict with me, and she replied, Tell him I am much obliged to him." After he had uttered of this word of this quotation, he presently swelled to such a prodigious size, and grew so lofty in stature that it verily seemed as if he would burst the bonds of nature, and strutting about he reared his sublime eye almost to the clouds, with these movements and a few haughty gesticulations he resumed the reading of his letter. The next sentence was this "and when I told her how gratified you were at our early rising she said Tell him that is the only way to make vigorous children," before he had quite finished this sentence it was apparent to all that the ineffable delight inspired by the answer would cause him to make some mighty effort to free himself from the steam which was pent up within, and had come well nigh exploding him when his eyes had read the last word of the former sentence. And well did he prove that the previous indications had not been deceitful, for while the word "children" was even on his lips he roared out in such a *terrific, great, coarse horse-laugh* that the whole welkin rang, and the distant forests echoed back the awful din, then in his great vehemence, he drew up his monstrous foot and stamped the earth with the most terrible force, so great powerful was the concussion that the whole firmament was shaken, the whole planetary system was deranged, the stars twinkled, and the clouds fell from the heavens strewing the earth with a white feathery substance.

This was probably the *"imaginative* note" that Emily thanked him for in her letter of May 29, 1848. She was "highly edified . . . & think your flights of fancy indeed wonderful at your age!!"

"I think we miss each other more every day that we grow older," Emily wrote in 1853, when Austin was at the Harvard Law School, "for we're all unlike most everyone, and are therefore more dependent on each other for delight." Speaking of the Newman cousins whom her father (to add to his burdens) had just taken under his wing, she wrote Austin: "The Newmans seem very pleasant, but they are not *like us.* What makes a few of us so different from others? It's a question I often ask myself." And the few were very few indeed. Even Lavinia, according to Joseph Lyman, was not "inside the ring." Until Austin married and moved into the house next door (he was twenty-seven then and Emily twenty-five), he seems to have been her chief support, as her girl friends, like Jane Hitchcock, Abby Wood, Jane Humphrey, and Sophia Holland, married, or left town, or died. Her troubled relations with Susan Gilbert, to whom Austin became engaged in 1853, will concern us later.

Austin had the usual Amherst schooling (which meant, of course,

Amherst Academy) until his thirteenth year, when his father sent him to boarding school at Williston Seminary (now Williston Academy).[7] He was there for the term April–August 1842, and again for the year 1844–45. It was during the latter period, apparently, that he formed his warm friendship with Joseph Lyman, the distant cousin from Chester. They both were entered in the classical course for that year. In 1846 Austin entered Amherst College and, unlike his father, went through the full four-year course, graduating Phi Beta Kappa in the class of 1850.[8] He was a Commencement speaker, sharing that honor with his two close friends, George Howland and George Gould, frequent visitors at the Dickinson house and special friends of his sisters. The topic of his address (the title alone survives) was "Elements of Our National Literature," a long stretch from the post-Revolutionary fervor of Samuel Fowler's oration at Dartmouth, and an indication perhaps of the kind of subject that occupied these young people at least some of the time in their conversation. Since Emily shared his interest—she kept a sharp eye on literary developments and often shared books with him—she probably heard his speech.

Whether it was his literary inclinations or his loyalty to his grandfather's and father's concern for education, Austin tried teaching after graduation, first in Sunderland, a village ten miles north of Amherst, for a few months and subsequently in Boston for about a year (1851–52). The periods of teaching were interspersed with several months of reading law in his father's office (between Thanksgiving 1850 and June 1851). That he tried teaching again after such exposure to his father's training and influence is fairly good evidence of his ability to get out from under his father's wing when he wanted to. But he was not a born teacher: the routine bored him, and the problem of discipline irked him. From Sunderland he wrote to Susan Gilbert a characteristically unenthusiastic note, with a touch of Dickinson homesickness and an indication, perhaps, of why he stayed out of politics:

Of a dozen compositions to decipher and correct – of an hour or two a day spent in declamation – of a colloquy on my hands to prepare for exhibi-

---

7. He was sent there, Edward writes Austin on April 14, 1842, "to improve." His solicitude about his son's education is impressive and specific: "I want to have you improve in writing, as much as you can – If Mr. Wright thinks it best for you to study English Grammar, or Arithmetic, you may do it. I think you had better spend the most of your time, in studying Caesar. I want to have you very particular to be thorough in every thing you study – It is not much matter how little you go over, if you understand it well – learn all about every word you study.

"Take pains to read distinctly – and give every little word its full sound – and the correct emphasis" (*YH* I, 74). Emily and Lavinia were probably getting the same advice, or would when they were ready for it. (Emily, clearly, took it to heart.) Austin became a good Latinist. On the program of the Spring Exhibition of Amherst College, April 18, 1848, appears the following: "1. Translation. From Longinus on the Sublime. Austin Dickinson, Amherst" (*YH* I, 142).

8. At the Commencement three years later (August 11, 1853) Austin was awarded the degree of Master of Arts.

tion – of all the hard sums brought to me for solution – of the time occupied with scholars and others, who call at my room to interrogate me on literary and scientific points – of my being a whig and having to appear in the bar-room every day or two to answer to the *Free Soilers* for all the sins of omission as well as commission, of the whole whig party –

Just think of these and a thousand nameless little things which conspire to fill up the out-of-school hours. . . . But three weeks more and I am returned to my father's house – Three weeks to night and another of those gladdest, those saddest of all the days of the year to me – Another Thanksgiving is over –

From his teaching post in Boston, a few months later, the news was not much better, to judge from Emily's letters of commiseration and encouragement—with some concern for the Irish children (then flooding the Boston schools) who had incurred Austin's wrath. "Father remarks quite briefly," she wrote, "that he 'thinks they have found their master,' mother bites her lips, and fears you 'will be *rash* with them' and Vinnie and I say masses for poor Irish boys souls." Austin was happy neither in his work nor in his new surroundings. Both sisters urged him to be more sociable, to see more people, and warned him against loneliness. "I wish you'd go into society a little more Austin," wrote Lavinia, "t'would be better & happier for you I know. Just try it & see." Emily urged him to see more of his friend Edmund Converse, whom he had recently brought home for a visit:

Now Austin – you have no friend there – why not see Converse often, and laugh and talk with *him*? I think him a noble fellow – it seems to me so pleasant for you to talk with somebody, and he is much like you in many thoughts and feelings. I know he would love to have you for a comrade and friend, and I would be with him a good deal if I were you.

She also urged him not to deny himself new girl friends in Boston out of loyalty to those at home (clearly, by this time, the Gilbert sisters, Susan and Martha):

I am glad you like Miss Nichols, it must be so pleasant for you to have somebody to care for, in such a cheerless place – dont shut yourself away from anyone whom you like, in order to keep the faith to those you leave behind! . . . On the contrary, Austin, I am very sure that seclusion from everyone there would make an ascetic of you, rather than restore you brighter and truer to *them*.

This was fine advice (and a bit ironical, coming from the "Queen Recluse" herself), but it was unavailing. He seems never to have been happy in Boston. In July 1852 he came home, his teaching days over. In early March 1853, after another stretch of reading law in his father's office, he entered Harvard Law School. Graduating in July 1854, he accepted his father's offer of a partnership and practiced law in Amherst the rest of his life.

Exactly when Austin's buoyant youth clouded over, it is hard to say. His unhappiness in Boston was partly homesickness, surely; partly the loneliness that Emily and Lavinia warned him against; partly his tendency, sharpened by loneliness, to brood and worry. For one thing, he was in the wrong profession. His gestures at schoolteaching were obviously a mistake—and perhaps a bit below the current level of Dickinson dignity. There is no sign that any of his family encouraged him, and Emily herself took a skeptical view. Once, urging him to come home from Sunderland for the annual Cattle Show, she wrote: "School masters and Monkeys half price." She never could see why he wanted to waste his time on "those useless boys." But admitting his mistake could not have been easy for one of his pride. When he finally fixed on the law as a career, the question of moving away from Amherst was a real and perplexing one. Like many other young people of the time, he felt the impulse to go west, and a few months after graduating from law school he went to Chicago to explore possibilities. By this time he was engaged to Susan Gilbert, who apparently would have relished the move. That he decided against it has been attributed most often to the influence of his father, who added to the partnership an offer of a fine new house next the Homestead for him and Susan.[9]

9. In his decision to stay in Amherst (according to Millicent Todd Bingham), Austin followed "the course his father had charted" (*Home,* p. 255). Throughout, Mrs. Bingham makes much of Edward's authoritarian nature, especially in the home, where "no one openly opposed his decisions" (p. 3). She finds "traces of command" (p. 410) even in Edward's last letters to his son; in short, Austin stayed in Amherst because his father wanted him to. More recently, in Cody, *After Great Pain,* p. 19, Austin is said to have "capitulated" to his father after "teetering on the verge of emancipation." Perhaps. But there were many other reasons, and it is clear that Austin was perfectly free to move had he so desired. In the spring of 1854, he wrote his fiancée, Susan Gilbert, "I shall keep it in mind – & wait the result of my trip West, and a plain frank talk with father – & then perhaps, *perhaps* a little variation from the present plan –" (*YH* I, 305). That fall he spent a full month in Chicago. Susan, ambitious, eager, and certainly not rooted in Amherst, would have offered no objection to moving west. But Austin was a New Englander, an Amherst boy, a Dickinson. He had been homesick even in Sunderland. Later, on another trip west, he was repelled by what he saw and couldn't wait to get back to Amherst. There was much more than the strong will of his father operating in his decision to make his career in Amherst. On November 27, 1851, Austin wrote Susan: "I love this Thanksgiving day – Sue – it is so truly New England in its spirit – I love New England & New England customs & New England institutions for I remember our fathers loved them and that it was they who founded & gave them to us –" (*YH* I, 226). So, if in the "plain frank talk" Austin had with his father, Edward's wishes prevailed, it must be remembered that many of Austin's basic wishes went the same way. Sue, perhaps a little disappointedly, described the decision to her brothers (*YH* I, 332; mid-May ? 1855):

Austin's plans are now definite, as he is writing you – tho' they have resulted very differently from our previously formed expectations, we are both happy in them, and hope they may strike you as pleasantly – Austin's Father has overruled all objections to our remaining here and tho' it has been something of a sacrifice for Austin's spirit and rather of a struggle with his pre-conceived ideas, I feel

While his father's offers undoubtedly influenced Austin's decision, there were other factors, and Emily may have been one of them. It may be too much to say that he depended on her in these early years as he certainly did later, but there are hints that it came close to that. On the most superficial level, a young man of his tastes and talents might have hesitated to leave behind so fascinating a sister for what seemed to him the cultural wastes of the Midwest. But there were deeper levels. Emily's long, newsy letters to him during his teaching and law-school years show a constant concern for his morale: "Take care of yourself, Austin, and dont get melancholy." " 'Let not your heart be troubled' – . . . believe also in me!" "And Austin, dont you care about anything else that troubles you – It isn't anything – It is too slight, too small, to make you worry so." Austin was perfectly frank about his own tendency to brood and worry. Once, ill and home from Sunderland (which in retrospect looked better to him), he described his dark mood to Susan Gilbert, whom he had by then (December 1850) begun actively to court:

> My last week's indisposition, and consequent seclusion brought back to me my old companion Reflection – whose presence had not obscured the brightness of my course for ten weeks – He yet tarries with me – and his children, The Blues – who ever accompany their Father, frisk about me – to my exceeding discomfort and gloom. . . . While in Sunderland, my mind was engrossed in matters of business, exciting and agreeable [by] nature, and to be at once transferred from scenes of activity and health and enjoyment, to the lonely, cold, dark, dismal, north room, whose four blank, meaningless walls have shut me from the world for the most of the last eight days, with memory, officious to remind of all done amiss in the Past – with Imagination, ready to predict the Future – and severe Physical Pain to render tedious the Present. . . .

But there is little to indicate that Susan, at least in these early years and perhaps never, was much of a help to him in his moods. She had many fine qualities, but her nature was hardly *sympathique*. Even in this letter, Austin complained, "I never *did,* and don't *now think,* we understand one another." And Austin's need for understanding was great. Emily sensed this and gave him what she could. If he stayed in Amherst partly for her, it has been suggested (such was the bond between them) that the reverse might have been true:

> To know Emily's brother as well as her father is to understand much of her own behavior. For it was her life work "to make everything

---

satisfied that in the end it will be best and he will be fully rewarded for his filial regard – He goes into partnership on even terms with his Father, the first of June –

Earlier (*YH* I, 312, August 13, 1854), when her hopes were up, she had written her brother Dwight: "You may like to know that Austin is going to Chicago early in the Fall with a view to settling there – How would you like to dine with me there some fine day in about a year –"

pleasant for father and Austin," as she said, and when Austin's life turned to tragedy, his suffering forged yet another link in the chain which held her fast at home.

It was not until some years later that Austin's life could be said to have "turned to tragedy," and there were many other reasons why Emily stayed at home. But Austin was right (in this letter to Susan) in his gloomy imaginings about the future. The course of his courtship of Susan was anything but smooth and the degree of understanding between them at best erratic. It is clear that his parents could help him only in practical matters, like a job and a house. During these early years, he was a confused young man, emotionally, intellectually, spiritually. His courtship letters to Susan, and a notable one of the same period to her sister Martha, show him in torment and ecstasy—but mostly in confusion.

For all the "Miss Nicholses" he met in Boston or might have met in Sunderland or Cambridge, no one seems to have attracted him outside the Amherst circle; and the two to whom he was most attached from college days on were the "Gilbert Twins," as they were called, although Martha was a year (or more) older.[10] Both girls were born in Greenfield, Massachusetts, where their father kept a hostelry. In 1832 the family moved to Amherst, where for the next five years Mr. Gilbert ran the Mansion House, a tavern and livery stable not far from the Dickinson Homestead. Mr. Gilbert's reputation was not high—"his convivial habits were well known"—but there is no clear indication that the girls suffered any embarrassment in the town from their origins. At any rate, they were cut off from any parental influence, good or bad, when they were orphaned in their early teens. Their mother died in 1837, and their father in 1841. Following their mother's death, they lived for several years with an aunt in Geneva, New York, dividing their time, after 1832, between Geneva and Amherst, where they lived with their married sister, Harriet Gilbert Cutler. Both attended Utica Female Seminary, and in Amherst Susan went to Amherst Academy for a term (at least) in the fall of 1847, which was Emily's first at Mount Holyoke.[11] Susan joined the First Church in 1850, went to Baltimore to teach school in the fall of 1851, and returned to Amherst permanently the following summer, much to the delight of Emily, who by that time thought of her as her dearest friend. Emily seemed delighted, too, with the growing intimacy between Susan and Austin, who became engaged the next spring (1853). They were married in Geneva on July 1, 1856. Next year, in Amherst, Martha

10. Records differ about the date of Martha's birth. The dates on her tombstone in Geneva, New York, have her born on April 13, 1827, whereas the Greenfield church records say 1829 (*Home*, p. 496). Mrs. Bingham and Jay Leyda (*YH* I, xlviii) accept the former, Thomas Johnson and Theodora Ward the latter (*L* III, 954).

11. Records conflict (again) about the goings and comings of the Gilbert sisters during the decade of the 1840s. I have pieced together what seems most likely from *YH* I, xlviii–xlix; *L* III, 939; and *Home*, p. 110.

Commencement daguerreotype, 1850   About 1854, as law student (?)

Daguerreotype, about 1856

Austin as a young man

Susan Gilbert

Martha Gilbert

"THE GILBERT TWINS"
ABOUT 1851

married John Williams Smith and went to Geneva to live, where Smith was in the dry-goods business.

The Gilbert sisters, though close enough to be called twins, were very different. Whether, in Austin's mind, it ever came down to a choice between the two cannot be said; probably not; but even at the height of his courtship of Susan, his letters to Martha were warm and loving and remarkably frank. That, of the two, he married Susan, and *why* (provided, at this distance, motives on such delicate matters can be ascertained), is of the utmost importance. In the light of what happened, it seems to have been a tragic mistake for all concerned, including Emily. It would be nice to say that, after her first flush of enthusiasm for Sue, she tried to dissuade him, but there is no evidence that she did. The best that can be said for both Austin and Emily is that the rest of the family (with the possible exception of Lavinia) warmly approved of the match. Edward, he who had been so prudent and careful in his own choice of a wife, was especially delighted. Susan made herself one of his favorites. Her background may not have been up to Dickinson level, but she was handsome, bright, and ambitious, one of the acknowledged leaders of the younger set. When she got the catch of the town, there was general applause.

Apparently none of their intimates foresaw difficulties.[12] But in what survives of Austin's turbulent courtship letters (or rather drafts), signs of trouble ahead are unmistakable. The letters are so different in every way from the reasoned discourse and restrained affection of Edward's to Emily Norcross as to stand almost as a paradigm of a new era and a new sensibility. No wonder there was so little communication between the generations in the Dickinson home—they lived in different worlds. It is as if, in thirty-odd years, New England youth had swung from the Age of Reason, with its outward thrust and its concern for the Amelioration of Man, to the most intense kind of romantic introspection. We see Austin embarked upon his own "Campaign inscrutable," groping (especially in the letter to Martha) in the darkness of self-doubt and cosmic questioning and, in the drafts of his letters to Susan, baffled by the extremes of his own emotional nature and trying to fathom and to find rest—it seems in vain—in hers.

It is best to start with Austin's letter to Martha, to whom he entrusted a more sustained, and more composed, bit of self-analysis than anything that survives in the drafts to Susan. With Martha he was less tense, less on edge; her nature was more serene and sympathetic than her sister's. "Mat is very shy," Emily wrote Austin in May 1852, during his schoolteaching in Boston. "She was going to send you some flowers in a box, the other

12. I have found record of only one misgiving: Mrs. Harriet Cutler's. In the drafts of Austin's letters to Sue there are several references to sister Harriet's watchful eye. At one point, he writes: "Does Mrs. Cutler ever [suggest?] her fears now Sue, that 'you & Austin will have a falling out by & by – & then if you ever do it will be an awful one' – Does she ever hint any suspicions – or look knowing?"

day, but you had'nt answered her letter, so you see why you did'nt get them." A few months earlier, when Austin had sent her a bracelet, her "sweet face grew radiant [Emily wrote] and joyful that blue eye." Always Martha seems the gentle and submissive one, with Susan more forthright and self-possessed. Their brother-in-law, Samuel Learned, contrasted them about this time: Martha, he said, "may not be quite as handsome or as brilliant but is just as good a girl." Martha had flowers for Austin when he left for Boston, and one of his first letters home was to her. Though Emily surely encouraged Austin's relationship with Susan, even to the point of what she called "clandestiny," she repeatedly wrote him how much Martha inquired about him, missed him, and looked forward to his return. She wrote him once about a long soulful talk with Martha, when they both wept together. Apparently, at least in these early years, she would have welcomed either girl as a sister-in-law.

Austin's first letters to Martha from Boston are warm and affectionate, full of thanks for her attentions and for the memories of happy times they'd had together. Then, in the spring of 1852 (May 11), after a miserable winter, came a long, introspective letter, perhaps the most revealing we have from his formative years. He is entirely clear about his purpose—to give Martha "a tolerably fair idea of me . . . a glance, *only* a glance, at my inner life," a selection, at least, "of my varied thoughts & feelings & experiences, and hopes & fears. . . ." It is in no way a love letter, simply the outpouring of a troubled mind to a receptive listener. It is worth pausing over in some detail for the light it throws on the problems that beset these young people, especially on Emily's problems (at age twenty-one)—the kind of thing, perhaps, she and Austin discussed in those long talks when "the just" were asleep. On such matters, mostly religious and philosophical, she *could* be of help to him. She had done a good deal of pondering herself.

There is a lot of Emily in the letter, her problems and her tone, the sense of bafflement, the search for identity. There are the same extremes of mood, the light and dark, the ecstasy and despair, the heaven and the hell in the heart, that run through many of her poems and letters. After a brief preliminary, Austin begins:

> My moods are so changing from day to day (& sometimes even from hour to hour) and with them my views of all about me. . . . For the shadows of life, with me, are so constantly changing from light to dark, from dark to light, sometimes as bright as bright can be, & at others, dark as a starless night, sometimes full of only lights of beauty & sounds of joy, & fragrant perfume, and every delightful sensation, and I feel the warmest, kindliest sympathy with all mankind, and can imagine then how no one can be *less* than happy in this world of such beauty & grandeur, nor how a heaven can be more perfect than the one that fills my own heart. And, at *others,* as entirely cheerless—no scenes meet my eye, but those of sorrow & misery, no tales, but of woe, my ears, and not the faintest glimmer from the faintest star of Hope, to encourage, or bec[k]on to a Future of promise.

It was only a few days later that Emily wrote Austin of the "long, sad talk" she'd had with Martha (obviously occasioned by this letter) "about Sue and Michigan, and Life, and our own future, and Mattie cried and I cried," among other things, surely, about Austin's unhappiness.

In the next paragraph Austin goes deeper, and again there is a good deal of Emily in what he says, the sense of bewilderment, jostle, even the "frightened child" pose:

> Sometimes its [Life's] end [is] clear as light, & its manifold duties & relations, and, at others, all an awful, bewildering mystery. I startle in broad day, like a frightened child from sleep, as if I had just woke for the first time, to consciousness of my existence & the world around me, and wonder where I am, & *what,* and what my destiny, and the meaning of all this bustle & parade I see, and this jostling and crowding of all these ten thousand men, in every respect like myself, this way & that, and all these signs of *power* impressed on all around.

Then Austin becomes philosophical, setting his broodings in the context of the mysteries of Time and Space and the Infinite. He is appalled at the paradox of the human mind (here the impact of his scientific studies is clear) that understands so much and yet so little. He stares into "the profound darkness" and contemplates the possibility of "blank nothingness" as the reality of human destiny. Emily knew these same moments,

> With Midnight to the North of Her –
> And Midnight to the South of Her –
> And Maelstrom – in the Sky –   (*#721, about 1863*)

and brought these same themes to great intensity in her tragic poems years later. Two years before Austin wrote this letter to Martha, Emily, apparently in the midst of some such thoughts, had set her course for the open sea, crying buoyantly to a pious friend, "I love the danger!" Austin here describes himself as "still drifting."

> I feel the presence of that within me, unseen, yet indescribably mighty, that can comprehend worlds & systems of worlds & yet cannot comprehend itself. That with the aid of history, history, not as written in books, but imprinted on the everlasting hills, & deeply imbedded rocks, may last through long ages of a remote past, before Time began, and learn of the lives & changes & ends of races of beings before man was, and yet cannot assure me of a single event of the Future. That can estimate the distances and weights of burning suns, far off in the trackless wastes of space, & yet can find nothing to satisfy its own eager, restless longings for knowledge of itself, & its Infinite author – and I tremble & my brain reels as I think, with all this amazing power, *passing* wonder, and all the susceptibility to pleasure or pain, I am still drifting on I know not whither – I look around me, to see what others are doing, whether *they* too are suffering in the same anxious suspense, or whether it is to me alone Life is a sealed book. Here & there I behold a solitary *one,* groping on in the profound darkness unknowing

whether this course or that will lead him if indeed *any*where, if he may not, with the next step plunge into blank nothingness –

Perhaps all this was frightening to Martha, with her modest capacities and (at least there is no evidence to the contrary) orthodox piety. The specifically religious doubts that he went on to disclose may have been too much for her. Just as Emily in her distaste for creeds and doctrines parted spiritual company with her pious friends, so Austin charted a course that Martha could not follow. Except for the few "solitary gropers" like himself (and Emily?), he wrote:

> I see them [mankind] marshalled in mighty hosts, yet under different banners, and marching on to the word of their several leaders, whom they believe, each his own, have received from the Omnipotent himself the true, and *only* true chart of the route to knowledge, to happiness everlasting & to him. And now *new* doubts encompass me, for if *either,* and only *one, which* is *right?* I am besought on the one hand to join one standard & on the other, another – the advocates for the standard of the "Cross" appeal to me in the most solemn manner, as I value quiet from the gloomy doubts & fears within me – as I value perfect peace & perfect happiness through a life eternal, in *God's* name to join them, for so surely as God is God, all the rest are marching on to death & perdition – but when I survey their ranks, and observe their comparative thinness, I hesitate. I ask myself, Is it possible that God, all powerful, all wise, all benevolent, as I must believe him, *could* have created all these millions upon millions of human souls, only to destroy them? That he *could* have revealed himself & his ways to a chosen few, and left the rest to grovel on in utter darkness? I *cannot* believe it. I can only bow & pray, Teach me, O God, what thou wilt have me do, & obedience shall be my highest pleasure.

At this point Austin catches himself, realizing how painful his confession must have been to Martha: "But Mat, what am I writing you? Something I am afraid you will be sorry to read from me." But it would have been worse, he goes on, had he not written thus frankly about himself. He asks her pardon for hurting her but (showing a candor quite like his sister's) not for telling the truth:

> And now that you have a glance, *only* a glance, at my inner life, you can appreciate a little the reason for my not liking to write as I should were *I* more settled in my feelings. I despise untruthfulness to friends, and yet I hesitate to do anything that may tend, in the least, to dim their sun-light. –

Austin's next two (and last) letters to Martha are full of questions as to why she never wrote him any more. Perhaps she hesitated to navigate further on these troubled waters. Perhaps, knowing what was going on between Austin and her sister, she decided to bow out.

What seems the real source of the moodiness he described to Martha, and perhaps the occasion of the soul-probing and the cosmic questionings, was not so much his career problems or religious uncertainties as the vicissitudes of his relations with Susan Gilbert. Begun as a pleasant flirtation during the spring of his senior year in college, the romance by this time (spring 1852) was growing in intensity—at least on his side. His moods went up or down according to Susan's attitudes, which sent him into raptures or plunged him into the deepest gloom. Out of the strange jumble of the courtship documents,[13] at least one thing stands out clearly: Austin's extraordinary capacity for feeling. He loved Martha, but with Susan he was in love, passionately, even wildly (a word he used himself). With Sue, there are no long contemplative religious discussions; indeed, a recurrent theme is Sue's distaste for his heterodoxy, and he approached the subject gingerly. Once the early battle-of-the-sexes sparring was over, all is feeling, sentiment, passion, sometimes elevated and calm, sometimes anguished and desperate; and always there is the sense that Austin is reaching out for more than Susan was prepared to give. There are some periods of calm joy when he seems to be sure of her:

Oh the virtues of love! the vastness of life – How few know anything of it & how solemn a responsibility upon those to whom it has been disclosed –
   Oh Sue, *Sue* – not the pumping of air in and out of the lungs – eating lest the body fall away – sleeping at night from weariness of the flesh – Life Soul Life – I have read of it – I have *felt* it with you – you are the light & you the genial warmth that have made the closed germ within me to ex-pand & send up its tender shoot – & you the sweet influence that is to cherish it to its perfect flower.

In such moods he looks forward to the home they will one day share. "What a dear home ours will be. . . . What a world of things we shall have to say to each other while we are growing old together – Growing old! It hardly seems possible *we can* grow old – at any rate we shall never *feel* old –" Like Ik Marvel's Bachelor, whose *Reveries* was then making the rounds of the younger set, he dreams his enchanted dream of the perfect home, with husband and wife attentive to each other's every need, happy together through thick and thin: "What precious evenings we will have around our fireside Sue, & let the wind blow, & the rain pour – What

13. The letters are in the Dickinson Family Papers (Folder 8) in the Houghton Library, Harvard University. Leyda (*YH*, passim) printed some significant excerpts; Cody was the first to make extended biographical use of them. So far, they are the only source of even an approximately coherent account of this troubled romance from its beginnings about 1850 (Austin apparently destroyed Sue's letters to him). They present problems. Few are dated (although some can be dated fairly precisely from internal evidence), and it seems unlikely that they can ever be arranged in chrono-logical order that will meet general acceptance. They are full of revisions and can-cellations and are, in spots, almost illegible. It is impossible to tell how many of the drafts were put in final form and sent. Although they spell, all in all, confusion and turbulence, the course of the affair can be traced with some confidence, if not step by step, and certain major themes recur that illuminate both Austin's problems and probably Emily's. Although Dr. Cody's psychosexual analysis, especially of Austin's moods, often rings true, I do not follow his theory of the Austin-Sue-Emily triangle (brother and sister in love with the same girl) nor of Emily's being crushed when she lost Sue (by then her surrogate mother) to Austin.

care we?"—a thought not far, except in expression, from Emily's own (and famous)

> Wild Nights – Wild Nights!
> Were I with thee
> Wild Nights should be
> Our luxury! . . .   (#249, about 1861)

He could sentimentalize on the idea of home along with Ik Marvel and Emily at their best:

> A home, Sue! It's too beautiful a word for this world. It means too much – It's an ideal realized by not one in a thousand – for it's not a house & barn & orchard. . . . It is the type & symbol of a heaven promised the followers of him who went about doing good. It is the center & spring of all living. It is the choice blossom of love – the beautiful answering of the dearest dream.

(If Austin is here apostrophizing the home of his boyhood, this is a fine tribute. But in view of what actually happened in the home he and Sue established next door, it is sadly ironic.)

Another effusion shows him again dreaming his dream of perfect love. There is little evidence that Sue shared his feelings with anything like his fervor, and there is a good deal of evidence that she did not. In such moments he seems blissfully unaware of the *other*, so rapt he was in his own inward vision. (In one of his first letters to Sue—one of the few that can be dated fairly accurately and itself a very effusive one—he had woven a poetic fantasy about himself as Narcissus, he who fell in love with his own image.) Like his sister Emily, he was inclined to see in others what he wanted to see.

> I don't know what to say to you, Sue. Maybe I'm brimming full of what I have to have you know. Perhaps your own heart can tell it all. I feel so dreamy, Sue. So strangely, wonderingly dreamy, for I dreamed a dream – a dream of the sweetest, sweetest love – and though I seemed waken the dream went dreaming dreaming on. And the joy of it never ceases – and whether I waken or whether I sleep – and whether the days are real and the sun is really up – or whether only the calm moon is shining in upon my eyelids – and lighting up a fancy of more than earthly beauty I sometimes hardly know. I want you to be glad and happy darling, and hopeful darling. I love you so and want you so to be – and God's and each other's – we'll [trust?] with his love our hopes – and pray if we sleep we may never waken – we sleep so sweetly – and if we waken we may never sleep. . . .

He was like Emily, too, in asking more of others than they wanted to, or could, give. For all his moments of rapture, the prevailing tone of the courtship letters is uncertainty, doubt of Susan's love, and tension that at times seems intolerable. Twice he speaks of his nerves as ready to snap under the strain, even when he most exults in what he thinks to be the certainty of Sue's love. (He has Emily's sense of being able to "wade

Grief – / Whole pools of it," but tipping "drunken" at "the least push of Joy.")

> I am overwhelmed with my emotions.
> I can't write. I haven't slept.
> All the night has a crowd of strange, tumultuous feelings made wild riot in my heart.
> O my God I am worthy of nothing – thou hast granted me everything. I tremble in my very joy. But I thank thee. I thank thee and pray that thou wilt continue thy care over me, support me, calm me for my shattered nerves are ready to snap.
> The excess of my joy is very pain.

"I love you Sue up to the very highest strain my nature can bear," he wrote, " – the least tension would snap my life threads – as brittle glass – more – you could not ask – more man could not give – Love *me,* Sue – *Love* me – for its my life."

His pleading is perhaps sufficient measure of Sue's response. He was troubled by her moods, which ranged from "stately indifference . . . unapproachable dignity . . . rigid formality" (as he described her once, whimsically, in what appears to be an early letter) to the stormy and unpredictable. Here he discusses them composedly:

> You seem to live in a rather tempestuous latitude, where tis a common thing for a bright day to be suddenly overcast with dark clouds – where the conflicts of the various elements are severe, yet unheralded – But do you not, sometimes, endeavor to account for these sudden & fierce storms? You designated the one of Wednesday last an "Equinoctial" – What corresponds in your "inner world" to the sun's crossing the line in [the] material?

(Or, as Emily said years later, "Susan fronts on the Gulf Stream.") But when Sue chides him—often, it would seem, for his religious views and perhaps for his overly aggressive courtship—or when he has doubts about his ability to make her happy or whether she really loves him, he is frantic. Only a week or so after a most rewarding meeting with her at the Revere House Hotel in Boston (the date was March 23, 1853; Austin had just settled in at the Harvard Law School), where amid kisses and confidences they had, it would seem, plighted their troth, he is thrown into despair by an unexpected reversal in one of Sue's letters:

> I read under the sting of these lines that told me that almost within one short week – and while you sat by my side – & pillowed your head upon my bosom & felt my arm around your neck & my lips on your cheek & my heart beating in its great love for you – Even there & then – you were doubting – *doubting* – questioning if after all you had any love for me – while I all unconscious of where your thoughts strayed – was ascribing every not perfect moment to your fatigue from your journey.

He has an impulse to give the whole thing up (the thought struck him several times during the courtship, even toward its end):

[T]hen Sue, the sooner I know it the better – then let us think no more of ever marrying – let our past be only as a dream that is soon forgotten. . . .

The very next evening, he retreats a bit: "I can hardly see to night how I happened to fix so closely upon those few lines"; but another letter from Sue a few days later, this time (it seems) questioning his religious belief, plunged him down again. Why the theological issue should have been so important to Sue raises a question. Though she was never famous for her piety, it may have meant much to her at this stage, only three years after she had joined the church, a step Austin had not taken. (Not to have publicly accepted Christ as one's Savior was to be marked out, even among the younger set.) Or she may simply have been impatient with Austin's spiritual gropings. (Martha met them with silence.) Or she may have used her objections—and her moods—as ways of keeping Austin at bay. It may be unfair to say that she was still playing the Amherst field, but as late as January 1853 she was still writing to Edward Hitchcock, Jr., and Austin mentions a certain "Jim" several times as a rival. And once, in a draft written apparently well after their engagement, he asks, "Does it ever seem to you you could live happier – better – unmarried – or married to some of the many others whose hearts you have unwittingly won?" At any rate, Sue's criticism on this occasion tore him apart:

Your last letter Sue has almost killed me – *Did* you mean all you said? & may I never write you again one word upon that one subject that I hope & feel is only for a time to separate us? till I can write just *your* words will it cast me from you Sue, *now!* Oh why is this. Has God permitted me to set you in my heart & watch you & cherish you there, till you have grown into its very fibre – become a part of it, only then to tear you thence – & leave me mangled, bleeding – dying — Oh Sue – I love you with a love that has almost driven me wild – I have centered everything in you – every hope – every aspiration – I've given you everything I have – all I am – & all I can make myself – & will you forsake me now – will you forsake me for only loving you too much?[14]

14. Sometimes the shoe was on the other foot. In two letters, apparently written fairly late in the courtship (in both there are references to his being in the "office"), Austin apologized profusely for wounding Susan's feelings. Both show signs of strain, not only in the frequent cancellations, illegibilities, and garbled sentences but in the abjectness of Austin's humility as he throws himself at her feet again and again, swears that his intentions were good, begs forgiveness, and vows eternal love. One letter (or draft) concerns a remark of Austin's that Sue had interpreted as "trifling" with her love. She had written him "a beautiful, dear note" forgiving him—to which he replied (in some thousand words) that he never meant it in the first place. He wonders how "for a single instant" it could have crossed her mind "that I could have meant or could have looked the slightest, faintest shadow of ridicule toward you . . . towards you (———?) to you as my life . . . nay, my life itself . . . toward you – so great a gift I tremble while I call you mine . . . No my own Sue, no thought of trifling with anything connected with you ever ventured its shade upon my mind. . . ." He wonders how she could have suspected an attitude toward her who had brought him tenderness for the first time in his life: "Ten-

Apparently, Sue had accused him of willfully refusing conversion (he did not join the church until 1856, six months before they were married).

> Will you tell me it is only my *will* keeps me back – & if it is not – will you reproach me for not doing what you tell me of myself I cannot? Do I not believe in God – Do I not bow before the author of my being & do I not acknowledge His power – & worship Him for His goodness! Do I not know my own weakness – my own unworthiness of the many daily blessings of which He is the constant giver – Am I not ready to serve him in whatever He may command & yet am I so wicked Sue – you can't love me? *Am* I as wicked as you say, Sue – Oh I'm sick – I want to go home – I want to see Vinnie & Emily & father & mother & see if they'll notice me – if they will speak to me – if I shall not find the doors of my home closed on me –

Emily (it may be noted), showing a willfulness that worried her friends, *never* joined the church. Had she been aware of this impasse between Austin and Sue, there is no doubt whose side she would have been on. Austin concluded the letter with a burst of self-drama quite like some of Emily's early letters, the kind of thing that, at her best, she not only objectified but brought to new life in her poems. Here, quite explicitly, the clouds are gathering:

---

derness has not been so common a thing to me in the years that I have so far numbered as to have become valueless in my estimation. I have never before received any – from anybody – I never would. [He forgets, or ignores, Martha here, and his sisters.] I wanted to feel it all, in all its deliciousness, all its purity, all its vastly increased exquisiteness – from long fainting for it – I feel it for the first time from her from whom I am to receive all that I ever receive . . . from the only woman of all the world whom I 'could not chose but love'. . . ." No, he concludes, no such "trifling" from that "surpassingly great love that for two long years has so worn & worried me – . . ."

The other letter, shorter but even more frenzied, begins: "And I have made you cry Sue – you whom I have (told I?) (taken to?) love – and who have breathed out your love upon me. . . . Have made you cry – you whose every moment I ought to brighten . . . whose every sorrow to lighten – whose every joy to heighten [he shared this epistolary trick with Emily]. I have made you cry – and I have made you feel alone again in the world. . . ." All of which, of course, was farthest from his thoughts: "Can I have been unkind to you! The subject of all my love [written boldly over canceled "affection"] – and as fond a love as ever filled a man's heart!" The gist of the matter seems to have been the thought he came to next: her failure to understand him. She won't feel these hurts, he seems to be saying, "when you have learnt me as well as I know myself (then / when?) (dear Sue?) you have only fully (finally?) known me –"

For a young man supposedly engaged for some time, these letters show at the very least a precarious uncertainty. They protest too much. What Sue's attitude was can only be conjectured. She must have known how deeply Austin was in love. How could she have suspected him of being willfully unkind or of "trifling" with her affection? How long would it take for her to "know" him? It almost seems as if she had provoked the episodes behind these letters, perhaps to keep him off balance. While Austin seems almost lost in love, Sue could write the Bartletts in Hanover (July 7, 1853), "I have *not* forgotten you my dear friends, neither am I blind or sick or married but hale, single, eyes strong . . ." (*YH* I, 279).

Tell me again you love me Sue, tell me you *will* love me – tell me what love you have for Earth shall be mine – tell me God will bring us together in our religion – Tell me to be calm again – to study, to trust, to pray – tell me you will never leave me – but for God – or my star of hope has set – a blight has overspread my youth and a darkness has overshadowed my morning's Sun – the chill touch of Autumn has come upon me in the "April hour" of my life & the flower of my Spring has faded in its earliest blossoming –

I'm faint when I ought to be strongest & old while I'm yet young. Are you surprised, Sue, to read such a letter from me? Then you have not known how deeply an occasional reproach – an occasional doubting expression has sunk into my heart – then you have not known all the passion that has lain there.

On March 27, 1853, only a few days after the Revere House meeting, when Austin had felt so secure in Sue's love, he drafted a curious letter to Mattie, who had heard from Sue (apparently) about the engagement and had written her congratulations: "Heaven bless you – Mattie [Austin replied] for those kind . . . words that told me you were glad I loved Sue – & she loves me – " And then, strangely, he proceeds to explain their love. One gets the impression that he is explaining it to himself.

It seems strange to me too – does'nt it to you, Mattie – that just such characters should have chosen each other to love, that two so tall, proud, stiff people, so easily miffed, – so apt to be pert, two that could . . . stand under the "oak tree" just at the setting of a glorious Sunday's sun – & speak words – & look, look, so cold, – so bitter, as hardly the deepest hatred could have prompted a pair as would the guiltiest wretch – & his most wronged victim – that two who could love so well, or hate so well – that two just such *could* not choose but love each other! – but we *could not* Mattie –

We have loved each other a *long time* – longer than either has guessed, but we were too proud to confess it – How we at *last* broke down – I hardly know . . . Forgive me now Mattie will you for not writing you before – It is not because I have not thought of you – nor because I do not love you – I *do* love you Mattie – just as well as Emily and Vinnie . . . & you all enter into all Sue's & my plans for the future –

This hardly sounds like the agonizing, pleading, passionate young man of the courtship letters. The love-hate he confesses so frankly to Mattie tells more, perhaps, than he intended. He hardly seems to know his own mind. He may have been posing a bit—presenting himself as he would like Mattie to see him, "tall," "proud," giving in to love only because he had to. (Emily enjoyed this self-drama in her correspondence, often bafflingly.)

The question is, did he talk or write to Emily this way? and how much did she know about the ebb and flow of his feelings during this turbulent period? Her letters to him stay mostly on the surface of things, with only occasional warnings against melancholy and loneliness. But when he told Sue he wanted to come home to "Vinnie & Emily & father & mother," it is fairly safe to say, from what we know about the other three, that Emily was the one he wanted to talk to.

If we can trust the evidence of several letters to her brothers, Susan approached the marriage coolly and unromantically. Her attitude was eminently practical. After her unsettled youth she wanted a home of her own, and she was confident that Austin could provide one. She asked her brother Francis, "Why don't you write to me Frank and congratulate me, that I have found some one who is going, by and by, to encumber himself with me?" She thought he would like Austin: "I see no reason, viewing the subject as I try to, without prejudice why you won't like Austin and find in him all you could desire in the companion of your sister –" He is "poor and young," she wrote, "and in the *world's* eyes these are great weaknesses – but he is strong, manly, resolute – understands human nature and will take care of me –" Although she admitted that he had not yet decided where he would settle in business, she was sure that they would "have a cozy place some-where, where the long-cherished wish of my heart to have a home where my brothers and sisters can come, will be realized." Either she still failed to understand Austin or she was putting up a bold and somewhat false face to her brothers. At age twenty-five, son of one of Amherst's leading citizens, with a fine education, including a law degree, he could hardly be called "poor and young." On the other hand, how could Sue, knowing his painful indecision about a career, his spiritual bewilderments and emotional insecurity, have called him "strong, manly, resolute"? Perhaps she, too, was posing a bit.

In September 1854 Susan wrote to her brother Dwight that "Austin *now* expects our marriage to take place the following Fall" but, she added, "all earthly plans are so *mutable*." Though one of the reasons for putting off the marriage was a practical one—the completion of the new house—the fact is that by the time they were married (July 1, 1856) they had been engaged for three years. As dates were shifted and plans changed, the whole affair began to seem unreal to Sue. She wrote Dwight in this same letter: "I have always felt so like a *child* the idea of really being married seems absurd enough and if the event ever occurs I think I shall experience a feeling of odd surprise." With no proper home of her own, she hesitated about where to have the wedding, Amherst or Geneva. Only a few weeks before the wedding, she finally decided on Geneva and her Aunt Sophia (Mrs. William Van Vranken), but only "after mature deliberation on my part – a balancing of the gains & losses &c &c"—so she wrote to the Reverend Samuel Bartlett and his wife (Samuel Learned's sister) of Manchester, New Hampshire, formerly of Amherst, who had shown special interest in the Gilbert girls. Mr. Bartlett (later president of Dartmouth College) had been her choice to perform the ceremony—and to perform it in Amherst. She told the Bartletts that her aunt "through the Winter has been besieging me to come to her house to be married. . . . The decision made great shaking among the old plans, and thawing of fancy's frost-works, but for reasons I cannot explain, both for prudence and prolixity, it was advisable." What the word "prudence" concealed, we may never know precisely. But tensions were developing on several fronts.

If Sue was thought by her contemporaries to be a little cool and calculating, it was because—given her ambition—her background and precarious home situation demanded these qualities. The rest of her letter to the Bartletts shows her at her ingenious best, patching things up with them and taking a pleasantly nonchalant attitude toward the whole affair.

No Mr Bartlett to marry me – or Mrs Bartlett for guest – strange hands to tie the silken knot, and some strange eyes to look on the tying – so I have said good-bye to some of the sweet old plans and pretend to believe the new ones are best – Yes my dear friends I am to be married the fourth week in June if God so wills and after a little jaunting, by way of matrimonial preface to return to Amherst to the new house Austin is building as fast as possible – I shall have a quiet wedding – a very few friends and my brothers & sisters a little cake – a little ice-cream and it is all over – the millionth wedding since the world began –

The wedding took place on July 1, the ceremony being performed by Professor Haven of Amherst. Apparently none of Austin's family made the trip to Geneva. On July 6 Austin made a curiously uncharacteristic request of a friend in New York, Gordon Ford: "May I ask if you will do me the kindness to see to the notice of my marriage in the New York 'Tribune' & 'Times.'" Both papers carried notices of the wedding in their issues of July 9. In both, Austin's bride is listed as "Miss Susan H. Gilbert, of Geneva." Why Sue's lifelong association with Amherst, much of it in residence, was thus slighted is not known. She was an "Amherst girl," like Emily.

By the middle of the month the two were settled in the new house— the Evergreens—next the Homestead. This was a fateful proximity, as it turned out. But all Amherst seemed pleased. Jane Hitchcock, the president's daughter, wrote a friend in September of the "beautiful new house" Austin and Sue moved into. Indeed, the Dickinson houses (she wrote) were "now quite as attractive" as any in Amherst.

With Austin and Sue established next door and little need for letters between the Homestead and the Evergreens, contemporary evidence is scant for a coherent, step-by-step account of the marriage. It was not until a full twenty-five years later, with the advent of Mabel Loomis Todd, that Austin unburdened himself; or, if he had confided in anybody before then (how he could have kept his troubles a secret from Emily is hard to see), no one recorded his confidences. Like his father, he grew more taciturn as he grew older. Until Mrs. Todd entered his life, there were no such outpourings as in the letter to Martha or the impassioned drafts to Sue. That strange late romance in his life, and what we can piece together of Susan's part in the marriage and its bearing on her long relationship with Emily, are reserved for later chapters.

Susan Gilbert Dickinson

The Evergreens

"The Other House" and its Mistress

Amherst, about 1875. The Dickinson Homestead in center, just above the word "Main"; the Evergreens to the left; First Church at far left, across Main Street; hat factories in foreground

But, first, a look at the externals of Austin's career, since it is important, with these introverted Dickinsons, to be reminded that they lived busy, active lives—including Emily, in her own way. We may begin with one general comment: as with both his grandfather and his father, Austin's public success—his steadily growing stature in the affairs of town, church, and college—was in ironic contrast to his personal frustrations and private tragedy. Such a situation, repeated in the three generations, seems almost to have been a Dickinson pattern. Emily shared in it, and escaped it—again, in her own way.

Austin's story is one of increasing burdens and responsibilities, both domestic and professional. Domestically, his and Sue's life was complicated by the arrival in 1858 of the orphaned Newman sisters, Clara and Anna, who were to spend the next ten years with them in the Evergreens. The arrangement was not entirely harmonious. But the girls were useful, especially when Sue's first child, Ned, was born in 1861 and her second, Martha, five years later—sufficiently so that when Clara married in 1869 and Anna went to live with her, a family friend wrote acidly: "So Marm D—— will have to wait on her own children – "

Socially, Sue set up a lively establishment. The Evergreens, rather than the Homestead, became the center of attraction. When Emerson spoke in Amherst in 1857, he was entertained by the Austin Dickinsons, an event of which Sue has left a rapturous record.[15] Emily was a frequent visitor during the first few years after Austin and Sue were married and in 1859 felt that they were all she wanted of society: she called them "my crowd." This happy state did not last long, however. Sue's temperament, tastes, and social ambition created an atmosphere in which the Dickinson qualities, at least Austin's and Emily's—given more to the creative and speculative, and requiring solitude—found less and less sustenance.

There is no doubt about Sue's success in what she set out to do. She became the chief hostess of Commencement Week; Samuel Bowles, who regularly reported the festivities in the *Springfield Republican,* wrote her after the Commencement of 1877: "You & Judge Spofford & Dr. [Edward] Hitchcock [Jr.] won the honors of the week – You ought to have a de-

---

15. Emerson's first lecture was on December 16, 1857. His topic was "The Beautiful in Rural Life." The *Hampshire and Franklin Express* (in an article that helps explain Aunt Elisabeth's satiric stanzas to Austin about Transcendentalism) said in its issue of December 18: "Ralph Waldo Emerson's lecture greatly disappointed all who listened. It was in the English language instead of the Emersonese in which he usually clothes his thoughts, and the thoughts themselves were such as any plain common-sense person could understand and appreciate" (*YH* I, 351). Sue wrote in "Annals of the Evergreens" (see Appendix I): "I remember very little of the lecture except a fine glow of enthusiasm on my own part. . . . I felt strangely elated to take his transcendental arm afterward and walk leisurely home. . . . he was our guest at the time." It is not clear where he stayed on his next visit to Amherst, when he gave a course of six lectures (October 1865) on "Social Aims" (*YH* I, 351; II, 102), perhaps with the Lucius Boltwoods. (Mrs. Boltwood, his cousin, was frequently his hostess on his Hampshire County lecture trips.)

gree." There are many tributes to her social leadership, perhaps the most famous being from Professor John Burgess, who graduated from Amherst in 1867 and taught there from 1873 to 1876:

> The society of Amherst . . . was, though limited, really charming in its simplicity, geniality, and intellectuality. In my day there were six chief social rendezvous in Amherst: the Austin Dickinsons', the Mathers', the Clark Seelyes', the Tuckermans', the Joneses', and the Stearns'. The social leader of the town was Mrs. Austin Dickinson, a really brilliant and highly cultivated woman of great taste and refinement, perhaps a little too aggressive, a little too sharp in wit and repartee, and a little too ambitious for social prestige, but, withal, a woman of the world in the best sense, having a very keen and correct appreciation of what was fine and admirable. Her imagination was exceedingly vivid, sometimes so vivid that it got away with her and she confounded its pictures with objective things. If she had had sufficient application, she would have rivaled Cervantes as a writer of romance and adventure. . . . Here at commencement time were to be met the élite of alumni: Henry Ward Beecher, Richard Salter Storrs, Frederic D. Huntington, Alexander H. Bullock, Edward B. Gillett, John E. Sanford, and the like. . . .
> Mrs. Dickinson was, I suppose, by descent a Puritan, but she was not much of a Puritan in her mentality. She was decidedly aristocratic in her tastes, and her friends among the alumni were generally scions of the best American families or men who had distinguished themselves highly.

This confirms what Mabel Todd found to be true of her in the early 1880s: "the most of a real society person here," as she described her in a letter home. But for Austin, not only was Sue's "salon"—the teas, the musicales, the dancing parties (oyster stew at ten)—expensive, and for this reason alone a burden, but the whole affair rang increasingly hollow. In his diary for these later years, he spoke often of "Sue and her crowd" and absented himself frequently from their functions. He spent more and more time in the Homestead. "We almost forget," Emily wrote in 1883, "that he ever passed to a wedded Home."

What sustained Austin, besides Emily and the retreat the Homestead offered, was his absorption in his work, his hobbies (his paintings, his fine horses), and especially his love of nature as displayed in the Amherst countryside. This last deserves a special word. The beauties and mysteries of nature had been opened up for him in his boyhood by Professor Hitchcock [Sr.], whose lectures and writings influenced several generations of young people in Amherst, Emily most surely among them. The inciting event that led Austin for nearly a half century to incorporate some of this natural beauty into his beloved town was a series of lectures Hitchcock gave in 1850 after a five-month tour of Europe, during which he was particularly impressed with shade trees and shrubs in the continental cities and towns. One of the major steps in Austin's campaign to beautify Amherst came in 1874 with the draining and planting of the village common, still the handsomest feature of the town. During his tenure as treasurer of the college from 1873 until his death, it was his peculiar pleasure to see to the landscaping of the college grounds and especially the several buildings whose construction he supervised. His delight in nature was an enthusiasm that Emily, of course, understood and shared, and it became one of the strongest bonds between him and Mabel Todd. Sue's interests, apparently, went in quite different directions.

The list of Austin's civic projects and responsibilities reads much like his father's. He moderated the town meetings from 1881 to the time of his death. He was president of the Village Improvement Association. In 1874 he drafted the articles of incorporation for the Amherst Library Association and served on its board. He was on the board of Amherst Academy, the Amherst Savings Bank, the First National Bank of Amherst, the Amherst Water Company, and the Amherst Gas Light Company. He helped found Wildwood Cemetery and directed the laying out of its grounds. One of his most notable contributions to the community was his part in promoting and supervising the construction of a new building for the First Church in 1867–68. He was at his best in the task of uniting the congregation behind the project and then in the practical problems of the construction itself. There is a legend that Emily "crept out one evening with her brother as far as a certain tree in the hedge in order to see the new church," perhaps a measure of how reclusive she had become by that time—even toward an affair in which her family was deeply involved. Her father gave the dedicatory speech (on September 23, 1868) to an audience "filled to overflowing with the worthy people of Amherst."

All this, plus his law practice, his duties as treasurer, and the management of a difficult family which, after Edward Dickinson died in 1874, included the three next door—Emily, Vinnie, and (until 1882) their invalid mother—stretched Austin's endurance to the breaking point. Mabel Todd teased him about being the indispensable man in Amherst. "I suppose nobody in the town could be born or married or buried, or make an investment, or buy a house-lot, or a cemetary-lot or sell a newspaper, or build a house, or choose a profession, without you close at hand." But it was no joke; Austin had earlier written her: "I am crowded with work and can with difficulty keep abreast of the demands upon me. I seem to be too convenient for too many people, in too many ways." He once remarked to Mrs. Todd: "I have a very expensive family." Austin seriously overtaxed his strength, and it was generally agreed that his final illness was brought on by exhaustion.

In this crowded life, the early literary inclinations Austin shared at least to some extent with Emily never flourished. He was interested enough in the epistolary style of both his sisters to comment in an older-brotherly way. He knew, certainly, that Emily wrote poetry; but there is no sure evidence that he was aware of its quality. His sense of what he was to call her "genius" came late, probably stimulated by Mabel Todd's influence. At one point, apparently during the very week of his engagement to Sue, he sent Emily some of his verse. Emily's reply, dated March 27, 1853, hailed him as "Brother Pegasus" and teased him properly in a letter that shows their relationship at its sprightliest. He must have sent a considerable sample of his work to have evoked such a response, though Emily gives no hint of its substance. (Her last sentence, it is to be noted, shows that she had begun thinking of herself as a poet well before this episode.) After some preliminary fooling, she writes:

> And Austin is a Poet, Austin writes a psalm. Out of the way, Pegasus, Olympus enough "to him," and just say to those "nine muses" that we have done with them!
> Raised a living muse ourselves, worth the whole nine of them. Up, off, tramp!
> Now Brother Pegasus, I'll tell you what it is – I've been in the habit *myself* of writing some few things, and it rather appears to me that you're getting away my patent, so you'd better be somewhat careful, or I'll call the police!

Only one scrap of what has been called, perhaps too charitably, "a tentatively light poem" of Austin's has survived. It was sent to Sue (visiting in Grand Rapids) on October 19, 1882:

> Oil is no name for it,
> Peace is not
> Quiet is not – nor
> Rest.
> Serene doesnt ma[t]ch(?) to it,
> Tranquil doesnt.

(A postscript adds: "All and more but feebly convey the ineffable – The utterly utter dumbness and smoothness of life on the magical Terrace since Tuesday.")

Although Austin's one publication—his address at the one hundred and fiftieth anniversary of the First Church in 1889—was strictly local, written in the line of duty, it is worth notice, like anything from a Dickinson pen so near Emily's. The topic was a large one, certainly for the twenty minutes he was given on the program and for the short time he was given (he complained) to prepare. But when "Representative Men of the Parish, Church Buildings and Finances" was published next year by the press of the *Amherst Record* in a volume containing the proceedings of the occasion, it came to a full 7,500 words and obviously had involved research and careful composition. It contains indispensable background material for all Amherst—and for all Dickinsons.

There is little of the "Pegasus" in the essay and not much to suggest that he was the brother of a poet. The writing is hardheaded, forthright and firm, sure in its command of fact. The most striking family resemblance is a kind of wry humor toward the past and its dignitaries, reminiscent of Emily's (and Vinnie's) occasional reverent irreverence toward holy things. There is an occasional turn, also, to metaphor. The passage on the third meeting house (1829)—"The First Church in Amherst was built in the years 1867-8. . . . Before that we had meeting-houses and went to meeting"—has the tone and design of some of Emily's satiric letters:

> It was a substantial structure, is still, and may have fulfilled the hope and purpose of the building committee; though architecturally it could hardly have been thought an inspiration even then, and the discussions were many among the students as to the age and order which it represented. It was more commonly classed as Tuscan, that being the most elementary described in the books; but by some to be back of books – ancient Egyptian. This was the claim of Tutor March of the class of 1845, while one of the French professors in the early days pronounced it the Eighth Astonishment.

Austin made pleasant fun of the various stages by which the "meeting house" developed into the "church": the introduction of pews ("every man was buttoned tight in"); stoves ("As I remember them they stood within this circular wall, the pipes running the whole length of the side aisles directly over the centre, entering the chimneys at the west end, with tin troughs underneath to catch the creosote which dropped from the joints"); horse sheds, which came in 1838; a bell in 1839 ("Down to 1862 this bell rang at noon and at 9 in the evening as notice for dining and retiring"); and, also in 1839 (an event which made a lasting impression on Austin and, if on him, surely on Emily), the purchase of the double bass viol, "the first musical instrument ever owned by the parish."

> With my first recollection Josiah Ayres managed it, and the tones he drew from its lower chords in his accompaniment to the singing of some of Watts' Favorite Hymns, haunt me even now. Such lines as
>
> > "That awful day will surely come,
> > That last great day of woe and doom,"
>
> and
>
> > "Broad is the road that leads to death," etc.,
>
> seemed to me sufficiently depressing in plain print; sung with the accompaniment, they were appalling – to a boy.

In 1854 a movement was started among the young people to replace the bass viol with an organ ("a small second-hand" one). Austin reports:

> There was a great deal of doubt about this: there was a suggestion of Rome and Episcopacy in this instrument not brought up by the double bass viol,

but some of the young people were very urgent, and it was decided to let it be tried.

"Things were running now on rather a high key," Austin resumes; and in 1857, when there was a proposal to raise seventy-five dollars for four kerosene chandeliers, the liberals had a rough time of it. The "hunkers," as he calls them, asserted themselves.

This [the chandeliers] was too much, a step too far for those who held religion rather as a matter for the practice of fine economy. They said it portended the theatre: they thought – as some of us believed – it would add to the burden of maintaining public worship; and threats of signing off were loud if the unsanctity were persisted in: the air was thick; there was concern on the part of the movers in the project and hesitation, but somehow the breakers were cleared and the chandeliers hung.

Once the parish recovered from the "shock of this innovation," things proceeded quietly until 1864, when the matter of the new building, often brought up in meeting but successfully quashed, would not down. Finally, after "numberless meetings" about plans and sites, the new church became an accomplished fact—"not without effort, not without opposition, not without sacrifice."

And here Austin embarks on a series of sketches of the leading men of the parish, past and present, to whom the First Church stood as a monument. He pays tribute to all those "strong and earnest men" who had been prominent in Amherst from the beginning, "when town and parish were the same": "The Bakers, Boltwoods, Clarks, Churches, Cowles, Dickinsons, Eastmans, Hawleys, Kelloggs, Montagues, Smiths, Strongs"; and others, "unrepresented among us now," the "Chaunceys, Colemans, Fields, Ingrams, Nashes, Porters, Warners"—an Amherst honor roll. The style in which he describes them is strong and earnest, like the men. We have already seen his tribute to his grandfather, Squire Fowler. Coming down the generations to his father, Austin shows the same bold Dickinson front to the world, excluding for public purposes all that was warm and personal, or amusing. Here again is the "River God," standing perpendicular in the community:

Edward Dickinson, proud of being of Amherst soil, of the sixth generation born within sound of the old meeting-house bell, all earnest, God-fearing men, doing their part in their day toward the evolution of the Amherst we live in; in the front from earliest manhood, prompt with tongue, pen, time, money for anything promising its advancement, leading every forward movement, moral or material, in parish and town; holding many positions of trust and responsibility, never doubted, the soul of integrity and honor, fearless for the right, shirking no duty, and dying at his post as representative of his district in the Massachusetts Legislature where, in his seventy-second year, he had gone to help in shaping legislation proposed affecting the interests of the Central railroad.

First Congregational Church, erected 1867–8. Construction and landscaping supervised by Austin Dickinson

Rev. Aaron Merrick Colton, pastor
of the First Church, 1840–53

Rev. Jonathan Leavitt Jenkins, pasto
of the First Church, 1867–77

Dr. Timothy Gridley, physician
Austin: "strange, queer, eccentric, fascinating"

Deacon David Mack
Austin: "I thought I had seen God

Austin's sketches of other Amherst notables gain in humor and immediacy the farther he moves from his family. One of the town worthies, William Cutler, was "naturally slow and cautious, more apt to see objections than advantages – the course of events never quite to his mind – finding much to condemn, little to approve outside Daniel Webster and the old Whig party." Sidney Adams was "amiable, seeing only the sunny side, useless in a tempest, but using a good oar in smooth water." Dr. Timothy J. Gridley, the Amherst physician of Austin's and Emily's youth (he died in 1852), was one of the town's leading eccentrics:

. . . that strange, queer, eccentric, fascinating man; doctor, politician; hated, admired, distrusted, believed to carry life in his hand; apparently not knowing day from night, that Sunday came the same day every time, his own house from another's; who wouldn't go straight if he could go across; regular only in being irregular; a most picturesque character.

And finally (his masterpiece) a tribute to Deacon David Mack, who with his family had lived in the west side of the Homestead during Austin's and Emily's childhood:

. . . a man to command attention anywhere, tall, erect, of powerful build, with a fine head finely set, clear, exact, just, a believer in law and penalty for its breach; strong as a lion, pure as a saint, simple as a child, a Puritan of the Puritans: I remember my first sight of him – I was four years old – I thought I had seen God.

His review of the heroes of the parish leads Austin to some melancholy thoughts: "Has manhood gained?" he asks. "We cannot fail to perceive that we are counting fewer and fewer in numbers of the kind of men that save cities." The small country towns are being drained of those "independent, strong characters – men of mark – who used to be scattered over our hills." They have heard the call and have gone to the cities to join in "the struggle for wealth and power and fame – a struggle as fierce and desperate as the struggle of battle." Amherst and towns like it, he warned, must look to themselves.

Austin concludes on a curious, apologetic note, explainable in part by the chivalry demanded of the occasion but also perhaps by a fact of his biography. For all his qualities as leader and as spokesman for the parish, the color and texture of his later life was determined by women. After his father's death in 1874 the Dickinson enclave was dominated by females, and he felt himself more and more enmeshed. "Women," he wrote a friend, "you may or may not know, are very unreasonable, and very unmanageable, at times, and a man had better stand from under, if he can, and as far as he can." In the light of such a remark, his tribute to the women of the parish becomes all the more ironic:

But the women count in our modern census. They have appeared above the surface in the last generation, and become a power, nowhere more than in parish affairs, where they have found a congenial field for their activities and displayed them to good advantage. We no longer go home and tell them what we have done at parish meeting; they tell us what they have done at the sewing society. They are hardly longer the power behind the throne; they are a good part of the throne itself.

It is not quite easy for a masculine man to admit all this; but if he will live in the country, he might as well – and thank God for salvation even so.

As we shall see shortly, the situation in Austin's private life in 1889 (the year of the address) was such that there could hardly have been a person in the audience who would not have perceived the irony. But there is still another, and final, irony to be perceived in his address, also of unhappy implications.

Although Austin touches upon his grandfather's and father's service in the Massachusetts Legislature—that is, their part in affairs *outside* Amherst—it is curious that he omits his father's term in the House of Representatives in Washington, the high-water mark of Dickinson public achievement. The purely local aspect of his own career would have become, by contrast, all the more obvious, and he may have wanted to play it down. A document recently come to light shows him quite conscious of his provincialism and, for so dedicated an Amherst man, curiously frustrated by the limitations of small-town life. This, in spite of the fact that since young manhood he seems to have been ill at ease away from home—in Sunderland, Boston, and Cambridge. He could have settled in Chicago as a young lawyer, but he did not. He traveled infrequently, and seldom for the sake of traveling—his scorn of people going hither and yon was like Emily's (and Thoreau's). Although, when he became treasurer, he went often to Boston and New York in the service of the college, there is record of only one extended trip made for its own sake, a six-week journey to the West and South with his friend, John Sanford, in 1887. He got to New Orleans and as far west as St. Louis. His letters home (the only ones we have are to Mabel Todd) complain of almost everything: the noise, confusion, discomfort, people. One of his remarks sounds like a shaft from Emily herself: "I wouldn't give a volume of Emerson for all the hogs west of the Mississippi." In short, to this complete New Englander, one might think that success in his beloved Amherst would have been enough. But a draft of a letter to a friend in Omaha, dated August 8, 1893, shows him thinking quite different thoughts. While his domestic troubles may have eroded by then whatever joy he took in his work for the town and the college, his discontent apparently went deeper. However much, in his church address, he may have lamented the departure of so many good men to the cities to join in "the struggle for wealth and power and fame," he apparently wished he had gone, too. The letter shows the frustration in which he lived, the sense of unused talents and energies that might have carried him far in a larger community. One interesting fact also emerges: he attributed these same longings to his father.

William Austin Dickinson

Amherst, Mass.
August 8th, 1893.

[Hon James Clark]
DEAR SIR

I have received yours of 3rd inst – and again carefully considered your several propositions for my joining you in Omaha.

I have thought more than ever in the last six months of trying to get away from Amherst, where so many unpleasant animosities surround me, and I am strongly inclined to feel that, with the opening you offer to make for me, now is the time and Omaha the place.

It would ordinarily be thought a little late to pull up old and put down new stakes – at sixty, but according to Depew, Vanderbilt made the larger part of his fortune after he was seventy, and I have always held that it is never to[o] late to attempt the right thing. Besides[,] the lines you lay out for me – while in accordance with my general training and experience are even more congenial to me than what I have been accustomed to, and on those I should see more men – men of the world and affairs, which I greatly miss here, as my father did before me. The same lack which drove our mutual friend Gibbs from Norwich [?] to New York.

Unless then something which I do not now foresee occurs to prevent, I think I will plan to come out about the 21st, look the matter all over on the ground, and decide then. I will have my business here in such shape that I can leave by that time.

[P.S.]
Of course you will say nothing about this anywhere at present.

The "unpleasant animosities" mentioned in the second paragraph and the secrecy enjoined in the postscript are part of the story of his involvement, then nearing a crisis, with Mabel Loomis Todd. It is possible that these animosities may have soured his attitude toward Amherst only temporarily; but the letter throws a sad light over his whole career. Emily could have understood this, too. Like her father and brother, she too at one time had her eye on a larger world than Amherst. All three knew frustration of this sort.

Externally, save for what in the Mabel Todd affair became public knowledge, Austin's life during its final few years was more of the same, the endless duties of any pillar of a small-town community. Looking back over his life—from the famous "hurra" of his boyhood, through the passion of his romance, to the intense dedication to his work—one is struck, perhaps chiefly, by his enormous vitality. The years of his relations with Mabel Todd reveal but a late manifestation of it, remarkable in a man half his age. Though not explaining, it enables us to approach with less surprise the miracle of his sister's extraordinary creative power.

Another fact of Austin's character and experience makes a similar trait in Emily more understandable—his response to the phenomenon of death when it struck close to him. Emily's poems and letters are full of the shock of death and its mystery, sometimes to the point of obsession. Each death seemed to her, as it apparently did to him, unprecedented, over-whelming, unfathomable. It was as if, each time, the old, grueling questions were opened all over again; each time she had to "regulate" her faith. And Austin had, at least once, to cling to his very life.

Although Austin has left little in writing, we have record of at least four occasions when his reactions were noted by others: the death of his friend Frazar Stearns, son of the president of Amherst College, in the Battle of Newbern (N.C.) in 1862; the death of his father in 1874; his beloved son Gilbert's death, at the age of eight, in 1883; and Emily's in 1886. These experiences appear to have been almost equally shattering. After Frazar's death, even Emily was distressed by Austin's behavior. (Perhaps there was a sense of guilt involved; he had paid for a substitute, while Frazar had joined up.) She described him as "stunned completely," and wrote to their friend Samuel Bowles:

> Austin is chilled – by Frazer's murder – He says – his Brain keeps saying over "Frazer is killed" – "Frazer is killed," just as Father told it – to Him. Two or three words of lead – that dropped so deep, they keep weighing – Tell Austin – how to get over them!

After his father's death he was similarly undone, about as little use to the family and their close friends as was Emily, who hid away upstairs. (It was Vinnie who bore the brunt.) Austin, wrote a friend, "is apparently the most shocked, stunned by the loss of his father." When Gilbert died, two close witnesses feared for Austin's life. Vinnie wrote some friends in Newport, "Of course you knew little Gilbert has disappeared & Emily & I have had hard work to keep Austin from following him –" Mabel Todd wrote in her diary the day after Gilbert died that Vinnie "says her brother looks like death" and later she wrote of the event in her journal: "Mr. D. nearly died too. Gilbert was his idol, and the only thing in his house which truly loved him, or in which he took any pleasure." It was weeks before he was himself again.[16] In a sense, Austin never got over Gilbert's

16. Gilbert was not only Austin's idol, and much cherished by Emily; he was already, at age eight, something of an idol of the town's, beloved by all. A striking obituary appeared in the *Amherst Record* for October 17, 1883, some two weeks after his death.

DEATH OF A PROMISING BOY.

Gilbert Dickinson youngest son of Wm. A. Dickinson died on the afternoon of Friday, October 5th, after a very short but severe attack of fever. He was at school on Thursday of the week before. He was only eight years old, and yet we are astonished to find how many Gilbert interested. His frankness and simple-heartedness were charming, but these are the common charms of childhood. There was in him also, a self-reliance, rare in a boy so gentle and sensitive, which seemed, somehow, to lift him into the sphere of men. He became not only interesting but companionable. People not only played with him to see the child-life show itself, but they talked with him for their own pleasure. When the village heard of his death we felt as if one had gone who had established a place for himself among us. We loved him as one in whom the qualities that men "Tie to" were freshened by the dew of childhood. Nor did this lessen his hearty

loss, nor did Emily. It was about this time (autumn 1884) that she wrote, "The Dyings have been too deep for me, and before I could raise my Heart from one, another has come – ." When Emily herself died a year and a half later, the loss was another fearful shock for Austin, even though there had been many premonitions. Mrs. Todd wrote in her diary on May 14 (Emily died the next day): "He is terribly oppressed." And the entry in his own diary for May 15 speaks for itself:

It was settled before morning broke that Emily would not wake again this side.

The day was awful. She ceased to breathe that terrible breathing just before the whistles sounded for six.

Mrs. Montagu and Mrs. Jameson were sitting with Vin.

I was nearby.

There is no entry at all for May 16, an unusual blank in the eight volumes of his diary that survive. When he picked it up again on the seventeenth, he was his usual laconic self, "I attending to some necessary things, seeing a number of people, and was at my office an hour in forenoon and a little more than that P.M." What sustained him this time was Mabel Todd, who wrote in her journal for September 1, 1886:

---

enjoyment of all that children delight in. He was a real child only his interests were very broad for such a little fellow. As if by intuition, he found the real stuff of humanity beneath all sorts of garbs and in persons old as well as young. The best in people he brought to the surface, and it met his friendship. His circle of friends therefore was wide and varied. That he liked a person was enough. Whatever others might think of his friends he was loyal always. He liked so many that he took it for granted that many liked him and when he stopped an older person in the street to see him ride his velocipede, it was not because he thought he rode better than other boys but because of a common interest he supposed people had in each other. The richest kind of democracy had taken possession of that little heart. But his affection was not less intense because it was broad. At times he could not bear to see even the picture of one of his little friends who had left town. It must be turned to the wall. And this wide and intense affection found abundant, even delicious expression in his words to those he loved. How this giving of his love evoked a rich return those who received it well understand. He taught how blessed it is to give as well as to receive. Hopes are always buried with children but not often do we lose in the death of so young a boy so much of actual fruition. He not only promised much but he already had provided much.

Or as Emily put it, a year later, in a letter to Sue (*L* III, 842; October 1884):

Twice, when I had Red Flowers out, Gilbert knocked, raised his sweet Hat, and asked if he might touch them –

Yes, and take them too, I said, but Chivalry forbade him – Besides, he gathered Hearts, not Flowers –

> Some Arrows slay but whom they strike –
> But this slew all *but* him –
> Who so appareled his Escape –
> Too trackless for a Tomb –

[#*1565*]

EMILY –

It [Emily's death] was a very great sorrow to Austin, but I have lived through a greater with him – when poor little Gilbert died. He and I are so *one* that we comfort each other for everything perfectly.

This final remark is a measure of Austin's need in the presence of death. He was well into his maturity when Frazar was killed, a leading figure in Amherst and seemingly all-in-all sufficient by the time his father died, and fifty-four when Gilbert died. And yet, each time he was "stunned." Emily was not the only one in the family for whom the "Dyings were too deep."

One can only speculate about causes. A fearful mother or a father who had made both children overly dependent on him are hardly sufficient explanations. Vinnie apparently escaped such parental influences. One recalls Austin's gropings into "the profound darkness" in his letter to Mattie and the "maelstrom" poems by Emily. "Eternity," she said after her mother died, "sweeps around me like a sea." Or one has recourse simply to the heightened sensitivities of the poet, or the man of poetic nature, and to the imagination which is at once the poet's glory and his curse.

When Austin himself died (August 16, 1895), the Amherst shops were closed during his funeral as they had been during his father's. "The woods and fields and mountains," said the report in the *Springfield Republican* (August 20), "which were so dear to Mr. Dickinson . . . seemed to his mourning friends never more beautiful." The obituary in the *Republican* the day after his death presented the main outlines of his career accurately enough and caught some of the nuances of his character, probably because of the long association of the Bowles family with the Dickinsons (young Samuel had become editor of the paper when his father died). "Amherst Loses a Strong Man," ran the headline, "A Useful and Worthy Life Devoted to Amherst College and Town," and the first sentence called him "the most influential citizen of Amherst."

Much was said in the obituary that might have been expected—tributes to "his tremendous will power" in his final fight for life, to the sacrificial nature of the work that brought on his last illness ("There is no doubt that his death was hastened by overwork, and that by a long rest at the right time he might have been spared for years of usefulness"), to his "universal" service in town affairs, especially his leadership in beautifying Amherst. He "exerted a potent influence with the faculty and the trustees in the administration of the internal affairs of the college" and showed "excellent judgment and fine taste" in his care of its buildings and grounds. It was noted that as a lawyer he "never attained prominence as a practitioner before the courts"; as a speaker "he had not much gift" and tended to avoid court cases. But he was an "excellent" Town Moderator and "he could condense into a sentence what would take others minutes to express"—a point of style shared by another member of his family. Politically, he had "usually acted with the republicans" but latterly had become independent of party politics. Mention was made of his charming home in Amherst, "embowered in trees and surrounded with lovely shrubs and flowers," and of the many prominent men he had entertained there. "He was exceedingly fond of fine pictures and had many of his own. He was also a most appreciative reader of the best literature."

What is most striking about the obituary is its sensitivity to certain shadings in Austin's character amounting, almost, to the same paradox that the *Republican* had found in Edward Dickinson years before: the public vs. the private figure. Such perception could have come only from firsthand observation; one suspects the hand of a Bowles in both documents. Again, it is the strong, austere exterior in contrast to the "real" man within.

> Mr. Dickinson was a strong and forceful personality. He had an open, frank and vigorous way of speaking to and looking out at the world that commanded respect and confidence from the moment that he appeared on any scene. But his nature was all gentleness and refinement, and there were a shyness and reserve in his composition, coupled with an intensity of feeling, that were almost pathetic at times. . . . [He was] best liked by those who knew him best. Many thought him austere in his nature, but with closer intimacy that idea would vanish.

The obituary spoke, too, of his superior abilities that fitted him "to fill a larger sphere," but it missed the sad truth as Austin had put it in the letter of 1893 to his friend in Omaha. The obituary merely said, piously, that he was

> content to devote his life to the local institutions and interests, amid which he had been born and which he loved with a deep and abiding affection. . . . His love for Amherst was so strong he did not care to spend a vacation elsewhere, and he always expressed the satisfaction he had on returning to the town from a trip of even a few days' duration. . . .

So far into the Dickinson interior the eulogist went—but no further—and we are in the presence of those same qualities we have seen developing since Samuel Fowler: the love of Amherst; the sacrificial dedication; the angular exterior ("the face of flint") belying the passion within. A later section, "War between the Houses," will reveal more not only about Austin and Dickinsons in general but about that figure to whom the obituary paid this passing tribute:

> One of his sisters was the late Emily Dickinson, the literary recluse whose singular life and wonderful writings in prose and verse have only recently become known to the world.

7

Lavinia Norcross Dickinson

Lavinia Dickinson (1833-1899) outlived all her family, and her comments during later years on the Dickinson scene have done much to clarify, color, and in some important ways distort our view of it. Summing up the inmates of her houshold, she said of Emily that "she had to think – she was the only one of us who had that to do," and added of the others: "Father believed; and mother loved; and Austin had Amherst; and I had the family to keep track of." Of the five, she came closest to the truth about Emily, her mother, and herself. From what we have seen of the family so far, she had Austin and her father the wrong way around. It was Edward Dickinson who "had Amherst"—and the railroad, and the college, and politics. His "belief" seems to have been more of an inherited discipline than a living spiritual experience. It guided him in his duty and set the tone of his public utterances, whether in leading family prayers (a phenomenon which must have impressed Lavinia as it did Emily) or in speaking at the dedication of the new church building. He left no record of any such spiritual anguish as Austin went through. Austin was more of a believer by temperament; at least, he was more expressive about spiritual matters, which is all we have to rely on. He "had Amherst," to be sure, and gave himself to it. But his loyalty to it was more like Emily's than his father's was; he was *in* it but not quite *of* it; his values and style of life were not identical with it, as (so far as we can see) Edward's—and Lavinia's—nearly were.

As an observer, Lavinia was never noted for her profundity; there were things about all her family she missed. If she was right that Emily "had to think," she seems to have been unaware of how much she had to write. At least, the surprise she expressed at finding, when Emily died, such a vast amount of writings tucked away in her room seems to have been genuine. As to her mother, it was to Vinnie's credit that she saw (for all the dark stories she told later about early days in the family) that her mother "loved," even though Vinnie's tenderness toward her came late. And it is to her credit, too, that she saw her own role in the family about right, though in this summary she did not do herself justice. She "kept track" of them, surely, but she was more than the family watchdog or drudge. As Emily's closest associate for more than fifty years, she became indispensable to her in many ways, if not in the same way Austin was. As a personality, she was indispensable to the family's solidarity. And in one final way she was indispensable to posterity. Her complete belief in Emily during her life was transferred to the poems after Emily died. Without that belief, which approached fanaticism, we might never have had them.

The questions will be asked: Who was Lavinia? What did she mean to Emily more than the guardian's role she is usually given? It cannot be insisted too much that, in Emily's limited circle, everyone counted. "Area – ," she once remarked, "no test of depth." To adopt an image from one of her poems, she "measured" people with "narrow, probing, Eyes," and she focused as closely on those nearest her as she did on the new visitor. She measured her father and mother with tender precision. She could make mistakes, and at times she could be impatient with people, especially bores. Sue, for instance, never bored her; but her misjudgment of Sue's future in the family circle shows how far wrong she could be, especially in this instance, about the character and needs of her own brother. It was an early mistake about "depth."

Lavinia, though in many ways the least of these, came under the same scrutiny. Fortunately, she involved Emily in no such problems as the others did. She was not by nature a griever. Though Austin was closer to Emily in temperament and mentality, she turned to Vinnie, the "uncomplicated" Dickinson, for daily living and the long pull. Vinnie functioned most notably in what might be called the comic side of the family drama. She early developed enough spunk and wit to make her a formidable figure even in a family of wits. Emily, older by two years and two months, kept a sisterly eye on her during their youth and, when Vinnie was fifteen, boasted to a friend that she had been "instilling many a lesson of wisdom into the budding intellect of my only sister." But neither the solicitude nor the humor was all one way. A few years later the roles were reversed. Vinnie wrote to Austin:

I think Emilie is very much improved. She has really grown *fat*, if youll believe it.
    I am very strict with her & I shouldnt wonder if she should come out bright some time after all.

There was the usual family bickering. "Emilie tells storys about me," Vinnie complained to Austin. "Dont believe her." She preceded this charge with a few comments on Austin's complaint about her handwriting. She is in fighting trim:

If you cant read my writing, Austin, perhaps twill do no good to say any thing to you. I really dont understand your inability to read what has always been called *plain*. I think you must be growing blind. I would advise you to consult Dr. Reynolds speedily, else secure a pair of Fathers glasses which have proved themselves *"uncommon"*.

(Austin's complaint, incidentally, could justly be leveled by generations of editors and biographers against the whole family, his own handwriting especially. It is sometimes almost indecipherable.)

As the sisters grew older, Emily became dependent on Lavinia in many practical ways, and there is no sign of discord. Emily loved her, respected her abilities, even felt a little humble, perhaps, in the presence of one so well adjusted to the world and confident in it. That she outgrew her was inevitable and no disparagement to Vinnie. But it did mean that above a certain level there was little communication between them. Vinnie was simply unequipped to function on her level.

As one who knew both girls during their formative years, Joseph Lyman sensed this difference, implicit in his remark about Vinnie's not being "inside the ring" as Emily was. She was "very pious and very pretty," and Joseph enjoyed his evenings with her. But it was Emily whom he took seriously. A letter of January 23, 1851, from his classmate, Daniel Bonbright, shows that even then the difference between the girls was common gossip among the young people. Bonbright, speculating on Lyman's activities during a short vacation, writes, "Or it may be, and I think this the more probable supposition, you are in Amherst, playing – what? 'spooney,' I suppose with Vinnie, or sitting up late of nights to talk with Emily, when less spiritual beings, such as watchful parents, are fast asleep."

Austin saw this difference, too, and Lavinia was occasionally miffed by his clear preference for Emily, who once scolded him for his favoritism: "Vinnie says she thinks you dont pay much attention to her." They all put much of the practical matters of the household on Vinnie's shoulders, and even Emily could be a little patronizing. She wrote to Austin that she would leave "all the matter o'fact to our practical sister Vinnie" and reserve for herself the interesting things to write about. Once she complained: "I dont see much of Vinnie – she's mostly dusting stairs!"—and sometimes to her annoyance:

> We cleaned house all last week – that is to say – Mother and Vinnie did, and I scolded, because they moved my things – I cant find much left anywhere, that I used to wear, or know of. You will easily conclude that I am surrounded by trial.

In this situation, as the only other daughter, Vinnie understood and accepted her role. But she sometimes wrote about it plaintively, as in her apology, when she was nineteen, to Austin for filling her letters with matters of business: "the folks make me do all the errands, else I should sometimes say some thing different." That she was capable of something different soon became clear. A little later, Austin spoke of a letter from her that surprised him: it was "more beautiful," he wrote to Sue, "than I supposed she *could* write." Emily never gave her full credit; even in later years, she summed her up too quickly as "happy with her duties, her pussies, and her posies."

But Vinnie had talents and a style of her own, and Emily was aware of them. Beyond some minor flaws, the relationship between the sisters was warm and vital. Once Emily did the personal side of it full justice in a late letter to a friend who had just lost his brother. In these later years she recognized not only her indebtedness to Vinnie as a protectress—by then Vinnie had become her "Soldier and Angel" carrying "a 'drawn Sword' in behalf of Eden"—but she paid tribute to a quality not often remarked in Vinnie: "Your bond to your brother reminds me of mine to my sister – early, earnest, indissoluble. Without her life were fear, and Paradise a cowardice, except for her inciting voice."

It would be interesting to know precisely what Emily meant by "her inciting voice." She may have had in mind what I have called Vinnie's style, a quality of bearing and attitude as well as her manner of expressing herself. It is clear from Vinnie's letters, from her witty sayings that have come down to us, and from descriptions of her by her contemporaries, that she *had* a style and that it was pungent, racy, very much her own. These qualities were noted in a eulogy of her that appeared, shortly after her death, in the *Springfield Republican,* by a friend of her later years, Professor Joseph Chickering of Amherst:

> I suppose people called her peculiar, a favorite term in the vocabulary of mediocrity. To me she was unique, rather than peculiar. She never said things as other people said them. I think she abhorred the commonplace in speech almost more than the vulgar. . . . Her views of life were those of an onlooker, not a participator in the affairs of men, and they were at once shrewd and amusing to a remarkable degree. Her conversational and literary gifts would have been more highly appreciated and more widely known, but for the extraordinary powers of her famous sister.

It is clear from Emily's many comments that her pleasure in Vinnie's style was important in her life. What the Dickinson family needed for its day-to-day health and good spirits was a leaven, someone to offset its tendency toward introspection and brooding. Father never played, and Mother, so the tradition runs, was more solicitous about the dust on the piano than about the music it could make. Emily complained that when Austin was away, there was no fun any more; and when he "went East," as she described his marrying, all she had left for daily fare was Vinnie and that inciting voice.

What is impressive about Vinnie, certainly in her youth and until the 1880s and 1890s, when her involvement in the trouble emanating from the Evergreens made her devious and bitter, is her forthrightness. It is the basis of her style as a conversationalist and correspondent. She was the most outgoing and the least inhibited in the household. As a girl, she was not only pretty, she was "pert." Emily, writing to Austin, saw her at eighteen as growing *"perter* and *more* pert day by day,"* a word that in her lexicon meant not only "lively, brisk, smart," but "forward, saucy, bold, indecorously free." She had wit and a talent for mimicry. According to Jane Hitchcock, her roommate at Ipswich Female Seminary, it was she who made life bearable at school. In a letter to Austin, Jane all but despaired over the stuffiness of the Seminary:

> Now such things would crush me, and take away every bit of spirit and life I ever had, and I should become a blue-stocking, or book-worm, were it not for your dear sister Vinnie. . . . Vinnie writes all the funny letters that go from this room. . . . Fortunately she still retains her ability to "take off" people. You have seen her, enough to know how well she does it. I assure you it is a real comfort. And now and then we have a good laugh together.

Several years later, during her visit with her father at the Willard Hotel in Washington in 1854, Vinnie was just as successful before a larger audience, sufficiently so to be commented on many years later, again by Professor Chickering:

> [Lavinia] was a clever raconteur, and when in Washington during her father's term in Congress, was quite the center of a little circle at Willard's, who were refreshed by her unique wit and impersonations.

Vinnie often used her talent to refresh the members of her family, conversationally and in her letters, and this may be part of what Emily meant by her inciting voice.[1] For her brother Austin, drudging away in Boston at his schoolteaching, she embellished her report of some pleasant Amherst news with a description of the complaints of a certain Mrs. James. She had Emily's excellent ear for the idiom and rhythm of local speech.

> There was a pleasant little gathering at Tempe [Linnell]'s, Friday eve, Martha [Gilbert] is better, Mrs "James' lungs are all tied up in a knout & she haint got nothin to hitch her breath on to & her vitals are struck." This is a true statement Austin, the poor lady really thinks she does suffer & "if it had'nt a been for [Dr.] Gridley she'd a went," that time.

Her letters have color and pace. Her forthrightness, whether naïve or calculated, is the most refreshing thing about them. She never wasted words, or minced them. In a family that went in for the slant, or oblique, approach, Vinnie's attack was direct and frontal. About a picture she had just had taken, she wrote to Austin:

> I will send you my picture, but I dont like it at all & should be sorry to have you or any one else think I look just like it. I dont think my real face is quite so stupid as the picture, perhaps I'm mistaken however.

1. For Vinnie's style, conversational and epistolary, for her reading and her (limited) prowess as a poet, see Appendix I.

A little later, sending Austin some mail, she enclosed a scatter-shot note that covers in fourteen abrupt sentences subjects that would have kept her brother and sister, at that time in their discursive period, busy for many pages. She marches swiftly through such important matters as Austin's neglect of his friend and her sweetheart, Joseph Lyman; the state of her health and her sanity; news of Father, Sue, and Emily, and of "that pretty cousin Lizzie" and her approaching wedding:

These documents came last night & I opened Joseph's thinking there might be some thing for me in it. I guess you won't care. You *must* write to Joseph. I think he feels badly that you dont. I've recovered from my head-ache. Father is coming this noon. It's dreadful lonely with out you Austin. Sue spent yesterday afternoon here. I've been thinking lately how easily I could become *insane*. Sometimes I feel as though I should be. Emilie & I had cards from Mr White, too. I am tired of receiving wedding cards, they come from some where, every day, that pretty cousin Lizzie sent me hers Monday. Now Austin, write to Joseph right off.

Write to us when you can.

Good bye.
VINNIE

Vinnie cultivated the staccato pace. An earlier note exceeds even the one above and ends with a flourish.

Martha is sick. Emilene is sick too. Mrs Nash goes there often. Mr. Godfrey is visiting New York now. Thompson was here last week. I. F. Conkey has a new span of the blacks, rides out &c. Jane is at home. Kate will be married soon. Weather cold, corn high. Metaphysics clear, other things to match, Sir.

In 1852, when she wrote these letters, Vinnie was nineteen and at something of a crisis in her life. Joseph Lyman was in the deep South and (it seemed to Vinnie) losing interest in his Northern friends, including her. Only a few months before, she recorded in her diary,[2] "Received offer of *marriage*," presumably from "Tutor [William] Howland," mentioned twice in the same brief entry. But that, too, came to nothing. And, although Lyman wrote his mother as late as 1855 that he still had serious intentions toward Lavinia, he was a long way off, and Austin was doing nothing to help her, by way either of brotherly advice or of intercession. No wonder she felt frustrated by the steady flow of wedding cards. If her thoughts of insanity have more to do with Dickinson rhetoric than with Dickinson neurosis—Emily's similar thoughts were sheltered in her poems—they show that she too knew what pressure was and sensed a breaking point, even at this buoyant age.

Vinnie's way of coping with it, however mildly it burdened her, was through activity, seemingly ceaseless and mostly non-intellectual. She was the permanent "head of the committee on arrangements," the planner and doer about the house. Domestically, Emily was kept busy with her plants

2. Vinnie's tiny line-a-day diary, now in the Dickinson Papers, Houghton Library, covers only the year 1851 and a few days of 1852.

and flowers, her cooking and sewing and tending her mother's frequent illnesses. The prickly part of housekeeping was left to Lavinia, to whom the family and the house and the garden (Emily called it "Vinnie's sainted Garden") became a vocation. At twenty she was already beginning to take over: "I feel unusually hurried just now," she wrote to Austin, "so many plans suggest themselves to my mind for improving the house & grounds." Emily later warned their less robust cousin, Frances Norcross, against trying to keep up to such a pace: "I fear you are getting as driven as Vinnie. We consider her standard for superhuman effort erroneously applied." And still later she described Vinnie's harried life to Mrs. Holland: "Vinnie is under terrific headway, but finds time to remember you with vivid affection"; and to young Ned, vacationing in the Adirondacks: "Vinnie is still subsoiling, but lays down her Spade to caress you."

If Emily's rhetoric is a little patronizing, she never underestimated Vinnie's usefulness to the family and to herself, no little of which lay in Vinnie's being what she was, a phenomenon, remarkable in her own way in a remarkable family. The whimsey does not preclude real admiration:

> Vinnie is far more hurried than Presidential Candidates [she wrote Mrs. Holland during the election year of 1880] – I trust in more distinguished ways, for *they* have only the care of the Union, but Vinnie the Universe –

Next year, complaining about some little contretemps in the house, Emily concluded her letter by urging the Norcross cousins not to worry, either about herself or about Vinnie, who "was only sighing in fun":

> Vinnie [is] spectacular as Disraeli and sincere as Gladstone. . . . When she sighs in earnest, Emily's throne will tremble . . . [but, as of now] Vinnie "still prevails."

Before Vinnie began "prevailing," she led a gay social life, probably the most active of the three children. She had many affairs of the heart. At what point she ceased being the pert, popular figure in Amherst circles and gave herself up to her "duties, her pussies, and her posies" cannot be determined any more precisely than Emily's withdrawal. Both girls drifted into their eventual ways of life gradually, although Emily sensed her vocation earlier and made a much more complete withdrawal. Vinnie was an inveterate caller to the end, went on trips, and made long out-of-town visits until she was well into middle age. A letter to Joseph Lyman congratulating him on his engagement to Laura Baker in 1856 showed that at that time she was still entertaining thoughts of getting married, and when she wondered in 1853 what their father would do "when *we* are *all* gone," she apparently thought that Emily would get married, too. She eventually said of Emily's withdrawal that it "was only a happen," springing from family circumstances. It was more than this, of course, but there was a good deal of happen in it; and there may have been even more in Vinnie's own ultimate way of life, into which she settled only after several doors were closed to her, perhaps by Howland, certainly by Lyman, and presumably by several others. Whether in some instances she herself closed the doors, it is hard to tell. Her letter to Lyman on his engagement gives the impression that she still held the initiative, but she may simply have been maintaining a bold front. She was nearly twenty-four, and she had her pride:

> You asked me who I will marry, Joseph. I wish I knew. I have some dear friends. I have promised to decide *the* question before winter is all gone. Perhaps I may give them all up. I shall always love to hear from you, Joseph, & trust you will be *good* & prosperous. God bless you! Joseph,
>
> Good bye
Vinnie

The affair with Joseph Lyman, by far the best documented of all the youthful Dickinson romances, tells us most about Vinnie; and since Joseph was an intimate friend of both girls, and often compared them, it reveals much about Emily as well. The story begins with the friendship of Joseph and Austin at nearby Williston Seminary, where Joseph had gone to school from his home in Chester, Massachusetts, some forty miles west of Amherst. The two boys roomed together, and Joseph paid an extended visit at the Dickinson home in the mid-1840s. (Edward Dickinson, in a gesture of thoughtfulness not usually considered characteristic of him, suggested the visit so that Austin could have a friend to keep him company during a term he had to be at home.) We know from Joseph's accounts that he enjoyed himself hugely, especially the family conversation. It was then that he found the Dickinson household "that charming second home of mine in Amherst," and later prized his friendship with the Dickinsons above all others. During his long visit Joseph became fond of Vinnie and began the "spooney" in which, according to his descriptions, she distinguished herself by quite un-Dickinsonian behavior. He never forgot her kisses, which he was fond of describing in the language of his favorite poem, *Maud,* as " 'sweeter, sweeter than anything on Earth.' " On both the first and later visits during his college years at Yale, he had long talks with Emily, helped her with her German, and joined the family and their Amherst friends in festivities like the annual sugaring-off parties.

One of these, during his last spring in New England, he later described in nostalgic detail to his fiancée, Laura Baker. Here, too, Vinnie distinguished herself as anything but shy. She was in love with him and wanted to display her love for all to see. But he was on the point of leaving Amherst and New England, and his own mind was far from made up about Vinnie. He recorded, for Laura's benefit, a snatch of their conversation on that last afternoon. When it came time to go home in the carriages, Vinnie begged him to ride with her. He held back. Vinnie came to him, took his hand, and said:

'O Joseph I havn't seen much of you today. Howell has been with me all the afternoon but I would so much rather have been with you.' I say 'My dear Vinnie, I thought it best under the circumstances not to pay you very marked attention before all these people. I would avoid every thing like gossip.' Vinnie loq. 'I know Joseph, but I love you, and I'm proud of you and of your love – I want people to know that you love me – come, Joseph, they are all going to the carriages. Let me take your arm and we will sit together in the carriage. – O Joseph *must* you go tomorrow!'

To Vinnie's sorrow, New England (and Yale, from which he had graduated in 1850) had made him restless. His farewell to Vinnie that day turned out to be for good. He left a few weeks later for the West and South. Vinnie wrote in her diary on March 26, 1851:

Letter from E.[liza] Coleman [Joseph's cousin]. Walked with Joseph. Now he is gone! Attended meeting, made calls, visited John Sanford, met Storrs there. Had maple Sugar. Joseph has gone, two years is a long time!

As Joseph later wrote to Laura, "Poor little soft-lipped Vinnie Dickinson."

The next stage in the story began in 1856. Lyman was in New Orleans, a rising young lawyer and engaged to Laura Baker, of Nashville, the two having met during Lyman's sojourn there on his way south. In the many and voluminous letters he wrote Laura between then and their marriage in 1858, he told her all about himself, his past, his present, his aims. He harked back frequently to his wonderful New England youth, not so much to his boyhood in Chester, or his years at Yale, but mostly to his memories of Amherst, particularly the Dickinson girls. Of all the girls he ever knew (and by that time his list was formidable), they understood him best. Of all his friends and many relatives in New England (in Chester, Amherst, Pittsfield, New Haven), it was they he wanted most to see again. As the story of his affair with Vinnie unfolds, with frequent references to the household in general and to Emily, some of our stock notions about the town, the family, and the girls are reversed, or at least heavily qualified. From hot and steaming New Orleans, Amherst seemed like a lost paradise to Joseph. He remembered the Dickinson house (it was the one on Pleasant Street that he had visited) as set in a "garden of roses." Far from being a prison dominated by an ogre father, he remembered the Dickinson home as one of freedom, love, gaiety, and good talk. We hear nothing about the depressing presence of parents; indeed, they seem tactfully to have retired, evenings, to leave the field open for the young. We see Emily as the good housekeeper—and Vinnie scarcely deigning to soil "her little fat hands." Indeed, Vinnie, not Emily, seems the delicate and protected one, unequipped for the "central strenuous life" that Lyman had chosen for himself.

The differences between the girls develop sharply in the course of Joseph's comments to Laura—Emily "inside the ring," Vinnie not; Emily platonic and intellectual, Vinnie warm and pliant. Perhaps by way of rationalizing his none-too-gentle rejection of Vinnie, he played her down

Lavinia Norcross Dickinson, about 1852

Joseph Bardwell Lyman, about 1850

The North Pleasant Street house occupied by the Dickinsons 1840–55
Lyman: ". . . my charming second home in Amherst"

a little heartlessly in the letters to Laura. She was "gentle" and affectionate (in this respect he several times held her up to Laura as a model), but she was otherwise not only unimpressive but had "radical defects":

I was very happy once in Vinnies arms – very happy. She sat in my lap and pulled the pins from her long soft chestnut hair and tied the long silken mass around my neck and kissed me again & again. She was always at my side clinging to my arm and used to have a little red ottoman that she brought & placed close by my chair and laid her book across my lap when she read. Her skin was very soft. Her arms were fat & white and I was very, very happy with her. But that was all. Vinnie hasn't brains at all superior. She is a proud, wilful, selfish girl. The only thing she wanted was to have me with her that she might be happy. She never forgot herself. She viewed everybody and every plan only as it might affect her happiness. All this in a quiet lady like way – "for Nelly was a Lady" but none of her blandishments could keep my calm impartial intellect from seeing all those radical defects of character. I never thought she would make me a good wife.

His "calm impartial intellect" may have told him at this point that she would not make him a good wife, but for a period of several years he had serious thoughts of marrying her. If not, he told his mother a downright lie, for he had twice within a year been very explicit. On May 23, 1854, he wrote his mother:

You ask me about my Amherst attachment. It is all right. Vinnie loves me and I love Vinnie and mean to marry her God willing – God and her old folks – and I have reason to think they do not object very much.

And again on February 12, 1855:

Vinnie Dickinson continues to love me very truly and writes me beautiful letters from Washington where she now is staying with her Father. She is a Christian girl and begs me to be very good. I think her parents object to her coming South but Vinnie declares that she can never love anybody else and I think I shall go on and marry her some of these summers if we live.

Joseph's meeting Laura and another remarkable girl, Araminta Wharton, in Nashville during 1856 apparently altered his perspective on Vinnie, whose stock steadily declined from then on. "Vinnie was not very noble or accomplished," he wrote Laura. "She could hardly be called 'a woman of superior merit.'" But no sooner had he written this than he was lost in memories of the little red ottoman and of Vinnie's "beauty . . . grace & gentleness," of "the simple unalloyed happiness of those sunny hours," the "beauty & purity & grace & gentleness that we may dream of but rarely see under the sun."

As Vinnie loses favor, Emily gains. Although Vinnie provided the romantic idyl in his life, it was Emily he admired. She saw the ambition in him and was aware, as Vinnie was not, that he was destined for a greater world than Amherst and that he even then was eager to be on his way. Emily had conveyed her impression to Lyman in a figure he later passed on to Laura:

> Emily Dickinson, who by the bye was the most appreciative lady friend I ever had till you, in those years of late boyhood when she knew me used to say of me that I seemed ever to carry an arrow in my hand so distinctly and persistently did my whole nature point to what was before me.

Several times he associated Emily with Araminta Wharton, "one of those [as he described her to Laura] to whom God gave a white soul, and she, beside that natural endowment is in the number of those who have been made perfect through suffering." He asked Laura's permission to continue to write, after their engagement, to "such friends as our sweet Mintie and to Emily Dickinson"—not, be it noted, Vinnie. He enclosed a blue slip on which he had written the famous verses from Revelation (III: 4-5) which may have some bearing on Emily's later habit of wearing white:

> . . . and they shall walk with me in white: for they are worthy.

> *He that overcometh* the same shall be clothed in white raiment; and I will not blot out his name out of the book of Life. . . .

It is possible that even then Lyman thought of both Emily and Araminta as in the "white company" of those born pure and made perfect through suffering, although Emily's suffering was surely not from physical causes like Mintie's, who died of tuberculosis when she was twenty-seven. This spiritual quality—however achieved, and something he never found in Vinnie—is the theme of his most significant comparison of Emily and Mintie:

> My friendships for Emily Dickinson & Mintie Wharton are much alike. They are both noble women – neither one of them will probably ever marry tho' both would make most true & devoted wives while they lived and both are deeply imbued with the essential spirit of the New Testament and of our Lord & Savior Jesus Christ.

His last glimpse of Emily had been during the morning of the sugaring-off party in March 1851, when he had said goodbye to Vinnie. He "had been with Emily a good deal." It is worth noting that even this early—Emily was only three months past her twentieth birthday—her character was sufficiently formed for Joseph to carry away this lofty view of her. (And, in fairness to Vinnie, it must be remembered that she was barely seventeen.) Although he sensed the essence of Emily's spirituality, he apparently did not know that she had refused to join the girls at Mount Holyoke who recognized Christ as their Savior and that she had not joined her family's church in Amherst (and never did). He would have been surprised, perhaps, to hear her call herself a pagan. But his impression of her as "noble," his notion that she would make a "true & devoted wife" even though she would probably never marry—all this helps to offset the traditional notion of her as fragile and timid, a moth-like creature who lived apart.

Lyman made another point of contrast between the girls—their verbal expression, a matter of interest to him as one who had literary ambitions. There is no indication anywhere that he knew that Emily wrote poetry, although in the "long and beautiful letters [as he wrote his mother]" which came to him from "Miss Emily Dickinson in Amherst" he had ample evidence of her power with language. As she did with many of her intimate friends, she may have sent him some of her poems. But, if only from her letters and from her talk, he had a strong sense of her style, and he admired it tremendously. He found in it another example of her superiority to Vinnie. On the eve of his marriage to Laura, he received congratulatory letters from both girls and, in an upsurge of the old feeling for the Dickinsons, sent Laura some excerpts. Writing to her from New Orleans, he expressed the hope that both girls would accept her "into the fold of their esteem & love. . . . Emily I know will. Vinnie somewhat reluctantly unless she marries soon & happily." He knew Laura would be interested in how differently the girls expressed themselves:

Emilys letter is very fine & has some rare delicate touches – let me copy some of them. She commences – "May. We parted in the spring, Joseph. It is natural that we should meet in months of the same name. I dare not count the crocuses that have sprung since then. It would bring us all nearer than we are fit to the Eternal Gardens. The "Kingdom by the Sea" never alters, Joseph but the "children" do – meeker and wistfuller on our part and more athletic-minded I believe on yours. . . . I suppose the grass is growing over much that is dear to us both but we'll leave that till we meet. . . . Are you well, dear Joseph? I am afraid of those Great Suns. I give his Tropics charge! Shall you not be carefull. When you know that the fires never burned low on the hearth stone of remembrance you will forgive us. Write to us again, dear Joseph, keep us in your prayer and in strong vesper we will bear you up – Good night – 'Good night' grows weary. I long to cry "Good Morning" so! Affecty Emilie" –

Vinnie talks more human like and passionately in this wise. Amherst May 1858 "Dear Joseph. Vinnie has not forgotten you in all these months of silence. Old times and old friends are still fresh in my memory and dear to my heart. Come back to us Joseph and you will then be assured that we love you still! Our new house [on Main Street, to which they had moved in the spring of 1855] is beautiful, Joseph, not so modest as the old one but *so pleasant*. I walk about in my garden in the bright mornings and then I think about the dear absent ones "– What is gone & what is left." My flowers dont know how far my thoughts wander away sometimes. Amherst is improved since you were here. Come & see for yourself. I wonder if we would know each other if we chanced to meet! Perhaps you are in your own home now. How queer it will seem to know that you are married! I would like to see you before that event takes place. I expect you have become very dignified & experienced but I guess we – we would be children again for a little while if we were together! Austin & Sue are close by us. Sue is a dear Sister, etc.

etc. . . . do come & see us before we are old people & wear caps and spectacles. Believe me always your true friend – Vinnie.

The two styles are distinguished accurately: Emily's "rare" and "delicate," Vinnie's "more human like" and passionate. Joseph's estimate of their letters corresponds roughly with his estimate of them as people, Emily noble and spiritual, Vinnie worldly and pleasure-loving.

Directly following the excerpts, Joseph embarked again upon the theme of Vinnie's inadequacies, which would seem in actuality to have been not so much radical defects of character as symptoms of a girl's first love encouraged a little irresponsibly by an older and more worldly young man. (He was Austin's age.) And now, to Laura, he put the blame for the failure of the affair on Vinnie. He rationalized his own conduct outrageously and attributed to Vinnie much of his own frank hedonism:

How much like "Maud in her Garden of Roses!" If Vinnie had been fit to be the wife of a self-made man I would have married her some time ago. But she is only a 'milk white fawn' – But her kisses – those kisses! – It is 7 years ago now since I kissed her among the crocus flowers. *They* and the daffodils and the little arbutus had left their sweetness on her lips! No wonder when she walks among her flowers that Maud 'remembers'. "I remember – I remember". I wish 'Maud' would forget that spiritual faced student boy that loosened the earth with his spade around the roots of her roses in the springtime so long ago! She has been up and down in the world – spent a winter in Boston – in Philadelphia – at Washington while her father was in Congress but no body talks as he talked – whispers as he whispered – kisses as he kissed! Poor Maud. If she had not thought so much of that fine house & carriage & roses her student lover would have 'come back' long ago. I was afraid she would miss them. So I left her with them. . . .

However unfair, it is remarkable that this portrait could have been written at all about a Dickinson. Vinnie hardly sounds like the scion of Puritan stock; nor do we recognize "our practical sister Vinnie," the planner and doer of the household, the "Soldier and Angel" with her " 'drawn Sword' in behalf of Eden." There is little trace of Vinnie the wit and mimic, the pert and peppery one. Although the letter shows that Joseph kept in touch with the family—he notes the visits in Boston, Philadelphia, and Washington—the Vinnie he depicts is still the Vinnie in her sentimental girlhood, well before she started "prevailing."

Five years later Joseph would have found a very different person, ready to take on, as Emily said, the "Universe." Far from developing as a Maud in her garden of roses, Lavinia became the family's front line of defense against the world. She ordered, shopped, bargained. Vinnie "cruises about some to transact the commerce," as Emily put it. She developed a combative streak that, with her wit, made her one of the most respected and feared tongues in town, to be surpassed (and this may have been a source of the later ill feeling between them) only by her sister-in-law, Sue.

When Vinnie was only twenty, she contemplated a passage-at-arms with the important Mrs. Luke Sweetser and her accomplice, Mrs. Fay, in a matter touching the family honor. The ladies in their gossip had accused the Dickinsons of slighting their four orphaned cousins, the Newmans, who had been living with their aunt, Mrs. Fay, for the past year. Her letter to Austin about the matter shows her fighting style at its best. (The letter begins "Dear *Rooster*" and is signed "Vinnie Alias, Chick.")

Sue was here this afternoon & told us a long story that Mrs Sweetser had told Harriet [Cutler] about us this morning. I have not been able to go out since Friday, but hope to get out again tomorrow & then Mrs Luke will get such a lecture from me as she never heard, I guess. She says we dont treat the Newmans with any attention & that Mrs Fay has talked with her about it & all such stuff. I shall first go to Mrs Luke & give her a piece of my mind, then Mrs Fay another piece & see what effect will come of it. Mrs Sweetser has interfered with my business long enough & now she'll get it, I tell you. I'll bring up all past grievances & set them in order before her & see what she'll say for herself. I hope to start by 11 oclock in the morning to deliver my feelings. I *certainly shall*. She has watched me long enough in meeting & her bonnet has bobbed long enough & now I'll have a stop put to such proceedings, I will indeed.

Austin, replying two days later from Cambridge, congratulated her on "rather the *smartest* note I have in your hand," and tried to soothe her spirit. He started with a bit of whimsey characteristic of the family's way of taking each other down:

Will those desiring have an opportunity to view the *remains* of the mischievous lady of the woods [the Sweetsers lived in the grove back of the Homestead on Main Street] when you get through with her, what few there may be left!

His counsel from then on was sober and judicious. The matter was a serious one. Besides the good advice he gave her, it is worth noting that he cleared with *her* (not Father, or Mother, or Emily) all the practical details of his expected trip home the following Saturday: the trunks, meeting him at the depot, his laundry. But it is his advice to Vinnie that tells most about himself, and Vinnie, and their relationship—and about certain realities of Amherst life:

My own notion would be, Vinnie, not to say a single word to Mrs Sweetser on the subject. She is not our master, nor are we in any way responsible to her for anything we are, or have. Let the woman talk if it makes her any happier. She cant hurt us, we dont care for her, and seems to me it would be making her of rather too much importance to take all the trouble to go up there & give her such a pommeling as you propose. I dont doubt your *ability* to raise an *awful* breeze around her ears, but is it on the whole best? Wont it be very apt to please her very much to know she has put you into such a fever?

I dont believe, Vinnie, that you could possibly tickle her so much as by just the course you promise yourself. If you want to punish her the severest, just let her alone severely. Let her passion for slandering & insinuating against you, or any of us, fall upon herself alone. Do nothing which shall divert it from her for a single moment. Keep quiet & let it burn away there as long as it will, and it will burn nobody but her own dear self. And that miserable, fretful, old maidish widow [Mrs. Fay], let her alone too. Dont say a single word to her, only if she barks too loud, & troubles your sleep, tell father & have him inform her her services are no longer needed, and hire some more serviceable girl to take charge of those children. We can turn her out of the house any day and she cant say one word.

Vinnie probably took the advice; at least we hear no more of the affair. But Joseph Lyman would have been surprised to see his "milk white fawn" eager to enter the lists as the sole representative of the family against two ladies twice her age, and entirely confident of her ability to put them down. She might have been more useful to him in the "central strenuous life" than he thought. Professor Chickering, in his eulogy of Lavinia in the *Republican*, spoke of her "heart of adamant" and of her courage: "Did ever so valorous a spirit lodge in so frail a tenement?"

As she grew older, Vinnie's loyalty to her family became her vocation. Much has been made of her uncritical devotion to Emily, but it extended farther. She would tolerate no criticism whatever of any member of the family. Even Professor Chickering, her admirer, saw it as an obsession:

It seemed impossible for her to realize that any other estimate than hers could be held of their gifts and graces, their abilities and achievements. Her fiercest denunciations were reserved for those who ventured to oppose or even call in question the opinions of her father and brother on matters of public concern. No other opinions were either conceivable or allowable.

Emily was amused by this quality in Vinnie, but she was grateful for the protection. She may have been grateful in still another respect. Although she herself shunned open battles and "fierce denunciations" as she did august assemblies, she was impressed by qualities in others that made them fit for such confrontations. The rhetoric she used in describing Vinnie—Gladstone, Disraeli, the Guardian Angel—was not necessarily facetious. There was something sharp and clear and tonic about Vinnie's belligerent loyalty, her dividing the world into Friends and Foes of Dickinsons. "Vinnie demurred," Emily once said, "and Vinnie decides." Once she described her in action:

Vinnie is full of Wrath, and vicious as Saul – toward the Holy Ghost, in whatever form. I heard her declaiming the other night, to a Foe that called – and sent Maggie to part them –

Emily was a little like Keats in this—the Keats who relished the display of human passion even in such sordid affairs as street fights. What she heard that night in Vinnie's tussle with the Foe may have been another aspect of what she had in mind when she spoke of her "inciting voice."

Lavinia in the 1860s

A later picture of the Homestead on Main Street

Floor plans of the Homestead

Plan of the ground floor
of the Dickinson homestead
(before remodeling in 1916 by
Howe & Manning, Boston).

SHED

WASH ROOM

KITCHEN

BACK PARLOR

PANTRY

DINING ROOM

FRONT PARLOR

HALL

LIBRARY

CONSERVATORY

Plan of the second floor
of the homestead; the third
floor was an unfinished
attic before the remodeling.

BEDROOM

BEDROOM

HALL

EMILY DICKINSON'S
ROOM

BEDROOM

The degree of Emily's so-called dependence on her sister deserves some scrutiny. Rhetoric here as elsewhere has too often been taken at its face value. When Vinnie was off for the winter taking care of her aunt, Mrs. Loring Norcross in Boston, Emily wrote a friend in what would seem to be a state of minor panic:

I would like more sisters, that the taking out of one, might not leave such stillness. Vinnie has been all, so long, I feel the oddest fright at parting with her for an hour, lest a storm arise, and I go unsheltered.

She once referred to Vinnie as her father confessor: "if she says I sin, I say, 'Father, I have sinned' – If she sanctions me, I am not afraid." We have already heard her speak of Vinnie as her "parents," although here she suggested that the dependence was mutual: "[Vinnie] has no Father and Mother but me and I have no Parents but her." Yet Emily probably was never so dependent on anyone as these remarks would suggest. Vinnie came nearer to what seems the truth when she said that the family lived together like "friendly and absolute monarchs, each in his own domain."

One action, however, speaks louder than any of Emily's rhetoric and suggests the true nature of her need of Vinnie. When Emily was about to come home from Cambridge after a long stretch of treatment for her eyes in 1864, she wrote Vinnie a brief note which concluded with a significant request: "I shall go Home in two weeks. You will get me at Palmer, yourself. Let no one beside come." A few days later she repeated it: "Vinnie will go to Palmer for me certainly?" Months before, she had written Vinnie from Cambridge, "I miss you most," and perhaps she had. But her singling Vinnie out for the lone meeting at Palmer should be viewed in the light of the possibilities she was excluding. While it is understandable, knowing what we know of her, that she would not want a delegation, Austin was available, and Sue, and her father and mother; and presumably all would have been eager to go. Her choice suggests, perhaps, not that she was so dependent on Vinnie, or loved her most, but that she felt most at ease with her. Vinnie's nature was the least likely to key her up. What she needed at this juncture, and to a certain extent all her life, was a stabilizing influence and someone to look after the details. Of all members of the household, Vinnie was best suited to fulfill this function. This was what she had in mind, perhaps, when she said that Vinnie had been "all" to her for so long.

What Vinnie's calming influence meant to her, and what it meant to the whole family in the Homestead after Edward Dickinson died, is nowhere better illustrated than in Emily's account, in a letter to the Norcrosses, of the fire that destroyed the business center of Amherst early in the morning of July 4, 1879. The letter—and I give it in full as the work of art that it is—is the most intimate glimpse we have of the family constellation during the later years. Vinnie is the heroine. Emily's narrative powers were never better, or her descriptive eye, or her humor, or her sense of character in action, or her command of sound and rhythm—all qualities, it should be said, that argue against the notion that her powers sadly declined after the miraculous production of the early 1860s.

> Did you know there had been a fire here, and that but for a whim of the wind Austin and Vinnie and Emily would have all been homeless? But perhaps you saw *The Republican*.
>
> We were waked by the ticking of the bells, – the bells tick in Amherst for a fire, to tell the firemen.
>
> I sprang to the window, and each side of the curtain saw that awful sun. The moon was shining high at the time, and the birds singing like trumpets.
>
> Vinnie came soft as a moccasin, "Don't be afraid, Emily, it is only the fourth of July."
>
> I did not tell that I saw it, for I thought if she felt it best to deceive, it must be that it was.
>
> She took hold of my hand and led me into mother's room. Mother had not waked, and Maggie was sitting by her. Vinnie left us a moment, and I whispered to Maggie, and asked her what it was.
>
> "Only Stebbins's barn, Emily;" but I knew that the right and left of the village was on the arm of Stebbins's barn. I could hear buildings falling, and oil exploding, and people walking and talking gayly, and cannon soft as velvet from parishes that did not know that we were burning up.
>
> And so much lighter than day was it, that I saw a caterpillar measure a leaf far down in the orchard; and Vinnie kept saying bravely, "It's only the fourth of July."
>
> It seemed like a theatre, or a night in London, or perhaps like chaos. The innocent dew falling "as if it thought no evil," . . . and sweet frogs prattling in the pools as if there were no earth.
>
> At seven people came to tell us that the fire was stopped, stopped by throwing sound houses in as one fills a well.
>
> Mother never waked, and we were all grateful; we knew she would never buy needle and thread at Mr. Cutler's store, and if it were Pompeii nobody could tell her.
>
> The post-office is in the old meeting-house where Loo and I went early to avoid the crowd, and – fell asleep with the bumble-bees and the Lord God of Elijah.
>
> Vinnie's "only the fourth of July" I shall always remember. I think she will tell us so when we die, to keep us from being afraid.
>
> Footlights cannot improve the grave, only immortality.
>
> Forgive me the personality; but I knew, I thought, our peril was yours.

Curiously, "our peril" did not involve, at least by name, that of Sue and the children next door. Or perhaps "Austin" was a sufficient summary. Curiously, too, there is no mention of any help from the Evergreens. Vinnie prevailed.

Emily's most extended and most poignant comment on Vinnie is in the letter to Joseph Lyman in which she had so much to say about her father and where she documents, in family terms, her famous complaint, "All men say 'What' to me." The theme of the letter, or that part of it which Joseph preserved, is the failure even of her intimates to understand her. Here Vinnie joins her father (and, we can assume, her mother) among the bewildered ones. She acknowledges her dependence on Vinnie in one vital matter and at the same time indicates the level on which she functioned in complete independence of her:

And Vinnie, Joseph[,] it is so weird and so vastly mysterious, she sleeps by my side, her care is in some sort motherly, for you may not remember that our amiable mother never taught us tayloring and I am amused to remember those clothes, or rather those apologies made up from dry goods with which she covered us in nursery times; so Vinnie is in the matter of raiment greatly necessary to me; and the tie is quite vital, yet if we had come up for the first time from two wells where we had hitherto been bred her astonishment would not be greater at some things I say.

Concluding the letter, she declares her independence of Space and Time and in a phrase hits off what might be properly called the motto for her life: "My Country is Truth." But she adds a wry note: "Vinnie lives much of the time in the State of Regret."

The remark is not only a measure of the extent to which Emily outgrew her sister; it explains much about Vinnie's later development, the fanatic family loyalty, the sharp tongue, the bitterness. What did Vinnie "regret" besides her idyllic childhood and lost youth? Howland? Lyman? At any rate, there seems to have been a vacuum in her life, not to be adequately filled with domesticities, not at least for a person of her emotional capacity, her energy and abilities. This, along with her father's lonely and austere life and Austin's domestic misery, Emily had to witness, too. That she was extraordinarily sensitive to the vicissitudes, physical and spiritual, of every member of her family needs no more proving. Once, writing to the Hollands about Vinnie's difficulties with a headache, she made a classic statement:

Vinnie is sick to-night, which gives the world a russet tinge, usually so red. It is only a headache, but when the head aches next to you, it becomes important. When she is well, time leaps. When she is ill, he lags, or stops entirely.

Sisters are brittle things. God was penurious with me, which makes me shrewd with Him.

Vinnie's life had its tragic side, too, and its deep frustration. And happening "next" to Emily—no one closer—it became important.

On the whole, Vinnie did well, considering the disappointments in her life. At least she never became melancholic or hangdog. If, according to Joseph Lyman's impression, she was made for marriage (though not with him), at least she adapted herself to her spinster's life with good grace, until the pressures became too much for her. She identified herself with her family, both in Amherst and in distant places like Boston, when for a winter she helped with her ailing Aunt Lavinia. She was at her best in time of crisis. When Edward Dickinson died and Austin was too stunned to be of much use and Emily was hidden away upstairs, it was Vinnie who took charge. "The world seemed coming to an end," Martha Bianchi wrote later. "And where was Aunt Emily? Why did she not sit in the library with the family if he [Austin] could? She stayed upstairs in her own room with the door open just a crack, where she could hear without being seen." Vinnie's conduct on the occasion so impressed Professor Chickering that he mentioned it twenty-five years later in his eulogy:

> She who because she was sure her father would have wished it, denied herself to no one in the hours that succeeded his death, could weep with those who wept, and tried in gentlest ways to ease the burden.

And the Dickinsons' Amherst friend and neighbor, J. L. Skinner, wrote to his wife three days after the funeral:

> Spent half an hour with Austin at his office this morning, and half an hour with Vinnie. . . . I thought Vinnie's character as it shone out in her face today was beautiful.

Nine years later when Gilbert died, it was Vinnie again who provided the main support. Vinnie's letter to some friends in Newport is one of the fullest accounts we have of the effect of the death on the family. Her own essential function was never more clearly illustrated. The letter is dated November 16 (1883), just six weeks after Gilbert's death.

> MY DEAR FRIENDS:
> A Newport paper was a gentle reminder of you, some weeks ago, but now Susan has come & I have been so absorbed trying to comfort Austin that all else has been neglected though not forgotten – Of course you knew little Gilbert has disappeared & Emily & I have had hard work to keep Austin from following him – His fever was short & fierce & little more than one week ended his happy, brilliant life – His home is greatly changed for Gilbert was "the Child of the Regiment" as you well know – Emily received a nervous shock the night Gilbert died & was alarmingly ill for weeks – She is much improved at present but still very delicate – You can imagine my anxiety for all that's left of this home – Emily was devoted to Gilbert & was there the night of his death – I have longed for you both in these last weeks – why did you go away – Please write to me & I wish you would write to Austin.

There is much to be noted in this letter. Austin's grief was nearly mortal, we know, and it is clear from the letter that, among the members of the family, the burden of keeping him from complete despair fell mainly on Vinnie. How much Emily helped is hard to tell. Vinnie's account of her nervous shock on the night of Gilbert's death, and of her delicate condition for weeks following, is borne out in more detail by the report of a friend and neighbor, Mrs. John Jameson, who wrote to her son John:

> Miss Emily Dickinson . . . went over to Austin's with Maggie the night Gilbert died, the first time she had been in the house for 15 years – and the

odor from the disinfectants used, sickened her so that she was obliged to go home about 3 A M – and vomited – went to bed and has been feeble ever since, with a terrible pain in the back of her head –

So it was Vinnie as usual who was the most active in keeping together "all that's left of this home." Her energy was tried to the limit. A week after Gilbert died, she was treated by Dr. Cooper for exhaustion, a detail which she does not mention to her friends in Newport.

After Gilbert's death, Lavinia was more preoccupied than ever with looking after her home. Her mother had died the year before after years of incapacity, and Emily never fully recovered her vitality. Vinnie's life was not a happy one as Emily's health declined. Although there is record of a pleasant visit with Mrs. Holland in Northampton the spring of 1884, of sleighing with Austin that winter—"'Tom' whirls us over the white country at a flying pace"—about the only solid pleasure in her life during these years seems to have come from her friendship with Mrs. Mabel Todd, who had arrived in Amherst in the fall of 1881. This, in light of events shortly to be discussed, turned out to be a mixed blessing. The trouble came from next door. The impact of the arrival of this young lady, beautiful, sociable, talented, and half the age of the Dickinsons, will concern us next. It is a complicated story, climaxing and documenting the tensions between the two houses long sensed by biographers. It led directly to Vinnie's later woe.

For Vinnie the story begins with a perplexing conversation Mabel had with Sue in early September 1882. Sue, for reasons to be discussed later, warned her about the loose morals of the sisters in the Homestead and urged her not to call on them. Mabel, however, called immediately, and Vinnie apparently was grateful for her act of defiance. Within a few months after that first call (surely by the following spring) the relationship had become more than merely social. "I'm surprised at my missing you so much, for I have seen you only a little," Vinnie wrote Mabel in Washington. Eight months later she wrote again (Mabel was once more in Washington), this time more fervently and even a little desperately:

I miss you every day & your companion also, whom I consider *gold* in character.

Winter is here & Sunday was a dreadful day for gloom & cold. How I did wish you were in reach of my summons. Austin is so oppressed by these "glad days" [the Christmas season] & I hardly know how I shall cheer him so many weeks without you to help him. Write to him often. I have almost forgotten how joy feels, anxiety for others beside my own sorrow has for the time hidden all light. "Without hope" is a doomed thought. . . . I know what Washington life is & sometimes I wonder if *I* could be whirled into forgetfulness by social excitement. Pardon my way of talking & make no allusion to it when you reply as your letters are read by more than me. . . .
Emilies love

The phrasing might have been her sister's—"I have almost forgotten how joy feels" and " 'Without hope' is a doomed thought"—but the problem was hers: how to keep up Austin's morale without Mabel Todd and with Emily in delicate health, and how to keep up her own spirits in so gloomy a situation. Her thought of being "whirled into forgetfulness by social excitement" is a touching throwback to the days when Lyman knew her and the Amherst boys were courting her. Mabel, who was having her usual busy and exciting time in Washington, was a reminder of all that she had missed.

It is easy to see how Mabel cheered Vinnie's gloom, but there was more to their friendship than that. As Mabel's relationship with Austin grew more intense, Vinnie was at the center of it, offering her house as a meeting place and acting as go-between in many ways. She was confidante, messenger, and scribe, often addressing envelopes to avoid telltale handwriting. Mabel was grateful for her loyalty; and Vinnie, on her part, welcomed a new ally against Sue. In the innumerable diary entries recording her calls on Vinnie from about 1883 on, not once does Mabel speak of meeting Sue at the Homestead, or of seeing Sue and Vinnie together.[8] Sue could hardly have helped knowing about their friendship—and hating them both for it—a fact which must have drawn them closer together. When, after Emily's death, and despairing of Sue, Vinnie finally took Emily's poems to Mabel Todd for editing, the reason for her secrecy, for the nocturnal visits and clandestine arrangements we will hear about, was fear of Sue's anger. And when Sue found out, she was furious; but the conspirators, then as in the early years of this drama (according to Mabel), kept their heads high.

Although Vinnie was often impatient with Mabel's progress during the long and difficult task of editing, their association seems to have been amicable. From the late 1880s until Austin's death in 1895, the calls and

3. Vinnie's relations with Sue seem to have been at best erratic, even during Austin's courtship, when at one point Vinnie apologized to Austin: "I love *Sue* most dearly & will try & never do her injustice again" (May 6, 1853; *Home,* p. 282). Firm evidence is scanty for the long years between Austin's marriage and Mabel Todd's arrival in Amherst. Vinnie gave Sue a copy of "H.H." 's *Verses* for her birthday in 1870 (*YH* II, 160). But by 1878 things were bad enough to start gossip in town. A "faculty wife" wrote to her son, abroad, on June 11: "I dont think [the Mathers] are quite as thick with the Dickinsons as they used to be – They are very sorry for Miss Vinny – Mrs Austin rides it rough shod over her – Prof M. says Ned D_____ grows lordly and cynical –" (*YH* II, 294). So, five years later, it is not surprising to find Vinnie taking Austin's and Mabel's part against Sue. In a letter to Mabel of September 25, 1883, Vinnie wrote: "I *know* there is no change of feeling toward you, save one house & there I never hear your name & am never there!" (*YH* II, 405). In *AB* (p. 59), Mrs. Bingham described the situation seven years later (1890): "Without at this time going further into the matter of her relationship to her brother's wife—whom she called 'the Old Scratch,'—it is at present enough to say that they were at swords' points"—mainly (in 1890) over the publication of the poems. The distressing (and perplexing) events of Vinnie's last years are considered in Chapter 13.

visits continued at an average, according to Mabel's diary, of two or three a week. If Vinnie (as Millicent Todd Bingham has suggested) all this while was growing jealous of Mabel's success with the poems,[4] both as editor and as lecturer, there is nothing in the letters or journals of either to show it. There are signs, however, of a rift between the women in the spring of 1895. It may have arisen from Vinnie's resistance to Austin's suggestion that Mabel be compensated for her editorial work by the gift of a strip of land which they owned in common from their father's estate. Vinnie apparently resented this public acknowledgment of indebtedness to Mabel, who, she felt, was sufficiently recompensed by the literary fame the work brought her. Evidently Vinnie gossiped, for Mabel (in her diary for June 2, 1895) accuses her of "treachery." After Austin's death on August 16 there is an unmistakable change. Mabel mentions not so much as a chat with Vinnie until October 1. Her entries for weeks after Austin's death are short, often only a sentence, and given over almost entirely to her own grief. There is no sign that she turned to Vinnie for comfort, or Vinnie to her. Then, on October 6, there is a disturbing entry, followed by silence until the very end of the year. The entry reads:

I went to see Vinnie in the morning, and I find she is going to ignore Austin's request to her – that she shall give to me his share of his father's estate. She is, as he always told me, utterly slippery and treacherous, but he did not think she would fail to do as he stipulated in this. Oh, it is pitiful! He had an entire contempt for her; but we talked it over, and it seemed the safest way to leave it. If he knows, how sorry he must be!

It is hard to tell how much Mabel's statement is colored by what seems to be her justified indignation. Austin had indeed made this request (although why, as a lawyer and with such an opinion of Vinnie's trustworthiness, he failed to put it in legal form is also hard to see); but whether he had always thought of Vinnie as "utterly slippery and treacherous" is open to question. He was often critical of her, but there is no evidence, except this statement of Mabel's, that he ever thought of her so harshly. He had welcomed her assistance, and trusted her, in his secret communications and meetings with Mabel, and so had Mabel. There is one redeeming note in Mabel's entry for December 29, 1895: "I went to see Vinnie just before tea – and had a talk with her. She is going to do one lovely thing." She concluded the entries for what she called her "tragic year" without specifying what the "lovely thing" was.

Vinnie thoroughly deserved Austin's harshness when she sued the Todds three years later for the land. To put it briefly, in bringing suit she was disloyal to Austin's wishes and to her friendship with both the

4. But Mrs. Bingham concludes her analysis of Vinnie's complicated attitude (and by this time Vinnie was a most "complicated" Dickinson) with a despairing " 'Jealousy' is too simple a word to apply to her feelings" (*AB*, p. 213). "For Emily belonged to her" (*AB*, p. 211).

Todds; she lied to her lawyer; and in the course of the trial she perjured herself in court. She may have been induced to do all this by Sue, who wanted nothing more than Mabel's public humiliation. She was in her mid-sixties, living alone, and full of fears. Even then, it is hard to understand her almost complete collapse of character. For years she was so devoted to her family that her loyalty became a byword, and she had stood up bravely against Sue in the matter of the poems. What seems like the failure of all her fine qualities gives some notion of how powerful the forces were in this tense family situation.

One further thought suggests itself: there may have been some truth in Austin's distrust of Vinnie, even though Mabel's report of it may be extreme. If there was, then his isolation in the family circle was more complete than other evidence suggests. And did Emily share his distrust of Vinnie? Emily seems to have been the only one in the family whom he trusted completely. This final revelation about Vinnie, however ambiguous, brings Austin and Emily closer together. It is obvious where the spiritual refreshment of his daily calls on his sisters really came from.

But Vinnie must have her due both as a person and as a source of insight into the baffling problem of her sister.

If the image she gives us of Emily is far from complete—and colored by her idolatry, her possessiveness, and her desire to protect—certain truths about Emily, or facets of her life, become clearer because of her. We see how independently life could be pursued by the inmates of the household, containing as it did, in a fair degree of harmony, people of such different natures. Edward Dickinson, traditionally thought of as the tyrant, does not seem to have cowed Vinnie's spirit any more than Emily's. Vinnie's busyness was often Emily's, too. They had to work hard. Against this background, Emily's literary production, her determination and energy in the pursuit of it are all the more striking. Vinnie's gradual retirement after the sociable life of her girlhood makes Emily's more understandable, even if Vinnie never secluded herself so completely. Vinnie's feud with Sue uncovers a trouble in which Emily shared. Her belligerent defense of the members of her immediate family had its counterpart in Emily's anxious love. Her style may have been unliterary, but, written or oral, it was tough-minded, direct, down to earth. She made herself heard in her own way. Bereavements did not desolate her as they did Emily and Austin; she was more resilient, but she knew their meaning. After her mother's death, Vinnie wrote to Mabel Todd: "I still envy your possession of Father & Mother. Realize the joy to the full for memory is a poor substitute for reality. I *know* what *each* means."

Vinnie even wrote a few verses, a handful of which survive.[5] They show almost no talent; but it is reassuring to know that she felt the urge

5. See Appendix I.

for such expression and could thus bring some understanding to Emily's lifelong vocation. The verses are on subjects that Emily made poems of, the things of nature (trees, stars, fireflies), pain, the indifference of friends, bits of gnomic wisdom. There are four epigrams, or attempts at the form: "New pleasures bring new anxieties" is perhaps the best. The slim collection shows a kind of rugged angularity—and no sense at all of how to round out a quatrain neatly. Perhaps its greatest virtue is its independence (though not quite complete) of the mawkish popular verse of the day,[6] a virtue she shared with Emily. And, although she was no "Sister Pegasus," her furious determination to get Emily's poems published, every one of them and immediately, may have come in part from her having shared, however humbly, in the practice of the art. The fact is that Vinnie threw herself into the project as Austin did not. His busy life with the college, the town, his legal practice, the demands of an expensive family, and his absorbing relationship with Mabel Todd—none of this explains why he left this important matter almost entirely to Vinnie. The question arises: Mabel Todd is rightly regarded as the savior of the poems, but what would have happened to them without Vinnie? There is no evidence that Mrs. Todd, fired by the poems Emily had sent her, rushed to the Homestead after Emily's death to inquire about her literary remains. And Austin made no move. It is possible that Vinnie knew more about Emily's literary work all along than she has been given credit for, so much has been made of her as the uncomprehending, Philistine sister.

So, when Emily says of her, as she did to Joseph Lyman, that "if we had come up for the first time from two wells . . . her astonishment would not be greater at some things I say," some discount must be made for Dickinson rhetoric. Emily never would have tolerated obtuseness, nor did she have to, in any member of her family. The more one looks into Vinnie, the quality of her character during the years of her prime, the texture of her mind as seen in her letters, in her recorded sayings, and even in these few fragments of verse, the more her stature grows. She had her admirers, a long line, from Tutor William Howland and Joseph Lyman in the early days to Professor Chickering and Mr. Melvin Copeland, bank president of Middletown, Connecticut, who sent flowers to her funeral. Lyman's negative estimate of her character (after his ardor had cooled) and the eccentric old-maid image that still clings to her must be qualified by the tribute of John Franklin Jameson (his family lived across Main Street from the Dickinsons), who was then on his way to academic fame as a historian. He writes in his diary:

> Went to call on Miss Vinnie. . . . I know her very little, but I do like her. She is a noble, good and kind woman in spite of her occasional sharpness of sarcasm, of which in talking with me there was little.

6. See Appendix IV.

That she became bitter and deceitful toward the end of a life that had in some ways been parallel in its frustrations to her sister's is a comment on the superior resources Emily brought to her problems. There was something of the loser in this generation of Dickinsons, a quality that in all of them except Emily evokes pity. They all, including Emily, suffered heartbreaking disappointments, and in this sense, perhaps, Emily like the others could be pitied. But none had a fulfillment like Emily's, and pity is hardly the dominant response to one who wrote what she wrote.

With Vinnie the pity is dominant, especially after Austin died and left her defenseless. Her life is what Emily's might have been, nurtured similarly as they were, had it not been for Emily's extraordinary gifts. This is not to say that Vinnie was a poet *manqué* who needed only some talent to transcend her troubles; it is simply to acknowledge that she had enough of Emily in her to understand her sister, if not deeply, at least better than has been thought. For one thing, she had sense enough to see how important it was for Emily to live her life in her own way, and in this, like Austin, she was way ahead of the Amherst gossipers who turned Emily into a hopeless eccentric, or those who, following Thomas Wentworth Higginson, could regard her as a "partially cracked poetess." As early as Emily's twenty-fourth year, her friend Eliza Coleman wrote to John Graves, Emily's handsome cousin, in concern even then for Emily's fate at the hands of those who failed to understand her:

Emilie . . . sends me beautiful letters & each one makes me love her more. I know you appreciate her & I think few of her Amherst friends do. They wholly misinterpret her, I believe—

It is notable, and to their credit, that both Austin and Vinnie took Emily exactly as she wanted to be taken. Mabel Todd said that Austin was merely amused at the gossip. Vinnie defended Emily from it and from all other intrusions. Not only this, but somehow or other, by affinities or perceptions she has been thought incapable of, she saw that Emily's poetry must be published.

A final example of her insight and devotion has come to light recently. A letter of January 29, 1895, is her answer to what she considered the growing misrepresentation of Emily's character and career. The myth-makers had been at work, and Vinnie was shocked to read the account of Emily in the *Boston Transcript* for December 22, 1894, by Mrs. Caroline Healey Dall. The article dealt in part with Emily's *Letters*, published that fall. Here is the passage that offended Vinnie:

Some years ago a relative of Emily's came to see me. . . . "It was in Washington," said her friend to me, "that Emily met her fate. Her father absolutely refused his consent to her marriage for no reason that was ever given." It was probably, as he once said, when she wanted to go away and make a visit, because "he was used to her and did not wish to part with her!" When such a motive was urged, Emily could not resist. She would wait, hoping, once, as we see in the pathetic little poem, "Almost". The lover came to see her and just missed her. His "soft, sauntering step" did not overtake hers. "Hope," she once wrote, had never "asked a crumb of her." It needed no sustenance, so immortal was her love, so elastic her spirit. And this answered until death came. In a few years her friend passed out of sight. I think from various indications that she never knew where his body lay, only he had gone after she had given her heart to him, and before her father would consent to ratify the contract.[7]

This has all the elements of the familiar story—indeed, several of the stories—said to explain Emily's "fate." Mrs. Dall's informant seems to have confused at least two, those involving her friendships with George Gould and (later) with Charles Wadsworth (whom, presumably, she met in Philadelphia, not Washington, but it was on the same trip). Here are the stock notions of the stroke of fate that cut her life in two, the possessive father, the life sustained on sad, sweet memories. Vinnie's reply to Mrs. Dall, as we have it from a typescript, signed by Vinnie, is a polite but earnest "You are wrong on every count":

> Will Mrs. Dall pardon intrusion if I correct false statements that have been made *to her* concerning my sister and our noble father?
> Emily never had any love disaster; she had the choisest friendships among the rarest men and women all her life, and was cut to the heart when death robbed her again and again. We were very fond sisters and, though I was the younger, I always took care of her, and we were never separated more than three months at any one time.
> I was in Washington with her where we found the most delight-[ful] friends. Emily's so called "withdrawal from general society", for which she never cared, was only a happen. Our mother had a period of invalidism, and one of her daughters must be constantly at home; Emily chose this part and, finding the life with her books and nature so congenial, continued to live it, always seeing her chosen friends and doing her part for the happiness of the home.
> Our father was the grandest of men, and never hindered our friendships after we were children. Emily had a joyous nature, yet full of pathos, and her power of language was unlike any one who ever lived. She fascinated every one she saw. Her intense verses were no more personal experiences than Shakespeare's tragedies, or Mrs. Browning's minor-key pictures. There has been an endeavor to invent and enforce a reason for Emily's peculiar and wonderful genius. This is not the first occasion that has forced me to right this cruel wrong (and, I think, always from the same source), the motive of invention being, I suppose, personal notoriety.
> I am sure you will endorse my determination to extinguish all untruth relating to my beloved sister who is not here to speak for herself; if her life

7. *AB*, p. 319. Mrs. Dall (1822–1912) was a prolific author, lecturer, and advocate of women's rights. The "relative of Emily's" who visited her has not been identified. The poem she calls "Almost" is #90 ("Within my reach!"). The title was given by Higginson (for *Poems,* 1890).

had been a tragedy I should never speak, but I should appreciate the brutality of lighting a subterranean passage for curious eyes.

Will Mrs. Dall be so kind as to *tell* me if these words find her,

And believe me earnestly,

Emily's sister, –
Amherst, Mass.,
  January 29, 1895.

Underneath, beginning at the left and in Vinnie's sprawling hand, is written: "Very Earnestly / Lavinia Dickinson / Amherst Mass – / January 29th '95."[8]

Most notable about the letter is that it squares perfectly with Austin's sense of the naturalness of Emily's way of life; and Sue, at least in the obituary of Emily she wrote for the *Republican,* seems to have held the same view. Vinnie's "only a happen" is too simple. Many of Emily's eccentricities—the long, intense seclusion; the refusal to call even next door; the interviews from behind doors or around corners or from the head of the stairs; her refusal to let doctors or dressmakers come near her or to let Mabel Todd see her when she called to sing—all this could hardly be called natural by any standard, nineteenth or twentieth century. Apparently what led those closest to Emily to call her retirement natural was its gradualness. Either that, or a family protectiveness that became all but conspiratorial. They seem, at least, not to have been disturbed by the eccentricities, so long and slow was the process of their development. But the rest of the world, waking up late to what had happened, saw them as very unnatural indeed and, as with all such phenomena, wanted an explanation. So the mythmaking began.

At the very least, I think we can agree with Austin and Vinnie that Emily's life is not to be explained by any one "love disaster." In the obituary, Sue attributed the withdrawal to Emily's "sensitive nature," insisting that she was "not disappointed with the world" but simply found in her own home "the fit atmosphere for her worth and work." Vinnie's reference to the series of losses from among Emily's "choisest friendships" seems more likely, if (which is hardly necessary) one looks to Emily's personal losses for an explanation of her withdrawn life. It is notable, also, that Vinnie considered the myth of the love disaster a "cruel wrong," the result of "false statements . . . always from the same source . . . the motive being, I suppose, personal notoriety." The source sounds like the Sue of the later years, who (Vinnie seems to be saying) was trying to get her share of the glory of being related to Emily, once the poems and letters had caused such a stir. The wrong was "cruel," one

8. The MS of the letter is in the Emily Dickinson Collection, Clifton Waller Barrett Library, University of Virginia Library, and is reproduced by permission. The typing was probably done by Mary Lee Hall, who later helped Vinnie with the transcripts of the poems, to be published long after Vinnie's death in *Further Poems of Emily Dickinson* (1929). See *AB*, pp. 371 ff. It is not known whether Vinnie ever got the reply she asked for.

gathers, both to Edward Dickinson and to Emily by making a tyrant of the one and a victim of the other.

Vinnie's comments about Emily's power with words need qualifying—save for the unexceptionable statement, "her power of language was unlike any one who ever lived." This remark sounds like a reference to Emily's spoken language and hence must long antedate Vinnie's full access to the poems. It alone would call in question the idea that her adoration was blind and uncomprehending. If, as Vinnie says, "she fascinated every one she saw," she fascinated Vinnie, too, and with the power of her language. Vinnie's remark about the poems—"Her intense verses were no more personal experiences than Shakespeare's tragedies, or Mrs. Browning's minor-key pictures"—is the same disclaimer that Emily herself had made years before to Higginson when she wrote him in July 1862, "When I state myself, as the Representative of the Verse – it does not mean – me – but a supposed person." Neither remark does justice to the whole truth, the truth of metaphor, Emily's characteristic vehicle, by which she could say a great deal about herself without seeming to. (She never lost a guinea in the sand, nor asked a merchant for Brazil, nor drowned at sea. But it is just as clear that at one time or another she felt *as if* she had done all three; and her life, even the simple, quiet life in the Homestead, was full of occasions that might have produced those feelings.) Both remarks are typical of Dickinson reticence, the fear of embarrassment, of "auctioning the mind," of exposing the soul *"at the White Heat."* The Dickinsons were not only reticent themselves; they respected each other's reticence, and protected it. Once in later years when Vinnie was asked if she could not get Emily to go out sometimes, she replied: "But why should I? She is quite happy and contented as she is. I would only disturb her."[9] An even more striking example of her respect for Emily's privacy is in one of her remarks recorded by a friend after Emily's death. She was asked whether she had studied her sister's poems extensively. She replied, "Certainly not. I never looked at Emily's poems except those she herself showed me. Had she wished me to do so, she would have made her wishes known."[10] Apparently she felt that even to

9. *YH* II, 273. This remark is quoted from Clara Bellinger Green's article on ED in *The Bookman,* November 1924, and dated as having been made in the spring of 1877. Mrs. Green's memories of Vinnie are as vivid as of Emily herself:

As young girls we used often to drop in after school to have a chat with "Miss Lavinia" as we called her, sure to be entertained by her droll, vivacious, and in-dividual views on men and things. . . .

"I, you must know," she remarked one day, "am the family inflater. One by one the members of my household go down, and I must inflate them." . . .

10. *AB,* p. 146 n. The remark is from a conversation between Millicent Todd Bing-ham and Mrs. Edward Robinson. (The entire memorandum is in the Todd-Bingham Archive.) A subsequent letter from Mrs. Robinson contained this further comment on Vinnie: "Your letter has set me remembering Miss Lavinia who, I feel, was the im-portant character of the family. A *dire* person! Perhaps she partly explains her sister." The reference is obviously to Lavinia in her declining years. See Appendix II, section 6, for a vivid glimpse of Vinnie in her later years, as Mrs. Bingham remembered her.

look at them after Emily's death would be disloyal. From all these remarks by Vinnie about the poems, it can be gathered how much Vinnie knew—Emily *did* show her some of the poems—and how much she did not know, not only about Emily's poetry but about the nature of poetry in general.

Finally, in the letter to Mrs. Dall, comes Vinnie's insistence that Emily "had a joyous nature, yet full of pathos," and that her life was not a tragedy. The joyousness is, of course, a major theme in Emily's letters and poems; it is nowhere more explicit, perhaps, than in her rejection of Higginson's solicitude about her starved and narrow life in Amherst: "I find ecstasy in living – the mere sense of living is joy enough." Then, as to want of employment and visitors, she told him, "I never thought of conceiving that I could ever have the slightest approach to such a want in all future time." Sue, in the obituary, and Mabel Todd, echoing Austin, both spoke of the "blossoming" of her nature, surely not a term denoting tragedy. Whether her life, for all its joy and richness, was, in a sense, a tragedy depends upon the reading of the whole. If, in spite of Vinnie and Austin, the love-disaster theory is insisted upon, her life could be called a tragedy; but even then the stress should be on her achievement as a poet, in spite of her tragic loss as a person. The same would be true if we accept the theory that her life was irretrievably warped by the inadequacies of her mother or the cruelties of a domineering father. If we accept the notion that her failure to publish her poetry blighted her life, then Bowles and Higginson become the antagonists in her tragedy, and her life after the age of thirty-one or thirty-two becomes a fifth-act denouement, a tapering off of unresolved tension. (If her rejection by Bowles was twofold, personal and professional, the tragedy deepens.) All these possibilities must be left open. So must Vinnie's formula that her withdrawn life was "just a happen," the result of nursing her mother through a spell of illness and liking the quiet life with nature and books. But Vinnie's explanation sounds too simple—as do all the single-cause theories, although each may contain a portion of the truth. All her intimates spoke at one time or another of her disenchantment with "the world" or "society." Such a large category could conceivably include a love disaster, a rejection by some representative of the world, or society; but it sounds more like a general rejection on her own part of a way of life in which she could not be happy and productive. There is something of Thoreau in the rejection, as has often been suggested. One surmises that he would have understood her better than Higginson did, and perhaps better than we can. We will come back to this problem many times.

One facet of it, and a major one, we shall now confront directly. I have already sketched some aspects of the distressing situation that developed in the family next door during the last five years of Emily's life. Although Vinnie certainly played a part in the situation, its origins go far back into the history of her generation of Dickinsons, and she was just as certainly its victim in many ways. Its virulence had a great deal to do with

Austin's premature death and even, in its long beginning (so Vinnie suggested darkly), with Emily's own. Its bitterness eventually spread into the town most divisively. Years later it was given a name, dramatic but descriptive, by Mary Lee Hall, Lavinia's friend and neighbor—"War between the Houses"—and it warrants a section to itself.

"*War between the Houses*"

8

Early Hostilities

THE ILL FEELING between the Homestead and the Evergreens had its origins in personal incompatibilities that go back to the time of Austin's troubled courtship and end only with Lavinia's death. It involved all three of the younger Dickinsons, plus two outsiders, Susan Gilbert Dickinson and (beginning in 1882) Mabel Loomis Todd. By Mabel Todd's time it had sufficiently advanced so that, at her first encounter with the Dickinsons, she realized that she was entering "a family quarrel of endless involutions." By the mid-1880s what had heretofore been kept under cover was all but open warfare, with Susan Dickinson and Mabel the chief antagonists. The quarrel by then, of course, was over Austin, whose affair with Mabel was being talked about in town; but this new development served merely to exacerbate old animosities and widen existing gaps.

We look in vain for explicit comment from Emily. But there are many reasons to believe that, in this situation as always, her sympathies were with Austin. In the 1890s it was Vinnie who got the worst of it, as the domestic tensions heightened and the personal problems involved in the editing of Emily's poems made matters worse. After Austin died in 1895, Vinnie and Sue were still at swords' points, until, by a curious switch whose rationale we can only guess at, Vinnie shifted to Sue's side and instituted the suit in 1898 against the Todds for the strip of land Austin had deeded Mabel Todd for her work on the poems. Vinnie died the next year, the last survivor in the Homestead; the Todds moved to the other side of town; and Sue and Martha (her loyal daughter) were left in possession.

But the real possessors were the bitterness and vindictiveness from which all have suffered, participants and posterity. To follow this story and sense its meaning is to gain new perspective on much that perplexes us about the Dickinsons, especially Emily: her withdrawal; the tragic, often violent tone of many of her poems; even, perhaps, her failure to publish. Seeing her against a background of anguish, frustration, and cruelty, we no longer have to ask how, in her quiet life, she came to know these things. Here is the real "Vesuvius at Home." All the characters in her limited circle take on new dimensions. Austin's story alone, now at last documented, shows him again passionately in love but this time a mature man, in firm control, glorying in a love that was fully reciprocated, and doing so in bland defiance of convention—and Amherst convention at that. Susan Dickinson emerges as one of the most impressive and formidable people in Emily's life, perhaps a decisive one. We see why the poems and letters were so long delayed and given to the world piecemeal and (for long) inaccurately. We see also why (by another curious switch) Emily's life and character were so sentimentalized by her niece Martha as to obscure for decades their stern and powerful reality.

As with any story of intensely private lives, of passions to which none of the participants ever publicly gave a name, the problem of the narrator is (again) delicate. The story must be pieced together from many sources, none of them free from bias. Sides are still taken, passionately. Often one must proceed by inference and intuition; and, as in all judgments of character and motive, conclusions must be tentative. But the story must be told, at whatever risk. Emily Dickinson did not write in a vacuum. The tangled relationships that developed into this final tragedy were a reality in her life, and an agonizing one, from her girlhood to the day she died.

One of the major themes in our treatment so far of the Dickinsons has been the closeness of the family, the interdependence of its members, and ultimately a pride that amounted to arrogance. Tradition may have exaggerated Edward Dickinson's petty tyrannies in the family, but there is no doubt that he kept a careful eye on the young men who came to call on his daughters. He was protecting the Dickinson name. He might have kept an equally careful eye on the young ladies who attracted his son. But, like Emily and all of Amherst, he was charmed by the dynamic young Susan Gilbert, who was clearly one of his favorites. He escorted her home on various occasions and called on her in Baltimore[1] (where she was teaching) when he went to the Whig Convention in June 1852. They joined the First Church on the same day, August 11, 1850. What Edward failed to see was that in encouraging the match between Susan and Austin, he was inviting into the family an alien and disruptive element. This is not a moral judgment; it is simply a fact.

To understand the disharmonies that soon arose, the nature of the conflict they developed into, and its effect on Emily as well as Austin, we

---

1. "Susie and I went to meeting last evening and Father went home first with Susie and then with me. I thought the folks would stare. I think Father feels that she appreciates him, better than most anybody else" (*L* I, 250; ED to Austin, May 16, 1853). "Father writes [from Baltimore] that he's called on Sue, twice, and found her very glad to see him" (*L* I, 213; ED to Austin, June 20, 1852).

must return to the early records for hints of trouble over and above the obvious frictions of Austin's courtship. Emily's early letters to Sue (there are none extant from Sue to Emily in this period and only one later) disclose a relationship which, on the face of it, seems rapturous. From the first letter (December 1850), Emily poured out her heart to her friend, showered her with affection, pined for her when she was absent, scolded her when she was offish. Her letters to many of her girl friends, like Abiah Root and Jane Humphrey, are insistent and effusive enough; the letters to Sue, even discounting the romantic style then in fashion and her own flair for rhetoric, are nothing less than love letters.

Even in its early stages, however, this relationship explains much that happened later. It has usually been taken at its face value—a girlish infatuation that developed, according to Martha Dickinson Bianchi's account, into lifelong devotion, with no rifts or seams. But there were difficulties from the start and rifts that opened wide in later years.

The question is: What is the truth behind the romantic rhetoric of the early letters? What did Sue really mean to Emily? It is clear, for all the gushiness, that she meant a great deal. By her twentieth year, Emily was consciously narrowing her circle, as one by one her friends, male and female, died or departed. More and more she saw Sue and Austin—and Vinnie in her own way—as supplying all the society she needed. As she looked forward to Austin's marriage, she saw Sue as her second sister, living only a hedge away. Discussions of life and love and literature would go on endlessly as they had begun in the letters. We "please ourselves with the fancy that we are the only poets, and everyone else is *prose*," she proclaimed to Sue when they were twenty. She knew Martha as the sweeter of the two sisters and apparently would have been happy had Austin married her. But Sue was the fascinating one—more "brilliant," as their brother-in-law had said—and for Emily the future lay with her.

Perhaps the closest we can come to explaining, if not explaining away, the fervor of the letters is by way of a literary parallel known to both girls. Several times Emily referred to Longfellow's *Kavanagh*, a novel published in 1849 and smuggled into the house despite Mr. Dickinson's watchfulness.[2] It was one of those books that he feared would "joggle the Mind." In the novel, the relationship between Alice Archer and Cecilia Vaughan might well have been taken by Emily as an idealized statement of what she hoped, at least, was true of her and Sue. She could have seen herself as Alice Archer:

She had a pale, transparent complexion, and large gray eyes, that seemed to see visions. Her figure was slight, almost fragile; her hands white, slender, diaphanous. . . . She was thoughtful, silent, susceptible; often sad, often in tears, often lost in reveries. She led a lonely life.

2. So Higginson wrote his wife (*L* II, 475, August 17, 1870): "Her father . . . did not wish them to read anything but the Bible. One day her brother brought home Kavanagh hid it under the piano cover & made signs to her & they read it: her father at last found it & was displeased."

Cecilia was in as sharp a contrast as, in real life, Sue was to Emily: beautiful, confident, outgoing, much sought after by young gentlemen. Longfellow pointed up the contrast in a passage that predicts precisely the theme and imagery of a poem Emily later sent to Sue (early in 1862), "Your Riches taught me Poverty".[3]

> . . . what a contrast was there between the two young friends! The wealth of one and the poverty of the other were not so strikingly at variance, as this affluence and refluence of love. To the one, so much was given that she became regardless of the gift; from the other, so much withheld, that, if possible, she exaggerated its importance.

If Emily's letters to Sue sound like the sentimentalizing of a second-rate romantic heroine, *Kavanagh* was just one model: the sighing and the kisses, the heart-to-heart talks and the "long and impassioned letters" are

---

3. The poem (#299) illustrates the difficulty of assigning ED's apparently occasional poems to any one set of circumstances. It exists in several versions. One was sent with three other poems to Higginson in July 1862, identical with the "packet" copy (see *P* I, 219 n.). A third copy was sent to Sue early in 1862, with this concluding note:

Dear Sue –
You see I remember –
        Emily.

In his note in *P* I, 220, Johnson tentatively accepts George Frisbie Whicher's suggestion (*This Was a Poet*, p. 92) that the poem was written in memory of Benjamin Franklin Newton, a law student in Edward Dickinson's office and an early friend and admirer of Emily's. Johnson goes further and suggests, in the light of ED's "unfailing" memory of anniversaries, that the poem was written on the ninth anniversary of Newton's death (March 24, 1853). However, the editors of the *Letters* (Johnson and Theodora Ward) three years later opened up another possibility (*L* II, 401–2): "On the other hand the poem may not be an elegy, but written about a person living whom ED feels that she has lost, perhaps Sue herself." The lines that echo (whether it was ED's intention or not) the situation and imagery of *Kavanagh* are:

> Your – Riches – taught me – poverty!
> Myself, a "Millionaire"
> In little – wealths – as Girls can boast –
> Till broad as "Buenos Ayre" –
> You drifted your Dominions –
> A Different – Peru –
> And I esteemed – all – poverty –
> For Life's Estate – with you! . . .
>
> At least – it solaces – to know –
> That there *exists* – a *Gold* –
> Altho' I prove it, just in time –
> It's distance – to behold!
> It's far – far – Treasure – to surmise –
> And estimate – the Pearl –
> That slipped – my simple fingers – thro'
> While yet a Girl – at School!

all there. To this extent, Emily and Sue, like Alice and Cecilia, were (as Longfellow describes them) "in love with each other":

They were nearly of the same age, and had been drawn together by that mysterious power which discovers and selects friends for us in our childhood. They sat together in school; they walked together after school; they told each other their manifold secrets; they wrote long and impassioned letters to each other in the evening; in a word, they were in love with each other.

Or (and this is the point) at least Emily was in love with Sue. By her early twenties, Sue was something of a woman of the world. As an orphan, she had known uncertainty and a good deal of knocking about. She took the teaching job in Baltimore as a gesture of independence and to make things easier for her sister, Mrs. Cutler. Her practical and matter-of-fact letters to her brothers before her marriage show that she knew where she was going. Austin's letter to Martha announcing the engagement described Sue as anything but sentimental: "tall," "stiff," "proud" were the words he applied to her as well as to himself. It is hard to believe that Sue responded to Emily's fervor in kind; the likelihood is that she was repelled by it or, at the very least, found it too demanding.

After she and Austin became engaged in 1853, it goes without saying that Sue could not have sustained anything like the relationship Emily wanted. Early in September 1854, ten months before Sue and Austin hoped to be married (the original wedding plans were for the summer of 1855), a letter of Emily's to Sue indicates a break that was by then inevitable. The letter starts bluntly, goes straight to the point, and ends with finality:

Sue – you can go or stay – There is but one alternative – We differ often lately, and this must be the last.

You need not fear to leave me lest I should be alone, for I often part with things I fancy I have loved, – sometimes to the grave, and sometimes to an oblivion rather bitterer than death – thus my heart bleeds so frequently that I shant mind the hemorrhage, and I only add an agony to several previous ones, and at the end of day remark – a bubble burst! . . .

Sue – I have lived by this. It is the lingering emblem of the Heaven I once dreamed, and though if this is taken, I shall remain alone, and though in that last day, the Jesus Christ you love, remark he does not know me – there is a darker spirit will not disown it's child.

Few have been given me, and if I love them so, that for *idolatry,* they are removed from me – I simply murmur *gone,* and the billow dies away into the boundless blue, and no one knows but me, that one went down today. We have walked very pleasantly – Perhaps this is the point at which our paths diverge – then pass on singing Sue, and up the distant hill I journey on.

The letter is an extraordinary one for Emily, the nearest approach to surliness and dismissal of any that survive. She is, quite simply, telling Susan off—her brother's fiancée and supposedly the darling of her heart.

Her own offense: "idolatry." The mysterious metaphor of the "darker spirit [that] will not disown it's child" is of a piece with similarly veiled prophecies she had been making for some time in letters to Jane Humphrey and Abiah Root but never with such an implied threat. What the substance of this immediate quarrel was we can only surmise. Religious differences between the two girls may have had something to do with it.[4] In a letter written a few weeks earlier, in August, Emily had said, "I was foolish eno' to be vexed at a little thing," and she asked God to forgive her—"as he'll have to many times, if he lives long enough." But the main point seems to have been Sue's neglect ("I have not heard from you"). With the September letter she sent a poem—"I have a Bird in spring"— that may have taken some of the sting off, since the poem says that the Bird (Sue?), though flown, will return some day with "Melody new for me." Then will come a time when "Each little doubt and fear, / Each little discord here" will be "Removed." But the doubts and discords were at that time real—and ominous.[5]

Whatever the cause of the quarrel, this apparently was not the first. Sometime in the early 1850s Austin drafted a strange letter to Sue. It is dated "Boston Sept. 23." In *The Years and Hours,* Leyda, associating it with the September "go or stay" letter, ascribes it to the year 1854, while the editors of the 1958 *Letters* place it in 1851. It is a chaotic scribble of nine pages, with many false starts, cancellations, and repetitions. Austin himself was apparently in trouble with Sue. First, he apologized profusely "for any reflections" he may have unconsciously made on her "honesty and honor," spoke acidly about not liking to hear "my plans ridiculed," and in conclusion put himself solidly on Emily's side in the impasse to which their relations had apparently come:

As to your deprivation of "Spiritual converse" with my sister – I Know Nothing – I was aware that you had been in correspondence for some time, but had never had an intimation that the correspondence was at an end –
I have full confidence in her good sense – as guide in this respect – So you

4. This is Thomas Johnson's explanation: "The letter . . . bears every evidence of telling Sue that she cannot honestly declare her faith, and therefore will not do so; and that if Sue's friendship is contingent upon such a declaration, the tie must be broken" (*Emily Dickinson: An Interpretive Biography,* p. 17). The falling out may have had some such origin, but it seems to have gone far beyond the religious issue, at least with Emily. Was the "darker spirit" the devil—or her own "pagan" Muse and its temptations?

5. Here (P #5), too, one hesitates to assert an absolute, one-to-one relationship between the poem and any specific person or experience. There almost always are other possibilities. For instance, Inder Nath Kher, *The Landscape of Absence: Emily Dickinson's Poetry* (1974), identifies the bird in the poem with Emily's Muse, her poetic inspiration. Certainly such bird symbolism can be seen in many later poems. Though the reference to Sue in "I have a Bird in spring" seems all but unmistakable, it is entirely possible that ED was writing on both levels at once: the Bird was Sue; Sue was her inspiration—her Muse—of the moment; with Sue out of her life, her poetry, for the time, dried up. The poem can be about both Sue *and* ED's poetry.

will not suspect me of having interfered with your epistolary intercourse with her –

Her choice of friends and correspondents is a matter over which I have never exerted any control –

Knowing therefore that you will not suspect me of having interfered with your epistolary relations & assuring you of my sentiments of regard for yourself – my respect and admiration for the President of the United States and the Gov Gen of Canada – I remain yours truly – Wm A Dickinson[6]

Sue herself had a reputation for being cool and self-possessed, but this (if we can take it even half seriously) goes beyond anything we have of hers from the early days. The line-up is significant: brother and sister versus the outsider.

Among the early hostilities that were later to develop so disastrously must be counted Lavinia's. Like all the family, she seems at first to have been charmed by Susan, half in love with her herself. Emily made a special point of it in a letter to Sue of April 1852:

Mother sends her best love to you. It makes her look so happy when I give your's to her. Send it always, Susie, and send your respects to father! And much from Vinnie. She was so happy at her note. After she finished reading it, she said, "I dont know but it's wrong, but I love Sue better – than Jane, and I love her and Mattie better than all the friends I ever had in my life."

Vinnie was then nineteen. A year later, March 1853, she was "vexed" with Sue for neglecting Emily—a sign, among other things, of how the Dickinsons rallied to each other's support and, in particular, of Vinnie's growing sense of guardianship of Emily. Susan had been away and had failed to keep up her share of the correspondence. Vinnie complained to Austin:

I think shes staid a long time & during it all she has written but a short note to Emilie. It has made E. very unhappy & me vexed. I dont understand what it means.

Two months later she wrote Austin the apologetic note about her quarrel with Sue, a premonition (as we can see now) of the later years of wrangling that came in the end to open warfare.

6. *YH* I, 316. The printed text of this draft gives a most inadequate idea of the MS. It is a curious mess. What it indicates about Austin's state of mind—or whether it was just another example of how seriously these young people took the discipline of epistolary composition—is problematic. It may have been a joke, pure and simple— but it has a sharp edge. At one point, Austin writes: "If you have occasion to address me on any subject again – please direct to the care of J. W. Norcross or if you are this way your card will find me at 19 Hancock St." The earlier date for this strange epistle (it was apparently never sent) seems more likely. During his first weeks as a teacher in Boston, Austin lived with the Norcrosses, then moved to a boardinghouse. In September 1854 he was in Amherst, preparing to go west in October. If the letter is serious, it is as little reassuring about the early relationship of Austin and Sue as about that of Sue and Emily. (The dating in the 1958 *Letters* [I, 307 n.] reverses Thomas Johnson's 1855 ascription in *Emily Dickinson: An Interpretive Biography*, p. 18.)

I saw *Sue* this afternoon, & everything is right between us now. We shall never have any more troubles. I confess I did wrong to suspect her, but sometimes I feel rather depressed & then I see every thing through cloudy spectacles. I love *Sue* most dearly & will try & never do her injustice again.

Actually, Vinnie saw more clearly through her "cloudy spectacles" than she did with them off. Her complaints against her sister-in-law in the later years were venomous, although for a while "so delicate," according to Mrs. Adelaide Hills, a close neighbor who often spoke critically of both Dickinson families. Mrs. Hills wrote to her husband (December 9, 1866):

Vinnie called here the other day – she said she had not seen Mrs. [Austin] Dickinson yet or the baby [Martha.] It had been nearly a week since the baby was born. I think if it had been me I should have felt quite badly – they try to be so delicate –

Mabel Todd was probably right when she said later that Vinnie and Sue came to "hate each other black and blue."

Between the "go or stay" letter and Austin's wedding there are only two letters from Emily to Sue, one at Thanksgiving that same year (1854) and the other the following January. There are the usual protests of loneliness and love, and only one mention of the previous quarrel.

I miss you, mourn for you, and walk the Streets alone – often at night, beside, I fall asleep in tears, for your dear face, yet not one word comes back to me from that silent West. If it is finished, tell me, and I will raise the lid to my box of Phantoms, and lay one more love in; but if it *lives* and *beats* still, still lives and beats for *me*, then say me *so*, and I will strike the strings to one more strain of happiness before I die.

Mostly, the two letters are concerned with sensible, gossipy matters, a welcome change from the saccharine (the September letter excepted) of the earlier ones. Perhaps Emily was consciously taking off the high sentimental style. Walking the streets alone at night and falling asleep in tears seems pure *Kavanagh*. But the words "If it is finished" and the "box of Phantoms" (a metaphor she used to conclude another friendship about that time) ring true. Later developments in Sue's character, in her marriage with Austin, and in Emily's own way of life bear out the prophetic hints here.

A poem Emily sent to Sue two years after the wedding, usually taken as a sign of Emily's total devotion to her sister-in-law, should be reexamined in the light of these early frictions. In the poem, Sue is again a Bird, and this time she has come to stay.

> One Sister have I in our house,
> And one, a hedge away.
> There's only one recorded,
> But both belong to me.

One came the road that I came –
And wore my last year's gown –
The other, as a bird her nest,
Builded our hearts among.

She did not sing as we did –
It was a different tune –
Herself to her a music
As Bumble bee of June.

Today is far from Childhood –
But up and down the hills
I held her hand the tighter –
Which shortened all the miles –

And still her hum
The years among,
Deceives the Butterfly;
Still in her Eye
The Violets lie
Mouldered this many May.

I spilt the dew –
But took the morn –
I chose this single star
From out the wide night's numbers –
Sue – forevermore!   (*#14, late 1858*)

Is the poem a pledge of eternal loyalty—or an elegy on a youthful friend-ship and a bitter reminder? From what we know about the "Dickinson difference" and about the relationships that were developing in this tightly knit group and even then worsening dramatically in the Evergreens, the lines that need stressing are the first two of the third stanza. The ironic implications of the images that follow the nostalgic stanza 4 are clear enough, a far cry from the kisses and comforting embraces of the early letters.

In view of the animosities that developed in the ensuing years, and in view of the possibility that Austin (or Mabel) exaggerated his early ex-perience, a comment in Mabel's journal for December 16, 1885, may be too melodramatic a conclusion to this first stage of the "War between the Houses." But it is part of the record: Susan, wrote Mabel, "made him marry her, in spite of his terrible repugnance to doing it (he said he felt as if he were going to his own execution the day he was married) . . ."

9

Mabel Loomis Todd and Austin

There seem to have been only two people in the world to whom Austin Dickinson, in his maturity, at one time or another poured out his heart. One was Emily, who, if she recorded the results at all, did so in her poetry, obliquely. The other was Mabel Loomis Todd (1856–1932), who for thirteen years was Austin's confidante in a relationship of complete intimacy. She has left us three major records: her daily diary from 1881 on; her journal, in which she wrote from time to time more fully than the size of the diary would permit; and her letters to and from Austin, from 1881 to the time of his death.[1]

Mabel Todd has appeared peripherally in our pages so far, but it is time now to bring her to the center. She not only precipitated the climactic conflict between the households, in both of which she was at one time intimate, but her records provide the materials for a striking new view of Austin and his private sorrow, of Sue and Lavinia, and ultimately of Emily as seen against the thirty-year background of family tensions. Furthermore, to follow the course of the complicated relationship she developed with both families is to see how she achieved the peculiar intimacy with things Dickinson that led her, finally, to edit the poems. True, she was technically the best-equipped person in town to do the work. But other qualities and insights and knowledge were needed. Jay Leyda's brief reminder gets at the heart of the matter.

If David Peck Todd had not been appointed director of the Amherst College Observatory in 1881 we might not today know that a poet named Emily Dickinson ever wrote a poem. It is possible that Lavinia Dickinson's persistence in keeping her beloved sister's memory alive might have found someone, somehow, to watch over the publication of the poems, but it is

---

1. These materials, as noted above, are in the Todd-Bingham Archive, Yale.

170]

extremely unlikely that she would have found an editor with the faith, sensitivity, and industry of Mabel Loomis Todd.

As we proceed with the story, unfolding as it does mainly from Mabel Todd's records, certain caveats are necessary. No one can claim that Mabel was an unbiased observer. She was every inch a participant, deeply in love with Austin, taking his side on every issue, and (in her journals and letters) defending her love against the world; and even if her reports of what Austin told her were truthful, it must be remembered that he, too, was in love, openly defying convention; and to justify himself to Mabel he may have exaggerated, knowingly or unknowingly, his previous difficulties with Sue—as in his remark about his wedding as his "execution." Nevertheless, the remark is not without some meaning, and, like everything she records, must be given its due. If nothing else, her account is by far the most complete we have, and impressively detailed. She was a veteran diarist, hardly missing a day from early girlhood on, and to read her daily entries is to gain confidence in her respect for fact and accuracy. She was twenty-seven years younger than Austin, she revered him, and she gives the impression, at least, of trying to put down on paper what he told her, even if in her youth and passion she made no discount for what may have been his colorations. And Austin's letters to her and to others over the thirteen years confirm, in general, her reliability, though with a lawyer's discretion he was seldom explicit on paper about details. Other observers corroborate her views of character and situation, although (again) no one of them is unprejudiced.[2] Mabel often rationalized her own behavior naïvely, and in the self-consciously literary manner of the day tended to overdramatize situations. But it seems to have been her sincere purpose to record the truth as she saw it, youthful, passionate, self-centered as she may have been.

Mabel Todd came to Amherst on August 31, 1881, with her husband, David Peck Todd, who had graduated from the college six years before. They had been married on March 5, 1879, in Washington, D.C. Their daughter, Millicent, was born on February 5, 1880. Mr. Todd had just been appointed, at the age of twenty-six, instructor in astronomy and director of the Amherst College Observatory. His wife was twenty-four, full of spirit and ambition, and fresh from a vibrant, social girlhood in Washington, where she had been brought up, we are told, "among distinguished scientists and men of letters."

Mrs. Todd made an immediate impression on Amherst, as did Amherst on her. Her journal and her letters to her family record exuberant enthusiasm over her first impressions of her new life. Her early tributes to the town, its blend of natural beauty with cultural and social amenities, should be put side by side with the dour comments of other observers, like Higginson, who found the atmosphere stifling. Her enthusiasm recalls the

2. The pertinent documents are assembled in Appendix II.

vivacious comments Emily made about the stir and bustle of Amherst in her youth ("Amherst is alive with fun this winter"), although the tone is quite different. In her journal for October 26, 1881, Mabel wrote:

> Do you know, I think Amherst is in many respects quite ideal. I always did like a college town, with its air of quiet cultivation, & by living in such an one it is possible to combine two things which are otherwise generally not found together. I mean the possibility of living in the country, amid the luxuriance of nature, and yet of having refined & educated society at the same time. . . . I have been entertained with a great deal of quiet elegance here, and I have had a really very brilliant experience. I was "taken in" at once, and have been constantly invited, for weeks.

Mabel Todd brought zest and color to this quiet elegance, and soon became a leading figure in many branches of the town's activity. She was the central attraction at parties and outings and the star of amateur the-atricals, like the performance in 1883 of Frances Hodgson Burnett's *A Fair Barbarian,* a piece which Emily had read with amusement in *Scrib-ner's,* and which, she said, amused "even the Cynic Austin." She became the leading soloist in the First Church and sang the lead in a performance of Handel's *Esther* in 1887. She held musical evenings, gave music lessons (she had studied piano for two winters in the New England Conservatory of Music in Boston), and according to the custom of the day was con-stantly calling and being called upon.

From girlhood on, she had literary ambitions; in later years, writing and lecturing became her major pursuits. She tried her hand at short stories and novels, she wrote and lectured about her travels with her husband on his scientific expeditions and, following her work on the *Poems,* about Emily Dickinson.[3] Her charm as a lecturer put her in wide demand. At the height of her career, her speaking schedule, which took her all over the East and once to San Francisco, was little short of profes-sional. She became a steady reviewer for Wendell Phillips Garrison's *Nation,* carried on a book column for *Home Magazine,* and was a frequent contributor to other journals. A major frustration of a life sprinkled with minor successes was her failure to achieve the first-rate literary success—as a novelist—she had always dreamed of.

One of her compensations, besides music, was her love of nature and her flair for painting it. Since childhood she had lived in its influence. Her

3. For Mrs. Todd's speaking schedule on Emily Dickinson for the years 1891–98, see *Ancestors' Brocades,* pp. 211–12. Her publications include a short story ("Foot-prints," *The Independent,* September 27, 1883; reprinted separately, Amherst, 1883); two volumes of poetry (*A Cycle of Sonnets,* 1896; *A Cycle of Sunsets,* 1910); three serialized novels, *Home Magazine,* Washington, D.C., and Minneapolis, Minnesota ("Stars and Gardens," 1899–1900; "A Better Part," 1902–03; "Polly in Japan," 1904); three books on travel (*Corona and Coronet,* 1898; *Coronet Memories,* 1899; *Tripoli the Mysterious,* 1912); two popular works on science (*Total Eclipses of the Sun,* 1894; *Steele's Popular Astronomy,* revised by David Peck Todd and Mabel Loomis Todd, 1899); and two essays, one posthumously published ("Witchcraft in New England," 1906; "The Thoreau Family Two Generations Ago," 1958).

MABEL LOOMIS TODD

Senior year, Amherst College, 1875
Professor of Astronomy, 1884

DAVID PECK TODD

father, Eben Jenks Loomis, of Concord, was a friend of Thoreau—indeed, was invited by him at one point to go on a camping expedition in Maine, an invitation that had, sadly, to be refused. On her visits to Concord as a girl, she was constantly in and out of the Thoreau household, and called Maria and Sophia Thoreau her "aunts." As she grew older, she began to paint and sketch with an eye trained to the closest observation. The panel of Indian pipes she sent Emily (in September 1882) is an example of her art—but crudely represented, it should be said, in the cover design she later used for the first edition of the *Poems*. (Emily thanked her for "the preferred flower of life" and sent her the famous *quid pro quo,* the poem "A Route of Evanescence," with the remark, "I cannot make an Indian Pipe but please accept a Humming Bird."[4]) The most impressive public recognition of Mabel's art came when Samuel Scudder, the great entomologist, used her full-color study of the monarch butterfly as the frontispiece of the prospectus for his *Butterflies of the Eastern United States and Canada* (1889). Her talent was (again) of professional quality and her production voluminous.

With all these gifts and her abounding energy, it is no wonder that her impact on Amherst was felt immediately, and especially in the Evergreens, where Susan by that time had established Amherst's closest approach to a salon. Very soon after their arrival in Amherst, the Todds were entertained by the Austin Dickinsons and taken up by them. Or rather, since the ladies were the socially aggressive ones, Mrs. Todd was taken up by Mrs. Dickinson. In the early weeks, Mabel wrote several times to her family about her first impressions of the Dickinsons. This was when she found Mrs. Dickinson "the most of a real society person here." "Her presence," she added, "filled the room with an ineffable grace and elegance." She was impressed by the Dickinson affluence—"they are quite wealthy"—and by their style (letter of October 2, 1881):

We met her [Mrs. Dickinson] the other morning driving with a handsome double carriage & pair, & coloured driver. . . . She is said to give extremely elegant little entertainments and musicales.

In her next letter to her parents (October 4, 1881), her enthusiasm soared:

Last evening . . . we went to return the Dickinsons' call. I told you I admired Mrs. Dickinson at first, but I am thoroughly captivated with her now. She does, as I supposed, live very handsomely, & she is so easy and charming, & sincere – and she understands me completely. She has a beautiful new upright piano, & her young daughter and I played some duetts, & then I sang. . . . Her husband was not at home last night – but I was very much impressed with him in various ways. He is fine (& very remarkable) looking – & very dignified & strong and a little odd.

4. ED had already sent copies of the poem (#1463, about 1879) to Helen Hunt Jackson, Mrs. Edward Tuckerman, and Higginson. Evidently one of her favorites, it went this time as a tribute to a fellow artist. Some sixty of Mabel Todd's nature paintings (oils and watercolors) are now in the Hunt Institute for Botanical Documentation, Carnegie Mellon University, Pittsburgh, Pennsylvania.

By October 12 she was spending "the morning with Mrs. Dickinson," playing and singing "three hours to her." Five months later she wrote in her journal (March 2, 1882) : "I have been at Mrs. Dickinson's a great deal since my return. . . . She appreciates me completely, and I love and admire her equally. She is a rare woman, & her home is my haven of pleasure in Amherst." Five months later (diary, July 18, 1882), the Dickinson home had become her "ideal place" and the Dickinsons her "ideal people."

Thus the Todds were well launched, to the delight of all. The relations between the two families ran smoothly for at least the first year and a half. But this pleasant state of affairs did not last. Mabel soon learned that Susan Dickinson was known in town for her violent but short-lived enthusiasms. She took people up—and dropped them capriciously, a fate (Mabel was warned) that might befall even Sue's "darling Toddy."[5] Sue, however, was not the immediate cause of trouble. What led to an open break was that Ned, Austin and Sue's twenty-year-old son, in his enthusiasm over this brilliant newcomer fell in love with her, all within the first few months of the Todds' arrival. Mabel's diary, during her first year in Amherst, records frequent visits from Ned, whom she found charming and chivalrous and whose attentions she welcomed, especially the long rides in the fall, the sleighing in the winter, the waltzing lessons (Ned taught her the new steps) at the Dickinsons'. By mid-winter 1882 Ned was calling on her almost every day, and by spring Mabel was disturbed. She admitted later that she should have seen what was coming; but she was only twenty-five herself, used to many suitors, and devoted to her husband ("I love him better every day," she concluded the entry in her journal for March 23, 1882, "I have made *the perfect marriage*"). So she planned a two-month visit with her parents in Washington, among other things to give Ned a chance to cool off. But as she wrote in her journal (April 10, 1882), she was not at all sure, knowing his character as she did, that his feelings would have changed much when she returned in June. She was troubled:

> We left Amherst on Wednesday, the twenty-ninth of March. Ned went with us as far as Palmer, on his way to Boston. The dear boy felt more badly about my leaving with every mile. He to all appearance was talking in a lively mood to me, on the train, but I could see that he felt dreadfully. I never had a more intense lover, and I don't know what to do about it. . . . he is in character a very determined and steadfast person, and I mistake him very much if his feelings will have changed at all toward me by June. Of course, I am a woman, and I am older than he, and I know more of life than he, and I can help him somewhat against himself, and I will try. But that is all I can do. . . .
>
> Well, time alone can extricate him – if he is to be extricated.

5. Mabel wrote in her journal, September 16, 1883: "It was a matter of wonder with my friends that there had been no break before. It was Mrs. D's way to have some 'fuss' on hand most of the time." When things were going right, Sue called Mabel her "darling Toddy," according to Mrs. Bingham (in conversation).

When she returned, Ned had not changed. All seemed serene on the surface. The gay outings and cheerful parties continued; but when he persisted to the point of openly declaring his love, saying that "if he should let go his fierce hold of himself, he could not answer for anything" (journal, September 15, 1882), she realized that she had to call a halt. So she added, "Ned and I have tacitly abandoned our little affair."

But it was not all that easy. Obviously, the affair was anything but little to Ned. He felt jilted and aggrieved; and (sometime in the late fall of 1882 or the early winter of 1883) in his bitterness he went to his mother with some startling accusations. In the journal for February 3, 1883—the first entry since a most happy one of December 11—Mabel is distressed:

> The root of all my trouble is that I allowed that affair with Ned to pro-gress too much. I got over all especial feeling for him in the summer, and supposed he did for me. But . . . he cared more for me than ever when I came back in November, & said he had given up the struggle to get over it. I talked very wisely & sensibly to him – & out of it might have sprung a pleasant & lasting friendship. But he is of a very jealous disposition, & began to think I must care more for his father than himself. So he got angry, and went to his mother with some very mean things – among other things telling her that I was an awful flirt – & having allowed him to fall in love with me, I was now tired of him & was trying the same thing with his father. Of course this troubled her very much, & she began to look about.

The root of the trouble was not simply Ned, of course, for by then her affair with Austin was well advanced; but she was right that he was the immediate cause. When she returned from another visit to Washington on January 6, the atmosphere had changed. Her February 3 entry continues:

> She [Sue] had always known that her husband was fond of me, & was very glad; but at Ned's soreness, and anger, she – being utterly devoted to him – began to think perhaps I *was* a flirt, & so she got jealous, too. When I came back from Washington in January her manner was so different that I had to ask an explanation, and we had a long conversation, which was conducted with fairness (in general) on both sides.

"Since then," she went on, "things have been better," and, indeed, the diary records pleasant doings—rides, calls, teas—between the families for the next year or so. But she was right when she concluded the entry by admitting, "The old cordial, frank relations I am afraid can never be resumed."

These mild words do not begin to convey the seriousness of the situation then developing, with herself at the center. Though she blamed herself for the affair with Ned, and rightly, there is in the journals and letters scarcely a word of self-reproach for her part in her affair with Austin, by this time five months under way, and potentially much more explosive.

In fact, Mabel was inexcusably naïve not to see this danger. By the winter of 1883 she and Austin were deeply committed, and tensions were rising. The course of their relationship and its effect on the families can be traced almost step by step in their letters and in her journal and diary. Austin's own laconic diary yields only one reference, but it is momentous.

Mabel's presence in the Evergreens had at first been a joy to all, including Sue. Perhaps Sue saw that Austin, fifty-two when the Todds arrived, was at a kind of dead center in his life and needed sprucing up. At any rate, he did respond to this vivid new personality, and there are numerous references in Mabel's diary, during the first year, to happy family gatherings and to walks and rides with "dear Mr. Dickinson." The Amherst countryside provided a special bond. She wrote in her journal for May 12, 1885, "His love for nature is as intense & necessary to him as mine is, & we see things just alike."

It was during one of their excursions to the country—on September 11, 1882, just a year after the Todds came to Amherst—that they recognized the full truth. Austin's diary for that day contains, along with some neutral items, one otherwise inexplicable word: "Rubicon." On that day seven years later, he wrote Mabel:

> A full 7, rich – and richer with every one –
>   Recall – remember – supply
>   Nor rose –
>   Nor earth –
>   Not Heaven –
> September 11 1889
> September 11 1882   It was so ordained

Mabel reciprocated in a letter of November 7, 1889:

> —how I live without you I do not see. Of course it is not living, but every moment of my life has been waiting ever since September eleventh, 1882. I had my vision then, and it has never wavered or faltered or grown dim since.

Following the day of days, their intimacy grew steadily, encouraged by circumstances. For three weeks beginning on October 19, 1882, Sue and daughter Martha were out of town attending a wedding in Grand Rapids. On November 10 David Todd left for the Lick Observatory in California to be the official photographer of the transit of Venus on December 6. He was gone two months. Mabel Todd became practically a member of the Dickinson family after he left, constantly in and out of the Evergreens and spending many nights there. One plaintive comment about that late autumn in Amherst has come down to us from David: "I never should have left her."[6]

The first few months of the romance, before suspicions were aroused,

6. Again, this was told me by Mrs. Bingham as her memory of what her father said. See also Appendix II, 5. Section 6 of this appendix assembles some striking sketches (from Mrs. Bingham's memoirs) of Austin, Vinnie, Mabel, and David.

seem to have been blissful. Twenty-two letters from Mabel to Austin, written between November (1882) and the following February, tell the idyllic story. One of them, written in mid-December, described the famous September 11 and set the tone—with one exception—for all the others:

. . . You thought you were all alone in the "by paths" – You loved the grass and the blue sky and the birds and the crickets – And you said you wanted the crickets to chirp about you when you were finally sleeping – You did not know then to whom you were saying that exquisite thing. But she loved those lonely walks too, only now they were not lonely – and she is thrilled with every bit of lichen on an old stone wall, and the scent of dead leaves, and the passive little buds that know so wondrously when to awake and breathe the rapture of spring.

And we walked toward the sunset – and leaning on an old fence, began to reach [each] other a very, very little – It was very peaceful, and very bright – but it was the beginning, unmistakably. . . . You reached out your hand without knowing it, almost – in the darkness – and you met another – warm and tender. You clasped it – knowing it was your fate – and it staid with you. It will never be withdrawn. . . .

Good night, beloved . . . Love me. Love me every minute, and think of me. The stars are shining brilliantly. I see many bright things for us in the future. Good night.

As the other letters pour out their protestations of love, the one exception to the idyllic tone emerges. Though their love "grows and grows . . . wondrously and beautifully," certain anxieties appear: "I hope everything was in a lovely and serene state upon your return," she wrote on December 5. "How is the Home atmosphere? I am anxious to know that." She hesitated to send some of her more passionate letters in the mail. In Washington, where she had gone for the Christmas holidays, she worried about not hearing from Austin:

. . . I am wondering too how the "Powers" are talking and acting and feeling – I hope it is not they – in any way – who keep you from writing. . . . It may be some idea of danger to us that keeps you from writing to me – and so it may not be safe for me to write to you even in the manner you suggested. . . .

Back in Amherst to greet her husband's return from California on January 6, she wrote in alarm over an evening at Sue's (Austin was in Boston):

The evening was too horribly chilling – The whole atmosphere was cruel – I felt as if all the surroundings were pitiless – What new thing has occurred to make everything so dreadful? I must see you – It is necessary for me to see you soon. . . .

Things were better a few weeks later (January 29), "but still the constant air of watchfulness is very uncomfortable."

It was in this letter that she urged Austin to burn all her letters. "But

[*177*

above everything, *do* be careful of this note. It frightens me when I think of your having it with you when you come home." It apparently frightened Austin, too. He burned them, all twenty-two of them—but not (curiously) before making copies. These, in his own hand, he placed in an envelope and entrusted it to Vinnie. On the envelope he wrote a surprising directive:

Vin –

If anything happens
  to me
     Burn this package
at once –
     without opening.
Do this as you love me.

    W A Dickinson

The "War between the Houses" was on in earnest.

Lavinia directed operations from the Homestead, addressing envelopes, delivering messages, arranging meetings. Austin's real center was there, too. In 1861 Emily had written a friend that Austin "married—and went East"; it was about this time (March 1883) that she wrote: "My Brother is with us so often each Day, we almost forget that he ever passed to a wedded Home." Whatever Emily's part was in all these doings, she had ample opportunity to hear about them. On July 12, 1885, Austin wrote Mrs. Todd about a custom of his that had obviously been going on for some time. It is a crucial one.

> I have two or three little visits with my sisters every day, and we talk you over, always. . . . I see Vin and Em more than I did and you are the constant theme.

By then Austin's alienation from his own home seems to have been complete. The loss of his son Gilbert in the fall of 1883 had been all the more grievous because Austin, according to Mabel, looked upon him as the only member of his household who understood and loved him.

The remaining years of this ill-fated love affair present a harrowing story of frustration and despair that in the end were almost too much for both Austin and Mabel. At first, when Sue's hostility became apparent, they were defiant. Two notes from Austin sounded the trumpet. The first (April 6, 1883) called for courage and belief in themselves (the envelope is addressed by Vinnie):

> . . . Hope you are holding up. It is the part of a man or a woman, to meet what they must in a noble way, even if it kills. Honor and nobleness are far beyond life.
>   Besides what is there from which either should shrink!

The next, written on July 12, when Mabel was vacationing at Hampton, N.H., is more militant. The spring in Amherst had been difficult:

Cast of *A Fair Barbarian,* November 23, 1883
David and Mabel Todd, sitting, center

DIVERSIONS IN AMHERST, 1882–3

"The Shutesbury School of Philosophy" (after a picnic, July 1882)
Mabel Todd, center, standing; David Todd, far right; Susan Dickinson, with
Gilbert on her lap, seated, center; Mattie Dickinson, seated, right; Ned
Dickinson, front right, with tennis racket

Indian Pipes, on black gilt-edge panel, by Mabel Todd. Sent by her to ED, September 24, 1882

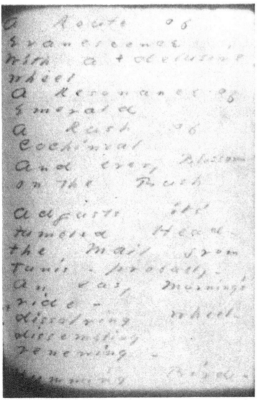

A final version of this poem, here in worksheet draft, went to Mrs. Todd in return. This is the only known version without the word "revolving" in line 2. The variants show the care with which ED arrived at her final choices

A FAMOUS EXCHANGE

. . . I hope the summer may be most pleasant to you, that the brightness of the passing days at Hampton may crowd down all memory of the unpleasantness of the days here, and that circumstances may so change as to make your return here in September easy and agreeable. I cannot but believe they will.

I suffer for every wound you have received from my family, but for the time have seemed powerless to prevent them.

What strength I have however will be pitted against any more of them.

I will straighten the matter out before the summer is over or smash the machine –

I had rather be under the wreck than under what I am. There would be several other broken heads, certainly, and I would take the chance of coming out on top.

Nothing in Austin's actions bears out these brave words. Perhaps Gilbert's sickness and death in October took the heart out of him. What eventuated, in spite of repeated protests of defiance in their correspondence, were twelve years of double living—with this notable exception: they made no attempt to conceal their love for each other from their spouses. In his July 1883 letter, Austin described the following scene in the Evergreens:

. . . At breakfast . . . the question came square, after leading up properly, "Did you see Mrs. Todd?" I had anticipated it and said at once, "Certainly, that was what I went to Boston for." This unhesitating frankness was somewhat stunning, and the rally wasn't prompt. When it came, it was, "She told me she was to spend a few days in Boston before going to Hampton, and I concluded you would see her." I replied, "Yes, I *said* I did." This ended it. There has been no allusion to it or you, since. I don't know whether on the whole I am supposed to have lied about it or not, but *you* know I spoke the Truth.

David Todd was equally aware of the relationship but tolerated it in his gentle way. A man deeply engrossed in science, he wanted nothing more than to have his brilliant Mabel happy. His role in this extraordinary affair was, of course, crucial. It could be said that, by his very virtues of restraint and tolerance, he contributed to the prolonged frustration and agony of all concerned, including himself. But he was a man of mild temper and of such devotion to his wife that her will was his will, even if it was her will to love another man. Of his feelings toward Austin, twenty-six years his senior, two things must be said. First, he revered him and loved him. In later years, he told his daughter, "I loved him more than any man I ever knew."[7] Second, in the early 1880s, Austin Dickinson was

7. This, too, was communicated to me by Mrs. Bingham. Since she died, its accuracy has been verified by three entries in David Todd's diary at the time of Austin's death: "My best friend died tonight, and I seem stranded." Next day, he wrote: "Impossible to do anything today. The loss of our dear friend is unspeakable – he touched and pervaded everything." On August 19: "The saddest day of my life – the funeral of our best friend." These entries were called to my attention by Polly Longsworth, currently engaged in a study of Mabel Loomis Todd.

one of the most powerful men in Amherst College. President Merrill Gates was neither a very forceful nor an entirely well man and depended on him a great deal. Young Professor Todd's tenure was far from secure. Part of his hesitancy to interfere with his wife's relationship with Austin might have been due to his regard for Austin's influence.

But the larger truth seems to have been that David Todd was deeply impressed by Austin from the start, delighted and flattered by his frequent visits to his house, and came to be very fond of him, as Austin came to be of him. In 1885, when Mabel was in Europe for the summer, while the two men consoled each other's loneliness, Austin actually speculated on a *ménage à trois*[8] to solve their problems. The three spent much time together—on outings and drives, at theater parties in Boston, with occasional meetings in New York, and a trip to the Chicago World's Fair in 1893. David Todd might at one point or another have taken a firm stand—or bowed out. But he did neither, nor did Austin ever seek a divorce. When he came at last to realize how deeply his wife was involved, he made up his mind to live with it, which he did with grace and magnanimity. But it was a design for living that ultimately satisfied no one. His daughter Millicent, during her girlhood, remembers hearing her father whistling a tune from *Martha* when he came home from the Observatory late at night. Only later did she realize that this was a signal to forewarn Austin and Mabel of his coming. Only later did she realize, too, why so many Amherst citizens refused to speak to her on the street. And she later saw that it was the strain of this trying and irregular relationship that contributed to her father's ultimate mental breakdown and hospitalization.

Often in her journal Mabel faced the anomaly of her situation but declared herself capable of loving two men at once, though each in a different way. A few sentences from a passage to be quoted in full later provide an example of how she thought it out to herself:

> I thank God again and again for him [Austin]. I do not love David less – he is sweet & gentle & tender – but I have found my very own. That is all. . . . And yet I will never make David unhappy. He has been wondrously generous & noble, and I appreciate, & will make his life just as happy as every possible sweetness & attention can make it. But I cannot be untrue to myself & shut the door on my real self for conventionality. I know that Austin belongs to me, & I to him.

Five years later (journal, May 13, 1890) came an even bolder defiance of convention. She had just visited her friend Mrs. Chant's "Refuge" for

8. On July 12, 1885, Austin wrote Mabel, traveling with her friend, Mrs. Caro Andrews:

> . . . I look after David – as a part of my charge. He seems to like me – to rely upon me – and to confide in me to a remarkable degree. I think we three would have no trouble – in a house together – in living as you and I should wish. He admires you more than Caro – but with you away and Caro present he would be filled – while I should die – and would^{nt} you without me!

fallen women in Chicago and found herself unable to condemn any of the inmates who had acted out of true love: "If it is something they have done for the love of a man, then it is a sweet and pure thing. . . . Mrs. Chant thinks so too, & she is the only person I ever saw – no, not quite, but nearly – who looks on such things as I do." So much for the "Dimity Convictions" of the gentle folk who surrounded her at Amherst. Apparently, what kept Austin and Mabel sustained during the long years of frustration was the idea (as far as one can see from hints and suggestions in the letters and journal) that they would somehow miraculously outlive their spouses, or (a thought shared between them many times) that they would be joined together forever in Eternity.

David Todd might acquiesce, and Mabel might justify, but neither Sue nor the community were prepared to understand. Despite their protestations of divinely sanctioned love and their contempt for town gossip, Austin and Mabel decided at an early stage to keep visible signs and public encounters to a minimum. They habitually met in the dining room in the Homestead and had private places of rendezvous for drives and walks. They concocted code names and code messages for communication by telegram. Austin had self-addressed, stamped envelopes printed for Mabel's use, to divert attention from her handwriting. David Todd addressed most of the letters that went from Austin to Mabel in Europe during her summer abroad. They adopted, in short, what Mabel called a "policy"—"that wretched, hateful, loathsome word!" she blurted out in a letter of January 17, 1888.[9] The strain was great; but such were the times, or such were their natures, that they could never bring themselves (as Austin put it) to "smash the machine."

The dominant note in their letters throughout the thirteen years is one of utter, absolute devotion. Their passion transcended all obstacles. They wrote each other almost daily, and voluminously. With both of them living full professional lives, the wonder is that they had time for it all—Austin with his law work and the college, Mabel with her music and painting lessons, her writing and lecturing. Starting with the simple discovery (to quote from widely separated parts of the journal) that "we had a great many ideas in common" and the announcement of a "friendship which is the most true and satisfying I ever had," the rhetoric soars to crescendo after crescendo. Toward the end it had a religious cast. Their love lifts them "solemnly to God." "You are my Christ," Austin writes in August 1887. "Oh! my love, my king! My star and guide and heaven-sent

9. The "policy" involved many levels of deception, one of which Polly Longsworth discovered in her work on the Austin-Mabel correspondence. For many months during the early stages of the affair, they wrote each other two sorts of letters: one, staid and respectable, harmless if read by Sue or David; the other, love letters, intense and passionate. These were transmitted by various means of subterfuge—in self-addressed envelopes; tucked into books; or exchanged during casual encounters on the street. These they agreed to burn (although Mabel couldn't bring herself to destroy all of Austin's), and it was these that Austin copied in his own hand before burning the originals.

light," declares Mabel a year later (June 28, 1888). "Do you not know that my soul is knit to yours by an Almighty hand? Through you I see God."

Their mutual love of nature is a recurrent theme. There is seldom a letter without some reference to the weather, or flowers, or the hills. In an early letter (September 25, 1883), to bolster Austin's low spirits, Mabel reminded him of this great resource:

> How the crickets are chirping today, and how the asters shine from the roadside! There is surely no place for unhappiness of any kind in so beautiful a world. I think it is a mistake when there is any – the elements of joy are so simple: Could you not make a perfectly uncomplicated combination which would bring joy to you? I have been so busy all day, and now I am resting – under a rare sky, breathing an air full of quiet peace. . . .

Since meetings in town were risky, they took to the country for long walks and rides, as far from "the Powers" as they could get. Mabel wrote in her journal on May 12, 1885:

> Through all the crises & chaoses how tender & restful has been my dear Mr. Dickinson! He takes me off for long quieting drives under the trees & by brooks & through the sweet home of wild flowers. And I see such blue, blue skies & such thrilling clouds with him, and we hear the half-melancholy notes of wee frogs in the boggy fields, & ecstatic bird-songs in the woods.

Another major theme in the letters and especially in the journals is Austin's life before he met Mabel, its sadness and frustration. Several times she asked him to put in writing the story of his life, partly, perhaps, for her own protection. He came close to answering her request in 1883, probably in March; but what resulted was a love letter, one of the most ardent in the long correspondence. It deserves quotation in full for many reasons, but here it speaks simply for "Austin in love," fifty-four-year-old husband and father, a pillar of the community, orator at church celebrations, first in honoring his Puritan forebears—and the brother of the "Queen Recluse." When the Dickinson dam burst, the flood was a mighty one.

> Yes, my darling, I did promise you that sometime I would put into your hands the story of my life, to use as a shield, if ever, when I am not here to answer for myself, any attack should be made upon my love for you, or yours for me, or our relations to each other.
> And yet is it not better and nobler that I say nothing which involves any other, reflects upon any other! may offend or wound. Is it not better to begin with my meeting you, and for the first time feeling clear sunshine! What is the past in the face of the present and the future, as we now see it! Is it not better, and enough, for me to say simply, what I have said so many times before, that I love you, love you, love you with all my mind and heart and strength! and that I know what I mean when I say this, that with you my real life began! that with you I have found what life may mean! that in you I have found the sweetest, richest dreams of my boyhood, youth, and early manhood more than realized! That I have found in you what a woman may

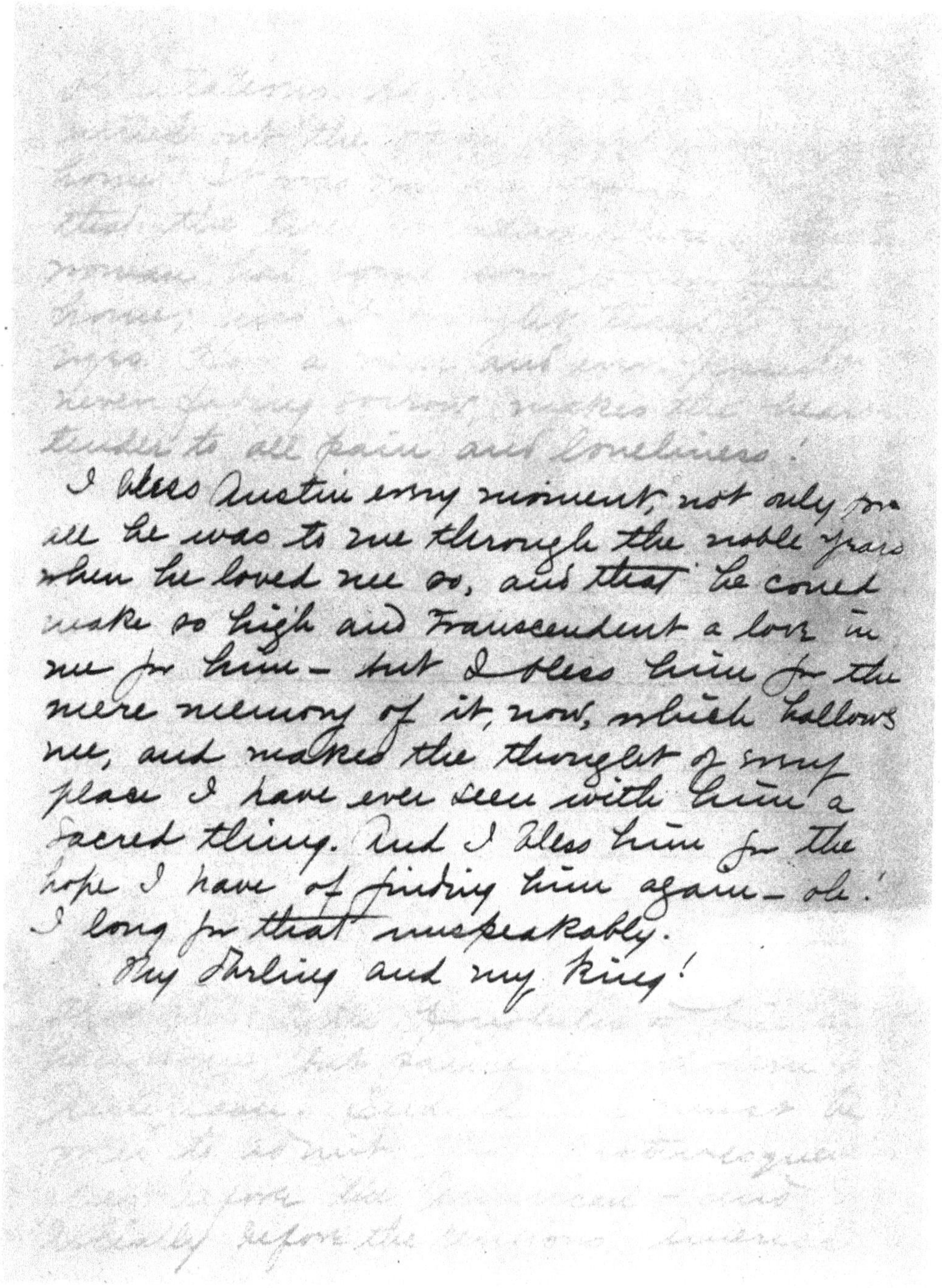
tender to all pain and loneliness!
I bless Austin every moment, not only for
all he was to me through the noble years
when he loved me so, and that he could
make so high and transcendent a love in
me for him – but I bless him for the
mere memory of it, now, which hallows
me, and makes the thought of every
place I have ever seen with him a
sacred thing. And I bless him for the
hope I have of finding him again – oh!
I long for that unspeakably.
My Darling and my King!

A page from Mabel Todd's journal, on board yacht *Coronet,* 1,600 miles from Honolulu, June 4, 1896

David and Mabel Todd, at the Observatory House, their last home in Amherst, May 1907

be to a man, hope, courage, joy, inspiration, companionship, rest, peace, religion! That in you I have found my perfect soul-mate, for time and eternity! That in you I have found my longing satisfied – that through you my ideals have been excelled! That you are to me a constant wellspring of delight! more than any throne – than any fame! That I have come to live in you – and by you – and for you – that I admire you as well as love you. That I trust you implicitly, and feel with you my most complete freedom. That I have given myself to you, or rather that I have found myself yours! outside of all will or intent. That with you I breathe a new air, move in new realms, that by you I am enlarged, enriched, uplifted. That I thank God for you every hour. That I find in you everything most beautiful, most dear, most rare, and in you the promptest response to every subtilest feeling and movement of my nature – or do we not rather move toward each other by a common impulse! and in perfect unison! No words can express, dearie, the depth and strength of my love for you, its sacredness, its holiness. You can know it only by looking into your own heart and seeing there the love you have for me, for we have learned that there is no difference in the quality or quantity of the love which fills us both, and that is the Glory of it. I am yours, yours wholly, and only, living or dying. I didn't will it. I simply recognized it, and recognizing it, I could not, and would not deny it. The highest truth is above and beyond common forms and formulas. The spirit is greater than the letter. Conventionalism is for those not strong enough to be laws for themselves, or to conform themselves to the great higher law where all the harmonies meet. I love you, love you, now and forever, and it is my great joy that my love is as much to you as yours to me. The fulness and stoutness and brightness – and excellent happiness – and hope, and thrill, and ecstasy of the days since in that sudden flash of light when we stood revealed to each other, through and through, and saw that each was, in the divine order, the other's world – one part of one existence forevermore.

How much we have to be grateful for, even though we have been obliged to defer some of our hopes – everything will come in good time.

> Once more I love you,
> and again, I love you
> my dearest, dearest Mabel,
> and without my will, and
> with my will am your
>   own Austin.

The sustained elevation, the almost awesome fervor of Austin and Mabel's love appear in letters throughout its thirteen-year course. The rhetoric becomes repetitious, but it is never exhausted. Mabel, of course, thought Austin's letters, if published,[10] would be "immortal," and wrote in her journal (September 14, 1886): "I have read a great many stories, & I

---

10. Many of them, it is to be hoped, will be published soon in a volume of selections from the Austin-Mabel correspondence now being assembled by Polly Longsworth and myself. A much more detailed account of the relationship will be possible there.

have had a good many love-letters, and I have heard a good many lovers talk, but I never heard or read or imagined such a wonderful putting-into-words. . . ." But Austin had little of his sister Emily's gift. What makes the letters remarkable is the completeness of the commitment they reveal, the outpourings of a heart too long frustrated and denied. One can only conclude that his hopes for happiness with Sue, stated with such fervor in the courtship letters, had long since come to nothing. Nor can one help thinking of Emily next door, at that very time pouring out her heart—also vainly, as it turned out—to Judge Otis Lord of Salem, pillar of the Massachusetts bar and eighteen years her senior.

As, month after month and year after year, the bright future that Austin and Mabel envisioned failed to materialize, signs of strain accumulated. The "Powers" became ever more formidable. The moods of the two lovers fluctuated more severely from hope to despair. "I have a strange sort of life," Mabel wrote in her journal on December 15, 1885, "it is not a bit like anybody else's . . . often far unhappier, it is sometimes infinitely happier." A hint of the martyr creeps into her complaints to Austin (and to her journal) about not being able to stand the strain much longer. By the late 1880s she was near the breaking point.

> I am so tired of *bearing* [she wrote to Austin on November 7, 1889]. If I could be once more happy – I have not quite forgotten how it feels – I could take breath for more pain. . . . I hope – I anticipate all. Some day it is coming.

The hope, or whatever it was, sustained her for another three years; but by then she was utterly exhausted. In a letter of July 28, 1892, she told Austin that she had reached her limit. She implied strongly that he had better *do* something:

> Your letter written on Tuesday, after getting my Sunday note, came this morning. I have just reread it, and I appreciate all you say. Whether I can live up to it or not I cannot say. There are qualities in me worth saving, I am sure. But I was not fitted to stand the kind of strain I have had, and it seems to have taken out from me the joyous, enthusiastic happiness in everything with which I was endowed by nature. I know it is nothing now but a question of will, as you say – but I have lived on will for ten years – even you do not know to what extent – and it has nearly used me up. Things must be happier soon, or my power of mental recuperation will give out. I could get back – *now*. . . .

It was soon after this, and probably in response to it, that Austin wrote to his friend in Omaha about the possibility of establishing himself there. One can hardly doubt that he had in mind a complete break with Sue and his family—and perhaps taking Mabel with him. But, like so many other frustrations in his life, nothing came of it. The letter to Omaha is only a draft; there is no proof that it was ever sent. The tensions continued. Austin showed more and more signs of fatigue. Two years later he was dead.

Mabel's grief demands a postscript. Whatever the verdict of history on her part in this whole troubled affair, there can be little doubt of the depth and sincerity of her love for Austin. Young, inexperienced, and incorrigibly romantic she may have been when she first came to Amherst, but once in love, she was in deep. She never wavered, and she never regretted it.

The entries in the journal for the months after Austin's death are short and stark. She did not indulge herself, as she sometimes had previously, in romantic rhetoric and posing. Three days after Austin died, she wrote (August 19, 1895): "I am utterly crushed. . . . I kissed his blessed cold cheek." Two months later (October 31): "It does not grow in the least easier." A month later (November 15): "I miss him so that I cannot adjust my life at all. . . . Well, my beloved Austin, there is no need to say good-night – you do not go away at all." And as late as the following January (the sixth): "I am so tired with grief that I am worn out." Early that spring, when the Todds were about to start on a scientific expedition to Japan in Arthur Curtiss James's yacht, *Coronet,* she was more composed, more literary, but still deeply involved. Writing of a prospect that would once have utterly delighted her, she had only one thought (March 30, 1896):

Yet nothing on earth has power to really thrill me any more – one old brown coat and a big hat used to be enough to set every drop of blood in my body tingling and racing through the veins in tumultuous rush. The sound of his well-beloved knock almost stopped my heart with joy – and the singular part of it is that it was always so – after fourteen years I thrilled to his coming or his voice or his distant figure just as in the first wonderful months when we were finding out that each was for the other *forever.*

10

Austin's Marriage

Aʟᴛʜᴏᴜɢʜ ᴍᴏsᴛ of Mabel Todd's correspondence with Austin is taken up with their mutual love and though most of her journal, when she is writing about personal things, concerns that same all-absorbing topic, she touched frequently on a matter about which much has been implicit, and not a little explicit, in earlier chapters: Austin's marriage. It has long been known that the marriage was unhappy, if only on the evidence of the affair with Mabel. The gossip began in earnest in the mid-1880s, but there were murmurings before then. What Mabel says about it, along with other comments that have recently come to light, allows the fullest view so far, and it is a bitter one.

Mabel's account, of course, tends to justify her own part in a highly unconventional relationship by sharpening the outlines of the story, with Sue the villain, Austin the victim, and herself the one who rescued his life from disaster. What Austin told her, even if she reported it truthfully, must (again) be taken with caution, since he, too, must have been under some compulsion to justify his relationship with Mabel. What cannot be denied is Mabel's privileged position. At one point in her journal (September 14, 1886) she described Austin as having been "self-contained and reticent all his life" (a good description of the Dickinson front to the world). But as their intimacy increased from that crucial September day onward, his reticence diminished. On April 5, 1890, he wrote her, "You are my only confidante – the only one I ever had"—an exaggeration, surely, in view of his outpourings to Sue during the courtship, the long confessional letter to Martha Gilbert, the "kitchen talks" with Emily, and his almost daily visits to the Homestead in the early 1880s. But by 1890 Emily had been gone four years, the courtship days were a bitter memory, and this late but perfect intimacy with Mabel may have made her seem the first. Certainly Austin had ample opportunity to tell her everything there was to tell. Mabel's diary records his innumerable calls, their day-long walks and rides when, apparently, he spoke more freely about Sue and his home life than he ever did in his letters. Only a fraction of his confidences, it seems clear, ever reached the pages of Mabel's journal or diary. What *did,* for all its obvious bias, is always revealing (in one way or another) and sometimes startling.

Austin's description of his feelings on his wedding day—as if he were going to his execution—is a sample. Mabel's account makes it sound as if Sue pressured him into marriage to satisfy her social ambitions and her longing for security. The thrust of the courtship letters, in which Austin is the passionate, pleading suitor, is reversed. While Mabel wrote in her journal for December 16, 1885, that Susan "made him marry her," and while it is conceivable, of course, that if an accurate dating of the court-ship letters were possible, Austin's passion might be shown to have ebbed· gradually as the wedding approached, Mabel's phrase about Austin's "terrible repugnance" cannot be otherwise documented and tells, perhaps, more about Austin's accumulated bitterness over the years than about his feelings on his wedding day. Mabel's account of his motives in choosing Sue also seems overcolored, although she purports to be quoting him. Austin thought (she wrote in this same entry) that by marrying Sue, a tavern keeper's daughter, he would be introducing "bodily vigor" into the Dickinson line, more so than if he married a "gentle lady"—a revelation that moves Mabel to comment: "It does not do for persons of entirely different social grade to marry." She continued with a panegyric on "the most intimate and tender friendship . . . the most delicate chivalry and courtesy" she has always enjoyed with Austin—all those blessings, she implies, that Sue failed to give him.

On one important point she is positive. In the same passage that described Austin's repugnance toward his marriage, she continued: ". . . he found himself wofully mistaken in it all – at once." If this is true, or even approximately so, it shows how soon the shadow fell over Austin's life, and it throws a somber light over those gay evenings in the Ever-greens we hear about during the late 1850s. What it meant for Emily we can only speculate.

In the journal, shortly after the first rift in the relations between the families in the winter of 1883, Mabel touches on the specifics of Austin's wretched domestic life. Other details, some of them harrowing, appear off and on throughout the next seven or eight years. Her account begins in a long journal entry for April 10, 1883:

> Mr. Dickinson has told me a great many things since I last wrote. . . .
> It seems he & his wife have not been in the least happy together, although for the sake of appearances & the children, they have continued to live to-gether. Notwithstanding the utter lack of love between them, the fact that he is so interested in me has stirred her beyond the power of words to ex-press. And she makes it pretty dreadful for him at home. I have seen some

developments in her character which are very startling. . . . Mr. Dickinson's life has been very barren.

What these startling developments were can be inferred from subsequent entries. On September 16, 1883, Mabel described Sue's behavior on a drive in the country, in which both families joined, as "still very chaotic and not sweet," and added that she has given Austin "a wretched life at home, in spite of the perfect house & grounds, the carriages & horses, pictures & luxuries generally." Relations between the families were now threatened with a permanent break, with the two ladies as antagonists. The journal commented:

> Mrs. D. is so well understood in Amherst that the fact of her breaking with us cannot redound to her credit. . . . Mr. D. says she fears me – the first woman who ever really crossed her path.

What Mabel meant by the "chaotic" in Sue's behavior soon becomes apparent. As the entries accumulate, Sue's character gradually takes on darker and darker colors. In this same entry, Sue's present anger and frustration appear (to Mabel) as the inevitable result of her failure as a wife from the beginning.

> I cannot blame her for her frantic efforts to regain the respect & love of her husband – which she has not had for more than twenty years. . . . Though she has gone her own way all these years, & never tried to keep him, doing all the time things morally certain to do worse than alienate him from her – yet now when she sees he has turned to me . . . she chafes & raves & cannot endure it. The greatest joy in life lay beside her for years, & she never moved to retain it, even pushed it from her. Now it has left her irrevocably, & she sees the awful loss & void. She has the husk, from which the soul has departed. And I cannot blame her, nor do other than deeply pity her.

Sue, added Mabel, has tried "coldness, hauteur, affectionateness, commanding, indignation" but "nothing succeeds."

All this made for unhappiness at home and social unpleasantness abroad, but it was superficial compared with the much deeper incompatibilities from which it apparently sprung. Not only had Austin's romantic dreams (as he had poured them out to Sue in the courtship letters) come to nothing; but, according to Mabel's account, Sue was an unwilling partner in his more realistic hope of strengthening the Dickinson line, or even perpetuating it. What he discovered—and "at once"—wrote Mabel in her journal (December 16, 1885) was Sue's "morbid dread of having any children." In her final summing up, in 1932, of her relations with the Dickinsons,[1] Mabel returned to this theme of Sue's distaste for marital relations. Sue, she wrote, called them "low practices" and kept Austin from her for many months after the wedding. Sue's attitude "hurt and distressed his life to the quick. . . . His life has been in all home things a terrible failure." Ned, the first child, was born a full five years after the

---

1. See the document "Scurrilous but True," reproduced fully in Appendix II, 4.

wedding and only after Sue (according to the journal entry) had "caused three or four to be artificially removed" and had failed in repeated attempts to prevent his birth. Years later (journal, October 18, 1891), Mabel reiterated that statement. Speaking of Austin's life of "bitter pain and disappointment," she wrote, "Sue's unnatural, cowardly horror of having any children turned all life dark to him for years – she had four killed before birth." To add to Austin's miseries, Ned became an epileptic (the result, thought Mabel, of Sue's efforts to "get rid of him"). Here, too, Sue turned out to be no tough and capable daughter of the soil. According to Mabel, she cowered in terror while Austin dealt with Ned's nocturnal fits, whose thrashings fairly shook the house. This "night horror" (as Mabel called it) was a severe strain on Austin, whose "nervous system [is] so exquisitely delicate and high strung."

These revelations may all be factual; they may not be; they may be partly so. In "Scurrilous but True," Mabel set them in the broad perspective of Sue and the town and brought in another witness to Austin's confidences, her husband David.

> While never saying anything unjust of his family, Austin told us, gradually, the entire tale of his life's utter disappointment, not only in the affected and pretentious Sue, but of her having caused his son Ned and his daughter Mattie to assume the attitude of utter superiority to the town and all his neighbors which they preserved through life and which caused profound anger in many persons quite as good in family and attainments as the two young people. Their mother had so instructed them that neither could act naturally or honestly toward the world. He also told us the real cause of Ned's delicacy – which cannot be repeated here.

A penciled scrap in the Todd-Bingham Archive, in Millicent Todd Bingham's handwriting and apparently a memorandum of a conversation with her mother, adds some specifics to the charge of the abortions and Ned's poor health:

> Sue had several abortions. Dr. Breck of Springfield, as she thought it disgusting to have children. She tried to get rid of Ned but he was born in spite of her but was an invalid, epileptic fits in his sleep. . . . His mother afraid of him so father had to go to him & he thought it gave him (Austin) heart disease. Ned woke on such mornings with a sore mouth from having bitten his tongue.

The darkest revelation of all is recorded in the long entry of December 16, 1885. It gives disturbing substance to Mabel's rhetoric—the "wretchedness" and the "horrors" of Austin's home life, Sue's "chafing" and "raving" and her "chaotic" behavior. As to its credibility, it at least is in line with a cluster of facts, near-facts, and allegations about Sue that all point to something ruthless and ungovernable in her nature: her bursts of temper, people leaving town because of her cruelty, her alleged alcoholism (supposedly inherited from her father), Vinnie's mortal fear of her after Austin died, and Vinnie's charge that Sue by her "cruel treatment" shortened Emily's life ten years. The crucial passage from Mabel's December 16 entry, furthermore, contains the very wording of Austin's cryptic directive to Vinnie on the packet of letters: "If anything should happen to me. . . ." The difference is that it specified the reason for his alarm:

> Her [Sue's] fits of horrible & entirely unrestrained temper have put Austin several times in danger of his life, & he says if anything should happen to him suddenly we may be tolerably sure she has killed him in a sudden wrath.

Then, as if to sum it up, there is a scrap in Mabel's hand that has survived in the family papers. Enclosed in an envelope labeled "Austin's statements to me," it is Austin's life as he described it to Mabel Todd. The items are numbered.

1. Fly in spider's web
2. Entire disappointment in all so-called married life
3. Destruction of various children (not intimated but expressed)
4. Carving knife thrown at you & other fits of diabolical temper
5. The spoiling of your life until you found me – that is, only coming to your own, after years of mistake & endurance.

There is little to corroborate these charges in Austin's letters and diary, though there are the directive to Vinnie, the repeated insistence that he knew no happiness until he met Mabel, the references to his family's behavior that made him want to "smash the machine," and the "animosities [that] surround me" of the letter to his friend in Omaha. We have seen how, in the impassioned letter to Mabel of March 1883, he did *not* write the story of his life, as he set out to do, thinking it would be "better and nobler that I say nothing which involves any other, reflects upon any other! may offend or wound." Once Mabel Todd praised him for his restraint. "He knows his life has been all but spoiled," she wrote in her journal on September 14, 1886, but he is "gentle and generous in his feeling toward the Spoiler." He often admitted to her that the original mistake had been his. "He says she was not made to understand him – so far she could not help." He blamed her only to this extent: "If she had done even as well as lay in her, he could never have blamed her, but not doing even that, & going through life wholly selfishly, & worse. . . ."

It is this last theme—Sue's selfish, pleasure-seeking life—that is reiterated in the surviving volumes of Austin's diary. Even here, whether through reticence or a lawyer's shrewdness, he is terse and detached. His infrequent comments seldom go beyond irritation with Sue's ways, or weariness with the social gatherings in his house. From 1880 on, the references are frequent to "Sue and her crowd," their outings, dances, "sprees," "riots": "A riot in the house till 10½" (June 17, 1880). On June 19, 1882, the party for Ned's twenty-first birthday lasted until one in the morning "in a wild tear and revel, everything being turned inside out and upside down, and one dancer jamming right through a register." At another time he declared himself "tired to death" with his family's pursuit of pleasure and called his house (June 20, 1882) "my wife's tavern." On May 11, 1883, two friends of Ned's arrive "to commence a series of orgies here." But there is no indication anywhere in the diaries of the kind of pressure or fear that Mabel Todd reported; compared with her rhetoric, Austin's is neutral indeed. The many entries about Ned's epileptic seizures make no complaint about Sue's lack of cooperativeness—nor, for that matter, do they mention her help. All that can be gathered from the diary is the impression of a busy man whose tastes, interests, and friends differed diametrically from those of his wife. He loved nature—his daily entries never failed to mention the weather and the look of things—while Sue loved society. He worked, while Sue (as he saw her) played. Emily hit off at least this superficial difference between them in an epigram in 1877: "[Austin] is overcharged with care, and Sue with scintillation."

Mabel Todd's youth, involvement, egocentrism, her turn for the dramatic—all these must be considered in evaluating her account. Her own behavior was not above reproach, and there were those in town who reproached her severely. During its thirteen-year history, in spite of all precautions, her affair with Austin became public knowledge, and gossip flew. On one side, she was branded as flirt and troublemaker (as Ned had accused her to his mother); on the other, there were those who blamed Sue for making Austin's life miserable and wished him joy of Mrs. Todd. (The second Mrs. Mather, wife of Professor Richard Mather and close neighbor of the Dickinsons, is reported to have said, "If after all his years of misery, Austin can get any joy from Mrs. Todd, he deserves it.") Still others thought that Austin was shockingly irresponsible and self-indulgent. In the eyes of the town, none of the three principals was blameless, and one would gladly dismiss the affair as another village quarrel were its implications not so important.

At the very least, the gossip that has come down in bits and snatches has tended to erode the notion of "Sweet Sue" as surely as the notion of "Our Emily" must now be relegated to myth. Life in the Evergreens can no longer be regarded in the idyllic light of the early biographies of Emily Dickinson. Though Austin had enemies, he was generally respected and loved and hence was less the target of gossip than the others. Young Mrs. Todd was much criticized at first for her "modern" ways but only later came in for vindictive gossip. Socially, Sue was a ruling power for sixty years in the town. (She was so good at it that Samuel Bowles would have given her a degree.) But she made many enemies. "Never have I lived where one family ruled as the D[ickinson]'s did in Amherst," wrote Lavinia's friend Mary Lee Hall, who came to the town shortly before Emily died and lived there twenty years. By "Dickinsons," she meant Sue. It will be clear later how far from benign she thought that rule was.

The recurrent themes in the gossip about Sue are snobbery and love of dominance. When the orphaned Newman sisters came to live in the Evergreens in 1858, Sue seemed to enjoy "treating them like poor relatives."[2] Clara reported that, for punishment, Sue made her study entire evenings "in a lighted bay window with the shades up," an indignity she remembered the rest of her life. A faculty wife wrote to her son in 1876 that Mrs. Jenkins, wife of the minister, at first a great favorite of Sue's, had become "disgusted – with the patronizing and the flattery and the hollowness." It was this same faculty wife who described the Mathers two years later as being "very sorry for Miss Vinny – Mrs Austin rides it rough shod over her – "

There are many other scratchy comments in the annals. Two more will suffice. They point, in different language, to the same thing. Professor John Burgess, whose praise of Sue's social talents we have already heard, admitted that she was "a little too aggressive, a little too sharp in wit and repartee, and a little too ambitious for social prestige." Alfred E. Stearns, recalling in 1946 his boyhood in Amherst, put it less politely:

> In my boyhood days and in common with my friends I had heard stories of a mysterious woman who with her less gifted but equally peculiar sister lived in the house next to that occupied by Austin Dickinson, the treasurer of the college. I knew that these spinsters were sisters of the treasurer and, for this was common gossip, that his wife and daughter Mattie, commonly regarded as the town's outstanding snobs, were a bit ashamed to acknowledge the relationship and treated them as strangers or worse.

As he continued with his reminiscences, Stearns's treatment of what he called the "Todd-Dickinson episode" is decidedly comic, as it must have seemed to a young man who knew very little about it. Austin, thought Stearns, liked Mabel because she was the only one in town who shared his interest in landscape gardening, and the love affair had been blown up by the gossips because someone had seen them out driving together. All smoke and no flame, he concluded.

Whether or not Sue brought her troubles on herself, there is no doubt that she had plenty to bear, much of it far from comic. Life in the Evergreens became unbearably tense, for Sue and the children as well as for Austin. On December 7, 1884, Sue wrote to her daughter: "I carry very many burdens, so heavy that I sometimes feel that you and Ned will be left ere very long without any one but each other"—the assumption being that they had already lost a father. Austin regarded Ned and Mattie as on their mother's side and said as much in his will. That short document left the Homestead and Austin's share in his father's estate to Lavinia, two pictures to Mabel Todd, and all the rest "real and personal" to Sue;

2. From Millicent Todd Bingham's penciled notes on an interview with Mrs. Clara Newman Pearl (Mrs. George E.), Clara Newman Turner's niece, in Haverhill, Mass., September 13, 1932. The whole passage reads:

> [After the death of their parents] the two younger girls [Clara and Anna] were put into Austin's family after his marriage and had a hard time of it. Though they had money, Sue took pleasure in treating them like poor relatives, and made Clara look out for Ned and Anna for Mattie. She was ingenious in cruelties. They went to the Amherst public schools. Sue had a very difficult disposition.

Edward Dickinson (Ned)
Martha Dickinson (Mattie)

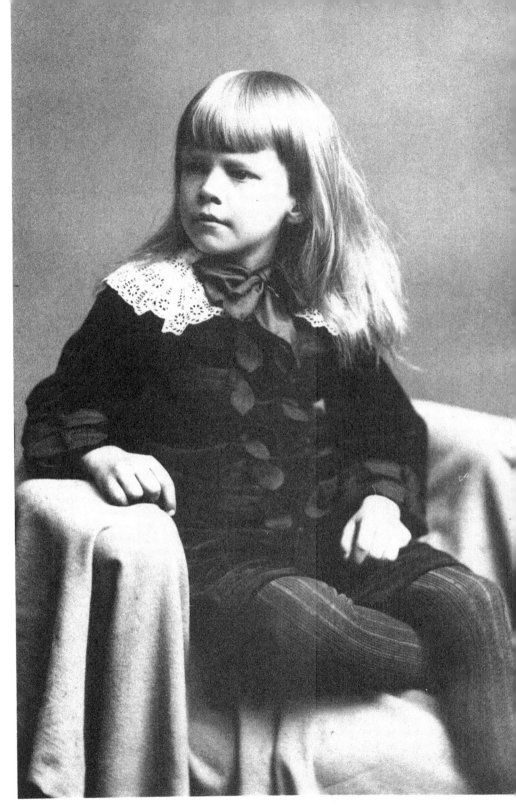

Gilbert Dickinson (Gib)

then: "I make no special mention of Ned and Mattie because they are practically one in interest and feeling with their Mother, and would I presume prefer it in this way to any division." He was completely right about Martha, who was very much her mother's child (as Gilbert was Austin's) and carried on her mother's battle to the end. Ned's loyalties seem to have been mixed. One of his letters shows compassion for his mother; on March 5, 1885, he wrote Martha:

> If there is any beautiful, peaceful, restful place hereafter and [Mother] dont have a seat among the Saints & martyrs – I dont care to go there – Such superhuman efforts to keep up & cheerful, for those around her – mortal eye never witnessed. . . . My only ambition in life . . . is to have a quiet, pleasant little house somewhere – with you and Mother in it, where things can be *pleasant* – No fame, no brains, no family, no scholarship, *No Anything* amounts to anything beside that. . . .

But if this seems to place him completely on his mother's side, later testimony puts it in question. Mary Lee Hall's letters to Mrs. Bingham in the early 1930s several times touch on Ned's attitude toward the family situation. Ned, apparently, became a frequent caller at the Halls' and gave them a sad picture of life in the Evergreens:

> Ned told us that his life had been a "hell on earth," & that the early hour that he daily spent in reading really worth while things, was what kept him sane, and half decent.

In another letter (three years later) Miss Hall returned to the "hell on earth" theme, with a pathetic Austin-Sue scene and more than a hint of Ned's attitude:

> I have wondered if Sue and Mattie knew that he [Ned] came to the house, and talked freely about the home life. He told of the friendship of Austin and your Mother, said he could not blame his father, altho' he called the attention indiscreet because of the terrible scenes it caused in the family. There were weeks when Sue would not speak to Austin, and when Austin would not speak to her. Ned had seen his Mother kneel at his father's feet, and beg him to speak to her. I truly believe that in his heart, Ned put most of the blame upon his Mother. He said that he and Mattie had grown up in an atmosphere of Hell.

In another of Ned's comments his feelings are put more precisely. He told Miss Hall that he "had always admired [Mrs. Todd], and had never changed in his feelings for [her], but he felt obliged to hide his feelings, and to stand by his Mother even though he considered her to be entirely responsible for what had happened."

Such comments seem sufficient, at least, to rule out the possibility that Mabel Todd willfully falsified her account of Austin's marriage. And it should be said that she, like Ned, had sympathy for Sue and (to her credit) recognized Sue's abilities from the beginning and never ceased admiring them. Even during the painful months of 1883, when the affair with Ned opened the first rift between the families, Mabel wrote to Austin in February, just after the distressing evening:

> Can you see how I can still love her very much? But I do – she stimulates me intellectually more than any other woman I ever knew. She is fascinating to me. I would do *anything* to make her like me again. . . . I do care a great deal for her – and I am inexpressibly sorry for her –

Seven months later, when things were even worse, she noted in her journal (September 16, 1883): "Notwithstanding all that I hear about her, I do admire her mind."

By the time of Susan's death in 1913, much had happened to fix forever the hostility between the two women. Sue had been furious when she heard that Lavinia had engaged Mabel to edit the poems. No one in the Evergreens was allowed to speak to Vinnie for months; Sue forbade the mention of her name—and Emily's—in the household. Mabel wrote (journal, November 30, 1890):

> [Vinnie] is constantly exasperated and outraged at Susan – as well as hurt and wounded to death by her cruelties. She seems at times to be curiously in fear of her, and she used to wish not to offend her. Of course she knew that Susan would want to kill her as soon as she found out that I had brought out the poems.

Her "crowning atrocity," as Mabel called it, was to claim that Emily had bequeathed the poems to *her* and that Vinnie's actions were illegal, a charge, however, that Sue never pressed. When Vinnie took legal action in 1898 against the Todds for the strip of land Austin had deeded them, Mabel, of course, saw Sue's hand in the operation, and all chance of reconciliation was gone. So it is noteworthy that in her diary (May 13, 1913) for the day after Susan died, Mabel, though still critical of Sue, was capable of some admiration and compassion. At least she seems to have understood, as Emily did, the paradox and the power of Sue's nature:

> Poor old Susan died last night. A very curious nature, full of (originally) fine powers most cruelly perverted. She has done incalculable evil, and wrought endless unhappiness. At times she seemed possessed of a devil – yet could be smoothly winning & interesting. Close to the surface was always the Tartar.

Mabel's final deposition, the document "Scurrilous but True," came nineteen years later, the year, as it happened, of her own death (1932). To one familiar with the journal and letters, it presents few surprises. The old charges are there: Susan's aggressiveness in getting Austin to marry her, her attitude toward having children, Austin's mistake in thinking that, by marrying out of his social class, he would strengthen his family line, Sue's cruelty to people in the town and the town's "thorough distrust" of her. There are some interesting additions, however, to certain aspects of the situation already familiar to us. She described her first impression of Austin and Susan:

. . . when these two called upon me, as they did shortly after my arrival in Amherst, I was much impressed with both. He was a truly regal man, tall and magnificent in bearing, and she well-dressed with an India shawl over her shoulders, which became her dark beauty.

She recorded her first intimations of trouble, intimations in the form of warnings from both Vinnie and Sue:

"I hope you will not go very much to the other house," said Vinnie one day shortly after my visits there had become regular and expected; "I have seen too many hearts broken there," she went on, "and always to those liked and loved at first."

It was on this occasion that she saw herself becoming involved in "a family quarrel of endless involutions," the "mazes of feeling between the two houses." Vinnie warned her about the Evergreens; Sue warned her away from the Homestead. The battle lines between the houses were well established by the early 1880s:

About this time Sue, as she was called in the village, began to tell me about a remarkable sister of Austin's who never went out, and saw no one who called. I heard of her also through others in town who seemed to resent, somewhat, her refusal to see themselves, who had known her in earlier years. Then came a note from this mysterious Emily's housemate, her sister Lavinia, demanding that I call 'at once, with my husband'. Sue said at that, 'You will not allow your husband to go there, I hope!' 'Why not?' I asked innocently. 'Because they have not, either of them, any idea of morality,' she replied, with a certain satisfaction in her tone. I knew that would interest my good husband, and pressing her a little farther, she added, 'I went in there one day, and in the drawing room I found Emily reclining in the arms of a man. What can you say to that?' I had no explanation, of course, so I let the subject drop, notwithstanding which I went to the ancestral mansion in which the two lived a few days later.

Sue's disparagement of Emily here brings up the entire problem of the Sue-Emily relationship later described so confidently by Martha as a "romantic friendship" that extended "from girlhood until death."[3] The

3. *The Single Hound* (1914), ed. Martha Dickinson Bianchi, "The Editor's Preface," p. v. Cf. Martha also in her *Life and Letters of Emily Dickinson:* "Her sister Sue recognized her genius from the first, and hoarded every scrap Emily sent her from the time they were both girls of sixteen. Their love never faltered or waned" (p. 64). In *Emily Dickinson Face to Face,* Martha becomes even more lyric; speaking of the notes Emily sent in a continuous stream across the lawn, she writes (p. 176):

Scores of such short notes were also given in the text of "Life and Letters," as they best flash a quick hint of the varied sympathies always existing between Aunt Emily and my mother – from their first girlish wonderings about life, on through the books they shared, the flowers they tilled, the friends they loved, their culinary wizardry, their domestic crises, their absorption in us children, their fun and fears, their gay whimsies and tragic realities; all their deepening experiences uniting to weld the confident and profound devotion enduring unto death.

following passage from "Scurrilous but True," however biased it may be, at least shows how questionable Martha's description is. During her first talks with Vinnie, Mabel continued:

It quickly came out that Vinnie was herself nearly heart-broken over Sue's treatment of Emily, and herself too, only she never counted anything done to herself in comparison with anything involving her adored Emily. She often said she knew that Emily would die years before she ought owing to the cruelties practiced upon her almost ever since poor Austin was "taken in" and made to marry outside of his normal class, socially. Her account was really sad and terrible. At first Emily had tried to make her only brother like and marry her early friend, Sue Gilbert, and for some years she aided and abetted the match, which had made Austin at first melancholy to an unprecedented degree. . . . For years before I came to Amherst Emily had not had any affectionate relations with the Sue once so loved, and Vinnie had not been to her brother's house for years. . . . Every day he visited them, and it was really a genuine refreshment of spirit to him.

Here is Mabel's summing up of Sue, the marriage, the "War between the Houses" and Austin's role in it:

"Sue" was a person full of certain kinds of ability, never used in any noble manner as help or affection for her fellow townsmen, but practically always in their detriment; for many years before my coming to Amherst there had been no real communication between the two Dickinson homes. The two sisters lived their own life entirely independent of the "other house" and Austin was the only link between. He went to see his sisters every day, and they loved and revered him all the more since his profound unhappiness in his marriage had left him few satisfactions in his home. The story of his disenchantment with Sue was told me, first by indifferent persons in town, and then more in detail by Lavinia with a few comments by Emily in her curiously interrogative voice from the next room.

The tone, compared with the letters and journal, is detached; but the position is the same. Sue, the alien element, had brought on the war and wrecked their lives. There is no word of self-reproach, no sense that she, Mabel Todd herself, had entered the situation as an alien element and had precipitated its worst phase. Her position was simple: Austin had been hers by divine right; Sue had forfeited him.

11

Susan and Emily

S USAN," said Emily, "fronts on the Gulf Stream." "What depths of Domingo in that torrid Spirit!" Whatever these two remarks (both in notes to Sue during the last three years of Emily's life) may imply in a moral way about Emily's estimate of Susan's character or behavior, they are tributes, if nothing else, to her power. To have lived next door to such a person for thirty years was an experience, and what Sue saved of the notes that crossed the narrow strip between the Homestead and the Evergreens fairly tingle with it. What Emily made of the experience, what it did for her or to her are vital questions. At the very least, her relation- ship with Sue was one of the controlling influences in her life. The girl- hood phase did not last long and ended sadly for Emily. What scars it left can only be guessed at. Emily in her maturity was seldom discursive on any aspect of her personal life and never on this.

The materials to go on are few and ambiguous. The most important, of course, are the dozens of notes that Sue kept. These are mostly very brief (Emily's early effusive style disappears soon after Sue's marriage); many of them are cryptic, or gnomic, or Delphic; and many can be dated only approximately. There are a few comments by observers, like Lavinia's as passed on by Mabel Todd and Mary Lee Hall, and then there is Martha Dickinson Bianchi's account, which gives only the happy side. There is a brief, troubled letter from Sue to Emily. There are a few poems that mention Sue by name and a cluster of others that by imagery, metaphor, and similar phrasing seem fairly surely to be about her or to have come out of their relationship.

Even a casual run through the notes makes the problem clear. In spite of all we know about the "War between the Houses" and what it tells about Emily's estrangement from Sue, terms of endearment persist to the end.

There is no clear evidence of a break—nothing as forthright as Emily's youthful pronouncement: "Sue – you can go or stay." There are some edgy notes and signs of strain. There is one bit of verse about a rejection that may be a cry from the heart. But, though not always loving, the tone of the thirty-year correspondence is mostly cordial. One wonders if Emily was being characteristically reticent, or hiding her true feelings behind irony and wit, or trying to keep the surface of things smooth for Austin's sake. Or Martha Bianchi, to give the impression of a love that never faltered, may have suppressed evidence or altered dates in her zeal to defend her mother.[1] The problem may never be solved, but it is important that its terms be understood.

A few general truths seem beyond question. We have seen that Emily had an all but obsessive concern for every member of her family. She kept an anxious eye not only on their private concerns (Father's loneliness or Vinnie's headache), but she was interested all her life in their public lives—whether her father's associates in Washington understood him, or how Austin was getting along with his students in Boston. Even when her withdrawal was most complete, her letters are peppered with gossip and personal matters. We know how close she and Austin were from the beginning; she had early spotted him as a worrier, and she worried about him. We know that she felt herself a part of his courtship, and it is inconceivable that she did not become involved in the much more intense drama of his marriage. When the Homestead became Austin's spiritual home, at the very least a refuge from the tensions of the Evergreens, Emily would hardly have tolerated his daily conversations about Mabel Todd (as he described them in the summer of 1885) if she had not long understood his situation and sympathized with him.[2] And there is the report by Mrs. Jameson that on the night of Gilbert's death Emily had come to Sue and Austin's house for the first time in "15 years." On an even more general level, the "Dickinson difference," an axiom of Emily's youth, reflects her hope that Sue would join the inner circle and be one of them, a true sister. But the fact is that the loving and fruitful relationship Emily hoped for did not materialize.

It may have been just as well for Emily's poetry, if not for her happiness, that Sue turned out to be a very un-Dickinsonian Dickinson. She

---

1. Cf. David Higgins, *Portrait of Emily Dickinson: The Poet and Her Prose* (1967), p. 37: "Sue's daughter, Martha Dickinson Bianchi, fostered the image of 'Sister Sue,' Emily's *alter ego* with a 'sixth sense for Emily's real meaning.' In doing so, she misdated poems and letters until it seemed that Emily had praised Sue in prose and verse from the mid-eighteen forties to the end of her life." Higgins appends a revealing note: "The misdating began with Sue. In March 1853, when both Sue and Emily were twenty-two, Emily sent Sue [the poem] 'On this wondrous sea.' Mrs. Bianchi wrote on the manuscript, 'The first verse Aunt Emily sent to Mamma – (She *thought* when both were sixteen or so.)' Sue's later transcript of the poem survives; on it she wrote '1848.' See *P* I, 6–7."

2. For "the little visits with my sisters" (letter of July 12, 1885), see Chapter 9, p. 178.

expanded Emily's horizon and was a vital part of her education. In 1882 (late enough to be a summing up), Emily put the matter to Sue in her usual ambiguous way: "With the exception of Shakespeare, you have told me of more knowledge than any one living – To say that sincerely is strange praise."[3] "Strange praise," surely, if she implies what seems obvious: a Shakespearian range of temperament and qualities, evil as well as good—as Mabel Todd (and, as we shall see later, Mary Lee Hall) summed them up, the "originally fine powers," the charm and wit, the touch of the devil and "the Tartar." Clearly, Emily reveled in the wit and the fine powers; it also seems clear that she felt at times the touch of the devil—the "Gimblets – among the nerve – " She learned from both.

For two years after the wedding (July 1, 1856) there were no letters— at least there are none extant. Whether Emily knew that Austin realized his mistake in marrying Sue—"at once," as Mabel Todd said—is impossible to say. At least his alleged unhappiness did not prevent Emily's frequent visits to the Evergreens. It was in 1859 that Emily called Austin and Sue "my crowd." When the correspondence resumed in the fall of 1858, there was some, but not much, of the old feeling and a good deal of verbal play. On September 26, a brisk, cheerful, gossipy letter went off to Sue, then visiting sister Martha in Geneva.

> I hav'nt any paper, dear, but faith continues firm – Presume if I met with my "deserts," I should receive nothing. Was informed to that effect today by a "dear pastor." What a privilege it is to be so insignificant! Thought of intimating that the "Atonement" was'nt needed for such atomies! . . .
>
> Ah – Dobbin – Dobbin – you little know the chink which your dear face makes. We would'nt mind the sun, dear, if it did'nt *set* – How much you cost – how much Mat costs – I will never sell you for a piece of silver. I'll buy you back with red drops, when you go away. I'll keep you in a casket – I'll bury you in the garden – and keep a bird to watch the spot – perhaps my pillow's safer – Try my bosom last – That's nearest of them all, and I should hear a foot the quickest, should I hear a foot – . . .
>
> God bless you, if he please! Bless Mr John and Mrs Mat – Bless two or three others! I wish to be there – Shall I come? If I jump, shall you catch me. . . .

And so on, with some tender farewells to the whole household. It is a cordial letter, surely, but the old passion and the yearning are gone. Emily, it seems, has learned that Sue the married woman was not to be the soul mate and confidante so longed for in the early years. Rather, Sue emerges as someone with whom, at a safe distance, she could at least play at wit and love. Such, at any rate, appears to be the meaning of the strained

3. The editors of the 1958 *Letters* (III, 733 n.) comment as follows on this remark, a complete letter in itself: "The strain between the two houses about this time had perhaps a temporary fission. . . . It is probable that Sue's resentment concerning the attachment of Emily to Judge Lord was made clear to Emily, and may account for this note of 'strange praise.'"

metaphors—the piece of silver, the red drops, the casket, her pillow, and her bosom. It can hardly be imagined that Sue took them seriously.

On the social level, Emily learned much from Sue, and much that was good. Her parties helped keep Emily in circulation, at least for a while. There were lively evenings at the Evergreens, during one of which Edward Dickinson himself arrived at the indecent hour of midnight to fetch his daughter home. Emily played and sang (we are told) her inimitable songs, and there was much laughter. Often there were interesting people at Sue's, and, much as she was inclined to run from them, Emily enjoyed their talk. She described a typical evening in a letter to Mrs. Holland (about February 20, 1859):

> . . . sitting next evening with S[ue],[4] as I often do, some one rang the bell and I ran, as is my custom.
> What was my surprise and shame, on hearing Mr. Chapman ask for "Mrs. D!" K[ate] S[cott], a guest of [Sue]'s, was my confederate, and clinging fast like culprit mice, we opened consultation. . . .

They were "detected" and Emily "gasped a brief apology":

> I do not mind [offending] Mr. Hyde of Ware [whom, with Mr. Chapman, the Edward Dickinsons had entertained the evening before], because he does not please me, but Mr. Chapman is my friend, talks of my books with me, and I would not wound him.

At least at Sue's she could talk books and get away from the austerity that, with Austin gone, was settling in at the Homestead. Whatever she said later about Sue's scintillation, at this point she delighted in it.

Intellectually, Sue was as lively as anyone in town. The two exchanged books, gave them to each other as presents, and (presumably) discussed them. Although, after the early years, Emily never unbosomed herself on important, personal matters in her extant letters to Sue (she *did* to other intimates, like the Hollands and the Norcross cousins), there is enough in her tiny notes to Sue to show rapport on many levels, if not the deepest. They enjoyed Biblical and literary allusions, usually with a whimsical turn and often so private as to be a kind of code language between them. (In the "Gulf Stream" note Emily comments on a coincidence that gave her pause: "Do you remember what whispered to 'Horatio'?") They

4. L II, 348-49. Sue's name was originally deleted by Austin. Millicent Todd Bingham (*Home*, p. 54) gives the following explanation:

Mr. Dickinson stipulated that if Emily's letters to him were to be used [in the publication Mrs. Todd was then preparing in the early 1890s], the name of one of her girlhood friends must be left out – that of Susan Gilbert, his wife. But omitting her name was not enough. Before turning over the letters he went through them, eliminating Susan Gilbert's name and in some instances making alterations to disguise a reference to her. He asked my mother to make sure he had overlooked nothing. In the published volumes Sue's name does not appear. It has been said that her name was omitted at her own request. This is not the case. Mrs. Dickinson was not aware that publication of Emily's letters was in prospect.

indulged their private skepticisms and being quizzical together. Emily called it "the clandestine Mind" and practiced her gnomic style on Sue. "In a Life that stopped guessing," she wrote, "you and I should not feel at home – "

The extent of Sue's help with Emily's poetry is impossible to document, except for the one instance of the poem "Safe in their Alabaster Chambers." She praised the poem, with reservations:

I am not suited dear Emily with the second verse – It is remarkable as the chain lightening that blinds us hot nights in the Southern sky but it does not go with the ghostly shimmer of the first verse as well as the other one – It just occurs to me that the first verse is complete in itself it needs no other, and can't be coupled – Strange things always go alone – as there is only one Gabriel and one Sun – You never made a peer for that verse, and I *guess* you[r] kingdom does'nt hold one – I always go to the fire and get warm after thinking of it, but I never *can* again – . . .

The note, besides being remarkably perceptive criticism, shows Sue as a mentor of some standing. In reply, Emily composed two alternates for the second stanza, chose one, and sent it to Sue with the question, "Is *this* frostier?" She appended a note that is as close as she got to announcing her literary ambitions in these years (the time was about 1860 or 1861) and is a measure of her confidence in Sue's judgment:

DEAR SUE –
    Your praise is good – to me – because I *know* it *knows* – and *suppose* it *means* –
    Could I make you and Austin – proud – sometime – a great way off – 'twould give me taller feet –[5]

After the "Alabaster Chambers" episode there is no record of Emily's asking Sue's opinion again. Emily may have sensed a barb in Sue's "You never made a peer for that verse, and I *guess* you[r] kingdom does'nt hold one – " The emphasis in Emily's reply—"*suppose* it *means*"—might imply a doubt of Sue's kindly intentions. Only a few months later she turned to another mentor, Thomas Wentworth Higginson. At any rate, her respect for Sue's mind, and style, never wavered. In two separate notes of about 1881 she wrote: "Balm for Susan's Voice – Could sooner spare the Nightingale's – " and "Your impregnable syllables need no prop, to stand – "

Sue was not only capable of impregnable syllables, she brought out some of Emily's best. If Emily's audience had all been Sues—at least Sue of the "Alabaster Chambers" exchange—the history of her publication might have been different. Emily's virtuosity is seldom as brilliant as in these messages that sped from one house to the other. They are in a style she particularly (though not exclusively) reserved for Sue: tight, elliptical, almost always figurative.

5. The story of this exchange is told in full, and the episode dated summer 1861, in *P* I, 151–55, n.

The dominant tone is clear: it is one of admiration and gratitude for the privilege of living near such a person as Sue. The language is almost never neutral. Hyperbole is the rule, and images of uniqueness, size, power, totality abound. "Only Woman in the World, Accept a Julep – " "That Susan lives – is a Universe which neither going nor coming could displace – " "To thank one for Sweetness, is possible, but for Spaciousness, out of sight – " Sue is at one time her "vast" and at another her "great" sister. "I must wait a few Days before seeing you – You are too momentous. But remember it is idolatry, not indifference." Ten years earlier (about 1868) it had been: "Susan's Idolator keeps a Shrine for Susan." "To miss you, Sue, is power. The stimulus of Loss makes most Possession mean." The qualities in Sue that irritated many people in town—her social ambition and worldliness—Emily apparently cherished as welcome change from the usual Amherst fare. "To see you," she wrote Sue, "unfits for staler meetings. I dare not risk an intemperate moment before a Banquet of Bran." Whatever else she might have been, Sue was not pure Amherst. "Susan breaks many Commandments," Emily wrote her about 1879, "but *one* she obeys – 'Whatsoever ye do, do it unto the Glory' – " And once, thanking Sue for a visit: "Thank her dear power for having come, an Avalanche of Sun!"

If all this time Sue (as Vinnie charged) by her "cruel treatment" was shortening Emily's life, there is little in the notes to suggest it. There may be some ill feeling in a cluster ranging over a period of a dozen years (beginning in 1869) that play on the notion of Sue as Cleopatra. One complete note of about 1874 is typical: " 'Egypt – thou knew'st' – " "Tell the Susan who never forgets to be subtle, every Spark is numbered – " wrote Emily about 1884 and included a poem that may have implied a reproach to the "torrid Spirit":

> The farthest Thunder that I heard
> Was nearer than the Sky –
> And rumbles still –
> Though torrid Noons –
> Have lain their Missiles by – . . .   (#1581)

And in 1878: "Susan knows she is a Siren – and that at a word from her, Emily would forfeit Righteousness – " Again (about 1869): "Dont do such things, dear Sue – The 'Arabian Nights' unfit the heart for it's Arithmetic – " She called Sue her "pseudo Sister" in a letter to Higginson about 1881—perhaps a rebuff, but possibly only a good-natured pun.[6] For Christmas 1876, Sue sent Emily a copy of *Of the Imitation of Christ,* inscribed "Emily with love," and in 1880 a copy of Disraeli's *Endymion*

---

6. Thomas H. Johnson, *Emily Dickinson: An Interpretive Biography,* p. 41, sees in it a hint "at some kind of alienation."

SUSAN GILBERT DICKINSON
From a medallion now hanging in ED's room, the Homestead.
Date and artist unknown. Perhaps taken from Sue's pose in
picture of "Shutesbury School of Philosophy"

Facsimile of "Safe in their Alabaster Chambers"
Emily to Sue, early summer 1861(?)

with the inscription: "Emily / Whom not seeing I still love,"—ironic in view of the proximity of the two houses. By this time, apparently, both women realized the distance between them. In late 1885, Emily concluded a brief note with the sentence: "The tie between us is very fine, but a Hair never dissolves." This may relate to a more explicit comment by Mary Lee Hall: "Emily turned against Sue, when Sue deceived her, and was not friendly toward her for more than a year before her death. . . ." What the deception was is not stated.

Two documents from the early 1860s, perhaps an exchange, indicate a much earlier breach than Miss Hall thought. The editors of the 1958 *Letters* suggest that the one from Emily to Sue was written shortly after Ned's birth (June 19, 1861) and is a complaint about Sue's neglecting her for the new baby. The note is a stanza of three lines:

SUE –

> Could *I* – then – shut the door –
> Lest *my* beseeching face – at last –
> Rejected – be – of *Her?*   (#*220, and L II, 381 n.*)

Perhaps Emily felt neglected while Sue was preoccupied with the new baby; but one wonders. Sue had plenty of domestic help (the Newman girls, both able and in their mid-teens, were in residence). Emily was fond of children, welcomed all of Sue's into the world and became devoted to them, as they to her. The note is characteristically ambiguous. It may be Emily's way of leveling an accusation: "Could *I* ever reject you as you have rejected me?" Or it may be part of a dialogue, an answer to an accusation that Emily herself has been aloof, or offish: "I could not possibly have rejected you, as you charge, if only for fear that you will some day ('at last') reject me." At the very least, it indicates trouble; there is no play here. But it is curiously isolated among the steady stream of friendly communications. One can only suspect that others of a similar nature have disappeared.

The other document is a note from Sue to Emily, written in late October of that year.

> *Private* I have intended to write you Emily to day but the quiet has not been mine – I should send you this, lest I should seem to have turned away from a kiss –
>
> If you have suffered this past Summer I am sorry [*cut*]. *I* Emily bear a sorrow that I never uncover – If a nightingale sings with her breast against a thorn, why not *we?* [*cut*] When I can, I shall write –
>
> SUE –[7]

7. The MS (Dickinson Papers, Houghton Library, Harvard) is in three scissored pieces, as indicated by the bracketed *"cut."* The scissorings seem to have been made for the purpose of deletion; but by whom, and why, is unknown.

There is no hint as to the cause of all this suffering—whether, for Sue, it had something to do with Austin and their marriage, or the birth of an unwanted child, or something in her relations with Emily. As for Emily's suffering "this past Summer," our only recourse is to other and not very clearly established facts of her life about this time. This was the year (1861, as far as can be determined from her handwriting) of the second and most anguished of her "Master" letters, drafted but never sent, recipient unknown, and whose theme is passionate and unrequited love. Many of the poems of this time are about loss and rejection. The search for specifics has led to many suggestions, ranging from personal and professional disappointment to anguish over the Civil War and back to premonitions of trouble with her eyes—whatever it was that in a letter of April 25, 1862, to Higginson she had in mind when she wrote, "I had a terror – since September – I could tell to none – "[8] And, according to this note of Sue's, *she* had a sorrow she could tell to none. Sue's nightingale with her "breast against a thorn" makes one suspect a romantic pose. But if Emily's verse note can be related to the withdrawn life that was shortly to intensify, there may be something more to it. As early as the quarrel in 1854, Emily had spoken of their "diverging paths," and now Sue, with her family and social life, was going a way which was clearly not Emily's. At the very least, the idea of rejection was in the air; and from what we know of Emily's sensitive relations with Sue, it would have taken only a hint. And it could have been either way: Sue might have rejected Emily, or Emily might have rejected Sue.

So, for fifteen years, according to the local estimate, Emily withdrew to the Homestead, not once venturing to the Evergreens until Gilbert's death, October 5, 1883. Had he lived, this remarkable child might have brought about some reconciliation between his parents and the two houses. Though there is no record of any loving, conciliatory meeting between Emily and Sue in their grief, the letters that Emily wrote Sue during the next months are among the tenderest since their girlhood. One is perhaps the finest she ever wrote anybody:

Dear Sue –
The Vision of Immortal Life has been fulfilled –
How simply at the last the Fathom comes! The Passenger and not the Sea, we find surprises us –
Gilbert rejoiced in Secrets –
His Life was panting with them – With what menace of Light he cried "Dont tell, Aunt Emily"! Now my ascended Playmate must instruct *me*. Show us, prattling Preceptor, but the way to thee!
He knew no niggard moment – His Life was full of Boon – The Playthings of the Dervish were not so wild as his –
No crescent was this Creature – He traveled from the Full –

8. I have reserved full discussion of these matters for subsequent chapters.

Such soar, but never set –
I see him in the Star, and meet his sweet velocity in everything that flies –
His Life was like the Bugle, which winds itself away, his Elegy an echo –
his Requiem ecstasy –
Dawn and Meridian in one.
Wherefore would he wait, wronged only of Night, which he left for us –
Without a speculation, our little Ajax spans the whole –

> Pass to thy Rendezvous of Light,
> Pangless except for us –
> Who slowly ford the Mystery
> Which thou hast leaped across!   [#1564]
> EMILY.

But beautiful as the letter is, Sue, the grieving mother, is hardly in it at all.[9] In most of her letters of condolence—and no one surpassed her in that delicate art—Emily offered comfort and help and love to her bereaved friends. Here there is only the wonder and beauty of the lost child and the mystery of death. Within a few days of Gilbert's death, Emily sent a flower with a tiny note to "the dear, grieved Heart"; and another note of about the same time spoke more to Sue's grief: "Hopelessness in it's first Film has not leave to last. . . . Intimacy with Mystery, after great Space, will usurp it's place –" But a poem that went with the note is all about the dead boy.

> Expanse cannot be lost –
> Not Joy, but a Decree
> Is Deity –
> His Scene, Infinity –
> Whose rumor's Gate was shut so tight
> Before my Beam was sown,
> Not even a Prognostic's push
> Could make a Dent thereon –

9. Mrs. John Jameson, a neighbor "intimate with both Dickinson households" (*YH* I, lvii), wrote her son Frank three weeks after Gilbert's death. Sue's grief, though apparently not so devastating as Austin's, is sharply etched. (So is the village gossip. Sue's period of formal mourning was indeed, at least in the eyes of Austin and Mabel, unduly prolonged. In their letters she was often called "the great big black mogul.")

> I called on Mrs Dickinson this week and she *kissed* me when I went and when I came away. She is a sad woman – and in fact the whole family are changed. . . . Mrs. D. has seen no one except Madam Stearns and myself – says she cannot, she will break down – and yet – someone said to Helen [Mrs. Jameson's daughter] today that Mrs D. would probably "make a parade of her grief." What an abominable place, a village is, for defamation of character and how easily the worst will be believed of folks – (*YH* II, 411).

The World that thou has opened
Shuts for thee,
But not alone,
We all have followed thee –
Escape more slowly
To thy Tracts of Sheen –
The Tent is listening,
But the Troops are gone! (#1584)

Emily never fully recovered from Gilbert's death. It was a staggering loss. Indeed, in sharing their grief, Emily and Sue might have done much for each other; but there is no sign that they did. When Vinnie described the shock and grief in the two households and confessed her anxiety "for all that's left of this home," it was Austin, not Sue, whom she described as the stricken one. She spoke of her own and Emily's "hard work to keep Austin from following" Gilbert. Not once did she mention Sue as sharing in their efforts. There is no record that Emily's single visit that sad night led to any others.

Searching the poems for what they reveal about the relationship between Emily and Susan also has its problems. A few poems, like the two discussed in an earlier chapter—"I have a Bird in spring," sent in the "you can go or stay" letter in 1854, and "One Sister have I in our house," a letter poem of 1858—are clearly to the point. Both contain elements that qualify the adoring tone of the early letters and foreshadow later rifts. One other early poem that contains Sue's pet name, Dollie, and was probably sent to her, seems even more clearly to reflect early tensions. It is of a piece, surely, with the tone and idiom of that plaintive letter Emily wrote Sue in January 1855 shortly after the quarrel of the preceding September. The theme, we recall, was: "Tell me that you still love me." She missed Sue (then visiting in Michigan), mourned for her, walked the streets "alone – often at night":

If it is finished, tell me, and I will raise the lid to my box of Phantoms, and lay one more love in; but if it *lives* and *beats* still, still lives and beats for *me,* then say me *so,* and I will strike the strings to one more strain of happiness before I die.

The poem seems to come so directly from this state of mind and heart (or from one very much like it) that it is tempting to suggest an earlier date for it than the 1860 assigned in the 1955 *Poems:*

You love me – you are sure –
I shall not fear mistake –
I shall not *cheated* wake –
Some grinning morn –
To find the Sunrise left –
And Orchards – unbereft –
And Dollie – gone!

I need not start – you're sure –
That night will never be –
When frightened – home to Thee I run –
To find the windows dark –
And no more Dollie – mark –
Quite none?

Be sure you're sure – you know –
I'll bear it better now –
If you'll just tell me so –
Than when – a little dull Balm grown –
Over this pain of mine –
You sting – again!   (#*156*)

The girlishness of such poems soon gives way to sterner stuff. The tense "Could *I* – then – shut the door – " is of a different order. While two hundred and seventy-six poems are indicated in the 1955 *Poems* as having been sent to Sue, two more that mention her by name are worth noting. The shorter, a letter poem, is a throwback to the theme of idolatry, puzzling (as usual) in view of the background. It is dated about 1877.

To own a Susan of my own
Is of itself a Bliss –
Whatever Realm I forfeit, Lord,
Continue me in this!   (#*1401*)

At least it is "Susan" now, and not "Susie" or "Dollie." The longer poem presents a peculiar problem centering in Emily's striking alteration of the two concluding stanzas. As the poem appears in the 1955 *Poems,* the concluding stanzas sum up the theme of the mystery of Nature, developed in the poem through the metaphor of the well. It has been a favorite of the anthologists, mostly, perhaps, for its last two stanzas—the final one a little too neat for Emily Dickinson at her best:

What mystery pervades a well!
The water lives so far –
A neighbor from another world
Residing in a jar

Whose limit none have ever seen,
But just his lid of glass –
Like looking every time you please
In an abyss's face!

The grass does not appear afraid,
I often wonder he
Can stand so close and look so bold
At what is awe to me.

Related somehow they may be,
The sedge stands next the sea –
Where he is floorless
And does no timidity betray

But nature is a stranger yet;
The ones that cite her most
Have never passed her haunted house,
Nor simplified her ghost.

To pity those that know her not
Is helped by the regret
That those who know her, know her less
The nearer her they get.   (#*1400*)

The 1955 *Poems* assigns no date to the poem, not even an approximate
one, since there is no autograph of the entire poem to provide a handwriting clue. It is grouped among the late poems on the evidence of the
two variant concluding stanzas, written in the handwriting of 1877, sent
to Sue, and signed "Emily –." Here the name "Susan" replaces "Nature."
The change suggests a good deal about the long tension between the two
women:

But Susan is a Stranger yet –
The Ones who cite her most
Have never scaled her Haunted House
Nor compromised her Ghost –

To pity those who know her not
Is helped by the regret
That those who know her know her less
The nearer her they get –

The change from "nature" to "Susan" raises many questions and
possibilities. Which, in Emily's thinking, came first, nature or Susan?
There may be a clue in a worksheet draft of a seventh stanza written in
the handwriting of about 1871.

> How adequate the Human Heart
> To it's emergency –
> Intrenchments stimulate a friend
> And stem an enemy

In the light of this stanza, the well and its mystery would seem to be figurative of the mystery of *human* nature and the poem as a whole originating in her thoughts about the complexities of a human relationship, though whether Sue was the friend stimulated by Emily's "intrenchments" or the "enemy" stemmed by them must remain a question. Much of the figurative language of the letters to Sue describe her as a force of nature ("Gulf Stream," "torrid Spirit," "Avalanche"), and for Emily it was an easy step from there to a poem about Nature and its mystery. This personal origin, if it is so, may explain the clipped and tart tone of the last stanza of the version as it is usually printed. It has the snap of a retort, and may tell much about the strained relations between the two. But the stanzas still pay their compliment: Sue may have enjoyed being known as a mystery.

In approaching the many other poems possibly about Sue, we must walk warily. It is clear that in her poems and letters, Emily tended to associate certain images, or clusters of images, with specific people, experiences, ideas. Bees, birds, the sea, the crescent, "circumference" or the circle, names of faraway places, images of battle, victory and defeat, even the hour of noon and certain colors—each of these in her writing has a discernible frame of reference. But she was neither systematic nor consistent. She never set up private symbolic structures as Blake or Yeats did. Thus one shrinks from uniformly equating the sea with death, the sky with immortality, noon with perfection and fulfillment—or images of rejection, the sting of loss, and birds of passage with Sue.

Nevertheless, certain connections seem unmistakable. Emily sent "I have a Bird in spring" to Sue in the "go or stay" letter of 1854 and then four years later wrote a poem on a "missing friend" (the date may well have been earlier than the assigned "about 1858") whose second stanza begins:

> I had a crimson Robin –
> Who sang full many a day
> But when the woods were painted,
> He, too, did fly away – . . .   (#23)

We can be fairly sure that the later one is a variant of the first and prompted by the same experience. Nor is it improbable that a poem assigned to the next year (or near it) is still another variant:

My friend must be a Bird –
Because it flies!
Mortal, my friend must be,
Because it dies!
Barbs has it, like a Bee!
Ah, curious friend!
Thou puzzlest me!   (#92, about 1859)

The "barbs" here recall not only the "sting" of the last line of "You love
me – you are sure – " but "the barbed syllables" of another poem also sent
to Sue and of the same period. Here too, one recalls Emily's respect for
Sue's "impregnable syllables" and the sense of loss in "Could I – then –
shut the door":

There is a word
Which bears a sword
Can pierce an armed man –
It hurls it's barbed syllables
And is mute again –
But where it fell
The saved will tell
On patriotic day,
Some epauletted Brother
Gave his breath away!

Wherever runs the breathless sun –
Wherever roams the day –
There is it's noiseless onset –
There is it's victory!
Behold the keenest marksman –
The most accomplished shot!
Time's sublimest target
Is a soul "forgot!"   (#8, about 1858)

If Emily could think of Susan as she plumbed "the mystery that pervades
a well," it is not too much to suggest that she could think of herself here
as the one "forgot." Again, the "epauletted Brother," slain by the barbed
syllables of the word "forgot," recalls the "defeated – dying – " of the
famous poem Emily sent Sue about the same time, the purport of which
Sue could hardly have missed:

Success is counted sweetest
By those who ne'er succeed.
To comprehend a nectar
Requires sorest need.

Not one of all the purple Host
Who took the Flag today
Can tell the definition
So clear of Victory

As he defeated – dying –
On whose forbidden ear
The distant strains of triumph
Burst agonized and clear!   (*#67, about 1859*)

What looks like an intentional summing up of their early relationship occurs in a poem dated "about 1862" but which may have been written much earlier. A copy was sent to Sue and signed "Emily – ." The first four lines recall the metaphor Emily used in the "go or stay" letter of 1854: "We have walked very pleasantly – Perhaps this is the point at which our paths diverge – then pass on singing Sue, and up the distant hill I journey on." The last two lines echo the theme, rhythm, and language of "Could *I* – then – shut the door." The identification seems almost unavoidable:

I showed her Hights she never saw –
"Would'st Climb," I said?
She said – "Not so" –
"With *me* – " I said – With *me*?
I showed her Secrets – Morning's Nest –
The Rope the Nights were put across –
And *now* – "Would'st have me for a Guest?"
She could not find her Yes –
And then, I brake my life – And Lo,
A Light, for her, did solemn glow,
The larger, as her face withdrew –
And *could* she, further, "No"?   (*#446*)

One could move down a long list of further poems about loss, rejection, separation, defeat. Of course, Sue was not the only cause of such sorrow for Emily; her early years were filled with numerous, if not such grievous, separations and losses. But, living next door for much of Emily's life, Sue was a continuous reminder of old wounds that never entirely healed. If these resulted from the "Gimblets – among the nerve," that image suggests another poem of about 1862 in which Sue's social methods at least, as many others besides Mabel Todd experienced them, are nimbly hit off:

She dealt her pretty words like Blades –
How glittering they shone –
And every One unbared a Nerve
Or wantoned with a Bone –

> She never deemed – she hurt –
> That – is not Steel's Affair –
> A vulgar grimace in the Flesh –
> How ill the Creatures bear –
>
> To Ache is human – not polite –
> The Film upon the eye
> Mortality's old Custom –
> Just locking up – to Die.   (#479)

If reports are true, however, Sue's motives were not so pure: she *knew* she hurt. A grim little poem of about 1863 may commemorate, if not the nadir of Sue and Emily's friendship, at least a moment of utter disenchantment. And here, even if the connection must remain problematic, we must keep in mind not only the divergent paths the young women had already taken, but all that Emily, by this time, had probably learned about Sue from Austin's disastrous marriage and his increasing defection from "Sue and her crowd."

> It dropped so low – in my Regard –
> I heard it hit the Ground –
> And go to pieces on the Stones
> At bottom of my Mind –
>
> Yet blamed the Fate that fractured – *less*
> Than I reviled Myself,
> For entertaining Plated Wares
> Upon my Silver Shelf –   (#747)

One final poem, a later one, will serve as coda to this sequence of possibilities. In a way, recapitulating as it does so many of the themes and motifs of the notes and poems that went to Sue or were almost certainly about her, it is the most tempting, as it is the most moving, of them all. Here are the idolatry, the rejection, the strangeness and remoteness, the "Foreigner" living just a hedge away:

> Now I knew I lost her –
> Not that she was gone –
> But Remoteness travelled
> On her Face and Tongue.
>
> Alien, though adjoining
> As a Foreign Race –
> Traversed she though pausing
> Latitudeless Place.

Elements Unaltered –
Universe the same
But Love's transmigration –
Somehow this had come –

Henceforth to remember
Nature took the Day
I had paid so much for –
His is Penury
Not who toils for Freedom
Or for Family
But the Restitution
Of Idolatry.   (#*1219, about 1872*)

It may have been that, while Emily "told the Truth" about Sue sufficiently "slant" in the poems she sent her to obviate an open breach
between them (but with ruthless directness in the poems she wrote for
herself), she kept up a pleasant surface relationship in the letters and
notes in the later years. If this is so, she was true to a frequent theme in
poems since the early years: the theme of the barb, or sting, or inner hurt
not perceived by others, and the protective covering assumed by the one
who has been hurt:

A *Wounded* Deer – leaps highest –
I've heard the Hunter tell –
'Tis but the Extasy of *death* –
And then the Brake is still!

The *Smitten* Rock that gushes!
The *trampled* Steel that springs!
A Cheek is alway redder
Just where the Hectic stings!

Mirth is the Mail of Anguish –
In which it Cautious Arm,
Lest anybody spy the blood
And "you're hurt" exclaim!   (#*165, about 1860*)

If this poem is really about Sue, her cruelties, and Emily's response, it
would alone go a long way toward explaining the cheerful face that
Emily put on their relationship throughout her life. It might explain
Martha Dickinson Bianchi's picture of Emily as humorous, whimsical,
roguish and of the relationship between Emily and Sue as idyllic throughout. It is possible that young Mattie never saw any other side, or was so
dazzled by her aunt's play-acting that she concluded the other side was
unimportant. At any rate, Emily's pose, if such it was, is essential New
England, pure Dickinson from Samuel Fowler to Edward to Emily and

Austin (Vinnie escaped)—the Puritan discipline of restraint. She may have suffered an early and painful rejection by Sue; or she may have rejected Sue and all she stood for. Some such hypothesis, more than Emily's shyness and eccentricity, seems necessary to explain the extraordinary fact that for "15 years," beginning sometime in the 1860s, she did not enter Sue's house only three hundred feet away. And this after a girlhood affection so warm, at least on Emily's part, as to evoke some of the most adoring letters she ever wrote.

12

Publication of the Poems:

Mabel and Austin

THE SAD COMPLEXITIES of Austin's marriage and his involvement with Mabel Todd had effects that lasted long after Emily's death in 1886, his own in 1895, and Lavinia's in 1899. The first, and by far the happiest, came in the late 1880s, when Mabel undertook the editing of the poems and (later) the collecting and editing of as many of Emily's letters as she could locate. This, in turn, led to the final and most public skirmish in the "War between the Houses," the trial about the strip of land deeded to the Todds, in which Susan may have played an important if invisible role. In any case, her treatment of the bereaved Lavinia was the subject of considerable gossip.

Mabel Todd's experience of Emily Dickinson from the beginning of their relationship, both as poet and as person, is important in more than one respect. First, her developing awareness of this strange sister of Austin's is figurative of the experience of all those who succeed in making the journey from the legend to the poet. Even though she never saw her face to face, it could be said that Mabel Todd penetrated, ultimately, to the "real" Emily Dickinson more surely than did any of Emily's close associates. Although she came to Amherst, and to things Dickinson, as the complete ingénue, susceptible to every wisp of sentiment and legend, the more romantic the better, her involvement with the family in the Evergreens led her steadily from youthful enchantment to realities almost too much for her to bear, in the light of which Emily as poet figured ever more powerfully in her consciousness. Second, on a more practical level, her intimacy with the Dickinsons, especially Austin, was essential to her undertaking the editorial task in the first place, and then, in spite of all her interests and distractions, bringing at least a good portion of it to completion. Without her intense loyalty to Austin and the insight and information he provided, it is hard to imagine her persevering in the enormous responsibility of transcribing the poems, a task often of cryptographic proportions, and then of persuading reluctant men of letters and editors that they were worth publishing.

How much practical help Austin gave her is hard to tell. He was continually at hand, in and out of her house on almost daily calls. At one point he presented her with a handsome quartered-oak desk to work on. There is evidence, in manuscript notes and jottings in the Todd-Bingham Archive, that they discussed Emily often. One disappointment, however, in reading through their thirteen-year correspondence is to find so little about Emily and especially about the poems. Apparently, their relationship and the difficulties attending it were too absorbing. What little we have from Austin on Emily comes from fleeting references, with one extended comment in a manuscript note presumably from the period of the editing. But his influence appears in many of Mabel's remarks in various contexts—her letters to her parents, her diary and journal, her prefaces to the *Poems,* her many lectures on Emily following their publication, and in the summary statement "Scurrilous but True"—and these are essential to our understanding of both the poet's retreat from the world and its discovery of her.

Mabel's first reference to Emily came in a letter to her parents of November 6, 1881, only two months after she arrived in Amherst. It had not taken her long to pick up the gossip. Unfortunately, the passage has become a *locus classicus* for most of the elements that make up the still-current myth:

> I must tell you about the *character* of Amherst. It is a lady whom the people call the *Myth*. She is a sister of Mr. Dickinson, & seems to be the climax of all the family oddity. She has not been outside of her own house in fifteen years, except once to see a new church, when she crept out at night, & viewed it by moonlight. No one who calls upon her mother & sister ever see her, but she allows little children once in a great while, & one at a time, to come in, when she gives them cake or candy, or some nicety, for she is very fond of little ones. But more often she lets down the sweetmeat by a string, out of a window, to them. She dresses wholly in white, & her mind is said to be perfectly wonderful. She writes finely, but no one *ever* sees her. Her sister, who was at Mrs. Dickinson's party, invited me to come & sing to her mother some time and I promised to go & if the performance pleases her, a servant will enter with wine for me, or a flower, & perhaps her thanks; but just probably the token of approval will not come then, but a few days after, some dainty present will appear for me at twilight. People tell me that the *myth* will hear every note—she will be near, but unseen. . . . Isn't that like a book? So interesting.

No one knows the cause of her isolation, but of course there are dozens of reasons assigned.

In her diary three months later (February 8, 1882) Mabel recorded her first experience of the poetry: "Went in the afternoon to Mrs. Dickinson's. She read me some strange poems by Emily Dickinson. They are full of power"—a response, incidentally, that joins Mabel with Helen Hunt Jackson as among the very few during Emily's lifetime who left on record unqualified approval of her poetry. Next month (March 26, 1882) she recorded proudly: "Miss Emily Dickinson sent me some exquisite flowers, with a verse."

A few months later (September 15, 1882) Mabel spoke again (this time in her journal), enlarging upon what she had written her parents about Emily. She repeated many of the details—the white dress, the fifteen-year retirement, the idea of "the Myth." In the meantime, however, she had actually visited the Homestead, sung for Emily, and been rewarded with a glass of sherry and a present; so it is not surprising that the Myth had taken on flesh and blood and that, such being Mabel's ear for gossip, the "dozens of reasons" for Emily's retirement were reduced to a few specific ones:

His [Austin's] sister Emily is called in Amherst "the myth." She has not been out of her house for fifteen years. One inevitably thinks of Miss Haversham in speaking of her. She writes the strangest poems, & very remarkable ones. She is in many respects a genius. She wears always white, & has her hair arranged as was the fashion fifteen years ago when she went into retirement. She wanted me to come & sing to her, but she would not see me. She has frequently sent me flowers & poems, & we have a very pleasant friendship in that way. So last Sunday I went over there with Mr. Dickinson. Miss Vinnie, the other sister, who does occasionally go out, told me that if I had been otherwise than a very agreeable person she should have been dreadfully tired of my name even, for she says all the members of her brother's family have so raved about me that ordinarily she would hate the sound of Mrs. Todd. But when I left her on Sunday she took my hand in the shyest, quaintest way, and said she saw plainly that she should have to yield to the same fascination which had enthralled her family; & when I come back [from Washington] she wants me to have stated & regular days for coming there to sing & play. It was odd to think, as my voice rang out through the big silent house that Miss Emily in her weird white dress was outside in the shadow hearing every word, & the mother, bed-ridden for years was listening up stairs. When I stopped Emily sent me in a glass of rich sherry & a poem written as I sang. I know I shall yet see her. No one has seen her in all those years except her own family. She is very brilliant and strong, but became disgusted with society & declared she would leave it when she was quite young. It is hinted that Dr. Holland loved her very much & she him, but that her father who was a stern old New England lawyer & politician saw nothing particularly promising or remarkable in the shy, half-educated boy, & would not listen to her marrying him. Of that I am of course not sure, but it might be so, for I know Dr. Holland has always been an intimate friend of the family. I have heard a great deal about Mr. Samuel Bowles who was the most intimate friend of both Mr. and Mrs. Dickinson. How they did love him!

It is unfortunate that the poem Emily sent in to Mabel with the sherry got less comment than the sentimental picture of Vinnie ("shy," "quaint") and the gossip about Dr. Holland and Samuel Bowles, but it at least gave Mabel another example of the "strange" and "remarkable" poetry that she was later to devote much of her life to:

> Elysium is as far as to
> The very nearest Room
> If in that Room a Friend await
> Felicity or Doom –
>
> What fortitude the Soul contains,
> That it can so endure
> The accent of a coming Foot –
> The opening of a Door –   (#1760, about 1882)

It would be interesting to know how Mabel Todd knew that this poem was "written as I sang." Did Emily tell her, through Vinnie? If the statement is true, it could tell much about the nature of Emily Dickinson's poetry and her method of composition, especially its speed. (The 1955 *Poems,* for instance, assigns an almost unbelievable 366 poems to a single year, 1862.) It might substantiate the theory that more poems than is usually thought came out of specific situations. But it may well be nothing but the product of Mabel's romantic imagination. Years later, in a little black notebook auspiciously labeled "Emily" but containing only the following entry of significance, Mabel again insisted upon the impromptu nature of Emily's composition. But she inserted some qualifying adverbs:

I used to sing to Emily frequently, in the long, lonely drawing-room. But she never came in to listen – only sat outside in the darksome hall, on the stairs. But she heard every note. When I had finished she always sent me in a glass of wine on a silver salver, and with it either a piece of cake or a rose – and a poem, the latter usually impromptu, evidently written on the spot.

It was during the editing of the poems and the letters that Mabel came closest to Emily Dickinson. The story of that undertaking, told by Millicent Todd Bingham in *Ancestors' Brocades,* is a tribute to Mabel's conviction and resourcefulness, though Mrs. Bingham gave only a few hints of the long personal background that made Mabel's involvement so intimate. If her sensitivity to the Dickinson style was not strong enough to keep her (as she explained in her journal, November 30, 1890) from changing "words here and there . . . to make them smoother"—an editorial license for which she has been sufficiently criticized—it is nevertheless safe to say (with Jay Leyda) that without the spiritual kinship she felt with the poet and with the poems we might have had no poems (or letters) at all.

This spiritual kinship is more important than it might seem. What the poems needed was somebody besides Lavinia to believe in them. Except for Helen Hunt Jackson, the professionals had been cool and unreceptive, and no one in Emily's immediate circle, except Vinnie, was moved to do much about them. Vinnie knew that she herself was incompetent. She tried vainly, with "fierce insistence" (according to Mabel), to get Sue to edit them. Mabel described the situation further in her journal (November 30, 1890):

> Susan is afflicted with an unconquerable laziness, and she kept saying she would, & she would perhaps, until Vinnie was wild. At last she announced that she thought nothing had better be done about it, they would never sell – there was not money enough to get them out – the public would not care for them, & so on – in short, she gave it up. Then Vinnie came to me. She knew I always had faith in the poems, and she begged me to copy and edit them – put them all into shape. Then she was sure Col. Higginson would write a preface, and somebody would be willing to publish them, and the desire of her heart would be accomplished. So I took them.

Thus Vinnie turned to Mabel not only as a friend of the family and a literary lady who knew something about publishing but as one who "had faith in the poems." There were many reasons why Mabel might have turned her down. She was deeply involved in her own literary affairs, in Amherst activities, and with Austin. She was giving art and music lessons, teaching school, and painting pictures. When Vinnie came to her, she was on the point of going to Japan with her husband. If she said yes to Vinnie, she knew she could count on Sue's antagonism—and that was something to reckon with. Then, too, the mere size of the task, the difficulties of the handwriting, the endless problem of the variants and the scraps, presented, as she wrote in her journal, an "appalling" outlook. But the years of anguish and frustration, with Austin so near and yet so far, had made her psychologically vulnerable. She too had begun to think of herself as something of a Queen of Calvary. As early as 1885 she wrote in her journal (November 10) of her "very happy & very unhappy" life: "I and my soul are becoming very well-acquainted." For all her intense sociability, she began to feel isolated. "I have a strange sort of life," she wrote (journal, December 15, 1885), "it is not a bit like anybody else's. . . ." She enlarged more and more upon "the ills which press upon me through small, narrow-minded people" (journal, April 30, 1889). Amherst, once so thrilling with its quiet elegance, became almost intolerable, especially when Austin was not there to sustain her. She became disgusted with the "cant" and "hypocrisy" of the preachers at the college church, and told her journal in blunt terms what Emily implied in many an irreverent poem: "Narrow, uncharitable, self-righteous, are the chief characteristics of the shining lights in this faculty" (November 30, 1890). She turned increasingly to her writing. There is even a faint echo, in a confession to her journal (July 15, 1889), of Emily's notion of the therapeutic value of writing—as Emily put it, the "palsy here, – the Verses just relieve –": "I feel more and more," Mabel wrote, "that I must write or die. A literary career is my only relief."

In such a state of mind (it was in the late 1880s that the words "martyr" and "suffering" began to appear in the journal), Mabel was ready to believe in the poems as no one else was. She recognized in them a suffering yet resilient spirit, a tumultuous inner life in sharp contrast to a placid exterior, a defiance of convention and orthodoxy suggestive of the attitude her own relations with Austin had forced her to adopt. As she worked, the sense of spiritual kinship grew (entry of November 30, 1890):

> The poems were having a wonderful effect on me, mentally and spiritually. They seemed to open the door into a wider universe than the little sphere surrounding me which so often hurt and compressed me – and they helped me nobly through a trying time. Their sadness and hopelessness, sometimes, was so much bitterer than mine that

> > "I was helped
> > As if a Kingdom cared."   [#260, about 1861]

> . . . I was strengthened and uplifted.

If the poems could help her so, she felt that others could be helped, too. The project became a mission. She became convinced that Sue was wrong in thinking that there would be no public for the poems. She contrasted her conviction to Vinnie's "blind sort of faith," which came, she thought, from uncomprehending adoration, "not in the least from any literary appreciation of their power."

Mabel's long journal entry for November 30, 1890, provides a full account of the many obstacles (at least they seemed so to her) to be overcome. The first was Thomas Wentworth Higginson, whom Vinnie, knowing that Emily had sent him dozens of poems, had already approached without success. Higginson had always admired Emily's dazzling thoughts but had consistently deplored the form of her poems and had never urged publication. Mabel described his conversion when, early in November 1889, she discussed the poems with him in Cambridge:

> He did not think a volume advisable – they were too crude in form, he said, and the public would not accept even fine ideas in such rough and mystical dress – so hard to elucidate.

> But I read him nearly a dozen of my favorites, and he was greatly astonished – said he had no idea there were so many in passably conventional form, and said if I would classify them all into A B and C he would look them over later in the winter.

When, some months later (he was ill that winter), he finally got around to studying the typescripts Mabel had prepared for him, he declared himself "much impressed"—though not to the extent of backing them all for publication and letting them speak for themselves. He accepted Mabel's "A" list, promoted a few from her "B" and "C" lists which she subsequently rejected, made still further editorial changes, and, against Mabel's judgment, insisted on giving the poems titles, some of which were so clearly mistaken that she later had to intercede with the publishers to make changes.

Nevertheless, Higginson's general approval, as Mabel acknowledged, was essential in persuading the publisher to go ahead at all, and this he finally gave. Even here the route was not easy. Mrs. Bingham tells of her father's report that Higginson first submitted the poems to Houghton Mifflin, for whom he was a reader, only to have them rejected as "queer – the rhymes were all wrong," and his own judgment ridiculed. Higginson, apparently, then endorsed Mabel's suggestion that she take them to Thomas Niles of Roberts Brothers, he himself (so David Todd surmised) being reluctant to take them to another Boston publisher so soon after Houghton Mifflin's rejection. Niles was a likely publisher, but at first he too was reluctant. For several years after Helen Hunt had persuaded Emily to include "Success is counted sweetest" in Niles's No Name anthology, *A Masque of Poets* (1878), Emily had corresponded with him and had sent him seven more poems. But he did nothing with them for reasons he later described to Higginson during the negotiations (June 10, 1890): "It has always seemed to me that it would be unwise to perpetuate Miss Dickinson's poems. They are quite as remarkable for defects as for beauties & are generally devoid of true poetical qualities." But an appraisal from Arlo Bates, a poet himself, and frequent reader for Roberts Brothers, recommended publishing a highly selected group in a small edition (five hundred copies). Its faults, Bates said, would be "colossal," but it would have "the real stuff in no stinted quantities." Bates's list of exclusions (among them the poems "I died for Beauty" and "I shall know why") infuriated Mabel, and she again had to assert herself. Niles agreed to the publication, provided "Miss [Lavinia] Dickinson will pay for the plates." When the book proved successful beyond the expectation of anyone but Mabel—even Vinnie had urged her to hurry before all of Emily's friends died or else there would be "no one left to welcome" the poems—it should be said to his honor that Niles withdrew the final proviso.

All this took time, courage, and faith. Aside from Austin, Mabel had much to overcome even in Amherst, what with Vinnie's passionate but unhelpful devotion and Sue's personal hostility and indifference to the poems (her daughter Martha was even then showing signs of talent that Sue was beginning to take more seriously than Emily's). And even Austin's help was limited. Although he could give her insights into Emily's character and way of life, he seems to have been curiously blind— or deaf—to the poetry. Millicent Todd Bingham says flatly that "he died without suspecting that his sister had been a great poet." Even after the first edition was well launched, his attitude was grudging and tentative. He wrote Higginson (October 10, 1890) to thank him for his article in the *Christian Union* (September 25, 1890) in praise of the *Poems,* just published:

> It struck me, as I read, that you had hit and revealed her exactly, and with great skill, taste, and good judgement. I do not see how she could have been brought before the world, if she were to be brought at all, more aptly and more favorably, and if the little volume meets with any success, I shall attribute it in the main to the labor of love which you and Mrs Todd have given to it, and of which I shall have something more to say hereafter.
>
> Whether it was, on the whole, advisable to publish is yet with me, a question, but my Sister Vin, whose knowledge of what is, or has been, outside of her dooryard is bounded by the number of her callers, who had no comprehension of her sister, yet believed her a shining genius, was determined to have some of her writing where it could be read of all men, and she is expecting to become famous herself thereby, and now we shall see.

If the editing of Emily's poems was to him no more than "a labor of love," of questionable permanent value, Mabel's persistence seems little less than inspired devotion.

Although Austin apparently held aloof from the process of the editing and publishing and never seems to have discussed Emily's poetry with Mabel or anyone else, there are two penciled documents in his hand in the Todd-Bingham Archive (with some scribbled notes in Mabel's on one of them) which show some understanding of what he called her "genius" and her chosen way of life. The first, with Mabel's notes, compares Helen Hunt Jackson and Emily as personalities. The closest he comes to Emily's writing is her schoolgirl compositions.

> It is a little remarkable that two girls – of the Genius of Helen Hunt and Emily Dickinson should have been within three or four years of each other in the same quiet New England village the one the daughter of a minister and professor in the College – the other daughter of a lawyer and Treasurer of the College – both attracting general attention in their childhood the one more by her wild romping rebellious Spirit and ways – the other by her intellectual brilliancy – the one as she grew up meeting the world fearlessly – and triumphantly – adding increasing fame with every year – moving through the country like a Queen – the other, after 18 or 20, gradually withdrawing herself from society till she saw very few except members of her own family – and was known only through memory or tradition – and her letters to those who especially interested her. In her school days – at the primary – at [word illegible] Amherst Academy and at South Hadley – she was not of the best scholars – but the brightest of any social group. Her compositions were unlike anything ever heard – and always produced a sensation – both with the scholars and Teachers – her imagination sparkled – and she gave it free rein. She was full of courage – but always had a peculiar personal sensitiveness. She saw things directly and just as they were. She abhorred sham and cheapness. As she saw more and more of society – in Bos-

ton where she visited often – in Washington where she spent some time with her father when he was a member of Congress – and in other places [*The following is crossed out:*] she could not resist the feeling that it was [ter-ribly] painfully hollow. It was to her so thin and unsatisfying in the face of the Great realities of Life although no one surpassed her in wit or bril-liancy. [*The text resumes:*] notwithstanding the fact that she was every-where sought for her brightness – originality & wit –

Far as Austin may be here from Emily as poet, this sketch deserves a word of comment. In the summer of 1878, there had been a lively discus-sion in the local press (Springfield and Amherst) about the possibility that Emily Dickinson had collaborated with Helen Hunt Jackson in the writing of the "Saxe Holm" stories. "Saxe Holm" was an obvious pseudo-nym, and the stories were immediately (and correctly) attributed to "H.H.," or Helen Hunt. But an anonymous contributor to the *Springfield Republican* (July 25) found the stories much too "morbid, and morbid to the last degree," too "weird and improbable," for the Helen Hunt every-body knew—practical, sociable, "a woman of every day life." The style was altogether (thought the contributor) that of a recluse, timid, quaint, "exquisitely sensitive to the feelings produced by birds and flowers . . . a person long shut out from the world and living in a world of her own. . . . We cannot refrain, also, from picturing her robed in white, like Draxy Miller, whether it be a mourning for a friend, a religious notion like that of Hawthorne's Hilda, or, perchance, the result of some decree of fate. . . ." Before a week was out, the papers of the region (the *Spring-field Union,* the *Amherst Record,* and the *Amherst Transcript*) had narrowed the field to one who "answers in private life to the honored name of Dickinson." This suggestion was promptly quashed by an edi-torial note in the *Republican:* ". . . we happen to *know* that no person by the name of Dickinson is in any way responsible for the Saxe Holm stories."

Despite the *Republican*'s welcome denial, many of the elements of the Myth (and some of the unfortunate ones) were now out in the open. Austin's sketch, with its insistence on Emily's wit and brilliance, her courage, her realistic view of things "just as they were," sounds like a direct answer to the statements in the *Republican*. Perhaps his sketch was an attempt to block out some ideas for Mabel's preface to the *Poems,* second series (1891), since by that time the interest in the poems had stirred up gossip about the Myth all over again. At any rate, the preface contained the gist of Austin's views. "Emily Dickinson scrutinized every-thing with clear-eyed frankness. . . . She had tried society and the world, and found them lacking." She was "never morbid or melancholy. . . ." Mabel went beyond Austin's sketch to add two other assertions, undoubt-edly picked up from Austin (or Vinnie) in conversation: "She was not an invalid, and she lived in seclusion from no love-disappointment." Mabel's penciled notes on the manuscript of Austin's sketch show how closely she followed his lead. They show also the degree of her own empathy with her great subject:

It all seemed to her so cheap and thin & hollow as she saw it, with the solemn realities of life staring her in the face, that she wanted none of it. Never made any difference what sort of day it was – every day was a red-letter day. The greatness mystery & depth of life was so great & overwhelming to her that she could not see how people could go into all this littleness. No suggestion in all her life that she had done anything they did not know about.

And a final, detached jotting on another page:

> Breezy & clear, opposite of morbidness.
> Good judgment and adviser.

The second document in the Todd-Bingham Archive that may throw some light on Austin's view of Emily is a series of jottings on the subject of genius. It seems inescapable that he had Emily in mind. Perhaps some of the items are snatches from his reading, but most seem to be his own, the kind of thing he and Emily discussed together, or later, he and Mabel, when the talk turned to Emily and her genius. They show him in a rare, detached, contemplative mood, more like his sister Emily than the harassed figure we have seen. From the very first, we can almost hear Emily's remark to Joseph Lyman, "So I conclude that space & time are things of the body. . . . My Country is Truth":

Genius is Veracity

With Genius there is always youth and never the obituary eloquence of memory

Talent is Vice president and presiding officer never the King –

Truth is sensibility to the laws of the world and Genius is always governed by truth

Genius deals with the Elemental
the roots of things and takes nothing
second hand

Then, after a space, there are some jottings about "Fancy" and "Imagination." It is hard to resist suggesting that, in what follows, Austin had in mind not only Emily and the imagination to which (as he had written) she gave "free rein" but the two worlds of his own divided life—the world of the Evergreens with "Sue and her crowd" (the delights of Fancy) and the world of the Homestead, where he encountered true Imagination:

Everybody can do his best work easiest

Fancy is full of accidental surprises and amuses the vacant or idle mind –

Imagination silences Fancy –

Fancy becomes speechless in its presence –

Imagination deals with the identity of things

It is more central, Tragic –[1]

If this last is indeed a comment on Emily's imagination, it is one of the best of its generation. One would like to think that Austin is here putting more briefly, and better, what he had written in the sketch—that Emily preferred contemplating the "Great realities of Life" to mixing in society. Mabel expanded upon the idea in her preface; for Emily Dickinson, she wrote:

Every subject was proper ground for legitimate study, even the sombre facts of death and burial, and the unknown life beyond.

She denied the charge that Emily had no humor and reverted to the impression of the "strange power" she had felt in Emily's poems when Sue had first read them to her years before:

She touches these themes sometimes lightly, sometimes almost humorously, more often with weird and peculiar power; but she is never by any chance frivolous or trivial.

Or, as Austin had written, "Imagination silences Fancy."

These comments of Austin's, however, still leave us far from Emily as poet. And yet he must have seen many of her poems, both those that came into his house addressed to Sue and the profusion of manuscripts that Mabel was working on. Early in her journal (September 15, 1882), Mabel called him a "silent poet" whose outlet was nature, not art; and though she later thought his letters publishable, she liked them for very different qualities from those she found in Emily's poems. They were ardent and strong, but she never mentioned any "weird and peculiar power." Austin was pleased, of course, by the popular success of the poems, but there is no evidence that he ever understood it. It can only be concluded that, like many of his more literary contemporaries, he had no ear for Emily's poems, much as he marveled at her "genius." The cadences of Tennyson and Longfellow and their hosts of imitators all but deafened, it would seem, not only Austin but a number of others, like Higginson, who might have helped her.

It was here, perhaps, that Mabel made one of her most important contributions. Though nothing she wrote ever came close to Emily's

1. On the reverse of the torn doubled sheet (9″ x 6½″) on which Austin jotted these remarks, he wrote the following:

"Page 275. Scruples are for common souls – The mark of a lofty heart is to desire all and to dare all – "

The page reference suggests that all these jottings were from his reading. But the remark on "scruples" seems to have been written at a different time and in a different context, probably that of his and Mabel's defiance of convention.

poetry, she heard Emily's subtle music as the others did not. In a day that sought message and uplift and the charm of lilting meters, she was ahead of her time in sensing and articulating the rhythmic and melodic qualities that, among other things, make Emily's poetry remarkable. It is notable that Higginson was not converted to the poems until he heard her read them aloud. If she was first drawn by Emily's strange power and then, as she immersed herself in the editing, found spiritual support "as if a Kingdom cared," she came eventually to see, quite precisely, why it was the poems moved her so. In the preface to *Poems,* second series, she wrote:

> Like impressionist pictures, or Wagner's rugged music, the very absence of conventional form challenges attention. In Emily Dickinson's exacting hands, the especial, intrinsic fitness of a particular order of words might not be sacrificed to anything virtually extrinsic; and her verses all show a strange cadence of inner rhythmical music. Lines are always daringly constructed, and the "thought-rhyme" appears frequently, – appealing, indeed, to an unrecognized sense more elusive than hearing.

If any important figure of Emily's early years had brought this kind of sensitivity to her poetry, her life and her literary career might have been quite different. It is notable, too, that by the time Higginson came to write the preface to the first group published (1890), he had moved far beyond the negative advice he had given Emily in the early 1860s. Although his first praise (always sufficiently guarded to preserve his critical reputation) was for her insights and thoughts that "take one's breath away" and for her "words and phrases exhibiting an extraordinary vividness of descriptive and imaginative power," he spoke admiringly of "an ear which had its own tenacious fastidiousness." His suggestion that the closest literary parallel to Emily Dickinson was the poetry of William Blake must have been based on more than his sense of their sometimes kindred spirit. This new insight, it can be said with some assurance, he owed to Mabel Todd. Whether she was ever as successful in sensitizing Austin's ear to the "inner rhythmical music" of his sister's poetry, we do not know.

Where Austin obviously helped Mabel was in his knowledge of Emily's secluded life and the reasons for it, as he saw them. He took for granted what the community built legends about, and he brought Mabel down from her early lofty, romantic notion of the Myth. She, too, in her preface to *Poems,* second series, had come a long way. The gossipy speculations of the early letters to her parents and of her journal were replaced by a normalized view of Emily's life. She rejected the notion of a "love-disappointment" and described Emily's career as "the normal blossoming of a nature introspective to a high degree, whose best thought could not exist in pretence." In her journal for October 18, 1891, just a few weeks before *Poems,* second series, was published, there is a hint of how much of these opinions she owed to Austin. That month, Higginson had published an article on Emily in the *Atlantic,* with some of her letters. There had been much criticism, including Amherst President Seelye's remark to

Mabel that it was "horrible" to publish the letters and even the poems of "that 'innocent and confiding child.'" Mabel dissented in her journal, and cited Austin's opinion:

> Yet my own opinion is that she thought sometime her own verses might see the light of print, only by other hands than hers. As to the letters, that is different. Those to Mr. Higginson are not of a private nature, and as to the "innocent and confiding" nature of them, Austin smiles. He says Emily definitely posed in those letters, he knows her thoroughly, through and through, as no one else ever did. He tells me many things quite unsuspected by others.

Millicent Todd Bingham, in *Ancestors' Brocades,* questioned her mother's conclusion about Austin's judgment here: "With the fate of her poetry at stake, it hardly seems likely that Emily Dickinson would have attitudinized in front of Colonel Higginson."[2] But it hardly seems likely, either, that among the "many things quite unsuspected by others" Austin told Mabel about Emily, he would have withheld any fact of sufficient importance to invalidate his "normal blossoming" idea of Emily's youth and his theory of her withdrawal. In "Scurrilous but True," Mabel's final comment on the subject is entirely consistent with her remarks in the preface forty years before:

> Her [Emily's] curious leaving of outer life never seemed unnatural to him [Austin]. He told me about her girlhood and her normal blossoming and gradual retirement, and her few love affairs. Her life was perfectly natural. All the village gossip merely amused him.

It is possible, of course, that New England reticence prevailed even over Austin's complete rapport with Mabel; but it is worth noting that

2. *AB*, pp. 166–67. Some slight corroboration for the "normal blossoming" view, at least as it discounts the notion that Emily's life was blighted by a hopeless love affair, comes in an item in the Todd-Bingham Archive. Although Ned Dickinson said he never lost his devotion to Mrs. Todd, he became engaged (a few years before his premature death at the age of thirty-seven) to Alice Hill (later Mrs. Franklin Harris). In a letter to Mrs. Bingham (June 1, 1945) thanking her for the "faint but convincing outline of Ned" in *Ancestors' Brocades,* Mrs. Harris added, "I wish I might have given him something of youth and joy, before he left his unhappy life"; and ten years later she wrote again to agree with one of the main theses of *Emily Dickinson's Home,* which had just been published (letter of June 14, 1955 ?):

> I never believed in any thwarted love affair, except perhaps in the vaguest sense.
> Martha [Dickinson Bianchi] once asked me if Ned had ever mentioned any man to me in connection with Emily – of course he never had – quite naturally she was never a subject of conversation between us – I wish she had been – . . .

In view of the certainty with which Martha Bianchi in *Life and Letters* told the story of Emily's frustrated romance, her quizzing Ned's fiancée seems curious. A final comment by Mrs. Harris, in view of the infinite involutions of the Dickinson family feud, is not surprising at all:

> I was in Amherst that summer Lavinia died [1899] – but [was] only told what they wanted me to know – I was vaguely troubled all the time by what I suspected –

Emily's closest associates agree. Sue's obituary of Emily in the *Springfield Republican* (May 18, 1886), three days after Emily's death, made the same point:

> As she passed on in life, her sensitive nature shrank from much personal contact with the world, and more and more turned to her own large wealth of individual resources for companionship, sitting thenceforth, as some one said of her, "in the light of her own fire." Not disappointed with the world, not an invalid until within the past two years, not from any lack of sympathy, not because she was insufficient for any mental work or social career – her endowments being so exceptional – but the "mesh of her soul," as Browning calls the body, was too rare, and the sacred quiet of her own home proved the fit atmosphere for her worth and work.

But by then the blighted-romance theory was abroad—perhaps, as some think, concocted by Sue for her own purposes and certainly, though much later, given to the world as gospel by daughter Martha for hers (now with the name of Charles Wadsworth publicly attached). The fact that Sue gave no hint of it in the obituary may be a clue to the element of artifice in it. One may be warned, in passing, against taking at face value Sue's assertion that Emily was "not disappointed with the world." What Emily might have been disappointed with, and might have withdrawn from, was precisely the kind of thing Sue would not have been inclined to understand—or, if she understood, to say anything about in public.

Such complexities Mabel ignored as, with Austin's views uppermost in her mind, she prepared to present Emily to the world. Whatever effects her efforts may have had in toning down the Myth, perhaps her greatest distinction was being among the first to "hear" Emily Dickinson and, far from being put off by her irregular form, to sense its creative power. Then she convinced Higginson, in itself a major achievement.

13

Last Phase of the Quarrel

and a Late View of Susan

MANY OF THE COMPLEXITIES that Mabel sidestepped came grimly to light during Lavinia's legal battle about the strip of land deeded to the Todds in return for Mabel's work on the poems. If Alfred E. Stearns, as we have seen, recalled the earlier stages of the Todd-Dickinson episode as comic, he took the trial in 1898 more seriously. It rocked the town, he wrote, dividing it into two irreconcilable camps. But even this, to Stearns, had its ridiculous side—the gossip it evoked and the dinner parties it spoiled. He sobered up when he came to Vinnie's curious reversal toward her old friend and ally, Mabel Todd:

> What means were employed to bring her change of heart to pass can only be guessed. Town gossips played with the topic, suggesting such devious devices as hypnotism, threats, blackmail, and deceit, but these notions were the products of minds too much accustomed to thinking in terms of unsupported evidence and hence were not generally taken seriously. But whatever they were they proved immensely effective, and Lavinia, turning against her former friend and helper, allied herself with her belligerent relatives.

The suggestion here of unscrupulous methods, even if Stearns dismissed it as gossip, recalls other comments closer to the scene of action: Sue "riding rough shod" over Vinnie; Vinnie "curiously in fear" of Sue; Vinnie's charge that Sue shortened Emily's life by her cruelties. And Stearns's report that Sue and Mattie were "a bit ashamed to acknowledge the relationship [with Emily and Vinnie] and treated them as strangers or worse" has the ring of something more than gossip.

Yet it is almost impossible to determine the facts here. Among the "cruelties" which Vinnie reported to her friends were Sue's setting her dogs on Vinnie's cats, appropriating Vinnie's cherished store of manure, and letting her horse trample Vinnie's lawn. Such incidents may be quite on the comic side, but Mary Lee Hall confirms their more somber implications in a late (1935) comment:

> Sue was relentlessly cruel to Miss Vinnie in every possible way, and they hated each other with a deadly hate. . . . I was called to Miss Vinnie's many times to quiet her nerves, and help her recover from Sue's *verbal* blows.

In assessing the situation, especially as Sue's character is brought under the most critical scrutiny, one can only invoke personal opinions and hope that the biases will even up. Mary Lee Hall's letters of the early 1930s are the richest source.[1] Although her friendship with Vinnie indicates her bias, she makes it clear that she lived quite outside the limits of Sue's influence and hence to that extent could write without prejudice. She observed Amherst life for nearly twenty years and wrote about it from the distance of some thirty years, enough time for feelings, it would seem, to cool. Her estimate of Sue, much darker than Mabel Todd's, is recorded with a vehemence that appears to come from deep conviction. "Sue was a jealous woman," she began in one of her milder charges; "she hated Vinnie because Vinnie knew too much about her." Writing to Mrs. Bingham, then collecting materials for the new edition of Emily's letters, she took a clear stand on the problem of the trial and its motivating force:

> Sue did everything in her power to *down* your adorable mother. . . . It must have been Sue who held a sword over Vinnie's head. . . . It was not Vinnie who started the trouble, I am sure of that. . . . she *dared not* do what would madden the enemy. . . . Sue was bitter, and cruel, & revengeful.

A little later, Miss Hall amplified her theory about Vinnie's part in the quarrel:

> During your Mother's absence in Japan, Sue found the opportunity of getting her chance for revenge, by telling Miss Vinnie about the strip of land, and she influenced her to do as she did, in order to get *in* with Miss Vinnie, that she might use her to get back the land, and to get control of her for the remainder of her life. For one thing, she feared that Miss Vinnie might make a will favorable to others, giving Ned & Mattie only what the law obliged her to give.

There are many difficulties here, although it is worth noting that Clara Newman Pearl agreed with Miss Hall's view: "I can remember hearing my father say that that last suit 'never should have happened,' but Cousin

1. For selections, see Appendix II, 1.

Susan Dickinson in 1897

Vinnie in 1896

Vinnie was just a tool in others' hands." Vinnie did not need to be "told" about the land. In signing the deed of gift, she had broken her promise to her legal and financial adviser, Mr. Hills, not to sign anything without first consulting him, and she may have decided to sue for the land as a way of redeeming herself with him, for whom she seems to have had a special regard. At any rate, Sue's part in the proceedings is difficult to ascertain. She kept herself aloof from the trial itself, sending Ned and Martha to sit beside Vinnie in the courtroom. It was probably from Vinnie, whose habits of exaggeration were then fully developed, that Miss Hall heard about the matter of the bequests to the children. The passage is significant mainly as it shows how completely Miss Hall distrusted Sue. She subscribed to the local gossip about Sue's alcoholism (her comment recalls Austin's complaint about Sue's fits of temper): "I think Sue inherited her father's love of liquor, and that there were times when she actually did not know what she was doing, or saying."

Miss Hall's general estimate of Sue's character hardly allows even the ambivalence of Mrs. Todd's view—the fine abilities wrongly used. It is much less charitable. The contradiction in her nature, as Miss Hall saw it, would seem to make Sue—and not Emily—the object of psychiatric investigation. The charming exterior and the "black" interior could be reconciled only in terms of the demonic theme carried out in Vinnie's favorite term for Sue, "the Old Scratch"—at least so Miss Hall's rhetoric suggests:

. . . you never will know what an evil minded person Sue was. You cannot imagine such a fiend, for Sue could appear like "an angel of light," when it served her purpose to do so.

Such epithets persist in her invective—"black devil," "fiend," "Satan, or Sue"—and come to a head in her most extended characterization:

To me Sue was abnormally self-centered; an egotist; arrogant; haughty; pretentious; and, to give the Devil her due, she could be gracious, clever, entertaining on the surface, and black as the blackest ink inside, where truth is generated, and where it lives, if it lives at all.

In one important passage, Miss Hall brings all the scattered themes together: Sue's character, Austin and Mabel, the family conflict, and Emily's involvement:

Vinnie told me . . . that Emily was furious at Sue on account of her deceptions, and had little, if anything to do with her a year or two before her death. It may be that Emily became too much interested in your Mother [Mrs. Todd], that she defended your Mother. That probably enraged Sue.

"Furious" seems hardly the epithet for Emily, and what Sue's "deceptions" were is another of those charges hard to document. They may have had something to do with Emily's relationship with Judge Lord, which seems to have been very distasteful to Sue. When Sue warned Mabel

Todd away from the Homestead because of the "immorality" practiced there—she had found Emily "in the arms of a man"—the man (if any) must have been Lord. It has been suggested that at this time she started the rumors of Emily's early love for the Reverend Charles Wadsworth to deflect gossip, both from Emily's involvement with Lord and from the trouble in her own home. "So successful was the stratagem, if such it was," wrote Millicent Todd Bingham in 1954, "that until now the existence of an ardent attachment between Emily Dickinson and the venerable Judge has not been suspected." Much more could be said about this strange ramification of the family quarrel, even if all analysis must remain hypothetical. In her distaste for Emily's late romance, Sue may simply have been siding with Judge Lord's niece, Abbie Farley, who had kept house for him after his wife died in 1877. (Abbie was a special friend of Sue's and "Vinnie's special aversion." She thought her uncle's and Emily's friendship disgusting[2] and years later called Emily a "little hussy. . . . Loose morals. She was crazy about men. Even tried to get Judge Lord. Insane, too.") Also, Sue may have been jealous of the attention Judge Lord was paying to the other house. It is conceivable that she may for years have been storing up resentment at Emily's withdrawal from her sphere of influence: a brilliant, even if eccentric sister-in-law would have been an asset at her teas and receptions and musicales, and Emily's absence might have drawn comment not always favorable to Sue. An early, frustrated love affair and a broken heart could have served as an appealing explanation for Emily's withdrawal. The legend, given such currency in Martha Dickinson Bianchi's *Life and Letters of Emily Dickinson*, may have had just such an origin.

Of all these complications Miss Hall seems to have been ignorant. What made her "furious" was Martha's suppression, in her various writings on Emily, of the dark realities of the family situation, of Emily's uneven relations with Sue, of any hint that life in the Evergreens was anything but idyllic. She hoped that Martha's "deceptions" and "falsehoods" would be *"stabbed* with the true history of the lives of all the D. family" and in a notable passage made her meaning clear:

> I do hope that someone will write "The Life of Shadows," or the "House of Shadows," a book giving some of the *awful pressure* under which Austin, Emily, and Vinnie lived; the stern, austere, unaffectionate character of Edward D., and the soft, yielding, rather unstable one of his wife. I shudder as I recall the stories Vinnie told me of their little deceptions in order to get a drop of joy out of their gloomy home life. . . . Sue had a fearful influence over the three, as each one found her out to his and her sorrow.

2. "Abbie," writes Mrs. Bingham, "sensed power in the relationship . . . and, my mother thought, wanted to disguise it, to cover it up, feeling that it was somehow disloyal to her dead aunt. At any rate, she made sarcastic comments on the 'sweet' letters she thought 'Uncle Lord' was sending to the 'mansion'" (*Revelation*, p. 60). Jay Leyda adds: ". . . marriage was further discouraged by the Farleys, Mrs. Lord's family, who continued to live in Lord's Salem home" (*YH* I, lix).

There is no need to accept Miss Hall's Vinnie-inspired version of life in the Homestead, or her moral verdict on Sue, to agree with her about Sue's influence in the lives of all the Dickinsons, even if the word "fearful" does not cover all the cases, all the time. For Emily it had moments of exaltation and delight, certainly, as well as disappointment and bitterness. There was perhaps one thing about Sue that Emily and Mary Lee Hall would have agreed upon: her power.

So much (although the final word can never be said on such delicate and sensitive matters) for what Miss Hall herself called "war." For us, the problem is not one of moral judgment but of determining as precisely as we can the effect of it all on Emily Dickinson. To this end, every scrap of information or opinion, even gossip, emerging from the heat of the conflict or coming to light years later, becomes relevant. How does the accumulated evidence illuminate the setting, help re-create the atmosphere in which she wrote her poetry, and thus illuminate the substance of the poetry itself? Of few poets could the claim be made more confidently that her life was her work. To repeat: Emily, even "Our Emily," did not write in total isolation, shut off from the world, meditating among her flowers. Vesuvius was at *home,* Gethsemane "but a Province – in the Being's Centre –" And at the center of Emily Dickinson's being must have been the gnawing realization of an early mistake in judgment, hers as well as Austin's; a youthful affinity that came to nothing; the lifelong suffering to which that mistake had condemned her brother; and the tension and anxiety it had brought them all.

> Remorse – is Memory – awake –
> Her Parties all astir –
> A Presence of Departed Acts –
> At window – and at Door –
>
> It's Past – set down before the Soul
> And lighted with a Match –
> Perusal – to facilitate –
> And help Belief to stretch –
>
> Remorse is cureless – the Disease
> Not even God – can heal –
> For 'tis His institution – and
> The Adequate of Hell –   (#744, about 1863)

Whether it was her fault, or his, or Sue's, or, in its final stages, Mabel Todd's, is now beside the point. The tragedy only a hedge away had to be, and was, lived through. The paradox of its final stage must now be clear: without it, we might never have had the poems.

There may be comfort in the paradox, but it is chilly. The conflict took a long toll. It may be true that without Mabel Todd and her involvement with the Dickinsons, we might never have had the poems (she edited a third series, without Higginson's help, in 1896). And it was she alone who saw the importance of collecting the letters that made up her pioneer edition in 1894—an achievement ranking close to her work on the poems. Her lectures in the 1890s undoubtedly made many readers of Emily Dickinson, even if she was inclined to put a disproportionate emphasis on the mystery of Emily's life and personality. But when the trial over the strip of land ended disastrously for the Todds, she determined to have nothing more to do with things Dickinson, put all the manuscript materials, including some 665 of Emily's poems, in the famous camphorwood chest and shut the lid, as she thought, forever. Her withdrawal left Martha Dickinson Bianchi with a clear field, with what results we have seen. There was no possibility of cooperation between the two women. The poems came out piecemeal, unprofessionally edited, with Mabel's holdings, of course, still in the camphorwood chest, not to be opened until 1929, when Mabel, finally relenting, entrusted their editing to her daughter. But it was sixteen years before *Bolts of Melody* (1945) and another ten before all of Emily Dickinson's poems were brought together in a single edition, professionally edited, with variants, an approximation of Emily Dickinson's unique punctuation, and a tentative chronology. There is hardly a more erratic publishing record of a major poet in literary history. Finally, with the *Letters* of 1958, we were enabled to view Emily Dickinson in what seems close to entirety. This long, tortuous delay exposed her, of course, to many partial judgments and misconceptions; and much of it must be attributed to the tensions and ill feeling between the families—the "war," with its long beginnings and disastrous finale.

14

The Dickinson Rhetoric and

the Structure of a Life

However far from center the preceding chapters may at times have seemed, their purpose has been to present in reasonably full detail the givens of Emily Dickinson's life, what she was born into, what in a sense she could not avoid, the complex and powerful forces of her heredity and environment that she had to cope with as she shaped her life. Of course, we have seen much that she could have avoided. The story of Sue, in its early years, certainly shows her making choices; but Sue's thirty-year presence next door was an inescapable fixture of her maturity, as (for her) were her home, her family, and Amherst. We are by no means done with such matters, for her childhood, her schooling, her intellectual surroundings, and the hard facts of mid-century America (including the literary situation) are all part of her ecology. The aim has been, by first showing what she reached out from, to prepare the way for a better understanding of what she reached out toward and of her extraordinary achievement in evolving out of both a structured and creative life.

In the course of our chapters, a number of stock notions should have been laid to rest or so qualified as to lose the insistence they have often had in accounts of Emily Dickinson: that Amherst was no place for a poet to be born in; that she was the lone star in a colorless and insignificant family; that her home was either a prison to her spirit or, at the other extreme, a cozy retreat irradiated (after July 1, 1856) by the attentions of a loving confidante; that she lived apart from the passions and bitterness that plague the rest of humanity and, not knowing such things firsthand, made them up for the purposes of poetry; that a love tragedy is the only way of explaining her withdrawal from society (Austin and Lavinia denied its existence, and Sue in the obituary gave no hint of it); that she spent her day "meditating majestically among her flowers."

On the contrary, what should be emerging is a perceptive, critical, self-propelling person working hard in the midst of a busy town and a busy family and taking the measure of both. We have seen her through the eyes of her intimates, but mostly we have seen them through hers—which is as sure a way as any, perhaps, of getting to know her. We have had glimpses of her in action: outmaneuvering her father, coping with the housework during her mother's illness, advising her brother, depending and not depending on her sister, living out a curious love-hate relationship with her sister-in-law—and trying out her style on them all. There is much more of all this to come—the qualities and the actions, what she was born into and what she made of it. And most important, of course, the major action, her vocation, which gave the structure to her life.

In retrospect, one matter emerges that requires a further word: a phenomenon of temperament and need—and hence style and hence vocation—that subsumes certain themes touched upon so far and prepares for encounters and problems to come. This too was a family character-istic—hardly inherited but certainly shared by all three of the young Dickinsons, and thus, in a sense, part of the world Emily grew up in. So distinct is it from anything recorded in Dickinson annals before this generation, and so unparalleled in Emily's immediate cultural environ-ment, that it deserves a special term: the Dickinson Rhetoric.

The baffled Higginson once said, ruefully, "It is hard to steer safely among Dickinsons!" He found them a subtle and circuitous family, with Emily, of course, his first and central enigma. He complained that she surrounded herself with a fiery mist. What he meant, presumably, was her bewildering language, the slant and elliptical style of the poems and letters she sent him. Or perhaps what made the mist fiery was her ex-travagance, the hyperbole he found hard to believe, a tendency to exag-gerate of the sort we have seen in operation frequently in the preceding chapters, whether it was Vinnie telling Mary Lee Hall lurid tales of her youth, or Austin calling Mabel Todd his "Christ," or Emily saying that Vinnie was "all" to her. Heightened rhetoric seems in this generation to have been a family phenomenon, and it presents a particular problem: the problem of *pose*. When can we trust these Dickinsons? When are they posing, or dramatizing—or speaking simply, directly, as we would say "truthfully"?

To the biographer, these questions are crucial in regard to many of Emily's statements in her letters, the richest source we have of positive, concrete information about her life. What did she mean, for instance, when she told Higginson, twice, that he had "saved [her] Life"? that, by 1862, she had written "but one or two" poems? One does not look first for hard biographical data in the hyperbolic and figurative language of the poems, although their truth becomes more available the more we understand her medium, an understanding that must come gradually (and may never be complete). But Emily as she presents herself in the letters, where (we would like to think) we see her face to face, is a constant problem. She could adopt a persona or don a mask as readily here as in the more obvious art constructs of the poems. It is too easy to dismiss such tendencies as merely protective. Viewed more closely, and in their historical context, they may be related to the large creative effort of Emily Dickinson's life.

To go back: until Samuel Fowler Dickinson, there was nothing in Emily's lineage to account for the flair for language peculiar to her generation of Dickinsons; and he did little more than establish directions toward ideas, education, literary expression. Although he and his son Edward made reputations as orators, their public rhetoric was quite conventional. Edward's courtship letters were, for the most part, models of rational control, with only an occasional burst of feeling and then in a style that has nothing surprising about it, nothing misty or fiery. At home, in his soberer years, Edward was inclined to be taciturn. By Higginson's standard he probably *was* "speechless," though he could at times be moved to argumentative bouts with Austin, as Emily records, and her quotations from his conversation show a turn for terse, wry humor, mostly ironic and understated. All his children inherited some of this, especially his satiric bent and his gift for mimicry, but in general their tendency went in the other direction, toward a freer, more colorful rhetoric. Much of this could be attributed to the tendencies of the times, the loosening of the old formalism by writers like Emerson and Thoreau, to whom Emily and Austin responded immediately, or to the influence of contemporary popular literature, like Ik Marvel's *Reveries* or Longfellow's *Kavanagh,* in which the young Dickinsons indulged heavily in spite of their father's disapproval.

There must have been an inner need for verbal expression without which these influences would have had little effect. These Dickinsons, certainly Austin and Emily, faced a spiritual crisis unknown, or at least not articulated, by their elders. The old forms and formulations were losing their sustaining power. Austin's letters to Martha Gilbert are a case in point; he was bewildered and groping, and he was impelled to an expression unprecedented in the Dickinson line. Apparently, his heterodoxy was a real obstacle in his early relations with Sue; he, a Dickinson, had to plead with her not to dismiss him as an atheist. Emily spoke of at least one theological discussion she had with him, and it is likely that the nocturnal talks that both she and Joseph Lyman referred to when "the ancient people" were away, or asleep, covered many such problems. They discussed their difficulties in a way not recorded of their elders, who presumably found their answers in church—or, if not, kept up appearances in silence. None of the three children was especially pious or churchly. Although Vinnie dutifully joined the church during the Revival of 1850, there is nothing in anything she said or did, certainly not in the years when she needed it most, that shows she got much help from it. Austin worked hard for the church as an institution, but it hardly seems to have been a major source of spiritual comfort for him either. He turned to his intimates, at first Sue and Martha and then Emily (who became a constant); then to nature, to his passion for art, to his work for the college and the town; and finally to Mabel Todd, who as his "Christ" released in him the flood of rhetoric that had the fervor and many of the phrases of the old piety. That Emily stopped going to church regularly by the time she was thirty is a sign of more than mere reclusiveness; she refused to follow her pious friends to the ark of safety when she was a girl, and later she openly confessed a scorn of doctrines. She took it upon herself to fill the void left by these rejections with all the verbal resources she could muster. She would triumph by the word—her own Word.

Each one of these younger Dickinsons, at one time or another, took a stance that required new, fresh expression. It showed in such everyday but significant ways as their conversation. They were well known as talkers. If Higginson was struck by Edward Dickinson's speechlessness, he was all but overwhelmed by Emily's intense, electric talk. As girls, Emily and Vinnie were famous as wits, a little on the prickly side. Neither of them, or Austin, tolerated fools gladly, and they could sometimes be abrasive or abrupt. The Dickinson snobbishness had its rhetoric, too—cultivated, I think, by Emily for defensive purposes, as when she called her Aunt Elisabeth "the only male relative on the female side," or when she directed an elderly and tiresome lady, inquiring at the Homestead about lodgings in Amherst, to the cemetery, as Emily later said, "to spare expense of moving." Austin's brusqueness was notorious. Vinnie was peppery. Her safety valve became increasingly her sharp tongue. She could "raise an *awful* breeze," as Austin observed, and in later years she exercised her considerable talents defending her family against the world. It seems that all three set out at one time or another to surround themselves, if not all with fiery mists, at least with some degree of impenetrability, as if to fend off ordinary, boring human nature. There is more than a trace of it in Emily's poetry, as in her famous jibe at gentility:

> What Soft – Cherubic Creatures –
> These Gentlewomen are –
> One would as soon assault a Plush –
> Or violate a Star –
>
> Such Dimity Convictions –
> A Horror so refined
> Of freckled Human Nature –
> Of Deity – ashamed –

It's such a common – Glory –
A Fisherman's – Degree –
Redemption – Brittle Lady –
Be so – ashamed of Thee –   (*#401, about 1862*)

But Emily's fiery mist, her rhetorical virtuosity, was more than protective. Her problem was constructive, and ours is to penetrate the mist to the outlines of what it was she was constructing. Her poems employ the language of almost every conceivable action, from the most gentle to the most violent—passionate love, torture, shipwreck, battle, murder, and, as in the poem just quoted, rape. Not that a poet must fight in a battle or commit murder before he can legitimately use the language of such actions in his poems. But the perennial misgiving about Emily Dickinson, the Amherst recluse, comes from what appears to be the unexplained gap between rhetoric and reality.

What we have seen so far of the vital and often agonizing relationships by which Emily's life was crisscrossed should have bridged some of that gap. As her purpose and method as poet become clearer in what follows, the gap should close further. Once understood, the career she fashioned for herself can be seen in the light of a grand metaphoric design—a design that puts everything else, including her baffling private life and her rhetorical eccentricities, into believable perspective. As we follow her on her way, I propose one important criterion as a guide.

The task, as one confronts the recalcitrant and often paradoxical materials, is not unlike that of the novelist as he approaches his imagined situations. Indeed, this is why her life has been such a tempting subject for the writers of fiction and fictionalized biography. One is confronted with many questions that are unanswerable, and as clue after clue ends in an impasse, the temptation is to hypothesize and improvise. One is reminded of Joseph Conrad's struggle to bring into focus his romantic young hero Lord Jim. It is worth noting that both Marlow (Conrad's fictional narrator and control) and Higginson (who functions somewhat similarly in our early pages) used the image of mist to describe their difficulty: Higginson's fiery mist and the fog, or mist, that shrouded Marlow's enigmatic young protégé. Several times Marlow (like Higginson) confesses his bafflement: "I don't pretend I understood him. The views he let me have of himself were like those glimpses through the shifting rents in a thick fog—bits of vivid and vanishing detail, giving no connected idea of the general aspect of a country. . . . how incomprehensible, wavering, and misty are the beings that share with us the sight of the stars and the warmth of the sun. . . ." Sometimes Marlow's vision is dimmed by the dazzle of too much sun: "My eyes were too dazzled by the glitter of the sea below his feet to see him clearly; I am fated never to see him clearly." Some such thoughts must have plagued everyone, beginning with Higginson, who has assayed the life of Emily Dickinson. For Marlow, it was not until the action was complete, with Jim's final heroic stand at

Patusan, that his life assumed coherence and meaningful shape. What one concludes is that, with people who guard their inner natures so successfully, either with reticence or rhetoric, we must look to their actions, or rather their life actions taken as wholes, for their overarching truth. This is the way Conrad solved his problem, as, under his treatment, the life action of his hero became metaphoric.

We would look, then, for Emily Dickinson's life action and its metaphoric purport. The early letters, especially, show that she, too, had a problem of organization and coherence. They abound in energy and zest for living, but they show her groping for direction and meaning. She tried all the standard routes in vain and ran the gamut of the current sentimentalities. She pummeled and browbeat her correspondents, or bathed them in the tender emotions. (No wonder they dropped off, unwilling or unable to keep up.) The wit, the whimsey, the turn for drama and exaggeration, the rhetorical tricks picked up at school or in reading or listening to sermons—all these entered into her brilliant young virtuosity, and all had, ultimately, to be brought under control. Her own word was "organized," as when she answered Higginson's charge that her poems lacked form: "When I try to organize – my little Force explodes." And often it did explode, especially though not exclusively in the early letters, into bathos, or rhapsody, or sheer indulgence. Later on, we detect her, in her rhetoric, stretching the truth, or posing, or just plain lying, as when she pictured herself as an ingénue to Higginson, with "one or two" verses to her credit, when we know that she had written hundreds, among them some of her finest. And many of the poems make denials or affirmations that seem startlingly at variance with the known facts of her life. We wonder what truth there is behind this seeming fantasia; we wonder where the ultimate meaning is.

Poets like Emily Dickinson may "lie" in their hyperbole and exaggerated rhetoric. They may strike poses and don masks and speak through personae. But in their basic structures, where they begin, where they end, and how they got there, they do not lie. Certainly it was Emily Dickinson's constant aim, her life action, to make her "truth" clear. Her poems, those "short sharp probings at the very axis of reality," show her in a continual effort to expand, deepen, clarify, and be ever more precise. That is why, perhaps, she tried her hand again and again at similar materials, sometimes forging new meaning, sometimes adding little or even slipping back (the curve is not always up), but in general continuing her course toward what she called "Circumference."

To watch her at work in one instance is a good way to get a sense of the configuration of her career. As poet, she worked from specific to general, concrete to universal. The phenomena of experience that surged more or less uncontrolled through the early letters came under increasingly sharp scrutiny. She became preoccupied with essence; the accidents (who? when? where?) did not concern her. The example at hand shows her moving from a specific early encounter and the rhetoric it evoked to what she ultimately made of much the same materials. Here, though hardly its finest achievement, is the type of her career as a whole.

The encounter, described in an early letter to Susan Gilbert, involved a bit of moon-gazing. She was twenty and at the height of her infatuation for Sue, at that time teaching school in Baltimore. She thinks of her friend as she gazes at the moon. In her fantasy, the moon becomes a fairy, sailing in a gondola, who coolly ignores her request for a ride to Baltimore and Sue, and sails serenely on. It is all very sad.

> I wept a tear here, Susie, on purpose for *you* – because this "sweet silver moon" smiles in on me and Vinnie, and then it goes so far before it gets to you – and then you never told me if there *was* any moon in Baltimore – and how do *I* know Susie – that you see her sweet face at all? She looks like a fairy tonight, sailing around the sky in a little silver gondola with stars for gondoliers. I asked her to let me ride a little while ago – and told her I would *get out* when she got as far as Baltimore, but she only smiled to herself and went sailing on.

Years later, after she had learned to disentangle essences from personal sentiment, the " 'sweet silver moon' " functions in two poems, "I watched the Moon around the House" and "The Moon upon her fluent Route," only in both poems far from sweetly. In the first poem, the moon, which in the letter played the stock role of uniting loving hearts only to prove fickle, becomes a symbol of much more than nature's coyness:

> I watched the Moon around the House
> Until upon a Pane –
> She stopped – a Traveller's privilege – for Rest –
> And there upon
>
> I gazed – as at a stranger –
> The Lady in the Town
> Doth think no incivility
> To lift her Glass – upon –
>
> But never Stranger justified
> The Curiosity
> Like Mine – for not a Foot – nor Hand –
> Nor Formula – had she –
>
> But like a Head – a Guillotine
> Slid carelessly away –
> Did independent, Amber –
> Sustain her in the sky –
>
> Or like a Stemless Flower –
> Upheld in rolling Air
> By finer Gravitations –
> Then bind Philosopher –

No Hunger – had she – nor an Inn –
Her Toilette – to suffice –
Nor Avocation – nor concern
For little Mysteries

As harass us – like Life – and Death –
And Afterward – or Nay –
But seemed engrossed to Absolute –
With Shining – and the Sky –

The privilege to scrutinize
Was scarce upon my Eyes
When, with a Silver practise –
She vaulted out of Gaze –

And next – I met her on a Cloud –
Myself too far below
To follow her superior Road –
Or it's advantage – Blue –   (#629, about 1862)

For all the ladylike imagery and the detached, contemplative mood of the poem, the preoccupation is with a moon whose cold indifference implies an absolute break between man and nature—the guillotined head, the stemless flower: nothing less than the isolation and terror of man's place in the universe, where his "little Mysteries . . . like Life – and Death – " are of no concern whatever to anyone or anything but himself. In such moods, Emily Dickinson is as far as can be imagined from Emerson and the Transcendentalists. The snub she felt from Susie's moon and the sentimental cry it wrung from her young heart have been developed into a Pascalian contemplation of immensity and (poetically) into a coolheaded, beautifully controlled statement of alienated man. No poetic cliché is more weary than the moon, and yet every detail is new, every image precisely visualized. She has brought her ideas, her perceptions, and herself under firm control. One has the feeling that, having confronted the destructive element fearlessly and frankly, and having painted it where it stands, she can live with it.

The other, later moon poem (she wrote still others, and in varying moods) shows her in another stage of contemplation. This time she has, to some degree, distanced the sense of alienation and is on the verge of revelation. It is an austere little statement, gnomic and oracular.

The Moon upon her fluent Route
Defiant of a Road –
The Star's Etruscan Argument
Substantiate a God –

> If Aims impel these Astral Ones
> The ones allowed to know
> Know that which makes them as forgot
> As Dawn forgets them – now –   (*#1528, about 1881*)

The distance is not complete or the revelation fulfilled. The conditional "If . . ." and the sense that full knowledge is achieved only by those who have joined the Astral Ones—that is, died—show her still groping for a firm and abiding faith. But the orderly wheeling of the moon and stars provide an Etruscan argument (primal? sturdy? and hence encouraging?), and we are nearer knowledge than before, if only in the sense of its possible revelation after death. This is not new in her poetic or spiritual development. She experimented with the thought many times—for instance, the agonizing cry of the early poem:

> I shall know why – when Time is over –
> And I have ceased to wonder why –
> Christ will explain each separate anguish
> In the fair schoolroom of the sky –
>
> He will tell me what "Peter" promised –
> And I – for wonder at his woe –
> I shall forget the drop of Anguish
> That scalds me now – that scalds me now!   (*#193, about 1860*)

Here the lyric outburst of the young heart is everything, only more controlled and (one feels) much less staged than the moon letter to Susan. "I watched the Moon around the House" and "The Moon upon her fluent Route" do not seem staged at all. No one is likely to exclaim, "Mere rhetoric." Their truth stands clear and powerful. They are a measure of the growth of the poet in breadth of vision and in organizing power.

In miniature, such was the journey, the life action, of Emily Dickinson. It required extraordinary discipline and concentration. While Austin apparently submerged his early bewilderments in his profession and his good works, and Vinnie made a career of the Dickinson home and taking care of Dickinsons, Emily had other work to do. "She had to think," said Vinnie; "she was the only one of us who had that to do." Seeing her life and her work and what she accomplished this way makes the disparity between the quiet life and the tumultuous rhetoric understandable. The intense inner life she was born to lead, as the others were not, required no less a rhetoric for its full expression. For her there came to be no such thing as mere rhetoric. Every word was an experiment in meaning, a route toward the discovery of new meanings in the perceptions and thoughts that entered her teeming consciousness. This was her career, her journey toward Circumference.

Appendixes for

VOLUME ONE

I

Vinnie as Stylist, Mimic, Reader,
and Poet

VINNIE'S PROSE STYLE, both written and oral, deserves attention. Like her mother, she did not enjoy writing. But she tried hard—if only to keep up with her brother and sister—as we know from a letter to Austin written when she was nearly seventeen (*Home,* pp. 87–89, January 11, 1850): "I thank you, for your good advice, concerning letter writing, & hope to profit by it. I have written one & generally two letters, evry Saturday, since I left home, &, though I've allways had a great aversion to writing, I hope, by consent practice, the dislike will wear away, in a degree, at least. . . . Write soon & dont ridicule this will you?" If in her letters she stuck to the "matters of fact" (which Emily relegated to her) and cultivated a staccato style, it was probably in reaction to the "metaphysics"—the "air"—she saw inflating the discursive paragraphs of her more literary siblings. "Emilie has fed you on air so long, that I think a little 'sound common sense' perhaps wouldnt come amiss[.] *Plain english you know* such as Father likes" (*Home,* p. 148; to Austin, June 30, 1851). She jammed her letters tight with gossip and crisp, sometimes enigmatic comments: "Emilie is pensive just now recollections of 'by gones' you know, 'Old un' &c." (*Home,* p. 206, December 29, 1851). She had a good ear and a keen eye. Her gift was for the satiric and combative, examples of which we have already seen. Mabel Todd described it as follows (*AB,* p. 6): "Lavinia was a brilliant exponent of ancient wit and comment not involving any superfluous love for one's fellow man. . . . I could not help a liking for the fierce denunciations which sprung forth from Vinnie's nimble tongue." Mabel once started a collection of Vinnie's sayings. To a woman who complained that Vinnie's cats were killing birds, Vinnie replied, "You must blame the Creator" (*Home,* p. 29). Hearing some working men cursing, she remarked, "At least they've heard of our Redeemer." After a tedious visit from Uncle Joel Norcross: "I have got tired of hearing about *Ego altogether.* He is never informed on any other subject" (*Home,* p. 297). She had other moods. "Vinnie says there is a tree in Mr. Sweetser's woods that shivers," wrote Emily to the Norcrosses (*L II,* 495, early May 1872). When a caller later, in 1895, urged her to look at the light on the Pelham Hills, she turned away and said, "There is no landscape since Austin died" (*AB,* p. 331).

The best account we have of Vinnie's gift for impersonation and imitation is in Susan Dickinson's monograph, "Annals of the Evergreens," a twenty-five-page, typewritten document (Dickinson Papers, Houghton Library, Harvard) written for her children as a memorial of the great days in the Evergreens when the Dickinsons entertained such notables as Bowles, Emerson, Wendell Phillips, Colonel Benton, Bishop Huntington, and Judge Lord. Susan exercises her own not inconsiderable style on each of these. One of her most entertaining passages is on Judge Lord, with Vinnie playing a strong supporting role—indeed, stealing the show. The episode—a Sunday dinner—might have taken place sometime in the late 1870s. Mrs. Lord is not present—she died on December 10, 1877; Vinnie and Sue seem on still cordial terms; Emily, of course, is not there; Austin is sick in bed, upstairs. Sue begins with an unflattering sketch of the Judge,

. . . a perfect figure-head for the Supreme Court, from his stiff stock to his toes; never seem[ed] to coalesce with these men, although he was often here with them as the guest of your Grand Father – But his individuality was so bristling, his conviction that he alone was the embodiment of the law, as given on Sinai so entire, his suspicion of all but himself, so deeply founded in the bed rock of old conservative Whig tenacities, not to say obstinacies, that he was an anxious element to his hostess in a group of progressive and mellow although staunch men and women. At an informal dinner with him once we saw him at his best. Your Father was ill, and he kindly took the head of the table, your Aunt Vinnie, sat at his right, the other guests I do not seem to remember. Perhaps because it was Sunday, we naturally got upon the subject of hymnology in New England. The Judge remarking that he was brought up on "Watts and Select" unabridged, asked if any of us were familiar with the hymn beginning

"My thoughts on awful subjects roll
Damnation and the dead."

In astonishment we answered, no! where upon he layed down his fork, made himself a little more stiff, and erect, behind his old-fashioned silk stock, than usual, if that were possible, and recited with an energy worthy himself and the subject, the whole hymn. There was really a horrible grandeur about it, although our nervous laughter might have misled one in the next room as to our real emotions. Your Aunt was inspired by this to give us one of her famous representations of the early choir, with bass viol accompaniment, as familiar to us in the Village church a generation ago when they worshipped in what is now called "College Hall." She sang stoutly and with real minor threat and pathos the first two lines of

"Broad is the road which leads to death."

but in the third line, where "Wisdom shows a narrow path," the melody running too high for the superannuated Village soprano, she dropped off in a cracked subsidence from the key, leaving the bass-viol to moan in harrowing discord, rejoining it again, after an interval in the fourth line, where they each, somewhat spent, strove to deepen the gloom of "Here and there a traveler" – ! the viol quite outstripping its rival and prolonging the last few notes in such grating woe, that I remember in the old days, the little boys used to look round furtively after sitting down to the prayer, to see if anything was the matter, with the good old man who bullied this kingly, misplaced instrument. The imitation was a most remarkable artistic performance on your Aunt's part, arousing such applause that your Father's bell rang, requesting us to remember that it was Sunday. The suggestion of unmusical, quavering voices was remarkable in the imitation, without the astonishing reproduction of the sullen bass-viol.

As to Vinnie's reading, her diary (see Chapter 7, note 2) shows what she was up to at age eighteen.

Jan. 16 finished Adirondack. [Joel Tyler Headley, *The Adirondack, or Life in the Woods,* 1849]

Jan. 21 Received my usual magazine [*Harper's.* This was a monthly entry]

Feb. 4 Attended the Lyceum.

Feb. 7 Read this eve.

Feb. 14 Read some in "Woman in America" [*Her Work and Her Reward,* by Maria J. McIntosh, 1850]

Feb. 20 Commenced Reveries of Bachelor. [Ik Marvel, 1850]

Feb. 22 Finished *Bachelors Reveries.*

March 1 Tutor Holland . . . Lent me "French Revolution." [Carlyle, 1837]

March 19 Commenced *David Copperfield* [1849–50]

March 21 The reading circle commenced this evening

April 18 Finished *"David Copperfield."* Commenced German Story.

April 20 Read "Literary attractions of the Bible." [Not identified]

May 30 Attended *reading club* in evening.

May 31 Received *Music* and Magazine [June *Harper's*]

June 3 Attended Reading Society.

June 4 Arranged books in morning.

June 13 Emilie Fowler spent morning reading Shakespeare here.

July 5 Went to preparatory lecture.

July 8 Went to reading club.

Aug. 13 Heard Mr. Beechers *address* [on "Imagination"]

Aug. 17 Read "House with seven gables" [1851]

Sept. 9 Heard Othello at Museum [in Boston]

Oct. 9 Borrowed Upham's phylosophy. [Thomas C. Upham, *Elements of Mental Philosophy,* 1838]

Oct. 17 Begin reading "Second Love" [by Martha Martell]

Oct. 18 Finished Second Love.

Oct. 19 Commenced "Memoir of Lady Colquhoun." [James Hamilton, *A Memoir of Lady Colquhoun,* 1851]

Nov. 23 Finished Lady Colquhoun.

Dec. 7 Commenced reading Miss Lyons memoir. [Edward Hitchcock, *The Power of Christian Benevolence Illustrated in the Life and Labors of Mary Lyon,* 1851]

Dec. 16 *Read all evening.*

As Mrs. Bianchi remarks of Vinnie's diary (*Face to Face,* p. 108, n.): "It is significant that books and the names of books read, as well as allusions to the 'reading club', are to be found on almost every page"; and (p. 113): "For even then their home was a house of books and the talk of them." And (in *Life and Letters,* p. 13): "It was Lavinia who knew where everything was, from a lost quotation to last year's muffler." Emily writes to Austin (November 16, 1851, L I, 157): "Vinnie is eating an apple . . ., and accompanying it with her favorite [New York] Observer, which if you recollect, deprives us many a time of her sisterly society."

Although later evidence is scanty, we can assume that she shared the young people's interest in books like *Kavanagh,* that she kept up with the magazines (*Harper's,* the *Atlantic,* and *Scribner's*) that came to the house, and that, as with Emily, the Bible and Shakespeare were staples, even if as busy house-keeper she spent much of her time being "Atlas."

Although Vinnie as poet is hardly a topic of broad or deep dimensions, one document survives to show that, whatever posterity might think, she thought of herself as sometimes visited by the Muse. The document (Dickinson Papers, Houghton Library, Harvard) is a gathering of seventeen 5 x 8 sheets, each sheet containing a poem (or fragment), typewritten, with a title sheet as follows:

Poems

by

Miss Lavinia Dickinson

Amherst, Massachusetts

1898

The final sheet, signed "Lavinia Dickinson," is on different paper from the rest, and the writing is in what appears to be Vinnie's *youthful* hand. It is difficult to explain this—indeed, one wonders how these verses ever got type-written. Surely not by Vinnie. Perhaps by her friend Mary Lee Hall, who earlier had helped transcribe Emily's MSS.

NIGHT

The stars kept winking and blinking,
    as if they had secrets to tell;
But as nobody asked any questions,
    Nobody heard any tales.

*   *   *

The ingenuity of pain
    Groping for tenderest nooks
Then plants its fangs in quivering flesh.

*   *   *

The pines let drop their needles
    As noiseless as the snow,
They carpet all the woods with plush
    And light the darkest paths.

*   *   *

New pleasures bring new anxieties.

*   *   *

Pain and I fought for the mastery
    But oh! the bleak, bleak battlefield
Before the victory.

*   *   *

Indifference is as sure to kill
    As smokeless powder's mark,
So be cautious how you trifle
    With a heart of any size.

      *   *   *

Why should we hide our friendship
    From those who've earned the claim?
Is it disgrace to recognize
    A kindred heart and soul?

      *   *   *

FIRE-FLIES

The fire-flies hold their lanterns high
    To guide the falling star,
But, if by chance the wicks grow short
    The stars might lose their way.

      *   *   *

The bells clang out the notice
    That the holy time has come, –
And man must cease from labor,
    And beasts may roam at will.

      *   *   *

Challenge makes contrast swift to hurt or heal.

      *   *   *

The wind hung high in the trees last night
    And threw the branches down,
And sang weird tunes the elfins made,
    And then the world was still.

      ["threw" is written in Vinnie's *late* hand]

      *   *   *

Appreciation is as rare as pearls in dusty streets.

      *   *   *

Forgetting to remember is such a little thing,
    But sometimes it snaps the heartstrings
And that's a little thing.

      *   *   *

Encouragement is like the dew
    That saves the breath of flowers,
Discouragement is drought
    That parches all their hopes.

      *   *   *

How easy 'tis to meet
   The wrongs to others done,
But when we are hurt
   The christian grace is not so manifest.

      *   *   *

Circumstances shatter vows, as autumn wind, the leaves.

      *   *   *

"And yet", is such a simple phrase, –
   It hardly seems worth mending;
But many a bliss has tripped just here,
   Because this fatal footing.

II

"War between the Houses": Documents

THE TODD-BINGHAM ARCHIVE is rich in gossipy memoranda. Much of it—interviews and correspondence—dates from the early 1930s, when Mabel Todd and her daughter were preparing the new edition of the letters, and later, after Mrs. Todd's death in 1932, when Mrs. Bingham was preparing *Bolts of Melody, Ancestors' Brocades,* and *Home.* Some of it is in Millicent Todd Bingham's hand; some of it typed, probably by her; some of it from other sources. The historical validity of such material, of course, is always open to question; but it is part of the written record.

To comment on the items in order: 1) Mary Lee Hall's bias is clear; she hated Sue and was fond of Vinnie. 2) Miss Jordan is also hostile to Sue, but, it should be noted, ambivalent toward Vinnie and Mabel Todd. (Mary Augusta Jordan was librarian at Vassar College following her graduation there in 1876. She taught English at Vassar from 1880 to 1884, when she went to Smith, where she remained a member of the English department until her retirement in 1921. She brought out editions of *The Vicar of Wakefield, Burke on Conciliation, Milton's Minor Poems,* and *Ten Essays of Ralph Waldo Emerson.* She received the honorary degree of L.H.D. from Smith in 1910. She died in New Haven in 1941.) 3) Mrs. Turner's memories of the Dickinsons in "My Personal Acquaintance with Emily Dickinson," edited by her niece Clara Newman Pearl, were drawn upon by Mrs. Bingham in *Emily Dickinson's Home,* by Jay Leyda in *The Years and Hours,* and are frequently mentioned in my own chapters; but the document, to my knowledge, has never been printed in full. It gains in color and, perhaps, in authenticity when one reads the whole of it. One can see, in action, the making of a myth. While not so acrimonious as Miss Hall or Miss Jordan, Mrs. Turner's bias for the Homestead over the Evergreens is clear. She can be inaccurate or sentimental, especially when she comes to the poems, to the earliest anecdotes about ED, to the last days, and to ED's funeral. But it is to be noted that she insists on the gradual nature of Emily's withdrawal and rejects the notion of a single traumatic love experience. 4) I have also frequently referred to the document, written or dictated by Mabel Loomis Todd the year before she died, "Scurrilous but True." It, too, has appeared elsewhere in part; but, again, it seems well to present the document in its entirety. Mabel Todd's bias, her suppressions, her vanity and snobbishness, are obvious enough. The document is important, however, for the kernel of truth in her side of the story. 5) Millicent Todd Bingham's report of her interview with her father in his declining years illuminates one of the saddest aspects of this drama of the Houses; and finally, 6) her sketches for her projected autobiography give revealing insights into the drama's setting, and glimpses of some of its important personages.

I

THESE EXCERPTS from the voluminous correspondence between Mabel Loomis Todd, Millicent Todd Bingham, and Mary Lee Hall during the years (1929–39) of the work on the 1931 *Letters* and beyond give the context, and more of the color, of Miss Hall's animadversions on the "War between the Houses." In spite of Miss Hall's plea for confidentiality, and sensitive as the issue may still be, it seems best now to put this material in the public domain. Its biases, indeed its furies, have long existed underground, to surface occasionally and tantalizingly, as in the brief selections in Mrs. Bingham's *Ancestors' Brocades* and Jay Leyda's *Years and Hours*. The processes of history, new material and new witnesses, will correct what is purely temperamental or untrue in them. Several of Miss Hall's fixed ideas have long since been questioned, or are questioned in my text: her notion of George Gould as the Lover and her melodramatic view of life in the "House of Shadows" in the early years. And when she writes Mrs. Bingham that "the awful spirit rises in me whenever Sue and Mattie are in my thoughts," she exposes frankly her own emotional bias, still powerful after all those years.

Excerpts, first, from a letter from Miss Hall to Genevieve Taggard will explain Miss Hall's involvement with Vinnie. It also establishes an important priority: it was Miss Hall who got in touch with Mabel Todd, rather than vice versa. The letter is dated November 4, 1929. Miss Taggard's biography of ED appeared the following year.

MY DEAR MISS TAGGARD:

A friend sent me notice of the "Emily Dickinson Meeting" soon to be held, and I am *very* anxious that Mrs Todd may add something quite interesting to her contribution on this special occasion.

How I wish I could follow my spirit, and be "present in the flesh", to hear the truth about Emily Dickinson.

Please tell Mrs Todd – and she *knows* that I do not stand for falsehoods – that Miss Vinnie brought the one hundred and fifty poems to my home, and putting them in my hands asked me to copy them for her, and to let no one know excepting my mother. I kept her secret until the "Further" poems were published, when I broke my silence, and wrote to personal friends about this incident.

Miss Vinnie asked me if it would "Hurt Emily" if the poems were published. I told her that *she* must decide that question, or ask some friend of Emily's who knew her in life.

I kept the poems six months, copied them as well as I could, and gave them back to Miss Vinnie who was not at all well at the time. (She did not live more than four months afterwards.) I asked her to put the poems in a *safe* place, or send them to a reliable firm to be published when she was able to attend to the matter. . . .

My heart and I rejoice that Mrs Todd is living, and will speak at this remarkable meeting – Give Mrs Todd my love, and ask her to let me know where the report of the meeting will be published, in what paper, that I may send for a copy. There are so many statements in the "Life of Emily Dickinson" written by her niece who wrote what she wished the world to believe, that I shall pray the good Lord to let me live to read your book. . . .

I am not sure of reaching Mrs. Todd in any other way, so I will be most grateful to you if you will share this with my dear friend of Amherst days, whom my mother and I admired tremendously, and trusted implicitly.

Most cordially yours

(*Miss*) MARY LEE HALL

1313 South Roan Street.
Johnson City, Tenn.

By late that month (November 1929), the correspondence between Miss Hall and Mabel Todd was in full swing. We begin with one of Miss Hall's typical blasts against Martha Dickinson Bianchi's alleged misrepresentations. (I have omitted from these excerpts the major passages appearing in the text.)

Nov. 24, 1929

MLH TO MLT

No, never have I fallen so desperately low as to follow Mattie's black flag of spiritual illiteracy.

When Ned died Mother and I allowed his sister to come to the house and cry out her anguish in complete seclusion; that is all. Never did we accept any of the invitations from the two women behind the hedge of utter insincerity & deceit, which were showered upon us. A friend sent me the "Life of Emily Dickinson" to read and return – a book made with the undivine purpose of painting Sue's portrait for the world – that did not know her – to gaze on and admire.

Poor Vinnie received blow after blow, and Emily's love affair was mangled beyond all possible recognition.

Had Mattie taken her pen to paint her own character, as the object of her work, she could not more truthfully have portrayed her lack of righteous standards, her false judgement, and her intentional betrayal of trust.

. . .

Feb. 26th, 1930

MLH to MLT

. . . The book [Josephine Pollitt, *Emily Dickinson: The Human Background of Her Poetry*, 1930] is interesting, and far superior in every respect to Mattie's "Life of *Sue*", as it ought to be called, yet it does not satisfy my hungry soul.

You know far more than any other person, probably, about the inner, personal history of the D. family. When you are at liberty to let your sparks fly, they will blaze a trail that will make other little by-paths look like spider tracks. Write it before I become immortal.

June 25, 1930

MLH to MLT

. . . I knew Vinnie intimately, and I knew the dreadful warfare that kept her mind unsettled, but I did not know Emily excepting as I knew her through her poems that you edited, and I am sure the world owes you an everlasting debt. . . .

July 29, 1930

MLH to MLT

A letter from you is an event and a most welcome one.

The "lover" of whom I wrote was not Emily's, but Vinnie's, a Mr Copeland – of the Copeland family of Northampton – and he was a banker at Middletown, Ct. at the time of Vinnie's death. . . .

The poems cannot be interpreted solely by Emily's love affairs, the *shadows* drove her into herself. She found much elation in the men who came into her horizon, and they seemed to be the matches that ignited her mental oil tanks. She was a poor, lonely soul, and so were the others. Each one had one or more romances, and they needed them. . . .

Sept. 14, 1930

MLH to MLT

Vinnie gave me the "Further" poems to copy just after Christmas of 1898, and I had them until the last of May, or first of June 1899. When she became ill I felt that it was better that she should have the poems in the house, especially as she was having some serious battles with "the other house". She said she would hide them where prowlers could not discover them. Of course I did not ask about them after they left my hands. Mattie has claimed to have found them in an old box, where deeds & mortgages were kept, also between the leaves of a large book that was usually in Vinnie's sitting room – perhaps in various other places built for the purpose by her vivid imagination. Vinnie intended to publish the poems, but was never well enough to do so, & I did not want to have any part in such an undertaking.

Vinnie suggested that Mattie's poems were manufactured out of some of Emily's. I told her I thought *not*.

Vinnie made no pretence to me ever of having any affection for Sue or Mattie. She was bitter in her denunciations of them. She told me Sue had been cruel to Emily and herself, and they each had suffered keenly from her insincerities, her insane jealousies, as well as her intentional deceit. I know that Vinnie told Mrs Stockbridge that Sue never ceased to annoy her in every possible way, and that she felt she was trying to *kill* her, as she knew her heart was weak.

In one of Mr Copeland's letters to me, written during Vinnie's last illness, he asked if "the other house" was fighting Vinnie, or leaving her in peace to be cared for by Maggie: he wanted to assure Vinnie that if he could be of comfort or assistance to her, he was ready to go to Amherst at any time. Vinnie often said that Emily's life was shortened by at least ten years, by Sue's cruel treatment. I know Vinnie's life was a tragedy after Ned's death. Sue & Mattie claimed that his heart was weakened by his determination to "stand by Vinnie", during the trial at Northampton. She had a bad adviser, and there were times when she regretted the step she took, also the publicity. . . .

What a novel could be written about the D. family. . . . Only the absolute truth need be revealed, and that would be startling, & sensational enough for the most rabid devourer of novels. . . .

Oct. 12, 1930

MLH to MLT

. . . Mrs. Davis came to see me one evening, and she was greatly agitated over a request from Mrs. Donald – that she "take a stand" against you, in favor of Sue D. Martha and Mrs. D. emphatically declared that Mrs Donald had been greatly mistaken if she expected any real friend of yours to be less a friend when you were under trial, and they decided that Sue was the one to be treated with disdain. Mrs. Davis said, "Why Sue drove Austin out of the house more than once when she was flirting with Mr. Sam Bowles, and *I* shall stand by Austin & Mrs Todd, and I am not afraid to show my colors either. I told Mrs Donald she was not setting a good example as a clergyman's wife, and I also told her that I could tell her a thousand things about Sue that would shock her." . . .

We refused to meet Sue for three years, and never accepted her invitations. One evening my brother and I went to the house to hear Mattie play, on Ned's invitation, & Mattie said she preferred to talk, and would not play. Sue & Mattie must have had a drink for they imitated Pres. Seelye, Dr. Wm Tyler, John Tyler and many others, spoiling the evening for us. When we left we vowed never to enter the house again unless to attend the funerals of Ned & his father. We kept the vow.

After Austin's death Ned came to the house a number of times, and, to our surprise he told us that the day of his father's funeral he arranged that you should be in the house at least ten minutes while the family was at lunch, & he told the nurse never to let his mother or sister know you had been there. He said the nurse told him you had put something in the casket, and he remarked, "Whatever Mrs Todd placed in the casket remained there – and I am glad she had the comfort of that last few minutes with my father"—When Sue knew that some pictures had been left you, by Austin's will, she swore you never should have them. Ned said, "Father loved Mrs Todd, and desired her to have the pictures, so I shall see that she receives them, if I have to send Mother and Mattie to Europe in order to carry out father's wishes."

Ned said he had always admired you, and had never changed in his feelings for you, but he felt obliged to hide his feelings, and to stand by his Mother even though he considered her to be entirely responsible for what had happened. He said he and Mattie had lived in *hell*, and he believed no one could possibly suffer more than he had in trying to be loyal to family traditions. This is for you alone, & not to be used for publication.

July 29, 1933

MTB TO MLH

. . . I want to know anything, everything that is true regarding Emily and every member of her family. Speculation does not interest me. I have no theory to prove. . . . I want solely to prevent a tortured and grotesque picture of Emily Dickinson from being foisted upon posterity. . . .

You ask me to write you what I want to know. The trouble is, I want to know everything, every little nugget of truth. For instance; Between what dates did you know the Dickinsons? Did you ever see Emily? Did you know Sue? What did you think of her? What were her characteristics? Was she pretentious? On what sort of terms was she with Emily and Lavinia? What did Lavinia say about her? What was Emily's attitude toward her? Was there ever any harmony between the two households? What was the attitude of each to each? How can Mrs. Bianchi say that Emily adored Sue up to the moment she died, when Emily called her her "pseudo-sister"?

Aug. 5, 1933

MLH TO MTB

Soon I will answer your other questions. I only hope you will gather some pebbles from all the sand I have scattered on the beach. I feel as you do, that the falsehoods, and deceptions, and insincerities that fill the books Mattie has written ought to be *stabbed* with the true history of the lives of all the D. Family.

Aug. 5, 1933

MLH TO MTB

Your Mother's heart is strong in you, and I want to tell you all you wish to know because of my faith in her, and because of my faith in you. Then, too, I want the truth to be known in regard to the kind of life that was lived behind the hedges, – both hedges! . . .

Mrs. Hills invited us a number of times to meet Austin & Sue, but we had heard so much about the arrogance, and insincerity of Sue, that we were determined *not* to meet her, & we avoided her for several years, but we consulted Austin about some business matters, and really liked & enjoyed him. . . .

Of course I kept meeting Mattie D. at parties, & receptions, and one morning half way between the First Church, and the Town Hall, I met Austin. He stopped me, and said, "I want to ask you a question. Mattie says you do not always recognize her – Why not?" To this I replied, "Having been introduced to your daughter twenty-six times, and having been snubbed by her quite as often, I have decided that I do not care to know her." Austin laughed, and so did I. He told me that I had a clear case against Mattie, one that he could endorse. Soon after, Mattie joined me after church service, and she said, "Ned and I are going to call on you some evening this week –" Hesitating a moment I said – "Oh, are you?" She tossed her head and replied, "You will soon find out." They called Wednesday evening, remained until half past ten, and we liked Ned. He was so outspoken and sincere, so courteous, and entertaining that we kept his friendship as long as he lived. Sue and Mattie did their best to dominate her [Vinnie], in every possible manner, especially after Ned's death. I have always thought that Vinnie never would have turned against your dear mother had not her mind been poisoned by "the two black devils," as Mrs. Tuckerman, the Esty boys' aunt, called Sue and Mattie. . . .

Vinnie did not dare say aught against your mother to me and she knew that I loved and admired the friend who really introduced Emily to the great literary world. I think *in her heart* Vinnie admired and loved your mother, but dared not admit it on account of some dire threat held over her head.

Vinnie told me of the lawsuit, and Ned talked it over with us, but it is not very distinct in my memory. I remember that Ned said, "If my aunt wins the suit, Mattie and I may join the church, as that would be the biggest thing we could do in this small college town."

The attitude between "the two houses" was one of war, and Sue was the cause of all the discord and strife as far as I could learn. . . .

. . . I copied many of them ["Further Poems"], and intended helping Vinnie to do as she wished me to, and there was "war between the houses", especially severe, and so much was done to cruelly hurt Vinnie, that she became seriously ill, and I returned the precious manuscript after keeping same for four or five months, giving them into Vinnie's hands, & telling her to hide them well. She hid them so well that they were not discovered for – was it twenty years, or thirty? If I am not mistaken Mattie has mentioned two, if not three places where she found them. In a box with old deeds, mortgages, etc. In a large book, and I can't tell where the third hiding place was. The Manuscript given me was *all* in Emily's handwriting. When Vinnie was so ill, Mattie came to see me one morning, and said, "By the Dr's orders, no one is to see Aunt Vinnie so please do not try to see her again." Vinnie had asked me to see her daily, and to write to her old lover, telling him of her condition. In the first letter that I received from Mr Copeland, he asked "Is there a battle going on between the two houses? Can I be of any help to Vinnie, if I visit Amherst?" As soon as Mattie was out of sight, I went to Miss Vinnie's, and met Dr Haskell, at the door. I asked if I might see Vinnie, or if he had given orders for me to keep away. He said, "Miss Vinnie wants you here as often as you can arrange to come – and, so do I." Before my visit ended that morning, Mattie came in with a handful of red roses, and she was furious when she found me there. She asked Vinnie if she was tired, and poor Vinnie who whispered all she had to say, managed to tell her that my little visits rested, and comforted her.

Never have I lived where one family ruled as the D's did in Amherst, and, as the Oliver Hunt family ruled in the First Church. And why? Was it because people were afraid of Sue's tongue, of what she might say? My brother and I went just once to the Austin D. house by invitation. That sufficed. . . .

You certainly will *feel* the awful spirit that rises in me whenever Sue or Mattie are in my thoughts, and I believe that generally speaking, Amherst people feel as I do, yet pretend otherwise for fear of the sulphur fumes of Mattie's condemnation. . . .

March 13, 1934

MLH TO MTB

The *cause* of her [Vinnie's] last illness was Sue who terrified her, and treated her shamefully. It began in the fall of '98. Vinnie always had Emily's rose bushes, and other shrubs carefully attended to before cold weather. When the day came for having the work done, the man told Vinnie that all the "dressing" had been taken from under the barn, and Maggie found out that Sue had ordered it put on her flower beds and shrubs. That stunned Vinnie. She sent for me, and I found her hardly able to speak. When I learned the reason for her condition, I laughed, and said, "Miss Vinnie, just get Mr Lindsay to bring you a load of fertilizer, and say nothing to Sue. Let her find you equal to the battle, and *don't* let her hurt you". Her heart was so rapidly beating that I cautioned Maggie to watch her. Mr Lindsay came to the rescue, and then Sue began to send "Sport" over to Vinnie's, and he worried the pussies. Finally Vinnie could endure no more, and she went to bed. She asked me to write to Mr. Copeland, and he wrote beautiful letters of tender sympathy, offering to come to her if she so desired, and he wrote me, asking if "the other house" was causing any trouble. . . .

Vinnie was not well all winter, and was not up during the summer – it was "the Dickinson heart" as she called it, and Dr. Nelson Haskell was her physician. . . .

Vinnie did not see much of Sue for several years, and rarely after Austin's death. Ned was kind to his aunt, and did all he could to cheer her, and she was fond of him. . . .

I may have written your Mother, or told her, of my visit one Sunday, after service, when Austin was ill. I saw him alone on the piazza, and he greeted me most cordially, asked me if I thought it would do him any harm to take a trip by water. I felt that Sue was not far away, invisible though, and I said I thought, with a jolly good friend to go with him, the trip might do him good. "Getting away might give you a brace", I told him. Then Sue came out and asked if I intended to imply that leaving his family would help recovery. I said, "Sometimes it does. It might in this case." Sue left, and I did not remain long. That was the last time I saw Austin. How he *suffered*. . . .

[259

March 20, 1934

MTB to MLH

   . . . Did Miss Vinnie ever talk to you about her suit against my mother? *Why* did she sue mamma for that piece of land – after all that mamma had done for her? Do you know why she did it? What was the real motive? I have wondered and wondered about it. Though it has warped my life, I never have fully understood it. Was Vinnie happy after she got the land back? If it does not tire you, please tell me sometime all you remember about it, and Sue's part in it.

   The more you tell me about Vinnie the more profoundly sorry I am for her. Poor, lonely, loyal, terror-stricken last of her race in the grip of a relentless alien like Sue! What a tragedy! But my father still speaks of her with affection. Why did she turn away from her best friends – my mother and even more my father who was devoted to her? All you say is heartbreaking.

April 10, 1934

MLH to MTB

   . . . Yes Vinnie spoke several times to me of "the suit," and I thought that she greatly regretted having been forced into it. Really, if Sue had kept her finger out of Vinnie's pies, there would not have been trouble of any depth. Vinnie never was loved by Austin as Emily was, and had he lived, there would not have been a suit. Ned talked very freely about the matter but only in regard to Vinnie appearing in court. We have thought his death was hastened by the friction at home over the suit. He felt by "the traditions of the family," to stand by his aunt. . . . Sue did everything in her power to *down* your adorable mother, and it made her furious that she had absolutely no influence over "the Halls". Mrs. A.B.H. Davis told me that Mrs Neill, & Mrs Donald – whose husband was rector of the Church of the Ascension, in N.Y. City, at the time – urged her to take sides with Mrs D. against your Mother, and Mrs Davis told them that she admired your Mother very much, & always enjoyed meeting her, and saw no reason whatever for hurting her. She also said she had known Sue D. for many years, and she did *not* admire her, and she blamed *her* for having made so much trouble in town among people whom she pretended to like, and whom she had treated shamefully. It must have been Sue who held a sword over Vinnie's head, ready to let it drop if she did *not* get that land back. It was not Vinnie who started the trouble, I am sure of that.

   Ned told us that his father left your Mother a picture, possibly two, that had hung in their parlor. Sue declared that the pictures never should be taken from the house, but Ned said he planned to take his mother & sister abroad for a few months, and would send them to N.Y. City for a few days while he closed the house. He planned to have the pictures boxed, and taken to your house, before leaving Amherst, and I suppose he did. He was loyal to Austin's memory, & especially after his father's death he was particularly fine.

Of course Vinnie missed your father – your mother also – but Satan, or Sue, was her deadly foe, and she *dared not* do what would madden the enemy. She had no one to defend her, and Sue was bitter, and cruel & revengeful. . . .

Feb. 20, 1935

MLH TO MTB

. . . If I remember correctly, Austin died in 1895, and of course Miss Vinnie was in the depths of loneliness; she had depended much upon her brother, and was ready to do whatever he wished her to regarding your Mother, and she did carry notes to him from your Mother during his illness, taking care never to be seen by any member of the family.

During your Mother's absence in Japan, Sue found the opportunity of getting in her chance for revenge, by telling Miss Vinnie about the strip of land, and she influenced her to do as she did, in order to get *in* with Miss Vinnie, that she might use her to get back the land, and to get control of her for the remainder of her life. For one thing she feared that Miss Vinnie might make a will favorable to others, giving Ned & Mattie only what the law obliged her to give.

Millicent, you never will know what an evil minded person Sue was. You cannot imagine such a fiend, for Sue could appear like "an angel of light", when it served her purpose to do so. . . . Miss Vinnie was devoted to Ned, and he was really a friend to her, but he was influenced by Sue, in the desire to get back the land, although he did his best to avoid the publicity of a law-suit, and it was one of the hardest things he ever did to go to Northampton with her, and remain by her side during the trial. Ned spoke freely to us about it, and he felt that his Mother was going too far in making such an exhibition of Miss Vinnie. . . .

My dear, your Mother never did anything to Miss Vinnie that caused her to act as she did. In her heart, she missed your Mother, but she *dared* not defy Sue. Sue was relentlessly cruel to Miss Vinnie in every possible way, and they hated one another with a deadly hate; even I was treated in the most offensive manner by Sue, but I simply ignored her, for I could do what Miss Vinnie felt she must not, on account of Ned. After Ned's death there were tragic battles between the two houses, and I was called to Miss Vinnie's many times to quiet her nerves, and help her recover from Sue's *verbal* blows.

Dec. 29, 1939

MLH TO MTB

I do not think Emily was a victim of Amherst social life. Instead I think her home life, its atmosphere, and her father's austere and stern character had a large part in the kind of life she chose to live.

May 3, 1940

MRS. S. S. PRESTON TO MTB

. . . dear Miss Hall left us Feb 17 – . . .

May 13, 1940

Mrs. Preston to MTB

Your letter inquiring about Miss Hall's letters, yes I can tell you about them she destroyed most of them before she passed away, and I destroyed what she left. The things (letters) she left was her late mail. But when she found her eye sight was failing so fast she went through her things and destroyed them. . . .

2

Mrs. Bingham included, in *Ancestors' Brocades,* Miss Jordan's account of the trial much as it appears here, an obvious polishing up of what Miss Jordan recounted in conversation. The other gleanings from the interview with Miss Jordan seem to be from notes taken at the time, or hurriedly written up shortly after. In *Ancestors' Brocades* (p. 359), Mrs. Bingham describes Miss Jordan as an "eyewitness" at the trial. Her interest in the trial, her detailed memory of it over the years, and her seemingly intimate knowledge of Dickinson gossip indicate, if nothing else, the impact of the doings of this extraordinary family on that whole Connecticut Valley area. (It is to be recalled that Maria Whitney was a member of the Smith College faculty from 1875 to 1880.)

Mary A. Jordan to Millicent Todd Bingham, interview of November 3–4, 1934

Miss Jordan remembers the trial, the relations of the Dickinsons, the attitude of the public to my mother and father, all in the greatest detail. She says mamma had a rather superior way with people and they were rather pleased to see the verdict go against her. Moreover, they enjoyed the trial exceedingly, it was very amusing. In fact, it was *opera bouffe.* It was generally recognized that Lavinia was putting up a ludicrous testimony.

"Miss Dickinson, is not this your signature?"

"Yes – that is to say, that's my autograph. I understood that someone in Boston wished my autograph, and thought that was what I was doing when I wrote it."

"Did you know that this was a release?"

"Isn't that business? I know nothing of business."

"Did you not know that this was a contract?"

"Isn't that business, too? Father always attended to business."

"Miss Dickinson, did you never employ labor?"

"No."

"Do you mean that you never hired servants?"

With lifted, inquiring eye-brows, "Does he mean Maggie?"

The judge had the greatest difficulty to control himself.

Miss Jordan thinks that the decision went in her favor not at all because of facts, for everybody knew that she had known what she was doing, but because it was felt that she had changed her mind about wanting mamma to have the property, and she should be allowed to change her mind.

Miss Jordan thinks mamma was greatly to blame for having attempted to get her to carry through her promise and to sign the deed, even though it had long been her intention to do so.

Miss Jordan thinks that Sue did not intimidate her, because nobody could, not her man of business either, as Miss Buffum thinks. Besides that, she was a complicated and adroit liar. She lived entirely in fiction and in her own imagination.

According to Lavinia, via Miss Jordan, when Miss Lyon said to Emily, "Have you said your prayers?" Emily replied, "Yes, why shouldn't I? Though it can't make much difference to the Creator." Emily was not unsympathetic, indeed, she was very affectionate according to Lavinia. She gave this as an instance. Emily asked the milk-boy one morning, "How did the great grey cat strike you?" "She didn't strike me."

When it comes to Sue, she was a lady who was known to have doubtful relations with other men besides Samuel Bowles. Had county-family manner, which is exaggerated in her daughter. Miss Jordan understands Mattie perfectly, calls her vain and pompous, an accomplished liar and a seducer of youth. She described a dinner party when she took the actor, Mr. Harrison, an Englishman, to dinner at Mattie's and his horror when, trying to place the date when something happened, she said, "Oh, that must have been when I was lying in with my first book." She throws around names and facts with equal abandon, and always supplied a sensation in Amherst which relieved the monotony. I questioned whether there is any interest which is real in her life, one which keeps her going. Miss Jordan thought she must sometimes get tired of pose, of nothing else.

Once she came over to Northampton and tried to vamp George McCallum. She came with a maid, in lordly manner, to make sure that it was all right. She talked at length about the "Count" [Bianchi] and his ancestral jewels. Miss Jordan thinks she bought them herself. Though he posed as Russian, he was Austro-Italian. Professor Tyler tried to save her, for "After all, she is a Dickinson." Bianchi used up all her money, and only Professor Tyler saved her mother's money from going the same way.

At the time of the 1898 trial, Field brought the correspondence between Dr. Dickinson and mamma to Miss Jordan and asked her to read it, and she kept it from coming up in the trial. They intended to use it as evidence that this land was payment by Austin for services other than the editing of Emily's poetry. This of course I doubt, inasmuch as they had none of Austin's or mamma's letters in their possession.

Miss Jordan begs me to let the whole thing alone. If I attempted to deny anything she may say in print, I couldn't prove a thing. It would be her word against my word and she is enormously clever, and entirely unscrupulous. And as for Amherst, I couldn't count on anybody. People do not like to get mixed up in such things. She concluded with, "I wouldn't get between the upper and lower jaws of that tradition, if I were you."

Thinks mamma made Emily – calls it creative editing – says that a woman who couldn't choose among half a dozen words, was mostly juggling with the Dictionary. Thinks Emily artificial & living in imagination entirely.

[The following is a transcript of Mrs. Bingham's penciled notes apparently from the same interview, followed by some jottings on separate, small scraps of paper.]

[Miss Jordan quoting Austin (?)]:

"People talk a lot about the play spirit. Never heard about the play spirit when I was a boy. When I was restless my mother put me in the wood-box and gave me an onion. Lavinia used to say, 'There ought to be an executive in every family. Father was always the executive in ours – After he died, [I] tried to be. I tried to be constructive. They said I should clean house. So I appointed the fourth of July – And had it done then. No calamity happened. So, if we got through it all right once, that ought to prove it can be done. And it did.' "

They were all remarkable. Was Sue? Oh yes, in her aplomb – She & her son & daughter put on all the airs of a county-family. They wanted to have a salon in Amherst with Samuel Bowles & his questionable relationship to Mrs. Austin as a background. They and their adjectives did not impress me. Mansion. Their statements of fact I sometimes questioned. (Miss Margaret Whitney in Farmington with Mattie. But Mattie didn't stay long) Mattie referred to her mother as "Dolly." In fact calling people by their first names was part of the technique of the salon – (Hitchcocks w[ith] all their integrities & all their angularities) Jealousies bet. Amherst & Smith – Bowles feminist & tried to get the Smith money to make Amherst coed and "a really 1st class institution" Resented the implication. Split the town – Over our dead bodies said the old timers. Seelye in particular – So Smith was founded, with L. Clark, who believed in the gentlewoman but not in feminism, at the helm – So close was he that Smith has more ready money than Amherst which added to the rift. Ned told Miss Jordan that she [Emily?] was a left-over of the Brontës. . . .

Miss Margaret, Emily & Maria Whitney, 186 Edwards St. – Miss Maria Whitney destroyed all her correspondence before she died as she wished to leave nothing to burden any relatives. Reserved, a great student & friend of prominent men. Loved teaching.

Further Poems in Atlantic not Emily
Sue a woman who despised her husband and was the soul mate of Sam
    Bowles.
Mrs. Bowles ill, [word illegible] for Republican & woman suffrage.
Miss Whitney an aristocrat who was conscious of it.
Lavinia said there ought to be someone in every family who would say
    Damn. Father did, but now up to her. "Damn, d.d." . . .

3

MY PERSONAL ACQUAINTANCE WITH EMILY DICKINSON*
by Clara Newman Turner

Edited by Clara Newman Pearl

SOON AFTER THE FIRST PUBLICATION of the Letters of Emily Dickinson in 1894, Mrs. Sidney Turner (Clara Newman) of Baltimore, a niece of Edward Dickinson, wrote for her friends a rather intimate account of Emily Dickinson's life. It was for them alone, for she felt that it would be sacrilege to give to the world the details of the private life of that shy, retiring personality. She remembered Emily's own words that she did not deem it "feminine" to publish. But after a lapse of more than thirty-five years I feel that I may be forgiven for publishing that account.

In March, 1852, Mary, a sister of Edward Dickinson, died. Mark Newman, her husband, followed her a few months later, and left his children and estate in the care of Edward Dickinson. He took the children to Amherst soon after the death of their parents, and after Austin Dickinson's marriage, placed the two younger children, Clara and Anna in Austin's family. Anna was my mother. She died when I was a child, but Clara, my aunt, the author of this account, born in 1844, married Sidney Turner, and lived to be seventy-eight years old. Mrs. Austin Dickinson was a woman of very peculiar disposition and the life of the two girls in the family of their cousin, Austin Dickinson, was far from happy. After my aunt was seventy years old I heard her say that she could not understand why Uncle Edward made them stay there when he knew how unhappy they were. For instance, my aunt to the end of her long life never willingly sat in a lighted room unless the shades were drawn for a favorite punishment of Cousin Sue's had been to make her study an entire evening seated in a lighted bay window with the shades up. It was my aunt's duty to take care of little Ned Dickinson, and my mother's to care for Mattie. My mother depended upon her sister always and my aunt in turn upon her Cousin Emily for counsel and support. As soon as an older sister, who had been placed in the family of William Dickinson of Worcester, married, both my mother and aunt went to live with her. My mother never went back to Amherst. My aunt went back each year to the old home and was married from Austin Dickinson's home. For many years the two orphan girls were in and out of their uncle's home almost every day. His two nieces never wavered in their love and loyalty to their Uncle Edward. . . .

Edward Dickinson has always been a very real person to me. His wife has not. As a child I remember standing beside my mother's sewing table and asking, "What was Aunt Emily like, Mother?" And her reply, "Aunt Emily was a Norcross." For years I wondered just what a Norcross could be.

I, personally, was brought up to believe that there never was what one would call a serious love affair. However, women of the old school, so

* Printed by permission of the Jones Library, Amherst. (Again, I have omitted the major passages appearing in the text or notes.)

called, like my aunt, did not discuss private family affairs with their "in-laws", nor a love affair before a young girl. I feel sure that the love and loyalty of the older generation were such that they never would have discussed the story of Emily's love affair with any outside person, even had there been such an experience in her life.

I never saw Emily Dickinson. In my childhood remembrance she is a dearly loved cousin who wore white in winter, as well as in summer, and who never would have her picture taken. This letter to my mother (the Madonna Anna) was rescued by my father when other personal letters from Emily were destroyed.

> "It hardly seems credible that the brave little Boy and the celestial little Girl are Anna's, and yet would we not expect her to be the Mother of Poets and Prophets, were she the mother of anyone at all, as the Mail so sweetly assures us.
>
> The bestowal of two such Fairies upon a sordid World, is of itself Prowess, and we give our hallowed congratulations to the Madonna Anna.
>
> The picture of the pretty home is very warm and vivid and we half "touch" it too, unless softly forbidden-not with mortal Fingers, but those more Tidy, mental ones which never leave a blot. Thanks, dear, for the beatific Package, a murmur of the Saints, and never hide so long again from

your seeking Cousins,

EMILY."

I knew and loved Lavinia, her sister. I shall always remember Cousin Vinnie as she arrived at my aunt's home in Norwich, Connecticut. With her was Professor Todd of Amherst whose friendship and reliability never failed her. He used even to wind her clocks on Saturday night. Family and friends were gathered there at Norwich to pay their last respects to Sidney Turner, my aunt's husband. A slight figure wrapped in an old squirrel-lined circular flew up the steps and into the house. A rusty crepe veil fluttered in the wind as she hurried to my aunt's side. It was the first time that she had been out of Amherst for twenty years, and she was the center of attraction as long as she stayed. My fifteen year old curiosity made me ask why she did not leave Amherst more often. I remember well her reply. "Because, my dear, I do not like to travel. One sees so many people and things that one does not wish to see."

This letter to my aunt from Maggie speaks of the visit.

"MY DEAR MRS. TURNER

How kind of you to give me a thought in youre large Hart Where there is So Much Sorrow just Now. I wish I were big enough to have some of the outer Sorrow that Seround you. Bleve me that if my Sympaty could only Bring you back youre love again youre hart would never Know What Pain ment. I hope the dear one whome you grive for is Safe in that Heavenly home Where he is Master of Pain and dont remember

the past you were So thoughtfull of dear dear Vinnia When she went to
you that she Never Will for get, how beautifull every thing looked in
youre lovely home and that nice vissit that you had with her in bed
that morning She So ofton Spakes of it I hope you will come to Amherst
some time this summer and have a nother Picknick with us in this
dear old home We Will make you happy if we can Vinnia has not being
Very Well this last few Weeks I hope she will sone be better The Doctor say she will to tell the truth of it She is not strong and cant get a
long with things that She have no write to be troubled with it Will always be so as far as I see all are well around here / But a few are happy
I hope the summer will give you a grate dale of Strenth and Some
Plasure dont work for others have little thought for yourself

We have 5 cats 2 in the house and 3 in the Barren all well and good
apetited so far again I think you for all youre kindness to me I hope
youre hart will always remain here as there is not many more like it as
I have reason to remember long, long, a go

Some time I will Write to you on
other Subjects
youre servent
Miss Emely.s and
Vinnia.s

Maggie"

My aunt went occasionally to Amherst for a visit with Cousin Vinnie. For
years I think she was the only overnight guest in that household and I was
always interested to hear about faithful and devoted Maggie and the
humorous cats, each with its own saucer. During my aunt's visits she and
her hostess always ate at two small tables, a not too sociable arrangement
that alway excited my youthful interest. With a hesitancy bred by an association so intimate and yet so bound by decorum my Aunt Clara begins
her article.

Since Death has loosened the clasps and opened the volume of Emily
Dickinson's poetic life and the world is turning its pages back and forth—
first with curiosity, then with curious interest—and closing the volume
always with wondering admiration, perhaps it may interest you to take a
little nearer look into that life, from the standpoint of one who was in and
out of her home nearly every day for many years. You will pardon my own
personal intrusion, as a necessary background to personal recollections.

I say *Poetic life* speaking as a whole, for from her mixing the bread her
father preferred—in the kitchen—to her mingling of the sunbeams, the
birds, and the flowers in the realm of her poetic thought, it was Fantasy
all the way. Had not others preceded me, I should have hesitated long before
bringing before any even private-public one so modest, so retired, so sensitive, who lived, as she said,

"I'm Nobody! Who are you?
Are you nobody, too?

[267

> Then there's a pair of us – don't tell!
> They'd banish us, you know.
>
> How dreary to be somebody!
> How public, like a frog
> To tell your name the livelong day
> To an admiring bog!"

I am *not* the first, however, to draw aside the curtain, and enter the "Sanctum Sanctorum" of her lovely life, and can only hope her pardon will not have been quite exhausted before she reaches my offense, for I cannot but feel a little guilty, knowing her extreme retirement of nature, and remembering her own remark that she did not deem it "feminine to publish." The only warrant, as you know, which her publishers offer, is this little Prelude to the 1st Series.

> "This is my letter to the world,
> That never wrote to me –
> The simple news that Nature told,
> With tender majesty
>
> Her message is committed
> To hands I cannot see;
> For love of her, sweet countrymen,
> Judge tenderly of me!"

Perhaps this is sufficient, when you place with it the fact that there were found—after she went—over 700 of these little poems, tied in tiny booklets of six pages each. I feel impelled to say just here, however, as my own opinion, that I find no warrant, not even in the world's interested curiosity, or curious interest (as you will) for the first publication of her personally-private letters to a personal friend, on strictly personal, private, and home details. I cannot but feel the friend must ask very humble pardon at the door of her "Mansion", before he be quite acquitted. . . . [*Of Edward Dickinson, she writes:* In our National and State Congress, and holding high positions of public trust for over 40 years, the newspapers spoke of him, after his death, as leaving a name without a stain upon its memory. While making a speech in the Massachusetts Legislature upon the "Hoosac Tunnel bill" one hot day in June '74, he suddenly became faint and sat down. The House adjourned, and he went directly to "The Tremont House", where he died in three hours. It is one of the facts we call *strange,* that although in apparently perfect health, he had sat for his picture only a week or two before for the first time in many, many years, and the finished photographs surprised his home after he had been borne beyond its doors forever.

Mrs. Dickinson was a quiet, sweet, practical, unpretentiously-modest woman, with the sweetly-hushed voice of her daughter's inheritance, to whom I think Emily was a great mystery and constant surprise. The family would have died for each other, in their loyalty to, and pride in one another, but in my many years of daily intercourse with them, I never saw exchanged any marked *demonstration* of affection. I speak thus in detail, to give you a little glimpse of the characteristics of the atmosphere into which the daughter Emily was born in Amherst, December 10th, 1830. She was not born in the house in which she died, but was laid to rest—the light of her Day just set—only a few steps from where she opened her eyes upon her day just begun.

It is not what the world would call an *eventful life,* of which we ask. Her childhood and youth were as joyous as the birds she loved. Amherst was the home of her whole life and education, with the exception of one year, into which she crowded a two years' course of study in South Hadley under Miss Mary Lyon and a short stay in Washington while her father was in Congress. She was, while in South Hadley, the idol of the school and its Preceptress, and her appointment for a composition marked a "Red Letter Day." To illustrate the independence and honesty of her convictions, —Miss Lyon, during a time of religious interest in the school, asked all those who wanted to be Christian to rise. The wording of the request was not such as Emily could honestly accede to and she remained seated—the only one who did not rise. In relating the incident to me, she said, "They thought it queer I didn't rise"—adding with a twinkle in her eye, "I thought a lie would be queerer." This letter to my aunt, my *aunt* would never have published.

"The cordiality of the Sacrament extremely interested me when a Child, and when the Clergyman invited 'all who loved the Lord Jesus Christ to remain', I could scarcely refrain from rising and thanking him for the to me unexpected courtesy, though I now think had it been to all who loved Santa Claus, my transports would have been even more untimely.
                                                                      EMILY"

Her father's house was always the resort of the most cultured and refined, and such were her surroundings always. His home and grounds were thrown open annually for a Lawn Reception to the Alumni of the College and their friends, and at these gatherings Emily was accustomed, at first, to take a daughter's place. Later she was seen for shorter and shorter times, until in the latter years, her appearance was but a prelude to her disappearance, after just a word to one or two favored friends. She was full of fun and had a keen sense of the ludicrous, although I do not think you gather this from her poems.

To repeat, the world would not call her's an eventful life. *Her events* were the coming of the first bird;—the bursting of a chrysalis;—the detection of the fascinating spring fuzz of green in the air—the wondering opening on the new world of every little flower; an unusual sunset; the autumn changes—and the inexhaustible life. Her *Tragedies*—the wild storm:—the bruising of a plant;—the falling of a young bird from its nest;—a hurtful slight to an animal;—the falsity of a friend—a surprise upon her retreat;— an unfriendly act to *her* friend. The death of one she loved was to her the saving of them for her, I think, a little later on, and not so much a tragedy as would be a possible perfidy in life. . . .

Winter was the absence of Nature's Panorama, and was filled with excited anticipation of the renewal of her miracles. *Then*—her pictures, changed every morning, in the infinite resources of an Infinite Artist—were the "undressed hills";—the stalactites of Nature's enclosing circles;—and the

[269

Frost-King in his studio—Monarch only while the opposing sceptre of the Sun was withheld.

Her Opera was the trilling of the birds outside her window;—the buzzing of the bees;—the flitting in and out of the butterflies in their gauzy costumes. The crickets, and the frogs, and the breeze in its orchestra;—the many tinted trees, the sky and the clouds, the God-painted scenery—and though there were nothing to count to assure the fact, the auditorium was always full, because her great appreciative heart was all there.

Of her loves you can judge somewhat by this little tribute to her sister, in a letter to a friend whose brother had just gone. She says, "Your bond to your brother reminds me of mine to my sister—early—earnest—indissoluble. Without her, life were tears, and Paradise a cowardice, except for her inciting voice."

She was a great reader and a dainty reader. You remember her questioning the need of any other book after she had found Shakespeare. Her selections were the choicest—I should have as readily believed of her reading anything but the best, the purest, the most uplifting, as I should dream of the snow falling any other color than white. Her books? To quote her own words, "For poets—I have Keats and Mr. and Mrs. Browning. For prose—Mr. Ruskin, Sir Thomas Browne, and the Revelations. When a little girl I had a friend who taught me Immortality; but, venturing too near himself, he never returned. Soon after—my tutor died, and for several years my Lexicon was my only companion." Had her "Lexicon" been of her own making, we should not have called her poverty-stricken.

Listen to a few of her uncompiled definitions:—

"*Presentiment* is that long shadow on the lawn
Indicative that suns go down:
The notice to the startled grass
That darkness is about to pass.

Hope is the thing with feathers
That perches in the soul,
And sings the tune without the words,
And never stops at all.

Experiment – to me – is every one I meet. If it contain a kernel?

Home – is the definition of God.

Sunset. Where ships of purple gently toss
On seas of daffodil,
Fantastic sailors mingle
And then – the wharf is still.

Remorse is memory awake
Her companies astir;
A presence of departed acts
At window and at door.

The Humming-bird. A route of evanescence
With a revolving wheel:
A resonance of emerald
A rush of cochineal.

The Sea – An everywhere of silver
With ropes of sand
To keep it from effacing
The track called land.

Prayer is the little implement
Through which men reach
Whose presence is denied them."
(I think I'll finish this)
"They fling their speech
By means of it in God's ear,
If then He hear.
This sums the apparatus
Comprised in prayer."

(Webster, and Worcester, and Johnson, and the rest seem a little like prosaic Monday morning, do they Not?)

My own personal acquaintance with Emily Dickinson began when I was a young school girl, and many were the interests I took to her at our trysting-place, on the top stair of the flight leading down to a side hall. It was almost dark but opened into many retreats for my fawn-like friend. On a few never-to-be-forgotten occasions she read to me there a verse or two before enclosing in some friendly letter asking me to tell her what it meant to me and calling me her little *World*. I think I can never feel more proud than when she honored me by thinking I understood her. . . .

In one of her letters, you may remember, she says, "While my thought is undressed, I can make the distinction; but when I put them in a gown, they look alike and numb." And this was the reason for her asking at all, as she states in her first letter to Mr. Higginson. "My life," she says, "has been too simple and stern to embarrass any. 'Seen of Angels' scarcely my responsibility." In another place—"I do not cross my father's ground to any house or town." (To my knowledge she did not own a bonnet for 25 years or more.) Her own testimony elsewhere "I oftenest stay with myself", is, to me, a sad little knell of the absence of sympathy in her own peculiar introspective world. "Of shunning men and women," she says, "They talk of hallowed things aloud, and embarrass my dog. He and I don't object to them, if they'll exist their side."

In the first years of my knowing her, she would sometimes come across the grounds to her brother's home and spend an hour in chatting with us all. Gradually these "angel visits became few and far between" indeed, and more and more quaint like herself. For instance—I remember, as I confided my hopes and fears to her ever-sympathetic listening ear before the severe examinations (taken alone) for entrance to the High School—then equal to the College examination—she would only repeat "I am sure of success, I see nothing else," until I met it brave in her courage. The morning of the dreaded ordeal came a little note on this wise,—"A little flower is sitting beside me waiting to be a Crown."

Released from my hard day only just before supper, I had no time to take her word that her kind prophecy was true, but I had no need, for, being summoned from the table, I found Emily in the dark just outside the door holding out the fair flower, and her sweet voice said, "Nobody came to tell us, and the little flower was so impatient to be a crown, it insisted upon bringing me over."

As this retirement grew upon her she rarely saw anyone outside her immediate home circle, although one and another of the Literati of the country have come—at times far—to see her. A glass of wine and a flower, accompanied with a note or line (as in one instance with a Cape Jessamine, the quotation "I, Jesus, send mine angel") and the visitor must be sufficed, if the Spirit within that strange little self did not move her to be seen.

I have been asked repeatedly what led to this withdrawing of herself from the world—was it some disappointment? If, by this, disappointment in love is meant, implying love unrequited, I answer almost an indignant *No*. If disappointment in *Life* is meant, consider her intensely sensitive nature, and exceeding individual mind and its longings, and you will readily accept my reply that I am sure there were *many*—but Life is not all Love, you know, although Love may be the sweetest part of all life. It began by simply not joining in some things which were not congenial and a gradual withdrawing from many things which we none of us hardly realized so subtly did it come, until *others* spoke of her as a Recluse. You know how imperceptibly such changes *can* approach.

One or two more little home incidents. Her little nephew, boy-like, had a way of leaving anything superfluous to his immediate needs at Grandma's. After one of these little "Sins of Omission", over came his high-top rubber boots, standing erect and spotless on a silver tray, their tops running over with Emily's flowers. At another time the little overcoat was returned with each velvet pocket pinned down, and a card with "Come in" on one, and "Knock" on the other. The "Come in" proved to be raisins;—the "Knock", cracked nuts. Do you blame the little fellow for leaving his things round over there? The boy was my care, but I never could be generous enough to discourage the failing.

She was very fond of music, and at one time played not a little on the piano. When I knew her, her Repertoire was quite limited—consisting of but three tunes. One of these she called "The Devil", and it was weird and quaint enough to warrant the title. She had learned it on an old-fashioned piano, two octaves shorter than the modern "Chickering" which then stood in her home parlor, and always before seating herself to play, she covered these superfluous octaves, that the keyboard might accord with her education. After she became more reclusive, and gave up the piano entirely I had the pleasure of playing for her and quite often would come to me just some little word as, "Emily is tired, and the sweet voice in the parlor cannot speak to her alone," or "There's a voice in the down-stairs; I call, but it does not answer." I answered the summons when I could, and never without some acknowledgement. Sometimes a flower on the piano stool, again a little plate of fresh cookies, or, best of all, a word written out for me. How I regret we had not known the Angel-Genius we were entertaining, and so had preserved these little missives! Is it always "Unawares"? What hourly caution lies in the answer!

Returning each year after my marriage, for short stays to her own home, so long as my Uncle lived, my visits with Emily were always in her own room after the evening was done below stairs, and by appointment her door was left ajar. "I don't speak things like the rest" was her apology and her "speaking things" like herself would delight my very soul often far into the night, or even early morning. I was not present at Mr. Dickinson's funeral. The following Christmas when I enclosed a Christmas wreath for his grave with the little remembrances for the living, Emily wrote thus in acknowledgement, "I am sure you must have remembered that Father had become 'as little children' or you would never have dared send him a Christmas gift, for you know how he frowned upon Santa Claus, and all such prowling gentlemen."

The next time I saw her was at the burial of her Mother. Arriving only in time for the service, I saw nothing of Emily, save a line asking for a word as I went away. On our way to the train, we stopped at the door just a moment and Emily, calling me *behind* the door, looking pale and worn with her anxious watching and grief, said she just wanted to thank Mr. Turner and myself for coming so far "to speak to Mother. She cannot thank you herself today, you know, but some other day," and this was the last time I ever saw her sweet face.

She *died* (as we say) quite suddenly May 15th, '86, of a disease which owing to her extreme reticence and retirement of disposition, and reluctance to confer with a physician, was hastened, no doubt, when it might possibly have been retarded, though not cured. Two years before—breaking through all reserve, and at night—she had had a chill while ministering to death in her brother's house, and was taken home unconscious. Three times during those two years she had similar attacks, and from little casual remarks doubtless she knew within herself that her note of warning had been sounded and she had heard. On Thursday, May 13th, '86, the message came very tenderly, for she became unconscious almost at once and so remained until Saturday afternoon, when Death gave her Life "the other side." I think it must have been during these two years, (although there is no date) that she wrote these poems.

Greatly to my regret, I was unable to attend Emily's funeral, being called to sickness by a telegram received the same hour with that which called me to her. They folded her in a little white wrap* I had sewed for her myself the last Christmas, little dreaming I was weaving her shroud, and she lay in her white casket in the hall of her father's house, while the bees and the butterflies she had immortalized, buzzed a Requiem without the open door. A knot of field blue violets lay at her throat, and a wreath of the same modest flower was the only decoration on her casket. The ser-

---

* Compare "Emily Dickinson, Face to Face," p. 61, Mrs. Powell.

vice was very simple. The Pastor of the Congregational Church of Amherst read from the Scriptures. Rev. Mr. Jenkins of Portland led in prayer, and Col. Higginson followed with the reading of Emily Brontë's last Poem, prefacing the reading by this introduction, "I will read a poem, our friend who has just now put on Immortality, and who seemed scarce ever to have taken it off, used to read to her sister."

The brief service concluded, six stalwart men, with whose faces she had been familiar, and who had rendered glad service as she toiled among her out-door friends—the flowers—lifted her on their shoulders and bore her—into the street? Ah no! That would have been a way almost as strange and unknown for her, to pass, as is to us today that upon which she has entered, while we stand without, as yet unbidden to follow.

The Cemetery lay three fields away, and the bars being lowered between —the light little burden led the way through meadows *filled* with buttercups and daisies, and they stood sentinels of her path, or bowed their heads as the funeral train brushed them by. Place these facts by her poem.

> "Let down the bars O Death!
> The tired flocks come in
> Whose bleating ceases to repeat
> Whose wandering is done."

Following the benediction, they turned away to leave her numbered now with those of whom she had so beautifully said,

> "Deep in their alabaster chambers
> Untouched by moon, and untouched by noon;
> Sleep the mute members of the Resurrection,
> Roof of satin, and Rafter of stone."

And we spoke of her as *Dead!* How later facts have reproved our mistake! Like the butterfly she had shown to the children in her conservatory, she had burst the chrysalis only to find wings for a wonderful delight-giving life. The Recluse is entering stranger homes all over the land. The quiet sweet voice calls even across the great waters.

Although there is no "Mould of her"—pen pictures leave her no stranger. Her secluded home life is eagerly asked and entered by the wondering Many. The dainty Poems of the modest little woman who deemed it "unfeminine" to publish have reached edition after edition in publication. Can we say she *died?*

Beside her bequest of these Poems to her only sister, there was but one other, viz.:—

> "If I shouldn't be alive
> When the Robins come,
> Give the one in red cravat
> A Memorial crumb."

and to the executor of this bequest,

> "If I couldn't thank you,
> Being just asleep,
> You will know I'm trying
> With my granite lip."

I cannot but ask again and again, for what service beyond was this sweetly strange life a preparation? What has she found awaiting her in the fulfilled promise that we shall be *satisfied*? She, who so shrank from people —is she among the multitude who have gone before, and yet *satisfied*? Are there birds, and bees, and clover for her there? Does she go on "making verses", or was her gift only for *this side?* and on and on I question.

Surely since her going Heaven holds a new mystery, and I can only answer in her own words,

> "There are that resting – rise,
> Can I expound the skies?
> How still the riddle lies!
>
>   *   *   *
>
> Faith faints to understand."

4

THE FOLLOWING IS A SYNTHESIS of three separate, brief MSS in the Todd-Bingham Archive. They are all in typescript, with a few penciled corrections in Mrs. Todd's shaky hand (the result of her stroke in 1913), and were enclosed in a manila envelope labeled, in Mrs. Bingham's writing, "Scurrilous but True," after a comment written by Mrs. Todd at the head of one of them. The three repeat one another often, sometimes at length, but each contains material not found in the others. The aim of this synthesis is to avoid repetition (although some still remains) while excluding no detail, not even the opening paragraphs about Mabel Todd's life in Washington, legends of Emily, animadversions on Vinnie, and the accounts of Mabel's work on the editing and of her stroke. All are relevant in some way, I think, to the "War between the Houses." The word "scurrilous" applies, of course, only to the paragraphs dealing with Susan Dickinson. (Words and phrases in brackets indicate, mostly, alternate readings in the MSS. In this instance, I have retained passages that appear in the text, since it is important that they be read in their original context.)

Our life in Washington was especially delightful. I had lived there ever since I was a small child, and my father's particular friends were chiefly the scientific men connected with the Observatory. He had gone from Cambridge where he had been associated with Professor Benjamin Pierce, Asa Gray the botanist, Louis Agassiz and other distinguished men connected with Harvard, James Russell Lowell, Professor Longfellow, and a unique combination of those in his own chosen subjects, and where he had helped to establish the American Ephemeris as distinguished from the British Nautical Almanac. His profession was really mathematics and astronomy, but that did not exclude him from the great interest he always felt in natural sciences as well as English literature, in both of which he was an authority. My grandmother was friendly already with some members of the Cabinet, Senator Hoar as well as Judge Rockwood Hoar, and from the beginning our life there was brilliant and satisfying. I was always on friendly terms with the young men who came to the Observatory from different colleges, to stay temporarily, or permanently as their gifts might develop, and among them was young David Todd, who had been invited to Washington as soon as he graduated from Amherst College (at the age of twenty) by Professor Simon Newcomb, a leading astronomer of America. He was engaged at once on the computations resulting from the last transit of Venus in 1874, and for some years he continued that congenial work. He meantime wrote numerous papers on allied subjects,—a continuation of De Damoiseau's tables of Jupiter's satellites to 1900, on an "Attachment for equatorial mountings to facilitate sweeping in right ascension", two upon his theoretical position of the possible trans-Neptunian planet, and many others which brought his name prominently before the astronomical world.

He soon became of all the young astronomers my best friend, and almost before I was aware of it I found myself engaged to marry him, and I was proceeding with wedding preparations, which culminated on March the fifth, 1879. For two years our brilliant Washington life continued, we made our home with my father and mother at their charming house on College Hill Terrace, where our constantly increasing number of friends augmenting every month gave me genuine happiness and satisfaction. My painting, piano-forte playing which I had pursued for years both in Boston and with Anton Gloetzner in Washington were of course continued, and our life was carried on with much satisfaction to us both. Then our daughter was born, and the days glowed with contentment and achievement.

Into the midst of this eminently happy experience came one day a letter from my husband's old professor at Amherst, Mr. Esty of the mathematics department, inviting him at the President's instigation, to return to Amherst and become Director of the Observatory there. He remarked that his especial student, David Todd, would remember that there was really no professor of astronomy, although his own chair was called "mathematics and astronomy", but what they now desired was an astronomer really, which they knew he was, and they both hoped that he would see the matter in the light they both regarded it, and come to his *alma mater* forthwith.

Of course we discussed this matter for several days. We really did not want to leave Washington even for distinguished consideration from Amherst. To be sure there was no great future in Washington, unless the appointment ultimately of "Professorship in the Navy" where the salary was settled and gradually increasing by slow degrees, but without great financial advantages. My husband had received invitations from one or two western colleges to become their professor of astronomy, which he had refused at once. But his own *alma mater* was slightly different.

At last, weighing advantages and drawbacks with perfectly honest study, we decided to go. Even now I can hardly say that our decision was a wise one. But the result caused our life to proceed on utterly different lines. A small village was henceforth to be our background. My husband's brilliant study of solar eclipses, throughout his life, founded as a basis on his constant expeditions to different parts of the world to observe the phenomena connected with those dramatic happenings in the heavens, made a specialty of the sun, which perhaps gave him wider reach than he could have had in Washington.

At all events, we were established in Amherst with our interest increasing in astronomy constantly, and with the hope that a friend of the college would soon give the funds for a new Observatory—as President Seelye had promised when we came to the little town.

The difference between life in the national capital and in a small New England village was very marked. At first we stayed at the Amherst House, a fairly good New England country hotel, and spent our time for a week or two in looking about the town for a permanent home. After many curious experiences we finally took rooms in a new and somewhat boxy large house "at the end of the village concrete sidewalk," as told us by the philanthropist who had presented the walks to the town. The door was opened upon our ringing by a very tall man in an unusually long linen coat, formerly a clergyman, with the air of a duke. He had been paralyzed to the extent that his left hand was peculiarly lifeless, only the right possessing initiative enough to put the left where it was required; after it was placed in position it could grasp anything wanted. His manner was unexpectedly courteous, and his language polished and elegant. For a time our meals were furnished by a dear old couple in the next house; also an ex-clergyman, as most of the dwellers in Amherst were, those not connected with the college. It was a quaint experience, and interesting to a degree, and almost at once we were invited to the homes of the college faculty so frequently that luncheons and dinners were nearly all taken in the homes of the professors.

Of course there were degrees of cultivation in the various homes, and I speedily made my choice of especial friends. One of the first places I particularly enjoyed was Professor Tuckerman's delightfully English mansion, and I continued to go there frequently all winter. The other was at the Dickinsons' charming home. Mr. and Mrs. Dickinson called on us very soon after we were established in the big new house. He was immensely impressive to me; and she was handsome, with a scarlet India shawl over her shoulders, which became her dark beauty.

That was the beginning. With her accustomed precipitancy she took an immediate fancy to me and to my experiences of life, and she followed me up with invitations until life began to take on a glamorous tint and to glow with colours beyond this existence. She talked to her son Ned and daughter "Mattie" of me until I should have thought they would despise the very sound of my name. But they too fell under the same spell, if so it could be called, which affected their mother, and I was the tutelary deity of their household. Unfortunately for me the son, Ned, fell violently in love with me, and just how to manage that romantic episode escaped my tact. I did not know how to take it. After a while Sue, Mrs. Dickinson, began to tell me about Austin's two sisters, who lived in the old family mansion, alone with a servant of ancestral manners and achievement and years a servant with them. Until that time I had not yet met them, Lavinia, the sister retaining her place in the world yet not frequenting its haunts; and Emily having been described to me as the "myth" and the "shadow lady." For nearly twenty years she had not left the house and grounds, for the last ten years the house was her only abode, and her curious habits formed the text for a hundred queer sermons and talks. There was a legend that she had crept out one evening with her brother as far as a certain tree in the hedge in order to see the new church which her brother had been the most instrumental in building. Old College Hall had been the church which she knew before the new stone Gothic building had arisen; so she went out actually from the house as far as would allow her a view of what she had heard about for months, but had not seen until the wonderful night which took her out into its view. And that was the only time, according to the eager gossips of the town, that Emily went out of the door of her dwelling in many years.

Poor Emily! To be the subject of so much speculation, so much "certain information" through all those years! She did not care—she was secluded from any pain of knowing what was said, and her curious, original life went peacefully onward as she came more and more into her own line of living.

The college, town and general life in Amherst were decidedly different in the early eighties from those in nineteen-thirty-one [nineteen-thirty]. People at that time were much more absorbed in the severities of living than in its gayeties. The faculty were elderly men, their wives estimable ladies of quiet tastes, dressing in dark colours, having their supper at six o'clock, dinner at one, or earlier, not playing cards nor dancing nor doing any of those things which I had been taught in Washington were a part of a lady's equipment; my first thoughts on entering this somewhat peculiar environment were rather amazed, even troubled.

Of course they were all courteous, called duly upon this young woman whose husband, notwithstanding his youth (then twenty-six) had acquired a great reputation for his scientific papers at the Observatory in Washington, had achieved a fine distinction by his observations of the sun's eclipse in Dallas, Texas, when he had been out of college only three years, and was bent upon making the little observatory at Amherst as noteworthy as possible.

My own opinion is that they did not wholly approve of me; the students were beginning their "promenades" and some fraternity dances, and they seemed delighted to have a member of the faculty for a chaperone, one who could also dance! They always supplied me with a dance programme completely filled out with names quite as if I had been a girl.

Every one began by telling me of town matters, explaining relationships, showing how this one and that one might be considered thus and so, and many other matters filled out my list of information quite completely within a short time of my arrival. I quickly learned that Austin Dickinson, the leading lawyer of the region and Treasurer of Amherst College, was deeply reverenced and loved, though slightly dignified in bearing; that his wife, Susan, was [quite generally disliked and] thoroughly distrusted. Notwithstanding, when these two called upon me, I was greatly [much] impressed with both. He was a truly regal man, tall and magnificent in bearing, and she well dressed.

Apparently they were not entirely congenial, a fact which appeared during the short call unmistakably. But I soon saw that life in the New England college town was not to be wholly circumscribed by the orthodox ideas of the majority of the faculty. We were soon invited to—not supper with scalloped oysters as in the majority of entertainments offered us (coming as we did from the native haunts of the oyster at home, oysters were not as foreign a delicacy to us as to the inland givers of suppers in Amherst)—but to dinner, and at half after six o'clock. This was like home, and I revelled in familiar surroundings.

The Dickinson home was very beautiful, planned after a generous Italian villa fashion, and fitted up delightfully inside. The pictures were especially lovely, and I learned soon after that Austin's chief extravagance, it could be so called, was in buying fine pictures. He had gradually accumulated through the past few years a splendid collection, greatly impressive to strangers or persons of susceptible taste [tastes].

About this time Sue, as she was [universally] called in the village, began to tell me about a remarkable sister of Austin's who never went out, and saw no one who called. I heard of her also quite constantly through others in town, who seemed to resent, somewhat, her refusal to see themselves, who had known her in earlier years. Then came a note from this mysterious Emily's housemate, her sister Lavinia. The writing resembled most perfectly the crawlings of a demented house fly, after having lain awhile in the family inkstand. As far as it was translatable I made out that Lavinia was demanding that I call "at once, with my husband."

Discussing this missive with Sue, she said quickly, "You will not allow your husband to go [there] to that house, I hope!"

"Why not?" I asked innocently.

"Because they have not, either of them, any [faintest] idea of morality," she replied, with a certain satisfaction in her tone. I knew that would interest my good husband, and pressing her a bit farther for information [a little farther] she continued, "I went in to the drawing room there one day a few years ago, and found Emily reclining in the arms of a man. What can you say to that?"

I had no explanation, of course, so I let the subject drop, notwithstanding which I went a few days later to the ancestral mansion in which the two [maiden ladies] lived. And then began the picturesque series of encounters which made life in Amherst far from commonplace to me.

Lavinia was a brilliant exponent of ancient wit and comment not involving any superfluous love for one's fellow men, and although I had as yet formed no active likes or dislikes in the town, I could not help enjoying [a liking for] the fierce denunciations which sprung forth from Vinnie's nimble tongue. Her two passions were cats and [her sister] Emily. Her wrath over any person, child or grown-up, who attempted to molest her cats was only equalled by anyone trying to impose upon Emily, for whom she was vigorously alert to protect.

"I hope you will not go very much to the other house," said Vinnie, once, soon after I had made her acquaintance; "I have seen too many hearts broken there," she went on—"And always of those loved and admired [liked and loved] at first." I speedily saw that I should become involved in a family quarrel of endless involutions if I inquired too much into the mazes of feeling between the two houses. The break between them was notorious in Amherst, and persons dropped by Sue used to fly at once to Vinnie, who comforted them after her own unique fashion, by her terrible diatribes against Sue, which grew more and more denunciatory as years went on.

It quickly came out that Vinnie was herself nearly heart-broken by [over] Sue's treatment of Emily, and of course [of] herself, also, only she never counted anything done to herself in comparison with those things [anything] involving her adored Emily. She often said that she knew that Emily would die years before she ought, owing to [the] cruelties practiced upon her almost ever since poor Austin was "taken in" and made to marry outside his normal class, socially.

Her account was really sad and terrible. At first, in earliest years, Emily had tried to make her only brother like and marry her old friend, especially while he was away, after graduation from Amherst, at the Harvard Law School, and for some years she aided and abetted the match [which had made Austin at first melancholy to an unprecedented degree]. When Austin returned, a graduate, he heard himself spoken of every where in town as "engaged" to Sue Gilbert. At first amazed, he denied vigorously any such idea, but finding that she also told "the lie" as he called it, he became so melancholy that life held very little to him with this incubus hanging over him. After a time he foolishly [finally] yielded, really a boy at heart, and consoling himself with the idea [hoping] that possibly his children [from such a match] might have stouter and stronger bodies from their mother being so much nearer the soil than his own inheritance could be [might inherit some strength of body from being so much nearer the soil in their mother's inheritance]. But that idea speedily vanished in her dread of having any children, and her determination to allow no indulgence [not to indulge] in those "low practices" of the average married couple. Finally she gave in, after a fashion, and then those without children [who did not have] were terribly denounced.

[One of the three MSS at this point gives a sufficiently differing version of Austin's courtship and early married life to warrant separate entry:]

At this time Austin was studying law at the Harvard Law School, and as will be remembered by his correspondence with Emily (her letters I published in the first volume of her *Letters*) he was on a really intimate footing with his dear sister. When he returned, flushed with his success at Harvard, he was spoken of in town as "engaged" to Sue. A complete surprise and not entirely a pleasant one, he denied it wherever he heard the assertion. Continual denials, however, seemed to do no especial good, and busy in establishing himself as a young lawyer he finally let the talk of him go, worrying no more about what he termed "silly gossip" about himself.

As it kept on with increasing volume, he was at last forced to pay some attention to the opinions of his neighbors. He comforted himself with the thought that if he really was obliged to marry in that unexpected way, at least he might anticipate that his children would come into the world with fine constitutions, that their health would be assured from the nearness to primitive conditions in their mother's heritage, and his own more delicate ancestry would thus be offset by the toilworn fingers of maternal inheritance. A sort of fatalistic feeling began to flow over him. His sister Emily talked strongly of her friendship with Sue and her wish·that he should not disappoint her, of what she assured him was her great devotion, and of how pleasant it would be if he did marry her good friend.

He said he had never offered himself in marriage to Sue, or anybody else, and when the day of his wedding actually dawned he felt far more as if he were going on to his hanging than to a supposable happy bridegroom's fate.

And very soon he found that the bride of former meek feelings changed utterly. As for children she would have none; she began that loftiness of demeanor which characterized her ever after. Many months elapsed before she would allow "the low practices" of married couples to approach her citadel. The possible ameliorations he had promised himself faded into thin air, and he had to make up his mind to live his own life untouched by any understanding or wish to aid in any of the large thoughts with which he had come back to his native village.

It was certainly a very unwise attitude which Sue assumed as soon as she had a fine husband safely secured from Amherst's best family, that of unutterable superiority to old friends and neighbors, and all new comers in the village. It caused such indignation among the simpler order of persons in town that they continued to repeat every story, real or fancied about her beginnings, and prevented any lapsing of tales of her childhood and girlhood—tales which under a different management of her manner might have been allowed to die a natural death. But her scorn of most of her neighbors kept alive the distressing stories, added to and enlarged as the narrators' imagination might suggest. They even told of her flirtations with delightful Sam Bowles, and of how she sent her husband off for a few hours occasionally in order that she might pursue her foolishness with him, untrammelled. Mr. Bowles was a man full of magnetic personality, and his relations with all his friends were full of this quality of responsiveness and appreciation. A pretty little aunt of mine [in margin: Colette Loomis], who had died shortly after I was born, had felt his affectionate interest in her poems until she had become one of the chief contributors of verse to the well-loved *Republican,* Mr. Bowles's splendid monument. Her friendship with the famous editor and proprietor had formed a bright spot in her short and promising life, which ended before she had passed her twentieth birthday.

A relative who came to the town to make a short visit to Austin, in leaving congratulated him on his most beautiful place, "a real Paradise," said the old man, and then, hesitating a bit "But why, Austin, *why* have you introduced the serpent already?"

Austin's father, the Hon Edward Dickinson, was an old-fashioned gentleman who used to answer the door bell in the evenings carrying a lighted lamp in his hand. In his own newly established home a fine hall lamp was always lighted. "Oh! Yes", said Austin to me in one of his early and heart-broken confessions, "Yes, everything was conducted on modern lines in my establishment. At first it pleased me, of course. The outward adherence to accepted kinds of life was just along my own thought, only I did not want to be so absorbed in the attempts to have the outward seeming instead of the real thing that I should ever forget the real thing." He never could, of course.

For years before I came to Amherst Emily had not had any affectionate relations with the Sue once so loved, and it was years since Vinnie had frequented her brother's house with any freedom. But he loved both his sisters, and his loyalty was always theirs. Of course his genuine love was Emily's, and his half humourous admiration for Vinnie was hardly in the category of real love. Every day he visited them, and it was really a genuine refreshment of spirit to him.

The whole situation was another illustration of the impossibility of a marriage between different grades of society ever becoming a perfect fusion. Sue's father was a "tavern keeper" of decidedly convivial habits, and Austin's father was a dignified gentleman, a lawyer of the old school. The two could hardly have known of each other's existence, mentally, at least. In those early days the democratic mixing of upper and lower classes was, to be sure, much more easily accomplished than in these later and stricter days of preserving family and training carefully. And Sue always made a point of associating principally with daughters of the better class. She was a bright girl, who knew how to put herself on confidential terms with daughters of the upper class in Amherst, and for some years she and Lavinia and Emily were trusting friends.

Town gossip said that Sue inherited all her father's fondness for strong drink. He, poor man, had died in the poor house after his experiences in keeping a tavern; "or in the gutter," said Vinnie, as she first told me Sue's history, with a certain grim satisfaction. One of his sons [Dwight] came to the rescue of the old man's name, and paid back to the town all that had been spent. [Both Todds assumed the worst about Thomas Gilbert. The Greenfield, Mass., records, of which Mrs. Bingham had a search made in the summer of 1930, give a different impression. Gilbert had a good military record in the War of 1812. He was elected to many positions of trust in the town. The titles "Esquire" and "gentleman" recur in the records. The researcher (Lucy Cutler Kellogg) concludes: "I have failed to find anything anywhere that was of an adverse nature to an upright character"—letter to Mrs. Bingham, August 4, 1930.]

Austin's attachment to Emily was a serious matter. She to him was the embodiment of family devotion. Her curious leaving of outer life never seemed unnatural to him. He told me about her girlhood and her normal blossoming and gradual retirement, and her few love affairs; her life was perfectly natural. All the village gossip merely amused him.

For Vinnie he seemed to have a half humorous, half absurd feeling not to be compared to his real feeling for Emily.

Sue had taken me up as her intimate friend at first and then, as usual, dropped me. Austin was, of course, deeply grieved by Sue's abandonment of me as her special friend. "Oh, well," he said almost resignedly, "It is only like other affairs of similar character. There are many persons of admirable qualities still in town, many of them, who have been as violently taken up and as violently dropped. But a great many have left town, grieved to the heart and sadly going elsewhere. Try not to have her defection cause you to leave."

"Indeed no," I replied with spirit, which kept me on my chosen path instead of weakly losing it and so leaving.

David had one or two delightful offers to go elsewhere, but he did not care, really, to leave Amherst before he should have had the happiness of establishing the new observatory, and leaving the astronomical interest of the College well advanced. He had also been appointed professor of astronomy at Smith College, and was just building in Northampton a fine little observatory of which he was to be director for the next year or two, until he could train some member of the Smith faculty to assume that position; so our interests were for the time concentrated in the vicinity [region] of Amherst. President Seelye no longer talked of "the new observatory", but my husband did not give up hope, and my own pleasure was to remain in the beautiful old town [nor did I care to depart yet from the charming place], albeit my chief happiness [delight] was blurred by the changed attitude of Sue. I had to choose newer friends owing to that development. Yet her very abandoning me was the cause of many more friends flocking toward me than had come before.

Lavinia once said to me "Oh, I have seen many hearts broken in Sue's house—many!" and she went on with names of half the town who had been ardently liked at first, and then dropped or neglected or worse. It was Sue's genius to make each former friend feel that she or he or they were too despicable to be retained on the list of respectable people. Alas, I could never feel that way.

One lady, wife of an older professor, had come to me in very friendly fashion [way] during my first year in Amherst, and begged me to consider how really dangerous to my future peace of mind would be [was] my blindly following Sue and her prejudices [likes and dislikes]. This lady was respected in town [Amherst] despite her lack of taste in furnishing her home [house]. On that occasion, later in the conversation, she told me, as I was about to furnish [starting my own housekeeping in] the noble D K E mansion, that my bill for shades would amount to almost more than a young professor could stand [too high for a young professor to stand].

"But I am not going to have any shades," I replied, with mischief intent. The good lady evidently thinking me crazy, looked with amazement at me for a moment, while I explained that the thin silk curtains I was getting were quite as opaque as shades, and far prettier. Evidently a completely new idea to her, and one requiring profound [quite an expenditure of] thought. But at all events, she meant well and kindly, and I was grateful.

The daily life of Emily Dickinson would be a very innocent story of making cake and cream puffs, bread and all sorts of pretty sweets, largely to please the numerous friends who frequented the house, partly, doubtless, in the vain hope of seeing her, and perhaps as much to hear her sister Lavinia break into her familiar diatribes against those who, sometimes only temporarily, had excited her verbal wrath. This virulence could be matched only by Emily's own ability in the use of words—in her case simply used as a literary vehicle for the conveyance of intimate ideas. Her "lexicon" was her most intimate companion. Lavinia's only talent lay in this use of violent words to describe those, once friends, now withdrawn from that pleasant state and transformed into enemies who never by any chance could begin to use words as their present virulent enemy would describe them. People generally told all sorts of curious facts or supposable facts to her, perhaps only to hear her characterization. Town gossip penetrated to the quiet house under the pines in carefully expressed sentences, subsequently transformed into vituperative descriptions told as fact by the mistress of the closed [rooms] and silent halls of the big house. Once or twice Lavinia almost got herself into decided trouble by her frequently baseless tales told with dramatic realism to some enemy of the person described. It was averted however, as the Dickinson family was too important to be lightly accused of anything, especially in the person of its representative, the "old maid" resident of the dignified mansion. Probably she was well aware of this immunity; at all events she never learned to suppress her tongue of its well loved activities.

During all the years when I was working on Emily's poems, after that dearly loved character had passed beyond praise or blame, Lavinia, coming always late at night to our home across the meadow, used to enliven us with scandalous tales of well known persons in town. After she left I used to remark to my husband, who quietly listened to Lavinia's outpourings, that if I only chose I could make the town ring with scandal beyond anything imagined in its scholarly shades. But of course I never did!

When I first arrived in Amherst I was greeted with scores of tales from one and another about persons I had come to know; perhaps no more than any other small town might show to a new comer, but certainly spicy and interesting. Absorbed as I was in the details of my husband's profession, these bits of information came as a sort of high relief from the assistance I was giving to astronomical research, and I do not remember now that I ever asked my informers not to retail to me their tales. At all events they never did forbear. One of the first series of stories naturally related to the Dickinson family, apparently the target of many small and critical tongues. Possibly it was a normal subject for talk, and principally it dealt with "Sue" the handsome wife of the Treasurer of Amherst College, successor of his father in that office as well as leading lawyer of that part of Massachusetts. A man loved and respected by friends as well as by enemies if he had any, in their strong sense of pity for his noble reticence.

Sue was a person full of certain kinds of ability, never, however, used in any noble manner as help or affection for her fellow townsman, but practically always in their detriment. For many years before my coming to Amherst there had been no communication between the Dickinson homes. The two sisters lived their own life entirely independent of the "other house," and Austin was the only link between them. He went to see his sisters every day. [They] loved and revered him all the more since his profound unhappiness in his marriage had left him few satisfactions in his own home. The story of his disenchantment with Sue was told me, first by indifferent persons in town, and later more in detail by Lavinia, with a few comments by Emily in her curiously interrogative voice from the next room.

From the beginning Austin had formed an odd fondness for my husband which grew with the years into genuine love and respect on both sides. While never saying anything unjust of his family, Austin told us gradually the entire tale of his life's utter disappointment, not only in the affected [pretentious] Sue, who very unwisely had assumed an attitude of vast superiority to all her surroundings, but of her having caused her son Ned and his daughter Mattie [especially] to assume the attitude of utter superiority to the town and all his neighbors which they preserved through life, and which caused not only profound anger in many persons quite as good both in family and attainments as the two young people. Their mother had so instructed them that neither could act naturally or honestly toward the world. He also told us both the real cause of Ned's delicacy of body—which cannot be repeated here. He was an epileptic with frequent attacks. Mr. Dickinson had had a third child, little Gilbert, who received his unutterable devotion. He often said this child would make up to him for his great disappointment in both the others. He was trying as carefully as any parent possibly could to train the boy to right ways of looking at life, and of regarding his acquaintances with affection, or at least appreciation. But the dear child died. Henceforth Austin was distinctly alone in the world.

[More than ever before] his attention was given even more than before to his love for the trees and shrubs of the region, preferably those which grew naturally there. The College grounds blossomed more beautifully than ever in their wealth of fine oaks, pines, hemlocks, ashes and the barberries and wigelia which made the paths radiant.

Few college grounds of institutions starting as many years in the past as Amherst College did—over a hundred years ago—can show as cultivated a development of their outdoor surroundings as the Hampshire County college. And this is virtually owing to the work and effort of one man, whose poetic taste was developed in as practical ways as if it were merely buildings or museum collections. And few institutions have any official as painstaking and generous as Amherst's treasurer.

Knowing how constantly I was working on Emily's somewhat confused and difficult manuscripts, he decided that my husband and I ought to build our own home, having lived as we did after the first three months with our ducal host in a large and beautiful house since being made over into the home for the D K E fraternity. So he gave us toward that home a lot in his "meadow" and we built a little house of thirteen rooms, in which we lived for ten years. Here it was that Vinnie used to come across the meadow to talk to us about the poems, to hurry me in my work upon them, and to spice these requests with tremendous "facts" about her neighbors.

The meadow had belonged to Austin's father, rich farming land, and where an immense number of hay cocks appeared every summer, later with almost as many monuments of "rowan," and to me it became a fairy land of sweet scents and the constant labours of many men. Unfortunately at one side, below the meadow itself, was erected the massive brick building of one of the two hat "factories," only industries of the village, making some little smooth rolling of machinery, heard to be sure only when all our windows were open, but showing its massive walls despite the high hedge of hemlock and pine which were at once planted below our artistic house. This meadow which Austin loved intensely contained many acres, and he always expected that other houses would appear in its fine precincts. But none came, and when we moved afterward to the big "Observatory House" given us by my cousin Mr. Wilder of Boston, it was still only the "meadow". But it was dear to me always.

It was very soon apparent to me at least that Austin Dickinson was quite as much a poet as his sister Emily. Only the poetry in his nature took the form not only of his love of fine pictures, but no less of the views to be seen all about Amherst and its environs. His love for nature was exact and cultivated, and his joy over the lovely scenes to be seen from every hill-top was passionate and never failing. The multitude of trees and of blossoming shrubs surrounding us on every hand formed his poems—and the grounds of Amherst College show a beautiful procession of growing things which could have been arranged only by a genuine lover of all outdoor beauty, and of one who could command necessary assistance to consummate so harmonious a picture. For years this beautification went on, and when the practical-minded Trustees deprecated any more money being "wasted" just for trees, then workmen of his own choosing and paid from his own willing pocket would complete his plans. The College grounds today bear lovely witness to his taste and wise expenditure; and not they only, but the private grounds of many of the earlier faculty too, of people who wished for beauty perhaps in a vague sort of way, but who did not know just what to plant, or how to preserve exotic growths through the long and cold winters. Flowers he left to themselves, devoting himself to native trees, or blossoming shrubs which kept decorative red berries during the winter, or remained evergreen through the cold and icy months. This community of interest deepened his friendship with Emily, whose poetry was expressed not only in writing verse, but in care for the rare flowers which bloomed so lavishly for her, at first in her garden, and when she no longer stepped outside, in her conservatory off the dining room.

When Lavinia brought the mass of manuscript to me with her request that I get it "printed" as soon as possible, I objected at first, feeling that Sue should have the first right to give the poems out, if she wanted it. Vinnie's repudiation of any effort on Sue's part was really terrific. She told me again of her treatment of Austin, of her ruining her two children, and lastly, probably most damning description of all, her procrastination in any literary work whatever. She went over again the weeks when she left the poems with Sue to look over, and when the only result had been her leisurely reading them to her callers, and subsequent description of them to those presumably interested. Finally her announcement that she doubted if any printing would be wise, for various reasons adduced; chiefly that one could not expect any public to be really interested, until Vinnie, who had left them there with a mistaken idea that it would be "decent" knowing Sue's reputation for literary interest, was utterly discouraged and had come to me with renewed zeal. So I finally consented, and began on them at once.

She must have had some kind of desire for outward friendship with Sue, notwithstanding that no real conversations or any intimate connection had existed for many years, between them, for knowing that by this time Sue's once devotion to me had changed as most of her enthusiastic likings had done, and that her hatred only equalled her former love of me, she tried, futilely as it happened, to keep the knowledge of my work on the poems from persons in the town lest, I suppose, Sue should learn of it; she also sent a request to T. W. Higginson not to let my name be used in connection with the poems, and this at the same time that she was supposedly most anxious that I should proceed as rapidly as possible with the editing. Her handwriting was an impossible kind of scrawl, which dear Mr. Higginson could by no means read. Several times he had sent me notes from Lavinia, asking me to assist him in making out their meaning, which usually I could do, but without their containing anything definitely to be answered. About the time that I was almost through with the actual copying and editing, she wrote again to him, this time evidently with the intention of keeping me completely out of the region of the poems at all; and as usual the good friend sent the note to me, with the request that if I possibly could make anything out of it, would I do so, adding that he supposed there would be nothing of any importance in it. After a few days, meantime being most busily at work on the last of the poems, I took up the note. It was even more unintelligible than her writings usually were, and I gave up, returning to the poems with zeal overflowing. Some time after I took it up once more making out the impossible word to be "co-worker". The whole line read "I dare say you are aware our 'co-worker' is to be 'sub rosa,' for reasons you may understand."

That was a species of treachery beyond my imagining, and I asked Mr. Higginson what we should do about it. Meantime the title-page had been set up, and the printing was going on. He tossed it off airily. "Nothing is going to be done about so foolish a request", he answered; "It does not amount to anything." I was well contented to let it remain as he had arranged it already, and the book proceeded merrily on its way.

My earliest years in Amherst had been passed in increasing intimacy with Sue. Every one tried, I see now, to make me cautious in my relations with her, and even the best people in Amherst, not by any means gossips, had tried in vain to make me see the unreliability of Sue and the danger to a young and somewhat trusting woman of a friendship with her, pointing out her having quarreled with every one once friendly to her, and most notorious of all her break with Lavinia and Emily. Thinking no evil I see that I tried, innocently enough, to find excuses in my own mind for her, not regarding the public estimates [the friendly advice I received].

During the years 1881–1886 I was very often in the ancestral mansion, where Emily begged me to come repeatedly, enjoying to a great degree my singing and playing, both of which I had pursued ardently for many years. As Sue grew farther from me Emily came closer, and her notes and messages grew more frequent and more intimate. After the recitals of this single [singular?] artist were over, would come in to her the usual silver tray, always with a different dainty, expressive of Emily's appreciation and affection.

Their mother, quiet, gentle little lady, died during the middle of November 1882, without causing a perceptible ripple on the surface of any one's life, or giving concern to any of her family. Austin told us that her chief claim to attention had been her constant attempts to bring something to any caller which he or she could possibly require, and continual questionings had almost exhausted their patience. "Won't you have this or that to make you more comfortable?" or "Can't I bring you another chair?" had been the basis of her poor little attempts to make anyone within her circle happier, which failed sadly, as she never seemed to realize. Well, she departed this life with little ostentation, and life flowed on as before.

[287

Emily had become a very dear and intimate friend to me, and Vinnie conveyed to me quite constantly Emily's loving feeling. Her little notes were the acme of each day. My housekeeping had become alluring, and much company was flowing all about me. My whist parties, with a little water-colour for each guest, became quite an institution, and my musicales were celebrated. We did not hear any more about "the new observatory," but we still hoped. Day after day brought me joy.

Emily formed the brightest spots in my day. I painted several panels for her, the indian pipes, fantastic witch hazel, a great mass of brilliant orange trumpet vine which she called "the Soudan", and several tall stalks of mullein; her notes of appreciation and thanks made epochs in the day. The quaint tales told me by Vinnie of Emily's vagaries in attempting to elude the family routine were curiously amusing yet somewhat pathetic to me as showing the lack of understanding of Emily by her nearest and most devoted friends. On one Sunday in particular the dignified lawyer had assembled his family for divine worship in the village church and Emily was summoned with the rest of the group. But she had disappeared, nor could search reveal her hiding place. Late in the afternoon Vinnie discovered her rocking away peacefully in the cellar bulkhead, reading a favourite book. "Oh yes," she replied calmly, to exclamations of wonder at her chosen place of immolation, "Why should I argue? I did not wish to go to church." Edward Dickinson had not yielded and joined the church as soon as most of his acquaintances in the village, and his rather late giving in to the town habit had resulted as usual in a somewhat tighter rein on his family than was generally held.

We had taken an absurd little house for the intervening time before our artistic one in "the Dell" should be ready for us, but even there life in the village flowed on happily, and my numerous activities progressed [normally]. One summer I went abroad. That really seemed to bring real grief to Emily. Despite her many poems upon the great world, "Teneriffe, receding mountain," Tunis, "an easy morning's ride", "Dneiper wrestlers run" and other far-away [remote] regions [but nearby beauties] [still] she seemed to feel always that a European summer was always a danger to her dear friends. The great world after all was far-off and not "easy" to Emily. She had once written [Writing] to Mr. Bowles under similar [like] disquieting circumstances, "My friends are my estate. . . . Good night, dear friend. You go away, and where you go we cannot come. You sleep so far, how can I know you hear?" "I tell you Mr. Bowles, it is a suffering to have a sea—no care how blue—between your soul and you." "I am taking lessons in prayer, so to coax God to keep you safe." "How sweet it must be to come home, whose home is in so many houses, and every heart a 'best room!' I mean you, Mr. Bowles."

All the far-fetched and imaginative reasons for Emily having become a recluse, a white-draped and spectacular household ghost, are as unnecessary as they are false. It was merely a normal blossoming of her own untouched spirit. The revelations of the hundreds of her letters show this exactly, to those who can read between the lines and feel the trend of her inner movement. As long ago as while she was studying at Mount Holyoke Seminary, in writing of some school gayety which she did not attend, she says "Almost all the girls went; and I enjoyed the solitude finely."

Mrs. Ford seemed to think other explanations possible when she writes "I think in spite of her seclusion she was longing for poetic sympathy, and that some of her later habits of life originated in this suppressed and ungratified desire. As a prophetic hint she once asked me if it did not make me shiver to hear a great many people talk—they took all the clothes off their souls." Emily herself writes of the boarding place in Cambridgeport where she stayed with her cousins while her eyes were receiving special treatment in Boston, "A. N. lives here since Saturday, and two new people more, a person and his wife, so I do little but fly, yet always find a nest." Always disliking to have "new" people about her person, she [could] say anent the leaving her of an old servant, "I winced at her loss, because I was in the habit of her, and even a new rolling pin has an embarrassing element."

To her cousin Louisa Norcross, she wrote as long ago as 1859,—"For you remember, dear, you are one of the ones from whom I do not run away." "Odd that I, who say 'no' so much, cannot bear it from others. Odd, that I, who run from so many, cannot brook that one turn from me." Other intimations quite as definite could be adduced of her own inclinations, from Emily's own letters—which form the only prose available to us now. This is shown by a letter to her brother, which says, "I sat in Professor Tyler's woods and saw the train move off, and then came home again, for fear somebody would see me or ask me how I did." And when Edward Dickinson asked his son Austin to bring his mother and Vinnie to Washington, while he was a member of Congress, he added, "And Emily too, if she will, but that I will not insist upon her coming." Her disinclination was already manifest. She did, however accompany her family to Washington that spring [1855] for three weeks, and after the Washington experience two weeks more were spent in Philadelphia, in all five weeks, which was the longest time she stayed from home during her life, except her sojourns in Boston to have her eyes treated. Several of the "lives" of poor Emily speak of her as visiting whole seasons, in Washington, perhaps, or other centres of fashion, giving the impression of her as quite a young lady of the world, who might have had a dozen love affairs to change the current of her life; but those ideas are not borne out by fact. Emily did enjoy her few weeks in both Washington and Philadelphia, and it is quite certain that in the latter city she met the clergyman who felt her unusual character and to whom she turned for years afterward.

That she felt distinctly the urge of genuine love, that her love-poems were by no means theoretical outpourings, but actual experiences of her own, we must admit, however contrary they may be to a preconceived notion of her heavenly remoteness from earthly happenings. She knew perfect love, however she may have retreated from its more practical manifestations. And this was her inspiration for many of her exquisite lines.

When I had finally decided to yield to the popular demand that Emily's letters should be published, and Vinnie and I had begun the collection of some remote notes to almost forgotten friends, I had to deal constantly with the wide-spread notion that Emily was "irreverent." To me that seemed a really cruel animadversion. Full of the opposite idea of Emily's almost uncanny intimacy with the great father, and of her reverence for the infinitely glorious creator of the wonderful universe, I could hardly understand the questions which came to me in hundreds of letters, and verbal questions as well which assailed me after every one of the hundreds of talks which I gave for eight or ten years after the poems and letters were issued. Constantly I had to deal with the, sometimes intelligent, often quite the reverse, demands to know all about her interior life, her most intimate thoughts. People quoted to me line after line which would almost seem to prove their contentions. I argued on the other side and occasionally succeeded in convincing doubting readers of the truth of my belief that Emily was far from being irreverent.

"God is a distant, stately lover," was one poem invariably quoted to me as proof positive. That poem I had sent to *The Christian Register* and it was joyfully accepted by the editor, Samuel J. Barrows. But alas, my good friend the Reverend Brooke Herford, then pastor of the Arlington Street church, spoke most slightingly of that poem, calling it "One of the offensive pieces of insistent unitarianism ever published."

"Why, Mrs. Todd," he asked me in real friendliness, "Oh, *why* did you give that to any magazine to publish?" The editor, Mr. Barrows, was much hurt at this estimate, and wrote me that it was far less objectionable than many other utterances of well-known persons. Vinnie and I had considered it together for a considerable time before I sent it away, and she was mischievously happy to have it published.

This poem, I am told, is included in "Further Poems" of Emily, heretofore supposedly unpublished; a note says that "Mattie" printed its opening stanza somewhere, but it really saw the light first on April 2d, 1891, in the magazine mentioned above.

This subject, Emily's irreverence, seemed to worry many worthy persons, and all my numerous talks for several years had to deal with the subject, at least in passing to other aspects of her curiosity-provoking personality. I always told my deeply interested audiences that she was *not* irreverent, that she lived in retirement not at all from any love-disappointment, and that she was not an invalid. Those simple, self-evident facts seemed to fill any audience with surprise, and I have no doubt with some lingering suspicions that I did not probe to the bottom of Emily's mysteriously engaging self. But such were the facts. And no less today while the world is busily searching industriously for the supposed lover, and the story of the "break" which left her a disappointed maiden on the verge of ignominious insanity. The world cannot accept any story which does not gratify its love of the spectacular.

"Mattie," as she was known to the village, was not yet fifteen years old when I reached the town, and she had had no real communication with her aunt at that time, nor since six or seven years before, which was the time about which MacGregor Jenkins wrote his winning little sketch entitled "Emily Dickinson; friend and Neighbor." The children at that happy year were Mattie and her brother Ned, the invalid boy, and the two Jenkins children, "Mac" and his pretty little sister "Did"; their father was pastor of the village church until 1877, when he resigned. Two little Mathers, across the street, children of the professor of Greek, were occasional additions to the quartette of children, for whom Emily used mysteriously to lower baskets of delectable eatables out of her window, as told by Mr. Jenkins in his article. Mattie was receiving instruction about this time from one of the professors in College, her Latin being very good, so much so that the professor said he only wished poor Ned was half as good as his young sister in the Latin tongue. Ned kept on bravely enough with the class of 1884 in College, but he could not graduate, and only studied enough to make the friendships of the class a background in his life. Mattie was given after this time a year in Miss Porter's well-known school at Farmington, by one of her relatives.

These were the years when she was often asked to join in the students' merry makings, and her mother tried vainly, we must admit, to keep her back to her normal years of life. Ned's friends, much older than she, became her own especial friends, and their life her *metier*. If she could have been taken then, during her formative years, and instructed in right ways of looking at life, she was bright enough to have gained inestimable benefit from a saner outlook than her mother's prejudiced point of view. I have always regretted her not having been entrusted then to some woman of fine character and noble aspirations as well as brilliant characteristics.

Ned was a fine horseback rider, and he and Mattie—never a "sport" where physical attainments were concerned—used to go out, she riding a bicycle beside the gallant charger of her brother. Bicycles were very much the fashion in those years. But my grandmother, a handsome old lady of vast experience who looked at life with the sane calmness of long years of efficiency behind her, used to say with the indulgence of old age, "Why doesn't Mattie *do* something? Why does she always play only? Is there nothing she could get interested in?" And that was the trouble. It was Sue's trouble as well. Supposedly a judge of matters literary, she yet never did anything to prove that interest. And the Dickinson house was synonymous with gay junketings morning noon and night, poor Austin working also all the days through to keep pace with the luxurious living imposed on him. We admired him all the years through, when his sad face haunted us, as we knew how much he desired to live quietly.

After Emily's poems were finally published, and when they were tremendously appreciated, when my mail was filled with admiring and interrogative letters about the mysterious author, when scores of talks were demanded everywhere, some one said to Mattie how proud she must be to have her aunt so much admired, but she, her nose in the air, said she had never been interested in those poems; indeed had never even read many of them, turning away with scorn from their conversation. And so she remained until she decided to publish the early poems sent years before to her mother, during the affectionate days when Emily trusted Sue and admired her—long before the later poems were even written.

Always I had been more than well—carrying out long pieces of work without even fatigue; but in the spring of 1913 Susan Huntington Dickinson had died. She was my most bitter enemy, no one in the world except possibly her daughter Mattie held such unchanging hatred toward me as she. After a fashion I felt a bit relieved, and freer in my mind and occupations for her departure. For several days, even weeks, I was much more completely myself than before.

Then suddenly I started up the College Hill one intensely hot morning in order to take a swim in the College pool now that the students were away, and ladies were admitted. On my way up the hill I felt the hot sun supposedly on the back of my neck, though never before had sun or winter winds affected me even slightly. It was distinctly an unfriendly push or hand laying-on which startled me. I got into the pool feeling more and more under the hatred of some near-by influence, and I swam up to the end of the pool, ninety feet away, becoming there very helpless—very different feelings from any other I had ever felt. I managed to swim back to the point of entering the pool, when I got out and tipped over, completely in the power of any unfriendly influence being exercised against me. Becoming unconscious then, I must have lain there for half an hour before any one noticed my predicament. Finally David was sent for, and he brought Doctor Herbert Rockwell and his automobile up to rescue me.

During my severe illness from "heat stroke" as I lay for weeks in bed and afterward when I was taken to a veranda outside, I frequently thought of "Sue" and her possible power to injure me, and although I knew for certain that she had no further power to hurt me, as she had exercised her power against me in one fierce stroke not again available, I could not help feeling certain she had stricken me in her pleasure to be able to work her will upon me. I felt equally certain that Austin, who had died many years before, had just learned of Sue's cruel "getting even" with me, and during six or eight months, while I was slowly recuperating, determined to walk and be myself so far as possible, when I could scarcely stand without falling, many times when I did fall, some kind hand prevented me from injuring myself, and many times I knew of his neverceasing watchfulness.

5

Notes taken by Millicent Todd Bingham in an interview with her father, David Peck Todd, at Hector, New York, September 29–October 3, 1933.

THIS DOCUMENT CONTAINS THE FULLEST ACCOUNT we have of David Todd's part in the Austin-Mabel-Sue situation and his attitude toward it. At the time of the interview, long after his first breakdown in 1917, Todd was seventy-eight years old and in the care of an attendant, William Field, in the home of a relative of Field's in Hector, near Elmira, N.Y. Todd was by no means a well man mentally, although physically he was very vigorous. To his visitors (Field told Mrs. Bingham) he appeared entirely normal; but he was subject to occasional irrational outbursts, several of which occurred during his daughter's visit. The jottings below are Mrs. Bingham's notes on his answers to her questions about the people and events in Amherst in the 1880s and 1890s. The jottings show how digressive and sometimes bitter Todd was. (For coherence, I have arranged them under headings and eliminated a few irrelevancies.) His judgments, though often cruel and of course undocumented, are at least rational and allow for some redeeming ambiguities. Thus, Sue may have been a "drunkard" and a "superhypocrite," but she was an "exquisite housekeeper." Lavinia was "snappy" and "had rows" but "she must have been an enchanting young woman." Austin was a "wonderful" man but "very unmoral." Some of Todd's remarks (worked into formal prose by Mrs. Bingham) on his part in the publication of the poems appear in *Ancestors' Brocades*, pp. 31, 51, 52, 134. (The parentheses below are Mrs. Bingham's; the material in brackets are additions of my own.)

Sue, Austin, Mabel, and the *"War between the Houses"*

"Little Dud Todd" Sue's name for me.

Sue drunkard.

Sue's father an inn-keeper in Greenfield.

Never knew whether two houses were friendly or not when I went over.

L[avinia] brilliant, witty, snappy—rows all the time between her and Sue. A[ustin]. He was very unmoral.

[To MTB's suggestion that DPT might have been attracted to her:] They (DPT and Sue) didn't like each other. What help could that have been? She never attracted me. Because an adultery has been[,] cancels it to have another? Well, it (adultery) ruined my life.

He (WAD) was [a] lawyer. Doubtless she (Lavinia) did make will. [On the Todds' return from Japan in 1896:] Town buzzing with gossip [about the quarrel with Vinnie over the strip of land]. "Todds can't live in Amherst." I said, "We'll see about it. Came here to build observatory and I'll build it."

Did not inquire (about gossip). Facts were so staggering to me didn't want to inquire.

Sue jealous because (mamma) succeeded. Nobody in Amherst who had a name outside.

Sue always making fun of A[ustin]'s going to church. She was a super-hypocrite. But an exquisite housekeeper. Began to wipe my feet on the grass all the way up from the gate, before I went into house.

With regard to adultery, "That's the trouble. Austin wonderful man, loved him more than any man I ever knew."

"I shall know why when time is over". DPT quotes it [Poem #193] and weeps.

Burst out: "Don't know what it all means—sometimes like a ghastly dream."

Preparing the poems for publication

Lav. says "What shall I do." I said, "Don't burn 'em. Don't burn any-thing."

Used to spend hours and hours looking at poems. Vin used to bring over bushel basket of poems and dump it on floor in front of fireplace in back parlor. After she (MLT) had finished I compared with original and she did it all over again.

Some poems L[avinia] wouldn't let out of house. Mamita [Mabel Todd] had to copy them there. L. would sit there and watch and if Sue was com-ing the poems all hustled out of sight. This all distasteful to me as it seemed so underhanded but Mamita wanted me to and that was enough.

Typewriter made no speed then (for copying ED's poems).

TWH [Higginson] recommended them to H[oughton] Mifflin. They said "Too queer—rhymes are wrong." Thought H[igginson] must be get-ting out of his mind to recommend such stuff. "H-M will be very sorry some day," I said. TWH thought so too. "But what can I do." I went to see Niles. TWH too ashamed to go, reader for H-M couldn't go to another publisher.

On [Arlo] Bates [reader for Niles]: "Didn't amount to 3 tail puffs in a gale of wind."

Niles accustomed to using his own judgement in literary matters. Suggested hectograph 50 copies. Blue ink. Niles scared to death about printing a *printed* edition. Said he'd pay for 500 copies on hectograph. I walked out. They would either be published in best dress possible or nothing. Came to my way of thinking. (Went in May [1890], first.)

We used to sit up all night to read proofs.

Made ABC lists [of poems, for Higginson's consideration] independently.

[In answer to question about financial remuneration for work on poems:] That was the satisfaction of doing it, great poetry, and great leader [Emily Dickinson] without caring whether they followed her or not.

On the Dickinsons

Austin had more power than all trustees put together. Never mentioned (my) salary. He raised it from time to time as he thought appropriate. I never asked him to.

His (WAD's) office—little building opposite Foster Cook's when I was in college. I paid my term bill [there]. Ed Dickinson a grim old fellow, never allowed you to see him smile.

Ned a weak minded fellow. Can't imagine the treasurership of the college could ever have been offered Ned.

6

THERE IS MUCH EVIDENCE in the Todd-Bingham Archive that Millicent Todd Bingham intended a full-length autobiography. There are many fragmentary beginnings in the archive, mostly reminiscences and impressions of her early days in Amherst. A recurrent theme is the oppressive air of the feud between the houses, her dimly felt sense of her mother's guilt, and the hatred that exuded from "the other house." The following excerpts come from one of the preliminary, incomplete chapters. It appears in the archive in two forms: (1) A penciled draft of fifty-three pages of 5″ x 8″ stenographer's copybook paper, sixteen 6″ x 9″ brown sheets, and five pages of yellow half sheets. The dates on these sections span the period between February 27 and August 30, 1927. (2) The same, typed, dated "August 1962," with frequent but minor stylistic changes and an occasional marginal note indicating a change of heart or attitude during the thirty-five-year interval.

The first excerpt is as good a near-contemporary view of the Dickinson houses and grounds as we have, while giving the child's reaction to the aura of tension and hate that surrounded them. The second is a composite view of Emily—part, perhaps, from actual experience but part, as the marginal comment admits, secondhand—a good example of how legends gain currency. The sketch of Vinnie is in startling contrast to the "tender, soft-lipped" girl Joseph Lyman knew; it is a measure, in part, of the toll the feud had taken. Austin's aristocratic, contemptuous bearing, as it impressed—or intimidated—young Millicent, bears out the legend of Dickinson snobbery. Mrs. Bingham's account of its effect on her mother is but one of her devastating criticisms of her mother: the shame of Mabel's behavior with Austin; her apparent insensitivity to the attitudes of the town or the effect of her behavior on her husband and her daughter; her vanity and love of applause. (A detached scrap in the archive reads, "Mamma's tendency to exaggeration & overstatement." Millicent's unquestioning loyalty during her childhood grew into a highly ambivalent attitude.) Another document in the archive (eleven pages, typed, headed "Mitchells, Stamford, Conn. December 14–15, 1935") contains this passage: "When mamma chose her course of action, she chose along with it the ignominy which such a New England community heaps upon that sort of behavior. I must not enter into any mother-defense like Mattie. . . ." Again: "Austin and Mamma. What could they have done? Crisp condemnation of one side with blanket approval of the other side is impossible. This also applies to the feud. How were they conditioned? What forces made the thing happen? This can be done better than you can pass judgment." Finally, David Todd's position in the affair is given a blunt and unequivocal statement, as is his "weakness" or "sin" with women. In Mabel's journal for November 26, 1911, she wrote: "I have even allowed misrepresentations and reproach to attach to myself, to be thought the gay and flirtatious one of the two; and never a word, written or spoken, has come from me to show I had the faintest justification for anything I have been supposed to do. David is innocently unmoral. . . ." (The next ten pages, probably containing incidents, have been cut from the journal.) Millicent's implied rejection of any such argument is notable, although she could not bring herself to remind her mother of her part in David Todd's tragedy.

The Dickinson Enclave on Main Street

The two great Dickinson houses stand under tall trees between dense hedges confined by a fence, both before and behind, on a narrow strip of land along Main Street. There are clumps of rhododendron and other exotic shrubs which blossom gorgeously at certain seasons. The ground behind this strip of property slopes up to a great oak grove and a street which crosses its top. On the Dickinson side of that street there was throughout its length but one house of the early 1800s, a large affair, known as the Owen house at one time used as a girls' school, and for long periods of time unoccupied, or rented in the summer to Dr. E. W. Donald, an opulent and elegant Episcopal clergyman from New York (later Rector of Trinity, Boston).

There is a front gate to both mansions, also a carriage gate, which swings together behind the service wagon which has made its exit, or the light buggy and high stepping sorrel horse named "Ned," the Squire's [Austin's] pride when they are safely lodged in the barn. Through them [the gates] one catches a glimpse of a gravel walk bordered by hollyhocks joining the two houses, otherwise invisible.

The Squire's own house, a gaunt, smooth, wooden, tan-colored structure of the black-walnut mid-Victorian era, has all the forbidding solemnity of that era. It had a square tower. A walk of granite slabs leads up a few granite steps and again up a few more to the mansion portal.

I can say no more of that house as I never really looked at it. If I walked along Main Street, which I always avoided if possible, because I might meet a member of the Squire's family if I did; so I kept my eyes straight to the front and walked as steadily as possible till I was safely past. To be sure, they always walked up town on their side of the street, although it was only a gravel walk. On the other side it was a tar walk where the common herd walked.

But the other house, the older of the two, had been built at a more genial epoch in the early 1800s. It was of brick, near Georgian, and painted a warm yellow with white trimmings and green blinds. On either side of the swinging gate stood a giant pine whose great roots spread out under the hedge and under the gravel walk. Here they abruptly reached the light and air, where the street had been cut down ten feet or so long after the house was built to temper the grade of the hill. A flight of solid granite blocks spanned this distance up from the highway to the front gate. But I never used that gate. There was another, a few feet distant to the right, whose granite walks led past the Conservatory around to the back. The carriage gate was off toward the left. The fenced-in hedge led on toward the right a few hundred yards concealing from passersby the garden which was said to exist behind it. As there were no houses very close behind the property, only a grove of giant oaks, on the higher ground, one could not see within.

On the opposite side of the street, throughout the entire length of the Dickinson property, there were but three buildings. Across from the Squire's house, with the parsonage behind it, stood the granite-built village church whose construction he had supervised. To the east of it, two village houses, and then a wide flowery open meadow leading down to a little brook into the dell at the lower end. Across this open field, filled with daisies in June before haying time, the Dickinsons might, through closed blinds, look across to the blue hills of Belchertown, where Pelham and Holyoke hills blend in a dip in the horizon. Half way across his meadow (for the Squire owned it all), he cut through a street, crossing it from east to west, in the middle eighties; but it remained a private road, with square stone posts at the further entrance to mark it as a private road. It was called "Fowler Place," named in honor of his grandfather. Not until much later did it become an extension of Spring Street, the commonplace name of the public part of the thoroughfare leading from the center of town. This street was cut through in order to enable my father and mother to build a house upon it, which they did in the late eighties. . . .

Emily

In the old homestead there were two occupants, Lavinia Dickinson and Maggie. Emily had died just before we built our house. I was just six when they carried her back across the fields to the village cemetery. Though she saw no one grown, a small child might sometimes step inside the doorway to receive a cookie fresh from the oven, or a flower to hold in his hand. My only remembrance of her, as I was but six when she died, is of a brown silk net in which her auburn hair was held, with a brown silk tassel behind each ear. Once, from behind a closed blind, she lowered a cream-puff at the end of a string. [Mrs. Bingham's marginal note: "Some one told me this. No!"] The taste lingers today. But sweet Emily, who had inherited from some remote ancestor her love of beauty, was only a legend to me. The harsh qualities of her forebears which had passed her by had been incorporated in Lavinia. . . .

Vinnie

There she sat in her apple-green kitchen or on the back porch, a trim little figure in a black cashmere dress of the style of the '60s. The knife pleatings which decorated it were always a marvel to me. Her sour, shrivelled face with its long nose was wrinkled like a witch of the fairy tale, her hands gnarled and knotted like the faggots in the wood-box. But her hair—her marvellous dark luxuriant hair streaked with grey!—it seemed to concentrate all the juices of her wizened body, the focus of interest in her person. Sometimes it was tied in a sort of bow-knot at the back of her head, held fast by two great pins thrust from each side. But usually she sat there with it hanging, while, with her knotty hands, outspread fingers rigidly extended, she thrust them through it, slowly lingering along from root to farthest tip. Pussy sat near by washing her face, fat Maggie billowed about the kitchen, as Miss Vinnie sat slowly combing her hair with her knotty fingers.

Sometimes she would open the door into the dining-room, windows closed, shades drawn so that the pattern of the dark-blue china on the sideboard could hardly be seen. (It was the Landing of Lafayette.) If I tip-toed in, it was sometimes to receive an apple which I might consume behind the closed door—for Miss Vinnie could not bear the sound of crunching. One other sound she could not bear—the rustling of a newspaper.

Austin

But oftener, when the door was opened, there sat my mother and Mr. Dickinson. I cannot remember that I ever stayed—nor can I ever remember that he addressed a word to me. He referred to me, if ever he did refer to me, as "child," but that was to Miss Vinnie. What a figure! A tall lean man, sitting rigidly erect in his chair. His clean-shaven face, except for red side-whiskers, was without a smile. I could not have imagined how he would look if he should smile. It would never have occurred to me to try to imagine. But his hair! A great shock of coppery fine silken hair, standing out like a halo in a soft aureole about his austere face. Squire Austin Dickinson, spare form faultlessly dressed, about his neck a long gold chain of olden days, and long slender feet in soft kid shoes of curious ancient cut. Aristocratic, contemptuous, yes, but to me just the somewhat terrible center of the universe, though why he was such I could not have said. He was. No human being ever mentioned his name to me, nor did I ever mention his. I doubt whether he would have acknowledged my presence by so much as a nod had I met him on the street. But I never did. . . .

Through the long winter days in the little red house a fire was always burning on the hearth. Usually when I came home from school Mr. Dickinson was sitting there beside the fire with my mother. He wore a brown velvet cap which we kept in our music case in the back parlor. He knew all about a fire—just how a bright coal upon the top of two smouldering logs would pull the flame up through. One did not venture to touch the fire in his presence—but one might brush the hearth.

A presence he was, an awful omni-presence, whether upstairs behind closed doors or sitting in plain view. I cannot remember that I ever voluntarily stayed in a room in which he was sitting. He was there, a core of the scheme of things. I cannot remember that I ever consciously questioned myself why he was the center of my universe. But I felt the weight of him and carried it throughout my childhood, and until, when I was fifteen, he died. . . .

Austin and Mabel

I watched him and my mother walking in the meadow when the haycocks gave off their sweet smell. When I was very small, I remember a certain stretch of road on the top of the Pelham Hills, with fragrant pine woods on one side and a blueberry pasture on the other. The beginning and end of that drive is lost in memory. But that little stretch of road is as vivid today as it was then. Each tree, each stone in the wall, the position of each bush and each cloud in the sky is etched in my remembrance. We were driving along in the shiny buggy, Ned stepping along with head and ears erect, aware of all that passed. I was sitting between mamma and Mr. Dickinson. I felt them lean together behind me. What transpired I do not know. I could have been borne rigid to a burning pyre before I would have turned my eyes from the tip of Ned's quivering ears. Unaware they thought me! . . .

One day I was starting down the stairs when I heard his voice in the lower hall. As usual, I stopped and waited. I did not go where he was, especially if mamma was there, if I could help it. And to his low voice I heard her reply, "My King"—and I tiptoed back to my room and shut the door. It was disloyal to even think about it—I would not—and yet—how strange! . . .

In the last few years I have been speculating somewhat upon the course of events and why things have turned out as they have. There was but one repugnant thing which did positively unnerve me. It was a sore which never healed and which got me in the middle like solar plexus nausea each time I looked at it. That was a diamond engagement ring and wedding ring which mamma wore on her left hand—her others, almost identical, which had preceded the union resulting in my birth, were now worn upon her right. The feeling never became a resentment, it was never even so much as speculation. Though as I think back upon it, I felt numbly degraded by the sight of those rings, and in a way disinherited. . . .

I say there was no visible result in childhood. There was: the disapproval and concern expressed themselves in trying to protect mamma. Of course I didn't know what from. Nor did I ever try to find out. But she needed someone to take care of her. I assumed the burden. It was an almost unbearable one, because there was so little sphere for action. I could not tell her not to sit in Miss Vinnie's parlor with Mr. Dickinson by the hour, not tell her not to go riding with him alone by the hour, nor to stay by the upstairs fire alone behind locked doors by the hour. No one of course knew of that but me. I never thought of my father. I never thought of him in that connection nor in any other. Nor did I think of that possibility— speaking to her, I mean. Usually it was not my own sensibilities that were offended. It was fear that those of the Amherst public would be, and my responsibility for making them see that it was all right, making them understand, that was all I needed to do. But, that locked door upstairs. That was hard to explain, or rather, no, I came up against it with a bang, if I thought of trying to make them understand. For I couldn't understand that myself. That formed a very substantial part of the weight I was carrying. . . .

My father did not mystify me. About him I then felt little concern. So it comes back again to my mother. What had been the result of her intimacy with the spare old Squire who despised the common herd? What was his influence on the tender, beautiful, talented young woman, who had been capable, under wise and generous care, of being a power of goodness and beauty not only in her community but throughout the land? Worse than the blight of hate which fell upon me from unknown sources, was the blight which came upon me from him by way of mamma as a medium. I just asked her a few moments ago what Mrs. Brown would think of something or other. Her reply was to stick out her tongue and simulate nausea at the mere mention of a good, simple woman who is her friend. And that is the essence of Mr. Dickinson's influence. He with his preeminence in the small world in which he lived, a survival of the days when men were not considered equal, enabled him to carry off his snobbery to the end, and yet be taken seriously by the community. Anything he chose to do was right by virtue of the fact that he did it. To the last, he and his gold-headed cane were looked up to in awe by every child in town, though secretly they laughed at his red wig, and imitated his important stride—Not in my presence, however! I also was his protector!

Mabel

My attitude toward her [my mother] has always been one of concern—ever since I was conscious of any attitude, and long before—why was she the object of the disapproval of the town? If I try to analyze those childish unacknowledged anxieties, they are thereby given a rational form, which they never had. They were dumb, inarticulate concern—concern—always concern. What could I do about it? Nothing, but be concerned, never allow her dashing, brilliant beauty to get far from my enveloping concern, but confine myself to that. Never speak to anyone about it, least of all to her, nor allow anyone to speak to me—though the possibility of *that* never could have been entertained by me for one instant. I recall the abhorrence with which I heard my grandmother refer, once or twice, to her disapproval of mamma and her sorrow because of it, though this merely referred to external things, such as love of dress. . . .

But her life and her talents? What became of them after their nurture in such a nursery? Her industry always and still is prodigious. From a young girl when she devoted herself with such zeal to painting and playing and singing and the theoretical study of music, her industry never flagged. But to what end was it all, and were all her talents directed? Alice Freeman Palmer, mamma's dear friend, with a fraction of her talent, is a national patron saint of the college girl. Artistically she was not gifted at all. In speaking and writing mamma was her superior. Mamma held audiences of thousands spell-bound for as long as she chose to wield her brilliant, picturesque tongue. But the loftiest motive that could be ascribed to her talks was the desire for self-expression and the sense of power she felt in holding the world at her feet. Her love of beauty was her only religion, and to that sum-total of beauty she has largely contributed. But the good of mankind, or village improvement, or the advance of knowledge—were farthest from her scintillating thoughts. The blight of self-interest and self-glorification had fallen upon her, which left her efforts worthy of oblivion instead of endearing her to half a nation. With all her energy and industry, what throwing away of talents—what prodigal waste of them because the scope of their use did not reach beyond herself! [In 1962, Mrs. Bingham inserted a marginal note at this point: "Not true."]

The War between the Houses

What about his [Austin's] household? The family in the forbidding house behind the hedge? I tremble as I think of it. To meet one of them in the street was a sufficient shock for the day. That they could be human beings, made of flesh and blood, never occurred to me. They were a race apart. They walked about the village streets scattering venom as they walked. It fell upon and withered me, dropping down from their haughty gaze above my head as I passed by. Could anybody be more humble and more negligible than I? Especially since half the town seemed to agree with the Dickinsons. But that atmosphere was the one I breathed, my environment to which my small life was to be adjusted.

Out of the miasma of their presence which filled their house and extended its pestiferous aura across the street and as far as the eye could reach toward it, it was hard for me to pick out individuals. But that there were individuals I knew, because they could be met separately and could separately exhale their poison.

Mrs. Dickinson, known as Sue, though I never heard that word mentioned more than twice in my life, was a low being, the daughter of a stable keeper [elsewhere, "inn keeper"] whom the Squire had married by mistake. These facts I knew, but to me she was only a nebulous figure overshadowed by her virulent daughter. That individual, tall and spare like her father, contemptuous like him, intensified all his exaggerations and embodied the terror of the family; for her brother [Ned], though with all of the snobbery, had none of the power of his father, not enough indeed to carry it off. There had been a younger son, "Gildud" [Gilbert], I called him as a baby, who had died. The other son [Ned], also, died early. Instead of mother's milk, I was nourished on the hate of Martha Dickinson —"Mattie D." as she was derisively known by the townsfolk. To make the connection between the brown-velvet capped man sitting by our fire, or in Miss Vinnie's dining-room with mamma, and the blight which fell from that unyielding proud dame, was beyond my power or wish to do. I accepted it. If I had been questioned, unthinkable though that is to this day, I should have replied, "Why should he not talk with my mother?"—if the breath with which to reply had not been stricken from me by the question. A bolt from heaven would have been no surprise to me if a living mortal had dared to address me on the subject.

David Todd

I didn't think much about my father, in fact chiefly I can remember helping at night to thaw out his hands as he came back from observing the stars, or walking with him up to Vespers, when he told me to lift my feet, not scuffle, or his hiding my hat and coat, which made me late to school, in order to teach me to put them where they belonged. Yes, and once or twice he took me to skate on a frog pond on the outskirts of the town and often up to the great cow barns of the Agricultural College or the orchards and vineyards. But usually, I didn't think much about him, except as he glanced at me—doubtless without seeing me at all, but I didn't know that—each time he put fork or spoon into his mouth. . . .

And it was not until after I was married [1920] and papa was in Bloomingdale Insane Asylum that it ever occurred to me to think of what his [Austin's] influence on papa might have been. He, the youthful, serious young scientist—how could he have accepted the situation—an old aristocrat twice his age, who looked down upon him as a plebeian, and preempted his wife as by the divine right of his august preference?

Only last year, for the first time, did mamma refer to papa's attitude toward women. It is his fundamental weakness, it seems. They had hardly been married three years when he began to make love to anybody that would accept his advances. He had most of the women guests who came to our house, even beginning on my friends when I grew up. As mamma expatiated upon this inherent weakness of his, I saw him sitting behind his barred windows. And again the legacy of Mr. Dickinson closed down upon me like a vacuum bell shutting out the air which would be for me life to breathe. And all I could do was to sit and listen, while she, unconscious of any shortcoming of her own, revealed to me my father's sin. It would have taken a harder heart than my own to suggest to her that she perhaps was not without fault—and that her scathing denunciation of him was unbecoming, considering, perhaps, the part she played in staging the tragedy.

*   *   *

After these long and often anguished documents—all-too-human in their mixture of indignation, bitterness, venom, and confession—the reader may well ask, "Why?" Ambience? atmosphere? the harsh realities of a situation long varnished over? Perhaps the best short, if incomplete, answer is an entry in Millicent Todd Bingham's diary for March 27, 1951:

> The effect on Emily? She was glad that Austin had found some comfort after his all but ruined life. In my mother's words, "Emily always respected real emotion."

To right the balance, we have only to remember how much Emily respected Sue's emotion, too—Sue, her "torrid" sister-in-law, she who "fronts on the Gulf Stream."

References for

VOLUME ONE

CHAPTER 1

PAGE
3 "Tell all the Truth . . ." *P* #1129, about 1868.
4 "I am Judith . . ." *L* I, 92 (February 1850).
4 "The Riddle . . ." *P* #1222, about 1870.
4 "In a Life . . ." *L* II, 632 (to Susan Gilbert Dickinson, about 1878).
5 "It is true . . ." *L* II, 559 (to Louise and Frances Norcross, August 1876).
5 "[I] pause, and ponder . . ." *L* I, 98–99 (to Abiah Root, May 7 and 17, 1850).
5 "All men say . . ." *L* II, 415 (to Thomas Wentworth Higginson, August 1862).
5 " 'shunning Men . . .' " Ibid.
5 "My life has been . . ." *L* II, 460 (to Higginson, June 1869).
5 "I find I need . . ." *L,* I, 229 (to Susan Gilbert, March 12, 1853). Emerson's comment on Thoreau is in the essay, "Thoreau" (1884).
5 "I have the greatest desire . . ." *L* II, 461 (May 11, 1869).
5 "I never was . . ." *L* II, 476 (August 16, 1870).
5–6 "She was much too . . ." "Emily Dickinson's Letters," *Atlantic Monthly* LXVIII (October 1891), 453.
6 "my eccentric poetess," etc. *L* II, 518–19 (to his sisters, December 9, 1873), and *L* II, 570 (to his sister Anna, December 28, 1876).
6 " 'spasmodic' " *L* II, 409 (to Higginson, June 7, 1862).
6 "robbed of me" *L* II, 450 (to Higginson, early 1866).
8 "I do not cross . . ." *L* II, 460 (to Higginson, June 1869).
9 "My friends . . ." *L* II, 338 (to Samuel Bowles, late August 1858?).
9 seeing "New Englandly" *P* #285, about 1861.
10 "So I conclude . . ." Letter to Joseph Lyman, about 1865? (*The Lyman Letters,* p. 71).
10–11 "Is it really possible . . ." "Late Thaw of a Frozen Image," *The New Republic* (February 21, 1955), p. 24.
11 "cuts a figure . . ." Hyder E. Rollins, *The Letters of John Keats,* II (1958), 67 (to George and Georgiana Keats, February 19, 1819).
11 "Nothing in nature . . ." Letter to Friedrich Preller, April 4, 1826, freely translated.

CHAPTER 2

17 "nothing in the parentage . . ." *The Life and Letters of Emily Dickinson,* p. 3.
18 the Amherst assessment list E. W. Carpenter and C. F. Morehouse, comps., *The History of the Town of Amherst, Massachusetts* (1896), pp. 598–99.
18 "It is a high honor" George Sheldon, *Lucius Manlius Boltwood* (1905), p. 3.

PAGE

19 "Without some understanding . . ." Perry Miller, *The American Puritans: Their Prose and Poetry* (1956), p. ix.

19 If Hawthorne . . . Allen Tate, "Emily Dickinson," from *Collected Essays*, 1932, reprinted in *Emily Dickinson: A Collection of Critical Essays*, ed. R. B. Sewall (1963), pp. 16–27.

19 "I do not respect 'doctrines'" *L* II, 346 (to Mrs. Joseph Haven, February 13, 1859).

19 "While the Clergyman . . ." *L* II, 508 (to Mrs. J. G. Holland, early summer 1873).

19 "Ancestors' Brocades" *L* II, 491 (to Higginson, November 1871).

19 the ideal time for a poet Tate, "Emily Dickinson," pp. 21, 23.

20 ". . . the community was . . ." Theodora Ward, *The Capsule of the Mind*, pp. 4, 9.

21 "thin dry & speechless" *L* II, 475 (Higginson to his wife, August 17, 1870).

22 "She did not reason . . ." Tate, "Emily Dickinson," p. 25.

22 "Man is put . . ." Miller, *The American Puritans*, pp. 171–72.

23 "ecstasy in living" *L* II, 474 (Higginson's letter to his wife, August 16, 1870).

23 " 'Consider the Lilies' " *L* III, 825 (to Mrs. Frederick Tuckerman, June 1884).

23–24 "Almost every Puritan . . ." Miller, *The American Puritans*, pp. 225–26.

24 Miller on Edwards and Stoddard Ibid., pp. 221, 222.

25 "The shore is safer . . ." *L* I, 104 (to Abiah Root, late 1850).

26 "the Flood subject" *L* II, 454 (to Higginson, June 9, 1866).

26 "The final direction . . ." Charles R. Anderson, *Emily Dickinson's Poetry: Stairway of Surprise*, p. 283.

26 "My dear Mr. Higginson . . ." Millicent Todd Bingham, *Ancestors' Brocades*, pp. 169–70.

26 "the most remarkable criticism . . ." Ibid.

26 "Unlike her contemporaries . . ." Tate, "Emily Dickinson," pp. 23, 25.

27 "Vesuvius at Home," *P* #1705, undated.

27 Erik Erikson on origins Cf. "Identity and Uprootedness in Our Time," in *Insight and Responsibility* (1964), p. 95.

CHAPTER 3

28 Carpenter and Morehouse on Samuel Fowler Dickinson *History of Amherst*, p. 187.

29 "He was trained . . ." *Reunion of the Dickinson Family at Amherst, Mass., 1883* (1884), pp. 172–74. The article is signed "The loving daughter," pretty clearly Elisabeth Dickinson [Currier].

31 "holds – so – " *L* II, 406 (to Mrs. Samuel Bowles, spring 1862).

31 "To see the little Tippler . . ." *P* #214, about 1860.

31 "these stirring words . . ." *Home*, p. 7, n.

33 "disillusioned, neglected . . ." H. F. West, "Forgotten Dartmouth Men," *Dartmouth Alumni Magazine*, XXVII (February 1935), p. 62.

34 the "original object . . ." Article 13 of the constitution of the "Collegiate Charity Fund" (see W. S. Tyler, *History of Amherst College*, 1895 ed., p. 9).

35   Edward Hitchcock's description of Fowler *Reminiscences of Amherst College,* pp. 5, 6. Hitchcock adds, "From all that I can learn, I have no doubt that Samuel F. Dickinson and Col. Graves had more to do in forming and executing plans for the founding of Amherst College than any other men."

35   "urged by the command . . ." Preamble to the constitution of the Charitable Fund.

35   William S. Tyler on Fowler—"head"; "hand"; "one of the most . . ." *History of Amherst College* (1873 ed.), pp. 49, 120–21.

36   The *Hampshire Gazette* on Fowler *YH* I, 7.

36–37   The *New-England Inquirer* on Fowler *YH* I, 6.

37   Fowler on female education *YH* I, 17–18 (October 27).

37   Fowler at Western Reserve Frederick Clayton Waite, *Western Reserve University, the Hudson Era, 1826–1882* (1943), p. 315; quoted in *Home,* pp. 17–18.

37–38   Catherine Dickinson on Fowler's last years *YH* I, 28; *Home,* pp. 21–22.

38   "Everything looks beautifully . . ." *Home,* pp. 16–17.

38–39   Edward Dickinson on home *YH* I, 14 (May 20, 1830), 29 (September 7, 1835).

39–40   ED on travel
"The world is full . . ." *L* I, 137 (October 1).
"rich in disdain . . ." *L,* I, 141 (October 5).
"all is jostle . . ." *L* II, 317 (to Susan Gilbert, February 28).
a "Wilderness" *L* II, 433 (to Lavinia, July 1864).
"to see the Grass . . ." *L* II, 434 (to Susan Dickinson, September 1864).
"I never thought . . ." *L* II, 474 (Higginson to his wife, August 16, 1870).
"I don't care . . ." *L* II, 551 (spring 1876).
"I do not go away . . ." *L* III, 716 (about 1881).
"To shut our eyes . . ." *L* II, 482 (to Mrs. J. G. Holland; early October 1870).

40   "Back to myself" *Journals,* ed. Edward Emerson & W. E. Forbes (Boston, 1909–14), III, 199.

40   "fiery mist" *L* II, 461 (Higginson to ED, May 11, 1869).

41   "our rye field . . ." *L* I, 48 (October 21, 1847).

41   Austin on his grandfather "Representative Men of the Parish, Church Buildings and Finances, an Address delivered at the one hundred and fiftieth anniversary of the First Church of Christ in Amherst, November 7, 1889," published with other proceedings on that occasion, Amherst, 1890, p. 63.

41   *"Si monumentum requiris . . ."* *Reunion,* p. 173.

42   a "Beautiful Incident" *YH* II, 175.

42   "outran his capacity . . ." *YH* I, xxxvii.

C H A P T E R   4

44ff.   Early correspondence of Edward Dickinson The Dickinson Papers, Houghton Library, Harvard University. Letters not dated in the text are as follows:

     44   "rational happiness" March 19, 1828.

PAGE

46 "Don't let your natural liveliness . . ." November 16, 1822.
46 "I know well enough . . ." April 24, 1824. Baker's quotation is from *An Essay on Man*. Edward used it years later in an address to the House of Representatives in Washington. See note 4, p. 53.
47 "I suppose that you are applying . . ." June 9, 1824.
47 "My life must be . . ." June 4, 1826.
47 "as far as in our power . . ." August 9, 1827.
47 "in having assisted . . ." November 30, 1827.
47 "Let us prepare . . ." March 19, 1828.
48 "Females, also . . ." April 10, 1826.
48 a "new novel" July 10, 1827.
48 "the dwelling place . . ." November 27, 1826.
48 Edward on deaths of ex-Presidents July 12, 1826.
48 "It is very late . . ." September 26, 1827.
48 "the wind whistles . . ." December 10, 1827.
48 "and let our prayers . . ." January 27, 1828.
49 "the subject, as I always . . ." October 22, 1826.
49 "Judge Howe . . ." June 4, 1826.
49 "industry, frugality . . ." October 29, 1826.
49 "a warning to all young men . . ." March 19, 1828.
49–50 "Continue in the path . . ." October 17, 1827.
50 "I will plainly tell you . . ." March 2, 1828.
50 "after the business of the day . . ." August 9, 1827.
51 "And now, My Dear . . ." September 24, 1827.
51 "I have already waited a year . . ." January 21, 1828.
49 "Father [is] . . ." *L* II, 404 (to Higginson, April 26, 1862).
52 "The best financier . . ." Tyler, *History of Amherst College*, 1873 ed., p. 540.
52 "unbending firmness . . ." Ibid., p. 539.
53 "Father and Mr. Frink . . ." *L* I, 128 (July 27, 1851).
53 northern lights *Home*, pp. 172–73.
54 "Gen. and Mrs. . . ." *YH* II, 139.
54 "both were our royal guests" *YH* I, 351.
55 "At the age . . ." Tyler, *History of Amherst College*, p. 540.
55 The *Boston Journal* on Edward *YH* II, 209–10 (entry of November 8, 1873). The *Republican,* then under the editorship of Dickinson's friend and trustee of Amherst College, Samuel Bowles, captioned the article:

TRIBUTE TO A VETERAN
ONE OF THE OLD "RIVER GODS."

55 "remote" *L* II, 475 (Higginson to his wife, August 17, 1870); *LL*, pp. 70–71, ED to Joseph Lyman.
55 "the low, enjoying power" *Moby-Dick*, Chapter 37.
55ff. ED on Edward
55 ". . . he never played . . ." *L* II, 486 (to Louisa Norcross, spring 1871).
55 "I am not . . ." *YH* II, 482 (as reported by Ellen E. Dickinson, wife of ED's cousin Willie, in an article in the *Boston Evening Transcript,* October 12, 1895).
55 "among men . . ." *L* I, 213 (to Austin, June 20, 1852).
56 "Father is really *sober* . . ." *L* I, 173 (February 6, 1852).
56 "marching around the town . . ." *L* I, 254 (to Austin, June 13, 1853).

PAGE

56   "his pantaloons tucked . . ." *L* I, 148 (October 17, 1851).

56   "Father steps like Cromwell . . ." *L* II, 470 (early spring 1870).

56   "the Barn . . ." *L* II, 464 (to Susan Gilbert Dickinson, autumn 1869).

56   "Father looks very grand . . ." *L* I, 188 (March 7, 1852).

56   "we young ones . . ." *L* I, 119 (June 29, 1851).

56–57   "When I know of anything funny . . ." *L* I, 161 (December 15, 1851).

57   "He buys me many Books . . ." *L* II, 404 (to Higginson, April 25, 1862).

57   "We're rejoiced . . ." *L* I, 190 (March 24, 1852).

57 "world of parental tyrannies . . ." Clark Griffith, *The Long Shadow,* p. 279.

57 "No one openly . . ." *Home,* p. 3.

57 "Tutor Howland . . ." *L* I, 111.

58 "Mat came home . . ." *L* I, 190 (to Austin, March 24, 1852).

58 "like friendly and absolute . . ." *Home,* p. 413.

58 "where each member . . ." *L* II, 473 (Higginson to his wife, August 16, 1870).

58 "We have no statutes . . ." *L* II, 606 (to Mrs. Edward Tuckerman, about March 1878?).

58 "that charming second home . . ." *LL,* p. 1.

58 "Now you have got . . ." *LL,* p. 12.

59ff. ED on home

59   my "very dear home" *L* I, 53 (to Abiah Root, November 6, 1847).

59   "my *own* DEAR HOME" *L* I, 58 (to Abiah Root, January 17, 1848).

59   "We rode . . ." *L* I, 58 (to Abiah Root, January 17, 1848).

59   come back "to freedom . . ." *L* I, 146 (October 10, 1851).

59   "I am so sorry . . ." *L* I, 162 (December 24, 1851).

59   "I'm afraid . . ." *L* I, 197 (about April 1852).

59   "Home is the definition of God" *L* II, 483 (to Perez Cowan, late October 1870).

59   "Home is a holy thing . . ." *L* I, 150–51 (to Austin, October 25, 1851).

59   "Infinite power of Home" *L* III, 782 (to Mrs. J. Howard Sweetser, summer 1883).

60 "Went to Vinnie's . . ." from Mrs. Todd's diary for August 26, 1893 (reprinted in *AB,* p. 231).

61 "The father was terrific . . ." *AB,* pp. 232–33.

61 "Miss Vinnie told me . . ." *YH* II, 231 (letter from M. L. Hall to M. T. Bingham, December 29, 1938).

61 "There, father . . ." *AB,* p. 233 (letter from M. L. Hall to M. T. Bingham, August 5, 1933).

61 "I have never *before* . . ." *YH* I, 315 (early September? 1854).

62 "You know home . . ." *Home,* p. 305.

62 "very funny indeed . . ." *L* I, 230–31 (March 18, 1853).

62 "an Eclipse" *L* II, 404 (to Higginson, April 25, 1862).

62 "standard of good workmanship" *Home,* p. 112.

62 "One day . . ." Ibid.

63 "Oh! dear! . . ." Ibid., p. 235.

63 "Father was the only one . . ." *Home,* p. 413.

PAGE

63 "quite a hand . . ." *L* I, 66 (to Abiah Root, May 16, 1848).

63 "as gentle . . ." *L* II, 439 (to Louisa Norcross, early 1865).

63 "Father was *thoughtful* . . ." *Home,* pp. 312–13.

63 "in the habit of me" *L* II, 450 (to Higginson, early 1866).

64 "this is a lonely house . . ." *L* I, 233 (to Austin, March 24, 1853).

64 "the letters of suspected . . ." *L* II, 346 (to Mrs. Joseph Haven, February 13, 1859).

64 "such papers only . . ." *L* I, 157 (to Austin, November 16, 1851).

64 "militant Accent" *L* II, 537 (to Mrs. Holland, late January 1875).

64 "Father sat all the evening . . ." *L* I, 121 (July 6, 1851).

65 "Her father was not severe . . ." *L* II, 475 (Higginson to his wife, August 17, 1870).

65 "We are having a pleasant . . ." *L* I, 125 (July 20).

65 "the Mail of Anguish" *P* #165, about 1860.

65 "I dont love to read . . ." *L* I, 243 (to Austin, April 16, 1853).

66 "My father seems . . ." *LL,* pp. 70–71.

66 "While Hon. E.D. . . ." *YH* I, 178 (entry of early August 1850).

66 "I am standing alone . . ." *L* I, 94 (to Jane Humphrey, April 3).

66 "the ark of safety" *L* I, 60 (to Abiah Root, January 17, 1848).

67 "Old Neighbor – . . ." *P* #623, about 1862.

67 "lasts a Solid Year –" *P* #569, about 1862.

67 Edward's death *YH* II, 224 (entry for June 16, 1874) gives Mabel Loomis Todd's account of the event. "These facts," she concluded (in a letter to Higginson), "have just been re-told me by Mr. Austin Dickinson, so I am sure of their accuracy."

67 "even more respected . . ." *YH* II, 224.

67 "He was, indeed . . ." *YH* II, 224–25.

67 "It is a condition . . ." *YH* II, 226–27.

69 "Memorial service . . ." *YH* II, 227 (J. L. Skinner to his wife).

69ff. ED on Edward's death

69 "I cannot recall . . ." *L* II, 526 (summer 1874).

69 "The last Afternoon . . ." *L* II, 528 (July 1874).

69 "I dream . . ." *L* II, 559 (August 1876).

69 "accustomed . . ." *L* II, 591 and n. (to Harriet and Martha Dickinson, about 1877?).

69 ED refers to "the mighty dying" of her father in *L* III, 716 (to Higginson, about 1881).

71 "When I think . . ." *L* II, 551 (to Higginson, spring 1876).

71 "beautiful Hymn" *L* II, 528 (to Higginson, July 1874).

72 "She wrote it . . ." Higginson to Mrs. Todd, *AB,* p. 130.

73 "*My* business . . ." *L* II, 413 (to Dr. and Mrs. Holland, summer 1862?).

CHAPTER 5

74 "I never had . . ." *L* II, 475 (Higginson to his wife, August 17, 1870).

74 "I always ran . . ." *L* II, 517–18 (January 1874).

75 Austin on ED's "posing" *AB,* p. 167.

75 "I have been in a savage . . ." *YH* II, 77 (April 18?, 1863).

76 Emily Norcross's letter to her sister *Home,* p. 25.

PAGE

76ff. The courtship letters are in the Dickinson Papers, Houghton Library, Harvard. The dates of letters not included in the text are given below.

    76 "amiable disposition," etc. April 10, 1826.

  76–77 "I suppose you are now . . ." January 27, 1828.

    77 "invitations without number" February 8, 1828.

    77 "I find that . . ." Ibid.

    77 "All I wish . . ." April 29, 1828.

    77 "I think it best . . ." Ibid.

  77–78 "I was much pleased . . ." January 10, 1828.

    78 "A woman, you know . . ." January 27, 1828.

    78 "May we be virtuous . . ." April 29, 1828.

    78 "My Dear, my heart . . ." April 18, 1828.

    78 "I have many friends . . ." April 25, 1828.

    78 "The time is short . . ." May 2, 1828.

79 "situated pleasantly" *YH* I, 6 (May 21, 1828).

79 "The Hon. Mr. Bliss . . ." *YH* I, 7 (September 23, 1828).

79 "It is enough . . ." *YH* I, 9 (February 12, 1829).

79 "I have retired . . ." *YH* I, 17 (June 1, 1831).

79 "grieved life" *L* II, 578 (to Mrs. William A. Stearns, early 1877 ?).

79 "tremulous fear of death" *Home*, p. 4.

81 "I have only a moment . . ." *L* III, 675 (about September 1880).

81 "a holier demand" *L* III, 716 (to Higginson, about 1881).

81 "Only the night . . ." *L* III, 748 (to Mrs. J. Howard Sweetser, November 1882). The reference is to Dick Matthews, the Dickinson stableman.

81 "The habit that grew . . ." Theodora Ward, *The Capsule of the Mind*, p. 7.

82 "Mother drives . . ." *L* II, 476 (to the Norcrosses, late summer 1870?).

82 apples to Samuel Bowles *L* II, 426 (to Bowles, autumn 1863).

82 bouquet to President Stearns *YH* II, 81 (July 12, 1863).

82 the parties *L* I, 59 (to Abiah Root, January 17, 1848); 288 (to Austin, March 16, 1854).

82 "Mother pines for you . . ." *L* II, 593 (to Mrs. Holland, September 1877).

82 "There are a great variety . . ." October 27, 1827.

82 Mrs. Dickinson's committee work and commendations

    In 1852 she was on the Fruit Committee; 1853, the Fine Arts Committee; in 1859, the Flowers Committee (*YH* I, 255, 282, 373). On September 2, 1853, the *Hampshire and Franklin Express* printed the following acknowledgment (*YH* I, 282): "We have received from Mrs. Edward Dickinson, a choice sample of Figs, grown under her cultivation. Also, from the same lady, a sample of apples, of the Russet variety, grown last season, looking as fresh as when gathered in the field."

83 ED on her mother's intellect *L* I, 287 (to Austin, March 14, 1854); 180 (February 18, 1852); 11, 404 (April 25, 1862).

83 Mrs. Dickinson's books *YH* I, 4 (May 6, 1828); 330 (March 3, 1855).

83 Mrs. Dickinson's reading *L* I, 157 (to Austin, November 16, 1851); *L* II, 604 (to Mrs. Holland, early 1878).

83 Mrs. Dickinson as a letter writer

    "write her *name* . . ." *YH* I, 31 (January 16).

    "Mother was much amused . . ." *L* I, 257 (June 19, 1853).

    "to put you in mind . . ." *L* I, 124 (July 13, 1851).

Her excuse for not writing *L* I, 240 (April 8, 1853), and cf. Cody, pp. 155–56.

84 "making most desperate efforts . . ." *L* I, 185 (to Austin, March 2, 1852).

84 Mrs. Dickinson quoted

"Mother had a nice time . . ." *Home,* p. 249 (July 15, 1852).

"Mother says it seems . . ." Ibid., p. 282.

"Mother tells how gently . . ." *L* II, 421 (to the Norcrosses, late January 1863).

"Jennie Hitchcock's mother . . ." *L* II, 425 (late May 1863).

"– and mother – oh she thought . . ." *L* I, 274 (December 13, 1853).

"Mother feels quite troubled . . ." *L* I, 151 (October 25, 1851).

"would be a very good Boy" *L* II, 454 (to Susan Gilbert Dickinson, about August 1866).

"Mother wants . . ." *L* I, 116 (June 22, 1851).

"The horse . . ." *L* I, 137–38 (to Austin, October 1, 1851).

85 "Mother is warming . . ." *L* I, 111.

85 ED's later remarks on her mother

"Mother went rambling . . ." *L* II, 470.

"She has no Father and Mother . . ." *L* II, 508 (early summer 1873).

"I ask Mother 'what message' . . ." *L* III, 689.

"Had he a tenderer eulogy?" *L* III, 713 (October 1881).

85–86 Mrs. Dickinson's understanding of family's complexity

"a mystery . . ." Clara Newman Turner, as quoted in *Home,* p. 5. Later (p. 265), Mrs. Bingham refers to the source of her reference, Mrs. Turner's "My Personal Acquaintance with Emily Dickinson," referred to in Chapter 4, note 6.

86 "Austin and I were talking . . ." *L* III, 667.

86 Mrs. Dickinson as loving and attentive mother

"Mother makes nicer pies . . ." *L* I, 127 (July 27, 1851).

"– what with fruit . . ." *L* I, 133 (to Austin, September 23, 1851).

"Mother and Margaret . . ." *L* II, 439 (to Louisa Norcross, early 1865).

87 ED's baking *L* II, 474 (to his wife, August 17, 1870).

87 "Vinnie's mother . . ." *LL,* p. 14.

88 Mrs. Dickinson's lessons

"Soon the carriage . . ." *L* I, 58 (to Abiah Root, January 17, 1848).

"Mother got a great dinner . . ." *L* I, 270 (November 14, 1853).

"Two things I have lost . . ." *L* III, 928–29 (Prose Fragment #117; in the MS, Emily crossed out the last sentence).

88–89 ED on her mother's death

"I hoped to write . . ." *L* III, 749–50.

"Blow has followed blow . . ." *L* III, 754 (to Mrs. Holland, mid-December 1882). The repeated blows probably include the death of Samuel Bowles in 1878, Dr. Holland in 1881, and Charles Wadsworth in 1882.

"Her dying feels to me . . ." *L* III, 752 (to James D. Clark, late 1882).

"We were never intimate . . ." *L* III, 754–55 (to Mrs. Holland, mid-December 1882).

"To have *had* a Mother . . ." *L* III, 892 (to Mrs. James C. Greenough, late October 1885).

"All is faint . . ." *L* III, 771 (to Maria Whitney, spring 1883).

89 "As Freezing persons . . ." *P* #341, early 1862.

PAGE
89–90 Lavinia on her mother
    "The days are beautiful . . ." *YH* II, 397 (to Mabel Loomis Todd,
      April 30, 1883).
    "and mother loved" *Home,* p. 414.

C H A P T E R 6

91 Mrs. Dickinson as "carrier of Dickinson traits" *Home,* p. 4.
92 Austin's friends
    Henry Hills *YH* II, 295 (July 17, 1878).
    Mrs. Todd Journal, January 6, 1885; Todd-Bingham Archive, Yale.
92 Skinner on Austin *YH* II, 228–29, 172 (March 31, 1871). The first in-
    cident occurred on August 2, 1874—as Leyda remarks, only six weeks
    after Austin's father's death and hence a period of great strain for him.
93 Austin and art
    "in a feverish excitement . . ." *YH* II, 41 (to Samuel Bowles, Decem-
      ber 25, 1861).
    "bought a water color . . ." *YH* II, 425. The diary, now in the Todd-
      Bingham Archive, Yale, is for the years 1880, 1882, 1883, 1884, 1886,
      1888, 1889, 1890.
95 "that Campaign inscrutable" *P* #1188, about 1871.
95–96 Austin's "Hurrah" *L* I, 3 (April 18, 1842); 123 (July 13, 1851); 83
    (January 23, 1850); 174 (February 6, 1852); 276 (December 20, 1853).
96 Aunt Elisabeth on Austin *YH* I, 75 (April 21, 1842).
96 ED's and Austin's long talks *L* I, 245 (April 21, 1853).
96–97 Austin's drafted note *Home,* pp. 82–83.
97 the *"imaginative* note" *L* I, 68.
97 ED on the Dickinson difference *L* I, 239; 245 (April 21, 1853).
97 Joseph Lyman on "the ring" *LL,* p. 48. Vinnie was Joseph's sweetheart as
    Emily was not; but Emily was in the small elite group of those who
    "understood," as Vinnie was not.
98–99 Austin to Susan Gilbert *YH* I, 182 (November 9, 1850).
99 ED to Austin *L* I, 113 (June 15, 1851); 151 (October 25, 1851); 160
    (December 15, 1851).
99 Lavinia to Austin *YH* I, 217 (October 10, 1851).
99 "Queen Recluse" *YH* I, 76 (Samuel Bowles to Austin, March? 1863).
100 "School masters . . ." *L* I, 101 (October 27, 1850).
100 "those useless boys" *L* I, 162 (to Austin; December 24, 1851).
101 ED's concern for Austin *L* I, 289 (March 16, 1854); 239 (April 2,
    1853); 248 (May 7, 1853).
101 Austin to Susan Gilbert *YH* I, 184–85 (December 11, 1850).
101–2 "To know Emily's brother . . ." *Home,* p. xiv.
102 Mr. Gilbert's "convivial habits" *AB,* p. 219.
103–4 ED on Martha Gilbert *L* I, 205; 135 (September 23, 1851).
104 Samuel Learned on the Gilbert sisters *YH* I, 280 (July 27, 1853).
104 Emily's "clandestiny" *L* I, 228–29 (to Susan Gilbert; March 12, 1853).
104–6 Austin to Martha Gilbert *Home,* pp. 240–42 (May 11, 1852).
105 ED on her talk with Martha *L* I, 205 (May 13, 1852).
105 "I love the danger!" *L* I, 104 (late 1850, to Abiah Root).
108–9 "wade grief" *P* #252, about 1861.
109 "Susan fronts . . ." *L* III, 895 (to Susan; early 1886).

PAGE

109–10   Austin to Susan   *YH* I, 268, 269–70.
112   Austin to Martha   *YH* I, 266 (March 27, 1853).
113   Susan Gilbert to her brothers   *YH* I, 293–94 (January 6, 1854); 315 (September 4).
113–14   Susan Gilbert to the Bartletts   *YH* I, 342 (May 19, 1856).
114   Austin to Gordon Ford   *YH* I, 343.
114   Jane Hitchcock on the Dickinson houses   *YH* I, 344 (September 24).
115   "So Marm D – . . ."   *YH* II, 143 (Mrs. Samuel Bowles to her son; October 29, 1869).
115   "my crowd"   *L* II, 358 (to Mrs. Samuel Bowles; December 10).
115–16   Samuel Bowles to Sue   *YH* II, 276 (June 29).
116   John W. Burgess on Sue   *Reminiscences of an American Scholar* (1934), pp. 60–61.
116   Mrs. Todd on Susan   Letter to her parents, *YH* II, 353 (October 2, 1881).
116   "We almost forget . . ."   *L* III, 765 (to James D. Clark, mid-March 1883).
117   "crept out one evening . . ."   *YH* II, 133.
117   "filled to overflowing"   *YH* II, 132.
117   Austin's overwork   Mrs. Todd's letter to Austin, April 20, 1890; Austin to Mrs. Todd, March 6, 1890 (Todd-Bingham Archive, Yale).
        Austin on ED's "genius"   See Chapter 12, pp. 222–25.
118   "Brother Pegasus"   *L* I, 235.
118   Austin's "poem"   *YH* I, xxxix; II, 380.
118–22   "Representative Men . . ."   In *An Historical Review: One Hundred and Fiftieth Anniversary of the First Church of Christ in Amherst, Massachusetts, November 7, 1889.* Amherst, Mass.: Press of the Amherst Record, 1890, pp. 50–66.
121   "Women . . ."   Postscript in a letter to William Hayes Ward, who sent it to Mabel Loomis Todd, March 3, 1897.
122   "I wouldn't give . . ."   Austin to Mrs. Todd, November 16, 1887 (Todd-Bingham Archive). Other recorded trips by Austin: to Washington, D.C., 1854; to the Centennial Exposition, Philadelphia, 1876; to the Chicago World's Fair, 1893.
123   Austin to James Clark   Todd-Bingham Archive.
124   to "regulate"   *P* #1100; about 1866.
        ED on Austin   *L* II, 398 (to Louise and Frances Norcross, late March 1862); 399 (late March 1862).
124   Austin at his father's death   *YH* II, 226 (J. L. Skinner to his wife, June 22, 1874).
124   Vinnie's letter   MS, University of Virginia Library. (See Chapter 7, note 8.)
124   Mrs. Todd on Austin   Diary, October 6, 1883; Journal, November 11, 1883. Todd-Bingham Archive.
125   ED on "the Dyings"   *L* III, 843 (to Mrs. Samuel E. Mack, autumn 1884).
126   ED on eternity   *L* III, 750 (to Louise and Frances Norcross, late November 1882).

CHAPTER 7

128   "she had to think – . . ."   *Home,* p. 414.
129   "Area – no test of depth"   *L* III, 767 (to Mrs. Jonathan L. Jenkins, date unknown).

PAGE

129 "narrow, probing, Eyes" *P* #561, about 1862.
129 "instilling many a lesson . . ." *L* I, 66 (to Abiah Root, May 16, 1848).
129 "I think Emilie . . ." *Home*, p. 174 (October 1, 1851).
129–30 "Emilie tells storys . . ." Ibid., p. 203 (December 1851).
130 "inside the ring" *LL*, p. 48.
130 "very pious and very pretty" *LL*, p. 54.
130 Daniel Bonbright to Joseph Lyman *LL*, p. 59.
130 "Vinnie says . . ." *L* I, 174 (February 6, 1852).
130 ED on Vinnie and practical matters *L* I, 213 (June 20, 1852); 310 (November 27–December 3, 1854); 297 (early June 1854).
130 "the folks . . ." *Home*, p. 234 (March 24, 1852).
131 "more beautiful . . ." *YH* I, 274 (draft of a letter to Susan Gilbert, May 10?, 1853).
131 "happy with her duties . . ." *L* III, 862 (to Maria Whitney, early 1885?).
131 "Soldier and Angel . . ." *L* III, 794 (to Harriet Austin Dickinson, mid-August 1883).
131 "Your bond . . ." *L* III, 779 (to Charles Clark, mid-June 1883).
131 Chickering's eulogy *Home*, pp. 490–91 (from the *Springfield Republican*, November 30, 1899).
131 "went East" *L* II, 377 (to Mrs. Samuel Bowles, about August 1861).
132 *"perter* and *more* pert . . ." *L* I, 127 (July 27, 1851).
132 "lively, brisk, smart . . ." Noah Webster, *An American Dictionary of the English Language*, Springfield, 1851.
132 Jane Hitchcock to Austin *Home*, p. 90 (January 11, 1850). (I have not followed the order of the sentences in the letter.) Jane Hitchcock was the daughter of Professor Edward Hitchcock, at that time president of the college.
132 Lavinia in Washington *YH* I, 302 (from the *Springfield Republican*, November 29, 1899).
132 "There was a pleasant . . ." *Home*, p. 211 (January 26, 1852).
132 "I will send you . . ." Ibid., p. 237 (April?, 1852).
133 Vinnie's letters Ibid., pp. 249 (July 8, 1852); 214 (January 28, 1852).
133 "Received offer of *marriage*" *YH* I, 216 (October 8, 1851).
133 Vinnie as head of the committee . . ." *Home*, p. 303.
134 "Vinnie's sainted Garden" *L* III, 812 (to Mrs. Henry Hills, February 1884?).
134 "I feel unusually hurried . . ." *Home*, p. 283 (May 6, 1853).
134 "I fear you are . . ." *L* II, 397 (March 1862?).
134 "Vinnie is still subsoiling . . ." *L* III, 880 (August 1885).
134 "Vinnie is far more hurried . . ." *L* III, 676 (about September).
134 "Vinnie is under terrific headway . . ." *L* III, 693 (spring 1881).
134 who "was only sighing . . ." *L* III, 695 (1881?).
134 "when *we* are *all* gone" *Home*, p. 313 (to Austin, November 9).
134 "was only a happen" See p. 153.
135 Vinnie to Lyman *LL*, p. 34 (December 29, 1856).
135 "that charming second home . . ."; "spooney" *LL*, pp. 1, 59.
135 " 'sweeter, sweeter . . .' " *LL*, p. 35.
136 "O Joseph I havn't seen . . ." *LL*, p. 18.
136 Vinnie's diary entry *YH* I, 196.
136 "Poor little . . ." *LL*, p. 21 (November 25, 1852).
136 "garden of roses" *LL*, p. 42.
136 "her little fat hands" *LL*, p. 14.
136 "central strenuous life" *LL*, p. 43.
137 Lyman on Vinnie *LL*, pp. 50–51 (mid-March 1858); 21, 22, 42–43.

PAGE

138   Lyman on ED *LL*, p. 60.

138   Lyman on ED and Araminta Wharton
        "one of those . . ." *LL*, p. 66.
        permission to write *LL*, pp. 58, 66.
        "My friendships . . ." *LL*, p. 67.

138   "had been with Emily . . ." *LL*, p. 18.

139–40   Lyman on ED's and Vinnie's epistolary styles *LL*, pp. 1, 51–53 (June 13, 1858; the ellipses are Joseph's).

140   Lyman on Vinnie *LL*, p. 53.

140   Vinnie "cruises about . . ." *L* I, 311 (to Sue, November 27–December 3, 1854).

141–42   Vinnie vs. Mrs. Sweetser *Home*, pp. 358, 359.

142   ED on Vinnie's belligerence *L* II, 612 (to Mrs. Holland, June 1878); 592 (to the Rev. and Mrs. Jonathan L. Jenkins, September 1877).

143   ED on her dependence on Vinnie *L* II, 346 (to Mrs. Joseph Haven, February 13, 1859); 348 (to Mrs. Holland, about February 20, 1859); 508 (to Mrs. Holland, early summer 1873).

143   "friendly and absolute . . ." *Home*, p. 413.

143   ED's return from Cambridge *L* II, 435 (early November 1864); 436 (November 13, 1864); 430 (about May 1864).

144   "Did you know . . ." *L* II, 643–44.

144   "All men say . . ." *L* II, 415 (to Higginson, August 1862).

145   "And Vinnie, Joseph . . ." *LL*, pp. 70–71.

145   "Vinnie is sick to-night . . ." *L* II, 353 (September 1859).

146   Martha Dickinson Bianchi on Vinnie *Emily Dickinson Face to Face*, p. 13.

146   Skinner on Vinnie *YH* II, 226 (June 22, 1874).

146   Vinnie on Gilbert's death The MS of the letter, heretofore unpublished, is in the Library of the University of Virginia and is reproduced here by permission. (For acknowledgment, see note 8.) The recipients are as yet unidentified.

146–47   Mrs. Jameson on Gilbert's death *YH* II, 406 (October 14, 1883).

147   Reunion with Mrs. Holland *L* III, 814, 816.

147   " 'Tom' whirls us . . ." *YH* II, 416 (to Mrs. Todd, February 5, 1884).

147; 150   Vinnie to Mrs. Todd *YH* II, 397 (April 30, 1883); 413 (December 27, 1883); 416 (February 5, 1884).

151   "Went to call . . ." *YH* II, 402 (July 23, 1883).

152   "partially cracked poetess" *L* II, 570 (Higginson to his sister Anna, December 28, 1876).

152   Eliza Coleman to John Graves *YH* I, 319 (October 4, 1854).

154   Sue's obituary of ED *Springfield Republican*, May 18, 1886 (*YH* II, pp. 472–73).

155; 156   ED to Higginson *L* II, 412; 474 (August 17, 1870).

155   "auctioning the mind" *P* #709, about 1863.

155   *"at the White Heat"* *P* #365, about 1862.

156   "blossoming" Mabel Loomis Todd, preface to *Poems*, second series (1891), p. 8.

157   "War between the Houses" This phrase first appears in Mary Lee Hall's letter to Mrs. Bingham, August 5, 1933 (Todd-Bingham Archive, Yale), which is quoted in *AB*, p. 371. For selections from this correspondence, see Appendix II, 1.

CHAPTER 8

PAGE

161 "a family quarrel . . ." From the document "Scurrilous but True"* (see Appendix II, 4).

163 we "please ourselves . . ." *L* I, 144 (October 9, 1851).

163–65 *Kavanagh* (1849), pp. 36–37, 77–78, 39.

165 "Sue – you can go or stay – . . ." *L* I, 305–7.
    Leyda (*YH* I, 317) suggests the date of *late* September.

166 "I was foolish . . ." *L* I, 304.

167 "Mother sends . . ." *L* I, 203.

167–68 Lavinia to Austin *Home*, pp. 268, 282.

168 Mrs. Hills on the Dickinsons *YH* II, 119 (December 9).

168 Mrs. Todd on Vinnie and Sue *AB*, p. 61.

168 "I miss you . . ." *L* II, 315. A third letter written from Washington that February is addressed to *both* Sue and Mattie and concerns mostly her trip.

CHAPTER 9

170–71 Jay Leyda on Mrs. Todd *YH* I, lxxiii–lxxiv.

171 "among distinguished scientists . . ." *AB*, p. 4.

172 "Amherst is alive . . ." *L* I, 80 (to Joel Norcross, January 11, 1850).

172 "even the Cynic Austin" *L* III, 690 (to Mrs. Holland, early spring 1881).

173 "aunts" Mabel Loomis Todd, *The Thoreau Family Two Generations Ago,* Thoreau Society Booklet #13 (1938), p. 11 and passim.

173 "the preferred flower of life" *L* III, 740 (late September 1882).

173 "I cannot make . . ." *L* III, 740 (October 1882).

176 "I never should have left her" As told me by Millicent Todd Bingham.

178 Austin "married – " *L* II, 377 (to Mrs. Samuel Bowles, about August 1861).

178 "My Brother is – " *L* III, 765 (to James D. Clark, mid-March 1883).

181 "Dimity Convictions" *P* #401, about 1862.

CHAPTER 10

189 "cruel treatment" *AB*, p. 374 (letter of Mary Lee Hall to Millicent Todd Bingham).

191 [Austin] is overcharged . . ." *L* II, 575 (to Mrs. Holland).

191 "If after all his years . . ." Todd-Bingham Family Papers.

191 "Never have I lived . . ." Letter to Mrs. Bingham, August 5, 1933.

192 "in a lighted bay window . . ." This is Clara Newman Pearl's comment in a document entitled "My Personal Acquaintance with Emily Dickinson, by Clara Newman Turner, edited by Clara Newman Pearl." A

PAGE

copy is in the Todd-Bingham Archive, Yale. See *Home*, p. 265, and Appendix II, 3.

192 "disgusted . . ." *YH* II, 257.

192 "very sorry for Miss Vinny . . ." *YH* II, 294.

192 "a little too aggressive . . ." *YH* II, 124.

192 "In my boyhood . . ." Alfred E. Stearns, *An Amherst Boyhood* (1946), pp. 72, 76.

192 "I carry very many burdens . . ." *YH* II, 438.

192–93 Austin's will Copy in the Todd-Bingham Archive; and see *AB*, p. 338.

193 "If there is any . . ." *YH* II, 445.

193 "Ned told us . . ." *AB*, p. 372 (September 14, 1930).

193 "I have wondered . . ." Letter of August 5, 1933.

193 "had always admired . . ." Letter of October 12, 1930, to Mabel Loomis Todd.

CHAPTER 11

197 ED on Sue *L* III, 895 (to Sue; early 1886), 791 (to Sue; about 1883).

198 Mrs. Jameson's report *YH* II, 406 (letter to her son, October 14, 1883).

199 "Gimblets . . ." *P* #244, about 1861.

199 "my crowd" *L* II, 358 (to Mrs. Samuel Bowles; December 10, 1859).

199 ED to Sue at Geneva *L* II, 339–40 (September 26, 1858).

200 Edward at midnight *YH* I, 367.

201 "the clandestine Mind" *L* III, 790 (to Sue; about 1883).

201 "In a Life . . ." *L* II, 632 (to Sue; about 1878).

201 "Safe in their Alabaster Chambers" *P* #216. The episode is described in full, with the exchange of letters, in *P* I, 151–55.

201 "Balm for Susan's . . ." *L* III, 700 (about 1881).

201 "Your impregnable . . ." *L* III, 707 (late summer 1881).

202 "Only Woman . . ." *L* II, 546 (about 1875).

202 "That Susan lives . . ." *L* III, 659 (spring 1880).

202 "To thank one . . ." *L* III, 699 (about 1881).

202 "vast" *L* III, 672 (about 1880).

202 "great" *L* III, 791 (about 1883).

202 "I must wait . . ." *L* II, 631 (about 1878).

202 "Susan's Idolator . . ." *L* II, 458.

202 "To miss you . . ." *L* II, 489 (September 1871).

202 "To see you . . ." *L* II, 477 (about 1870).

202 "Susan breaks . . ." *L* II, 652.

202 "Thank her dear power . . ." *L* III, 733 (about 1882).

202 " 'Egypt . . .' " *L* II, 533.

202 "Tell the Susan . . ." *L* III, 831.

202 "Susan knows . . ." *L* II, 612.

202 "Dont do . . ." *L* II, 465.

202 "pseudo Sister" *L* III, 716.

202–3 Sue's gifts to Emily *YH* II, 263, 336.

203 "The tie . . ." *L* III, 893.

203 Mary Lee Hall on Sue and Emily *YH* II, 440 (to Genevieve Taggard; December 8, 1932).

PAGE

203   "Could *I* – then . . ."   *P* #220, and *L* II, 381 and n.: "The tension which developed between ED and Sue, when the infant Ned began to absorb Sue's attention, is hinted at in this note, which is in the handwriting of about 1861."

203   *"Private . . ."*   *YH* II, 38.

204   "I had a terror . . ."   *L* II, 404.

204–5   ED to Sue   *L* III, 799 (early October 1883), 800, 800–1 (and *P* #1584).

206   "If it is finished . . ."   *L* II, 315.

CHAPTER 12

219   "fierce insistence"   Mrs. Todd's journal, November 30, 1890.

220   "palsy here, – . . ."   *L* II, 408 (to Higginson, June 7, 1862).

221   "queer – . . ."   *AB*, p. 51 n.

221   "It has always seemed . . ."   *AB*, p. 53.

221   "colossal," "the real stuff . . ."   Ibid.

221   "Miss [Lavinia] Dickinson . . ."   *AB*, p. 67.

221   "no one left . . ."   *AB*, p. 33.

221–22   "he died . . ."   *Home*, p. 374.

222   "It struck me"   *AB*, p. 66.

223   "we happen to *know* . . ."   *YH* II, 295 ff.

224   "So I conclude . . ."   *LL*, p. 71 (ED to Joseph Lyman, about 1865?).

227   "horrible . . . 'innocent . . .' "   *AB*, p. 166.

CHAPTER 13

229   "What means . . ."   Alfred E. Stearns, *An Amherst Boyhood*, p. 76.

229   "curiously in fear"   Mabel Loomis Todd's journal, November 30, 1890.

229   "a bit ashamed"   *An Amherst Boyhood*, p. 72.

230   "Sue was relentlessly . . ."   Mary Lee Hall to Millicent Todd Bingham, February 20, 1935.

230   "Sue was a jealous . . ."   Letter to Mrs. Bingham, August 5, 1933.

230   "Sue did everything . . ."   Letter of April 10, 1934.

230   "During your Mother's absence . . ."   Letter of February 20, 1935.

230–31   "I can remember . . ."   Letter of April 15, 1945.

231   "I think Sue inherited . . ."   Letter of September 14, 1930, to Mabel Loomis Todd.

231   "the Old Scratch"   *AB*, p. 59.

231   " . . . you never will know . . ."   Letter of February 20, 1935, to Mrs. Bingham.

231   "To me Sue . . ."   Letter of August 5, 1933, to Mrs. Bingham.

231   "Vinnie told me . . ."   Ibid.

232   "immorality," "in the arms of a man"   *YH* II, pp. 375–76.

232   "So successful . . ."   *Emily Dickinson: A Revelation* (1954), p. 61.

232   "Vinnie's special aversion"   Ibid., p. 60.

232   "little hussy . . ."   Ibid., p. 23.

PAGE

232   "deceptions," "falsehoods," *"stabbed* . . ."   Mary Lee Hall to Mrs. Bingham (August 5, 1933).

232   "I do hope . . ."   *AB,* p. 374 (Mary Lee Hall to Mabel Loomis Todd, July 29, 1930).

233   Gethsemane "but a Province . . ."   *P* #553, about 1862.

CHAPTER 14

236   "meditating majestically . . ."   *YH* I, p. xx.

236   "It is hard to steer . . ."   Cf. *AB,* p. 62.

236   "saved [her] Life"   *L* II, 460 (June 1869) and *L* II, 649 (about 1879).

236   "but one or two" poems   *L* II, 404 (April 25, 1862).

237   "the ancient people"   *LL,* p. 12.

238   "the only male relative . . ."   *L* II, 561 (to Mrs. Holland, August 1876).

238   "to spare expense . . ."   *L* II, 427 (to Louise and Frances Norcross, October 7, 1863).

238   "raise an *awful* breeze"   *Home,* p. 359.

239   "I don't pretend . . ."   *Lord Jim,* Sun Dial ed., p. 76.

239   "how incomprehensible . . ."   Ibid., p. 180.

239   "My eyes were . . ."   Ibid., p. 241.

240   "When I try to organize . . ."   *L* II, 414 (to Higginson, August 1862).

240   "short sharp probings . . ."   Melville on Shakespeare, in "Hawthorne and His Mosses," *The Literary World,* August 17 and 24, 1850.

240   "Circumference"   *L* II, 412 (to Higginson, July 1862).

241   "I wept a tear . . ."   *L* I, 143 (October 9, 1851).

243   "She had to think . . ."   *Home,* p. 414.

THE LIFE OF

Emily Dickinson

VOLUME TWO

15

Childhood

WHATEVER TRUTH there may be to the legend that on December 10, 1830, Mrs. Edward Dickinson's room was papered against her husband's express wishes, it is certain that on that date Dr. Isaac Cutler officiated at the birth of their second child.[1] Edward entered his new daughter's name in the family records as "Emily Elizabeth" and the time of her birth as "5: o'clock A.M." Thus began a childhood of which little is known and much surmised.

Before adding to the speculation, we would do well to ponder a few hard facts. Emily was born during a time of family trouble, when the era that had been dominated by her distinguished grandfather was coming to an end and the new one, of which her father was to be the central figure, was by no means securely established. She was born into a prominent family but not into opulence or luxury. When Edward brought his bride from Monson in May 1828, they had settled in half of the Widow Jemima Montague's house and taken in student boarders to eke out Edward's yearly professional income, listed at that time in the town clerk's office as $250. Only eight months before Emily was born, Edward bought one half—the west half—of the Homestead, the fine brick mansion on Main Street that his father had built in 1813 but had been forced to sell to John Leland and Nathan Dickinson (a cousin), at the same time maintaining residence as tenant. Edward paid the new owners $1,500, gave them a mortgage for $1,100, and moved in with his parents and their still-large family in (or shortly after) April 1830.

For three years the two families lived together in the house—thirteen

---

1. Dr. Cutler had delivered the last of Samuel Fowler's children and was to deliver all of Edward's. Only two months before, he had presided at the birth of another baby girl—Helen Fiske, who as Helen Fiske Hunt Jackson ("H.H.") was to become one of Amherst's two most famous daughters. (See *YH* I, xxx, 15, 16.)

people in all, although with goings and comings (Lucretia was married in 1832 and Lavinia was born in 1833), the number varied. The year of Vinnie's birth, there were other disturbing changes. The mortgage was foreclosed and the place sold to General David Mack, Jr., of Middlefield, Massachusetts, who was moving to Amherst to undertake the manufacture and sale of straw hats. (He was the one whom Austin, in his early youth, remembered as "God.") Squire Fowler, his wife, and their youngest child, Elisabeth, took their sad way west, while the other brothers and sisters dispersed variously, except Frederick, the youngest son, who stayed on under Edward's care. Edward promptly rented the east half of the Homestead from General Mack, who with his wife and two children (a daughter of twenty-eight and a son of nineteen) moved into the west half sometime late in 1833 or early in 1834.

It was not until 1840 that Edward's improved finances enabled him to remove to a house of his own on North Pleasant Street. This was the house that Austin described in the late 1840s to Joseph Lyman as the "mansion" over which he and Emily presided as "lord and lady" during the absence of their parents. And so it must have seemed to them after the crowded life of their early childhood. This was the house, too, that Joseph called "that charming second home of mine in Amherst."

The circumstances of Emily's childhood seem to have been about normal for Amherst at the time, at least for the professional and academic group. No one in Amherst, with its many farms, a few light industries, and fledgling college, was rich. But one does not often think of Emily, the Queen Recluse, as spending the first ten years of her life in a situation that, if not exactly deprived, involved a good deal of close living among fellow members of the human race. Such must have been the case in a house that, for all its fine exterior, had only four good-sized bedrooms, with only two of those available to the Dickinsons.[2] The little children were apparently bundled together; Emily's first letter to Austin when she was eleven complains of missing "My bedfellow very much." (In her mid-thirties she still spoke of Vinnie as sleeping "by my side.") Such circumstances indicate limitations other than merely financial. Two-family living is seldom carefree for parents of small children, and at least one reason Edward early acquired a reputation for sternness is not far to seek. If Emily's stanza

> They shut me up in Prose –
> As when a little Girl
> They put me in a Closet –
> Because they liked me "still" – . . .   (#613, about 1862)

2. Jean Mudge, "Emily Dickinson and the Image of Home," Yale dissertation, 1973, unpublished, says that the original rectangle of 1813 was enlarged, "probably by Edward," in 1855 to include the two-story east wing, the conservatory, the rear ell, and veranda.

does not literally describe her childhood, it perhaps tells something about the inevitable parental discipline. But from Emily's accounts of the stir and bustle in the house, and of Austin's presence especially, it appears that the discipline was, at least after a certain stage, anything but perfect.

We know that Edward, for one, chafed under the restrictions. In June 1835 his sister Catherine wrote to their parents in Ohio that he "seems very sober & says but little." But some weeks later, writing to his wife in Boston, he exploded in a very uncharacteristic way: he wanted money, and lots of it; he had had enough of living in half a house. He told his wife to "tell y^r father I wish he would speculate a little for me in *'Maine land'* – as I can't go myself, until October, at the earliest. . . ." He went on:

I must make some money in some way, & if I don't speculate in the lands, at the "East," I must at the "West" – and when the fever next attacks me – nothing human shall stop me from making one desperate attempt to make my fortune – To be shut up forever "under a bushel" while hundreds of mere Jacanapes are getting their tens of thousands & hundreds of thousands, is rather too much for my spirit – I must spread myself over more ground – half a house, & a rod square for a garden, won't answer my turn – Don't think me deranged so soon – altho' my regulator is gone – I am in earnest.

This reveals an Edward as excited as any ambitious young American by the lure of an expanding economy, something of a change from the idealist of the courtship letters. His mood is an indication, among other things, of one more tension under which he was raising his young family. Actually, he turned "West," not "East," buying a thousand acres of Michigan land early in 1836.

We first hear about Emily—at first called by her middle name, Elizabeth—from her Aunt Lavinia Norcross. She appears as a model child. During Mrs. Dickinson's illness following the birth of Vinnie, Aunt Lavinia, to make things easier for her sister, took little Emily for an extended visit to Monson. The twenty-mile trip was eventful for at least this fact; it occasioned Emily Dickinson's first recorded comment (age two and a half) on natural phenomena. There was a fierce thunderstorm when they reached Belchertown, about halfway to Monson. Lavinia wrote to her sister:

I believe I mentioned before that she slept most of the way to B——— We heard it thunder several times but tho't we should not have a shower where we were – We stopped at the tavern in B——— . . . Just after we passed Mr Clapps – it thundered more & the thunder & lightning increased – Elizabeth called it *the fire* – the time the rain wind & darkness came we were along in those pine woods – the thunder echoed – I will confess that I felt rather bad . . . We tho't if we stopped we should not get home that night – Elizabeth felt inclined to be frightened some – she said "Do take me to my mother" But I covered her face all under my cloack to protect her & took care that she did not get wet much –

The visit was a success. Lavinia wrote glowingly to her brother-in-law:

> I have but a few moments of leisure but I will just let you know that Emily is perfectly well & contented – She is a very good child & but little trouble – She has learned to play on the piano – she calls it the *moosic* She does not talk much about home – sometimes speaks of *little Austin* but does not moan for any of you – She has a fine appetite & sleeps well & I take satisfaction in taking care of her –

This high opinion of her guest not only weathered a call on "Grandmother Fay [Norcross]," who said that Emily looked "precisely as our brother Austin did when he was a child"; it even survived an uneasy morning in church:

> I took her to meeting yesterday morning – She behaved very well – Once in a while she would speak loud but not to disturb any one – she sit between Pa & me – he would slap her a little occasionally when she was doing wrong – not to hurt her or make her cry –

Emily established herself as a favorite in the household. "There never was a better child," wrote Lavinia. "Father came home the Saturday after – said he was glad I brought her home – He is much amused by her sports . . . She is very affectionate & we all love her very much." Lavinia begged to keep her as long as possible; and when the visit ended after about a month, she felt bereft.

> I cant tell you how lonely I was – it seemed so different & I wanted to weep all the time – the next Morning after Emily was gone I saw a little apron that she left & you cant think how I felt . . . I took pleasure in taking care of her – she thought every thing of me – when any thing went wrong she would come to me – When she went to bed I used frequently to lie on the bed for I felt weary & so I suppose she did not forget it after she went home – You must not let her forget me –

Aunt Lavinia's warmth and affection deserve a comment. Her "when any thing went wrong she would come to me" recalls a little ruefully Emily's remark that she "never had a mother. I suppose a mother is one to whom you hurry when you are troubled." We remember Austin's confession to Sue that he had never known tenderness in his family and (later) Clara Newman Turner's observation that she had never seen any outward sign of affection between members of the Dickinson family in all her experience with them. Whether or not the atmosphere of Emily's home was as dour as tradition maintains, it hardly offered such lavish affection as this from young Aunt Lavinia (she was then just twenty-one). Emily wrote, years later, "The ravenousness of fondness is best disclosed by children. . . . Is there not a sweet wolf within us that demands its food?" Aunt Lavinia's devoted attentions provided at least one time when such hunger was satisfied. As substitute mother she apparently did all too well. In one of her letters she wrote that Emily "speaks of her father & mother occasionaly & *little Austin* but does not express a wish to see you – Hope this wont make you feel bad – "

Unfortunately, we know little more about Emily's relationship, thus so happily begun, with her favorite aunt. Their correspondence apparently perished in the general destruction of letters following their deaths. Emily's letters to her cousins, Frances and Louise (or Louisa) Norcross, at the time of their mother's last illness show how close the tie was, perhaps as close as any Emily established with members of the outer family circle. Lavinia was fond of books, wrote verse, had an independent turn of mind, and was sprightly in a way her older sister, Emily's mother, was not. A year and a half after Emily's visit she married her cousin Loring Norcross against her family's wishes and (incidentally) Edward Dickinson's. Emily always felt close to the family, staying with Frances and Louise in Cambridgeport during her periods of eye treatment in Boston in 1864 and 1865 and exchanging books and gifts and tender sentiments throughout their long relationship. It is a special loss that we know so little about what Aunt Lavinia thought of her remarkable niece in her maturity.

At least we know what she thought of that early visit. Indeed, the main theme of her letters to Amherst—Emily's model behavior—may point to the very reason we know so little about Emily's childhood. Extraordinary children usually make themselves felt at once. Emily's almost exact contemporary in Amherst, for instance, Helen Fiske (Hunt Jackson), was known from the start as a robust and open rebel. Her mother described her as an "everlasting talker" at the age of two and a half, and at six as "quite inclined to question the authority of everything; the Bible she says she does not *feel* as if it was true." Once she ran away when she was very small, and startled the whole neighborhood. One of her contemporaries described her as "tough & hardy, & would wrestle or fight at almost any time or any body." She soon was a legend. Emily was no legend at all—at least not until school days. Then she became known as a wit, and in religious matters, at least, something of a problem to her friends. Although her vivacious early letters (at age eleven) hardly show it, she may have been something of the "sombre Girl" she later called herself in a poem—and somber girls seldom get talked about.

Whether it was because of possible repressiveness in the Dickinson atmosphere, or a disinclination to assert herself, or simple timidity, we know little more than that Emily was a good child and gave little trouble. When Edward, on his frequent business trips, wrote home, he singled her out for special comment only when she had been ill. Usually he gave general instructions for health and conduct:

My Dear Little Children, I am glad to hear that you have been so good little children, since I left home – I want to have you see which of you will be the best – the one that is the best, I shall give the best present to. Be kind & pleasant to Mother, & each other – do exactly as she tells you – & be pleasant to [Aunt] Catharine, too. . . . Now you must learn, & study, to do as

Mother wants you to – She will always do exactly right by you. Good night.
Your dear father, E. Dickinson

If Emily's genius was apparent in her early childhood, no one seems to
have been aware of it or bothered to record its signs. The nearest Aunt
Lavinia came was Emily's fondness for music, which, to be sure, was to
develop into a considerable talent. But no one paid attention to it until she
was fourteen, when her father at last bought her a piano. Neither in these
years nor at any time thereafter did either parent, or any of the numerous
aunts and uncles, give evidence of seeing anything unusual, let alone
genius, in Emily. Aunt Lavinia's correspondence might have proved an
exception. Edward's household, it seems, was all too typical of late-Puritan, small-town New England families in their insensitivity to extraordinary abilities in their children, especially those of an imaginative or artistic turn. Life was real, earnest, and mostly "Prose."

One recalls Emily's famous comment: "Fathers real life and *mine*
sometimes come into collision." But this remark came long after Emily's
childhood and tells little about what she thought of her earliest years. She
was never discursive about them. In her letters and prose fragments, she
left only a few tantalizing reminiscences, mostly in irrelevant contexts. In
a letter of 1873 to the Norcross cousins, she indulged in this whimsey at
the expense of Louise:

> Tell Loo when I was a baby father used to take me to mill for my health.
> I was then in consumption! While he obtained the "grist," the horse looked
> round at me, as if to say " 'eye hath not seen or ear heard the things that'
> I would do to you if I weren't tied!" That is the way I feel toward her.

There is the fragment recalling the rapture of losing her shoe in the mud
and her mother's gentle reproof—"she frowned with a smile." She remembered going to a funeral "when a few years old" and being disturbed
by the clergyman's question, "Is the Arm of the Lord shortened that it
cannot save?" (She detected an emphasis on "cannot" and years later
asked Higginson if he, once a clergyman himself, could "explain" it to
her.) There is another fragment, without date, that gives some sense of
the religious discipline of her childhood, though whether it refers to an
episode at home or at school is not clear—nor is the reason for the
punishment:

> We said she said Lord Jesus – receive my Spirit – We were put in sepa-
> rate rooms to expiate our temerity and thought how hateful Jesus must be
> to get us into trouble when we had done nothing but Crucify him and that
> before we were born –

Once (to Higginson) she recorded another bit of mystification at adult
behavior. Why, she asks, did her elders frighten her with their dire
warnings?

When much in the Woods as a little Girl, I was told that the Snake would bite me, that I might pick a poisonous flower, or Goblins kidnap me, but I went along and met no one but Angels, who were far shyer of me, than I could be of them, so I hav'nt that confidence in fraud which many exercise.[3]

This may cover up much that was dour and somber in her childhood—she was inclined to take poses in her letters to Higginson—but it seems a kind of benediction on those early years. At any rate, it is such glimpses as these that provide the only firsthand evidence about Emily's childhood. When her letters begin, they overflow with good spirits and the joy of young life.

And yet the notion persists that Emily's childhood was bleak and gloomy. Vinnie's stories, transmitted by Mabel Todd and Mary Lee Hall, were perhaps the origin of such a view; and many of Emily's poems about childhood, or poems using childhood as a metaphor, may seem to confirm it. A look at a few of them will show, I think, that they also point in other directions.

The poem "They shut me up in Prose" may seem at first glance to be a complaint against repression:

> They shut me up in Prose –
> As when a little Girl
> They put me in a Closet –
> Because they liked me "still" –
>
> Still! Could themself have peeped –
> And seen my Brain – go round –
> They might as wise have lodged a Bird
> For Treason – in the Pound –
>
> Himself has but to will
> And easy as a Star
> Abolish his Captivity –
> And laugh – No more have I –   (*#613, about 1862*)

But clearly her concern here is more with herself as poet than with herself as child. Like every child, she had had a taste of parental discipline; perhaps she had even been shut in a closet for making too much noise (we have just seen her and the others put "in separate rooms"), though it was Austin who raised the "Hurrah" around the house. The figure of the

---

3. Norman Talbot, "The Child, the Actress and Miss Emily Dickinson," *Southern Review* (Adelaide, June 1972), p. 105, calls attention to this passage as an expression of "joyous optimism" and suggests that it be "written out some hundreds of times by such critics of Miss Dickinson's poetry as wish to see her besieged by a monstrously alien universe. . . ." The warning is a good one, especially regarding her early years; but it is hardly an adequate answer (nor is it presented as one) to the complicated problem of her later and quite explicit alienations.

little girl in the closet seems almost unmistakably the young poet struggling to assert herself against the "prosaic" influences around her—the "real life" world of her father's house and of Amherst. Perhaps, too (since the poem was written when she was about thirty-one) she had in mind the failure of her literary advisers, like Higginson, to encourage her to write poetry. By this time she could indulge in a bit of petulance and even (in that last laugh) defiance—but not, I think, at the expense of her parents.

There is another poem often thought to describe her bleak childhood—in this instance, her sense of the failure of maternal love.

> A loss of something ever felt I –
> The first that I could recollect
> Bereft I was – of what I knew not
> Too young that any should suspect
>
> A Mourner walked among the children
> I notwithstanding went about
> As one bemoaning a Dominion
> Itself the only Prince cast out –
>
> Elder, Today, a session wiser
> And fainter, too, as Wiseness is –
> I find myself still softly searching
> For my Delinquent Palaces –
>
> And a Suspicion, like a Finger
> Touches my Forehead now and then
> That I am looking oppositely
> For the site of the Kingdom of Heaven –   (#959, about 1864)

But again, the poem might have a quite different, at least an additional referent. Her religious anxieties came early and went deep. As the only one in her group of pious friends who could not (as she thought, from some strange spiritual lack) accept Christ as her Savior, she felt like an outcast. The "Dominion," "the only Prince cast out," the "Delinquent Palaces," and the whole last stanza suggest, at the very least, something more than merely the failure of her parents to love her enough. The concluding thrust of the poem, the theme it leaves us with, is the danger of nostalgia, of looking back to some distant golden time for the solution to problems of the present. She chided her sister Vinnie for living "much of the time in the State of Regret." "My Country," she wrote, "is Truth." And it is never reached, she says here, by "looking oppositely."

Another poem that has been taken as a lament on her childhood seems also to have a very different thrust:

I cried at Pity – not at Pain –
I heard a Woman say
"Poor Child" – and something in her voice
Convicted me – of me –

So long I fainted, to myself
It seemed the common way,
And Health, and Laughter, Curious things –
To look at, like a Toy –

To sometimes hear "Rich people" buy
And see the Parcel rolled –
And carried, I supposed – to Heaven,
For children, made of Gold –

But not to touch, or wish for,
Or think of, with a sigh –
As so and so – had been to me,
Had God willed differently.

I wish I knew that Woman's name –
So when she comes this way,
To hold my life, and hold my ears
For fear I hear her say

She's "sorry I am dead" – again –
Just when the Grave and I –
Have sobbed ourselves almost to sleep,
Our only Lullaby –[4]   (#588, early 1862)

There is enough here to wring pity from the stoniest heart—"'Poor Child,'" the want of "Health, and Laughter," no presents, the sobbing "Lullaby." But the poem is not an appeal for pity; it is a warning against it, particularly here the kind of sentimental, uninformed pity (the "Woman" is clearly an outsider) that brings out the worst in the one pitied. Again she uses childhood as a metaphor for conveying an attitude toward a kind of pain that may have nothing to do with childhood—frustration of any sort, the experience of being excluded, or even, as has been suggested, frustration as poet.[5] Indeed, the poem is more about pity than

4. I have accepted ED's changes as indicated in the editor's note, and I have corrected line 15 ("And" to "As") following Ralph Franklin, *The Editing of Emily Dickinson*, p. 104.
5. Ruth Miller, *The Poetry of Emily Dickinson*, p. 164, links this poem to ED's reaction to the pity her Amherst friends felt for her after they had read Samuel Bowles's (?) article in the *Springfield Republican* attacking the "literature of misery," whose authors are "chiefly women, gifted women may be, full of thought and feeling and fancy, but poor, lonely and unhappy." ED, thinks Miller, saw this as an attack on herself. The poem, then, would be a rejection of her friends' pity. Whether or not Miller's theory is accepted, it seems more likely that the poem came out of some such context than from ED's broodings over a sad and bereft youth. (See Appendix IV.)

about pain. Pain can be endured, she says; but she would "hold her ears" against the kind of pity that leads only to the debasement of self-pity.

One poem is often regarded as traumatic:

> I was the slightest in the House –
> I took the smallest Room –
> At night, my little Lamp, and Book –
> And one Geranium –
>
> So stationed I could catch the Mint
> That never ceased to fall –
> And just my Basket –
> Let me think – I'm sure
> That this was all –
>
> I never spoke – unless addressed –
> And then, 'twas brief and low –
> I could not bear to live – aloud –
> The Racket shamed me so –
>
> And if it had not been so far –
> And any one I knew
> Were going – I had often thought
> How noteless – I could die –   (*#486, about 1862*)

To take the poem at the literal level first, Emily probably was, in point of fact, the "slightest," the least robust of the family, although we know that, in her prime, she worked as hard as anyone, went to bed latest, and got up earliest. She may actually have had the smallest room, but she shared it with Vinnie and in the early years perhaps with Austin, too. The third stanza can hardly be taken literally, since we know that, for all her denials, she "lived aloud" with the boisterous Austin and the "pert" Vinnie and was known as a talker and a tease among her young friends. Her mother seems to have had neither the physical strength nor the strength of character to be a stern disciplinarian. And her father was, by Emily's description, "too busy with his Briefs – to notice what we do," except, we may be sure, to demand quiet at meals, at family prayers, and during exhausted evenings at home.

To say that the poem is a poem and not autobiography is not, however, to say that Emily is not in it at all. She simply need not be regarded as bemoaning her repressed childhood. The poem seems an attempt, again, to recapture the conditions and circumstances of herself as poet. The second stanza describes the advantages of her situation: inconspicuousness was just what she wanted to "catch the Mint / That never ceased to fall –" We recall her complaint to Higginson about her embarrassment when people talked of "Hallowed things" aloud. So she shunned the

"Racket," bided her time, and kept her counsel. Her lamp, her book, her geranium, her basket are symbolic of all that she needed to become a poet, even if this meant—a fancy that often crossed her mind—how "noteless," or unrecognized, she could die. (Why talk aloud when "all men say 'What' to me"?) Many of the attitudes of her maturity are caught up in this poem ostensibly about her childhood. As she said to Higginson about this time, again using the metaphor of childhood: "If fame belonged to me, I could not escape her – if she did not, the longest day would pass me on the chase – and the approbation of my Dog, would forsake me – then – My Barefoot-Rank is better – "

What confronts us in these poems is not the vagaries of the Dickinson rhetoric, the family tendency toward hyperbole and self-drama, but the symbolic use of the materials of childhood and domestic living for the purposes of poetry. Emily's experience of childhood, what she was like as a child, what she actually felt and thought in the earliest years, can best be inferred from other sources, aside from those few firsthand glimpses; the atmosphere, or feel, of the Dickinson household with its mixture of solicitude and austerity (with Vinnie's later, lurid tales heavily discounted); refractions from her ebullient early letters; her reiterated love of home in letter after letter of her youth and maturity; and all that can be deduced from the observations of outsiders like Aunt Lavinia. We can assume that there was enough discipline in the Dickinson home (and in all such homes) to give her clues to the nature of parental discipline; it was a natural step for her to heighten and expand these clues into the symbolic and metaphoric patterns of her adult poetry.[6]

As always, her concern was with essence. One thing is certain: Emily Dickinson took childhood seriously. She gloried in all the children in her neighborhood and was their favorite (as Martha Dickinson Bianchi says often) because she listened to what they had to say and talked to them on even terms. Her notes to her nephews and niece contain some of her happiest flights of fancy.[7] As she herself outgrew childhood, the wish crept several times into her letters that she could return to childhood. She

6. Talbot's article (see note 2) is a perceptive study of Emily Dickinson's use of childhood, both here as a kind of protective mask with Higginson and in many of her poems as an "analogue of all human experience. . . . [t]he five crucial subjects of Miss Dickinson's poetry [Death, Love, Poetry, Nature, and Eternity] are constantly seen in terms that make the present finite life analogous to the life of a child. . . . Our life in this limited world . . . is the life of a child yet to grow up" (pp. 108–9). The article defends Emily Dickinson's use of the persona of the child against the disparagements of Yvor Winters (who accused her of "a kind of poetic nursery jargon"), Richard Chase, R. P. Blackmur, and Clark Griffith.

7. Like this one to nephew Ned on his third birthday (*L* II, 432 and n.):

My little Uncle must remember me till I come Home a Hundred miles to see his Braided Gown –

Emily knows a Man who drives a Coach like a Thimble, and turns the Wheel all day with his Heel – His name is Bumblebee. Little Ned will see Him before

His Niece.

praised one friend for being "more of a woman than I am, for I love so to be a child." When she was twenty-one, she longed to "ramble away [with Sue] as children, among the woods and fields, and forget these many years, and these sorrowing cares, and each become a child again." To Austin the next year she longed for the old days, for the "things we did when children. I wish we were children now. I wish we were *always* children, how to grow up I dont know." Sometimes, this is pure nostalgia; sometimes, as in 1856 when her mother's illness frightened her, she felt an urge to escape: "I don't know what her sickness is, for I am but a simple child, and frightened at myself. I often wish I was a grass, or a toddling daisy, whom all these problems of the dust might not terrify – " But this *is* Dickinson rhetoric, not reality. She never rambled away her time with Susan, and she never shirked the care of her mother.

The essence, as we might expect, came in the later letters and in the poems. What Emily liked was the frank, fresh gaze of childhood, its powers of complete absorption, the immediacy of its vision. She might carp at the restrictions of her youth and the household chores, but the essence of childhood, its glory, was to her its freedom from the commitments and clutter of adulthood. "Don't let your free spirit be chained," she wrote to the pious Abiah Root at fourteen. She liked to listen to children because their talk was free and uninhibited. She exploited their privilege often in her poems, where some of her most irreverent or radical thoughts come as if from a child who, innocently, speaks the truth.

There is a good deal of romantic sentimentalism in her attitude toward children, surely, but more perhaps of the Christian ideal of the simplicity and innocence of childhood that, for redemption, must somehow be regained. Emily's thought is most explicit in a letter of about 1870 to Joseph Lyman, in answer to one about his growing family. The letter is both a congratulation and, in view of Lyman's streak of vanity and ambition (well known to Dickinsons), a gentle rebuke. It finishes with her own curious combination of Luke 18:17 and Matthew 18:3.

> You speak Joseph of a young Anak and of a little Seraph. It may be that he *is* the Hercules & she the true Seraph – stronger *he* than you w[ith] your manhood – sweeter she than living woman for I bethink me of a speech uttered by one who has much credit here & everywhere for perfect vision, "Except ye all become as little children ye shall in no wise enter the Kingdom."[8]

Ultimately she sentimentalized neither her own childhood nor childhood itself. She liked children because, as she once remarked, "Children's Hearts are large." "Please never grow up," she wrote to MacGregor

8. As often in her quotations, especially from the Bible and Shakespeare, ED did not bother to be exact. This is a good example of how she trimmed down the original (Luke), which reads, in the King James Version in her father's library: "Verily I say unto you, Whosoever shall not receive the kingdom of God as a little child shall in no wise enter therein." And Matthew: "Except ye be converted, and become as little children, ye shall not enter into the kingdom of heaven."

Jenkins (age twelve), "which is 'far better' – Please never 'improve' – you are perfect now." In a late letter (about 1883) she imparted some Words-worthian wisdom to a friend who was interested in the Children's Aid Society and had apparently taken a child under her care:

> I rejoice that it was possible for you to be with it, for I think the early spir-itual influences about a child are more hallowing than we know. The angel begins in the morning in every human life.

If she had dark thoughts about her own childhood, she seems never, unlike Vinnie, to have confided them to anyone. Looking back, as she does in this letter, she appears reconciled to the early spiritual influences of her own household—even to Father's addressing "an Eclipse, every morn-ing" in family prayers—those same influences under which she is sup-posed to have suffered. At least, she seems not to have held her parents' effort against them, even though she could not share their piety. When George Eliot died in 1880, she wrote of "the gift of belief which her greatness denied her." This gift, she said, comes in childhood, "earth's confiding time," and "perhaps having no childhood, she lost her way to the early trust, and no later came." Although Emily felt a certain identity with George Eliot ("Now, *my* George Eliot," she wrote in this same letter), their spiritual courses were not parallel. Emily *had* a childhood and one that she was grateful for.

If Emily's view of childhood is often sentimental, she knew the limita-tions of "earth's confiding time." One of her most buoyant summings up—a true poem of Innocence and of Experience—ends on an entirely realistic note. She knows how innocence ends, but for two stanzas she glories in it. How this poem could have come out of a blighted childhood is hard to see:

> The Child's faith is new –
> Whole – like His Principle –
> Wide – like the Sunrise
> On fresh Eyes –
> Never had a Doubt –
> Laughs – at a Scruple –
> Believes all sham
> But Paradise –
>
> Credits the World –
> Deems His Dominion
> Broadest of Sovreignties –
> And Caesar – mean –
> In the Comparison –
> Baseless Emperor –
> Ruler of Nought,
> Yet swaying all –

Grown bye and bye
To hold mistaken
His pretty estimates
Of Prickly Things
He gains the skill
Sorrowful – as certain –
Men – to anticipate
Instead of Kings –   (*#637, about 1862*)

16

Schooling

EDWARD DICKINSON's chief concern about his children during these early years (in addition, of course, to their health and their duty to be pleasant and obedient in the home) was their education. In this he was true to his father's lifelong dedication and to the atmosphere of the town in which he grew up. Even in the era before the college, Amherst had an unusual number of college graduates for so small a town. It had its men of parts, like Noah Webster, Lucius Boltwood (who helped in the founding of the college and whose wife was a cousin of Emerson's), and Samuel Fowler Dickinson, the young orator who had early become the county's leading lawyer. In his letters home Edward said less about the children's piety and Christian nurture than about how much they were learning at school. "Keep school, and learn, so as to tell me, when I come home, how many new things you have learned, since I came away," he wrote them when Emily was seven. His advice to his children was practical and worldly. He said nothing about fulfilling God's purpose or about the good of their souls:

My Dear little Children, Your mother writes me that you have been quite good since I came away – You don't know what a pleasure it is for me to have such good news from you – I want to have you do perfectly right – always be kind & pleasant, & always tell the truth, & never deceive. That is the way to become good – If you do right, & that every body will – every body will like you – I want to have you grow up & become good men & women – and learn all you can, so that you can teach others to do right. You have enough to eat & drink, & good clothes – & go to school – while a great many poor little children have to go hungry – and have ragged clothes – & sleep cold, & have poor green wood to burn, & can't have books or go to school. All you learn, now, when you are young, will do you a great deal of good, when you are grown up. Austin, be careful, & not let the woodpile fall on you – & don't let the cattle hurt you in the yard, when you go . . . after water. Take good care of Emily, when you go to school & not let her get hurt.

His next letter (four days later) returned to the subject, apparently much on his mind. His weeks in Boston that winter (1838) for the sessions of the General Court gave him a chance to view it in some detachment. This time he gave some thought to his children's souls, but it came curiously late. "The duty which devolves upon us," he wrote his wife, "of bringing up our little children as they should be, is an important one – and we can not realise too deeply, our obligation to study the best course – and adopt the best methods of instruction & government – & set before them the best example for imitation." But always, he finally reminded himself, to prepare them for the life to come:

> To take a rational view of life, & the object of it, is, at once, to place almost any thing we value here, in the light of little importance – and if, as you believe and I can't doubt, this life is a mere preparatory state for another period of existence, how important, to act with reference to such a state – & yet how little we really do seem to consider it.

Of course, Edward Dickinson did *not* place things of this world "in the light of little importance," and his last sentence is a significant confession, a reminder that he was first of all an ambitious man, busy with quite worldly affairs. Three years earlier, after he learned that his brother Samuel had become a Christian, he had made a similar admission:

> Truly I cannot but rejoice at such news from a brother so dear to me as he is, and for whom I have so high an opinion – and I hope he is really prepared for that happy future state of existence, for which we all ought to be ever in readiness, but which I am sensible I have always neglected – and fear I always shall.

When Emily, in her fifteenth year, wrote her friend Abiah Root, "I feel that the world holds a predominant place in my affections," she reflected in her own way the main thrust of her father's life (he was forty-seven before he brought himself to join the church, and then only after he had "been long struggling with his feelings"), even though what she meant by the "world" had little to do with "Maine land" and those "Jacanapes" making their tens of thousands while he, a man of spirit, lived in half a house. Edward may have been conventionally pious, but it could hardly be said that he walked in daily fear of his Creator, or that he created such an atmosphere in his home. He wanted his children's feet planted firmly on the ground, and he set out to see that they had a fine, solid education that would "do them good" in many senses of the word. On one occasion he sent them a copy of *Parley's Magazine* with its cover depicting a little girl with a book, and the inscription:

I wish you all a happy New Year,
Plenty of books, and very good cheer.

The school that, prior to 1840, Edward urged his children to "keep" was the district school, ungraded, one-room. No one has much good to say of it, though it was a great improvement .(such was the growing concern in Amherst for the proper education of the young) over its predecessor, the miserable affair described by a contemporary (Noah Webster's youngest daughter) as "forlorn, unpainted, and unshaded . . . no maps or pictures . . . or equipments for the assistance of the teacher. . . ." By the time Emily Dickinson started going to school (the first reference is in Edward's letter to his wife of September 7, 1835), the children were provided with a two-story building of whitewashed brick, situated on a plot of land bought from Samuel Fowler Dickinson on Pleasant Street opposite the house to which Edward moved his family in 1840. Emily was silent in later years on her experience in this "Primary School." It is probably true that the school "contributed nothing to her mental stores except the power to read, write, and cipher."

By contrast, Emily could hardly say enough in praise of Amherst Academy, which she and Lavinia entered together, in the "English Course," each for the first time, at the beginning of the fall term, September 7, 1840. If ever there was a blossoming period in her life, full and joyous, the years at the Academy—seven in all, with a few terms out for illness—were it. This remarkable school, with its enlightened curriculum, its young and enthusiastic administrators and teachers, and its close association with Amherst College, was an influence of first importance in Emily's formative years.

Subscriptions for the establishment of Amherst Academy were first opened in 1812 under the leadership, among others, of Samuel Fowler Dickinson, who, with Noah Webster as president *pro tem,* sat on the first Board of Trustees. The school was formally opened December 6, 1814. It was conceived on liberal principles (theology excepted) and from the first offered a wide variety of studies. Its founders are properly celebrated by its historian, Frederick Tuckerman:

> The projectors of Amherst Academy were men of vision and practical wisdom. Earnest, resolute, self-sacrificing, they were animated by a high purpose. As friends of education they were determined to provide better educational facilities in the county of Hampshire than then existed. With this end in view they . . . set up a school [which soon became] successful beyond their most sanguine expectations, with a superior corps of teachers, and an average attendance of more than a hundred pupils, and which was second to none in New England.

It is worth noting that Amherst College, which opened seven years later, grew out of the Academy (not vice versa, as is often true in such situations today) and was projected by this same group of dedicated men. The two institutions moved along closely together; indeed, for the first four years of the college, its records and the Academy's were kept together. Once well under way, the college supplied the school with a steady stream of young, devoted, well-educated instructors, and opened its lectures to Academy students.

A letter sent by the Academy to parents in 1827 described some of these advantages and gave an idea of the tone and purpose of the school. After telling of recent improvements to the building (three-story, brick), now "finished in convenient rooms for Students," the letter dealt with curricular matters:

> There is both a Classical and English department. The learned languages will be taught in such a manner, as to make the study of text-books a study of interesting facts and sentiments, as well as of words and their grammatical relations. Instead of confinement to the dry details of agreement and government, there will be constant endeavours to excite interest, by adverting to ancient literature, politics, manners and customs.
>
> The English Department will receive special attention. Besides the advantages ordinarily enjoyed in Academies, its members will be allowed to attend Lectures in the College, on History, Chemistry and Natural Philosophy.

A list of the extraordinary men whose lectures were available to students in the Academy shows how remarkable these advantages were. Each one of the men mentioned in the following tribute by Tuckerman was an acknowledged leader in his field; each had published, some of them widely:

> The opportunities at Amherst during the early years of the College for the study of the natural sciences were exceptional. The teachers in the scientific branches were second to none in New England, even if Harvard and Yale be included in the comparison. Among them were Amos Eaton in chemistry, botany and zoology, Edward Hitchcock in chemistry, geology and natural history, Ebenezer S. Snell in mathematics and natural philosophy, Charles U. Shepard in chemistry and natural history, and Charles B. Adams in zoology and astronomy.

The emphasis here may seem more on the scientific side than would be likely to provide nurture for a poet. But as science was taught in the school and in the college (Edward Hitchcock's influence pervaded both), it may have been precisely the nurture best suited to Emily Dickinson's development. Another letter to parents (this one in 1843) placed more emphasis on the literary side:

> The Trustees are able to secure the best of instruction. Besides the Principals of the departments, in whom the Public can place the highest confidence, as respects both character and literary competence, such assistance as the multiplicity of classes may require, can at all times be commanded from among

Brick School-house on Pleasant Street

EARLY AMHERST: EMILY'S TWO SCHOOLS

The Common, looking southwest, about 1842
From left to right: Baptist Church(?), Merchants' Row, Amherst House
(at intersection of roads), Amherst Academy

Leonard Humphrey, ED's first "Master'

Amherst Academy (at left) in 1847

the best scholars in College. Hence the instruction in each Department, and of every class, is thorough, and the standard of literary attainment always high.

Special attention was given in this letter to the "Female Department." In Emily's time there were about a hundred girls enrolled, although few attended every one of the four terms. They were "under the charge of a competent and accomplished Preceptress," who was to give "particular attention to the formation of the moral and social, as well as intellectual character of her pupils"—and, of course, the religious:

The instructors shall be persons of good moral character; of competent learning and abilities: firmly established in the faith of the Christian religion, the doctrines and duties of which they shall inculcate as well by example as precept. They shall instruct their pupils whether male or female in the several arts and sciences which may be necessary or proper to an accomplished education of either. The Preceptor shall open and close the school each day with prayer. All the students shall uniformly attend upon the public worship of God on the sabbath. The tuition shall for the present be, *five dollars* in the classical department, and *four dollars* in the English department, for each term of eleven weeks.

Besides the religious observances here indicated, the students were expected to attend Bible class Saturday evening, but the degree of piety seems to have been no more than Emily was used to from the daily prayers (led by her father) at home. The college, many of whose students were destined for the ministry or missionary work, was much more evangelical than the Academy. If the world began about this time to hold a predominant place in Emily's affections, part of the reason was the rich and humane education she was receiving in Amherst Academy.

It is important not to judge Amherst Academy by secondary education in New England of the last few decades of the century, when the first flush of the private academy movement had worn off and enthusiasm had been replaced by discipline, routine drudgery, and undeclared war between students and teachers. The students were no doubt held to account, but neither Emily nor any of her contemporaries, as far as can be determined, ever breathed a word about being put upon or abused or bullied, in class or out. The concern in the 1827 letter to parents to "excite interest" in the study of language has a downright progressive ring. So has a paragraph on the use of the blackboard ("visual aids") to get the students to *see* their errors. The school even provided for what we now call teacher training:

There will also be, during each fall term, a Class for School Teachers, whose studies are conducted with special reference to the business of teaching.

This Class will be permitted to attend familiar Lectures from one of the College Professors on the subject of School Instruction.

[*339*

But most important for Emily Dickinson's blossoming was the school's policy on the relations between teachers and students. It goes far to explain why she spoke of her teachers so often and with such affection:

> The Instructors will mingle daily with their pupils in cheerful conversation and gymnastic exercises. The Government will be of an affectionate, paternal character.

The only disciplinary note in the letter seems mild enough: "And such as cannot be influenced by honourable motives, will not be suffered to remain to corrupt others."

The most striking things about the teachers and administrators of Amherst Academy are, to us, their extreme youth and (in view of our emphasis upon academic tenure) their rapid turnover. Apparently this too was policy, and it worked. Members of the staff were recruited every year from the graduating classes of New England colleges, most of them from Amherst and Mount Holyoke. After a year or so of teaching, the young people would move on to graduate study or professional work. There were eight principals (they all taught, too) during Emily's seven years in the Academy, and all but two of them took the post directly after graduating from Amherst. The preceptresses were somewhat older—there were six during Emily's years—but at least two were under thirty. Rebecca Woodbridge was twenty and, according to Emily's description, very pretty. "We all love her very much," Emily wrote Abiah Root. Helen Humphrey was twenty when she became preceptress in 1842. She was the older sister of Emily's great friend and correspondent, Jane, and so had much more than a professional relationship with Emily. Elizabeth Adams was in her early thirties. She married the year she left the Academy (in 1847) and was the one of whom Emily spoke most often and was perhaps the most fond. During her school days and for years after, Emily wrote of these people in her letters as one would of intimate friends, certainly not teachers for whom she felt awe or fear. When she wrote Abiah toward the end of her Academy days, "you know I am always in love with my teachers," we can understand why.

An example, and one with no slight bearing on her development as a poet, was her regard for Leonard Humphrey, principal of the Academy for the two years following his graduation from Amherst in 1846, where he had been valedictorian of his class. Tuckerman describes him as "a young man of rare talents and great promise." Emily revered him but knew him also as a friend. During her first winter in Mount Holyoke, Humphrey and Mary Warner, one of Emily's group in Amherst, called on Emily, who promptly told Abiah Root, "we had a delightful time." Two years later, after a very brief illness, he died. The news was a shock to the whole community, and he was much elegized.

While there was little or no romantic attachment between Humphrey and Emily—we know from his correspondence with a friend named Brigham that he was interested in several other Amherst girls—the sudden loss of this friend and former teacher gave her cause for deep and melancholy thought. This was an instance, too, of how vulnerable she was (like her brother Austin) to each new death among her intimates. Often the blow required her utmost resources for recovery. Characteristically, she turned to some kind of literary expression. ("We – tell a Hurt – to cool it –" she wrote in a later poem, and to Higginson she spoke of the "palsy, here – the Verses just relieve.") When Humphrey died, she relieved her melancholy by writing a letter to Abiah Root. It is her first sustained elegiac effort, full of mortuary clichés (as might be expected), and more concerned with herself than with Humphrey. But she is writing about one she revered and (in her own way) loved. She called him "master," a term she reserved for only the very few men in her life (all of them older men) whose wisdom, advice, or love she sought.

> I write Abiah to-night, because it is cool and quiet, and I can forget the toil and care of the feverish day, and then I am *selfish* too, because I am feeling lonely; some of my friends are gone, and some of my friends are sleeping – sleeping the churchyard sleep – the hour of evening is sad – it was once my study hour – my master has gone to rest, and the open leaf of the book, and the scholar at school *alone,* make the tears come, and I cannot brush them away; I would not if I could, for they are the only tribute I can pay the departed Humphrey.
>
> *You* have stood by the grave before; I have walked there sweet summer evenings and read the names on the stones, and wondered who would come and give me the same memorial; but I never have laid my friends there, and forgot that they too must die; this is my first affliction, and indeed 'tis hard to bear it.

As a matter of fact, Humphrey's death was not her first affliction. She had suffered one before and had written about that, too. In April 1844, she was deeply affected by the death of her friend Sophia Holland, to the point (as she described it two years later to Abiah Root) of "a fixed melancholy." Her worried parents sent her to visit her beloved Aunt Lavinia for a month. She confessed to Abiah that, at the time, "I told no one the cause of my grief, though it was gnawing at my very heart strings." The experience must have haunted her; her letter to Abiah after the two-year lapse told about the hurt in vivid detail, perhaps to cure it. Sophia's death was much closer to her than Humphrey's, and her style shows it:

> My friend was Sophia Holland. She was too lovely for earth & she was transplanted from earth to heaven. I visited her often in sickness & watched over her bed. But at length Reason fled and the physician forbid any but the nurse to go into her room. Then it seemed to me I should die too if I could not be permitted to watch over her or even to look at her face. At length the doctor said she must die & allowed me to look at her for a moment through the open door. I took off my shoes and stole softly to the sick room.
>
> There she lay mild & beautiful as in health & her pale features lit up with

an unearthly – smile. I looked as long as friends would permit & when they told me I must look no longer I let them lead me away. . . .

This little elegy stands out sharply from the rest of the letter, which is even richer in mortuary clichés than the piece on Humphrey. The two passages show her finding her voice and developing a style. Later, when the matter of death became more "organized" in her mind (to use her own term again), it inspired some of her finest poems.

She never spoke of another of her teachers, Daniel Taggart Fiske, who was principal of the Academy in 1842 at the age of twenty-three. But he spoke of her and has the distinction of being the only one whose recollections we have. When Mrs. Todd was collecting material for the *Letters* in 1894, he answered her inquiry:

> I would say that I have very distinct and pleasant impressions of Emily Dickinson, who was a pupil of mine in Amherst Academy in 1842–43. I remember her as a very bright, but rather delicate and frail looking girl; an excellent scholar, of exemplary deportment, faithful in all school duties; but somewhat shy and nervous. Her compositions were strikingly original; and in both thought and style seemed beyond her years, and always attracted much attention in the school and, I am afraid, excited not a little envy.

Though these young teachers—along with an extraordinary group of young friends—set the tone of Emily's day-by-day life at school and contributed much to her blossoming, the source of the school's most profound and lasting influence on her was quite different. This was the "large, noble looking man" who set the educational tone for the whole community: the Reverend Professor, and (from 1845 to 1854) President of Amherst College, Edward Hitchcock. He warrants a section of his own in any account of Emily's early years.[1]

Hitchcock was a remarkable man, the "pace setter," man of God and man of Science, who inspired a whole generation with a love of nature that combined a sense of its sublimity with an accurate knowledge of its

---

1. William S. Tyler, the eulogist at his funeral, described him as follows: "He was a large man. His frame was large, his mind was large, his heart was large. He sympathized with all, because he comprehended all; and he comprehended all . . . because he had all in himself. . . . He had naturally great physical strength and powers of endurance . . . few could climb mountains or break rocks with him – few could endure so much fatigue as he on a geological excursion. . . . Large as was the framework of bones, and strong as was the texture of muscles and sinews, it was pervaded and over-mastered by a still more remarkable nervous development. . . . Every bone and muscle and sinew was alive with sensibility. Every organ thrilled to its extremity with the excitement of his mind, when it was roused to action, every nerve and fibre of his body quivered with pain or pleasure, as his heart sank with sadness or leaped for joy within him" (*The Wise Man of the Scriptures; or, Science and Religion. A Discourse delivered in the Village Church in Amherst, March 2d, 1864, at the Funeral of Rev. Prof. Edward Hitchcock*, DD., LL.D., Samuel Bowles and Company, Springfield, 1864, pp. 31–32).

parts and processes, as far as the natural sciences of the day knew them. His early history is a fascinating story of a born scientist gradually becoming a devout apologist for revealed religion but never once relinquishing his dedication to the discovery and propagation of scientific knowledge.[2] Coming to Amherst in 1825 from Benjamin Silliman's laboratory at Yale, Hitchcock was largely responsible for attracting the science faculty that put Amherst on even terms with Harvard and Yale and opened up such unusual opportunities for students in Amherst Academy.[3]

He was also part poet. When he was twenty-two, he wrote a verse tragedy of five hundred lines, "The Downfall of Bonaparte," and there was a touch of the poet in everything he did. Although his voluminous scientific writing is for the most part strictly disciplined and factual, in his prefaces and introductions and wherever the text gives him the slightest opportunity, his style becomes rhapsodic. His Inaugural Address as president of the college shows him in characteristic form, tempering the moralizing and piety demanded by such occasions with lyric tributes to the Amherst countryside. Compared with similar addresses in the New England colleges of the time, his is unique in this respect. It is hard to imagine that Emily Dickinson, with her father as treasurer and her brother about to enter the college, did not attend the ceremony. And so, undoubtedly, did the other students and the staff of Amherst Academy. (Whoever did not attend could have read the address later, for it was promptly published.)

How rich the gentle slopes of yonder distant mountains, that bound the Connecticut valley on either side! How striking Mount Sugar Loaf on the north, with its red belted and green tufted crown: and Mount Toby too, with its imposing outline of unbroken forest! Especially, how beautifully and even majestically does the indented summit of Mount Holyoke repose against the southern sky! What sunrises and sunsets do we here witness; and what a

2. Hitchcock's pre-Amherst career may be summed up briefly. He was born in Deerfield, Massachusetts, in 1793. His father was a hatter, a farmer, and a deacon of the Congregational Church. As a boy he worked as a farmer, carpenter, and surveyor. He was self-educated, studying at night, and once nearly ruined his health and his eyesight by lying on his back too long studying the stars. He was early attracted to Unitarianism but after a cover-to-cover reading of the Bible went over to the orthodox evangelical faith. He was principal of Deerfield Academy from 1815 to 1818 (*they* believed in youth, too), a Congregational minister from 1821 to 1825, but at heart and always a scientist. During his months in the Yale Theological Seminary just prior to his ministry, his happiest days were in Benjamin Silliman's laboratory, to which he returned after resigning from his church in Conway, Massachusetts. It was from there that he went to Amherst as Professor of Chemistry and Natural History, a title he soon had changed to Professor of Natural Theology and Geology.

3. He literally brought science to Amherst, in men, in enthusiasm, in equipment. Before he came, Tyler wrote "the chemical apparatus was . . . not worth ten dollars. Cabinet there was none. Not even a beginning had been made of those magnificent scientific collections, which now adorn college hill" (*The Wise Man,* p. 24). Within a few years Amherst was an acknowledged center of activity in all the sciences.

multitude of permutations and combinations pass before us during the day, as we watch from hour to hour, one of the loveliest landscapes of New England. Surely if there is any poetry in the student's soul, – if any love of nature, – they must be here developed. And how can he but cherish enobling thoughts and purposes, whose eyes are continually feasted with such noble prospects![4]

With a little of Emily's own hyperbole, one might say that such "permutations and combinations" made up her day, as she later described it to Higginson: "You ask of my Companions Hills – Sir – and the Sundown – " It is hard to imagine her not having been touched, like Austin, by this vibrant spirit in the community. While Mark Hopkins at Williams was deploring the effects of the new sciences on religious faith, Hitchcock set about leading his students to God through the study of His works. He did this not only in his college lectures, frequent sermons, and other public orations, but on botanical and geological field trips with his students and young people of the town.

Many of his lectures were published, including a series he gave in the 1840s that appeared in 1850 under the title *Religious Lectures on Peculiar Phenomena in the Four Seasons*. It has particular relevance, I think, to our study. Based on talks "delivered to the students in Amherst College, in 1845, 1847, 1848 and 1849," and hence open to students in Amherst Academy during Emily's years there, it is Hitchcock at his best, combining mystical fervor and pure aesthetic delight with sharp scientific observation. Many a passage could have prompted a later poem of Emily's. (Again, if she missed the lectures, she could have seen the little volume at its publishers, J. S. & C. Adams of Amherst, whose bookstore Tuckerman called "for many years the gathering place of the learned clan of the village.")

Emily always gloried in the changing seasons and was sensitive (as what New England poet is not) to their individual qualities and characteristics. Hitchcock, devoting a lecture to each season, goes a step further: each season has not only its peculiar beauty and meaning but its own chemistry and physics. In his lecture called "The Euthanasia of Autumn," he is both scientist and poet to that yearly glory of New England hills, often celebrated in Emily's poems, the autumn foliage:

> With us, then, the fading leaf is not a mere example of decay, producing sadness, if not melancholy, in other lands. When autumn approaches, some slight frosts chill the vegetable fluids and weaken the power of their delicate organs to produce the various proximate principles in proper proportions. In other words, a diseased action supervenes in the vessels, and the result is, an

4. *The Highest Use of Learning: an Address delivered at his Inauguration to the Presidency of Amherst College,* by Rev. Edward Hitchcock, LL.D., published by the Trustees. Amherst: J. S. & C. Adams, Printers: 1845, p. 45. The "highest use," of course, was religious. Most of the other inaugural addresses of the time, like that of Hitchcock's predecessor in Amherst, Heman Humphrey, are so taken up with moral and spiritual verities that they might have been written—and delivered—anywhere.

excess of acid or alkali. These substances, it is well known, produce most striking effects upon vegetable colors; changing sometimes those that are dull into a brilliancy often gaudy, and sometimes oppressive. Ere long the effects of these chemical changes become manifest upon the foliage of our forests, as the autumn advances; and then follow weeks, in which the eye is met by prospects the most brilliant and imposing that can be conceived of, whose description the inhabitants of other lands regard as caricature. The richest and most diverse hues that nature can produce by the separation and blending of all the prismatic colors, meet us in every grove, and hill side, and mountain. Red of every shade, from crimson to cherry, – yellow, from bright sulphur to orange, – brown, from clove brown to liver brown, – and green, from grass green to oil green. . . .

It is hard to believe that Emily would not respond to Hitchcock's fine sense of the specific here, if to nothing else than his eye for precise shades of color. Her own sense of precision was already showing itself, for instance, in one of the delights of her girlhood, her herbarium, with its carefully printed Latin name for each item; and she was known among her friends for her detailed knowledge of the flora around Amherst. Certainly one of the strengths of her nature poems lies in their firm substratum of knowledge and accurate observation. But more than this, her poems show a knowledge of chemical process, of botanic and especially geologic lore far beyond the usual nature poet's stock in trade. There are more earthquakes and volcanoes in her poems—phenomena which then were central in all geological inquiry, especially Hitchcock's—than in the poetry of Keats, Emerson, Browning, and Shelley combined. Gems, minerals, just plain rocks, and even alloys abound, together with a sense of their properties and of the process involved in their creation: "A Quartz contentment, like a stone"; ". . . a finer Phosphor / Requiring in the Quench – / A Power of Renowned Cold"; an "Anthracite" temperature; the "Columnar Self" firm on its "Granitic Base."[5]

5. The poems quoted here are #341, #422, #789. Once, whether intentionally or not, she made a poem out of Hitchcock's religious application of the law of the conservation of matter, a subject he had broached in *Religious Lectures* (1850) and argued vigorously in his later book *The Religion of Geology* (1851), which we know was read by Austin (see letter to Sue, November 7, 1851) and almost certainly by Emily. The passage (p. 7) deserves ample quotation as a fine example of Hitchcock's matter and method as he strove to use his scientific knowledge to confirm his religious faith:

It is probably the prevailing opinion among intelligent Christians at this time, and has been the opinion of many commentators, that when Peter describes the future destruction of the world [II Peter 3:10–11], he means that its solid substance, and indeed that of the whole material universe, will be utterly consumed or annihilated by fire. This opinion rests upon the common belief that such is the effect of combustion. But chemistry informs us, that no case of combustion, how fiercely soever the fire may rage, annihilates the least particle of matter; and that fire only changes the form of substances. Nay, there is no reason whatever to suppose that one particle of matter has been annihilated since the world began. The chemist moreover asserts that all the solid parts of the globe have already under-

Emily Dickinson

All this is "Hitchcockian" to a degree, and the kind of thing (being a poet himself) he may have envisioned as the result of his educational policy. In the preface to his famous *Elementary Geology*, which was published the year Emily entered the Academy (1840) and which went through thirty editions, he argued:

> In Institutions of a lower grade [i.e., secondary schools], it [geology] receives far less attention than its merits deserve. Why should not a science, whose facts possess a thrilling interest; whose reasonings are admirably adapted for mental discipline, and often severely tax the strongest powers; and whose results are, many of them, as grand and ennobling as those of Astronomy itself; . . . why should not such a science be thought as essential in education as the kindred branches of Chemistry and Astronomy?

> gone combustion, and that although heat may melt them, it cannot burn them. Nor is there any thing upon or within the earth capable of combustion, but vegetables, and animals, and a few gases. Has Peter, then, made a mistake because he did not understand modern chemistry? . . .
>
> Scarcely any truth seems more clearly taught in the Bible than the future resurrection of the body. Yet this doctrine has always been met by a most formidable objection. It is said that the body laid in the grave is ere long decomposed into its elements, which are scattered over the face of the earth, and enter into new combinations, even forming a part of other human bodies. Hence not even Omnipotence can raise from the grave the identical body laid there, because the particles may enter successively into a multitude of other human bodies. I am not aware that any successful reply has ever been given to this objection, until chemistry and natural history taught us the true nature of bodily identity. . . .

Here is how ED reduced Hitchcock's long and fervent argument to her own characteristic size—and perhaps with a touch of irony.

> The Chemical conviction
> That Nought be lost
> Enable in Disaster
> My fractured Trust –
>
> The Faces of the Atoms
> If I shall see
> How more the Finished Creatures
> Departed me!   (#954, about 1864)

In another poem she took Hitchcock's side (knowingly or not) in the geologic controversy between the "igneous" and the "aqueous" theories of origins. Benjamin Silliman in his *Geological Lectures,* published in New Haven in 1829, had argued against "the fashion of the day to attribute almost everything to igneous agency." Hitchcock and Emily (she for poetic purposes, at least) disagreed—or did she straddle both theories?

> Though the great Waters sleep
> That they are still the Deep,
> We cannot doubt –
> No vacillating God
> Ignited this Abode
> To put it out –   (#1599, about 1884)

And why, he asked, should it not be taught to children in the earliest grades? Hitchcock had apparently won his case for geology, at least in Amherst, long before 1840. Harriet Martineau, visiting Amherst in 1835, left an account that shows him in vigorous action:

Mr. Bancroft drove me to Amherst [from Northampton] this afternoon. . . . We mounted the steep hill on which Amherst stands, and stopped before the red brick buildings of the college. When the horse was disposed of, Mr. Bancroft left me to look at the glorious view, while he went in search of some one who would be our guide about the college. In a minute he beckoned me in, with a smile of great delight, and conducted me into the lecture-room where Professor Hitchcock was lecturing. In front of the lecturer was a large number of students, and on either hand as many as forty or fifty girls. These girls were from a neighbouring school [Amherst Academy], and from the houses of the farmers and mechanics of the village. . . . We found that the admission of girls to such lectures as they could understand (this was on geology) was a practice of some years' standing, and that no evil had been found to result from it. It was a gladdening sight, testifying both to the simplicity of manners and the eagerness for education.

It is not too much to imagine Emily's enjoying the same privilege during the 1840s, when Hitchcock was at the top of his powers. If she heard or read the *Religious Lectures,* she must have been struck by "The Coronation of Winter," a lecture describing a dazzling ice storm of recent memory in Amherst, when the sun, refracted by the ice on the trees and bushes, produced colors unimaginable by one who had not actually seen them. Hitchcock invoked Emily's favorite chapter in Revelation (XXI)— she called it the "Gem chapter"—to do them justice, but he added much from his own acute and practiced observation.[6] The world, he wrote, seemed ablaze with the colors of sapphire, chalcedony, emerald. His joy mounted to near ecstasy.

. . . I began to notice the prismatic colors; now exhibiting a gem of most splendid sapphire blue; next one of amethystine purple; next one of intense topaz yellow; then a sea green beryl, changing by a slight change of posture, into a rich emerald green; and then one of deep hyacinth red. As the sun approached the meridian, the number and splendor of these colored gems

6. On October 17, 1847 (*YH* I, 125), during Emily's first term at Mount Holyoke, Hitchcock preached a sermon there on the "Gem chapter," using the key verses (18–24) as his text; so Emily heard the sparkling passage read—in a voice, we are told, famous for its sonority:

18 And the building of the wall of it was of jasper: and the city was pure gold, like unto clear glass.
19 And the foundations of the wall of the city were garnished with all manner of precious stones. The first foundation was jasper; the second, sapphire; the third, a chalcedony; the fourth, an emerald;
20 The fifth, sardonyx; the sixth, sardius; the seventh, chrysolite; the eighth, beryl; the ninth, a topaz; the tenth, a chrysoprasus; the eleventh, a jacinth; the twelfth, an amethyst. . . .

increased; so that on a single tree hundreds of them might be seen, and sometimes so large was their size and intense their color, that at the distance of fifty rods, they seemed equal to Sirius, nay, to the morning star! and of hues the most delicate and rich that can be conceived of, exactly imitating, so far as I could judge, the natural gems; and not partaking at all of those less delicate and gaudy tints, by which a practiced eye can distinguish genuine from supposititious precious stones. . . . I have seen many splendid groups of precious stones, wrought and unwrought, in the large collections of our land; and until I witnessed this scene, they seemed of great beauty. But it is now literally true, that they appear to me comparatively dull and insignificant. In short, it seemed to me as if I was gazing upon a landscape which had before existed only in a poet's imagination. It is what he would call a fairy land; but a more Christian designation would be, a celestial land.

Throughout the *Religious Lectures,* and in a hundred different ways, Hitchcock stressed the Christian theme of the Resurrection. Life is imperishable, its seed never extinct. Winter is but a harbinger of spring. The lecture on "The Resurrections of Spring" gave him fullest scope. It has as its frontispiece an engraving, in color, by Mrs. Hitchcock, who illustrated many of her husband's books. (As Orra White she had been the second preceptress of Amherst Academy.) It depicted an idealized landscape, a little pond with trees and bushes, all burgeoning with the emerging life of spring—a butterfly coming from a cocoon, a frog from pollywogs in the pond, a bird hovering about her nest, and spring flowers all about. The caption under the picture reads, "Emblems of the Resurrection." Emily (we have seen) had no respect for doctrines, but this is the kind of doctrine, and the kind of preaching, she could accept. Years later she wrote to Higginson, "When Flowers annually died and I was a child, I used to read Dr Hitchcock's Book on the Flowers of North America. This comforted their Absence – assuring me they lived."[7]

The curriculum that awaited Emily when she entered the Academy at age nine was varied and interesting, well beyond the reading, writing, and arithmetic we associate with those supposedly unenlightened days. Hitchcock's influence was pervasive. Almost half the studies Emily spoke of particularly, and always with enthusiasm, are scientific. In May 1842 she wrote Jane Humphrey, "I am in the class that you used to be in in Latin – besides Latin I study History and Botany I like the school very much indeed." Three years later she boasted to Abiah Root of her four studies—"They are Mental Philosophy, Geology, Latin, and Botany. How large they sound, don't they? I don't believe you have such big studies"— and declared, "We have a very fine school." Except for the required

7. *L* II, 573 (early 1877), and n., where the editor suggests that ED may have had in mind Hitchcock's *Catalogue of Plants Growing Without Cultivation in the Vicinity of Amherst College* (1829). It was published in Amherst by J. S. & C. Adams at the request of forty of Hitchcock's students "now attending your lectures [so the dedicatory note goes] on the subject of botany, in the belief that their knowledge of the science, and the interest of their botanical tours, may be increased by the possession of such a work." The names of the forty are subscribed.

Edward Hitchcock
"Pace-Setter"

EMBLEMS OF THE RESURRECTION.

Illustration for chapter, "The Resurrections of Spring," from Edward
Hitchcock's *Religious Lectures on Peculiar Phenomena in the Four Seasons*, 1850

ED on the same subject:

> The dreamy Butterflies bestir!
> Lethargic pools resume the whirr
> Of last year's sundered tune!
> From some old Fortress on the sun
> Baronial Bees – march – one by one –
> In murmuring platoon!
>
> from *P* #64, about 1859

Wednesday afternoon exercises in composition and declamation—one of which was the occasion of her first recorded witticism[8]—there is no way of knowing precisely what courses she took. Other studies offered in the Second Division (for the younger students) in the "English Department" were History, Geography, Grammar, Arithmetic, Natural History, Physiology, and English. (For an extra charge, one could take lessons in Drawing, Painting, and French.) What was meant by English, apparently, was "analysis of Cooper's Task" and Young's *Night Thoughts* and exercises in composition and orthography based on Ebenezer Porter's *Rhetorical Reader* and the New Testament. The older students ("First Division") studied *Paradise Lost,* did more advanced work in composition, and took the following courses: Algebra, Chemistry, Natural Theology, Ecclesiastical History, Anatomy, Astronomy, Geology, and Logic. "The Classical Department," which Emily entered in 1842, offered studies that began with Nepos and Caesar and took the usual route through Vergil, Cicero, Sallust, and the Greek Testament. Work in Mathematics, Geography, Ancient History, and English Grammar and Composition continued.[9]

8. The witticism, characteristically, had a bite to it. Even this early, she showed the family bent toward satire (*L* I, 6, to Jane Humphrey, May 12, 1842):

– this Afternoon is Wednesday and so of course there was Speaking and Composition – there was one young man who read a Composition the Subject was think twice before you speak – he was describing the reasons why any one should do so – one was – if a young gentleman – offered a young lady his arm and he had a dog who had no tail and he boarded at the tavern think twice before you speak. Another is if a young gentleman knows a young lady who he thinks nature has formed to perfection let him remember that roses conceal thorns he is the sillyest creature that ever lived I think. I told him that I thought he had better think twice before he spoke –

9. For further information concerning the Academy's curriculum see Tuckerman, pp. 100, 107, and passim. ED's use of Porter's *Rhetorical Reader* (1842) has been the occasion of recent controversy. Edith Perry Stamm ("Emily Dickinson: Poetry and Punctuation," *Saturday Review,* March 30, 1963, pp. 26–27) first advanced the theory that ED used dashes in her poems as elocutionary guides according to Porter's system (dashes slanting upward to indicate rising inflection, etc.). Miss Stamm later elaborated on the theory (Edith Perry Stamm Wylder, *The Last Face: Emily Dickinson's Manuscripts,* 1971). Objections were raised by (among others) Theodora Ward, *Saturday Review,* April 27, 1963, p. 25, and Ralph Franklin, *The Editing of Emily Dickinson,* pp. 118–20, 121. While I do not find ED's use of dashes mere eccentricities of penmanship, the elocutionary theory seems untenable. A passage from another composition book used at the Academy may throw some light on the problem. Richard Green Parker, *Aids to English Composition,* 1845 (1846 ed.), p. 30, discusses the dash as follows:

The proper use of the dash is to express a sudden stop, or change of the subject; but, by modern writers, it is employed as a substitute for almost all of the other marks; being used sometimes for a comma, semicolon, colon, or period; sometimes for a question or an exclamation, and sometimes for crotchets and brackets to enclose a parenthesis.

I think it more likely that ED followed such liberal advice as this rather than so confining a system as Porter's. The opening paragraph of Parker's preface sets a tone that

How much of all this stuck in Emily Dickinson's consciousness is hard to say. She was never pedantic, nor did she have a particularly historical imagination. She made fun of a good deal of her formal learning, as in the famous verse valentine she sent William Howland in 1852, with its Latin tags, classical references, and historical allusions.

> "Sic transit gloria mundi,"
>   "How doth the busy bee,"
> "Dum vivimus vivamus,"
>   I stay mine enemy!
>
> Oh "veni, vidi, vici!"
>   Oh caput cap-a-pie!
> And oh "memento mori"
>   When I am *far* from thee! . . .   (#3)

and so on for seventeen stanzas (including a climb up the "Hill of Science"). Many years later she wrote about her reduced family—her mother, Vinnie, and herself—to Mrs. Holland: "Three is a scant Assembly, but Love makes 'One to carry –' as the Children say – That is all of my Learning that I recall." But at least she was sufficiently impressed by *Night Thoughts,* even in these carefree days, to quote in a letter to Abiah the famous line "O! what a miracle to man is man." Had she added "nature" to Young's line, she would have defined with some accuracy Hitchcock's spirit—and the spirit of learning in Amherst Academy.

But such a definition would have left out the spirit of orthodox piety that, for better or worse, governed education in Amherst. Unlike Edward Dickinson's wavering attention to ultimate ends, Hitchcock's was con-

---

ED at that age would have found congenial: "Genius cannot be fettered, and an original and thinking mind, replete with its own exuberance, will often burst out in spontaneous gushings, and open to itself new channels, through which the treasures of thought will flow in rich and rapid currents. Rules and suggestions, however, are not wholly useless." They may help the young writer, Parker concludes in a phrase ED was fond of, "in his laborious ascent of the hill of science." (Austin and Lavinia, incidentally, used the dash profusely in their letters.) In her poems and often in her prose the dash became a sensitive instrument to regulate rhythm and gain emphasis. A remarkable instance in her letters is the sentence: "How is the love of Christ done when that – below – holds – so –" Parker also has some advice on the use of capital letters that may have interested ED: "Any words, when remarkably emphatical, or when they are the principal subject of the composition, may begin with capitals" (p. 26). Here too is a suggestion she may have picked up during her school days to incorporate with precision and control into her mature aesthetic.

Extracurricular activities of a literary nature included a literary society (with weekly meetings) and a school publication called "Forest Leaves," issued by the pupils of the Academy. We know that one of Emily's friends, Emily Fowler (Ford), contributed to it, and in view of the comments that have come down to us about her compositions, Emily must have, too. But no copy of the publication has come to light, a challenge to all searchers of attics.

stant. His Inaugural Address made explicit what he no doubt had been practicing for years in the college and encouraging in the Academy. The address specified nine "uses of learning"—eight of them secular, which, to give him his due, he praised with great eloquence: arts and sciences, communication, travel, health. The ninth hardly needed arguing, but he argued it:

> I need not argue before such an audience as this, the superior importance of religious principles to all others. This will be admitted; for all other truths have reference to time, these to eternity: all others regard man's mortal, these his immortal interests: all others are limited by created natures; these centre in the uncreated God.

Such a philosophy of education meant, for the Academy, not only that its teachers "must be firmly established in the faith of the Christian religion" but so must its books. Nor could this latter insistence have been entirely bad, even for Emily's rebellious spirit. Two of her texts will suffice as examples. Both set their subjects (history and botany) in the widest possible perspective. For all its moralism, such an introduction to the study of history (Worcester's *Elements of History*) might have had an inspiring effect on a young student beginning to be aware of talents of her own.

> [History] tends to strengthen the sentiments of virtue. In its faithful delineations, vice always appears odious, and virtue not only desirable and productive of happiness, but also favorable to true honor and solid glory. The reader of history learns to connect true glory, not with the possession of wealth and power, but with the disinterested employment of great talents in promoting the good of mankind.
> True history has numberless relations and uses as an exhibition of the conduct of Divine Providence. . . .

Emily's botany text, the enormously popular *Familiar Lectures on Botany* (Hartford, 1829), by Mrs. Almira H. Lincoln (Phelps) of the Troy Female Seminary, may well have been one of the most important of her school books. Here were no lessons to be learned by rote, but (for Emily) a life-giving source. Although it was written for beginners, there is nothing condescending about it. It, too, was dedicated to the Divine Purpose, but its piety is gentle and humane. It is rigorous, tightly packed, systematic, but imaginative enough to throw off at many points hints for the devoted amateur that Emily became. Again, like Hitchcock and Worcester, Mrs. Phelps set her sights high. She concluded her introduction:

> The *vegetable world* offers a boundless field of inquiry, which may be explored with the most pure and delightful emotions. Here the Almighty seems to manifest himself to us, with less of that dazzling sublimity which it is almost painful to behold in His more magnificent creations. . . .
> The study of Botany naturally leads to greater love and reverence for the

[*351*

Deity. We would not affirm, that it does in reality always produce this effect; for, unhappily, there are some minds which, though quick to perceive the beauties of nature, seem blindly to overlook Him who spread them forth. They can admire the gifts, while they forget the giver. But those who feel in their hearts a love to God, and who see in the natural world the workings of His power, can look abroad, and, adopting the language of a christian poet, exclaim,

"My Father made them all."[10]

Whatever is to be said about these people—Hitchcock, Worcester, Phelps—there was nothing small about them or their books. Their style had richness, often grace. Their piety lent fervor and zest to their undertakings. "Sublimity" was a favorite word, especially to the scientists. Always there was care to relate the subject to man in all his possible dimensions, mortal and immortal, physical and spiritual, utilitarian and aesthetic. And, perhaps most important to Emily Dickinson's developing imagination, these books were animated with a sense of wonder and love in the contemplation of their great subjects.

There was nothing small, either, about other books on the Academy's list, such as Joseph Butler's *The Analogy of Religion;* Isaac Watts's *The Improvement of the Mind;* Oliver Goldsmith's *History of England;* and William Paley's *Natural Theology.*[11] With how many of these (and many others of equal stature) Emily came in contact, it is impossible to say; but they were part of the curriculum and were certainly in the school's library, which by Emily's time contained some four hundred volumes.

Another aspect of Hitchcock's piety, this time applied to what he called "polite literature," may not have been so beneficent. In the same Inaugural Address that invited the poetic student to contemplate the beauties of the Amherst landscape, Hitchcock declaimed at some length on the dangers of certain kinds of poetry and certain kinds of poets. Even if Emily had not been present at the inauguration or had never read the published address, what he had to say was important to her, since it represented a position she had to combat the rest of her life. He merely articulated what, clearly, her father felt and what the community felt— that "majority" against which she demurred.

10. A copy of the *Familiar Lectures* in the Yale University Library has Benjamin Silliman's bookplate and this inscription on the flyleaf: "Prof. Silliman, with the respects of Mrs. Lincoln."

11. Some other books used in the school, as recorded in Tuckerman and in Carpenter and Morehouse (*History of Amherst,* pp. 147, 153), were: William Smellie, *The Philosophy of Natural History;* Denison Olmsted, *A Compendium of Natural Philosophy;* John Abercrombie, *Inquiries Concerning the Intellectual Powers;* Thomas Cogswell Upham, *Elements of Mental Philosophy;* Samuel Phillips Newman, *A Practical System of Rhetoric;* John Marsh, *Ecclesiastical History;* Charles Augustus Goodrich, *History of the United States;* Archibald Alexander, *Evidences of Christianity;* Lord Kames, *Elements of Criticism;* Francis Wayland, *Elements of Moral Science.*

It was when, in the address, he came to the uses of literature that he showed the restrictive and *un*liberating side of his position. There were good poets and bad poets, and the criterion was their orthodoxy:

> . . . not a little of the influence of modern polite literature has been very disastrous to religion. For much of it has been prepared by men who were intemperate, or licentious, and secretly or openly hostile to Christianity. . . . And their writings have been deeply imbued with immorality, or infidelity, or atheism. Yet the poison has been often so interwoven with those fascinations of style, or thought, characteristic of genius, as to be unnoticed by the youthful mind, delighted with smartness and brilliancy.

Emily was just then (age fourteen) showing signs of smartness and brilliancy herself and enjoying them in others. Hitchcock's words were a rebuke and a warning. He drew a very clear line. Among the acceptable poets were Milton, Watts, Cowper, and Young; but Pope tended in his writings to "wantonness and indecency," and even Shakespeare, for all "his splendid moral sentiments was undoubtedly a libertine in principle and practice." Care, too, must be taken in regard to the more literary writers of history: among the "atheists" were Bayle, Voltaire, Hume, Gibbon; the "believers" were Goldsmith, Smollett, Russell, and Ramsay. A measure of Hitchcock's influence on the Academy is the precision with which the curriculum honored his categories.

In view of such attitudes, it is not surprising that Emily Dickinson was later to approach her vocation, like her near-contemporary Hawthorne, with a sense of guilt. New Englanders, especially the Connecticut Valley breed, were uneasy about "artists of the beautiful," and official pronouncements like Hitchcock's gave their prejudices a powerful mandate. No wonder Emily complained to Austin a few years later that "we do not have much poetry" here at home, and no wonder they had to smuggle *Kavanagh* into the house. Five years after Hitchcock's address, Emily wrote a long and mysterious letter to her friend Jane Humphrey, in which she said, "I have heeded beautiful tempters, yet do not think I am wrong," a confession on which Hitchcock's moral view of poetry may shed some light. Still later, and on several occasions, she called herself a "pagan," once adding to her bereaved Norcross cousins, "Let Emily sing for you because she cannot pray." The life of a "singer," or so Hitchcock's teaching as it pervaded the community presented it to her, was beyond the pale, somehow sinful. It was only when she had achieved complete poetic independence that she could write confidently and, it would seem, in open defiance of the local piety:

> I reckon – when I count at all –
> First – Poets – Then the Sun –
> Then Summer – Then the Heaven of God –
> And then – the List is done –

But, looking back – the First so seems
To Comprehend the Whole –
The Others look a needless Show –
So I write – Poets – All –

Their Summer – lasts a Solid Year –
They can afford a Sun
The East – would deem extravagant –
And if the Further Heaven –

Be beautiful as they prepare
For Those who worship Them –
It is too difficult a Grace –
To justify the Dream –   (#569, about 1862)

It is perhaps just as well that Hitchcock and the rest never saw this poem.

What the Academy—with Hitchcock, this one attitude excepted, as the living embodiment of its positive values—did for her was to open her eyes, give her a discipline, and set her studies in the largest possible frame of reference. Perhaps the most important was opening her eyes. If Emily learned of the grander things of nature from Hitchcock and his fellow geologists and astronomers, she learned about the "minims" from Mrs. Phelps and her like (although Hitchcock too was a devoted botanist). And, again, she learned about both with enough precision to put (for instance) such phenomena as "parallax" and "perihelion"—unlikely words for a poet of her day[12]—to vivid poetic use. "Parallax" occurs in a poem which may be a tribute to her absorption in her nature studies in these early years:

I thought that nature was enough
Till Human nature came
But that the other did absorb
As Parallax a Flame – . . .   (#1286, about 1873)

"Perihelion" (and a good deal of astronomy) comes with equal ease into the final stanza of a poem on one of her familiar themes, the superiority of anticipation to fulfillment:

Enchantment's Perihelion
Mistaken oft has been
For the Authentic orbit
Of its Anterior Sun.   (#1299, about 1874)

12. William Howard, "Emily Dickinson's Poetic Vocabulary," *PMLA* LXXII (March 1957), shows that out of the 770 words ED used from special sources, the largest group is from contemporary technology or science. (The second largest is housewifery.) ". . . 328 words are technical terms of one sort or another or words generally found only in scientific or academic discourse . . ." (p. 230).

She knew that marl was white and chrysolite yellowish-green. She knew about "corollas" and "calyxes" and "capsules" and set them, quite non-chalantly, in a lilac to achieve one of her most striking sunset metaphors:

> The Lilac is an ancient shrub
> But ancienter than that
> The Firmamental Lilac
> Upon the Hill tonight –
> The Sun subsiding on his Course
> Bequeathes this final Plant
> To Contemplation – not to Touch –
> The Flower of Occident.
> Of one Corolla is the West –
> The Calyx is the Earth –
> The Capsules burnished Seeds the Stars – . . .[13]

(*#1241, about 1872*)

When Edward Hitchcock died in 1864, Amherst knew it had lost a great man. William Tyler, the historian of the college, preached the funeral sermon, a notable attempt to define Hitchcock in all his phases. Emily's life was by then too withdrawn to warrant even the suggestion that she heard it; but it was soon printed, and she could have read it. In a passage that might have caught her eye, Tyler subsumes Hitchcock's achievements as scientist, teacher, and man of God under the general concept of language.

Figurative language is not a mere play of the imagination. It is not by some accidental discovery or human invention that all words in all languages originally and properly signify objects, actions and events in the outward world. The material world was *made for this purpose*. It is a universal *language*. The elements of nature are a universal alphabet. . . . We often hear of the language of flowers. There is much of fancy in the details, but the idea is based on a profound truth. There *is* a language of flowers. There is also a language of plants and animals, and it is the language of God. . . . "Consider the lilies". . . . "I am the true vine". . . . *All* science . . . is of God and from God.

13. The concluding lines of the poem may well be a slanting reference to Hitchcock (the "Scientist of Faith") and his work, with a challenge to go beyond "Time's Analysis":

> The Scientist of Faith
> His research has but just begun –
> Above his synthesis
> The Flora unimpeachable
> To Time's Analysis –
> "Eye hath not seen" may possibly
> Be current with the Blind
> But let not Revelation
> By theses be detained –

Were it not for Hitchcock's deeply imbedded Congregational orthodoxy, one might conclude from this passage that he was an Amherst Emerson (whose chapter, "Language," in *Nature* Tyler clearly echoes). Actually, the two were far apart, and not only theologically. As professional scientist, Hitchcock set out to classify, describe, and explain natural phenomena, especially geologic, and he gained an international reputation. As teacher, his mission was to pass on his knowledge—and, as Emily would call it, the "phosphorescence" of his knowledge—to his students and to glorify God by opening their eyes to the wonders of the created universe. As president, he did all he could to lead the young men of Amherst to accept Christ as their Savior; and in this capacity he was more concerned about their souls than their Emersonian self-reliance. What he seems to have shared with Emerson was a kind of serene optimism—and this in spite of ill health, from youth on, that handicapped him severely. While he stuck to orthodoxy, Emerson departed from it; but they both believed in "the confident quest." Ultimately, Emily Dickinson followed neither way, but they both were lions in her path, major influences encountered early, opening new realms, and providing perceptions and values that became living parts of her own unique synthesis.[14]

To Hitchcock her debt was perhaps mostly perceptual (granted, of course, that there *was* a debt; she might have developed as she did without him; but Tyler's words indicate a community awareness that she could hardly have missed). She too heard the language of plants and flowers. She could hear the "noiseless noise in the Orchard"; she set out to be the birds' "Expositor," to tell the secret of the crocus, to interpret the flowers, "which [she wrote] without lips, have language – " When she was thirty-two, the year before Hitchcock died, she summed up the gist of his teaching in one sentence and a couplet, concluding with a remarkable optical metaphor:

> I was thinking, today – as I noticed, that the
> "Supernatural," was only the Natural, disclosed –
>
> Not "Revelation" – 'tis – that waits,
> But our unfurnished eyes –   [#685]

Certainly Hitchcock and the education he inspired were among the influences that "furnished" her eyes—taught them how to look at nature

14. William Robert Sherwood, *Circumference and Circumstance: Stages in the Mind and Art of Emily Dickinson* (1968), points out correctly, I think, that, ultimately, ED accepted wholly neither Emerson's optimistic Transcendentalism nor Hitchcock's "religion of geology." She evidently concluded "that the gulf between nature and man was too great for nature to offer meaningful analogies" (p. 27). Perhaps. But we have already noted how hard it is to say that such-and-such a view, certainly on matters of spiritual import, was ever ultimately true of ED. If anything, and in the earlier years, she may have felt more of an affinity for Hitchcock than for Emerson. She had moments in which she seems to have felt the truth of both.

and what to look for. One of his great qualities was the spirit of love, amounting at times to rapture, which animated his studies. "No language can express," wrote Tyler, "what he enjoyed, when body, soul, and spirit were all in harmony, and all seemingly filled with the charms of nature, the delights of science, or the love of God." But while Hitchcock loved and studied this earth for God's sake (with him, Tyler wrote, *"All science . . . is of God and from God"*), she loved it and wrote about it for its own. "Oh Matchless Earth – " she wrote Sue about 1870, "We underrate the chance to dwell in Thee." As she grew older, a note of urgency crept into her love: " – the time to live is frugal – and good as is a better earth, it will not quite be this." The devout Hitchcock might have been troubled by her question, "How is the love of Christ done when that – below – holds – so – " but he would have gloried in her dedication and in her achievement.

The text of Tyler's funeral sermon was the description of Solomon in I Kings 4:33 "And he spake of trees from the cedar tree that is in Lebanon even unto the hyssop that springeth out of the wall; he spake also of beasts, and of fowl, and of creeping things, and of fishes"—to which Tyler added: "He [Hitchcock] spake also of rocks and soils, of which, so far as appears, Solomon did *not* speak. He dealt also in songs, and proverbs, to say nothing of sermons. . . . He might have made a great poet." He never did, but there are many reasons to believe that he contributed immeasurably to the cultural climate that produced one.

Emily's final term at the Academy came to an end on August 10, 1847. The occasion was appropriately celebrated by an "Exhibition," with declamations, singing, and prayer.[15] On September 30 she started what

15. William Gardiner Hammond, then a sophomore in the college, described the affair in his diary (*Remembrance of Amherst: An Undergraduate's Diary, 1846–1848,* ed. George Frisbie Whicher, 1946). It is an amusing valediction to ED's school days.

There was an exhibition at Amherst Academy this afternoon; when I went in Charley Fowler (one of the "graduating class" of sub-freshies, six in number) was getting off a Salutatory, in tolerable Latin. Then came any quantity of declamations, good, bad, and indifferent, from scholars of all sizes. . . . Members of the graduating class all had *orations:* very decent. . . . Little Willy Fowler, though among the very smallest, declaimed most *beautifully,* even so as to attract universal notice and admiration. To serve as music, the place of a band was most beautifully and to my mind most appropriately filled by a choir of young girls and several youths, led by *Emerson;* they sang most *beautifully,* and I thought the music far better adapted to a literary exhibition than the loud notes of martial music. The performances closed with a pretty fair oration, on the "scholar's object attainable," and neat Valedictory addresses, from Sanford. Not caring to hear a prayer from Leonard Humphrey, I rushed out . . . [pp. 167–8].

If Emily performed, either Hammond missed her or he was not impressed. But she probably sang in the choir (her music was then well along). Charley and Willy Fowler were brothers of Emily's friend Emily Fowler (Ford). Their father, William Chauncey Fowler, was Professor of Rhetoric and Oratory at the college. (John) Sanford later became one of Austin's best friends and a leading trustee of the college.

turned out to be a ten-month—or two-term—sojourn at Mount Holyoke Female Seminary in South Hadley, then beginning its tenth year under the leadership of its founder and guiding spirit, Mary Lyon. There were three classes, Junior, Middle, and Senior. Emily entered as a Junior, hoping to qualify shortly for the Middle class.

That Emily never got beyond the first two terms has been explained variously by her poor health, her father's wanting to have her home, her rebellion against the evangelical fervor of the place, her dislike of the discipline and the teachers (Vinnie, overdoing it as usual, is reported by Mabel Todd as saying that "there were real ogres at South Hadley then"), and simple homesickness. Much of this is as legendary as the still-current notion that she hated it. She had a bad cough that winter, sufficient to take her home for a few weeks in late March, much against her will, but she returned in good shape for the summer term. Part of her six-week stay at home included spring vacation (April 27–May 11). She had spells of homesickness, but she described them jauntily in her letters and boasted of being their master: "I had a great mind to be homesick after you went home, but I concluded not to, & therefore gave up all homesick feelings. Was not that a wise determination?"[16]

As to the continuous religious pressure, it could hardly be said that Emily stood in lonely rebellion. She went to the assemblies (Miss Lyon spoke to the school three times a week) and listened to the sermons, some of which thrilled her while others bored her.[17] She was saddened to find

16. *L* I, 48 (to Austin; October 21, 1847). Similarly, to Abiah Root, November 6 (*L* I, 53–54): "I was very homesick for a few days & it seemed to me I could not live here. But I am now contented & quite happy, if I can be happy when absent from my dear home & friends. You may laugh at the idea, that I cannot be happy when away from home, but you must remember that I have a very dear home & that this is my first trial in the way of absence for any length of time in my life. . . ." By mid-February, however, her mood was less buoyant. Writing to Austin two weeks after she returned from winter vacation (February 17; *L* I, 62–63), she had already begun the traditional student pastime of counting the weeks until it was all over. Here, too, she indicates a truth that the Mount Holyoke experience brought into sharp focus for her: just how important home was for her:

> I have been quite lonely since I came back, but cheered by the thought that I am not to return another year I take comfort & still hope on. My visit at home was happy, very happy to me & had the idea of in so short a time returning, been constantly in my dreams, by night & day I could not have been happier. "There is no rose without a thorn" to me. Home was always dear to me & dearer still the friends around it, but never did it seem so dear as now. All, all are kind to me but their tones fall strangely on my ear & their countenances meet mine not like home faces, I can assure you, most sincerely. Then when tempted to feel sad, I think of the blazing fire, & the cheerful meal & the chair empty now I am gone. I can hear the cheerful voices & the merry laugh & a desolate feeling comes home to my heart, to think I am alone. But my good angel only waits to see the tears coming & then whispers, only this year!! Only 22. weeks more & home again you will be to stay.

17. This is as good a place as any to consider briefly an important aspect of ED's cultural environment: sermons. About this time she began to listen critically, and her

herself incapable of the commitment to Christ that many of her friends were making, including her pious cousin and roommate, Emily Norcross

---

comments show sharp discernment. Her most explicit statement about the sermons at Mount Holyoke is in the February 17 letter to Austin. Here she makes a sharp distinction:

> Professor. [Henry Boynton] Smith. [of Amherst College] preached here last Sabbath & such sermons I never heard in my life. We were all charmed with him & dreaded to have him close. I understand the people of S. Hadley have given Mr. Belden [pastor of the East Parish church in Amherst] a call to settle here. If he accepts, I hope it *will*, WILL not be until my year is out.

Smith was a brilliant man, and Emily's enthusiasm was justified. He had studied in the universities of Halle and Berlin, which "had given him what no earlier disciple of New England theology had enjoyed: a mastery of Kantian philosophy and an understanding of the conflict of religion with modern philosophy" (Thomas Le Duc, *Piety and Intellect at Amherst College,* p. 42). He came to Amherst in 1847 and left three years later for a long and distinguished career in Union Theological Seminary. Contrary to the notion that Emily hated sermons, she was capable of being transported by a good one. When Professor Edwards Amasa Park of Andover Theological Seminary preached in the First Church in Amherst on November 20, 1853, she could hardly restrain her enthusiasm in her letter the next day to Austin: "I never heard anything like it, and dont expect to again. . . . And when it was all over, and that wonderful man sat down, people stared at each other, and looked as wan and wild, as if they had seen a spirit, and wondered they had not died. How I wish you had heard him." Again her enthusiasm seems to have been justified. Park was one of the famous preachers of his day.

But, as she said, she had no use for "doctrines" and, during the sermons that bored her, she thought of other things. Like her father and brother, she was hard to please. During his stay in Cambridge at the Harvard Law School, Austin found the sermons in the local churches not worth listening to. From Washington, Edward wrote his son (*Home,* p. 385, July 23, 1854) that "there was no preaching that [I] cared to hear. It is the driest of all places, to attend church – there is hardly enough of mentality here to hold the place together –" It was not that Austin or Edward demanded orthodoxy of the strictest sort; they looked for ability and integrity. Emily the same— and woe to the preacher who failed her:

> He preached upon "Breadth" till it argued him narrow –
> The Broad are too broad to define
> And of "Truth" until it proclaimed him a Liar –
> The Truth never flaunted a Sign –
>
> Simplicity fled from his counterfeit presence
> As Gold the Pyrites would shun –
> What confusion would cover the innocent Jesus
> To meet so enabled a Man! (*#1207, about 1872*)

Among the Amherst preachers (or faculty members who occasionally preached) whom she admired were Aaron Colton, Professor William Tyler, and Edward S. Dwight, who seems to have been a favorite. "I never heard a minister I loved half so well," she wrote Austin on May 16, 1853. She commented many times on how "beautifully" and "wonderfully" the Reverend Mr. Dwight preached. It was his sermon on "unbelief" that elicited her famous comment: "Sermons on unbelief ever did attract me" (*L* I, 311, November 27–December 3, 1854). One sermon "scared" her, as she confessed to the Hollands (*L* I, 309, about November 26, 1854). The effect on her of these weekly (at Mount Holyoke more frequent) invasions on her spirit, for good or ill, was profound.

of Monson, who, after three months at Mount Holyoke, expressed her concern about Emily's spiritual apathy in a letter to a friend:

> Emily Dickinson appears no different. I hoped I might have good news to write with regard to her. She says she has no particular objection to becoming a Christian and she says she feels bad when she hears of one and another of her friends who are expressing a hope but still she feels no more interest.[18]

But in this she had plenty of company. Piety at the school was never complete. Even in the best of times there were many who remained unconverted. In a letter Miss Lyon wrote to a friend (in April of Emily's second term) she rejoiced that some fifty had "expressed hope" of accepting Christ; "still," she added, "there are about thirty without hope." Indeed, what Miss Lyon called the "established Christians" were usually

18. That month (January 1848) Mrs. Porter, an ardent supporter of Mount Holyoke, received two other letters showing concern for Emily Dickinson's spiritual state. On January 17 Miss Lyon had held a meeting for the unconverted. Her text was "Choose ye this day whom ye will serve." Mary Whitman, one of the teachers, wrote: "Seventeen attended. . . . it was a very solemn meeting. Emily Dickinson was among the number" (YH I, 136). Sarah Jane Anderson, a senior and Mrs. Porter's niece, wrote: "I believe Emilie [Norcross] wrote you last week, and probably she told you about her room-mate. She still *appears* unconcerned. Emilie [N] seems quite engaged, much as when you were here. I do hope her example will be such as it ought" (YH I, 136).

The above material appeared first in Sydney R. McLean, "Emily Dickinson at Mount Holyoke," *New England Quarterly* (March 1934), pp. 25–42. Here, among other matters, the famous anecdote is examined about Emily Dickinson's recalcitrance when Miss Lyon, according to the story as told in Martha Dickinson Bianchi, *The Life and Letters of Emily Dickinson,* demanded from the students a rising vote of acquiescence in her decree that the next day, Christmas, be celebrated by fasting and prayer. Miss McLean found the Bianchi account "inaccurate in its details" and concluded that Emily Dickinson's "dramatic defiance is legend." She is surely right when she says, "Both Mary Lyon and Emily Dickinson have been misunderstood." Miss Lyon was neither so dictatorial nor Emily so rebellious as tradition would have them. One further bit of testimony comes from within the family circle, this time quoting Emily herself. Clara Newman Turner, "My Personal Acquaintance with Emily Dickinson," says nothing about the Christmas decree. She has Miss Lyon requesting that all students rise who wanted to be Christians (see Appendix II, 3):

> To illustrate the independence and honesty of her convictions, – Miss Lyon, during a time of religious interest in the school, asked all those who wanted to be Christians to rise. The wording of the request was not such as Emily could honestly accede to and she remained seated – the only one who did not rise. In relating the incident to me, she said, "They thought it queer I didn't rise" – adding with a twinkle in her eye, "I thought a lie would be queerer."

In the Bianchi account, Emily Norcross at first joined her cousin in remaining seated but, terrified by Miss Lyon's repeated request, rose the second time, leaving Emily Dickinson the lone rebel. Miss McLean proves beyond doubt that Miss Lyon carefully sounded out the mood of the students before making her request (about being Christians or fasting on Christmas?) and left their response to it optional. The incident, surely, seems to have some basis in fact; the error has been in overdramatizing it.

in the minority, the school being divided into "No-hopers" (of whom Emily was one), "Hopers," and Christians.

Miss Lyon met with each group separately once a week. Every year, the incoming students presented her and her teachers with a new challenge, and the success of the year was gauged by the number of converts they made. Apparently, they kept fairly accurate track of the numbers in each group. Of the two hundred and thirty students enrolled during Emily's year, it would appear from Miss Lyon's letter that nearly half of them, at the beginning of the year, were not established Christians. That thirty finished the year without hope should be assurance enough against the notion of Emily's isolation.

Emily may have resented such efforts, but there is nothing in her letters from Mount Holyoke to indicate it. One written toward the end of her final term expresses no bitterness or resentment against the piety of the place, only a sad realization that perhaps she had missed a chance:

> Father has decided not to send me to Holyoke another year, so this is my *last term*. Can it be possible that I have been here almost a year? It startles me when I really think of the advantages I have had, and I fear I have not improved them as I ought. . . .
>
> I tremble when I think how soon the weeks and days of this term will all have been spent, and my fate will be sealed, perhaps. I have neglected the *one thing needful* when all were obtaining it, and I may never, never again pass through such a season as was granted us last winter. . . . I am not happy, and I regret that last term, when that golden opportunity was mine, that I did not give up and become a Christian. It is not now too late, so my friends tell me, so my offended conscience whispers, but it is hard for me to give up the world.

No one of these reasons—health, father, hatred of the regime, or homesickness—fully accounts for Emily's short stay at Mount Holyoke, though each one of them may have played a part. Another probability, and an important one, is that Amherst Academy gave her all the formal education she needed or wanted. At least there is no record of her pleading for more, and she was quite content to return to her "feast in the reading line" (as she called it) at home. When she wrote Higginson in 1862 that "I went to school – but in your manner of the phrase – had no education," there was no note of deprivation in her words—if anything, perhaps a hint of irony. Later still, after twenty more years of living in a college town, she came to look on the professorial breed a little scornfully. "Most such are Manikins," she wrote Mrs. Holland, "and a warm blow from a brave Anatomy, hurls them into Wherefores – " But it was hardly the manikins in the youthful Academy or in zealous Mount Holyoke that led her to cut short her academic career. The fact is that the Amherst community—the Academy and the college, not to mention her library at home—offered richer opportunities than Mount Holyoke at that time possibly could have. And in many ways she must have found Mount Holyoke frankly repetitious. Except for its missionary spirit, it was

[*361*

another Hitchcockian institution. Even among the textbooks there were many duplications.[19]

What she could not have found repetitious was its principal. Although Miss Lyon's name occurs frequently in Emily's letters from Mount Holyoke, she never spoke at length about this remarkable person. But in so small an institution (all under one roof), which, as one of her friends wrote, was truly "an expansion of herself," Mary Lyon's influence was inescapable. She herself had been a student at Amherst Academy (in 1818) and later studied science with Hitchcock during his ministerial days in Conway, Massachusetts, in the early 1820s. During her student years she was known as "all intellect," always first in her class; and as a teacher in various Massachusetts academies she soon became famous for her high standards of scholarship, discipline, and piety. As the idea of a college for the higher education of women took shape in her mind, it was Hitchcock who strengthened her resolve and helped her formulate principles. During the planning stage, she spent many weeks at his home in Amherst. What emerged (in 1836) was an expansion not only of herself but of Hitchcock. Like him, she was at once a born scientist and a spiritual leader. She led her pupils to Christ—and taught chemistry. She never failed (wrote one of her colleagues) to impress "on the minds of her pupils the power, wisdom, and goodness of God, as displayed in his works." Only, at Mount Holyoke the missionary zeal seems to have been more intense than at Hitchcock's Amherst. Miss Lyon "sought not merely their [the students'] conversion, but their enlistment in the great work of saving a lost world. It was the end and aim of all her efforts to make the seminary a nursery to the church."

So much has been said (or assumed) about Emily's antipathy to the religious intensity of Mount Holyoke as to obscure certain ways in which the woman at the center of it might have helped shape her life. When

19. It was inevitable that Miss Lyon should have imported materials as well as ideas from Amherst. She gave her own book list in an address describing her ideas and curriculum to the friends of the school in 1835. The address was distributed in pamphlet form that year and was reprinted (for the first time) in *Old South Leaflets* (1904), pp. 425-35.

TEXT BOOKS

The Bible, Worcester's Abridgement of Webster, or some other English Dictionary, the Eclectic Reader, by B. B. Edwards, Porter's Rhetorical Reader, Colburn's First Lessons, Adams's Arithmetic, Smith's and Murray's Grammar, Simson's or Playfair's Euclid, Woodbridge's Larger Geography, Sullivan's Political Class Book, Goodrich's United States, Worcester's Elements of History, with Goldsmith's England, Greece, and Rome, Mrs. Phelps's Botany, Olmstead's Natural Philosophy, Wilkins's Astronomy, Abercrombie on the Intellectual Powers, Newman's and Whateley's Rhetoric, Baily's Algebra, Marsh's Ecclesiastical History, Paley's Natural Theology, Smellie's Philosophy of Natural History, Butler's Analogy, Alexander's Evidences of Christianity.

By 1847-48, Emily's year, the list was undoubtedly larger. Hitchcock would surely be there; and Emily herself mentions Milton, Pope, and Silliman's *Chemistry* in her letters.

Mary Lyon
"We may become almost what we will"

Mount Holyoke Female Seminary
"All under one roof"

Miss Lyon died at the height of her powers, just seven months after Emily left Mount Holyoke, the whole community was shocked and saddened. The *Springfield Republican,* which Emily read daily, printed the following obituary notice in its issue for March 7, 1849:

> Miss Lyon. – We record to-day with sincere regret, the death of Miss Lyon, the well-known teacher at the Mount Holyoke Female Seminary. She was a person of uncommonly strong intellect, of devoted piety, and of most indomitable energy. She gave to that Seminary its peculiar character and its high reputation; and it is pleasant to remember that the good she has done lives after her, to embalm her memory in perennial fragrance.

That no mention of Miss Lyon's death appears in Emily's extant letters is a reminder that we have only a small fraction of the letters she wrote. Certainly she must have read a memorial volume, inspired and compiled by Hitchcock, when it appeared in August 1851: *The Power of Christian Benevolence Illustrated in the Life and Labors of Mary Lyon,* published in Northampton. It was a labor of love; and it is clear evidence, if any more be needed, of how closely Hitchcock and Miss Lyon worked and thought together. We know that Vinnie read it, and it appears in the list of books in Edward Dickinson's library. Emily could have found in it many things that would have brought her closer to the dynamic leader who for ten months presided over her destiny.[20]

20. In a Monday morning feature called "New Publications," the *Republican* for August 11, 1851, gave the book the leading position and the longest review in many months:

> We feel ourselves entirely unqualified for writing anything like a critique upon this book. The subject of this work was so unselfish in her nature, so self-sacrificing in her Christianity, and holds so sacred a place in the affections and memory of her cloud of friends that it would seem almost heartless to pass judgment upon the book as a literary performance or question the taste of some portions of the compilation. In the first place, in a book like this, we do not look for a discriminating estimate of the character of the subject, because such an estimate would be well nigh unattainable by the personal friends who wrote it. In the second place, we cannot expect that rigid rejection of unimportant and diffuse material necessary to conciseness and clearness from those with whom every word of the deceased was so wrapped up in sisterly and Christian affection, and is now so radiant with the glory which it catches from the beatified spirit which originally gave it utterance, that though meaningless to the world it is to them an apple of gold in a picture of silver. Premising thus much, we enter heartily into the spirit of the work, sympathizing in the enthusiastic love betrayed in every comment upon the character, labors, trials and triumphs of one of the noblest of all New England's daughters.

The reviewer, following the information given in President Hitchcock's preface, indicated the authorship of the parts of the book: Part I by "Miss White and Mrs Banister, confidential friends of Miss Lyon"; Part II by "Mrs Cowles, another friend"; Part III by Hitchcock himself "from materials furnished him by Miss Whitman." The reviewer concluded:

> . . . we cannot but feel that the book is well calculated to gratify the wants of personal friendship and to diffuse through a selfish world the pure and Christian spirit which breathed in the words, shone in the labors and ordered the aims of

[*363*

And she might have found surprising things in the book, in view of the seemingly invulnerable piety Miss Lyon must have presented to her pupils, especially to the "No-hopers." It is clear from the early letters with which the first part of the volume is sprinkled that young Mary Lyon had had a problem not unlike Emily's own. "I have a strange, rebellious, wicked heart. . . . I cannot trust myself," she wrote when she was twenty-six. When this book appeared, Emily had for some time been calling herself "one of the lingering *bad* ones" and speaking of her evil heart and the "beautiful tempters" she had been listening to. Again and again Mary Lyon agonized over her own "treacherous," "wicked heart." During her intellectual youth it was her constant fear "that she loved human science [Emily was calling it "the world"] more than divine truth." Saddened as Emily was that she could not share in the spirit of the revivals (there had been a famous one in Amherst in 1850), she might have been surprised to find that Miss Lyon herself confessed to a similar lack:

> Her mind, she often said, was of such a cast, that she could not look for much religious fervor or enjoyment. She often remarked to her intimate friend and religious adviser, "I think it very doubtful whether I ever see heaven myself, but I mean to do all in my power to prepare others for that blessed world."

In short, Miss Lyon kept as careful a watch over her own heart as she did over those of her students: "I find my best promises violated, my best resolutions broken."

Nor was the institution that Miss Lyon established to further her cause so dour as legend (and Vinnie) would have it. Along with its combination of science and piety, Miss Lyon imported the friendliness and humanity of Amherst Academy. The atmosphere here, too, was one of love, even if at Mount Holyoke its scriptural basis was more explicit: "Love God and thy neighbor as thyself" were the two Commandments kept constantly before the students. And the spirit was practiced, not merely preached. The memorial volume describes Miss Lyon as she greeted students at the opening of term—each one getting a warm welcome. "Heart met heart instantly. Teacher and pupil were one." "One thing is certain," Emily wrote Abiah Root during her second month at Mount Holyoke, "& that is, that Miss. Lyon & all the teachers, seem to consult our comfort & happiness in everything they do & you know that is pleasant."

Other snatches from this letter to Abiah, to whom she confided so much in these early years, show her busy and contented. The examina-

---

the strong and noble-hearted woman whom it commemorates, and whose bright example it commends. That it will be widely purchased and widely read there is no doubt, and it possesses a double value in giving the history of an institution peculiar and original in its features which has had, and is still to have, an important influence in shaping the educational system of the country.

The book was also reviewed by the *Northampton Courier* ("more precious than rubies") and the *Hampshire Gazette* ("no *true* New England household ought to be without it").

tions, she admits, were a strain: "I am sure that I never would endure the suspense which I endured during those three days again for all the treasure of the world." But once settled in, she is happy with her room-mate, Cousin Emily ("You can imagine how pleasant a good room-mate is, for you have been away to school so much"), and surprised to find how homelike the atmosphere is: "Everything is pleasant & happy here & I think I could be no happier at any other school away from home. Things seem much more like home than I anticipated & the teachers are all very kind & affectionate. They call on us frequently & urge us to return their calls & when we do, we always receive a cordial welcome from them." Her day was a busy one, but she makes no complaint as she sketches a typical one for Abiah:

> I will tell you my order of time for the day, as you were so kind as to give me your's. At 6. oclock, we all rise. We breakfast at 7. Our study hours begin at 8. At 9. we all meet in Seminary Hall, for devotions. At 10¼. I recite a review of Ancient History, in connection with which we read Goldsmith & Grimshaw. At .11. I recite a lesson in "Pope's Essay on Man" which is merely transposition. At .12. I practice Calisthenics & at 12¼ read until dinner, which is at 12½ & after dinner, from 1½ until 2 I sing in Seminary Hall. From 2¾ until 3¾. I practise upon the Piano. At 3¾ I go to Sections, where we give in all our accounts for the day, including, Absence – Tardi-ness – Communications – Breaking Silent Study hours – Receiving Company in our rooms & ten thousand other things, which I will not take time or place to mention. At 4½. we go into Seminary Hall, & receive advice from Miss. Lyon in the form of a lecture. We have Supper at 6. & silent-study hours from then until the retiring bell, which rings at 8¼, but the tardy bell does not ring until 9¾, so that we dont often obey the first warning to retire.

Nor did she complain of the domestic work, which for her consisted in "carrying the Knives from the 1st tier of tables at morning & noon & at night washing & wiping the same quantity of Knives." She tells Abiah not to believe the reports she may have heard about the food:

> . . . I can tell you, that I have yet seen nothing corresponding to my ideas on that point from what I have heard. Everything is wholesome & abundant & much nicer than I should imagine could be provided for almost 300. girls. We have also a great variety upon ou[r] tables & frequent changes.

Miss Lyon assembled a staff apparently as devoted as she was. They worked for tiny salaries and for the joy in what "seemed to them [wrote Hitchcock] a miniature paradise." She looked upon them all, staff and students, as "the family" (a recurrent term in the memorial volume), with herself in the maternal role, even to the cooking, a large part of which, at least at first, she did herself. (The policy of the seminary was against domestic help of any kind. The girls and the staff did all the work.) She was ubiquitous—planning, teaching, addressing assemblies, administering, advising, working in the kitchen. She worked "sixteen to eighteen hours out of the twenty-four." Her mission was not only spiritual. She hated snobbery and idleness and unused abilities of any kind. At a time when Emily was finding herself in less and less sympathy with certain aspects of the social life of Amherst, Miss Lyon's words might have come as an encouragement: "My heart is sick," she is quoted as saying, "my soul is pained with this empty gentility, this genteel nothingness." As Hitchcock wrote in the memorial, "By precept and example she showed the duty and dignity of labor," her charge to the girls being that, when the last word was pronounced on their lives, let it be said of each one of them, "She hath done what she could." And Emily, with her own emerging notion of the "Columnar Self," could hardly have missed such a ringing statement as this: "We have great powers over ourselves. We may become almost what we will."

Emily, too, hated "Dimity Convictions." If a girl came to Mount Holyoke a "Brittle Lady," she soon got over it, or left. Whether you hoped, or had no hope, or were "saved," you worked and you thought. Emily's schedule to Abiah does not mention specifically the two half-hour periods given each day to solitary meditation and prayer. Miss Lyon "set life and death before her pupils"; and whatever their degree of piety, they could hardly escape her influence. One need only call in witness the rest of Emily's life—her preoccupation with the "Flood subject" (as she called it), her love of solitude, her "having to think" (as Vinnie called it)—to show how deeply this early meditative discipline and the daily reminder, under such leadership, of ultimate things must have impressed her.

To soften the traditionally harsh outlines of Miss Lyon's character, other aspects of her approach to students must be kept in mind. We are told that she never browbeat the girls but talked quietly and sympathetically with them. She met every Sunday with those who "were destitute of the Christian hope," and apparently in the kindliest way, having known hopelessness herself. We know that Emily attended one of those meetings, and she probably was present at many more. In her talks to the whole school Miss Lyon "preserved the friendly, sincere tones of conversation"— a manner she may have adopted from Hitchcock, who was famous for his "simple, off-hand" style. She had a remarkable speaking voice: "She could fill the whole of the hall with her voice, without seeming to speak loud or to make an effort."

There was laughter at Mount Holyoke (Miss Lyon was witty) and a great deal of good sense that could have helped any girl, especially one who at an early age began to look inquiringly at her fellow beings. Miss Lyon, we are told,

at this time had a familiar and practical acquaintance with mind. Few could take the measure of hers; she measured every one she met. She had studied her scholars until she instinctively read and analyzed every character that came under her observation.

In no one's life is there any one source for qualities such as these, but here in Emily's most impressionable time—her first away from home—was the

New England, Puritan concern for character in most powerful and public operation. It was only a step from here to her own formulation (the passage may even have supplied the words): "I measure every Grief I meet / With analytic Eyes –" And no Mount Holyoke girl ever made more of Miss Lyon's excellent injunction: "Never write a foolish thing in a letter or elsewhere; 'what is written is written' "—or, as Emily put it in her famous poem, "A Word dropped careless on a Page" may live for centuries, to cure or kill. Emily's own words came to "chill and burn" her so that, at one point, she "had no grace to talk"; she pondered often what words could do to human beings, whom a mere syllable "can make to quake like jostled tree"; and she wrote years later to Higginson,

> What a Hazard a Letter is!
> When I think of the Hearts it has scuttled and sunk, I almost fear to lift my Hand to so much as a Superscription.

Except for Abiah's benefit, she said little about her formal studies, perhaps (again) because she had had most of them in Amherst Academy. Ancient History ("Goldsmith & Grimshaw") was a review. She had certainly met Pope at the Academy. In December, when she reported to Austin that she was "getting along well" in "Chemistry, Physiology & quarter course in Algebra," the books she was studying (" 'Silliman's Chemistry' & Cutter's Physiology") were well known in Amherst, though not surely in the Academy's curriculum. "In both of [them]," she told Abiah, "I am much interested." To Austin she admitted that she was even "engrossed in the history of Sulphuric Acid!!!!!" (though what is implied by the five exclamation points is not entirely clear), and she boasted about a skill not usually associated with her: "We are furnished with an account-book, here & obliged to put down every mill, which we spend & what we spend it for & show it to Miss Whitman every Saturday, so you perceive your sister is learning to keep accounts in addition to the other branches of her education."

In conclusion, if she felt bullied by the "ogres" or harassed by Miss Lyon's piety, there is little in the record—her *own* record—to show it. She had moments of homesickness and loneliness, but the experience seems on the whole to have been positive and good. She wept when Austin came to take her home in March because of her cough and was sad when the time came to leave for good in August. But Mount Holyoke wasn't Amherst, and toward the end she got impatient for her home—"my *own* DEAR HOME"—where she soon settled down, happily acquiescent (as far as can be seen) in her father's decision. She lost little emotional energy in nostalgia or regret. What she took from Mount Holyoke was the invaluable self-knowledge of a year more or less on her own, some more book learning, and a new sense of discipline; but chiefly (one can only surmise this; she never said it) the example of a brilliant and loving woman who had found her work and had given her life to it.

17

Early Friendships I

ALTHOUGH EMILY liked the girls at Mount Holyoke, she made no lasting friendships there. The trouble was not that she had difficulty in making new friends or felt lost in the multitude. Simply, the girls at Holyoke were not Amherst girls—a distinct category in the Dickinson mind, to judge by a remark Vinnie later made to Austin from Ipswich Seminary: "Do you care to know about the girls, here? They are not *Amherst girls,* yet some are pretty & fine scholars." A touch of this Amherst-Dickinson snobbery can be found in Emily's surprise at finding so many nice girls (as she wrote Abiah) at Holyoke:

> When I left home, I did not think I should find a companion or a dear friend in all the multitude. I expected to find rough & uncultivated manners, & to be sure, I have found some of that stamp, but on the whole, there is an ease & grace a desire to make one another happy, which delights & at the same time, surprises me very much.

"I love many of the girls," she went on, but "I find no Abby. or Abiah. or Mary." Two months later, in mid-January, she admitted to Abiah: "There are many sweet girls here & dearly do I love some new faces, but I have not yet found the place of a *few* dear ones filled, nor would I wish it to be here."

In a way, she was right. The girls she left behind in September 1847 and rejoined in Amherst the following August were a remarkable group. It is hardly too much to say that they played as important a part in her development as did her formal schooling. A great deal of self-education went on among all the Amherst young people, but mostly, in this generation, among the girls. There was a steady stream of bright young men coming into the town by way of the college, and the town itself was not destitute of young male talent, with Edward Hitchcock, Jr., and Austin

Dickinson, both of an age, as a nucleus. (Hitchcock became a physician and "a teacher as pivotal in Amherst's character as his father had been.") But it was the girls among the children of the faculty and administration—the stable population—who excelled in the lively arts of conversation, verse making, letter writing, music, school compositions, and the rest. Certainly it was from the group of girls that the greatest literary achievement was later to come—from Helen Fiske, Emily Fowler (Ford), and Emily herself.

The only considerable account we have of the group comes from Mrs. Ford. It was written in response to Mrs. Todd's inquiry in 1893 at the time of the editing of the *Letters*. By then, Mrs. Ford was an established author, with essays, stories, a book of verse (*My Recreations*, 1872), and a two-volume biography of her grandfather, Noah Webster, to her credit. She had long since been out of touch with Emily Dickinson and Amherst. She had married in 1853, had eight children, and was living in Brooklyn. The document she wrote for Mabel Todd, used in part in the first edition of the *Letters* (1894) and in full in the edition of 1931,[1] gives a sentimental view of Emily but is true in the main to Emily's distinguished group:

> There was a fine circle of young people in Amherst, and we influenced each other strongly. We were in the adoring mood, and I am glad to say that many of those idols of our girlhood have proved themselves golden. The eight girls who composed this group had talent enough for twice their number, and in their respective spheres of mothers, authors or women, have been notable and admirable.

Just what eight Mrs. Ford had in mind is not clear. She mentioned a few by name: Mary Humphrey (older sister of Emily's special friend, Jane), Helen Fiske, and Emily. But Mrs. Ford was four years older than Helen and Emily, and it would be surprising had the younger and older girls mingled in quite such intimate association as her glowing account suggests. (Also, Mary Humphrey was not an Amherst girl; she came to Amherst Academy from Southwick, Massachusetts, some thirty miles to the southwest.) Mrs. Ford was writing after a span of fifty years, enough to blur such distinctions. A likely eight can be pieced together from other sources. Kate Hitchcock, daughter of the president and exactly Mrs. Ford's age, was undoubtedly one of them. Two other probabilities are mentioned in Alice M. Walker's *Historic Homes of Amherst* (1905): Louisa Bridgman and Fanny Montague, the first an artist and poet and the other known for her "acute mind and vivid sense of humor." Both are coupled with Emily Dickinson, whom Miss Walker describes as "very bright and original," as "classmates." But they seem to have been in Emily Fowler's generation. Emily herself, in a letter to Abiah Root in March 1846, spoke of a "five," her own special group: they were (besides herself

1. See *Letters*, 1894, pp. 126–32, and *Letters*, 1931, pp. 124–32.

and Abiah), Abby Wood, Harriet Merrill, and Sarah Tracy—all of an age, it should be said, and classmates.

It may have been, in a school like Amherst Academy, where the teachers were only a few years older than the pupils, that age did not matter. Mrs. Ford speaks of hilarious times in a secret society called the Unseen Trap, "which brought out talent in its dozen members" and held meetings in a favorite grove. There was a Shakespeare Club—"a rare thing in those days"—and "after we left school," frequent meetings to discuss books. There were evening parties and of course the annual to-do about verse valentines. "Emily Dickinson and Mary Humphrey were the wits of the school," Mrs. Ford wrote, and contributed the liveliest pieces to "Forest Leaves," the little paper of which no copy survives. Years later, Abiah Root (Strong) told Mrs. Todd that she had never forgotten Emily's compositions in the Academy and (luckily for Mrs. Todd and posterity) had cherished her letters all these years.[2]

It was an idyllic time for Emily—or at least Mrs. Ford makes it sound that way. And the verve and dash of Emily's letters of the period, extending into the early 1850s, make it sound that way, too. "There was nothing of the recluse about her," wrote Mrs. Ford. "She was a free talker about what interested her." She was a free writer, too, the letters careering through matters mighty and minuscule, noting occasionally that there is "no rose without a thorn," but plunging on in glorious acceptance of it all.

Indeed, letters were an important part of the self-education among these young people. In his "Prologue" to William Gardiner Hammond's undergraduate diary for the years 1846-48, George Frisbie Whicher writes: "It was the fashion . . . to exchange letters for the sake of mutual improvement. Throughout his college course Hammond was carrying on an extensive correspondence with his former chums and with the girls of his acquaintance," apparently for educational as well as romantic purposes. We have already seen how seriously Austin and Joseph Lyman took the art of letter writing and how Emily and Austin bantered each other about their letters. As Emily grew older and saw fewer people, letters became not only indispensable for communication but a more and more carefully practiced art form. In the early letters she is obviously trying out her skills and, through the sharing of confidences and confessions, exploring life and herself. It is a shame, of course, that the surviving correspondence (a fraction of what she wrote) is only one-way.

The very length of Emily's letters—fifteen hundred words is common and some of them are twice that—shows exuberant energy; and still she

2. *AB*, p. 188. Mrs. Todd described the episode in *Letters*, 1931, pp. xv–xvi: "After I had finished [a lecture on ED], a little lady in a black bonnet came up to me, told me she had been a schoolmate of Emily at Amherst Academy, that she had never forgotten her extraordinary compositions, and *where* might she read some of Emily's prose? . . ." Mrs. Strong then told about the letters in her keeping and arranged to make them available to Mrs. Todd.

complained (to Abiah), "My pen is not swift enough to answer my purpose at all," or (to Jane Humphrey), "Seems to me I could write all night, Jennie, and then not say the half, nor the *half of the half* of all I have to tell you." These were the days (age fourteen) when she could write, "I am growing handsome very fast indeed! I expect I shall be the belle of Amherst when I reach my 17th year." These were the years (age eighteen) when she could say, "Amherst is alive with fun this winter," and (again), "The last week has been a merry one in Amherst, & notes have flown around like, snowflakes"—with "Tableaux at the President's . . . a Sliding party close upon it's heels – and several cozy sociables [bringing] up the rear." There was healthy competition (Emily wanted her letters to be the "smartest") but warm hearts—the "adoring" age Mrs. Ford called it, and continued:

> Emily was part and parcel of all these gatherings [and doings]. . . . She mingled freely in all the companies and excursions of the moment, and the evening frolics. . . . When "we girls" named each other flowers, and called her sister the Pond Lily, she answered so quickly, "And I am the Cow Lily," referring to the orange lights in her hair and eyes.

There *were* thorns, however, and even Mrs. Ford recalled a "prophetic hint" in her early talks with Emily: ". . . she once asked me if it did not make me shiver to hear a great many people talk – they took 'all the clothes off their souls' – and we discussed this matter. . . . At this time she had a demure manner which brightened easily into fun where she felt at home, but among strangers she was rather shy, silent, and even deprecating." Lively and talented as Emily's friends were, and much as she loved them, it is clear that they represented, or came to represent in her mind, much that frustrated her and, ultimately, drove her inward. As Abiah and Abby and Jane and the rest came to maturity, they accepted with cheer and energy the values and the challenge of mid-nineteenth-century American life—the outgoing piety, the missionary spirit (at home and abroad), the expansionism in every phase of national life. When President Hitchcock wrote, "Great and invaluable was the influence of Miss Lyon in *training up active and efficient women*," he was describing a nurture better fitted to the Abiahs and the Janes than to Emily Dickinson. The Humphrey sisters (Helen, Mary, and Jane) all taught school after leaving Mount Holyoke—Helen and Jane at Amherst Academy. Within a decade they were all married to businessmen. Helen settled in Wisconsin Territory, Mary in Alabama, and Jane in nearby Southwick. Abiah Root and Abby Wood were both married by the time they were twenty-five, Abiah to a clergyman (Samuel Strong of Westfield) and Abby to the Reverend Daniel Bliss, with whom she went to Beirut and there helped him found the Syrian Protestant College (American University). Harriet Merrill, daughter of Calvin Merrill, one of the original trustees of Amherst Academy and active in the founding of the college, taught at the Academy and later at Pittsfield. She was among the first to leave the group. In a letter of January 1846, Emily referred to her as one of the "lost sheep."

Another "lost sheep," but one deserving special comment, was Sarah Tracy, the "Virgil" of the group (Abiah was "Plato" and Emily "Socrates"). She soon faded out of what, as early as 1846, Emily called the "ancient picture," when the five had been in their glory. Her placid and serene nature was of particular interest to Emily. "Sarah alias Virgil is as consistent and calm and lovely as ever," she wrote Abiah in 1845. By this time, Emily's letters were revealing certain anxieties and tensions, ostensibly religious (at least this is what she wrote most about), but symptomatic also of her growing sense of alienation from many things about Amherst, including her old friends. Increasingly she saw that their ways were not her ways, and she was troubled. When she saw Sarah again in 1851, what still impressed her was Sarah's serenity and peacefulness. She described her to Abiah a little wistfully:

> Is'nt it very remarkable that in so many years Sarah has changed so little – not that she has stood still, but has made such *peaceful* progress – her thot's tho' they are *older* have all the charm of youth – have not yet lost their freshness, their innocence and peace – she seems so pure in heart – so sunny and serene, like some sweet Lark or Robin ever soaring and singing –

Emily herself was at that time making progress, certainly, but it was hardly peaceful. She seems to be wondering here how peaceful progress is made. How do you grow up "serene"? But Sarah departed, along with the others, and never told her secret.

Of the peripheral figures, those outside the five, we know only what can be gleaned from Emily's passing references, from village annals and casual reminiscences. Chief among the last is the diary of William Hammond, whose lively picture of Amherst life in the late 1840s is worth pausing over. Although he never mentions Emily, he knew and commented on almost all her friends, went to the same parties (at least the same *kinds* of parties), and shared the same cultural amenities (we have already seen him at Emily's Amherst Academy Commencement). From him we can see not only what it was that, up to a point, Emily shared in, but, increasingly, what she separated herself from.

Hammond was from Newport, Rhode Island, an excellent scholar, and a born enthusiast. He was interested in everything (but mostly language and literature; although he admired President Hitchcock, his science and piety bored him). He led an active social life, with teas and evening calls at the Hitchcocks', the Tylers', and the Gridleys', promenades, parties, levees, and rides without end. He courted, more or less seriously, almost every likely girl in town and assessed their merits and defects with confident precision. Jane Gridley, daughter of the eccentric doctor whom Austin described in *Representative Men of the Parish,* was the prettiest (Emily said she "strutted"; she returned from boarding school, Emily added, "to honor us poor Country folks"). Anna Tyler, wrote Hammond, was "a queer looking young lady with a face not pretty, but such as you could not help looking at: half child and half sage, half genius and half fool. Very agreeable and said to be very *smart*." (Emily's comment: "Anna Taylor is on the single.") There was the "pleasing, commonplace Tempe Linnell"[3] (who never married) and the "pretty would-be belle Miss [Emeline] Kellogg" (who did). Neither was very close to Emily. Emily attended a party (which she called a *"confidentiale"*) at Tempe's in January 1850, sat next to her at meeting in March 1854 and asked her bluntly if she was "engaged to Sam Fiske" (she said she was not). We hear no more of her in Emily's letters. Emily seems to have kept in closer touch with Emeline, who once spent a night in the Homestead when Mr. Dickinson was away and Emily and Vinnie were in Boston, and worried them all during a protracted illness in the winter of 1852. But by that time she was all but engaged to Henry Nash, whom she married on October 9, 1855. Another of Emily's friends whom Hammond saw a good deal of was Sabra Howe, daughter of the landlord of the Amherst House and mentioned several times in Emily's earliest letters. She was another one of those who were sent away to school (Baltimore, in this instance) and was similarly accused by Emily of condescending to the country folks. Hammond took her to lectures, the Cattle Show, a country wedding, and for a time called on her almost daily for chess, whist, and pleasant chats. Emily's last reference to her (in January 1852) described her as "very happy indeed" in some distant place, perhaps married.

At a party given by his classmate Theodore French during Hammond's first term in the college, he met "many young ladies I never saw before and never wish to see again," but he made exceptions of a few: "Miss Emily Fowler, one of the reigning belles, with rather a pretty face, but a figure like a jar of sweetmeats; also Miss Livia Coleman, another belle and the prettiest girl [except Jane Gridley] I have seen in Amherst." "The evening passed quickly in talking, promenading, music, and *feeding*." Olivia, sister of Eliza who later married Emily's friend John Dudley, died in Princeton, New Jersey, the next year, a loss to which Emily gave three sentences in a letter to Abiah: "You probably have heard of the death of *O. Coleman*. How melancholy!! Eliza. had written me a long letter giving me an account of her death, which is beautiful & affecting & which you shall see when we *meet again*."

For us, the most striking fact about Hammond's reporting of the Amherst scene is his failure to mention its two most important young ladies: Helen Fiske and Emily Dickinson. He was a year and a half older,

3. John Burgess, whose *Reminiscences* I have quoted before, had kindlier memories of Tempe Linnell. He described her at forty as "one of the prettiest, most refined, and genial of women." She ran a student boardinghouse with her mother (to whom she devoted her life). There was a story that she had been "cruelly treated by a student," and Burgess remembered the "sad, appealing look in her beautiful gray eyes as she went uncomplainingly about her duties" (p. 39). Emily described her as "very dear to me", *L* I, 194 (to Susan Gilbert, April 5, 1852).

to be sure, and came to college when they had a year to go in the Academy. Also, during one of the years covered by his diary, Emily was in Mount Holyoke. But Emily was a known wit, and Helen even then a local character. Hammond says nothing, either, about Austin, who was only a class ahead of him in the college and whom he must have met frequently in Amherst gatherings. It should be said, however, that the silence is mutual: Hammond appears in none of the Dickinson annals.

This is difficult to explain in view of Hammond's literary interests, and even more so since he paid such attention to Mary Warner, Emily's exact age and one of her dearest friends outside the five. Hammond found her, at first meeting, "a pretty, modest, pleasant girl with beautiful hair." Later she was to emerge as "La Bijou," Hammond's first choice, a musician, a chess player, a good cook, and a magnificent companion on a sleigh ride. He saw her constantly. His entry for February 2, 1848, shows him at the height of his enthusiasm (and engaging in a favorite Amherst winter sport):

> This over [a rhetorical exercise at the college], went off for a sleigh ride with Mary Warner. Oh ye Gods, what a glorious time! The snow smooth and hard, the sky clear, the horse spirited, the sleigh of Cook's best, and *La Bijou* snugly by my side, her rosy pleasant face beaming with smiles. What wonder that I enjoyed my rambling ride through all the byroads of the North Parish! And what wonder – not to dilate – that coming back I should sometimes be looking at my partner instead of my horse?

The ensuing accident, tumbling them both into a snowbank in "a mingled mass of red cloak and dishevelled curls," only added to the excitement and to his admiration for Mary. Later Hammond's friend Edward Olcott proposed to her three times; John Sanford (Austin's friend) proposed to her; Hammond came near it himself; at one time she had a suitor named Thurston; and she finally married Edward Crowell, '53, professor of Latin in the college from 1864 to 1908. In Emily's letters from Mount Holyoke, she had seldom failed to send her love to Mary; they exchanged books (*Kavanagh* was one of them) and calls. But it was inevitable that their ways should part—Mary pious, popular, and headed for matrimony. When she was finally married (on August 13, 1861), a cool little note tells the story—and a good deal about Emily's youth:

DEAR MARY –
    You might not know I remembered you, unless I told you so –
                                            EMILY –

In her early friendships, at least in the letters that record them, Emily Dickinson was quite consciously taking the measure of herself. Although (she later said) she learned most from her lifelong relationship with Sue, even her earliest letters were not only exercises in style but, with their introversions and their increasingly critical animadversions on people and

Abiah Root, about 1847

Emily Fowler Ford, about 1875 (?)

Mary Warner, about 1861

Early Friendships I

ED to John L. Graves, occasion and date uncertain

Emily Dickinson's watch

things, exercises in the discovery of herself and her world. In measuring everything she met, she was constantly assessing "with analytic eyes" and typical Puritan introspection her own being in relation to others and to what she later called "Ourself behind ourself." She asked a great deal of her friends, flooding them with letters (the words must have come more quickly to her than to most) and scolding them when they failed to respond in kind. She probably asked too much. Many of them apparently lacked the skill, or the will, to follow her. All we know is that, one by one, the early group fell away, and she was left in her early twenties with her "Lexicon" (as she put it with characteristic exaggeration) as her "only companion."

There are three correspondences emerging from the years before Sue arrived on the scene that invite closer examination than the others. From one, Emily seems to have learned nothing at all; in the course of another, we can see her learning who she was not; the third, if my reading is correct, shows her learning who she was. The first, with Emily Fowler Ford, is most important because of its long aftermath, extending into the time of the publication of the poems in the 1890s. The second (the letters to Abiah Root) shows her at the point of striking out on her own. To Jane Humphrey (in the third) she seems to be revealing the secret of her new vocation.

The fourteen letters to Emily Fowler, beginning in the spring of 1850 and extending briefly beyond her marriage to Gordon Ford in December 1853, are written in a sub-"dear Susie" style (Emily once included Emily Fowler in a list of girls who were "very dear" to her) and represent as vacuous a correspondence as Emily ever conducted. Eight of the letters gave excuses for not coming to visit, one included a lock of hair, and one went with a flower. There was much sentiment after the wedding in 1853; a one-sentence note acknowledged a letter of condolence after the death of Mr. Dickinson in 1874; and three sentences in 1882 acknowledged the gift of Mrs. Ford's *My Recreations* (ten years after it was published):

DEAR FRIEND,
   The little Book will be subtly cherished –
   All we secure of Beauty is it's Evanescences – Thank you for recalling us.
                                             Earnestly,
                                                EMILY.

The two were never very close, even at a time when the young people of Amherst were pouring out their hearts to one another about religion during the winter and spring of 1850 (when the correspondence began). This was the year of an unusually fervent revival in Amherst, when, according to Emily Dickinson, "Christ is calling everyone here, all my companions have answered." Emily Fowler was caught up in it, and Abby Wood, and Jane Hitchcock, and Mary Warner, and Susan Gilbert. "Even my darling Vinnie," wrote Emily, "believes she loves, and trusts him, and I am standing alone in rebellion, and growing very careless."

[*375*

(Vinnie took it upon herself, from faraway Ipswich Seminary, to convert her brother and sister. "How beautiful," she wrote Austin, "if *we three* could all believe in Christ, how much higher object should we have in living! . . . Does Emilie think of these things at all? Oh! that she might!") Emily Fowler, who had joined the church on profession of faith when she was sixteen, was sufficiently moved by the missionary spirit to send Austin a long letter remarkable for little more than its almost complete dependence on the clichés of the revival—"the sense of sin, the joy of pardon, the holy strength, the happiness, they will all come, dear Austin, in time." (That they did not, at least then, we know from Austin's confessional letter to Martha Gilbert a little later.) There is no indication in the existing correspondence that Emily Fowler was concerned over the spiritual state of Austin's sister Emily, and one wonders whether her first interest was actually the state of his soul.[4] She seems to have had as little understanding as Vinnie did of what was going on in the minds of Austin and Emily.

But more important, Emily Fowler seems to have had as little understanding of Emily's literary proclivities and talents as she did of her spiritual problems. After the popular success of the *Poems* in the early 1890s, she was glad enough to share with Mabel Todd (and the public) her knowledge of Emily Dickinson's formative years. What she sent Mrs. Todd, however, were reminiscences from fifty years back; and her contribution, like Higginson's impression of his "partially cracked poetess," did little more than encourage the stock images of Emily that have been so stubbornly persistent—in this instance, the sentimental ones. Typical of the first critical reaction to the *Poems,* Mrs. Ford was preoccupied with the person, not the poet. She told about Emily's love of "the great aspects of nature" and how "She knew the wood-lore of the region round about," how "she could name the haunts and the habits of every wild or garden growth within her reach"—true enough, and a tribute, among other things, to the thoroughness of botanical studies in Amherst Academy. We hear that her eyes were "lovely auburn, soft and warm," that "her hair lay in rings of the same color all over her head," that "her skin and teeth were good." And we see her in the classic pose, a flower among the flowers:

I have so many times seen her in the morning at work in her garden where everything throve under her hand, and wandering there at eventide, that she is perpetually associated in my mind with flowers – a flower herself. . . .

4. Emily Fowler's letter to Austin is undated. Mrs. Bingham writes that it was "written during the aftermath of the revival [and] is a good illustration of the concern felt by young people for the spiritual welfare of their friends" (*Home,* p. 97). But why was Emily not included in her concern? There were many reasons, and good ones, why Emily Fowler should have been interested in Austin. The two were of an age; she was a "reigning belle" in Amherst, and Austin the catch of the town. In a letter to Austin of April 2, 1853, ED wrote: "Emily Fowler spent yesterday afternoon here. She *inquired for you*" (*L* I, 238; emphasis hers).

Again, this picture may be true enough, in that Emily Fowler may
have seen Emily often in her garden. Emily Dickinson, she wrote, was
"several years younger, and how and when we drew together I cannot
recall"—not, apparently, until their interests had matured. "We often
walked together . . . and I remember especially two excursions to Mount
Norwottock, five miles away, where we found the climbing fern, and
came home laden with pink and white trilliums, and later, yellow lady's-
slippers." While one cannot doubt the cordiality of the relationship, one
regrets what Mrs. Ford left out—the real Emily Dickinson and her part in
the busy Dickinson day, the cooking, the cleaning, the nursing when
needed, the callers and the calling, and (for Emily) the "thinking" and
the writing. It is obvious how much Mrs. Ford's account, appearing when
and under the auspices it did, encouraged the already well-developed
legend.

This would not be serious, were it not for the fact that Mrs. Ford's
lack of discernment was one of the series of such failures that kept Emily
Dickinson's poems from being published in her lifetime. Mrs. Ford
merely repeated the larger failures of Samuel Bowles and Higginson in
the 1860s—but she did so at a critical moment when a different attitude
might have altered history. With no sense of the irony of what she was
revealing, Mrs. Ford wrote in her letter to Mabel Todd:

> Once I met Dr. Holland, the Editor then of *Scribner's Magazine,* who
> said, "You know Emily Dickinson. I have some poems of hers under con-
> sideration for publication – but they really are not suitable – they are too
> ethereal." I said, "They are beautiful, so concentrated, but they remind me
> of orchids, air-plants that have no roots in earth." He said, "That is true, – a
> perfect description. I dare not use them"; and I think these lyrical ejacula-
> tions, these breathed out projectiles sharp as lances, would at that time have
> fallen into idle ears.

Perhaps Mrs. Ford and Dr. Holland were right in their estimate of the
literary climate of the time (the conversation is not dated; Holland
founded *Scribner's* in 1870 and was editor until his death in 1881); but in
view of the success of the poems in the early 1890s—six printings of the
first edition in as many months—it may have been that the only thing
needed at this earlier time was the vigorous backing of a few literary
leaders.

A glance at Mrs. Ford's life and work explains her failure here. If in
the mid-1840s Hammond called her "one of the reigning belles" of
Amherst, she apparently achieved that eminence (in the minds of some)
at a price. According to Leonard Humphrey (Emily Dickinson's revered
"Master"), she was much too worldly. She was "planned for a noble
woman," he wrote to a friend in February 1846, "but College & flattery
have interfered amazingly with the design. . . ." Emily recorded a few
calls from her after the Holyoke year, but after 1853 their ways parted for
good. *My Recreations,* a volume thick enough to show that Mrs. Ford had

been writing verses for many years before 1872, shows also how far apart the two were, aesthetically and in every other way. She told Dr. Holland that Emily's poems had "no roots in earth"; her own poems are so deeply rooted in the moral and religious platitudes of the day as to have little life of their own. She was hardly the one to stiffen Dr. Holland's spine and give him courage. Another comment to Dr. Holland shows how far from the mark they both were in judging Emily Dickinson's poetry. Singly, said Mrs. Ford, the poems are baffling, but ". . . gathered in a volume where many could be read at once as her philosophy of life, they explain each other and so become intelligible and delightful to the public." She may have assessed the market correctly, but "philosophy of life" will hardly do. And it was easy to heap praise on the poems *after* the popular success of the first editions.

Mrs. Ford's final words in the letter to Mabel Todd attempt an explanation of Emily's withdrawn life:

> I think in spite of her seclusion, she was longing for poetic sympathy and renown, and that some of her later habits of life originated in this suppressed and ungratified desire of distinction. She wore white, she shut herself away from her race as a mark of her separation from the mass of minds. I only wish the interest and delight her poems have aroused could have come early enough in her career to have kept her social and communicative, and at one with her friends.

This time she may not have been so far from the mark. After Emily Dickinson's discouragement with Higginson, it may have been that she had decided against pursuing fame vigorously; but she was surely posing when (in the third letter she wrote Higginson in the spring of 1862) she said that publication was "foreign to my thought, as Firmament to Fin –" Why else had she sent him six poems, four in the first letter, two in the second? On several occasions in her early letters the truth slipped out—the youthful pride she took in her schoolgirl compositions; the literary ambitions she shared with her talented schoolmates; and her most explicit remark to Sue on the occasion of the "Alabaster Chambers" exchange: "Could I make you and Austin – proud – sometime – a great way off – 'twould give me taller feet –" Mrs. Ford, a professional herself, understood what the "longing for poetic sympathy and renown" was. In her own busy life, she was too far out of touch with Amherst to give her friend the poetic sympathy she needed; but the talk with Dr. Holland shows how easy it would have been for her to help Emily Dickinson to the renown she at one time longed for.

As for her wish that Emily had remained "social and communicative, and at one with her friends," Mrs. Ford had once felt herself snubbed by Emily and may have spoken with some pique. When she visited Amherst in July 1882, she saw many of her old friends—Mrs. Snell, the Sweetsers, the Tylers, and the Dickinsons. But Emily declined to see her. When the *Poems* made their instantaneous success in 1890, Mrs. Ford memorialized this incident in an effusion she sent to the *Springfield Republican*. It was published in the issue of Sunday, January 11, 1891, and is unimportant except for one thing: it shows the Myth in action. It was given a prominent place, under the masthead on the second page:

EHEU! EMILY DICKINSON!

Written by Emily E. F. Ford for *The Sunday Republican*.

> Oh, friend, these sighs from out your solitude
>   But pierce my heart! Social with bird and bee,
>   Loving your tender flowers with ecstacy,
> You shun the eye, the voice, and shy elude
> The loving souls that dare not to intrude
>   Upon your chosen silence. Friend, you thought
>   No life so sweet and fair as hiding brought,
> And beauty is your song, with interlude
> Of outer life which to your soul seems crude,
>   Thoughtless, unfeeling, idle, scant of grace;
>   Nor will you touch a hand, or greet a face, –
> For common daily strife to you is rude,
>   And, shrinking, you in shadow lonely stay
>   Invisible to all, howe'er we pray.

Brooklyn, January 3, 1891.

While the letters to Emily Fowler, though affectionate enough, are lean and mostly dull, the letters to Abiah Root—twenty-two of them, from 1845 to 1854—are lively and full to overflowing. Abiah came to Amherst Academy (she had cousins in Amherst, the Palmers) from Feeding Hills, just southwest of Springfield. The first meeting of the two friends was an immediate success. In one of the numerous stylistic flourishes that sprinkle the letters, Emily, now twenty-one, described the meeting:

You and I have grown older since school-days, and our years have made us soberer – I mean have made *me* so, for you were always dignified, e-en when a little girl, and *I* used, now and then, to cut a timid caper. That makes me think of you the very first time I saw you, and I can't repress a smile, not to say a hearty laugh, at your little girl expense. I have roused your curiosity, so I will e-en tell you that one Wednesday afternoon, in the days of that dear old Academy, I went in to be entertained by the rhetoric of the gentlemen and the milder form of the girls – I had hardly recovered myself from the dismay attendant upon entering august assemblies, when with the utmost equanimity you ascended the stairs, bedecked with dandelions, arranged, it seemed, for curls. I shall never forget that scene, if I live to have gray hairs, nor the very remarkable fancies it gave me then of you, and it comes over me now with the strangest bygone funniness, and I laugh merrily. Oh, Abiah, you and the early flower are forever linked to me; as soon as the first green grass comes, up from a chink in the stones peeps the little flower, precious "leontodon," and my heart fills toward you with a warm and childlike fullness! Nor do I laugh now; far from it, I rather bless the flower which sweetly, slyly too, makes me come nearer you.

Abiah soon became one of "the five," an honor, perhaps, since with Sarah Tracy she was the only other non-Amherst girl in the group. She was one of the two girls, in Amherst or out, with whom Emily discussed freely the matter that bore so heavily on all these young people, their spiritual condition. In her last letter to Abiah from Mount Holyoke, Emily wrote about Abby Wood, her only other confidante.

> I had quite a long talk with Abby while at home and I doubt not she will soon cast her burden on Christ. She is sober, and keenly sensitive on the subject, and she says she only desires to be good. How I wish I could say that with sincerity, but I fear I never can. But I will no longer impose my own feelings even upon my friend. Keep them sacred, for I never lisped them to any save yourself and Abby.

Jane Humphrey and Susan Gilbert were to share many of Emily's innermost thoughts—but not many on the "all-important subject." And since only Abiah's letters have survived, she, rather than Abby, must be regarded as the chief sister-confessor.

When after a year (in 1845) Abiah left Amherst Academy for a school nearer home (Miss Campbell's in Springfield) and communication had to be by letter, the tone was anything but serious. "So leave everything," Emily wrote in her first letter, "and sit down prepared for a long siege in the shape of a bundle of nonsense from friend E."[5] And so the letters go, six of them in the first year, at intervals of a few weeks to three months, filled with (often) brilliant fourteen-year-old nonsense, gossip, flights metaphoric and "poetical" ("and you know," Emily wrote, "that is what young ladies aim to be now-a-days"), quotations from the Bible and Shakespeare, boasts (about "my abilities, which you know are neither few nor small"), and pledges of undying friendship. The whole exuberant flow slowed down only once for a moment of genuine pathos, the death of "S Norton's" mother. In the first five letters there was scarcely a cloud on the horizon, unless one chooses to see prophetic hints in Emily's thrice

5. All these letters to Abiah are signed "Emily E. Dickinson" or "Emily E D." until the last one from Mount Holyoke (May 16, 1848), when the spelling becomes "Emilie." Beginning with the short letter of October 29, 1848, the signatures (with one exception) are shortened to "Emilie" or "Emily" or "Emily E." or (once) "E." For the "-y" vs. "-ie" debate, see Ruth Miller (*The Poetry of Emily Dickinson*, pp. 125–26), who feels that an article by Samuel Bowles [?] in the *Republican* (July 14, 1860), ridiculing the custom of ending girls' names in "ie," moved Emily to give it up. John Evangelist Walsh, *The Hidden Life of Emily Dickinson*, p. 266, disagrees. For whatever reason, the last of the extant letters signed "Emilie" was to Louise Norcross, December 31, 1861. (It might be noted that Vinnie referred to her as "Emilie" in a letter to Mabel Todd, July 12, 1883.)

urging Abiah not to let anyone see her letters, or a slight streak of competitiveness that emerges several times (Emily jokes about Abiah's getting ahead of her in smartness, wisdom, and playing the piano[6]), or some New Year's blues (at age fifteen):

> How many good resolutions did I make at the commencement of the year now flown, merely to break them and to feel more than ever convinced of the weakness of my own resolutions! The New Year's day was unusually gloomy to me, I know not why, and perhaps for that reason a host of unpleasant reflections forced themselves upon me which I found not easy to throw off. But I will no longer sentimentalize upon the past, for I cannot recall it.

It is in the sixth letter, written a fortnight later (January 31, 1846), that the New Year's meditations come to a focus on spiritual matters. Save for a gossipy postscript, the letter, a long one, is entirely given over to religion. Emily confesses to Abiah that she did not become a Christian during the revival the previous winter in Amherst. She has seen "many who felt there was nothing in religion . . . melted at once," and it has been "really wonderful to see how near heaven came to sinful mortals." Once, "for a short time," she had known this beatific state herself, when "I felt I had found my savior." "I never enjoyed," she wrote, "such perfect peace and happiness." But "I soon forgot my morning prayer or else it was irksome to me. One by one my old habits returned and I cared less for religion than ever." At Abiah's recent announcement that she was close to conversion, Emily "shed many tears." She herself longs to follow after: "I feel that I shall never be happy without I love Christ." But midway through the letter she makes a striking admission, a real bit of self-discovery. Putting aside the revival rhetoric, she seems to be speaking in her own voice (even to the misspelling):

> Perhaps you will not beleive it Dear A. but I attended none of the meetings last winter. I felt that I was so easily excited that I might again be deceived and I dared not trust myself.

This revelation is followed by a long passage on the dreadful thought of Eternity, by a set piece on her own death ("I cannot imagine with the farthest stretch of my imagination my own death scene"—and then she proceeds to imagine it), and by thoughts on the Last Judgment and the Resurrection, when she hopes to be united with her friends in "one unbroken company in heaven." It seems clear that her absence from the revival meetings was not because she was unmoved, or alienated, or bitter.

6. Such hints are probably no more than a normal, youthful love of secrets and a desire to excel. But it is true that the former became obsessive. As to the latter, only a few years later Emily was warning her "Brother Pegasus" (Austin) that he could expect some competition from her in the matter of writing poems. She kept a shrewd eye on the literary scene and knew the quality of her work as compared with what was being published. From the bravado of these early letters, it seems clear that she knew her worth from the start.

She was afraid of being too much moved and, her imagination overstimulated, lured into a commitment she knew from experience she could not live up to.

Just when and under what circumstances Emily had once known the peace of submission to Christ we will probably never know. But its evanescence had apparently frightened her. She had been "easily excited" once, and she would not subject herself to the experience again—or, as she put it (lapsing into revival talk but keeping her own spelling and grammar): "Many conversed with me seriously and affectionately and I was almost inclined to yeild to the claims of He who is greater than I." So, she confessed to Abiah, "I am continually putting off becoming a christian. Evil voices lisp in my ear – " Later on, these "evil voices" were to become "syren" voices, and still later, "beautiful tempters" whispering to her; but what she meant precisely she did not say.

By the time of the next letter (March 28, 1846), Abiah has made her decision, causing Emily again to "shed many a tear" and wish that she "had found the peace which has been given to you." She looks back on the "perfect happiness I experienced while I felt I was an heir of heaven as of a delightful dream, out of which the Evil one bid me wake & again return to the world & its pleasures." Again there was a revival going on in the college (for the second year in a row), and again she resists it:

I know that I ought now to give myself to God & spend the springtime of life in his service for it seems to me a mockery to spend life's summer & autumn in the service of Mammon & when the world no longer charms us, "When our eyes are dull of seeing & our ears of hearing, when the silver cord is loosed & the golden bowl broken" to yield our hearts, because we are afraid to do otherwise & give to God the miserable recompense of a sick bed for all his kindness to us.

The rest of the letter is about death: the funeral of "Judge Dickinson's wife" she saw yesterday from her window; the death of a friend of Abiah's; and then the description of her visit to Sophia Holland's sickroom, remarkable if for no other reason than that it is remembered so vividly over a period of two years. The postscript contains an admonition: "Please not let S. or any one see this letter. It is only for you."

With Abiah safely in the fold and Emily out, the tone of the letters changes, and the intervals between them, certainly from the Mount Holyoke period to the end of the correspondence in 1854, lengthen considerably. The two were no longer facing the same problem, and the differences between the friends widened:

I am not unconcerned Dear A. upon the all important subject, to which you have so frequently & so affectionately called my attention in your letters. But I feel that I have not yet made my peace with God. I am still a s[tran]ger – to the delightful emotions which fill your heart. I have perfect confidence in God & his promises & yet I know not why, I feel that the world holds a predominant place in my affections. I do not feel that I could give up all for

Christ, were I called to die. Pray for me Dear A. that I may yet enter into the kingdom, that there may be room left for me in the shining courts above.

A year and a half and three good, gossipy letters intervene before Emily comes back to the subject, and then only in two sentences at the end of a postscript. She is writing from Mount Holyoke:

There is a great deal of religious interest here and many are flocking to the ark of safety. I have not yet given up to the claims of Christ, but trust I am not entirely thoughtless on so important & serious a subject.

We have already heard her regretting, in her last letter to Abiah from Mount Holyoke, her failure during the preceding term to seize the "golden opportunity," as she put it, to "give up and become a Christian." Six months later the first signs of a real break appear. Abiah had not answered her letter and did not speak to her during the Commencement exercises at Mount Holyoke in August, when Emily had caught a tantalizing glimpse of her. A short, tense letter in late October is very much like the "you can go or stay" letter to Susan Gilbert a few years later. (Emily could be peremptory with her friends when she sensed any slackening in the original fervor.) But the friendship survived, happily, even after this:

Why did you not come back that day [Commencement], and tell me what had sealed your lips toward me? Did my letter never reach you, or did you coolly decide to love me, & write to me no more? If you love me, & never received my letter – then may you think yourself wronged, and that rightly, but if you dont want to be my friend any longer, say so, & I'll try *once* more to blot you from my memory. Tell me very soon, for suspense is intolerable.

It seems clear that, in Abiah, Emily saw a way she could not follow: she was learning from her who she was not. Even from the first, there is a slight sense in her letters that the two are functioning on different planes. From time to time Emily wonders whether Abiah would laugh at her nonsense, or be bored by her sentimentalizings, or offended by her "speaking so lightly of so solemn a ceremony" (a wedding Abiah had attended). Of a certain Mr. Eastcott who had given Abiah concert tickets, she writes, "He is a young man I suppose. These Music teachers are always such high souled beings that I think they would exactly suit your fancy." Abiah was the dignified one, proper and pious, while Emily posed as the scapegrace, listening to Evil Voices. Rather than confidences, the letters are more and more spiced with entertaining set pieces, exercises in style—and some good ones. One letter is given over almost entirely to her trip to Boston. She described her visits to Mount Auburn Cemetery, to the Chinese Museum, where she saw the reformed opium eaters (whose "self *denial*" was "peculiarly interesting to me"), to the top of the State House, and to a horticultural exhibition. Besides the accounts of her studies and her daily routine at Mount Holyoke, there is a lively (and loving) description of

EMILY DICKINSON

the first sight of her parents as they came to visit, and a rapturous one of her first homecoming.

One letter (January 29, 1850) represents, with other compositions of the same time, a kind of stylistic milestone. It begins with spiritual matters but in no time has embarked on an extended bit of whimsey regarding a cold from which Emily is suffering. The cold is personified as a being from the Alps who had heard of the traditional hospitality of New Englanders and had made itself quite at home, "slept in my bed, eaten from my plate, lived with me everywhere, and will tag me through life for all I know." Having built heroically on the fantasy (no one has ever done better on the genus *cold*), Emily suddenly breaks off, fearing (or pretending to fear) that she is leaving Abiah behind:

> Now my dear friend, let me tell you that these last thoughts are fictions – vain imaginations to lead astray foolish young women. They are flowers of speech, they both *make,* and *tell* deliberate falsehoods, avoid them as the snake, and turn aside as from the *Bottle* snake, and I dont *think* you will be harmed.

To leave Abiah (and Emily's warnings) for a moment: Just two weeks before, she had written her Uncle Joel Norcross in much the same vein. It was a long, whimsical letter about a man who "told a lie to his neice"—a gorgeous bit of fooling and the most sustained bit of virtuoso writing (of what survives) she had yet done:

> DEAREST OF ALL DEAR UNCLES.
> Sleep carried me away, and a dream passed along, a dream all queer, and curious – it was a dream of warning – I ought not to hide it from whom it concerns – God forbid that you trifle with vision so strange – the Spirit of love entreat you – the Spirit of warning guide – and the all helping hold – and prevent you from falling! And I dreamed – and beheld a company whom no man may number – all men in their youth – all strong and stout-hearted – nor feeling their burdens for strength – nor waxing faint – nor weary. Some tended their flocks – and some sailed on the sea – and yet others kept gay stores, and deceived the foolish who came to buy. They made life one summer day – they danced to the sound of the lute – they sang old snatches of song – and they quaffed the rosy wine – One promised to love his friend and one vowed to defraud no poor – and *one* man told a lie to his neice – they all did sinfully – and their lives were not yet taken. Soon a change came – the young men were old – the flocks had no sheperd – the boat sailed alone – and the dancing had ceased – and the wine-cup was empty – and the summer day grew cold – Oh fearful the faces then! The Merchant tore his hair – and the Sheperd gnashed his teeth – and the Sailor hid himself – and prayed to die. Some kindled the scorching fire – some opened the earthquake's mouth – the winds strode on to the sea – and serpents hissed fearfully. Oh I was very much scared and I called to see who they were – this torment waited for – I listened – and up from the pit *you* spoke! You could'nt get out you said – no help could reach so far – you had brought it upon

yourself – I left you alone to die – but they told me the whole of the crime – you had broken a promise on earth and now t'was too late to redeem it. . . .

And so on for many "vain imaginations" more, and "flowers of speech" and "deliberate falsehoods" of the sort she showered on Abiah. She was as solicitous about her uncle's perceptions as she was about Abiah's. "Do you take any hints I wonder – can you guess the meaning of things – not yet aroused to the truth[?]" Although in the early letters to Abiah she had developed conventional personifications—Father Time, Jack Frost, herself as Eve ("alias Mrs. Adam"[7])—she had never let her fancy run like this. Here within a fortnight are her two most daring experiments in style so far. More important, she seems to have discovered a way of structuring certain thoughts that to express otherwise would have left her vulnerable in a way she was increasingly trying to avoid.

The warning to Abiah about the snake is developed in mock serious-ness but so elaborately as to suggest that she is hinting at something else. When we see her doing much the same thing in the letters to Jane Humphrey that began this same month, the suspicion grows that this something may be momentous. Here she seems, deliberately, to be throw-ing dust in Abiah's eyes:

> Honestly tho', a snake bite is a serious matter, and there cant be too much said, or done about it. The big serpent bites the deepest, and we get so ac-customed to it's bites that we dont mind about them. "Verily I say unto you fear *him*." Wont you read some work upon snakes – I have a real anxiety for you! *I* love those little green ones that slide around by your shoes in the grass – and make it rustle with their elbows – they are rather my favorites on the whole, but I would'nt influence *you* for the world! There is an air of misanthropy about the striped snake that will commend itself at once to your taste, there is no monotony about it – but we will more of this again. Something besides severe colds, and serpents, and we will try to find *that* something. It cant be a garden, can it, or a strawberry bed, which rather belongs to a garden – nor it cant be a school-house, nor an Attorney at Law. Oh dear I dont know *what* it is! Love for the absent dont *sound* like it, but try it, and see how it goes.

Perhaps Abiah decoded this without difficulty, but some remarks toward the end of the letter must have left her guessing:

> If you were here I would tell you something – *several* somethings which have happed since you went away, but time, and space, as usual, oppose themselves, and I put my treasures away till "we *two* meet again." . . . I have been introducing you to me in this letter so far – we will traffick in "joys" – and "sorrows" some other day. Colds make one very carnal and the spirit is always afraid of them.

7. *L* I, 24 (January 12, 1846): "I have lately come to the conclusion that I am Eve, alias Mrs. Adam. You know there is no account of her death in the Bible, and why am I not Eve? If you find any statements which you think likely to prove the truth of the case, I wish you would send them to me without delay."

With the next letter (May 7 and 17, 1850), a strange mélange, the mystery deepens. Mother is sick, Vinnie is at Ipswich, and Emily is doing the housework: "Father and Austin still clamor for food, and I, like a martyr am feeding them." The letter begins archly and in the high style:

DEAR REMEMBERED.

The circumstances under which I write you this morning are at once glorious, afflicting, and beneficial – glorious in *ends,* afflicting in *means,* and *beneficial* I *trust* in *both.* Twin loaves of bread have just been born into the world under my auspices – fine children – the image of their *mother* – and *here* my dear friend is the *glory.*

Domestic duties ("God keep me from what they call *households"*), her mother's illness, and illness in general ("Father Mortality") all get the light touch; but a new tone emerges—and something else—as she embarks upon an episode involving the refusal of an invitation. She tells it in near-perfect narrative form. In all her domestic trials, she writes, "I hav'nt repined but *once,* and you shall know all the why":

While I washed the dishes at noon in that little "sink-room" of our's, I heard a well-known rap, and a friend I love *so* dearly came and asked me to ride in the woods, the sweet-still woods, and I wanted to exceedingly – I told him I could not go, and he said he was disappointed – he wanted me very much – then the tears came into my eyes, tho' I tried to choke them back, and he said I *could,* and *should* go, and it seemed to me unjust. Oh I struggled with great temptation, and it cost me much of denial, but I think in the end I conquered, not a glorious victory Abiah, where you hear the rolling drum, but a kind of a helpless victory, where triumph would come of itself, faintest music, weary soldiers, nor a waving flag, nor a long-loud shout. I had read of Christ's temptations, and how they were like our own, only he did'nt sin; I wondered if *one* was like mine, and whether it made him angry – I couldnt make up my mind; do you think he ever did?

This is clearly a conscious stylistic effort; she wants to entertain Abiah. But the tears and the frustration—and something else—seem real. She has said no to the young man—has "struggled" and "conquered"—and, in the telling, out comes a full-fledged martial metaphor, precisely modulated: not a "glorious victory Abiah, where you hear the rolling drum, but a kind of a helpless victory . . ." From there it is an easy step to Christ's victory over temptation, with a quick application to herself: "Was *he* angry, as I was?"

And from there (the whole imaginative complex in which she is now involved) it seems clear that the next step is to the poems, "whose jingling," she told Higginson years later, "cooled my Tramp." To Abiah at this time she can only say, "Dont be afraid of my imprecations, they never did anyone harm, and they make me feel so cool, and so very much more comfortable!"[8]

8. In the third letter to Higginson (*L* II, 408–9, June 7, 1862), ED "thanked [him] for his justice" – his criticism of her poems – "but could not drop the Bells

In this account of a trivial frustration while she was washing dishes (after all, she was not renouncing the young man forever), Emily is not far from one of her finest poems on frustration. The poem tells of defeat, not victory. The victorious though "weary" soldiers of the letter become the "defeated – dying" soldier of the poem; "faintest music" becomes "distant strains." But, with allowances for the differences between a half-serious letter and a completely serious and finely wrought poem, the sense of untasted joys and life's inequity is the same. This was one of the poems that Emily sent to Sue in 1859 with (as we surmised) obvious bearing on their friendship. The poem, whose germ we see in the letter, cut across a wide swathe of her experience, then and later:

> Success is counted sweetest
> By those who ne'er succeed.
> To comprehend a nectar
> Requires sorest need.
>
> Not one of all the purple Host
> Who took the Flag today
> Can tell the definition
> So clear of Victory
>
> As he defeated – dying –
> On whose forbidden ear
> The distant strains of triumph
> Burst agonized and clear!   (#67)

Again, the letter's moment of wonderment about the temptation of Christ is not far from the last few lines of "I measure every Grief I meet":

> A piercing Comfort it affords
> In passing Calvary –
>
> To note the fashions – of the Cross –
> And how they're mostly worn –
> Still fascinated to presume
> That Some – are like My Own –   (#561, about 1862)

Emily concludes the letter to Abiah, still mysteriously. She has just compared herself with Abby Wood, now "a sweet, girl christian . . . full of radiance, holy, yet very joyful," while she, Emily, is "one of the lingering *bad* ones, and so do *I* slink away, and pause, and ponder, and ponder, and pause, and do work without knowing why –" And then, a full ten days having elapsed since she started the letter:

---

whose jingling cooled my Tramp –" It is in this letter also that she spoke of her verses as relieving the "palsy" when "a sudden light on Orchards, or a new fashion in the wind troubled my attention –"

[387

Where do you think I've strayed, and from what new errand returned? I have come from *"to* and *fro,* and walking up, and down" the same place that Satan hailed from, when God asked him where he'd been, but not to illustrate further I tell you I have been dreaming, dreaming a *golden* dream, with eyes all the while wide open, and I guess it's almost morning. . . .

With no further explanation, she takes her leave of the good Abiah—"I presume you are loving your mother, and loving the stranger, and wanderer, visiting the poor, and afflicted, and reaping whole fields of blessings"—but not before she has asked her to "remember, and care for me sometimes, and scatter a fragrant flower in this wilderness life of mine by writing me. . . ."

By late 1850, the time of the next letter, and the last one of importance, Emily is frank about the distance that now separates them: "we are growing away from each other, and talk even now like strangers." Of Abby Wood, also, she writes: "We take different views of life, our thoughts would not dwell together as they used to when we were young." But it is Abiah she favors with the most explicit statement so far of her own emerging "view of life." The metaphors of Job's Satan, the snake, the garden, the Evil Voices are now softened to a metaphor of bud and blossom; but the "wilderness life" becomes life on the open sea, with its dangerous winds and bitter wrecks, compared with the safe shore of Abiah's life:

> . . . You are growing wiser than I am, and nipping in the bud fancies which I let blossom – perchance to bear no fruit, or if plucked, I may find it bitter. The shore is safer, Abiah, but I love to buffet the sea – I can count the bitter wrecks here in these pleasant waters, and hear the murmuring winds, but oh, I love the danger! You are learning control and firmness. Christ Jesus will love you more. I'm afraid he don't love me *any!* . . . Write when you *will,* my friend, and forget all amiss herein, for as these few imperfect words to the full communion of spirits, so this small giddy life to the *better,* the life eternal, and that *we* may live this life, and be filled with this true communion, I shall not cease to pray.

The direction seems as clear "as if the chart were given," even if the goal remained indeterminate in her mind (and in ours, speculative).

If Emily was envisaging and hinting at the life of a poet through all these indirections, she was simply following the strategy recommended in a later poem:

> Tell all the Truth but tell it slant –
> Success in Circuit lies
> Too bright for our infirm Delight
> The Truth's superb surprise
> As Lightning to the Children eased
> With explanation kind
> The Truth must dazzle gradually
> Or every man be blind –   (#*1129, about 1868*)

It may have been the fashion for young ladies to be "poetical," but to be a poet, which meant for Emily Dickinson a bitter break with the "sweet, girl christian" life she was brought up to lead, was something else. To have announced anything of the sort to her young friends or her family would have dazzled them blind; the shock would have been too great. And she herself may have had intimations only.

She returned to the subject, or something approaching it, only once in the subsequent letters to Abiah, which are filled mostly with news, nostalgia, and charming descriptions of this and that. In a letter written shortly after the Commencement in August 1851 when Abiah had unexpectedly come to town, she scolded her for giving her so little time. Like all their youthful intimacies (she wrote), "too quickly *flown* my Bird, for me to satisfy me that you *did* sit and sing beneath my chamber window!" The phrasing here looks forward, surely, to the poem sent to Sue in the "you can go or stay" letter of early September 1854: "I have a Bird in spring / Which for myself doth sing." Again we have a parallel between the growing distance between Emily and Abiah and the later, more agonizing quarrel (and ultimate break) with Sue. By missing a heart-to-heart talk with Emily on this occasion, Abiah had perhaps missed some important confidences:

> I was *disappointed* Abiah – I had been hoping much a little visit from you – when will the hour *be* that we shall sit together and talk of what we were, and what we *are* and may be – with the shutters closed, dear Abiah and the balmiest little breeze stealing in at the window?

What Emily would have told her, had she opened her mind, we can only guess. But whatever else was shaping in her mind, this was certain: she could not be an Abiah, or an Abby Wood, or what Miss Lyon (or her family) would have wanted her to be. She was on the point of making a choice; and in her thinking, which was taking on an increasingly absolutist tinge, it had to be either/or. The commitment—and what better example than Miss Lyon herself, even if the commitment was to a different goal—had to be total. This was not a pleasant experience, for all its "golden dreams." In the letter of late 1850 there is a moment of what looks like agony before the brave words about venturing out into the sea:

> . . . my rebellious thoughts are many, and the friend [Abiah] I love and trust in has much *now* to forgive. I wish I were somebody else – I would pray the prayer of the "Pharisee," but I am a poor little "Publican." "Son of David," look down on me!

Abiah, and all the Abiahs in Amherst and everywhere, had indeed much to forgive. While the Publican humbled himself, saying "God be merciful to me a sinner," the prayer of the Pharisee was sheer pride, and Emily knew it: "God, I thank thee, that I am not as other men are." She had much to feel guilty about. Not only was she a Publican wanting to be a

Pharisee, but she was, in a sense, being disloyal to her two dearest friends and to her family ("They are religious – except me," she wrote Higginson).

We recall that in his Inaugural Address, Dr. Hitchcock had publicly warned against the "fascinations of style, or thought" in modern literature, fascinations that hide "infidelity, or atheism" from the youthful mind delighted with "smartness and brilliancy." No wonder, as she set out in "this wilderness life," that Emily asked Abiah to pray for her. Much time had to elapse before she could say with confidence: "There is always one thing to be grateful for – that one is one's self & not somebody else." Not until about 1863 could she write the poem that, owing so much to Hitchcock in other ways, came close to reconciling those two disparate phases of her being: her love of the God of her fathers and her belief in herself:

> On a Columnar Self –
> How ample to rely
> In Tumult – or Extremity –
> How good the Certainty
>
> That Lever cannot pry –
> And Wedge cannot divide
> Conviction – That Granitic Base –
> Though None be on our Side –
>
> Suffice Us – for a Crowd –
> Ourself – and Rectitude –
> And that Assembly – not far off
> From furthest Spirit – God –   (#789)

If we can only guess that Emily, by all these devious means, was suggesting to Abiah the still vague outline of a career—the career of a poet—the hypothesis (it must remain that) is strengthened by Emily's letters to Jane Humphrey. Jane brought out her best humor and, at least once, what looks like high seriousness. The relevant letters start in January 1850, a few months before Emily's "golden dream" letter to Abiah, and end in 1855. Before then, there is only one, written when Emily was eleven.

The friendship was an old one, probably beginning when Jane came to Amherst to attend the Academy for a brief time and lived with the Dickinsons. The first letter (May 12, 1842) suggests that Jane was a fairly recent and very welcome visitor:

. . . I miss you more and more every day, in my study in play at home indeed every where I miss my beloved Jane – I wish you would write to me – I should think more of it than of a mine of gold . . . what good times we used to have jumping into bed when you slept with me. I do wish you would come to Amherst and make me a great long visit –

Their next contact seems to have been at Mount Holyoke, from which Jane graduated at the end of Emily's year there. During the next academic year (1848–49) Jane was preceptress of Amherst Academy and must have seen much of the Dickinsons. But we know little of their relationship until the correspondence resumes in 1850, when Jane was in her first year of teaching at Warren. Her teaching career, which took her west to Willoughby, Ohio, then back to Groton for the last three years, ended with her marriage in 1858.

In general, the letters are high-spirited, somewhat less moody than the ones to Abiah, and laced with Amherst gossip and doings. They show a developing talent for satire that Emily apparently felt free to indulge with Jane more than with the others. There are some neatly turned passages, like this nostalgic bit, half whimsical, half serious, beginning *in medias res,* on how much she misses Jennie and the old days:

And what will dear Jennie say, if I tell her that selfsame minister preached about her again *today,* text and sermon, and all; morning and afternoon: why, the minister must be mad, or else *my* head is turned, I am sure I dont know which – a little of both, may be! Yet it is'nt Sunday *only,* it's all the days in the week, the *whole seven* of them, that I miss Jennie and re-member the long, sweet days when she was with me here. I think I love you *more* when spring comes – you know we used to sit in the front door, after-noons after school, and the shy little birds would say chirrup, chirrup, in the tall cherry trees, and if our dresses rustled, hop frightened away; and there used to be some farmer cutting down a tree in the woods, and you and I, sitting there, could hear his sharp ax ring. You wont forget it, Jennie, Oh no, I'm sure you wont, for when you are old and gray, it will be a sweet thing to think of, through the long winter's day!

The two most important letters were written in the early months of 1850 (January and April), the year of the revival that caused so much of the anxiety apparent in the letters to Abiah. During the Mount Holyoke year and earlier, Emily may have been merely saddened by her inability to partake in the revival spirit, which was more or less constant in the community; but there are signs in the January letter to Jane that she was beginning to resent it. It emerges here as a threat, if not to her integrity, at least to her privacy, and perhaps to her growing sense of vocation. The January letter carries the theme of her "wickedness" much further than the letters to Abiah, but the tone to Jane is humorous. It is directed, satirically, at the by-products of the religious fervor in the community, the charitable projects, the Sewing Societies, the visits to the sick, and so on—all the good works by which practicing Christians identified them-selves.

Emily starts, as in the January letter to Abiah, with her own plight in the home, with Vinnie away at Ipswich "and my two hands but *two* – not four, or five as they ought to be – and so *many* wants – and me so *very* handy –" But what follows is no semi-tearful account of a romantic disappointment; rather, she takes the offensive in what could stand, for all its high spirits, as her Manifesto against the Age, or New England Piety, or (more precisely) Mary Lyon's doctrine of Work as it had begun to interfere with certain work of her own. And perhaps, in the sense of her own notion that "Mirth is the Mail of Anguish," it is all this. She enlarges on how busy she is:

> . . . and really I came to the conclusion that I should be a villain unparralleled if I took but an inch of time for so unholy a purpose as writing a friendly letter – for what need had *I* of sympathy – or very much less of affection – or less than they all – of friends – mind the house – and the food – *sweep* if the spirits were low – nothing like exercise to strengthen – and invigorate – and help away such foolishness – work makes one strong, and cheerful – and as for society what neighborhood so full as my own? The halt – the lame – and the blind – the old – the infirm – the bed-ridden – and superannuated – the ugly, and disagreeable – the perfectly hateful to me – all *these* to see – and be seen by – an opportunity rare for cultivating meekness – and patience – and submission – and for turning my back to this very sinful, and wicked world. Somehow or other I incline to other things – and Satan covers them up with flowers, and I reach out to pick them. The path of duty looks very ugly indeed – and the place where *I* want to go more amiable – a great deal – it is so much easier to do wrong than right – so much pleasanter to be evil than good, I dont wonder that good angels weep – and bad ones sing songs.

In all her extant letters, she had never complained this way before, so specifically or so extendedly. As she proceeds, very little escapes, even the fun of Amherst that winter. She would exchange all the social hubbub—the *"universale* at the house of Sydney Adams" and the *"confidentiale* at Tempe Linnell's"—for "one evening's talk with the friends I love." Prayer (for Jane's presence) will not be answered, a thought that leads her into blithe irreverence, a tendency to which, like her penchant for satire, she was giving ever freer rein:

> If every prayer was answered, there would be nothing left to pray for – we *must* "suffer – and be strong." *Shall* we be strong – wont suffering make weaker this human – it makes stronger not *us* – but what God gave, and what he will take – mourn our bodies ever so loudly. We do not know that he is God – and *will* try to be still – tho' we really had rather complain. . . . Kavanagh [in Longfellow's novel] says "there will be mourning – mourning – mourning at the judgment seat of Christ" – I wonder if that is true?

For all its light touch, there is a strain of guilt in this letter, which returns to the theme no less than four times. Even the burlesque of the local charity workers is not, as the final two sentences show, without a twinge (at least a simulated one):

Sewing Society has commenced again – and held its first meeting last week – now all the poor will be helped – the cold warmed – the warm cooled – the hungry fed – the thirsty attended to – the ragged clothed – and this suffering – tumbled down world will be helped to it's feet again – which will be quite pleasant to all. I dont attend – notwithstanding my high approbation – which must puzzle the public exceedingly. I am already set down as one of those brands almost consumed – and my hardheartedness gets me many prayers.

Earlier in the letter she rejoices that Jane was teaching in far-off Warren, "out of the way of temptation – and out of the way of the tempter – I didn't mean to make you wicked – but I was – and am – and shall be –" Then, after bemoaning her loneliness without Vinnie and excoriating Fate for taking Jane from her, she sums up: "Is it wicked to talk so Jane – what *can* I say that isn't? Out of a wicked heart cometh wicked words –"

With this bow to Scripture, she turns to cheerful matters free from taint: "There is a good deal going on just now – the two last weeks of vacation were full to the brim of fun": the "uproar" to celebrate Austin's finishing Hume's History, a sleigh ride, the New Year's Eve party at South Deerfield, "comprising charades – walking around *indefinitely* – music – conversation – and supper – set in most modern style; got home at two o'clock – and felt no worse for it the next morning –" So she exorcised the demon of wickedness—and with suspicious ease. Perhaps she had really felt guilty with Abiah but had hesitated to offend her with her confessions. Jane was of tougher stuff, a year older than Emily and Abiah, a graduate of Mount Holyoke, a preceptress, and a teacher. She could pour out her prejudices to Jane, confess her wickednesses with impunity, and feel better for it.

Emily never talked to Abiah, or to anyone else, in quite the way she addressed Jane in the April letter: "my trusty Jane – my friend encourager, and sincere counciller, my rock, and strong assister!" This letter is serious and, taken with similar implications of the one to Abiah written in May, may be crucial. In the January letter to Jane, comparing her life with the life of good works, she had said, "Somehow or other I incline to other things –" She would pick Satan's flowers and sing songs with the bad angels. In April, she goes further, but still tantalizingly.

It takes her some time to get to the point, but two matters induce a serious mood from the outset. She had just heard of the illness of Jane's father (he died the day Emily wrote the letter), and her first paragraphs are full of conventional condolence. She hears "the voice of affliction" and puts on the "wings of affection"; she would "sing, sing sad music" for her distressed friend, would lift her "above this cumbering," could she "speak with a right of Heaven." But she cannot, and this brings her to the second reason for the long preliminary: the Revival and its claims on her, this year particularly intense. At the very time she was inclining toward Satan's flowers and the bad angels, a very different scene, according to her pastor, Aaron Colton, was taking place in the town:

[*393*

. . . the work of God broke forth on the right hand and left. Such a shaking among the dry bones is not often beheld. . . . Evening meetings for prayer and hearing of the Word were crowded to overflowing and pervaded by a death-stillness except as broken by sobs that *could* not be wholly suppressed. . . . Proud and hard hearts that had hitherto resisted every call of God's mercy were now humbled and broken for sin.

As she proceeds in the letter to Jane, Emily gives her own description of the Revival. She shows at once her sympathy for what was going on, her distance from it, and how different her conception of it was from the Reverend Mr. Colton's. There are no "dry bones" here, or sobs in the death-stillness, or proud hearts broken for sin. Nor, be it noted, is there any tendency to make fun of it. She is quite sober:

Christ is calling everyone here, all my companions have answered, even my darling Vinnie believes she loves, and trusts him, and I am standing alone in rebellion, and growing very careless. Abby [Wood], Mary [Warner], Jane [Hitchcock], and farthest of all my Vinnie have been seeking, and they all believe they have found; I cant tell you *what* they have found, but *they* think it is something precious. I wonder if it *is?* How strange is this sanctification, that works such a marvellous change, that sows in such corruption, and rises in golden glory, that brings Christ down, and shews him, and lets him select his friends! In the day time it seems like Sundays, and I wait for the bell to ring, and at evening a great deal stranger, the "still small voice" grows earnest and rings, and returns, and lingers, and all the faces of good men shine, and bright halos come around them; and the eyes of the disobedient look down, and become ashamed. It *certainly* comes from God – and I think to receive it is blessed – not that I know it from *me,* but from those on whom *change* has passed. They seem so very tranquil, and their voices are kind, and gentle, and the tears fill their eyes so often, I really think I envy them.

But if she is sympathetic with all these spiritual manifestations, she cannot share in them. And in such a mood, all she can do for Jane's grief about her father is to "tell you how dearly I love you, if *this* will make you happier."

But she has other things to tell, and now she turns to Jane as "my rock, and strong assister":

I would whisper to you in the evening of many, and curious things – and by the lamps eternal read your thoughts and response in your face, and find what you thought about me, and what I have done, and am doing; I know you would be surprised, whether in pleasure, or disappointment it does'nt become me to say – I have dared to do strange things – bold things, and have asked no advice from any – I have heeded beautiful tempters, yet do not think I am wrong. Oh I have needed my trusty Jane – my friend encourager, and sincere counciller, my rock, and strong assister! I could make you tremble for me, and be very much afraid, and wonder how things would end – Oh Jennie, it would relieve me to tell you all, to sit down at your feet, and look in your eyes, and confess what *you only* shall know, an experience bitter, and sweet, but the sweet did so beguile me – and life has had an aim, and the world has been too precious for your poor – and striving sister! The winter was all one dream, and the spring has not yet waked me, I would *always* sleep, and dream, and it never should turn to morning, so long as night is so blessed. What do you weave from all these threads, for I know you hav'nt been idle the while I've been speaking to you, bring it nearer the window, and I will see, it's all wrong unless it has one gold thread in it, a long, big shining fibre which hides the others – and which will fade away into Heaven while you hold it, and from there come back to me.

"What do you weave from all these threads . . ." indeed! This was the same year in which she taunted her Amherst student friend: "That's what they call a metaphor in our country. Don't be afraid of it, sir, it won't bite." Two questions confront us, as they must have confronted Jane: What was the "one gold thread . . . the long, big shining fibre which hides the others"? And why should she talk in riddles to her trusty friend?

The second question is the easier to answer. Emily's growing fascination for words and their uses can be traced from her eleventh year on. Had we some of her celebrated schoolgirl compositions, we would undoubtedly see the process at work more clearly. When she wrote to Joseph Lyman in the sixties, "We used to think, Joseph, when I was an unsifted girl and you so scholarly that words were cheap & weak. Now I dont know of anything so mighty," she was referring to a change in her attitude from that of the mid-forties, the period of Joseph's visit in the Pleasant Street "Mansion." Emily's early letters squander words prodigally, but with an ever-increasing use of original figure and metaphor. The clichés gradually diminish: Father Time, Jack Frost, tempest in a teapot, the Hill of Science, the rose without thorns, the ceaseless flight of the seasons, and the stock religious phrases that saturated her early vocabulary. On the one hand, the style tightens, as in little satiric thrusts like this one to Austin from Mount Holyoke: "Has the Mexican war terminated yet & how? Are we beat? Do you know of any nation about to besiege South Hadley?" On the other, it gets more lavish but more controlled, as in the elaborate fantasy to her Uncle Joel Norcross or the fantasy on her cold to Abiah. Especially in the former, she reeled out the figures and metaphors, hardly taking breath; but clearly she knew what she was doing. Such a sophisticated piece of writing is a compliment to her uncle's understanding and sense of humor. And toward the conclusion, she momentarily sobered up. Having asked about his health, "bodily, and mentally," and added an irrelevant "no harm done I hope," she thought a long thought:

Harm is one of those things that I always mean to keep clear of – but some-how my intentions and me dont chime as they ought – and people will get hit with stones that I throw at my neighbor's dogs. . . .

What seems to be happening is this: in a world with which she is increasingly feeling at variance, with friend after friend not so much forsaking her as, like Abby Wood, taking such "different views of life" that communication was fruitless, she begins to exploit more and more, even with trusted friends like Abiah and Jane, her powerful new protective weapon of metaphor. Hence the golden dream, the snake, the flowers of Satan, the gold thread, and the beautiful tempters.

The question of what Emily was specifically hinting at through these metaphors may perhaps be answered (however provisionally) in terms of the answer to the second question. She had found a way, through the language of figure and metaphor, to protect herself and to work around and ultimately transcend all that was frustrating her emerging view of life, not only her sense of reality and truth but all her minor irritations, like the Sewing Society. There is ample evidence that by the time she wrote the riddling letters to Abiah and Jane (she was nineteen) she had begun to write poems.

In the "Brother Pegasus" letter to Austin (March 27, 1853) she spoke of being "in the habit *myself* of writing some few things." The verse valentines, which we know come from this period (March 4, 1850, and "*St. Valentine*—'52"), show a versatility and command that indicate considerable practice in versifying. She was finding, first, a way not only to "cool the hurt" by telling it but to tell it so slant that no one would know she had been hurt. Second, she was finding a way (to use the figure in the letter to Joel Norcross) of throwing stones without hurting people. She was getting to the point when everything she said was "wicked," as she told Jane Humphrey. But, unlike her Amherst contemporary, Helen Fiske, a robust and open rebel "quite inclined [at age six] to question the authority of everything," she was not geared to rebellion. She had been a model child, a good girl in school, a dutiful daughter. She had to find another way.

The language of the passage in the letter to Jane—"I have dared to do strange things – bold things, and have asked no advice from any . . . and life has had an aim, and the world has been too precious"—suggests that she had found it. The passage ends in a lyric burst, not always coherent, on the theme of the joy of a new dispensation. And in the last few phrases she seems to be groping—fittingly, it would seem—for a poem.

The lyric conclusion begins with the idea of "belief," but belief in general, surely not the "belief" urged by the Revival, whose insistent claims she had rejected. The whole passage, of course, may refer to a love affair, and the object of her belief may be a young man. But, in a postscript, she relegates to oblivion a certain James Kimball, whom she called "our 'Theologian,'" and adds a notable comment: "Something else has helped me forget *that,* a something surer, and higher, and I sometimes laugh in my sleeve." The impersonal *something* and the words *surer* and *higher* do not suggest a romantic attachment. In what follows she seems to be stating her belief in *this* world (as opposed to the otherworldly concern of the Revival), her belief in human nature (the "Columnar Self"), and her joy in the prospect of a poetic vision—a vision of a world that she as poet could create—that has made all things new for her.

I hope belief is not wicked, and assurance, and perfect trust – and a kind of twilight feeling before the moon is seen – I hope human nature has truth in it – Oh I pray it may not deceive – confide – cherish, have great faith in – do you dream from all this what I mean? Nobody *thinks* of the joy, nobody *guesses* it, to all appearance old things are engrossing, and new ones are not revealed, but there *now* is nothing old, things are budding, and springing, and singing, and you rather think you are in a green grove, and it's branches that go, and come.

Though Emily Dickinson can hardly be counted among those romantic poets, like Wordsworth, who were quite explicit about when and how they discovered they were poets, she seems to be coming close to it here. One looks for corroboration elsewhere in her writing. At least two poems come to mind that, through theme and metaphor, seem related to what she was hinting at to Jane. First, the famous one we have already encountered, "I reckon – when I count at all – / First – Poets – " In the April letter to Jane, she said she felt as if she had been in a dream that lasted all winter; she says that in this exalting new experience "there *now* is nothing old," and "you rather think you are in a green grove," where "things are budding, and springing, and singing"—all ways of suggesting the nature of the created world of the artist, permanent like Keats's Grecian Urn. The last two stanzas of the poem tell why "I write – Poets – All – " and why she prefers their world to the heaven (of the revivalists):

> Their Summer – lasts a Solid Year –
> They can afford a Sun
> The East – would deem extravagant –
> And if the Further Heaven –
>
> Be Beautiful as they prepare
> For those who worship Them –
> It is too difficult a Grace –
> To justify the Dream – (#569, about 1862)

The second poem uses the metaphor of the thread (and needle) to indicate what seems to have been a temporary pause in her writing, perhaps through illness or fatigue. Surely she is talking about more than her domestic handiwork.

> Dont put up my Thread & Needle –
> I'll begin to Sow
> When the Birds begin to whistle –
> Better Stitches – so –
>
> These were bent – my sight got crooked –
> When my mind – is plain
> I'll do seams – a Queen's endeavor
> Would not blush to own – . . .

In saying that she couldn't "see" well enough to write poems she thought were true, Emily may be referring to an agitation of spirit, or the blurring of inward vision resulting from a crisis in her life, or an actual physical difficulty with her eyes, a premonition of the ailment that sent her to Boston in 1864 for extended treatment. This, as she wrote Joseph Lyman sometime in the mid-sixties, was the only "woe . . . that ever made me tremble."

We know that Emily had a great store of metaphors for her poems: flowers, songs, psalms, perhaps the "little green snakes" she warned Abiah about, even dancing, as in the poem she sent Higginson, "I cannot dance upon my Toes – " In the letter to Jane the "one gold thread . . . the long, big shining fibre" may well be the dedication to the life of poetry that (as she told Jane) gave her life "an aim," and (in the poem) the "seams – A Queen's endeavor / Would not blush to own" may refer to the hundreds of poems she knows she has it in her to write when her "sight" gets adjusted and her mind is "plain" again. In both letter and poem it is the spring that is the period of creativity, and in both the creativity is associated with a dream. The poem concludes in an almost arrogant assertion of her confidence in her returning power, with an aside (slightly abrasive?) at the expense of the "Lady" (of the Sewing Society?) who would not be up to the fine and close work Emily will do when she gets back to it:

> Hems – too fine for Lady's tracing
> To the sightless Knot –
> Tucks – of dainty interspersion –
> Like a dotted Dot –
>
> Leave my Needle in the furrow –
> Where I put it down –
> I can make the zigzag stitches
> Straight – when I am strong –
>
> Till then – dreaming I am sowing
> Fetch the seam I missed –
> Closer – so I – at my sleeping –
> Still surmise I stitch – [9]   (#617, about 1862)

9. Another poem involving the metaphor of sewing may also be about her writing poems. Ostensibly it is about a spider; but she worked at night, too, and often, it seems, with little or no light, a reason (it has been suggested) to account for the fact that sometimes her lines went right off the page. She was quite capable of writing on both at once.

> A Spider sewed at Night
> Without a Light
> Upon an Arc of White.
>
> If Ruff it was of Dame
> Or Shroud of Gnome
> Himself himself inform.

Speculations of this sort are no more than this poet's guarded life demands at almost every important juncture from this point on. Jane Humphrey seems to have been made privy in this letter to one of the most important of them all. Emily was at the parting of many ways. Her schooling was over, the "ancient picture" was dissolving, many of her friends were going ways she could not or would not follow. Her last few letters to Jane show her saddened by the death of another of her early friends, Abbie Haskell, in 1851. Jane herself was by then all but out of Emily's life. Emily wrote her the next year at Willoughby, Ohio: "Why so *far*, Jennie, was'nt there room enough for that young ambition, among New England hills?" And she lost her completely, even as a correspondent, when on August 26, 1858, Jane married William H. Wilkinson, a harness manufacturer, and settled in Southwick.

> Of Immortality
> His Strategy
> Was Physiognomy.   (*#1138, about 1869*)

Her "strategy" by this time (about 1869) was her poetry. She more and more used the word "immortality" in this generalized, semiliterary sense.

18

Early Friendships II

I F WE WOULD KNOW more about the Amherst girls in Emily's circle, our ignorance about the young men is even more tantalizing. The problem, of course, is documentation. It has been estimated that we have about a tenth of all the letters Emily Dickinson wrote, and probably less than a thousandth of those written to her. The letters to Abiah, Emily Fowler, Jane Humphrey, and Susan Gilbert allow us to talk fairly confidently about these young ladies, although we would give a great deal to know what they wrote to her. But as for the young men who we know came almost daily in and out of the Dickinson house, spent many an evening in talk and currant wine, escorted the Dickinson girls to lectures, concerts, sleigh rides, promenades, and all the other functions a college town with its inexhaustible supply of young males can provide—as for these, the source of much of the color of Emily's young life, we have little more than bits and scraps, an invitation here and there, a few valentines, and brief, often cryptic, messages.

And where the allurements of romance coincide with a knowledge vacuum, legends flourish. They have flourished, unfortunately, here. Most of the rumors center on Edward Dickinson as chief spoiler of his daughter's chances of romantic happiness, and speculation has been active from the first as to who among the dozen or so frequenters of the Dickinson household broke Emily's heart and cut her life in two. The dubious assumption behind it all is that Emily was staking her life on romantic happiness and, when that failed her, gave up and withdrew. At this point we would do well to look at the leading contenders and assess what we actually do know about them. This process may, in turn, help resolve the problem.

One certainty is that Benjamin Franklin Newton, a law student in Edward Dickinson's office from 1847 to 1849, was important in Emily's formative years. She herself said so. The evidence is firm, although it comes not from any surviving correspondence between the two but mainly from a letter Emily wrote, shortly after Newton's death early in 1853, to his minister in Worcester, the Reverend Mr. Edward Everett Hale. Newton was nine years older than Emily, a young man of rare qualities and the first (with the possible exception of Leonard Humphrey) whom Emily regarded as one of those older men she called variously her tutor, preceptor, or master. Her letter to Hale, of whom she inquired as to Newton's spiritual state at the time of his death, is one of the few we have addressed to a complete stranger. It is formal, yet simple, direct, and almost entirely free from the sentimental pose of the elegiac passage on Humphrey. This time, she is more concerned with the deceased than with herself, and her account of Newton is objective and discerning. The style is under full control.

REV MR HALE –

Pardon the liberty Sir, which a stranger takes in addressing you, but I think you may be familiar with the last hours of a Friend, and I therefore transgress a courtesy, which in another circumstance, I should seek to observe. I think, Sir, you were the Pastor of Mr B. F. Newton, who died sometime since in Worcester, and I often have hoped to know if his last hours were cheerful, and if he was willing to die. Had I his wife's acquaintance, I w'd not trouble you Sir, but I have never met her, and do not know where she resides, nor have I a friend in Worcester who could satisfy my inquiries. You may think my desire strange, Sir, but the Dead was dear to me, and I would love to know that he sleeps peacefully.

Mr. Newton was with my Father two years, before going to Worcester – in pursuing his studies, and was much in our family.

I was then but a child, yet I was old enough to admire the strength, and grace, of an intellect far surpassing my own, and it taught me many lessons, for which I thank it humbly, now that it is gone. Mr Newton became to me a gentle, yet grave Preceptor, teaching me what to read, what authors to admire, what was most grand or beautiful in nature, and that sublimer lesson, a faith in things unseen, and in a life again, nobler, and much more blessed –

Of all these things he spoke – he taught me of them all, earnestly, tenderly, and when he went from us, it was as an elder brother, loved indeed very much, and mourned, and remembered. During his life in Worcester, he often wrote to me, and I replied to his letters – I always asked for his health, and he answered so cheerfully, that while I knew he was ill, his death indeed surprised me. He often talked of God, but I do not know certainly if he was his Father in Heaven – Please Sir, to tell me if he was willing to die, and if you think him at Home, I should love so much to know certainly, that he was today in Heaven. Once more, Sir, please forgive the audacities of a Stranger, and a few lines, Sir, from you, at a convenient hour, will be received with gratitude, most happy to requite you, sh'd it have opportunity.

Yours very respectfully,
EMILY E. DICKINSON

P.S. Please address your reply to Emily E. Dickinson – Amherst – Mass –

Why Emily should have worried about Mr. Hale's thinking it strange of her to ask if Newton were "willing to die" is itself strange, since the question was a common one in her day. It was a test of faith. Such a question need not mean that she was obsessed or overburdened with thoughts of death. Her inquiry was the first of many similar ones she directed to men, mostly ministerial and always older than she, whom she regarded as able to help her with ultimate questions—the sort of questions, according to the letter, Newton must have talked to her about when he was her "grave Preceptor."

The letter clearly defines Newton's role as older brother, criterion intellect, friend and guide in matters aesthetic and spiritual. We see Emily, in her mid-teens, already reaching out for the qualities of a mind "far surpassing" her own, and responding to its "gentle, yet grave" instruction. She loved him—he "was dear to me"—but whatever romantic hopes she may have had are not apparent in her restrained rhetoric. It was Newton who, the year after he left Edward Dickinson's office, sent her a copy of Emerson's poems,[1] and it is generally thought that he was the "friend [she wrote Higginson in 1862] who taught me Immortality – but venturing too near, himself – he never returned –"[2] Twice she spoke of

1. On January 23, 1850, Emily wrote to Jane Humphrey (L I, 84): "I had a letter – and Ralph Emerson's Poems – a beautiful copy – from Newton the other day. I should love to read you them both – they are very pleasant to me. I can write him in about three weeks – and I *shall*."

2. L II, 404 (April 25, 1862). Leyda (*YH* I, liv) thinks it likely that Emily was referring to Jacob Holt, a student in Amherst Academy in the early 1840s who had come to practice dentistry in Amherst in August 1845 after a period of study and practice in Boston. He had published several verses in the *Northampton Courier* that Emily must have seen. His health was poor, and Emily inquired about him three times in letters to Austin from Mount Holyoke. He died of tuberculosis on May 14, 1848, and was memorialized by some verses in the *Hampshire and Franklin Express* for May 18. On June 8 the *Express* printed "the following brief but expressive lines written by Dr. Holt during his sickness:"

THE BIBLE

'Tis a pure and holy word,
'Tis the wisdom of a God,
'Tis a fountain full and free,
'Tis the Book for *you* and *me;*
'Twill the soul's best anchor be
Over life's tempestuous sea,
A guardian angel to the tomb,
A meteor in the world's dark gloom;
'Tis a shining sun at even,
'Tis a *diamond dropt from heaven.*

Emily copied the poem on the back leaf of her Bible and pasted an obituary notice beside it (*YH* I, 147). Whether it was Ben Newton or Jacob Holt who taught Emily Dickinson immortality is a question that may never be answered with certainty. It may be worth pointing out that the "friend" mentioned in the letter to Higginson is pretty clearly the same as "My dying Tutor" of the next letter to Higginson (L II,

him as her earliest friend. Three days after he died (March 24, 1853) she wrote a brief postscript to a long and cheerful letter to Austin (perhaps another instance of telling "no one the cause of my grief"):

> Love from us all. Monday noon. Oh Austin, Newton is dead. The first of my own friends. Pace.

The letter to Hale, for whatever reason, waited a full nine months. His reply, if any, has not survived. She wrote him again, "several springs" later (1856?):

> My dear Mr. Hale.
>   Perhaps you forget a Stranger Maid, who several springs ago – asked of a friend's Eternity –, and if in her simplicity –, she still remembers you, and culls for you a Rose and hopes upon a purer morn, to pluck you buds serener – please pardon her, and them.
>
> With sweet respect
Your friend,
Emilie E. Dickinson[3]

Twenty years later, Newton was still on her mind (to Higginson, spring 1876):

> My earliest friend wrote me the week before he died "If I live, I will go to Amherst – if I die, I certainly will."

Newton's greatest distinction is that among all her early friends, male or female, he seems to be the only one who understood her poetic promise—or the only one, at least, for whom there is evidence that this is so. There are two scraps, slim but convincing. The first is an inscription he wrote in Emily's autograph album before he left Amherst:

> All can write Autographs, but few paragraphs; for we are mostly no more than *names*.

The second is a remark of Emily's in her third letter to Higginson thanking him for his criticism of her poetry. The passage indicates not only Newton's influence in shaping her career but how early it was (at least 1853, when Newton died) she began thinking of herself as a poet.

> My dying Tutor told me that he would like to live till I had been a poet, but Death was much of Mob as I could master – then –

Newton's discernment underscores, of course, the lack of it in her other friends and advisors like Higginson, Emily Fowler Ford, Dr. Holland,

---

408; June 7, 1862). There is no record of any association with Holt such as Emily enjoyed with Newton, who had been "much in our family." The *Express* for May 18, 1848, says that Holt was twenty-six when he died (*YH* I, 144), which would make him eight years Emily's senior.

3. The MS of this letter, recently discovered in Hale's papers, is in the Lilly Library, University of Indiana, and is printed here by permission.

Samuel Bowles. His death, coming at a time when the distance between Emily and all her young friends was growing, cut off her most promising hope for literary guidance and encouragement. Looking back, she may have seen how serious his loss was, and our wonder lessens at her hyperbole when she told Higginson in 1862 that "for several years, my Lexicon – was my only companion –"

Nevertheless, to take this remark to Higginson literally and regard Emily as lonely and bereft for the several years following March 24, 1853, is to succumb to her hyperbole and slip into a stock aspect of the Myth. The annals of the town and her family record enough activity, social and otherwise, for the next year or so to make any such simplification of her life impossible. Her friendship with Sue was still warm; they were seeing a great deal of each other. She wrote to Sue in September 1854 about having "a great deal of company"—the suggestion is, too much. And there were at least two young men, her distant cousin John Graves and his friend Henry Vaughan Emmons, who paid her much—and welcome—attention until they graduated from the college (Emmons in 1854, Graves in 1855) and went their ways.

Perhaps John Graves, simply because of his cousinship (Emily habitually addressed him as "Cousin John"), should not count as a romantic possibility, although he was an exceptionally handsome and capable young man. Born in Sunderland, he was a year younger than Emily and related to the Dickinsons through the Gunn family. He made his first call on his kinsfolk early in his freshman year and was a frequent visitor from then on. Emily went to a concert with him, knitted wristlets for him, played music for him, asked him in (with Emmons) for currant wine. During the family's Washington visit in 1854, Emily and Susan Gilbert were left behind in the Pleasant Street house under Graves's protection. When he and Emmons quarreled during his junior year, Emily was much concerned for his happiness and rejoiced at their reconciliation.

Her letters to him, except two, are mostly brief messages, arch and sprightly. One, an invitation, is in ingenious verse—her favorite "8's" and "6's," but strung out in four long lines of "14-ers" to look like prose; the rhymes are only approximate, and there are no capital letters to set off the lines. (I have added slash marks to indicate verse divisions.)

A little poem we will write/unto our Cousin John,/to tell him if he does not come/and see us very soon,/we will immediately forget/there's any such a man,/and when he comes to see us,/we will not be "at home."

Such fooling might lead one to write off the relationship as merely casual were it not for several other indications, one from an outside source and two from Emily herself. The first is Eliza Coleman's remark in a letter to

Graves (October 4, 1854), cited earlier as a sign of the growing breach between Emily and the Amherst community. Here it shows that she was not without some understanding friends:

> *Emilie* . . . sends me beautiful letters & each one makes me love her more. I know you appreciate her & I think few of her Amherst friends do. They wholly misinterpret her, I believe –

Who these friends were who misinterpreted her, and what Eliza's evidence was, we would like to know, unless her remark is simply an indication of the general response of the community to Emily's increasingly offish attitude toward Amherst piety and good works. In such a situation a loyal and handsome cousin was good to have. About the time Eliza wrote to Graves, Emily wrote quite happily to Sue:

> Father and mother were gone last week, upon a little journey, and we rioted somewhat, like most ungodly children – John came down twice from Sunderland, to pass a day with us.

The two letters in which Emily put her heart out to John came toward the end of their association. He graduated with high honors in August 1855, giving the Philosophical Oration at Commencement (on "Philological Philosophy"). Next spring, in late April, Emily wrote him a letter of the sort we have seen paralleled in several of her early correspondences. It was tender, nostalgic, poetical—a little elegy on the end of things, strange in the April setting, but appropriate to what she saw, perhaps, as the end of their relationship. The day was Sunday, the family had gone to church. She set the scene (the Dickinsons were now in the house on Main Street, with its greater space and evergreen trees and "crumbling wall" that divided their land from the Sweetsers') and began to tell John what she saw from her vantage point and "what I would that you saw – " In the account, she seems to be reaching for a poem, or poems; details of the scene take on instant symbolism, the lyric impulse surges, and with the sentence beginning "Much that is gay," the language becomes metrical. The climax (in the final sentence, set off in a paragraph) shows her triumphing over the mortuary theme.

> You remember the crumbling wall that divides us from Mr Sweetser – and the crumbling elms and evergreens – and *other* crumbling things – that spring, and fade, and cast their bloom within a simple twelvemonth – well – *they* are *here,* and skies on me fairer far than Italy, in blue eye look down – up – see! – away – a league from here, on the way to Heaven! And here are Robins – just got home – and giddy Crows – and Jays – and will you trust me – as I live, here's a *bumblebee* – not such as *summer* brings – John – earnest, manly bees, but a kind of a Cockney, dressed in jaunty clothes. Much that is gay – have I to show, if you were with me, John, upon this April grass – then there are *sadder* features – here and there, *wings* half gone to dust, that fluttered so, last year – a mouldering plume, an empty house, in which

a bird resided. Where last year's flies, their errand ran, and last year's *crickets fell!* We, too, are flying – fading, John – and the song "here lies," soon upon lips that love us now – will have hummed and ended.

To live, and die, and mount again the triumphant body, and *next* time, try the upper air – is no schoolboy's theme!

That Emily did not attend church that morning with her family probably gained her no good will either from her family or from the congregation—one of the reasons, perhaps, for Eliza's concern about her being misinterpreted. Only John Graves could have known what she was up to. And few besides John (and Austin?) in Amherst would not have been shocked by the way she carried on (in the next passage of the letter) with a veritable burlesque of the Resurrection—and this during the Easter season:

It is a jolly thought to think that we can be Eternal – when air and earth are *full* of lives that are gone – and done – and a conceited thing indeed, this promised Resurrection! *Congratulate* me – John – Lad – and "here's a health to *you*" – that we have each a *pair* of lives, and need not chary be, of the one "that *now* is" –
Ha – ha – if any can afford – 'tis *us* a roundelay!

The rest of the letter tapers off into nostalgia: "Mid your momentous cares [as schoolteacher in Orford, New Hampshire], pleasant to know that 'Lang Syne' has it's own place – " She speaks of "those triumphant days – Our April," the spring when she and Sue and John were alone in the Pleasant Street house, and she recalls one particularly haunting memory of those days, or rather nights, when she entertained John (and woke up Sue) with her piano.

If Newton was one of the very few to understand her poetic promise, John Graves was among the few who, of all her contemporaries who must have heard her play, has left on record his impression of her music, a major interest, especially in her early years, and one worth a brief comment. Many years later, his daughter wrote the following account of her father's visits with the Dickinsons:

Oftentimes, during these visits to the Dickinson relatives, father would be awakened from his sleep by heavenly music. Emily would explain in the morning, "I can improvise better at night." On one or two occasions, when not under their friendly roof, my father, in paying his respects at the house, would receive a message from his cousin Emily, saying, "If you will stay in the next room, and open the folding doors a few inches, I'll come down to make music for you." My father said that in those early days she seemed like a will-o-the-wisp.[4]

4. YH I, 301–2. The quotation is from an article by Gertrude M. Graves in the Boston *Sunday Globe*, January 12, 1930. See *L* I, 19 n.: "No reliable account of her playing has been preserved, though Mrs. Bianchi recorded [*Emily Dickinson Face to Face*, p. 157] her mother's memory of ED's improvisations." Just how musical she

Emily's letter describes one of those haunting moments:

I play the old, odd tunes yet, which used to flit about your head after honest hours – and wake dear Sue, and madden me, with their grief and fun – How far from us, that spring seems –

This was not the only time she played for him, since John was often asked to spend the night in the Dickinson house when Mr. and Mrs. Dickinson were away. The tunes she played for John were apparently her own. She had outgrown the "beautiful pieces" she boasted to Abiah about learning when she was fourteen—"The Grave of Bonaparte," "Lancers Quick Step," and "Maiden Weep No More"—just as she was outgrowing (the parallel may not be too extravagant) the kind of poetry that was then in vogue. Her particular talent, it seems, was for improvising, and she did it better at night—a clue, perhaps, to her literary habits, since her letters often refer to her writing when all the others were asleep. (She wrote Austin on March 14, 1854: "Then I wrote a long letter to Father . . . then crept to bed softly, not to wake all the folks, who had been asleep a long time.")

At any rate, the nocturnal sessions that John was privileged to hear are of no little significance in what they tell us about her music and the part it played in her developing poetic career. In the early days she enjoyed most of the musical opportunities of the neighborhood. She took lessons in voice and piano. She heard Jenny Lind in Northampton in 1851 (*"Herself*, and not her music," she wrote Austin, "was what we seemed to love"); in 1853, Graves took her and Vinnie to a concert by the famous Germania Serenade Band, then on a national tour (she called them *"brazen Robins"*); she spoke of a pleasant meeting of the "girls 'Musical' " at her house in April 1853 and (perhaps) of being unable to attend another some six years later.

But all this time she was getting deeper and deeper into a music of a different sort. In her second letter to Higginson she wrote that "the noise in the Pool, at Noon – excels my Piano." As her practical interest in music declined, her metaphoric interest increased. In trying to capture in her poetry the "music" of nature, she put to use all she had learned about music as a child, and in college, and from the hymns she heard in church, whose metrical schemes were to become her chosen and all but exclusive

---

was (*Home,* p. 153) is "hard to say. . . . One [Clara Newman Turner; cf. Appendix II, 3] who heard her strange, limited repertoire said that before seating herself at the piano Emily covered the upper and lower octaves so that the length of the keyboard might correspond to that of the old-fashioned instrument on which she had learned to play." At least twice, in later years, she asked friends to sing for her (Nora Green and Mabel Todd) and listened to them, in her odd way, from upstairs (*YH* II, 273, 357). Kate Scott Anthon, in a letter to Martha Bianchi, October 8, 1917, recalled those "blissful evenings at Austin's" (in the late 1850s) when Emily was "often at the piano playing weird & beautiful melodies, all from her own inspiration . . ." (*YH* I, 367).

form.[5] At a crucial point in her career, her "business," she said, was to *"sing"*; she wished for her nephew's sake that the Bible had a "warbling Teller"; she asked the Norcross cousins, during a time of bereavement, to "Let Emily sing for you because she cannot pray"—all metaphors that grew out of a lifetime's association with the thing itself. She had shifted from the old music to the new, but the old lived on as part of her poetry.

A poem of about 1860 shows the change. All the early part is here—the hymns, carrying the "treble" in the choirs at the Academy and Mount Holyoke, even the Germania Band in full regalia. But the poem concerns another kind of music:

> Musicians wrestle everywhere –
> All day – among the crowded air
> I hear the silver strife –
> And – waking – long before the morn –
> Such transport breaks upon the town
> I think it that "New life"!
>
> It is not Bird – it has no nest –
> Nor "Band" – in brass and scarlet – drest –
> Nor Tamborin – nor Man –
> It is not Hymn from pulpit read –
> The "Morning Stars" the Treble led
> On Time's first Afternoon!
>
> Some – say – it is "the Spheres" – at play!
> Some say – that bright Majority
> Of vanished Dames – and Men!
> Some – think it service in the place
> Where we – with late – celestial face –
> Please God – shall Ascertain!   (#157)

5. For ED's use of the hymn meters, see Thomas H. Johnson, *Emily Dickinson: An Interpretive Biography*, pp. 84 ff. Copies of Isaac Watts's *Christian Psalmody* and *The Psalms, Hymns, and Spiritual Songs* were in Edward Dickinson's library. David T. Porter, *The Art of Emily Dickinson's Early Poetry* (1966), p. 55, speaks of her lifelong use of hymn meters as "a constant occasion for irony," as she used the orthodox form to express unorthodox views. (He discusses the subject at length in his fourth chapter.) Leonard Conversi brought to my attention the similar practice of Thomas Hardy, who used "Common Measure" (as John Crowe Ransom points out) for heretical poems: "There are no churches, nor hymns, which will embody or publish Hardy's peculiar views." Ransom speculates on Hardy's early experience of the hymns, in many ways applicable to ED's: "Hardy would have known it [the common measure] very well from the many hymns he had sung as a youth. Their tunes lingered nostalgically in his mind even after he had lost his faith, and we find him writing poems about them. At any rate, the scruple of good workmanship shows just as clearly in hymnology as in architecture; and in the visual and aural versions of a poem as in the meaningful" (*Selected Poems of Thomas Hardy*, 1961, pp. xiv–xv). "Common Measure" (or Meter) is the "8's" and "6's" referred to above.

Even the hint of ambivalence in her reminiscence to John Graves about the old tunes that "maddened" her is present here in the "wrestling" musicians and the "silver strife," a motif which recurs in many phrases and figures in her later writing. In 1873 the pianist Anton Rubinstein made her think of "polar nights," and in a poem of about 1879 she wrote of "The fascinating chill that music leaves." In the poem "There's a certain Slant of light," the light of the sun on the landscape late winter afternoons "oppresses, like the Heft / Of Cathedral Tunes – " Once she remarked to Higginson that the change of the seasons "hurt almost like Music – shifting when it ease us most." Curiously, the words "melody" or "harmony" usually had no such association for her; but "music" *hurt*. It may not be too farfetched to say that in her poetry she found a medium more viable in a quite literal sense. She could live with it—it was her true medium, as music was not, no matter how "heavenly" her music sounded to the appreciative John Graves.[6]

But the "triumphant days" and the musical evenings were soon over. After graduation and several years of teaching at Orford Academy, where he married Frances Britton on September 1, 1858, Graves studied for the ministry and was ordained pastor of a new Congregational church in Boston on January 4, 1860. He soon gave it up and went into business. When Edward Dickinson died suddenly in Boston in 1874, Graves came to Amherst to help with the family and give what information he could about the circumstances of the death. If he saw Emily and talked with her, there is no record of it. His daughter wrote that whenever he spoke of her in later years "there was about him a kind of glow," and he would say, "unlike anyone else – a grace, a charm . . ."

What she thought about him, how deep her feeling went, can only be conjectured. A hint that it was more than casual is in her last, or next-to-last, letter to him (the date is uncertain).[7] It is a brief note and may have been written well before he left Amherst. It may have arisen from some minor contretemps and thus have been partly playful. Or, as with many of her early friendships about this time, it may have meant the end.

6. That, at a certain point, she made a professional decision about music is suggested in Clara Bellinger Green's memory of her conversation with ED after Nora Green sang for her: "She told us of her early love for the piano and confided that, after hearing Rubinstein [?] – I believe it was Rubinstein – play in Boston, she had become convinced that she could never master the art and had forthwith abandoned it once and for all, giving herself up then wholly to literature" (*YH* II, 273).

7. *L* II, 330. Here, on the basis of the handwriting, the conjectured date is "about 1856," and the letter printed *after* the "Lang Syne" letter. *YH* I, 327, however, suggests mid-January 1855 as the date and prints it well *before* the "Lang Syne" letter, juxtaposing it with the "box of Phantoms" letter to Sue. But neither the handwriting nor the duplication of phrasing can be regarded as conclusive. At best, the evidence of the handwriting is imprecise within a year or so, and frequently ED used similar phrases in letters and poems years apart. I print the shorter letter last because we know that, historically, the friendship did come to an end about this time (although Graves never lost touch with the Dickinsons and cherished his memory of Emily). The shorter letter can stand, at least symbolically, as a *Hic finis est*.

Ah John – *Gone?*

Then I lift the lid to my box of Phantoms, and lay another in, unto the Resurrection – Then will I gather in *Paradise,* the blossoms fallen here, and on the shores of the sea of Light, seek my missing sands.

Your Coz –
E M I L I E .

The phrase "my box of Phantoms" occurs—or recurs—in the letter to Sue written during their quarrel early in 1855, where the phrase does signify an end, or the possibility of one. The image is a strong one, with perhaps a touch of bitterness. Was she beginning to think that the way of all friendships was phantasmal? Many had failed her, they were melting away; and John's appears to be another one. In these years, surely, she was reaching out for something that would not fail her—"something surer, and higher," as she had written Jane, the "one gold thread . . . a long, big shining fibre which hides the others – " A little later she could write, with more assurance than she seems to have had in the early 1850s:

> I shall keep singing!
> Birds will pass me
> On their way to Yellower Climes –
> Each – with a Robin's expectation –
> I – with my Redbreast –
> And my Rhymes –
>
> Late – when I take my place in summer –
> But – I shall bring a fuller tune –
> Vespers – are sweeter than Matins – Signor –
> Morning – only the seed of Noon –   (*#250, about 1861*)

By then she had found her vocation, and from the early disappointments learned the "fuller tune" that would one day (she is confident) give her a place among the poets.

There was not even an observant daughter to tell us what Henry Vaughan Emmons thought of Emily Dickinson. The gap is peculiarly tantalizing; for, except for Newton, her relationship with Emmons was the closest to a literary one among her early friends of any on record. It was not exclusively that, of course. In a letter to Sue Gilbert late in February 1852, she told of finding "a beautiful, new, friend," in all probability *"Sophomore Emmons"* with whom (as she wrote to Austin a few weeks earlier) she had been to ride "alone." She promised to tell Austin "all about it when I write again," but the closest she got to it was a remark in a letter a year and a half later about a similar excursion that had been repeated many times in the interim: "I am glad you are glad that I went to ride with Emmons." Also by then there had been (or were soon to be) many calls and sociable evenings, a gift of arbutus, a valentine, an exchange of books and (perhaps) manuscripts.

Emmons first enters the Amherst annals by way of William Gardiner Hammond's diary, under circumstances that are colorful indeed for a young man who later became an active evangelical preacher. In his entry for March 18, 1848, two years before Emmons entered Amherst College, Hammond described a mission with his friend Jacob Ide:

> After dinner, accepted Ide's invitation to ride to Easthampton with him, but met [in] Northampton the boy he was going to see, a bright, black-eyed son of Judge Emmons, of Hallowell [Maine]: the same who ran away from home, some time ago. He had a letter of introduction to a family of young ladies in Hadley, and was going over there to spend Sunday, so after staying long enough in Northampton, to have our hair cut, etc., we took him with us on our return.

The young ladies turned out to be beautiful but "guarded by a perfect dragon of a cross old father" (an opprobrium Edward Dickinson seems to have escaped). Two years later, Jacob Ide, '48, introduced this same ex-runaway to Professor Aaron Warner, Mary's father:

> Mr Henry V. Emmons, the Bearer, has expressed a preference for Amherst as the place of his education. . . . He is a young gentleman of an amiable disposition & engaging manners. He has promising talents, is a bright scholar, & sustains a fair moral & religious character.

It was not long before Emmons had established himself in the good graces of the Dickinsons—probably through Cousin John Graves—and as a leader in the college. When Daniel Webster died on October 24, 1852, Emmons and Rufus Choate, Jr., were among the five students who drew up a set of resolutions in his honor, the college voting to wear a badge of mourning for thirty days. In scholarship, Emmons justified Ide's recommendation. He presented a "Dissertation" at the Spring Exhibition of the college, on the subject "Sympathy in Action"; and he gave two orations during his college course, both on weighty subjects: "Influence of the Belief in a Resurrection on Law" and (at his Commencement) "Sources of Originality."

It would be pleasant to think that some of his ideas on originality (or on sympathy, or the Resurrection) came from his association with his friend Emily Dickinson. There was plenty of opportunity, either in conversation or in correspondence. Her few surviving notes to him show that they must have communicated a good deal on such matters. The notes begin, presumably, in the spring of 1853, the date of the first on the assumption that she referred in the first sentence to Emmons' essay on Sympathy. But there seems to be another and more important reference in the letter.

MR EMMONS –

Since receiving your beautiful writing I have often desired to thank you thro' a few of my flowers, and arranged the fairest for you a little while ago, but heard you were away –

I have very few today, and they compare but slightly with the immortal blossoms you kindly gathered me, but will you please accept them – the "Lily of the field" for the blossoms of Paradise, and if 'tis ever mine to gather those which fade not, from the garden we have not seen, you shall have a brighter one than I can find today.

EMILIE E. DICKINSON

Whatever the "beautiful writing" was (the essay or something else), "a few of my flowers," in view of Emily's increasingly metaphoric mode, are pretty clearly her poems. Certainly the "immortal blossoms you kindly gathered me" are the beautiful thoughts he sent her; and the flowers (in the last sentence) "which fade not, from the garden we have not seen" are as clearly the poems she will one day write. The "Lily of the field" which she sends him now, though dated "about 1862" in the 1955 *Poems*, may have already been in her portfolio.

> Through the Dark Sod – as Education –
> The Lily passes sure –
> Feels her white foot – no trepidation –
> Her faith – no fear –
>
> Afterward – in the Meadow –
> Swinging her Beryl Bell –
> The Mold-life – all forgotten – now –
> In Extasy – and Dell – (#392)

The theme of the poem, at least, is appropriate to the early date, with Emily having finished her schooling and Emmons nearing the end of his.[8]

More flower talk came in a little note written presumably that same spring, but this time the association with some writing (her own?) is closer:

Thank you, indeed, Mr Emmons, for your beautiful acknowledgement, far brighter than my flowers; and while with pleasure I *lend* you the little manuscript, I shall beg leave to claim it, when you again return. I trust you will find much happiness in an interview with your friend, and will be very happy to see you, when you return.

EMILIE E. DICKINSON

8. Although this is a suggestion only, it brings up the difficulty of dating the poems by their position in the packets (or "fascicles"). The date of #392 in *Poems* is inferred from its position in packet No. 21, which contains poems written in the handwriting of that year. But for this packet ED may have copied poems written much earlier. (For an explanation of the "packets" or "fascicles," see below, pp. 537–8.)

And still later (next spring?) came some more flowers, with another Lily in question: "I said I should send some flowers this week. I had rather not until next week – My Vale Lily asked me to wait for her. I told her if you were willing –" Since there is no reason to believe that Emmons was a horticulturalist or even much interested in the real thing, we can only assume that this was metaphoric talk, a special language between them.

A project Emmons led during the fall of his junior year shows what in Emily Dickinson would have attracted him most. As chairman of a committee, he reported:

> We would earnestly recommend the revival of a college magazine – for the following reasons – First – Because Amherst College needs it – The new interest awakened in the litterary societies demands every opportunity for the cultivation of the ability of their members. . . .

Emily was by no means aloof from such activities in the early 1850s and may have been in Emmons' mind as he continued:

> [Amherst's] great want imperatively demands it – that the impression – so fatal to many of our great interests – which now prevails so generally in a large portion of the community – be done away with – we mean the impression that Amherst College – lacks cultivation – literary power – literary advantages. . . .

The *Amherst Collegiate Magazine,* which resulted from these efforts, printed in its July 1854 issue (the summer Emmons graduated) an essay by him entitled "The Words of Rock Rimmon," ending with three lines of verse. In the last of her (extant) letters to him, Emily gracefully applied these lines to the "journey" whose beginning his Commencement celebrated.

> A pleasant journey to you, both in the pathway home, and in the longer way – *Then* "golden morning's open flowings, *shall* sway the trees to murmurous bowings, in metric chant of blessed poems" –

—the last phrase perhaps a tribute to their strongest mutual interest.

A puzzling note, with further literary applications, appears in the earlier paragraphs of this letter, where something new—gems—is added to the flower motif:

> I find it Friend – I read it – I stop to thank you for it, just as the world is still – I thank you for them all – the pearl, and then the onyx, and then the emerald stone.
> My crown, indeed! I do not fear the king, attired in this grandeur.
> Please send me gems again – I have a flower. It looks like them, and for it's bright resemblances, receive it.

The ingenious suggestion has been made that she is thanking Emmons for a farewell gift of a book, perhaps Poe's poems because of the initial letters of pearl, onyx, and emerald. But there are difficulties. Years later Emily wrote Higginson, "Of Poe, I know too little to think," the only time on record she broke her silence on the subject of Poe. It hardly seems as if his poems ever could have been her "crown." Perhaps the gift was a sheaf of Emmons' own poems, and when she asked him to "Please send me gems again," she may have been asking for more. This seems more likely than "send me more Poe" and perhaps accounts for the "flower" (a poem?) she asked him to receive in return.[9]

Finally, the last, one-sentence paragraph of this letter—"Have I convinced you Friend?"—continues the riddling. The letter is signed "Pleasantly, Emily." Emily wrote to Sue, shortly after, about the "sweet Commencement week" just past and the many long talks she had had with Emmons and the "charming farewell ride" they had together. "He stayed more than a week," she added, "after Commencement was done, and came to see me often." She told Sue about Emmons' friend whom he brought "to pass the day with me . . . Her name is Susie too. . . ." The day passed "very sweetly." But this was not so of Emmons' engagement to Susan Phelps of Hadley. It was broken five years later, on May 8, 1860, amid general sorrow. Emily had kept in touch. She wrote a one-sentence note to Susan Phelps that month: " 'When thou goest through the Waters, I will go with thee.' " But no note to Emmons has survived. What part (if any) Emily had in the breakup of the engagement must remain problematical. Questions, however, have been asked.[10] But, for all the long talks at Commencement and the sweet farewell ride and the mutual interest in literature, there is no hint that their relationship ever approached marriage. Emmons was interested in other girls from his junior year on. He studied in the Bangor Theological Seminary from 1856 to 1859 and married Ann Shepard, daughter of George C. Shepard, longtime friend of the Dickinsons and Mrs. Boltwood's niece, on September 6,

---

9. *L* II, 649 (December 1879). Helen H. Arnold (" 'From the Garden We Have Not Seen': New Letters of Emily Dickinson," *New England Quarterly* XVI, September 1943, p. 370) suggested: "The volume of poems which he lent her was perhaps his choicest collection, or . . . one of the 'Gift Volumes' in vogue at that time." Aurelia G. Scott ("Emily Dickinson's 'Three Gems,' " *NEQ* XVI, December 1943, pp. 627–28) suggested Poe on the basis of "a not uncommon custom" to give presents of rings set with gems whose initial letters spelled a name. (She cites Goethe's gift of such a ring to Rosette Städel.) Most commentators seem tacitly to have accepted this suggestion.

10. See Leyda, *YH* I, xlv: ". . . the documents of Emmons' years immediately after graduation are so unsatisfying that we cannot answer the questions they raise: Why did Susan Phelps break her engagement with Emmons? Did ED's friendship with Emmons develop after his graduation to become a factor in that crisis?" It is true that Emmons seems to have paid Emily somewhat more attention during the days after graduation than was fitting for an engaged man; but the first record of any communication between them after that period does not come until May 25, 1859, when Sarah Phelps (Susan's sister) records in her diary: "The Dickinsons from Amherst called to see Henry [Emmons] and the girls just before tea . . ." (*YH* I, 369). Emmons had been studying theology in distant Bangor for three years—a long enough stretch to test any engagement to the limit.

1865, and continued on an active ministerial career until his retirement in 1902. As for Emily, the closest she came to confiding her feelings was a single sentence in the letter to Sue after Commencement: "I shall miss Emmons very much"—another friendship for her box of Phantoms.

There were many others besides John Graves and Henry Emmons to keep Emily from solitude after her "Tutor" left. Vinnie's diary for 1851 (the only year she kept it) mentions social calls to be numbered in the hundreds. Very few days went by without the girls' either receiving or making calls, and most such occasions involved college students, or tutors, or associates in Mr. Dickinson's law office. And they did not all come to see Vinnie, nor was she the only Dickinson girl to make calls, although she was the only one, as far as we know, to get an offer of marriage (from the persistent Tutor William Howland). In those days when a young lady could fall in love with her future husband by watching him put on his gloves in church, the ways of courtship were not so strenuous as today. The formal "Emilie E. Dickinson," as she signed her letters, the use of the title "Mr." in mixed company even with undergraduates, and the zealous parental surveillance we hear so much about (which in the Dickinson family seems not to have been very rigid anyway) need not put us off. Both Austin and Vinnie, in their comments on Emily's early years, said she had the usual number of romantic attachments, and the tone of even the surviving scraps of correspondence indicates that she was probably in and out of love, after her fashion, a good many times.

How many of the young men involved in all those calls, and in the daily activities in which she shared, interested Emily romantically we will probably never know. It is clear that, like all the rest of her family, except possibly her mother, she was highly selective toward her fellow mortals. The family talent for satire (Edward Dickinson set the tone) was expended mainly on bores, fools, or egotists; and the Amherst complement of young men contained the usual percentage of all three. From the time she told her young classmate to "think twice before he spoke," Emily's attitude was anything but melting and romantic. Even her valentines were sharp and shrewd, as in the remark to the Amherst senior that metaphors wouldn't bite. When Elbridge Bowdoin, her father's law partner and ten years her senior, came to call on her at Mount Holyoke, his conversation, apparently, was somewhere this side of electric. Emily wrote Austin:

> Bowdoin, tells me of no news, excepting the following. Cherries are fast getting ripe & the new generation attended the Senior Levee, a short time since, both of which facts, were received by me, with proper resignation. Surely, things must have changed in quiet, peace loving Amherst.

Though older and an all-but-confirmed bachelor, Bowdoin was not so vacuous, it seems, as Emily suggests. He lent the Dickinson girls novels

(Emily returned *Jane Eyre,* with a note, in December 1849), to Mr. Dickinson's displeasure, and further troubled his partner with his liberal politics. (The course of the partnership was anything but smooth and was dissolved in 1855.) Emily thought enough of him and of his sense of humor to send him, in 1850, an exuberant verse valentine urging marriage. It is her earliest known poem and one of the happiest, presenting the Law of Life as *mating.*

> Oh the Earth was *made* for lovers, for damsel, and hopeless swain,
> For sighing, and gentle whispering, and *unity* made of *twain.*
> All things do go a courting, in earth, or sea, or air,
> God hath made nothing single but *thee* in His world so fair!

And so on, for twenty-four rollicking hexameters on the anomaly of Bowdoin's single state, until it arrives at a catalogue of eligible young ladies, with herself last:

> There's *Sarah,* and *Eliza,* and *Emeline* so fair,
> And *Harriet,* and *Susan,* and she with *curling hair!*
> Thine eyes are sadly blinded, but yet thou mayest see
> *Six* true, and comely maidens sitting upon the tree . . .

The poem ends in a glorious exhortation to choose one:

> Then bear her to the greenwood, and build for her a bower,
> And give her what she asketh, jewel, or bird, or flower –
> And bring the fife, and trumpet, and beat upon the drum –
> And bid the world Goodmorrow, and go to glory home!   (#*1*)

Bowdoin was unmoved; he remained a bachelor to the last—in Iowa, where he dealt in real estate and became known as one of the shrewdest politicians in the State Legislature. But he kept the valentine for forty years.[11]

Another associate in Mr. Dickinson's law office did not fare so well. John Milton Emerson, who graduated from the college a year ahead of Austin and came back to Amherst to study law with Mr. Dickinson, apparently bored Emily in advance. She wrote to Austin on July 20, 1851, concluding with an arch Shakespearean reference:

11. Finally, shortly before his death, he gave the valentine to Anna Kellogg, sister of Rufus Kellogg, Amherst '58 and the first alumni trustee. She sent it to Vinnie during the gathering of materials for the 1894 *Letters* (*AB,* pp. 205-6). The six "comely maidens" have been identified as Sarah Tracy (?), Eliza Coleman, Emeline Kellogg, Harriet Merrill, Susan Gilbert, and Emily. For the confusion about Sarah Tracy's name (it is "Sarah Taylor" in the note to *P* #1), see *YH* I, lxxv. The trouble arose from Mrs. Todd's difficulty in reading Emily's early handwriting.

John Emerson has come, and has entered himself as a student in Father's office – he carries about the sail of a good sized British vessel, when he has oped his mouth I *think* no dog has barked.[12]

He was known to have been interested about this time in Emily Fowler and Eliza Coleman. Vinnie once focused her sharp eye on him and wrote Austin:

I'm in the kitchen writing. John Emerson is in the sitting room with Emilie reading parts of Eliza Colemans letters. I wonder if he thinks t'will do him any good. Poor fellow is [a] little deluded I fear.

Whatever Vinnie's fears, he had been valedictorian of his class and was a tutor in the college from 1851 to 1853. He lectured at the Citizen's Lyceum in Amherst on March 9, 1852, on the subject "Protestantism and Catholicism in Their Influence Upon Civilization," noted before-the-fact and without comment by Emily. Indeed, most of the references to him, in Vinnie's diary or in letters from the sisters to Austin, are mere notes of the fact that he called. Only once did Emily expand: "John Emerson just went away from here – he has been spending the evening, and I'm so tired now, that I write just as it happens, so you must'nt expect any style." It was probably Emerson who tired her out. Whether or not she let her boredom show and thus discouraged future calls, this is the last reference to Emerson in the Dickinson annals. He practiced law in Amherst until 1856 and then in New York City, where he died in 1869, "an able lawyer, a ripe scholar, and an honorable man." His obituary proceeds:

But his life hid a rare and romantic constancy which his death has revealed. He was once to have been married to a young and beautiful woman, whose sudden sickness and death left this true lover lonely through life.[13]

The young woman was probably Olivia Coleman, Eliza's sister, who died in 1847 (Emerson's junior year) of "galloping consumption," suddenly, in

12. *L* I, 126. Cf. *Merchant of Venice* I, i, 90 ff., where Gratiano, trying to induce Antonio to talk about the cause of his low spirits, burlesques those who

> . . . do a wilful stillness entertain,
> With purpose to be dress'd in an opinion
> Of wisdom, gravity, profound conceit;
> As who should say, "I am Sir Oracle,
> And, when I ope my lips, let no dog bark!"

13. *Springfield Republican,* August 10, 1869 (*YH* II, 141). George Frisbie Whicher, in the "Epilogue" to William Gardiner Hammond's diary, *Remembrance of Amherst,* p. 279, calls Emerson "a favorable specimen of the type known to later generations as a 'grind.' There was nothing vivid or colorful about him. Hammond liked him, but with reservations. He was undeniably hard to talk to, a reserved young man with unadventurous mind. After an evening's call from him Emily Dickinson once wrote her brother Austin that she was completely exhausted." But Emerson beat out Hammond for top place in the class, an honor strenuously competed for and made much of in campus circles.

a carriage. It has been suggested that Emily's famous· poem "Because I could not stop for Death" was based on the circumstances of Olivia's death. Perhaps during that long evening, witnessed by Vinnie, when Emerson was reading Eliza's letters with Emily, he also told her of his early love for Olivia, now transferred to sister Eliza. But, like the precise nature of Emily's response to Emerson's hidden romantic nature, the matter remains obscure.

Many other names dot the family annals, mostly peripheral figures, although the discovery of a long-lost batch of letters might bring any one of them into the center at any time. There was Henry Martyn Storrs, Amherst '46, who came in "quite often to see us" before he married the president's daughter, Kate Hitchcock, in 1852, and became a famous preacher. (Emily's comment: "I dont envy her that Storrs.") Henry Root and Brainerd Harrington were frequent callers in the early 1850s.

Somewhat closer to the center were the Howland brothers and George Gould. George Howland, the younger of the brothers, had the distinction of bringing out the worst (or the best) of Emily in one long and tiresome evening:

AUSTIN –
George Howland has just retired from an evening's visit here, and I gather my spent energies to write a word to you – "Blessed are they that are persecuted for righteousness' sake, for they shall have their reward"! Dear Austin – I dont feel funny, and I hope you wont laugh at anything I say.

After being a tutor for five years, George left Amherst for Chicago, where he became superintendent of the Chicago public schools and was made a trustee of Amherst in 1879. He never married. His brother William, the one who proposed to Vinnie, was the probable recipient of the only other verse valentine of Emily's that survives and the first of her verses to be printed (*Springfield Republican,* February 20, 1852, though how it got there is a mystery). It is in seventeen trimeter quatrains, never stops for breath, shows no concern for logical connections, and is utterly successful, from the first pastiche from her book of quotations (the "Sic transit gloria mundi" cited above) to the final resounding farewell:

> Good bye, Sir, I am going;
>   My country calleth me;
> Allow me, Sir, at parting,
>   To wipe my weeping e'e.
>
> In token of our friendship
>   Accept this "Bonnie Doon,"
> And when the hand that plucked it
>   Hath passed beyond the moon,

> The memory of my ashes
>   Will consolation be;
> Then, farewell, Tuscarora,
>   And farewell, Sir, to thee!   (#3)

What Howland had done to deserve such attention is another mystery. He evidently bored Vinnie, and Emily says little about him. But he got along splendidly in Mr. Dickinson's law office, to the point where Emily memorialized the relationship in near-poetic style (to Austin):

> Howland is here with father – will stay a while I guess. They go to Northampton together, as it is court there now and seem very happy together in the law. Father likes Howland grandly, and they go along as smoothly as friendly barks at sea – or when harmonious stanzas become one melody. Howland was here last evening – is jolly and just as happy – really I cant think now what *is* so happy as he.

He was admitted to the bar in 1851, set up practice in Lynn in 1852, married in 1860, and died in 1880.

Of George Gould, who (it is thought) was favored with another of Emily's valentines, this one in prose, there is more to say. A daguerreotype of the time shows him as a lean-faced young intellectual; but he was of a different sort from Emerson the Valedictorian. He was a close friend of Austin's, a classmate, in the same fraternity (Alpha Delta Phi), and his rival on the Amherst oratorical platforms. When they appeared together in their Commencement exercises, it was Gould's speech ("Relation of Self Reverence to Christianity") that attracted notice. The *Hampshire and Franklin Express* caught the flavor of his style:

> Among the Orations we remarked that of Mr. Gould. It abounded in glowing thought, which shone and sparkled like the gem, outshining the rich and costly setting.

Such talent may account for the enthusiasm Emily put into the valentine she (presumably) sent him that same year (1850). He was at that time chairman of the editorial board of a new student publication, the *Indicator*, published, as he announced in his first statement as editor in June 1849, with the prime object of "our own literary advancement." The following February, the *Indicator* was flooded with valentines from female admirers—and *"one, such* an one" they chose to publish. Since Gould was the only member of the board we know of so closely associated with the Dickinsons, the valentine probably was sent to him.

It was his colleague Henry Shipley, however, who wrote the comment on it: "I wish I knew who the author is. I think she must have some spell, by which she quickens the imagination, and causes the high blood 'run frolic through the veins' "—an appreciation not surpassed for decades. The *Indicator* printed the whole tumultuous affair.

Magnum bonum, "harum scarum," zounds et zounds, et war alarum, man reformam, life perfectum, mundum changum, all things flarum?

Sir, I desire an interview; meet me at sunrise, or sunset, or the new moon – the place is immaterial. In gold, or in purple, or sackcloth – I look not upon the *raiment*. With sword, or with pen, or with plough – the weapons are less than the *wielder*. In coach, or in wagon, or walking, the *equipage* far from the *man*. With soul, or spirit, or body, they are all alike to me. With host or alone, in sunshine or storm, in heaven or earth, *some* how or *no* how – I propose, sir, to see you.

And not to *see* merely, but a chat, sir, or a tete-a-tete, a confab, a min- gling of opposite minds is what I propose to have. I feel sir that we shall agree. We will be David and Jonathan, or Damon and Pythias, or what is better than either, the United States of America. We will talk over what we have learned in our geographies, and listened to from the pulpit, the press and the Sabbath School.

This is strong language sir, but none the less true. So hurrah for North Carolina, since we are on this point.

Our friendship sir, shall endure till sun and moon shall wane no more, till stars shall set, and victims rise to grace the final sacrifice. We'll be in- stant, in season, out of season, minister, take care of, cherish, sooth, watch, wait, doubt, refrain, reform, elevate, instruct. All choice spirits however distant are ours, ours theirs; there is a thrill of sympathy – a circulation of mutuality – cognationem inter nos! I am Judith the heroine of the Apoc- rypha, and you the orator of Ephesus.

That's what they call a metaphor in our country. Don't be afraid of it, sir, it won't bite. If it was my dog *Carlo* now! The Dog is the noblest work of Art, sir. I may safely say the noblest – his mistress's rights he doth defend – although it bring him to his end – although to death it doth him send!

But the world is sleeping in ignorance and error, sir, and we must be crowing cocks, and singing larks, and a rising sun to awake her; or else we'll pull society up to the roots, and plant it in a different place. We'll build Alms-houses, and transcendental State prisons, and scaffolds – we will blow out the sun, and the moon, and encourage invention. Alpha shall kiss Omega – we will ride up the hill of glory – Hallelujah, all hail!

Yours, truly,

C.[14]

Although reckless and non-sequential, this is more than a young virtu- oso's show-off piece. Like the verse valentines, it sometimes deviates into remarkable sense and gives surprising insights, among other things, into the range of Emily Dickinson's awareness of her times, their idiom and chief concerns. Besides the classical tags and Biblical lore and the obvious caricature of current oratory, there is much of mid-century American ferment here—the growing tension between North and South, the impact of Carlylean idealism, the new energies being exhibited by the pulpit and the press, the new spirit of science and invention, the social criticism of Emerson and Thoreau. Like her great contemporaries, she had the Orphic

14. I know of no speculation about the meaning of the signature "C." Nothing in the valentine comes near it—except Carlo (!).

John L. Graves ("Cousin John") about 1851

Henry Vaughan Emmons, about 1854 ". . . a beautiful, new, friend . . ."

EARLY FRIENDSHIPS II

George Gould, 1850 "Sir, I desire an interview"

James Parker Kimball, about 1860(?) ". . . our 'Theologian' "

Charles Humphreys Sweetser, about 1863,
of Amherst and New York City
First publisher of "Some keep the Sabbath going to Church" (*P* #324)

TWO DISTANT COUSINS

Perez Dickinson Cowan ("Cousin Peter"),
1866, of Tennessee

urge to wake up a sleeping world, to arouse her fellow mortals to the joys of living. She soon found, apparently, that these stirring strains were not her permanent voice. But there is more than a hint of the Orphic in her later attitudes. She wanted to let persons hear the "noiseless noise in the Orchard," to catch the light that never was on sea or land as Wordsworth (she implies) couldn't, to be truth's "warbling Teller": "Orpheus' Sermon captivated – / It did not condemn –" "How do most people live without any thoughts," she complained to Higginson years later. ". . . How do they get strength to put on their clothes in the morning[?]" At this point, she challenges her young friends to assault, with her, the ills of the world head-on.

The *Indicator* made a brave but not very impressive *riposte:* "Now this is, after all, a very ingenious affair. If it is not *true,* it is at any rate philosophical. It displays clearly an inductive faith; a kind of analytic spirit. . . ." One remark, however, was entirely correct: "The author . . . has not (it is plain to see) told the half of her feelings. It were impossible!"

What Gould himself thought of all this we do not know. Nor can we be certain about a story connecting him and Emily that has given rise to elaborate biographical speculation. The story was told in the 1920s by Mrs. Aurelia Hinsdale Davis to Mary Lee Hall, who reported it (in a letter of November 4, 1929) to Genevieve Taggard, who based her biography, *The Life and Mind of Emily Dickinson,* upon it. Supposedly, Edward Dickinson, thinking to protect his daughter from an unfortunate marriage, refused to let her see or correspond with Gould, who was beginning "to show a decided fancy for Emily." The crisis came at Gould's Commencement reception at the Dickinsons', when Emily, dutifully obedient, sent word to him to meet her "in a part of the grounds, after the reception was over." Here, "dressed in white," she told him the bad news and "declared that love was too vital a flower to be crushed so cruelly."[15]

Much could be said, and has been, about this tearful episode. I find it hard to see why Edward Dickinson should have forbidden Emily one of the most brilliant men of the class of 1850, Austin's intimate college friend, a frequent visitor before and after Commencement, and (later) a successful minister of such intellectual stature that Amherst College offered him a professorship in 1876, which he refused, partly because his Worcester congregation wanted him to stay with them. There is no hint of a quarrel or misunderstanding between Mr. Dickinson and young Gould.

When Mabel Todd, with Austin's help, was assembling material for the 1894 *Letters,* she wrote Gould in Worcester to inquire about Ben Newton (who had lived in Worcester), never thinking that Gould himself might have any of Emily's letters. Surprisingly, he wrote that he had

15. The quotations are from Mary Lee Hall's letter to Genevieve Taggard, which is printed in full in *The Life and Mind of Emily Dickinson,* pp. 107–9. Since Mary Lee Hall requested that her name be withheld "while I am living," the letter, with a "sworn statement," is signed "X."

"quite a cherished batch of Emily's letters myself kept sacredly in a small trunk," lost some fifteen years before. Had Austin suspected that the relationship was any more than a pleasant meeting of minds between two witty young people, surely he would have directed Mrs. Todd to Gould at once.[16]

Nor does the story fit the two Dickinson principals. Edward Dickinson may well have been a protective father, and at one point or another he may have discouraged an unlikely suitor; but on the whole he seems to have been decently respectful of his children's wishes, and there is no other parental action nearly so tyrannical recorded against him. Emily was a dutiful daughter; but she had been away from home a year, and she had learned to function on her own. Her letters show a growing sense of her own power. One can say with some confidence that had her heart been set on Gould or anybody else, nothing would have stopped her.

The story sounds a little too much like Vinnie in her later days telling Mary Lee Hall—and perhaps Mrs. Davis—those lurid tales about life in the Dickinson household, although even her own letters and diary give a happier picture. But when Emily once became public property, there was considerable pressure to produce the clue that would solve the mystery. Of Aurelia Davis we know little, except that she was an Amherst girl, sister of Harriet Hinsdale (Hubbell), who roomed with Sue Gilbert in Baltimore when, as two displaced Yankees, they taught school there in 1851–52. Mrs. Davis was a near enough neighbor to be on hand and helpful during Edward Dickinson's funeral; she was known as "Saint" Aurelia. But she appears in the early annals of the family only once, when Sue and Harriet Hinsdale visited her (from Baltimore) in Havre de Grace in April 1852. How she came by the story about Gould and Emily is itself a mystery, unless we can attribute it to Vinnie's love of the dramatic. But then there is Vinnie's flat denial in the 1895 letter to Caroline Healey Dall of similar allegations about Mr. Dickinson and about Emily in regard to someone Emily met in Washington. Here Vinnie was unequivocal: "Emily never had any love disaster."

From such mysteries we turn back with some relief to Joseph Lyman, Vinnie's suitor, whose friendship with Emily is refreshingly free from such complexities, especially romantic ones. This friendship began earlier and lasted longer than those we have been considering and in a sense recapitulates them, confirming the meaning for Emily's heart and mind the others, together, seem to have.[17]

Throughout his visits to the Dickinsons in the 1840s, Joseph, besides "playing spooney" with Vinnie (as his friend accused him), walked and

16. Cf. *AB*, p. 255. Of course, Emily could have been in love with Gould without Austin's knowledge. But Austin would surely have known of any such dramatic event as Mr. Dickinson's refusal to let his daughter marry a perfectly eligible suitor.

17. For a full treatment of Lyman's relations with the Dickinsons, see my *Lyman Letters: New Light on Emily Dickinson and Her Family* (1965).

talked with Emily often. They read German plays together, and Emily (so he wrote his fiancée, Laura Baker) "sat close beside me so as to look out words from the same Dictionary – " For many years after he left New England in 1851, he corresponded with her; and when he came back in 1863, he undoubtedly renewed his associations with the Dickinsons, especially with Emily, whom he came to admire much more than he did Vinnie. Whether he ever understood her as well as she understood him may be doubted, but at least he was an observant young man, intimate with Dickinsons as few contemporaries were. In his many comments on the Dickinsons and on Emily in his letters to Laura Baker, he was far enough away (New Orleans) from the Amherst scene to be dispassionate and near enough in time (five years) for his impressions to be fresh. The passages he saved from her letters (he called them "snatches") are good evidence of the nature of their friendship. Emily appears at her best, not posing, talking neither up nor down nor in riddles, communicating directly and sincerely with a good friend.

Once she touched on a subject that echoes the central theme in the letters to Abiah Root and Jane Humphrey and shows, perhaps, that Lyman played some part, as he read German with her and looked up words and talked literature, in her developing sense of vocation—the "gold thread." To Joseph, rather than telling it through symbol and dream as she had to Abiah and Jane, she puts it in terms of her discovery of the power of the individual word:

> We used to think, Joseph, when I was an unsifted girl and you so scholarly that words were cheap & weak. Now I dont know of anything so mighty. There are [those] to which I lift my hat when I see them sitting princelike among their peers on the page. Sometimes I write one, and look at his outlines till he glows as no sapphire.[18]

When Joseph first visited at the Dickinsons', he was hardly old enough (he was only a year older than she) to qualify as a "grave Preceptor," but at least he seemed "scholarly" to her then and may have given her something like the encouragement and help she had from Ben Newton.

As he developed beyond the schoolboy stage, however, he seems the sort one would have supposed her to be utterly bored with. In New Orleans, before he was caught up in the war, he was an aggressive young lawyer and man about town. His career in the South (he felt cramped in New England) shows him increasingly ambitious and worldly. In his letters he is a typical young American idealist-materialist and romantic dabbler in fashionable ideas. Yet Emily was *not* bored with him. She saw the "arrow in his hand"—his ambition—and rather relished the world-shine he acquired. (She had a penchant for such people: Higginson as

18. *LL*, p. 78. For Emily's "unsifted girl": *Hamlet* I, iii, 102–3 (Polonius to Ophelia):

. . . you speak like a green girl,
Unsifted in such perilous circumstance.

colonel, Bowles the editor, Kate Anthon the traveler, Judge Lord the jurist, Dr. Holland, editor and lecturer.) And she was fond of him. When he left on his adventures in 1851, she wrote Susan in Baltimore: "Dear Susie, Dear Joseph; why take the best and dearest, and leave our hearts behind?"

Perhaps their greatest common bond was literature. The seven passages he saved from her letters were obviously chosen for their style and opinions, often literary—on Shakespeare, the Bible, "princelike" words. When he came back North after the war, he had given up his career as a lawyer and was determined to be a writer. "The sole instrument," he wrote, "with which I sought to carve my way . . . was my PEN." He had shown signs of the professional long before this. In his letters to Laura Baker, written during their engagement between 1856 and 1858, he is obviously trying out his style in his long descriptions of New Orleans and his lyric longings for New England (and the Dickinsons). Once a venture into theology evoked some purple prose:

> This natural Religion, my Laura, is indeed very beautiful. It is taught purity by the lilly, industry by the bee, faith by the Sparrow, mercy by the gentle dew of heaven and charity by the summer rain; while the far-floating downy cloud and the over-arching blue are not without their sublime suggestions of the immortality of the spirit and of the boundless Love of God.

Since his correspondence shows him repeating himself often to different recipients, something like this may have gone to Emily. One wonders how she could have stood it. Perhaps she didn't. The following early bit of her own sounds like a riposte:

> In the name of the Bee –
> And of the Butterfly –
> And of the Breeze – Amen![19]   (#18, about 1858)

By the mid-1860s Joseph was well established in New York as editorialist and feature writer for *The New York Times,* and later, as expert on agricultural matters, columnist for the *World* and the *Tribune.* His marriage to Laura Baker in 1858 was happy and productive: seven children in ten years. He died suddenly in 1872 of smallpox. But, according to Laura, he never forgot the Dickinsons; and when Emily died in 1886, Laura wrote a friend: "I wonder if they have met up yonder. . . ."

Our gratitude to Lyman begins, of course, with the passages he saved from Emily's letters. Their range of style and subject suggests, perhaps, that as professional journalist he may have been collecting them for some kind of literary treatment. He had a good eye. Here is a passage he entitled "Dull days" that a less discerning reader might have missed:

19. But of course these lines are the last three of a nineteen-line poem on the death of summer, with its tone of pathos not true of Joseph's surging optimism. The parallel shows merely the two friends touching a similar theme, "This natural Religion"—Joseph sentimentally, ED with whimsey and perhaps a hint of irony.

I specially love them because, [by] the kindly thirst they give, I can drink deeper from the sun: just now for instance I would be glad of a little mist, a furlough, for June has been bombarding us, boom after boom of summer glory – a very cannonade of splendors.

But he was more than a good anthologist. Once, probably in the mid-1860s, he tried his hand at a pen portrait. It is a brief sketch, most of it in the high romantic mode, but a few sharply realized details bring it (and Emily) down to earth. And it rises to a climax on the quality in her that always impressed him most: her power with words.

EMILY
"Things are not what they seem"
Night in Midsummer

A library dimly lighted, three mignonettes on a little stand. Enter a spirit clad in white, figure so draped as to be misty[,] face moist, translucent alabaster, forehead firmer as of statuary marble. Eyes once bright hazel now melted & fused so as to be two dreamy, wondering wells of expression, eyes that see no forms but gla[n]ce swiftly to the core of all thi[n]gs – hands small, firm, deft but utterly emancipated from all claspings of perishable things, very firm strong little hands absolutely under control of the brain, types of quite rugged health[,] mouth made for nothing & used for nothing but uttering choice speech, rare thoughts, glittering, starry misty figures, winged words.

It may be just as well that Lyman as journalist never developed this little sketch to the point of publication; the myth of Emily as the fragile, white-clad Nun of Amherst might have had an earlier start than it did. The sentimentalists could be depended upon to overlook the swift-glancing eyes, the hands "small, firm, deft . . . very firm strong," the impression of absolute intellectual control and "quite rugged health." Higginson's similar sketch, written to his wife after his meeting with Emily in 1870, shows hardly more than the "little plain woman," the white dress, the lilies, and "the soft frightened breathless childlike voice." It is redeemed only by some of the "winged words" that Higginson caught and recorded for his wife. Apparently, Emily never posed before Lyman.

But also we are grateful to Lyman for the few simple, homely things he said in other contexts about Emily. Though far from the whole truth, they seem at least the honest truth as seen by this capable young man. None of her contemporaries assayed the complexities of her nature with such confidence or, in a few passing comments, said so much. The first remark came in a letter to Laura after he had quoted the following passage from Emily's note congratulating him on his engagement:

I am glad you are well & of that other tidings. I give you more joy than of all the rest. It is the nearer Heaven & tho' the Angels do not so it makes the bliss none the less. Give *one* of your kisses in *my* name and tell her we are glad. You will work faster Joe – you wil[l] find time shorter. God bless you – & bless her! –

To this he added the comment (with the quotation from *Maud*) comparing Vinnie and Emily:

> Emily you see is platonic – She never stood "tranced in long Embraces mixed with kisses sweeter, sweeter than anything on Earth."

He called her "rather morbid and unnatural" in another passage, but he called even Laura "morbid" when she was chilly to him. Such adjectives may have deeper implications; but what, in context, they seem to have meant to him was that Emily was not interested in the kind of dalliance he enjoyed with Vinnie and the New Orleans belles he described to Laura. At least this young worldling had the discernment to see Emily's distinction; she was neither "partially cracked" nor a flower among flowers. One of his finest tributes to her came in a letter to Laura about a mutual friend, Araminta Wharton of Nashville, "to whom," he wrote, "God gave a white soul." Emily and she were much the same: "They are both noble women – neither one of them will probably ever marry tho' both would make most true & devoted wives. . . ." If Emily ever entertained the idea of becoming *his* wife, she apparently kept it secret from him and from everybody else. As with the other young men in her life, she enjoyed what appealed to her in him, absorbed his meaning, saw him happily married, and continued on her own way.

"Her own way," if we can trust the gist of some isolated and widely separated remarks to Joseph and others, demanded freedom. This is the theme of one of her few frank comments on the subject of matrimony, this one to Sue early in June 1852, a subject on which, she wrote, "You and I have been strangely silent." The new bride must look on our single lives, she said, as dull; but the neglected wife must envy our freedom: her life is "henceforth to him [her husband]. . . . It does so rend me, Susie, the thought of it when it comes, that I tremble lest at sometime I, too, am yielded up." Although she enjoyed domestic chores like baking bread, she asked to be preserved from "what they call *households*" and the "prickly art" of housekeeping. The year after Joseph married, she called herself a "Bachelor"—in fun, but the remark is worth noting. (She is writing Mrs. Holland to congratulate her on Dr. Holland's return from a three-month lecture tour, noted in the *Springfield Republican* for February 28, 1859.)

> I gather from "Republican" that you are about to doff your weeds for a Bride's Attire. Vive le fireside! Am told that fasting gives to food marvellous Aroma, but by birth a Bachelor, disavow Cuisine.

The letters to Abiah and Jane and Uncle Joel, even the whirlwind valentines, the elaborate love letters to Sue during the early 1850s, and certainly the poems which were in composition about this time—all show her experimenting in styles and making deeper and deeper excursions into the realm of the imagination. Some years later she defined that realm more precisely to Joseph Lyman, again with an insistence on freedom.

So I conclude that space & time are things of the body & have little or nothing to do with our selves. My Country is Truth. . . . I like Truth – it is a free Democracy.

What sustained her in the years ahead was no fulfilled romantic relationship; that seems to have eluded her permanently. She lived increasingly in her own chosen country, where she was free. Her home was the setting, with a family that learned not to intrude. Her companions were her Lexicon; the things of nature; her books; her letters, which became increasingly the measure of her fulfilled relationships; but especially her poems, in which she explored the truth of her fulfillments and her unfulfillments—with nature, man, and God. Not that she shut herself up in the iron solitude of her own imagination. Her family and her friends, young and old, were always important to her. But (to sum up these early years) it is clear—although neither she nor Lyman nor anyone else said so—that it would have taken a much more powerful attraction to have swerved her from her course than anything the young men of Amherst had to offer. Perhaps Lyman came close to saying it in a letter to his brother Timothy, written sometime during his Yale years (1846–50). Complaining of the dullness of the conversation in his circle of lady friends, he made a notable exception: "Em. Dickinson is a year younger it is true but older than all in mind and heart." Older, and increasingly remote from Lyman's world. Perhaps a measure of how far beyond him she came to be is the one glaring omission in all he had to say about her: he honored her prose and he delighted in her talk; but nowhere does he even hint that she was, or was going to be, a poet.

19

Brother and Sister

As THESE early friendships flowed and ebbed, brother Austin was perhaps Emily's greatest resource. In temperament and tastes they were the closest in the family (Vinnie being not quite inside the ring) and stood together against Father's "real life" world in the household. Emily's letters to Austin during his periods of teaching in Sunderland and Boston and during his study at the Harvard Law School show how much she did for him, how she worried about his health and spirits, and cheered on his courtship of Sue. But just how much he did for her, how sustaining a force he was on matters that troubled her most during these early years and later, can only be surmised. Certainly she depended on him for humor and gaiety about the house. "Well Austin," she wrote at the end of a holiday, "– you are gone, and the wheel rolls slowly on – nobody to laugh with – talk with, nobody down in the morning to make the fun for me!" as, on this occasion, she was making the breakfast for the family. Father, be it said, was not without humor; once after they had all been mimicking a poor sermon, Emily wrote Austin, "I never heard father so funny. How I did wish you were here. I know you'd have died laughing." And Vinnie was pert. But it was Austin who lifted her spirits. During the general rejoicing (in February 1852) over the successful funding of the proposed railroad, Father was proud and happy, but, wrote Emily, "I miss your big Hurrahs, and the famous stir you make, upon all such occasions." In spite of the innumerable diversions and warm friendships she enjoyed during the early 1850s—the calls, the parties, the walks and rides, the intimacy with her then darling Sue—she could write to Austin in April 1853, just as it was becoming clear that he and Sue were engaged to be married: "I think we miss each other more every day that we grow older, for we're all unlike most everyone, and are therefore more dependent on each other for delight."[1]

There are problems here, as in almost every one of Emily's important relationships. Except for what Austin told Mabel Todd and the scraps about Emily he left in writing, the major source of information is his letters from Emily. The letters he wrote her (with two minor exceptions) apparently went in the general conflagration. Furthermore, of the eighty-six she wrote him, eighty-three are from the early period—between April 1842 and the summer of 1854, two years before his marriage—and the three others (about 1861, Thanksgiving 1884, and about 1885) are one-sentence notes (one note includes a poem). It is hard to believe that these are all the letters she wrote to him, and it is equally hard to account for the almost complete absence of letters from the later years. There are obvious reasons why there should be fewer after 1854. Once Austin had taken his law degree (on July 19, 1854) and come home for good, and especially after he and Sue moved in next door, there was less need for them. But as Emily withdrew more and more from social life in Amherst, including Austin and Sue's, she depended increasingly on letters. One hundred and twenty-eight went to Sue from 1858 on. To be sure, Sue was often away from home, frequently on extended visits; but a great many of Emily's letters merely traversed the few hundred feet between the houses. Perhaps Emily and Austin renewed the long talks mentioned in the early letters and so had no need to write. But it was Emily's way, increasingly,

1. One of the delights they shared, if Emily's side of the correspondence may be taken as evidence, was poking fun at men and things. Emily enjoyed playing, at least, with subversion, a mild current of which runs through the correspondence. A letter from Mount Holyoke hopes, ironically, that Austin is "gratified that I am so rapidly gaining correct ideas of female propriety & sedate deportment"; and she herself is gratified at finding "nothing which savored of rebellion or an unsubdued will . . . no dangerous sentiments," in a letter just received from him (*L* I, 62; February 17, 1848). She boasts in the same letter of thwarting Miss Lyon's edict against valentines. Later, at home, she describes one of her father's visitors, a Mr. Marsh, as a " 'man of cares' . . . I think he's for 'law and order' " (*L* I, 112–13; June 15, 1851). Making fun of Father is a favorite sport in the letters—Father and the railroad, Father at Jenny Lind's concert, Father and the "amazin raw" weather, Father wagging "his head profound" when no letter comes from Austin, Father at the Kimberly barn fire, and so on and on (*L I,* 254, 121–22, 110, 119, 128). No wonder she censored one of Austin's letters before reading it to Father: "I reviewed the contents hastily – striking out all suspicious places, and then very *artlessly* and unconsciously began" (*L* I, 136; October 1, 1851). Another letter records coming in from church "very hot, and faded, having witnessed a couple of Baptisms, three admissions to church, a Supper of the Lord, and some other minor transactions time fails me to record," including the Reverend Mr. Colton's sermon: "No doubt you can call to mind his eloquent addresses, his earnest look and gesture, his calls of *now today* . . ." (*L* I, 120; July 6, 1851). To Austin teaching school in Boston and facing a possible confrontation with the administration, she wrote: ". . . if they raise the wind, why let it blow – there's nothing more excellent than a breeze now and then!" (*L* I, 187; March 7, 1852). Aside from the sheer fun in all this, there was moral support; and the support was probably mutual.

to *write*. When little Gilbert died, for instance, Emily wrote Sue several letters, one of them her greatest; but we have no written word from her to Austin, who was almost prostrated in grief. The scarcity of surviving letters from Emily after the marriage is as mysterious as the fact that between 1851 and 1877 there is record of Emily's having sent him—her "Brother Pegasus"—only five poems, while some two hundred and seventy-six, between 1853 and 1885, are supposed to have been sent to Sue. One suspects that many letters were destroyed, perhaps by Austin as too intimate, or by Sue, who survived him by many years.

All this intensifies our interest in the letters we do have. They reveal much about the day-to-day relationship between brother and sister—how she joked with him, worried about him, sent him fruit, mended his shirts and socks, asked him to do errands for her, kept him up on the town gossip and doings at home, tried out her style on him. Compared with her other early correspondences, there is very little of the confessional in this one, at least in what remains of it. She is more outgoing, more reportorial, since it was her purpose to send him in faraway Sunderland or Boston or Cambridge as much of home as she could. She seldom gives way to her moods, as she often did to Abiah Root or Jane Humphrey. With only a few exceptions, she avoids the large subjects she discussed so intensely with the girls—religion, death, and the conduct of life. Perhaps she was keeping up a good front for Austin, to cheer him up in what for a Dickinson was foreign land. Perhaps he destroyed the more personal or somber letters. If he wrote her anything like the long, soul-searching letter he wrote Martha Gilbert in May 1852, nothing in her letters indicates such an unburdening. Still, the structure of the correspondence, its beginning, middle, and end, follows a pattern all too like the other correspondences of the early years, the flow and the seemingly inevitable ebb. In a sense— her own sense—Emily lost Austin, too.

But in general, Emily's spirits were never higher, her eye never keener, her style never more varied and pungent than in these lively letters. From the big "Hurrah" of the first letter (age eleven) to the last of the series in the summer of 1854 when, she wrote, all the folks at home "allude to you as to a missing Saint," she flattered Austin, pampered him, assured him of her and the family's continued love as if she were really concerned lest he doubt it, and re-created for him scenes of home and Amherst with loving care.

There is more about Emily's days and hours here than in any other source. We hear the family snoring as she writes letters late at night and the fire crackling while she gets breakfast as the others sleep. She tells Austin whether the hens are laying or not, and who is currently taking care of the horse. We see Father in "neglige," and misbehaving at Jenny Lind's recital, and "giving commands" at the Kimberly fire. Mother returns from a lecture "too high for her unobtrusive faculties." Both parents "sit in state" in the sitting room reading their *un*carnal books, and Father gives Emily a "trimming" on the folly of modern novels. Vinnie comes home faint and bandaged from a dog bite at the Kelloggs', and both girls are busy to distraction during Mother's illness. The callers come endlessly, until Emily cries out for "this beleaguered family." We see her defenses go up as she resists, even at age twenty, the drain on her resources through too much socializing. Consoling Austin on the loneliness of his little room in Boston, she points out an important Emersonian compensation:

> . . . but if you talk with no one, you are amassing thoughts which will be bright and golden for those you left at home – *we* meet our friends, and a constant interchange *wastes tho't* and feeling, and we are then obliged to *repair* and *renew* – there is'nt the *brimfull* feeling which one gets *away.*[2]

The *"brimfull* feeling" depended on sufficient solitude, which was becoming more and more necessary to her and which in later years she guarded obsessively. But, paradoxically, a repeated theme in the letters to Austin was her loneliness. It was not for lack of human companionship in general—"the high and the low, the bond and the free," whom she once rather acidly described as filling her father's house. She was lonely for *him,* she said again and again, and for Susie, as that friendship grew. She indulged herself in this mood perhaps too often for our taste, unless it was a strategy to cheer him up: "I dont think I should mind the weather if Susie, and you were here, but I feel so very lonely now, when it storms – and the wind blows." But such lyric effusion—we are only a step or two away from the famous poem "Wild Nights – Wild Nights!"[3]—was not, in

2. Cf. Emerson in "Friendship" (*Essays,* first series, 1841): "The soul environs itself with friends that it may enter into a grander self-acquaintance or solitude; and it goes alone for a season that it may exalt its conversation or society."

3. The "effusion" is in a letter of April 21, 1852 (*L* I, 199). The poem has been dated about 1861:

> Wild Nights – Wild Nights!
> Were I with thee
> Wild Nights should be
> Our luxury!
>
> Futile – the Winds –
> To a Heart in port –
> Done with the Compass –
> Done with the Chart!
>
> Rowing in Eden –
> Ah, the Sea!
> Might I but moor – Tonight –
> In Thee!   (#249)

This has been variously interpreted as religious or erotic. It may be both. But its central tensions—storm / calm, danger / security, separation / reunion—and their hoped-for resolution may go back emotionally to such relatively simple origins as appear in this letter—loneliness and longing for her friends during a bad spell of early spring weather. The poem, of course, intensifies the mood and focuses on *one* object of longing. As often, the early letter shows the incipient poet—indeed, may suggest an earlier date than 1861 for the poem.

the letters to Austin, her characteristic resource. Rather, when she felt put upon, bored, or out of sorts with humanity in general, she slipped into irony and satire, often far from kindly. We have seen how she dealt with the young and boring Mr. Emerson, the Valedictorian. In her letter to Austin about her loneliness when the wind blew, and immediately following that chilling phrase, she disposes of a whole family of relatives in a passage that may have relieved her loneliness (one surmises) more than her tearful words of self-pity. The social scene is described with the precision of a novelist.

> I will tell you about the cousins. You have heard father speak of his cousin, Pliny Dickinson, of Syracuse. He has had two daughters in Hanover, at Mrs Austin Dickinson's school – there is a vacation there, and he has been on to Hanover for the girls. Cousin Harriet [Montague] heard he was coming, and she and Zebina [Montague] wrote – urging him and his daughters to visit them. They arrived on Saturday noon, passed that night at Cousin Harriet's, and then proposed coming here. Of course, we told them they might – and having got our permission, they came home with us from meeting – and stayed until yesterday noon [Tuesday], when they went back to Cousin Harriet's.
> Cousin Pliny says he "might stay around a month, visiting old acquaintances – if it was'nt for his business."
> Fortunate for us indeed, that his business feels the need for him, or I think he would *never* go. He is a kind of compound of Deacon Haskell, Calvin Merrill, and Morton Dickinson, so you will easily guess how much we enjoy his society. The girls are pretty girls, very simple hearted and happy – and would be very interesting, if they had any body to teach them. The oldest, Lizzie, is nineteen – looks exactly like Sarah Pynchon, and is very lively and bright, Sarah, the younger – fifteen, a sober little body – and has quite a pensive air, and a cough.[4]

A more sustained bit, and one of the most contrived of the many miniature narrations she spun out for Austin, came in a letter some weeks

4. Jay Leyda (*YH* I, lxii–lxiv) has given the fullest account of Cousins Harriet and Zebina Montague, brother and sister, whose mother was Samuel Fowler Dickinson's sister, Irene. ED held them high; and, oddities as they were in the Amherst scene, we would know more about her communications with them. Zebina, Amherst classmate ('32) and lifelong friend of Otis Phillips Lord, was at one point delinquent in his undergraduate work because of "the peculiar circumstances of his mother's family during the vacation" (so runs the faculty record for October 12, 1831), but what those circumstances were is not known. Harriet was forbidden the communion of the church for six months in 1845 for an unspecified sin. "ED's correspondence with Zebina and Harriet was continuous," writes Leyda, "but no trace of it has appeared." In the late 1830s Zebina was paralyzed and from then on "debarred," as he wrote in 1860 (*YH* II, 5), "from actively participating in the enjoyments and pleasures of life." He wrote many sprightly contributions for the local press and thus, as Leyda writes, gave ED "at least one literary cousin."
Just what Emily had in mind by a "compound of Deacon Haskell [Abby's father], Calvin Merrill [Harriet's father], and Morton Dickinson [a remote cousin?]" will have to be left to future investigators. But it can be imagined.

earlier. If the Cousin Pliny letter shows her in the satiric vein of Jane Austen or George Eliot, here she achieves the action and pace of drama. It was a cold evening—March 1, 1852. The dramatis personae include a blundering senior, Brainerd Harrington; a distant cousin and tutor, William Cowper Dickinson; Benjamin Thurston, another senior, not famous, apparently, for his conversational gifts; and Father, around whom the drama swirls. The *deus ex machina* appears in the arrival, in full regalia, of the "Hadley cousin," Thankful Dickinson Smith (the unmarried daughter and only child of Samuel Fowler Dickinson's youngest sister, Anna). James, her attendant and apparently another cousin of some sort, has not been identified.

Emily warms up in mock-heroic style: "I would have given most anything to have had you here, last evening – the scene was indeed too rich, to be detailed by my pen, and I shall ever regret that the *world* has lost such a chance to laugh." She concludes the preliminaries with a word on Father's rheumatism (he is getting better) and his kind thoughts of his son. Then the drama begins:

> Soon after tea, last night, a violent ring at the bell – Vinnie obeys the summons – Mr Harrington, Brainerd, would like to see me at the door. I come walking in from the kitchen, frightened almost to death, and receive the command from father, "not to stand at the door" [for the cold?] – terrified beyond measure, I advance to the outside door – Mr. H. has an errand – will not consent to come in, on account of my father's sickness – having dismissed him hastily, I retreat again to the kitchen – where I find mother and Vinnie, making most desperate efforts to control themselves, but with little success – once more breathe freely, and conclude that my lungs were given me, for only the best of purposes. Another ring at the door – enter Wm Dickinson – soon followed by Mr Thurston! I again crept into the sitting room, more dead than alive, and endeavored to *make conversation*. Father looked around triumphantly. I remarked that "the weather was rather cold" today, to which they all assented – indeed I *never witnessed* such *wonderful unanimity*. Fled to my mind again, and endeavored to procure something equally agreeable with my *last happy remark*. Bethought me of Sabbath day, and the Rev. Mr Bliss, who preached upon it – remarked with wonderful emphasis, that I thought the Rev. gentleman a very remarkable preacher, and discovered a strong resemblance between himself & Whitfield, in the way of remark – I confess it *was rather* laughable, having never so much as seen the ashes of that gentleman – but oh such a look as I got from my rheumatic sire. You should have seen it – I never can find a language vivid eno' to portray it to you – well, pretty soon, another pull at the bell – enter *Thankful Smith,* in the furs and robes of her ancestors, while *James* brings up the rear.
>
> Austin, my cup was full – I endeavored to shrink away into primeval nothingness – but sat there large as life, in spite of every effort. Finally Father, accompanied by the cousins, adjourned to the kitchen fire – and Vinnie and I, and our friends enjoyed the rest of the evening.

[433

Another theme in the letters, and perhaps the most insistent, is Emily's longing for Austin to come home. Ostensibly it was for his sake—the precariousness of his health, which she seems to have exaggerated; the dullness of his work and his loneliness, which she assessed accurately, perhaps, but sentimentalized unduly. She rang the changes on the theme so often as to tax the resources of even her rhetoric, and the more she persisted, the more her efforts appear to have been for her own sake rather than his. Her loneliness is the most frequent claim on him, and her constant appeals to his loyalty to the family make it seem that they all were fairly languishing for him: Father depended on him, and Mother wept when he failed to show up. (Vinnie, as might be expected, bore up best.) How much strategy there was in all this is hard to tell, but the letters are scarcely the selfless attempts one might expect from a sister encouraging a young man to face the world on his own—the kind of encouragement Austin needed. At one point when Father was away, she made a frank admission: "If I am *selfish* Austin, I tell you you *must come home.*"

To get Austin home, Emily tried many devices. She took the part of the solicitous sister worrying about his eye trouble, his facial neuralgia, or his laundry (all real enough problems). She spoke in the siren's voice: "Duty is black and brown – home is bright and shining." Or, shifting from the satiric and dramatic, she became the pastoral poet, with a touch of the lover. Her letter of October 17, 1851, concludes in a hidden poem.

Dont think that the sky will frown so the day when you come home! She will smile and look happy, and be full of sunshine *then* – and even *should* she frown upon her child returning, there is *another* sky ever serene and fair, and there is *another* sunshine, tho' it be darkness there – never mind faded forests, Austin, never mind silent fields – *here* is a little forest whose leaf is ever green, here is a *brighter* garden, where not a frost has been, in its unfading flowers I hear the bright bee hum, prithee, my Brother, into *my* garden come!

The letters of October 1851 are particularly intense, and the one written one week after this (on the twenty-fifth) shows her in still other modes and moods, including the nostalgic and homiletic:

You had a windy evening going back to Boston, and we thought of *you* many times and hoped you would not be cold. Our fire burned so cheerfully I could'nt help thinking of how many were *here* and how many were *away*, and I wished so many times during that long evening that the door would open and you come walking in. Home is a holy thing – nothing of doubt or distrust can enter it's blessed portals. I feel it more and more as the great world goes on and one another forsake, in whom you place your trust – here seems indeed to be a bit of Eden which not the sin of *any* can utterly destroy – smaller it is indeed, and it may be less fair, but fairer it is and *brighter* than all the world beside. I hope this year in Boston will not impair your health, and I hope you will be as happy as you used to be before. I dont wonder it makes you sober to leave [this] blessed air – if it were in my power I would on every morning transmit it's purest breaths fragrant and cool to you. How I wish you could have it – a thousand little winds waft it to me this morning, fragrant with forest leaves and bright autumnal berries. I would be *willing* to give you my portion for today, and take the salt sea's breath in it's bright, bounding stead.

Several matters may explain the intensity of her mood that month. Susie was away in Baltimore (this was the month of the "sweet silver moon" letter); Joseph Lyman had just left, to Vinnie's sadness; Abiah Root had been offish at the Commencement in August. Emily and Vinnie had had in some ways a most successful visit with Austin in Boston during September, but, apparently, Emily had come home from the trip sadder and wiser. They "had some capital times together," Austin wrote Sue, " – Vinnie enjoyed herself, as she always does among strangers – Emily became confirmed in her opinion of the hollowness & awfulness of the *world.*" Perhaps the theme in the letter—home as "fairer" and *"brighter* than all the world beside"—reflects this experience, a sobering one as she saw the "world" threatening her home, with Austin started on his profession and Vinnie involved with a distant suitor. Or perhaps she was pursuing the "one gold thread" of the letter to Jane Humphrey, and home, like so many other aspects of her life, was taking on ever deeper, more symbolic—and more somber—meaning. A further explanation may lie in the fact that 1851 had been a year of deaths among the young people of Amherst, some of them Emily's close friends. Abby Haskell died in April, age nineteen. In October, John Spencer, Amherst '48, principal of Amherst Academy 1848–49, who had once climbed Mt. Holyoke with Emily and Vinnie, died of consumption. Jennie Grout died on October 27 and "merry Martha Kingman" on the thirtieth, both about Emily's age. "It *cannot* be – yet it is so," Emily wrote Austin that day, " – Jennie Grout was buried yesterday – Martha Kingman died at four o'clock this morning – one and another, and another – how we pass away!"[5] And there was no Austin around to lighten the atmosphere in the Dickinson household, sober enough without him in the best of times.

The mortuary theme appeared most strikingly in a letter of November 11, climaxing Emily's mood of the time. (The two-week interval between letters was average, although at certain times she wrote Austin once a week, or even more.) At first it followed the familiar route of love and loneliness but soon took a new and more hopeful turn. Austin had left for Boston the day before, and that night, "when the chilly wind went down,

5. *L* I, 153 (October 30, 1851). In *Home,* pp. 179–80, Millicent Todd Bingham documents the depressing incidence of death among the young people of Amherst in the early 1850s. In this chapter ("Funerals and Fears") she also documents vividly the primitive state of mid-century medicine and the day-to-day anxiety that must have been the lot of the less robust. On the trip to Boston in the fall of 1851, Emily had consulted the famous homeopathic physician Dr. William Wesselhöft; but why, we do not know. Vinnie and Austin also consulted him about this time. At one point, Vinnie and Emily ran up a bill for sixteen dollars for medicine (*Home,* pp. 213–14).

and the clear, cold moon was shining," she had been very lonely. She thought of Hawthorne's Hepzibah—"how sorrowful *she* was, and how she longed to sleep, because the grave was peaceful," and how she "wearied on" for Clifford's sake. ("I dont mean that you are *him*," she hastened to add, "or that Hepzibah's *me* except in a relative sense, only I was reminded.") Then, thinking of Austin as she went to sleep, she dreamed a dream—real or fictitious, a veritable beatific vision:

> . . . Lo, I *dreamed,* and the world was no more *this* world, but a world bright and fair – no fading leaves, no dying friends, and I heard a voice saying there shall be no more tears, neither any crying, and they answered, *nevermore,* and up from a thousand hearts went a cry of praise and joy and great thanksgiving, and I awoke, yet I know the place was heaven, and the people singing songs were those who in their *lifetimes* were parted and separated, and their joy was because they should never be so any more. Good bye, dear Austin, yet why Good bye, are you not with me always – whether I wake or sleep? "And tho *all others* do, yet will not *I* forsake thee"!

This bit of apocalypse, in the same vein as the dream visions to Uncle Joel, Jane Humphrey, and Abiah, is unique in the letters to Austin, the closest to an intimate confidence. The question is, why do not more such letters survive?

Mostly, she gossiped or bantered or satirized, or wrote him matchless genre pieces on life in Amherst: the fire in the Kimberly's barn or the Sweetser house; the Jenny Lind concert; Professor Park's wonderful sermon—"people stared at each other, and looked as wan and wild, as if they had seen a spirit"; how Mr. Pierce was fined two dollars and costs for beating a servant girl ("Vinnie and I heard the whipping, and could have testified, if the Court had called upon us"); and so on.

Whether Austin was concerned over his sister's retreat from the "hollowness and awfulness of the *world*," her "fleeing to her mind," or if he found anything to worry about in the Hepzibah comparison or the dream vision, cannot be said. Such an effusion may have prompted him (as she accused him once) to recommend a "simpler" style. It would be particularly interesting to know what he thought of one of her most sustained bits on Amherst, one that tells us, at least, a great deal about her growing withdrawal from the Amherst scene. In this passage, she quite literally flees to her own mind.

On June 9, 1853, a trainload of celebrants came from New London, Connecticut, to honor the completion of the Amherst & Belchertown Rail Road. It was Edward Dickinson's big day, with appropriate pomp and circumstance. Emily describes it—and her own part in the proceedings.

> The New London Day passed off grandly – so all the people said – it was pretty hot and dusty, but nobody cared for that. Father was as usual, Chief Marshal of the day, and went marching around the town with New London at his heels like some old Roman General, upon a Triumph Day. Mrs Howe got a capital dinner, and was very much praised. Carriages flew like sparks,

hither, and thither and yon, and they all said t'was fine. I spose it was – I
sat in Prof Tyler's woods and saw the train move off, and then ran home
again for fear somebody would see me, or ask me how I did.

Knowing his sister, Austin was probably neither surprised nor worried.
We, perhaps, can see Emily's taking to the woods (while the Amherst
and New London leaders celebrated Industry, Trade, and Progress) as a
neurotic escape, a portent of stranger behavior to come. But, in another
view, her fleeing to her mind may have been a well-calculated way of
mastering a phenomenon that obviously disturbed her deeply. As with
loneliness, loss of friends, death, and fear of a disintegrating home, she
had to come to terms with this public display of aspects of contemporary
life she distrusted and in which her father, whom she loved and revered,
gloried. Her way was simply to detach herself from it, think about it,
write about it to Austin, and later, perhaps, in her poem:

> I like to hear it lap the Miles –
> And lick the Valleys up –
> And stop to feed itself at Tanks –
> And then – prodigious step
>
> Around a Pile of Mountains –
> And supercilious peer
> In Shanties – by the sides of Roads –
> And then a Quarry pare
>
> To fit it's sides
> And crawl between
> Complaining all the while
> In horrid – hooting stanza –
> Then chase itself down Hill –
>
> And neigh like Boanerges –
> Then – prompter than a Star
> Stop – docile and omnipotent
> At it's own stable door –[6]   (#585, about 1862)

6. The 1955 *Poems* rejects the variant reading "hear it" for "see it" in line one.
But what seems to have thrilled her most about the new railroad was its *sound*. On
May 16, 1853, she had written to Austin: "While I write, the whistle is playing, and
the cars just coming in. It gives us all new life, every time it plays. How you will love
to hear it, when you come home again!" And later (November 10, 1853): "You asked
me about the railroad – Everybody seems pleased at the change in arrangement. It
sounds so pleasantly to hear them come in twice. I hope there will be a bell soon."
The sense of ambivalence in such details in the poem as the "horrid – hooting stanza,"
in such words as "prodigious," "supercilious," "complaining," "omnipotent," and in
the image of the monster with its sinister "docility," perhaps came later, after she had
thought the whole phenomenon over and was able to give her uneasiness a more
precise statement. At the very least, both letter and poem show the growing distance
between ED and the Amherst community.

It is doubtful if many of the participants in the New London Day saw in quite this way what it was they were celebrating: the ambiguity of power, the excitement of this new monster and yet its threat. But such insights, she might have told Austin, come from the "brimfull feeling," which requires solitude and thought.

Our knowledge of what Austin thought is limited, of course, by the one-sidedness of the correspondence. But there is another aspect of her nature that, in human terms, might have been even more disturbing to a solicitous brother, had he noticed it, than those tendencies which put her increasingly out of the reach of Amherst folk. A recurrent if muted theme in the letters suggests that even Austin gave her the same difficulty she later complained about to Higginson—"All men say 'What' to me"—a problem reflected in her earlier description of her father staring in bewilderment, and Vinnie in astonishment, at "some things I say." If, in the letters to Austin we have, she never unburdened herself as she did to Abiah and Jane, the reason may have been—for all their mutualities, their humor and spirit—a kind of reserve between brother and sister. Twice Emily referred to long sessions of talk with Austin: those "interviews with you at the *Barn*" and "the long talks . . . upon the *kitchen stone hearth,* when the just are fast asleep," but what transpired in them is probably lost forever. The fact is that Austin was an older brother in a male-dominated household, and he could be critical. "If I had'nt been afraid that you would 'poke fun' at my feelings," she wrote on June 8, 1851, "I had written a *sincere* letter, but since the 'world is hollow, and Dollie is stuffed with sawdust,' I really do not think we had better expose our feelings." It was only a little later (March 12, 1853) that she wrote Susan Gilbert: "I find I need more vail – " At least in the surviving letters to Austin, she kept at a safely ironic distance, a device she found unnecessary with the girls. On June 22, 1851, referring to the interviews in the barn, which in his absence she found "frought with a saddened interest," she whetted his appetite for renewed conversations by promising to be more intelligent and mature when he got back from Boston:

> . . . I suppose I am a fool – you always said I was one, and yet I have some feelings that seem sensible to me, and I have desires to see you now that you are gone which are really quite intelligent. Dont take too much encouragement, but really I have the hope of becoming before you come quite an *accountable being!*

Even in this mostly jocular passage, where her soundings seem anything but deep, one can see basic differences between the two. For all the flights of fancy of her "romantic" Brother Pegasus, Austin's ways of thinking and standards of judgment were not those of an emerging poet. After all, he had just graduated from college with honors, he was teaching school, and he was headed for the law. Feelings that seemed sensible and intelligent to her she feared he would think foolish. Writing to Jane Humphrey, she could expand on the figure of the "one gold thread," the "long, big shining fibre," and merge it into others—the spring, the buds, the green grove—freely and joyfully. She could share with Abiah her feelings about the challenge of the open sea and the "danger," about the fancies she was letting blossom, even if their fruit should be bitter. But she could not talk this way to Austin, at least not in the letters we have—the dream vision being the nearest approach.

In her next letter (June 29, 1851), the issue is squarely joined, even if the tone is still light. She (or the family) had just received a long letter from Austin. "I like it grandly – very – because it is so long, and also it's *so* funny – " It delighted them all: ". . . we have all been laughing till the old house rung again at your delineations of men, women, and things"— delineations in the Dickinson satiric style, it can be assumed, the same that mimicked the preacher and mocked Jenny Lind's performance, the norm being good Dickinson common sense. During the laughter over his letter,

I feel quite like retiring, in presence of one so grand, and casting my small lot among small birds, and fishes – you say you dont comprehend me, you want a simpler style. *Gratitude* indeed for all my fine philosophy! I strove to be exalted thinking I might reach *you* and while I pant and struggle and climb the nearest cloud, you walk out very leisurely in your slippers from Empyrean, and without the *slightest* notice request me to get down! As *simple* as you please, the *simplest* sort of simple – I'll be a little ninny – a little pussy catty, a little Red Riding Hood, I'll wear a Bee in my Bonnet, and a Rose bud in my hair and what remains to do you shall be told here- after.

What she meant by "all my fine philosophy" and what precisely Austin had in mind by the style he found too complicated are questions hard to answer. One must go back at least eight months among the letters that survive (to October 27, 1850) to find a single passage that might bother the most rationalist of brothers; and this is no more than the whimsical teasing she sent Uncle Joel Norcross or the raillery of the valentines—throwing stones, as she put it, without hurting people. Austin was on his first job, teaching at Sunderland. Apparently, he was feeling his superiority and beginning to condescend. The letter begins with no salutation:

Suppose "Topknot" should come down, and speak to his brothers, and sisters, or bind up the broken hearts of divers deserted friends, suppose he should doff his crown, and lay down his lofty sceptre, and once more a patient child receive reproof, and correction, salute the insulted rod, and bow to the common Lord!

An affection of *nin*[e]teen years for the most ungrateful of brothers jogs now and then at my elbow, and calls for paper and pen. Permit me to tie your shoe, to run like a dog behind you. I can bark, see here! Bow wow! Now if that is'nt fine I don't know! Permit me to be a stick, to show how I will not beat you, a stone, how I will not fling, musquito, I will not sting. Permit me to be a fowl, which Bettie shall dress for dinner, a bantam, a fine,

fat hen. I will crow in my *grave* if you will, Chanticleer being still, tho'
sleeping. Herein I "deign to condescend to stoop so low," what a high hill
between me, and thee, a *hill,* upon my word, it is a *mountain,* I dare not
climb. Let's call it "Alp," or "*Ande,*" or yet the "Ascension Mount." I have
it! – you shall be "Jove" a sitting on great "Olympus," a whittling the light-
nings out, and hurling at your relations. Oh, "Jupiter"! fie! for shame!
Kings sometimes have fathers and mothers. Father and I are going to have
a Cattle Show Wednesday. School masters and Monkeys half price. I guess
you had better "come down." They've appointed *you* joint committee on the
"Beast with the seven horns.["] If time, and ability fail you, they'll omit
the remaining horn. There's an old hand they call "Revelation." I dare say
he will give you a lift!

There are other minor stylistic flings in the letters, but nothing to account
for Austin's saying he could not understand her, certainly nothing so
riddling as the letters to Abiah and Jane. Either the exchange between the
two about "simple style" was pure joke, or some letters have been lost. At
the very least, the fact that Emily brought the matter up at all, on whatever level, shows a degree of constraint between them.

The constraint was not serious, however. If it inhibited Emily's confessional tendencies, it stimulated, happily, her more extroverted ones,
toward Amherst doings and gossip. The letters for the most part trip
merrily on. There are sighs of loneliness and longing, not, apparently,
very profound. But a somber and prophetic tone gradually develops.

To recapitulate: When Sue first came into the life of the family shortly
after Emily returned from Mount Holyoke (Austin's courtship began
more or less seriously about 1850), she was a great bond between brother
and sister. Until about 1854, the most precise date so far for the troubled
"you can go or stay" letter from Emily to Sue, all seems to have been
harmonious between the two girls. Sue was the dear sister; increasingly
Emily was lonely for Austin *and* Sue; she rejoiced in a successful
maneuver by Sue when the engagement was settled but still secret: "Sue's
outwitted them all – ha-ha!"; she defended Sue and Austin against the
gossips: "Dont mind them," she wrote Austin. "Nobody'll dare to harm
dear Susie, nobody'll dare to harm you"; she rejoiced that Mother and
Father were taking Sue unto their own. But the time came when she
seemed to have realized that the new intimacy between Sue and Austin
meant, if not the end, at least the lessening of their intimacy with her. I
return to my earlier observation that Emily demanded a great deal of her
friends. In the early love letters to Sue, she as much as asked that they be
all-in-all to each other; it was as if she thought she could absorb Sue to
herself. Higginson's complaint comes to mind again: "I never was with
any one who drained my nerve power so much." The rift with Sue (over
what specific issue we do not know) is clearly documented in the letter of
late August 1854 complaining of neglect. The "go or stay" letter points out
that "We differ often lately, and this must be the last," and in late January
1855 she wrote with seeming finality, though softened by the sweetness of

the rest of the letter, of raising "the lid to my box of Phantoms," to "lay one more love in." From then on, despite all the jolly evenings we hear about in the Evergreens in the late 1850s (when, as she said, Austin and Sue were her "crowd"), the old intimacy seems never to have been restored. Sue was not to be absorbed, and the increasing complexities of Austin's involvement made the old intimacies impossible.

There are signs in Emily's letters to Austin about the time of the engagement (spring 1853) that she saw the inevitable. In the very letter (April 8, 1853) in which she remarked upon their dependence on each other for delight, she concluded: "I shall never write any more grand letters to you, but all the *little* things, and the things called *trifles,* and the crickets upon the hearth, you will be sure to hear." Four days later, she wrote of a long talk with Sue on a certain Saturday night, apparently a customary meeting time: "I have taken *your place* Saturday evening, since you have been away, but I will give it back to you as soon as you get home"—an inevitable exchange, of course, but a sad one for Emily. She slipped at once into nostalgia, concluding with a bit of confession, unusual at this stage in her letters to Austin. She sighs for the old days when "the nails hang full of coats," and the chairs hang full of hats, and she could "count the slippers under the kitchen chair":

> Oh Austin, how we miss them, and more than them, somebody who used to hang them there, and get many a hint ungentle, to carry them away. Those times seem far off now, a great way, as things we did when children. I wish we were children now. I wish we were *always* children, how to grow up I dont know.

Growing up meant change and change meant loss. Her moodiest letter in some time came the next month (May 16, 1853). Whether the tone is mortuary (Newton had died in March) or nostalgic, or whether it arose from her sense of the end of an era in their relationship—perhaps a bit of all three—the letter contains one of the most touching of all those passages in the early letters to her friends which signalize the end of intimacy, the parting of ways. Perhaps this sense of poignancy would be lessened if we knew that those long talks in the kitchen or the barn had continued to exert their tonic effect on her spirits. They did for some months, anyway. But although the letter brightened up as it went along, there is little in the early correspondences to equal this somber prophecy:

> Somehow I am lonely lately – I feel very old every day, and when morning comes and the birds sing, they dont seem to make me so happy as they used to. I guess it's because you're gone, and there are not so many of us as God gave for each other. I wish you were at home. I feel very sure lately that the years we have had together are more than we shall have – I guess we shall journey separately, or reach the journey's end, some of us – but we don't know.

As Sue and Austin's engagement progressed, the letters were shorter and given over mostly to news. The last substantial one we have was written in the summer of 1854, two years before the marriage. It is inconceivable that the correspondence (save for the three later trifles) ended there. Emily wrote Sue from Washington in February 1855 and spoke of having heard from Austin. It would have been strange had she not answered him. Perhaps her letters were too trivial, or too intimate, for Austin to save. In spite of the signs of disharmony during the latter months of the engagement, and the tensions between Sue and both the Dickinson girls, and the troubled course of the engagement itself, it is hard to understand why none of the family went with Austin to his wedding in Geneva, New York, on July 1, 1856. And his bitter remark to Mabel Todd that on that day he felt as if he were going to his execution remains haunting, even if it owes something to Dickinson rhetoric, to the accumulated bitterness of years, and to his desire to justify himself to Mabel. If he and Emily shared their inmost thoughts—and in writing—Emily's letters may have gone the same way as did Mabel's during the early months of that relationship. Such an action would have been true to Dickinson secretiveness, but it is unprovable.

Emily's prophecy in 1853 seems to have been sadly accurate: "I guess we shall journey separately." Her remarks about Austin in her other correspondences after 1856 are infrequent and curiously casual. Austin's absorptions were many and demanding—his law practice, town and college affairs, his complicated home. The Newman girls came to live in the Evergreens in 1858, and from the start Sue and he maintained an active social life, in which after a certain point Emily did not share. It is true that during his years of greatest stress in the early 1880s Austin came more and more to the Homestead and to Emily (". . . we almost forget that he ever passed to a wedded Home"). What pleasant references there are come mainly in the early years. To Mr. and Mrs. Samuel Bowles she wrote in June 1858: "I rode with Austin this morning. He showed me mountains that touched the sky, and brooks that sang like Bobolinks. Was he not very kind?" We hear of his dining at the Homestead that September, in Sue's absence; of the "blissful" evenings in the Evergreens with Kate Scott and the Bowleses in 1859; and of a brotherly scolding Austin gave Emily in 1862 when she refused to receive a call from Mr. Bowles.[7] But as time went on, Emily journeyed so separately, not only

---

7. In a letter (conjecturally dated late 1859), Emily wrote to Kate Scott (Anthon), Susan's friend from school days in Utica, New York, and occasional visitor at the Evergreens: "How do you do this year? I remember you as fires begin, and evenings open at Austin's, without the Maid in black, Katie, without the Maid in black. Those were unnatural evenings. – Bliss is unnatural –" (L II, 355). As to the scolding, she had it from Vinnie, too. "Because I did not see you," Emily wrote Bowles in late November 1862, "Vinnie and Austin, upbraided me –" (L II, 419). Another indication of Austin's irritation at her increasingly eccentric behavior came earlier, during one of those evenings in the Evergreens. It was on the occasion of the unexpected call from Mr. Chapman and Mr. Hyde of Ware. ". . . some one rang the bell," Emily wrote Mrs. Holland, "and I ran, as is my custom. . . . Austin said we [Emily and Kate Scott, "my confederate"] were very rude, and I crept to my little room, quite chagrined and wretched . . ." (L II, 348, about February 20, 1859).

from the Evergreens but from all Amherst, that it is hard to construct a coherent relationship between brother and sister from the scattered references after 1860.

One of the most puzzling, and perhaps a measure of the distance between the two during the middle years, comes after Edward Dickinson's death, when Austin's new responsibilities were weighing on him and when—if there is any credence at all in the account of his marriage we have from Mabel Todd—his life with Sue was becoming intolerable. Late in January 1875, Emily wrote Mrs. Holland:

> Austin's Family went to Geneva, and Austin lived with us four weeks.
> It seemed peculiar – pathetic – and Antediluvian. We missed him while he
> was with us and missed him when he was gone.
> All is so very curious.

Whatever she had in mind precisely, the old spirit was gone. One wonders whether it was Sue's long absence that struck her as peculiar, or Austin's taking his father's place in the Homestead, or the change in her once uproarious brother. Was Austin's loneliness "pathetic," or was it the failure of the old intimacy between brother and sister, or did she have in mind the failure of the marriage? At any rate, she is obviously lamenting the end of an era, now so long gone that it seemed antediluvian.

The one thing certain is that Austin, to say the very least, was not one of those Phantoms she put back in her box of memories. He was a very solid reality right to the end. He paid the bills, saw to the chores, kept the machinery running. The advent of Mabel Todd, though it split the Houses irrevocably in one way, in another brought them together. "I see Vin and Em more than I did," Austin wrote Mabel in July 1885. It was Austin and Vinnie (and not Sue) whom Emily saw standing by her bedside—"all so kind and hallowed"—as she came to consciousness after her first fainting spell in the summer of 1884. But when Austin married Sue, the break in Emily's life was real; 1856 did mark the end of an era, for all her efforts to prolong it. A remark in a letter to Mary Bowles about August 1861 has a symbolic finality, or at least it is tempting to read one in, however whimsical its context. Vinnie, she tells Mrs. Bowles, would send her love, "but she put on a white frock, and went to meet tomorrow – " Mother would, too, but she is in the " 'Eave spout,' sweeping up a leaf, that blew in, last November." As for Austin, he "would send his – but he dont live here – now – He married – and went East."

20

Charles Wadsworth

DURING HIS TENURE as Representative from the Tenth Congressional District of Massachusetts, Edward Dickinson twice arranged for members of his family to visit him in Washington. Both times they stayed at the Willard Hotel; but it was only the second visit, February–March 1855, that included Emily.[1] During the first one, in April 1854, she stayed at home, with Susan Gilbert and cousin John Graves for company and protection. This was the time that Emily called "Our April" in her letter to Graves, and it was then that John heard Emily's heavenly music that enchanted him and woke up Sue.

Apparently Emily had fought shy of the first trip, and her father had given in to her. On March 13, 1854, he had written Austin from Washington, "I have written home, to have Lavinia come with yr mother & you – & Emily too, if she will – but that I will not insist upon her coming." As the time approached for the second visit, Emily wrote Sue (who was away) that she "would give the whole world if I could stay, instead" in Amherst for Sue's return. But she went, probably in late January or early February, perhaps with Vinnie as her only companion (Mrs. Dickinson and Austin stayed home), and with no further recorded reluctance. Except for the sojourn in Boston because of her eyes nine years later, it turned out to be her longest trip away from Amherst and certainly a major experience. This much can be said even though Martha Dickinson Bianchi's claim that it was then that Emily "met her fate" must be questioned.

1. The date of Emily's visit to Washington was long thought to be 1854 and her letters written during the visit dated accordingly (see *Home*, pp. 342 ff.). But this was under the assumption that there was only one Dickinson family visit. It is now certain that there were two and that Emily went only on the second. (See *L* I, 289 n., II, 318 n., and 319 n.; David Higgins, *Portrait of Emily Dickinson*, p. 80.)

The trip had two phases, three weeks in Washington with Father and two in Philadelphia with the Colemans, whose sole surviving daughter Eliza (after Olivia's death) was Emily's special friend and admirer. Most of our knowledge of what happened on the trip comes from two of Emily's letters, one from Washington to Sue and Martha Gilbert on February 28 and one from Philadelphia to Mrs. Holland on March 18. They are not very helpful, either as to external details or inmost thoughts. The thoughts in the first are mostly home thoughts, tinged with Dickinson homesickness, perhaps in this instance real. "I have not been well since I came here," she wrote the Gilberts, "and that has excused me from some gaieties, tho' at that I'm gayer than I was before." At least we have her response to her only Southern spring:

> Sweet and soft as summer, Darlings, maple trees in bloom and grass green in the sunny places – hardly seems it possible this is winter still; and it makes the grass spring in this heart of mine and each linnet sing, to think that you have come [back to Amherst].

This is in fact quite at variance with the chilly meteorological data of Washington at that time, but she was a New England girl and had known only Amherst springs.

In the letter to Mrs. Holland she told of a notable trip she took with Vinnie to Mount Vernon. Her description of the day shows, among other things, a sense of history she is seldom credited with. She responded warmly to this hallowed spot, singing a requiem (as her Grandfather Fowler had done) for the soul of General George Washington. It is true that she was never discursive on historical matters; her imagination was more prophetic, or apocalyptic, looking more to the end of things than to the beginnings; but here for once, at least, she was caught in the spell of the past. She soon disposes of the fripperies of Washington:

> I will not tell you what I saw – the elegance, the grandeur; you will not care to know the value of the diamonds my Lord and Lady wore, but if you haven't been to the sweet Mount Vernon, then I *will* tell you how on one soft spring day we glided down the Potomac in a painted boat, and jumped upon the shore – how hand in hand we stole along up a tangled pathway till we reached the tomb of General George Washington, how we paused beside it, and no one spoke a word, then hand in hand, walked on again, not less wise or sad for that marble story; how we went within the door – raised the latch he lifted when he last went home – thank the Ones in Light that he's since passed in through a brighter wicket! Oh, I could spend a long day, if it did not weary you, telling of Mount Vernon – and I will sometime if we live and meet again, and God grant we shall!

Beautiful and moving as such experiences were, Emily nevertheless persisted in her sense of the "hollowness and awfulness" of the world that Austin had noted when she came to Boston, even if it was moderated in Washington and Philadelphia by the graciousness and kindliness she met on every hand. There is no word about what Father did for them in

Washington, or where he took them. Perhaps he was too busy, for the record shows that he was active in the House during those weeks. The sisters were much on their own. "Vinnie is with me here," Emily wrote Mrs. Holland, "and we have wandered together into many new ways. . . . We have had many pleasant times, and seen much that is fair, and heard much that is wonderful – many sweet ladies and noble gentlemen have taken us by the hand and smiled upon us pleasantly – and the sun shines brighter for our way thus far." They had pleasant converse with Rufus Saxton, a cousin of the Gilberts, met by chance in the hotel. (He later became a general and visited Sue and Austin in the Evergreens.) "We walked in the hall a long while [she wrote the Gilberts] talking of you, my Children, vieing with each other in compliment to those we loved so well." Despite all this, much of both of Emily's letters from Washington is taken up with longing for reunion with family and friends, or thoughts of home, or assurances of love, or—perhaps the basic theme, however muted—her distaste for the glitter and the worldliness:

> Dear Children – Mattie – Sue – for one look at you, for your gentle voices, I'd exchange it all. The pomp – the court – the etiquette – they are of the earth – will not enter Heaven.

Poets, as Robert Frost once remarked of Emily Dickinson, need not go to Niagara to write about the force of falling water. Apparently Emily had seen enough of the world in Washington to last her a lifetime. She was not moved to describe any more of it, at least in the letters we have. The only other clues to further activities of the visit come from Vinnie's late reminiscences or those of other guests at the Willard who responded to Emily's later fame by searching their memories for whatever they could recall. Thus it is that we hear about Vinnie's wit as reported by Professor Chickering, and of Mrs. Jeanie Greenough's kindly but imprecise memory of Emily:

> My first acquaintance with Emily D. was in Washington many years ago. Her father was in Congress. He, with his two daughters, my father & mother & myself were together at Willards Hotel. Emily impressed me as a girl with large, warm heart, earnest nature & delicate tastes, & we soon became friends.

Emily's remark to a judge who sat next to her at dinner, when the flaming plum pudding was passed, has come down somehow or other: "Oh, Sir, may one eat of hell fire with impunity here?" We know that the girls made the friendship of a certain Mrs. James Brown of Alabama who later sent them a novel, and that Vinnie walked with "some ladies here" and got tired out. We know that the two girls, according to Mrs. Henrietta Mack Eliot's memory of Vinnie's reminiscence, met and admired Mr. Thomas D. Eliot of New Bedford, Mrs. Eliot's husband's uncle (and T. S. Eliot's granduncle), who as member of Congress was also at the Willard with his family.[2] Except for the trip to Mount Vernon, however, there is nothing about how the girls passed their days, whether they visited other monuments or the seats of government, whether they saw their father in action, or what they thought of the whole rugged display of democracy at work. All we know is that, about March 4, they arrived in Philadelphia, probably escorted there by Edward Dickinson on his way back to Amherst.

It is this second phase of the trip that has long been thought the crucial one, for here is supposed to have come Emily's encounter with the Reverend Charles Wadsworth, famous minister of the Arch Street Presbyterian Church, the Colemans' church, where Eliza would surely have taken her visitors. And yet we know even less about what the girls did in Philadelphia than about what they did in Washington, let alone anything specific about an encounter with Wadsworth. The only surviving letter from Philadelphia is the one to Mrs. Holland, and in it Emily makes no mention of having heard Wadsworth preach or even, for that matter, of having gone to church. The omission is curious in view of Emily's frequent mention in earlier letters of sermons that impressed her, like Henry Boynton Smith's when she was at Mount Holyoke or Edwards Amasa Park's when he was guest preacher in Amherst in 1853 ("I never heard anything like it, and dont expect to again"). But she must have heard Wadsworth at this time if her lifelong though distant and sparsely documented friendship with him is to have any ascertainable origin at all. There is as yet no other possibility.

For it is clear that such a friendship existed, that other people knew about it (though they disagreed widely as to its nature), and that it lasted until Wadsworth's death in 1882. Disagreement is still far from being resolved, if indeed it is resolvable. At the romantic extreme is the notion of love at first sight, mutually recognized but renounced in deference to Wadsworth's married state. This version has Emily returning to Amherst in despair, writing her poems of passion and frustration, and, soon after, retiring in white from the world.

The flaws in this interpretation have often been pointed out. Current dating of the poems by handwriting (however tentative) makes it probable that the poems of frustrated love did not begin until four or five years after the Philadelphia visit. The one scrap of correspondence that survives is a brief note, undated and unsigned, from Wadsworth to "My Dear Miss Dickenson" offering consolation and comfort for an unspecified sorrow or anxiety about which Emily had written him. The note was first published

2. The hell-fire story is reported in Martha Dickinson Bianchi's *Life and Letters* (p. 46) as a story "handed down in the family." For Mrs. Brown's gift (*The Last Leaf from Sunny Side,* by Elizabeth Stuart Phelps, 1854) and Mrs. Eliot's reminiscence, see *YH* I, 328. Vinnie was especially impressed by Mr. Eliot's affectionate ways with his daughters, the good-night kisses, and so on. She was moved by such displays to speak of her own father thus: "He never kissed us goodnight in his life – He would have died for us, but he would have died before he would have let us know it!"

in *Emily Dickinson's Home,* where it is reproduced in facsimile and fully discussed. It is an earnest but formal pastoral reply. Suggested dates start at 1858 (when Emily's anxiety may have been her mother's health); move on to 1862, to square things with the so-called "Master" letters; and go as far as 1877, when Emily was distressed over the illness of Samuel Bowles. As to 1858, one must assume that her distress was great enough to make her seek beyond Amherst for help. (The evidence is not conclusive.) 1862 must face the many and cogent arguments recently made against the theory that Wadsworth was the Master of the letters,[3] while 1877 reduces to something quite professional and remote the friendship that Emily described so tenderly, after Wadsworth's death, in her letters to his friends the Clark brothers.[4]

In the note, Wadsworth begged to hear more about the "affliction which has befallen, or is now befalling you [could this refer to her eye trouble of 1863–64?]," and concluded, "In great haste," "Sincerely and most Affectionately *Yours.*" It is to be noted that he misspelled her surname and failed to sign his own. More important than any inference that can be drawn from such a document is the nature of Emily's life, insofar as it can be pieced together from scanty knowledge, for the four or five years after Philadelphia. It seems clear that her withdrawal was neither abrupt nor dramatic. In 1859 and 1860, she was still going to church, if irregularly, "doing her courtesies," and enjoying evenings of gaiety at the Evergreens. Many letters of the period describe moments, at least, of laughter and delight. Vinnie's explanation of the withdrawal, though far from the whole truth, seems more likely: "[it] was only a happen," a way of life gradually induced by domestic cares and the needs of her own temperament. As to the immolation in white, it is well known that she wore white a good deal, but the custom was probably not fixed until after her father's death.[5]

3. The main arguments, including the argument from the handwriting, are summarized by David Higgins, *Portrait,* pp. 81 ff.

4. *YH* I, xxxiv. James and Charles Clark were natives of Northampton who later moved to Brooklyn, where James established a school with Charles Brownell ("Clark and Brownell"), to both of whom she had been introduced by her father, probably at a Commencement tea about 1859. Her correspondence with the brothers began shortly after Wadsworth's death.

5. Precisely when the white dresses became habitual is hard to tell. She was "a spirit clad in white" when Joseph Lyman saw her in the mid-sixties. The suggestion about her wearing white after her father's death (as told me by Millicent Todd Bingham) came from Mabel Todd, who got it from Austin. As to the happy letters, some spirited ones were going, for instance, to Mrs. Joseph Haven, from whom (*L* II, 336–37, early summer 1858) she wishes to borrow De Quincey's novel, *Klosterheim,* and *The Confessions of an English Opium-Eater* ("for tho' the hours are very full, I think that I might snatch here and there a moment, if I had the books"). Her remark in this letter that "I do not go out at all, lest father will come and miss me" is in curious contradiction to her remark to Mrs. Haven six months later about "doing her courtesies" with Vinnie. "We have hardly recovered laughing," she wrote (February 13, 1859) from a "jolly" letter from Mr. Haven (*L* II, 346). A breezy letter went off

Another view has the Wadsworth meeting growing into an all-encompassing fantasy in her mind, much as the lovers in the medieval Courts of Love are supposed to have idealized their beloveds. In this rich and romantic tradition, the enemy of true love, paradoxically, was marriage. To know the truth of love, the lover must languish in despair, savor the reality of fulfilled love by living through its opposite, rejection and loneliness. So Emily (according to the theory), enchanted by her preacher (Wadsworth was forty-one in 1855, at the height of his remarkable powers) and knowing that he was forever forbidden her, returned to Amherst to nourish her dream, to live in her imagination through the whole course of love, fulfilled and unfulfilled, and to re-create in her poems its every phase and meaning. Thus Wadsworth was not so much the man in her life as the one who provided the idea of what a man in her life would have been like. He may have been other things to her, her "Shepherd from 'Little Girl'hood,'" as she wrote James Clark, but according to this theory, he was her Muse, the source and inspiration of her greatest love poems.[6]

No one can deny that something of this sort may have operated in Emily's consciousness. We have seen how her younger friends, Newton and Gould and Graves and the others, either left or died or disappointed her. As Joseph Lyman said, she seemed *older* than the rest. The excitement of the visit to Washington and Philadelphia, with new experiences and impressions every day, must have made her already acute sensitivities all the sharper. She was beginning to grapple with questions and problems that her younger friends, male and female, could not help her with. She was capable of being greatly moved by sermons, and it was to become her habit to turn to older men for spiritual guidance, especially clergymen. A single sermon by Wadsworth, a gifted preacher and a somewhat mysterious personality, might well have had a deep and lasting effect.

Certainly Wadsworth could have provided spiritual sustenance beyond the usual Amherst fare. He was a man of impressive stature. He had graduated from Union College in 1838, taught two years in Canajoharie, New York, spent two years in the Princeton Theological Seminary, and was pastor of the Second Presbyterian Church of Troy, N.Y., from 1842 to 1850. He accepted the call to Philadelphia in 1850, and in a few years raised the Arch Street Church from a dwindling affair of twelve families to a position of prominence and even fame. His popularity in Philadelphia has been compared to Henry Ward Beecher's in Brooklyn and his preaching was ranked second only to Beecher's in the country. In April 1862, he accepted a call from the Calvary Presbyterian Society in San

---

to Sue in Michigan on September 26, 1858 (*L* II, 339–40); and the letters of the period to the Hollands, the Norcrosses, and Kate Scott are sprinkled with gossip, fun, flowers, young ambition, and satiric or philosophic shafts that counterpoint and lighten the somber themes.

6. This theory is argued at length by William Robert Sherwood, *Circumference and Circumstance.*

Francisco at a salary of $7,000, a move which was long thought (in keeping with the romantic theory of the relationship) to account for Emily's complaint in her letter to Higginson of April 25, 1862, of her "terror since September," the chronological difficulty being resolved by the suggestion that Wadsworth must have told her of his intentions as early as September 1861. In 1869 he refused a call to the Third Congregational Church of New Haven and returned to Philadelphia (the Alexander Church). In 1871 he refused still another call, this time from Chicago. Many of his sermons were published, in pamphlet form, in periodicals, and collected in four volumes, two during his lifetime (1869 and 1882) and two after his death (1884 and 1905).[7]

Emily seems to have paid as little attention to Wadsworth's worldly fame as she did to her father's. In her letters to James Clark he was simply "the beloved Clergyman," "my Shepherd . . . so noble . . . so fathomless – so gentle," "my dearest earthly friend." In a letter to Higginson a few months after Wadsworth died, he was "my closest earthly friend"; to Judge Lord about the same time, "My Philadelphia." It is not even clear whether Higginson and Lord were supposed to have known whom she meant; she did not mention Wadsworth's name. In a letter to James Clark a year after Wadsworth's death, she spoke pointedly of Clark's being the only one, "with the exception of my Sister," to whom she had ever spoken about Wadsworth, adding "though the great confidences of Life are first disclosed by their departure – "

Fortunately, we have a firsthand account of Wadsworth in the pulpit near enough in time to Emily's visit to give a good idea of what she would have seen and heard had she attended the Arch Street Church on one of her Sundays in Philadelphia. On October 22, 1850, the *Springfield Republican* reprinted an article on him from the *New York Evening Post,* which, incidentally, gives ample reason why the Colemans might have insisted that their guests hear Wadsworth preach and why Emily, sensitive to great preaching and emotionally susceptible (having recently dropped a lost love or two in her box of Phantoms), might have been deeply moved.

> *A New Lion.* – Philadelphia is greatly interested just now by the preaching of the Rev. Charles Wadsworth, of the Arch-street Church, lately of Troy, in this State. It is said that his church is besieged by persons anxious to hear him, long before the hour for the services to commence. His person is slender, and his dark eyes, hair and complexion have decidedly a Jewish cast. The elements of his popularity are somewhat like those of the gifted Summerfield – a sweet touching voice, warmth of manner, and lively imagination. But Wadsworth's style, it is said, is vastly bolder, his fancy more vivid, and his action more violent. . . . A correspondent says, "that the subjects which the Arch-street pastor selects for his pulpit discussions are

7. Wadsworth has had no biographer. Even the biographical dictionaries neglect him in favor of his more famous son, Charles Jr. Jay Leyda's penetrating sketch (*YH* I, lxxvi–lxxviii) is the most useful single document available.

Charles Wadsworth
as a young man

Jane Locke Wadsworth

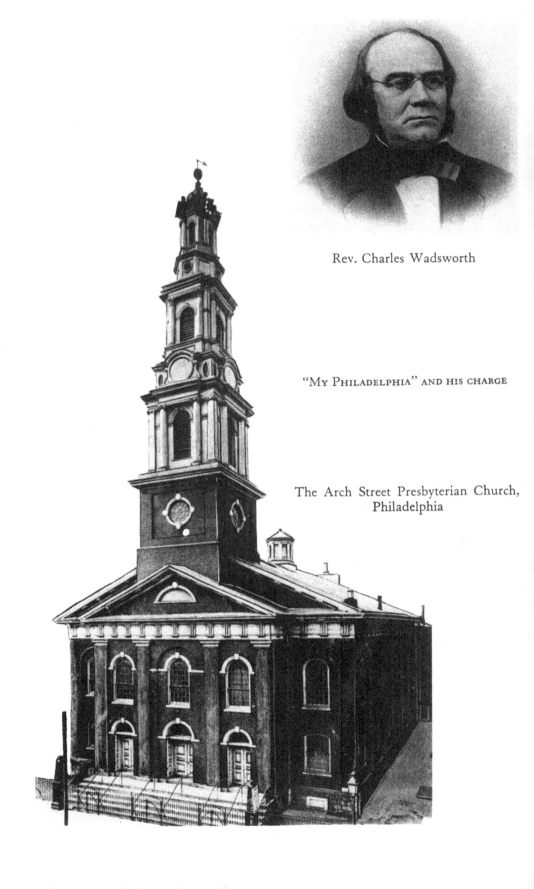

Rev. Charles Wadsworth

"My Philadelphia" and his charge

The Arch Street Presbyterian Church,
Philadelphia

peculiar, and quite out of the usual line. His texts are short. . . . In illustrating such phrases as "Jesus wept," and "watching the dying Savior," the plaintive wail of his tremulous voice is singularly subdued and effective. . . . In argumentation, Mr Wadsworth is rapid, unique and original, often startling his audience, like Dr Bushnell, with a seeming paradox. How long his imagination will sustain such adventurous flights, and how long his feeble frame will bear such pressure, it is impossible to conjecture."[8]

Transferred to Emily's poetry, many of these phrases describing Wadsworth's style fit exactly; and it is not surprising to find that Wadsworth himself started out as a poet, that he disliked Tennyson,[9] and that his humor toward revered things was not unlike Emily's own. Apparently, he could strike a whimsical pose, even in the pulpit; Mark Twain, who heard him in San Francisco in 1866, recorded an instance:

Dr. Wadsworth never fails to preach an able sermon; but every now and then, with an admirable assumption of not being aware of it, he will get off a firstrate joke and then frown severely at any one who is surprised

8. *YH* I, 181. About Wadsworth's homiletic style and appearance in the pulpit, reports differ. While the *Post* article spoke of his plaintive voice and feeble frame, George F. Whicher (*This Was a Poet*, pp. 101 ff.), who had talked with a member of Wadsworth's congregation, stressed his "deep voice and sturdy frame – he was five feet ten inches tall," his "dynamic power," his "strength that was not of this world only." Whicher wrote: "his sheer moral intensity penetrated the most sealed and obdurate hearts, and his congregations were shaken as if by a whirlwind. As Emily Dickinson put it, he wrought upon his hearers gradually, then with increasing hammer strokes, and when the stupendous moment came, dealt 'one imperial thunderbolt that scalps your naked soul.' " Whicher apparently assumed that the poem "He fumbles at your Soul" (#315, about 1862), from which these lines are taken, is about Wadsworth; but Emily had heard other great preachers and had been "scalped" by them. Both the *Post* and Whicher leave out Wadsworth's humor. Another quality, his intellectual power, was emphasized in an article of September 8, 1875, in the *Metropolitan* (*YH* II, 236): "In the pulpit he is remarkable for force of argument, beautiful imagery, and an impressive manner. He is earnest and eloquent as a speaker, clear as a thinker, concise and powerful as a logician. . . ."

9. Another view of Wadsworth, quite different from the *Post*'s account of him but pointing at least to his early love of poetry (and distaste for Tennyson), appears in the diary of James Hadley, tutor and professor of Greek in Yale College from 1845 to 1872, who described a "long talk" with Wadsworth in New Haven in the summer of 1850. "He has given up his poetry," wrote Hadley, "neither reading nor writing the article, did not know that Tennyson [on whom Hadley was writing an article] was a great poet, has been accustomed to laugh at his wife for admiring him, but on my recommendation promised to read a little of him. Showed his depoetization still more by the very matter-of-fact, commonplace, and prosaic advice and counsel which he was kind enough to give me on the subject of matrimony" (*Diary, 1843–1852, of James Hadley,* ed. Laura Hadley Mosely, 1951, pp. 94–95; and *YH* I, 178–79). The "depoetization" and the "prosaic advice" hardly augur well for the romantic theory of the Wadsworth-Dickinson relationship, nor does Hadley's description in a previous entry (August 20) of Wadsworth as having been "too rheumatic to go about" (!). Wadsworth was a man of moods, and Hadley must have caught him during one of his less enthralling. The two were obviously unsympathetic, Wadsworth religious, Hadley a philologist with scientific leanings. As to his "depoetization," Wadsworth's sermons will have to speak for themselves (excerpts will follow).

into smiling at it. . . . Several people there on Sunday suddenly laughed and as suddenly stopped again, when he gravely gave the Sunday school books a blast and spoke of "the good little boys in them who always went to Heaven, and the bad little boys who infallibly got drowned on Sunday," and then swept a savage frown around the house and blighted every smile in the congregation.

Emily, always on the side of "the bad little boys," may have at last found in Wadsworth a preacher who, as she put it later, did not make "the love of God . . . seem like bears," or the Bible like "an antique Volume / Written by faded Men," or youngsters feel that "Boys that 'believe' are very lonesome – / Other Boys are 'lost' – " Wadsworth may have been the "warbling Teller," the Orphic preacher, she sought. Shortly after he died, when James Clark sent her a copy of his sermons, her letter of thanks echoed the phrase from the poem.

> To thank you is impossible, because your Gifts are from the Sky, more precious than the Birds, because more disembodied. I can only express my rejoiced surprise by the phrase in the Scripture "And I saw the Heavens opened." I am speechlessly grateful for a friend who also was my friend's, and can scarcely conceal my eagerness for that warbling Silence.

But other qualities of his, to judge by what she said in her letters to the Clarks, impressed her more. There are twenty-one of these letters, six to James Clark, beginning in August 1882, and fifteen to Charles, beginning in April 1883, when James was stricken with the illness from which he died in June. The letters tell us much but unfortunately only heighten the mystery. A few facts emerge: that Wadsworth called on Emily in the Homestead shortly after his mother died on October 1, 1859, probably early the following spring (March?); that he called again in August 1880; that the Clarks sent her at least two volumes of his sermons, one shortly after his death, by which kindly act the correspondence was begun; that Emily asked for his picture (it was sent by James) and for the pictures of his children (never a word about Mrs. Wadsworth); that Emily knew so little about him as to have to ask whether he had brother or sister ("He never spoke of himself. . . . He never spoke of his Home. . . .") and that she remembered enough of his conversation to record three brief examples of it.[10]

It is worth remarking that, in the course of the correspondence, Emily asked both Clarks to call on her in Amherst (and this when her withdrawal, presumably, was complete: she saw the people she wanted to see). A tradition in the Holland family has Emily sending letters to Wadsworth through Mrs. Holland between the time he returned to Philadelphia in 1869 and his death. But only four of Emily's letters to Mrs.

10. The "few facts" emerge as follows: the 1860 meeting, L III, 742, and see YH II, 7; the 1880 meeting, L III, 738; the sermons, L III, 737–38 and n., 762 and n.; the pictures, L III, 745 and n., and 857; brother or sister, L III, 742; the conversations, L III, 738, 742, 744.

Holland refer to any such mission, and even these do not begin until the summer of 1876. Wadsworth's name is never mentioned. Only one letter comes anywhere near being specific: "I ask you to ask your Doctor will he be so kind as to write the name of my Philadelphia friend on the Note within, and your little Hand will take it to him –" It was Jay Leyda who suggested that Emily started writing Wadsworth as early as 1858 to ask advice about her mother's illness. On January 4 of that year, one of his sermons had been sent her by Eudocia Flynt of Monson, whose friend Eliza Coleman may have started it on its way from Philadelphia. The sermon, like Higginson's famous *Atlantic* article in 1862, may have suggested to Emily where she could get help, Wadsworth's magnetic presence and spiritual power presumably being already known to her. But even if she had never seen him, the sermon may have initiated a correspondence, now lost, like the one she carried on with Higginson for eight years before he finally came to Amherst.

And so surmise follows surmise. If the relationship between Emily and Wadsworth is a mystery to us, an underlying theme of the letters to the Clarks is that Wadsworth was a mystery to Emily. Her first letter after his death contains a curious paradox. She wrote of an "intimacy of many years with the beloved Clergyman," and yet, "I have never before spoken with one [met one] who knew him, and his Life was so shy and his tastes so unknown, that grief for him seems almost unshared." This does not rule out the possibility that she heard him preach, but it makes it seem unlikely that she met him socially with the Colemans in Philadelphia. And if that is so, unless she made a trip alone to his house or ministerial study, it is hard to see how "an intimacy of many years," with its clear indication of warm personal acquaintance, could have begun there. Emily's insistence in this letter on Wadsworth's shyness, his fathomlessness, and (as the letter continues) the complete surprise of his visit in 1880 makes one wonder how intimate the intimacy was. The next letter contains a simple inquiry about Wadsworth's brother and sister, but in the one after that (late 1882) the sense of mystery deepens:

> The Griefs of which you speak were unknown to me, though I knew him a "Man of sorrow," and once when he seemed almost overpowered by a spasm of gloom, I said "You are troubled." Shivering as he spoke, "My Life is full of dark secrets," he said. He never spoke of himself, and encroachment I know would have slain him.

Apparently Wadsworth was as successful in keeping his secrets as Emily herself had been, years before, with Higginson, who had hesitated to question her for fear she would "withdraw into her shell." Emily summed up the rest of Wadsworth's disclosures quickly: he loved his mother and his son Willie, and when he visited Amherst in 1880 he had said, "I am liable at any time to die." "He was a Dusk Gem," Emily wrote James Clark, "born of troubled Waters, astray in any Crest below." In subsequent letters to Charles Clark, she spoke of Wadsworth's "mysterious face" and his "momentous nature"; to know him "was Life – " It would seem that mystery faced mystery in the meeting of these two people, and this may have been part of his fascination for her.[11]

There was more than his aura of mystery, however, that could have appealed to her. The humor that pleased Mark Twain was close to the "roguery" she herself cherished and often indulged in. Once, thanking Dr. Holland for an amusing letter, she wrote that she was "re-convinced by your arch note that Unless we become as Rogues, we cannot enter the Kingdom of Heaven – " One of her last comments to Charles Clark was about Wadsworth's "inscrutable roguery." Nor could she have missed the poet in him, either hearing him preach or reading his sermons. The *New York Evening Post* made much of his speaking voice, ranging from a "plaintive wail . . . singularly subdued and effective" to boldness and rapidity in argumentation; and his homiletic style is all that the *Post* said it was: vivid, imaginative, adventurous, with a tendency toward the startling and paradoxical. His published sermons show a firm control of cadence and pace, and from their richness in image and metaphor it is easy to see why the vocation of poet first attracted him. He had a wide literary range and he kept an eye on what was being written. Once, in a sermon, he blasted the periodical press in a way that, if she knew about it, must have pleased Emily Dickinson: "Three-quarters of our magazines are a poor conglomerate of pretentious platitude, pointless tales, fulsome reviews, and bedizened rhymes, made to do service as poetry."[12]

11. It is difficult to explain ED's stress on the "sorrow" and mystery of Wadsworth's life. A quite different picture of the man, his family life, and his career emerges from the Wadsworth family letters (see Appendix III).

12. *YH* II, 246 (sermon of April 2, 1876). But he did not confine his notion of poetry to the written word. A sermon of November 25, 1852, preached in the Arch Street Church, shows him reaching for "poetry" in young America's burgeoning utilitarianism:

> Imagination hath itself become practical in its energies. Poetry is not dead, for the word "poet" means a *creator,* and its power will cease only when a progressive race has attained the loftiest height of its possible strivings. Nor does poetry sleep even. Spite of all sentimental lamentations over the homely utilitarianism of this age, it is, after all, the most poetic and imaginative of all ages. But then imagination hath become practical. Samson hath sprung from the lap of Delilah, and gone forth against the Philistines. The poet, the creator of these later times, brings forth, not day dreams, but realities. The steam engine is a mightier epic than the Paradise Lost. The magnetic telegraph is a lovelier and loftier creation of true poetry than Spenser's Fairy Queen or Shakespeare's Tempest. Genius had flung the flowery garlands off, and gone forth with a bronzed cheek and a hard hand, to work for a race in the very van of advancing civilization.

One is reminded of Hitchcock's fervent attempts to reconcile his science with his faith—and of Emily's poem on the locomotive ("I like to hear it lap the Miles," #585, about 1862). More reassuring is an article in the *Presbyterian* of April 28, 1882, the month Wadsworth died (*YH* II, 365):

> In those days [at the Oneida Institute, near Utica, N.Y.] Dr. Wadsworth wrote much poetry, which he read to his admiring listener. I think he abandoned that kind of work soon after. If he subsequently destroyed the fugitive pieces of those

Indeed, there are enough similarities in figurative language, theme, and poetic conception to suggest that the literary influence between Emily and Wadsworth, if we can assume an intimacy of many years, could have gone both ways.[13] Some of the parallels between passages in the sermons and Emily's poems are striking, even though they prove no more than an affinity of mind and imagination. The similarities show the two at home, and together, in many moods. In an undated sermon published in the posthumous volume of 1884, Wadsworth is didactic and a bit roguish:

> And although Satan with his wonderful power might, if truly regenerated and reformed, become a most efficient teacher of morals, yet as for six thousand years he has proved himself still a devil, the Church, hopeless of his reform, will use other ministries. . . .

A poem of Emily's of about 1879 builds on the idea and keeps the same tone:

> The Devil – had he fidelity
> Would be the best friend –
> Because he has ability –
> But Devils cannot mend –
> Perfidy is the virtue
> That would he but resign
> The Devil – without question
> Were thoroughly divine   (#1479)

A sermon, "My Jewels," in the 1882 volume that James Clark sent Emily used the kind of geological analogy that Edward Hitchcock was fond of and Emily was nourished on (Wadsworth was also interested in "Scientifics," especially the work of Louis Agassiz):[14]

---

days – as I have no doubt he did – he did what I wish he had not done. . . . But Dr. Wadsworth was born a poet, and could not cease to be one, however much he avoided blank verse and rhyme.

13. Cf. Higgins, p. 82, and Leyda, *YH* I, lxxvii, for suggestions about a two-way literary influence.

14. See James Hadley's entry for August 24, 1850: "After tea had an hour's talk with Wadsworth on Scientifics, Agassiz, original unity of race, inspiration, etc. etc. He talks well, but it strikes me rather curiously to find myself able to cope on equal terms, at least so far as mere strength of intellect is concerned, with one whom my latest recollections represent to me as so immeasurably superior." As to the parallels between passages from the sermons and Emily's poems: Mary Elizabeth Barbot, "Emily Dickinson Parallels," *New England Quarterly* XIV (1941), pp. 689–96, following Whicher's suggestion (*This Was a Poet,* p. 112), found seven striking ones, of which I have quoted parallels to P #356, #550. David Higgins found another (*Portrait,* p. 82), and Jay Leyda has suggested to me still others, of which I have used those to P #1479, #201. Barbot also cites several images and metaphors from Wadsworth's sermons that recall similar uses in Emily's poems—"God's school-room," the conscience as "a spectral and unbidden guest," etc. "Diadem" and "adamant" were favorite words with both.

The value of a gem is not in its composition, but in its crystallization. Even the diamond is composed mainly of carbon, and differs from the black coal of our furnaces only in this mysterious transfiguration. . . . But the spiritual man has, through gracious crystallization, become a gem, reflecting Divine light, and thus fitted for a diadem.

The phenomenon of crystallization often attracted Emily, who wrote about "crystal Reticence" and "Quartz contentment," of the "Anthracite" life and the quiet stiffening to quartz. Another poem carries out Wadsworth's analogy in precisely his way (unless, of course, he had done it in hers):

> The Day that I was crowned
> Was like the other Days –
> Until the Coronation came –
> And then – 'twas Otherwise –
>
> As Carbon in the Coal
> And Carbon in the Gem
> Are One – and yet the former
> Were dull for Diadem –
>
> I rose, and all was plain –
> But when the Day declined
> Myself and It, in Majesty
> Were equally – adorned – . . .   (#356, about 1862)

Another "Resurrection" poem seems almost an answer to Wadsworth's "The Gospel Call," a sermon delivered on April 11, 1858, and published in his first volume (1869). The mood of the sermon is ecstatic, the pitch is high, and the sonorities resound.

Oh, what a call is this! The Spirit and the Bride call, and he that heareth calls. The voices of all God's bright and blessed things take up the utterance. The dear ones in your earthly homes – mother, and sister, and brother, and child – whose names are written in the Lamb's book of life, cry, "Come, come!" And the Church below, Christ's witness unto the world, in all her ordinances and utterances, cries, "Come, come!" And the Church above, with the rustling of white robes, and the sweeping of golden harps, cries, "Come, come!" And the angels of heaven, lo! rank above rank, the immortal Principalities, as they circle the eternal throne, they have caught up the sound, and cry, "Come, come!" And the Triune and Everlasting God – the Father, the elder Brother, the almighty Comforter – says, "Come, come!" And, behold, the battlements of the fair city are thronged with a great crowd of witnesses; and upon the ear of every fainting, dying soul in this earthly wilderness, breaks the glad call of the rejoicing universe, "Come, come, come!" *"And the Spirit and the Bride say, Come; and let him that*

*heareth say, Come; and let him that is athirst come, and whosoever will,
let him take the water of life freely!"*

It is hard to see how, in view of passages like this one, Samuel Bowles
could have described Wadsworth as "more of a scholar than an orator."[15]
    Emily could not have heard this sermon and may never have read it.
What she is answering in the poem is, if not Wadsworth's sermon, at least
his text, Revelation 22:17; and her reply shows not only her imaginative
affinities with him but how far she was from sharing his evangelical
fervor:

> Me – come! My dazzled face
> In such a shining place!
> Me – hear! My foreign Ear
> The sounds of Welcome – there!
>
> The Saints forget
> Our bashful feet –
>
> My Holiday, shall be
> That They – remember me –
> My Paradise – the fame
> That They – pronounce my name –   (*#431, about 1862*)

Although she caught the scriptural rapture—or the rapture of Wadsworth's sermon—in this tiny dialogue poem, its heaven is remote; and the
only immortality she sees is the immortality of being remembered,
presumably (a thought that preoccupied her about this time) for her
poetry.
    It is in his somber or tragic moods that Emily seems spiritually closest
to Wadsworth. A sermon, "The Great Query," in the 1884 volume uses
the central image of one of her most anguished early poems: "to the poor,
lost soul *there shall be no tomorrow,"* wrote Wadsworth, ". . . the spar
will be washed away from the grasp of the shipwrecked man ere the sun
rise up again to shine upon his sea-tossed head." If in their correspondence
Emily sent him poems as she sent Bowles and Higginson and the

15. Bowles's opinion appeared in the *Springfield Republican,* October 28, 1865, in
one of his letters "Across the Continent," dated San Francisco, August 31. He also
acknowledged that "Among the 'orthodox' preachers, Rev Dr Wadsworth from Philadelphia, perhaps ranks first," and went on to say that he was "greatly respected and
beloved." Whether Bowles had any notion that Emily might have read this with
especial interest, we do not know. But preachers and their sermons were standard
topics of conversation in the Dickinson circle, which we know Bowles joined on
many occasions in the years shortly after Emily Dickinson came back from Philadelphia. If she had heard Wadsworth and if she had been as impressed as the weight of
circumstantial evidence and legend would have her, it is hard to see how she could
have failed to discuss this "New Lion," the "Prince among Preachers" (as he was
called in the *Presbyterian* article), in the presence of Bowles or of someone who might
have conveyed her enthusiasm to him.

Hollands and many others, she must have sent him this one (she *did* send it to Bowles):

> Two swimmers wrestled on the spar –
> Until the morning sun –
> When One – turned smiling to the land –
> Oh God! the Other One!
>
> The stray ships – passing –
> Spied a face –
> Upon the waters borne –
> With eyes in death – still begging raised –
> And hands – beseeching – thrown!　　(# *201, about 1860*)

The metaphor of shipwreck was hardly original with Emily or Wadsworth; they might have come upon it separately (the morning sun is more distinctive). Both poem and sermon show an intimacy with despair, and their congruence may help limit the nature of the despair of the poem (which has been variously interpreted) as specifically religious. One is reminded of Emily's parting-of-the-ways letter to Abiah Root, who had chosen the safety of the shore, and Emily's fear of being lost to the love of Christ. Or, if Emily had heard Wadsworth preach before she wrote the poem (not this sermon but perhaps one like it), she might have thought of her clergyman as one who, though he himself turned smiling to the land, convinced her through passages such as this that he knew what it was to be lost:

> Why, look ye! Far away over the desert, up where the mountains are piercing the skies, shine the palaces of immortality! And if we attain to them in triumph at all, these deserts must be traversed, these stormy waters crossed, these mountains ascended!

In a poem of about 1862, the mountains and seas and deserts function in a remarkably similar way. There is the same challenge of the obstacle, and the envisioned triumph, or "Victory." Emily's anguished question mark corresponds to Wadsworth's qualifying "if . . .":

> I cross till I am weary
> A Mountain – in my mind –
> More Mountains – then a Sea –
> More Seas – And then
> A Desert – find –
>
> And My Horizon blocks
> With steady – drifting – Grains
> Of unconjectured quantity –
> As Asiatic Rains –

Nor this – defeat my Pace –
It hinder from the West
But as an Enemy's Salute
One hurrying to Rest –

What merit had the Goal –
Except there intervene
Faint Doubt – and far Competitor –
To jeopardize the Gain?

At last – the Grace in sight –
I shout unto my feet –
I offer them the Whole of Heaven
The instant that we meet –

They strive – and yet delay –
They perish – Do we die –
Or is this Death's Experiment –
Reversed – in Victory?   (#550)

The letters to the Clarks suggest that, in Wadsworth, Emily found, above all, a fellow sufferer, the quality of whose suffering had in common with hers that it was borne in silence. Wadsworth, we are told, had a curious reputation in his parish. Though an utterly dedicated preacher and cordial and frank with his friends, he arranged his pulpit to avoid greeting his congregation after the service and would go out of his way at other times to avoid casual contacts. His mornings were strictly reserved for study. He too, it seems, was something of a recluse, and what Emily called his shyness seems to have been characteristic. This, along with his early poetic ambitions that came to nothing, may have some bearing on the "dark secrets" he spoke of to Emily. At the very least, it is significant that Bowles thought of him primarily as a scholar. Very different in all his professional duties from the gregarious, wide-ranging Beecher, Wadsworth "never conciliated any one." This intransigence, too, Emily could have understood. Clearly, it had not made life easy for him.[16]

16. Whicher, pp. 101–2, describes Wadsworth's personal habits and his unconciliatory ways, presumably from the testimony of a parishioner. All such efforts, here and in the paragraphs to follow, to explain the "dark secrets" in Wadsworth's life may be wide of the mark. He was obviously a great success in his profession; he was happily married; he had three children, one of whom, Charles Jr., became a famous preacher and national leader. And yet the impression he gave in the pulpit, according to still another view, corresponds precisely to Emily's later descriptions of him in the letters to the Clarks. The Reverend George Burrows of San Francisco wrote an extended account of him shortly after he went to Calvary Church ("Impressions of Dr. Wadsworth as a Preacher," San Francisco, 1863). Burrows pointed to the great success Wadsworth was having in San Francisco, the crowds at his church, many people coming miles to hear him. And yet the newcomer or casual visitor, wrote Burrows, is often disappointed. He is not flowery, or rhetorical, or metaphysical. He abhors

Well before 1861, Emily had known sorrows—and probably sorrows (if something short of "terror") she "could tell to none." In a world that to her young perception was increasingly hollow, a world of self-righteous sewing circles and "Dimity Convictions," she may have seen in this startling young preacher (but old enough in 1855 to have the kind of authority she sought out frequently in the course of her life) the spiritual insight and integrity that she was coming to believe only suffering could give:

> I like a look of Agony,
> Because I know it's true –
> Men do not sham Convulsion,
> Nor simulate, a Throe – . . .   (*#241, about 1861*)

She had a firsthand instance of this quality in him when she saw him in 1880, and she may have sensed it long before. It is remarkable that thirty years earlier the *Post* correspondent had been particularly impressed by his sermons on the suffering and dying Christ; he had even wondered if Wadsworth's feeble frame could hold up under the pressure of his impassioned empathy.

Apparently, from what Emily wrote James Clark, the empathy was not simulated. As she grew older, she became keenly conscious of "the fashions of the Cross," measuring every grief she met to see if it weighed like hers. The Christological theme which runs through much of her

---

cant and claptrap. "His argumentation is peculiar, close, compact, and strong . . . with a powerful condensation, till it glows like a diamond . . ." (p. 15). His voice has "a musical plantiveness in harmony with the feelings of his heart" (p. 6). His humor is remarkable: "Never have we seen these things [his "polished wit and effective sarcasm"] used with such propriety in the pulpit." Addison, said Burrows, could not have been "more polished, nor in better taste" (p. 16). Apparently Mark Twain was right. "Like lightning from a clear sky, when least expected there is a flash and a smash . . ." (p. 17) and the "empty fooleries of the day" lie demolished. He breaks all rules of homiletics, but "he has courage and sober sense enough to be evangelical, to hold to the sound old truth, without regard to the fashionable sneers from 'philosophy and vain deceit'" (p. 21). But above all is the impression he gives of "deep, tender, humble-hearted love to Jesus" (p. 6) and a sense of the suffering of Christ, the Man of Sorrows:

> You feel that behind all he says there must be lying years of conflict and agony, of trials and sorrows, of deep gloom and despondency, of strong cries and tears, of heavenly fellowship and confidential friendship with God. . . . All this blended with deep study and meditation on the Scriptures . . . finds utterance through the molding control of a brilliant, original, powerful mind, of a soul whose lips have been touched with a coal from Isaiah's hallowed fire. . . . He preaches consolation like a man who knows how to succor others, because he has himself been compassed with suffering. . . . All is sobered by deep penetration and sound common sense. . . . A humility so unfeigned, allied with so much greatness, and mellowed, no less than deepened, by divine grace, throws a great charm around the character [pp. 5, 7–8, 11, 15]. [Like Shakespeare] "He gives us . . . profound abstractions in the guise of living things [pp. 12–13].

anguished poetry and seems obviously self-directed was eventually, in a four-line elegy, directed toward Wadsworth. She saw him not only as a "Man of sorrow[s]" but in her imagination as one who had earned in life and gained in death an immortality, a kind of godhead, that she compared to Christ's. "Heaven might give him Peace," she wrote James Clark in late 1882, "it could not give him Grandeur, for that he carried with himself to whatever scene—

> "Obtaining but his own extent
> In whatsoever Realm –
> 'Twas Christ's own personal Expanse
> That bore him from the Tomb." [#*1543*]

In a letter of about 1884 to Mrs. Henry Hills (whose husband Austin had saved from bankruptcy), Emily said in two sentences (the entire letter) a great deal about her own religious position, which in turn may explain why she turned "for many years" to Wadsworth for spiritual guidance:

When Jesus tells us about his Father, we distrust him. When he shows us his Home, we turn away, but when he confides to us that he is "acquainted with Grief," we listen, for that also is an Acquaintance of our own.

Here are her dislike of doctrines; her sense of the remoteness of that "Further Heaven" of the poem "I reckon – when I count at all"; her often skeptical, sometimes quizzical attitude toward the Deity; but most important, her sense of kinship with the Man of Sorrows, the Suffering Servant of Isaiah, the prefiguration of Christ.

By 1855 Emily had been subjected to many preaching styles, ranging from the comfortably orthodox, which bored her, to the hell-fire, which frightened her. In her own church she had been restless under the Reverend Aaron Colton's evangelical *"now today"* style as she described it to Austin, "his earnest look and gesture." She was very fond of the Reverend Edward Dwight, who succeeded Colton in 1853; and she apparently consulted him often in his study. He was kinder, more understanding, and his message was one of love and the abundant life.[17] At

17. Emily satirized Colton's style in her letter of July 6, 1851 (*L* I, 120): ". . . no doubt [she added] you can call to mind the impetus of spirit received from this same gentleman and his enlivening preaching –" In a letter to Dwight shortly after his wife died, Emily wrote: "I suppose your friend – the Stranger [Matthew 25:35] – can comfort more than all of us – but that is Dusk – to me – and so I knock tonight – on that far study door – that used to open kindly – but if you'd rather see no one – you need not say 'Come in'" (*L* II, 383–84). On February 22, 1857, Dwight preached on John 10:10 ("life . . . more abundantly"): "The word so prominent here – 'life' – is one whose value varies as much as its signification. . . . Take two men, for instance. . . . Both of these men are *alive* . . . but how much *more* life has this one than that! . . ." (*YH* I, 347); or, as Emily put it a few years later to the wonderfully

Mount Holyoke she heard Miss Lyon's missionary charge, and of course both there and in Amherst there was a steady stream of visiting preachers and Reverend Professors, including Edward Hitchcock with his insistence on the wonders and meaning of the created world. But "The loveliest sermon I ever heard," she wrote Frances Norcross early in 1873, "was the disappointment of Jesus in Judas. It was told like a mortal story of intimate young men. I suppose no surprise we can ever have will be so sick as that. The last 'I never knew you' may resemble it." Clearly she preferred sermons that spoke to her very human condition. On December 3, 1854, she wrote Susan Gilbert about two "precious" sermons by Mr. Dwight: "One about unbelief, and another Esau. Sermons on unbelief ever did attract me." It may have been the undercurrent of unbelief in Wadsworth, the "years of conflict and agony" that at least one observer felt "behind all he says," or a spiritual uncertainty he was too honest to hide from her completely (perhaps his darkest secret) that attracted her. "On subjects of which we know nothing," she once wrote, ". . . we both believe, and disbelieve a hundred times an Hour, which keeps Believing nimble."

There is no doubt that Charles Wadsworth was an important figure in Emily Dickinson's life. Otherwise, the letters to the Clarks would have to be rejected as sheer Dickinson rhetoric, a step that even the most skeptical commentators have not taken. There is the strong possibility that Susan Dickinson, and later her daughter Martha Bianchi, exaggerated the relationship into a thwarted but lifelong love to explain Emily's withdrawal and to divert attention from her affair with Judge Lord and from domestic troubles in the Evergreens. Perhaps the documents will sometime be found to explain all. Meanwhile, all we can say with confidence is that she needed someone all her life with whom she could share her spiritual problems and disbeliefs honestly and on her level—"to keep Believing nimble." And at a crucial point, the very time when their first meeting was most likely, she would have been especially susceptible to the kind of Christianity Wadsworth preached and to the kind of man he was.

---

vital Samuel Bowles, then recovering from illness: "So few that live – have life . . ." (*L* II, 418; mid-November 1862). As to sermons that scared her, she wrote to the Hollands in late November 1854 about a sermon on "death and judgment, and what would become of those, meaning Austin and me, who behaved improperly – and somehow the sermon scared me . . ." (*L* I, 309).

21

Samuel Bowles

THE ANNALS of Emily Dickinson's life up to and including the Washington-Philadelphia visit are full and factual compared with what lies ahead. Fortunately, it has been possible to speak with some confidence about the major phases of her life so far: the Amherst background and her home, her family and early friends, her schooling in the Academy and at Mount Holyoke. And this latest sojourn, at least the Washington part, occasioned some unusually specific comment by her. Except for the mystery of what happened in Philadelphia, these matters seem, in outline, fairly clear. There they *are,* external, real, even if one must speculate, sometimes strenuously, about what was most important in them for Emily, the ". . . internal difference, / Where the Meanings, are –"

This situation changes radically after Emily reaches her mid-twenties. She admittedly withdrew more and more ("my Lexicon – was my only companion – "), and not only does the information about the externals of her life become sparser and less determinate but the metaphoric expression that was developing in the letters to her young friends intensifies to such a degree that it becomes an almost private code. At times one wonders whether the recipients themselves may not at some points have been almost as puzzled as we are. Unfortunately, in no case is this more true than in her letters to Samuel Bowles, ebullient editor of the *Springfield Republican* and special friend of Austin's and Sue's. Since those letters to him and the poems she sent him are by far the most important, indeed almost the only, surviving evidence about the nature of their friendship, surely one of the most important in her life, the situation is especially tantalizing.

Almost four years elapsed between Emily Dickinson's return from Philadelphia and the time Samuel Bowles entered the Dickinson circle on anything like an intimate basis. They were crucial years in her developing poetic purpose, and yet her surviving correspondence for those years is peculiarly sparse. Only ten letters survive, for instance, from the period between January 1855 and January 1858; the dates of two of these are conjectural, and none at all can be ascribed with any certainty to 1857. But of precisely these years, so lean for the historian, Emily could write to her Uncle Joseph Sweetser in the summer of 1858: "Much has occurred, dear Uncle, since my writing you – so much – that I stagger as I write, in its sharp remembrance." Any normal uncle might expect, after this, some help as to what staggered her. Loss of friends? Disappointment in love? What he got was a mystifying compound (or so it must have been to a dry-goods merchant living in New York and not in very close touch with the family) of fact and fancy, prose veering into poetry, ecstasy of life and thoughts of death, so mystifying, indeed, that she even seems mystified at herself and ends the letter in a flutter of apology. The letter is an emblem of the mood and style of the late 1850s, alternately transparent and opaque, and evasive where we (and perhaps Uncle Joseph) would most seek enlightenment. It is a sobering introduction to this phase of her life.

. . . Summers of bloom – and months of frost, and days of jingling bells, yet all the while this hand upon our fireside [Mrs. Dickinson's ill health?]. Today has been so glad without, and yet so grieved within – so jolly, shone the sun – and now the moon comes stealing, and yet it makes none glad. I cannot always see the light – please tell me if it shines.

I hope you are well, these many days, and have much joy.

There is a smiling summer here, which causes birds to sing, and sets the bees in motion.

Strange blooms arise on many stalks, and trees receive their tenants.

I would you saw what I can see, and imbibed this music. The day went down, long time ago, and still a simple choir bear the canto on.

I dont know who it is, that sings, nor *did* I, would I tell!

God gives us many cups. Perhaps you will come to Amherst, before the wassail's done. Our man has mown today, and as he plied his scythe, I thought of *other* mowings, and garners far from here.

I wonder how long we shall wonder; how early we shall *know*.

Your brother [the Luke Sweetsers were the Dickinsons' nearest neighbors] kindly brought me a Tulip Tree this morning. A blossom from his tree.

I find them very thoughtful friends, and love them much. It seems very pleasant that other ones will so soon be near.

We formed Aunt Kate's acquaintance, for the first – last spring, and had a few sweet hours, as do new found *girls*.

I meet some octogenarians – but men and women seldomer, and at *longer* intervals – "little children," of whom is the "Kingdom of Heaven." How tiny some will have to grow, to gain admission there! I hardly know what I have said – my words put all their feathers on – and fluttered here and there. Please give my warmest love to my aunts and cousins – and write me, should you please, some summer's evening.

Affy,
EMILIE.

Perhaps the last paragraph means what it says: that she was reducing her social life to elderly people, small children, and ever fewer people of her own age or thereabouts: it was a year later (December 10, 1859) that she called Susan and Austin her crowd. Her thoughts on salvation may be of a piece with her growing aversion to the kind of adult society she saw herself becoming a part of—one reason, that is, for her withdrawal. The apology for her flutter may reflect some fear of having offended Uncle Joseph. At any rate, the thoughts that give the letter its somber tone ("so glad without . . . so grieved within – "; "I cannot always see the light – "; "*other* mowings"; "how long we shall wonder") and what seems like a genuine if minor panic at the end strike the mood of these years and foreshadow the deeper disturbances and often breathless style of the letters that began about this time, both to Bowles and to the "recipient unknown," her beloved "Master," be he Bowles or someone else, or a figment of her imagination.

If the increasing frequency of mature and sometimes distraught religious gropings noticeable in the letters of this period are any indication, formidable pressures were beginning to build up, signs of which we saw in the early confessions to Abiah Root. And always, of course, there was the pressure of a formidable talent demanding expression. According to the (tentative) chronology of the Harvard edition, Emily was only four years away from a year's production averaging a poem a day; so that the productive pressure of these earlier years was probably greater than we can document. Even if her words (as she wrote Uncle Joseph) "put all their feathers" on and flew, the strain on her constitution must have been great. No wonder she reduced her commitments outside her household and even resented those within, as when she protested to Mrs. Holland about having to "regulate" the house with Vinnie during their mother's illness and longed to be clear of "these problems of the dust." In this letter to Mrs. Holland, signed "From your mad Emilie," the playful diction may not be altogether in fun: ". . . and should my own machinery get slightly out of gear, *please,* kind ladies and gentlemen, some one stop the wheel, – for I know that with belts and bands of gold, I shall whizz triumphant on the new stream!"

Other sources of information throw at least oblique light on these puzzling years: the annals of the family, town, and nation. Although they have to do with externals, some of which we have encountered before, it is good to be reminded of them, if only to be reminded that her life *had* externals during this time of what seems like her almost exclusive preoccupation with that "Campaign inscrutable / Of the Interior." This period of her life—roughly, the years 1858–62—is rightly regarded as crucial, a time of extraordinary stress and inner turmoil. But so much of the rhetoric of agony and despair has been used, in the writing about these years, that it has all but obscured the quotidian of her life; the comings and goings of her family, whose every action and mood were vital to her; the daily, sustaining routine of a busy home.

The entrance on the scene of Samuel Bowles, whose journalist's eye was forever on the external life of his times—politics and preferment, the buzz and stir of the marketplace, the sights and sounds of America and Europe—makes this reminder all the more appropriate. Bowles was good for the non-traveling Dickinsons. Not that they were uninformed; Edward Dickinson was still politically active, and they all read the *Springfield Republican*. But Bowles more than any other visitor brought the sense of this "yeasty time" into their very living rooms. They seem even to have depended on him, close to the news as he was and the confidant of men in high places. He took the shock, for instance, out of the bad news in the early years of the Civil War. "We used to tell each other," Emily wrote him in late November 1862, shortly after he had returned from a seven-month sojourn in Europe, "when you were from America – how failure in a Battle – were easier – and you here – " And, it should be said, the Dickinsons were good for Bowles. At their home he found momentary peace and a change of tempo from the busiest life any man can lead—that of editor of a flourishing one-man daily newspaper. Once, at ease in the Evergreens (he was habitually the guest of Austin and Sue, but he did not neglect the Homestead), he is said to have remarked, "This, I guess, is as near heaven as we shall ever get in this life!"

When his regular visits to the Evergreens started about 1858, what Bowles saw—and clearly relished—was a lively family circle, still harmonious (as far as can be discerned) in the two houses, prospering materially and apparently in every other way. A month after Emily's return from Philadelphia in March 1855, Edward Dickinson bought back the Homestead from Samuel Mack, put in another $5,000 (according to local gossip) to make it "one of the most pleasant places in Amherst," and moved in with his family in mid-November, one member registering piteous complaints:

> I cannot tell you how we moved. I had rather not remember. I believe my "effects" were brought in a bandbox, and the "deathless me," on foot, not many moments after. I took at the time a memorandum of my several senses, and also of my hat and coat, and my best shoes – but it was lost in the *mêlée,* and I am out with lanterns, looking for myself.
>
> Such wits as I reserved, are so badly shattered that repair is useless – and still I can't help laughing at my own catastrophe. I supposed we were going to make a "transit," as heavenly bodies did – but we came budget by budget, as our fellows do, till we fulfilled the pantomime contained in the word *"moved."* It is a kind of *gone-to-Kansas* feeling, and if I sat in a long wagon, with my family tied behind, I should suppose without doubt I was a party of emigrants!
>
> They say that "home is where the heart is." I think it is where the *house* is, and the adjacent buildings.[1]

1. *L* II, 323–24 (to Mrs. Holland, about January 20, 1856). The possibility that the move brought Emily more than temporary discomfort is developed by Jean Mudge,

(All this, after a move of a short mile, literally just around the corner from Pleasant Street to Main! But at least the agony added a classic passage to the literature of moving day.) In October, Edward Dickinson and Austin had formally announced their law partnership, and about this time work on the Evergreens began. Between July 1854 and July 1856, Edward Dickinson's tax assessment rose from $5,360 to $13,095. By 1859 it was $19,000. He ran for Congress again but was defeated in the November election, the month of the moving. On June 2, 1856, sixty-four students and thirty-two oxen (according to a jocular account in the *Springfield Republican*) moved a ten-ton boulder from the Edward Dickinson estate to a position in front of the Woods (Geological) Cabinet. The Dickinson Commencement Tea went on that year as usual. Sometime in 1857, Edward Dickinson bought a set of Shakespeare.[2]

Mrs. Dickinson's health had remained poor during 1856, which meant more housework for Emily and Lavinia. (She went to Northampton for the water cure in September.) Austin joined the church in January of that year and, with Sue, spent some time in the late spring in Geneva, New York, preparing for the wedding on July 1. By mid-summer, social life was well under way in the Evergreens, with Emily a frequent participant (at least for the first few years), joining in the jolly times when Bowles's visits began and (early in 1859) Kate Scott Anthon's (Sue's classmate in Utica Female Seminary), much to Emily's delight.

Austin's stature and influence in the town grew steadily. He served on committees for the annual Cattle Show (with Commencement, one of the two major events in the Amherst calendar), helped in a drive to resuscitate the languishing Amherst Academy early in 1857, and was appointed by Governor Gardner a Justice of the Peace in January of that year. This last event was signalized by a congratulatory note to "our young friend" in the *Hampshire and Franklin Express:* ". . . Mr. Dickinson is a gentleman of industry and ability, and will discharge the duties of his new appointment with credit to himself, and even handed justice to all parties." Late in the year the *Express* published an interesting cultural note; it is hardly conceivable that Austin was not involved, perhaps with an assist from his literary sister:

---

currently residing in the Homestead, who feels that the experience was traumatic, that Emily always had ambivalent feelings toward the Homestead—which was "my father's house," while, in the Mount Holyoke letters, for instance, she habitually spoke of the Pleasant Street house as "my home." In her Yale dissertation (1973) on ED's use of the imagery of house and home, Mrs. Mudge finds veiled references, for instance, to the Pleasant Street house in the earlier version of *P* #609 (about 1862), "I Years had been from Home." But it is clear that Emily's deep loyalty to her home—the household, the family circle and her own privileged place in it—survived the shock, if such it were. The humor, at least, of the letter to Mrs. Holland indicates a certain mastery of the situation.

2. All these matters, from Edward's buying back the Homestead to his buying the Shakespeare, are chronicled in *YH* I, 331–52 passim.

A half dozen of our young men, determined upon varying the monotony of the hard times by something that should remind us that we have minds and tastes too as well as pockets, formed themselves into a club, pledging each other for a first class lecture here as often as once a fortnight, with tickets of admission so low that no one who had the least desire to attend could find fault. . . .

Wendell Phillips inaugurated the series on December 11, speaking to a mere 150 people on the "Lost Arts," the community being roundly scolded by the *Express* for the poor turnout. Ralph Waldo Emerson followed on December 16 (on "The Beautiful in Rural Life"), apparently with better success, and, to Sue's pride, ate and slept "under our roof." There is no reason to believe that Emily did not hear both Phillips and Emerson. It may have been on this occasion that Emily (according to Sue) gave her famous impression of Emerson: "As if he had come from where dreams are born."

For 1858, the family annals are slim. Vinnie seems to have remained *in situ* much of the time, her romance with Joseph Lyman once and for all concluded by Joseph's marriage to Laura Baker in July, and the Homestead, with Mrs. Dickinson's illness, more and more (if we can believe her and Emily's random comments) under her firm managerial control. Emily had won second prize (75¢) for her rye and Indian bread in the Cattle Show for 1856 and had found herself on the committee for rye and Indian bread for 1857, an appointment not renewed, apparently, in 1858 or subsequently. Jane Humphrey was married in August, Cousin John Graves in September, and Austin had a mild case of typhoid fever in October.

Samuel Bowles's regular visits to this apparently placid scene, sometimes with his wife Mary, sometimes alone, began about this time. The exact dates are difficult to determine, but it seems that the warm friendship between the families developed then, or shortly after Austin and Sue's marriage. Bowles had long been familiar with Amherst. He had begun reporting Commencements for the *Springfield Republican* as early as 1849 and may have heard Austin's Commencement Address in 1850. Not a college graduate himself (a deprivation he is said to have regretted all his life), he relished such occasions. "Amherst," he wrote of the Commencement in 1860, "furnishes the beauty – the world comes to adore." But the mood was not all adoration, as his often amusing accounts in the *Republican* show. When he was in Europe during the summer of 1862, Emily wrote, "We shall miss you, most, dear friend, who annually smiled with us, at the Gravities." Whether or not Sue Dickinson was right in claiming him as their first visitor after their marriage, the families, including Emily, were sharing their joys and sorrows—Austin's illness, the sadness of Mrs. Bowles's stillborn children (three between 1855 and 1860)—well before the end of the decade.

On the face of it, the friendship between Samuel Bowles and Austin, a preliminary to whatever that mysterious relationship was between Bowles and Emily, was an unlikely one. A brief inquiry into it may throw some light on the impasse Emily later faced. Except for their similar origins in western Massachusetts, Bowles differed from Austin almost diametrically in background, training, and temperament. Austin's leisurely youth and careful schooling, most of it in the quiet college town of Amherst, was very different from Bowles's working life from seventeen on. While Austin was given to brooding and speculation and dabbled in schoolteaching and literature, Bowles was from the first a practical man, a product of the worldly, workaday side of the developing Connecticut Valley culture. George Merriam's great biography of Bowles, published in 1885, close to the man and the times, described Bowles's early preoccupation: "At the time of life when a young man is most liable to questioning and mental unrest, Mr. Bowles was held too closely by work and responsibility to have any leisure for exploring excursions into the infinite."

Three years older than Austin, Bowles came of Puritan but more recently Unitarian stock and was working full time for his father on the *Republican* at an age when Austin was just entering college. During his second year on the job he persuaded his father to change the paper to a daily on the promise that he would take the main responsibility and do most of the work. From then on, the paper became his life; and, quite literally, he gave his life to it. There was no thrashing around, as with Austin, in search of a vocation, or a wife, or religious certainty. "I married early," he said later, "and I worked with all my might."

Bowles was everywhere, doing everything, poor at delegating responsibility and exacting maximum results from himself and from everyone who worked for him. He expanded far beyond his own community, as Austin never did. His journalistic efforts took him deep into local, state, and national politics. As a matter of principle, he never ran for office himself, but he was close to many who did, from the lowest to the highest. He enjoyed the political world and became an important influence in it. It may have been Edward Dickinson's political activities that first made him aware of the Dickinson family; from the earliest times the *Republican* took note of Edward's public life and spoke of him respectfully, if not always in agreement.[3] Bowles covered all the national and state conventions himself, shuttling back and forth from Springfield to Washington, Boston, and New York with air-age frequency. He was a child of the young democracy, socially as well as politically, as Austin was not. He "was always ready to hob-nob," Merriam wrote, "with any man, saint or

---

3. Bowles was deeply interested in the formation of a new party, to be called the Republican Party, a coalition of all the factions opposing the Kansas-Nebraska Bill, passed in May 1854. The day after the passage of the bill, the meeting to form the party was held "at the rooms [in Washington] of Edward Dickinson and Thomas D. Eliot, of Massachusetts" (Merriam I, 117; and see *Home,* p. 380).

sinner. . . . His mode of growth was by absorption. Other people were to him sponges out of which he deftly squeezed whatever knowledge they could yield"—knowledge, that is, that could be turned into news items or editorial material. Dr. Josiah Holland, his colleague on the *Republican* for years and close friend of the Dickinsons, must have thought him, Merriam writes, "irreverent, not to say heathenish." "I think," said Holland, "that his strongest passion was the love of power"—the power, that is, of manipulating men and influencing decisions.

In his few leisure times, which were all but forced on him as his health weakened under the strain, he sought out the most interesting people he could find for talk and gaiety. Once he tried the solitude of Mt. Desert in Maine, but it did not work; as Merriam wrote: "This man had no taste for solitude, no genius for lonely contemplation." It is a tribute to Austin—and indeed to Bowles himself, since the Dickinsons were so differently gaited—that he came often to the Evergreens with (as Emily put it) his "vivid Face" and his "besetting Accents." Although much of Bowles's best work was done after 1857, a series of sharp headaches in the fall of that year were a prelude to a constant battle with ill health. The trips to Amherst were supposed to be rest cures, but even here he squandered his vitality and had to learn to be more frugal. In the fall of 1861, almost prostrated with sciatica, he took the water cure at Dr. Denniston's in Northampton, where Mrs. Dickinson had been, and, according to a fellow patient, a woman, was "the life of the whole company."

> Bent over with sciatica, suffering day and night, he gave cheer to us all, though probably no one of us was suffering more than he. He helped in all the common amusements, and was quick at all games. He had a happy and delicate way of receiving kindly attentions from women, without any sentimentality. To everybody his manner was gracious, but especially to plain and unattractive people, – he had a knack of drawing them out, so that they became agreeable and entertaining. . . . He had in him a great deal of the boy, – sportiveness and playfulness. There was a genuine reverence and seriousness, but it was his habit to mask it. . . .

These fine gregarious qualities seem quite un-Dickinsonian, or at least more like Sue, one of Amherst's leading hostesses, than like Austin. It may have been that Sue was the chief attraction for Bowles. In 1848 he had married Mary Schermerhorn, of Geneva, New York, who in her childhood had come to Springfield to live with relatives, and this connection with Geneva, where Sue had spent much of her girlhood, provided an early point of contact, perhaps even the starting point of the friendship between the families. Many of his letters to the Evergreens were addressed to Sue. He seldom failed to pay her tribute, and at one point tongues began to wag.[4]

4. The following sentence, at least, appears in a penciled memorandum by Millicent Todd Bingham of her interview in 1934 with Miss Mary A. Jordan, who taught

This brings us to an aspect of Bowles's character of more than gossipy importance, since it may have involved Emily Dickinson and may have accounted for a strain in his relations with Austin and Sue. Bowles was known for his partiality for women of spirit and brains. Merriam, who stoutly defended his integrity, nevertheless described him as "quick," "subtle," "magnetic," "charming," one who conquered hearts (male and female) "like a charming woman, and with a feminine sense of power and pleasure in his conquests." The columns of the *Republican,* for instance, were famous for their hospitality to lady poets, like young Colette Loomis, Lizzie Lincoln of Hinsdale, N.H., Luella Clarke, Ellen P. Champion, and "Fannie Fern" (Sarah Willis Parton).

Perhaps Bowles's most intimate friend, man or woman, was Maria Whitney, of the New Haven Whitneys, distantly related to his wife, a frequent visitor in his household, and onetime instructor in languages in Smith College. Merriam's description of the kind of woman Bowles was attracted to was probably based on this friendship, which was well known among Bowles's friends and involved a long correspondence, some of which Merriam reproduces; but as he proceeds, one is tempted to see another reference.

He was a man who could unite an entire and life-long loyalty to one woman, the partner of his life, the mother of his children, and the mistress of his home, with intimate and mutually helpful friendships with other women. . . . His closest intimacies were with women of a characteristic New England type. . . . [of] fine intellect, an unsparing conscience, and a sensitive nervous organization; whose minds have a natural bent toward the problems of the soul and the universe; whose energies, lacking the outlet which business and public affairs give to their brothers, are constantly turned back upon the interior life, and who are at once stimulated and limited by a social environment which is serious, virtuous, and deficient in gayety and amusement. There is naturally developed in them high mental power, and almost morbid conscientiousness, while, especially in the many cases where they remain unmarried, the fervor and charm of womanhood are refined and sublimated from personal objects and devoted to abstractions and ideals. They are platonic in their attachments, and speculative in their religion; intense rather than tender, and not so much soothing as stimulating. By the influence of such women Mr. Bowles's later life was colored – his views were broadened, his thoughts refined, his friendships exercised in offices of helpfulness and sympathy. . . .

From Merriam's benign and uncomplicated point of view, this description fits Emily Dickinson even more precisely than it does Maria Whitney, who was well-traveled, scholarly, cosmopolitan like many of her illustrious family—in short, she hardly seems to be one of the circumscribed,

English at Smith College from 1884 to 1921: "They [Sue, her daughter Martha, and her son Ned] wanted to have a salon in Amherst with Samuel Bowles and his questionable relationship with Mrs. Austin as a background." The memorandum is in the Todd-Bingham Archive at Yale (see Appendix II, 2).

introspective ladies here described. The difficulty is that Emily Dickinson is never once mentioned in Merriam's long and detailed biography.

A remarkable passage in a letter written late in 1862 by Bowles to Austin is an indication, at least, of disturbances and anxieties of a sort that do not trouble the placid surface Merriam maintains on all such matters. Bowles had just returned from Europe and had made a homecoming call at Amherst:

> I give thanks anew for the pleasant day with you. The gift of friendship is a holy one, & its proofs stimulate and sadden, as the most delicate of responsibilities. It annoys me that I cannot show more my appreciation & enjoyment, – that I cannot do more – write oftener, visit more frequently, & stay longer – as you would wish. – Some of the reasons for my incapacity, & the consequent disappointment to you, you know because I have told you. – I have many cares & small power. The price of life & health to me is clearly abstinence "from all which does intoxicate" – from work, excitement, even earnest feeling; from irregularities in eating, drinking & exercise. Sometimes life seems not worth the keeping at such egotistical cost. It would not for self, but we all give bonds that must be respected. – Other causes for my reticence – of which you seem sometimes oppressed, – you ought to know without my explaining. – I thought to write you of them fully; but I cannot. You certainly are not ignorant of them. I must respect them; so must you. They are not unconquerable – it has seemed to me the correct thing to put them aside. But that [belongs?] not to me, nor to you. So long as they exist, however, I pray you to be indulgent to my short-comings in the duties & delights of friendship. I know you must feel that my circle has none more to me, in the suggestions of the past, & in the hopes of the future, than you. I could not afford to lose you, to go on without you, & I do not mean to – if I can hold you. Our intercourse & exchange may not be so free & abundant, as it was, as I at least would have it; but it may & I think will be deeper and richer for its very limitations – Can you take less of me in time & word, & feel you have as much as ever, or rather more, in eternity?
>
> This is somewhat [*word illegible*] & morbid, perhaps; but I am rather sensitive to your more or less open suggestions of dropping away from the frequency of older intercourse. I thought to say more – I could not say less, & I know you will understand & appreciate it all. –

The hints of overwork and ill health here are familiar enough; the rest— actually, the end of a certain phase of their friendship for unspecified reasons—is new. An earlier letter (May 15, 1861) had apologized to Austin for Mary Bowles's odd behavior on a recent visit:

> . . . you must make some allowances for her peculiarities, – & judge her by what she means, rather always than by what she says. Her very timidity & want of self-reliance gives her a sharper utterance. . . . I think she was somewhat disappointed in her Amherst visit – it did not turn out so pleasantly, as she meant to have it.

Whether in the 1862 letter it was Mary's "peculiarities" that threatened the friendship or something else about which he refused to be specific, we

472]

cannot tell. At any rate, the letter shows that Emily was not the only Dickinson who asked from this vibrant and charming visitor more than he was able, or willing, to give.

Several times in her life Emily Dickinson showed poor judgment. She encouraged Austin's courtship of Sue, she sought literary help from Thomas Wentworth Higginson, and she tried to inject herself into the busy, utterly committed, and domestically complicated life of Samuel Bowles. But when the heart has reasons, common sense and judgment, which should have warned her, are hardly relevant categories. For if her words mean anything at all—thirty-five of her letters to Bowles survive and nearly fifty poems went to him (some of them to his wife)—she was deeply in love with him for several years and never ceased loving him, at a distance, for the rest of her life. If, as some think, the "Master" letters were written to him, her love must have been desperate. At any rate, it was misguided. Bowles was out of her reach in every way, professionally, domestically, morally.

And she was out of *his* reach, had she seen him clearly, in matters of the mind and spirit. For one thing, his taste in poetry was completely conventional; he seems to have delighted in all that had gone dead in the mid-to-late-Victorian tradition—as the kind of poem the *Republican* printed should have warned her.[5] He was not even, for a literary man, very bookish. "Newspapers," writes Merriam, "were his chief literary food; and newspapers, with all they teach, teach but little of the heights and depths of humanity, and hint but scantily at its sublimity and tenderness." He read other things, of course, Dickens, books of sermons, Macaulay's history, Renan; and he shared Emily's enthusiasm for *Aurora Leigh*. He wrote occasional reviews and comments on literary matters for the *Republican*. But the poems Emily sent him—some of her best—seem to have given him no more than momentary pause.

In spite of what Merriam says about his taste for introspective, platonic women, when he sought female companionship beyond the confines of his home, he turned to women like Sue and her brilliant friend Kate Scott Anthon, or to his "fair logician," as he called her, Maria Whitney, whose discursive, academic mind was much more akin to his own than were Emily Dickinson's lightning-like apprehensions. He would propound to Maria his views on ambition and progress, or chart for her (in a way, one might assume, that Emily would hardly have tolerated) the course of his uninspired religious thinking:

> So I have seemed forced to be content to grow in goodness in my more practical way, and to leave theories and faith to time. I try to make my life

5. Although the *Republican* frequently reprinted selections from standard English poets—a likely source, as has often been pointed out, for ED's familiarity with the seventeenth-century metaphysicals—its taste in contemporary verse shows what ED had to contend with. A few samples from the years of her closest association with Samuel Bowles will be found in Appendix IV.

show the result of Christianity and godliness, if I have not the thing in its theoretical form. Patience, charity, faith in men, faith in progress, have been lessons that I have been learning these many years.

He kept the subject, that is, at a safe distance. A reading list of Maria's on religion shows a scholar's interest—books on Judaism, Buddhism, historical aspects of the Old Testament, the Oxford Reformers. Neither Bowles nor Maria, if their letters are any evidence, lived with this "Flood subject" as a constant, harassing presence. Neither seems to have felt its unrelenting pressures, the "yearning for a oneness" (as Emily described it), the overriding quest of her own life and the mark of her religious imagination.[6] In all the surviving letters, the only religious questions Emily asked him were in one of the first (1858 or 1859):

> . . . Our Pastor says we are a "Worm." How is that reconciled? "Vain – sinful Worm" is possibly of another species.
> Do you think we shall "see God"? Think of "Abraham" strolling with him in genial promenade!

How far Bowles was from perceiving the seriousness behind her whimsey came out somewhat later in a message to her he relayed through Austin:

> . . . To the girls & all hearty thoughts – Vinnie ditto, – & to the Queen Recluse my especial sympathy – that she has "overcome the world." – Is it really true that they ring "Old Hundred" & "Aleluia" perpetually, in heaven – ask her; and are dandelions, asphodels, & Maiden's [*vows?*] the standard flowers of the ethereal?

If the message ever reached Emily, it might well have hurt her deeply. By this time (1863) in his friendship with the Dickinsons, unless his insensitivity was invulnerable, he should have known something of her mind and heart toward him. Yet in this message he treated her simply as one among the others, to be singled out only for a special bit of ribbing.

It seems clear that neither Emily's idiom nor her concerns were congenial to Bowles; or, to say the very least, he was never sufficiently moved to take decisive action, certainly not about the poetry. Since we have no letters from him to her, about the only clues to his attitude toward her lie in her persistent and often impassioned letters to him, her thanks for his letters and other kindnesses, and the fact that he thought enough of her letters to save them, or some of them. It is a hazardous task, in view of the uncertain dates of the letters, to trace her developing feeling for him.

We can start, at least, with this same early letter in which she presented her homemade theology and put the religious questions to him. It is likely that he made as little of certain other odd passages in the letter as

---

6. Maria's reading list is in a tiny diary, now in the Whitney Papers at Yale, of her trip abroad in 1890. It may not be a true indication of her lifelong attitude. Bowles once wrote to her of a religious experience of some sort that he wished he could have shared with her. But it need hardly be argued that her approach to such matters was scholarly and academic compared with Emily Dickinson's.

Samuel Bowles
"Would you like Summer? Taste of our's—
Spices? Buy, here! . . ."
P #691

Kate Scott Anthon
". . . the old blissful evenings at Austin's! . . . Emily at
the piano playing weird & beautiful melodies . . ."

Maria Whitney
Bowles's "fair logician"

he did her questions, or perhaps in his busy life he simply brushed them all aside.

> My friends are my "estate." Forgive me then the avarice to hoard them! They tell me those were poor early, have different views of gold. I dont know how that is. God is not so wary as we, else he would give us no friends, lest we forget him! The Charms of the Heaven in the bush are superceded I fear, by the Heaven in the hand, occasionally. . . .
>
> Good night, Mr Bowles! This is what they say who come back in the morning, also the closing paragraph on repealed lips. Confidence in Daybreak modifies Dusk.
>
> . . . We want to see you, Mr Bowles, but spare you the rehearsal of "familiar truths."
>
> Good Night,
> EMILY.

The personal feeling here, later to bring her such anguish, seems unmistakable. It must at once be set against another and perhaps deeper impulse in her relationship with Bowles. For years, at least on a superficial level, she had made no secret to her intimates of her literary interests and skills, clear enough in the early valentines, in the poems she had sent to Sue and others, and in the "Brother Pegasus" letter to Austin. Deeper thoughts may have been masked in the *"golden* dream" letter to Abiah Root and the "gold thread" letter to Jane Humphrey, to come out more frankly when she chatted with her sixteen-year-old cousin, Louise Norcross, one October morning in 1858:

> . . . I have known little of you [Emily wrote], since the October morning when our families went out driving, and you and I in the dining-room decided to be distinguished. It's a great thing to be "great," Loo, and you and I might tug for a life, and never accomplish it, but no one can stop our looking on, and you know some cannot sing, but the orchard is full of birds, and we all can listen. What if we learn, ourselves, some day! Who indeed knows? . . .

What she seems to have expected from Samuel Bowles was assistance in the fulfillment of what by now may have been a consuming passion: the publication of her poems.[7] Thus the relationship may have been a mixture of the personal and the professional, with Emily Dickinson trying vainly in her oblique, metaphoric way to get him to accept her as person and as poet, and Bowles, chivalrous but preoccupied, or unmoved, or simply obtuse, accepting neither, at least as she wanted to be accepted. As a person, she could hardly have been pleased with his breezy remembrances to his "Queen Recluse," or, as poet, with an occasional message to Austin or Sue to "tell Emily to give me one of her little gems!" "Little gems" or no, the hospitality of the *Republican* was anything but cordial. Only five of her poems were printed (beginning with the 1852 valentine), all anonymously, all with manufactured titles, most with petty alterations

7. Ruth Miller's *The Poetry of Emily Dickinson* develops this theory in full.

toward conventionality, and in the final instance, "The Snake," not only altered but "robbed." She complained to Higginson:

> Lest you meet my Snake and suppose I deceive it was robbed of me – defeated too of the third line by the punctuation. The third and fourth were one – I had told you I did not print – I feared you might think me ostensible.[8]

She wrote this in March 1866, long after she had resigned herself, apparently, to Bowles's indifference. But in the early years of the friendship, the intensity of her purpose and mood is unmistakable, not only in the letters she wrote him and the poems she sent him, but also in many poems of this period so close in image and feeling to those she sent him as to be considered part of her dialogue (or here, unfortunately, monologue) with him.

The poems Emily sent to Bowles can be divided into two groups: those that served as letters or parts of letters, with formal salutation and, usually, valediction, and those she copied on separate sheets to be enclosed with the letters. These latter may be regarded, in general though not always, as less personally directed, more as samples of her work she wanted her publishing friend to see, such as two autumnal pieces sent in a letter of 1859: "These are the days when Birds come back – " and "Besides the Autumn poets sing." Both of these are so superior to the verses the *Republican* habitually honored as to defy comparison; nor are they so unconventional as to shock a conservative editor. It is conceivable that, had Emily asked Bowles bluntly to publish them, she might have been successful. But such was not her way, whether through shyness, or fear of refusal, or New England reticence; and he failed to take the hint. If one wonders why she even tried with a publisher like Bowles, it must be remembered that only a few years previously she herself had copied out a ten-stanza bereavement poem by John Pierpont to send to her friend Mary Warner, who had lost a sister. The opening three lines are enough to indicate its quality:

> "I cannot make him dead!
> His fair sunshiny head
> Is ever bounding round my study chair – . . ."

She thought it "very sweet." One of the mysteries of Emily Dickinson, from our point of view, is how she could enjoy such stuff and yet write

8. *L* II, 450 and n. The story of the publication in the *Republican* (February 14, 1866) of the poem "A narrow Fellow in the Grass" is told both here and in *P* II, 712–14, where the *Republican*'s changes are indicated. The poem apparently got to Bowles through Sue. The one thing about it that struck Bowles seems to have been the first lines of the third stanza: "He likes a Boggy Acre – / A Floor too cool for Corn – " His remark is recorded by Martha Dickinson Bianchi, *Emily Dickinson Face to Face*, p. 27: "How did that girl ever know that a boggy field wasn't good for corn?"

the way she did. Whatever saved her—the Bible, or Shakespeare, the seventeenth-century poets, or Emerson, or her scientific training—it was not Samuel Bowles.

Nor could she save him, although there is a sign that he may have become more receptive a few years later, perhaps through the encouragement of Sue, who was a much more perceptive reader of Emily's poetry than he was, or perhaps merely out of friendship for the family. But this too may be legendary. Emily wrote Higginson on April 25, 1862, that "Two Editors of Journals came to my Father's House, this winter – and asked me for my Mind – and when I asked them 'Why,' they said I was penurious – and they, would use it for the World –" The editors are generally assumed, with no proof, to be Bowles and Holland, but by then, so the theory runs, it was too late. Bowles, she felt, had rejected her. During these years she was gradually withdrawing from the complications in the Evergreens, especially as they focused on Sue, and by now Bowles was part of them. Perhaps her refusal to the two editors was symptomatic. Bowles (if indeed he was one of the two) failed to overcome her qualms. As to Holland (if he was the other), his failure here is of a piece with his failure in the 1870s when, as editor of *Scribner's,* he agreed with Emily Fowler Ford that the poems were too "rootless" to be published.

Thus, what appears to have been one of the major drives in Emily's relationship with Bowles, the need for publication, came to little. Of the other, her love for Bowles, the evidence seems sure that it existed, was intense, and was unfulfilled. We cannot even be sure that it was the primary sorrow of these troubled years. A break with Sue; Austin's troubles; a religious crisis of her own; or a frustration, still to be uncovered, with an entirely different person, may have contributed.

Of the intensely personal poems incorporated in the letters to Bowles, or sent as letters, an early one of about 1860 is typical. The Harvard editors link it to her "turbulent emotional disturbance" of about this time, suggest its connection with the "Master" letters, and point ahead to a similar letter poem of 1862 as a sign that she made Bowles a confidant in her love secret. Current opinion—it is only that—links the turbulence, the "Master" letters, and the 1862 poem with Bowles himself. I have already cited the poem, but not the salutation:

I cant explain it, Mr Bowles.

> Two swimmers wrestled on the spar
> Until the morning sun,
> When one turned, smiling, to the land –
> Oh God! the other One!
> The stray ships – passing, spied a face
> Upon the waters borne,
> With eyes, in death, still begging, raised,
> And hands – beseeching – thrown!   [*#201, about 1860*]

What she couldn't explain—and, of course, what we would most like to have explained—is left unspecified. This is the letter in its entirety; it has no valediction. Nor should it be dismaying to find in this context the shipwreck metaphor that was earlier linked to a passage in a sermon by Wadsworth. The "it" of her salutation could as well refer to a religious as to a romantic frustration or disaster. Such multi-leveled metaphoric implication, or application, is entirely characteristic (as, for instance, the poem "What mystery pervades a well!"—#1400—with its two variants involving "Susan" and "nature").

The problems this letter raises are a prelude to the more complicated problems of several subsequent and apparently crucial letters and poems to Bowles. In these the interchangeability of frames of reference is far more baffling. For instance, the language of marriage that permeates many of the poems—"wife," "bride," "husband"—can be read with credibility as pointing either up or down, to a celestial relationship or to a human. And the human fulfillment for which she yearns may be either one of erotic passion or the joy of "greatness" as a published poet (this last in spite of her protests to the two editors).

An example of how carefully all of Emily's poems and letters of this period must be read in the light of these possibilities is another short letter of about 1860:

DEAR MR BOWLES.
    Thank you.

>"Faith" is a fine invention
>When Gentlemen can *see* –
>But *Microscopes* are prudent
>In an Emergency.   [*#185, about 1860*]

You spoke of the "East." I have thought about it this winter.
Dont you think you and I should be shrewder, to take the *Mountain Road?*
That *Bareheaded life* – under the grass – worries one like a Wasp.
The Rose is for Mary.

                                        EMILY.

This, indeed, is a test case, and as such worth dwelling on. Every sentence except the last needs explication, including the quatrain. "Thank you"—for what? The quatrain itself—from the 1891 edition of the *Poems* onward, it is printed quite apart from the letter—has usually been taken as her tiny critique of a theology that neglected the evidence of science, perhaps a bow to Hitchcock and her early training in Amherst Academy and Mount Holyoke. But other and more immediate implications arise when it is viewed in the context of the letter. If the letter is seen as part of Emily's dialogue with Bowles about publishing her poems, it becomes an appeal to read her poems with more perception. In this reading,[9] she

9. Cf. Ruth Miller, p. 127.

cannot live on the "faith" that somehow, someday, some editor will see her work for what it is and publish it. She has run out of patience; this is an "Emergency." Get a microscope! The "East," about which Bowles had spoken to her, may be the world of the Boston and New York publishers. But she urges Bowles not to wait for them. Would it not be "prudent," "shrewder," for her poems to take the *"Mountain Road"* (the pass between the range of hills that separates Amherst and Springfield) for publication in the *Republican?* Time is running out. There may be a sense of urgency because of Bowles's health, which had been precarious for several years. "That *Bareheaded life* – under the grass – worries one like a Wasp."

This is a tempting interpretation, and it may be valid. But other possibilities cannot be excluded. The letter may be part of a dialogue on religion. The main intent of the quatrain may be theological. It might be a variant of Emily's idea that faith, or belief, must be kept "nimble," that we must keep an ever-watchful eye on "that religion / That doubts as fervently as it believes" (from a poem incorporated in a letter to Bowles) —that is, we need *spiritual* microscopes.

As to the "East" of the first sentence after the verses, here is a fine example of the multiple possibilities of her metaphors. In poems from the beginning to the end of her career, "East" is a word charged with symbolic significance, often with no regard to geography. Sometimes it suggests paradise or heaven, earthly or celestial. In a poem of about 1862 the marriage metaphor points both ways, and the "East" could signify either human or celestial fulfillment:

> A Wife – at Daybreak I shall be –
> Sunrise – Hast thou a Flag for me?
> At Midnight, I am but a Maid,
> How short it takes to make it Bride –
> Then – Midnight, I have passed from thee
> Unto the East, and Victory –
>
> Midnight – Good Night! I hear them call,
> The Angels bustle in the Hall –
> Softly my Future climbs the Stair,
> I fumble at my Childhood's prayer
> So soon to be a Child no more –
> Eternity, I'm coming – Sir,
> Savior – I've seen the face – before!   (*#461*)

It is almost as if the East had become a private symbol among the group that assembled for those evenings in the late 1850s in the Evergreens— Bowles and Kate Scott Anthon, Sue, Austin, and Emily. "Dare you dwell in the *East* where we dwell? Are you afraid of the Sun?" Emily asked Kate Anthon in a letter of about March 1859, the "East" here being a challenge to an unconventional, unorthodox, dangerous life. She went on:

"All *we* are *strangers* – dear – The world is not acquainted with us, because we are not acquainted with her. And Pilgrims! – Do you hesitate? and *Soldiers* oft – some of us victors. . . . We are hungry, and thirsty, sometimes – We are barefoot – and cold – " In a poem of about 1865 the "East" is the promise of human passion (as when Emily said of Austin: "He married – and went East," when, of course, everyone knew that the Evergreens was due west of the Homestead):

> Said Death to Passion
> "Give of thine an Acre unto me."
> Said Passion, through contracting Breaths
> "A Thousand Times Thee Nay."
>
> Bore Death from Passion
> All His East
> He – sovreign as the Sun
> Resituated in the West
> And the Debate was done.   (#*1033*)

Shortly after Mrs. Dickinson died, Emily incorporated a poem about her in a letter to Maria Whitney. Here the "East" is clearly the celestial heaven, the life to come:

> To the bright east she flies
> Brothers of Paradise
> Remit her home,
> Without a change of wings,
> Or Love's convenient things,
> Enticed to come. . . .   (#*1573*)

It may be that the word "shrewder" of the next sentence in the 1860 letter is an echo of the word "prudent" in the quatrain, thus "locking together"[10] the stanza and the prose part of the letter. But the *"Mountain Road"* may refer to something quite different from the road that connects Amherst and Springfield. The "mountain of the Lord" is a phrase that reverberates through the Old Testament, usually with the exhortation to "come up unto His mountain." There must have been many sermons on the theme of the mountain road. And in the next sentence it may be the thought of death—"That *Bare-headed life* – under the grass – " that locks together the letter and poem in a *religious* unity. Or, preposterous as it may sound, the letter, quatrain and all, may be a *carpe diem* appeal, quite on the romantic side.

This merely points up what has been said often before, that one must

10. Cf. Miller's phrase. Ibid.

walk warily among Dickinson metaphors. Nor does it refute the contention that she looked to Bowles as a prospective publisher of her poems
and (however the word is to be interpreted) as a lover. It is a reminder
that, from here on, Emily's figurative language and the allusions often
defy precise explication. It is as if, as may well be the case, she consciously
phrased letters that, should they fall into alien hands, would be all but
undecipherable.

Those letters discussed so far, generally agreed to be the early ones in
the friendship, are comparatively relaxed in tone, with only a few signs of
growing tension, as in her embarrassment about writing him so much—"I
write you frequently, and am much ashamed"—and in the "Two swimmers" message. The next letter that can be dated with some accuracy is
one of early August 1860, perhaps written within a few months of "Two
swimmers." It is generally relaxed, but with a further note of embarrassment, this time for "misbehaving," as she called it, perhaps at a family
gathering: "I am sorry I smiled at women"—not at the "holy ones," she
hastened to add, "like Mrs Fry and Miss Nightingale," but perhaps at the
lady poets Bowles was giving space to in the *Republican,* or perhaps at the
ladies of the Amherst sewing circles. At any rate, she asked forgiveness:
"My friends are a very few. I can count them on my fingers – and besides,
have fingers to spare." The tone is light, but the concern seems real: "God
will forgive me – Will you please to *try?*"

In the winter or early spring of 1861, an arduous trip to Amherst by
sleigh during a heavy snowstorm left Bowles with a chill and the severe
sciatica that sent him to Dr. Denniston's in Northampton that fall. The
three of Emily's letters to him that can be assigned with some assurance to
that year all show a concern for his health that went far beyond the
requirements even of close friendship. There is a hint of deep anxiety. The
pace becomes staccato, and twice she is moved to verse. Sometime shortly
after Bowles was stricken, she writes what purports to be a committee
letter (Sue, Vinnie, and herself), but it is clearly dominated by her own
intense feeling.

Dear friend.

You remember the little "Meeting" – we held for you – last spring? We
met again – Saturday – 'Twas May – when we "adjourned" – but then Ad-
journs – are all – The meetings wore alike – Mr Bowles – The Topic – did not
tire us – so we chose no new – We voted to remember you – so long as both
should live – including Immortality. To count you as ourselves – except
sometimes more tenderly – as now – when you are ill – and we – the haler
of the two – and so I bring the Bond – we sign so many times – for you to
read, when Chaos comes – or Treason – or Decay – still witnessing for
Morning.

We hope – it is a tri-Hope – composed of Vinnie's – Sue's – and mine –
that you took no more pain – riding in the sleigh.

We hope our joy to see you – gave of it's own degree – to you – We pray for your new health – the prayer that goes not down – when they shut the church – We offer you our cups – stintless – as to the Bee – the Lily, her new Liquors –

> Would you like Summer? Taste of our's –
> Spices? Buy, here!
> Ill! We have Berries, for the parching!
> Weary! Furloughs of Down!
> Perplexed! Estates of Violet – Trouble ne'er looked on!
> Captive! We bring Reprieve of Roses!
> Fainting! Flasks of Air!
> Even for Death – a Fairy Medicine –
> But, which is it – Sir?   [#691]
>   EMILY

For all her intense concern about his health, Emily is also saying something that has much to do with her poetry. In the letter, especially in its last paragraph and in the poem that follows, she covers, in metaphor, almost every point in her own personal poetics. Indeed, she seems to be showering him with metaphors to convince him of the value of metaphors (and of her poems) and of their specific value, right now, to help him get well. A poem is a kind of prayer, she seems to be saying, as when she wrote her Norcross cousins when their father died, "Let Emily sing for you because she cannot pray." And poems are life-giving: she spoke once of the "balsam word" as having more power to heal than doctors. In a later poem she wrote, "If I can ease one Life the Aching / Or cool one Pain. . . ." So here the "stintless cups," the liquors of the lily, the spices and berries, are at once her poems and the healing power she hoped they contained. She is only a step here, where it is the Poet who makes possible the "Furloughs of Down" and the "Reprieve of Roses," from the great statement of the poet as Creator (soon to come in "I reckon – when I count at all –"). She wanted Bowles to get well, she suffered in his suffering; but she seems eager to have him see and feel what she *as poet* could do for him. In another letter close to this (suggested dates range from March to October 1861), she is still grieved "till I cannot speak, that you are suffering," and again she offered him the kind of medicine that only she could give:

. . . Cant I bring you something? My little Balm might be *o'erlooked* by wiser eyes – you know – Have you tried the Breeze that swings the Sign – or the Hoof of the Dandelion? *I* own 'em – Wait for *mine!*

Whether Bowles took this as any more than advice to get fresh air and sunshine is dubious.

Her letter of early December 1861 found Bowles, convalescing but not well, in New York with Mrs. Bowles, who was under a doctor's care prior to the birth of her son Charles. The letter is about suffering and its uses, purportedly about Bowles's suffering but perhaps as much about her own suffering as about his, and, to press her intention further, perhaps to establish a kinship with him more than literary or social, a kind of bond (she had used the word in the previous letter) in suffering. The concluding poem, in its appeal to the crucified Christ, seems to encompass a range of feeling far beyond her concern for the final throes of Bowles's sciatica. Indeed, the whole letter provided him with another exercise in Dickinson metaphor.

DEAR MR BOWLES.

It grieves us – that in near Northampton – we have now – no friend – and the old-foreigner-look blurs the Hills – *that* side – It will be bravest news – when our friend is well – tho' "Business" leaves but little place for the sweeter sort.

The hallowing – of pain – makes one afraid to convalesce – because they differ – wide – as *Engines* – and *Madonnas*. We trust no City give our friend – the "Helena" feeling.

The Cages – do not suit the *Swiss* – well as steeper Air.

I think the Father's Birds do not all carol at a time – to prove the *cost* of *Music* – not doubting at the last each Wren shall bear it's "Palm" –

To take the pearl – costs Breath – but then a pearl is not impeached – let it strike the East!

Dear Mr Bowles – We told you we did not learn to pray – but then our freckled bosom bears it's friends – in it's own way – to a simpler sky – and many's the time we leave their pain with the "Virgin Mary."

> Jesus! thy Crucifix
> Enable thee to guess
> The smaller size –
>
> Jesus! thy *second* face
> Mind thee – in Paradise –
> Of Our's. [#225]

Though no narrative of this relationship can be any more precise than the dating of the letters and poems, the crisis seems to have come in the late weeks of 1861 and the first of 1862, before Bowles sailed for Europe in April. A letter, probably of early January 1862, was addressed to him in New York. There is much in it about his continued suffering, and at least a postscript for Mrs. Bowles ("We never forget Mary – "), to whom, it should be said, Emily had written a hearty letter of congratulation shortly after Charles's birth on December 19. The first paragraph is as packed with puzzles as it could well be:

DEAR FRIEND.

Are you willing? I am so far from Land – To offer *you* the cup – it might some Sabbath come *my* turn – Of wine how solemn – full!

The rest of the letter is clear enough—about naming the baby "Robert" (after Browning), about Bowles's coming to Amherst in February, about the moon that night and her sadness that he is ill so long: "When did the Dark happen?" Then another apology for writing him so often; and then a note, if not new, at least insistent in the letters of these months, of pleading and appeal. (A letter as far back as October had begun: "Perhaps you thought I did'nt care – because I stayed out, yesterday, I *did* care, Mr Bowles.") Here she concluded: "When you tire with pain – to know that eyes would cloud, in Amherst – might that comfort – *some?*" But the first paragraph remains a problem. "Are you willing?"—to read this letter? to listen to me? to *die?* (This was a traditional question in her time: Emily asked it of Ben Newton's pastor, and after Bowles's death she wrote Higginson: "Mr Bowles was not willing to die.") "I am so far from Land" is her frequent phrase for depression or bewilderment or inner turmoil, but, again, she does not "explain it." Is she echoing in the next sentence the words of her previous letter, in which "cups" referred to the "Spices," the "Berries," the "Furloughs of Down"—that is, her healing poems? Then why *the* cup here?—"Of wine how solemn – full!" The Communion cup? And what is her "turn" that might come "some Sabbath"? Death? Physical suffering like Bowles's? Or something quite the reverse, a great blessedness, like fulfilled love, or redemption, or the successful publication of her poems?

If this last suggestion is valid, all these dire and mortuary interpretations could be abandoned and the full and solemn cup could be a confessional poem we know Emily sent Bowles about this time and may have included in this letter. (Size, folds, and handwriting all fit: there is no salutation or valediction, another clue that it may have been enclosed with the letter.) A prose postscript suggests its confessional nature, and its urgency.

> Title divine – is mine!
> The Wife – without the Sign!
> Acute Degree – conferred on me –
> Empress of Calvary!
> Royal – all but the Crown!
> Betrothed – without the swoon
> God sends us Women –
> When you – hold – Garnet to Garnet –
> Gold – to Gold –
> Born – Bridalled – Shrouded –
> In a Day –
> "My Husband" – women say –
> Stroking the Melody –
> Is *this* – the way? [#*1072*]

Here's – what I had to "tell you" – You will tell no other? Honor – is it's own pawn—

The "title" Emily assumes here may be that of the imagined wife of Samuel Bowles, a title denied her in reality. Or, as the Bride of Christ, she may be sharing with Him the martyrdom of Calvary. Finally, there is the possibility that she has here taken her ultimate stand, conferring upon herself the "Acute Degree" of Poet. Viewed in this light, the poem may be seen as the most striking and dramatic of a cluster of poems of similar suggestion written about this time, the climax of her developing sense of vocation. All three possibilities are present in the poem, and they are not mutually exclusive. She may have intended a renunciation of Bowles as well as a declaration of love: since, by a direct "no" or by implication, he spurned her human appeal, she has taken the "divine" way, the only way left her, the way of the poet. And just as, years before, when the pain of refusing a young man's invitation to take a walk suggested to her the martyrdom of Christ, so now, in this dedication which is at the same time a renunciation, she sees herself as Empress of Calvary.[11] The same ambiguities may be operating in another ecstatic poem of about 1862, often looked upon as a love poem only. Here again she becomes "titled":

> Mine – by the Right of the White Election!
> Mine – by the Royal Seal!
> Mine – by the Sign in the Scarlet prison –
> Bars – cannot conceal!
>
> Mine – here – in Vision – and in Veto!
> Mine – by the Grave's Repeal –
> Titled – Confirmed –
> Delirious Charter!
> Mine – long as Ages steal!   (#528)

Such analysis does not exclude meanings; it adds to them, although opinions may differ as to the emphasis accorded any one. It shows, among other things, how what appears to have been a climactic experience produced climactic poetry, how in this instance the agonizing failure of a friendship impelled her to a new vision of herself and her work. Coming at about the same time as her growing disenchantment with Sue, it

11. It is on this poem that Ruth Miller (p. 134) takes her most positive stand in her argument about Emily's consuming desire to publish. She posits an encounter during which Emily "called him [Bowles] to her side in order to defend her poetry." When Bowles, thinking she was offering love, rejected her, she answered (in this poem) "with a deflating scorn, with a ringing declaration that her devotion is to God. The emphasis here is more on poetry, on the poet and her affiliation with Christ. Emily Dickinson takes her own title . . . she gives herself redemption as a living soul and immortality as a poet." Something of the sort may have happened, but there is no evidence to confirm it. "Deflating scorn" does not seem adequately to describe the tone of the poem and its postscript. But she may indeed have been announcing here, to Bowles, her new dedication.

presented a stark choice: either she must re-form her life according to the creative powers surging within her or, such is the implication of the desperate rhetoric of the poems and letters of this period, she must perish. Years later, writing to Higginson of his help at this time, she said, "You saved my Life."

A more sober statement of her new "title" is in a poem whose second stanza was sent to Bowles:

> For this – accepted Breath –
> Through it – compete with Death –
> The fellow cannot touch this Crown –
> By it – my title take –
> Ah, what a royal sake
> To my nescessity – stooped down!
>
> No Wilderness – can be
> Where this attendeth thee –
> No Desert Noon –
> No fear of frost to come
> Haunt the perennial bloom –
> But Certain June!
>
> Get Gabriel – to tell – the royal syllable –
> Get Saints – with new – unsteady tongue –
> To say what trance below
> Most like their glory show –
> Fittest the Crown!   (#195, about 1860)

(In the stanza sent to Bowles, the punctuation was eliminated and the last two words underscored in the first line, and "this" in the second line was underscored.) Again, the poem may look two ways, or both at once. The "accepted Breath" can signify her poetic inspiration, or the God-given breath of life, or both, since to her, the power to write poetry *was* life and the source of life; and it was the gift of God. "Where *this* [the accepted Breath] attendeth thee—" there need be no fear of change or death. She is only a step here from perhaps her clearest, most composed statement of the function of the poet. It is an amplification, in serener tone, of the second stanza above:

> I reckon – when I count at all –
> First – Poets – Then the Sun –
> Then Summer – Then the Heaven of God –
> And then – the List is done –

But, looking back – the First so seems
To Comprehend the Whole –
The Others look a needless Show –
So I write – Poets – All –

Their Summer – lasts a Solid Year –
They can afford a Sun
The East – would deem extravagant –
And if the Further Heaven –

Be Beautiful as they prepare
For Those who worship Them –
It is too difficult a Grace –
To justify the Dream –   (*#569, about 1862*)

But such assurance was not easily won, nor, for that matter, did it ever ride serene for long. By this time, the rebelliousness of the girlhood letters had developed into a clear-eyed notion of just how wide and deep the chasm was between her and what she called the World. She could talk about her state of mind calmly and with some humor in the letter to Kate Scott Anthon, and she could come back to it later that year (1859?), again to Kate and again whimsically: "Insanity to the sane seems so unnecessary – but I am only one, and they are 'four and forty,' which little affair of numbers leaves me impotent." This is echoed in the poem of about 1862 ("Much Madness is divinest Sense – ") where the one who demurs is "straightway dangerous – / And handled with a Chain – " She could say to Kate in this same letter, "I am pleasantly located in the deep sea." But in a letter to Bowles of late 1861 or early 1862 the mood has changed. Here the sea is a place where people drown, and other images of extremity convey nervousness and tension amounting to a crisis. Unfortunately, the manuscript is torn away on the outside edges; reconstructions (by Jay Leyda and the editors of the 1958 *Letters*) differ; but the purport seems clear enough, and we are back again with the profoundly personal side of her appeal to Bowles. This seems nothing short of a declaration of love (apparently she had done something else to apologize for, perhaps another refusal to see him when he called):

DEAR FRIEND.
    If I amaze[d] your kindness – My Love is my only apology. To the people of "Chillon" – this – is enoug[h] I have met – no othe[rs.] Would you – ask le[ss] for your *Queen* – M[r] Bowles?
    Then – I mistake – [my] scale – To Da[?] [Leyda reads *David*] 'tis *daily* – to be gran[ted] [Leyda reads *grand*] and not a "Sunday Su[m] [En]closed – is my [d]efence –
    [F]orgive the Gills that ask for Air – if it is harm – to breathe!
    To *"thank"* you – [s]hames my thought!

[487

[Sh]ould you but fail [at] – Sea –
[In] sight of me –
[Or] doomed lie –
[Ne]xt Sun – to die –
[O]r rap – at Paradise – unheard
I'd *harass God*
Until he let [you] in!   [#226]

EMILY.

Clear as the purport may be, some of the details are baffling but important. The verbal connections of the letter with the "Master" letters alone warrant the fullest examination; but even without them the letter seems crucial.

Here is a tentative reading: "If my seeming ingratitude has shocked you, I can only plead my love for you, which has somehow fettered my proper expression. This is all I can say from my prison. Prisoners can do little else. Nor would you, Mr. Bowles, were I your queen, ask less for me. If you would, then I have misunderstood what I thought I meant to you – my 'scale.' " If the "Da[?]" of the next sentence can be read "Daisy" instead of Leyda's "David," a major problem can be considered solved; for in the "Master" letters she habitually refers to herself as "Daisy," obviously the recipient's pet name for her. If it can be so read, the rest of the paragraph would read thus: "This 'scale,' or 'rank,' is my *daily* blessing, not just a sum of blessings reserved for Sunday. I enclose my '[d]efence,' a poem to prove my love. Loving you is the breath of life to me. Is it harmful [or a sin] to breathe? Surely you can forgive *that*. I am ashamed even to use the words 'thank you,' so large is my indebtedness to you [for some specific favor, or simply for being himself and allowing her the privilege of knowing him?]."

The poem that follows needs no explication (provided the reconstruction is acceptable) as a statement of ultimate loyalty. There does, however, seem to be a lingering fear that the loyalty is only one-way: would *you* do this for *me*? The poem is strikingly like the verse letter she sent to Sue about this time, which, as we saw, may have signalized a crisis in that relationship, too:

Could *I* – then – shut the door –
Lest *my* beseeching face – at last –
Rejected – be – of *Her*?   (#220, *about 1861*)

Rejection of one sort or another, mutual or one-sided, and on several fronts, seems to have been in the air.

Of the surviving letters, the "Chillon" letter and the "Two swimmers" are climactic. Close to them is one more of early 1862. There is a sense of finality in it, as if she felt that words had done what words could do—which in this instance was nothing:

Dear Mr Bowles.

I cant thank you any more – You are thoughtful so many times, you grieve me *always – now*. The old words are *numb* – and there *a'nt* any *new* ones – Brooks – are useless – in *Freshet-time* –

When you come to Amherst, please God it were *Today* – I will tell you about the picture – if I *can*, I will –

> *"Speech"* – is a prank of *Parliament* –
> *"Tears"* – a trick of the *nerve* –
> But the Heart with the heaviest freight on –
> Does'nt – always – move –   [#688]

Emily.

Of course, the letter may be only her hyperbolic way of saying that she cannot thank him enough for some favor rendered, perhaps for having sent her the picture mentioned in the next-to-last sentence. But the "heaviest freight" of the poem seems more than mere unexpressed gratitude. From now on, as she realized the hopelessness of her cause, both personal and professional, the curve of feeling in the letters went down and eventually leveled off in a correspondence with both Bowleses that lasted to the time of Samuel's death in 1878 and with Mary for several years beyond.

One imagines the first step in the process as a decision to have nothing more to do with any concerted effort in the direction of the *Springfield Republican*. After three years during which she sent many poems to Bowles, he had printed only one before the winter of 1862: "I taste a liquor never brewed," which was given the title "The May Wine," and was printed anonymously, with two lines altered to get an exact rhyme and one line changed in the interest of a more understandable metaphor. This had come out on May 4, 1861. Then, a month before he sailed for Europe, and perhaps as a gesture of friendship before leaving, the *Republican* printed "Safe in their Alabaster Chambers" (issue of March 1, 1862), called it "The Sleeping," and regularized punctuation, capitalization, and lineation. Articles, comments, and reviews in the paper of about this time, as well as the utterly routine verse it regularly printed, may have helped persuade her to stop trying.[12]

12. Ruth Miller (pp. 128, 163–64) regards an article in the *Republican* (July 7, 1860), perhaps by Bowles, on "When Should We Write," as the ultimate rejection of all ED stood for and a staggering blow. "It seems inevitable," Miller writes, "that Emily Dickinson should have interpreted these words as a public rebuke to her":

There is another kind of writing only too common, appealing to the sympathies of the reader without recommending itself to his subject. It may be called the literature of misery. The writers are chiefly women, gifted women may be, full of thought and feeling and fancy, but poor, lonely and unhappy. Also that suffering is so seldom healthful. It may be a valuable discipline in the end, but for the time being it too often clouds, withers, distorts. It is so difficult to see objects distinctly through a mist of tears. The sketch or poem is usually the writer's photo-

If the "two editors" to whom she refused her poems sometime in the winter of 1862 were in fact Bowles and Holland, this refusal may be linked to two other documents of about this time, linked by a common metaphor referring, certainly in the first instance, to her poetry. The first is a poem possibly sent to Bowles, and the second is a letter known to have been written to him. The poem is her familiar renunciation of publication:

> Publication – is the Auction
> Of the Mind of Man –
> Poverty – be justifying
> For so foul a thing

---

graph in miniature. It reveals a countenance we would gladly brighten, but not by exposing it to the gaze of a worthless world. We know that grief enriches the soul, but seldom is this manifest until after its first intensity is past. We should say to our suffering friends, write not from the fullness of a present sorrow. It is in most cases only after the storm is passed that we may look for those peaceable fruits that nourished by showers, grow ripe and luscious in the sun. There are those indeed who so far triumph over their own personal experiences as to mould them into priceless gifts to the world of literature and art. Like the eider duck bending over her famished young, they give us their heart's blood and we find it then a refreshing draught. But there are marked exceptions. Ordinarily the lacerated bosom must first be healed, 'ere it can gladden other natures with the overflowings of a healthful life.

"It takes little imagination," continues Miller, "to reconstruct the effect of such an article, reminding ourselves that Susan would read it, Lavinia would read it—well, all of Amherst that counted for Emily Dickinson would read it—and perhaps laugh, or what would be worse for such a proud and so self-conscious a woman, pity her."

It seems inevitable, but of course it wasn't. There were many other, and much grosser, examples at hand of the literature of suffering than the few poems, conceivably deserving the label, that Emily Dickinson sent him. Of the thirty-odd poems she sent him before the time of the article, only nine had much to do with suffering, twelve were as "healthy" and happy as Bowles could have wished, and some eleven were analytic, or neutral, or appealing as any love poem would appeal. Bowles seems to be talking about the tearful lyrics on early death and sorrow, on frustrated love and loneliness, that flooded the market. Whatever Emily wrote "through," even Bowles should have seen that it was not through a "mist of tears." Bowles knew that Emily was not "poor" and if she was "lonely," it was in the style of a "Queen Recluse" who had "'overcome the world.'" I cannot see it as inevitable that Bowles was rebuking Emily Dickinson in his article or that she, her family, and the town would have identified her as his target. But I agree with Ruth Miller that the article reveals the limits of Bowles's taste in poetry and helps explain why Emily gave him up. (Following the lead of Bowles's crude distinctions, I have grouped these poems, among those she sent him, as relatively on the happy or healthy side: #33, 44, 130, 131, 161, 200, 204, 227, 329, 330, 331, 691. The following reflect considerable "suffering" of various sorts, although the "mist of tears" idea is irrelevant, I think, by any standard: #83, 84, 85, 121, 201, 225, 688, 690, 792. In the middle ground would come #114, 162, 185, 186, 195, 223, 224, 284, 312, 494, 683. But such listings are highly subjective and must by their nature be more or less blind to occasional Dickinson irony.)

> Possibly – but We – would rather
> From Our Garret go
> White – Unto the White Creator –
> Than invest – Our Snow – . . .   (#709, *about 1863*)

If we can take the metaphor of snow as referring in both instances to her poems, the letter may be imagined as clinching the nail—that is, she will bother Bowles no more with the poems. It ends in a poem on martyrdom, a statement, however elevated, of the only way she may then have seen out of her anguish:

DEAR FRIEND

If you doubted my Snow – for a moment – you never will – again – I know –

Because I could not say it – I fixed it in the Verse – for you to read – when your thought wavers, for such a foot as mine –

> Through the strait pass of suffering –
> The Martyrs – even – trod.
> Their feet – upon Temptation –
> Their faces – upon God –
>
> A stately – shriven – Company –
> Convulsion – playing round –
> Harmless – as streaks of Meteor –
> Upon a Planet's Bond –
>
> Their faith – the everlasting troth –
> Their Expectation – fair –
> The Needle – to the North Degree –
> Wades – so – thro' polar Air!   [#792, *about 1863*]

It is impossible to document with any precision Emily's state of mind during this anguished time. Almost all the poems must be dated by handwriting alone, in which process there is often a subjective element; and most of the letters must be dated by internal clues, not always precise. (In my discussion, I have recorded the dates assigned in the 1955 *Poems* but have assumed the possibility of considerable leeway.) If the dating in the Harvard edition is even approximately right, her writing of some 366 poems in 1862 shows that her anguish, however great, did not prostrate her, a fact which should be kept in mind when one is tempted to pity her. Her production alone, with all the other things she had to do about the house, shows how firmly she kept her faculties under control during a time when many commentators have seen her on the edge of madness and when the theme of poem after poem is humanity at the limits of its sovereignty: "Dare you see a Soul *at the White Heat?*" "After great pain, a formal feeling comes – " "Of Course – I prayed – " " 'Twas the old –

road – through pain – " and many more. It should be noted also that, if Emily in fact came near a breakdown during this period, no mention of it in the annals of her family or friends has so far come to light. Apparently, as far as the world could see, she went about her business as usual.

She may have recovered from the *Springfield Republican*—as shown, perhaps, by her turning elsewhere a week after Bowles had left for Europe—but her personal attachment to Bowles, regardless of his attitude to her, was permanent. She could dodge and dissemble in her riddling poems and letters to him, and she could perhaps admit in her own heart that nothing more would come of their relationship. But the experience had gone deep. In a curious letter written shortly before he left, she used Austin's name for her own throughout, either to be arch or for purposes of disguise. "Will you be kind to *Austin* – again? . . . He could not thank you – Austin is disappointed. . . . He is sure you wont go to Sea – without first speaking to Him. I presume if Emily and Vinnie knew of his writing – they would entreat Him to ask you – not – . . ." And then comes a paragraph close to the message ("Here's – what I had to 'tell you' – ") that followed the "Title divine" poem:

> He is very sorry you are not better – He cares for you – when at the Office – and afterwards – too – at Home – and sometimes – wakes at night, with a worry for you – he did'nt finish – quite – by Day – He would not like it – that I betrayed Him – so you'll never tell. . . .

A letter poem, addressed "Dear Mr Bowles" and signed "Emily," which is variously considered in the handwriting of late 1861 and in that of late March 1862, may be regarded as in some sense signaling the end, or near it, of her hopes. Opinions also differ about its intention. According to the Harvard editors, it may be an elegy for Frazar Stearns, the president's son and Austin's friend, who was killed in battle on March 14, 1862, at Newbern, North Carolina (a Union victory). Others find it Emily's expression of controlled exasperation at Bowles's and the *Republican*'s meager and belated reception of her work. Again, it may be her reminder to Bowles, especially in the last line, that she can exist on whatever bit (crumb) of love he chooses to bestow on her. That is, she will endure. All three of these suggestions may be relevant in some degree, and even they are only ways of indicating major thrusts; the minor implications, including the religious, are myriad. What Samuel Bowles made of it is not on record.

DEAR MR BOWLES.

> Victory comes late,
> And is held low to freezing lips
> Too rapt with frost
> To mind it!
> How sweet it would have tasted!

Just a drop!
Was God so economical?
His table's spread too high
Except we dine on tiptoe!
Crumbs fit such little mouths –
Cherries – suit *Robins* –
The Eagle's golden breakfast – *dazzles them!*
God keep his vow to *"Sparrows,"*
Who of little love – know how to starve!   [#690]

The experience of these crucial years—roughly, from the time Samuel Bowles entered the Dickinson circle about 1858 to his departure for Europe in April 1862—reverberated in Emily Dickinson's poems and letters for a long time. Whether Bowles was at the exact center of it, or whether he was only a part of it, a catalyst in a mixing of many elements, cannot yet be said with certainty. One hestitates to formulate lives as complicated as Emily Dickinson's. But it is fully apparent that Bowles was a powerful presence on whom for a while she focused with extraordinary intensity both her ambition and her love. Shortly after he left for Europe, she wrote a strange letter to Mrs. Bowles, purporting to console her for the absence of her husband. But she seems to be speaking for herself as much as for her friend. What Mrs. Bowles made of this is not on record either:

Dear Mary –
When the Best is gone – I know that other things are not of consequence – The Heart wants what it wants – or else it does not care –
You wonder why I write – so – Because I cannot help – I like to have you know some care – so when your life gets faint for it's other life – you can lean on us – We wont break, Mary. We look very small – but the Reed can carry weight.
Not to see what we love, is very terrible – and talking – does'nt ease it – and nothing does – but just itself.
The Eyes and Hair, we chose – are all there are – to us – Is'nt it so – Mary?
I often wonder how the love of Christ, is done – when that – below – holds – so – . . .

A letter to Bowles in Europe that summer is more composed, with news from home and pleasant longings to have him back: "I tell you, Mr Bowles, it is a Suffering, to have a sea – no care how Blue – between your Soul, and you." And in this letter the home to which she would have him come back is in Amherst as well as Springfield:

How sweet it must be to one to come Home – whose Home is in so many Houses – and every Heart a "Best Room." I mean you, Mr Bowles.

Three letters on the occasion of his return in mid-November are the last we have that bear on this phase of the relationship. In general they, too, are more composed, as if she were adjusting herself to the inevitable. She was solicitous about his health: "So few that live – have life – it seems of quick importance – not one of those – escape by Death." In a brilliant stroke, anticipating (or echoing) the theme of a poem she sent him, she hit off the nature of what she called his "power":

How extraordinary that Life's large Population contain so few of power to us – and those – a vivid species – who leave no mode – like Tyrian Dye.

The poem which went to him about a year later may explain a good deal about the process by which she got involved in this ill-starred love:

> The Zeroes – taught us – Phosphorus –
> We learned to like the Fire
> By playing Glaciers – when a Boy –
> And Tinder – guessed – by power
> Of Opposite – to balance Odd –
> If White – a Red – must be!
> Paralysis – our Primer – dumb –
> Unto Vitality! (#689, early 1863)

The next paragraph in the letter is an admission that such vitality must live unto itself; she asked only for the sparrow's crumb, "Who of little love – know how to starve":

Remembering these Minorities [the "so few of power"] – permit our gratitude for you – We ask that you be cautious – for many sakes – excelling Our's. To recapitulate the Stars – were useless as supreme. Yourself is Your's – dear friend – but ceded – is it not – to here and there a minor Life? Do not defraud These – for Gold – may be bought – and Purple – may be bought – but the sale of the Spirit – never did occur.

And with this gentle admonition that he had better not forget what her "minor Life" might offer him—not the Gold of material success nor the Purple of worldly power—she urged him to prolong his rest cure. For all her rhetoric of humility, Emily Dickinson never underestimated herself. She may have loved Bowles, but she never confused her values with his. After this tiny sermon, she talked to him like a solicitous mother: "Do not yet work. No Public so exorbitant of Any – as it's Friend – and we can wait your Health. Besides – there is an idleness – more Tonic than Toil."

The other two letters in this group have to do mainly with her refusal to see him on his first visit to Amherst after his return. In the first, she wrote, very briefly:

I cannot see you. You will not less believe me. That you return to us alive, is better than a Summer. And more to hear your voice below, than News of any Bird.

Samuel Bowles
ED: ". . . the most triumphant Face out of Paradise"

Mrs. Samuel Bowles
ED to SB: "We never forget Mary – "

Her refusal has usually been attributed to overwhelming emotion and turbulence of spirit. She may indeed not have trusted herself. But she may simply have been ill; or, having accepted her "minor Life," she may have decided, quite composedly, not to expose herself again. In the final letter, which tells of Austin's and Vinnie's "upbraiding" her for her discourtesy, she gave her ostensible reason: "They did not know I gave my part that they might have the more – but then the Prophet had no fame in his immediate Town – My Heart led all the rest," indicating that, at least in retrospect, she could talk in perfect control. The rest of the letter further protests her good intentions: "Did I not want to see you? Do not the Phebes want to come?"; chides him for not believing in her: "Oh They of little faith!"; and tells of her joy in his health and her hope to see him often in Amherst.

And come often he did, although the next recorded visit was not until July of 1863 and after that not until he called in 1868 to tell the Dickinsons about his plans for a trip west. But he probably missed few Commencements. From 1868 until his health failed in 1877, he came at least once a year—in 1873, as a guest in the Homestead—and maybe oftener. He walked in Edward Dickinson's funeral procession in June 1874 and was thanked by Emily in a letter that tells much about her loyalty to him over the years. There is no salutation:

I should think you would have few Letters[,] for your own [perhaps one about her father?] are so noble that they make men afraid – and sweet as your Approbation is – it is had in fear – lest your depth convict us.

You compel us each to remember that when Water ceases to rise – it has commenced falling. That is the law of Flood. The last Day that I saw you was the newest and oldest of my life.

Resurrection can come but once – first – to the same House. Thank you for leading us by it.

Come always, dear friend, but refrain from going. You spoke of not liking to be forgotten. Could you, tho' you would? Treason never knew you.

EMILY.[13]

A letter the next year referred to her father's funeral again: "If we die, will you come for us, as you do for Father?" She urged him (again) to take care of his own life, so precious to them all, and she put better than she had before the peculiar vitality and power he brought to her and to the routine Dickinson life:

13. Ruth Miller (pp. 187–88) finds this letter as referring "still to this past [the past of their relationship], but now with utter coldness behind her mask of hyperbole." Compared to the earlier letters, it is indeed formal and cool; but equally clearly, she is preoccupied with her father's death. I do not find the tone one of "utter coldness," nor can I see the last sentence (as Miller suggests) as hinting at Bowles's "treason." Couldn't she be saying, "No one—myself included—could be treasonable to you"?

We miss your vivid Face and the besetting Accents, you bring from your Numidian Haunts.

Your coming welds anew that strange Trinket of Life, which each of us wear and none of us own, and the phosphorescence of your's startles us for it's permanence. . . .

. . . "Not born" yourself, "to die," you must reverse us all.

There are scores of poems from the late 1850s, many of them clearly love poems, that Emily did not send to Bowles. Many of them are obvious variants of the poems she sent him or extensions of ideas or figures in the letters she wrote him. To do justice to them all would involve a critical anthology of the work of her middle years. They are in many modes and moods, from the suggested despair of "Two swimmers" to her own version of Mrs. Browning's similar question, at once a poetic amplification of her remark in the letter to Mary Bowles about love ("The Heart wants what it wants – ") and (perhaps) a more lighthearted way of saying, "I cant explain it, Mr Bowles":

> "Why do I love" You, Sir?
> Because –
> The Wind does not require the Grass
> To answer – Wherefore when He pass
> She cannot keep Her place.
>
> Because He knows – and
> Do not You –
> And We know not –
> Enough for Us
> The Wisdom it be so –
>
> The Lightning – never asked an Eye
> Wherefore it shut – when He was by –
> Because He knows it cannot speak –
> And reasons not contained –
> – Of Talk –
> There be – preferred by Daintier Folk –
>
> The Sunrise – Sir – compelleth Me –
> Because He's Sunrise – and I see –
> Therefore – Then –
> I love Thee –   (#480, about 1862)

No amount of verbal parallels and biographical hints can prove that Bowles was the man here addressed, but so much evidence has been gathered to support the guess about this and similar poems of the period that the burden of proof seems to be shifting to those who would deny it.

The temptation, of course, is to piece together poems like this one with all those that address a man, or depict a situation involving a man, into a continuous narrative of her love for Samuel Bowles, and thus to construct a pattern of the relationship, logically satisfying but chronologically (and otherwise) impossible to verify, replete with meetings, confrontations, and sad partings. The story can take Emily Dickinson all the way from the tentative beginnings, through moments of wholehearted affirmation, as in the poem above, through the agony of frustration and the reassessment her failure demanded, and finally to the consequent rededication of her life. Every one of these major phases, and many minor ones, can be documented persuasively by its own cluster of poems, the only caveats being in the order of occurrence and the degree of uncertainty as to the whereabouts of Bowles. Sometimes he seems very near; at other times she seems to have so sublimated her feelings as to put him at far remove, if he is in the poem at all. The following poems may stand as typical of the various stages of their friendship as it has been reconstructed and, indeed, as we have already seen these stages suggested in the letters and in the letter poems.

To begin with the timid beginnings. Fairly early, perhaps in the summer of 1860, she may have sent Bowles this poem, although it is not in any of the surviving letters. Here her love (it is hard to see how anyone could have otherwise interpreted the "Hound within the Heart") is rendered as a whimpering dog longing to get to its master. If she let the dog loose, would its master receive him?

> What shall I do – it whimpers so –
> This little Hound within the Heart
> All day and night with bark and start –
> And yet, it will not go –
> Would you *untie* it, were you me –
> Would it stop whining – if to Thee –
> I sent it – even now?
>
> It should not tease you –
> By your chair – or, on the mat –
> Or if it dare – to climb your dizzy knee –
> Or – sometimes at your side to run –
> When you were willing –
> Shall it come?
> Tell Carlo –
> *He'll* tell *me!*[14]   (#186)

14. In the 1955 *Poems*, this poem is listed as "to an unidentified recipient." One of the two manuscripts of the poem is signed "Emily." The poem is one of those found by Samuel Bowles, Jr., among the family papers and transmitted to Austin Dickinson during the period in the early 1890s when Austin and Mabel Todd were gathering materials for the 1894 *Letters*. It was not published, however, until it was

The little pleasantry about Carlo, the dog her father had given her in 1850(?), would have been reassuring enough to this busy and preoccupied man; and she herself could enjoy anatomizing her feelings (then and later) in such a poem as " 'Why do I love' You, Sir?" Such may have been the beginnings, after the first of those lively evenings in the Evergreens and about the time the note of pleading entered the letters.

The poem that follows is a good example of her least troubled mood. There are no suggestions of overwhelming power as in the wind and the lightning of " 'Why do I love,' " only the soft sun, the increasing nearness, the peace, the "possibility." It may have nothing at all to do with Bowles. But if the date (about 1859) is correct, she had already seen a good deal of him and was certainly thinking about him. The "Daisy" is, of course, a tempting clue.

> The Daisy follows soft the Sun –
> And when his golden walk is done –
> Sits shily at his feet –
> He – waking – finds the flower there –
> Wherefore – Marauder – art thou here?
> Because, Sir, love is sweet!
>
> We are the Flower – Thou the Sun!
> Forgive us, if as days decline –
> We nearer steal to Thee!
> Enamored of the parting West –
> The peace – the flight – the Amethyst –
> Night's possibility!   (#*106*)

About this time, flowers and letters were going to both Bowleses (she was apologizing for the number), but to what avail? She may in this poem have recorded her sense of strain and uncertainty:

> By a flower – By a letter –
> By a nimble love –
> If I weld the Rivet faster –
> Final fast – above –
>
> Never mind my breathless Anvil!
> Never mind Repose!
> Never mind the sooty faces
> Tugging at the Forge!   (#*109, about 1859*)

---

included in *Bolts of Melody* (1945) by Millicent Todd Bingham. Mrs. Bingham—I think correctly—regarded all the poems found by Bowles's son to have been addressed to Samuel Bowles, or to a member of the family. (The Harvard editors were more conservative in their decision to leave the recipient unidentified unless specifically indicated by Emily Dickinson.)

In another, the mood is melancholy and the source of "irritation" unspecified. This one she sent to him, for whatever reason:

> Heart, not so heavy as mine
> Wending late home –
> As it passed my window
> Whistled itself a tune –
> A careless snatch – a ballad –
> A ditty of the street –
> Yet to my irritated Ear
> An Anodyne so sweet –
> It was as if a Bobolink
> Sauntering this way
> Carolled, and paused, and carolled –
> Then bubbled slow away!
> It was as if a chirping brook
> Upon a dusty way –
> Set bleeding feet to minuets
> Without the knowing why!
> *Tomorrow*, night will come again –
> Perhaps, weary and sore –
> Ah Bugle! By my window
> I pray you pass once more.

(#*83, about 1859*)

Although the tone of unease and strain becomes steadily more pronounced and may have come from her growing frustration with Bowles alone, it must be remembered (again) that there were other anxieties in her life: her mother's health, Vinnie's troubles, Austin's marriage, her difficulties with Sue, perhaps her disappointment with Sue's vivid friend Kate Scott Anthon, and her gradual estrangement from the Evergreens group in general. In several poems it is "they" whom she identifies as having rejected her, or disappointed her, and whom in the end she defies. The following poem has been seen as a "whining" complaint against the editors of the *Republican* for their insensitivity to her poems, but it may have a more general reference. It was addressed "Mrs Bowles –" and signed "Emily."

> "They have not chosen me," he said,
> "But I have chosen them!"
> Brave – Broken hearted statement –
> Uttered in Bethleem!
>
> *I* could not have told it,
> But since *Jesus dared* –
> Sovreign! Know a Daisy
> Thy dishonor shared!

(#*85, about 1859*)

This is the time, as we have seen, when rejection was in the air. The mood did not produce Emily Dickinson's best poetry, but the poems reflecting it—the following are examples—must be regarded as preliminary to some of the great ones to come. In one poem, the pose at first is that of the helpless, abandoned little creature; but the surge of confidence in the end is true to what actually happened in her life:

> Poor little Heart!
> Did they forget thee?
> Then dinna care! Then dinna care!
>
> Proud little Heart!
> Did they forsake thee?
> Be debonnaire! Be debonnaire!
>
> Frail little Heart!
> *I* would not break thee –
> Could'st credit *me?* Could'st credit me?
>
> Gay little Heart –
> Like Morning Glory!
> Wind and Sun – wilt thee array!   (#*192, about 1860*)

Another builds on the idea of the "rejection" verses she sent to Bowles and to Sue: how she'd *"harass God"* for his sake and never shut the door on Sue's "beseeching face."·

> Why – do they shut Me out of Heaven?
> Did I sing – too loud?
> But – I can say a little "Minor"
> Timid as a Bird!
>
> Would'nt the Angels try me –
> Just – once – more –
> Just – see – if I troubled them –
> But dont – shut the door!
>
> Oh, if I – were the Gentleman
> In the "White Robe" –
> And they – were the little Hand – that knocked –
> Could – I – forbid?   (#*248, about 1861*)

The pose of the "poor little heart" or the timid bird should not obscure, however, Emily Dickinson's infinitely deeper probings. Chronologically, the two kinds of poems appear side by side in the 1955 *Poems;* for that matter, the pages for these years are well mixed with poems of neutral or whimsical tone, objective nature bits, and the like. Since it is demonstrable that the anguished poems came about this time in her life and that the poems of her later years, while never ignoring for long the problem of suffering and loss, seldom give this sense of crucial, intense involvement, we can look upon such poems as the following as arising from the darkest center of the 1858–62 experience, regardless of whether Bowles, or someone else, or some personal disturbance involving no one else, was the cause of it. First, "about 1860," it is the "drop of Anguish":

> I shall know why – when Time is over –
> And I have ceased to wonder why –
> Christ will explain each separate anguish
> In the fair schoolroom of the sky –
>
> He will tell me what "Peter" promised –
> And I – for wonder at his woe –
> I shall forget the drop of Anguish
> That scalds me now – that scalds me now! (#*193*)

By "early 1862" it is "Earthquake" and "Maelstrom":

> At least – to pray – is left – is left –
> Oh Jesus – in the Air –
> I know not which thy chamber is –
> I'm knocking – everywhere –
>
> Thou settest Earthquake in the South –
> And Maelstrom, in the Sea –
> Say, Jesus Christ of Nazareth –
> Hast thou no Arm for Me? (#*502*)

If in this poem she showed how far she was from the comfort of the Gospel injunction to "Knock and it shall be opened unto you," another shows how far in her extremity she was from the comfort of prayer. She never made a starker statement of a deprived existence:

> Of Course – I prayed –
> And did God Care?
> He cared as much as on the Air
> A Bird – had stamped her foot –
> And cried "Give Me" –
> My Reason – Life –
> I had not had – but for Yourself –
> 'Twere better Charity
> To leave me in the Atom's Tomb –
> Merry, and Nought, and gay, and numb –
> Than this smart Misery. (#*376, about 1862*)

The following poem, where Reason "breaks," may be a tortured requiem on her hopes for Bowles both to love her and to accept her poetry; or it may commemorate a period of stagnation as a poet, when her mind, as she looked back, almost gave way under the weight of her despair; or it may refer to a mental or spiritual crisis of the sort she predicted (in the letter to Mrs. Holland) when she asked the "kind ladies and gentlemen" to be indulgent. She seems as close to touching bottom here as she ever got. But there was nothing wrong with her mind when she wrote the poem:

> I felt a Funeral, in my Brain,
> And Mourners to and fro
> Kept treading – treading – till it seemed
> That Sense was breaking through –
>
> And when they all were seated,
> A Service, like a Drum –
> Kept beating – beating – till I thought
> My Mind was going numb –
>
> And then I heard them lift a Box
> And creak across my Soul
> With those same Boots of Lead, again,
> Then Space – began to toll,
>
> As all the Heavens were a Bell,
> And Being, but an Ear,
> And I, and Silence, some strange Race
> Wrecked, solitary, here –
>
> And then a Plank in Reason, broke,
> And I dropped down, and down –
> And hit a World, at every plunge,
> And Finished knowing – then –[15].   (#280, about 1861)

Another poem, side by side with this one in the 1955 *Poems* and (by Emily Dickinson's own arrangement) in one of those gatherings, or

15. Miller, whose insistence on the proliferation of "variant" poems in the ED canon is a highly useful one, cites (p. 128) the following as a variant of "I felt a Funeral, in my Brain."

> I felt a Cleaving in my Mind –
> As if my Brain had split –
> I tried to match it – Seam by Seam –
> But could not make them fit.
>
> The thought behind, I strove to join
> Unto the thought before –
> But Sequence ravelled out of Sound
> Like Balls – upon a Floor.   (#937, about 1864)

fascicles, in which she bound together groups of her poems, renders in a sense the obverse of this experience, or its complement. She has come back to "knowing" again. She can look back on the terror and the suspense of the action in the preceding poem and can now look it coldly in the face. She has even extracted a kind of exhilaration from the experience, suggesting an "aesthetics of terror."[16] In the therapeutic view, she has come near mastering her affliction and is on the way to health:

> 'Tis so appalling – it exhilirates –
> So over Horror, it half Captivates –
> The Soul stares after it, secure –
> To know the worst, leaves no dread more –
>
> To scan a Ghost, is faint –
> But grappling, conquers it –
> How easy, Torment, now –
> Suspense kept sawing so –
>
> The Truth, is Bald, and Cold –
> But that will hold –
> If any are not sure –
> We show them – prayer –
> But we, who know,
> Stop hoping, now –
>
> Looking at Death, is Dying –
> Just let go the Breath –
> And not the pillow at your Cheek
> So Slumbereth –
>
> Others, Can wrestle –
> Your's, is done –
> And so of Wo, bleak dreaded – come,
> It sets the Fright at liberty –
> And Terror's free –
> Gay, Ghastly, Holiday!   (*#281, about 1861*)

To fit this poem, perhaps too neatly, into our narrative: the Truth of the third stanza is her failure to elicit response from Bowles (or whoever or whatever); the Death of the fourth stanza is the death of her hopes. The exhilaration from recognizing the truth is the mark of her recovery.

But an even surer sign of recovery is the reiteration in poems of this period of the notion of "Title divine," the "Degree" somehow conferred upon her, by herself, or some Being unknown. One poem comes very

16. The phrase is Inder Nath Kher's, whose study of Emily Dickinson's poetry shows how terror, horror, all that "appalled her," became a creative part of her personal poetics.

close to "For this – accepted Breath," discussed earlier. Here in essence is a new kind of poem for her, one in which she leaves the things of this world—space and time, the wind and the grass and the lightning and the sunrise of " 'Why do I love' "—and pictures herself as the center of a heavenly scene.[17] Her old pose of timidity and helplessness is gone; she is no longer a beggar for alms, or a starving sparrow, or a drowning swimmer, or "The Drop [as she wrote in a poem she sent Bowles] that wrestles in the Sea – " She assumes a new stature. She is still bound to her "Master," whose "face" she will present in heaven as her credential to claim equality of rank (one is reminded of her identification with Bowles's suffering and of her remark in the "Chillon" letter: "Would you – ask le[ss] for your *Queen* – M[r] Bowles?") :

> The face I carry with me – last –
> When I go out of Time –
> To take my Rank – by – in the West –
> That face – will just be thine –
>
> I'll hand it to the Angel –
> That – Sir – was my Degree –
> In Kingdoms – you have heard the Raised –
> Refer to – possibly.
>
> He'll take it – scan it – step aside –
> Return – with such a crown
> As Gabriel – never capered at –
> And beg me put it on –
>
> And then – he'll turn me round and round –
> To an admiring sky –
> As one that bore her Master's name –
> Sufficient Royalty!   (# 336, early 1862)

In another poem her independence is complete. Here again she claims a "second Rank," a new baptism, this time of her own choosing. This may render at once her emancipation from a hopeless love and her declaring herself a Poet. Poem after poem of this period seem "poet poems"—the celestial imagery, besides its conventional religious suggestions, representing the fulfillment she has found in her new dedication. In her own mind she joins the Immortals; in the words of her famous poem she "selects her own Society":

17. Ruth Miller, pp. 198 ff., defines this new kind of poem as "the allegory of the disjunctive mode" and distinguishes it from the earlier poems on nature—"the lyrics of flowers, of birds, of gardens, hills, spring, or sunrise"—which are structured on "the single logically expanding metaphor."

I'm ceded – I've stopped being Their's –
The name They dropped upon my face
With water, in the country church
Is finished using, now,
And They can put it with my Dolls,
My childhood, and the string of spools,
I've finished threading – too –

Baptized, before, without the choice,
But this time, consciously, of Grace –
Unto supremest name –
Called to my Full – The Crescent dropped –
Existence's whole Arc, filled up,
With one small Diadem.

My second Rank – too small the first –
Crowned – Crowing – on my Father's breast –
A half unconscious Queen –
But this time – Adequate – Erect,
With Will to choose, or to reject,
And I choose, just a Crown –   (#*508, early 1862*)

In her growing confidence—if we can give a chronological sequence to what may have been sporadic—she does indeed do a bit of "crowing," as if to answer those who would "shut her out of Heaven" or "shut her up in prose":

I shall keep singing!
Birds will pass me
On their way to Yellower Climes –
Each – with a Robin's expectation –
I – with my Redbreast –
And my Rhymes –

Late – when I take my place in summer –
But – I shall bring a fuller tune –
Vespers – are sweeter than Matins – Signor –
Morning – only the seed of Noon –   (#*250, about 1861*)

She does not despair of some day "awakening them"—the insensitive ones—by her music; but the way will not be easy:

Put up my lute!
What of – my Music!
Since the sole ear I cared to charm –
Passive – as Granite – laps My Music –
Sobbing – will suit – as well as psalm!

Would but the "Memnon" of the Desert –
Teach me the strain
That vanquished Him –
When He – surrendered to the Sunrise –
Maybe – that – would awaken – them!   (#261, about 1861)

Two poems, out of many that could be chosen, may be seen as the climax of this sequence. Although the first, about 1861, may be viewed as looking two ways, religious and secular, it seems to reflect her realization of the price of her commitment to her vocation. The "pearl," the "gem," the "diadem," though never without their religious resonance for her, are by now well-established metaphors for her poetry. She is saying here that the price is worth it. It is tempting to see the last stanza as her ironic comment on the lady poets whose verses graced the columns of the *Republican* and as her prediction of the ultimate verdict of time:

One Life of so much Consequence!
Yet I – for it – would pay –
My Soul's *entire income* –
In ceaseless – salary –

One Pearl – to me – so signal –
That I would instant dive –
Although – I *knew* – to *take* it –
Would *cost* me – *just a life!*

The Sea is full – I know it!
That – does not blur my Gem!
It burns – distinct from all the row –
Intact – in Diadem!

The life is thick – I know it!
Yet – not so dense a crowd –
But *Monarchs* – are *perceptible* –
Far down the dustiest Road!   (#270)

The second poem, cited earlier in the context of her family and social problems, takes on a new dimension in the light of her professional struggles of these years. It is a later statement, about 1863, but it seems to come from the same complex of feeling we have been examining. She still feels her isolation, but she is calling neither upon Christ, to whom she turned in extremity, nor upon "Master," nor for some kind of celestial compensation. She has found power in herself to withstand "Tumult" or "Extremity." The "Assembly" of the next-to-the-last line may be the saints of heaven—or it may be the poets whom she counted "All," an Assembly of which she is now a member:

On a Columnar Self –
How ample to rely
In Tumult – or Extremity –
How good the Certainty

That Lever cannot pry –
And Wedge cannot divide
Conviction – That Granitic Base –
Though None be on our Side –

Suffice Us – for a Crowd –
Ourself – and Rectitude –
And that Assembly – not far off
From furthest Spirit – God –   (#789)

It would be pleasant to report that the curve of Emily Dickinson's spirits went steadily up, leveling off after these turbulent years into the mellowness of a productive maturity, the storm and stress over. But the line was never steady; it had many ups and downs; and it is not quite enough to say that she mastered the experience in the sense that it did not destroy her. It released her creative powers as nothing else had—except the possible confrontation in Philadelphia. In another sense, however, she never got over it:

They say that "Time assuages" –
Time never did assuage –
An actual suffering strengthens
As Sinews do, with age –

Time is a Test of Trouble –
But not a Remedy –
If such it prove, it prove too
There was no Malady –   (#686, late 1863)

The Malady here may refer to her experience with Bowles, or someone else, or she may simply be applying her microscopic eye and general experience to a vulnerable adage. As usual, she kept the specifics to herself, as if it were a point of honor not to let even those closest to her know.

Even Austin and Vinnie could say confidently that she never had a "love disaster" and that her withdrawn life was just a "happen." But her poems of these years and later are full of silent suffering. "Many a bitterness – had been," she said in a poem of about 1862, presumably after the major stress was over and many bitternesses remained. But she was true to an earlier insight into herself:

I can wade Grief –
Whole Pools of it –
I'm used to that –
But the least push of Joy
Breaks up my feet –
And I tip – drunken –
Let no Pebble – smile –
'Twas the New Liquor –
That was all!

Power is only Pain –
Stranded, thro' Discipline,
Till weights – will hang –
Give Balm – to Giants –
And they'll wilt, like Men –
Give Himmaleh –
They'll Carry – Him!   (*#252, about 1861*)

Looking back, she could even imagine a final dramatic encounter with her lover, a meeting held after both had realized the cold truth. She could savor the strange mixture of joy and pain at his coming and imagine a final hour with him in the moonlight:

Again – his voice is at the door –
I feel the old *Degree* –
I hear him ask the servant
For such an one – as me –

I take a *flower* – as I go –
My face to *justify* –
He never *saw* me – *in this life* –
I might *surprise* his eye!

I cross the Hall with *mingled* steps –
I – silent – pass the door –
I look on all this world *contains* –
Just his face – nothing more!

We talk in *careless* – and in *toss* –
A kind of *plummet* strain –
Each – sounding – shily
Just – how – deep –
The *other's* one – had been –

We *walk* – I leave my Dog – at home –
A *tender* – *thoughtful* Moon
Goes with us – just a little way –
And – then – we are *alone* –

> *Alone* – if *Angels* are "alone" –
> *First time* they *try* the *sky!*
> *Alone* – if those "vailed faces" – be –
> *We* cannot *count* – on High!
>
> I'd give – to live that hour – *again* –
> The *purple – in my Vein* –
> But *He* must *count the drops – himself* –
> *My price* for *every stain!*   (#*663, about 1862*)

So she could tell herself, in sum, that talk had come to nothing—it was mere "careless" and "toss"; that during their hour under the moon they were together only as bodiless angels are; that the anguish of their original encounter and its failure would never leave her; that *he* must make himself aware of the price she had paid, drop by drop, of her heart's blood.[18]

"Tell Him the page I did'nt write – " So she addressed the "Happy letter" in a poem she sent Bowles about 1862. This is the page many have tried to write and will continue to until there is new evidence. After Bowles died in January 1878, she wrote poignant letters to Mary Bowles and Maria Whitney, making herself almost co-equal in their grief. More and more, Bowles became elevated in her mind to a place beside her father. "He is without doubt with my father," she wrote Mrs. Bowles; and to Maria Whitney some five years after Bowles's death: "The past is not a package one can lay away. I see my father's eyes, and those of Mr. Bowles – those isolated comets. If the future is mighty as the past, what may vista be?" There is no trace of bitterness—at least I can detect none— in these letters, although one can never be sure about this master ironist. Shortly after his death, this note went to Maria:

I have thought of you often since the darkness, – though we cannot assist another's night. I have hoped you were saved. That he has received Immortality who so often conferred it, invests it with a more sudden charm. . . .

His "beautiful face . . . graphic as a spirit's"[19] was the theme of the letter

18. Ruth Miller (pp. 200–4) finds this poem a striking example of the disjunctive mode, with its stress on the metaphor of the heavenly meeting of the last two stanzas. The "old *Degree*" of line 2 is contrasted with *"this life"* of line 7, the new life, that is, entered upon when she took the "Title divine" of poethood. Miller sees the *"He"* of the final stanza as God, a suggestion I do not find inevitable.

19. Bowles was an extraordinarily handsome man. What seems to have impressed Emily Dickinson most were his eyes. Shortly after his death, she wrote Mrs. Bowles: "Dear 'Mr. Sam' is very near, these midwinter days. When purples come on Pelham, in the afternoon we say 'Mr. Bowles's colors.' I spoke to him once of his Gem chapter [Revelation XXI], and the beautiful eyes rose till they were out of reach of mine, in

to Mrs. Bowles just quoted, with this tribute to Mrs. Bowles herself:

> ... To forget you would be impossible, had we never seen you; for you were his for whom we moan while consciousness remains. As he was himself Eden, he is with Eden, for we cannot become what we were not.

Thus she paid homage to the "Great Spirit" (as she called him in another letter to Maria) whose presence in her life seems nearly to have wrecked it and, paradoxically, perhaps made it.

One should not read this account apart from the "Master" letters, the most poignant and the most searing documents in all of Emily Dickinson's correspondence, which will be our next concern. But it may not be inappropriate to end this phase of the discussion on a note of serenity, when, in calm of mind, Emily Dickinson wrote her last letter to Samuel Bowles, probably a year or so before his death. It stresses an aspect of their friendship often lost sight of in our preoccupation with all that was frustrating and anguishing for her. One cannot help being impressed with the discipline of these New England people, so that, whatever went on beneath the surface, life could proceed unruffled, with the giving and receiving of gifts, the literary talk, the humor. This final letter, and the episode it refers to, are pleasant examples.

To put the letter in its setting: Bowles had apparently just visited the Dickinsons (the suggested date of the letter is "about 1877"), had hesitated between borrowing a book about Theophilus Parsons and borrowing a copy of *Junius*—or perhaps they had been offered him as gifts. This is the time when, according to a familiar story, Emily had at first declined to see him, and he had shouted upstairs, "Emily, you damned rascal! No more of this nonsense! I've traveled all the way from Springfield to see you. Come down at once." Down she came, we are told, and was charming and sociable.[20] (Clearly, she needed more Bowleses in her life.) The whole letter reads:

DEAR FRIEND.

Vinnie accidentally mentioned that you hesitated between the "Theophilus" and the "Junius."

Would you confer so sweet a favor as to accept that too, when you come again?

---

some hallowed fathom" (*L* II, 601). Her greatest tribute came in one of the last letters she wrote him: "You have the most triumphant Face out of Paradise – probably because you are there constantly, instead of ultimately –" (*L* II, 574, about 1877).

20. For the anecdote, as told by Gertrude M. Graves, "A Cousin's Memories of Emily Dickinson," *Boston Sunday Globe,* January 12, 1930, see *L* II, 589–90 n., where Bowles's first words are "Emily, you wretch!" The change to the more vigorous salutation, suggested by the Harvard editors, makes sense of Emily's valediction and postscript in the letter. Gertrude Graves concluded her description of the episode: "To Cousin L[avinia]'s utter astonishment her sister appeared. . . . 'I never knew Emily to be more brilliant or more fascinating in conversation than she was that day.'"

I went to the Room as soon as you left, to confirm your presence – recalling the Psalmist's sonnet to God, beginning

> I have no Life but this –
> To lead it here –
> Nor any Death – but lest
> Dispelled from there –
> Nor tie to Earths to come –
> Nor Action new
> Except through this extent
> The love of you. [#*1398*]

It is strange that the most intangible thing is the most adhesive.

Your "Rascal."

I washed the Adjective.

A worksheet draft of the last line of the poem reads "The loving you."

22

The Master Letters

THREE DRAFT LETTERS, unusually long for her maturity, were found among Emily Dickinson's papers after she died, two in ink with corrections in pencil, one in pencil throughout, and all directed to a man she called Master, otherwise unidentified. The two in ink seem ready for posting, although there is no evidence that any of them ever was. They are in the handwriting of the late 1850s and early 1860s, and a mention of the dog Carlo in one of them confirms the date as of that period. Austin and Vinnie winnowed out six sentences from one of them for Mabel Todd to publish in the 1894 *Letters,* where the recipient was indicated by the customary "To ———." Whether Austin and Vinnie knew who he was is itself not known. They suppressed the rest of the letters for protective reasons, giving their selection a deliberately misleading date, 1885. For whatever reason, Mabel followed suit in her 1931 edition of the letters.[1] It was not until 1955 that the complete texts of all three letters were made available by Millicent Todd Bingham in *Emily Dickinson's Home*—an example of the slow and circuitous route by which many vital matters pertaining to Emily Dickinson have come to light. No wonder our view of her has been partial and distorted.

There is no doubt of the importance of these three letters. They are vital indeed. Two of them, the longer ones, are among the most intense and fervent love letters she ever wrote, and all three are extraordinary human documents, at once baffling and breathtaking. They raise innumerable questions, of which the identity of the recipient, however in-

---

1. *Letters of Emily Dickinson,* edited by Mabel Loomis Todd, p. 411. The six sentences selected by Austin and Vinnie were from the longest of the three letters. They are the first and third sentences of the letter and the four that begin, "Vesuvius dont talk . . ." This was as much, writes Mrs. Bingham (*Home,* p. 421), as Austin and Vinnie thought "decorous."

triguing, is among the least important. Far more important is what they tell us about Emily Dickinson at this crucial point in her life. That she went through a crisis, and probably a love crisis, about this time has long been known. We have just seen the part that Samuel Bowles may have played in it. What is new about the letters is their sustained revelation of the intensity, depth, and power of her love and the agony of its frustration. As few have, she shows what it is to "suffer" love. We see her coping with the experience with all her imaginative and verbal power and thus partially, at least, transcending it.

The letters show Emily at the height of the metaphoric style that had its inception in the letters to Abiah Root, Jane Humphrey, and others. Many passages defy precise explication, although since 1955 there have been many attempts. The usual precaution about dates must be stated; the first letter I shall discuss, for instance, has been assigned dates ranging from 1858 to 1861. Even the order of the three letters has not been determined. The 1958 *Letters* prints this one, the shortest, first, dating it "about 1858," but Mrs. Bingham prints it last and with no attempt at dating. This letter, one of the two in ink, is the least confessional, the least intense, of the three. It is a tender "get well" letter written to her ailing Master, with whom, it appears, Emily has been in correspondence for some time. The words in parentheses are her penciled deletions.

DEAR MASTER

I am ill, but grieving more that you are ill, I make my stronger hand work long eno' to tell you. I thought perhaps you were in Heaven, and when you spoke again, it seemed quite sweet, and wonderful, and surprised me so – I wish that you were well.

I would that all I love, should be weak no more. The Violets are by my side, the Robin very near, and "Spring" – they say, Who is she – going by the door –

Indeed it is God's house – and these are gates of Heaven, and to and fro, the angels go, with their sweet postillions – I wish that I were great, like Mr. Michael Angelo, and could paint for you. You ask me what my flowers said – then they were disobedient – I gave them messages. They said what the lips in the West, say, when the sun goes down, and so says the Dawn.

Listen again, Master. I did not tell you that today had been the Sabbath Day.

Each Sabbath on the Sea, makes me count the Sabbaths, till we meet on shore – and (will the) whether the hills will look as blue as the sailors say. I cannot talk any more (stay any longer) tonight (now), for this pain denies me.

How strong when weak to recollect, and easy, quite, to love. Will you tell me, please to tell me, soon as you are well.

The letter begins in a note of surprise that her Master has written her after a considerable lapse, and she plays with the notion of having consigned him to heaven in the interim. But heaven is *here*—"*these* are gates of Heaven"—now, in the spring. She breaks into a tiny dithyramb as if to explain to those who ask "Who is she – going by the door – " what spring is. She would paint it, like Michael Angelo, were her words (her poems) not enough. He apparently had not understood the poems—"my flowers" —she had sent him, and she explains that they say only what all nature says, the sunset and the dawn, to those who listen. Then she asks him to "Listen again" while she tells him how jealously she guards the Sabbaths still allotted to them on earth and, continuing her play on the idea of heaven, wonders if when they meet there ("on shore") it will be as beautiful as "the sailors" (the religious ones? the preachers?) say it is. She herself is ill; she "cannot talk any more" because of the pain (so her talk of death might not have been altogether playful). But illness, or weakness, she says in closing, makes memory keener and love stronger. She asks him to tell her when he is well.

It is a beautiful, gracious letter, perhaps a little too insistent for perfect propriety, as in the gently chiding note in her surprise at hearing from him ("Listen again, Master") and in the repetition of "tell me" in the last sentence. She is composed and in command. Only, there seems a disturbing one-sidedness in the relationship; she is making an effort to get him to understand more, one feels, than her poems. The tone is one of muted entreaty.

The tone of the longest letter, printed in *Home* as the first of the three and in the 1958 *Letters* as the second, is anything but muted. Its entreaty is direct, urgent, and unabashed. The style for the most part is nervous and staccato, but there are many changes of pace and mood as Emily pleads or chides or jokes or dreams of what might have been or might be. (The letter was written in ink, heavily corrected in pencil. I have bracketed her deletions and put her alternative readings in parentheses.)

MASTER.

If you saw a bullet hit a Bird – and he told you he was'nt shot – you might weep at his courtesy, but you would certainly doubt his word.

One drop more from the gash that stains your Daisy's bosom – then would you *believe?* Thomas' faith in Anatomy, was stronger than his faith in faith. God made me – [Sir] Master – I did'nt be – myself. I dont know how it was done. He built the heart in me – Bye and bye it outgrew me – and like the little mother – with the big child – I got tired holding him. I heard of a thing called "Redemption" – which rested men and women. You remember I asked you for it – you gave me something else. I forgot the Redemption [in the Redeemed – I did'nt tell you for a long time, but I knew you had altered me – I] and was tired – no more –

No Rose, yet felt myself a'bloom,
No Bird – yet rode in Ether.[2]

2. In the MS, there is a symbol "†" over the word "more." The symbol is repeated at the end of the letter, where the couplet occurs. She thus showed where she wanted the couplet to be inserted—that is, as a celebration in verse of the new exhilara-

[so dear did this stranger become that were it, or my breath – the Alternative – I had tossed the fellow away with a smile.] I am older – tonight, Master – but the love is the same – so are the moon and the crescent. If it had been God's will that I might breathe where you breathed – and find the place – myself – at night – if I (can) never forget that I am not with you – and that sorrow and frost are nearer than I – if I wish with a might I cannot repress – that mine were the Queen's place – the love of the Plantagenet is my only apology – To come nearer than presbyteries – and nearer than the new Coat – that the Tailor made – the prank of the Heart at play on the Heart – in holy Holiday – is forbidden me – You make me say it over – I fear you laugh – when I do not see – [but] "Chillon" is not funny. Have you the Heart in your breast – Sir – is it set like mine – a little to the left – has it the misgiving – if it wake in the night – perchance – itself to it – a timbrel is it – itself to it a tune?

These things are [reverent] holy, Sir, I touch them [reverently] hallowed, but persons who pray – dare remark [our] "Father"! You say I do not tell you all – Daisy confessed – and denied not.

Vesuvius dont talk – Etna – dont – [Thy] one of them – said a syllable – a thousand years ago, and Pompeii heard it, and hid forever – She could'nt look the world in the face, afterward – I suppose – Bashful Pompeii! "Tell you of the want" – you know what a leech is, dont you – and [remember that] Daisy's arm is small – and you have felt the horizon hav'nt you – and did the sea – never come so close as to make you dance?

I dont know what you can do for it – thank you – Master – but if I had the Beard on my cheek – like you – and you – had Daisy's petals – and you cared so for me – what would become of you? Could you forget me in fight, or flight – or the foreign land? Could'nt Carlo, and you and I walk in the meadows an hour – and nobody care but the Bobolink – and *his* – a *silver* scruple? I used to think when I died – I could see you – so I died as fast as I could – but the "Corporation" are going too so Heaven [Eternity] wont be sequestered – now [at all] – Say I may wait for you – say I need go with no stranger to the to me – untried [country] fold – I waited a long time – Master – but I can wait more – wait till my hazel hair is dappled – and you carry the cane – then I can look at my watch and if the Day is too far declined – we can take the chances [of] for Heaven – What would you do with me if I came "in white?" Have you the little chest to put the Alive – in?

I want to see you more – Sir – than all I wish for in this world – and the wish – altered a little – will be my only one – for the skies.

Could you come to New England – [this summer – could] would you come to Amherst – Would you like to come – Master?

[Would it do harm – yet we both fear God –] Would Daisy disappoint you – no – she would'nt – Sir – it were comfort forever – just to look in your

---

tion just described. The 1958 *Letters* prints the couplet at the end, ignoring the signs. Ruth Miller, in *The Poetry of Emily Dickinson* (p. 173), follows this reading of the MS and sees the metaphor of the bird—first, the bird shot down, then a "transfigured" bird—as ending the letter "at affirmation, strong affirmation." I have followed what seems to me the clear direction in the MS (Jay Leyda's reading, *YH* II, 22, agrees), even at the expense of removing what would have been a dramatic conclusion in the affirmative vein.

face, while you looked in mine – then I could play in the woods till Dark –
till you take me where Sundown cannot find us – and the true keep coming
– till the town is full. [Will you tell me if you will?]

I did'nt think to tell you, you did'nt come to me "in white," nor ever
told me why.

In this letter she seems intensely personal, tossing propriety aside,
confessing all. She is her Master's "Daisy," his "Queen," his companion in
old age. She tells how her love started and how long she endured it before
speaking out. From the first image of the stricken bird bleeding to death,
so that anyone could see, and her emphatic "then would you *believe?*,"
she seems to be saying again and again, "How can I make you understand?" She starts with the mystery of her own nature ("God made
me – Master – I did'nt be – myself") and the long fatigue that became
intolerable ("like the little mother – with the big child – I got tired holding him"). She had asked him for "Redemption" to rest her, only to fall
in love with the Master of whom she asked it. But that was long ago: "I
am older – tonight." The pathos of the lovely lyric passage that follows, on
the theme of the "holy Holiday," the "prank of the Heart at play on the
Heart," is her realization that, even as she plays with the idea, fulfillment
is impossible. It was *not* "God's will." It was "forbidden me." But for a
moment, in her imagination, she puts herself in "the Queen's place," the
"love of the Plantagenet" her only apology. She comes nearer to him than
"presbyteries," nearer than "the new Coat – that the Tailor made. . . ."
She seems to be challenging him to understand the power of such love;
indeed, does he understand love at all? "Have you the Heart in your
breast – Sir – is it set like mine . . . ?" She fears that he laughs at her
behind her back; she reminds him that prisoners in dungeons ("Chillon")
are not funny. Twice, continuing her scolding mood, she wonders why he
has accused her of not telling him of her love; but she *had,* if he had only
listened: "Daisy confessed – and denied not." "These things are holy,
Sir"—we don't laugh at them. But then she laughs at herself: in her
confession she "spoke" like Vesuvius, only to retreat in bashful silence, the
Pompeii of her own eruption. And then follow three quick metaphors by
which she tries to make him feel what she has felt: the bloodsucking
leech, the unattainable horizon, the menacing sea. Again she seems to be
saying, "Can't you understand?"

Before she embarks on the little fantasies that follow, Emily chides the
Master once more, as if to say: "If you were in my place, you couldn't
stand it!" But then she is off walking in the meadows with him and Carlo
and the bobolink, the only one to "care"—one way, perhaps, of dismissing
Amherst gossip. In an imaginative leap we have seen her make before, she
recalls how she "died" for him once to meet him in Heaven; now that she
contemplates doing it again, however, she realizes that there will be no
privacy in Heaven with everybody else, the "Corporation," there. So,
giving up that notion, her next bit of fantasy imagines waiting for him
until they both are old, when they can "take the chances for Heaven"

together and she will come to him a spirit "in white." And in a remark that may continue the note of chiding, she seems to say, "You couldn't bury me, a living spirit, *then,* could you?"

Finally there is the invitation to New England and Amherst, the longing for him to come, the promise not to disappoint him, the fantasy of the child playing unafraid in the woods till dark, and the reunion with the "true" in the celestial city. The poignancy of all this, certainly for us and probably for Emily, is its unattainability. She seems to realize that none of it will ever happen. Her last sentence signifies, at the very least, another failure, another rejection. Much could be said about what *his* coming "in white" might mean. Is she merely saying, "You didn't come to see me this winter"? Or is the "white" symbolic: "You never came to me as I have now come to you, in the purity of my complete confession of love"? Or, "You never came to me as a sufferer, you never told me your sorrows"? Or, "You never 'died' for me as I died for you"? There is valid meaning at each level. But whatever the phrase means, the last clause in the sentence is the most poignant of all: ". . . nor ever told me why." And, so the whole letter seems to say, he never will. That it was probably never sent may be a sign of her hopelessness. Only a very few draft letters, including those to Judge Lord written twenty years later, were found among her papers; most of the others were either sent or (perhaps) destroyed.

Like many a scene in one of Shakespeare's more tightly knit tragedies, this letter may be regarded as a microcosm of the whole. Emily Dickinson's whole life is here, the history of what could be called its failures and the reason for them and the prevision of its triumphant success and the reason for *that*. Her failures, certainly, were with people. Throughout her life, she never achieved a single, wholly satisfying relationship with anybody she had to be near, or with, for any length of time. Vinnie was the closest, perhaps; but even she spoke of her family as living together like "friendly and absolute monarchs" (Higginson, we recall, likened them to federated states in a commonwealth, where "each member runs his or her own selves"); and to Emily it seemed often as if she and Vinnie had "come up for the first time from two wells where we had hitherto been bred. . . ." As for Emily's correspondents, affectionate as she might have been in her letters, they were always at a safe distance. Her Master in this letter is remote and unreal. Not a single descriptive phrase identifies him unmistakably among the men in her life we know anything about. All we can be sure of is his failure to understand her and to respond to her love.

The reason seems not far to seek. All her life she demanded too much of people. Her early girl friends could hardly keep up with her tumultuous letters or, like Sue, could not or would not take her into their lives as she wanted to be taken. They had other concerns. The young men, save for a few who had amusing or edifying intellectual exchanges with her, apparently shied away. Eliza Coleman's fear that her friends in Amherst "wholly misinterpret" her, was a polite way of saying, perhaps, that they would not respond with the intensity she apparently demanded of everyone. She seemed unable to take friendship casually, nor could she be realistic about love. The result was excessive tension at every meeting, so that meetings themselves became ordeals. One such meeting was enough for Higginson ("I am glad not to live near her"); in her own economy, she found that she had to ration them very carefully. And when she fell in love, all this was further intensified. The one meeting recorded in this letter, when she asked her Master for Redemption, spelled at once her joy and her tragedy. It exalted her—she bloomed like the rose, she soared like the bird—but it plunged her into "Chillon," the captive of her own soaring fantasy about love.

The remaining Master letter, dated in the 1958 *Letters* "about 1862?", contrasts with the other two in several respects. They address a man to whom Emily can speak eye-to-eye, but here she writes in abject humility, "smaller," "lower," an offender and a blunderer, not even knowing her fault. She will gladly submit to any punishment except banishment. In the first letter, she spoke to a fellow sufferer in illness; in the second, she was his Daisy, his Queen, his companion, but only once his little girl playing in the woods. Those letters scolded and joked and indulged in fantasies; here the tone is almost entirely self-abasing and apologetic.

Oh, did I offend it – [Did'nt it want me to tell it the truth] Daisy – Daisy – offend it – who bends her smaller life to his (it's) meeker (lower) every day – who only asks – a task – [who] something to do for love of it – some little way she cannot guess to make that master glad –

A love so big it scares her, rushing among her small heart – pushing aside the blood and leaving her faint (all) and white in the gust's arm –

Daisy – who never flinched thro' that awful parting, but held her life so tight he should not see the wound – who would have sheltered him in her childish bosom (Heart) – only it was'nt big eno' for a Guest so large – *this* Daisy – grieve her Lord – and yet it (she) often blundered – Perhaps she grieved (grazed) his taste – perhaps her odd-Backwoodsman [life] ways [troubled] teased his finer nature (sense). Daisy [fea] knows all that – but must she go unpardoned – teach her, preceptor grace – teach her majesty – Slow (Dull) at patrician things – Even the wren upon her nest learns (knows) more than Daisy dares –

Low at the knee that bore her once unto [royal] wordless rest [now] Daisy [stoops a] kneels a culprit – tell her her [offence] fault – Master – if it is [not so] small eno' to cancel with her life, [Daisy] she is satisfied – but punish [do not] dont banish her – shut her in prison, Sir – only pledge that you will forgive – sometime – before the grave, and Daisy will not mind – She will awake in [his] your likeness.

Wonder stings me more than the Bee – who did never sting me – but made gay music with his might wherever I [may] [should] did go – Wonder wastes my pound, you said I had no size to spare –

You send the water over the Dam in my brown eyes –

I've got a cough as big as a thimble – but I dont care for that – I've got a Tomahawk in my side but that dont hurt me much. [If you] Her master stabs her more –

Wont he come to her – or will he let her seek him, never minding [whatever] so long wandering [out] if to him at last.

Oh how the sailor strains, when his boat is filling – Oh how the dying tug, till the angel comes. Master – open your life wide, and take me in forever, I will never be tired – I will never be noisy when you want to be still. I will be [glad] [as the] your best little girl – nobody else will see me, but you – but that is enough – I shall not want any more – and all that Heaven only will disappoint me – will be because it's not so dear

Only once in the letter does she allow herself a virtue: her courage during "that awful parting." The only image that suggests stature and strength is that of the sailor pulling desperately for the shore. If the second Master letter is unsurpassed as an expression of love that overpowers, exalts, releases the imagination, this final one shows the despair into which a sensitive person can sink when such a love is rejected or, worst of all, seen by the loved one as an offense or an intrusion.

Again the letter harks back to a past. There must have been a moment in which "Daisy offended it" (a strange but not unprecedented use by Emily of the neuter pronoun), in which, as she says in a passage she deleted, she "told it the truth," probably the simple truth that she loved him. Was it at the moment of "that awful parting"? She asks what to do to redeem her misdemeanor. But she wonders at the same time how any offense could have come from a love as great as hers. Or was it simply her gracelessness, her "Backwoodsman ways"? She asks for instruction from her Master, now her "preceptor," and recalls a moment of "wordless rest" on his knee. She remembers the days before this grief "stung" her, when the bee, "who did never sting me – " made "gay music" wherever she went. Now she is ailing, she has "a Tomahawk" in her side, she weeps, her love is so big it "scares her." Again, as in the previous letter, she looks to the future. Will he come to her, or let her come to him? Again the "little girl" image, not as before a symbol of the need of companionship and protection, but here carrying out the theme of Daisy the offender, who now promises to be his "best little girl," to be seen only by him. That is all she wants; "that is enough." After it, heaven itself will be a disappointment. And again there is the pathetic probability that the letter was never sent: the chances with this one are least of all, since it is the roughest draft of the three and is entirely in pencil.

Assuming that the order in which I have discussed the three letters is the right one, it could be said that the first represents the early stages of her love, the second the climax, when she could at least still imagine herself as having hope, and the last a final cry of despair following a rejection which her Master never explained. Of course, the possibility of a pervasive irony throughout all three letters cannot be denied. To what extent was Emily phantasizing? daydreaming? imagining the whole

thing or willfully overdramatizing it? employing her extraordinary rhetorical powers by way of exploring a realm of experience she had only
nibbled at the fringes of? While the Dickinson rhetoric in her hands, as
we have seen, was quite capable of carrying her to imagined heights with
the slightest stimulus, these letters cannot, I think, be looked upon as
fictions, even though passages in them show her artfulness. It is clear, for
instance, that her self-abasement in the third letter was quite out of character. She knew her ways were not "Backwoodsman" and she knew that
her sensitivities were infinitely superior to her Master's. She knew she had
no more to learn from him than she had later from Higginson, whom she
also called master and preceptor, and, after a certain point, she was no
one's "little girl," except, as here, for rhetorical purposes.

Certainly the letters must be examined skeptically. They show an artist
at work at every point, choosing words, images, metaphors with fine
precision; establishing rhythms and cadences with a most delicate ear;
arranging materials (however she might have rearranged them in final
drafts) for subtle dramatic effect. It is tempting to see the arrangement as
"just coming," the images and metaphors as pouring out willy-nilly, with
no contrivance, the release of an overburdened heart. But clearly the
letters are the work of a supremely conscious artist. And, as with any
artist, to bring her materials under such control was, in a sense, to distance
and command them. We find her here coming to terms with a turbulent
experience ("real," or imagined, in whole or in part). She reduces her
thoughts and feelings to a kind of form—with a beginning, a middle, and
an end—and, in the process, she distances them, commands them, triumphs over them, and prepares to move on. It is by no chance that these
three letters are the seedbed, the matrix, of dozens of her poems—"final
drafts," as it were, of thoughts and themes appearing here, but further
pondered over, developed, made into poetic wholes.[3] Probably no poem
she wrote after the experience recorded in the three letters was entirely
unrelated to it. After it, she had to go somewhere, or perish. Fortunately,
she knew where to go and was fully equipped for the journey.

Since 1955, when the letters first appeared, students of Emily Dickinson have puzzled over the identity of their recipient. The field was soon
narrowed, perhaps prematurely, to the Reverend Charles Wadsworth and
Samuel Bowles. Mrs. Bingham mentioned both men but left the matter
open. In the 1958 *Letters,* Thomas Johnson and Theodora Ward cautiously suggested Wadsworth, who had been Emily Dickinson's "muse"
in Johnson's biography of 1955. In 1961 Winfield Townley Scott strongly
supported Bowles, and in David Higgins' full-length study of 1967 the
Master appears as "almost certainly" Bowles. By 1968 William Robert

3. Ruth Miller finds in the Master letters her whole poetic process in little, a
revelation of "the operation of Emily Dickinson's poetic imagination," her attempt
"to explain herself and her poetry" (p. 144).

Sherwood was arguing that Emily Dickinson constructed, out of her slight contact with Wadsworth, "a drama of passion, transgression, defiance, punishment, damnation, and despair, assimilating, as Hawthorne may have taught her to do, the conventions of medieval romance within a Calvinist framework." He went on to claim that "One can say, to paraphrase Voltaire, that if life had not presented a Reverend Charles Wadsworth, Emily Dickinson would have had to invent him, and then add that to a great extent she did." Yet in that same year Ruth Miller's analysis, the most extensive of the Master letters yet made, based its case for Bowles on the many striking parallels between them and the letters and poems known to have been sent him. She found equally persuasive the intensity with which Emily Dickinson's personal and professional aims both focused, she feels, on Bowles.[4]

Hardly a hint or clue in any of the letters has been overlooked. Much meaning has been uncovered in the search, with our notion of how Emily Dickinson developed as a person and poet expanding in the process. The detailed "microcosmic" aspects of the letters have ramifications of feeling, thought, and phrasing that extend far and wide, and over many years, throughout all the writings we have from her. Of course, one must always keep in mind that the exclusion of any other candidates besides Wadsworth and Bowles might one day, in the light of new discoveries, turn out to be presumptuous.

To begin with the letter I discussed first, Bowles's poor health after 1857 makes him the more likely recipient of this letter than Wadsworth, especially in view of Emily Dickinson's solicitude about his health from the time of her early acquaintance with him. Nothing in all she said about Wadsworth shows any such concern for him, nor do the records of his life show any need for it.[5] Her urging her Master here to "Listen again" and her care to interpret the spring and to explain her poems for him parallel the procedure in several letters and poems to Bowles discussed earlier; for

4. To fill out the references in this paragraph: Cf. *Home*, p. 421: "One is tempted to link the . . . letters to one of the names just mentioned [Wadsworth, Higginson, and Bowles], but it is wiser to wait awhile longer. For it is not impossible that some hitherto unidentified correspondent might turn up, one whose power to arouse such fine frenzy as that which throbs in these letters has not as yet been suspected." *Letters*, 1958, p. 332: "Whether he [Charles Wadsworth] or another is the one she addresses as 'Dear Master' . . . may never be surely known. At present one conjectures no other whom she might thus have designated." Johnson, *Interpretive Biography*, p. 80: "Whereas [Benjamin] Newton had awakened her to a sense of her talents, Wadsworth as muse made her a poet." Winfield Townley Scott's advocacy of Bowles first appeared in "Emily Dickinson and Samuel Bowles," *Fresco: the University of Detroit Quarterly* (Fall, 1959). Higgins (*Portrait*) proceeds, as his evidence mounts, from probability (p. 16) to near certainty (p. 84), and finally to a barely qualified ". . . Samuel Bowles was 'Master,' the man she loved when she became a poet" (p. 118). For Sherwood's remarks, see *Circumference and Circumstance*, pp. 81–82.

5. The Wadsworth family letters show him as occasionally bothered by colds and fatigue; but the emphasis is on an extraordinarily active career sustained by dependable if not rugged health. (See Appendix III.)

instance, the letter beginning, "I cant explain it, Mr Bowles," and then the "explanation" in verse. The metaphor of the flowers (her poems) parallels the "stintless cups," the spices, the berries, she offered him in that other get-well letter we have seen.

If indeed this first letter is to Bowles, it is consistent with Emily's other attempts to test his busy intelligence with her figurative language. Wadsworth, a poet in his youth and in his sermons a master of image and metaphor, would hardly seem to require such treatment. Another crux, "Each Sabbath on the Sea, makes me count the Sabbaths . . .," seems to indicate an ocean traveler. Bowles sailed for Europe in April 1862;[6] Wadsworth sailed for San Francisco that May. If either of these facts is pertinent, the date assigned the letter in the 1958 *Letters* ("about 1858") must be moved ahead. And yet the handwriting suggests this year or near it; certainly well before the spring of 1862.

But it may be that the "Sabbath on the Sea" is entirely metaphoric, as the "shore," the "sailors," and the "hills" of that same sentence surely are. She is writing on Sunday, clearly enough; but Sunday, or Sabbath, is the day of the week commemorating the Resurrection, a meaning noted in her Lexicon, and thus may carry out the theme of the lyric passage on the spring earlier in the letter, where spring is the very gate of heaven.[7] So the idea of the Sabbath takes her to heaven, too, and she asks whether the "hills" there will be as beautiful as the "sailors" say they are, a variant of the sentence in the "Vain – sinful Worm" letter to Bowles: "The Charms of the Heaven in the bush are superceded I fear, by the Heaven in the hand, occasionally," and a variant also (to show how frequently she played with the idea) of the lines in the poem "I reckon – when I count at all – " when she wonders whether ". . . the Further Heaven – / Be Beautiful as they prepare / For Those who worship Them – "

Emily Dickinson repeatedly thought of the sea as an emblem of life itself—not only its risks and dangers but its alluring mysteries. About 1859, in a poetic rendering of her early words to Abiah Root, she set out in high spirits:

> Exultation is the going
> Of an inland soul to sea,
> Past the houses – past the headlands –
> Into deep Eternity –

6. In a letter to Bowles of about August 1862, Emily spoke of the sea that then separated them, of the Amherst hills, and of Carlo, all quite literally: "I tell you, Mr Bowles, it is a Suffering, to have a sea – no care how Blue – between your Soul, and you. The Hills you used to love when you were in Northampton, miss their old lover, could they speak – and the puzzled look – deepens in Carlo's forehead, as Days go by, and you never come" (*L* II, 416).

7. Cf. Miller, p. 147.

> Bred as we, among the mountains,
> Can the sailor understand
> The divine intoxication
> Of the first league out from land?   (#76)

About a year later, another poem shows how readily she put the sea, the sailors, the shore to metaphoric use, only here her "exultation" is darkened by a sense of awe tinged with terror. She feels

> . . . as One returned, . . .
> Odd secrets of the line to tell!
> Some Sailor, skirting foreign shores –
> Some pale Reporter, from the awful doors
> Before the Seal! . . .   (#160)

We saw how alien to Bowles's imagination this "divine intoxication" was; "odd secrets of the line" did not draw him. He was content, as he wrote Maria Whitney, "to grow in goodness in my more practical way." And Emily, as we saw, soon gave up plying him with her "Sabbath" thoughts. The next two Master letters are more earth-bound—another sign, perhaps, that if this one was to Bowles, it was an early one.

Finally, the last sentence of the letter—"How strong when weak to recollect . . ."—seems to echo a poem she sent Bowles "about 1858," a bit of word play from, perhaps, the lighthearted time of their friendship:

> If recollecting were forgetting,
> Then I remember not.
> And if forgetting, recollecting,
> How near I had forgot.
> And if to miss, were merry,
> And to mourn, were gay,
> How very blithe the fingers
> That gathered this, Today!   (#33)

But the parallel is slight and proves nothing in itself.[8] She often sent the same poem to several people, and similar phrases appear in letters to widely diverse correspondents. It does, however, add to the conviction that the letter speaks more loudly of Bowles than of any other known candidate.

Two cruxes in the second letter have been thought to point to Wadsworth: the phrase "nearer than presbyteries" and the invitation to come to New England. Wadsworth was a Presbyterian and lived in

8. Cf. Miller, p. 148.

Philadelphia; Bowles was a Unitarian and lived in Springfield. Further, regarding the earlier sentences in the letter, why should Emily ask for Redemption from a newspaper editor? These matters have been dealt with in several ways, notably by proponents of Bowles. As early as 1955, Mrs. Bingham warned against taking "presbyteries" any more literally than Emily Dickinson's metaphorical "Himmaleh" or "Calvary." Bowles's sojourn in New York with Mrs. Bowles in the winter of 1861–62 could possibly explain Emily's hope that he would come back to New England. As for "Redemption," she often used religious terms secularly; "Immortality," for instance, meant as often for her the immortality of the poet as it did the immortality of the soul, and sometimes a combination of both. Redemption here might mean what Bowles could give her (the fulfillment of being a published poet),[9] although the emphasis on fatigue and rest suggests a less worldly fulfillment. She speaks of the "Corporation" going to Heaven, a more likely term to use to a man of affairs like Bowles, whose SAMUEL BOWLES AND COMPANY topped the masthead on every issue of the *Republican,* than to a minister. David Higgins noted that Emily's "if I had the Beard on my cheek" further indicates Bowles, since he was notably hirsute, while at least one picture of Wadsworth in his maturity shows him with sideburns only. But in both these instances Emily's references may have been unspecific: the "Corporation" may be simply the Redeemed and the beard a way of indicating a male.[10]

Pursuing her theory of Emily Dickinson's concern with publication, Ruth Miller sees the first sentence in the letter, "If you saw a bullet hit a Bird," as a reference to Bowles's(?) article in the *Republican* on "When Should We Write," his attack on the "literature of misery"—which Emily saw as the end of all her hopes. This, Miller feels, may also be behind the reference, later in the letter, to Vesuvius and Etna; the "bullet" now becomes a volcano, with Emily herself as the bashful Pompeii who heard what the volcano said and hid forever. Emily's "Could you forget me in fight, or flight – or the foreign land" suggests the embattled editor and traveler more than the minister, and Emily's coming " 'in white' " to him may be a trope for her longed-for rank as a published poet. Here one recalls those poems in which Emily Dickinson used the color white possibly to render the exaltation of her self-appointed rank among the poets, "A solemn thing – it was – I said / A Woman – white – to be," and the

9. An example of ED's free use of the term appears in a letter to Higginson of February 1879. She congratulated him on his marriage to Mary Thacher: "To congratulate the Redeemed is perhaps superfluous for Redemption leaves nothing for Earth to add – " (*L* II, 635).

10. Cf. David Higgins on Bowles's beard, *Portrait,* p. 116. Rebecca Patterson, "Emily Dickinson's 'Double' Tim: Masculine Identification," *American Imago* (Winter, 1971), p. 362, pressing her theory of ED's homosexuality, accuses "a generation of biographers" of being "bemused by pencilled-in mustaches." But the biographers (including this one) press on.

"White Election" of the poem whose possible connection with Bowles has already been examined. Such arguments assume that Emily Dickinson's drive for publication was obsessive, that she could not rid herself of it even in a letter that confesses an utter and absolute love. It may well be that she hoped for publication from Bowles; the wound she complains of here, however, seems a rejection more by a lover than by an editor.

But this neither denies nor exhausts the case for Bowles. Two other cruxes point to him: the use of the pet name Daisy, and the reference to "Chillon" similar to the one in the mutilated letter of "early 1862" already discussed. Who of all her friends called her Daisy? The Chillon letter is torn at the crucial point: all we have is "To Da[?]." Nowhere in the surviving correspondence between Bowles and any of the Dickinsons has a reference to Emily as Daisy been found. When Bowles sent messages to her by way of Austin, it was to "Emily" (and once to the "Queen Recluse"). There are "Daisy" poems, however, that went to the Bowleses, the most convincing in this regard being the one to Mary Bowles:

> "They have not chosen me," he said,
> "But I have chosen them!"
> Brave – Broken hearted statement –
> Uttered in Bethleem!
>
> *I* could not have told it,
> But since *Jesus dared* –
> Sovreign! Know a Daisy
> Thy dishonor shared!   (#85, about 1859)

Two other poems of about 1859, neither of them, as far as we know, sent to Bowles, carry out ideas or metaphors so close to what we know she sent him as to be pertinent here. In both, the speaker, likened to a daisy, addresses a man. In the first, "The Daisy follows soft the Sun," the daisy "sits shily at his [the sun's] feet – . . . Because, Sir, love is sweet!"; and in the second the contrast is between the "Immortal Alps" and "A Myriad Daisy" at play at their feet: ". . . Which, Sir, are you and which am I / Upon an August day?" Another Mountain-Daisy poem in this same vein renders the same attitude of humble devotion that "Daisy" adopts toward her "Master," "Lord," or (by implication) "king" in the Master letters:

> The Himmaleh was known to stoop
> Unto the Daisy low –
> Transported with Compassion
> That such a Doll should grow
> Where Tent by Tent – Her Universe
> Hung out it's Flags of Snow –   (#481, about 1862)

[525

There may be a clue in Bowles's apparently offhand remark to Austin about the "Queen Recluse." "Would you ask – le[ss] for your *Queen* – M[r] Bowles?" Emily had asked him in her Chillon letter. The recurrence of both Chillon and the queen image in the second Master letter ("if I wish with a might I cannot repress – that mine were the Queen's place . . .") is persuasive if not convincing.

Still another poem, sent to Bowles, contains a significant clue first pointed out by David Higgins. Probably composed nearer the latter part of 1861 than the 1864 assigned it in the 1955 *Poems*, the poem employs a grammatical device—the use of the neuter "it" instead of the expected "you"—that occurs several times in the third Master letter. The poem also picks up a theme we have noted in her letters to Bowles—her embarrassment over writing him so much, with (presumably) so few replies:

> If it had no pencil
> Would it try mine –
> Worn – now – and *dull* – sweet,
> Writing much to thee.
> If it had no word,
> Would it make the Daisy,
> Most as big as I was,
> When it plucked me?   (*#921, about 1864*)

The poem was written on a slip of paper which was pinned around the stub of a pencil and signed "Emily." The last four lines are puzzling. For all the pronominal difficulties, they seem to say, "If I don't hear from you, does that make me the little girl I was when I fell in love with you?"— that is, taking the poem as a whole, it is another, though muted, complaint that he has ignored or rejected her. The assumption is that Bowles would know what she meant by "the Daisy."

In a poem of "early 1862"—one is tempted to say it was written shortly after Bowles sailed for Europe in April—she again addresses a man, telling him,

> I tend my flowers for thee –
> Bright Absentee! . . .

In seventeen lines she takes the census of her spring garden; her "Fuschzia," geraniums, daisies, hyacinth, carnations, "globe roses," whose bright crimson "ill becometh," she says, the sadness of her Lord's absence. So, she concludes,

> I'll dwell in Calyx – Gray –
> How modestly – alway –

Thy Daisy –
Draped for thee!   (#339)

Appealing as such hints and parallels are, they cannot be regarded as proving that Bowles was Master. The third letter is similarly inviting but still elusive. There may be a clue in the similar use of the impersonal "it" of the first sentence ("Oh, did I offend it – ") and in the first line of the poem "If it had no pencil," which she sent Bowles. Another poem uses the same device and, indeed, has the same theme and tone as the third Master letter. It addresses "Master" directly in the last line. The last clause of the second Master letter (". . . nor ever told me why") appears almost verbatim in the next-to-last line of the poem.

> Why make it doubt – it hurts it so –
> So sick – to guess –
> So strong – to know –
> So brave – upon it's little Bed
> To tell the very last They said
> Unto Itself – and smile – And shake –
> For that dear – distant – dangerous – Sake –
> But – the Instead – the Pinching fear
> That Something – it did do – or dare –
> Offend the Vision – and it flee
> And They no more remember me –
> Nor ever turn to tell me why –
> Oh, Master, This is Misery –   (#462, about 1862)

And yet there is no evidence that the poem ever went to Bowles or to anyone else.

Other hints in the letter—"that awful parting" and the "odd-Backwoodsman ways"—are equivocal. The parting may have been Bowles's departure for Europe or the conclusion of Wadsworth's visit to Amherst in 1860. Either Bowles's life in Springfield or Wadsworth's in Philadelphia may have made her own life in Amherst seem "Backwoodsman." One can only suggest that Bowles's famous cosmopolitanism, the worldliness he brought so frequently to the Dickinson circle, makes him—if the choice is to be between these two men—the likelier.[11]

Emily's "Low at the knee that bore her once unto [royal] wordless rest" brings up a host of possibilities, from the idea that the Master might have been someone she had known since childhood to something like the romantic scenes in the Dickinson home that Joseph Lyman described,

---

11. Cf. ED to Bowles, about August 1862: ". . . I have heard, that in large Cities – noted persons choose you" (*L* II, 416). But the adjective "finer" ("perhaps her odd-Backwoodsman [life] ways [troubled] teased his finer nature") would seem to suggest Wadsworth, as ED saw him.

when Vinnie sat in his lap and wound her chestnut hair around his neck. We think of those happy evenings in the Evergreens during Bowles's and Kate Anthon's visits and, of course, of Bowles's famous penchant for the companionship of ladies. Joseph Lyman, referring to the late 1840s, called Emily "platonic" and found his friendship with her "too sacred to be called a flirtation." But ten years later, and with Bowles, she may have been quite different. We have already seen what happened with Austin when the Dickinson floodgates opened. We recall Sue's charges of "immorality" against both Emily and Vinnie when she warned Mabel Todd against calling on them. David Higgins sees the "knee that bore her once" as probably Bowles's in a moment of "fun," since Wadsworth at the time of his visit was still in mourning for his mother (a fact worth pointing out but hardly conclusive). The scene is at least credible. It is quite conceivable that, looking back on those late-Puritan days, it is *we* who have been overly fastidious.[12]

One can only add that, whatever the circumstances, the moment went far beyond mere fun for Emily. The theme of fatigue in the last two Master letters: the Redemption that "rested men and women"; the little mother who got "tired" holding the big child; and now the memory of the "wordless rest" on her Master's knee and (in the last paragraph) "I will never be tired"—all this shows, perhaps, the tension she was living through, the culmination of many years of frustrations of various sorts, rejections (as we can see them) large and small. The moment of wordless rest she here commemorates seems to have come as a climax to a relationship of some duration and with someone (to return to the Bowles or Wadsworth question) who was more accessible than the distant Philadelphian. The evidence in all three letters of a long-established dialogue, of restful moments together and disturbing confrontations, makes propinquity, if the choice is limited to the two men, almost decisive. And finally, if such a choice must be made, the intensity of feeling in the letters to Bowles would seem to exclude Wadsworth almost automatically. She could hardly have loved both at the same time, at such a pitch.

And yet we look in vain in all three letters for the living presence of either one of them. Toward the end of the second letter, Emily longs merely to look in her Master's face rather than into Bowles's remarkable eyes, those "isolated comets" she spoke of in her letters. Nowhere do we hear the sound of his voice, those "besetting Accents," or see his "vivid Face." In almost all the letters we know she wrote him, his name—"Mr Bowles"—resounds; its absence in the Master letters is conspicuous. There is nothing to identify him as newspaper editor or friend of the family or unmistakably the man of national importance she knew him to be. The same generalizations could be made about Wadsworth, even to the crux

12. The suggestion advanced by John Evangelist Walsh (*The Hidden Life of Emily Dickinson*, pp. 184 ff.) that the "knee that bore her once" was Judge Lord's is discussed in Chapter 27.

of the "presbyteries." Twice in the second letter she speaks as if a meeting with her Master might cause harm or embarrassment of some sort. But she concludes that if they walked in the meadow, only the bobolink would care, and she rests in the thought, "yet we both fear God." It hardly helps the search for the Master's identity to be reminded that both Bowles and Wadsworth were married men.

Emily (it seems clear) loved Samuel Bowles, and that frustrating experience carried her toward a new sense of her own strength, the strength of the "Columnar Self," one source of which was religious. Many poems of the period show her turning more and more to her God and her Christ, as if to substitute a celestial for an earthly Master. And there was obviously some bitterness as she made her great adjustment. A poem of "about 1862" weaves many of these strands into one. She rejects the heaven she longed for in the Master letters; it is up to *him* to apologize now; his courtesies can make little difference to her as she comes to him "in white." The tone is almost strident:

> Take Your Heaven further on –
> This – to Heaven divine Has gone –
> Had You earlier blundered in
> Possibly, e'en You had seen
> An Eternity – put on –
> Now – to ring a Door beyond
> Is the utmost of Your Hand –
> To the Skies – apologize –
> Nearer to Your Courtesies
> Than this Sufferer polite –
> Dressed to meet You –
> See – in White! (#388)

It is tempting to see Bowles as Master here, even to his obtuseness in the line "Had You earlier blundered in," and the "Door beyond" as a suggestion that he should confine his calls from now on to the Evergreens. She refused to see him when he called after his return from Europe in the fall of 1862, and she made it difficult from then on. But this is supposition. It is conceivable that in this poem she was talking of someone quite different, perhaps a preacher whose "Heaven" disgusted her and whose calls she would no longer accept. Or, the sex of the addressee being indeterminate, it may have been Sue. Or she may have been talking to herself.

To sum up, Emily Dickinson appropriated the experience with Bowles to her own creative uses, and this (whoever the Master was) she clearly did with the experience recorded in the Master letters. For all her intense

[529

feeling for the present—what she called the "ecstasy" either of pain or of joy—she never lost her Puritan sense of life as a preparation. The bitterness gone, she saw such experiences in perspective, even with pleasure, as tests of one's humanity. "You have felt the horizon hav'nt you," she asked in the second Master letter, and fixed the metaphor in a later poem:

> These tested Our Horizon –
> Then disappeared
> As Birds before achieving
> A Latitude.
>
> Our Retrospection of Them
> A fixed Delight,
> But our Anticipation
> A Dice – a Doubt –   (*#886, about 1864*)

The cost was severe—if we are to trust her rhetoric at all, almost fatal. She was honest to every step of the way, as her many poems of anguish and suffering testify. She never blinked the hard facts, and even in moments of composure admitted the precariousness of the journey:

> I stepped from Plank to Plank
> A slow and cautious way
> The Stars about my Head I felt
> About my Feet the Sea.
>
> I knew not but the next
> Would be my final inch –
> This gave me that precarious Gait
> Some call Experience.   (*#875, about 1864*)

She moved, with many intermittences, toward what she called in a poem of about 1863 "the perfected Life." She revised the poem slightly in 1869 and sent it to Sue, a sign perhaps of her regard for it. Knowing now something of the route as she experienced it, and something of the resonance for her of the poem's commonplace images (Augur, Plank, Nail, and Scaffold[13]), we can perhaps see in the poem her own final adjustment to those anguished years of the Master letters:

---

13. Cf., for instance, the "Gimblets – among the nerve – " of Poem #244; "And then a Plank in Reason, broke," in the poem "I felt a Funeral, in my Brain" (#280); the martyrs in Poem #295 whose "young will" was "Bent to the Scaffold." David Higgins (*Portrait*, pp. 150–51) sees "that old nail in my breast," of which Emily complained in a letter of May 1863 to the Norcross cousins, as a reference to the "Master" experience. Certainly the metaphor recalls the "Tomahawk in my side" of the third Master letter, although there the reference seems to be to a physical ailment, and may be here.

The Props assist the House
Until the House is built
And then the Props withdraw
And adequate, erect,
The House support itself
And cease to recollect
The Augur and the Carpenter –
Just such a retrospect
Hath the perfected Life –
A past of Plank and Nail
And slowness – then the Scaffolds drop
Affirming it a Soul.

(#*1142*)

23

Thomas Wentworth Higginson

IT SHOULD COME as no surprise by now that there are at least two Emily Dickinsons. There may in fact be as many as there are biographers, but for expository purposes at this juncture, two will do. There is the "real" Emily Dickinson, the object of all sober inquiry, and there is the figure of legend, the somewhat mellowed version of "the village mystery" her friend Abby Wood Bliss found when she revisited Amherst in 1873 and the "Myth" described by Mabel Todd when she came to Amherst in 1881. This version darkened with Vinnie's stories of her youth and the legends of blighted love but lightened in Martha Dickinson Bianchi's reassuring memories of her aunt.[1] Martha helped create the figure of whimsey and fun, fond of children, full of gnomic wisdom, and of barely sufficient awe, mystery, and talent to remain a poet—or if a poet, one who celebrated the gladsome aspects of nature and human life, leaving their darker aspects to sterner spirits. In spite of the pleas of scholars, critics, chroniclers, and other poets, this Emily Dickinson lives on.

It should also be clear by now that the "real" Emily Dickinson, even if ultimately inaccessible, is hardly the lovable but eccentric genius, the fragile, secluded flower, of the many-phased myth. We have already seen her in an impressive range of experience—high passion, loss, frustration, doubt, the perplexities and anxieties of the common lot—and the whole pervaded by a redeeming humor, a powerful zest for living, a piercing sense of beauty, and given form by a restless search for identity and

---

1. Martha Dickinson Bianchi, *The Life and Letters of Emily Dickinson* (fifth printing with corrections, 1929), and *Emily Dickinson Face to Face: Unpublished Letters with Notes and Reminiscences.* Martha's contributions have been variously assessed, mostly harshly. We have seen how much she left out of her account of life in the Evergreens and of the relations between the two houses. Her account of her aunt suffers similarly; she either failed to see, or subordinated, the sterner realities.

vocation. We have seen her, as she reflected on her experience, developing steadily in disciplined verbal expression remarkable even in her casual utterances and superb in her greatest.

In a biography where the approach is necessarily piecemeal, moving stage by stage, friendship by friendship, it is difficult to give the proper sense of complexity—of the many stresses and strains, thoughts and counter-thoughts, of all that was going on at any one time in the life and consciousness of this very complicated person. Limited as her sphere of action may have been by the spring of 1862 (where our narrative now continues), she had a full quota of daily encounters. For all her rhetoric of loneliness and isolation, it is misleading to imagine her as a walled-in Chillon prisoner during these years. No one—poet or lover or poet in love—is ever completely engrossed, or trapped, in a single aim or passion or person. Emily's letters to Thomas Wentworth Higginson, which began with her now historic note of April 15, 1862, contributed much, in their degree of pose and coyness, to the figure of the legend. But they are also among the most thoughtful (as they are certainly the most literary) of her correspondences, and tell us much of what we know about the spiritual and artistic problems with which the "real" woman was struggling throughout her middle and later years.

During the period when Emily Dickinson was deliberately withdrawing from the wider world, she regularly saw her parents and the indefatigable Vinnie in the Homestead and the two formidable personalities next door at the Evergreens, augmented since 1858 by the two Newman cousins. For a person of her sensitivities, no encounter would have been trivial. Fortunately, for balance, she had her chores, her cooking, her sewing, whatever cleaning she could not pass off on Vinnie, and always, of course, Nature and her writing. Her mother's health, never robust, took constant watching. She had not entirely lost the run of the roads and was still being called on, though she was becoming more and more selective about those she would receive. During the crucial years 1858–62, letters (we should be reminded again) were going out to her Norcross cousins, to the Hollands, to scattered correspondents like Mrs. Joseph Haven and the Reverend Edward Dwight and Kate Scott Anthon —letters of wit and inventiveness and friendly solicitude seemingly as free from the kind of agony that pervades the Master letters as her friends could wish.[2]

2. The mention of these friends points up, of course, the highly selective aspect of my choice, for full discussion, of only six of the friendships of ED's maturity (Bowles, Higginson, "H.H.," the Hollands, the Norcrosses, and Judge Lord). Others come to mind: Rev. John Langdon Dudley, whose marriage to Eliza Coleman in 1861 may have caused ED some pain (see *YH* I, xli–xlii); Kate Anthon, the subject of Rebecca Patterson's full-length study; Perez Dickinson Cowan, ED's cousin; Rev. and Mrs. Jonathan L. Jenkins, ED's favorite pastor; the Tuckermans; Charles Sweetser, cousin, editor of *The Round Table;* and others. Mrs. Bingham's "Relatives, Friends

We see her sympathizing with her correspondents' illnesses, complaining a bit of her own, and, when the occasion arose, yielding to the old mortuary mood, which led her to hold her friends closer and cherish them more: as she wrote Mrs. Holland in March 1859, "Pointed attentions from the Angels, to two or three I love, make me sadly jealous." She lived to regard the "Master" experience as but an instance of a vaster problem; indeed, I think she saw it so all the time or she could never have written about it as she did. The vaster problem was time and mortality, and a particular instance of it among her relatives or friends brought her out of whatever secret sorrows might have been hers into hard external realities and the thoughts that death always occasioned. A fine example is her letter of April 1860 to the Norcross family (sent to Vinnie, who was staying with them) on the death of her favorite Aunt Lavinia. Though not without self-pity, the letter shows concern for more than her own anguish, whether over the loss of an aunt or a Master:

VINNIE –
I can't believe it, when your letters come, saying what Aunt Lavinia said "just before she died." Blessed Aunt Lavinia now; all the world goes out, and I see nothing but her room, and angels bearing her into those great countries in the blue sky of which we don't know anything.

Then I sob and cry till I can hardly see my way 'round the house again; and then sit still and wonder if she sees us now, if she sees *me,* who said that she "loved Emily." Oh! Vinnie, it is dark and strange to think of summer afterward! How she loved the summer! The birds keep singing just the same. Oh! The thoughtless birds!

Poor little Loo! Poor Fanny! You must comfort them.

If you were with me, Vinnie, we could talk about her together.

And I thought she would live I wanted her to live so, I thought she could not die! To think how still she lay while I was making the little loaf, and fastening her flowers! Did you get my letter in time to tell her how happy I would be to do what she requested? Mr. Brady is coming to-morrow to bring arbutus for her. Dear little aunt! Will she look down? You must tell me all you can think about her. Did she carry my little bouquet? So many broken-hearted people have got to hear the birds sing, and see all the little flowers grow, just the same as if the sun hadn't stopped shining forever! . . . How I wish I could comfort you! How I wish you could comfort me, who weep at what I did not see and never can believe. I will try and share you a little longer, but it is so long, Vinnie.

We didn't think, that morning when I wept that you left me, and you,

and Neighbors: Biographical Notes" (*Home,* pp. 481–513) was a pioneering attempt to show how wide ED's circle actually was. Jay Leyda's "The People around Emily Dickinson" (*YH* I, xxvii–lxxxi) went further, adding valuable critical estimates to welcome (and often new) factual material. His mention of some twenty missing or incomplete correspondences, simply among the people he discusses, widens the circle still more and opens up dramatic possibilities. (See Appendix V.)

for other things, that we should weep more bitterly before we saw each other.

Well, she is safer now than "we know or even think." Tired little aunt, sleeping ne'er so peaceful! Tuneful little aunt, singing, as we trust, hymns than which the robins have no sweeter ones.

Good-night, broken hearts, Loo, and Fanny, and Uncle Loring. Vinnie, remember

SISTER

It is worth pausing over this recurrent mortuary theme. Every death, every illness she heard about among her friends, set Emily Dickinson wondering about "those great countries in the blue sky of which we don't know anything," and no love disaster entirely preempted her feeling or thought. In spite of the concluding picture of the "tuneful little aunt" singing hymns in heaven, this wonder, the same wonder that had haunted her since Mount Holyoke days and the early letters to Abiah Root, and always would, is the overarching theme not only of this letter but of many of her finest poems. It gives the transcendent dimension to the Master letters themselves. And, although it may be right to say that her chief concern in her first letters to Higginson was her poems, these larger thoughts became more and more prominent as the correspondence progressed. She saw loss of any sort, whether of a lover, a friend, her flowers in the fall, or (of crucial importance in the Higginson letters) her power and will to write poetry, as an emblem of the perennial mystery, all the more excruciating because she loved the people and things of this world so intensely. And not to be able to write about them, to distill their essence in poems, meant, simply, death. She once described the Gospel theme to Joseph Lyman as the "yearning for a oneness." It could be called the theme of her life. Sooner or later she saw every experience in its light, every relationship, almost everything, it seems, that impinged upon her consciousness. One of the many ironies in her letters to Higginson is her description of her family: "They are religious – except me. . . ." She may at times have felt emotionally walled in—or walled out—but her mind and her sympathies recognized no limits, or limitations.

Save for a few poignant references, it is characteristic that, in her letters to Higginson, she all but ignored the stirring events of the time and said nothing at all about the great national causes with which he had for years been publicly identified—Abolition, women's rights, the plight of the Northern poor. Long before the spring of 1862, his name had appeared frequently in the *Springfield Republican* in connection with such matters; she could hardly have helped reading about him, and them.

To go back a bit: during the period of the Master letters the threat of war was growing steadily more ominous, to break into open conflict with the attack on Fort Sumter on April 12, 1861, approximately the time Emily Dickinson was composing the second Master letter. She has been accused of holding herself aloof from all such matters, as befits Emily

[535

Dickinson the legendary recluse; and certainly her way was not the way of causes or reforms or national movements, of Higginson the militant Abolitionist or of Emerson who could say at the news of Sumter, "Sometimes gunpowder smells good." We do not know what she thought of her father's published plea in 1855 that "by the help of Almighty God, not another inch of our soil *heretofore consecrated* to freedom, shall *hereafter* be polluted by the advancing tread of slavery. . . ." Nor do we know what she thought of her brother Austin's buying a substitute for $500 to send to the army. Shortly after Higginson went to South Carolina in the fall of 1862 to take command of a black regiment, she said only that she wished she had seen him before he became "improbable," that "War feels to me an oblique place," and that "when service is had in Church, for Our Arms, I include yourself – " These are her most extended comments on the war as such. Her letter to Bowles about the death of Frazar Stearns had nothing to do, it will be remembered, with issues or causes. It was full of the shock of death and its effect on her brother. Three months before Frazar's death, on the last day of 1861, when, as far as we can tell, her anguish over her personal problems was at its height, she wrote one of her most moving elegies in a letter to Louise Norcross, this time about two other boys—the Adams boys—who had died in the war, one of a wound, one of typhoid fever.

> Mrs. Adams had news of the death of her boy to-day, from a wound at Annapolis. Telegram signed by Frazer Stearns. You remember him. Another one died in October – from fever caught in the camp. Mrs. Adams herself has not risen from her bed since then. "Happy new year" step softly over such doors as these! "Dead! Both her boys! One of them shot by the sea in the East, and one of them shot in the West by the sea." . . . Christ be merciful! Frazer Stearns is just leaving Annapolis. His father has gone to see him to-day. I hope that ruddy face won't be brought home frozen. Poor little widow's boy, riding to-night in the mad wind, back to the village burying-ground where he never dreamed of sleeping! Ah! the dreamless sleep!

This letter with the one about Stearns and a few random remarks[3] comprise her total comment on the Civil War. Nothing about issues, about slavery or the Union, nothing specific about victory or defeat or any of the heroes on either side. It was not that she shut these matters out of her life; she had to come to terms with them in her own way. And when Amherst boys were killed, the tragedy of the times emerged in her marvelous little elegies on these young men lost in the dreamless sleep, like this one about Francis H. Dickinson ("the first man on Amherst's quota to give up his life for his country"), killed in action at Ball's Bluff, Virginia, on the Potomac, near the Maryland border, October 21, 1861:

3. Recall the one to Bowles in November 1862: ". . . failure in a Battle – were easier – and you here – " (*L* II, 420).

When I was small, a Woman died –
Today – her Only Boy
Went up from the Potomac –
His face all Victory

To look at her – How slowly
The Seasons must have turned
Till Bullets clipt an Angle
And He passed quickly round –

If pride shall be in Paradise –
Ourself cannot decide –
Of their imperial Conduct –
No person testified –

But, proud in Apparition –
That Woman and her Boy
Pass back and forth, before my Brain
As even in the sky –

I'm confident that Bravoes –
Perpetual break abroad
For Braveries, remote as this
In Yonder Maryland –   (*#596, early 1862*)

Another concern during these crucial years puts still further in question the notion of the all-absorbing nature of her love situation, or at the very least shows that, even as she was in it, she was forging a way out of it, a way of survival. This concern, or project, may also have bearing on her motives for writing Higginson in the first place. About 1858, according to the best estimates, she began to assemble her poems into groups, averaging about eighteen to twenty each, which she carefully bound by threading the folded sheets, four or five sheets to each group. There are thirty-nine groups so threaded and four held together with brass fasteners, probably put there by Lavinia. Mabel Todd called them "fascicles." The 1955 *Poems* calls them "packets," a term most recently used to differentiate them from twenty-five other gatherings, not threaded, eight of which appear to have been intended for binding, with seventeen too loosely assembled to judge.

Emily Dickinson followed this procedure for about seven years, spanning the period of her greatest productivity. It has been argued that if at first she had in mind the preparation of copy for a possible publisher—a Bowles or a Higginson—she came to regard the procedure, after (and perhaps before) these men failed her, as her private substitute for publication or, most important for us, her notion of the way her poems should be presented to the world when and if the world should be receptive. For many years the fascicles were regarded as haphazard gatherings to be broken up at will by editors for purposes of arranging poems by theme, as in the earliest Todd-Higginson divisions ("Life," "Love," "Nature," "Time and Eternity"), or chronologically, as in the 1955 *Poems*. But it is possible that the gatherings were not haphazard and that the editorial freedom so far taken with them may have violated Emily Dickinson's profoundest intentions. Ruth Miller has perceived a rationale, a calculated structure, in the fascicles that no critic or future editor, she feels, can ignore. According to this theory, Emily Dickinson arranged the fascicles as long link-poems, with the parts, the individual lyrics, bound together by intertwinings of imagery, metaphor, theme, and mood into a sustained, emblematic narrative, with the poems arranged to present, dissect, lament, or celebrate the stages of a progression from "quest" through "suffering" to "resolution." Each link-poem shows the design and scope of a mature poet, sure of herself and her theme. Whether or not one accepts this theory *in toto*, as applicable in every instance, the fascicles are clear evidence that Emily Dickinson was extraordinarily busy during these years *as poet*, whatever she may have been as frustrated lover. They also show that she was hardly the ingénue she presented herself to Higginson as in the famous introductory letters of April 1862.[4]

It will be remembered that, shortly before Mabel Todd's edition of the *Letters* was to come out in 1894, President Seelye of Amherst spoke strongly to her against making public the letters of that "innocent and confiding child." Mrs. Todd defended herself and Emily in her journal:

> As to the letters. . . . Those to Mr. Higginson are not of a private nature, and as to the "innocent and confiding" nature of them, Austin smiles. He says Emily definitely posed in those letters, he knows her thoroughly, through and through, as no one else ever did.

Although Seelye may be pardoned for not penetrating the pose, from our vantage point its elements seem obvious enough, even in the first, short letter to Higginson occasioned by his article in the April 1862 *Atlantic Monthly*, "Letter to a Young Contributor."

The article itself, it might be said, was not without pose, that of a busy editor weary and a little sad with having to write so many rejection letters

---

4. The most recent and the most careful work on the fascicles appears in Ralph Franklin, *The Editing of Emily Dickinson: A Reconsideration*, and Ruth Miller, *The Poetry of Emily Dickinson*, Chapter 10 and Appendix II. Ruth Miller's theory of the fascicles as link-poems, resembling the structured sequence of Francis Quarles's *Emblems, Divine and Moral*, is still to be demonstrated to general satisfaction. One difficulty is that almost any random grouping of eighteen or twenty of ED's stronger poems can be shown to have similar coherence, so recurrent are her major themes, images, and symbolic structures. Nor is it easy to demonstrate, without straining credibility, the progression in each fascicle from "quest" to "resolution" that Miller sees with "blueprint" certainty. Nevertheless, a copy of the *Emblems* (1824 edition) was in the Dickinson library, and the parallels are striking. The virtue of such speculation is that it opens up a question long ignored by editors. It will be much facilitated by a printing of the fascicles exactly as ED arranged them.

to young writers impatient to publish. (Higginson was not an editor of the *Atlantic;* the article had been commissioned.) There was much in it that might have caught Emily Dickinson's eye. In the first sentence Higginson paid his respects to women writers—"My dear young gentleman or young lady . . ."—and there were signs, throughout, of his longstanding feminist position. She may have noted his hospitality to "new or obscure contributors" and his insistence that editors are "always hungering and thirsting after novelties." His feeling for language must have seemed close to her own; his remarks on "the magnificent mystery of words"; his praise of sentences that "palpitate and thrill with the mere fascination of the syllables"; his application to literature of Ruskin's notion of the "instantaneous line"; his praise of Keats's "winged wonders of expression" unsurpassed even by Shakespeare. He spoke of the single word in a way she must have approved of. "Oftentimes a word," he wrote, "shall speak what accumulated volumes have labored in vain to utter: there may be years of crowded passion in a word, and half a life in a sentence." Or she may have been attracted by the assurance from this well-known activist, even then becoming militarist, that actually the pursuits of peace are "real" and war is "accidental." "In all free governments, especially," wrote Higginson, "it is the habit to overrate the *dramatis personae* of the hour." And quoting "the brilliant [Rufus] Choate," he added " 'a book is the only immortality.' "[5] Higginson concluded the article with some thoughts that must have come to Emily Dickinson with alienated grandeur, they were so much like her own during these anguished years:

> . . . we may learn humility, without learning despair, from earth's evanescent glories. Who cannot bear a few disappointments, if the vista be so wide that the mute inglorious Miltons of this sphere may in some other sing their Paradise as Found? War or peace, fame or forgetfulness, can bring no real injury to one who has formed the fixed purpose to live nobly day by day. I fancy that in some other realm of existence we may look back with a kindly interest on this scene of our earlier life, and say to one another, "Do you remember yonder planet, where once we went to school"? And whether our elective study here lay chiefly in the fields of action or of thought will matter little to us then, when other schools shall have led us through other disciplines.

5. There are many parallels in ED to Higginson's remarks in the "Letter." She spoke of the "lovely . . . wiles of Words," how her own sometimes "chill and burn me," how a single syllable can make a "human heart . . . to quake like jostled tree." Again: ". . . Earth's most graphic transaction is placed within a syllable . . ." "A Word," she said, "is inundation, when it comes from the Sea." She spoke of books as "those enthralling friends, the immortalities . . ." (*L* II, 612; III, 758, 700, 802, 858, 771). But Higginson's feeling for language may have seemed, to her, closer to her own than it was. For what might have attracted ED in Higginson's views on the "real" vs. the "accidental," see Tilden G. Edelstein, *Strange Enthusiasm: A Life of Thomas Wentworth Higginson* (1968), p. 250.

As she put it in one of the four poems she sent him with the first letter:

> We play at Paste –
> Till qualified, for Pearl –
> Then, drop the Paste –
> And deem ourself a fool –
>
> The Shapes – though – were similar –
> And our new Hands
> Learned *Gem*-Tactics
> Practicing *Sands* –   (*#320, about 1862*)

    Though "Letter to a Young Contributor" was surely not the first Emily had heard of Higginson, there is nothing in the family records to tell how much she knew of his many activities before this time, of his steady progression from the liberal young Harvard divinity student to the radical Unitarian minister in Newburyport, Massachusetts (from 1847 to 1852), to the revolutionary Abolitionist who twice tested the new Fugitive Slave Law in Boston, once by a conspiracy that failed in 1851 and again in 1854 by conspiracy and violence in the famous case of Anthony Burns. In that action Higginson was wounded and one man was killed. Both of these episodes were fully covered and editorially applauded by the *Springfield Republican;* and since both were prime examples of the clash between individual moral ideals and the sanctity of the law, the two lawyers of the Dickinson family were undoubtedly aware of them and may have discussed them in the presence of the others. Emily could not have known of Higginson's membership in the Secret Six who conspired with John Brown in planning the Harper's Ferry raid on October 16, 1859; but the *Republican* was full of the episode and she must have known Higginson's leanings. His move to Worcester, Massachusetts, as minister of the Free Church in 1852, had brought him and his ideas that much nearer Amherst. "We need more radicalism in our religion and more religion in our radicalism," he said in his installation sermon, printed that year in Worcester. (Later, as he wrote in the 1891 article in the *Atlantic,* he was to meet Emily's uncle William Dickinson in Worcester and discuss with him Mr. Dickinson's puzzling niece.) Emily could hardly have missed an item in the *Republican* for December 3, 1861, under news of Worcester:

> Rev T. W. Higginson of Worcester, it is said, will be appointed lieutenant colonel of the 29th regiment. He has seen some military service in Kansas, and showed good pluck at the time of a fugitive slave [Anthony Burns] case in Boston. The appointment would be a good one.

What made her reading of Higginson's "Letter" inevitable, regardless of her previous knowledge of him, was an enthusiastic notice in the *Republican* for March 29, 1862:

Colonel Thomas Wentworth Higginson
First South Carolina Volunteers
ED to TWH: "War feels to me an oblique place – "

Thomas Wentworth Higginson
man of letters

The Atlantic Monthly for April is one of the best numbers ever issued.
. . . Its leading article, T. W. Higginson's Letter to a Young Contributor,
ought to be read by all the would-be authors of the land. . . . It is a test
of latent power. Whoever rises from its thorough perusal strengthened and
encouraged, may be reasonably certain of ultimate success.

Emily Dickinson was sufficiently strengthened and encouraged to
write the following letter. In the larger envelope that contained it, she
enclosed her signature in an envelope of its own.

MR HIGGINSON,
Are you too deeply occupied to say if my Verse is alive?
The Mind is so near itself – it cannot see distinctly – and I have none to
ask –
Should you think it breathed – and had you the leisure to tell me, I
should feel quick gratitude –
If I make the mistake – that you dared to tell me – would give me sin-
cerer honor – toward you –
I enclose my name – asking you, if you please – Sir – to tell me what is
true?
That you will not betray me – it is needless to ask – since Honor is it's
own pawn –[6]

The pose is delicate here, and one hesitates to assign the degree to which it
was calculated. The absence of epistolary formalities is striking, though
the detached signature and the plea for secrecy may have come not only
from her own distaste for publicity but from genuine worry about involving the Dickinson name in ways that might have brought embarrassment
to her family or the town. Edward Dickinson was a figure in state politics. Samuel Bowles, with whom she had just failed, was known to
Higginson and Higginson to Bowles. Perhaps she wanted to make sure
they would not compare notes. The artifice of the letter lies in what seems
like her conscious effort to achieve the "instantaneous line," syllables that
palpitated and thrilled even in this workaday little note. Perhaps she
hoped Higginson would pick up the Shakespearean echo in the final
clause.[7] To that extent, the artifice worked. Thirty years later Higginson
was to recall the day and occasion: "On April 16, 1862, I took from the
post office in Worcester, Mass., where I was then living, the following
letter. . . ."

One wonders, too, about Emily's diffidence. She was thirty-one. She
had written hundreds of poems. The fascicles show, perhaps, that she
knew herself to be master of more than the isolated lyric, although why

6. Besides the poem "We play at Paste," three others went with the letter: "Safe
in their Alabaster Chambers," "The nearest Dream recedes unrealized," and "I'll tell
you how the Sun rose."
7. Cf. ". . . her honor's pawn" (*Two Gentlemen of Verona* I, iii, 47); ". . .
mine honor's pawn" (*Richard II,* I, i, 74; IV, i, 79); "my honor is at pawn"
(2 *Henry IV,* II, iii, 7); ". . . pawn mine honor for their safety" (*Cymbeline* I, vi,
194), etc.

she did not send Higginson a complete fascicle as a demonstration of her organizing power (if that is what the groupings show) is a mystery. Two editors had already inquired about her poems. When she wrote, "I have none to ask," she was not quite telling the truth. She had already asked Sue's opinion, during the previous summer, of "Safe in their Alabaster Chambers," although, to her, the relationship may not have been cordial enough at this time for more such exchanges. Most striking of all is the spareness of the letter, six sentences, with not a word to give this busy man of affairs the kind of leads one would normally look for in such an introductory letter.

No wonder he wrote her almost at once to find out who she was. We can infer from her second letter to him the series of questions he asked: How old are you? How much have you written? What books do you read? What has been your education? Who are your friends? Have you a family? (Clearly, Higginson had not identified her as Edward Dickinson's daughter; there were many Dickinsons in Amherst.) Will you send me more poems? She answered all his questions in approximately this order, and so evasively that he later compared her to an accomplished coquette.[8] The letter is dated April 25, 1862, in the 1958 *Letters,* but it may have been written a few days later.

Mr Higginson,
Your kindness claimed earlier gratitude – but I was ill – and write today, from my pillow.
Thank you for the surgery – it was not so painful as I supposed. I bring you others – as you ask – though they might not differ –
While my thought is undressed – I can make the distinction, but when I put them in the Gown – they look alike, and numb.
You asked how old I was? I made no verse – but one or two – until this winter – Sir –
I had a terror – since September – I could tell to none – and so I sing, as the Boy does by the Burying Ground – because I am afraid – You inquire my Books – For Poets – I have Keats – and Mr and Mrs Browning. For Prose – Mr Ruskin – Sir Thomas Browne – and the Revelations. I went to school – but in your manner of the phrase – had no education. When a little Girl, I had a friend, who taught me Immortality – but venturing too near, himself – he never returned – Soon after, my Tutor, died – and for several years, my Lexicon – was my only companion – Then I found one more – but he was not contented I be his scholar – so he left the Land.
You ask of my Companions Hills – Sir – and the Sundown – and a Dog – large as myself, that my Father bought me – They are better than Beings – because they know – but do not tell – and the noise in the Pool, at Noon – excels my Piano. I have a Brother and Sister – My Mother does not care for

8. In his *Atlantic Monthly* article for October 1891, p. 445, Higginson described his first exchange with ED: "I remember to have ventured on some criticism which she afterwards called 'surgery,' and on some questions, part of which she evaded . . . with a naïve skill such as the most experienced and worldly coquette might envy."

thought – and Father, too busy with his Briefs – to notice what we do – He buys me many Books – but begs me not to read them – because he fears they joggle the Mind. They are religious –except me – and address an Eclipse, every morning – whom they call their "Father." But I fear my story fatigues you – I would like to learn – Could you tell me how to grow – or is it uncon-veyed – like Melody – or Witchcraft?

You speak of Mr Whitman – I never read his Book – but was told that he was disgraceful –

I read Miss Prescott's "Circumstance," but it followed me, in the Dark – so I avoided her –

Two Editors of Journals came to my Father's House, this winter – and asked me for my Mind – and when I asked them "Why," they said I was penurious – and they, would use it for the World –

I could not weigh myself – Myself –

My size felt small – to me – I read your Chapters in the Atlantic – and experienced honor for you – I was sure you would not reject a confiding question –

Is this – Sir – what you asked me to tell you?

Your friend,
E – Dickinson

Hardly a letter in literary history has been more heavily annotated than this one, a tribute to Emily Dickinson's ability to say so much and yet so little, and all so tantalizingly. We have already explored, though hardly decisively, many of its cruxes—the terror since September (Wads-worth's imminent departure? the first hint of trouble with her eyes? some frightening nervous or mental disturbance?); her education; the friend who taught her immortality (Ben Newton?), and her second friend, who "left the Land" (Wadsworth? Bowles, who had sailed for Europe that very month?). We have made something, at least, of her remarks on her family, especially her father and mother; of those "companions," her Lexicon, the Hills and the Sundown; of the two Editors and her curious penury, when only recently, if we read the situation correctly, she had been trying to interest Bowles in her poems.

Emily's reading list (Keats, the Brownings, Ruskin, Browne, "the Revelations") is as misleading, in what it says and what it omits, as anything in the letter. Ruskin and Browne seem to have been of minor importance to her; perhaps she mentioned them because Higginson did in his article. Where is Thoreau, for whom her few tantalizing references show a kinship greater than she ever acknowledged? Where is Emerson, a major influence, whose *Poems* (1847) Ben Newton had given her in 1850? Above all, where is Shakespeare, of whom she was later to ask Higginson, "Why is any other book needed?"

Though the letter is sparse in vital statistics and evasive in details, it says a great deal. With it she sent three more poems (so now Higginson had at hand seven of her best): "There came a Day at Summer's full,"

"Of all the Sounds despatched abroad," and "South Winds jostle them." It will be remembered that he later complained of the "fiery mist" with which Emily surrounded herself, and it may have been asking too much of him to have understood at once all she was telling him. Yet, as an admitted connoisseur of the "magnificent mystery of words," he might have been expected to understand a little more than he did. The two letters and the poems together tell enough, it would seem, to have impelled even this busy man to the next train to Amherst.

The second letter speaks of illness, loneliness, terror; of family distances and frustrated love; of her turning to the things of nature in her despair over humans: "They are better than Beings – because they know – but do not tell – " Higginson may be pardoned if he did not at once perceive what it was "they knew and did not tell," though for a friend of Emerson and a reader of Wordsworth the thought should not have seemed too extravagant. We accuse Emily of reticence; and it is true that she withheld her age, the names of her tutors and the editors, and lied about the number of poems she had written. Yet to a total stranger she confessed fear, prejudice, irreligion, and her own isolation—for a Dickinson, a degree of self-exposure that was almost embarrassing—and one would think she had displayed enough of her verbal power, in prose and verse, as to be irresistible to a man who had just confessed himself to be deeply interested in the cause of American letters. Perhaps it was a touch of embarrassment or a premonition of failure that made her say, toward the end, "But I fear my story fatigues you – "

If Higginson had felt himself inadequate to deal with the letter and the seven poems, one wonders why he did not hurry off to Emerson or any one of his literary friends with whom he had fraternized in the Boston Town and Country Club (Longfellow, Lowell, Bronson Alcott, among others). All he did, besides sending Emily a letter of cautious praise sometime during the next six weeks, was to exclaim to the *Atlantic* editor, James T. Fields, the day after he got Emily's first letter: "I foresee that 'Young Contributors' will send me worse things than ever now. Two such specimens of verse as came yesterday & day before – fortunately *not* to be forwarded for publication!" The next day (April 18, 1862) he wrote his mother much the same: "Since that Letter to a Young Contributor I have more wonderful effusions than ever sent me to read with request for advice, which is hard to give. Louise [his sister] was quite overwhelmed with two which came in two successive days." History does not record the name of the other hopeful young contributor.

The seven poems were apparently not chosen at random. Emily may have sent the two short ones by way of introducing her poetry and perhaps as comment on the major insistence of the "Letter." "We play at Paste" agreed, on one level, with his emphasis on the necessity of constant revision, or practice, in literary composition and, on a higher level, echoed the idea in his final paragraph that the whole human exercise was merely preparation for the divine. The second short poem presented her poems to him as she frequently had presented them to others; that is, as flowers, things of nature that had come with no practice at all:

> South Winds jostle them –
> Bumblebees come –
> Hover – hesitate –
> Drink, and are gone –
>
> Butterflies pause
> On their passage Cashmere –
> I – softly plucking,
> Present them here!   (*#86, about 1859*)

She had asked him in the letter, "Could you tell me how to grow—or is it unconveyed—like Melody—or Witchcraft?" and included an incomparable example of her own mantic art:

> Of all the Sounds despatched abroad,
> There's not a Charge to me
> Like that old measure in the Boughs –
> That phraseless Melody –
> The Wind does – working like a Hand,
> Whose fingers Comb the Sky –
> Then quiver down – with tufts of Tune –
> Permitted Gods, and me –
>
> Inheritance, it is, to us –
> Beyond the Art to Earn –
> Beyond the trait to take away
> By Robber, since the Gain
> Is gotten not of fingers –
> And inner than the Bone –
> Hid golden, for the whole of Days,
> And even in the Urn,
> I cannot vouch the merry Dust
> Do not arise and play
> In some odd fashion of it's own,
> Some quainter Holiday,
> When Winds go round and round in Bands –
> And thrum upon the door,
> And Birds take places, overhead,
> To bear them Orchestra.

I crave Him grace of Summer Boughs,
If such an Outcast be –
Who never heard that fleshless Chant –
Rise – solemn – on the Tree,
As if some Caravan of Sound
Off Deserts, in the Sky,
Had parted Rank,
Then knit, and swept –
In Seamless Company –   (#321, about 1862)

What is especially important about the poems sent in these first letters to Higginson is Emily's singleness of purpose in sending them. Many of the poems to Bowles carried personal as well as professional messages; the first poems sent to Higginson are samples of her work, presumably chosen to show its variety and range and something, as in the short poems, of its purpose and method. She had come a long way from the early years, when she was experimenting recklessly and joyously with words in fantasy letters and verse valentines. Her style took shape as she outgrew her youthful extravagances, as she came closer and closer to a sense of vocation and found a form suited to her gait. Her growing sense of the healing power her verses had for others now joined with her awareness of how necessary they were to her own health of mind and spirit; how (as she wrote Higginson in her third letter, June 7, 1862) "the Verses just relieve" the palsy, how their "jingling cooled my Tramp –"; and technically she felt her poems ready for professional assessment. All this was to emerge triumphant in her conception of the poet as Creator, on a par, as she was to suggest in moments of audacity almost incredible in one so reared, with Deity Itself. The poem "Of all the Sounds despatched abroad" shows extraordinary confidence. Eight years later she put a question to Higginson that seems strange in view of the many times she answered it herself not only here but in poem after poem of about this time: "You told me Mrs Lowell was Mr Lowell's 'inspiration' What is inspiration?" In "Of all the Sounds," there is no doubt about what inspiration is. It cannot be "earned," nor (*pace* Higginson and his "Letter" and in spite of her pleas for further instruction) can it be learned. It is "inner than the Bone." It is a "charge," a solemn command direct from Nature, ". . . that old measure in the Boughs – / That phraseless Melody –" and—again the audacity—"Permitted Gods, and me –"

Not that Higginson himself was deaf to such Melody. Prior to April 1862, he had published four nature studies in the *Atlantic*. Following the failure of John Brown's raid in the fall of 1859, militant Abolitionism was for a while in retreat. As he had done after he was ousted from Newburyport for his radical views, Higginson returned for a period to his beloved nature. He had visited Thoreau in 1850, in whose way of living he found at least a temporary solace after the disheartening experience in Newburyport. Now he was ranging the woods and streams again, with an eye sharpened by (among other authorities) Thoreau and Professor Edward Hitchcock, whose report on Massachusetts flora and fauna he cited approvingly. Much of his nature work was the product of these months of withdrawal between John Brown and the colonelcy that came to him in the fall of 1862. Emily Dickinson had probably read all four essays before she wrote her first letter to him that April. She told him later that she had read everything he had written; and when he came to see her in 1870, he saw in the Dickinson parlor a copy of his book *Out-Door Papers* containing them.

A comparison of Higginson's treatment of nature with Emily's will tell much, I think, about the relationship between the two, what drew them together in the first place and what helped sustain the friendship of two such disparate temperaments, so close in some ways and so far apart in others.

One of the essays, "April Days" (*Atlantic* for April 1861), begins with a metaphor, or several of them, which, if not up to her style, is at least in Emily Dickinson's vein. It is a celebration of the months.

God offers us yearly a necklace of twelve pearls; most men choose the fairest, label it June, and cast the rest away. It is time to chant a hymn of more liberal gratitude.

Although Emily never counted them out, as here, or gave them labels, the months were distinct personalities to her. She wrote poems about many of them, five about her favorite, March, among them: "We like March. / His Shoes are Purple"; "March is the Month of Expectation"; and the chatty "Dear March," where Higginson's favorite, April, gets short shrift:

> Dear March – Come in –
> How glad I am –
> I hoped for you before –
> Put down your Hat –
> You must have walked –
> How out of Breath you are – . . .
>
> Who knocks? That April.
> Lock the Door –
> I will not be pursued –
> He stayed away a Year to call
> When I am occupied – . . .   (#*1320, about 1874*)

Years earlier, about the time of Higginson's "April Days," April got a poem to itself:

I cant tell you – but you feel it –
Nor can you tell me –
Saints, with ravished slate and pencil
Solve our April Day!

Sweeter than a vanished frolic
From a vanished green!
Swifter than the hoofs of Horsemen
Round a Ledge of dream!

Modest, let us walk among it
With our faces vailed –
As they say polite Archangels
Do in meeting God!

Not for me – to prate about it!
Not for you – to say
To some fashionable Lady
"Charming April Day"!

Rather – Heaven's "Peter Parley"!
By which Children slow
To sublimer Recitation
Are prepared to go!   (#65, about 1859)

To Higginson there was no such mystery in an April day. He was content to luxuriate in its warmth and sweetness, its parade of wild flowers, its promise of new life on every hand:

> There are no days in the whole round year more delicious than those which often come to us in the latter half of April. On these days one goes forth in the morning, and finds an Italian warmth brooding over all the hills, taking visible shape in a glistening mist of silvered azure, with which mingles the smoke from many bonfires. The sun trembles in his own soft rays, till one understands the old English tradition, that he dances on Easter-Day. Swimming in a sea of glory, the tops of the hills look nearer than their bases, and their glistening watercourses seem close to the eye, as is their liberated murmur to the ear. All across this broad intervale the teams are ploughing. The grass in the meadow seems all to have grown green since yesterday. The blackbirds jangle in the oak, the robin is perched upon the elm, the song-sparrow on the hazel, and the bluebird on the apple-tree. There rises a hawk and sails slowly, the stateliest of airy things, a floating dream of long and languid summer-hours. . . . the buds are swelling, the birds are arriving; they are building their nests almost simultaneously . . . there is no such rapture of beauty and of melody as here marks every morning from the last of April onward.

If, compared with Emily's treatment, this is utterly earthbound, at least Higginson was writing in cadences that we can imagine as soothing to her troubled spirit. When she told him in later years that he had saved her life, she may have had more in mind than his friendly letters of advice about her poetry—advice to which, in practice at any rate, she apparently paid no attention whatever. It is certainly not surprising that several of the seven poems she sent him with these first letters dealt amply with nature. She must have recognized it as a firm bond between them.

She is more Higginsonian in one of those poems, "I'll tell you how the Sun rose." Indeed, it might have been in response to a notable early-morning scene of his own in the essay "Water-Lilies," where he is gliding on the lily-pond, absorbing the early warmth and watching the hills take shape:

> It is one of those summer days when a veil of mist gradually burns away before the intense sunshine, and the sultry morning only plays at coolness, and that with its earliest visitors alone. But we are before the sunlight, though not before the sunrise, and can watch the pretty game of alternating mist and shine. Stray gleams of glory lend their trailing magnificence to the tops of chestnut-trees, floating vapors raise the outlines of the hills and make mystery of the wooded islands, and, as we glide through the placid water, we can sing, with the Chorus in the "Ion" of Euripides, "O immense and brilliant air, resound with our cries of joy!"

We have seen examples of how Emily Dickinson enjoyed establishing a kind of dialogue with the things she read, picking up hints and snatches here and there and, as it were, answering them or expanding upon them. Like her answer to the invitation of Revelation 22:17 in the poem "Me – come! My dazzled face . . .," the first line of her sunrise poem might be a way of saying, "Here, Mr. Higginson, is how *I* do it."

> I'll tell you how the Sun rose –
> A Ribbon at a time –
> The Steeples swam in Amethyst –
> The news, like Squirrels, ran –
> The Hills untied their Bonnets –
> The Bobolinks – begun –
> Then I said softly to myself –
> "That must have been the Sun"!
> But how he set – I know not –
> There seemed a purple stile
> That little Yellow boys and girls
> Were climbing all the while –
> Till when they reached the other side,
> A Dominie in Gray –
> Put gently up the evening Bars –
> And led the flock away –   (*#318, about 1860*)

The last eight lines show her moving beyond Higginson—and (it might

EMILY DICKINSON

be added) beyond Thoreau, whose characteristic enthusiasm, like Higginson's, was for sunrise and the dawn.

Perhaps it was this sense of mystery ("But how he set – I know not"), of unanswerable questions here delicately put but coming into Emily Dickinson's major poems with tragic intensity, that kept Higginson at a distance. It was eight years before he finally reached Amherst, and even then he was miles away from her imaginatively. He had none of her inquiring, groping, experimental spirit. To judge from his words and actions, he seems never to have been "haunted" (to use a favorite word of hers) by mysteries or doubts. He knew frustration and loss, and his many causes did not always triumph. But he knew they were just. His life seems to have been one long and confident campaign against the evils he saw about him, clear and distinct. His friends at Newport, Rhode Island, where he went to live with his invalid wife after the war, called him the "muscular Christian," and everywhere he went he exuded health and buoyancy. The terrrible losses of the war, whose duration he had badly underestimated, he accepted with equanimity. In the presence of the death of a soldier, he wrote his wife, "I feel it scarcely more than if a tree had fallen." In a preface to a biographical memoir to Harvard men killed in the war, he wrote: "I do not see how any one can read these memoirs without being left with fresh confidence in our institutions, in the American people, and indeed in human nature itself."

The three other poems of the first seven Emily Dickinson sent him put their worlds even farther apart. Always in his nature studies, the feeling is of nature's abundance, of her marvelous intricacy or her simple plan for life's renewal. The thrust is positive and happy, with humans triumphing over her mild discipline or luxuriating in her delights or being calmed by her serenity. There is nothing that approaches the tone of one of the poems that went to him in the first letter, the one she had sent to Sue for criticism. Higginson got the revised version, with the version of the second stanza she hoped would "please [Sue] better."

Safe in their Alabaster Chambers –
Untouched by Morning –
And untouched by Noon –
Sleep the meek members of the Resurrection –
Rafter of Satin – and Roof of Stone –

Grand go the Years,
In the Crescent above them –
Worlds scoop their Arcs –
And Firmaments – row –
Diadems – drop –
And Doges – surrender –
Soundless as Dots,
On a Disc of Snow.   (#216, version of 1861)

There are doges in "Water-Lilies" and there are snowflakes under the microscope in his essay "Snow." But if she picked up doges from Higginson (the snowflakes came later), she put the image to a very different use.

Higginson's sermons were not noted for their spiritual flights. He preached the "Inner Light" and the "simple humanity of Jesus," the love of God rather than His power; and he rejected the doctrine of Election and Eternal Damnation. It was his social criticism that led to his leaving Newburyport, and in the Free Church in Worcester he seems to have maintained the same position. One of his parishioners called him an infidel and added approvingly: "He does not insult my reason." Emily Dickinson, who boasted of having no respect for doctrines, may have been attracted to him by his heterodoxy but hardly by his religious imagination; in this respect Wadsworth was closer to her than Higginson was. When Higginson wrote confidently in the last paragraph in "Letter to a Young Contributor" of the mute inglorious Miltons who should be comforted by the thought of singing their "Paradise as Found" in some other sphere (heaven), she may have been answering him in another of the poems sent in the first letter.

> The nearest Dream recedes – unrealized –
> The Heaven we chase,
> Like the June Bee – before the School Boy,
> Invites the Race –
> Stoops – to an easy Clover –
> Dips – evades – teases – deploys –
> Then – to the Royal Clouds
> Lifts his light Pinnace –
> Heedless of the Boy –
> Staring – bewildered – at the mocking sky –
>
> Homesick for steadfast Honey –
> Ah, the Bee flies not
> That brews that rare variety![9]   (*# 319, about 1861*)

Even if Higginson the minister failed to see this as a remarkable statement of the perennial human search for religious certainty, or certainty of whatever kind, Higginson the literary critic, who had just written an article of sympathetic advice to young writers, might have seen from it what cold comfort his concluding paragraph had given a young poet whose "nearest Dream" may have been publication.

Nor, as far as can be inferred from Emily's replies to his letters, did

---

9. It might be noted, too, that in Higginson's essay "My Out-Door Study" (*Atlantic*, September 1861) there is a boy who in his rustic rambles is quite clearly *realizing* the nearest dream—"a bliss," as Higginson describes it, "which no Astor can buy with money" (*Out-Door Papers*, 1863, p. 250).

Higginson respond in any substantive way to another of her longer poems that she sent him, this one in the letter of April 25. It, too, is a remarkable poem and has been set by scholars and critics in many contexts.

> There came a Day at Summer's full,
> Entirely for me –
> I thought that such were for the Saints,
> Where Resurrections – be –
>
> The Sun, as common, went abroad,
> The flowers, accustomed, blew
> As if no soul the solstice passed
> That maketh all things new –
>
> The time was scarce profaned, by speech –
> The symbol of a word
> Was needless, as at Sacrament,
> The Wardrobe – of our Lord –
>
> Each was to each The Sealed Church,
> Permitted to commune this – time –
> Lest we too awkward show
> At Supper of the Lamb.
>
> The Hours slid fast – as Hours will,
> Clutched tight, by greedy hands –
> So faces on two Decks, look back,
> Bound to opposing lands –
>
> And so when all the time had leaked,
> Without external sound
> Each bound the Other's Crucifix –
> We gave no other Bond –
>
> Sufficient troth, that we shall rise –
> Deposed – at length, the Grave –
> To that new Marriage,
> Justified – through Calvaries of Love –   (#322, late 1861)

This has been read as a love poem commemorating a farewell meeting, perhaps with Wadsworth (whose 1860 visit was, however, in March); or with Bowles, who at least came to Amherst for many a Commencement in August; or, going further back, with Ben Newton, her first Tutor. When first published in *Scribner's Magazine* for August 1890, it was given the title "Renunciation," although clearly it has as much to do with a commitment as with a giving up. The commitment has been seen as a religious dedication, the mystical marriage of the soul to Christ. Or, in an interpretation that unites the romantic and the religious in a theme of which we have already discussed many examples, the poem may be Emily Dickinson's way of dramatizing her ultimate determination to be a poet, the culminating moment, perhaps, of the long way she had come since the early premonitions in the letters to Abiah Root and Jane Humphrey. In this reading, the poem commemorates the moment of rebirth, the moment "That maketh all things new," a silent and holy time, a kind of preparatory sacrament of "The Sealed Church" at this meeting (or in this vision) "at Summer's full."

However the poem may be read (and there can be several ways), it is surely the culminating poem of the original seven, the one that should have interested Higginson most in his young contributor. Though in her letter to him of July 1862 Emily was to disavow her personal involvement in her lyrics ("When I state myself, as the Representative of the Verse – it does not mean – me – but a supposed person") it is hard to see how he could have missed the intense involvement here and the power of its expression, enough of both, one would think, to send him packing off to Amherst, only fifty miles from Worcester. As to the involvement, it is striking that she should have so exposed herself before a perfect stranger. For here she was, sharing with Higginson one of the "Soul's Superior instants," and he had every reason to assume, as we have, that it was her own. Whether the meeting described in the poem is entirely fictitious, whether it is between herself and a lover, or her own soul, or Jesus Christ, the experience was in essence hers—the poems and letters of the period corroborate this abundantly. Her later disavowal in the July letter seems like an attempt to cover up.

As to the form of the poem, it is as carefully wrought as even Higginson could have wished: the two stanzas of narrative introduction, with their beautifully modulated tonal setting and promise of revelation to come; the four stanzas describing the hushed and holy meeting, the pledge, and the parting; the final stanza with its vision of a celestial union. The total journey of the poem, from a lovely summer day with sun and flowers to the beatific vision won through loyalty and suffering, is achieved with modulation and control. Higginson and Mabel Todd included it in the 1890 selection with very few of the kind of changes they made when, as editors, they regularized Emily Dickinson's wayward syntax or grammar or rhyming. And yet it was on the basis of this and the six other poems, all of which stand up well under structural analysis, that he called her gait "spasmodic" and "uncontrolled" and urged her to delay to publish.

In her reply in the letter of June 7, 1862, Emily had made other disavowals that have contributed as much as anything ever said about her to the legend of the shy genius:

> I smile when you suggest that I delay "to publish" – that being foreign to my thought, as Firmament to Fin –
> If fame belonged to me, I could not escape her – if she did not, the

longest day would pass me on the chase – and the approbation of my Dog, would forsake me – then – My Barefoot-Rank is better –

Other passages in the letter show why, perhaps, she clung to him. Rather than "Mr Higginson," he becomes "Dear friend." He had apparently praised her poems. If her second letter thanked him for his surgery, this one speaks as if she were touchingly grateful for his praise:

> Your letter gave no Drunkenness, because I tasted Rum before – Domingo comes but once – yet I have had few pleasures so deep as your opinion, and if I tried to thank you, my tears would block my tongue –

Apparently, he had suggested that one day she might be a poet, the first such encouragement she had had since Ben Newton, it would seem from what she said next:

> My dying Tutor told me that he would like to live till I had been a poet, but Death was much of Mob as I could master – then – And when far afterward – a sudden light on Orchards, or a new fashion in the wind troubled my attention – I felt a palsy, here – the Verses just relieve –

His second letter was "Balm" after the surgery:

> Your second letter surprised me, and for a moment, swung – I had not supposed it. Your first – gave no dishonor, because the True – are not ashamed – I thanked you for your justice – but could not drop the Bells whose jingling cooled my Tramp – Perhaps the Balm, seemed better, because you bled me, first.

To repeat: Emily's disavowal about publishing can hardly be taken literally. After all, she had sent him the poems in response to his article on how young writers could get their work published. We know that for years she had thought of herself as a poet, that she had discussed with her cousin the possibility of one day being great, and that she hoped to make Sue and Austin proud of her sometime—to walk on "taller feet." What she said here about publishing and fame could perhaps mean that, in view of Higginson's hesitance, she was renouncing her ambition to be a public poet and was adjusting her mind to the "Barefoot-Rank" of a private poet, writing to relieve the palsy, and for the benefit of a few friends, and perhaps in the hope that some far-off Tribunal would render different and unequivocal judgment:

> You think my gait "spasmodic" – I am in danger – Sir –
> You think me "uncontrolled" – I have no Tribunal.

From the next passage in the letter, it is clear that Higginson had urged her to get a friend to give her counsel, an indication that he was not unresponsive to the deep personal appeal of the two letters and the seven poems. Though a man of causes and a reformer, he was also a minister of the Gospel and a shepherd of souls. But he may have been startled to find her asking that *he* be the friend:

Would you have time to be the "friend" you should think I need? I have a little shape – it would not crowd your Desk – nor make much Racket as the Mouse, that dents your Galleries –

If I might bring you what I do – not so frequent to trouble you – and ask you if I told it clear – 'twould be control, to me –

The Sailor cannot see the North – but knows the Needle can –

The "hand you stretch me in the Dark," I put mine in, and turn away – I have no Saxon, now –

Her "Saxon" prose having said all it can, Emily concluded the letter with a poem that elevated Higginson's efforts on her behalf way above what posterity has been inclined to grant them. He had stretched her a hand in "the Dark." Her "dark," at this point, was very great, and this was the kind of gesture she needed. She never thanked Bowles for his kindnesses in such terms as this.

> As if I asked a common Alms,
> And in my wondering hand
> A Stranger pressed a Kingdom,
> And I, bewildered, stand –
> As if I asked the Orient
> Had it for me a Morn –
> And it should lift it's purple Dikes,
> And shatter me with Dawn!   (*#323, about 1858*)

Higginson's hand had come to her during a dark night, and it brought, in the metaphor of the poem, the dawn. Again, this is part of what she might have had in mind when she thanked him later for saving her life.

After this, her final request, following immediately upon the poem, is at least partly understandable. She did not want him as Preceptor so much as friend; and she was enough of a coquette to flatter him, as she did later when she signed herself "Your Scholar" or "Your Pupil":

But, will you be my Preceptor, Mr Higginson?

> Your friend
> E Dickinson –

Throughout the correspondence Emily's signatures vary curiously. Once it is "Your Gnome," once "Barabbas." The few letters between 1864 and 1872 are mostly signed "Dickinson" or "E. Dickinson." Then there is a reversion to "Your Scholar," which became habitual, except for a few letters that had no signature. One senses in them all what Austin called her pose. Clearly, she sought Higginson's opinion of her poems and wanted to know what it was about them that bothered him and other readers. But in the qualities she cared about, certainly in her exalted conception of herself as poet and in her confidence in her powers, she had no more reason to be deferential to Higginson than she had to be to Bowles; and one cannot help feeling that she knew it.

[555

There are only three other letters during the crucial year 1862, one in July, one in August, and a tiny, puzzled one in October, occasioned probably by Higginson's preoccupation with his military commitments. Since mid-September he had been in barracks at Camp Wool, near Worcester.

> Did I displease you, Mr Higginson?
> But wont you tell me how?
>
> Your friend,
E. DICKINSON –

The July letter, the one in which she denied being the "I" of her poems, carried further some of the earlier themes and added a striking new one. Higginson had been sufficiently interested in her to ask for her portrait; she replied with a thumbnail sketch of herself that has done little more than provide material for the Myth:

> Could you believe me – without? I had no portrait, now, but am small, like the Wren, and my Hair is bold, like the Chestnut Bur – and my eyes, like the Sherry in the Glass, that the Guest leaves – Would this do just as well?
> It often alarms Father – He says Death might occur, and he has Molds of all the rest – but has no Mold of me, but I noticed the Quick wore off those things, in a few days, and forestall the dishonor – You will think no caprice of me –

Then, curiously, she reverted to the remark about the hand he had stretched her in the dark: "You said 'Dark.' I know the Butterfly—and the Lizard—and the Orchis—Are not those *your* Countrymen?" Was she cheering *him* up in the "dark" of war? Or had he used the word to suggest his own bewilderment, similar to the "fiery mist" of his later statement? In the August letter she quoted one of his phrases that disturbed her:

> You say "Beyond your knowledge." You would not jest with me, because I believe you – but Preceptor – you cannot mean it? All men say "What" to me, but I thought it a fashion –

This was her perennial complaint, and even Higginson, she was discovering, was not exempt.

Again (to continue the July letter) she asked for surgery: "Will you tell me my fault, frankly as to yourself, for I had rather wince, than die"—another hint as to what she meant by his saving her life. And then a curious moment of embarrassment, real or feigned, out of which came that striking and completely confident pronouncement: "Perhaps you smile at me. I could not stop for that – My Business is Circumference – " About this time, she wrote the Hollands in much the same vein: "Perhaps you laugh at me! Perhaps the whole United States are laughing at me too! *I* can't stop for that! *My* business is to love. . . . *My* business is to *sing –* " The word "Circumference" in the letter to Higginson seems to climax, as it comprehends, the other "businesses." She could hardly have found a more direct way of rejecting his cavils about her lack of control and her spasmodic gait, nor could she have found a more suggestive way of declaring her mature poetic purpose. And yet—perhaps it was the woman in her—she wanted to know why her poems were not welcomed like the innumerable effusions she read in the journals:

> An ignorance, not of Customs, but if caught with the Dawn – or the Sunset see me – Myself the only Kangaroo among the Beauty, Sir, if you please, it afflicts me, and I thought that instruction would take it away.

Again one suspects the pose in this. As she nears the end of the letter, one suspects it even more: "You spoke of Pippa Passes – I never heard anybody speak of Pippa Passes – before. You see my posture is benighted." But the gratitude with which she concludes seems heartfelt:

> To thank you, baffles me. Are you perfectly powerful? Had I a pleasure you had not, I could delight to bring it.
>
> Your Scholar

It is difficult to detect the strategy, if there was one, of the four poems Emily sent Higginson with the July letter: "Of Tribulation – these are They," "Success is counted sweetest," "Your Riches – taught me – Poverty," and "Some keep the Sabbath going to Church." The first two presented the paradox of victory in defeat in a way perhaps a military man (whom a friend described a few months later as marching proudly at the head of his troops in Worcester "like a piece of caste-iron happiness") would understand. Whether Emily intended any irony cannot be known; she may have picked up something of this view of Higginson from the public prints. More likely, she chose "Success" as an example of her work at its formal best—it is perfect by Higginson's standards, or any other—and both poems as reflecting her own somber mood at the time, with the last two stanzas of "Of Tribulation –" perhaps another way of thanking him for his saving hand in the dark:

> "Surrender" – is a sort unknown
> On this Superior soil –
> "Defeat", an Outgrown Anguish,
> Remembered – as the Mile
>
> Our panting Ancle barely passed,
> When Night devoured the Road –
> But we – stood – whispering in the House –
> And all we said – was
>
> SAVED!   (*#325, late 1861*)

EMILY DICKINSON

The other two poems are far from her best: "Your Riches – taught me – Poverty," a tribute to a friend she lost [Sue?]; and "Some keep the Sabbath going to Church," a tuneful bit of "natural religion," quite in the convention:

> Some keep the Sabbath going to Church –
> I keep it, staying at Home –
> With a Bobolink for a Chorister –
> And an Orchard, for a Dome –
>
> Some keep the Sabbath in Surplice –
> I just wear my Wings –
> And instead of tolling the Bell, for Church,
> Our little Sexton – sings.
>
> God preaches, a noted Clergyman –
> And the sermon is never long,
> So instead of getting to Heaven, at last –
> I'm going, all along. (#324, about 1860)

Perhaps she was testing Higginson's humor, or perhaps, in view of her delight in Higginson's nature essays, she was telling him in a way suited to his taste how much nature meant to her.[10]

In the August letter she sent two more poems, with the question "Are these more orderly? I thank you for the Truth –" They seem neither more nor less orderly than those she had already sent him; but they are, if anything, more cryptic. The poem "Before I got my eye put out" carries further the theme of nature, this time with striking originality.

> Before I got my eye put out
> I liked as well to see –
> As other Creatures, that have Eyes
> And know no other way –
>
> But were it told to me – Today –
> That I might have the sky
> For mine – I tell you that my Heart
> Would split, for size of me –
>
> The Meadows – mine –
> The Mountains – mine –
> All Forests – Stintless Stars –
> As much of Noon as I could take
> Between my finite eyes –

10. It is a comment on the taste of the times that this was one of the seven poems that found their way into print during Emily's lifetime. Charles Sweetser, her cousin by marriage, published it in his short-lived New York journal, *The Round Table*, in March 1864. Whether it got to him by Emily's wish or was sent by some other hand is not known. It was selected by Higginson and Mabel Todd for the 1890 *Poems*.

The Motions of The Dipping Birds –
The Morning's Amber Road –
For mine – to look at when I liked –
The News would strike me dead –

So safer Guess – with just my soul
Upon the Window pane –
Where other Creatures put their eyes –
Incautious – of the Sun –   (*# 327, about 1862*)

Higginson was a devoted lover of nature, and his observation of it was careful and precise; but compared with this, his love was a flirtation. Nor did his favorite Romantic poets, who, like himself, emphasized nature's soothing or healing effects (he mentioned Wordsworth frequently), often come so close to the overwhelming, even mortal, experience when, for the supremely sensitive soul, mere observation becomes possession and man and nature are one. There is a suggestion here of the Old Testament notion of Godhead, whom to see is to die.[11]

The second poem, "I cannot dance upon my Toes," could be said, with a few minor exceptions, to bring to an end one aspect of the correspondence. Especially since the letter is the last one in which she discussed at any length her verse and its technique, the poem may be a comment, as Charles Anderson has suggested, on Higginson's attempts to get her to write according to his prescriptions. She said in so many words that it was impossible for her to follow his advice. The kind of "orderliness" he looked for was beyond her:

I had no Monarch in my life, and cannot rule myself, and when I try to organize – my little Force explodes – and leaves me bare and charred –
I think you called me "Wayward." Will you help me improve?

With a conception of poetry so different from his, she could not possibly write as he would wish. In a series of metaphors that must have baffled him, sandwiched as they were between matter-of-fact remarks, she hinted at her own conception of poetry, continuing from the poem "Of all the Sounds despatched abroad" the idea of her mantic inspiration:

I suppose the pride that stops the Breath, in the Core of Woods, is not of Ourself – . . .
. . . I think you would like the Chestnut Tree, I met in my walk. It hit my notice suddenly – and I thought the Skies were in Blossom –
Then there's a noiseless noise in the Orchard – that I let persons hear – . . .
When much in the Woods as a little Girl, I was told that the Snake

11. Ruth Miller (pp. 276–79), emphasizing the visionary experience recorded in the poem, sees it as one of the sequence poems in Fascicle 32, where it introduces "the poet and her soul," the whole fascicle resembling the structure of Quarles's Emblem 10.

would bite me, that I might pick a poisonous flower, or Goblins kidnap me, but I went along and met no one but Angels, who were far shyer of me, than I could be of them, so I hav'nt that confidence in fraud which many exercise.

The passages between these ellipses, when assembled, show how far she was from his world of discourse, let alone from following his advice:

You say I confess the little mistake, and omit the large – Because I can see Orthography – but the Ignorance out of sight – is my Preceptor's charge – . . .
All men say "What" to me . . .
I shall observe your precept – though I dont understand it, always.

Emily did not observe Higginson's precept, and the poem may be her polite way of saying, "Thank you just the same." It becomes, in this reading, an example of those of her poems that should be seen as part of a dialogue or conversation (whether or not Higginson saw it as such).

> I cannot dance upon my Toes –
> No Man instructed me –
> But oftentimes, among my mind,
> A Glee possesseth me,
>
> That had I Ballet knowledge –
> Would put itself abroad
> In Pirouette to blanch a Troupe –
> Or lay a Prima, mad,
>
> And though I had no Gown of Gauze –
> No Ringlet, to my Hair,
> Nor hopped for Audiences – like Birds,
> One Claw upon the Air,
>
> Nor tossed my shape in Eider Balls,
> Nor rolled on wheels of snow
> Till I was out of sight, in sound,
> The House encore me so –
>
> Nor any know I know the Art
> I mention – easy – Here –
> Nor any Placard boast me –
> It's full as Opera –   (#326, about 1862)

If the "Ballet knowledge" and the pirouettes and the hopping for audiences, with their suggestion of pose and artificiality, are to be taken as standing for the kind of poems Higginson would have her write, her scorn must have been deep. "I hav'nt that confidence in fraud," she wrote in the letter, "which many exercise." The implication is strong that she could play at that game if she chose. On this slightly minor note, whether or not detected by Higginson, the first phase of the correspondence ended.

When the letters resumed early next year (February 1863), probably on Emily Dickinson's initiative, Higginson was with his black regiment in South Carolina. "I found you were gone," she wrote, "by accident . . ." The letter she sent him was to the "Dear friend" she addressed him as—not a word about "Preceptor" or "Scholar," and no poems enclosed. Again she was remarkably forward for a shy recluse. She asked him to visit her at Amherst "should there be other Summers," and included him among the friends she could not afford to lose—this to a man she had never seen, a national figure even then emerging as a hero: "Perhaps Death – gave me awe for friends – striking sharp and early, for I held them since – in a brittle love – of more alarm, than peace." In a postscript, she mentioned his essay "The Procession of the Flowers" (*Atlantic* for December 1862) and referred to it obliquely, perhaps, in the body of the letter, although what she says is more like the preaching of Edward Hitchcock than anything in Higginson's essay:

I was thinking, today – as I noticed, that the "Supernatural," was only the Natural, disclosed –

Not "Revelation" – 'tis – that waits,
But our unfurnished eyes –

She spoke of praying for his safety and concluded the letter with a mock formality on a subject that for a soldier is anything but an amusing possibility, his own death. As for her signature, he had probably at one time or another called her verse or her letters "gnomic."

Should you, before this reaches you, experience immortality, who will inform me of the Exchange? Could you, with honor, avoid Death, I entreat you – Sir – It would bereave

Your Gnome –

The tone of this letter is typical of the new phase of the correspondence, which continued, often with long gaps, to the month she died. During this time she sent him some ninety more poems, sometimes on separate sheets enclosed with the letter, sometimes within the letters themselves. Once or twice she asked for more instruction and about 1874 reverted to the signature "Your Scholar." She even began calling him "Master" about then. She became more and more solicitous about his family affairs, especially during the illness of his wife in the mid-1870s.

The deaths in his family, or hers, brought letters haunted with the question that never ceased bothering her. Her letter to Higginson the month after her father died in June 1874 is the finest example. Although we have seen parts of it, a look now at the whole letter shows how much this strange, all but unilateral friendship had come to mean to her. (The "beautiful Hymn" she mentions in the last sentence is Higginson's "Decoration," whose seven stanzas she reduced to the elegy on her father.)

The last Afternoon that my Father lived, though with no premonition – I preferred to be with him, and invented an absence for Mother, Vinnie being asleep. He seemed peculiarly pleased as I oftenest stayed with myself, and remarked as the Afternoon withdrew, he "would like it to not end."

His pleasure almost embarrassed me and my Brother coming – I suggested they walk. Next morning I woke him for the train – and saw him no more.

His Heart was pure and terrible and I think no other like it exists.

I am glad there is Immortality – but would have tested it myself – before entrusting him.

Mr Bowles was with us – With that exception I saw none. I have wished for you, since my Father died, and had you an Hour unengrossed, it would be almost priceless. Thank you for each kindness.

My Brother and Sister thank you for remembering them.

Your beautiful Hymn, was it not prophetic? It has assisted that Pause of Space which I call "Father" –

Although Higginson had written her warmly, even tenderly, after his visit to Amherst in 1873, he might have been surprised at the intimacy with his strange Amherst friend, indeed with the whole Dickinson family, that this letter almost naïvely, it would seem, assumes. He had seen her only twice, both times briefly, and was glad "not to live near her." But in this letter he is almost a member of the family and admitted to her deepest grief and inmost thoughts.

Emily's experience of her father's death, coming as the hardest of all those with which she had had to grapple since the days of her earliest losses, led at one point in the correspondence to an interesting reversal of roles. Three years to the month after her father died, she asked help from Higginson both as friend and as former clergyman. She recalled an incident of her youth:

Since my Father's dying, everything sacred enlarged so – it was dim to own – When a few years old – I was taken to a Funeral which I now know was of peculiar distress, and the Clergyman asked "Is the Arm of the Lord shortened that it cannot save?"

He italicized the "cannot." I mistook the accent for a doubt of Immortality and not daring to ask, it besets me still, though we know that the mind of the Heart must live if it's clerical part do not. Would you explain it to me?

I was told you were once a Clergyman. It comforts an instinct if another have felt it too.

Three months later (September 2, 1877) his wife Mary died after a long illness. Emily Dickinson, who had traveled this road many times, as he had not, was now in a position to stretch him the saving hand in the Dark:

DEAR FRIEND.
If I could help you?

Perhaps she does not go so far
As you who stay – suppose –
Perhaps comes closer, for the lapse
Of her corporeal clothes –

Did she know she was leaving you? The Wilderness is new – to you.
Master, let me lead you.

Four letters of condolence—an art in which she had few equals—followed
during the fall. Two of them were signed "Your scholar" when in reality
she was instructing him:

DEAR FRIEND,
I think of you so wholly that I cannot resist to write again, to ask if you
are safe?
Danger is not at first, for then we are unconscious, but in the after –
slower – Days –
Do not try to be saved – but let Redemption find you – as it certainly
will – Love is it's own rescue, for we – at our supremest, are but it's trembling Emblems –

Your scholar –

The high point of the relationship, at least for Emily Dickinson, was
Higginson's trip to Amherst to see her in August 1870. She had suggested
many times in her letters that he visit, and she had declined his invitations
to come to literary gatherings in Boston. That she was finally to see him,
as she said in a note of greeting sent to the Amherst House, was, simply,
incredible:

DEAR FRIEND
I will be at Home and glad.
I think you said the 15th. The incredible never surprises us because it
is the incredible.

E. DICKINSON

The meeting was apparently breathless and tense. It was after this
encounter that Higginson confessed that he had never been with anyone
"who drained my nerve power so much." (His letters home from Southern battlefields seem relaxed in comparison.) All he could do, as he wrote
later in the 1891 *Atlantic* article, was to "sit still and watch" while Emily
talked. In a letter that night to his wife, he set the scene of the hour's
interview:

I shan't sit up tonight to write you all about E. D. dearest but if you had
read Mrs. Stoddard's novels you could understand a house where each
member runs his or her own selves. Yet I only saw her.

A large county lawyer's house, brown brick, with great trees & a garden – I sent up my card. A parlor dark & cool & stiffish, a few books & engravings & an open piano – Malbone [Higginson's novel] & O D [Out-Door] Papers among other books.

A step like a pattering child's in entry & in glided a little plain woman with two smooth bands of reddish hair & a face a little like Belle Dove's; not plainer – with no good feature – in a very plain & exquisitely clean white pique & a blue net worsted shawl. She came to me with two day lilies which she put in a sort of childlike way into my hand & said "These are my introduction" in a soft frightened breathless childlike voice – & added under her breath Forgive me if I am frightened; I never see strangers & hardly know what I say – but she talked soon & thenceforward continuously – & deferentially – sometimes stopping to ask me to talk instead of her – but readily recommencing. Manner between Angie Tilton & Mr. Alcott – but thoroughly ingenuous & simple which they are not & saying many things which you would have thought foolish & I wise – & some things you wd. hv. liked. I add a few over the page.

The impression Emily gave of being childlike may be understandable from Higginson's point of view; but it should be placed at once beside Joseph Lyman's similar description, based on a meeting only a few years earlier, that emphasized quite different features and qualities: the firm forehead, the expressive eyes, the hands "small, firm, deft . . . very firm strong . . . ," the mouth "made for nothing & used for nothing but uttering choice speech, rare thoughts, glittering, starry misty figures, winged words." That Lyman was an almost exact contemporary and Higginson seven years her senior could explain some of the difference. Further, Higginson had not grown up with the family as Lyman had, had not talked with Emily far into the night, knew nothing of what to Lyman had been the gaiety and charm of the Dickinson household. Nor had he had the benefit of the letters Emily had written Joseph in her near-normal, relaxed, lighthearted style.[12]

12. Higginson was not alone, however, in his impression of ED as childlike. Clara Bellinger Green's impressions of her visit to the Homestead in June 1877, when she, her brother Nelson, and sister Nora sang for Emily (who listened upstairs), were much the same (*The Bookman,* November 1924; and see YH II, 272–73):

At the close of the singing a light clapping of hands, like a flutter of wings, floated down the staircase, and Miss Lavinia came to tell us that Emily would see us – my sister and myself – in the library. . . . In the library, dimly lighted from the hall, a tiny figure in white darted to greet us, grasped our hands and told us of her pleasure in hearing us sing.

"Except for the birds," she said, "yours is the first song I have heard for many years. I have long been familiar with the voice and the laugh of each one of you, and I know, too, your brother's whistle as he trudges by the house." She spoke rapidly, with the breathless voice of a child and with a peculiar charm I have not forgotten.

. . . As she stood before us in the vague light of the library we were chiefly aware of a pair of great, dark eyes set in a small, pale, delicately chiseled face, and a little body, quaint, simple as a child and wholly unaffected.

Higginson seems to have come prepared for oddity and found it. How much of pose there was in Emily's breathlessness and fright we cannot know. Her reluctance to see strangers had been growing at least since her early twenties; and the long-awaited meeting with Higginson, a man of such consequence in her life, must have been a major experience. Once she started talking, however, she seemed under no restraint to monopolize the conversation with her distinguished visitor. (Bronson Alcott, it should be noted, was notoriously verbose.) When Higginson called her "thoroughly ingenuous & simple," he seems to have come closer to revealing his own bafflement than to describing the "real" Emily Dickinson. At least he was sufficiently impressed to describe his visit as "a remarkable experience, quite equalling my expectation."

It is to his credit that, as he sat still and watched, he noted enough of what Emily said to give his wife a good sampling. This is the source of most and certainly the best of Emily Dickinson's obiter dicta. Joseph Lyman praised her "winged words" but, except for a comment or two by Emily on himself, preserved only snatches of her letters. Martha Bianchi drew on the family stock of Emily's remarks mostly for the elfish or whimsical ones. Vinnie, Father, Mother, the aunts and uncles seem to have been deaf to what they must have been hearing, some of them daily, so meager is the record they left of Emily's conversation. Vinnie's remark that Emily was always on the lookout for the rewarding person, by whom she meant someone who could listen without apparent bewilderment and respond approximately in kind, applied to a very few people. Among them surely were Bowles, Kate Scott Anthon, the Hollands, Judge Lord, perhaps Lyman, and Helen Hunt Jackson. Certainly Higginson, from Emily's point of view, must have been one of the most rewarding. She talked to him about her home and family with a lack of restraint explainable in part, perhaps, by the fact that she had already introduced the subject in her second letter to him. Apparently keyed up by his presence, she seems to have strained for aphorisms, to have posed here as she did in the first letters to him. "Could you tell me what home is," she asked—although she herself had defined it beautifully and lovingly many times. "I never had a mother. I suppose a mother is one to whom you hurry when you are troubled"—sentiments that do not at all square with her mature thoughts about her mother. Her remark about her father's reading *"lonely & rigorous* books," and those "only on Sunday," seems more credible than the anecdote (if Higginson recorded it correctly) about not being able to tell time by the clock until she was fifteen because as a child she had been afraid to tell him that she had not understood his instruction. We can believe in part, at least, Higginson's report that "she makes all the bread for her father only likes hers," and we get a rare slant of her humor when he quoted her as adding " '& people must have puddings' this *very* dreamily, as if they were comets – so she makes them."

She talked, too, about general matters. "Women talk: men are silent: that is why I dread women," a remark with no precise parallel in anything else recorded of her, but perhaps an echo of the poem "She dealt her pretty words like Blades" with its possible reference to Sue. She talked about how important thought was to her: "How do most people live without any thoughts. There are many people in the world (you must have noticed them in the street) How do they live. How do they get strength to put on their clothes in the morning [?]" Such remarks may have occasioned Higginson's misplaced pity for her cramped life in Amherst, with her sharp rejoinder that she never once felt the "slightest approach" to a want of employment or friends, that "the mere sense of living is joy enough."

She talked of books, including her delight, as a child, in discovering her first one: "This then is a book! And there are more of them!" She delivered herself of her thoughts on Shakespeare, culminating, apparently, in a remark she repeated in substance several times during her life, notably in her letter to Joseph Lyman about her ecstatic return to Shakespeare after the trouble with her eyes. Higginson records: "After long disuse of her eyes she read Shakespeare & thought why is any other book needed." She gave her own test of literary excellence, at which Higginson, with his sense of what he called (in "Letter to a Young Contributor") "the majesty of the art," could only have smiled.

If I read a book [and] it makes my whole body so cold no fire ever can warm me I know *that* is poetry. If I feel physically as if the top of my head were taken off, I know *that* is poetry. These are the only way I know it. Is there any other way.

These, apparently, were the high points of this first conversation. Higginson recorded only one remark as the result of his second visit three years later on a lecture trip to Amherst: "She says, 'there is always one thing to be grateful for – that one is one's self & not somebody else.'" This seems excellent doctrine for one who during her troubled youth had thought precisely the opposite, but to Higginson, sadly, it was all too typical of "my eccentric poetess," as he described her in his letter to his sisters after the visit, and added: "I'm afraid Mary's other remark 'Oh why do the insane so cling to you?' still holds." This, after two visits, fifty-two poems, and twenty-one letters. Perhaps he, too, was posing a bit with his sisters. When he told Mary of the things Emily had said that "you would have thought foolish & I wise," his admiration seems to have been genuine.

If the visit is to be measured by any future effort on Higginson's part toward furthering Emily Dickinson's poetic career, it must be regarded as a failure. For all the oddity he was prepared to find at Amherst, he apparently thought he could be to her, in his gentle, paternal way, what he had been to three other lady poets—Harriet Prescott Spofford, Rose Terry, and Helen Hunt Jackson—a literary comrade and an instructor whose advice would be taken.[13] But his final comment to his wife, "I am glad not to live near her," signified the end of whatever hope he might have had of making a poet out of Emily Dickinson. He later recorded his shock at her undemocratic notion about the people in the streets who have no thoughts and her "wantonness of overstatement" about almost everything they discussed, especially her physiological test of poetry. The Dickinson rhetoric, the "fiery mist," the pose, were too much for him.

For all his doubts and hesitations, Higginson as literary mentor was important in Emily Dickinson's life. Many years later, she turned to him for advice about someone who had asked her for a few of her poems for "a Charity" and described herself as "utterly guideless." For all her protestations about the self-sufficiency of her life in Amherst, she did need friends—and literary friends—she could talk to. Sue, her greatest hope, had apparently long since failed her. The gap between the houses seems to have been too wide for the long, intimate discussions Emily had looked forward to. Sue never, during Emily's life, led anything that could be called a crusade (with Bowles or anyone else) for the poems; and after Emily died, she maddened Vinnie by her indifference toward them. (During the 1890s she was more interested in the poetic future of her daughter Martha.) Emily turned to no one in town, and of her correspondents, Higginson was the one she talked to most about books. In 1884, she sent a valentine gift of a book to his small daughter, Margaret, saying, "It would please me that she take her first Walk in Literature with one so often guided on that great route by her Father – "[14]

Though Emily Dickinson talked to Higginson only twice in person and never in her letters at any length about books, she held literary converse with him in her own way through his writings. It was not only his nature studies that delighted her. In coverage, she was a complete Higginsonian; it disturbed her once to run across two of his essays she had not read. His buoyant pages, full of good sense and polite learning, apparently gave her something she needed, as Longfellow's *Kavanagh* and Ik Marvel's *Reveries of a Bachelor* had when she was younger. Several times she thanked him explicitly. When his "A Plea for Culture" appeared in the *Atlantic* for January 1867, she responded to his Emersonian call for a genuine American literature. ("Between Shakespeare in his cradle and Shakespeare in Hamlet," he had concluded, "there was needed but an interval of time, and the same sublime condition is all that

---

13. For Higginson as literary mentor to these ladies, see Edelstein, *Strange Enthusiasm*, pp. 342–44.

14. Anna Mary Wells, *Dear Preceptor: The Life and Times of Thomas Wentworth Higginson* (1963), shows convincingly how important his friendship was for Emily Dickinson, however much we may wonder at his failures with her. If in his busy life she was just another fascinating and perhaps sometimes troublesome concern, he was obviously a mainstay to her. And it should not be forgotten that she favored him with her most famous remark on literature: "Nature is a Haunted House – but Art – a House that tries to be haunted" (*L* II, 554, spring ? 1876).

lies between the America of toil and the America of art.") Emily wrote him, as if in answer, the following complete letter, perhaps intended as a couplet:

> Bringing still my "plea for Culture,"
> Would it teach me now?

There was no signature. Another answer-poem was her elegy on her father, "Lay this Laurel . . .," in response to his "Decoration." And the poem "I sued the News" must be read as her comment on his first book, *Out-Door Papers:*

> It is still as distinct as Paradise – the opening your first Book –
> It was Mansions – Nations – Kinsmen – too – to me –

> I sued the News – yet feared – the News
> That such a Realm could be –
> "The House not made with Hands" it was –
> Thrown open wide to me –   [*#1360, spring 1876*]

How many of her poems were developed out of passages, or metaphors, or phrases in his writings is difficult to establish with certainty; we have seen a few already. She told him in the August 1862 letter, "I never consciously touch a paint, mixed by another person," but the New England writers of the time, for all their individual differences, were products of the same cultural matrix, and Higginson and Emily Dickinson were among them. In the essays that most appealed to her, Higginson was writing in the shadow of Thoreau and Emerson. Though she herself wrote in no one's shadow, many passages in his essays, dilutions of these masters, could have started her off on poems of her own.

Nor was Higginson all dilution. He observed nature closely and independently; she must have been impressed by the extensive and precise botanical knowledge that everywhere appears in his nature studies. "That it is true, Master, is the Power of all you write," she wrote him in 1876. How far it was from being the whole truth she herself showed when she carried his delightful world of sunrises and lily ponds and April flowers into new dimensions of wonder, mystery, and sometimes terror. But the Truth, as she said in a poem she had written a few years before, ". . . must dazzle gradually / Or every man be blind – "

And the "truths" of this benign and gracious man apparently helped her, up to a point. In 1877 she wrote him:

> Often, when troubled by entreaty, that paragraph of your's has saved me – "Such being the Majesty of the Art you presume to practice, you can at least take time before dishonoring it" . . .

Like most of her quotations, this one was not exact, and the capitals are hers. It is from the passage in "Letter to a Young Contributor" in which he insists on the necessity of exactness and constant revision. Balzac, who demanded four proof sheets from his printers, was his model for thoroughness. Some of Emily Dickinson's manuscripts, with their many alternate readings, show that she may have taken his advice seriously; when "my Brook is fluent [one of her poems begins] I know 'tis dry."[15] But, while Higginson spoke for literary polish and grace, she thought in more basic and vital terms. She saw words as infinitely powerful to heal or to kill. She gloried in them as they sit "princelike among their peers on the page." No wonder the poet must choose them with infinite care. Once she wrote a poem about the process. The method begins as if with the discipline Higginson required but ends in a stage beyond his scope. The poem might well have been written to answer, or supplement, his good Horatian advice.

> Shall I take thee, the Poet said
> To the propounded word?
> Be stationed with the Candidates
> Till I have finer tried –
>
> The Poet searched Philology
> And when about to ring
> For the suspended Candidate
> There came unsummoned in –
>
> That portion of the Vision
> The Word applied to fill
> Not unto nomination
> The Cherubim reveal –   *(#1126, about 1868)*

For all his shortcomings, Higginson was to her what Emerson was to many, "a friend and guide of those who would live in the spirit," or in this instance, the Word. He failed her as a critic of her poetry; but at least he answered her letters, came (at last) to see her, and was perceptive enough to see something "remarkable" in her. He saw, too, that, eccentric as she may have seemed to him, she was a poet. Her ultimate tribute to him came late, extreme even for her hyperbole: ". . . your Pages and Shakespeare's, like Ophir – remain – "

The list of the books Emily mentioned in her letters to Higginson is remarkable neither for range nor for novelty. Her references, even to Shakespeare, are few and brief. She seldom quoted him and never rhapsodized about him as she did to Joseph Lyman. To the reading list she sent him in her second letter only a relatively few names and titles are

15. Cf. Henry W. Wells (*Introduction to Emily Dickinson*, p. 208): "In another piece she says that whenever her words are fluent she knows them to be false." A bit of advice she certainly did *not* take seriously came in one of his injunctions to the young writer: "Reduce yourself to short allowance of parentheses and dashes" (*Atlantic Essays*, p. 83).

added in the length of the correspondence. She noted Hawthorne's death in 1864 and said later he "appalls, entices." Of Poe she knew "too little to think – " "Of Howells and James, one hesitates – " She called Helen Hunt Jackson's poems (which Higginson had urged her to read) "stronger than any written by Women since Mrs – Browning, with the exception of Mrs Lewes –" She quoted Tennyson once, and Henry Vaughan, and made a cryptic remark on Emerson: "With the Kingdom of Heaven on his knee, could Mr Emerson hesitate?" She rejected Higginson's advice to read Joaquin Miller, "because I could not care about him." She asked him if she could send him *Daniel Deronda* when it appeared in 1876; and that same year, two years after her father's death, she asked if she could send two books her father had given her—Frothingham's *Theodore Parker* and George Eliot's poems—strange choices, it would seem (the life of a famous radical and the works of a lady poet) for the "ogre father" to give his daughter; but her father could have rested easy:

> The last Books that my Father brought me I have felt unwilling to open, and had reserved them for you, because he had twice seen you. They are Theodore Parker, by Frothingham, and George Eliot's Poems. If you have them, please tell me – If not, you will not forbid mine?

There was something naïve and even pathetic about her solicitude for Higginson's reading: she in her backwoodsman's life, he in the center of New England literary activity. Probably it was her way of keeping in touch, of starting literary talk. In 1883, she hastened to make sure he had a copy of the new life of George Eliot:

> May I ask the delight in advance, of sending you the "Life of Mrs Cross" by her Husband, which the Papers promise for publication? I feared some other Pupil might usurp my privilege. Emblem is immeasurable – that is why it is better than Fulfillment, which can be drained –

The pupil-teacher roles were being reversed, it seems, in literary matters, too. By the time of the second interview (December 1873), Higginson had given up the preceptor's role. About all he could do was offer continued assurance of friendship and concern. After this second visit he wrote her a note that makes more understandable, perhaps, the intimacy of the letter she wrote him after her father died:

> DEAR FRIEND
> This note shall go as a New Year's gift & assure you that you are not forgotten. I am glad to remember my visit to Amherst, & especially the time spent with you. It seemed to give you some happiness, and I hope it did; – certainly I enjoyed being with you. Each time we seem to come together as old & tried friends; and I certainly feel that I have known you long & well, through the beautiful thoughts and words you have sent me. I hope you will not cease to trust me and turn to me; and I will try to speak the truth to you, and with love.

That was the tone, friendly and solicitous, of the nearly fifty letters she sent him from that time on. They tapered off, after the death of Mary Higginson and his remarriage in 1879, to two or three a year. Forty more poems went to him in batches of three or four, sometimes embodied in letters. His part of the correspondence can be estimated only by inference; apparently there were long lapses. The relationship, it has been said, became of "haunting importance" to him. It followed him long after she died. During the period of the editing, which he undertook only after some prodding and Mabel Todd's assurance that she would do most of the work, his enthusiasm was slow to develop. Finally, with some two hundred poems at hand, neatly typed by Mrs. Todd, he made a handsome acknowledgment in a letter to her of November 25, 1889:

> I can't tell you how much I am enjoying the poems. There are many new to me which take my breath away & which have *form* beyond most of those I have seen before. That one descriptive of the shipwreck for instance! ["Glee – The great storm is over –"] My confidence in their *availability* is greatly increased. . . .[16]

He blocked out the categories under which they were finally printed ("Life," "Love," "Nature," "Time and Eternity"), a device characteristic of his way of thinking about poetry and quite unsuited to Emily's complex symbolism and, often, her clear purpose. The titles given many of the poems (whether Mabel Todd's or his[17]) are often reductive, indicating a single meaning or message and ignoring important possibilities. For instance, the famous "Because I could not stop for Death" appeared in the 1890 *Poems* with the title "The Chariot," apparently the sort that carries people to heaven (Elijah's chariot? the chariot that "swings low"?). Thus the reader is directed to read the poem as an account of the soul's journey to eternity. Actually, it may have as much to do with life and the poet's purpose as with death. Emily Dickinson seems to be commemorating the moment (the "Day" of the last stanza) when the thought of eternity

16. Higginson's enthusiasm mounted steadily. On August 26, 1890, he wrote Mabel Todd: "How wonderfully strong are some of these later ones! Surely they must find readers." Although in a letter of September 19 he warned Mabel against William Dean Howells' prediction of a large sale ("I do not expect this"), he added: "[I] feel like you increased confidence in the real power thro' this intimacy which editing gives." On November 12, his confidence soared: "How could we ever have doubted about them," and added a postscript: "Books just arrived – bound. I am *astounded* in looking through [them]" (*Ancestors' Brocades*, pp. 62, 65, 72).

17. In her journal (quoted in *AB*, pp. 57–58) Mabel Todd recorded her disagreement with Higginson on the matter of "naming" the poems, a subject they discussed "at intervals." Higginson favored titles to assist the "reading public"; Mabel Todd "was exceedingly loath to assign titles to any of them which might not be unmistakably indicated in the poem itself. I had found, I believe, ten altogether to which she herself had given names." The discussions ended in a compromise favoring Higginson. In a letter of December 15, 1890, he congratulated them both on "this extraordinary thing we have done in revealing this rare genius. I feel as if we had climbed to a cloud, pulled it away, and revealed a new star behind it." He added: "I wish I could remember who suggested each title; some of the best, I know, are yours. On the whole, they help" (*AB*, p. 81).

struck with full force and, glimpsing "Circumference," she saw her poetic mission (her "Business") unfolding before her. In this reading, the fourth stanza (omitted by the original editors and not restored until the 1955 *Poems*) gives the sense of chilling awe as she contemplates the task and her own slim equipment.

> Because I could not stop for Death –
> He kindly stopped for me –
> The Carriage held but just Ourselves –
> And Immortality.
>
> We slowly drove – He knew no haste
> And I had put away
> My labor and my leisure too,
> For His Civility –
>
> We passed the School, where Children strove
> At Recess – in the Ring –
> We passed the Fields of Gazing Grain –
> We passed the Setting Sun –
>
> Or rather – He passed Us –
> The Dews drew quivering and chill –
> For only Gossamer, my Gown –
> My Tippet – only Tulle –
>
> We paused before a House that seemed
> A Swelling of the Ground –
> The Roof was scarcely visible –
> The Cornice – in the Ground –
>
> Since then – 'tis Centuries – and yet
> Feels shorter than the Day
> I first surmised the Horses Heads
> Were toward Eternity –   (#712, about 1863)

It may be too much to say that the poem commemorates the birth of the poet in her, the time of poetic awakening, although surely there were ample precedents among poets she knew and loved, like Wordsworth, Keats, and Shelley; but there can be little doubt that the poem commemorates her recognition of her all-encompassing theme, the "flood subject," the meaning of eternity in the light of which all things, from childhood to the grave, must now be seen. Higginson knew her concern; she had even asked him as a former clergyman for help. And yet the title, ignoring these implications, reduces the poem to a conventional death-piece. Perhaps he did not know about the fourth stanza; it might have changed his mind.[18]

18. Ruth Miller, pp. 193–94, sees the poem as ED's "heraldic cry of commitment," when, emerging from her harrowing failure with Samuel Bowles, she dedicated her

In his later remarks on Emily Dickinson, even after the popular success of the poems (eleven editions in the first two years), Higginson still clung to his doctrine of form. Helen Hunt Jackson remained his model for the woman poet in America. In her poems, he found emotion thoroughly under the control of form. Though publicly he grouped Emily Dickinson with her and Elizabeth Barrett Browning, he privately conceded that Emily's poems were "not valued by the finest minds." In his *Reader's History of American Literature* (1903), written with Professor Henry Boynton of Harvard, only two slim pages, mostly biographical, go to her. "Emily Dickinson," he wrote, "never quite succeeded in grasping the notion of the importance of poetic form." He predicted that she would be best known by the poem which, in the 1891 *Poems,* appeared with the title "Vanished." His choice speaks for itself:

> She died – *this* was the way she died.
> And when her breath was done
> Took up her simple wardrobe
> And started for the sun.
>
> Her little figure at the gate
> The Angels must have spied,
> Since I could never find her
> Upon the mortal side.   (#*150, about 1859*)

He and Mrs. Todd rejected, perhaps as too esoteric, an alternative reading for lines 5–6:

> "Bernardine" Angels, up the hight
> Her trudging feet espied –

It is ironic that a man so prominent in his time—Abolitionist, reformer, preacher, army officer, litterateur with a bibliography of some five hundred items—should now be known principally as the friend and editor of Emily Dickinson. We may wonder at his inadequacies in both roles toward her; but it must be remembered that she first approached him at the most difficult possible time. The war fever was at its height, and he was on the point of undertaking an important and dangerous mission.

---

life to poetry and, as a Bride of Christ, "shut her door" on man. "Only she herself was allowed inside her room where she sat down for the rest of her life to contemplate her meaning" (p. 190). One need not see her commitment as quite so exclusive to read the poem as her dedication to the deepest of all themes, the one that subsumes all others in her poetry. It is not the ecstatic cry of Keats's Hyperion, or Wordsworth's detailed account of his boyhood experience of "dedication" in *The Prelude*, or Shelley's "shriek" of ecstasy as "The awful shadow of some unseen Power" fell upon him ("Hymn to Intellectual Beauty"). ED couched her experience in simple, familiar terms—a carriage ride through a country landscape—but the awe and the portentousness of all three of the great Romantics are here.

And many years later, at the time of the editing, his attitude toward these strange new poems was, compared with that of many sober heads in the publishing world, sympathetic and liberal. It is at least understandable why he and Mabel Todd concluded that Emily's eccentricities must be cleaned up a bit if the publication was to have any success at all with the reading public of the 1890s. Probably the texts fared as well with them as they would have with any comparable editors of the time.

And he did his best, to give him his due, to understand his odd protégée. She would have been a problem with any outsider, as she was with most insiders. It is tempting to see the two Emilias who appear in Higginson's fiction as reflecting his experience with Emily Dickinson. Emilia in the short story "The Haunted Window" (*Atlantic,* April 1867) is beautiful but withdrawn, with a "childlike look" that told of "sorrow, and the wreck of a life." The Emilia in his novel *Malbone* (1869) is passionate, sorrowful, with a "pathetic lost sweetness in her voice." Both have only a shadowy resemblance to Emily Dickinson, but there is just enough mystery and enigma about them to suggest the frustrations of his attempt at understanding her. It was a case, of course, of two all-but-incompatible sensibilities. While he sought structure, message, and uplift in poetry and what he called "passion" (but thoroughly under the control of form[19]), she asked him if her poems "breathed," if they were "true." Some of his literary opinions will show how far apart they were. During the decade after she first wrote him, when he might have been of most help to her, he insisted in his essays again and again on the values he stressed in "Letter to a Young Contributor": thoroughness, form, and simplicity. *"Simplicity,"* he wrote in "Literature as an Art" (*Atlantic,* December 1867), "must be the first element of literary art," and it is achieved only through painstaking workmanship and constant revision. He quoted Dr. Johnson approvingly about turning over "half a library to make one book." When he mentioned Emerson and Hawthorne, it was mostly to approve their form. "While Emerson lives," he wrote in "On an Old Latin Text-Book" (*Atlantic,* October 1871), "it will be still believed that literature means form as well as matter." He praised Hawthorne (whose many-leveled symbolism he apparently missed as badly as he did Emily Dickinson's) for his formal perfection, achieved through years of quiet work while the world ignored him. Whitman was an example of eccentricity never brought under control: "Art has . . . its law; and eccentricity, though often promising as a mere trait of youth, is only a disfigurement to maturer years. It is no discredit to Walt Whitman that he wrote 'Leaves of Grass,' only that he did not burn it afterwards and reserve himself for something better." In the essay "Americanism in Literature" (*Atlantic,* January 1870), Whitman is ignored. So is Melville,

19. Cf. *Strange Enthusiasm,* p. 351: "It was 'H.H.' whom Higginson viewed as the best kind of 'poet of passion,' one who tempered her waywardness and controlled her poetic impulses by being always ready to revise and correct her verse at his suggestion."

whose deeper meanings apparently eluded Higginson as surely as Hawthorne's and Emily Dickinson's. Higginson thought Margaret Fuller Ossoli and Thoreau "our most original authors," Irving and Hawthorne the best stylists. Our most "daring Americanism" is represented by Cooper and Harriet Beecher Stowe. He found Henry James "involved and often puzzling." Besides the stylistic models of history—the Greeks, the great English essayists of the eighteenth and early nineteenth centuries, and his own mid-century American heroes—he praised Lanier, and (to his credit) Stephen Crane and William Dean Howells, whose *Silas Lapham,* he thought, placed him with Turgenev.

I said in an earlier chapter that one of Emily Dickinson's failures of judgment was to turn to Higginson for literary advice. She could hardly have known from "Letter to a Young Contributor" how deep-seated his literary conservatism was. His cordiality to young writers, his sense of "the magnificent mystery of words," and all she had read of him, led her on. A shrewder eye might have seen how hopeless her cause was. But Higginson heard her and answered, and kept on answering throughout the long years of her persistence. At least he was interested and, in his way, loyal. He went to Amherst for her funeral and read Emily Brontë's "Last Lines," one of her favorite poems, at the ceremony. In his diary he commented on the death "of that rare & strange creature Emily Dickinson" and added, "How large a portion of people who have interested me have passed away." His poem "Astra Castra," published in 1889, reads like a final tribute to the "strange, solitary, morbidly sensitive" young woman whom he had tried to guide and failed:

Astra Castra

Somewhere betwixt me and the farthest star,
   Or else beyond all worlds, all space, all thought,
   Dwells that freed spirit, now transformed and taught
   To move in orbits where the immortal are.
Does she rejoice or mourn? Perchance from far
   Some earthly errand she but now has sought,
   By instantaneous ways among us brought,
   Ways to which night and distance yield no bar.
Could we but reach and touch that wayward will
   On earth so hard to touch, would she be found
   Controlled or yet impetuous, free or bound,
Tameless as ocean or serene and still?
   If in her heart one eager impulse stirs,
   Could heaven itself calm that wild mood of hers?

". . . if I could once take you by the hand I might be something to you," he had written her shortly before his first trip to Amherst. "Still, you see, I try." Perhaps in this sonnet on "that wayward will / On earth so hard to touch" he had in mind her own "Astra Castra"—a title (Mabel Todd opposed it) he had given a poem selected for the 1890 *Poems* and one of the fourteen he chose to present in an introductory essay in the *Christian Union* six weeks before the *Poems* were offered to the public:

ASTRA CASTRA

Departed to the judgment,
A mighty afternoon;
Great clouds like ushers leaning,
Creation looking on.

The flesh surrendered, cancelled,
The bodiless begun;
Two worlds, like audiences, disperse
And leave the soul alone.[20]

20. The poem as it appears in the Harvard edition of 1955 (#524, about 1862), with the punctuation approximating ED's as nearly as typography can and with the capitalization as she indicated it, is a striking example of the difference in tone achieved by modern editing.

Departed – to the Judgment –
A Mighty Afternoon –
Great Clouds – like Ushers – leaning –
Creation – looking on –

The Flesh – Surrendered – Cancelled –
The Bodiless – begun –
Two Worlds – like Audiences – disperse –
And leave the Soul – alone –

24

Helen Hunt Jackson

I N ONE OF THE LETTERS in which Emily Dickinson thanked Higginson for saving her life, she said, "Of our greatest acts we are ignorant." At that very time, during the late 1860s, Higginson was engaged, unwittingly perhaps, in one of the best things he ever did for her: he was sharing her poems with Helen Fiske Hunt Jackson, her childhood friend in Amherst and since 1866 the Higginsons' fellow boarder at Mrs. Hannah Dame's literary boardinghouse in Newport, Rhode Island.[1]

The reasons Emily and Helen were never close as children were more than temperamental, although it is easy to see why Emily was never intimate with the robust, tomboyish Helen. By the time Helen was eleven, Professor and Mrs. Fiske had decided that Amherst schooling would not be right for their daughter. Apparently Amherst Academy was having disciplinary problems in the early 1840s, at least in the girls' division, and Helen was proving to be a handful. By the time she was nineteen she had sampled six schools away from home—Hadley; Charlestown, which in its proximity to Cambridge she thought an "Eden" compared with Amherst; Pittsfield, where she shook hands with former President John Quincy Adams and wrote her mother that she was on the brink of conversion; Falmouth Seminary, where she gave up thoughts of going to Mount Holyoke (as she put it) "to learn to make hasty pudding and clean *gridirons!*"; Ipswich Female Seminary, where she hated the discipline and the isolation of the town, and left just as Lavinia Dickinson entered; and finally Abbott (later Spingler) Institute in New York City, founded in

---

1. This Newport "center" is described in lively detail by Ruth Odell, *Helen Hunt Jackson* (1939), pp. 70–71. Other boarders, "at one time or another," included Dr. Holland (Emily's friend), Bret Harte, Charlotte Cushman, and Sarah Willis Parton ("Fanny Fern"). For the most recent biographical study, see Evelyn I. Banning, *Helen Hunt Jackson*, 1973.

1843 as a pioneering and progressive school for girls by the Abbott brothers, old friends of the family. She went there from Ipswich two years after her father's death in 1847 left her an orphan, and lived happily in the home of her beloved "Mr. John" Abbott.[2] In August 1851, she met Lieutenant Edward Hunt during a visit in Albany, New York, with the family of her guardian's brother, the Reverend Ray Palmer, and married him next year.

Thus ended a girlhood that, compared with Emily Dickinson's, was wide-ranging and cosmopolitan. From the early 1840s on, her connection with Amherst was limited mainly to visits during the Commencement seasons. The Hunts lived in Washington until 1855, when the lieutenant was moved to Newport. It was from there that, during the Commencement season in August 1860, they called on the Dickinsons. The visit delighted Emily so much that she recalled it to Higginson ten years later and by her hyperbole started another—and by now rejected—theory as to the identity of the Lover. Higginson wrote to his wife:

> Major Hunt interested her more than any man she ever saw. She remembered two things he said – that her great dog [Carlo] "understood gravitation" & when he said he should come again "in a year. If I say a shorter time it will be longer.["]

Major Hunt's death by accident in the Brooklyn Navy Yard in 1863 was followed two years later by the death of Helen's only surviving son, nine-year-old Rennie. The two disasters were crushing. It was during the long period of recovery that she began writing, first poems for the *New York Evening Post* under the pseudonym "Marah," and then prose pieces, beginning in 1865, for which, at last, she was paid. By the time she reached Mrs. Dame's boardinghouse early in 1866, she had published nearly a dozen items, all except one in the *Post,* and had determined to be a writer.

That she found herself in the same boardinghouse with Thomas Wentworth Higginson seems providential. He took an immediate and active interest in her. He wrote his sisters on February 20:

> There is a new boarder here with two dainty rooms up stairs arranged by herself – Mrs. (Major) Hunt, a young widow. . . . She is in deep mourning for husband & child & I fancy has private depression to correspond with her high spirits in the family, wh. are so far invariable. She seems very bright & sociable & may prove an accession.

The relationship between the two literary friends thrived. By 1869 her poems began to appear in the *Atlantic.* The year before, Higginson had called her "one of the most gifted poetesses in America," and "H.H.," as she signed her first volume, *Verses* (1870), gladly admitted her indebtedness to him. In 1873 she wrote Charles Dudley Warner: "Col. Higginson, as you perhaps know, is my mentor – my teacher – the one man to whom

2. Cf. Odell, pp. 37–43.

& to whose style, I chiefly owe what little I have done in literature. . . ."
She was his perfect pupil, submitting her talents gladly to his discipline.
Years later, she wrote a friend:

> Have you ever tested the advantages of an analytical reading of some writer
> of finished style? There is a little book called *Out-Door Papers,* by Went-
> worth Higginson, that is one of the most perfect specimens of literary
> composition in the English language. It has been my model for years. I
> go to it as a text-book, and have actually spent hours at a time, taking one
> sentence after another, and experimenting upon them, trying to see if I
> could take out a word or transpose a clause, and not destroy their perfection.

And she later confessed to Higginson: "I shall never write a sentence, so
long as I live, without studying it over from the standpoint of whether
you would think it could be bettered."

By 1871, when the "Saxe Holm" stories began (in Dr. Holland's *Scribner's*), her fame was growing steadily. In the *Springfield Republican* for
January 1, 1874, Samuel Bowles echoed the opinion of the literary world
in a statement (for us) heavy with irony: "Mrs Hunt stands on the
threshold of the greatest literary triumphs ever won by an American
woman." Emerson joined in the praise. He had met her in the late 1860s
in Newport and was charmed by her, as were all. (He may have noted
her tributes to him in her *Verses*.) He paid her this high compliment in
the preface to his anthology, *Parnassus* (1874), in which he included five
of her poems:

> The poems of a lady who contents herself with the initials H. H. in her
> book published in Boston (1874) have rare merit of thought and expression,
> and will reward the reader for the careful attention which they require.

No lady poet could have had a more propitious introduction to the
American literary scene. But her thin volume of 1870, except for the
"enlarged edition" in 1873 (Emerson mistook the date), was the last book
of poems she published. She made her greatest reputation in prose, and
for a cause, another bond with Higginson the reformer. Today she is best
known for *A Century of Dishonor* (1881) and *Ramona* (1884), both on
America's treatment of the Indians. She died in 1885 (a little less than a
year before Emily Dickinson), happy that her books had stirred the conscience of America. There was national mourning at her death. The
Springfield Republican eulogized her. Higginson wrote a sonnet on her,
published it in the *Century Magazine* and perhaps sent an advance copy
to Emily Dickinson. However it got to her, she read it, called it "beautiful," and included in an appreciative letter to Higginson two quatrains of
her own on her by then dear friend.[3]

The friendship, though late blooming, was a vital one. It differed from
all the others in one particular: the frustration in this instance was not

3. The letter with the quatrains, which appear as #1648 and #1647 in the 1955
Poems, is given below, p. 592.

Emily Dickinson's. Higginson's letter to her shortly before his 1870 visit spoke of having seen "[a lady] who once knew you, but could [not] tell me much." In spite of their early association in Amherst and the cordial call in 1860, Helen was apparently unaware that Emily wrote poems until Higginson showed her some. Higginson wrote to Mrs. Todd: "H.H. did not know of her poems till I showed them to her (about 1866) and was very little in Amherst after that. But she remembered her at school."

It is not clear when, or how, the correspondence between the two began. There are two unmailed envelopes, both mysteriously empty, addressed to "Mrs. Helen Hunt," one in the handwriting of that period (1868) and another, from about 1872, addressed to her in Bethlehem, New Hampshire. A letter of late October 1875 begins what we have of the correspondence, when Emily wrote a cryptic note of congratulation (at least so it seemed to the recipient) on Helen's marriage to William S. Jackson of Colorado Springs:

> Have I a word but Joy?
>   E. DICKINSON

> Who fleeing from the Spring
> The Spring avenging fling
> To Dooms of Balm –   [#1337]

Helen Jackson, with more courage than most of Emily's correspondents, confessed her bafflement, not simply in terms of "fiery mists" but in specifics. She sent the letter back and asked for an explanation. It did not come, nor did the letter, which she had asked to have returned. This may have annoyed her, but the last paragraph of the letter she then wrote (March 20, 1876) got at the source of her major frustration. Helen began about the unreturned letter:[4]

> But you did not send it back, though you wrote that you would.
> Was this an accident, or a late withdrawal of your consent?
> Remember that it is mine – not yours – and be honest.
> Thank you for not being angry with my impudent request for interpretations.
> I do wish I knew just what "dooms" you meant, though!
> A very clever man – one of the cleverest I ever met – a Mr. Dudley of Milwaukee, spent a day with us last week, and we talked about you. So threads cross, even on the outermost edges of the web.
> I hope some day, somewhere I shall find you in a spot where we can know each other. I wish very much that you would write to me now and then, when it did not bore you. I have a little manuscript volume with a few of your verses in it – and I read them very often – You are a great poet – and it is a wrong to the day you live in, that you will not sing aloud. When you are what men call dead, you will be sorry you were so stingy.

4. ED must have returned the letter, eventually. It was found by Jay Leyda in the Jackson house in Colorado Springs.

Made on the basis of the poems she had on hand, either some Emily or Higginson had sent her or some she had copied from those Higginson had shown her, this is an extraordinary statement. Had it been made publicly a few years earlier by Bowles, or Higginson, or Emily Fowler Ford, or Dr. Holland of *Scribner's,* the course of Emily Dickinson's life might have been very different.

Helen Jackson did not stop there. By the time she wrote this letter, she was deeply involved in the publishing world, with seven books and well over four hundred magazine and newspaper pieces to her credit. She was no mere amateur enthusiast, and she pressed her point with Emily Dickinson hard. In 1876 Roberts Brothers of Boston, Helen's publishers, launched a venture known as the No Name Series, under the editorship of Thomas Niles, involving a series of stories and a volume of poems, all anonymous, each story and each poem to be "by a great unknown." On August 20, 1876, Helen tried to interest her "dear Miss Dickinson," so formal the relationship still was, in contributing. She anticipated her objections about the publicity involved—indeed, she could understand it herself, seeking shelter, as was her custom, in initials or pseudonyms, "Marah," or "Saxe Holm," or "Rip Van Winkle." She offered to do the clerical work herself:

> I enclose to you a circular which may interest you. When the volume of Verse is published in this series, I shall contribute to it: and I want to persuade you to. Surely, in the shelter of such *double* anonymousness as that will be, you need not shrink. I want to see some of your verses in print. Unless you forbid me, I will send some that I have. May I? – It will be some time before this volume appears. There ought to be three or four volumes of stories first, I suppose. – . . .
>
> Thank you for writing in such plain letters! Will you not send me some verses?
>
> > Truly your friend
> > HELEN JACKSON

Surprisingly, Emily said neither yes nor no; she asked Higginson's advice. It would be interesting to know if she asked advice from anyone else—Sue or Austin, both acquainted with her work and both people of the world. Higginson, thinking that Helen had asked her for stories, wrote her a delicate no; but at least he wrote as one literary person to another:

> Now as to your letter of inquiry; It is always hard to judge for another of the bent of inclination or range of talent; but I should not have thought of advising you to write stories, as it would not seem to me to be in your line. Perhaps Mrs. Jackson thought that the change & variety might be good for you: but if you really feel a strong unwillingness to attempt it, I don't think she would mean to urge you. The celebrated prison-reformer, Mrs. Fry, made it one of her rules that we must follow, not force, Providence; & there is never any good in forcing it.

[*581*

Emily could hardly have needed Mrs. Fry's wisdom on the subject of
Providence or to be told, at this late date, what her "line" was. Higginson
was fumbling badly.

Helen Jackson saw her more clearly. She had called on her in October
1876, to discuss the No Name Series further. The letter she wrote after the
call shows why she succeeded where Higginson failed. Among other
things, she did not cling to first impressions, either of Emily or of her
poems. She admitted the stupidity of her first snap judgments:

> I am very sorry if I seemed neglectful and I hope to hear from you
> again. I feel as if I had been very impertinent that day in speaking to you as
> I did, – accusing you of living away from the sunlight – and telling you that
> you looked ill, which is a mortal price of illness at all times, but really you
> looked so white and moth-like! Your hand felt like such a wisp in mine
> that you frightened me. I felt like a great ox talking to a white moth, and
> begging it to come and eat grass with me to see if it could not turn itself
> into beef! How stupid. –
>   This morning I have read over again the last verses you sent me: I find
> them more clear than I thought they were. Part of the dimness must have
> been in me. Yet I have others which I like better. I like your simplest and
> most direct lines best.
>   You say you find great pleasure in reading my verses. Let somebody
> somewhere whom you do not know have the same pleasure in reading
> yours . . .

Here at last was someone who did not condescend, who realized that the
obligation to understand both the person and the poet was up to her. It
was not until the very day of the publication of the *Poems* (November 12,
1890) that Higginson finally wrote Mabel Todd (and even then the "we"
was presumptuous): "How could we ever have doubted about them?" It
is sad that such perception (both his and Mrs. Jackson's) came so late.

Helen's success was real, if limited. She induced Emily Dickinson to
publish one poem, anonymously. Two years later (1878) the volume of
poems in the No Name Series, to be called *A Masque of Poets,* was still
awaiting publication. Late in April of that year Helen tried again, with
further suggestions for preserving Emily's anonymity:

> Would it be of any use to ask you once more for one or two of your
> poems, to come out in the volume of "no name" poetry which is to be
> published before long by Roberts Bros.? If you will give me permission I
> will copy them – sending them in my own handwriting – and promise
> never to tell any one, not even the publishers, whose the poems are. Could
> you not bear this much of publicity? only you and I would recognize the
> poems. I wish very much you would do this – and I think you would have
> much amusement in seeing to whom the critics, those shrewd guessers
> would ascribe your verses.

That October, the Jacksons called on Emily. She received them both
cordially. (By this time, for Emily to see a total stranger was, we are told,

Helen Hunt Jackson
"H.H." to ED: "You are a great poet . . ."

Thomas Niles

ED to TN: "I bring you a chill Gift – My Cricket and the Snow"

"unprecedented.") Emily described the visit, in a letter to Maria Whitney, as "a lovely hour." But Helen had not elicited the permission she sought. She tried once more, the day after the visit:

Now – will you send me the poem? No – will you let me send the "Success" – which I know by heart – to Roberts Bros for the Masque of Poets? If you will, it will give me a great pleasure. I ask it as a personal favor to myself. – Can you refuse the only thing I perhaps shall ever ask at your hands?

Late in 1878, *A Masque of Poets* appeared, with Emily's "Success is counted sweetest" occupying what Helen Jackson called, in a congratulatory letter to Emily that December, "a special place, being chosen to end the first part of the volume." We can only assume that Emily gave her permission. She soon received a copy of the book itself, for which she sent thanks. The editor replied:

DEAR MISS DICKINSON
    You were entitled to a copy of "A Masque of Poets" without thanks, for your valuable contribution which for want of a known sponsor Mr Emerson has generally had to father.
    I wanted to send you a proof of your poem, wh. as you have doubtless perceived was slightly changed in phraseology.
                                    Yrs very truly
                                    T. NILES

Much has been made of Emily Dickinson's fear of having her poems altered by editors—as her "Snake" had been in the *Springfield Republican*—even to the point of having it explain, in part, her refusal to publish. What she thought of Niles's editing we do not know, but it was close to the kind of revision Higginson might have recommended, the kind he actually gave the poems of "H.H." and to which Emily Dickinson was continually subjected by her posthumous editors. It is worth close inspection. Here is the text of the poem as it appears in the fascicle copy:

Success is counted sweetest
By those who ne'er succeed.
To comprehend a nectar
Requires sorest need.

Not one of all the purple Host
Who took the Flag today
Can tell the definition
So clear of Victory

As he defeated – dying –
On whose forbidden ear
The distant strains of triumph
Burst agonized and clear!

The changes made by Niles, or by someone in his office, are all true to contemporary taste. In line 2, "who" is changed to "that," presumably for alliteration. In line 3, "a" becomes "the," clearly to make the article refer to the specific nectar, "success," thus spoiling the original tight aphoristic couplet. In line 4, "the" is inserted before "sorest," thus adding another syllable to the line and spoiling its emphatic rhythm by forcing it to lilt. The word "clear" in line 8 is changed to "plain," to avoid, presumably, repetition of the word in line 12. This line is changed to read: "Break, agonizing clear." "Break" was probably regarded as a little less harsh than "burst," and the editor apparently wanted to keep the reference clear and reasonable: the *listener* was agonized, not the "distant strains of triumph." While the changes hardly kill the poem, they surely weaken it. The conclusion must be that it is better to let Emily Dickinson speak for herself. Had subsequent editors followed this simple truth, the history of the publication of the poems would have been much happier.

Again it is surprising to find no word of protest from her, to either Niles or Mrs. Jackson or Higginson. On the contrary, far from being displeased, she seems actively to have sought out Niles as publisher. As to when she began, whether in connection with the No Name Series or later, much depends on the dating of a very brief letter of thanks to Niles for a book he had sent her. She included two poems in the letter.

> DEAR FRIEND.
> I bring you a chill Gift – My Cricket and the Snow. A base return indeed, for the delightful Book, which I infer from you, but an earnest one.
> With thanks,
> E. DICKINSON

"My Cricket" ("Further in Summer than the Birds") was embodied in the letter; the earlier, "Snow" ("It sifts from Leaden Sieves"), written about 1862 and revised in 1864, was separate.[5] The letter may have been in thanks for *A Masque of Poets,* which would date it in January 1879 and put what may have been this late bid for publication during the time of Mrs. Jackson's enthusiasm and the general interest in the No Name Series. On the other hand, the letter appears in the 1958 *Letters* dated mid-

5. In her article, "Inner than the Bone: Emily Dickinson's Third Tribunal," *Proceedings of the Conference of University Teachers of English* held at the University of the Negev, Beer-Sheva, March 1971, pp. 36–49, Ruth Miller suggests that these and the other poems sent to Niles were part of ED's strategy in this third attempt at finding a publisher (Bowles and Higginson being the first two). In this reading, the seven poems sent to Niles may be seen as "the poet's final assessment of herself and of her poetry" (p. 37). Thus, if "the purple Host" is taken to mean "published poets," "Success" becomes "a sadly ironic comment on her lot" (p. 38). The song of the cricket is her "bardic avowal" of death and regeneration (p. 42)—that is, a demonstration of her subject matter; while "The Snow" is an example, "less elusive, more conventional," of her craft (p. 42). All three of these poems had been sent to Higginson in 1862.

March 1883, where it is assumed to be in thanks for Niles's sending her the new life of George Eliot by Mathilde Blind.

The letter makes sense in both contexts, but the latter seems more likely in view of several other communications with Niles that can be dated with some precision. In April 1882, Emily Dickinson had inquired of Niles about the forthcoming life of George Eliot by Mr. Cross and about Lowell's projected work on Hawthorne, solid evidence, if any is needed, of her continued and lively interest in the literary world even in these years of almost complete withdrawal. In responding, Niles concluded with an important statement:

"H. H." once told me that she wished you could be induced to publish a volume of poems. I should not want to say how highly she praised them, but to such an extent that I wish also that you could.

Emily's answer was evasive, as usual, and seems unduly modest for one who supposedly was so sure of herself as a poet: "The kind but incredible opinion of 'H. H.' and yourself I would like to deserve – Would you accept a Pebble I think I gave to her, though I am not sure." Though the manuscript of the poem included in the letter has not survived, her "Pebble" may have been her own way of declaring her independence, a whimsical way of putting Niles off and, if read analogically, anything but modest. "H.H." had liked her "simplest" and most direct lines best. These sound more simple than they are:

> How happy is the little Stone
> That rambles in the Road alone,
> And does'nt care about Careers
> And Exigencies never fears –
> Whose Coat of elemental Brown
> A passing Universe put on,
> And independent as the Sun
> Associates or glows alone,
> Fulfilling absolute Decree
> In casual simplicity –   (#1510)

It may be that a quatrain she added in a version of the poem sent to Higginson in late 1882 also went to Niles. If there is even the faintest autobiographical hint in the added lines, the modesty vanishes completely. This is not the first time we have seen her compare herself to Christ:

> Obtaining but our own extent
> In whatsoever Realm –
> 'Twas Christ's own personal expanse
> That bore him from the Tomb –

She added a note to another version of the poem, about 1881, which may have been sent to Sue: "Heaven the Balm of a surly Technicality!," one of her most pointed jibes at the Calvinist doctrine of Election—Election, that is, need not wait upon God's grace. Some few win it (and she certainly counted herself as one) by their own "expanse." The poem is serene and confident. And she sent it to one of the most influential publishers in the East; to Higginson; and probably to Helen Jackson, the hearty, friendly instigator of this late surge.[6]

We wonder what she was waiting for. Perhaps if Niles and Higginson and Mrs. Jackson had combined their efforts in a group descent upon Amherst, she might have been persuaded to let Niles have the poems he asked for again the next year. If we follow the chronology of the 1958 *Letters,* the next of her surviving letters to Niles was the "chill Gift" note, with the two poems. That same month (March 1883), to express her thanks further, she sent him her own copy of the Brontë sisters' poems—to keep him interested in poems by women?—a gift that embarrassed him and led to this:

If I may presume to say so, I will take instead a M.S. collection of your poems, that is, if you want to give them to the world through the medium of a publisher

Very truly yours
T. NILES

I return the precious little volume by mail.

Again no direct answer, only another poem, "No Brigadier throughout the Year," on her favorite bird, the blue jay; and then in April three more poems, "The Wind begun to rock the Grass," "A Route of Evanescence," and "Ample make this Bed." Niles liked them all:

I am very much obliged to you for the three poems which I have read & reread with great pleasure, but which I have not consumed. I shall keep them unless you order me to do otherwise – in that case I shall as in duty bound obey[.]

A fourth poem, "Her Losses make our Gains ashamed," was included in the letter, and hence Niles probably felt it to be his by right. It was Emily Dickinson's comment on Mathilde Blind's life of George Eliot. She wrote Niles, "The Life of Marian Evans had much I never knew – a Doom of Fruit without the Bloom, like the Niger Fig." Perhaps in the first line of the poem she made a slant reference to her own late recognition:

6. Cf. Miller, "Inner than the Bone," pp. 39–40, who sees in the poem ED's "affirmation of confidence in ultimate vindication. . . . There seems to be indifference to the question of immediate fame . . . but if one uses the line 'Fulfilling absolute Decree' as a stepping-stone to the stanza added for Higginson, one realizes Emily Dickinson wears a mask to disguise a towering self-esteem. . . . Just as divine resurrection was not a gift bestowed by God but was achieved by Christ's own personal expanse, his own powers and qualities, so too the poet achieves immortality by his own 'expanse.'"

Her Losses make our Gains ashamed –
She bore Life's empty Pack
As gallantly as if the East
Were swinging at her Back.
Life's empty Pack is heaviest,
As every Porter knows –
In vain to punish Honey –
It only sweeter grows.

(#*1562, about 1883*)

What Emily meant by the *empty* pack George Eliot bore through life may be obscure to us; on the surface, she seems to have enjoyed the fulfillment Emily Dickinson missed. Mathilde Blind described a life, however, that had been far from easy, especially in the early years, with much of the frustration and many of the spiritual anxieties Emily had suffered through. Apparently, Emily rose from the book encouraged. Like Helen Jackson's and Niles's enthusiasm for her poetry, the experience lifted her mood.

Again nothing came of it. Perhaps Niles's enthusiasm waned. He was a busy man and did not press her further. Certainly after Emily died he did not rush to get the poems for Roberts Brothers. When Mabel Todd came to him with the copy in 1890, he was curiously cautious, even negative, at first.[7] There was no "H.H." at hand to encourage him. Or perhaps the fault lay in Emily Dickinson's own eccentricity. No matter how strong the case is for her having been thwarted by Bowles, Higginson, Dr. Holland, and others in her earlier interest in publication, her written statements in both letters and poems show an ambivalence that she never entirely resolved. She *would* and she would *not*. External events at this point may have had a dampening effect. Wadsworth died in April 1882; Judge Lord, with whom she was by then deeply involved, suffered a stroke in May; her mother's prolonged illness—she died that November—was an obvious deterrent; her dear cousin Willie Dickinson died in the spring of 1883; and on October 5 of that year came the most distressing loss of all, one from which she never fully recovered, the death of her nephew Gilbert. She slipped into a "nervous prostration" that was to incapacitate her for many weeks.

Next spring (June 28, 1884), in Colorado Springs, disaster struck Mrs. Jackson also—a badly broken leg in a fall downstairs. Emily wrote a note of sympathy: "I shall watch your passage from Crutch to Cane with jealous affection." Helen replied with a vivid description—"two inches of the big bone smashed in – & the little one snapped"—but soon got to matters of more permanent interest:

What portfolios of verses you must have. –
It is a cruel wrong to your "day & generation" that you will not give

7. Cf. *AB*, p. 51, where Mabel Todd records Niles's views: ". . . to publish her 'lucubrations' had always seemed to him 'most undesirable.' "

them light. – If such a thing should happen as that I should outlive you, I wish you would make me your literary legatee & executor. Surely, after you are what is called "dead," you will be willing that the poor ghosts you have left behind, should be cheered and pleased by your verses, will you not? – You ought to be. – I do not think we have a right to with hold from the world a word or a thought any more than a *deed,* which might help a single soul.

There could hardly have been a handsomer tribute or a more generous offer. Emily Dickinson apparently ignored both. The letter she wrote in reply was lively and spirited, her "balsam words" at their best. But it was simply one convalescent (and poet) to another:

DEAR FRIEND –
I infer from your Note you have "taken Captivity Captive," and rejoice that that martial Verse has been verified. He who is "slain and smiles, steals something from the" Sword, but you have stolen the Sword itself, which is far better – I hope you may be harmed no more – I shall watch your passage from Crutch to Cane with jealous affection. From there to your Wings is but a stride – as was said of the convalescing Bird,

> And then he lifted up his Throat
> And squandered such a Note –
> A Universe that overheard
> Is stricken by it yet –   [*#1600, about 1884*]

I, too, took my summer in a Chair, though from "Nervous prostration," not fracture, but take my Nerve by the Bridle now, and am again abroad – Thank you for the wish –
The Summer has been wide and deep, and a deeper Autumn is but the Gleam concomitant of that waylaying Light –

> Pursuing you in your transitions,
> In other Motes –
> Of other Myths
> Your requisition be.
> The Prism never held the Hues,
> It only heard them play –   [*#1602, about 1884*]

Loyally,
E. DICKINSON

There was one more exchange about six months later, and only six months before Helen Jackson died. Helen's letter (February 3, 1885) was in thanks for the gift of a fan Emily had sent her. She wrote cheerfully about her convalescence and the delights of her surroundings, then Santa Monica, California, from which, she wrote, she looked "straight off towards Japan." Her reference to the poetry was limited to a single concluding sentence: "I hope you are well – and at work – I wish I knew what your portfolios, by this time, hold." There was no reference to the executorship. Apparently she had given up, or was too preoccupied with her own problems. Emily's reply survives in two drafts, in pencil, found among her papers. The drafts differ slightly, though neither says anything about poems or executorships. Both have imperfections and probably formed the basis of the final letter that presumably was sent. As an indication of the care with which Emily composed her letters, here are two sentences: *Draft 1:* "That you compass 'Japan' before you you [*sic*] breakfast, not in the least surprises me, clogged only with the Music, like the Wheels of Birds." *Draft 2:* "That you glance at Japan as you break-fast, not in the least surprises me, thronged only with Music, like the Decks of Birds." Emily's letter was cheerful, too: "Thank you for hoping I am well. Who could be ill in March, that Month of proclamation? Sleigh Bells and Jays contend in my Matinee, and the North surrenders, instead of the South, a reverse of Bugles." *Ramona* had been published the previous year. "Pity me, however," she wrote, "I have finished Ramona. Would that like Shakespeare, it were just published!"

Incorporated in the letter were two poems, the second complete only in Draft 2, but both indicating moods in sharp contrast to the anguished poems of the early years. The first poem may have been a comment on Helen's urging her to publish her poems for the sake of posterity, those "poor ghosts" she will leave behind. Or it may have been a tribute to Helen's courageous spirits during her long siege of ill health. But in its basic metaphor it reverses the despondent early poem, where the riches of someone else (Sue?) had "taught me poverty." Now her own riches make even the wealthy seem poor indeed:

> Take all away from me, but leave me Ecstasy,
> And I am richer then, than all my Fellowmen.
> Is it becoming me to dwell so wealthily,
> When at my very Door are those possessing more,
> In abject poverty?[8]   (*#1640, about 1885*)

8. This poem was incorporated in three letters during 1885: besides this, one went (*L* III, 854–55) to Mr. and Mrs. Eben J. Loomis (Mabel's parents), and one to Samuel Bowles's son, Samuel the younger (*L* III, 888), where it was written as prose, a striking example of ED's way with words. It is instructive to *see* the letter (she was probably thanking the Bowleses for a gift of flowers):

DEAR FRIENDS.

Had I not known I was not asleep, I should have feared I dreamed, so bliss-ful was their beauty, but Day and they demurred.

Take all away from me, but leave me Ecstasy, and I am richer then, than all my fellowmen. Is it becoming me, to dwell so wealthily, when at my very door Are those possessing more, in boundless poverty?

With joyous thanks,
E. DICKINSON –

[589

The second poem is a prayer for forgiveness; and in view of her earlier prayer poems, or poems on prayer, it represents another reversal. Before, her theme had usually been the inefficacy of prayer, and her tone had been whimsical or chiding, as in "Papa above! / Regard a Mouse . . .," or bitter as in "Of Course – I prayed – / And did God Care?," or anguished in "At least – to pray – is left – is left – " An undated poem, perhaps from this early period, is close to despair:

> There comes an hour when begging stops,
> When the long interceding lips
> Perceive their prayer is vain.
> "Thou shalt not" is a kinder sword
> Than from a disappointing God
> "Disciple, call again."   (#*1751*)

The poem that presumably went to Helen Jackson is a prayer for forgiveness for loving life too much. Perhaps she was responding to Helen's buoyant spirit, marvelously resilient in her misfortunes. The two were good for each other. "Knew I how to pray," she wrote, "to intercede for your Foot were intuitive, but I am but a Pagan." And then the poem:

> Of God we ask one favor,
> That we may be forgiven –
> For what, he is presumed to know –
> The Crime, from us, is hidden –
> Immured the whole of Life
> Within a magic Prison
> We reprimand the Happiness
> That too competes with Heaven   (#*1601, about 1884*)

No uninterrupted line of ascent can be traced in Emily Dickinson's treatment of this or any other theme. There is irony here still in the paradox of a God who encloses us in a magic prison and then holds it a crime to love it so much. But she is no longer seeking her lost "Delinquent Palaces" or asking for the beggar's crumb. The mood is serene, true to the prevailing vision of her last years. She concluded the letter (Draft 2):

> May I once more know, and that you are saved?
> Your Dickinson.

Helen Jackson died on August 12, 1885. Had she lived and regained her vigor, Emily Dickinson's poems might have fared much better in the world. Even if she had not been appointed executor (and she wasn't), it is hard to imagine her not inquiring at once into those "portfolios of verses" in Amherst. Her genuine and professional regard for the poems would surely have been influential. She had all of Mabel Todd's enthusiasm, with much more publishing experience and national prestige. Emily Dickinson was no "myth" to her but a flesh-and-blood reality with whom she had grown up and whom she had come to recognize as a great poet. A sad comment by one of her biographers may explain, in part, her determined attempts to get Emily to publish: she may have recognized that Emily had actually succeeded where she had, profoundly, failed:

> Upon occasion she had defied the tradition and written as she pleased. . . . All these [stories] proclaimed her the rebel and non-conformist she always was at heart, but her failure readily to place such pieces resulted in her abandoning them. When she began, however, to receive harsh and stinging criticism for her "Saxe Holm" and "No Name" novels . . . she saw that her own work was not much better than that of the Fanny Ferns and the Minnie Myrtles she had derided. Her success had been too easy, too early, too rapid. She had sold her birthright.

She had sold it, among others, to Thomas Wentworth Higginson. Emily never did, and perhaps Helen Jackson realized it.

Emily wrote Higginson that she was "unspeakably shocked" at the news that Helen was on the point of death. Late in August she wrote a brief note of condolence to Mr. Jackson, and drafted another, presumably to him:

> Helen of Troy will die, but Helen of Colorado, never. Dear friend, can you walk, were the last words that I wrote her. Dear friend, I can fly – her immortal (soaring) reply. I never saw Mrs Jackson but twice, but those twice are indelible, and one Day more I am deified, was the only impression she ever left on any Heart (House) she entered –

Next spring, she wrote Higginson that she had been "very ill . . . since November, bereft of Book and Thought, by the Doctor's reproof . . ." Two letters to Higginson during this her last spring were mostly about Helen Jackson. Recalling, imperfectly, Higginson's lines in his poem "Decoration"—"And no stone, with feign'd distress, / Mocks the sacred loneliness"—she changed "Mocks" to "Mars" and applied them to Helen. And then she recalled the tribute Heman Humphrey had written to Helen's father following Professor Fiske's death in Jerusalem: " 'Mars the sacred Loneliness'! What an Elegy! 'From Mount Zion below to Mount Zion above'! . . . Gabriel's Oration would adorn his Child –" She adapted for Helen (and Higginson) a quatrain she had written earlier, in which originally "Herself" read "the Dawn":

> Not knowing when Herself may come
> I open every Door.
> Or has she Feathers, like a Bird,
> Or Billows, like a Shore –   (#1619, about 1884)

"Herself/Dawn" could hardly have been a better way of indicating what this late friendship meant to her. The second letter thanking Higginson for his sonnet on Helen had two more quatrains and concluded with a question:

DEAR FRIEND.
   The beautiful Sonnet confirms me – Thank you for confiding it –

> The immortality she gave
> We borrowed at her Grave –
> For just one Plaudit famishing,
> The Might of Human Love –   [#1648, about 1886]

The sweet Acclamation of Death divulges it – There is no Trumpet like the Tomb –

> Of Glory not a Beam is left
> But her Eternal House –
> The Asterisk is for the Dead,
> The Living, for the Stars –   (#1647, about 1886)

Did you not give her to me?

                    Your Scholar.

   What Higginson had given her was—at last—an uncomplicated friendship, free from anguish, open, frank, delightful. Here she was no one's Scholar or Daisy or "Wife—without the Sign!" It was a relationship of equals. There was no posing, because none was needed. What Higginson also gave her was something she had not had, perhaps, since her friendship with Ben Newton, who had hoped to live to see her a poet. Here at last was a figure of high importance in the literary world who knew she was a poet, had sought her out, and had engineered for her an offer, with no prior qualifications, from a leading publisher. It had now been Emily's turn to accept or reject. Helen, whose distaste for publicity gave her a special feeling for the problem, had almost overcome Emily's resistance; in one minor instance she had succeeded. With a little more discernment, time, and patience, one has the feeling that Samuel Bowles, whose hearty way with Emily was closer to Mrs. Jackson's than to Higginson's, might have succeeded fifteen years earlier. Had he done so, whether the result would have been triumphant or disastrous, no one can say. It is hard to imagine Emily Dickinson as part of the publishing world, with all its stresses and inevitable compromises. Helen Jackson, knowing Emily's strength, thought she should risk it. After all, Helen knew that she came from a family of lawyers, that she was a New Englander, and that she could be cranky about her poetry. And Helen also knew, as history has proved, that she was a more truly popular poet than Minnie Myrtle or Fannie Fern or even "H.H." herself.

25

Dr. and Mrs.

Josiah Gilbert Holland

D<small>R. AND MRS. JOSIAH HOLLAND</small> have appeared frequently in these pages —Dr. Holland as Bowles's associate on the *Springfield Republican* and perhaps one of the two editors who came to ask Emily Dickinson for her "Mind" in the winter of 1862, Mrs. Holland as the one to whom Emily described her Washington trip in 1855 and (to speak only of the major references) to whom she complained so piteously, later that year, about moving from the Pleasant Street house to the Homestead. It was to the Hollands also, according to a Holland family tradition, that she entrusted for many years the forwarding of letters to the Reverend Charles Wadsworth.[1] To both of them, in the late 1850s or early 1860s, she proclaimed her "business": to "love" and to "sing"—that is, to be a poet.

So the Hollands were important to her, perhaps in ways and to a degree never made explicit in the ninety-four letters, from Emily to the Hollands, which is all we have of this correspondence. There are curious gaps in it, the strangest being between the years 1860 and 1865, crucial ones for Emily, when it is inconceivable that she did not turn at least to Mrs. Holland, whom by 1860 she called "Sister," for the kind of sisterly—or

1. Theodora Van Wagenen Ward, *Emily Dickinson's Letters to Dr. and Mrs. Josiah Gilbert Holland* (1951), p. 106, writes: "It has always been understood by the Holland family that for many years Emily made a practice of sending to Mrs. Holland the letters she wrote to Dr. Wadsworth, to be addressed and forwarded to Philadelphia." This is problematic. It has been the basis of speculation about Emily and Wadsworth for many years. But no documentary evidence is cited, here or elsewhere; and Mrs. Ward, who, as the Hollands' granddaughter, is close to family sources, assures me in a letter of January 27, 1972, that she recalls none.

[593

indeed, motherly—advice and comfort it had become her custom to seek from her and of which, it would seem, she stood then in especial need. In the letters we have, there is no mention of Samuel Bowles until 1878, when he was in his last illness, or of Higginson or Wadsworth by name, or of Susan Dickinson until 1877 (it was then that Emily described Sue to Mrs. Holland as "overcharged with scintillation"). Hints of crisis are infrequent and, except when she writes of the deaths of those close to her, so embedded in trivia or whimsey as to deflect alarm, which may have been her purpose. Parts of some of the letters are missing, and surely many have been lost or destroyed. Perhaps Mrs. Holland, one of Emily's closest and most trusted confidantes, took precautions to spare her friend any possible future embarrassment. It may well be that she knew more about Emily Dickinson's private troubles than anyone else. Or perhaps Emily maintained an ultimate reticence even with this dear friend.

The friendship differs in several respects from those we have examined so far. More than any relationship except those with her immediate family, it was a constant in her life for thirty-three years. It has no flavor of crisis, no sudden intensity of feeling or purpose only to diminish decorously over the years. It was warm, fruitful, reciprocal, from beginning to end, unmarred even by temporary misunderstandings or rejections. The deletions and gaps may conceal dark moments; and Mrs. Holland's half of the correspondence, if we had it, might have told a different story. One can only conclude that Emily delighted in the Hollands, especially in Mrs. Holland, and they in her. Only once, in the mid-1860s, did Emily scold her friend, and this, perhaps, mainly to show off her wit. Mrs. Holland had made the tactical error of sending a joint letter to Emily and Vinnie, of whom she was also fond. She never did it again.

SISTER,
    A mutual plum is not a plum. I was too respectful to take the pulp and do not like a stone.
    Send no union letters. The soul must go by Death alone, so, it must by life, if it is a soul.
    If a committee – no matter.

(Emily seems to have forgotten that she herself frequently wrote to both Hollands at once, and, for that matter, to both her Norcross cousins.)

The friendship began in the early 1850s, shortly after Dr. Holland joined Bowles on the *Republican* in the spring of 1849. No doubt Edward Dickinson was in some official way involved in Amherst's giving Holland an honorary A.M. at the 1851 Commencement, and both Hollands were probably entertained by the Dickinsons then. Early in June two years later, the Doctor stopped by for a call, "seemed very pleasant indeed," Emily wrote Austin, and, with Mrs. Dickinson's permission, invited her and Vinnie to visit him and Mrs. Holland in Springfield. The friendship seems to have been well launched by July 1853, when the Dickinsons

Josiah Holland

ED TO EH: "VIVE LE FIRESIDE!"

Elizabeth Holland

Dr. Holland of *Scribner's*

Elizabeth Holland

ED to EH: "It is the Meek that Valor wear too mighty for the Bold"

entertained the Hollands, during the Commencement festivities, at what would seem like a most un-Dickinsonian dinner. Emily wrote happily of the occasion to Austin:

> Dr Holland and his wife, spent last Friday with us – came unexpectedly – we had a charming time, and have promised to visit them after Commencement. They asked all about you, and Dr Holland's wife expressed a great desire to see you – He said you would be a Judge – there was no help for it – you must certainly be a Judge! We had Champagne for dinner, and a very fine time – We were so sorry you were not here, and Dr and Mrs Holland expressed their regret many times –

The promised visit came off early in September. In view of Emily's growing reluctance to travel, even then, it is worth noting that the visit was a rapturous success. When another invitation came the following September, the memory was still warm and she accepted joyfully:

> The cars leave here at nine o'clock, and I think reach Springfield at twelve. I can think just how we dined with you a year ago from now, and it makes my heart beat faster to think perhaps we'll see you so little while from now.
> To live a thousand years would not make me forget the day and night we spent there, and while I write the words, I don't believe I'm coming, so sweet it seems to me.

The home the two girls visited was in some ways a refreshing contrast to their own, especially for Emily, whose sense of "real life" frequently collided with her father's and who, with Austin gone, had (as she complained) no one to make jokes with. Mrs. Theodora Ward describes the atmosphere of her grandparents' home as having "a warmth and a sense of freedom . . . lacking in many a New England home . . . a quality of naturalness and spontaneity which kept it always fresh and vivid."

The secret was not far to seek. "Josiah Holland," writes Mrs. Ward, "was a happy man. His family life was one of rare harmony. . . ." His career (he was thirty-four at the time of Emily's first visit, and his wife thirty) had none of the arrow-straight directness of Edward Dickinson's. His father was no Squire Fowler Dickinson with a face of flint and fierce dedication but a perennially unsuccessful inventor and machinist, who led his family from town to town in western Massachusetts (Josiah happened to be born in Belchertown), always looking for something better to turn up. Josiah could not afford to go to college, thought for a while of becoming a minister, and then eked out a sketchy medical training in the offices of two Northampton doctors and in two terms of lectures at the Berkshire Medical College at Pittsfield. His years of practice in Springfield, from early 1844 to late 1846, convinced him that medicine was not his vocation. His first try at journalism—the *Bay State Weekly,* published in Springfield—lasted six months, the subscription list being sold to the *Republican.* Two years of schoolteaching, first in Richmond, Virginia, and then in Vicksburg, Mississippi, were more successful; but the work was uphill and unrewarding, especially in Vicksburg, both for him and for his wife Elizabeth, whom he had married in Springfield in 1845. He saw enough of Southern life, however, to be moved to write a series of articles, *Sketches of Plantation Life,* which Samuel Bowles readily accepted for the *Republican.* Also, during his Southern years, two of his poems had been published in widely read magazines. When he and Elizabeth arrived in Springfield in May 1849, the literary direction of his career seemed all but settled. It *was* settled at his first meeting with Samuel Bowles, who hired him on the spot.[2]

It could be said that he raised the tone of the *Republican,* not to any peak of intellectual prominence, but as a medium for thoughtful comment on matters literary, religious, and moral. He saw that the paper kept abreast of current books and periodicals. The reviews became longer and more informative. News of parishes, both local and distant, was reported and notable sermons summarized—a source of information that enabled Emily Dickinson, for one, to keep in touch with her clerical friends. He soon began a series of short articles, somewhat like lay sermons, on moral matters, directed in turn to young bachelors, unmarried girls, young married couples, and sometimes to long-married couples in need of advice. Under the pen name of Timothy Titcomb he became a national institution, and it was not long before he became one of the most sought-after lyceum lecturers in the country. It was his return from one of his long and fatiguing tours that Emily celebrated in her letter to Mrs. Holland of March 2, 1859:

> I gather from "Republican" that you are about to doff your weeds for a Bride's Attire. Vive le fireside! Am told that fasting gives to food marvellous Aroma, but by birth a Bachelor, disavow Cuisine.

The fireside that Emily and Vinnie visited on those two September trips must have restored her spirits in many ways. Mrs. Ward speaks of the literary talk in the Holland home, the laughter and the music. Dr. Holland (he never lost the title) had a fine tenor voice, and Mrs. Holland played the piano. To Emily and Vinnie, whose own home, much as they professed to love it, resounded infrequently with such delights, the Hollands, as Mrs. Ward suggests, must have seemed the perfect young married couple—he tall, dark, likened by one of his friends to an Indian chief; she little, lively, and radiant, the perfect mother and hostess.

It must be kept in mind that the early 1850s were not easy for Emily. Her girlhood confidantes—Abiah Root, Emily Fowler, Jane Humphrey, and the rest—were busying themselves with careers or matrimony, most of them far from the Amherst circle. Sue, very much in the Amherst circle, was less and less in Emily's as she, too, headed for matrimony.

2. Besides Mrs. Ward's notes and comments in her edition of the letters, there are two full-length studies of Holland, *Josiah Gilbert Holland,* by Mrs. Harriette Merrick Plunkett (1894), and *Josiah Gilbert Holland in Relation to His Times* (1940), by Harry Houston Peckham.

Ben Newton died in March 1853, "the first of my own friends," and she seems to have found little to interest her deeply or permanently in the other young men of the town, the students, the tutors, the apprentices in her father's office. Other problems were separating her more and more from the community. She saw her rebellious thoughts setting her apart from Amherst piety, and she seemed unable to talk about her growing sense of poetic vocation except in veiled metaphors and with a sense of guilt—the "evil voices" lisping in her ears—as if to be a poet were somehow improper or even blasphemous. She could write whimsically about this to Jane Humphrey, but it seems clear that she did not enjoy her rebellion. During the early 1850s, too, she had family worries. She worried about Austin, his career and his prospects for marriage. She probably worried about Vinnie and her affair with Joseph Lyman, that bird of passage. It was then that Mrs. Dickinson's health, after a dozen years or so of adequacy, began to become a problem. In short, by the time the Hollands entered the scene, life had begun to close in.

So the elation and lift of spirit with which Emily entered upon this new friendship become more understandable. However cautious we may be about her tendency toward hyperbole, her first letter to the Hollands (it is dated tentatively by Mrs. Ward as coming shortly after the first visit in September 1853) seems more than a demonstration of rhetoric. It was as if the Hollands had opened up a new world, or at least a world where the eyes of Amherst and her family were not on her and where, to use the figure in her first paragraph, she felt on holiday. The letter deserves quotation in full. It shows the release of spirit the Hollands always brought her, whether she was visiting them, or writing them, or just thinking about them. It is an example of her early style at its best.

Dear Dr. and Mrs. Holland – dear Minnie [Mrs. Holland's sister] – it is cold tonight, but the thought of you so warm, that I sit by it as a fireside, and am never cold any more. I love to write to you – it gives my heart a holiday and sets the bells to ringing. If prayers had any answers to them, you were all here to-night, but I seek and I don't find, and knock and it is not opened. Wonder if God is just – presume he is, however, and 'twas only a blunder of Matthew's.

I think mine is the case, where when they ask an egg, they get a scorpion, for I keep wishing for you, keep shutting up my eyes and looking toward the sky, asking with all my might for you, and yet you do not come. I wrote to you last week, but thought you would laugh at me, and call me sentimental, so I kept my lofty letter for "Adolphus Hawkins, Esq." [the sentimental poet in *Kavanagh*].

If it wasn't for broad daylight, and cooking-stoves, and roosters, I'm afraid you would have occasion to smile at my letters often, but so sure as "this mortal" essays immortality, a crow from a neighboring farm-yard dissipates the illusion, and I am here again.

And what I mean is this – that I thought of you all last week, until the world grew rounder than it sometimes is, and I broke several dishes.

Monday, I solemnly resolved I would be *sensible,* so I wore thick shoes, and thought of Dr Humphrey, and the Moral Law. One glimpse of *The Republican* makes me break things again – I read in it every night.

Who writes those funny accidents, where railroads meet each other unexpectedly, and gentlemen in factories get their heads cut off quite informally? The author, too, relates them in such a sprightly way, that they are quite attractive. Vinnie was disappointed to-night, that there were not more accidents – I read the news aloud, while Vinnie was sewing. *The Republican* seems to us like a letter from you, and we break the seal and read it eagerly. . . .

Vinnie and I talked of you as we sewed, this afternoon. I said – "how far they seem from us," but Vinnie answered me "only a little way" . . . I'd love to be a bird or bee, that whether hum or sing, still might be near you.

Heaven is large – is it not? Life is short too, isn't it? Then when one is done, is there not another, and – and – then if God is willing, we are neighbors then. Vinnie and mother send their love. Mine too is here. My letter as a bee, goes laden. Please love us and remember us. Please write us very soon, and tell us how you are. . . .

Affy,
EMILIE.

There is a good deal of play-acting here, of course: the Hollands' absence *that very minute* as a sign of God's injustice; the broken dishes and forgotten chores as she loses herself in the illusion of their presence; the cooking stoves and roosters and President Heman Humphrey's Moral Law[3] that call her back to reality. Such flights seem, and probably were, a conscious extension of the "Sue rhetoric"—too importunate, too fervent. (Indeed, in a later letter she duplicated whole sentences from a letter to Sue.) But the fervor is redeemed here by a pervasive humor not often true of the early Sue letters, by the reflective note on the *Republican* and the genre bit on Vinnie. Mrs. Holland, to whom she seems really to be writing (it was not long before she began to address letters to her alone), was seven years her senior; and it is probable that, sympathetic but level-headed, she kept Emily on balance. Even the little theological flight at the end does not spoil the tone. (What the ellipses leave out we may never know. They are the original editor's, Mabel Todd's, and the manuscript is missing.) Emily had the sense to realize that pure "Adolphus Hawkins" sentimentality would not be right for the Hollands.

Hence, perhaps, the motif in her early letters to the Hollands of embarrassment or apology, coming when she feels she has spilled over, or asserted herself too much. Even in this happiest of them she tells of suppressing a letter she had written the previous week, for fear "you would laugh at me." In the next major letter, a year later (1854), she apologized for wearying the Hollands with her importunities—how she

---

3. Humphrey was president of Amherst during Emily's childhood (he retired in 1845) and taught moral philosophy.

missed them, whether they were well and happy and, if so, *"how* happy, and why, and what bestows the joy? . . . do they [the Hollands] love – remember us – wish sometimes we were there?"—and so on, much like her imploring letters to Sue, except that she never said to Sue, as she says here, "perhaps my queries tire you." A year later (1855), when she described her experiences in Washington, her longing for reunion with her friends overflowed, and she looked back at their last meeting as if she only dreamed it:

> . . . as vague – as vague; and sometimes I wonder if I ever dreamed – then if I'm dreaming now, then if I *always* dreamed, and there is not a world, and not these darling friends, for whom I would not count my life too great a sacrifice. Thank God there is a world, and that the friends we love dwell forever and ever in a house above.

If the Hollands might have been confused as to which world Emily was placing them in, so was Emily, and again she apologized: "I fear I grow incongruous, but to meet my friends does delight me so that I quite forget time and sense and so forth"—a notable statement from one who was soon to become the Queen Recluse, notorious for an exclusiveness that never, it should be said, excluded the Hollands.

What we see in these letters is a style emerging from prolixity and sentimentality, which she did well to feel embarrassed about, to something more firm and self-confident. The next stage comes in a later letter, about August 1856, directed to Mrs. Holland alone, where Emily developed an elaborate fantasy of being with her friends in heaven. It is well composed and leavened with humor; and although she still apologizes, this time for a bit of theologizing, it is as if for form's sake only. In the letters to the Hollands, it is worth noting, she indulges in more whimsical speculation of this sort than usual in her correspondence, perhaps because the blessing of their friendship was a constant emblem to her of the divine reward, or simply because she felt freer to indulge her fancies with them than with her more orthodox and pious friends. Here, as frequently in these years, her gaze is alternately on this world and the next.

> Don't tell, dear Mrs. Holland, but wicked as I am, I read my Bible sometimes, and in it as I read today, I found a verse like this, where friends should "go no more out"; and there were "no tears," and I wished as I sat down to-night that we were *there* – not *here* – and that wonderful world had commenced, which makes such promises. . . . And I'm half tempted to take my seat in that Paradise of which the good man writes, and begin forever and ever *now,* so wondrous does it seem.

It is only mortality (she went on), where roses fade and frosts come, that makes heaven necessary: ". . . if God had been here this summer, and seen the things that *I* have seen – I guess that He would think His Paradise superfluous." She rejoiced that Mrs. Holland was not a rose that fades, or a bee that disappears with the summer, or a robin that flees "when the west winds come"; and she concluded her fantasy with a poetic

[*599*

paragraph whose first and last sentences slip (roughly) into the "8s" and "6s" meter of many of her poems (I have indicated the metrical lineation by virgules) and whose theme is "little Mrs. Holland" in the *here* and the *hereafter*:

As "little Mrs. Holland," then, / I think I love you most, / and trust that tiny lady will dwell below while we dwell, and when with many a wonder we seek the new Land, *her* wistful face, *with* ours, / shall look the last upon the hills, / and first upon – well, *Home!* /

The apology came at the end of the letter; but this time it is more like an apologia, quite in the spirit of her poem of a few years later, "Much Madness is divinest Sense." She wrote: "Pardon my sanity, Mrs. Holland, in a world *in*sane, and love me if you will, for I had rather *be* loved than to be called a king in earth, or a lord in Heaven."

In a world in which she was finding (in the words of the poem) that to demur was dangerous, the Hollands represented holiday from such restraints. She could be "insane" with them as she could not at home. Two years before (January 16, 1854), when Dr. Holland lectured in Amherst on "Manhood" to a capacity audience in Sweetser's Hall, a reporter in the *Hampshire and Franklin Express* scolded him sharply for his "creedless, churchless, ministerless christianity, so called," and warned all readers of the *Express* "against the adopting of any such notions. . . ." No wonder Emily, who for better or worse was headed much this way, found the atmosphere of the Holland home congenial. Many years later, a few weeks after Dr. Holland died (October 1881), Emily wrote to Mrs. Holland about one of her happiest memories of that first September visit. Her reminiscence tells much about the bond between her and the Hollands at the time—more than a matter of fun and music and literary discussion. Their congeniality was, among other things, religious. Their God was her God.

I shall never forget the Doctor's prayer, my first morning with you – so simple, so believing. *That* God must be a friend – *that* was a different God – and I almost felt warmer myself, in the midst of a tie so sunshiny.[4]

Her emphasis tells much, also, about the God she left behind in Amherst. If her tie with the Deity did not always remain so sunshiny, at least she had this warm and restorative memory of life with the Hollands. After the excitement of the new friendship had worn off and had spent itself in the rhetoric of the early letters, she found herself with the Hollands on what Mrs. Ward calls a "common ground of essential human experience." Before this happened—and with it a tightening and maturing of her

4. ED's informal ways with the Deity, and with doctrines generally, may go back to this early experience with the Hollands; e.g., in such poems as "Papa above!" (#61, about 1859) and "'Sown in dishonor'!" (#62, about 1859). Perhaps it was the Hollands who helped her see how "infinitely wise & how merry" the Bible is (*LL,* p. 73).

style unmistakable in the letters from 1865 on—she went through another phase with Mrs. Holland. I have spoken of her turning to Mrs. Holland for the motherly advice she clearly had to seek beyond her own home. It was not, I think, that she did not love her mother; she simply found her inadequate. As to the theory of "mother rejection," it is just as possible that it was Emily who did the rejecting. Her gently disparaging remarks about her mother may point merely to an all too common relationship between mothers and daughters, where perfect communication rarely exists. And when it is far short of perfection, daughters go elsewhere for sympathy and advice—to the mothers of their friends, to wise and understanding aunts, or, in this instance, to friends of the family. It was not that Mrs. Holland took Mrs. Dickinson's place in Emily's mind and heart; rather, she fulfilled tactfully and sympathetically certain functions Mrs. Dickinson's unobtrusive faculties and limited energy were not up to. Soon in their correspondence Emily began calling her "sister," as clear an indication as any, perhaps, of how she felt toward her. She and Emily were *en rapport* as Emily and her mother were not.[5]

The first instance of Emily's seeking Mrs. Holland's help came in a letter after the second September visit. Significantly, it concerned a theological matter—the sermon that "scared" her.

> The minister to-day, not our own minister, preached about death and judgment, and what would become of those, meaning Austin and me, who behaved improperly – and somehow the sermon scared me, and father and Vinnie looked very solemn as if the whole was true, and I would not for worlds have them know that it troubled me, but I longed to come to you, and tell you about it, and learn how to be better. He preached such an awful sermon though, that I didn't much think I should ever see you again until the Judgment Day, and then you would not speak to me, according to his story. The subject of perdition seemed to please him, somehow. It seems very solemn to me. I'll tell you about it, when I see you again.

The letter is addressed to both Hollands, whose sunshiny God she remembered, and it may be that here she turned to both equally. The family line-up is interesting: Austin and Emily on one side, Vinnie and Father on the other. Perhaps she got some fun out of it with Austin, her partner in sin. But her remark about Father and Vinnie, "I would not for worlds have them know that it troubled me," goes to the heart of her problem with her family. Mother is not mentioned, perhaps because she was not in church that day, perhaps because this was not the kind of trouble Emily took to her. At any rate, it was to the Hollands that she entrusted what seems to have been a real anxiety. Although later she could talk blithely about having no respect for doctrines, she could not shake this one of perdition, preached (as it seems to have been this time)

5. This reading of Emily's relationship with her mother does not exclude Dr. John Cody's theory in his *After Great Pain;* but it presents what to me is a more likely alternative. (See above, Chapter 5, note 2.)

with peculiar vehemence and the slightly sadistic touch—so Emily's comment suggests—of the typical Calvinist sermon. Clearly, such experiences (among other things) made church an ordeal for her; and she was fortunate in these early and more expansive years to have the Hollands, and their God of love, to turn to.

Indeed, this letter about perdition shows her at the beginning of the long, anxious process of making the decision about her "business" she announced to the Hollands a few years later. If it could be said that the note of apology still clings even in that later letter, when she had made her choice, it seems from habit only and is by now entirely whimsical: "Perhaps you laugh at me! Perhaps the whole United States are laughing at me too! *I* can't stop for that! *My* business is to love."

She turned to Mrs. Holland in little matters as well as big—the ordeal of moving from one house to another; Vinnie's headache; the trials of keeping house when her mother was sick; how she "winced" at the loss of the family servant (the first Margaret [O'Brien], who married); even the contretemps involving "Mr. Chapman and Mr. Hyde of Ware," the visitors at the Evergreens that winter evening in 1859, from whom Emily and Kate Scott fled in confusion at the first ring of the doorbell. The aftermath of the episode found Emily sufficiently troubled to write a note of apology at least to Mr. Chapman (Mr. Hyde got short shrift) and to seek Mrs. Holland's advice: "I do not mind Mr. Hyde of Ware, because he does not please me, but Mr. Chapman is my friend, talks of my books with me, and I would not wound him." With one sister in her own house and a sister-in-law next door who witnessed the scene, not to mention a mother to whom she could have turned, she wrote to her friend in Springfield, enclosing the note of apology:[6]

> Now will I ask so much of you, that you read it for me, judge if it is said as yourself would say it, were *you* rude instead of me – that if you approve, when you walk again, you will take it for me to Mr. Chapman's office, tell him for me, intercede as my sister should? Then if he forgives me, I shall write you quickly, but if he should not, and we meet the next in Newgate, know that I was a loving felon, sentenced for a door bell.

The episode obviously amused her, and she seems to have enjoyed telling Mrs. Holland about it—she tried out many styles on the Hollands; this was the mock heroic—how Kate Scott and she, "clinging fast like culprit mice . . . opened consultation," how she "proposed that we ask forgiveness," how Kate "was impenitent and demurred," and how they were discovered in clandestine conference by Sue. A little later, in a letter for the first time beginning " 'Sister,' " came a bit of fantasy—to exorcise, it

---

6. Mrs. Ward has suggested to me, however, why Emily's writing Mrs. Holland would have been quite appropriate: "When Emily asked Mrs. H's advice about her breach of good manners toward the two gentlemen, she was writing to a friend of Mr. Chapman" (letter of January 17, 1972).

seems, the uneasiness she felt in the absence of Vinnie, more and more the guardian at the gate:

> Vinnie is yet in Boston. Thank you for recollecting. I am somewhat afraid at night . . . and if the Chairs do prance – and the Lounge polka a little, and the shovel give it's arm to the tongs, one dont mind such things! From fearing them at first, I've grown to quite admire them, and now we understand each other, it is most enlivening!

So she worked out many a little woe, in whatever style took her fancy, with Mrs. Holland, the perfect listener. The letter included the first of the thirty-one poems we know about (there may have been others) that went to the Hollands, who became an important part of her private public. The tone of the poem is anything but playful. In the letter, the poem followed Emily's remarks on Dr. Holland's return from lecturing, a reunion which brought to Emily's mind, as such things often did, the ultimate parting and the ultimate reunion. Here the tone goes from girlish sentiment (in the prose part) to a finely controlled statement of the agony of loss:

> Meeting is well worth parting. How kind in some to die, adding *impatience* to the rapture of our thought of Heaven!

>> As by the dead we love to sit –
>> Become so wondrous dear –
>> As for the lost we grapple
>> Though all the rest are here –
>> In broken Mathematics
>> We estimate our prize
>> *Vast*, in it's *fading* ratio
>> To our penurious eyes.   [#88, 1859]

Only once (September 1859), in this first series of letters before the 1860–65 gap, did Emily slip into the pose of the child asking for help, and even here the style and context would seem to belie so-called "regressive" tendencies she has sometimes been accused of:

> We talk of you together, then diverge on life, then hide in you again, as a safe fold. Don't leave us long, dear friends! You know we're children still, and children fear the dark.
> Are you well at home? Do you work now? Has it altered much since I was there? Are the children women, and the women thinking it will soon be afternoon? We will help each other bear our unique burdens.

By the time she wrote this letter, she was nearly twenty-nine, and Vinnie, whom she included in her appeal, was, she knew very well, much too independent and peppery a character to need such help. The "dark" she fears is the dark of death, in the presence of which, she implies, we are all children.

In one letter, a little earlier (November 1858), the dark all but engulfed her. We have noted the theme of death in many of her early correspondences, but it seldom appears so poignantly or, indeed, with an ever-so-slight tendency toward panic. After her girlhood, she was never expansive about her griefs, or the griefs of others, even to the Hollands. Her mature medium was economical; apparently she could trust herself with no other; and the mask of humor in this letter seems easily penetrated. She does not modulate (as she frequently did with the Hollands) into visions of eternal companionship with her friends:

DEAR HOLLANDS,

Good-night! I can't stay any longer in a world of death. Austin is ill of fever. I buried my garden last week – our man, Dick, lost a little girl through the scarlet fever. I thought perhaps that *you* were dead, and not knowing the sexton's address, interrogate the daisies. Ah! dainty – dainty Death! Ah! democratic Death! Grasping the proudest zinnia from my purple garden, – then deep to his bosom calling the serf's child!

Say, is he everywhere? Where shall I hide my things? Who is alive? The woods are dead. Is Mrs. H. alive? Annie and Katie – are they below, or received to nowhere?

I shall not tell how short time is, for I was told by lips which sealed as soon as it was said, and the open revere the shut. You were not here in summer. *Summer?* My memory flutters – had I – was there a summer? You should have seen the fields go – gay little entomology. Swift little ornithology! Dancer, and floor, and cadence quite gathered away, and I, a phantom, to you a phantom, rehearse the story! An orator of feather unto an audience of fuzz, – and pantomimic plaudits. "Quite as good as a play," indeed!

Tell Mrs. Holland she is mine. Ask her if *vice versa?* Mine is but just the thief's request – "Remember me to-day." Such are the bright chirographies of the "Lamb's Book." Goodnight! My ships are in! – My window overlooks the wharf! One yacht, and a man-of-war; two brigs and a schooner! "Down with the topmast! Lay her a' hold, a' hold!"

EMILIE.

Few of her letters so clearly illustrate her notion of mirth as "the Mail of Anguish" (and here, perhaps, of terror) and the protective style she was developing. By way of the recreative play-world of the poet, she has worked her way here from the "world of death" to life again, and vigorous, hearty life at that. In the opening paragraph, the oppressive feeling of mortality is barely relieved, if at all, by the notion that death is somehow dainty and democratic.[7] There is a resurgence of energy as she

7. This seeming echo of Whitman is probably a coincidence. In her second letter to Higginson she had said, "You speak of Mr Whitman – I never read his Book – but was told that he was disgraceful –" (*L* II, 404). She might have been told this by Dr. Holland himself, who was probably the author of an editorial in the *Republican* (June 16, 1860) entitled " 'Leaves of Grass' – Smut in Them" (*YH* II, 10). It would be interesting to know what Higginson wrote to her about Whitman. Probably (in view of his later opinion) he warned her against his formlessness.

develops, in the central paragraph, her fantasy on summer, which becomes quite literally a "play," with stage and performers and audience and applause; even the Lamb's book has its *"bright* chirographies." Then, shifting the metaphor, she "brings her ships in" (perhaps "the yacht, the man-of-war, the two brigs and a schooner" are her family, the five of them), not to death but to harbor, a quiet moor after a stormy passage. The spirited rhetoric of *The Tempest* signalizes the victory. Here, if ever, is an example of what she meant when she said that she wrote her verses to relieve the "palsy." The poem has made the poet.

Then, or shortly after, came the five-year gap in the Holland correspondence, covering, ironically, the most crucial—certainly the most discussed—five years in Emily Dickinson's life. Mrs. Ward found "no single reason" to account for the gap. The friendship remained constant, and Emily continued to write letters to other people. Mrs. Ward suggests several explanations, ranging from such simple matters as the loss or chance destruction of letters when the Hollands moved in 1862, to such large national anxieties as the Civil War. In between (it might be well at this point to review the many suggestions) are Emily's personal involvement with Samuel Bowles; the turn of her primary attention to Higginson and her poetry; the "terror since September [1861]," perhaps caused by Dr. Charles Wadsworth's leaving for California, or by first hints of the eye trouble that developed later; or perhaps it was the product of "a deep psychic disturbance," as Mrs. Ward says, "marking the transition from a youthful phase to one more mature." We have seen Dr. John Cody's views, with "mother rejection" as a central thesis. There may have been times, he thinks, when her sanity, of which she wrote so blithely to Mrs. Holland, was quite literally in danger. Many pressures or compulsions may have contributed: the breach with Sue; the loss of Austin when he married Sue (perhaps a twofold sexual loss, however unconscious, explaining much about her trouble with Sue from the time Austin began his courtship); her rejection, according to Rebecca Patterson's theory, by Sue's brilliant visitor, Kate Scott Anthon, and Emily's recognition of her own (possible) homosexuality, and of the utter hopelessness that, in her society, such a relationship relegated her to; Ruth Miller's theory of Bowles's rejection of her poetry as well as her person and of Higginson's subsequent failure with her poetry; the suggestion that during this period she realized that she was not an original poet—indeed, a plagiarist—and could never meet the high ideal she set for herself; the theory that the "terror" came from her first full recognition of all that the dedication of her life to poetry implied, the discipline, the inevitable renunciations, and the perhaps appalling depths her poetic probings might reveal. All these theories have been vigorously argued, and at length.[8] Each may contain

8. The references should by now be (mostly) clear: Cody's *After Great Pain* (where, besides the "mother rejection," the notion of Sue as a sexual loss is developed); Rebecca Patterson's *The Riddle of Emily Dickinson,* which suggests that

its element of truth, although I fail to see any in the theory of Emily Dickinson as plagiarist, her accommodation of however many borrowings into her own rhythms and idiom being completely original. In our present context, all we can do is lament the loss of her letters, with their possible explanations, to the Hollands during these five years.

One fact must always be kept in mind: it was these years that marked her greatest poetic productivity. Although the dating of the poems in the 1955 *Poems* is, properly, tentative, the 916 poems assigned by the editors to these five years may not be far wrong, even if the 366 assigned to 1862 alone seems an incredible number. If during these years, or a substantial part of them, Emily Dickinson was in such a deplorable emotional condition as is often hypothesized, it is hard to see how she could have had the strength to put mind to matter or pen to paper, let alone write poems of such coherence and power. Dr. Cody frequently concedes this paradox. His intense Freudian analysis of the poem "My Life had stood – a Loaded Gun – " points to hypothetical aggressions, compulsions, and frustrations any one of which would be sufficient to account for the disintegration of a personality or, more simply, the crack-up of a mind. And yet he finds the mind of the woman who wrote the poem functioning clearly and efficiently; in other words, if the poem means what he makes it mean, Emily Dickinson's personality did not disintegrate nor did her mind fail under such stress. Mrs. Ward sums up her achievement by saying that "she took the artist's path to redemption." Ruth Miller, asking what Emily had left after Bowles and Higginson failed her, answers: "A thousand and more poems," and stresses the degree to which her redemption was religious, with Christ as savior, redeemer, lover—great themes she incorporated into her poetry. Though my own reiterated stress in previous chapters on the concept of self in the poem "On a Columnar Self – / How ample to rely / In Tumult – or Extremity – " suggests that she proceeded without special religious dependency or inspiration, her identifications with Christ, especially the suffering Christ, are frequent and impressive. Also, according to one theory, she may have had psychological help in 1864 from her Boston ophthalmologist, Dr. Henry W. Williams.[9] Many and mysterious

---

Mrs. Holland destroyed the 1860–65 letters to shield Emily from their intimate disclosures about her love for Kate Anthon—the poem "As by the dead we love to sit" actually being Emily's requiem over that affair (p. 156); Ruth Miller's theories (discussed above) about Bowles and Higginson; the "whisper" of plagiarism in John Evangelist Walsh, *The Hidden Life of Emily Dickinson*, p. 108; and the theory of the "terror since September" in Inder Nath Kher's *Landscape of Absence: Emily Dickinson's Poetry*.

9. The nature of Emily's difficulty with her eyes is still a mystery. There is a wide range of explanations. Dr. Cody feels that the ailment was psychosomatic and was treated accordingly by Dr. Williams. Other suggestions point to physiological disorders: the early manifestations of Bright's disease (as her final illness was diagnosed) or strabismus (the inability to direct both eyes to the same object) or glaucoma. The suggestion about strabismus came to me from Mrs. Patricia Sierra of Toledo, Ohio, whose husband detected the outward deviation of the right eye as he

elements enter into the forming, or the re-forming, of a self, and the most refined analysis cannot exhaust the possibilities. In this case, the simplest and most obvious should not be overlooked: the sustaining routine of household chores; a stable family situation that at least left her free to develop as she would; the constant joy of the Amherst countryside and of her flowers; a town and a college with which she had by no means lost contact; her reading—even to the *Springfield Republican,* a daily ritual that kept her in contact with the world beyond Amherst; and friends like the Hollands, especially Mrs. Holland, who, save for one blind spot, seems to have understood her best of all her friends. While Sue scintillated and became her "pseudo Sister," and while Vinnie, the "Atlas" and the busybody of the house, adored her but understood her no better (as Emily wrote Joseph Lyman) than if "we had come up for the first time from two wells where we had hitherto been bred," it was Mrs. Holland who became her true spiritual sister. In the correspondence from 1865 on, she is almost invariably called "Sister" or "Little Sister," or "Loved and Little Sister."

The one great exception—the blind spot—to the Hollands' understanding of their Amherst friend was their lack, all the more noticeable in a

---

was painting a portrait of ED from the 1848 daguerreotype. The deviation might not have been sufficient, however, to cause the long and apparently painful treatment in Boston for eight months, unless Dr. Williams operated. In that case, as he says in his book, *Recent Advances in Ophthalmic Science* (1866), which won the Boylston Prize at Harvard in 1865, glasses would have been mandatory, and there is no evidence that she ever wore them. There is no evidence to support the theory of Dr. Williams' possible psychiatric help. His book is rigidly physiological, its primary aim being to "assist the student and the general practitioner in acquiring a knowledge of the principles of the Ophthalmoscope and of its practical application" (p. v). Only once, in a passage on "Spasm of the Ciliary Muscle," is optical difficulty related to general health (p. 128):

> Distant objects are therefore seen very indistinctly; and although those near the eye are seen clearly for a short time, the effort of close attention soon fatigues.
> This morbid condition is oftenest met with in persons who use the eyes continuously for fine work. It sometimes comes on suddenly. . . .
> In combination with such treatment as may be indicated for lessening nervous sensibility and improving the general health, we should enjoin rest from fatiguing employment of the eyes; – and even, if necessary, place the accommodative power in repose by paralyzing the ciliary muscle by means of a solution of atropia. The use of convex glasses may often be advised for a time, in order to insure complete rest from accommodative efforts.

Dr. Williams was Ophthalmic Surgeon to the City Hospital, Boston, and University Lecturer on Ophthalmic Surgery at Harvard. His previous publication, *A Practical Guide to the Study of Diseases of the Eye: their Medical and Surgical Treatment* (1862), is similarly oriented. Here the strabismus operation is described as a simple office procedure. It seems that unless Dr. Williams' office records, or some such evidence, can be found, those "eight months of Siberia" as she described them to Joseph Lyman (*LL,* p. 76) must remain a mystery. So far, inquiries have been unavailing.

study of the relationship from 1865 on, of any conception of Emily Dickinson as poet, either of the quality of the poems she was sending them or of the magnitude of a vocation on which she was then fairly launched. Their failure in the latter respect was no worse, of course, than that of the members of Emily Dickinson's own household, who seem, at any rate, to have been oblivious of Emily's absorption in her literary work and completely surprised by the extent of the manuscript material found in her room at her death. (Vinnie, the guardian and housekeeper, must have known more than she let on; she may have agreed, for whatever reason, to keep Emily's confidence.) Nor was the Hollands' failure worse than Bowles's or Higginson's or Emily Fowler Ford's when she agreed with Dr. Holland, then editor of *Scribner's,* that the poems should not be published. Dr. Holland, a published poet and novelist, was as much a literary man as Higginson, and as editor had many occasions to advise young writers about their work, although his advice seems never to have gone much further than the salutary admonition to stop talking about themselves.[10] The Dickinsons subscribed to *Scribner's,* of course, at its inception. If Emily ever asked him for literary help, there is no record of it. Another question: Why was it that Helen Hunt Jackson, a frequent contributor to *Scribner's* from 1870 on, seems never to have urged Dr. Holland to publish Emily's poems at a time when Emily might have agreed? The entire phenomenon is mysterious. When anyone as close as a daughter or sister or intimate friend, or even one not so intimate, is writing poems of such quality (however odd they may have seemed) at the rate of one a day, or even one every other day as seems likely at her peak, the general silence is hard to explain. Mrs. Ward writes thus about her grandparents:

> One would like to feel that the Hollands recognized Emily's genius, but their taste was too limited by the conventional forms of their time to enable them to see the full worth of her poetry. Dr. Holland is quoted [by Emily Ford] as having said that Emily's verse was too ethereal for publication, and the personal nature of Mrs. Holland's feeling may have obscured her appreciation of the artist in her friend. Her poetry was set apart, as something special, not to be judged according to recognized standards, but warmly cherished as the individual expression of her stimulating, elusive, affectionate self.

It is difficult to see what is so ethereal or elusive or even contrary to recognized standards about the following joyful lyric included in a letter of early summer 1873:

10. "I'm a bit tired of *subjective* poems," Holland wrote Mrs. Cora Daniels, who had inquired about sending her poems to *Scribner's*. "Try going outside for topics, and get an interest in some thing beside yourself and your emotions. That is the way to grow. Construct more and evolve less" (*YH* II, 272; June 2, 1877).

The most triumphant Bird I ever knew or met
Embarked upon a twig to-day
And till Dominion set
I famish to behold so eminent a sight
And sang for nothing scrutable
But intimate Delight.
Retired, and resumed his transitive Estate –
To what delicious Accident
Does finest Glory fit! (#*1265*)

The form may be unconventional, but it is very regular—the six-beat, four-beat, three-beat iambic triplets thrice repeated. In an age that doted on bird poems,[11] this exuberant little piece, so much more distinguished than most, should not have daunted, one would think, the most timid editor. Was it the third line, or "his transitive Estate," or the "delicious Accident" that gave Dr. Holland pause? Or the broken syntax? (Logically, lines 3 and 4 should directly precede the last two lines.) The theme is transparent, the mood buoyant, the eye is directed outward according to Holland's most rigorous prescription. But, when Dr. Holland became editor of *Scribner's* in 1870, its pages were closed to Emily Dickinson. From 1865 on, her letters were addressed almost exclusively to Mrs. Holland.

The letters of this second stage of the friendship vary in mood and style. Even in single letters, and short ones at that, Emily could run the gamut from grave to gay, whimsical to sharply realistic. Some of her early preoccupations are still there, like the theme of death; but in general she is more objective; there are more references to the world of nature and affairs, and to books; she quotes more, especially from the Bible; her wit is sharper; and her tendency toward aphorism, especially in the early 1870s, becomes extreme.

The first letter (early November 1865) after the break starts with two jokes:

DEAR SISTER,
Father called to say that our steelyard was fraudulent, exceeding by an ounce the rates of honest men. He had been selling oats. I cannot stop smiling, though it is hours since, that even our steelyard will not tell the truth.
Besides wiping the dishes for Margaret, I wash them now, while she becomes Mrs. Lawler, vicarious papa to four previous babes. Must she not be an adequate bride?[12]

11. For the kind of bird poems Dr. Holland was accepting for *Scribner's,* see Appendix IV, 2. Some seven years before, she had sent him one of her best: "At Half past Three, a single Bird" (#1084, about 1866); but it too was editorially ignored.
12. A word is appropriate here about the Dickinsons' "Margaret" and "Maggie." Margaret O'Brien, to whom Emily makes frequent and fond reference in the letters,

EMILY DICKINSON

The anecdote about Father brings up a question about a matter that concerned her, and her poetry, deeply. To follow it for a moment leads us to the heart of what might be called her private poetics. The letter begins as if she and Mrs. Holland had been discussing, in letters that are lost, the problem of Truth and how seldom it is told. Back from the ordeal in Cambridge with her eyes, she is now restored to health and is able to help with the housework. She smiles with Olympian humor at Father's moral outrage and shares with her friend in Springfield her observation that truth is a rare commodity in Amherst. (Apparently by this time Mrs. Holland was well used to Emily's nonconformist thoughts.) Many years later Emily reverted again to the theme of telling the truth. Speaking of her childhood spelling of the word "phoebe," she wrote to Mrs. Holland (spring 1883): "Should I spell all the things as they sounded to me, and say all the facts as I saw them, it would send consternation among more than the 'Fee Bees'!" The emphasis in this letter of 1865, characteristic of the outward-turned letters of the mid-1860s, is the problem, not so much of the truth of what people tell each other as of the truth of nature as it impinged upon her sensibilities. She went on:

left the Dickinsons when she became Mrs. Lawler. She had been with them ten years. Whatever might be said about the Dickinson snobbishness as the town saw it, their domestic help, at least the two we know most about, were loyal and devoted. Maggie Maher was the more remembered, coming four years after Margaret O'Brien and staying until Vinnie's death in 1899. Maggie was a favorite of Mrs. Holland's, often sending her love or "respects" by way of Emily's letters. Emily once described her to Mrs. Holland as "good and noisy, the North Wind of the Family" (L III, 690, early spring 1881), and three years later Maggie was "with us still, warm and wild and mighty" (L III, 827, early August 1884). When Maggie was sick with typhoid Emily wrote her the following letter (L III, 741, October 1882):

The missing Maggie is much mourned, and I am going out for "black" to the nearest store.
All are very naughty, and I am naughtiest of all.
The pussies dine on sherry now, and humming-bird cutlets.
The invalid hen took dinner with me, but a hen like Dr. T[aylor]'s horse soon drove her away. I am very busy picking up stems and stamens as the hollyhocks leave their clothes around.
What shall I send my weary Maggie? Pillows or fresh brooks?
Her grieved Mistress.

As Jay Leyda wrote in his fine tribute to Maggie ("Miss Emily's Maggie," *New World Writing,* 3rd Mentor Selection, 1953, pp. 255–67), "few dared to be playful with the very ill." For an example of Maggie's epistolary style, see above, pp. 266–7.
A brief account of the entire Dickinson domestic staff over the years is in L III, 959–60. Emily, who left directions for her funeral, was borne to her grave by the six Irishmen who had worked on her father's grounds, Thomas Kelley, Dennis Scannell, Stephen Sullivan, Patrick Ward, Daniel Moynihan, and Dennis Cashman. "She asked to be carried out the back door, around through the garden, through the opened barn from front to back, and then through the grassy fields to the family plot, always in sight of the house" ("Miss Emily's Maggie," pp. 266–67).

The Dickinson domestics, about 1870
Left to right: Maggie Maher ("the North Wind of the Family");
Tom Kelley ("I ran to his Blue Jacket . . ."); Margaret Kelley

It is also November. The noons are more laconic and the sundowns sterner, and Gibraltar lights make the village foreign. November always seemed to me the Norway of the year.

In the next letter but one (March 1866) she condescended grandly (in this matter of light on landscape) to Wordsworth:

February passed like a Skate and I know March. Here is the "light" the Stranger said "was not on land or sea." Myself could arrest it but we'll not chagrin Him.

By this time she was something of a specialist on light. She had told Higginson that the "sudden light on Orchards" was one of the things that moved her to write verses, and she had already shown what she could do toward "arresting" such phenomena—that is, getting them "truly" in her poems:

> There's a certain Slant of light,
> Winter Afternoons –
> That oppresses, like the Heft
> Of Cathedral Tunes – . . .   (#258, about 1861)

Later in this March letter to Mrs. Holland, she gave some more hints as to the nature of her poetic purpose, with several examples:

My flowers are near and foreign, and I have but to cross the floor to stand in the Spice Isles.

The Wind blows gay today and the Jays bark like Blue Terriers. I tell you what I see. The Landscape of the Spirit requires a lung, but no Tongue. I hold you few I love, till my heart is red as February and purple as March.

There is a paradox here, of course. She knew very well that the landscape of the spirit—the inner life—needed a tongue, and no one surpassed her in getting at its truth. She is simply saying, "There's no need to *tell* you I love you; while I breathe, I do." It is when she says, "I tell you what I see," that she describes her purpose as a poet of both lives, inner and outer. As poet of the inner life, her dedication to this kind of truth led her to insights of the most penetrating kind, epiphanies of the moral and spiritual life; as poet of the external world, she caught its evanescences and its permanent realities with matchless precision. In the Holland letters she functions as both; but it may have been Mrs. Holland's hearty, outgoing nature that particularly stimulated her faculties in the latter direction. Passages from two letters of the mid-1860s (and the last before another curious gap in the correspondence, only partly explained by the Hollands' two-year sojourn abroad, 1868–70) are fine examples of the precision she was developing as an expositor of both domains, but especially (for Mrs. Holland) her sharp, pungent observation of the external world:

Friday I tasted life. It was a vast morsel. A circus passed the house – still I feel the red in my mind though the drums are out. . . .

The lawn is full of south and the odors tangle, and I hear today for the first the river in the tree.

You mentioned spring's delaying – I blamed her for the opposite. I would eat evanescence slowly.

Vinnie is deeply afflicted in the death of her dappled cat, though I convince her it is immortal which assists her some. . . .

"House" is being "cleaned." I prefer pestilence. That is more classic and less fell. . . .

A woman died last week, young and in hope but a little while – at the end of our garden. I thought since of the power of death, not upon affection, but its mortal signal. It is to us the Nile. . . .

I saw the sunrise on the Alps since I saw you. Travel why to Nature, when she dwells with us? Those who lift their hats shall see her, as devout do God. . . .

Today is very homely and awkward as the homely are who have not mental beauty.

> The sky is low, the clouds are mean,
> A travelling flake of snow
> Across a barn or through a rut
> Debates if it will go.
>
> A narrow wind complains all day
> How someone treated him;
> Nature, like us, is sometimes caught
> Without her diadem.   [#1075, about 1866]

(Again one might be permitted to wonder why Dr. Holland, if he ever saw it, should have neglected such a poem when he became editor of *Scribner's* four years later.)

Although many more letters must have been written, what we have of the correspondence does not resume until some five months after the Hollands returned from Europe in May 1870. One of the ways Emily Dickinson kept in touch with the world was through her friends who traveled. From Syria, Abby Wood Bliss sent her specimens for her herbarium and a section of polished olivewood;[13] Emily asked Bowles, when he was in England, to touch Mrs. Browning's grave for her—"put one hand on the Head, for me – her unmentioned Mourner"; Dr. Holland sent her a picture of Mrs. Browning's tomb, which she promptly gave to Higginson on his visit that August (1870). Obviously the Hollands came home loaded with photographs and anecdotes of their travels and their lengthy stays in five countries, England, France, Switzerland, Germany, and Italy. (They had left Paris for home just as the Franco-Prussian War was about to break out.) But all this seems merely to have confirmed

13. Now in the Todd-Bingham Archive, Yale.

Emily Dickinson in the rightness of her choice of her own way of life. The last half of the first letter after the break gives her own views, to her traveling friends, on how unnecessary travel is and where they should look for the true meaning in life (including the then formidable figure of Bismarck). Her aphoristic style is at its height.

> We are by September and yet my flowers are bold as June. Amherst has gone to Eden.
> To shut our eyes is Travel.
> The Seasons understand this.
> How lonesome to be an Article! I mean – to have no soul.
> An apple fell in the night and a Wagon stopped.
> I suppose the Wagon ate the Apple and resumed it's way.
> How fine it is to talk.
> What Miracles the News is!
> Not Bismark but ourselves.

> The Life we have is very great.
> The Life that we shall see
> Surpasses it, we know, because
> It is Infinity.
> But when all Space has been beheld
> And all Dominion shown
> The smallest Human Heart's extent
> Reduces it to none.   [#1162]

The passage is remarkably coherent, the seemingly detached aphorisms each contributing, however obliquely, to the theme that is given its summation in the concluding poem (another one, quite eligible, that Dr. Holland missed). The sentences on the Apple and the Wagon are perhaps a tiny parable on soul-less travel.

Two years later, so intense had become her focus, or so obsessive had become her rejection of travel of any sort, that she found it impossible to accept an invitation of Mrs. Holland's for a visit in Springfield: "Thanking you tenderly as a child for a sweet favor I can never go." Her letter of apology shows a guilty conscience. She denies being a traitor to their friendship, pleads for Mrs. Holland's love, and only once, toward the end, comes near offering a reason for her refusal. Her style is now so tight as to require explication, which I have suggested in the brackets.

> Some [I] must seem a Traitor, not because it is [I am], but it's Truth [my fidelity] belie it.
> Andre [the British spy whose hanging had been widely deplored as unjust] had not died had he lived Today.
> Only Love can wound –
> Only Love assist the Wound.
> Worthier let us be of this Ample Creature [Love].
> If my Crescent [my worldly part] fail you, try me in the Moon – [my spiritual part] . . .

In adequate Music there is a Major and a Minor –
Should there not also be a Private?

In her girlhood she had exclaimed simply, "I enjoyed the solitude finely."
Now, to Mrs. Holland, she felt compelled to give her preference (or her
compulsion) a rationale: privacy is as essential to her as the minor key is
to music.

In the seventy-odd surviving letters of the rest of the correspondence,
Emily shared some, but not much, of her privacy with Mrs. Holland and
a great deal of her wit and love. The love is constant, and the wit gives
way only to the somber mood of the periods of the deaths, notably her
father's in 1874, Dr. Holland's in 1881, her mother's in 1882, and little
Gilbert's in 1883. If we had Mrs. Holland's side of the correspondence, we
would probably find that she was a sturdy friend during Emily's sorrows.
But Emily also helped *her* through two crises, first when a long period of
eye trouble ended in the summer of 1872 with the loss, by operation, of
one eye; and next at her husband's death. Emily Dickinson is so often
thought of as the recipient of pity or condolence that her strength to aid
her friends in their troubles is often forgotten. Whatever were the cause
and nature of her own troubles in the early 1860s, she emerged stronger,
with sharper perceptions and broader sympathies. Her letter of August
1872, written shortly after Mrs. Holland's eye operation, shows one "Gibraltar's Heart" writing to another:

> To have lost an Enemy is an Event with all of us – almost more memor-
> able perhaps than to find a friend. This severe success befalls our little Sis-
> ter – and though the Tears insist at first, as in all good fortune, Gratitude
> grieves best.
> Fortified by Love, a few have prevailed.
> "Even so, Father, for so it seemed faithful in thy Sight."
> We are proud of her safety – Ashamed of our dismay for her who knew
> no consternation.
> It is the Meek that Valor wear too mighty for the Bold.
> We should be glad to know of her present Lifetime, it's project, though
> a little changed – so precious to us all.
> Be secure of this, that whatever waver – her Gibraltar's Heart is firm.
> EMILY.

The letters of condolence to Mrs. Holland at the time of the Doctor's
death in October 1881 show the same poetic precision, maintaining the
fine, always precarious balance necessary in such matters if sentiment is
not to be lost in bathos. Emily Dickinson was an artist here as elsewhere.
The discipline, it would seem, strengthened her—and we can assume that
its product strengthened Mrs. Holland. One of the letters is a poem;
several conclude in poems. Here is one, probably written within a few
days of the Doctor's death, that almost breaks into verse—the last sentence
("if I . . .") of the first paragraph is in her favorite meter ("8s" and
"6s")—and concludes with two tiny dramatic scenes, beautifully calcu-

lated to objectify her feelings, while conveying them to her friend obliquely and with restraint. (She had earlier confided to Mrs. Holland her preference for "the inferential Knowledge – the distinctest one.")

> Panting to help the dear ones and yet not knowing how, lest any voice bereave them but that loved voice that will not come, if I can rest them, here is down – or rescue, here is power.
>
> One who only said "I am sorry" helped me the most when father ceased – it was too soon for language.
>
> Fearing to tell mother, some one disclosed it unknown to us. Weeping bitterly, we tried to console her. She only replied "I loved him so."
>
> Had he a tenderer eulogy?
>
> EMILY..

If Emily ever told Mrs. Holland the whole truth about her friendships with those three men, Bowles, Wadsworth, and Lord, who must loom large, almost by default, in any account of her life, she did not do it in any of the letters that survive. Even at their deaths, when if ever her feelings might have spilled over in confidences, she is strangely laconic. A few days before Bowles died (January 16, 1878), came this comment in the midst of a letter devoted to many other matters: "Dear Mr Bowles is hesitating – God help him decide on the Mortal Side!" And a few days after, only this, similarly embedded: "Dear Mr Bowles found out too late, that Vitality costs itself. How mournful without him! I often heard the Students sing – delicious Summer nights, 'I've seen around me fall – like Leaves in wintry weather' – This was what they meant – " Some ten months after Wadsworth's death on April 1, 1882, came what seems to be a reference to the event, but even this is not certain. It is indirect, anonymous, and it climaxes a brief meditation on her mother's death and death in general. The letter was written shortly after Christmas of that year.

> Mother's Christmas Gift of another Life is just as stupendous to us now, as the Morning it came – All other Surprise is at last monotonous, but the Death of the Loved is all moments – *now* – Love has but one Date – "The first of April" "Today, Yesterday, and Forever" –
>
> > "*Can* Trouble dwell with April Days?"
> > "Of Love that never found it's earthly close,
> >   what sequel?"
>
> Both in the same Book – in the same Hymn – Excuse your Mourning
>
> EMILY –

"The first of April" has been assumed to clinch the reference to Wadsworth;[14] but, along with the two quotations from Tennyson (*not* from

14. Mrs. Ward, p. 169, makes this assumption, and in her note to the letter properly identifies the two quotations. The first is from *In Memoriam* (No. 83) and the second is from *Love and Duty*. "Today, Yesterday, and Forever" is from Hebrews 13:8.

the same poem), the date, like the Biblical quotation that follows—"To-day, Yesterday, and Forever"—may have a literary source, and the similarity in dates may be coincidental. "Your mourning Emily" may have been grieving for her mother and not Wadsworth at all. Again the baffling questions: Why did Emily, if she *was* mourning for Wadsworth, stop short of mentioning his name? Why is it never mentioned in the surviving Holland letters? Did Mrs. Holland destroy letters that named him, or delete references to him in the letters she kept? And if she did, why? The Hollands were conventional people; but the very conventions of the time, with their careful separation of "carnal" and "spiritual" love, allowed, as Mrs. Ward is careful to point out, for "an astonishing degree of freedom in friendship between men and women of fine feeling"—a freedom that Bowles, for instance, assumed with Maria Whitney, that Emily perhaps presumed upon in her fervent letters to Bowles, and a freedom that surely would have been allowed her, even by her most proper friends, in her many years of correspondence with her distant clergyman. Again, her tenderness when Judge Lord died, in view of what we know about the intimacy of their relationship, is remarkably restrained, although she at least mentions his name and a few of the circumstances of his death:

> When I tell my sweet Mrs Holland that I have lost another friend, she will not wonder I do not write, but that I raise my Heart to a drooping syllable – Dear Mr Lord has left us – After a brief unconsciousness, a Sleep that ended with a smile, so his Nieces tell us, he hastened away, "seen," we trust, "of Angels" – "Who knows that secret deep" – "Alas, not I –"[15]
> Forgive the Tears that fell for few, but that few too many, for was not each a World?

As often in these letters, we seem close to another fundamental aspect of Emily Dickinson's consciousness, this time suggested by her remark here concerning the nature of her friendships: ". . . *for was not each a World?*" We have seen the "World"—of holiday, and freedom, spiritual resource and a sunshiny God—she made out of her friendship with the

15. The Bible and (perhaps) *Paradise Lost* XII, 575–78, are in conjunction here (see *L* III, 817 n.):

I Timothy 3:16:
God was manifest in the flesh, justified in the Spirit, seen of angels, preached unto the Gentiles, believed on in the world, received up into glory.

PL XII, 575–78 (the Archangel Michael to Adam):

> This having learned, thou has attained the sum
> Of wisdom; hope no higher, though all the stars
> Thou knew'st by name, and all the ethereal powers,
> All secrets of the deep, all Nature's works . . .

"Seen of angels" was a favorite phrase of ED's. In an enigmatic remark to Higginson (*L* II, 460, June 1869), perhaps referring to a title of some bit of fugitive verse or prose, she wrote: " 'Seen of Angels' scarcely my responsibility."

Hollands. She seems also to have made a separate world of each of her other major correspondents. She was very selective; there were few enough, as she says many times. Each had its peculiar qualities and ambience, its flavor and meaning. She seems almost to have walled them off in her consciousness and from her friends. In what survives of these important correspondences, the letters to Higginson say nothing about Bowles; the letters to Bowles say nothing about Higginson; the letters to Helen Hunt Jackson say nothing about either of them, although Emily knew very well that they were all three active in the contemporary literary world and that at least two of them (Higginson and Mrs. Jackson) were mutually aware of her own literary activity. Unless the missing letters to Mrs. Holland (and others) might prove the contrary, we can only assume that she did not share, readily or fully, the intensity of these private worlds, at least in her letters, with anybody. She might have talked about them with Austin or Vinnie or Sue or, during her infrequent visits to Amherst, with Mrs. Holland; but it is likely that her characteristic reticence prevailed here, too.

Of course, all this heightens our sense of her isolation. Certainly no major poet ever lived so private an existence, with no circle, no coterie, almost no sustaining professional gossip. But the implications of this seemingly casual remark to Mrs. Holland go further. There is a hint here of her sense, not merely of the way she regarded her friends, but of the nature of reality itself and the methods she fashioned to cope with it. Her friendships were like her poetry, creations of her imagination—"worlds"— in which she could live the only kind of life possible for her and as necessary as her poetry to her survival. She endowed each of her friends— the important ones—with whatever qualities her own nature required and, regardless of reciprocity, lived, for longer or shorter periods, within an ambience largely of her own creation. First came essence, whatever it was in a new friend that would spark her imagination and to which she would penetrate with the intense concentration she devoted to the matter of her poems—like the essence of winter in "There's a certain Slant of light." Her chief medium with her friendships, of course, was the writing of letters, when, alone and undistracted, she could fill out in her imagination the gaps and blanks and frustrations with which actual human contact seems usually to have left her, and luxuriate in a "world" partly of her own creation. Occasionally, as in the remark to Mrs. Holland, she generalized on the whole procedure. Years earlier (May 1866) she had been even more revealing. She wrote Mrs. Holland:

After you went, a low wind warbled through the house like a spacious bird, making it high but lonely. When you had gone the love came. I supposed it would. The supper of the heart is when the guest has gone.

Essence, for her, required absence. Love comes after the guest leaves, because only then can it be disentangled from its "accidents" and truly

known. That she was not happy with this seems clear; absence is a kind
of death. She put the idea in a quatrain:

> Absence disembodies – so does Death
> Hiding individuals from the Earth
> Superstition helps, as well as love –
> Tenderness decreases as we prove –   (#860, about 1864)

She admitted an element of shame. Like Adam and Eve in the Garden
she had to hide herself from the Presence. She continued in the May 1866
letter:

> Shame is so intrinsic in a strong affection we must all experience
> Adam's reticence. I suppose the street that the lover travels is thenceforth
> divine [i.e., where reticence is unnecessary?], incapable of turnpike aims
> [i.e., where there is no threat of loss?].

If it can be said that she hid herself from her friends to understand
friendship, to create in her imagination the divine street the lover travels,
so, in her search for the essence of everything that came within her
consciousness, she hid herself to write her poems—and (for whatever
reason) hid her poems, except from a few. In a world of process and
evanescence, to which the bulk of her poems testify, the only way left to
her was to construct permanences of the mind—in the way of the poet,
whose "Summer – lasts a Solid Year." No wonder (in this same poem)
she called "Poets – All – " If in her daily life this meant isolation, even a
kind of destitution, it was a "sumptuous Destitution" that she had learned
to relish:

> In many and reportless places
> We feel a Joy –
> Reportless, also, but sincere as Nature
> Or Deity –
>
> It comes, without a consternation –
> Dissolves – the same –
> But leaves a sumptuous Destitution –
> Without a Name –
>
> Profane it by a search – we cannot
> It has no home –
> Nor we who having once inhaled it –
> Thereafter roam.   (#1382, about 1876)

Although she apparently did not send this poem to Mrs. Holland, it gives
another reason why she felt that travel was unnecessary.

Save for the letters about the other major deaths—Father's, Mother's, little Gilbert's—the correspondence, from the early 1870s on, ripples with humor, anecdote, slanting reference to current events, books (Biblical quotations abound, mostly whimsical), and friendly gossip about family matters like weddings, grandchildren, illnesses, examinations passed (by Ted Holland), and books published (by Dr. Holland). Austin appears occasionally, although he is reported as visiting "rarely as Gabriel" during the fall of 1882 (not surprising in view of the Rubicon he and Mabel Todd crossed that September). There is at least one cordial reference to Sue (this time in a letter to Dr. Holland), when, in 1881, she and Emily had a gay time in the Homestead talking of "Mr Samuel and you, and vital times when you two bore the Republican. . . . Sue said she was homesick for those 'better Days,' hallowed be their name." Vinnie, by far the most frequently mentioned, emerges as the comedy star of the letters— Vinnie who "thinks Vermont is in Asia"; Vinnie as "Atlas"; Vinnie "under terrific headway," "more hurried than Presidential Candidates" but with loftier aims (this in the election year, 1880); Vinnie and her pussies, for which Emily is seeking assassins; Vinnie and her "special Mind," which would have God overlook her flowers during a killing frost; Vinnie whose practical mind "prefers Baldwins" to fruits of the Spirit. Although it extended to all her family, Vinnie brought out the best of Emily's comic spirit; but the references show the distance as well as the affection between the sisters. Only occasionally does she sober down. During what she called Vinnie's "singular illness" (still unexplained) in the late 1870s Emily, describing her own feelings, said that she "felt like a troubled Top, that spun without reprieve." But there is no hint in the letters that she felt herself trapped in her home, or that she wished she were somewhere else. For the most part, she gives the impression of not having enough time in "our hurrying Home" for all she wants to do— "Time is short and full, like an outgrown Frock"—and her central theme, for all her somber thoughts during the periods of the deaths, is life's abundance and joy: "To live is Endowment. It puts me in mind of that singular Verse in the Revelations – 'Every several Gate was of one Pearl.' "

The larger world, too, appears in these later letters, although the slant and fleeting references scarcely convey what seems to be a vivid interest in matters of politics and contemporary history. She could relegate Bismarck to low priority in her list of essentials, but she knew when Albert Briggs, a friend of the Hollands and the Dickinsons, was appointed railroad commissioner in 1871: "Steam has his Commissioner, tho' his substitute is not yet disclosed of God." The stock-market crash of 1873 moved her to comment, "Owning but little Stock in the 'Gold of Ophir' I am not subject to large Reverses," and in the same letter she summed up in two sentences her attitude toward the controversy then raging about the Higher Criticism of the Bible:

Science will not trust us with another World.

Guess I and the Bible will move to some old fashioned spot where we'll feel at Home.

Later (August 1881) the Shakespeare-Bacon controversy got another two:

Shakespeare was never accused of writing Bacon's works, though to have been suspected of writing his, was the most beautiful stigma of Bacon's Life – Higher, is the doom of the High.

In a letter of January 1879, she makes figurative use of the "Mollie Maguires" and of the peace settlement of the Russo-Turkish War. ("The 'rectification of his Frontier,' " she wrote, "costs the Earth too much.") As Mrs. Ward writes, she seems "to have gone straight from her daily reading of the newspaper to her desk." She is sure, in 1881, that Mrs. Holland, too, is following the news of President Garfield's assassination, and twice she refers to the Sudanese crisis of 1883–85, again figuratively. In a letter in the fall of 1884 she stumbled on the phrase "an open secret," a cliché of the current Presidential campaign. She wrote:

What a curious Lie that phrase is! I see it of Politicians – Before I write to you again, we shall have had a new Czar – Is the Sister a Patriot?

She continued with a remark sometimes taken as her rejection of all interest in politics:

"George Washington was the Father of his Country" – "George Who?" That sums all Politics to me – but then I love the Drums, and they are busy now –

Actually, she seems merely to be indulging here in a bit of skepticism about the American democratic process, where the vote of an ignoramus counts as much as a Dickinson's.

The Holland letters, for the most part leisurely and relaxed, allowed for more literary references and quotations than was true of most of the other correspondences, especially from 1870 on. Mrs. Holland shared her friend's interests and, apparently, did her best to keep up with them in spite of difficulties:

I wish the dear Eyes would so far relent as to let you read "Emily Bronte" [the biography by A. M. F. Robinson] – more electric far than anything since "Jane Eyre."

Napoleon of the Cross! Try and read a few lines at a time – and then a few more later – It is so so [sic] strange a Strength, I must have you possess it –

Emily was as seldom discursive about books as about other such matters; indeed, this was the most extensive comment she made in these letters on any book; and although she had told Mrs. Holland that Mr. Chapman, the visitor at Sue's, had "talked of my books with me," it is hard to imagine her as participating in any sustained literary discussion, either in conversation or in correspondence. Titles, names of authors and characters, tags from plays or novels or poems make their brief appearances in the letters, seldom for the purpose, as above, of anything close to a critical comment, but almost always to evoke a mood, sum up a thought, or pay a compliment—as when Emily praised Mrs. Holland in the words Charlotte Brontë had used to describe her sister Emily ("gigantic Emily Brontë," Emily called her): "Full of ruth for others, on herself she had no mercy." Emily quoted a line from "the consummate Browning" a few years later ("But the last Leaf fear to touch" from "By the Fireside") to hit off for Mrs. Holland the deceptions of February weather—the poem's November mood altered to suit. Fictional characters appear with the familiarity of household names, apparently the stock in trade of these two devoted novel readers. Three words commemorate Charles Kingsley's death in 1875: "'Kingsley' rejoins 'Argemone' – " (his ill-fated heroine in *Yeast*). When Horace Church, the Dickinson's gardener, died in 1881, Emily called him "the 'Cap'n Cuttle' of Amherst" (*Dombey and Son*). Sometimes the source was given, more often not. Emily's "what Mrs Micawber would call 'remunerative' – " seems easier to us than "I have a Letter from 'Aunt Glegg' saying 'Summer is nearly gone'" (Aunt Glegg is Maggie Tulliver's dismal aunt in *The Mill on the Floss* and suggests Emily's formidable Aunt Elisabeth Currier). Mrs. Holland was apparently expected to respond at once to "Mr Wentworth's" question: "Where are our moral foundations?" (Henry James, *The Europeans*); to two references to "Brooks of Sheffield" (*David Copperfield*); and to fill in the complicated psychology behind "I find your Benefits no Burden, Jane," Rochester's way of telling Jane Eyre that he gladly accepts *her* help and not others'. Cathy, Heathcliff, and "Little Nell's Grandfather" are all familiar friends, but Mrs. Holland's range must have been tested by such phrase-dropping as "for those ways 'Madness lies'" (*Lear*), "Whips of Time" and "Crowner's Quest" (*Hamlet*), "Love's 'remainder Biscuit'" (*As You Like It*), and "Contention 'loves a shining Mark'" (Edward Young, *Night Thoughts*); or by the lines, "the 'Soul's poor Cottage battered and dismayed'" (Edmund Waller), and "The flower that never will in other climate grow," a reasonably accurate rendering of *Paradise Lost* II, 273, whose author Emily described only (and gloriously) as "the great florist."

The Bible is quoted most, then Shakespeare, then Milton. From Milton there is one echo, one quotation, and one near-quotation. Her "whole legions of Angels" and "that secret deep" may have been suggested by *Paradise Lost* II, 891 (or XII, 577) and VI, 655. Characteristic of her way of ignoring the context of her quotations, she used Manoa's words on hearing of Samson's death to describe her reaction to Mrs. Holland's gift of a photograph of her son and her two sons-in-law: "If the Spirits are fair as the Faces 'Nothing is here for Tears.'" The Bible is a constant; it is as if she were playing out in adulthood her remark to Abiah Root years before: "Excuse my quoting from the Scripture, dear Abiah, for it was so handy in this case I couldn't get along very well without it." Few letters are without their Biblical tags, some of them retaining the solemnity of the original context, like her comment on George Eliot's death: "It is deep to live to experience 'And there was no more Sea' – " and her tense, prophetic remark on the death of William Cullen Bryant, a close friend of Dr. Holland's: " 'It is finished' can never be said of us." At the time of Dr. Holland's death, she knew she could trust Mrs. Holland to fill out the verse (Matthew 25:40) she indicated by a single quoted word: " 'Inasmuch,' to him, how tenderly fulfilled!" But most of the Biblical quotations are whimsical, as if she enjoyed twisting the solemn phrases to her slightly impertinent uses: "Please 'consider' me [she concluded the letter on George Eliot] – An antique request, though in behalf of Lilies." When Annie Holland Howe (Mrs. Holland's daughter) went to Europe, her husband kept her walking the deck to avoid seasickness. Emily hoped that "Annie's Walk on the Water was a pedestrian success."[16] She played Deity: "I give my Angels charge" (Psalms 91:11)—over her beloved Hollands. Her reverence, certainly, is not in question:

> All grows strangely emphatic [she wrote in October 1884], and I think if I should see you again, I sh'd begin every sentence with "I say unto you –" The Bible dealt with the Centre, not with the Circumference –

But (again) she is true to the delightful discovery she wrote Joseph Lyman about in the mid-1860s: "Some years after we saw each other last I fell to reading the Old & New Testament. I had known it as an arid book but looking I saw how infinitely wise & how merry it is." Apparently Mrs. Holland shared in the merriment and relished it.[17]

16. Annie later recorded her impression of her "cousin Emily," as she called her, in a letter to Martha Bianchi (YH II, 115–16, entry of July 11/12, 1866):

> When I was a young girl visiting in Amherst I went to a Reception in your grandparents house, and met your Aunt Emily. She was so surrounded by people that I had no chance to talk with her, and she asked me to call on her the next morning.
> She received me in a little back hall that connected with the kitchen. It was dimly lighted. She asked if I would have a glass of wine or a rose. I told her I would take the rose, and she went to the garden and brought one in to me. This happened more than sixty years ago.
> I can recall very little of our conversation, and I did not think of her then as a great poet, but just a sister of cousin Vinnies that I called "cousin Emily." . . . She seemed very unusual, and her voice, her looks, and her whole personality made an impression on me that is still very vivid after all these years.

17. Although Emily's literary talk seemed mostly with Mrs. Holland, she sent Sue a copy of a "correspondence" with Dr. Holland, who, early in 1881, had secured William Dean Howells' new novel, "A Fearful Responsibility," for *Scribner's* (YH II, 344, March 23, 1881):

DOCTOR –
    How did you snare Howells?
                EMILY

EMILY –
    Case of Bribery –
    Money did it –
                HOLLAND

The aphorisms continue to the end, becoming perhaps more sententious as she saw things growing strangely emphatic, though often occasioned, like the following series, by nothing more portentous than a Christmas package (in 1882) from Mrs. Holland: "It came so long it knows the way and almost comes itself, like Nature's faithful Blossoms whom no one summons but themselves, Magics of Constancy – " Then (so her mind worked) the Christmas package led to thoughts of Santa Claus; then to what she called the "fiction" of Santa Claus; then, by way of her early question of "Who made the Bible," to the nature of Revelation and to a summing up: "Santa Claus, though[,] *illustrates* – Revelation." Finally, as if to make it up to the Bible, came this: "But a Book is only the Heart's Portrait – every Page a Pulse – "

The deaths brought out her somberest thoughts, of course, every one representing her characteristic leap from the specific to the general, as if she could not bear dwelling long on the particularity of her loss. One sentence about her cousin Willie's terminal illness led to an aphorism: "How deep this Lifetime is – One guess at the Waters, and we are plunged beneath!" And that was all. Little Gilbert's death that same year (1883) left her, as she wrote Mrs. Holland, with what the physician called " 'Nervous prostration,' " so, she said, she had to choose her words carefully (a discipline she spent her life cultivating), since she had strength for only a few. This was when she consoled herself by recalling that "Earth's most graphic transaction is placed within a syllable, nay, even a gaze." In what followed, she said nothing about what Gilbert's loss might mean to the family or to her, nothing about the marvelous little boy that had gone. She told only an anecdote of his last hours (she seems to have been the only one to record it) and asked at the end the deepest of all questions:

> "Open the Door, open the Door, they are waiting for me," was Gilbert's sweet command in delirium. *Who* were waiting for him, all we possess we would give to know – Anguish at last opened it, and he ran to the little Grave at his Grandparents' feet – All this and more, though *is* there more? More than Love and Death? Then tell me it's name!

But the thrust of the Holland letters is toward the love of life—the sound of the drums, the "taste" of the circus—tempered as her generalizations almost always are with the awareness of life's transiency and suffering. " 'This tabernacle' [II Corinthians 5:1]," she wrote during the time of Mrs. Holland's eye trouble, "is a blissful trial, but the bliss predominates." The aphorisms, even the most lighthearted, convey the sense of paradox. When Mrs. Holland sent some arbutus from New York City, Emily wrote:

> I thought that "Birnam Wood" had "come to Dunsinane." Where did you pick the arbutus? In Broadway, I suppose. They say that God is everywhere, and yet we always think of Him as somewhat of a recluse. . . .

What she was after was Life, it seems, its essence and marrow. As if to explain to Mrs. Holland her pungent, non-discursive summings-up, she rejected all this "talk" about life but left a portentous question in a sweeping aphorism:

> The vitality of your syllables compensates for their infrequency. There is not so much Life as *talk* of Life, as a general thing. Had we the first intimation of the Definition of Life, the calmest of us would be Lunatics!

"Life's Music" could be portentous, but it was nonetheless music. To live was still "Endowment." Her "business," as she had told the Hollands, was to love and to sing. Early in 1881, during a cold snap, she employed the same image she had used to announce her business—the bird singing in her garden, whether anyone listens or not. Now, writing in the depth of winter, she told of another bird, triumphing over the ravages of the frost:

> I knew a Bird that would sing as firm in the centre of Dissolution, as in it's Father's nest –
> Phenix, or the Robin?
> While I leave you to guess, I will take Mother her Tea –

This may have been a tribute to Mrs. Holland's courage that refused to be shaken by her eye trouble or by her husband's poor health that ended with his death later that year. Or she might have had in mind herself-as-poet, the same she described years earlier to her Norcross cousins in her surprise over Browning's writing a poem so soon after his wife's death, "till I remembered that I, myself, in my smaller way, sang off charnel steps."

Much has been made of Emily Dickinson's great years, when during the early 1860s she wrote, apparently, two or three hundred poems a year, only to find her creative powers (so the assumption seems to be) dwindling to almost nothing during the last two decades of her life. Perhaps the still-tentative dating of the poems needs revision. Perhaps much of her creative power went into her letters, only a fraction of which we have. At any rate, the Holland letters show no diminution in spirit or style to the very end. Emily remained as interested in the least detail of the Holland family as she was after the first rapturous visit in 1853. In the next-to-the-last letter (spring 1885), she is still playing her game with the Scriptures, still full of love for the whole family:

> To "gain the whole World" in the Evening Mail, without the baleful forfeit hinted in the Scripture, was indeed achievement – and I was led resisting to Bed, but Vinnie was firm as the Soudan – . . .
> Love for the "Holy Family," and say to the Son that the Little Boy in the Trinity had no Grandma, only a Holy Ghost –
> But you must go to Sleep, I, who sleep always, need no Bed.
> Foxes have Tenements, and remember, the Speaker was a Carpenter –

The last letter, probably written only a few months before she died and well after the symptoms of her final illness had become manifest, is as full as ever of interest and concern and wit. Mrs. Holland had gone to Florida for her rheumatism:

> Concerning the little sister, not to assault, not to adjure, but to obtain those constancies which exalt friends, we followed her to St. Augustine, since which the trail was lost, or says George Stearns [the Connecticut Valley humorist] of his alligator, "there was no such aspect."

She thanked her, with a quotation from "the great florist," for a gift of flowers, and begged for news of her friend—"any news of her as sweet as the first arbutus." The last sentence (the letter is unsigned) is a fitting benediction for the entire correspondence:

> Emily and Vinnie give the love greater every hour.

26

The Norcross Cousins

S TUDENTS OF DICKINSON annals have wondered why, in a correspondence that was continuous from 1859 to a few weeks before she died,
Emily Dickinson lavished such affection, wisdom, and wit on her two
cousins, Louise (or Louisa[1]) and Frances Norcross. Twelve and seventeen years her junior, they, of all her major correspondents, seem least to
merit such attention. Much of what we know about the sisters comes from
Mabel Loomis Todd's frustrating experience with them during the early
1890s when she was gathering materials for the *Letters* of 1894, and none of
it helps explain Emily's devotion. Mrs. Todd found them finicky, timid,
and dull; it was only through great tact and persuasion that she got them
to cooperate at all. An excerpt from her diary (August 9, 1894) during the
final stages of the work shows her irritation:

> Miss [Frances] Norcross here about 9:30, and we finished up the letters.
> She is alarmed at seeing her name in print, and thinks it will annihilate her
> sister – who is evidently attempting to copy Emily – and succeeding weakly.
> She has given me more fuss & trouble & silliness than all the rest of the
> book together.

In another entry she is at a loss to see what Emily ever saw in her
cousins:

> [August 11, 1894] At work on my miscellaneous chapter of E.D. . . . . The
> chapter came back from that dull, uninteresting, commonplace Miss Nor-
> cross. How Emily could have cared one particle for her I cannot imagine.

1. The name "Louise" appears in the 1955 *Poems* and the 1958 *Letters* throughout.
In all of Millicent Todd Bingham's writings on ED, it is "Louisa." Mrs. Bingham
apparently felt strongly about the matter and backed her opinion by a reference in
Austin's diary to "Louisa" (August 30, 1880); to a book of Whittier's poems presented to "Louisa" Norcross, February 13, 1861; and to several references to "Louisa"
in Edward Dickinson's letters (see *Home,* pp. 464, 469).

Summing up her experience in later years, she fairly exploded:

> They had the most intimate letters from Emily, but they wouldn't let any-body put their eyes on them. They copied them all. They would not send the originals. They made up their minds to destroy all they had of Emily's. They thought that they were the great patrons of Emily, but they were nothing of the kind. Louisa pretended to be a reticent person, out of the world like Emily. They adored her like a god. Vinnie wasn't devoted to the Norcrosses. They were such geese.

The letters Mrs. Todd finally got from them appeared in the 1894 volume heavily censored and addressed to "The Misses ———."

But Mabel Todd's words can hardly be the last. When she dealt with the Norcrosses, she was a vibrant, impatient young woman, with a project in which she was emotionally as well as professionally involved. Except for Austin, her relations with all Dickinsons and Dickinson connections were strained. She had met with many disappointments in gathering the letters, and this must have seemed the last straw. Further, she was free from many of the inhibitions of the older generation—especially, among the gentility of the time, its obsessive aversion to publicity. The Nor-crosses were well along in their spinsterhood, long since orphaned, and bearing to each other somewhat the same relation (as Jay Leyda points out) as Emily to Vinnie. Louise was small and "ethereal," as a friend described her, with ringlets all around her face. Fanny was "tall, stylish, quite like other people!" and "battled with the outer world" for both of them. She was the one who battled Mabel Todd. In answer to Mabel's inquiry, she wrote (August 1, 1894):

> I cannot send the letters, not because I fear they will be lost, but because my sister and I are not willing that any one even Vinnie should have the free reading of them; many of them have whole sentences which were in-tended for no eyes but ours, and on our account as well as Emily's no one else will ever read them.

In such a context Mrs. Todd's estimate of the Norcrosses must be qualified.

Clearly the first reason Emily turned so warmly to her young cousins was her devotion to their mother, the excellent Aunt Lavinia, who enter-tained the infant Emily at Monson during the weeks of Mrs. Dickinson's illness after Vinnie's birth. That visit was the beginning of a long and firm friendship. The correspondence that came of it, unhappily destroyed, would no doubt have told much about Emily's life through her twenties. When Aunt Lavinia died in 1860, Emily simply transferred her affection to the girls, then aged eighteen and thirteen. Her letter to Vinnie, who was with the Norcrosses in Cambridgeport after the death, shows, besides her own grief, how her heart went out to the cousins:

VINNIE —

I can't believe it, when your letters come, saying what Aunt Lavinia said "just before she died." Blessed Aunt Lavinia now; all the world goes out, and I see nothing but her room, and angels bearing her into those great countries in the blue sky of which we don't know anything.

Then I sob and cry till I can hardly see my way 'round the house again; and then sit still and wonder if she sees us now, if she sees *me,* who said that she "loved Emily." Oh! Vinnie, it is dark and strange to think of summer afterward! How she loved the summer! The birds keep singing just the same. Oh! The thoughtless birds!

Poor little Loo! Poor Fanny! You must comfort them. . . .

Louise, the older, had been Emily's special friend. It was with her, that October morning in 1858 in the Dickinson dining room, that Emily "decided to be distinguished"; she was "one of the ones [as Emily wrote in the letter that recalled the incident] from whom I do not run away!" But after their mother's death, most of Emily's letters went to both girls—she called them her "children," or "little children," or, in the last letter she wrote them (or anybody, as far as we know), "Little Cousins." Indeed, the first letter she wrote them after their mother died shows that part of the relationship which Mabel Todd failed to perceive (Eliza Coleman had chaperoned the girls at Commencement):

I knew she [Eliza] would guard my children, as she has often guarded me, from publicity, and help fill the deep place never to be full. Dear cousins, I know you both better than I did, and love you both better, and always I have a chair for you in the smallest parlor in the world, to wit, my heart.

In her own way, and at a distance, Emily assumed the role of mother, offering the girls complete, uncritical love and perpetual welcome. As Mabel Todd said, they "adored" her in return, and it is not surprising that they became protective when Mabel approached them about the letters.

In view of the many excisions the sisters made in the letters before releasing them, it is surprising to find as many intimacies in them as there are. Covering nearly twenty-seven years, they provide a more accurate barometer than the Holland letters of the fluctuations of Emily's inner life. Even here, however, she is seldom specific about causes, except about matters of general knowledge, like the war and deaths in the family circle. Her major relationships are scarcely mentioned. The Hollands enter only when Dr. Holland died and then only as "the dark man with the doll-wife." Bowles, Higginson, "H.H." go unnoticed. Judge Lord is vouch-safed only a tiny elegy:

Thank you, dears, for the sympathy. I hardly dare to know that I have lost another friend, but anguish finds it out.

> Each that we lose takes part of us;
> A crescent still abides,
> Which like the moon, some turbid night,
> Is summoned by the tides. [#1605]

The central concern of her life, the writing of her poems, is barely touched upon. Of course, it may have been assumed as common knowledge between them. Some twenty-five poems are sprinkled throughout the letters (or were sent with them), and Emily had confided to Louise in that dining-room conversation that it was "a great thing to be 'great' . . . [that] the orchard is full of birds, and we all can listen. What if we learn [to sing], ourselves, some day!" So Louise may have been in on the secret. Once, late in 1872, Emily wrote her about a request, perhaps for her poems, from a certain "Miss P———," identified tentatively as Elizabeth Stuart Phelps, editor of *The Woman's Journal,* a feminist, and a friend of Higginson's (who may have engineered the request). Apparently, Louise had been curious:

> Of Miss P——— I know but this, dear. She wrote me in October, requesting me to aid the world by my chirrup more. Perhaps she stated it as my duty, I don't distinctly remember, and always burn such letters, so I cannot obtain it now. I replied declining. She did not write to me again – she might have been offended, or perhaps is extricating humanity from some hopeless ditch. . . .

Such indifference to a matter so vital to her can be explained only by appealing to Emily's reticence, her tendency to hyperbole ("my chirrup more"), or, after the discouragements of the 1860s, perhaps to her determination (which weakened only slightly with Helen Hunt Jackson and Niles) to have no more to do with the publishing world. At least that part of the letter which has been preserved stops far short of taking Louise fully into her confidence. The only other possible reference to herself as poet (if we can take "work" to refer to her writing) came in a remark that concluded her little elegy on Judge Lord. Characteristically, the remark follows an ellipsis: ". . . I work to drive the awe away, yet awe impels the work." And that, in what we have of the letters, is all that bears upon the all-important subject.

Although Emily is never introspective for long in these letters, they give a sense of the range and quality of her moods. The tensions of the early 1860s come out clearly, if only in a phrase or two. She complains of friends who go and don't come back. "I've had a curious winter," she tells Louise in March 1860, "very swift, sometimes sober, for I haven't felt well, much, and March amazes me!" But the rest of the letter is about Louise as dear as the "apple of my eye," about the spring sleighing, Vinnie's absence, and about a carnation she is sending from her conservatory. A letter of the following December (the date is tentative) begins with a report that she feels "rather confused to-day, and the future looks 'higglety-pigglety,'" but the rest of it is, again, chatty and cheerful. It gives her longest declaration about matters of raiment—a salutary reminder to those who see her only as the Queen Recluse, dressed in white—by joking about a new cape the girls have made her:

> You seem to take a smiling view of my finery. If you knew how solemn it was to me, you might be induced to curtail your jests. My sphere is doubtless calicoes, nevertheless I thought it meet to sport a little wool. The mirth

it has occasioned will deter me from further exhibitions! Won't you tell "the public" that at present I wear a brown dress with a cape if possible browner, and carry a parasol of the same!

However uncertain the future may have looked, the tone of the letter is summed up in one of her final depositions: "We have at present one cat, and twenty-four hens, who do nothing so vulgar as lay an egg, which checks the ice-cream tendency."

Six months or so later, the tone was more somber. And so it remained for the better part of the decade: through the agonies of the Civil War, with its local losses in Frazar Stearns and the Widow Adams' boys; through the deaths of the girls' Aunt Lamira in 1862 and their father in 1863; through Emily's own trouble with her eyes in 1864 and 1865; and through various minor illnesses and vexations that Emily saw plaguing her "little children." A note dated tentatively 1868 (Louise is now twenty-six and Fanny twenty-one) shows the motherly concern that is the main theme of the letters:

> . . . Tell us all the load [of troubles]. Amherst's little basket is never so full but it holds more. That's a basket's cause. Not a flake assaults my birds but it freezes me. Comfort, little creatures – whatever befall us, this world is but this world. Think of that great courageous place we have never seen!

The somber tone of the decade is first manifest in a series of extracts from letters loosely dated by the Norcrosses as written in the spring of 1861. There are only two hints as to its source in Emily herself; mainly it seems to come from her concern over whatever it was that troubled her cousins. Although she fretted over "the seeing pain one can't relieve" and concluded that "Heaven is so cold!" and God parsimonious to deny "such little wishes" ("It could not hurt His glory, unless it were a lonesome kind"), exactly what the pain was, or even whose it was, the excerpt does not say. Apparently one of the girls, probably Louise, had complained of certain restrictions at home. In her reply, Emily fulfilled her own definition of a mother as "one to whom you hurry when you are troubled." Her comfort was to tell about two other girls who had known similar troubles:

> . . . Your letters are all real, just the tangled road children walked before you, some of them to the end, and others but a little way, even as far as the fork in the road. That Mrs. Browning fainted, we need not read *Aurora Leigh* to know, when she lived with her English aunt; and George Sand "must make no noise in her grandmother's bedroom." Poor children! Women, now, queens, now! And one in the Eden of God [EBB died June 29, 1861]. I guess they both forget that now, so who knows but we, little stars from the same night, stop twinkling at last? Take heart, little sister, twilight is but the short bridge, and the moon [morn?] stands at the end. If we can only get to her! Yet, if she sees us fainting, she will put out her yellow hands. When did the war really begin?

Just what she means by "the war"—specifically, whether she means anything larger by it than Louise's private war—is hard to tell. The possibly national, even cosmic, implications would indicate that she, too, was involved. The only other hint that the somber mood is her own is in one excerpt, set between ellipses, that may reveal more than the Norcrosses realized: ". . . Think Emily lost her wits – but she found 'em, likely. Don't part with wits long at a time in this neighborhood"—a remark which, if it has anything at all to do with her supposed breakdown of about this time (and it may), seems to tell more about the resilience of her wit and the sustaining discipline of the Dickinson home.

A moody letter, late in 1861, went to Louise, and this time the mood was Emily's, partly a touch of self-pity at Louise's announcement that she could not come to Amherst for a visit, partly the sorrow of the war brought home to Amherst by the death of the Adams boys. Emily "brushed away the sleet from eyes familiar with it" at Louise's announcement and indulged in a moment of unusual self-analysis (the ellipsis is the Norcrosses'): ". . . Odd, that I, who say 'no' so much, cannot bear it from others. Odd, that I, who run from so many, cannot brook that one turn from me." "Loo," she concluded, "I wanted you very much, and I put you by with sharper tears than I give to many." The elegy on Sylvester Adams (the "poor little widow's boy") that takes up much of the letter I have already cited as typical of the mortuary thoughts the war brought her. (She was only three months away from her first letter to Higginson and her involvement with the war on still another front.) As always, a particular death led her to death in general: "Ah! the dreamless sleep!" When Frazar Stearns was killed the following March (1862), she described the circumstances for the Norcrosses with a detail and an intensity of feeling that should lay to rest the notion of her indifference to such matters. The letter is one of her finest.

DEAR CHILDREN,

You have done more for me – 'tis least that I can do, to tell you of brave Frazer – "killed at Newbern," darlings. His big heart shot away by a "minie ball."

I had read of those – I didn't think that Frazer would carry one to Eden with him. Just as he fell, in his soldier's cap, with his sword at his side, Frazer rode through Amherst. Classmates to the right of him, and classmates to the left of him, to guard his narrow face! He fell by the side of Professor Clark, his superior officer – lived ten minutes in a soldier's arms, asked twice for water – murmured just, "My God!" and passed! Sanderson, his classmate, made a box of boards in the night, put the brave boy in, covered with a blanket, rowed six miles to reach the boat, – so poor Frazer came. They tell that Colonel Clark cried like a little child when he missed his pet, and could hardly resume his post. They loved each other very much. Nobody here could look on Frazer – not even his father. The doctors would not allow it.

The bed on which he came was enclosed in a large casket shut entirely, and covered from head to foot with the sweetest flowers. He went to sleep

from the village church. Crowds came to tell him good-night, choirs sang to him, pastors told how brave he was – early-soldier heart. And the family bowed their heads, as the reeds the wind shakes.

So our part in Frazer is done, but you must come next summer, and we will mind ourselves of this young crusader – too brave that he could fear to die. We will play his tunes – maybe he can hear them; we will try to comfort his broken-hearted Ella, who, as the clergyman said, "gave him peculiar confidence." . . . Austin is stunned completely. Let us love better, children, it's most that's left to do.

It was about this same time that she wrote Bowles, perhaps, as the Harvard editors suggest, using Austin's name as a cover, "Austin is chilled – by Frazer's murder – He says – his Brain keeps saying over 'Frazer is killed' – 'Frazer is killed,'" and she asked Bowles to help him get over the shock. Here, Austin is "stunned completely." The grief is deep but it is also composed; she herself is not "stunned"—a good example, perhaps, of how Emily could "work to drive the awe away." Perhaps even while writing her "little children," she could attain a higher level.

Emily was quite aware of her power in this regard, not only for herself but in her capacity to instill it in others. When Loring Norcross died in January 1863, her letters took much the same course, in their tenderness, tact, and gentle humor (the ellipses are mine):

Wasn't dear papa so tired always after mamma went, and wasn't it almost sweet to think of the two together these new winter nights? The grief is our side, darlings, and the glad is theirs. . . . When you have strength, tell us how it is, and what we may do for you, of comfort, or of service. . . . Good-night. Let Emily sing for you because she cannot pray:

> It is not dying hurts us so, –
> 'Tis living hurts us more;
> But dying is a different way,
> A kind, behind the door, –
> The southern custom of the bird
> That soon as frosts are due
> Adopts a better latitude.
> We are the birds that stay,
> The shiverers round farmers' doors,
> For whose reluctant crumb
> We stipulate, till pitying snows
> Persuade our feathers home. [*#335, late 1862*]

In later contexts of grief or illness she was more succinct: "Be sure you don't doubt about the sparrow." "Tell the doctor . . . I shall heal you quicker than he. You need the balsam word." After Mrs. Browning's death and Robert Browning's poem (the one which reminded her that she, too, sang off charnel steps), she ended a letter with a surge of spirit:

Adjutant Frazar Stearns

Main Street, looking [...] Phoenix Hall, Straw Works [...]

"Every day life feels mightier, and what we have the power to be, more stupendous." Much of this was no doubt motherly encouragement to the girls; some of it, perhaps, self-encouragement. In making the rough places smooth for her children, she may have smoothed out some places for herself. Assuming their burdens gave her an added strength. She wrote Louise in 1871: "Of the 'thorn,' dear, give it to me, for I am strongest. Never carry what I can carry, for though I think I bend, something straightens me."

The insistence in these letters and elsewhere on the need for play had its therapeutic side. It was during her father's illness in the spring of 1871 that Emily made, for Louise, the shrewd diagnosis of his trouble:

> Father was very sick. I presumed he would die, and the sight of his lone-some face all day was harder than personal trouble. He is growing better, though physically reluctantly. I hope I am mistaken, but I think his physical life don't want to live any longer. You know he never played, and the straightest engine has its leaning hour.

(It is worth noting that this letter preceded Edward Dickinson's death by three years; as most people saw it, his death was sudden, unexpected, coming at the height of his powers.) She recalled once her father's "militant Accent" when he led family prayers. Emily was perhaps the only one in the family who saw the Bible as a "merry" book, who insisted that it should have a "warbling Teller," and who believed (as she wrote Louise and Frances in 1861) "the love of God may be taught not to seem like bears." In the spring of 1881, which could hardly have been a lighthearted time for her, she wrote the girls the gayest of letters, concluding it with her famous Tenth Beatitude:

> We have had two hurricanes within as many hours, one of which came near enough to untie my apron – but this moment the sun shines, Maggie's hens are warbling, and a man of anonymous wits is making a garden in the lane to set out slips of bluebird. The moon grows from the seed. . . . Vinnie's pussy slept in grass Wednesday – a Sicilian symptom – the sails are set for summer, East India Wharf. Sage and saucy ones talk of an equinoctial, and are trying the chimneys, but I am "short of hearing," as the deaf say. Blessed are they that play, for theirs is the kingdom of heaven.

She seemed bent, too, on not letting her young charges miss the glories of the world around them. Part of this, surely, was the natural overflow of her own spirits, but some of it seems pure motherly concern. In July 1871 Louise received this rhapsody (actually, a lightly concealed poem) in a short letter otherwise occupied with minor details:

> This is a mighty morning. I trust that Loo is with it, on hill or pond or wheel. Too few the mornings be, too scant the nights. No lodging can be had for the delights that come to earth to stay, but no apartment find and ride away.

Whether the girls needed such prodding, we don't know. In late April 1873 they got it on two fronts, the glories of spring and another glory, of which they had apparently asked (timidly?) Aunt Emily's opinion:

Spring is a happiness so beautiful, so unique, so unexpected, that I don't know what to do with my heart. I dare not take it, I dare not leave it – what do you advise?

Life is a spell so exquisite that everything conspires to break it.

"What do I think of *Middlemarch?*" What do I think of glory – except that in a few instances this "mortal has already put on immortality."

George Eliot is one. The mysteries of human nature surpass the "mysteries of redemption," for the infinite we only suppose, while we see the finite. . . .

So, except for the periods of the deaths, she chatted and joked with her "little children" as blithely as if there were no clouds at all in her sky. Once, explaining a gap in her letters, she spoke of a "snarl in the brain which don't unravel yet" occasioned by domestic difficulties during Vinnie's absence; and, she added, "that old nail in my breast pricked me"—recalling the "Tomahawk in my side" of the third Master letter but with no more clue than she gave there. During the time of her trouble with her eyes, she wrote what she called "an ill and peevish" note to Louise, who censored all but the first sentence. But mostly she favored the girls with humor and wisdom and—more notably perhaps in these letters than in any except those to Austin—with some of her best satiric thrusts, mostly at the expense of members of the household, relatives, or near neighbors. Here, indeed, she "played." It was to the Norcrosses that she described Father as stepping "like Cromwell when he gets the kindlings"; Mother as Noah's dove coming in "with a burdock on her shawl, so we know that the snow has perished from the earth"; Vinnie as "spectacular as Disraeli and sincere as Gladstone"; and Maggie the cook as "warm and wild and mighty." A letter of October 7, 1863, opens in a melancholy way: "Nothing has happened but loneliness, perhaps too daily to relate"—but then she fairly scintillates, beginning with the dog Carlo and, before ending on a slightly plaintive note, covering almost everybody:

. . . Carlo is consistent, has asked for nothing to eat or drink, since you went away. Mother thinks him a model dog, and conjectures what he might have been, had not Vinnie "demoralized" him. Margaret [O'Brien] objects to furnace heat on account of bone decrepitudes, so I dwell in my bonnet and suffer comfortably. . . .

. . . No one has called so far, but one old lady to look at a house. I directed her to the cemetery to spare expense of moving.

I got down before father this morning, and spent a few moments profitably with the South Sea rose [Melville's *Typee?*]. Father detecting me, advised wiser employment, and read at devotions the chapter of the gentleman with one talent. I think he thought my conscience would adjust the gender.

Margaret washed to-day, and accused Vinnie of calicoes. I put her shoe and bonnet in to have them nice when she got home. . . . Cattle-show is to-morrow. The coops and committees are passing now. . . . Be good children, and mind the vicar. Tell me precisely how Wakefield looks, since I go not myself.

EMILY.

Later that month (October 1863, though the date is tentative) she wrote in the same vein, perhaps continuing her attempt to cheer up her cousins, who had lost their father that year, or perhaps to get over her own irritations by laughing at them. This time, Mother and the formidable Aunt Elisabeth Currier ("Libbie") bear the brunt:

. . . No frost at our house yet. Thermometer frost, I mean. Mother had a new tooth Saturday. You know Dr. S[tratton] had promised her one for a long time. "Teething" didn't agree with her, and she kept her bed, Sunday, with a face that would take a premium at any cattle-show in the land. Came to town next morning with slightly reduced features, but no eye on the left side. Doubtless we are "fearfully and wonderfully made," and occasionally grotesquely.

L[ibbie] goes to Sunderland, Wednesday, for a minute or two; leaves here at 6½ – what a fitting hour – and will breakfast the night before; such a smart atmosphere! The trees stand right up straight when they hear her boots, and will bear crockery wares instead of fruit, I fear. She hasn't starched the geraniums yet, but will have ample time, unless she leaves before April. Emily is very mean, and her children in dark mustn't remember what she says about damsel.

Aunt Libbie's visits were not a treat. Six years later, perhaps in the summer of 1869, she was almost surely the object of an even stiffer attack:

. . . J——— is coming to put away her black hair on the children's pillow.[2] I hoped she'd come while you were here, to help me with the starch, but Satan's ways are not as our ways. I'm straightening all the property, and making things erect and smart, and tomorrow, at twilight, her little heel boots will thump into Amherst. It being summer season she will omit the sleigh-bell gown, and that's a palliative. Vinnie is all disgust, and I shall have to smirk for two to make the manners even.

The last sentence is another good example, on the family level, of Dickinson discipline. But in essence it shares something with the discipline by which, on a higher level, Emily Dickinson achieved the perspective of the satirist, as in these letters, and, on the highest, with the discipline that produced her poems. As far back as school days, Emily was known for her wit, and she never lost it. But it needed cultivation. If she was glorying in a native skill in such passages, she was also exercising a control that in its highest manifestation saved her.

2. The Norcrosses transcribed the initial letter of the name of the expected visitor, whom they, or Emily, preferred to keep anonymous, as "J———"; but as the 1958 editors suggest, the "J" was probably a misreading of "L."

Only twice did Amherst piety come under the knife, the same piety against which Emily defended herself in the early letters to Jane Humphrey and Abiah Root. Then she had felt guilty and depressed at her rebellion; here, in her maturity, she showed no compunction. Her next-door neighbor, the pious (and ample) Mrs. Luke Sweetser, was simply comic: "Mrs. S[weetser] gets bigger, and rolls down the lane to church like a reverend marble." Three years later (April 1873) she is the star:

> . . . There is that which is called an "awakening" in the church, and I know of no choicer ecstasy than to see Mrs. [Sweetser] roll out in crape every morning, I suppose to intimidate antichrist; at least it would have that effect on me. It reminds me of Don Quixote demanding the surrender of the wind-mill, and of Sir Stephen Toplift, and of Sir Alexander Cockburn.

In the early 1880s Amherst was plagued with a series of fires. A serious one, in April 1881, did great damage to Phoenix Row, the main business section in town, where Austin had his office. Emily described for her cousins the "night of terror": ". . . I could not rise. The others bore it better. The brook from Pelham saved the town. . . . We are weak and grateful." But in the very next sentence she has recovered, with a satiric assist from Thoreau: "The fire-bells are oftener now, almost, than the church-bells. Thoreau would wonder which did the most harm."

Very little is known about Emily's sojourns with the Norcrosses in their Cambridgeport boardinghouse from April through November 1864, and again from April 1 to sometime in October 1865. During this dismal time the trouble with her eyes precluded much writing. Only ten letters, all brief, survive from the first visit; only two from the second. "Loo and Fanny," she wrote Vinnie shortly after she arrived for the first time, "take sweet care of me, and let me want for nothing, but I am not at Home, and the calls at the Doctor's are painful, and dear Vinnie, I have not looked at the Spring." Later: "Fanny and Loo are solid Gold, Mrs Bangs and her Daughter [who ran the boardinghouse] very kind, and the Doctor enthusiastic about my getting well – I feel no gayness yet. I suppose I had been discouraged so long." Without her writing, or housework, or the Amherst countryside, she felt imprisoned. A brief note to Higginson written in early June 1864 spoke in that metaphor. The doctor, she wrote, "does not let me go, yet I work in my Prison, and make Guests for myself—" She incorporated a poem in the letter:

> The only News I know
> Is Bulletins all day
> From Immortality.   [#827, 1864]

And added: "Can you render my Pencil? The Physician has taken away my Pen." Again one can assume that by "work" she meant writing poetry and that the "Guests" she made for herself and the "Bulletins from Immortality" are her poems, or ideas for them. Whether Louise and

Fanny were a party to this, we do not know; but someone, at least, must have supplied the pencil and paper. Once, Clara and Anna Newman came from Amherst and the Evergreens to see her, and once she wrote to Vinnie that, like Elijah and the ravens, "I have found friends in the Wilderness."

Perhaps the Norcrosses brought friends in to see her. For all Mabel Todd said about their dullness in the 1890s, the girls, in their prime, had interesting friends. Either then or later, the list included the John Dudleys, whom they visited in Middletown, Connecticut, and later in Milwaukee—he on the way to being one of the most successful and controversial preachers of his day, she the former Eliza Coleman, who understood Emily as few did; Daniel Chester French, the sculptor, known to the Dickinson circle when his father was president of the Massachusetts Agricultural College in Amherst from 1865 to 1876; and, above all, Maria Whitney, independent and bluestocking, the least likely to tolerate bores. As early as 1861, Maria was in correspondence with Louise, one of whose letters to Maria (in an interesting reversal of roles) Emily addressed and forwarded. The friendship may not have been intimate, but it was cordial. On March 1, 1875, Maria wrote her brother about an invitation "from Miss Fanny Norcross" to spend Sunday with them before the Concord Centennial—"which of course [she wrote] I shall be delighted to do. I am anticipating it all with the greatest pleasure." Apparently the expectation was high on both sides, and at least one was not disappointed. That summer, Emily wrote her cousins, adding a thought she wove into many poems: "I am glad that you loved Miss Whitney on knowing her nearer. Charlotte Brontë said 'Life is so constructed that the event does not, cannot, match the expectation.'" It was during those years, the mid-1870s, when Maria was established in Northampton, that Emily (or so reported Maria's niece, Miss Emily Whitney of New Haven) was in the habit of sending a carriage to Northampton to bring Maria to Amherst for visits, another indication that Emily's seclusion was not impenetrable. "I know each moment of Miss W[hitney]," she wrote the cousins in 1884, "is a gleam of boundlessness. 'Miles and miles away,' said Browning, 'there's a girl'; but 'the colored end of evening smiles' on but few so rare." She ended the letter with "a kiss besides for Miss W[hitney]'s cheek, should you again meet her." So, although there is no hint that Maria visited Emily in Cambridgeport, Emily and the Norcrosses enjoyed some friends in common, some of whom, perhaps, enlightened those dreary months in "the Wilderness" (which for Emily, of course, was any place not Amherst).

Nor were the Norcrosses as "dull" and "silly" as Mabel Todd found them when it came to what Emily called the "strongest friends of the soul – BOOKS." Emily quoted freely and happily to them, her allusions ranging from the Bible and Shakespeare to the latest poem by Mr. Lowell or Mr. Lathrop. She was solicitous, in a motherly way, about their reading. A month or so before she died, she ended a letter that included both kinds of friends: "Are you reading and well, and the W[hitney]s near and warm? When you see Mrs. French and Dan give them a tear from us." The curiosity was mutual: once Louise asked her what books she was "wooing now – " The Bible was handy at all times, but not (for whatever it may mean) used nearly as often as in the Holland letters. Nor are the allusions to reading of any sort quite so sophisticated and arch. She was more likely in these letters to label her quotations and, consciously or unconsciously, to shorten or simplify them. A paragraph from a letter of about 1880 gives good examples of all these devices:

> When Macbeth asked the physician what could be done for his wife, he made the mighty answer, "That sort must heal itself" [from "Therein the patient / Must minister to himself"]; but, sister, that was guilt, and love, you know, is God, who certainly "gave the love to reward the love," even were there no Browning [who wrote, in "Evelyn Hope," ". . . creates the love to reward the love"].

It is clear that the three cousins read the same magazines (*Harper's* and the *Atlantic*) and enjoyed the same novels—those mentioned are all contemporary except *The Vicar of Wakefield* and *Don Quixote*. While the allusions come less frequently than in the letters to Mrs. Holland—the correspondence is decidedly less literary—Dickens is there, and George Eliot several times (once Louise is called "Mrs. Ladislaw"). At one point Emily reports that "Vinnie has a new pussy the color of Branwell Brontë's hair." Bret Harte appears unexpectedly in an elaborate reference to "Miggles" and the character Oakhurst in "The Outcasts of Poker Flat"— all to explain Maggie's welcome decision to stay with the Dickinsons. Browning appears most often, Keats only once, and Mrs. Browning's *Aurora Leigh* is assumed to be common knowledge. The girls are once thanked for buying books for her at "Burnham,"[3] and Emily regrets that she could not share their delight in a reading of Shakespeare by Fanny Kemble and (much later) a recital by the pianist Anton Rubinstein.

The Norcrosses were not, then, such inconsiderable people as Mabel Todd and our ignorance traditionally have them. We would like to know more about them and someday we may, although the destruction of the manuscripts, on each side by request, has cut off the main source. Emily's fondness for her cousins went beyond the loyalty of kinship; she could cut a near relative out of her life as easily as a boring neighbor. They were a resource to her in many ways. They were adoring, uncritical, but perceptive enough to delight in her wit, enjoy her poems, and understand (up to a certain point, it seems) her problems. We can only lament the loss of those sentences that Fanny insisted were "intended for no eyes but ours."

---

3. The Burnham Antique Book Shop was "an established Boston store" (*L* II, 368 n.). Apparently, Fanny was a frequent shopper for Emily, who wrote: " 'Burnham' must think Fanny a scholastic female. I wouldn't be in her place! If she feels delicate about it, she can tell him the books are for a friend in the East Indies."

Emily thought enough of "her children" to favor them with some of her profoundest thoughts, which she would hardly have expended on "geese." On their Aunt Lamira's death in the spring of 1862—Aunt Lamira, who died young, leaving husband, babies, "big life and sweet home by the sea" (as Emily wrote)—Emily permitted herself one anguished cry, as purely tragic as anything she ever wrote: "I wish 'twas plainer, Loo, the anguish in this world. I wish one could be sure the suffering had a loving side." Mrs. Edward Hitchcock's death in 1863 moved her to a somewhat oracular statement, a test of the girls' comprehension. It was preceded by an episode of the funeral whose symbolic import Emily's aphorism may have been an attempt to sum up.

> Jennie Hitchcock's mother was buried yesterday, so there is one orphan more, and her father is very sick besides. My father and mother went to the service, and mother said while the minister prayed, a hen with her chickens came up, and tried to fly into the window. I suppose the dead lady used to feed them, and they wanted to bid her good-by.
> Life is death we're lengthy at, death the hinge to life.

Much depends here on whether the door—that is, death—is to be imagined as opening or closing on its hinge. The hen and chickens (it was spring) suggest life, surely, on this earth, which Mrs. Hitchcock helped prolong, and which insisted upon being prolonged even after her death. It was not much of a stretch to transfer such insistence to the notion of life beyond death. Ten years later, Emily wrote Frances: "A finite life, little sister, is that peculiar garment that were it optional with us we might decline to wear." Part of what she called the "skill of life," as she told both girls that spring, was to see this life in terms of the infinite:

> SISTERS,
> I hear robins a great way off, and wagons a great way off, and rivers a great way off, and all appear to be hurrying somewhere undisclosed to me. Remoteness is the founder of sweetness; could we see all we hope, or hear the whole we fear told tranquil, like another tale, there would be madness near. Each of us gives or takes heaven in corporeal person, for each of us has the skill of life.

One of her missions with her little cousins, then, was to cultivate in them the skill of life to see the door of death as hinging *open*.

When her own mother died in November 1882, her letter to the Norcrosses, besides being one of the most beautiful the event produced, contains one of her most explicit credos. Her own "skill" was obviously being tested severely. The letter hardly shows the "quiet confidence" that has been attributed to it; although the door to eternity is still open, she is far from peaceful about what lies beyond. But it is significant that one of her first attempts to write, as she says, "intuitively" about her mother's death went to the Norcrosses. One would give much to know what the ellipses (which are theirs) contained.

DEAR COUSINS,

I hoped to write you before, but mother's dying almost stunned my spirit.

I have answered a few inquiries of love, but written little intuitively. She was scarcely the aunt you knew. The great mission of pain had been ratified – cultivated to tenderness by persistent sorrow, so that a larger mother died than had she died before. There was no earthly parting. She slipped from our fingers like a flake gathered by the wind, and is now part of the drift called "the infinite."

We don't know where she is, though so many tell us.

I believe we shall in some manner be cherished by our Maker – that the One who gave us this remarkable earth has the power still farther to surprise that which He has caused. Beyond that all is silence. . . .

Mother was very beautiful when she had died. Seraphs are solemn artists. The illumination that comes but once paused upon her features, and it seemed like hiding a picture to lay her in the grave; but the grass that received my father will suffice his guest, the one he asked at the altar to visit him all his life.

I cannot tell how Eternity seems. It sweeps around me like a sea. . . . Thank you for remembering me. Remembrance – mighty word.

"Thou gavest it to me from the foundation of the world."

Lovingly,

EMILY.

After this, there is a gap of a year and a half in the letters we have, and there are only a half dozen to the end. Surely she must have written her cousins about Gilbert's death eleven months after her mother's, or about Willie Dickinson's—another cousin she loved—in May 1883, letters which the Norcrosses perhaps lost or refused to show to Mabel Todd. After the note about Judge Lord's death in March 1884, the few remaining are shadowed by her illness. One in mid-summer 1884 contains the most extended account, in any of her letters, of her first seizure, her blackout on June 14.

Eight Saturday noons ago, I was making a loaf of cake with Maggie, when I saw a great darkness coming and knew no more until late at night. I woke to find Austin and Vinnie and a strange physician bending over me, and supposed I was dying, or had died, all was so kind and hallowed. I had fainted and lain unconscious for the first time in my life. Then I grew very sick and gave the others much alarm, but am now staying. The doctor calls it "revenge of the nerves"; but who but Death had wronged them?

By Death, of course, she means the deaths, her mother's, Lord's, Gilbert's, and the rest—especially Gilbert's, it seems, in view of her concluding words, which follow. The poem at the end sums up the second of the major "skills" she would teach her children. After Frazar Stearns's death she had written them: "Let us love better, children, it's most that's left to do." One of her lessons to them had been the interdependence of human beings: "I suppose [she wrote in 1873] the wild flowers encourage themselves in the dim woods, and the bird that is bruised limps to his house in silence, but we have human natures, and these are different." So she concludes the letter:

The little boy we laid away never fluctuates, and his dim society is companion still. But it is growing damp and I must go in. Memory's fog is rising.

> The going from a world we know
> To one a wonder still
> Is like the child's adversity
> Whose vista is a hill,
> Behind the hill is sorcery
> And everything unknown,
> But will the secret compensate
> For climbing it alone?   [#1603]

The Norcrosses, younger, less gifted, hardly it seems in her world at all, nonetheless mitigated the loneliness of the climb. Their companionship, on whatever level, was steady and sure. One way of estimating its value to her is to imagine her collected letters with none to the "little cousins."

27

Otis Phillips Lord

THROUGHOUT THESE MANY CHAPTERS, we have seen so much of the Dickinson genius for keeping private affairs private that it should come as no surprise that the final, climactic, and by far the most securely documented of all Emily Dickinson's so-called love affairs contains almost as many mysteries as the others. At least in this instance it is clear that Emily Dickinson was in love and that she was loved in return. Her letters to Otis Lord, though only a few survive, and those in scraps and heavily censored drafts, prove this beyond doubt. Although we have no letters from him to her, there are enough comments by members of both families to show that the love was mutual. But none of them indicates when it began, by what stages it grew, or, in spite of several hints in Emily's letters, whether marriage was seriously contemplated. What is perhaps most mysterious of all is how Emily became so passionately involved with this distinguished public figure—Rufus Choate called him "one of the very ablest men in this State [Massachusetts]"—eighteen years her senior and in many ways her polar opposite.

We should approach these final mysteries from the perspective of all that has gone before. If we have met with little but bafflement as to the specifics of Emily Dickinson's affairs of the heart—the time, the duration, the degree of reciprocity, at times the identity of the beloved—it should be clear by now that, satisfying as it would be to have all such questions answered, by far the greater value lies in the letters and poems these relationships produced. Perhaps it was the woman in her, perhaps it was simply a basic human need, but all her life Emily Dickinson needed an object, a person, on whom she could focus her creative powers. (In this light, one hesitates to write off the recipient of the Master letters as only a figure of her fantasy.) Vinnie, probably with little idea of the full meaning of her remark, said that Emily was always on the lookout for "the rewarding person."

Vinnie may have been on the edge here of the ancient notion of the Muse, or whatever it was that "loosened the spirit." Emily could, and did, operate on her own a good part of her life; but she seems always to have been grateful to anyone who would spark a poem in her or inspire a letter. At first it was Sue or Austin or Abiah Root or Jane Humphrey or any of the young people, male and female, she wrote to with almost equal intensity. Later she turned to people of a quite different sort, most of them impossibly out of her reach—Samuel Bowles, "Master," Wadsworth, Higginson. In the many poems of inner dialogue from the middle years on, she turned increasingly to her own "Columnar Self." It sustained her, but often precariously. In moments of what seem like agony, when all else failed, she turned to "Jesus Christ of Nazareth." In moments of apparent ecstasy—whether of revelation or despair—she seems to have imagined herself in the ancient role of the Bride of Christ:

> Given in Marriage unto Thee
> Oh thou Celestial Host –
> Bride of the Father and the Son
> Bride of the Holy Ghost.
>
> Other Betrothal shall dissolve –
> Wedlock of Will, decay –
> Only the Keeper of this Ring
> Conquer Mortality –   (*#817, about 1864*)

Whether Emily lived out such an imagining to the end, whether she would have defined herself ultimately as one so dedicated, is a mystery and perhaps always will be. Only, as we come to this final chapter of her life, involving a very real ring and the possibility of a real marriage, we must keep everything in lively suspension. And most of all, of course, the one unfailing constant in her life, from beginning to end, her poetry. This was her ". . . Fortune – / Exterior – to Time – "

But the very real—and worldly—Judge Otis Phillips Lord of Salem, longtime friend of the family and the man Emily once referred to as "my father's closest friend," her last "Preceptor" (as she once called him), was, miraculously, *within* her reach. Miraculously, because to the casual observer the odds would seem to be so heavily against it.

Lord graduated from Amherst in 1832, when Emily was in the second year of her life. He went directly into the study of the law, reading in Oliver Morris's office in Springfield and later studying at Harvard. He was admitted to the Essex County bar in 1835 and set up practice in Ipswich. In 1843 he married Elizabeth Farley, a descendant of President Leverett of Harvard. The couple moved to Salem, where they lived for the rest of their lives. There were no children. Until his judicial duties interrupted it, Lord enjoyed there a "wide and lucrative" practice of the law. He was appointed judge of the newly formed Superior Court of

Massachusetts in 1859 and an Associate Justice of the Supreme Judicial Court of the State in 1875. From about 1846 until the early 1860s he was active in state politics, five years in the House of Representatives, of which he was Speaker in 1854, and one term in the State Senate. He developed a formidable reputation. In an article of March 29, 1853, the *Springfield Republican* saw him as "the acknowledged leader of the House," a man of "vigorous intellect . . . force of character . . . a powerful and pungent debater," who is "severe in his logic, blighting in his sarcasm, and audacious in his denunciations, and always armed, at all points, either for defense or attack."

Although none of Lord's periods of service in the General Court coincided with Edward Dickinson's, they were both die-hard Whigs, and it may have been this common bond, together with Lord's interest in Amherst College (he helped raise $25,000 in 1847), that brought the two together in close friendship. There is no evidence, though the possibility cannot be excluded, that there was any connection between Lord and the Dickinsons during his undergraduate years or until the fund-raising in 1847, which involved Edward Dickinson as treasurer. The thought that Lord might have dandled Emily on his knee during her early childhood, suggested by the line in the third Master letter—"Low at the knee that bore her once unto wordless rest Daisy kneels a culprit"—has no external support, tempting as it is as a solution to the identity of "Master."[1]

During the 1850s Lord established himself as the leading Whig in Massachusetts. His reputation as an orator grew steadily. He was the leading speaker at a "grand whig rally" on November 3, 1853, in Northampton, a meeting that Edward Dickinson may have attended. Later that year, an editorial in the *Republican* (for December 8) spoke of Lord's election as Speaker of the House "by apparently universal whig consent." He again addressed the Whigs at their State Convention in Worcester on October 2, 1855, which we know Edward Dickinson attended.[2] It was in this speech that, to "loud cheers," Lord made his famous utterance. "The great heart of Massachusetts is Whig to the core." Next year (October 8, 1856), he addressed a Whig rally in Faneuil Hall, Boston, in a long election-year speech—later separately printed—resounding with Whig principles and punctuated again and again by "cheers," "laughter and cheers," "applause," and "tremendous applause." Admitting the divided opinions among Whigs, Lord came out strongly, but of course hopelessly, for Millard Fillmore and "moderation." What might have been a brilliant political career was cut short by the disintegration, by then well along, of the Whig Party. In his stubborn loyalty, Lord was left, like Edward Dickinson, whose mind "ran in much the same groove," a man without a party. Four times, the last as late as 1874, his friends put him forward for

1. This theory is developed at length by John Evangelist Walsh in *The Hidden Life of Emily Dickinson.*
2. With Professor W. C. Fowler (Emily's father) and L. M. Hills, Edward Dickinson was one of the three delegates from Amherst (*YH* I, 335).

elective office; once he declined "on grounds of political principle," three times he was defeated.

But Lord remained, again like Edward Dickinson, a man of consequence in the state. When he was Speaker of the House in 1854, three bills had come up in which we can imagine the two men sharing an interest: the ten-hour-day bill, a reform that Representative Dickinson was then arguing in Washington for the national armory in Springfield, where, as in industry, the employees worked twelve hours a day, six days a week; the incorporation of the Amherst Savings Bank; and the Hoosac Tunnel bill, which Edward Dickinson was still urging, twenty years later, in Boston, on the day he died. In 1857 Lord and Dickinson sat in Northampton on a commission to adjudicate (according to the *Springfield Republican*) "matters at issue between the Connecticut River and the Canal railroads."

Lord's appointment to the Superior Court in 1859 brought him at least twice a year, in April and October, to Northampton; and it may have been then that cordial relations between the families began. What casts doubt about the intimacy of the families before then is an entry in Mrs. Lord's diary for June 9, 1860, recording a visit to Amherst from Northampton. She speaks as if she, at least, were meeting the Dickinsons for the first time (it is unlikely that Lord would have made all his previous visits to Amherst—he is said to have attended Amherst reunions faithfully—without her):

> Fine clear day – Got ready & started with Otis for Amherst at 1/4 to 9. Fine ride rather cool thick shawl necessary, buggy top down – Called on Bina [Montague] & sister, found them about as usual. Went over the colleges with Mr Dickinson, dined with him found his wife & daughter pleasant back to N[orthampton] at 5 1/2.

Which daughter Mrs. Lord meant and what that daughter's response was to the distinguished visitors are matters lost, it seems, to history. In view of Emily's current preoccupations and tendencies, Mrs. Lord probably meant Vinnie, though for either daughter the word "pleasant" is curiously colorless.

Two years later (July 9, 1862), Lord was one of the Commencement speakers at Amherst, an event—to indicate the importance of such matters at the time—announced in the *Springfield Republican* seven months in advance (December 16, 1861). Some time before this, there had been at least one sign that Lord's popularity in western Massachusetts was not solid, and apparently the speech did little to advance it. The *Republican* for May 18, 1859, had suggested that the unanimous approval by his fellow Essex County lawyers of Lord's appointment to the Superior Court was perhaps motivated less by admiration of Lord's qualities than by a desire to inherit his large and lucrative practice. The Commencement speech, as reported by Dr. Holland in the *Republican,* gave some indication of what those qualities were:

Mr. Lord is a graduate of the class of 1832, and is well known in the state and throughout the country as a prominent eastern Massachusetts politician of the old Whig school, and the disturbed state of the country placed public expectation on tiptoe to hear something connected with the war. Nor were the audience disappointed in the theme, though the radically conservative, not to say intensely hunkerish view of affairs, was unexpected, and did not elicit any very warm response either in the minds or heels of the hearers. . . .

A sample of Lord's hunkerism followed his description (summarized by Holland) of the good old days when the country was "a city set on a hill, a light to nations":

But . . . uneasy men, in all parts of the country, disturbed the peace. They saw spots on the sun, and would remove them even at the risk of blotting out that sun. There were tares among the wheat, and they would root them out even at the risk of pulling up the wheat. It is our duty to see that the wheat is not rooted up.

This "duty" was the vigorous prosecution of the war, the restoration of law and order under the Constitution. Ignorant civilian criticism of the military should cease. Lord "spoke most feelingly" (Holland reported) of the death of Frazar Stearns, but his praise of the "young and gallant McClellan" evoked "the only genuine and hearty applause of the occasion."

Another speaker that Commencement Day was Henry Ward Beecher. Holland found a striking contrast between the two. Beecher's speech (to the literary societies of the college) was

the exact counterpart of the forenoon's performance in every particular. Lord was hunkerish, unmagnetic, unpopular; Beecher was eloquent, earnest and right, and carried away the sympathies of the audience with him by storm.

It is difficult to explain Holland's vigorous preference for Beecher's speech, since both Lord and Beecher spoke on the same theme and both were strong for the war, the Union, and the Constitution. The difference, as Holland reported the speeches, was in emphasis and style—Lord emphasizing the need to return to the values of the past, Beecher the need to understand the problems of readjustment, even basic Constitutional ones, once the war was over and the slaves freed. Beecher's style was more personal, occasionally poetic. He defended his choice of subject, employing a phrase that, perhaps, found its way permanently into the consciousness of at least one poetic listener (or reader).

The speaker said it might be expected, perhaps, that he would choose a literary subject, but we are so near the edge of revolution that public questions must take precedence, and he must be indulged while he treated of the questions of the hour which are passing through a storm and an earthquake: the storm in the North, and the earthquake in the South. . . .

If Emily Dickinson's appeal to "Jesus Christ of Nazareth" actually owes a line to Beecher's rhetoric, her agonized poem can be read in a new and illuminating context:

> At least – to pray – is left – is left –
> Oh Jesus – in the Air –
> I know not which thy chamber is –
> I'm knocking – everywhere –
>
> Thou settest Earthquake in the South –
> And Maelstrom, in the Sea –
> Say, Jesus Christ of Nazareth –
> Hast thou no Arm for Me?[3] (*#502, early 1862*)

Lord's speech in the morning had reminded all Amherst of Frazar Stearns's death only four months before. Beecher's eloquence was powerful and could be upsetting. He had spoken of the threat of a draft—which would involve Austin. He was a clergyman and might have urged prayer (although Holland did not report it). The poem, itself a prayer, might have been Emily's answer.

Since Lord's speech came in the very center of the five-year gap in Emily's correspondence with the Hollands, her feelings about Dr. Holland's severe criticism are not known. The episode of that Commencement Day serves, if nothing else, to show how close she lived to the stirring events of her times. Amherst was no backwater. As to her feelings about Lord, had she been in love with her father's "hunkerish" friend at that time—even, as has been maintained, to the point of addressing the Master letters to him—Holland's opinions would have hurt her deeply. Although she must have been aware of the political differences between her two friends, no hint of such a hurt appears once the correspondence was resumed, and by the time Emily's surviving letters to Lord began, during the late 1870s, her relations with the Hollands were unclouded.

There is no doubt that Lord was a success as a judge, although the nature and degree of his success appear to have depended on what side of the political fence the observer sat. Edward Dickinson seems to have admired Lord extravagantly (for him), and Austin thought him the best judge in the Commonwealth. When he was elevated to the Massachusetts Supreme Court in 1875, the *Newburyport Herald,* in an article reprinted in the *Republican,* called him "the greatest common-law judge Massachusetts has ever had upon the bench of an inferior court" and deplored the "injustice which has kept [him] for 16 years" from the Supreme Court. But when it was suggested that his portrait be painted for the county court house in Salem to celebrate his elevation, a signed document of

---

3. If Emily's "Earthquake in the South" is an echo of Beecher's speech, then the date given the poem in the 1955 *Poems,* "early 1862," must be changed to the summer or autumn of 1862.

protest was submitted to the county commissioners by the District Attorney and "several other prominent lawyers," asserting [said the *Republican*] "that Lord's qualities are not such as fit him to be a judge, and that there is more complaint against him than against any other judge on the bench." A startling incident in 1872 had been reported by the *New York Independent*. Judge Lord sent "Dr James McDonough, a Catholic witness, to jail because he refused to kiss the Book, preferring to 'affirm' with the uplifted hand." The *Independent* was shocked to find that "barbarism of this sort was permitted in the courts of Massachusetts." Lord had long been known as a judge of strict principles and harsh sentences. In 1866, the House of Representatives in Boston viewed with "indignation" Lord's intended proceedings—"severe," "anti-Republican"— against those indicted in the Essex County riot case.[4] (The report of this anti-Lord sentiment appeared in the "Boston Letter" in the *Springfield Republican* on the very day, February 14, 1866, that the *Republican* carried Emily Dickinson's "The Snake"—"A narrow Fellow in the Grass"—on its front page.) Lord was notoriously hard on divorce seekers, and he could be a terror in cross-examination. An eyewitness reported:

> I remember to have heard him cross examine a defendant, who had offered himself as a witness in a criminal case, where he assisted the Government

4. The case involved the tarring and feathering of "a painter by the name of Stone," who "on the day when news of assassination of Pres. Lincoln reached S[wampscott] . . . said he was glad of it, and it was the best news he had heard for many a day, or words to that effect" (*Springfield Republican,* February 15, 1866). Stone sued the leaders and got a verdict of $800. Judge Lord reopened the case in the Superior Court in Salem, bringing indictments for riot. The *Republican,* through its Boston correspondent "Warrington" (William S. Robinson), discussed the case vigorously during the month of February. The paper was solidly against Lord, accusing him of party bias, of instituting a "bloody assize," of "feed[ing] fat his ancient grudges against the republicans" and determining to "put the culprits through at railroad speed" (*SR,* February 21). The popular sentiment against Lord's proceedings was echoed in the House of Representatives in Boston, and the issue became one of Legislative vs. Judicial authority. The furor subsided by the end of the month. In the February 26 issue, Warrington wrote: "A good deal might be said, and with reason, on both sides. . . . The mob was clearly wrong. . . . But the fact that the Swampscott people were wrong does not make it right to persecute them for political purposes." Lord's political bias, very different from Samuel Bowles's liberalism, which the *Republican* reflected, was only asserted, not proved. Warrington went so far as to say, in his February 26 statement, "But sometimes the mob is right." It can be said with some confidence that Lord never would have agreed to that. Warrington, incidentally, became a cherished writer for ED, not because of his political views, but for his confident belief in immortality. In a letter to Sue about 1884 (*L* III, 828 and n.) she speaks of a volume missing from "my Treasures." She calls it "the Warrington Words," probably a reference to his *Pen-Portraits* (1877), a posthumous collection of his writings. The editors of the 1958 *Letters* quote a sentence from *Pen-Portraits* (p. 162): "This life is so good, that it seems impossible for it to be wholly interrupted by death," and find it an apt explanation of Emily's concluding remark to Sue in the letter: "Remember, Dear, an unfaltering *Yes* is my only reply to your utmost question – "

Judge Otis Phillips Lord

Judge Lord

in the prosecution. That cross examination was terrific; his sudden and powerful mental grip so checked the witness' circulation that he fainted.

An editorial in the *Boston Transcript* the day after he died (March 14, 1884) described him as "a marked man in appearance, of a decidedly controversial taste, with sledge-hammer powers of expression, which he wielded relentlessly when moved thereto." Others pointed to his unimpressive learning ("his temperament was always too impatient for much research") but praised his sharp eye for fallacies, his overriding of procedural niceties when they impeded justice, and his "robust common sense." Like him or dislike him, they all agreed on his power and his authority. This was the man whom Emily Dickinson, in her late forties, called "My lovely Salem," "my Darling," "My Sweet One," "my Church."

As she had with her father, Emily Dickinson saw much more than the public side of Otis Lord, and, in both men, a paradox. "River God" as Edward Dickinson might have been to the people of western Massachusetts, to his daughter he was lonely, misunderstood, often bewildered, sometimes comical, and a little pathetic. In a letter shortly after Lord's death, Emily summed up the paradox in her "Salem": "Calvary and May wrestled in his Nature." Since we know of no other major source of suffering or tension in his life, what she meant by Calvary was probably close to the vulnerable point in her father's character, as she saw it: his too strict attention to duty and his tendency to overwork. We recall her remark about her father: "He never played, and the straightest engine has its leaning hour." About Lord she wrote: "Abstinence from Melody was what made him die." Apparently Lord was one of those vigorous, hearty men who work until they drop. He had almost dropped in the winter of 1876, his first on the Supreme Court. On April 28, the *Newburyport Herald,* as quoted in the *Republican,* welcomed his return to the court after "his recent severe illness" and gave an inkling, perhaps, of what Emily called the "Melody" in his nature when the writer rejoiced in "his returning animal spirits, his restless manner and bonhomie. . . ." In 1881, three years before he died, the *Republican,* which kept a careful eye on his health, reported him in such bad shape that "he can no longer read or write and his work is much behindhand," and yet a month later (April 17, 1881) he presided over the Supreme Court session in Northampton and spent a day at the Austin Dickinsons'. He recovered sufficiently from an "alarming illness" in the spring of 1882 (which threw Emily into a panic) to continue his judicial work for the better part of a year. While it cannot quite be said that he died in harness, like Edward Dickinson, he kept on nearly to the end. A stroke carried him off on March 13, 1884, aged seventy-two.

Besides his political speeches, there is one extended bit of writing by Lord that throws some light on his character and, perhaps, what it was that Emily found so compelling in him. In a Memorial Address of some thirteen thousand words delivered at the Essex Institute in Salem on September 5, 1871, he eulogized a much-beloved local dignitary, Asahel Huntington. Huntington was an Essex County lawyer, served the county as prosecuting officer and later as District Attorney, and was twice elected to the Massachusetts House of Representatives. In 1854 he became Mayor of Salem and served a short term. But his personal qualities were what interested Lord most. The address concluded with Washington Irving's description of Sir Walter Scott—that "golden hearted man."

The address was no mere sentimental eulogy. It was a careful estimate of a career and a character, from Huntington's origins in an "unmixed Puritan stock" and hard-working youth, through an education in Andover and Yale, a lifelong devotion to the practical application of the law (like Lord, Huntington was no scholar: ". . . he limited his labors to the exigencies of immediate duty"), to the position of honored citizen in the Salem community. Other qualities lighten the picture and bring us closer to qualities in Lord himself that Emily responded to. Lord quotes enthusiastically a boyhood friend of Huntington: "He was manly in his deportment, yet not, I am glad to say, without a vein of roguishness. . . . he had a most exuberant love of *fun*. His sense of the comic and ludicrous was very keen. . . ."[5] He loved literature and intellectual discussion, ". . . and the more earnest and excited it was, the more pleasurable was it to him." As a young man in Newburyport, he was the center of a "brilliant

5. Apparently Emily found this quality to be also one of Lord's most congenial traits. She could joke with him, as she had with Austin in their untroubled youth. In a penciled scrap that survives in the Amherst College archives, she wrote: ". . . you have a good deal of glee (many a glee) in your nature's corners . . ." (*L* III, 695, 1881 ?). Martha Dickinson Bianchi, *Emily Dickinson Face to Face*, p. 36, spoke of Emily's and Lord's enjoying their "adventures in conversation." In *Life and Letters*, pp. 69–70, she is more specific: "They saved scraps of current nonsense for each other, and these clippings flew back and forth between the grim court-house in Salem and the little desk by her conservatory window, where Emily oftenest sat. There was a certain kind of wit she labelled 'the Judge Lord brand.' One specimen of it especially relished by both remains still pinned to her tiny workbox. It is yellow with age, in a type quite bygone and evidently cut from the county paper. It is marked in her own handwriting – 'Returned by Judge Lord with approval!'

NOTICE! My wife Sophia Pickles having left my bed and board without just cause or provocation, I shall not be responsible for bills of her contracting.

SOLOMON PICKLES

NOTICE! I take this means of saying that Solomon Pickles has had no bed or board for me to leave for the last two months.

SOPHIA PICKLES

Another story which they repeated, relishing its portentous inference lacking fact, was this; the Nurse speaks first.

'Nurse,' says he, kind of high and haughty-like, 'what is your opinion?'
'Doctor,' says I, kind of low and deferential-like,
'I am of your opinion.'
'And what was his opinion?' asked the listener.
'Lord bless you, my dear, he hadn't any!' "

coterie." But the bent of his nature was practical, and by long, hard discipline he achieved a "strong, sterling, common sense," a virtue that Lord subjected to extended analysis—and again, curiously enough, we come close to Emily. The essence of common sense, he said, is not the humble and unpretentious thing the term usually implies:

It is more properly wisdom applied to conduct. The secret springs of action in one mind are not intuitively known to another. To discover them and to turn them to useful account demands more profound thought and more incessant study than to master the details of history or science. The mysteries of mind are more subtle than those of physics and much more readily elude pursuit and investigation; and he that becomes master of the human mind and human passions has achieved a greater triumph than he who has discovered a planet. "He understands human nature," can properly be said only of him who has been a long, severe and profound student; although when such power is attained, like the most marvellous discoveries in science or art, it seems so simple that we are inclined to deem it intuitive. . . . it was the subtle and more mysterious workings of the mind, the more difficult and multifarious rules of human conduct that claimed the study of Mr. Huntington. . . .

Whether it was Lord's teaching or not, Emily Dickinson shared this exalted view of Huntington's leading virtue. "Common Sense," she wrote, "is almost as omniscient as God." Lord's supreme example of common sense was not God but Shakespeare. Emily, who wrote her sister-in-law, "With the exception of Shakespeare, you have told me of more knowledge than any one living," would have understood this, too:

The great poet of nature wrote songs and sonnets, which would have given high place to another; but how insignificant they are in comparison with his magnificent exhibitions of human action!

Although Emily's letters to Lord contain fewer literary allusions than do most of her other correspondences, "the great poet of nature" was clearly a bond between them. Even in the few letters we have, there are quotations from *Othello, Antony, Hamlet,* and *Lear.* To Abbie Farley after Lord's death Emily wrote, "'An envious Sliver broke' was a passage your Uncle peculiarly loved in the drowning Ophelia." And in December 1880, probably for Christmas, Lord sent Emily Mrs. Cowden Clarke's *Complete Concordance to Shakspere* (Boston, 1877). Whether Lord prized Emily for her knowledge of "the subtle and more mysterious workings of the mind," whether indeed he admired or even knew the poetry in which she demonstrated such knowledge, is a question; but this eloquent tribute to his friend Huntington's skill in such matters—his "wisdom applied to conduct"—shows an ample and capable perception.

Emily Dickinson, we have seen, had no respect for doctrines. Huntington's religion, wrote Lord, "was a religion of thought and action rather than speech." His views were "tolerant and catholic . . . substantially in accordance with those with whom he was accustomed to worship – the orthodox congregationalists." (Lord himself, if we are to believe a remark of Emily's, was officially associated with no church. Emily assured her nephew Ned that Lord would not join a church just to be respectable: "I think he does nothing ostensible – Ned.") When Lord wrote that Huntington "never proclaimed that he was a lighted candle, but those who approached him saw the light, which could not be hid," he used a figure Emily had come close to in her poem "The Poets light but Lamps." Huntington's "light" was Revelation, the truth of the Scriptures and of the immortality of the soul. On these matters, Lord asserted, "Science was silent," philosophy nothing but "a 'pleasing hope'" and a "'fond desire,'" sentiments that he expounded vigorously in a long digression against a tendency in modern thought to reject "what was old in belief, because it was old":

> There is a class quite numerous now, and perhaps temporarily increasing in number, endowed above all others with inquiring and investigating minds. They receive nothing upon trust. Old truths are merely superstitions until tested by the touchstone of their unerring wisdom. They must put their finger into the print of the nails, and thrust their hand into the side of every truth before it can have their sanction. . . . They go for progress. To believe what has been believed a thousand years, is not progress.

What Emily made of hunkerism of this sort is not on record. She herself, certainly in her earlier years, was a great tester. She thought microscopes (spiritual or otherwise) were "prudent / In an Emergency," and her early studies, in spite of occasional jibes at the "savants" who classify and catalogue, had taught her to respect science. Such a poem as this put her close, at least in spirit, to the progressive thinkers Lord inveighed against:

> Experiment escorts us last –
> His pungent company
> Will not allow an Axiom
> An Opportunity   (#1770, about 1870)

Apparently Lord's conservative attitudes did not bother her. She accepted him *in toto*—as it were, religiously. Early in the correspondence she wrote him, "It may surprise you I speak of God – I know him but a little, but Cupid taught Jehovah to many an untutored Mind." By 1882 she could write. "While others go to Church, I go to mine, for are you not my Church, and have we not a Hymn that no one knows but us?" Austin and Mabel Todd talked to each other this way—he called her "my Christ" and she wrote: "Through you I see God." Though it may have been little more than a current rhetorical device, and a somewhat desperate one, it apparently neutralized conflicting attitudes or (with Austin and Mabel) helped the lovers face a world that looked upon their love as anything but holy. Only once in her letters to Lord did Emily reflect his skepticism about science. Mrs. Stearns (Frazar's mother) had been shocked, Emily reported, by Benjamin Butler's likening himself " 'to his Redeemer.' " Emily commented: "But we thought Darwin had thrown 'the Redeemer' away."

Lord brought out one other quality in Huntington that may illuminate one of his own—or at least one that he admired in others, and perhaps in Emily. A previous eulogy, by Huntington's pastor, had spoken of him as "a man of more than usual inertia." Lord agreed but took pains to define the term as "a quiet repose of mind – an indisposition to obtrude his own reflections upon others – an apparent inattention. . . ." As he had done with the notion of common sense, Lord raised this quality to a high place:

> He was a thinking man. His mind was constantly active. . . . He spoke only matured opinions. It was the incessant activity of his intellect – its presentation to itself of every question in so many phases and aspects which gave the idea of what is sometimes called inertia – more properly, perhaps, abstraction – but which is, in reality, the highest condition of mental activity.

Hunker or no, if Lord was perceptive enough to see and admire this quality in Huntington, he was well prepared to accept it and honor it in Emily, whose "inertia" puzzled her neighbors and even the sophisticated Higginson. Her family accepted it, and honored it. Said Vinnie (again), "[Emily] had to think—she was the only one of us who had that to do."

So, for all their temperamental differences, Lord was in many ways the supremely rewarding person for Emily. What we can properly call their love affair starts for us, inevitably, *in medias res*. The usual warning must be posted: of the fifteen letters that survive, only three can be dated precisely and those only by internal evidence. The first of these three was written April 30, 1882; the first five of the fifteen sometime (according to the handwriting) in 1878, the year following Mrs. Lord's death on December 10, 1877.

Apparently it was this latter event that released feelings in Emily that had been building up for some time. Her first letter (to follow the order of printing in the 1958 *Letters*) starts with a sense of glorious new freedom:

> My lovely Salem smiles at me. I seek his Face so often – but I have done with guises.
> I confess that I love him – I rejoice that I love him – I thank the maker of Heaven and Earth – that gave him me to love – the exultation floods me. I cannot find my channel – the Creek turns Sea – at thought of thee –
> Will you punish me? "Involuntary Bankruptcy," how could that be Crime?
> Incarcerate me in yourself – rosy penalty – threading with you this lovely maze, which is not Life or Death – though it has the intangibleness of one,

and the flush of the other – waking for your sake on Day made magical
with you before I went. . . .

Here the fair copy stops. A rough draft, which contains the above with a
few changes and some minor additions, continues—a situation that points,
of course, to another warning: there is no way of telling which of these
drafts and fair copies were posted. They were transmitted to Mabel Todd
by Austin in the early 1890s all in one envelope, with an indication by
Austin that they were "very special and personal," but with no indication
of how he came by them. One can only suppose that, himself experiencing
a glorious new freedom in a love, like Emily's and Judge Lord's, that met
with disapproval and hostility, he had snatched them from the burning
and kept them safe. It is conceivable that Emily herself entrusted them to
him. The censoring (by scissors) was probably done by Austin. It is
surprising that so much was left in. The rough draft continues, the
emphasis still on freedom:

> . . . to sleep – What pretty phrase – we went to sleep as if it were a coun-
> try – let us make it one – we could (will) make it one, my native Land – my
> Darling come oh *be* a patriot now – Love is a patriot now Gave her life for
> its country Has it meaning now – Oh nation of the soul thou hast thy free-
> dom now

The draft was written on an envelope addressed, in Lord's hand, to
Vinnie, who may have been acting as go-between, as she was later to do
for Austin and Mabel. But with Mrs. Lord's death, there was no need for
"guises." Emily's figure in the final sentences recalls her words to Joseph
Lyman: "My Country is Truth. . . . it is a free Democracy." (It is worth
noting that, contrary to her custom of getting others to address her letters
to her close friends, the few surviving envelopes to Judge Lord were
addressed by Emily herself.) It is as if, after years of reticence, she had
found someone in her maturity to whom she need not varnish the truth.
Nor need it be only about love. "I never seemed toward you," she wrote
about 1880. On December 3, 1882, she wrote:

> The Month in which our Mother died, closed it's Drama Thursday, and
> I cannot conjecture a form of space without her timid face. Speaking to you
> as I feel, Dear, without that Dress of Spirit must be worn for most, Cour-
> age is quite changed.

Whatever else he may have meant to her, he brought a release of spirit at
a difficult time in her life, with her father gone, her mother a hopeless
invalid requiring much of her time, Bowles dead, Sue apparently long
since lost except for delicate house-to-house missives, Austin overworked
and depressed, and her literary production and ambition well beyond their
peak.
    But neither her production nor her ambition, as witness the correspon-
dence with Thomas Niles that began in 1878 and lasted until 1885, was
over. It may be this that accounts for the tentativeness, even a clinging

sense of guilt, in these passionate letters to Lord. In the "My lovely Salem" letter, her gentle satire on his profession may be only that, but she plays a little insistently on the notion of guilt—"Bankruptcy," "Crime," "rosy penalty." The next letter (again, following the 1958 order) ends with a sharper statement:

Dont you know you have taken my will away and I "know not where" you "have laid" it? Should I have curbed you sooner? "Spare the 'Nay' and spoil the child"?

Oh, my too beloved, save me from the idolatry which would crush us both –

"And very Sea-Mark of my utmost Sail" –

(The final quotation is from Othello's fifth-act speech, "Behold! I have a weapon," with its despairing line, "Who can control his fate?") Then, still in these letters of about 1878, Lord becomes the guilty one, she the one resisting his advances:

. . . my Naughty one, too seraphic Naughty, who can sentence you? Certainly not my enamored Heart. Now my blissful Sophist, you that can make "Dont" "Do" – though forget that I told you so, [*Part of two pages is here cut out.*]

She begins another letter:

Dont you know you are happiest while I withhold and not confer – dont you know that "No" is the wildest word we consign to Language?

. . .

The "Stile" is God's – My Sweet One – for your great sake – not mine – I will not let you cross – but it is all your's, and when it is right I will lift the Bars, and lay you in the Moss – You showed me the word.

It may have been that "the idolatry which would crush us both" was Emily's realization that complete abandonment to their love would destroy each of them in their vocations, he as judge—"for your great sake"; she as poet. In these love letters, she is always the stylist—even in the rough draft she paused long enough to say, "What pretty phrase"— and the style is that of the poet: "the Creek turns Sea – at thought of thee – " The drafts show her at her work, and even in the fair copies she could apologize for her style: "Please excuse the wandering writing. Sleeplessness makes my Pencil stumble. Affection clogs it – too," although it is hard to see what was wandering or clogged in a passage she had just written, as lively a bit as she ever wrote:

The Air is soft as Italy, but when it touches me, I spurn it with a Sigh, because it is not you. The Wanderers [Austin's children?] came last Night – Austin says they are brown as Berries and as noisy as Chipmunks, and feels his solitude much invaded, as far as I can learn. These dislocations of privacy among the *Privateers* amuse me very much, but "the Heart knoweth its own" Whim – and in Heaven they neither woo nor are given in wooing – what an imperfect place!

So Austin, too, loved solitude, and Emily's amusement is both at his failure to establish, as she had long ago, a firm domain of privacy in his home and at her own inconsistency as she welcomes Lord's invasion of her privacy now—a privacy, one must say, it is hard to imagine her ever relinquishing for the complexities of married life with a distinguished member of the Massachusetts bar. Here she speaks of the heart's "Whim"; in another letter it is "Witchcraft" that is "wiser than we." In a scrap found with the Lord letters, it becomes "magic," and has its dangers (the brackets indicate deletions):

> We are always in danger of magic
> The perils of magic cannot be overestimated –
> [One] A single thrill can end a life or open it [anew] forever
> [And this my] This mystic territory then, is life –

In a fragment written on the back of a poem of about 1880, there is this disconcerting remark: "There is an awful yes in every constitution." Emily Dickinson knew the dangers of commitment; she had seen two men close to her—her father and Samuel Bowles—die, quite literally, of overcommitment. Austin seemed unable to say no to any personal or civic appeal; Mabel Todd's remark that no one in town could be born, marry, or die without him was not altogether humorous; and his death at sixty-six was generally attributed to overwork. At an early age (for whatever reasons) Emily had learned to say no. It became habitual and, as she became more and more dedicated to her vocation, an absolute necessity. Lord's notion of inertia came close to defining this quality. It had something in it of Keats's "negative capability." Certainly it was more than the lovely solitude she enjoyed even as a girl at Mount Holyoke, more than the "sumptuous Destitution" she later cherished. Perhaps she saw this late "idolatry" as a threat to a value she had established in her life at great expense. She had seen the issue clearly long before:

> Renunciation – is a piercing Virtue –
> The letting go
> A Presence – for an Expectation –
> Not now –
> The putting out of Eyes –
> Just Sunrise –
> Lest Day –
> Day's Great Progenitor –
> Outvie
> Renunciation – is the Choosing
> Against itself –
> Itself to justify
> Unto itself –
> When larger function –
> Make that appear –
> Smaller – that Covered Vision – Here –   (#745, about 1863)

By the late 1870s she was well used to "choosing against" herself. Years before, she had gone to Bowles and Higginson, and perhaps Wadsworth, with her poems and, to the first two, *for* her poems. Her relationship with Lord apparently had nothing to do with her poems, except perhaps to pose a threat that demanded another exercise in renunciation.

When the relationship began is impossible to tell precisely. There is nothing to link the Master letters (approximately 1858–62) necessarily to Lord; the slight parallels (such as her "Backwoodsman ways" of the third letter and her apology to Lord for "the trespass of my rustic Love upon your Realms of Ermine") are intriguing but not conclusive. Following Lord's Commencement Address in 1862, the recorded facts of his contacts with the Dickinsons during the decade of the seventies and his presence in or near Amherst are these: he was awarded an LL.D. by Amherst in 1869; he attended the alumni gatherings in July 1871 and 1873, and probably in other years during the decade; he presided at court in Northampton in the spring and fall; he invited Edward Dickinson, then in Boston, to visit him in Salem just two weeks before Edward's death in June 1874; in October 1875, he "was with me a week," Emily wrote Higginson (during the visit, Mrs. Lord witnessed Emily's will); the visit was repeated the following year; and, finally, a letter of 1877 survives from Lord to Vinnie inquiring of her health, Austin's, and Emily's. This is all that the present record reveals.

The letter to Vinnie deserves special comment. It is apparently the only one to any of the Dickinsons that survived the post-mortem burning which Lord himself ordered. It shows that by 1877 he had been intimately concerned with the Dickinsons, and especially Emily, for some time. He saw her character clearly, at least up to a point. And we owe him one insight that we have from no one else:

> Peccavi, my dear Vinnie, peccavi; but much more in fact than in purpose.
> I have had any quantity of the paving stones of that place, which we do not mean to dwell in. . . . There has not been a day since the receipt of your letter written in January (I am ashamed to say) that I have not had it in my mind to write to you; but I have been in court . . . or writing opinions and in the evening I have felt jaded with aching eyes and the listlessness and ennui of solitaire with one or more packs of cards has been the summit of my capacity; and still I have thought of you & of Emily, whose last note gave me a good deal of uneasiness, for knowing how entirely unselfish she is, and how unwilling to disclose any ailment, I fear that she has been more ill, than she has told me. I hope you will tell me particularly about her. . . . The pear scions shall be cut off & deposited in sand for your brother, whose health I trust is fully restored. He has had a long & painful and what is as bad almost a wearisome sickness [malaria] at a time . . . when he most needed to be in full strength & vigor. . . . I have felt anxious also about your health, for I know how wearing your in-

cessant cares and the necessary anxieties of your situation are, but I hope
that you will be able before a great while to run away from them and come
and see us.

Emily's reticence about her health comes as no surprise; but Lord's tribute
to her unselfishness is the only one of its kind we have and at last gives a
proper title to all those devoted labors for her family and the countless
acts of thoughtfulness for her friends that her correspondences, major and
minor, indicate. The image of the self-absorbed recluse has too long
dominated the conventional notion of her; Lord's perception seems truer.
And, be it noted, "one of the very ablest men in this State" is here addressing
a letter to sister Vinnie, too often dismissed as the least of these. But mostly
the letter shows the kindly paternal concern Lord had for all Dickinsons,
especially for the sisters in the Homestead; and, unless one is to read
romantic implications in Emily's remark in a letter to Higginson of late
October 1876, "Judge Lord was with us a few days since – and told me the
Joy we most revere – we profane in taking. I wish that was wrong," we
may assume that this was the spirit of the relationship, at least as far as he
was concerned, until sometime after his wife's death.

Whether Emily's regard for Lord was at first merely filial, whether it
was mixed with a "primitive kind of awe" for the man who had been
closer, geographically, to her father when he died than she was, or
whether she had been secretly in love with him for years, are questions
that cannot in the present state of our knowledge be answered. Her letters
to Lord are curiously contradictory. The letters assigned to 1878, if indeed
they were written in that year, show a depth of feeling that must have had
its origins well before Mrs. Lord's death in December 1877. "Idolatry"; the
notion of the "guises" she has at last cast off; a reference to "our dear
past" and "Anguish I long conceal from you" in still another 1878 (?)
letter—all these indicate a development of some duration. And yet, speaking of a "little Book" she had been reading, she says (in the "dear past"
letter):

. . . because it broke my Heart I want it to break your's – will you think
that fair? I often have read it, but not before since loving you – I find that
makes a difference – it makes a difference with all.

The "difference" here seems to have been a recent phenomenon. The
sentence about "Witchcraft" (quoted above) with which she concludes
the letter also suggests a recent, even a sudden onset.

The contradictions continue in later, and datable, letters. A single
passage from the one of May 1, 1882, indicates, first, that their love had a
long past, but then, in the concluding sentences, that it had come suddenly, and recently:

Our Life together was long forgiveness on your part toward me. The trespass of my rustic Love upon your Realms of Ermine, only a Sovereign could
forgive – I never knelt to other – The Spirit never twice alike, but every time

another – that other more divine. Oh, had I found it sooner! Yet Tenderness has not a Date – it comes – and overwhelms.

The time before it was – was naught, so why establish it? And all the time to come it is, which abrogates the time.

The last paragraph, it may be noted, is a perfect quatrain of "8s" and "6s." In an earlier poem in the same meter she had found that pain, like love, has "an Element of Blank." She was not concerned to establish for us the chronology of either in her life. Perhaps the best surmise is that, though the "overwhelming" tenderness came late, there was a long preparation for it, going back at least to Edward Dickinson's death;[6] certainly to the long visits in the mid-1870s; and given release, at least for Emily, by Mrs. Lord's death in 1877. At what point her "lovely Salem" began smiling at her in the way she cherished cannot be ascertained.

Nor do we know whether Lord knew much about her poetry or had any conception of the magnitude of her dedication to it. While she sent one hundred and two poems to Higginson and nearly fifty to Bowles (if we include here the ones she sent to Mary Bowles and those found by his son in the family papers), the envelope containing the Lord letters and scraps had only two poems, both rough drafts, and one two-line fragment, which we can only presume were ultimately sent. One of these is on the reverse of a fragment of a letter containing a passage on the *"carpe diem"* theme: "Lay up Treasures immediately – that's the best Anodyne for moth and Rust and the thief whom the Bible knew enough of Banking to suspect would break in and steal[.]" Both the passage and the poem may have some bearing on the surmise about the late coming of the tenderness:

> The Summer that we did not prize,
> Her treasures were so easy
> Instructs us by departing now
> And recognition lazy –

6. Millicent Todd Bingham (*Emily Dickinson: A Revelation*, p. 55) makes much of the probability that Judge Lord "had been nearer to him [Edward Dickinson] when he died than she had which, for Emily, would have invested him with a kind of sanctity." (Lord was holding court in Cambridge when Edward wrote his last letter home—June 5, 1874—telling of the Judge's invitation to visit him at his home. "I declined for this week," Edward wrote, "on account of things which detained me here.") Mrs. Bingham continues: "These are mysterious things, hard to understand. But we must recognize the fact that whereas she had always honored Judge Lord as her father's best friend, after his death she seems to have felt toward him a veneration, a primitive kind of awe." Such things, indeed, are mysterious and may, in this instance, be true; but if there is "awe" in Emily's letters to the Judge, there is little to indicate this particular source. To support her notion Mrs. Bingham quotes two tangential remarks of ED's—one to Higginson (*L* II, 583, June 1877): "Since my Father's dying, everything sacred enlarged so"; and a sentence to James Clark after Wadsworth's death: "The sharing a sorrow never lessens, but when a Balm departs, the Plants that nearest grew have a grieved significance and you cherished my friend" (*L* III, 742, 1882).

Bestirs itself – puts on it's Coat,
And scans with fatal promptness
For Trains that moment out of sight,
Unconscious of his smartness.   (#1773, about 1883)

The other poem picks up the theme of guilt begun, though faintly and whimsically, in another letter fragment (Lord's letters usually came on Mondays):

> My little devices to live till Monday would woo (win) your sad attention – (fill your eyes with Dew) – Full of work and plots and little happinesses the thought of you protracts (derides) them all and makes them sham and cold.

The first two lines of the poem were incorporated in the prose part of the fragment:[7]

How fleet – how indiscreet an one –
How always wrong is Love –
The joyful little Deity
We are not scourged to serve –   (#1771, about 1881)

("Train up a Heart in the way it should go," she once wrote, "and as quick as it can twill depart from it.")

What the "work" was that her anticipation of Lord's letter interferes with she does not specify. There is no hint here or elsewhere that it was with anything but housework, or nursing her mother. Nowhere in the letters or fragments does she speak of poetry, or the writing of poetry, or of herself as poet. Yet several of the letters (or the presumably intended letters) merge into verse, as we saw; and in the letter to Benjamin Kimball (Lord's cousin and executor) after Lord's death, she wrote, "He did not tell me he 'sang' to you, though to sing in his presence was involuntary, thronged only with Music, like the Decks of Birds." Since "singing" is so often a synonym with Emily Dickinson for the writing of poetry, she may be referring here to something Kimball had told her about Lord's interest in poetry, either his fondness for reading it aloud or perhaps for writing it. The letters Emily actually posted to Lord almost certainly contained more poems; it is unthinkable that she did not send him many more than the two discussed above. As it is, she enclosed, in this letter to Kimball, one of the finest poems to come out of the relationship. It is one of her best brief elegies:

Though the great Waters sleep,
That they are still the Deep,

7. See *Revelation*, p. 94.

We cannot doubt –
No vacillating God
Ignited this Abode
To put it out –[8]   (#*1599, about 1884*)

On the sheet containing the draft of this poem, there is a finished draft of another, which she apparently discarded in its favor:

A World made penniless by that departure
Of minor fabrics begs
But sustenance is of the spirit
The Gods but Dregs   (#*1623, about 1885*)

If Lord's death moved her to such poems as these, we can only assume that his life moved her to many more, especially among the many written during what has been called her "late prolific period." But we can only surmise about these. In the final pages of the book that first told us about the relationship, *Emily Dickinson: A Revelation* (1954), Millicent Todd Bingham prints, with little comment, twenty-three poems, presumably those she thought had something to do with this late experience.[9] The first, though assigned approximately to the year 1880 in the 1955 *Poems,* may well have been a poetic version of Emily's description to Lord, in a letter of May 14, 1882, of her "rapture" on learning of his recovery from illness:

To remind you of my own rapture at your return, and of the loved steps, retraced almost from the "Undiscovered Country," I enclose the Note I was fast writing, when the fear that your Life had ceased, came, fresh, yet dim, like the horrid Monsters fled from in a Dream.

Happy with my Letter, without a film of fear, Vinnie came in from a word with Austin, passing to the Train. "Emily, did you see anything in the Paper that concerned us"? "Why no, Vinnie, what"? "Mr Lord is very sick." I grasped at a passing Chair. My sight slipped and I thought I was freezing. While my last smile was ending, I heard the Doorbell ring and a strange voice said "I thought first of you." Meanwhile, Tom [Kelley, the

8. Emily sent this poem to Sue in the letter on the "Warrington Words" (*L* III, 828), where it commemorates Samuel Bowles. She had just said to Sue, "You remember his swift way of wringing and flinging away a Theme, and others picking it up and gazing bewildered after him, and the prance that crossed his Eye at such times was unrepeatable – " Emily may have been romantically in love with both men at one time or another; but what she seems to have cherished chiefly in both of them was their vitality, their range of responsiveness, and their extraordinary intellectual vigor.

9. The "late prolific period" is Mrs. Bingham's phrase (p. 107) and rightly questions, I think, the current notion that ED's creative powers slacked off badly after the early 1860s, when for several years she was supposedly writing an average of almost a poem a day. True, she did not keep up that pace. But the quality of these late poems and of the superb letters from these years shows undiminished power in all respects but quantity.

Dickinson handyman] had come, and I ran to his Blue Jacket and let my Heart break there – that was the warmest place. "He will be better. Dont cry Miss Emily. I could not see you cry."

Then Vinnie came out and said "Prof. Chickering thought we would like to telegraph." He "would do it for us."

"Would I write a Telegram"? I asked the Wires how you did, and attached my name.

The Professor took it, and Abby's[10] brave – refreshing reply I shall remember[.]

The poem may have recalled this moment of rapture, or, more generally, the late tenderness in her life:

> The Thrill came slowly like a Boon for
> Centuries delayed
> It's fitness growing like the Flood
> In sumptuous solitude –
> The desolation only missed
> While Rapture changed it's Dress
> And stood amazed before the Change
> In ravished Holiness –   (#*1495*)

Another poem gets the verve and excitement of the 1878 (?) letters and recalls the idea of "guises" (here "strategy") that she renounced in the first letter:

> I thought the Train would never come –
> How slow the whistle sang –
> I dont believe a peevish Bird
> So whimpered for the Spring –
> I taught my Heart a hundred times
> Precisely what to say –
> Provoking Lover, when you came
> It's Treatise flew away
> To hide my strategy too late
> To wiser be too soon –
> For miseries so halcyon
> The happiness atone –   (#*1449, about 1878*)

Two late poems use legal terms reminiscent of the letter beginning "My lovely Salem" and, like the letter, convey the notion of guilt, real or whimsical; and, in the second poem (the one she had sent Helen Jackson), the sense of "magic" that came with this late experience:

10. Abbie Farley, Lord's niece, whom we saw in an early chapter (Chapter 13) as vigorously opposed to a possible marriage of Emily and her uncle. See also *YH* I, lix.

Tried always and Condemned by thee
Permit me this reprieve
That dying I may earn the look
For which I cease to live –   (*#1559, about 1882*)

Of God we ask one favor,
That we may be forgiven –
For what, he is presumed to know –
The Crime, from us, is hidden –
Immured the whole of Life
Within a magic Prison
We reprimand the Happiness
That too competes with Heaven.   (*#1601, about 1884*)

Two poems written in rough draft on the back of a letter fragment found in the Lord envelope may be relevant, directly or obliquely, to Lord. The fragment can be dated March 2, 1884, eleven days before he died, and the poems were probably written shortly thereafter. In the first, with its echo of Shelley's "Epipsychidion," the notion of Circumference, a favorite and multivalenced word with her, may suggest Lord's worldly achievement in his life or even her own achievement in winning his love. (Later she sent the poem to her girlhood friend Daniel Chester French to celebrate the unveiling of his statue of John Harvard in Cambridge.)

Circumference thou Bride of Awe
Possessing thou shalt be
Possessed by every hallowed Knight
That dares to covet thee[11]   (*#1620, about 1884*)

11. There could be no better example of the way ED transformed her borrowings than her probable use here of the passage from Shelley. The hero of "Epipsychidion" is describing to his love (named Emily) the delights of the Ionian isle where he has prepared an idyllic abode. There they will

Be one: –
. . . linger, where the pebble-paven shore,
Under the quick, faint kisses of the sea
Trembles and sparkles as with ecstasy, –
Possessing and possessed by all that is
Within that calm circumference of bliss,
And by each other, till to love and live

lines 546–552

Of course, the parallels—"possessing and possessed" and the notion of "circumference" —may be accidental; but such a coincidence seems unlikely. Assuming the borrowing, note how ED has lifted the words from their lush and hedonistic setting in Shelley's flowing pentameters and has put them to work in her prim "8s" and "6s" to honor a thoroughly Puritan ideal. Her "circumference" does not (like Shelley's) signify delightful enclosure but bold expansion and awesome achievement.

The other poem, in very rough draft (I have accepted her variant for the last line), seems more nearly a characterization of Lord, her "lovely Salem":

> Arrows enamored of his Heart –
> Forgot to rankle there
> And Venoms he mistook for Balms
> Renounced their character –　　　(#1629, about 1884)

A poem of the mid-1870s recalls the notion of witchcraft and perhaps signals the kindling of her long dormant love:

> Long Years apart – can make no
> Breach a second cannot fill –
> The absence of the Witch does not
> Invalidate the spell –
>
> The embers of a Thousand Years
> Uncovered by the Hand
> That fondled them when they were Fire
> Will gleam and understand　　　(#1383)

A poem in worksheet draft whose handwriting, at least, indicates the year 1884 sounds as if it might have been written during Lord's last illness. Its final image of the sea suggests the elegy she included in the letter to Kimball, "Though the great Waters sleep," which, indeed, may have been written to follow this:

> Still own thee – still thou art
> What surgeons call alive –
> Though slipping – slipping I perceive
> To thy reportless Grave –
>
> Which question shall I clutch –
> What answer wrest from thee
> Before thou dost exude away
> In the recallless sea?　　　(#1633)

The question in the second stanza, we may presume, was the one she asked Washington Gladden, the Springfield minister, during Lord's illness in 1882. Gladden's answer, dated Springfield, May 27, 1882, a copy of which is the only survivor of the exchange, begins:

My friend:
　　"Is immortality true?" I believe that it is true – the only reality – almost; a thousand times truer than mortality, which is but a semblance after all. . . .

Finally, there is a poem of about 1884, one of her finest summations on death. By then she was reeling from loss after loss in quick succession: Dr. Holland, Wadsworth, her mother, little Gilbert, and now Lord. As she explained to the Norcrosses her own collapse that year, "The doctor calls it 'revenge of the nerves'; but who but Death had wronged them?" In the poem, her nerves seem still resilient:

> So give me back to Death –
> The Death I never feared
> Except that it deprived of thee –
> And now, by Life deprived,
> In my own Grave I breathe
> And estimate it's size –
> It's size is all that Hell can guess –
> And all that Heaven surmise –   (#*1632*)

The poem is about personal loss, surely, perhaps the loss of Otis Lord, but it does not stop there. It is more the product of that quality of "inertia" as Lord defined it: the capacity for "abstraction . . . the highest condition of mental activity." In the poem, she is estimating the "size" of death—distancing it, coming to terms with it, and finding no fear in it. In her two letters to Benjamin Kimball after Lord's death, she said, "I was only his friend . . . only a Scholar who has lost her Preceptor," and she quoted one of Lord's last admonitions:

I once asked him what I should do for him when he was not here, referring half unconsciously to the great Expanse – In a tone italic of both Worlds "Remember Me," he said. I have kept his Commandment.

One way of keeping his Commandment was never to give up her vocation, her gift for the highest condition of mental activity, which for her was poetry. She shared his courage. "Neither fearing Extinction," she wrote Kimball, "nor prizing Redemption, he believed alone. Victory was his Rendezvous – " And she celebrated the victory thus [still to Kimball]:

> Go thy great way!
> The Stars thou meetst
> Are even as Thyself –
> For what are Stars but Asterisks
> To point a human Life.   (#*1638, about 1885*)

We can only speculate, of course, about how many of these late poems have to do directly with Lord. Her love for him was tonic and his influence invigorating; but she kept them both on this side of the idolatry she feared. In a way, every one of the major relationships in her life, with all they cost her in anguish or ecstasy, was not only a stimulus, involving each time a new and very personal Muse, but also a threat to her life as a poet, an invasion of the privacy without which she could not function. She weathered every one and continued on as poet. She did the same with Lord.

I cannot think that she ever entertained seriously the notion of marriage to him, although twice her letters play with the idea: "Emily 'Jumbo'! Sweetest name, but I know a sweeter – Emily Jumbo Lord. Have I your approval?" This was about November 1882. A letter of December 3 contains a passage that could, perhaps, have been a reply to an actual proposal—or an invitation to visit:

> Your Sorrow was in Winter – one of our's in June and the other, November, and my Clergyman passed from Earth in spring, but sorrow brings it's own chill.[12] Seasons do not warm it. You said with loved timidity in asking me to your dear Home, you would "try not to make it unpleasant." So delicate a diffidence, how beautiful to see! I do not think a Girl extant has so divine a modesty.
>
> You even call me to your Breast with apology! Of what must my poor Heart be made? . . .

Whatever it was, invitation or proposal, she did not accept. Then there is the ring (now at Harvard) that, we are told, Martha Dickinson Bianchi showed to visitors as having belonged to Emily. On the inside is engraved "Philip." What is the connection here, we ask, with the "Little Phil" of the lighthearted letter of May 1, 1882, in which she described Mrs. Stearns's shock at Benjamin Butler and the spring air as "soft as Italy"?

> That was a big – sweet Story – the number of times that "Little Phil" read his Letter, and the not so many, that Papa read his, but I am prepared for falsehood.
>
> On subjects of which we know nothing, or should I say *Beings* – is "Phil" a "Being" or a "Theme," we both believe, and disbelieve a hundred times an Hour, which keeps Believing nimble.
>
> But how can "Phil" have one opinion and Papa another – I thought the Rascals were inseparable – "but there again," as Mr New Bedford Eliot used to say, "I may be mistaken."

What was she imagining here? What is implied by her question, ". . . is 'Phil' a 'Being' or a 'Theme' "? Was she imagining a fantasy child? Or the "sweet Salem" side of the hunkerish politician and stern judge, the youthfulness, the "glee," the "May" in his nature which in her presence he apparently never quite lost?[13] These questions, and many more, remain unanswered.

12. The losses referred to are: Lord's wife (in December), Emily's father (in June), her mother (November), and Wadsworth (my Clergyman).
13. The Lords (again) were childless. Abby Farley once referred to a gift of flowers coming from the "Mansion" (Homestead) to "dear Otis" (*YH* II, 396; to Ned Dickinson in the Evergreens, April 8, 1883).

Emily Dickinson complained that "All men say 'What' to me." She was mystified by their mystification, and withdrew. But in Otis Lord's presence—"thronged only with Music, like the Decks of Birds"—she "sang." That kind of singing, surely, was interrupted by the illnesses (his and hers) of 1882 and 1883, and ended forever in March 1884. Her own kind, the poems and the magical letters, stopped only when, two springs later, she herself was "called back." Higginson read Emily Brontë's "No coward soul is mine" at the funeral and later made this entry in his diary: ". . . the sister Vinnie put in [the coffin] two heliotropes by her hand 'to take to Judge Lord.'"

28

Books and Reading

THE WHOLE TRUTH about Emily Dickinson will elude us always; she seems almost willfully to have seen to that. The family, the early friends and the later, the mentors and the masters, the lovers or would-be lovers or fantasy lovers—each yields it modicum of meaning. In our present state of knowledge, however, no more than that can be claimed for any of them. There is a feeling of incompleteness, of areas still to be explored, of mysteries that still beckon. The aim must be to shore up what truth we have as firmly as possible in the never-ending dialectics of readings and counter-readings. To twist one of her later remarks, " 'It is finished' can never be said of us."

But to leave her with no more than passing glimpses into one major source of truth about her—her life in books and reading—would be to cut her short indeed. Here she herself gives the lead in the remark to Joseph Lyman about her fear of blindness: "Some years ago I had a woe, the only one that ever made me tremble. It was a shutting out of all the dearest ones of time, the strongest friends of the soul – BOOKS." Had she been a nature poet in the Romantic tradition, one would have expected her first thought to be the shutting out of flowers and hills and sunsets. Or, if frustrated love had brought her to the edge of collapse, she might have trembled over such woes—the loss of a Sue or a Kate or a Master. If her religious crisis was as great as some of the despairing poems seem to indicate, her trembling might have been over loss of faith. But of all these, she singled out the threat of the loss of books. Even allowing for Dickinson hyperbole, she seems to be speaking candidly.

And yet, in 1960, it was said of her, "the best informed guess is that no poet was ever less indebted to books." Although our guesses are better informed now, the statement is still, in one sense at least, true. She never, like Dr. Johnson, tore the heart out of many books to make a new one and seldom put classical legend, myth, or history—the stock in trade of the Romantic poets—to work in her poems; or if she did, the references are usually fleeting and peripheral. There are no imitations of Spenser or Milton in her canon. She was never the avowed disciple, as far as we know, of anyone.[1] When she disclaimed the conscious use of "a paint, mixed by another person," she distinguished herself from the tradition of learned poets who used whatever they wanted from their predecessors, often verbatim and for well-calculated effects—one thinks of Chaucer, Spenser, Webster, Milton, Coleridge, T. S. Eliot. Although in the early years she joined her friends in the "Reading Club," or "talked books" that night at Sue's with Reuben Chapman, such references are sparse. There is nothing in her annals like the literary exchanges recorded between the English Romantics or among the Concordians. A few incisive phrases were enough even for her greatest enthusiasms: the Bible "dealt with the Centre"; "While Shakespeare remains Literature is firm"; " 'What do I think of *Middlemarch?*' What do I think of glory?" She had no coterie, no publisher to keep her in touch with the literary world, not even a literary neighbor she could count on for day-by-day support—except Sue, perhaps, but her support seems to have diminished early and was at best intermittent.

So the conditions of her life, and her temperament, made her especially dependent on books. In this sense the best-informed guess of 1960 is wrong. She could hardly have lived without them. If, using a legal term she must have heard around the house a good deal, she called her friends her "estate," more often than not she used metaphors of eating and drinking—life-sustaining processes—to describe what books meant to her. As a girl she came home from Mount Holyoke to "a feast in the reading line." Thirty years later, she began her most famous poem about books, "He ate and drank the precious Words – / His Spirit grew robust – ." In the letter to Lyman (the most sustained statement we have from her about books), the metaphors are mostly vitalistic. When the doctor forbade reading, "He might as well have said, 'Eyes be blind', 'heart be still.' " Her "blood bounded" when the restriction was finally removed. "Shakespear was the first. . . . Give me ever to drink of this wine." She "devoured the luscious passages. I thought I should tear the leaves out as I turned them." Few poets have ever confessed so voracious a passion.

As the source studies of her poetry add to our knowledge of her reading, both what and how she read, several truths emerge. She can no

---

1. She came closest to it when she told Higginson (*L* II, 404, April 25, 1862) that "For Poets – I have Keats – and Mr and Mrs Browning"; but we have already seen how inadequate that statement is. The present chapter will attempt to fill out her statement (as we have already seen her do, to a certain degree, in her more literary correspondences), but not with the purpose of establishing anything approaching a discipleship or even "influences" in the traditional sense—though much more could be said, for instance, about Emerson and Thoreau. The emphasis is on process: Emily Dickinson *reading*—and writing.

longer be regarded, for all her withdrawn ways, as working in grand
isolation, all uniqueness and originality. She saw herself as a poet in the
company of the Poets—and, functioning as she did mostly on her own,
read them (among other reasons) for company. In another series of
metaphors, they become people. They are "the dearest ones of time, the
strongest friends of the soul," her "Kinsmen of the Shelf," her "enthralling friends, the immortalities." In a poem of about 1862 she takes a
"venerable Hand" and finds it warming her own:

> A passage back – or two – to make –
> To Times when he – was young –
>
> His quaint opinions – to inspect –
> His thought to ascertain
> On Themes concern our mutual mind –
> The Literature of Man –
>
> What interested Scholars – most –
> What Competitions ran –
> When Plato – was a Certainty –
> And Sophocles – a Man –   (#371)

She chatted, or argued, or agreed with these friends, it seems, quite as
she did with those of flesh and blood. Many of her poems appear to be her
end of conversations struck up with what she found on printed pages.
"Me – come!" we have heard her reply to the Evangelist (or Wadsworth),
and we find her continuing the conversation later, this time with the
Apostle Paul:[2]

> "And with what body do they come?" –
> Then they *do* come – Rejoice!
> What Door – What Hour – Run – run – My Soul!
> Illuminate the House!
>
> "Body!" Then real – a Face and Eyes –
> To know that it is them! –
> Paul knew the Man that knew the News –
> He passed through Bethlehem –   (#1492, October 1880)

2. I Corinthians 15:35: "But some man will say, How are the dead raised up?
and with what body do they come?" Ruth Miller, pp. 221 ff., was the first to stress
this aspect of ED's poetic practice: "She wrote her poems as a kind of practice of
skill, as her part of an argument which she carried on all her life with published
prose or verse. . . . When she reads something that is printed, she pits her skill
against that which has won the public stamp of approval, she does it over, leaving it,
as she thinks, with a finer finish, a greater relevance"—or, simply, turning it into a
poem.

We have seen her work Beecher's "earthquake in the South" into a poem and sum up Hitchcock's proof of immortality in her poem about "The Chemical conviction"—to show, perhaps, what a poet could do with an orator's phrase and a scientist's attempt at theology. Her response to Higginson's "Decoration" is the most famous of these conversation poems only because its nature is in no need of proof. Scholars have recently been pointing out her similar use of passages from such disparate sources as Hawthorne's stories, Ik Marvel's *Reveries,* Thoreau, Mrs. Browning's *Aurora Leigh,* Emerson's essays, Quarles's *Emblems,* and the endless string of fugitive verses in the periodicals (the *Republican,* the *Hampshire and Franklin Express,* the *Atlantic, Harper's,* and *Scribner's* were among those that came to her door).[3] The process can go on indefinitely as we explore the range of that prehensile mind and burrlike memory. In the obituary Sue wrote for Emily in the *Republican,* she spoke of her as turning more and more, as she grew older, "to her own large wealth of individual resources for companionship, sitting thenceforth, as some one said of her, 'in the light of her own fire.'" The metaphor is a good one. Much of the fuel for that fire came from her reading.

She read hungrily, uncritically, and with her whole being. In her recorded remarks about things she read, one of the few adverse comments we find is on Harriet Prescott [Spofford]'s "Circumstance," a story that appeared in the *Atlantic* in May 1860. She wrote Higginson that "it followed me, in the Dark – so I avoided her –" and that, in its way, was a compliment.[4] Her capacity for absorbing what we would consider banal-

3. Since the decade of the 1950s, which produced workable texts of the poems and the letters, source and "affinity" studies have multiplied. Many of them have already been mentioned (all of them, of course, preceded by Whicher's pioneering chapter in *This Was a Poet*): Charles Anderson's *Emily Dickinson's Poetry;* Jack L. Capps, *Emily Dickinson's Reading,* with its comprehensive sweep from the Bible to the *Springfield Republican;* Rebecca Patterson's essay on ED and Elizabeth Barrett Browning; Ruth Miller, *The Poetry of Emily Dickinson,* with its special emphasis on Quarles and the miscellaneous resources of Edward Dickinson's library; John Evangelist Walsh's stress on ED's debt to Brontë and Elizabeth Barrett Browning (*The Hidden Life of Emily Dickinson*); Miriam Baker's study (unpublished) of ED and popular verse ("Emily Dickinson and the Practice of Poetry"); Judith Banzer on ED and the English Metaphysicals. Jay Leyda's *Years and Hours* pointed to innumerable parallels, especially in contemporary fiction, essays, sermons, newspapers, and magazines. Although I still agree with Whicher that "Emily Dickinson's poetry is not derivable from her reading" (p. 224) and with Henry Wells (*Introduction to Emily Dickinson,* 1947, p. 278) that "her library, however important, was always secondary to her practice," the value of such probing into sources, parallels, and affinities is indisputable. She appears in ever-widening perspective, and her stature grows. She comes to us increasingly as the summation of a culture, not (as she was long regarded) a minor and freakish offshoot.

4. To Sue, after reading the concluding installment of Mrs. Spofford's "The Amber Gods" in the February 1860 *Atlantic,* Emily wrote: "You stand nearer the world than I do, Susan. Send me everything she writes" (Martha Dickinson Bianchi, *Emily Dickinson Face to Face,* p. 28; and see YH II, 6). The story is a frothy bit, involving a chattery heroine named Giorgione Willoughby, some mysterious amber

ities was apparently lifelong, not just an aberration of youth. At twenty-one, when she should have been outgrowing some of her girlish senti-mentalities, she wrote Susan Gilbert about some books that were not sentimental enough for her:

> I have just read three little books, not great, not thrilling – but sweet and true. "The Light in the Valley," "Only," and A "House upon a Rock" – I know you would love them all – yet they dont *bewitch* me any. There are no walks in the wood – no low and earnest voices, no moonlight, nor stolen love, but pure little lives, loving God, and their parents, and obeying the laws of the land; yet read, if you meet them, Susie, for they will do one good.

It is reassuring to find "Alton Lock" and "Bleak House" ("it is like him who wrote it – that is all I can say") mentioned in the next paragraph; but what she liked next year in the poems of Alexander Smith, the young Scottish writer who was making such a stir, was his "exquisite frensy" and "some wonderful figures, as ever I met in my life."[5] While she could

---

beads, and (for Giorgione) frustrated love. The concluding passage, where Giorgione imagines her own death, might have attracted ED:

> Half-past one? Why, then, did not the hands move? Why cling fixed on a point five minutes before the first quarter struck? To and fro, soundless and purposeless, swung the long pendulum. And, ah! what was this thing I had become? I had done with time. Not for me the hands moved on their recurrent circle any more.
> I must have died at ten minutes past one.

Mrs. Spofford's "Circumstance" (in the May *Atlantic* for that year) tells of a woman in the wilds of Maine, who, going home through the forest on a wintry night, is seized by the "Indian Beast," half human, half animal, and, about to be devoured, finds that the beast will desist as long as she *sings*. This she discovers after screaming in vain for her husband:

> . . . she knew, that, even if her husband heard it, he yet could not reach her in time; she saw that while the beast listened, he would not gnaw, – and this she *felt* directly, when the rough, sharp, and multiplied stings of his tongue re-touched her arm. Again her lips opened by instinct, but the sound that issued thence came by reason . . . when she opened her lips the third time, it was not for shrieking, but for singing.

She sings all night long – songs, ballads, hymns, passages from Scripture. Finally her husband comes, shoots the beast, and leads her to their log-cabin home – which (in the very last sentence) they find burned to the ground by Indians.

5. A copy of Alexander Smith's *Poems* (1853) is in the Dickinson Collection at Harvard. The opening soliloquy of Walter, the poet hero, will give a notion of the "wonderful figures" (and perhaps the theme) that attracted ED.

> As a wild maiden, with love-drinking eyes,
> Sees in sweet dreams a beaming Youth of Glory,
> And wakes to weep, and ever after sighs
> For that bright vision till her hair is hoary;
> Ev'n so, alas! is my life's passion story.
> For Poesy my heart and pulses beat,
> For Poesy my blood runs red and fleet.
> As Moses' serpent the Egyptians' swallow'd,
> One passion eats the rest. . . .

say of Whitman (in 1862), "I never read his Book – but was told that he was disgraceful," and of Poe (in 1879), "I know too little to think," she thought enough of John Pierpont's "very sweet" elegy on his son to copy its ten anguished stanzas for her friend Mary Warner in 1856, and of George Parsons Lathrop's very similar elegy, "The Child's Wish Granted," to tell Frances Norcross in 1881 that it was "piteously sweet."

The truth seems to be that what is banal to us was lifeblood to the "advanced" young people of Amherst, who vibrated sympathetically to Ik Marvel's *Reveries,* or Longfellow's *Kavanagh,* or the tearful effusions of the sub-poets. Perhaps they found compensation for the earnest, overly pious culture of their community and the rigors of their "real life" homes. Although Emily's reading sobered considerably as time went on (the allusions to sub-literature diminish rapidly after the mid-1860s), she never lost her taste for sentiment. Her very last letter (to the Norcross cousins) is, *in toto,* the title of Hugh Conway's *Called Back* (1883), a novel in the sentimental-melodramatic mode at its worst. And yet she found it "a haunting story, and as loved Mr. Bowles used to say, 'greatly impressive to me.'"

One aspect of her early, and perhaps later, reading deserves comment, since it illuminates certain aspects of her poetry, its subjects and form. She read, not just to pick up conversations with her authors or to quench her burning thirst at the Pierian spring, but competitively. This streak was apparent from the first. As a girl, she wanted her letters to be the brightest and best. She joshed Austin about his poetic pretensions, with a hint about the competition he'd meet in the family. She said that one day she hoped to make Austin and Sue proud of her. One way to begin was to do what other poets had done, only do it better. In this she had ample precedent in the custom of the day among the Minnie Myrtles and Grace Greenwoods, whose verses on birds and buttercups, sunsets and cemeteries, dotted the poetry departments of the journals and newspapers. The would-be poetesses (the vogue was notably female) were frankly imitative, which meant, we can assume, competitive. A theme or subject would go the rounds—frustrated love, early death, the seasons, the "little things" in nature—and the point would be to see who could do it best.[6] There seems a hint of this in Emily's attitude when she said of Mrs. Spofford's "The Amber Gods": "It is the only thing I ever read in my life that I didn't think I could have imagined myself!" There surely is a suggestion of competitiveness when she sent Higginson her redaction of his "Decoration," or in her refusal to embarrass Wordsworth about his "Light that never was, on sea or land": "Myself could arrest it but we'll not chagrin Him."

It seems likely, though nothing so sure as in the Higginson episode, that she similarly reduced an effusion of the Scottish bard Charles Mackay that had found its way into the *Springfield Republican* (January 23, 1858):

6. This is Miriam Baker's thesis; see note 3 above.

LITTLE NOBODY

When the tempest flies
O'er the cloudy skies,
And from crag to crag the frantic thunders ride;
When the lightning stroke
Has destroyed the oak,
Safely down below the little violets hide.
In the strife appalling,
When the proud are falling,
Little men can rest, or watch unheeded by;
Blow, ye storms of Fate,
On the rich and great,
I'm but little Nobody – Nobody am I.

Pebbles on the shore
Dread no billows roar,
But the mighty ships, deep-laden in the hold,
With a thousand men,
Steering home again,
Founder oftentimes with all their men and gold.
Feathers fall but slowly,
And the poor and lowly
Fall and are unhurt – while greatness falls to die;
Kings may wake to weep,
While their plowmen sleep;
Who would be a Somebody? – Nobody am I.

Emily's poem on the same theme, whether or not a conscious effort to chagrin Mackay, is far from her best:

I'm Nobody! Who are you?
Are you – Nobody – too?
Then there's a pair of us!
Dont tell! they'd banish us – you know!

How dreary – to be – Somebody!
How public – like a Frog –
To tell your name – the livelong June –
To an admiring Bog![7]   (#288, about 1861)

The poem strikes a pose, and a sentimental one; it could be called coy, or cute. But judged comparatively, and as an early exercise, it does not fare

7. Jack L. Capps, p. 65, follows George Whicher's suggestion (*This Was a Poet*, p. 223) that in this poem ED "may have been thinking of Desdemona's last words, 'Nobody; I myself; farewell.'" But ED's "I'm Nobody!" in no way shares the mood, theme, or rhythm of the passage from *Othello;* it is simply an infinitely superior "Little Nobody."

badly. Emily Dickinson at least keeps clear of thunder and lightning, mighty oaks and dread billows, kings and plowmen; the compact, homely, implied dialogue is surely superior to Mackay's swollen monologue; and although the frog and the puddle are hardly new to proverbial wisdom, she rejuvenates the cliché. The last stanza, at any rate, lives as nothing in the Mackay poem does.

If Emily read competitively and for companionship, she also read for inspiration—but inspiration in her own special sense. In one phase of her reading, she seems constantly to have been on the lookout for the nugget, the germ, some striking word or phrase that would set her mind going. Such at least seems the gist of a passage in the letter to Joseph Lyman about words and their effect on her. She speaks of literature here in terms not of wholes—the philosophy, or the moral, or the message embodied in the total work—but of parts, the single, glowing words:

> We used to think, Joseph, when I was an unsifted girl and you so scholarly that words were cheap & weak. Now I dont know of anything so mighty. There are [those] to which I lift my hat when I see them sitting princelike among their peers on the page. Sometimes I write one, and look at his outlines till he glows as no sapphire.

"In the beginning was the Word" has been said of her, and rightly. When she was fifteen she wrote Abiah Root, thanking her for a letter, "At every word I read I seemed to feel new strength." Many statements and certainly the practice of her later years indicate that the particularizing of "every word" was not casual. "A Word is inundation, when it comes from the Sea." "You need the balsam word," she wrote to her bereaved cousins. "How lovely are the wiles of Words!" she exclaimed to Mrs. Holland. Some such enthusiasm was surely the meaning behind her remark that for several years in the late 1850s her "Lexicon" was her only companion. As late as 1883, thanking Mrs. Holland for her "full sweetness, to which as to a Reservoir the smaller Waters go," she paused to say, "What a beautiful Word 'Waters' is!" She rejoiced in the sheer thrill of words wonderfully put together. She wrote Joseph Lyman, after the doctor said she could read again, that

> Shakespear was the first; Antony & Cleopatra where Enobarbus laments the amorous lapse of his master. Here is the ring of it.

> > "heart that in the scuffles of
> > great fights hath burst the
> > buck[l]e on his breast"

—a passage expressive of her own sense of liberation, surely, but the thrill seems to have come mainly from "the ring of it."

At least three poems deal explicitly (and many more implicitly) with the power of words for evil as well as good.

A word is dead
When it is said,
Some say.
I say it just
Begins to live
That day.   (#1212, about 1872?)

Words can be dangerous. A syllable "can make to quake like jostled tree":

Could mortal lip divine
The undeveloped Freight
Of a delivered syllable
'Twould crumble with the weight.   (#1409, about 1877)

A careless word can kill:

A Word dropped careless on a Page
May stimulate an eye
When folded in perpetual seam
The Wrinkled Maker lie

Infection in the sentence breeds
We may inhale Despair
At distances of Centuries
From the Malaria –   (#1261, about 1873)

Her manuscripts, sometimes with half a dozen variants for a single word, show how carefully she chose. She once begged off seeing a caller because, she said, "My own Words so chill and burn me."

Her feeling for words went far beyond the aesthetic response—"lovely" or "beautiful" or "ringing." In her sense of their power to heal or kill, we again come close to what she read for and how she used what she read. She could be said to have been in the tradition of Shelley's vitalism, when he implored the west wind to scatter his poems abroad to "quicken a new birth"; but the immediate, intimate power of the word, of the "jostling" syllable or the malarial sentence, is different from the nineteenth-century notion of winged words, message-bearing verses. There is something in her of Emerson's idea of each word as once a stroke of genius, a poem, but much more of the idea of the Incarnation as she transferred it from theology to poetics. She made two statements of it, one in prose and one in a poem. Both are undated.

The import of that Paragraph "The Word made Flesh" Had he the faintest intimation Who broached it Yesterday! "Made Flesh and dwelt among us."

In the poem she describes the experience of partaking the Word as a kind of communion. Of the first fourteen verses of the opening chapter of the Gospel according to St. John, she ignored the reiterated metaphor of the "light" that "shineth in darkness" and chose only the most explicit statement of the Incarnation.

> A Word made Flesh is seldom
> And tremblingly partook
> Nor then perhaps reported
> But have I not mistook
> Each one of us has tasted
> With ecstasies of stealth
> The very food debated
> To our specific strength –
>
> A Word that breathes distinctly
> Has not the power to die
> Cohesive as the Spirit
> It may expire if He –
> "Made Flesh and dwelt among us["]
> Could condescension be
> Like this consent of Language
> This loved Philology   (*#1651*)

It is the poet, of course, who brings about this mystical transmutation of word into flesh. She knew that the achievement was rare. "Sometimes," she wrote Lyman, "I write one." This is why, in her first letter to Higginson, she was eager to know if her verse was "alive," whether it "breathed" —that is, whether she had achieved the miracle of Incarnation. It is not surprising that Higginson, schooled in the Victorian virtues of form and message, did not understand what she meant. He was not ready, nor was nineteenth-century America, for so intensely sacramental a poet.

Her method was just that: the intensification, or concentration, of meaning in words until they glowed "as no sapphire"—until, that is, they became, in mutually supportive combination, the Word, a poem that could "dwell among us," alive, a corporate fusion of meaning and (like human life) mystery. This sense of life is the most difficult of all things to create—and she knew that, too. This is one reason, surely, why many of her poems seem cryptic, incomplete, barely reducible to coherent statement, as if she was conscious of an element of the ineffable, even in usual things, like hummingbirds or sunsets. Or perhaps it was the sheer magnitude of meaning that defied communication. This seems to be the gist of her remark to Mrs. Holland, "There is not so much Life as *talk* of Life, as a general thing. Had we the first intimation of the Definition of Life, the calmest of us would be Lunatics!" She read and heard plenty of talk about Life—the Victorian mode was not famous for its succinctness—and, as she told Higginson, it embarrassed her and her dog. It was not that she spurned the "Hallowed things" she read about or heard people talk about; she simply withdrew in order to give these things a life that so many of the writers and the talkers failed to give them. This took time, concentration, and solitude.

By a good chance, we can occasionally catch a glimpse of another phase of her reading. In a poem of about 1862 she wrote:

> A Book I have – a friend gave –
> Whose Pencil – here and there –
> Had notched the place that pleased Him – . . . (#360)

Apparently, the habit of notching passages was hers, too. A good number of the books that have come down to us from the library in the Homestead and a few from the Evergreens that she almost certainly shared with Austin and Sue have markings that seem to be hers: thin pencil lines in the margin, parallel to the column of print, and sometimes barely discernible. Sometimes a passage is marked with a tiny "x." The trouble is, other people in the Dickinson circle had pencils too, and followed the same practice. Sue's copy of *Aurora Leigh,* for instance, is marked, but with heavier lines than Emily's. *Of the Imitation of Christ,* given her for Christmas by Sue in 1876, is marked with much heavier lines than the marks, presumably hers, in two books of her youth, *Kavanagh* (1849) and Ik Marvel's *Reveries* (1850). Copies of both of these, with Austin's signature on the flyleaves, have come down to us from him by way of Mabel Todd. One can only guess that both the fine, thin lines and the later bold ones are Emily's.[8]

8. There are some thirty marked books in the Dickinson Collection in the Houghton Library, Harvard. In the library's short-title registry of the books, the markings are described as "probably" or "perhaps" by Emily Dickinson. Though the markings must be approached cautiously, the general scholarly agreement on their authenticity is impressive. The markings in a few of the volumes consist simply of several pages turned down at the corner. The marked volumes (dates indicate editions) are: Matthew Arnold, *Essays in Criticism* (1866 ed.); Elizabeth Barrett Browning, *Aurora Leigh* (1857), *Poems* (1852), *Prometheus Bound,* tr. (1851); Robert Browning, *Dramatis Personae* (1864), *The Ring and the Book* (1869), *Selections* (1884), *Sordello,* (1864); William Cullen Bryant, *Poems* (1849); Thomas Carlyle, *Heroes and Hero Worship* (1853); Arthur Hugh Clough, *Poems* (1869); Thomas De Quincey, *Autobiographical Sketches* (1853), *The Avenger* (1859), *Confessions of an English Opium-Eater* (1855), *Literary Reminiscences* (1854); George Eliot, *The Mill on the Floss* (1860), *Romola* (1863), *Scenes from Clerical Life* (1859); Ralph Waldo Emerson, *The Conduct of Life* (1861, 1879), *Society and Solitude* (1879), *May-Day* (1867), *Essays* (1861); Theodore Parker, *Prayers* (1862); Coventry Patmore, *The Angel in the House* (1856, 1857, 1877); Adelaide Ann Procter, *Legends and Lyrics* (1860); Jean-Paul Richter, *Titan* (1862); Shakespeare, *Comedies, Histories, Tragedies, and Poems* (1853); Alexander Smith, *Poems* (1853); Alfred

Assuming they are (and at least we can be fairly sure that they were done by one or another of the *young* Dickinsons), what kind of passage is marked? Not, usually (to take the *Reveries* first), the glowing word or ringing phrase so much as meditative passages on subjects mighty and minuscule: life and death, time and eternity, love frustrated or fulfilled; marriage versus the solitary life; silence; hiding one's feelings; home; Past and Present; dreams; letter writing; or the plight of a woman without Religion (much worse, says Ik Marvel, than that of a man!). Sentimentalities perhaps, but matters that the young people had to deal with on their own, with little help from father, mother, or the Sunday sermon. Apparently, Ik Marvel played the role (among others) of today's psychological counselors. Here he is, for instance, on marriage:

Shall this brain of mine, careless-working, never tired with idleness, feeding on long vagaries, and high, gigantic castles, dreaming out beatitudes hour by hour – turn itself at length to such dull task-work, as thinking out a livelihood for wife and children?

Where thenceforward will be those sunny dreams, in which I have warmed my fancies, and my heart, and lighted my eye with crystal? This very marriage, which a brilliant working imagination has invested time and again with brightness, and delight, can serve no longer as a mine for teeming fancy: all, alas, will be gone – reduced to the dull standard of the actual! No more room for intrepid forays of imagination – no more gorgeous realm-making – all will be over!

Why not, I thought, go on dreaming?[9]

Some such misgivings as these may have been behind Emily's anxieties about marriage in her letter to Sue in 1852, when (only a few months after reading the *Reveries,* and obviously engaged in something of a reverie herself) she confessed that "I tremble lest at sometime I, too, am yielded up." Time after time Marvel's dreamer broaches thoughts similar to her own. She boasted to Joseph Lyman that "space and time are things

---

Tennyson, *Poems* (1853), *The Princess* (1848); Thomas à Kempis, *Of the Imitation of Christ* (1857); James Thomson, *The Seasons* (1817); Henry David Thoreau, *Walden* (1863); John Wilson, *Noctes Ambrosianae* (1855)...

It will be seen from this list, which, it should be clear by now, by no means includes all of ED's literary enthusiasms, how selective my approach is in this chapter. I have centered my remarks on only five texts: the *Reveries, Kavanagh, Of the Imitation of Christ,* the Bible, and Shakespeare. They may be said to represent stages, or phases, of ED's reading as it may have informed her spirit or guided her choices. Pinpointing "influences" on ED is a precarious undertaking, so well she covered her tracks. "Affinities" are another matter. W. J. Buckingham's exhaustive *Emily Dickinson: An Annotated Bibliography* (1970) shows how much has been accomplished (through the year 1968), but also how much still needs to be done. How close was she to Emerson in certain ways, how far from him in others? And Thoreau, Hawthorne, Whitman, and the English Romantics, especially Keats and Wordsworth? The way is open for some important studies (e.g., "Emily Dickinson and the British Romantics: The Problem of Influence," Yale dissertation, 1974, unpublished, by Joanne Diehl).

9. This passage is not "notched," but it is close to a cluster of those that are.

of the body. . . . My Country is Truth." The Dreamer says of his imaginings,

> Are not these fancies thronging on my brain, bringing tears to my eyes, bringing joy to my soul, as living, as anything human can be living? What if they have no material type – no objective form? All that is crude, – a mere reduction of ideality to sense, – a transformation of the spiritual to the earthy, – a levelling of soul to matter.

Reading, says the Dreamer, is "a great, and happy disentangler of all those knotted snarls – those extravagant vagaries, which belong to a heart sparkling with sensibility," and he recommends, for solace, or sympathy, or "soul-culture" (his phrase), many of those "strongest friends of the soul" to whom Emily turned.

One can imagine the following (marked) passage disentangling a knotty snarl in Emily's consciousness at this crucial time in her development. For all that can be said about her Puritan heritage of Duty and Work, about Mary Lyon's exhilarating example, or even Emerson's insistence, of which she surely was aware, upon the Now, "the almost unbelievable miracle"[10] of the moment, the likelihood is that at a time when she was dreaming of fame Ik Marvel spoke most directly to her:

> Stop not, loiter not, look not backward, if you would be among the foremost! The great Now, so quick, so broad, so fleeting, is yours; – in an hour it will belong to the Eternity of the Past. The temper of Life is to be made good by big honest blows; stop striking, and you will do nothing: strike feebly, and you will do almost as little. Success rides on every hour: grapple it, and you may win: but without a grapple it will never go with you. Work is the weapon of honor, and who lacks the weapon, will never triumph.

These stirring words come toward the end of the section in *Reveries* called "Noon"—preceded, of course, by "Morning" and followed by "Evening," each with its appropriate thoughts. It may well be that Emily Dickinson's long-time fascination with the phenomenon of noon had its start here. (The section is marked in several places.) Marvel begins,

> The Noon is short; the sun never loiters on the meridian, nor does the shadow on the old dial by the garden, stay long at XII. The Present, like the noon, is only a point; and a point so fine, that it is not measurable by grossness of action. Thought alone is delicate enough to tell the breadth of the Present.

10. Cf. Francis Otto Matthiessen, *American Renaissance* (1941), p. 12, where he describes Emerson's discovery (after he had turned his back on the "pale negations" of Unitarianism) of "what, after long and quiet listening to himself, he knew that he really believed. The first and recurrent upsurge of his conviction was that 'life is an ecstasy,' that the moment was an almost unbelievable miracle, which he wanted, more than anything else, to catch and to record."

Or, as he puts it a few paragraphs later, "Thought ranges over the world, and brings up hopes, and fears, and resolves, to measure the burning NOW."

Such "measuring" was to become Emily Dickinson's life work, but she carried Marvel's notion of the "breadth of the Present" much further. Noon became a token of the instantaneous, arrested present which is timelessness, or eternity, or heaven, when all accident, or "grossness," is discarded and there is nothing but essence. In the poem "A Clock stopped," "Degreeless Noon" is the timelessness of death. Another poem equates noon with perfection, the ideal world of pure essence, or Heaven:

> There is a Zone whose even Years
> No Solstice interrupt –
> Whose Sun constructs perpetual Noon
> Whose perfect Seasons wait –
>
> Whose Summer set in Summer, till
> The Centuries of June
> And Centuries of August cease
> And Consciousness – is Noon.　　　(#*1056, about 1865*)

"When Water ceases to rise – [she once wrote] it has commenced falling. That is the law of Flood"—another statement of the idea of "Degreeless Noon." Much of what is often called the breathlessness of Emily Dickinson's poems comes from the urgency of her attempts to arrest the moment, to catch and preserve its essence. The exercise kept her nimble. "Forever – ," she began a poem that further dignifies Ik Marvel's exhortations, "is composed of Nows."[11]

11. Roland Hagenbüchle, "Precision and Indeterminacy in the Poetry of Emily Dickinson," pp. 10–11, elevates this idea into a major component of her poetics:

The . . . concentration on the "critical" moment [the "Now"] is a crucial element in Emily Dickinson's poetry. . . . It finds expression, first iconically, in the epigrammatic shortness of her poems, second thematically, in the numerous descriptions of unstable phenomena in nature such as the rising and setting of the sun or its precarious poise at the meridian hour of noon, the changing of the seasons at the solstices and certain fleeting effects of light in general. It can further be observed in the elliptical and often ambiguous syntax (including the hyphen), and finally in the use of polysemantic and often precariously unstable words and expressions. The world's drama is enacted before her eyes as a process or, to use her own words, as "God's Experiment" [*P* #300, about 1862]. The reversal from being into nothingness (and vice-versa) takes place anew at every moment, as "a gun . . . that touched 'goes off'" [*L* III, 670, to Louise Norcross, early September 1880]. This eminently *dialectic* principle foredooms every attempt to pursue the romantic quest by means of analogy or metaphor. The poet experiences each instant of life and, even more so, that of death as a "critical" turning point or crisis:

> Crisis is a Hair
> Toward which forces creep
> Past which forces retrograde　　　[#*889, about 1864*]

Reveries, of course, was only one of many books that fueled her youth. *Jane Eyre* inspired her by the example of a sensitive, intellectual girl holding to her convictions and triumphing. In *Aurora Leigh,* in Mrs. Browning herself, and in George Eliot, she saw examples of women whose literary ambitions were triumphantly fulfilled. Emerson, Thoreau, Hawthorne were living presences.[12] But nothing could have come much closer to what seem to have been her major preoccupations in the early 1850s than a passage in the "Evening" section in *Reveries,* more liberally marked than any other. Sooner or later, Ik Marvel touched on almost all her problems, at least those that concerned her relations with the outside world. In this passage he goes beyond the gospel of Work and Duty and Fame, and maps out a modus vivendi for Emily Dickinson—at least, a course of life and a rationale that, for whatever reasons, she later announced as her twofold "business" to the Hollands, to "sing" and to "love":

> But not alone does the soul wander to those glittering heights where fame sits, with plumes waving in zephyrs of applause; there belong to it, other appetites, which range wide, and constantly over the broad Future-land. We are not merely, working, intellectual machines, but social puzzles, whose solution, is the work of a life. Much as hope may lean toward the intoxicating joy of distinction, there is another leaning in the soul, deeper, and stronger, toward those pleasures which the heart pants for, and in whose atmosphere, the affections bloom and ripen.
>
> The first may indeed be uppermost; it may be noisiest; it may drown with the clamor of mid-day, the nicer sympathies. But all our day is not mid-day; and all our life is not noise. Silence is as strong as the soul; and there is no tempest so wild with blasts, but has a wilder lull. There lies in the depth of every man's soul a mine of affection, which from time to time will burn with the seething heat of a volcano, and heave up lava-like monuments, through all the cold strata of his commoner nature. . . .
>
> Love only, unlocks the door upon that Futurity, where the isles of the blessed, lie like stars. Affection is the stepping stone to God. The heart is our only measure of infinitude. The mind tires with greatness; the heart – never. Thought is worried and weakened in its flight through the immensity

---

The nature of a turning point is such that it simply eludes all our attempts to grasp it. . . .

If indeed existence proves to be a continuous crisis, we begin to understand why the poet preferably portrays moments of precarious poise between "advance" and "retrograde." . . . *Emerson Society Quarterly* XX (1974), pp. 38–9.

12. No brief note—or chapter—can do justice to the scholarly and critical studies, growing steadily in number, that show her many and sometimes profound affinities with these three. Even to Whitman she was closer than she thought, as Babette Deutsch pointed out in "Poetry at the Mid-Century" (*Virginia Quarterly Review,* Winter 1950): "Miss Dickinson's intense concern for the unique and the particular and her thrifty accuracy have nothing Whitmanesque about them. . . . [But] both were forerunners of those compatriots who returned poetry to its roots in common experience and the language of daily converse" (pp. 69–70).

of space; but Love soars around the throne of the Highest, with added blessing and strength.

Here was a career based on other values than fame—a problem which was
to give her more and more trouble as time went on. Marvel's Dreamer,
again, shows her a resolution she could have found in a dozen different
places but never so fetchingly. Home, he had said in an earlier passage
(marked), is a place where "you may be entirely and joyfully – yourself!"

> Your dreams of reputation, your swift determination, your impulsive
> pride, your deep uttered vows to win a name, have all sobered into affection
> – have all blended into that glow of feeling, which finds its centre, and hope,
> and joy in HOME. From my soul I pity him whose soul does not leap at
> the mere utterance of that name.

In 1862, after Frazar Stearns was killed, Emily wrote the Norcrosses: "Let
us love better, children, it's most that's left to do." This was a "business"
she could conduct at home. About the only thing Marvel left out was her
own peculiar and private method of confronting those "social puzzles"
(including oneself), whose solution he described as "the work of a life": a
ceaseless, lifelong dedication to the Word.

Kavanagh was the book, according to Higginson's report of his conversation with Emily in 1870, that Austin smuggled into the house for one
of those feasts of reading when they were all young together. The time
must have been about 1849, the year the book appeared and the date of
Austin's copy. We have already noted the passage in *Kavanagh* describing
a friendship between two girls—Alice Archer and Cecilia Vaughan—so
close to what Emily felt for Sue as, it would seem, to have been unmistakable, at least to Emily: "They sat together in school; they walked together
after school; they told each other their manifold secrets; they wrote long
and impassioned letters to each other in the evening; in a word, they were
in love with each other." The passage is marked, apparently by two
hands—first, by two faint, parallel, but slightly wavy lines next to the
column of print and following the length of the paragraph; and then by
one very short, straight line, also fine, outside the parallel ones. The book
went the rounds: no less than four kinds of markings are discernible—
short, heavy, firm; long, light, wavy; long, straight, intermittent light and
heavy; and the wavy parallels, which give the impression of being the
most emphatic of all.

At the very least, the markings show how carefully these young people
pored over the book and for much the same kind of sustenance they
found in *Reveries*. Longfellow's romance strings together in its loose
narrative the same kind of animadversions on life, love, and literature—
often little sententious bits that have only slight relevance to the story, like
these (marked with the parallel lines):

The same object, seen from the three different points of view, – the Past, the Present, and the Future, – often exhibits three different faces to us; like those sign-boards over shop doors, which represent the face of a lion as we approach, of a man when we are in front, and of an ass when we have passed. . . .

The rays of happiness, like those of light, are colorless when unbroken.

These are the thoughts of Mr. Churchill, the village schoolmaster, a would-be poet and novelist, whose projected romance never gets beyond the Casaubon stage and thus provides the theme of the story, summed up in Longfellow's epigraph on the title page,

> The flighty purpose never is o'ertook,
> Unless the deed go with it.
>
> Shakespeare.

Kavanagh, by contrast, the brilliant young preacher whose marriage to Cecilia Vaughan (the Sue figure in the story) leads to Alice Archer's brokenhearted death, represents achievement, the man who follows purpose with deed. On the outside of his study door is the "vigorous line of Dante, 'Think that To-day shall never dawn again!'" and on the inside some lines by "a more modern bard," including the following (marked by parallel lines):

> And days are lost, lamenting o'er lost days.
> Are you in earnest? Seize this very minute!
> What you can do or think you can, begin it!
> Boldness has genius, power, and magic in it!

Such stirring thoughts were lost, however, on Mr. Churchill, who had the soul but not the executive power of a poet. He is announced in the opening paragraph of the book (marked by a long thin line):

> Great men stand like solitary towers in the city of God, and secret passages running deep beneath external nature give their thoughts intercourse with higher intelligences, which strengthens and consoles them, and of which the laborers on the surface do not even dream!

To the villagers, he was only the schoolmaster. "They beheld in his form and countenance no outward sign of the divinity within," no "delicate golden wings, wherewith, when the heat of day was over, he soared and revelled in the pleasant evening air." Again the passage is marked by a wavy line; and a short, heavy one marks this description of Mr. Churchill's after-school release:

> . . . his soul seemed to float away on the river's current, till he had glided far out into the measureless sea, and the sound of the wind among the leaves was no longer the sound of the wind, but of the sea. . . .

The evening came. The setting sun stretched his celestial rods of light across the level landscape, and, like the Hebrew in Egypt, smote the rivers and the brooks and the ponds, and they became as blood.

"Soul-culture" surely, and as frenzied figures as Emily could want. We are not surprised to find (in a passage a few pages on) that "books seemed to him almost as living beings, so instinct were they with human thoughts and sympathies," and that as he thought about their authors, "he dreamed of fame, and thought that perhaps hereafter he might be in some degree, and to some one, what these men were to him."

Churchill and Kavanagh were good friends. They philosophized together in their walks. Once they heard in the distance the singing from a camp meeting:

> "O, there will be mourning, mourning, mourning, mourning, –
> O, there will be mourning, at the judgment-seat of Christ!"

—lines which Emily quoted in some alarm to Jane Humphrey a few months after she read them.[13] Kavanagh was moved by the hymn to an extemporaneous sermon, crowded with ideas for a future poet. (The passage is marked with those insistent parallel lines.)

> "And to thousands . . . this is no fiction, – no illusion of an overheated imagination. To-day, to-morrow, every day, – to thousands, the end of the world is close at hand. And why should we fear it? We walk here as it were in the crypts of life; at times, from the great cathedral above us, we can hear the organ and the chanting of the choir; we see the light stream through the open door, when some friend goes up before us; and shall we fear to mount the narrow staircase of the grave, that leads us out of this uncertain twilight into the serene mansions of the life eternal?"

Whatever Kavanagh's rhetoric might have done for Emily Dickinson, it did no good, as the story reveals, to Mr. Churchill. The closest Churchill got to literary fame was a few articles in the magazines and an invitation from an editor to write for a new journal to foster a national literature in America " 'commensurate with our mountains and rivers . . . altogether shaggy and unshorn, that shall shake the earth, like a herd of buffaloes thundering over the prairies!' " (The whole passage is marked by a single line.) Mr. Churchill protested (and here the line becomes almost imperceptibly double): " 'Literature is rather an image of the spiritual world, than of the physical, is it not? – of the internal, rather than the external.' " The project came to nothing, as did a similar request from a young lady, Clarissa Cartwright (of the school of Harriet Hyacinth and Minnie Myrtle), to write a preface for her poems, "Symphonies of the Soul," that were crying for publication.

13. "Kavanagh says 'there will be mourning – mourning – mourning at the judgment seat of Christ' – I wonder if that is true?" (*L* I, 85, January 23, 1850).

As in *Reveries,* Emily Dickinson could have found here almost anything her symphonic young soul wanted to hear. Two passages toward the end, marked with the parallel lines, may have given her something more solid. If *Reveries* indicated a "business" and a locale, *Kavanagh,* dealing with the problem of the writer, is more explicit. In an authorial aside, Longfellow meditated on the reasons for Churchill's failure.

How often, ah, how often, between the desire of the heart and its fulfilment, lies only the briefest space of time and distance, and yet the desire remains forever unfulfilled! It is so near that we can touch it with the hand, and yet so far away that the eye cannot perceive it. What Mr. Churchill most desired was before him. The Romance he was longing to find and record had really occurred in his neighbourhood, among his own friends. It had been set like a picture into the frame-work of his life, inclosed within his own experience. But he could not see it as an object apart from himself; and as he was gazing at what was remote and strange and indistinct, the nearer incidents of aspiration, love, and death, escaped him. They were too near to be clothed by the imagination with the golden vapors of romance; for the familiar seems trivial, and only the distant and unknown completely fill and satisfy the mind.

Emily Dickinson apparently never entertained the idea of writing a romance, although we have no way of knowing the subjects of what must have been the endless scribbling of her earliest years, the compositions that attracted such attention in her school days, or her possible contributions to "Forest Leaves," the school publication that has disappeared. The early valentines show an imagination fully capable of profitable wanderings in romantic groves; but by the time she began to save her poems, she had, at least officially, discarded that mode. Ik Marvel may have helped fix her attention on the burning NOW, and Longfellow may have helped dissipate "the golden vapors of romance," traces of which lingered long in her letters. His advice to focus on "the nearer incidents of aspiration, love, and death" was what she needed.

In his final conversation with Mr. Churchill, Kavanagh put the matter even more bluntly:

"My friend . . . that is not always excellent which lies far away from us. What is remote and difficult of access we are apt to overrate; what is really best for us lies always within our reach, though often overlooked. To speak frankly, I am afraid this is the case with your Romance. You are evidently grasping at something which lies beyond the confines of your own experience, and which, consequently, is only a play of shadows in the realm of fancy. The figures have no vitality; they are only outward shows, wanting inward life. We can give to others only what we have."

Mr. Churchill sighed: "And if we have nothing worth giving?" Kavanagh continued, in a figure Emily Dickinson was fond of:

"No man is so poor as that. As well might the mountain streamlets say they have nothing worth giving to the sea, because they are not rivers. Give what you have. To some one, it may be better than you dare to think."

The passage suggests another dimension to an early poem of Emily's, usually thought of as a love poem or a poem begging for personal acceptance only:

> My River runs to thee –
> Blue Sea! Wilt welcome me?
> My River waits reply –
> Oh Sea – look graciously –
> I'll fetch thee Brooks
> From spotted nooks –
> *Say* – Sea – Take *Me!*   (*#162, about 1860*)

(Although the poem was sent to Mrs. Bowles, the chances were that Mr. Bowles, the editor, would see it.)

Kavanagh lingered long in Emily's imagination. "Adolphus Hawkins, Esq.," the simpering village poet in love with Cecilia Vaughan, became the type of the sentimentalist. In the fall of 1853 she showed signs of consciously discarding the mode. She wrote the Hollands: "I wrote to you last week, but thought you would laugh at me, and call me sentimental, so I kept my lofty letter for 'Adolphus Hawkins, Esq.'" Earlier that year (February 24, 1853), a letter to Susan Gilbert, still thoroughly à la Hawkins, quotes the device Mr. Churchill once used for reckoning on what day of the week the first of December would fall: "'At Dover dwells George Brown, Esquire, / Good Christopher Finch and Daniel Friar!'" (As Emily has it, however, Christopher becomes Carlos, Daniel becomes David, and Friar becomes Fryer; her memory was burrlike but not photographic.) The experience of reading the book was still alive enough in her mind to come up in her conversation with Higginson in 1870; and in 1879 she compared Austin and Sue's driving off to the Belchertown Cattle Show to "Mr and Mrs 'Pendexter,' turning their backs upon Longfellow's Parish."

The reference to the Reverend Mr. Pendexter and the parish brings up another concern of Emily's—and, incidentally, another example of the novel's almost complete coverage of small-town New England culture at mid-century. (The town might have been Amherst, with its visiting circuses and dramatic troupes and the great stir when the railroad reached the town.) Pendexter was the strict orthodox preacher who had preceded Kavanagh in the village parish. Kavanagh, a convert from Catholicism, brought new life and a liberal theology to the community. Indeed, Alice's tragedy began when she fell in love with him as he preached his poetic sermons in the village church.[14] What might have lived in Emily Dickinson's mind as long as anything in the book was Longfellow's description of Kavanagh's spiritual quest:

> The search after Truth and Freedom, both intellectual and spiritual, became a passion in his soul; and he pursued it until he had left far behind him many dusky dogmas, many antique superstitions, many time-honored observances. . . .

—a succinct statement of Emily Dickinson's avowed purpose and major attitudes: "I do not respect 'doctrines.'" "My Country is Truth. . . . It is a free Democracy." And, after her late twenties, she left "many time-honored observances" far behind, including going to church.

To Emily Dickinson in her mid-twenties, already feeling estranged from certain aspects of things spiritual and temporal in her small, self-conscious community, *Of the Imitation of Christ* must have come with a jolt. Yet there is no word about the book in her surviving letters, early or late. The clue to the time of her first experience of it is a copy of an edition of 1857, though it is not certain that the book was acquired that year. It bore her name but was owned by Sue and apparently shared with her. Although it has markings similar to those in the 1876 copy that Sue gave Emily for Christmas that year, whether they are Sue's or Emily's or both, it is impossible to tell. It may have been that Sue, hearing of the new edition in 1876, presented Emily with a book that had long interested them both.[15]

Reveries and *Kavanagh* touched on many of Emily's problems and may have helped her to some resolutions, but the *Imitation* presented her with an all-or-nothing choice far more radical in its demands than the mild inspirations of Marvel's Dreamer or Kavanagh's literary advice to Mr. Churchill. The issue of choice was sharpening for her, as she saw her friends taking paths very different from anything she was inclined to follow—matrimony, or careers, or the kind of piety she saw in Abiah Root. She could explain her refusal to become "a christian" (in Abiah's sense) by saying that the world held her affections, but it was not the world of the Amherst sewing society or august assemblies or Boston and

14. Such was Sarah Jane Locke's experience (it will be recalled from our account of Wadsworth) at the Troy Female Seminary when she fell in love with her future husband. (See Appendix III.)

15. The copy of the 1857 edition is in the Dickinson Collection, Houghton Library, Harvard. The title page is inscribed "Emily Dickinson," in Sue's handwriting. The copy of the 1876 edition is in the Beinecke Library, Yale. It is inscribed, in Sue's hand, "Emily with love / Dec 26th 76." The translations differ slightly. I have followed the 1857 edition except for a few marked passages in the 1876 edition.

A few pages in the 1857 edition are uncut (Bk. II, ch. 11; Bk. III, ch. 3; pp. 147–48). Bk. III, ch. 5, and Bk. IV, ch. 7 and 12, are the most heavily marked, often in the same wavy parallel lines noted in *Kavanagh*. The passages marked in the 1876 edition are indicated later in my discussion.

Bostonians. For whatever reasons, normal or neurotic, she was withdrawing more and more from the community. The *Imitation* was the sternest kind of challenge to certain tendencies she felt in herself. Her remark to Higginson in 1869 that her life "has been too simple and stern to embarrass any," suggests the degree to which she had answered it. "By two wings," says the *Imitation,* "a man is lifted up from things earthly, namely, by Simplicity and Purity." The passage is marked in the 1876 copy.

"Despise the world." "Fly the tumultuousness of the world as much as thou canst." "Take refuge within the closet of thine heart." These and similar exhortations echo and reecho throughout the *Imitation.* For a girl with religious and social problems, with a burgeoning talent still unfocused, this manual for the dedicated life must have had an attraction quite apart from its doctrinal basis. Its insistence on innate depravity (the doctrine of "corruption" that the minister preached to Father and Vinnie), on the purging away of the sins of the flesh, on the dangers of succumbing to the wiles of the devil—all this she could deal with as she dealt with similar doctrines in the Amherst sermons. But its pattern of life was adaptable to purposes other than monastic. She had not yet, it seems, found a discipline, a way of implementing the "work of a life" she read about in *Reveries.* Here in the *Imitation* was the same urgency: "Why wilt thou defer thy good purpose from day to day? Arise and begin in this very instant, and say, Now is the time to be doing"—and here was a touch of Mary Lyon's teaching: "Do what lieth in thy power and God will assist thy good affection"; and here, even, was something of her own scorn of people (as Higginson recorded her conversation in 1870) who were only half alive ("How do most people live without any thoughts"). The *Imitation,* lamenting "lukewarmness of spirit," slothfulness and apathy, had an answer: "For that is the reason why there are few contemplative men to be found, because few have the knowledge to withdraw themselves fully from perishing creatures."

The *Imitation* prescribed a daily regimen and a locale. "Things private are practised more safely at home." "The more thou visitest thy chamber, the more thou wilt like it; the less thou comest thereunto, the more thou wilt loathe it." In "daily exercises" the cloistered one penetrates those "things internal"—Emily Dickinson's phrase was "the Being's Centre"— and (according to another passage in the *Imitation*) he "must diligently search into, and set in order both the outward and the inward man, because both of them are of importance to our progress in godliness." Then comes a verse, especially marked in the 1876 copy, much to her purpose: "Never be entirely idle; but either be reading, or writing, or praying, or meditating, or endeavouring something for the public good."

She never learned to pray, she said, and she persisted in calling herself a pagan. She interpreted the common good differently from the organized charity or sewing circles of her day and perhaps from what the *Imitation* here implied. Something closer to her notion of the common good came in another passage, where the *Imitation* urges that "we may learn to bear one another's burdens . . . to bear with one another, comfort one another, help, instruct, and admonish one another." This she did with the balsam word, the healing word, the wise word, but, above all, with the living word in hundreds of letters and poems. "Let Emily sing for you because she cannot pray," she wrote the Norcrosses in their bereavement. The *Imitation,* expanding on the Gospels, states her "business" and suggests her method:

> Love feels no burden, thinks nothing of trouble, attempts what is above its strength, pleads no excuse of impossibility; for it thinks all things lawful for itself and all things possible. . . . Love is watchful, and sleeping slumbereth not. . . . Let me sing the song of love. . . .

With one exception, the two chapters on love in the *Imitation* are the most heavily marked in the 1876 copy.

The exception is the chapter on the Cross. The marked passages in this section could be called glosses on a late remark of Emily's in a letter to Mrs. Hills: "When Jesus tells us about his Father, we distrust him. When he shows us his Home, we turn away, but when he confides to us that he is 'acquainted with Grief,' we listen, for that also is an Acquaintance of our own." There is little in the *Imitation* about heaven or about Emily's "Flood subject," immortality. We do not see Christ sitting at the right hand of God—indeed, there is little about God in the *Imitation;* what we see is Christ bearing the Cross, the emblem of human suffering and tribulation borne for a transcendent purpose. The *Imitation* chides those who would have it the other way around:

> Jesus hath now many lovers of His heavenly kingdom, but few bearers of His Cross.
> He hath many desirous of consolation, but few of tribulation.
> He findeth many companions of His table, but few of His abstinence.
> All desire to rejoice with Him, few are willing to endure any thing for Him, or with Him.
> Many follow Jesus unto the breaking of bread; but few to the drinking of the Cup of His Passion.
> Many reverence His miracles, few follow the ignominy of His Cross.[16]

This is very close to Emily's lifelong experience of the Cross and her sense of its meaning. An early poem set the theme of suffering and anguish.

> I shall know why – when Time is over –
> And I have ceased to wonder why –
> Christ will explain each separate anguish
> In the fair schoolroom of the sky –

16. This passage occurs in one of the uncut sections in the 1857 copy. As the opening passage of Book II, Chapter 11, however, it was not concealed among the uncut pages.

> He will tell me what "Peter" promised –
> And I – for wonder at his woe –
> I shall forget the drop of Anguish
> That scalds me now – that scalds me now!   (*#193, about 1860*)

Her references to Christ are seldom so eschatological—here, her vision of the explanation in heaven of suffering on earth. Mostly, her Christ is a very human figure: "when Christ was divine, he was uncontented till he had been human." She liked the sermon about the disappointment of Jesus in Judas, because it was "told like a mortal story of intimate young men." In a late poem

> The Savior must have been
> A docile Gentleman –
> To come so far so cold a Day
> For little Fellowmen – . . .   (*#1487, about 1880*)

and in the elegy on Wadsworth,

> 'Twas Christ's own personal Expanse
> That bore him from the Tomb –   (*#1543, about 1882*)

Christ's personal expanse meant for her his triumph over suffering, and in this she found identity with him, not so much in the Risen Christ, or in Christ the Consoler or Redeemer. An undated poem follows the emphasis of the *Imitation,* even to the note of chiding in its opening lines:

> One crown that no one seeks
> And yet the highest head
> Its isolation coveted
> Its stigma deified
>
> While Pontius Pilate lives
> In whatsoever hell
> That coronation pierces him
> He recollects it well.   (*#1735*)

What pierced her was the truth in a "look of Agony" and "the fashions – of the Cross – " as she "passed Calvary." According to her greatest crucifixion poem, this was a daily experience:

> One Crucifixion is recorded – only –
> How many be
> Is not affirmed of Mathematics –
> Or History –

One Calvary – exhibited to Stranger –
As many be
As Persons – or Peninsulas –
Gethsemane –

Is but a Province – in the Being's Centre –
Judea –
For Journey – or Crusade's Achieving –
Too near –

Our Lord – indeed – made Compound Witness –
And yet –
There's newer – nearer Crucifixion
Than That – (#553, about 1862)

Whenever she spoke of abstinence or endurance or renunciation—that "piercing Virtue"—or of the "'Thorns'" she'll wear "till *Sunset,*" or of "the strong cup of anguish brewed for the Nazarene," she went back, not so much to the Gospels as to the *Imitation,* with its powerful emphasis on renouncing the world, bearing the burden, shouldering the Cross—that is, the simple, stern life of the dedicated religious:

To put this World down, like a Bundle –
And walk steady, away,
Requires Energy – possibly Agony –
'Tis the Scarlet way

Trodden with straight renunciation
By the Son of God –
Later, his faint Confederates
Justify the Road – . . . (#527, about 1862)

In one of her phases, at least, it is clear that she identified herself as one of Christ's faint Confederates. She followed his suffering to its bitter end: "Even in Our Lord's 'that they be with me where I am,'" she wrote, "I taste interrogation."

The moral advice of the *Imitation* parallels much of what she said in letters to her friends and to herself in many poems. The chapter on Solitude is well marked. A quotation from Seneca she would have recognized as justifying her early advice to Austin to cultivate solitude: "One said, 'As oft as I have been among men, I returned home less a man than I was before.'" When she "selected" her own society—of one—she was carrying out the *Imitation*'s beatitude, "Blessed are the single-hearted; for they shall enjoy much peace." In the poem "One need not be a Chamber – to be Haunted," she pictures the terror of confronting oneself in the "Corridors" of the mind: "Wheresoever thou goest," says the *Imitation,* "thou carriest thyself with thee, and shalt ever find thyself." The "royal way," the "crown" are frequent images in the *Imitation* and in her poems. The idea of suffering as a test is also frequent. This passage, among many others, is marked: "In temptations and afflictions a man is proved, how much he hath profited. . . . Neither is it any such great thing if a man be dèvout and fervent, when he feeleth no affliction." Emily carried the idea further: "He deposes Doom / Who hath suffered him – " The speaker in the *Imitation* confesses to sadness and dejection because of "a small matter . . . sometimes a very trifle" (the passage is marked) and warns against succumbing to moods (again the passage is marked): "My son, trust not to thy feelings, for whatever they be now, they will quickly be changed towards some other thing. . . . so that thou art at one time merry, at another sad; at one time quiet, at another troubled; now devout, now undevout; now diligent, now listless; now grave, and now light"—a passage that needs no further documentation in the life of Emily Dickinson, especially in the early troubled years.

One phase of Emily's Christology is barely touched upon in the *Imitation:* the idea of Christ as the Beloved, the Divine Lover. After two chapters on suffering and misery, both liberally marked in the 1876 edition, there comes one, unmarked, on the theme of everlasting rest in Christ, in which the speaker establishes a kind of dialogue with his Lord:

> O thou most beloved spouse of my soul, Jesu Christ, thou most pure Lover, thou Lord of all creation; O that I had the wings of true liberty, that I might flee away and rest in thee![17]

The 1857 edition contains a reference here not to the Song of Songs, as one might expect, but to Psalms 55:6: "Oh that I had wings like a dove! for then would I fly away, and be at rest." In the *Imitation,* the Lord answers: "Behold, here I am. Behold, I come unto thee, because thou hast called upon Me." Although she had many other sources, the germ is here for her poems on the theme of the Bride of Christ.

> Given in Marriage unto Thee
> Oh thou Celestial Host –
> Bride of the Father and the Son
> Bride of the Holy Ghost.
>
> Other Betrothal shall dissolve –
> Wedlock of Will, decay –
> Only the Keeper of this Ring
> Conquer Mortality –   (#817, about 1864)

Precisely how much the *Imitation* had to do with Emily Dickinson's vocation in its formative stage is debatable, like so many important phases of her life. It may have provided at an early stage a shock and a model. It

17. In the 1857 copy, the passage beginning "Voice of the Beloved" (Book IV, Chapter 12) is marked with wavy parallel lines.

is hazardous to claim too much for markings and parallels, however striking. Her failure to comment directly upon the *Imitation* in what we have of her writings should stand as a caution; but she was often most secretive about what mattered most. All that can be said is that she had ample opportunity to read it during a crucial period in her life and could have found in it not only the perfect challenge to take the solitary way— the way she in fact took—but also a detailed manual of instructions and encouragement. And, coming back to the book after the stormy years had passed, she could have seen her way vindicated, the *Imitation*'s promise— of victory for those who endure—fulfilled.

In Emily Dickinson's community, the Bible was not only read always and at length from the pulpit and in family prayers (Edward Dickinson went through a chapter a day), it was the duty of the pious to keep a copy always at hand in case of spiritual need.[18] It was the parents' duty, also, to see that each child had a Bible. Emily's copy, inscribed to her, is an 1843 edition of the King James Version; so we can assume she had one of her own at least by the time she was twelve. How much she read it in the early years is a matter of conjecture; she certainly heard it a great deal. By whatever process, it was in and through her consciousness like no other book. When she told Higginson in the spring of 1862 that she had, for prose, "Mr Ruskin – Sir Thomas Browne – and the Revelations," she gave an utterly inadequate notion of her knowledge and use of it. The extraordinary range of the Biblical allusions in her letters and poems shows how arbitrary her selection here of Revelation is, although admittedly the "Gem chapter" (XXI) was a favorite, and in one of the few moments when we can actually catch her in the act of reading the Bible, she is deep in Revelation: "Don't tell, dear Mrs. Holland, but wicked as I am, I read my Bible sometimes, and in it as I read today, I found a verse like this"—and she strings together phrases from three widely separated chapters. But in the length and breadth of her letters and poems very few books of the Bible are not represented in some way, by word, phrase, reference, or allusion. She was saturated with it and could apparently summon it to her aid at will. She began early. At fourteen she wrote Abiah Root that she thought she could "keep house very comfortably" if she knew how to cook but admitted that her situation was a little like "faith without works, which you know we are told is dead" [James 2:26]. She apologized (we recall) for her pedantry: "Excuse my quoting from the Scripture, dear Abiah, for it was so handy in this case I couldn't get along very well without it." Next year, again to Abiah, she rolled together Matthew 13:15 and Ecclesiastes 12:6, with delightful imprecision, in a

---

18. There was no shortage in the Dickinson families. Jack L. Capps, p. 212, calls attention to the nineteen Bibles in the Dickinson Collection at Harvard.

brand-new Dickinson Version: " 'When our eyes are dull of seeing & our ears of hearing, when the silver cord is loosed & the golden bowl broken' "[19] —an indication perhaps that, so far, she was doing more listening than reading, that she heard the great phrases ringing in her ears rather than saw them in print before her eyes. (Her freedom with the text is characteristic of a lifelong habit. Her quotations are seldom exact.)

In point of doctrine, theology, and vision, in range of human emotion and experience and character, the Bible was infinitely richer, of course, than the *Imitation*. The great dimension that the *Imitation,* relatively speaking, left out was here fully realized: the apocalyptic vision, the vision of the Last Things, the time when (to use the verses Emily quoted to Mrs. Holland) friends shall "go no more out" and God shall wipe away all tears. In this sense, Revelation was perhaps her greatest inspiration, especially in her later years, when phrases from the book resound through the letters: " 'And there was no more Sea,' " " 'Every several Gate is of one Pearl,' " " 'And I saw the Heavens opened' " (a verse quoted twice within a few months). Although she never formally became a Christian, it was the promise of the Gospels and the vision of the Prophet that both strengthened her and, in long moments of doubt, haunted her throughout her life. This was the "Theme stubborn as Sublime" that she "grappled" with in poem after poem. Indeed, by implication or indirection, it is never far from any of them. Scorn doctrines as she would, she all but polled the preachers, or any older, wiser person she thought could help her, for their ideas on immortality. "The Clergyman says I shall see my Father," she said. She scorned the doctrines she did not like; and if the assurance of the preacher never seems to have convinced her, it was the Christian dispensation that gave form and meaning—ponder it and question it as she would—to her life. She lived, it seems, in a state of wonder and hope: "I wonder how long we shall wonder," she wrote, "how early we shall *know*." But it was the Bible and her Christian heritage that gave her the questions to wonder about and the destiny to hope for.

One further glimpse of her in the act (or near it) of reading the Bible tells much about how it became the resource it was for many phases of her life—artistic as well as personal—other than the matter of vision and belief. In a letter to Joseph Lyman, written probably in the mid-1860s, she describes an experience that seems to date about ten years back:

> Some years after we saw each other last I fell to reading the Old & New Testament. I had known it as an arid book but looking I saw how infinitely wise & merry it is.
>
> Anybody that knows grammar must admit the surpassing splendor & force of its speech, but the fathomless gulfs of meaning – those words which

19. Matthew 13:15: "For this people's heart is waxed gross, and their ears are dull of hearing, and their eyes they have closed. . . ." Ecclesiastes 12:6: "Or ever the silver cord be loosed, or the golden bowl be broken. . . ."

He spoke to those most necessary to him, hints about some celestial reunion – yearning for a oneness – has any one fathomed that sea? I know those to whom those words are very near & necessary, I wish they were more so to me, for I see them shedding a serenity quite wonderful & blessed. They are great bars of sunlight in many a shady heart.

This is a curious confession from one who on many occasions wrote of her longing for the Christian consolation. Perhaps at the time she was writing Lyman she felt more than usually self-confident. She had weathered the storm of the late 1850s and early 1860s and (if we read the signs right) had now found her vocation. It may be that her new confidence opened her eyes as if for the first time to other qualities in the Bible: "the splendor and force of its speech," "how infinitely wise & merry it is"—a quite secular response, not surely her first, but, coming at the time it did, important.

In letters and poems the rest of her life she put the Bible to whatever use fitted her mood, grave or gay, pious or impious, serious or whimsical. The Good Book has seldom been put under such wide-ranging obligation; there is little in the annals of any literary figure to equal it. In this at least she seems unique.

The famous poem about books sets the tone, as its last line contributes the key phrase. (I have already cited the poem in part; now it is good to see it all.)

> He ate and drank the precious Words –
> His Spirit grew robust –
> He knew no more that he was poor,
> Nor that his frame was Dust –
>
> He danced along the dingy Days
> And this Bequest of Wings
> Was but a Book – What Liberty
> A loosened spirit brings –   (*#1587, about 1883*)

The Bible loosened her spirit in ways that her devout contemporaries would hardly have deemed spiritual. At widely scattered intervals in her late correspondence, she referred to it as speaking to us "roguishly," or "joyously," or "boyishly." At least, after she had outgrown her youthful feeling that it was an "arid book," she made it speak to herself that way, as, confessed in the poem sent to her nephew Ned (aged twenty-one), it did *not* for most boys. The Bible of the poem is the Bible as it came to her out of the dour Puritan tradition.

The Bible is an antique Volume –
Written by faded Men
At the suggestion of Holy Spectres –
Subjects – Bethlehem –
Eden – the ancient Homestead –
Satan – the Brigadier –
Judas – the Great Defaulter –
David – the Troubadour –
Sin – a distinguished Precipice
Others must resist –
Boys that "believe" are very lonesome –
Other Boys are "lost" –
Had but the Tale a warbling Teller –
All the Boys would come –
Orpheus' Sermon captivated –
It did not condemn –   (*#1545, late 1882*)

Throughout her life, beginning with the Abiah Root days and the passage about faith, works, and cooking, she played Orpheus in a variety of ways. She delighted in giving the fine, old, deadly serious phrases a new life by working them into whimsical contexts. Once, at nineteen, she found Isaiah's exalted prophecy fulfilled during an evening of orations at the college's Eclectic Society. She jotted a cryptic memorandum to herself on the program: "New things have happened. 'The crooked is made straight.' I am confided in by one – and *despised* by an *other!* and another still!" She liked the witty conjunction of the trivial and the exalted, the domestic and the divine. In 1884 a late-spring frost had ruined the apple crop. The harvest, she wrote, was reduced to " 'Fruits of the Spirit.' " "But Vinnie," she added, "prefers Baldwins." " 'Day unto Day uttereth Speech,' " she wrote Ned—but no letter comes from his vacation spot in the mountains. Thrice she played on the verse "Consider the lilies," once impishly as "the only Commandment I ever obeyed." At least five times, with Godlike sweep, she "gave his [or "my"] angels charge," once (changing angels to "Tropics") for nothing more than to protect Joseph Lyman from the New Orleans heat. Once she threatened Austin with the "whip of scorpions" if he didn't come home on a certain weekend. Susan "breaks many Commandments, but *one* she obeys – 'Whatsoever ye do, do it unto the Glory' – Susan will be saved –" Once to Ned, only six months before she died, she turned a robbery at the Evergreens into a Biblical joke: "Burglaries have become so frequent, is it quite safe to leave the Golden Rule out over night?"

Sometimes the same verse is used in contexts of entirely different moods. "Eye hath not seen, nor ear heard" the wonders (in 1852) of her new friend, Susan Gilbert, or (in 1873) what a certain horse wouldn't do to its owner if it weren't tied. Once the opening words of the passage found their way into a poem where they are used to taunt the empirical scientists whose "theses" were disturbing the faithful:

"Eye hath not seen" may possibly
Be current with the Blind
But let not Revelation
By theses be detained – . . .   (#*1241, about 1872*)

But then, in a letter of condolence, in 1886, to a bereaved friend, she is true to the exalted original: " 'Eye hath not seen nor ear heard' " all that God has prepared for His sons: "What a recompense! . . . How ecstatic!"

She almost always clipped down the Biblical rhetoric or used a single word or phrase as shorthand for the original. I Peter 1:8 ("Whom having not seen, ye love") becomes a whole letter to Mrs. Holland: " 'Whom seeing not, we' clasp –" Matthew 25:40 ("Inasmuch as ye have done it unto one of the least of these my brethren, ye have done it unto me") becomes "Unto the little, unto me," and in another letter simply "Inasmuch –" "Consider the lilies" is reduced to "Consider," leaving her correspondent to fill in the rest.[20] She liked to roll the great phrases under her tongue—"the silver cord," "the golden bowl," the *weight* of glory," or (to bring Matthew 6:19–20 up to date), "Lay up Treasures immediately – that's the best Anodyne for moth and Rust and the thief whom the Bible knew enough of Banking to suspect would break in and steal." Matthew 10:29 ("Are not two sparrows sold for a farthing? and one of them shall not fall on the ground without your Father") is similarly glossed for a friend: "Gentlest of Neighbors, recall the 'Sparrows' and the great Logician –"

The Biblical characters, especially the Old Testament ones, lived for her as vitally, and often as secularly, as any out of Shakespeare or her favorite novelist, Dickens. About something disturbing her, she wrote Mrs. Holland (about 1881): "Jacob versus Esau, was a trifle in Litigation, compared to the Skirmish in my Mind." In an early poem, Jacob is the "bewildered Gymnast" who "found he had worsted God," and in two letters in the last few months of her life she has him wrestling with the angel, first (with fine disregard of the source) making the angel speak the line, "I will not let thee go, except I bless thee," and in the second having Jacob say it but keeping the altered pronouns. She felt the pathos, or tragedy, or merriment in these people and their situations—the love of Saul and Jonathan, "old Moses" and his disappointment, David grieving over Absalom, David as "Troubadour," and poor Noah who never got credit for saving the human race:

20. The remark to Sue, mentioned above, "Whatsoever ye do," is a characteristic shortening of I Corinthians 10:31: "Whether therefore ye eat, or drink, or whatsoever ye do, do all to the glory of God."

And so there was a Deluge –
And swept the World away –
But Ararat's a Legend – now –
And no one credits Noah –   (*#403, about 1862*)

She pinned a prudential moral on the story of Abraham and Isaac:

Abraham to kill him
Was distinctly told –
Isaac was an Urchin –
Abraham was old –

Not a hesitation –
Abraham complied –
Flattered by Obeisance
Tyranny demurred –

Isaac – to his children
Lived to tell the tale –
Moral – with a Mastiff
Manners may prevail.   (*#1317, about 1874*)

(Kierkegaard was not alone in questioning the divine morality in that story.)

She made many self-identifications, sometimes whimsical (especially at first), sometimes deeply serious. "I have lately come to the conclusion that I am Eve, alias Mrs. Adam," she wrote Abiah Root in 1846. "You know there is no account of her death in the Bible, and why am not I Eve?" (Thirty-eight years later, the identification was not so jaunty—the years had done their work. She apologized to some friends for not seeing them: "In all the circumference of Expression, those guileless words of Adam and Eve never were surpassed, 'I was afraid and hid Myself.' ") In the early valentine to her student friend she was Judith of the Apocrypha and he the orator of Ephesus. She could be Ruth ("My father will be your father, and my home will be your home"), and Rebecca at the well. Later on, whether or not suggested by the *Imitation,* identifications with Christ and his suffering abound; she became Queen, or Empress, of Calvary; she was "acquainted with Grief." Still later, toward the very end, she spoke not so much as the suffering Christ but as Christ the teacher and prophet. "All grows strangely emphatic," she wrote Mrs. Holland in the fall of 1884, "and I think if I should see you again, I sh'd begin every sentence with 'I say unto you – ' " Most of the late poems, those that can be dated with some assurance as in the late 1870s and 1880s, are wisdom pieces, distillations, summings up—"My Wars are laid away in Books"; "Who has not found the Heaven – below – / Will fail of it above"—or deal in some way or other with the ends of things, whether they be summers, sunsets, or human lives.

This was no new vein for her, of course, simply an intensified search for essences and a heightened sense of prophecy as the "dyings" followed one after the other and she saw her own end near. The Bible itself came in for a masterful, if enigmatic, summing up immediately after her remark to Mrs. Holland about everything growing strangely emphatic. "The Bible," she added, "dealt with the Centre, not with the Circumference – " Earlier she had stated her own "business" as Circumference, by which she probably meant (in 1862) her purpose to encompass the truth of life, the whole range of human experience, and somehow to arrest it in her poetry. She set out to be Expositor, Interpreter, Analyst, Orpheus—all in one.

This remark to Mrs. Holland may admit the need, toward the end, of a sharper focus. The problem of belief had always haunted her. In 1869, she wrote her cousin Perez Dickinson Cowan, "I suppose we are all thinking of Immortality, at times so stimulatedly that we cannot sleep." In 1884, the problem was coming very close. The Bible, with its ecstatic promise of what eye hath not seen nor ear heard, became central. But it never failed her as a "merry" book, either, and through it, for a lifetime, she explored the fringes as well as the center of being. It broadened and deepened her insights. She experimented with its language, its characters, its stories, its tremendous affirmations with a recklessness and humor quite unbecoming her time and station.

An earlier chapter explored the possible implications of Emily's remark to her sister-in-law in 1882: "With the exception of Shakespeare, you have told me of more knowledge than any one living." The supposition was that she meant: "I have *learned* more from you . . ." The question now is: What did she learn from Shakespeare?

A passage from Virginia Woolf's *A Writer's Diary* may set the tone here:

> A curious sense of complete failure. . . . I can't write this morning, can't get into the swing. Innumerable worries. . . . My head is all jangled. . . . Go back and get the central idea, and then rocket into it. And be very controlled and keep a hand on myself too. And perhaps read a little Shakespeare. Yes, one of the last plays: I think I will do that, so as to loosen my muscles.

Emily's description of her devouring Shakespeare after the long stretch of eye trouble suggests a degree of involvement that did more than merely loosen the muscles, but it would be pedantic to call either response an instance of literary influence. Such re-creative power, joy, and refreshment have more to do with the springs of life itself than with anything like the indebtedness, verbal or philosophical, usually associated with the notion of influence. When Emily asked Joseph Lyman, "Why clasp any hand but this?" and said to Higginson, "Why is any other book needed?" her hyperbole could hardly have been intended to convince either man of so exclusive a preference; she was simply pointing to Shakespeare's indispensability in her life, especially after the long, hard deprivation in Cambridge. As it did for Mrs. Woolf, reading Shakespeare meant new life and new energy.

It is hard to tell when Shakespeare became a potent factor in Emily's life. In her schooling, the plays were not the academic staple they later became, certainly not in Amherst Academy or Mount Holyoke, where the authors most studied in Emily's time were Milton, Pope, Cowper, Thomson, and Young. The Amherst community was dubious about Shakespeare. For all "his splendid moral sentiments," said President Hitchcock in his inaugural address, Shakespeare "was undoubtedly a libertine in principle and practice," and there is a persistent legend that her father wanted her to read nothing but the Bible. (Apparently, when he saw there was no help for it, he bought books for her, and added a new edition of Shakespeare to his library in 1853.) Meanwhile, the younger set was way ahead of him. They had a Shakespeare Club. Between September 1850 and June 1852 the following items are recorded: Vinnie (aged seventeen) read *Hamlet* to prepare for Richard H. Dana's lectures. Emilie Fowler spent a whole morning at the Dickinsons' reading Shakespeare, and Susan Gilbert bought the *Complete Works*. Probably the whole group, including Emily, went to hear "An Evening with Shakespeare: An Elocutionary Entertainment" by Miss Lizzie Johnson in Phenix Hall. It was in 1859 that Emily, speaking of Fanny Kemble, wrote Louise Norcross, "I have heard many notedly *bad* readers, and a fine one would be almost a fairy surprise." So it appears that much of the experience of these young people with Shakespeare was both extracurricular and auditory; they *heard* the plays. Years later Emily wrote Louise about a reading of her own that must have been extraordinary (we can only guess, and hope, that she read aloud): "I read a few words since I came home – John Talbot's parting with his son, and Margaret's with Suffolk. I read them in the garret, and the rafters wept."

She began referring to Shakespeare in her letters, or quoting him, when she was fourteen, and never stopped. Although all but a very few quotations come after the trouble with her eyes, she may have been quoting the plays steadily in letters that are lost, and certainly Shakespeare was omnipresent in her life. From 1865 on, the quotations multiply, surpassed only by those from the Bible.

She could play, or be merry, with Shakespeare, too. Some of her quotations are true to their serious, sometimes tragic, contexts, but most are in fun, or for decoration, or to display her wit. At first she is merely showing off (as she did to Abiah about faith and works) and uses the obvious counters one would expect of a teenager: the "sere and yellow leaf," "till 'we *two* meet again,'" and a mysterious reference to "Shakespeare's description of a tempest in a teapot." Later, in letters to Austin, she became more subtle. "Oh my dear 'Oliver'," she addressed him in 1853, perhaps a reference, by way of Oliver's remark in *As You Like It* about

Celia—"my sudden wooing . . . her sudden consenting"—to his secret engagement to Sue (or perhaps the reference is merely to the always handy Oliver Twist). Once, when Edward Dickinson was in Congress, she thought of franking a package to Austin. Vinnie, she says, would do it if *she* were in Congress ("She'd save something snug for us all, besides enriching herself"), "but Caesar [Father] is such 'an honorable man' that we may all go to the Poor House, for all the American Congress will lift a finger to help us – " Sometimes she is facetious, as when she remarked to the Norcrosses upon the death of an elderly lady in town: "Did you know about Mrs. J——? She fledged her antique wings. 'Tis said that 'nothing in her life became her like the leaving it.'" Once she twisted the quotation to suit a birth, not a death, and tucked in a phrase from *As You Like It* for good measure—all to congratulate Mrs. Holland on becoming a grandmother:

> The contemplation of you as 'Grandma' is a touching novelty to which the Mind adjusts itself by reverent degrees.
> That nothing in her Life became her like it's last event, it is probable – So the little Engrosser has done her work, and Love's 'remainder Biscuit' is henceforth for us –

Mrs. Holland tended to put her in the quoting mood. She hoped "the Airs were delicate" when her friend returned home from a visit. Thanking her for a note, she reduced Hamlet's "whips and scorns of time" to something more wieldy: "Your little Note protected, as it always does, and the 'Whips of Time' felt a long way off." And speaking (presumably) about the talk aroused by Cross's life of George Eliot, she put *Hamlet* and the New Testament in telling conjunction: "None of us know her enough to judge her, so her Maker must be her 'Crowner's Quest' – Saul criticized his Savior till he became enamored of him – then he was less loquacious – "

As with the Bible, she often pruned down the Shakespearean lines to fit her sense of economy—or perhaps it was simply that she did not have iambic pentameter to contend with, or perhaps, quoting from memory, she did not bother to be precise. The Physician's remark to Macbeth, "Therein the patient / Must minister to himself," becomes (she used it on several occasions) "That sort must heal itself." Antony's advice to his followers (she gave the speech to Enobarbus), "let that be left / Which leaves itself," becomes, "Leave that which leaves itself." Congratulating Samuel Bowles, Jr., on the birth of his son, she offered her help in a shortened (and improved?) version of Claudius's exhortation to Polonius ("O, speak of that! that do I long to hear"): "If ever of any act of mine you should be in need, let me reply with the Laureate, 'Speak that I live to hear!'"

Though all this is agreeable and witty, it was from Shakespeare, she said, that she learned more of *knowledge* than from anyone else. But even here, as she was playing with the great lines, it could be said that what she was learning was the power of words and ways of manipulating them to their utmost effect, solid knowledge for a poet. Sometimes it was the "ring of it" (Virginia Woolf called it "the tune of words") that excited her. She had Shakespeare's miraculous ear for language—she may have learned it from him. If the ring of the lines from *Antony* thrilled her ("heart, / Which in the scuffles of great fights hath burst / The buckles on his breast"), the words she used to introduce the passage are themselves a minor miracle: "where Enobarbus laments the amorous lapse of his master."

Many of her poems, otherwise undistinguished, achieve distinction by a word or phrase that "scalps your naked Soul." Sometimes a single word in one of the plays startled her with its enormous, implied drama. She wrote Judge Lord five years after the death of his wife: "Antony's remark to a friend, 'since Cleopatra died' is said to be the saddest ever lain in Language – That engulfing *'Since'* – " Sometimes she used a word or two from the plays—*Antony* was a favorite—as a quick way of conveying to a knowledgeable correspondent an immense thought she chose not to spell out. Antony complained to Cleopatra, "Egypt, thou knew'st too well, / My heart was to thy rudder tied by the strings." To Susan, apparently during a time of tension, went this note: " 'Egypt – thou knew'st – ' " When she concluded a letter to Otis Lord (the one asking that he "save me from the idolatry that would crush us both – ") with Othello's "And very Sea-Mark of my utmost Sail," she knew that she need say no more about the extent of her love, or her endurance, or both. Later, in a letter to his niece, Ophelia's "envious Sliver" conveyed the tragedy of his death. Once, a quick if inaccurate "for those ways 'Madness lies' " was a mild warning to Dr. Holland not to jeopardize his health by trying to increase the fame he had already won.

Shakespeare's characters lived for her much as did the people in the Bible, and she enjoyed using them to convey general sentiments. Here Othello was a favorite. She had not seen Maria Whitney for some time. "Othello is uneasy," she wrote, "but then Othellos always are, they hold such mighty stakes." A whole note, at Christmas time, to Mrs. Hills read: "When the 'Children' for whom the Cakes were founded are 'Merchants of Venice' and 'Desdemonas,' Santa Claus must tell me." Brabantio's reluctant gift of his daughter to Othello was a favorite paradox. When Bowles died, she wrote Maria Whitney, quoting this time with remarkable exactness, "Brabantio's resignation is the only one – 'I here do give thee that with all my heart, which, but thou hast already, with all my heart I would keep from thee.' " Antony, who paid "his Heart for what his eyes ate, only," three times represented unfulfilled desire. But, among many, her greatest summing up, occasioned by nothing more than a flower she feared would fade before it got to a sick friend, was this: "Hamlet wavered for all of us."

One of the very few appearances of Shakespeare in the poems puts Hamlet and Romeo to this same kind of use. Here, perhaps, is a clearer example of the knowledge she meant in the remark to Sue. It is more like what she learned from the Bible as "centre." If her contemplation of the

Crucifixion led her to see as many Calvaries as there are "Persons – or Peninsulas," here she sees the daily enactment of two of the tragedies:

> Drama's Vitallest Expression is the Common Day
> That arise and set about Us –
> Other Tragedy
>
> Perish in the Recitation –
> This – the best enact
> When the Audience is scattered
> And the Boxes shut –
>
> "Hamlet" to Himself were Hamlet –
> Had not Shakespeare wrote –
> Though the "Romeo" left no Record
> Of his Juliet,
>
> It were infinite enacted
> In the Human Heart –
> Only Theatre recorded
> Owner cannot shut –   (#741, about 1863)

A young poet with perceptions of this sort could do very well on the supposedly minimal cultural resources of a small New England town. "Quiet Amherst had its quota of violence"—the materials of tragedy; and there were ample materials, too, for comedy and satire and (with a look to the hills) rhapsody. There were plenty of books to season wisdom and set the words ringing. "While Shakespeare remains," Emily wrote pontifically to Higginson, "Literature is firm – " The full extent of her indebtedness to Shakespeare can never be known, for she never told us. "Experiment escorts us last," she said in her epigram of about 1870, and there was something of the experimentalist in her from the beginning, something of the spirit of the true Renaissance overreacher. This, perhaps, was why she called herself a pagan; this was what she liked in Sue's "torrid spirit" and what she found everywhere in Shakespeare. Her poems owe nothing in form to him; she was incapable of his grand organizing power ("When I try to organize," she told Higginson, "my little Force explodes"), and the few verbal echoes in her poems are insignificant. But the tone and spirit, the exhilaration and encouragement, were everything. In Shakespeare's robust, un-Puritan expression was a whole new world for her of feeling and fulfillment. In point of substance, or knowledge, what she found most to her hand in Shakespeare was what impressed Melville:

But it is those deep, far-away things in him, those occasional flashings forth of the intuitive Truth in him; those short, quick probings at the very axis of reality – these are the things that make Shakespeare, Shakespeare.

Even in point of method, what Melville added to this famous remark went, in a sense, directly to her purpose. If she, living in a world where the "majority prevail," found it necessary to tell the truth *slant,* so, says Melville, did Shakespeare:

> Through the mouths of those dark characters of Hamlet, Timon, Lear, and Iago, he craftily says, or sometimes insinuates the things which we feel to be so terrifically true that it were all but madness for any good man, in his own proper character, to utter, or even hint of them.

In all these ways, and in a world where the "divine madness" she felt stirring in her was hardly understood, much less welcomed, Shakespeare was a never-failing sustenance for her slim minority.[21] In certain moments she felt she needed nothing else. "Why clasp any hand but this?"

21. In any assessment of ED's position in her time, and of the use she made of books ancient and modern, her sense of frustration and isolation (as in the first letter to Higginson, "I have none to ask –") must be borne in mind. John J. Gross, "Tell All the Truth But . . ." (*Ball State University Forum* X, i, 1969, pp. 71–77), attributes her characteristic obliqueness of method to her sense that "no significant body of understanding readers was available to her." Certainly Melville himself, and Hawthorne, knew this frustration.

29

The Poet

"Just how good is she?" asked the Skeptic, a man of learning and culture, a college president. And this well into the era of enlightenment, long after the frozen image of "Our Emily" had begun to thaw, with the 1955 *Poems* and the 1958 *Letters* long since available and an impressive series of critical and biographical studies well on the way. But the question, shocking as it may be to the devotees, is still a good one and should be asked again and again—not only by the skeptical but by the devotees themselves.

There is solid evidence that the cult began early, as witness this prophetic note—not without its irony—in the *Springfield Republican* of June 10, 1891, only seven months after the appearance of the 1890 *Poems*:

"The Home of Emily Dickinson. Some Observations Concerning the Characteristics of Amherst." Written by A[lice] W[ard] B[ailey] for the Republican.

It would seem that admiration for Emily Dickinson's poems is assuming the proportions of a "cult." This morning as I stepped out upon the veranda of the Amherst house, three women of modest appearance but with keen, intellectual faces, inquired of the proprietor which direction they should take to find the home of Emily Dickinson the poet. They had come from a distance to visit the spot and to inquire into the conditions that produced and fostered so singular a genius; – the poet hunter is nothing if not scientific these days. Listening to their conversation brought something very like interest to my own breast. I followed their lead, strolled through the beautiful streets, studied curiously the physiognomy of those I met, and asked myself what part of all this belonged to the poet, – hers by appropriation and use? How much of it explains, as far as such things can be explained, the quaintness of diction, the peculiarity of thought, in poems which in a

twelvemonth after their first publication are reviewed by the leading magazines, read aloud in fashionable gatherings and discussed with only less
awe and acumen than are brought to bear upon the works of Browning
himself.[1]

As with all cults, there has been sentimentalism—sometimes snobbish,
sometimes a mere failure of communication, and often counterproductive.
Rapture, ecstasy, awe, delight, discovery—however one describes the
response of the devotee to Emily Dickinson's achievements in language—
are hard to communicate, especially when the response may combine all
these elements, and no doubt more. It is hard to convey a mystery, like
love or religion. For all her obliqueness and her secretive ways, Emily
Dickinson establishes an intimacy with her readers as do few other poets.
Such an intimacy leads to a possessiveness the skeptics find hard to deal
with. As Millicent Todd Bingham, something of a skeptic herself, once
said, "They all think they own her."

But such a phenomenon is still a blessing, however mixed. The cult
helped keep Emily Dickinson alive during the long years between the first
flurry of interest in the 1890s and the beginning (save for a few pioneer
essays) of solid work toward the middle of our own century. Myths have
their uses. The myth of the plowboy singing at his work did Burns no
permanent harm. It was the Myth of Amherst that first fascinated the
romantic Mabel Todd. The figure of the Isolato, the one who, for whatever reason, cuts himself off from society to live on his own nerve and
grandeur, is universally appealing, even if not always entirely true. (It is
said that Thoreau came in from Walden for Sunday dinners with his
sisters in Concord; Emily's "hurrying Home" was hardly a hermit's
hideout, and, in her own way, she had an "estate" of friends.) When the
Isolato is a woman, sensitive, fragile, with legends of blighted romance, of
suppressions external and repressions internal to give added piquancy to
the agony and ecstasy that all may read in her published poems, the
appeal is, for many, irresistible.

1. Alice Ward Bailey (I am indebted to Nolan Smith for the identification) was
born in Amherst in 1857; so, in this passage, her air of discovering the town is a
journalist's pose. She had a considerable literary career herself, publishing a volume
of poems (1899); some short stories (sometimes under the pseudonym, A. B. Ward);
and three novels, *Mark Heffron* (1896), *The Sage Brush Parson* (1906), *Roberta and
Her Brothers* (1906). There are presentation copies of the novels (and a few letters)
to Mabel Loomis Todd in the Todd-Bingham Archive. Alice Bailey's sense of ED's
immediate popular success is, of course, accurate: eleven printings of the 1890 *Poems*
led to the *Second Series* (1891), the *Third Series* (1896), and the *Letters* of 1894. The
unevenness of her critical reception, however, is documented in *The Recognition of
Emily Dickinson* (1964), ed. Caesar R. Blake and Carlton F. Wells. A remark by the
novelist Elizabeth Barstow Stoddard in a letter to her friend Lillian Whiting (February 27, 1892) fairly well sums up the opposition: "An eccentric arrangement of
words – or ebullition of feeling [–] do not constitute poetry" (quoted by James Mat-
tock, "Elizabeth Barstow Stoddard," unpubl. Yale diss., 1967, p. 470).

By now the Myth has done its work, good and bad; but the question "Just how good is she?" remains in many minds, in spite of some recent able and informed answers. Especially since the late 1950s, studies of her thought and style have proliferated, and the estimate, with very few dips, has gone steadily up. The Poet is at last replacing the Myth. One prediction, in which I concur, is that within another decade America's two seminal poets will be Whitman and Dickinson.

Whether I succeeded with my skeptical president, I know not; at least, busy man that he was, he stayed for an answer. I remember beginning with Shakespeare, at which came a cry of disbelief only to be quieted by my assurance that I was far from suggesting that she was capable of a *King Lear* or a *Hamlet* or even a cycle of sonnets ("When I try to organize – my little Force explodes – and leaves me bare and charred – "). My attempt was to find some high achievement of linguistic virtuosity, rhythmic control, resourcefulness of metaphor, the capacity, indeed, to refresh the language and create a genuinely new music, with which Emily Dickinson could meaningfully be compared.

The seventeenth-century Metaphysicals, with whom she has often been compared and to whom she was undoubtedly indebted, came, of course, to mind. Her love of colloquialism and wit; her feeling for precision and her tendency toward the analytic; her habitual economy of form—all these qualities invite comparison with the closely knit form and mode of the seventeenth-century lyric. She has been described as a seventeenth-century self, "poised between scepticism and faith, desire and renunciation, optimism and despair," and her natural expression as the poetry of "paradox, argument, and unifying conceits." (It is not surprising that two trim stanzas from George Herbert's "Matins" were found, copied in her own hand, among her papers; nor is it surprising that they were at first thought to be her own work.) In a perceptive chapter in his *The Poem of the Mind* (1966) Louis Martz points to the many qualities she shares with the so-called Meditative Poets of the century.

But these comparisons hold, I think, up to but not beyond a certain point. Her more precarious stance, her more self-conscious, detailed, and poignant exploration of the dark interior, her distant and often paradoxical God, set her apart from these poets and made for a different rhythm and language. She could not take the full meditative route (as Martz describes it) from "meditation" to "contemplation" of the very presence of God, even if an occasional poem shows her in the meditative mood or in a moment of vision. She lacked the sense of sin that plagued Donne, and the prevailing serenity of Herbert. Her spiritual gait, as we see it in the poems (Higginson may have provided the right word), is more spasmodic than theirs; but, at the same time, the unitary moments, what she called "The Soul's Superior instants," are more intense, the concentration of thought and feeling more severe.

Dare you see a Soul *at the White Heat?*
Then crouch within the door –
Red – is the Fire's common tint –
But when the vivid Ore
Has vanquished Flame's conditions,
It quivers from the Forge
Without a color, but the light
Of unannointed Blaze.
Least Village has it's Blacksmith
Whose Anvil's even ring
Stands symbol for the finer Forge
That soundless tugs – within –
Refining these impatient Ores
With Hammer, and with Blaze
Until the Designated Light
Repudiate the Forge –   (*# 365, about 1862*)

Such a poem sends us back, perhaps, not so much to Donne and Herbert and Vaughan as to Edward Taylor, their New England counterpart, their near contemporary and avowed follower. A moment's comparison between the two poets (although she could not have read him[2] and probably never heard of him) puts in sharp relief not only her affinities with the Metaphysicals and with New England Puritanism but her own unique qualities.

Taylor was a Puritan at or near the tradition's purest moment. He transmuted into poetry the Puritan life of the spirit, with its insistent dialogue of the soul and its untiring and confident reach toward God. With a shrewd Puritan sense of the realities of this world (and following the directions of that manual for Meditative Poets, Richard Baxter's *The Saints' Everlasting Rest*) he put to metaphoric use details of everyday life, from pots and pans to spinning wheels and bowling alleys, often constructing a whole poem around one homely detail, as here Emily Dickinson has with the forge. Like him, she continued the Puritan dialogue of the soul ("Soul, take thy risk," "Soul, Wilt thou toss again?") but without the confidence that sustained Taylor. He *does* move, as she seldom does, from meditation to the contemplation of the presence of God.

Take the metaphor of the flame, or fire, in "Dare you see a Soul" and in two of Taylor's poems. In Dickinson, only when the soul is at white heat can it be free of flame and "repudiate the Forge" (its worldly existence). The stress is on the struggle for release, what Melville would call "the fine hammered steel of woe." There is no God in the poem to comfort, sustain, or even pray to. Taylor, on the other hand, is a confident worshiper, certainly in these two poems. He asks the Lord to send down

2. The poems were found, in MS, among the papers of Taylor's grandson, Ezra Stiles, in the Yale University Library, and first edited by Thomas H. Johnson in 1939.

the flame of His divine love, to ignite his own "Lifeless Sparke," to "Enflame [Thy Love] in mee." He is at peace with himself—at once God's "tinder box" and His

> . . . Censar trim,
> Full of thy golden Altars fire,
> To offer up Sweet Incense in
> Unto thyselfe intire . . .

There is a century and a half of waning conviction between the two poets, of increasing tensions and (with Dickinson) the love of this world that "holds – so – " If it was George Herbert's advice that she followed: "Dare to look in thy chest, for 'tis thine own, And tumble up and down what thou find'st there," what she found in her rummaging called for a tenser language, expressive of crisis and near breakdown.

> It's Hour with itself
> The Spirit never shows.
> What Terror would enthrall the Street
> Could Countenance disclose
>
> The Subterranean Freight
> The Cellars of the Soul –
> Thank God the loudest Place he made
> Is licensed to be still.　　　　　(#1225, about 1872)

Herbert's "chest" is convenient, accessible, even inviting compared with these "Cellars of the Soul," the place of terror—and worse still, repressed terror. Emily Dickinson's language of the self is new. Neither the seventeenth century nor any other is speaking in poems like this, where both language and rhythm are uniquely hers:

> One need not be a Chamber – to be Haunted –
> One need not be a House –
> The Brain has Corridors – surpassing
> Material Place –
>
> Far safer, of a Midnight Meeting
> External Ghost
> Than it's interior Confronting –
> That Cooler Host.
>
> Far safer, through an Abbey gallop,
> The Stones a'chase –
> Than Unarmed, one's a'self encounter –
> In lonesome Place –

Ourself behind ourself, concealed –
Should startle most –
Assassin hid in our Apartment
Be Horror's least.

The Body – borrows a Revolver –
He bolts the Door –
O'erlooking a superior spectre –
Or More –   (*#670, about 1863*)

Perhaps the only century that the following poem brings to mind is our
own, with that telltale "they say" (in the seventh line) of the modern
hesitant and the "Midnight" and the "Maelstrom" of the spiritually lost:

Behind Me – dips Eternity –
Before Me – Immortality –
Myself – the Term between –
Death but the Drift of Eastern Gray,
Dissolving into Dawn away,
Before the West begin –

'Tis Kingdoms – afterward – they say –
In perfect – pauseless Monarchy –
Whose Prince – is Son of None –
Himself – His Dateless Dynasty –
Himself – Himself diversify –
In Duplicate divine –

'Tis Miracle before Me – then –
'Tis Miracle behind – between –
A Crescent in the Sea –
With Midnight to the North of Her –
And Midnight to the South of Her –
And Maelstrom – in the Sky –   (*#721, about 1863*)

Many centuries and many traditions speak in another phase of Emily
Dickinson—her Orphic phase, with which is combined a healthy amount
of Puritan didacticism, coming variously from her family training, from
the Biblical "I say unto you" vein, from the hymns and sermons of the
First Church of Amherst, and certainly from the late-Puritan, New
England literary climate. She inherited an obligation to do for others what
they cannot do for themselves—on the one hand (as we have seen), to let
them hear the "noiseless noise in the Orchard," to catch the light that
never was on sea or land; and, on the other hand, to comfort people with
the "balsam word" or the prayer that is a poem. In a poem too explicit for
Emily Dickinson at her best and, for obvious reasons, seized upon by
Higginson and Todd for a prominent place in their first winnowing, she
espoused the doctrine of poetry as message, or service, abhorrent to
modern ears but an operative and unabashed phase of her own aesthetic:

If I can stop one Heart from breaking
I shall not live in vain
If I can ease one Life the Aching
Or cool one Pain

Or help one fainting Robin
Unto his Nest again
I shall not live in Vain.   (#*919, about 1864*)

She felt impelled not only to comfort but to teach people how to live. We remember her, in her youth: "But the world is sleeping in ignorance and error, sir, and we must be crowing cocks, and singing larks, and a rising sun to awake her. . . ." And again, twenty years later, she was still worrying about her fellow citizens, as when she wondered (in the interview with Higginson) how all those people in the streets lived without any thoughts. If the Myth leads us straight to the lyrics of anguish and despair—and they are many and moving—fully half her canon could be called "wisdom pieces," thoughts on life and living, sometimes exhortations, sometimes warnings, sometimes pure clinical analyses, as in her anatomizings of hope (variously "the thing with feathers," "a subtle Glutton," "a strange invention"), of faith ("a fine invention"), or of secrets:

"Secrets" is a daily word
Yet does not exist –
Muffled – it remits surmise –
Murmured – it has ceased –
Dungeoned in the Human Breast
Doubtless secrets lie –
But that Grate inviolate –
Goes nor comes away
Nothing with a Tongue or Ear –
Secrets stapled there
Will emerge but once – and dumb –
To the Sepulchre –   (#*1385, about 1879*)

Such definition poems, mostly with a didactic turn, came frequently with her, as if she felt impelled to shape and clarify thoughts for the thoughtless. "A Letter is . . ." "Glory is . . ." "Crisis is . . ." "Exhiliration is . . ." "Remorse is . . ."—so begin many of her more explicit ones. Her first question to Higginson was whether her poems "breathed"; to Susan: "Do I paint it *natural?*" (a gloomy April day); and to "H.H." (about her poems on the oriole and the hummingbird). "I . . . hope they are not untrue." In the definition poems she seems bent on making moral or psychological distinctions for the benefit of those whose vision is not as clear as hers. With sublime arrogance she could write:

> I found the words to every thought
> I ever had – but One –
> And that – defies me –
> As a Hand did try to chalk the Sun
>
> To Races – nurtured in the Dark –
> How would your own – begin?
> Can Blaze be shown in Cochineal –
> Or Noon – in Mazarin?   (*#581, about 1862*)

Every poet except the pure expressionist feels to some extent, I suppose, the urge to try to "chalk the Sun / To Races – nurtured in the Dark – " The urge was especially intense in Emily Dickinson's New England, the schoolteacher of America. Emerson's lectures and poems were packed with moral distinctions, and Thoreau's clarion call blended with his to awake America from its ethical and aesthetic torpor. Her famous poem "This is my letter to the World," too often regarded as a tearful complaint about being neglected, is actually a statement (this time she is more humble) of the difficulty of conveying what she calls the "Message" of Nature—Nature that "never wrote to Me." Her concern is for communicating truth:

> This is my letter to the World
> That never wrote to Me –
> The simple News that Nature told –
> With tender Majesty
>
> Her Message is committed
> To Hands I cannot see –
> For love of Her – Sweet – countrymen –
> Judge tenderly – of Me   (*#441, early 1862*)

If there is a faint image of the schoolmarm behind the hand trying to "chalk" the sun, the address to her "Sweet – countrymen" is American and democratic. In such stances she is indigenous, home-grown, not out of seventeenth-century England. Her form (unless the fascicles are a "form") is not from Donne or Herbert or Vaughan or Quarles but from that hymnologist to New England Congregationalism, Isaac Watts. By miracle of metaphor, or rhythm, or sound, even her tightest little apothegms become poems. And she used the hymn forms so flexibly, with such rhythmic subtleties, that her formal sources went mostly unnoticed until Thomas Johnson's discussion in 1955.[3] It may come as a surprise, even now, to see how perfectly this typical wisdom piece lends itself to the great hymn tune "O God our help in ages past":

3. *Emily Dickinson: An Interpretive Biography*, pp. 86–88.

[713

> Experiment escorts us last –
> His pungent company
> Will not allow an Axiom
> An Opportunity   (#1770, late 1870)

In my search for a meaningful comparison to satisfy my skeptical friend, I did not pause long over the English Romantics or the Victorians, in spite of her own declaration that "For Poets – I have Keats – and Mr and Mrs Browning." Again, parallels and borrowings come to mind—the search should go on—but the rhythm, the beat, the new synchronism to which she fitted whatever matter she borrowed, set her apart. Her hymn forms create a new, often staccato music of her own, very different from the more sustained, sonorous tones of the prevailing iambic pentameter of these poets. Less discursive than they, less of an "organizer," less the bearer of any message more precise than Nature's (and that fleeting, evanescent, "committed / To Hands I cannot see – ") and far less positive than Emerson's or Thoreau's ebullient charge, she is the poet of the passing insight, the moment of vision, the unitary experience. She had no social or political program and was inclined to smile at those who did. (It is significant that she apparently never discussed with Higginson any of his numerous causes.) Higginson was perhaps closest when he suggested her affinity with Blake, presumably the Blake of the *Songs of Innocence and of Experience;* but her moods and rhythms are more varied than his, she is at once more introspective as she explores the "Cellars of the Soul" and yet more objective and precise, as in her nature poems, with their Hitchcockian respect for fact. She was closer to nature than was Blake, the city poet, and though his use of the ballad form to achieve varying effects may have encouraged her as she reduced her complicated meanings to fit Watts's simple structures, perhaps it was this regenerative source, always available in rural Amherst, that kept her from the somber sense of political and social injustice that Blake (and many of the other English Romantics) saw all about him. She read of disasters in the papers; there was trouble enough in quiet Amherst; and the Civil War was a living fact for her. But the evils of industrialism, the plight of the oppressed and of the urban poor, were plagues that never came nigh her dwelling.

She had Wordsworthian and even Byronic moments, but her similarities to these poets are hardly basic and tell little about how good she was or where she stands in the hierarchy of poetry in English. She had Romantic tendencies, surely. Her sense of self had Romantic origins— rebellious at first, developing into a kind of heroic individualism, but tempered always by the vestigial Christian mystery, whose awe she never ceased to feel. She had the Romantic sensitivity to nature, but always with a certain abstemiousness. She could become "Inebriate of Air" and "Debauchee of Dew" in one rapturous poem about summer, but she could never say with Keats, "O for a Life of Sensations rather than of

Thoughts!" Nor with Thoreau would she be "drunk, drunk, drunk, dead drunk to this world with it [the song of the wood thrush] forever." She was always wary of excess, even of joy.

> I can wade Grief –
> Whole Pools of it –
> But the least push of Joy
> Breaks up my feet – . . .   (*#252, about 1861*)

She was too Puritan, too severe with herself, too spiritually anxious to allow herself for long the luxury of the Romantic sensibility.

> Partake as doth the Bee,
> Abstemiously.
> The Rose is an Estate –
> In Sicily.   (*#994, about 1865*)

If many of her poems are in the confessional mode (the Rosenbaum *Concordance* to her poems shows the first-person "I" as her most frequently occurring word), she never wrote, in verse or prose, such sustained, explicit accounts of herself as, say, Wordsworth did or Rousseau, who established the mode for the Romantics. And even here she apologized, or covered up. "When I state myself, as the Representative of the Verse – it does not mean – me – but a supposed person." Romantic barings of soul would have embarrassed her.

Actually, of course, the sub-Romantic, or sub-Tennysonian, verse of her day was her worst enemy, although we have no word of hers against it and a good many to show that she enjoyed it. Her language and rhythms seemed "strange" and "weird" to Higginson and Mabel Todd (those were the words they used to describe their first reactions) and had little chance against the lilting euphonies favored by contemporary editors. It is significant that Alice Ward Bailey, speaking of the cult, mentioned Browning's vogue, then current, with its Browning Clubs throughout America earnestly searching for clear prose meaning in their enigmatic Master. Apparently Dickinson posed much the same problem, without the charm of Browning's narrative sweep and dramatic power to help sustain the search. Her tight, aphoristic, riddlelike qualities, the ellipses, the grammatical incoherences, the odd or missing punctuation even in some of her best poems, directed Higginson and Todd, in their first selection from the mass of manuscripts, toward the simpler pieces, and many of those they normalized. But even those held puzzles for readers; and so she came under the same kind of scrutiny as Browning.

There is much to sustain Mrs. Bailey's conjunction of the two poets. Between "Mr and Mrs Browning," Emily Dickinson's real affinities are, I think, mostly with the former. His *Men and Women* and *Dramatis*

Personae, published (1855 and 1864) when she was at the height of her powers, may have encouraged her latent sense of drama (imbibed from many sources), her recurrent use of monologue and dialogue, the core of action on which many of her lyrics turn. Many of her poems are dramatic monologues in little, with the speakers as "supposed persons":

> You're right – "the way *is* narrow" –
> And "difficult the Gate" –
> And "few there be" – Correct again –
> That "enter in – thereat" –
>
> *'Tis* Costly – So are *purples!*
> 'Tis just the price of *Breath* –
> With but the "Discount" of the *Grave* –
> Termed by the *Brokers* – *"Death"!*
>
> And after *that* – there's Heaven –
> The *Good* Man's – "Dividend" –
> And *Bad* Men – "go to Jail" –
> I guess –   (*#234, about 1861*)

The conversational tone, the broken rhythms, the sudden shift (from Scripture to the stock market), the dramatic development (from the speaker's agreements to his doubt)—for all these qualities she may have found encouragement in Browning's distinctive form. Her themes or preoccupations were different from his, her tone was habitually more lyric, and she had very little of his interest in creating characters. But through her "supposed persons," her varying personae in poem after poem, she projected phases of experience, thought, and feeling dramatically, as Browning did through his characters. Her notion of the identity of beauty and truth may have come from Keats, but the poem she put it in is a dialogue distantly Browningesque:

> I died for Beauty – but was scarce
> Adjusted in the Tomb
> When One who died for Truth, was lain
> In an adjoining Room –
>
> He questioned softly "Why I failed"?
> "For Beauty", I replied –
> "And I – for Truth – Themself are One –
> We Brethren, are", He said –
>
> And so, as Kinsmen, met a Night –
> We talked between the Rooms –
> Until the Moss had reached our lips –
> And covered up – our names –   (*#449, about 1862*)

In two other famous death pieces, "Because I could not stop for Death – " and "I heard a Fly buzz – when I died," attitudes and moods are objectified through setting, characters, and action. In neither poem does she sing a romantic song about death; rather, she assays through dramatic probing its nature and possibilities. "What does it feel like to die?" she is asking. In "Because I could not stop" she imagines a slow-paced carriage ride with a most civil partner, Death, who "kindly" stops for her. They ride past children at recess, past "Fields of Gazing Grain," and finally (the atmosphere growing chillier) come to the grave, the "Swelling of the Ground," the end of the long day of dying, and the thought of what Eternity must be. The poem has roots in many traditions, the seventeenth century (Metaphysical and Meditative), the Romantic (the long thoughts of the Grave Yard Poets, or the sentimentalities of the Death-and-the-Maiden theme), and the dramatic turn Browning gave to the romantic lyric. It may, as we have seen, commemorate the moment in her development in which she first realized the full implications, for her poetry, of the "Flood subject"—a Wordsworthian recognition of poethood. But the synthesis is hers, and unique—worth another scrutiny in this final summary.

> Because I could not stop for Death –
> He kindly stopped for me –
> The Carriage held but just Ourselves –
> And Immortality.
>
> We slowly drove – He knew no haste
> And I had put away
> My labor and my leisure too,
> For His Civility –
>
> We passed the School, where Children strove
> At Recess – in the Ring –
> We passed the Fields of Gazing Grain –
> We passed the Setting Sun –
>
> Or rather – He passed Us –
> The Dews drew quivering and chill –
> For only Gossamer, my Gown –
> My Tippet – only Tulle –
>
> We paused before a House that seemed
> A Swelling of the Ground –
> The Roof was scarcely visible –
> The Cornice – in the Ground –
>
> Since then – 'tis Centuries – and yet
> Feels shorter than the Day
> I first surmised the Horses Heads
> Were toward Eternity –   (*#712, about 1863*)

In "I heard a Fly buzz," there is the drama of the deathbed scene, the watchers by the bedside, the dying person—quite composed, signing away the "assignable"—and the buzzing fly accentuating the stillness. It is dying dramatized; but there is no shock, no lamentation, nothing mortuary. Few poets have dealt with this all-engrossing subject with such intense feeling under such perfect control.

> I heard a Fly buzz – when I died –
> The Stillness in the Room
> Was like the Stillness in the Air –
> Between the Heaves of Storm –
>
> The Eyes around – had wrung them dry –
> And Breaths were gathering firm
> For that last Onset – when the King
> Be witnessed – in the Room –
>
> I willed my Keepsakes – Signed away
> What portion of me be
> Assignable – and then it was
> There interposed a Fly –
>
> With Blue – uncertain stumbling Buzz –
> Between the light – and me –
> And then the Windows failed – and then
> I could not see to see – *(#465, about 1862)*

The point is (I might have continued with my skeptical president), not that she did better what all these others did, but that, out of all the modes and materials available to her, she shaped, at her best, something new. Even in her lesser poems, the verses that form parts of letters and seemingly written on the spur, her trial pieces, the fragments and scraps from her workshop that nevertheless occupy positions in the canon co-ordinate with her best—even here the language is invigorated by an uncanny ear for sound, by unexpected juxtapositions, by single striking adjectives or verbs of action used as never before. In this scrap (probably sent to Sue), the verbs "retired" and "obliged," the adjective "soft," the opening spondee and the concluding anapest of the first line and the delayed stress on "obliged" in the fourth, the beautifully controlled combination of dentals and sibilants throughout—all unite to redeem a commonplace subject:

> Some Days retired from the rest
> In soft distinction lie
> The Day that a Companion came
> Or was obliged to die *(#1157, about 1870)*

Or consider another play on "soft" (this time meaning "silent") in an extraordinary two-line bit, called a "fragment" when it was first published in *Bolts of Melody* (1945) but having the wholeness of a haiku. In ten words, their sound and rhythm under perfect control, the awesome silence of spectacular sunsets, intensified by the sense of terrifying cosmic power, is conveyed with rare completeness in this tiny-huge poem:

> Soft as the massacre of Suns
> By Evening's Sabres slain   (*#1127, about 1868*)

A prominent review of the 1958 *Letters*—beginning unequivocally: "Emily Dickinson was one of the great English poets"—traces the source of her power to what the reviewer called a vision that, "in spite of a certain appearance of sophistication, was essentially primitive. . . ." Primitive, one infers, in the sense of seeing things as if they had just been created, but sophisticated enough to know that all things pass, and possessing the "acute natural sensibility" (again the review) to detect the pathos, or terror, or beauty of the full human cycle. Her preoccupation with death, as in the poems just cited, and as reflected in scores of poems on the ends of things—days, flowers, summer, friendships—was to the reviewer (and I agree) a "natural complement of an intense love of life," with this very intensity, one might infer, being a mark of the primitive vision. Perhaps, possessing this primitive vision, fresh and clear, she shunned the "strange disease of modern life" (Arnold's phrase appeared when she was twenty-two) partly in the primitive's impulse to avoid whatever would blur or clutter it. She "selected her own society" and shut the door—not on life but on the non-life she saw about her.

Of course, I took a bad risk in mentioning Shakespeare at all to my skeptical friend. But if kept in the context of Brita Lindberg-Seyersted's remark (in the most exhaustive study yet attempted of Emily Dickinson's language), "What she does is to use freely the creative principles operating in the English language," in which "Shakespeare is her preceptor," the comparison may not seem so preposterous. I would add that she not only learned from Shakespeare in this area but achieved comparable results. If I had it to do over with my friend, I would add the language of the Authorized Version of the Bible. Not that her canon can be reasonably compared in other ways to these mighty monuments, nor can she match them image for image or metaphor for metaphor; but the quality of her figurative language, its range, inventiveness, its boldness and its primitive freshness (in our reviewer's sense), is similar. It is as if, in a phrase she liked, she saw "all things new." To the psalmist the "mountains skipped like rams, and the little hills like lambs." To the Poet of Job "the morning stars sang together, and all the sons of God shouted for joy"; his war horse "swalloweth the ground with fierceness and rage. . . . He saith among the trumpets, Ha, ha! And he smelleth the battle afar off, the thunder of the captains, and the shouting." Emily Dickinson could be just as reckless. Her Amherst-to-Belchertown Railroad—"prodigious," "supercilious"—"lapped the miles" and "licked the valleys up." It complained in "horrid hooting stanza" and "neighed like Boanerges." In a joyous poem, the world is her "Republic of Delight," where

> The Bird did prance – the Bee did play –
> The Sun ran miles away
> So blind with joy he could not choose
> Between his Holiday . . .   (#1107, about 1867)

In other poems, the shadows on the hills give "a mighty Bow . . . / To Neighbors doubtless of their own"; Eternity's "vast pocket" gets "picked"; summer "troubles," and "Eggs," in one creative flash, assume wings:

> What shall I do when the Summer troubles –
> What, when the Rose is ripe –
> What when the Eggs fly off in Music
> From the Maple Keep? . . .   (#956, about 1864)

Turn almost anywhere in the canon (as I have here) and the same surprises await. The cosmic jostles the everyday and each is illumined, as here, where eternity is like an unexpected guest at the Homestead (the guest is exalted; eternity domesticated, just a bit):

> The Infinite a sudden Guest
> Has been assumed to be –
> But how can that stupendous come
> Which never went away?   (#1309, about 1874)

Abstract and specific are brought together in often strange but rewarding combinations. Emily once said of Vinnie, "She has the 'patent action,' I have long felt!"—perhaps an echo of the advertisements of newly invented machines in the *Republican*. In this definition poem, Hope is a patent action, with improvements:

> Hope is a strange invention –
> A Patent of the Heart –
> In unremitting action
> Yet never wearing out –
>
> Of this electric Adjunct
> Not anything is known
> But it's unique momentum
> Embellish all we own –   (#1392, early 1877)

First edition of the 1890 *Poems*
(Design adapted from Mabel Todd's panel of Indian Pipes)

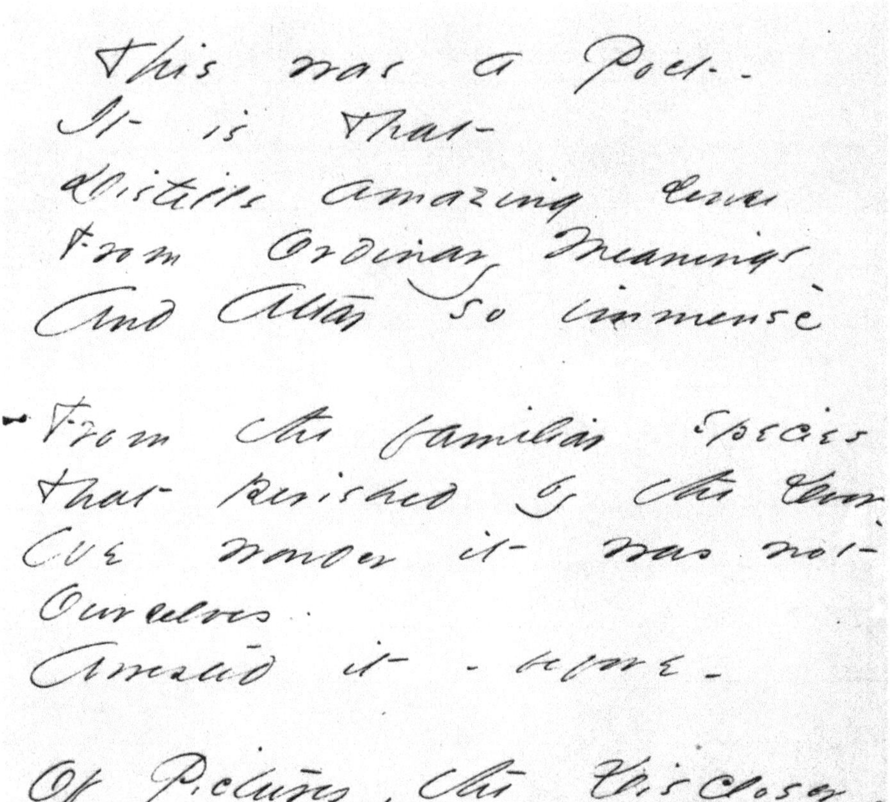

This was a Poet—
It is That—
distills amazing sense
From ordinary Meanings.
And Attar so immense

From the familiar species
that perished by the Door—
We wonder it was not—
Ourselves.
Arrested it—before.

Of Pictures, the Discloser.
the Poet—it is He.
Entitles Us. by Contrast.
to Ceaseless Poverty.

Of Portion—so unconscious
the Robbing—could not harm.
Himself—to Him—a Fortune—
Exterior—to time.

P #448, about 1862

The familiar, in one or two deft strokes, is shown in odd and revealing light, as in this bit about the color yellow:

> Nature rarer uses Yellow
> Than another Hue.
> Saves she all of that for Sunsets
> Prodigal of Blue
>
> Spending Scarlet, like a Woman
> Yellow she affords
> Only scantly and selectly
> Like a Lover's Words.   (*#1045, about 1865*)

"Selectly," of course, is the magic word that tops this tiny "stairway of surprise." It is a good example of Emily Dickinson's free use of the creative principles of the language. Mrs. Lindberg-Seyersted cites some others—they are legion: the "Daily Own" of love, the smile of fame that "meagres Balms," the happy lip that "breaks sudden – " Or take this *jeu d'esprit,* a penciled draft of about 1876, where pompous Latinisms and legalisms cavort with pure Saxon to present the case (which in mock helplessness she finally abandons to Nature) against the common fly:

> Those Cattle smaller than a Bee
> That herd upon the eye –
> Whose pasture is the passing Crumb –
> Those Cattle are the Fly –
> Of Barns for Winter – ignorant –
> Extemporaneous stalls
> They found to our objection –
> On eligible walls –
> Reserving the presumption
> To suddenly descend
> And gallop on the Furniture –
> Or odiouser offend –
> Of their peculiar calling
> Unqualified to judge
> To Nature we remand them
> To justify or scourge –   (*#1388*)

It would be idle to insist that this exuberance, this stretching of the language at point after point, was precisely Biblical or Shakespearean—flies as *"cattle"* that *"herd"* upon the eye," the *"extemporaneous* stalls," the image of the flies as they "gallop on the furniture," the comparative adjective "odiouser" suddenly transformed to an adverb and torturing the line rhythmically (for repugnance), the flies *"remanded"* to Nature for judgment. But the frequency in her letters of phrases from both Shakespeare and the Bible is far more impressive than from any other source.

Those from the Bible amount almost to saturation. We recall her delight over the "ring" of the words from *Antony and Cleopatra* after the siege with her eyes, and her reiterated opinion that after Shakespeare little else is needed. In spite of all those qualities that would seem to make her a private poet—her moments of exaltation and agony, seldom recorded by any poet with such intense self-concern; her convolutions and involutions, her strained syntax, warped grammar, and odd usages—in spite of all this, she is a popular poet, popular as her great sources are. She defies labels—Romantic, Transcendental, Metaphysical, Meditative; she defies boundaries—New England or America; she defies categories—female or lyric; religious, or existential, or nature poet. She is something of all these, and as investigations continue, we will undoubtedly find out more about her affinities, her sources and indebtednesses. But we are beginning to realize her uniqueness. Like only the greatest, she stands alone.

It is now time to revert to our original question (many chapters earlier) suggested by Keats's remark: "Lord Byron cuts a figure but he is not figurative." "The sense of the Scriptures," said the preacher, grappling with their diversity and contradictions, "is one." Could the same be said of the 1,775 poems, tentative poems, fragments and scraps of poems, the 1,049 letters and 124 prose fragments that make up Emily Dickinson's current canon? (There must be more somewhere; some of those lost correspondences will come to light and will contain poems.) Or must we leave her as a fascinating weaver of words, an impressionist of many moods and startling perceptions but with no clear direction, or central thrust, or unifying principle? Shaw scolded Shakespeare for not standing for anything; amazing insights, remarkable characters, but a little like his own Hamlet, with no political or religious conviction important enough for a man to risk his hat for in a shower. Shaw asked for the artist-philosopher and himself posed as one. Keats's notion of figurativeness is not so doctrinaire or demanding. It asks of the artist, as I see it, some kind of overarching dedication or commitment, or increasing purpose, so that posterity, looking long and hard on the total accomplishment, may discern some even remotely satisfying coherence, or order, or progression toward some transcendent idea or ideal, however vaguely articulated. My conviction, implicit and sometimes explicit in the preceding chapters, is that Emily Dickinson in this sense is figurative. I have answered the consequent question, "Figurative of *what?*" randomly in various contexts. What now remains is a clarification and summing up.

We have seen her in many phases, the confiding schoolgirl, the witty virtuoso and emerging poet; the perplexed ponderer building a self she could live with; the frustrated lover; the devoted friend and helper; the mature poet—rhapsodist and anatomist of heaven, nature, and man; near-mystic, Orpheus, and oracle by turn. She herself had a few things to say about what a poet is; but her passing remarks do less than justice to the whole and would hardly satisfy either Shaw or Keats: finding the words "to every thought I ever had," exploiting the "wiles of Words," getting "the ring" of them, hurling "Bolts of Melody," comforting the faint of heart, awakening America. Even her most sustained statement leaves much unsaid. (The "amazing sense" of the second line would hardly satisfy Shaw.)

> This was a Poet – It is That
> Distills amazing sense
> From ordinary Meanings –
> And Attar so immense
>
> From the familiar species
> That perished by the Door –
> We wonder it was not Ourselves
> Arrested it – before –
>
> Of Pictures, the Discloser –
> The Poet – it is He –
> Entitles Us – by Contrast –
> To ceaseless Poverty –
>
> Of Portion – so unconscious –
> The Robbing – could not harm –
> Himself – to Him – a Fortune –
> Exterior – to Time –   (*#448, about 1862*)

When she declared her "Business" to Higginson and the Hollands—"to sing," "to love," and apparently summing it all up in the enveloping word "Circumference"—she came closer. "Let us love better, children, it's most that's left to do," she wrote her cousins when Frazar Stearns was killed in action; and in a poem written well into her maturity she made a tremendous equation of Poetry and Love and God:

> To pile like Thunder to it's close
> Then crumble grand away
> While Everything created hid
> This – would be Poetry –
>
> Or Love – the two coeval come –
> We both and neither prove –
> Experience either and consume –
> For None see God and live –   (*#1247, about 1873*)

"We both and neither *prove* – " That is, try? test enough? and hence know love and poetry only slightly? But to know them fully is to experience the ultimate epiphany—like a confrontation with God, in "death." Hence (another poem) the "Truth" must be told "slant"; it must "dazzle gradually / Or every man be blind – "

So (it might be said) she set herself the task—a task that developed gradually into a vocation—to mediate to "every man" the infinitely varied facets and phases of the central "dazzling" truth as it was vouchsafed her in her moments (she had a hard time defining it) of inspiration. She mediated truths of nature and human nature, sights and sounds and meanings; she lit the poet's "vital lamp"; she did the poet's (and God's) primal work of creation:

> I reckon – when I count at all –
> First – Poets – Then the Sun –
> Then Summer – Then the Heaven of God –
> And then – the List is done –
>
> But, looking back – the First so seems
> To Comprehend the Whole –
> The Others look a needless Show –
> So I write – Poets – All –
>
> Their Summer – lasts a Solid Year –
> They can afford a Sun
> The East – would deem extravagant –
> And if the Further Heaven –
>
> Be Beautiful as they prepare
> For Those who worship Them –
> It is too difficult a Grace –
> To justify the Dream –   (#569, about 1862)

But the "Dream" was always there. Immortality was the "Flood subject." And it was the pursuit of this that gave form and coherence to her life and her work. Several times she referred to her "pilgrim" life, her "Puritan Spirit," and from childhood on, those "great countries in the blue sky of which we don't know anything" haunted her days and nights but at the same time fascinated her imagination and impelled her mind. Such preoccupation seemed not to distract or dim her immediate vision of worldly things—nature and people; rather, it sharpened it, as if she were in constant process of viewing all things in the ultimate perspective (like the sudden Guest at the Homestead) and with the intensity that comes from an unremitting sense of their evanescence. This was her pilgrimage: to "regulate" (her word) a faith that "doubts as fervently as it believes"— a faith that was everywhere tried, not only by personal sorrow and loss, but paradoxically by the very love of this world that "holds – so – " The pilgrimage had many intermittences. We would call it lonely; but she had many Guests, many "Bulletins . . . from Immortality," and, as poet, "a Fortune – Exterior – to Time – " Self-pity is not a major theme with her; quite the contrary. With the "ecstasy" she confessed to Higginson—"the mere sense of living is joy enough"—she felt herself "richer . . . than all my Fellow Men." It was a long way from her early pausings and ponderings to the following climactic letter, written only a few weeks before she died, to Mrs. Edward Tuckerman, who had just lost her husband:

> "Eye hath not seen nor ear heard." What a recompense! The enthusiasm of God at the reception of His sons! How ecstatic! How infinite! Says the blissful voice, not yet a voice, but a vision, "I will not let thee go, except I bless thee."

Jacob asked the Angel to bless *him*. Emily Dickinson, in a sublime inversion of Genesis 32:26, confers the blessing herself. Such breathtaking authority becomes credible only in the light of the long, slow, hard pilgrimage, with every step honored and all honestly.

Appendixes for

VOLUME TWO

III

Charles Wadsworth as Husband,
Father, and Poet

I

THE LETTERS APPEARING IN THIS APPENDIX were exchanged among the Wadsworth family members during the 1850s and 1860s and are made available through the courtesy of Mrs. John Sharman Zinsser of Poplar Grove, Sweet Briar, Virginia, granddaughter of the Reverend Charles Wadsworth; and Mr. John S. Zinsser, Jr., of New York City, his great-grandson. The scrapbook containing the letters is rich in memorabilia of Wadsworth—his school and college certificates, various professional testimonials, tributes by his parishioners, and obituaries. There are some items, also, concerning his remarkable wife, Jane Locke Wadsworth. Nowhere is there a mention of Emily Dickinson or Amherst.

In view of the widespread speculation concerning his friendship with ED—speculation which originally assumed a reciprocal relationship—it is notable that these letters show Wadsworth as completely happy in his family life, a loving and devoted husband and father. Jane Wadsworth's letters to him are full of admiration and comfortable intimacy, with no trace of tension. There is a constant concern for his health and happiness. His letters to her, although sometimes moody, with complaints of headaches and of overwork, and often signed "in haste," show the same tender devotion and dependence. And those to his children, filled with warmth and whimsey, reflect a gay and loving family circle: " 'Mamma – Edith Charlie & Willie' this is all my world."

Jane Locke fell in love with Charles Wadsworth much as Emily Dickinson is supposed to have (and as Longfellow's Alice Archer fell in love with Kavanagh): by hearing him preach. The story is told in a posthumous tribute to Jane, written for the alumnae record of her boarding school by one of her teachers (*Record of Pupils, 1842–52*, Emma Willard School, Troy, New York, p. 347):

> I remember that her beauty attracted universal admiration, while her character as a pupil and a lady secured the confidence and approval of all. No better proof of this could be given than the circumstance of her attending Dr. Wadsworth's Church. She had heard him in Boston, and charmed as all people were with his unique and impressive style, she desired to be one of his congregation in Troy. His church was some distance from the Seminary, and no boarders attended it. While a teacher usually accompanied Miss Locke, she was also permitted to go alone. Her seat was in the rear of the church, so that in reaching it she faced the audience. Her beauty and dignified bearing did not escape observation.

Later she met Dr. Wadsworth at tea at the house of one of the elders. Shortly after her graduation, she married him (on December 1, 1846). The account continues:

Her life was devoted to his family, and to the brightening and blessing of her home she consecrated the exceptional powers of her rich nature.

The Rev. Dr. Wadsworth, her husband, had a wonderful career as a minister. He lived to a ripe old age, and during the long years of his popularity, with all the toil, care, and burden which they brought, Mrs. Wadsworth inspired, helped, and strengthened him continually.

Said one who knew them well:

"Dr. Wadsworth owed his best success to his wife. Hiding herself away out of sight, she poured the light and strength and influence of her own spirit into her husband's life. . . ."

"Her life [her son, Charles Jr., wrote] was one of such pure consecration to her husband and children that data do not tell much about it." . . .

Her children brightened her last and lonely days with tender love and care. Never was mother more honored.

Mrs. Wadsworth died in 1891.

The following two letters of this promising young lady, now wife, show a fine balance of humor and tenderness. She is fully aware of her young husband's professional promise and (in the first letter) makes a shrewd prediction.

Bradford, [Massachusetts] August 6th, 1851

My dear Hubba,

Your most excellent and welcome letter came to me on Monday Afternoon when I was in the midst of packing and adieus; else I should immediately have had the pleasure of writing to you.

I left Hanover yester-morning and when I reached Boston, the family were all departed to Bradford; so I followed them to this *charming* place, where we *have not Dodge* [Hotel?] accomodations; quite the reverse. The – Ahem! – The Hanoverians were "astonied" at my *short* stay; expecting a visit of several weeks. But I said to myself "Short and Sweet" and ran away home again to see my good mother.

And now I dare not take the time to write a good long letter lest I keep it from Lake George till you are gone from there. Salute the hills in my name *as of old!* My *best* love to the fickle waters. By these commands, you see, I would make *you remember me.* Unfortunately my visit at Hanover was at commencement time, when that quiet little place is like a box of toys shook up by a great hand; and in the noisy confusion the little folk almost walk over each other. They expected the great Daniel [Webster] but he did not appear. But they had a Judge (*Gilchrist*) and a Poet (*Saxe*) and A Minister (*Swain*).

The Judge was a just, vain gentleman of common sense baptised in Latin, motoes and couplets of which seemed to hang upon him in little strips as he arose from the imersion – an *educated man,* a *scholar!* Bless me. I wish I were wise. The poet is a brother Jonathan, kind hearted (I guess) *versed* in simplicity and says his wife is not quite so tall as I. Indeed I think it very likely he may be Pope's, God's-noblest-work, – an honest man. The Minister! God bless the race and give them wisdom, for there is great want thereof. His Reverence discoursed a *very short* time. All from Aunt's house went to hear; but Alas! not one of us knew what was said and we had a solemn assembly when we got home, to decide *"What we should say if any-body asked us how we liked the address* before the Theological society." There is room enough above the humble heads of the clergy for you, hub[,] to tower like Mount Washington above the other *peaks.* So – May you have health, strength and heart and head and love the Lord and *in the world love me!*

Now you would have another full sheet if there were time (or if the sun rolled back an hour.) Write to me *soon very soon* Hubba for now I am within speaking distance (by lightning). I hope your plump companion will by good management make you a little more en bon point.

Ever, Affectionately Yours,

J.L.W.

[P.S.] If the other sheet were written I should add that I had a very pleasant visit at Hanover.

The second letter, with its glimpse of the elderly Daniel Webster and a con-cluding vignette of Charles in Philadelphia enjoying his "short-lived, single blessedness," is again critical of contemporary preaching. (This time she is in Boston; it is to be noted that her opinion coincides perfectly with Edward Dickinson's.)

Boston, Sept. 20th 1851

I sent my Dear Hubba a letter this morning, then went out and passed a few hours very happily.

I called on Mrs. Eustis – whose house was undergoing repairs when I first returned from Haverhill – She was very cordial and agreeable, regretted that you did not preach for them.

Called on Julia Rilham [?] and met Mary Dwight there; and as they were all going to see Healey's famous picture of Webster, I went with them. The Hon. Daniel himself being there, we had a very good opportunity to judge of the likeness, though it is younger than he now is. He behaved like an old patriarch among his children; enquired about and praised the por-traits of different persons in the picture. He tottered like a very old man when he walked. The picture, I noticed less than the original; I presume you have heard of it. It contains likenesses of many distinguished men; and of some of the *rich* ladies of Boston. It is perhaps eighteen by twenty feet. Webster stands out handsomely as the chief actor and the likeness seems to me the best I have seen of him. The other portraits I did not notice particu-larly.

I came home to get my dinner and got first, *two* letters from you. One was due yesterday; but the bustle of the jubilee hindered it, so they came one on top of the other.

You seem to be meeting charming people in the streets; no doubt the sight cheers your heart.

My love to Mrs. Wallace. And my affectionate regards to my share of the chickens and peaches and ice creams. Sabbath. I should like to hear my Hub preach this evening. Went to Bowdoin Street and heard Mr. Pomroy, as Dr. W. is unwell. Preaching is on the wane. When I sit in the Bowdoin Street church and listen to the preaching there, it seems to me that if any good is done or heard of within those walls it must be miraculous for the "dry bones" are not only in the aisles and pews but have stalked up into the pulpit. . . .

Now it is Evening. I suppose my Hubba is up in the third story eating, snoosing, reading or smoking and altogether having quite a cosey time; and I congratulate you on your short-lived, single blessedness. I am in the third story thinking I should like right well to see my Hub sitting in one of these chairs; and I should not wonder if I kissed him a *little bit*. But after waiting a minute and then examining, I find that wishing does not bring my Schallowague, for the chair is still empty. So good night and much joy to you, away over the "hills and a good way off" and a good way up in Filbert Street.

Ever yours truly
And "Honestly"

J.L.W.

The letters by Wadsworth to Jane and the children are undated but seem to be mostly from a later period. Daughter Edith was born in 1858; Charles, Jr., in 1860; and Willie (whom Wadsworth spoke of so affectionately to Emily Dickinson) in 1868. The following letter, from Philadelphia, was written, in part, on a Christmas day, "Tuesday 25," which gives a choice (if Wadsworth got the day of the week correctly) of 1853, 1860, or 1874 (in 1867 the family was in San Francisco). Since there is no mention of the children, the first seems most likely. The first part of the letter commemorates his loneliness for Jane in verse:

A very cold day – set out early to escape callers and put a letter to my dear wife in the mail, called for Mr. Agnew and with him went to a Puseyite Church, with stained windows and a stone floor – heard some fine music, and some pompous declamation – My companion's "fingers itching" to pull the white sleeved gentleman out of the pulpit and put *your husband* in it – that the audience might *be warmed* – so at least he avers –

Dined sumptuously at Mr Wallace's – whose wife is a nice cook – he has a large family – after dinner went to the Catholic Cathedral with two gentlemen – to see the pomp and vanities of a religion of ritualism – came home tired & cold to find cards on my table – and rejoice that I have escaped being *bored* & am going to bed to dream about my wife – and find myself *alone – alone*

"A Bark at midnight, left alone.
To float upon a moonlit Sea;
A wounded bird, that hath but one
Imperfect wing to soar upon;
Are like what I am WITHOUT THEE"

Good night – "Good night"

The second part, dated "Wednesday Evening," gives a notion of the increasing harassments of a busy clergyman, the endless interruptions of privacy, the demands on his time and for his services, "the many minds [as he puts it] to manage."

A Journal of my life were about as amusing as the Journal of a growing Tree – monotony – sameness – Soda water with the sparkle gone – And yet my life here is laborious and tiresome enough to be interesting – Tonight I am sadly jaded – I have had not a moment to myself today – And yet this is all I have done –

Servant made my fire at 6½ o'clock. Rose at 7 – Breakfast at 7½ – smoked a cigar with mine Host in his little snuggery called a Smoking Room –

Sat down to write a letter – Charles, the servant, announces a visitor –

– Mr. King – Begs leave to present me with a woolen comforter for my neck – Talks *half an hour* – says Judge Long our mayor was greatly pleased with my sermon Sabbath – Enquires kindly after "Mrs Wadsworth" – Enter Charles – another visitor – Mr. Dulty [?] – Talks *an hour* about X'mas – and then about the order and unanimity of the Second Church – Enter Charles – another visitor – Rev Dr Hughs [?] – talks *an hour* about God's providence in regard to the 2nd Church – Begs me to preach Sunday – to go with him to a tea party tomorrow – expresses the great interest of his people in my preaching – Enter Charles – "Rev Mr Owen" – Talks ¾ hour about his Church – urges me to preach – etc. etc. etc. – Enter Charles – "Rev Dr Lord" – talks 2 hours – about the desire of his church to obtain my services etc. etc. urges me to lecture this evening – to preach Sunday etc.

– By this time it is 2 o'clock – Dinner Bell rings – have not been able to shave [?] me – at 2¼ all my visitors gone – go down to dinner – soup finished – Eat a little chicken – Run up stairs and hurry out of doors to escape further visiting – go down 7th Street – a gentleman calls me – cant get away from him anyway – another joins us – walk an hour about town looking at many things – get away from all company – at last hurry home – determined to lock myself in and rest – find a gentleman sitting cozily in my rocking chair –

Talk till supper bell 6¼ – go down with a head ache – drink coffee – come up, put on gown – light a cigar, *hope* for a *little rest* – Enter Charles – "A Gentleman Sir" – D——I take all gentlemen – M. Enters – Talks till 9 oclock about Churches – *Churches* – CHURCHES – wish they were all burnt –

And now they are at last all gone – and I am so nervous and tired – tired – tired – This is my life – Don't you think it pleasant –

Nevertheless it is all right – I don't know what will come of it – I *have many minds to manage, and it requires all my skill* – and I wish you were here TONIGHT – *dont you think I do* –

But I'll get to bed – *"Good night"* . . .

The final section of the letter, dated "Dec. 26, 116 Arch St," recites more of the same. He apologizes, quite appropriately, for his handwriting:

You will excuse now and ever my abominable handwriting – I am too nervous to take pains – and if you can not read it, all the better –

Appendix III

How Emily Dickinson, coming to Philadelphia two years later (if our dates are correct), could have fiitted into this busy life—as busy in its own way as Samuel Bowles's—is hard to see. Even to his wife he wrote (as he did, at least once, to Emily) "in haste." Many years, and much success, went by before the following letter, written presumably on his return from San Francisco in 1869 and during the gap between his ministry there and his new church, the Third (Reformed) Dutch Church of Philadelphia. His family is evidently in Massachusetts for the summer with Jane's mother and father. (The episode of the unwitting elocutionist is evidently typical of the "roguery" Emily enjoyed.)

Philadelphia
August 31st

Dear Folks,

I have not time today to write separately. I have been with some gentlemen looking at the *Alexander Church* situate on that beautiful part of *Green Street* which we used so to admire – It is in the highest and most beautiful part of Philadelphia – splendid new stone Church. Lecture room etc. – all on the ground – They owe $45,000 – but think they can pay it all off within 90 days if I will go with them –

Meanwhile the Dutch Church is getting ready for me – So you see my hands are busy – Old friends as I meet them are more than cordial – I keep myself out of the way, but some find me out – very many are out of town. . . .

I am greatly exercised – perplexed – It seems almost as if we are never to have a home again – But God rules and reigns –

I was so glad to hear from you – It is the *first* letter – I feared a thousand things – do *not leave me in this state again.*

Dear *Charlie* and *Edith!* Kiss them for their letters to Papa – Dear *Willie's* picture is a gem – I do pray that I may not *always* be away from you all –

Comstock the Elocutionist is *dead* – By the way I went to another noted Elocutionist, telling him that I was *a minister,* on vacation – wishing to exercise my voice. He gave me an account of several ministers – *Rev Dr Stockton* & Rev *C. Wadsworth.* Of the *latter* he said his manner was awkward – like a man "digging *exquisite flowers* with his *elbows"* – But his *matter* was so exceedingly beautiful that he was carried away etc.

– Of course I had to tell him *who I was* – And it was funny – He had never seen me but at a distance in a pulpit – He bounded about like a grasshopper –

Told me that he had many a time spoken of me to *his classes* as a [word illegible] of the triumph of *matter over manner.*

I read with him an hour daily – I write sermons etc. to keep my hand in – . . .

But excuse all this gossip – *"Mamma – Edith Charlie & Willie"* this is all my world –

Give a thousand kisses to all – write at least some of you – *at least* every *two* days . . .

734]

If you can not read this – send for Mark Twain – my best love to your Father Mother Brother & Sister – I envy you your life in that beautiful house.

In great haste
Ever your

C WADSWORTH

Jane's reply, besides giving a notable tribute to her now famous husband and some charming glimpses of the children, responds pleasantly to the anecdote about the elocutionist.

Bradford, Sept, 2nd / 69

MY DEAR HUSBAND,

I received your most welcome and excellent letter this morning.

We have a fire today.

Every thing is disposed according to your wishes in this life, I think. You are a rare mortal. All the ado your friends make over you, does you good. I rejoice in it for your sake. And with us your wishes prevail; for we'll not go to Hanover at all. Whooping cough rages in Uncle Edwin's family. Cousin Kate wrote for her father an answer to my second letter, saying that even Mrs. Webster is beginning to cough.

It is just as well, now, that the Summer is gone. Then another visit of yours is "coming to pass". I shall stay here at present until you arrange for us or until the weather becomes winterish, as Mother wishes me to and thinks as I do that it would be better for Willie here at present. Whooping cough is so prevalent that I am almost frightened at the thought of it; these tenderlings have a Winter to face and I hope that is all.

Charlie is trying his "muscle" out in the yard.

I cannot wait to send their letters this time to you as I wish to hurry this to you in a few minutes.

I will send you word about them as often as twice a week so *rely* upon *that.*

The children say of themselves, without being asked, "How dreadful for Papa to go to Cal. again, so many thousand miles away from us!" "I *do* hope he won't."

How droll the elocutionist's introduction! How droll! I should like to have seen him tee-to-tum-ed.

It is a capital thought of yours, reading with him now you are out of preaching practice. I like to hear of your treating yourself so well.

I send another photograph of Willie. They are from Black's, Boston.

I hope you received Mr. Robert's letter mailed about a week ago in Boston.

I hope for all our sakes that our home together is not far in the future.

How is your heart? Mine yearns to "own a chair" again a strong one, a suitable one.

[735

I do not want you to lose the charming babyhood of dear Willie.
Write often and much.

> Affectionately,
> Yours
>
> Jane L. Wa.

Great love from the Children to dear Papa.

Perhaps that same (hot) summer, he wrote to Edith and Charlie, then about twelve and ten, a charming letter out of the depths of Philadelphia's 90° heat and a Job-like complaint of his own:

> *Philad. Monday*

Dear Edith & Charlie

Your kind, nice letters delight me greatly. It makes me happy to hear that you have pleasant times this hot summer.

Edith's pictures from the Old Catechism made me laugh till I cried. They carried me back to the old school house in Bradleyville where I had merry times. And, though I deserved it, never got whipped for I was a "Wadsor" and my father was "Lord of the Manor." I have showed the pictures to many to their great delight.

I can not write well today. For I am sick from yesterday's work – , *and* I took cold in Friday's sudden change of weather – *and* I have rheumatism all over me – *and* I have a great boil on my right hand with nobody to poultice it – *and* I took 4 Blue pills and 3 Ayres pills last night and all together feel very much like

"That idle fool (who)

Got whipped at school" . . . I have been hoping to send you a box of peaches but they are yet *not good* and very, very dear – The Joneses have come back . . . I preached to full houses [yesterday] – and the people are edified as the apes who snuff the East Wind. . . .

I want to see you all very much, but can not get away. Tell Mama to send me the *amount* of the Monthly Bills for Board and Riding, etc.

My hand and arm are very painful with *My Boil* – and I must close my delightful letter – and will go and study Edith's charming picture of the Boil-ed Job . . .

I think if he had one on his *right hand* – and had to write sermons and make *graceful* gestures – the while – with the thermometer at 90 – he would have remembered how *"Satan"* was the cause of them and

> Up and kicked
> The devil wicked.
>
> Most lovingly
> Your venerable Papa

I had sealed my charming epistle – But forgot to send my love to *Dear little Willie* – so here it goes with a cart-load of kisses –

Tell him papa loves Willie – Wont have any lack of [?] – wishes he could send Willie something from Philadelphia –

Willie must be a good boy – and love Papa – and not get another Papa
– and must send his love to Papa
  Love to Mama and unceasing veneration for the Crown of Glory –
  Write often and a little *longer* letters.

C W

A final letter, to Charlie, is a lesson on how to catch pickerel, with appropriate admonitions.

MY DEAR SON

If thy brave heart be set on catching *"pickerel"* – then attend unto the lessons of age and experience.

First – *Find* your fish – for you can not catch what *is not!*
Second – Find him in the *right place* – for if he be *on a tree,* or *under a stone wall* your hook will get broken
Third – Carefully note *at which End his head is* for fish will not bite with their *tail*.
Fourth – Provide thee with *a Rod* – for the wise man says – "A saddle for a horse a bridle for an ass and *a Rod* for Pickerel"
Fifth – For *"Bait"*
    1 – a *living minnow*
      or small fish
    2 – a Frog's hind leg
      skinned & white
    3 – Part of a fishes belly –
      (That is so)
Sixth – In fishing be careful not to get the hook caught on *your own breeches* – for then the fish will *catch you* – not you the *fish* You will become a Junior Jonah – and your Dad will be Charley-less –
Seventh – Move your *bait gently in sight of the fish* – and if he WONT *see* it throw him a pair of leather *spectacles!*
Eighth – In fishing you must keep your trousers free from *"huckleberry pie"* and *"butter"* else the bears in the wood will devour you for their "desert"
Ninth – If after all your labor the foolish fish *wont bite* (and they are *not* voracious in this warm weather) then try *stratagem* – creep carefully to the stream-side and sprinkle some *"fresh salt* – (mark, it must be *fresh*) on the fish's tail – then you have him!
Tenth – When you have secured him – *treat him gently* –
If he be a *young* fish – give him *soda-water,* and sing "shoo fly" to him. And put him back into the stream *to comfort his poor Papa;*
If he be *old* – and have a "crown of glory" – Polish his "grey head" with a *blacking* brush – and send him home out of respect to your *venerable Mama.*
Finally – If you can not catch him *at all* either by stratagem or "high art" – and your desire is intense to EAT a pickerel – then – Buy a "paper of pins" and fry them in *"Malton tallow"* and it will taste just like one.

– Seriously my dear boy I am sick from Sunday work in the heat – and your nice letters do me much good – I hope you are happy – and pray for me for I love you very much though I am often very *cross*.

2

SOME EARLY POEMS OF WADSWORTH'S, most of them clippings from local newspapers (Litchfield, Conn.; Utica, N.Y.; Palatine, N.Y.), and loosely stitched together, scrapbookwise, are in the New York Public Library. On the cover is written in Wadsworth's hand: "The Poems that are pasted into this book were written by Rev. C. Wadsworth of Conn. years ago." Except for "Christmas Hymn, 1854. Written for the Arch St. Church Sabbath School" (printed on a decorated leaflet with embossed edges), the poems are from the 1830s. The general tone, except for the hymn, is one of romantic melancholy. "My Birth Day," clipped from a newspaper ("Whitestone, 1833"), is preceded by these quotations:

> "The life of man
> Is summ'd in *birth days* and in sepulchres."
>   *H. K. White*

> Count o'er the joys thine hours have seen,
>   Count o'er thy days from anguish free,
> And know, whatever thou hast been,
>   'Tis something better not to be.

>   [*Anon.*]

The poem develops this lugubrious theme. It begins:

> A birth day! 'tis a mournful theme
>   To one whose hopes are fled;
> Whose spirit in a clouded dream
>   Lies desolate and dead . . .

and so on, for five nine-line stanzas. The fourth will suffice:

> For I have learn'd to veil my woe
>   With joyous smiles and free,
> And would not that the world should know
>   How *deep* that woe may be.
> I would not that the crowd I scorn,
> The weight of grief my heart hath borne,
>   With *careless* eyes should see;
> Or if they *felt*, I ill could brook
>   The coldness of a *pitying* look.

The final stanza suggests that this birthday may be his last.

Several of the poems lament the loss or breakup of home. One ("Utica, N.Y., Nov. 14, 1838") ends with a plea to

> Remember me as one who wears
>   A lengthening chain where'er he roams,
> And, sickening in these stranger airs,
>   Yearns like a wounded bird for *home*.

Another, "My Home," undated, takes off from Shenstone's lines, "The school-boy that expires / Far from his native home"; carries the wanderer through various phases of gloom and loneliness; and reveals his only solace as looking back from "life's weary track" to the joys of his boyhood home. A poem of 1837 (Palatine, N.Y.) addresses an absent lover, and another (Litchfield, Conn.) says farewell to a "bright girl with a laughing brow."

How much these melancholy verses are mere exercises, the reflections of moods popular among sensitive young people of the time, and what bearing they have on Wadsworth's character and life experience is impossible to tell. Certainly he seems to have outgrown such moods by the period of his active ministry and the family letters. But they may point to a phase, or dimension, of his character—the somber or tragic—noted in the newspaper report of his preaching and in the "man of sorrows" Emily Dickinson saw. Two other poems, the most ambitious in the collection and both undated, though more positive in their moods, show occasional technical subtleties and emotional heights and depths—anxieties, tensions, raptures—that bring him a little closer, as poet, to Emily Dickinson. At least, they show what he had to conquer, or give up, to become the famous preacher and the happy family man. (Both poems are clipped from the *Litchfield Religious Intelligencer*.)

DEATH

"And must they die – the young?"
—Childe Harold

How welcome those untrodden spheres!
How sweet this very hour to die!
To soar from earth and find all fears
Lost in thy light – Eternity!
—Lord Byron

"I cannot die"—thus came a soft tone breaking
    The stillness of the vines at summer's eve—
"O friends! sweet friends, your voices here are making
    A happiness—a heaven—I cannot leave."

"O, I would die!"—a high wild tone came swelling,
    Through the bright sky, with its triumphant tone;

"Oh! I would pass where bright free streams are welling
    Amid the flowers, thou spirit-home, my own."

"Oh, hold me back!" the soft tone murmur'd then.
    "Oh! hold me back from death—the summer's sigh,
Bearing rich rose-scents up from fount and glen,
    Comes through the vine leaves—can I, can I die!

"My heart hath loved earth's things—the tones that rise
    From the deep forest up at set of sun,
The summer vines, the spring time melodies,
    The gathered stars in heaven when day is done.

"Oh, fold me closer friends! the wild bird's wing
    Is soaring upward in the sunset sky;
The wandering bee amid the flowers of spring
    Hath *its* free joyous life—and must *I* die?

"Oh for the eagle's wings, to bear the thrilling
    With the heart's might—to one bright world—
        Love's own.
But come not, come not now—Earth hath a tone
    Sweet to my spirit—and a breath of joy
Each breeze is bearing from the mountains lone
    To the wild ocean—come not to destroy
        Youth's gladness from my heart."

The Spirit of Night

There is a spark within me that but needs
The fannings of thy pinions to blaze up
To an o'ermastering power.

Come not upon me in thy fearful power
    Thou thing of shadows! with the soft winds bringing
Fragrance around me from the vines and flowers,
    And music from the woods of night-birds singing
        To the bright stars above.

Come not upon me now, for I would hold
    Communion with earth's beings, and would fling
My young affections out in joy, to fold
    Unto my heart bright spirits, then to cling
        With an undying love.

Come not, for there is music on the air,
    Like prayer from the flower's lip—and rose scents blending
With the soft night breeze—and the heavens are fair

With summer stars, down thro' the ether sending
    Their quivering light to earth.

And my young pulse hath caught a fleetness, leaping
    In dream-like gladness to the fragrant air,
As if some spirit's wing were lightly sweeping
    O'er my hush'd thought to wake bright visions there,
        Visions of summer mirth.

Come not, oh come not now—I would not leave
    Earth's holiest things—the summer dew—the flowers,
Hush'd as with slumber—and the gentle eve,
    With all its balm and music, for the powers
        Of thy wild tempest-wing.

And yet there are dark hours when I would call thee
    From thy cloud-home on high, to wake my soul
From the bright dreams of earth that so enthral me,
    Clothing with fearfulness thy wild controul,
        Thou dark, deep, searching thing.

Oh, when my soul hath lost its dreams,
    And bent its wing in weariness—when flowers
In the bright star light, and the tone of streams,
    Come o'er my mind with nought of thrilling powers,
        O come, then come to me.

And in that lightning moment, when the mind,
    Loathing earth's sluggishness, would send away
From its proud wing the bond that hath confined
    Its mightiest soarings in the blaze of day,
        Come to me—come to me.

Come to me then, Oh come! The high power bearing
    To wrestle with the world—the deep love born
By the bright streams of heaven—the eagle daring
    Of the high heart, laughing proud death to scorn—
        Bless'd in such hours thou art.

Popular Poetry
Selections from the *Springfield Republican,* 1858–62

I

ALTHOUGH THE *Republican* frequently reprinted selections from standard English poets, its taste in contemporary verse shows what it was that ED had to contend with. A few samples (rather, a sampling of the samples) from the years of her closest association with Samuel Bowles will suffice.

Bowles (or whoever) may have had the following in mind in the piece on "the literature of misery"—to which for all its protestations, the *Republican* was remarkably hospitable. The poem is entitled "The Rose and the Nightingale" ("after the Persic and Hugo's 'Rose et Papillon' ") and was written by "Wendell L'Amoreux." It appeared in the issue of January 23, 1858.

> One day, the lovely rose said to the Nightingale,
> > Dear one! O! stay!
> Think on my lonely fate – I linger in this dale,
> > Thou goest away.
>
> Bright is the beam, said he, through crystal leaves descending;
> > Joyous, the breeze;
> The stream with birdling's note its happy song is blending –
> > Sport thou with these.
>
> Then answered she, My heart would fain forget its sadness,
> > But all is drear.
> The beam, the bird, the stream bring to me nought of gladness –
> > Thou are not here.
>
> See how I droop – my cheek grows pale with constant anguish,
> > Longing for thee.
> In vain the showers kiss my pallid brow – I languish,
> > Longing for thee. . . .

Here is another in the same vein, by Lucy Larcom, "Hannah Binding Shoes," *Republican,* March 6, 1858:

> Poor lone Hannah,
> Sitting at the window, binding shoes.
> > Faded, wrinkled,
> Sitting, stitching, in a mournful muse.
> > Bright-eyed beauty once was she,
> > When the bloom was on the tree:
> > Spring and winter
> Hannah's at the window, binding shoes. . . .

On March 12, 1859, came this elegy, by William Winter:

THE LAST SCENE

Here she lieth, white and chill;
　　Put your hand upon her brow!
For her heart is very still,
　　And she does not know you now.

Ah the grave's a quiet bed!
　　She shall sleep a pleasant sleep,
And the tears that you may shed,
　　Will not wake her – therefore weep:

Weep – for you have wrought her woe;
　　Mourn – she mourned and died for you;
Ah, too late we come to know
　　What is false and what is true.

On February 4, 1860, Sarah Shelley Clemmer contributed another:

"NORA"

Nora is dying, as well as the year,
　　And mine is the sad, sweet task
To smooth her pillow and sit by her side,
　　And tell what her soft eyes ask. . . .

A less melancholy Lizzie Lincoln longed for summer (in the issue of March 13, 1858):

"IMPATIENCE"

I am longing for the summer,
　　For the long glad summer days,
For the river's dreamy murmur,
　　And the wild birds' gushing lays;
For the breath of countless flowers
　　By the zephyr borne along,
Oh, joyous summer hours –
　　They can never seem too long! . . .

(It is to be noted that the poems were almost invariably given titles—"Nellie and I," "God's Next Best Gift," "A Song of Slumber," "Nameless Pain," "The Coquette," "The Crown of Love"—a custom ED honored in the breach.)

For Bowles's (or Holland's?) real enthusiasm for some of these verses, witness this comment, appearing in March 1859.

Gerald Massey has never written anything in our opinion, which surpasses in lyric power and fire, or equals in sweep and breadth of imagination, the following poem, contributed to our columns by a new correspondent:

"MORNING"

O, the dreary, dreary darkness; how it girds the
    stifled land!
How it falls in viewless torrents from the frowning
    midnight skies!
When shall Lucifer, resplendent on the eastern mountains stand!
    Will the morning never rise? . . .

That the *Republican* catered to popular taste is clear from this editorial note (March 12, 1859):

Such is the renewed interest in this sweet and touching poem, by our correspondent, Miss NANCY A. W. PRIEST of Hinsdale, N.H., that we can only supply the constant demand for copies by a second re-publication.—Editor Republican

"OVER THE RIVER"

Over the river they beckon to me –
    Loved ones who've crossed to the further side;
The gleam of their snowy robes I see,
    But their voices are drowned in the rushing tide.
There's one with ringlets of sunny gold,
    And eyes, the reflection of heaven's own blue;
He crossed in twilight, grey and cold,
    And the pale mist hid him from mortal view.
We saw not the angels who met him there;
    The gate of the city we could not see;
Over the river, over the river,
    My brother stands waiting to welcome me! . . .

Childhood death was a frequent theme. "The Withered Daisies," also signed N.A.W.P. and written for the *Springfield Republican*, appeared February 19, 1859.

She flitted like a sunbeam bright
    Around our cottage door;
Her footsteps, as a fairy's light,
    Made music on the floor.
On every flower of wood or glade
    She lavished childish praises,
She loved all things the Lord has made,
    But most she loved the Daises.

How many thoughts beyond her years,
    That then were all unheeded,
We think of now with blinding tears, –
    Sweet teachings that we needed.
Three happy years we led her feet
    Along life's thorny mazes;
The fourth, we laid her down to sleep
    Beneath the April Daises. . . .

Perhaps most of the verses were about blighted love, or lovers doomed to separation or death.

"LANG SYNE" by Maude (*June 29, 1861*)

She came to meet me at the tryst,
    The cool, night breeze around her blowing,
    Her sunny hair in tresses flowing,
Glad laughter on the lips I kissed.

Each heart-throb thrilled with sudden pain,
    As dimpled hands stretched forth to meet me,
    As rosy mouth upturned to greet me –
I knew we ne'er should meet again.

She looked at me in doubt and fear;
    The sweet smile died on dewy lips,
    While o'er her face spread pain's eclipse;
Ah, then *she* knew the end was near. . . .

That dear form lies in Death's embrace,
    White hands are crossed o'er pulseless breast,
    The weary heart has found its rest,
God's peace has crowned that angel face.

But grief and woe are all my part;
    I sit and dream those sweet days o'er,
    And cry aloud in anguish sore,
"O, May, give back *my* heart!"

Sydney Orfy's lover stands in proud defiance in this stanza from "Miriam" (February 5, 1859):

Stand haughtily there, proud Miriam,
    Under the cedar tree!
The words you have sent from your frozen heart,
    Are chilling and freezing me;
But I will not die for the scorn in your eye,
    Though bitter the scorning be! . . .

Mary Clemmer Ames's speaker (April 30, 1859) looks remorsefully to the past:

"I MIGHT HAVE DONE"
(written for the *Springfield Republican*)

Is there a sadder word than this,
    I might have done?
I might have filled life's cup of bliss,
    At least for one!

I might have done! So much have done,
    For her, now flown;
My own, my loved, my lovely one,
    Who left me lone. . . .

Matilda Burton's note of sympathy for the sorrows of the world (July 12, 1862) is typical of the didactic strain in much of this verse:

"KINDNESS"

Earth, though a lovely place,
    Teems with dark care;
Clasping each other comes
    Death and Despair;
Sorrows on ev'ry side
    Frowning we find;
Sad hearts need sympathy –
    Let us be kind. . . .

These were the verses, then, that the *Republican* favored during the years when Emily Dickinson was sending her most fervent letters and many of her poems to Samuel Bowles. Either he was tone deaf or, a cautious editor, yielded to what he assumed would be an adverse public response. It is ironic that only a generation later her poems were a great popular success. In fairness to Bowles, however, it must be remembered that ED herself was fond of such verses as these—occasionally, it seems clear, plundering them for wisps of thought or feeling she could make into poems. In the Dickinson Papers in the Amherst College Library, there is a clipping, dated in pencil July 1864 and presumably taken from the *Republican* by ED herself, of Adelaide Anne Procter's "A Woman's Question." Its theme of the questing heart and the willingness to risk all is a familiar one in ED's poetry but nowhere strung out, as here, in eight insistent stanzas.

Before I trust my Fate to thee,
    Or place my hand in thine,
Before I let thy Future give
    Color and form to mine,
Before I peril all for thee, question
    thy soul to-night for me.

I break all slighter bonds, nor feel
    A shadow of regret:
Is there one link within the Past
    That holds thy spirit yet?
Or is thy Faith as clear and free
  as that which I can pledge to thee?

Does there within thy dimmest dreams
    A possible future shine,
Wherein thy life could henceforth breathe,
    Untouched, unshared by mine?
If so, at any pain or cost, O, tell me before all is lost.

Look deeper still. If thou canst feel
    Within thy inmost soul,
That thou has kept a portion back,
    While I have staked the whole;
Let no false pity spare the blow, but in
  true mercy tell me so.

Is there within thy heart a need
    That mine cannot fulfil?
One chord that any other hand
    Could better wake or still?
Speak now – lest at some future day
  my whole life wither and decay.

Lives there within thy nature hid
    The demon-spirit Change,
Shedding a passing glory still
    On all things new and strange? –
It may not be thy fault alone – but shield
  my heart against thy own.

Couldst thou withdraw thy hand one day
    And answer to my claim,
That Fate, and that to-day's mistake –
    Not thou – had been to blame?
Some soothe their conscience thus; but thou
  wilt surely warn and save me now.

Nay, answer *not,* – I dare not hear,
    The words would come too late;
Yet I would spare thee all remorse,
    So, comfort thee, my Fate –
Whatever on my heart may fall – remember,
  I *would* risk it all!

2

Dr. Holland's taste in poetry was also thoroughly conventional. The bird poems he chose to include in *Scribner's* are good examples. Here are some from the early period of his editorship:

"A Bird-Song"

It's a year almost that I have not seen her;
Oh! last summer, green things were greener,
Brambles fewer, the blue sky bluer.

It's well-nigh summer, for there's a swallow;
Come on swallow, his mate will follow,
The bird-race quicken and wheel and thicken.

Oh, happy swallow, whose mate will follow
O'er height, o'er hollow! I'd be a swallow
To build, this weather, one nest together!

(January 1873)

"The Cuckoo"

Forth I wandered, years ago,
When the summer sun was low,
And the forest all aglow
            With his light;
'Twas a day of cloudless skies;
When the trout declines to rise,
And in vain the angler sighs
            For a bite.

And the cuckoo piped away –
How I love his simple lay,
O'er the cow-slip-fields of May
            As it floats!
May was over, and of course
He was just a little hoarse,
And appeared to me to force
            Certain notes.

Since mid-April, men averred,
People's pulses, inly stirred
By the music of the bird,
            Had upleapt:
It was now the close of June;
I reflected that he'd soon
Sing entirely out of tune,
            And I wept. . . .

(January 1873)

And so on for eight more stanzas describing a romance, a marriage, a child—all under the happy aegis of the cuckoo's song. In July 1873 came a salute to the song sparrow. Holland, it seems, preferred lyrics of some length, with easy narrative or (as here) didactic line:

"THE SONG-SPARROW"

Glimmers gray the leafless thicket,
  There, beside the garden gate,
Where so light from post to picket
  Hops the sparrow, blithe, sedate
    Who, with meekly folded wing,
    Comes to sun himself and sing.

It was there, perhaps, last year,
  That his little house he built;
For he seems to perk and peer,
  And to twitter, too, and tilt
    The bare branches in between,
    With a fond, familiar mien.

Once, I know, there was a nest,
  Held there by the sideward thrust
Of those twigs that touch his breast;
  Though 'tis gone now. Some rude gust
    Caught it, over-full of snow, –
    Bent the bush; – and stole it so.

So too our own nests are tossed,
  Ruthless, by the wreaking wind,
When, with stiffening winter's frost,
  Woods we dwelt in, green, are thinn'd
    Of leafage all, and grown too cold
    For wing'd hopes purely summer-souled.

But if we, with spring-days mellow,
  Wake to woful wrecks of change,
And the sparrow's ritornello
  Scaling still its old sweet range;
    Can we do a better thing
    Than, with him, still build and sing?

O, my sparrow, thou dost breed
  Thought in me beyond all telling;
Shootest through me sunlight, seed,
  And fruitful blessing, with that welling
    Ripple of ecstatic rest,
    Gurgling ever from thy breast!

And thy breathing, breeze-like, stirs
    In my veins a genial flood,
Such as through the sapwood spurs,
    Swells and shapes the pointed bud
        Of the lilac; and besets
        The hollows thick with violets.

Yet I know not any charm
    That can make the fleeting time
Of thy sylvan, faint alarm
    Suit itself to this rough rhyme:
        Still my ruder rhythmic word
        Stifles thy rare strain, dear bird.

And, however thou hast wrought
    This wild joy on heart and brain,
It is better left untaught.
    Take thou up the song again:
        There is nothing sad afloat
        On the tide that swells thy throat.

Clearly there was little place in such a setting for ED's "most triumphant Bird," the poem she sent Holland in 1873 (see above, p. 609).

V

A Note on the Missing Correspondences

It is clear that we have only a fraction, and probably a small one, of ED's correspondence. Most of the letters to her were destroyed in the burning of her papers after her death. In the introductory biographical sketches ("The People around Emily Dickinson") in *Years and Hours,* Jay Leyda provides the materials for a rough check list of those whose letters from Emily are missing totally or in part. The list is probably far from complete. (*The Lyman Letters,* for instance, appeared too late for *YH.* All we have of those "long and beautiful letters" from "Miss Emily Dickinson in Amherst" are the few passages Joseph Lyman copied out.)

To begin with family and relatives: Emily must have written many more letters than have survived to her father and to Austin on their frequent trips and to Vinnie when she was at Ipswich Female Seminary. The few we have to her cousin, Perez Dickinson Cowan, are clearly, as Leyda says, "fragments of a fuller and more continuous correspondence." Her letters to cousin William Hawley Dickinson ("Willie") and his wife Ellen apparently were mostly destroyed by Ellen; and *"scores* of letters, with some verses too" to cousin William Cowper Dickinson's sister Martha were destroyed at Martha's death in 1870.

(She wrote his other sisters, Mary and Harriet, too. See *YH* I, xli.) Her correspondence with cousins Zebina and Harriet Montague of Amherst "was continuous, but no trace of it has appeared." Nor have any of the letters she must have written to cousin Charles Sweetser, who published her "Some keep the Sabbath going to church" in his *Round Table* (March 12, 1864). The Norcross cousins, Louise and Fanny, deleted a good deal from the letters they allowed Mabel Todd to use in the 1894 *Letters* (she never saw the originals), and probably withheld others. Louise and Fanny were "doubtless responsible," writes Leyda, "for the destruction of ED's letters to her beloved aunt, their mother." And no doubt other family letters have gone the same way.

As to the friends of her youth, the boys and girls who married and moved away, what survives is probably a tiny fraction of what she wrote at a time when she was overflowing with words and when letter writing was a favorite pastime with them all. One thinks first of Jane Humphrey (Wilkinson); Eliza Coleman (Dudley), with whom ED maintained a regular correspondence, "no part" of which "has yet been found"; Sarah Tracy, Mary Warner (Crowell)—"only tokens escaped destruction"—and Abby Wood (Bliss); Ben Newton ("none . . . has been found"); Henry Emmons; George Gould ("I had quite a cherished batch of Emily's letters"—lost about 1880); and perhaps James Kimball and Elbridge Bowdoin. (Abiah Root, fortunately, seems to have saved all her letters from ED.) Mrs. Charlotte Sewall Eastman corresponded with both ED and Vinnie: "The Dickinson side of the correspondence has not been located—it hasn't even been looked for."

Undoubtedly, ED corresponded with her Amherst neighbors much more extensively than surviving scraps indicate—with, e.g., the Boltwoods, the Bullards, the Coopers, Professor Chickering, the Havens, Mrs. Henry Hills, the Hitchcocks ("ED is known to have corresponded affectionately with all members of the family, but nothing of this is now among the Hitchcock papers at Amherst College"), the Jamesons, the Edward Tuckermans.

It is hard to imagine her not writing to her early teachers of whom she was fond—Elizabeth Adams and perhaps Leonard Humphrey—but nothing has come to light; and the few letters we have to her ministers, Edward Dwight and Jonathan Jenkins, are probably a fraction of what she wrote.

The mystery of her supposed decades-long correspondence with Charles Wadsworth is still not solved; nor is the riddle of the claim (perhaps fraudulent) made by Gardner A. Fuller in 1891 that he had "about 19,000 words" of ED's letters received during the years 1861–64 when he was in "the publishing business" (Leyda suggests the possibility that he might have been referring to the lost Sweetser correspondence). We probably do not have all the letters she wrote Thomas Niles or Helen Hunt Jackson or Maria Whitney, who is known to have destroyed all her correspondence, as she "wished to leave nothing to burden any relatives" (see Appendix II, 2).

Such a list, tentative as it is, indicates how much searching is still to be done. (Leyda obviously realized this.) It also adds new dimensions to the scope and range of ED's social outreach and (most important) to our notion of the sheer magnitude of her literary production. It is sobering to contemplate the fact that her known correspondents number ninety-three. Except for the period of her eye trouble, her pen seems almost never to have been idle. And in her letters as in her verses, she was a poet all the time.

Emily Dickinson 1860

This is an enlargement of a 3″ x 1¾″ photograph reproduced here by the kind permission of Mr. Herman Abromson, who bought it "some years ago" from a bookseller in Greenwich Village, New York City, since deceased. The name and date (in handwriting unknown) appear on the back of the photograph. Opinions vary as to whether it is an authentic picture of Emily Dickinson, the poet. There were several other Emily Dickinsons in the vicinity of Amherst during ED's lifetime. (See *YH* I, lxxx–lxxxi.) The date of the photograph is probably approximate, but it accords well with ED's concerns of about that time. In her first exchange with Thomas Wentworth Higginson in the spring of 1862, he asked her for a picture. She replied that she had none.

References for

VOLUME TWO

CHAPTER 15

PAGE
321–22   the hard facts   See *YH* I, 4, 9, 13, 19–20, and *Home*, pp. 9, 62.
322   "lord and lady"   *LL*, p. 12.
322   "that charming second home . . ."   *LL*, p. 1.
322   ED to Austin   *L* I, 3 (April 18, 1842).
322   "by my side"   *LL*, p. 70.
323   Catherine on Edward Dickinson   *YH* I, 29 (June 22, 1835).
323   Edward to his wife   *YH* I, 30 (September 7, 1835).
323   Edward's speculation in Michigan land   *YH* I, 32, 89, 113.
323–24   Aunt Lavinia's letters (May–June 1833)   *YH* I, 20–22. See also Theodora Ward, *Capsule of the Mind*, p. 9.
324   "never had a mother . . ."   *L* II, 475 (Higginson to his wife, August 17, 1870).
324   "The ravenousness of fondness . . ."   *L* III, 777 (to Maria Whitney, May 1883?).
325   Helen Hunt's childhood   *YH* I, 19 (Mrs. Nathan Fiske to her Vinal family, February 7, 1833), 36 (Mrs. Fiske to Mrs. Hooker, April 28, 1837); *YH* I, xlvi (Edward Hitchcock, Jr.'s memoir, Amherst College Library, Hitchcock Room).
325   ED was independent   *YH* II, 477 ("I see that 'Emily' was very early a rebel" was Frederick Bliss's conclusion in 1913 after reading Abby Wood's letters, now missing, to Abiah Root).
325   "sombre Girl"   *P* #593, about 1862.
325–26   Edward to his children   *YH* I, 41 (January 13, 1838).
326   "Fathers real life . . ."   *L* I, 161 (to Austin, December 15, 1871).
326   ED to the Norcrosses   *L* II, 515; her mother's reproof   *L* III, 929 (Prose Fragment #117); the funeral   *L* II, 583 (June 1877); "We said she said . . ."   *L* III, 920 (PF #51).
326–27   Letter to Higginson   *L* II, 415 (August 1862).
328   "much of the time . . ." "My Country . . ."   *LL*, p. 71.
330   "too busy . . ."   *L* II, 404 (to Higginson, April 25, 1862).
330   "Hallowed things"   *L* II, 415 (to Higginson, August 1862).
331   "If fame belonged . . ."   *L* II, 408 (June 7, 1862).
332–33   ED on childhood   *L* I, 104 (to Abiah Root, late 1850); 211 (to Sue, June 11, 1852); 241 (to Austin, April 12, 1853); *L* II, 324 (to Mrs. Holland, about January 20, 1856); *L* II, 528 (to Mrs. Henry Hills, summer 1874); *L* III, 704 (to MacGregor Jenkins, about August 1881); 777 (to Maria Whitney, May 1883?).
332   ED to Abiah Root   *L* I, 13 (May 7, 1845).
332   ED to Lyman   *LL*, pp. 71–72.
333   ED on George Eliot   *L* III, 700 (to the Norcrosses, about 1881?).

CHAPTER 16

335–36   Edward Dickinson and his children   *YH* I, 40 (January 9, 1838); 42 (January 17, 1838); 43 (January 21, 1838).

PAGE

336 "Truly I cannot . . ." *YH* I, 26 (to Joseph Sweetser, as quoted in Sweetser's letter to Catherine Dickinson, his fiancée, November 10?, 1834).

336 "I feel that the world. . . ." *L* I, 38 (September 8, 1846).

336 "struggling with his feelings . . ." *YH* I, 176 (Mrs. Lucius Boltwood to her son, May 30, 1850).

336–37 *Parley's Magazine YH* I, 45 (February 16, 1838).

337 "forlorn, unpainted . . ." Mrs. Eliza Webster Jones, quoted in Frederick Tuckerman, *Amherst Academy: A New England School of the Past, 1814–1861* (1929), p. 10; George F. Whicher, *This Was a Poet*, p. 40.

337 "Primary School" Whicher, p. 41.

337 "contributed nothing . . ." Ibid.

337–40 Information on Amherst Academy comes from Tuckerman, *Amherst Academy*, pp. 27–28, 243, 87, 100, 106–7, 97, 243–44.

340 ED on her teachers *L* I, 45 (March 14, 1847).

340 "a young man of rare talents" Tuckerman, *Amherst Academy*, p. 214.

340 "we had a delightful time" *L* I, 60 (January 17, 1848).

340 Humphrey to Brigham *YH* I, 108.

341 "We tell a Hurt . . ." *P* #554, about 1862.

341 the "palsy, here . . ." *L* II, 408 (June 7, 1862).

341–42 ED to Abiah Root *L* I, 102–3 (late 1850); 32 (March 28, 1846).

342 "organized" *L* II, 414 (to Higginson, August 1862).

342 Fiske on ED *YH* I, 81.

342 "large, noble looking man" *YH* I, 8 (Mrs. Nathan Fiske to her aunt, November 18, 1828).

342 "pace-setter" *Home*, pp. 103–11.

344 "You ask of my Companions . . ." *L* II, 404 (April 25, 1862).

344 Tuckerman on the bookstore *Amherst Academy*, p. 202; and see ED's reference to the store, *L* I, 144.

344–45 Hitchcock on the autumn foliage *Religious Lectures*, pp. 91–92.

347 Harriet Martineau on Hitchcock *YH* I, 29 (from *Retrospect of Western Travel*).

347 the "Gem chapter" *L* II, 601 (to Mrs. Samuel Bowles, early 1878).

347–48 Hitchcock on the ice storm *Religious Lectures*, pp. 116–17. The lecture containing this passage was published separately in 1845 in Amherst by the Adamses within a few weeks of its delivery.

348 ED on her studies *L* I, 7, 13.

350 "Three is a scant Assembly . . ." *L* II, 604 (early 1878).

350 ED to Abiah Root *L* I, 31 (March 28, 1846).

351 "I need not argue . . ." *Address*, p. 6.

351 "[History] tends . . ." John Emerson Worcester, *Elements of History, Ancient and Modern*, Boston, 1838, p. 2.

351–52 "The vegetable world . . ." *Familiar Lectures*, p. 14.

352–53 Hitchcock on "polite literature" *Address*, pp. 8–11.

353 "we do not have much poetry . . ." *L* I, 161 (December 15, 1851).

353 smuggling *Kavanagh L* II, 475 (conversation with Higginson, August 1870).

353 "I have heeded . . ." *L* I, 95 (April 3, 1850).

353 "Let Emily sing . . ." *L* II, 421 (late January 1863).

355 "Figurative language . . ." *Sermon*, pp. 11–12.

356 "phosphorescence" *L* II, 540 (to Samuel Bowles, about 1875).

356 "confident quest" Paul Lauter's phrase, "Emerson's Rhetoric," Yale dissertation (1958), p. 1.

356 "noiseless noise in the Orchard" *L* II, 415 (to Higginson, August 1862).

356 the birds' "Expositor" *L* II, 464 (to Sue, autumn 1869).

PAGE

356 "which without lips, have language" *L* III, 881 (to Eugenia Hall, about 1885).

356 "I was thinking, today . . ." *L* II, 424 (to Higginson, February 1863).

357 "No language can express . . ." *Sermon*, p. 32.

357 "*All* science . . ." Ibid., p. 12.

357 "Oh Matchless Earth . . ." *L* II, 478.

357 "the time to live . . ." *L* II, 579 (to Mrs. Higginson, early spring 1877).

357 "How is the love of Christ done . . ." *L* II, 406 (to Mrs. Bowles, spring 1862).

357 "And he spake . . ." *Sermon*, pp. 11 and 24, 34.

358 "there were real ogres . . ." *YH* I, 131.

360 "Emily Dickinson appears . . ." *YH* I, 135 (to Mrs. Andrew Porter of Monson, January 11, 1848).

360 Miss Lyon's letter Edward Hitchcock, *The Power of Christian Benevolence, Illustrated in the Life and Labors of Mary Lyon*, 1851. (The quotation is from the second edition, 1858, p. 310.)

360–61 "established Christians" Ibid., p. 65.

361 "Father has decided . . ." *L* I, 66–67 (to Abiah Root, May 16, 1848).

361 "feast in the reading line" *L* I, 66 (to Abiah Root, May 16, 1848).

361 "I went to school . . ." *L* II, 404 (April 25, 1862).

361 "Most such . . ." *L* III, 824 (early June 1884).

362 "an expansion of herself" *Christian Benevolence*, p. 209.

362 "all intellect" Ibid., p. 24.

362 Miss Lyon's piety Ibid., pp. 37, 210.

364 Miss Lyon's spiritual doubts Ibid., pp. 29, 41, 42, 50, 66, 67, 72.

364 "one of the lingering . . ." *L* I, 98 (to Abiah Root, May 7 and 17, 1850).

364 "beautiful tempters" *L* I, 95 (to Jane Humphrey, April 3, 1850).

364 the two Commandments *Christian Benevolence*, p. 214.

364 "Heart met heart . . ." Ibid., p. 195.

364–65 Emily to Abiah Root on Mount Holyoke *L* I, 54–55 (November 6, 1847).

365 "a miniature paradise" *Christian Benevolence*, p. 222.

365 "sixteen to eighteen hours . . ." Ibid., p. 201.

366 "My heart is sick . . ." Ibid., p. 152.

366 "By precept . . ." Ibid., p. 350.

366 "She hath done . . ." Ibid., p. 87.

366 "We have great . . ." Ibid., p. 372.

366 "Dimity Convictions," "Brittle Lady" *P* #401, about 1862.

366 "set life and death . . ." *Christian Benevolence*, p. 157.

366 "Flood subject" *L* II, 454 (to Higginson, June 9, 1866).

366 "were destitute . . ." *Christian Benevolence*, p. 242.

366 "preserved the friendly . . ." Ibid., p. 239.

366 Hitchcock's "off-hand" style William Hammond's diary, August 8, 1847.

366 "she could fill . . ." *Christian Benevolence*, p. 239.

366 "at this time . . ." Ibid., p. 150.

367 "I measure . . ." *P* #561, about 1862.

367 "never write a foolish thing . . ." *Christian Benevolence*, p. 372.

367 "A Word dropped careless . . ." *P* #1261, about 1873.

367 ED on words *L* III, 758 (to Professor Chickering, early 1883); 700 (to the Norcrosses, about 1881?); 884 (August 6, 1885).

367 ED on her studies *L* I, 54 (to Abiah Root, November 6, 1847); 57 (to Austin, December 11, 1847) and 62 (February 17, 1848); 59 (to Abiah Root, January 17, 1848).

367 "We are furnished . . ." *L* I, 52 (November 2, 1847).

367 "my *own* DEAR HOME" . . ." *L* I, 58 (to Abiah Root, January 17, 1848).

CHAPTER 17

PAGE
368 Vinnie to Austin (January 11, 1850) *Home*, p. 89.
368 ED to Abiah Root *L* I, 55 (November 6, 1847); 59 (January 17, 1848).
368–69 Edward Hitchcock, Jr. *YH* I, liii.
369 Alice Walker on ED and friends *Historic Homes of Amherst*, p. 31.
369–70 the "five" *L* I, 30, 32.
370 "no rose without a thorn" *L* I, 27 (to Abiah Root, January 31, 1846).
370 Whicher on letter writing *Remembrance of Amherst*, p. 7.
371 ED's energetic letters *L* I, 23 (January 12, 1846); 198 (about April 1852);
       13 (to Abiah, May 7, 1845); 80 (to Joel Norcross, January 11, 1850);
       76 (to William Cowper Dickinson, February 14, 1849); 84 (to Jane
       Humphrey, January 23, 1850); 10 (to Abiah, February 23, 1845).
371 Hitchcock on Miss Lyon *Christian Benevolence*, p. 350.
372 ED on "lost sheep" *L* I, 24 (to Abiah, January 12, 1846); 10–11 (to
       Abiah, February 23, 1845): "We'll finish an education sometime, won't
       we? You may then be Plato, and I will be Socrates, provided you won't
       be wiser than I am. . . . Sarah alias Virgil . . ." etc.); 130–31 (August
       19, 1851).
372 "ancient picture" *L* I, 34 (to Abiah, June 26, 1846).
372 ED on Jane Gridley *L* I, 11 (to Abiah, February 23, 1845); 17 (to
       Abiah, August 3, 1845).
372–73 Hammond on Anna Tyler *Remembrance of Amherst*, p. 93.
373 ED on Anna "Taylor" *L* I, 11 (to Abiah, February 23, 1845); 25 (to
       Abiah, January 12, 1846).
373 Tempe Linnell and Emeline Kellogg Hammond, pp. 93–94 (describing
       the girls he met at the Gridleys'); *L* I, 84 (to Jane Humphrey, January
       23, 1850, describing the fun in Amherst that winter); 290 (to Austin,
       19, 21 March 1854). See *L* I, 133, 139, 165 ff. (on Emeline).
373 ED on Sabra Howe *L* I, 165 (to Austin, January 5, 1852). Emily is here
       reporting a remark of Sabra's mother.
373 Hammond on the "young ladies" and the party *Remembrance of Am-
       herst*, p. 41. The party (on November 10, 1846, for the whole class)
       was at the home of Theodore French, a classmate, who lived in
       Amherst and is not mentioned in Dickinson annals. This is Hammond's
       only reference to Emily Fowler.
373 ED on Olivia Coleman *L* I, 56 (November 6, 1847).
374 Hammond on Mary Warner *Remembrance of Amherst*, pp. 93, 220–21.
374 ED to Mary Warner *L* II, 378 (about August 1861).
375 "with analytic eyes" from *P* #561, about 1862.
375 "Ourself behind ourself" *P* #670, about 1863.
375 "Lexicon . . ." *L* II, 404 (to Higginson, April 25, 1862).
375 list of girls *L* I, 194 (to Sue, April 5, 1852).
375 ED to Emily Fowler *L* III, 747 (about November 1882).
375 ED on the revival *L* I, 94 (to Jane Humphrey, April 3, 1850).
376 Vinnie to Austin *Home*, p. 96 (March? 1850).
376 Emily Fowler to Austin Ibid., p. 99.
376 "partially cracked poetess" *L* II, 570 (to Anna Higginson, December 28,
       1876).
377 Leonard Humphrey on Emily Fowler *YH* I, p. 106 (February 26).
378 ED to Higginson *L* II, 408.

CHAPTER 18

PAGE

403 Newton's inscription *YH* I, 158 (August 1849).

403–4 ED to Higginson *L* II, 408 (June 7, 1862); 404 (April 25, 1862).

404 "a great deal of company" *L* I, 304 (late August 1854; *YH* I, 316, suggests September 24).

404 ED to John Graves *L* I, 244 (spring 1853). For obvious reasons, these verses have not been included in the canon (they are signed "Emilie – Vinnie – ").

405 Eliza Coleman to Graves *YH* I, 319.

405 ED to Sue *L* I, 305 (late August 1854; *YH* I, 316, suggests September 24). I have followed the reading in *YH*: "rioted" for "rested."

405 Graves's oration *YH* I, 334.

405–7 ED to Graves *L* II, 327–28.

407 ED's "beautiful pieces" *L* I, 18 (August 3, 1845).

407 ED to Austin *L* I, 286.

407 ED at concerts, etc. *L* I, 120–22 (to Austin, July 6, 1851); 245 (to Austin, April 21, 1853); I, 238 (to Austin, April 8, 1853); II, 347 (to Sue, about 1859).

407 "excels my Piano" *L* II, 404 (April 25, 1862).

408 ED on her "singing" *L* II, 413 (to Dr. and Mrs. Holland, summer 1862?); *P* #1545 (about 1882); *L* II, 421 (late January 1863).

409 ED on music *L* II, 507 (to Frances Norcross, late May 1873); *P* #1480; *P* #258 (about 1861); *L* II, 501 (late 1872).

409 Graves's daughter's comments *Home,* pp. 400–1.

410 ED on Emmons *L* I, 183; 174 (February 6, 1852); 260 (July 1, 1853).

411 Hammond on Emmons *Remembrance of Amherst,* pp. 241–42.

411 Ide's introduction of Emmons *YH* I, 178 (August 19, 1850).

411 Emmons and the Webster memorial *Home,* p. 253.

411 Emmons's orations *YH* I, 271, 288, 312.

412 ED to Emmons *L* I, 246 and n.

412–13 ED to Emmons *L* I, 247, 295 (May 1854?).

413 Emmons's report *YH* I, 283 (September 26, 1853).

413–14 ED to Emmons *L* I, 303 (August 18, 1854) and n.

414 ED to Sue *L* I, 304–5.

414 ED to Susan Phelps *L* II, 364 and n. (May 1860). The quotation from Isaiah 43:2 is, as often with ED, approximate: "When thou passest through the waters, I will be with thee."

415 "think twice" *L* I, 7 (to Jane Humphrey, May 12, 1842).

415 ED to Austin *L* I, 69 (June 25, 1848).

415–16 on Elbridge Bowdoin *YH* I, xxxi, 154, 160, 252, 260, 335. The novels we have record of were *Dombey and Son* and *Jane Eyre.*

417 Vinnie on John Emerson *Home,* pp. 282–83 (May 6, 1853).

417 Emerson's lecture Ibid., p. 232, n.; *L* I, 188 (to Austin, March 7, 1852). Once Emily referred to him, perhaps a little facetiously, as "the Valedictorian" (*L* I, 128; to Austin, July 27, 1851).

417 ED after Emerson's visit *L* I, 296 (to Austin, early June 1854).

417–18 ED on Olivia Coleman's death *Home,* p. 367, and *L* I, 56 (to Abiah Root, November 6, 1847: "You probably have heard of the death of *O. Coleman.* How melancholy!! Eliza. had written me a long letter giving me an account of her death, which is beautiful & affecting & which you shall see when we *meet again*"). The poem "Because I could not stop . . ." is dated "about 1863" in *Poems* (#712). But, again, this is a packet poem and could have been written earlier.

418 ED on H. M. Storrs et al. *L* I, 180 (to Austin, February 18, 1852).

418 ED on George Howland's visit *L* I, 280–81 (January 5, 1854).

419 ED on William Howland *L* I, 134 (September 23, 1851).

PAGE
436 ED's genre pieces *L* I, 127–28, 179, 120–22, 272, 259. Again, most of the passages have already been quoted in full.
436 "simpler style" *L* I, 117 (June 29, 1851).
436–37 ED on "New London Day" *L* I, 254 (June 13, 1853).
438 "All men . . ." *L* II, 415 (August 1862).
438 Vinnie's astonishment *LL*, p. 70.
438 ED to Austin *L* I, 116 (June 22, 1851); 245 (April 21, 1853).
438 Letter of June 8, 1851 *L* I, 112.
438 Letter of March 12, 1853 *L* I, 229.
438 Letter of June 22, 1851 *L* I, 116.
439 Letter of June 29, 1851 *L* I, 117.
439–40 Letter of October 27, 1850 *L* I, 100–1.
440–41 ED on Sue *L* I, 233 (March 24, 1853); 252–53 (June 9, 1853); 304–5; 305–7 (about 1854); II, 315.
441 ED to Austin *L* I, 240, 241.
441 Letter of May 16, 1853 *L* I, 249.
442 "we almost forget . . ." *L* III, 765 (to James D. Clark, mid-March 1883).
442 ED to Mr. & Mrs. Bowles *L* II, 334.
442 the "blissful" evenings Cf. *L* II, 355 (to Kate Scott, late 1859?).
443 ED to Mrs. Holland *L* II, 537.
443 ED's fainting spell *L* III, 826 (to the Norcrosses, early August 1884).
443 ED on Austin's marriage *L* II, 377.

CHAPTER 20

444 "I have written home . . ." *Home*, p. 339.
444 "would give the whole world . . ." *L* II, 315 (late January 1855).
444 "met her fate" *The Life and Letters of Emily Dickinson*, p. 46.
445 ED to the Gilberts *L* II, 316–17. For the actual weather, see Higgins, *Portrait*, p. 80 and n.
445–46 ED to Mrs. Holland *L* II, 318–19.
446 For Edward's Congressional activities, see *YH* I, 327–30, entries for January 4, February 20, 23, 26, and March 1.
446 "We walked in the hall"; "Dear Children . . ." *L* II, 316–17 (February 28, 1855).
446 Frost's remark is recorded by Millicent Todd Bingham *AB*, p. 322.
446 Mrs. Greenough's memory of ED *YH* I, 328.
447 "I never heard . . ." *L* I, 272 (to Austin, November 21, 1853).
447–48 Wadsworth's note to ED *Home*, 369–72; *L* II, 392–93.
448 "doing her courtesies" *L* II, 346 (to Mrs. Joseph Haven, February 13, 1859).
448 "only a happen" Vinnie to Mrs. Dall (see above, p. 153).
449 "Shepherd from 'little Girl'hood" *L* III, 747 (August 1882).
450 ED on Wadsworth to James Clark, *L* III, 737, 764; to Higginson, *L* III, 737; to Lord, *L* III, 727 (April 30, 1882).
451–52 Mark Twain on Wadsworth *YH* II, 112 ("Mark Twain contributes to the *Golden Era*, 'Reflections on the Sabbath'").
452 "the love of God . . . bears" *L* II, 372 (to the Norcross cousins, early March 1861?).
452 "an antique Volume . . . warbling Teller" *P* #1545, late 1882.
452 ED to James Clark *L* III, 761–62 (late February 1883).
452 "He never spoke of himself . . ." *L* III, 744–45.

PAGE

452   The invitations to the Clarks   *L* III, 745, 810.
453   "I ask you . . ."   *L* II, 648 (October 1879).
453   Leyda's suggestion   *YH* I, lxxvii, 352.
453–54 ED to the Clarks   *L* III, 737, 744–45, 738, 745, 779, 793.
453   "withdraw into her shell"   *L* II, 476 n.
454   "re-convinced by . . ."   *L* III, 703 (about 1881).
454   "inscrutable roguery"   *L* III, 901 (mid-April 1886).
455   "And although Satan . . ."   Charles Wadsworth, *Sermons*, 1884, p. 37; and
           cf. George Frisbie Whicher, *This Was a Poet*, p. 223.
456   "crystal Reticence"   *P* #778, about 1863.
456   "Quartz contentment"   *P* #341, about 1862.
456   "Anthracite"   *P* #422, about 1862.
456   stiffening to quartz   *P* #337, about 1862.
456–57 "Oh, what a call is this! . . ."   Charles Wadsworth, *Sermons*, 1869, pp.
           88–89.
460   "terror . . ."   *L* II, 404 (to Higginson, April 25, 1862).
460   "Dimity Convictions"   *P* #401, about 1862.
460   "the fashions of the cross"   *P* #561, about 1862.
461   ED to James Clark   *L* III, 745.
461   ED to Mrs. Hills   *L* III, 837. The words she has Christ saying are of course
           Isaiah's (53:3): "He is despised and rejected of men; a man of sorrows,
           and acquainted with grief . . ."
461   "I reckon . . ."   *P* #569, about 1862.
461   *"now today . . ."*   *L* I, 120 (July 6, 1851).
462   ED to Frances Norcross   *L* II, 502–3.
462   ED on Mr. Dwight's sermons   *L* I, 311.
462   For the one observer—George Burrows—see *Home*, p. 368.
462   ED on believing and disbelieving is in a letter—*L* III, 728 (to Judge Lord,
           April 30, 1882); she was speaking, lightheartedly enough, about the
           mysterious behavior of people, *"Beings,"* but it is proper, I think, to see
           in the remark more general, religious implications.

                                    C H A P T E R   2 1

463   ". . . internal difference . . ."   *P* #258, about 1861.
463   "my Lexicon . . ."   *L* II, 404 (to Higginson, April 25, 1862).
464–65 ED to Joseph Sweetser   *L* II, 335–36.
465   ED to Mrs. Holland   *L* II, 324 (about January 20, 1856).
465   "Campaign inscrutable . . ."   *P* #1188, about 1871.
466   "yeasty time"   George S. Merriam, *The Life and Times of Samuel Bowles*
           I (1885), 33.
466   "We used to tell . . ."   *L* II, 420.
466   "This, I guess . . ."   Merriam II, 79.
466   "one of the most pleasant . . ."   Mrs. Elizabeth Hannum to her brother,
           YH I, 339 (December 7, 1855).
467   "our young friend : . ."   *YH* I, 346.
468   "A half dozen . . ."   *YH* I, 350, December 25.
468   Emerson's visit and ED's remark   From Susan Dickinson's "Annals of the
           Evergreens," quoted in *YH* I, 351–52. (Austin's activities, from his join-
           ing the church to the lecture series, are listed in *YH* I, 339–50 passim.)
468   "Amherst," he wrote . . .   *Springfield Republican*, August 10, 1860.
468   "smiled . . . Gravities"   *L* II, 410 (to Samuel Bowles, early summer 1862).

PAGE
469   "At the time of life . . ." Merriam I, 34.
469   "I married early . . ." Ibid., 56.
469–70 "was always ready to hob-nob . . ." Ibid., 63, 101.
470   Dr. Holland's impression of Bowles   Ibid., 63, 68.
470   "This man . . ." Ibid., 306–7.
470   "vivid Face" . . . "besetting accents" L II, 540 (ED to Bowles, about 1875).
470   Bowles in Northampton   Merriam I, 311. The name of the lady is not given.
471   Bowles's charm   Ibid., 196, 208.
471   "He was a man . . ." Ibid., 216–17.
472   "I give thanks . . ." YH II, 71–72 (mid-December? 1862).
472   ". . . you must make some . . ." YH II, 28.
473   "Newspapers . . ." Merriam I, 217.
473   "fair logician" Ibid., 381. Letter to Maria Whitney, September 20, 1862, from Vevey, Switzerland.
473–74 "So I have seemed . . ." Ibid., 337. The passage comes from a long, discursive letter written to Maria in January 1862, the very time, as far as can be determined, when Emily Dickinson's feeling about Bowles was most intense.
474   "yearning for a oneness" LL, p. 73.
474   ". . . Our Pastor says . . ." L II, 339.
474   ". . . To the girls . . ." YH II, 76 (March? 1863).
475   "Brother Pegasus" L I, 235 (March 27, 1853).
475   "*golden* dream" L I, 99 (May 7 and 17, 1850).
475   "gold thread" L I, 95 (April 3, 1850).
475   ". . . I have known little . . ." L II, 345 (letter of about January 4, 1859).
475   "tell Emily to give me . . ." YH II, 68 (letter to Sue, September 1862).
476   "Lest you meet my Snake . . ." L II, 450.
476   "These are the days . . ." P #130, about 1859.
476   "Besides the Autumn poets sing" P #131, about 1859.
476   ED to Mary Warner L II, 325–26.
477   "Two Editors . . ." L II, 404–5.
477   "I cant explain it . . ." L II, 363 and n.
478   "Dear Mr Bowles . . ." L II, 364.
479   "That religion . . ." P #1144, about 1877.
479–80 ED to Kate Anthon L II, 349.
480   ED to Maria Whitney L III, 771 (spring 1883). "To the bright east . . ." P #1573, about 1883.
481   "I write you frequently . . ." L II, 352 (early April 1859).
481   "I am sorry I smiled . . ." L II, 366.
481–83 ED's letters of 1861 to Bowles L II, 371, 382–83.
482   "Let Emily sing . . ." L II, 421 (to the Norcrosses, late January 1863).
482   "balsam word" L II, 425 (to the Norcrosses, late May 1863).
482   "If I can ease . . ." P #919, about 1864.
482   "I reckon . . ." P #569, about 1862.
483–84 Letter of early January 1862 L II, 390.
484   "Perhaps you thought . . ." L II, 382.
484   "Mr Bowles was not willing . . ." L II, 611 (early June 1878).
484   "Title divine . . ." L II, 394 (early 1862).
486   "You saved my Life" L II, 460 (June 1869).
487   "Insanity to the sane . . ." L II, 356.
487   "Much Madness . . ." P #435.
487–88 "If I amaze[d] . . ." L II, 393. For Leyda's reconstruction of the MS, see YH II, 43.

PAGE

489   "I cant thank you . . ."   *L* II, 395.
489   "I taste a liquor . . ."   *P* #214, about 1860.
491   "If you doubted my Snow . . ."   *L* II, 394–95. The date assigned is "early 1862." If the poem "Publication – is the Auction" is the "Snow" referred to in the letter, then the date assigned the poem, "about 1863," must be advanced. See *YH* II, 47 n.
491   "Dare you see a Soul . . ."   *P* #365, about 1862.
491   "After great pain . . ."   *P* #341, early 1862.
491   "Of course – I prayed . . ."   *P* #376, about 1862.
491–92   " 'Twas the old . . ."   *P* #344, early 1862.
492   "Will you be kind to *Austin* . . ."   *L* II, 398–99 (late March 1862).
492–93   "Victory comes late"   *L* II, 399–400. The connection with Frazar Stearns is suggested in *L* II, 400. Ruth Miller (p. 143) suggests the connection with Bowles and the *Republican*.
493   "When the Best is gone – "   *L* II, 405–6 (spring 1862).
493   "I tell you, Mr Bowles . . ."   *L* II, 416 (about August 1862).
494   "So few that live – "   *L* II, 418.
494   "I cannot see you . . ."   *L* II, 419.
495   "They did not know . . ."   *L* II, 419–20.
495   Bowles's visits   *YH* II, 81, 131, 145, 183, 233, 260.
495   Bowles at Edward Dickinson's funeral   *Home*, p. 473.
495   "I should think . . ."   *L* II, 526–27.
495–96   "If we die . . ."   *L* II, 540.
499   "whining" complaint   Miller, p. 120.
504   "The Drop . . ."   *P* #284, about 1861.
504   "selects her own Society"   *P* #303, about 1862.
507   "Many a bitterness"   *P* #430.
509   "Tell Him the page . . ."   *P* #494.
509   "He is without doubt . . ."   *L* II, 621 (late summer 1878).
509   "The past is not . . ."   *L* III, 780 (late June 1883).
509   "I have thought . . ."   *L* II, 602 (early 1878).
510   "To forget you . . ."   *L* II, 620.
510   "Great Spirit . . ."   *L* II, 623 (late 1878).
510–11   "Vinnie accidentally mentioned . . ."   *L* II, 589.

C H A P T E R   2 2

513   "I am ill . . ."   *L* II, 333.
514–16   "If you saw . . ."   *L* II, 373–75.
517   "friendly and absolute monarchs"   *Home*, p. 413.
517   "each member . . ."   *L* II, 473 (to Mrs. Higginson, August 16, 1870).
517   ". . . come up . . . from two wells . . ."   *LL*, p. 70 (to Joseph Lyman, n.d.).
518   "wholly misinterpret . . ."   *YH*, I, 319 (to John L. Graves, October 4, 1854).
518   "I am glad . . ."   *L* II, 476 (to Mrs. Higginson, August 17, 1870).
518–19   "Oh, did I offend it . . ."   *L* II, 391–92.
522   "The Charms of the Heaven . . ."   *L* II, 338–39.
522   "I reckon – when I count . . ."   *P* #569, about 1862.
524   Mrs. Bingham on "presbyteries"   *Home*, p. 421.
524   "A solemn thing . . ."   *P* #271, about 1861.
525   The "Chillon" letter   *L* II, 393.

PAGE
525 "The Daisy follows . . ." *P* #106.
525 "Immortal Alps" *P* #124.
526 David Higgins on "If it had . . . ," p. 118.
528 "too sacred to be called . . ." to Laura Baker (May 9, 1858, Lyman Archive, Yale).
528 "isolated comets" *L* III, 780 (to Maria Whitney, late June 1883).
528 "besetting Accents," "vivid Face" *L* II, 540 (to Samuel Bowles, about 1875).

CHAPTER 23

532 "the village mystery" *YH* II, 205.
534 "Pointed attentions . . ." *L* II, 351.
534-35 "I can't believe it . . ." *L* II, 361-62.
535 "yearning for a oneness" *LL*, p. 73.
535 "They are religious . . ." *L* II, 404 (April 25, 1862).
536 "Sometimes gunpowder . . ." Tilden G. Edelstein, *Strange Enthusiasm: A Life of Thomas Wentworth Higginson*, p. 243.
536 Edward Dickinson's plea *YH* I, 333 (July 3, 1855).
536 "improbable . . ." *L* II, 423 (February 1863).
536 "Mrs. Adams had news . . ." *L* II, 386.
536 "the first man . . ." Carpenter and Morehouse, *History of Amherst* (1896), p. 478.
538 President Seelye and Mrs. Todd *AB*, pp. 166-67.
538-39 "Letter to a Young Contributor" was reprinted in Higginson's *Atlantic Essays* (1871), pp. 71-92. The quotations are from pp. 72, 75, 90, 91, 92.
540 "We need more radicalism . . ." *Strange Enthusiasm*, p. 131.
540 The 1891 *Atlantic* article "Emily Dickinson's Letters," *Atlantic Monthly* LXVIII (October), p. 445.
541 "Are you too deeply . . ." *L* II, 403 (April 15, 1862).
541 "On April 16 . . ." *Atlantic Monthly* (October, 1891), p. 444.
542ff. "Your kindness . . ." *L* II, 404-5.
543 "Why is any . . ." *L* II, 476 (Higginson to his wife, August 17, 1870).
544 Town and Country Club *Strange Enthusiasm*, pp. 91-92.
544 Higginson to Fields; to his mother *YH* II, 55.
546 "the Verses just relieve . . ." *L* II, 408.
546 "You told me Mrs. Lowell . . ." *L* II, 481 (about October 1870).
547 Higginson on Hitchcock *Out-Door Papers*, 1863, p. 258.
547 "God offers us . . ." Ibid., p. 225.
547 "We like March . . ." *P* #1213, about 1878.
547 "March is the Month . . ." *P* #1404, about 1877.
548 "There are no days . . ." *Out-Door Papers*, pp. 225-26.
549 "It is one of those . . ." Ibid., p. 273.
549 "Me – come! . . ." *P* #431, about 1862.
550 the "muscular Christian" "Newport Letter," by "Straws, Jr." (Kate Field), in the *Springfield Republican,* September 6, 1865 (*YH* II, 101).
550 "I feel it scarcely . . ." *Strange Enthusiasm*, p. 281.
550 "I do not see . . ." Ibid., p. 297.
551 "Inner Light," "simple humanity . . ." Ibid., p. 131.
553ff. Letter of July 1862 *L* II, 411-12.
553 "Soul's Superior instants" *P* #306, about 1862.
553-55 "I smile when . . ." *L* II, 408-9.

PAGE

"daring Americanism" p. 66.
On James, Lanier, Crane, Howells See *Strange Enthusiasm*, pp. 361, 356, 367, 363–64.
575 "of that rare & strange creature . . ." *Strange Enthusiasm*, p. 345.
575 "Astra Castra" Higginson, *The Afternoon Landscape* (1889), p. 58.
575 "strange, solitary . . ." Higginson, *A Reader's History*, p. 130.
575–76 ". . . if I could once . . ." *L* II, 461 (May 11, 1869).

CHAPTER 24

577 "Of our greatest acts . . ." *L* II, 460 (June 1869).
577 Cambridge an "Eden" Ruth Odell, *Helen Hunt Jackson*, p. 28.
577 "hasty pudding . . ." Ibid., p. 36.
578 "Major Hunt . . ." *L* II, 475–76 (August 17, 1870).
578 "There is a new boarder . . ." *YH* II, 110.
578 "one of the most gifted . . ." Higginson to Mrs. Lippincott ("Grace Greenwood"), *YH* II, 130 (March 21, 1868).
578–79 "Col. Higginson . . ." *YH* II, 213 (December 22).
579 "Have you ever tested . . ." Sarah K. Bolton, *Lives of Girls Who Became Famous* (1886), p. 23.
579 "I shall never write . . ." Ibid.
579 "Mrs Hunt stands . . ." *YH* II, 215.
579 "The poems of a lady . . ." *Parnassus*, p. x. See Odell, pp. 85–87; *YH* II, 159.
580 "[a lady] who . . ." *L* II, 461 (May 11, 1869).
580 "H.H. did not know . . ." *YH* II, 111 (December 15, 1890).
580 "Mrs. Helen Hunt" and the two envelopes *L* II, 544 n. and *P* #1168 n.
580 "Have I a word but Joy?" *L* II, 544.
580 "But you did not . . ." *L* II, 544–45.
581 "by a great unknown" *L* II, 564 n.
581 "I enclose to you . . ." *L* II, 563–64 (August 20, 1876).
581 "Now as to your . . ." *L* II, 564 (October 22, 1876).
582 "I am very sorry . . ." *L* II, 565; and see *YH* II, 259, where the letter is dated October 18, 1876.
582 "How could we . . ." *AB*, p. 72.
582 "Would it be . . ." *L* II, 624–25 (April 29, 1878).
583 "unprecedented" *L* II, 624 n.
583 "a lovely hour" *L* II, 623.
583 "Now – will you send me . . ." *L* II, 625 (October 25, 1878).
583 "Success is counted sweetest" *P* #67, about 1859.
583 "a special place . . ." *L* II, 626 (December 8, 1878).
583 "Dear Miss Dickinson . . ." *L* II, 626 (January 15, 1879).
583 The "Snake" episode *L* II, 450–51 n. (early 1866).
584 Niles's changes in poem *P* #67 and n.
584 "I bring you . . ." *L* III, 768.
584 "My Cricket" *P* #1068, about 1866.
584 "Snow" *P* #311.
585 ED's inquiries *L* III, 726.
585 " 'H. H.' once told me . . ." *L* III, 726 (April 24, 1882).
585 "The kind but incredible . . ." *L* III, 725 (late April 1882).
586 "Heaven the Balm . . ." *P* #1510 n.
586 "If I may presume . . ." *L* III, 769.

PAGE

586   "No Brigadier . . ." *P* #1561, about 1883.

586   "The Wind begun . . ." *P* #824, about 1864.

586   "A Route of Evanescence" *P* #1463, about 1879.

586   "Ample make this Bed" *P* #829, about 1864.

586   "I am very much . . ." *L* III, 770 (April 23, 1883).

586   "The Life of Marian Evans . . ." *L* III, 769 (April 1883).

587   "nervous prostration" *L* III, 840 (to Helen Jackson, September 1884).

587   "I shall watch . . ." *L* III, 840 (September 1884).

587–88   "two inches . . ." *L* III, 841 (September 5, 1884).

588   "I infer from your note . . ." *L* III, 840 (September 1884).

588–89   "straight off towards Japan" *L* III, 869.

589   drafts 1 & 2 *L* III, 866–67.

589   "taught me poverty" *P* #299, about July 1862.

590   "Papa above! . . ." *P* #61, about 1859.

590   "Of course – I prayed – . . ." *P* #376, about 1862.

590   "At least – to pray – . . ." *P* #502, early 1862.

590   "Delinquent Palaces" *P* #959, about 1864.

591   "Upon occasion . . ." Ruth Odell, *Helen Hunt Jackson*, p. 227.

591   "unspeakably shocked" *L* III, 884 (August 6, 1885).

591   "Helen of Troy . . ." *L* III, 889.

591   "very ill . . ." *L* III, 903 (spring 1886).

591–92   "Decoration" . . . *L* III, 903 and n.

591   "the Dawn" *P* #1619 and n.

592   "The beautiful Sonnet . . ." *L* III, 904.

592   "Wife—without the Sign!" *P* #1072, about 1862.

CHAPTER 25

593   "Mind" *L* II, 405 (to Higginson, April 25, 1862).

593   "business" *L* II, 413 (summer 1862?); but cf. Theodora Ward, *Emily Dickinson's Letters to Dr. and Mrs. Josiah Gilbert Holland*, p. 55, and *The Capsule of the Mind: Chapters in the Life of Emily Dickinson*, p. 61, where the date is 1859.

594   "A mutual plum . . ." *L* II, 455 (late November 1866?).

594   "seemed very pleasant . . ." *L* I, 254 (June 13, 1853).

595   "Dr. Holland and his wife . . ." *L* I, 262 (July 10, 1853).

595   "The cars leave . . ." *L* I, 308 (September 15, 1854).

595   "real life" *L* I, 161 (to Austin, December 15, 1851).

595   "a warmth and a sense . . ." Theodora Ward, *Letters* (to the Hollands), p. 15.

595   "Josiah Holland was . . ." Ibid.

596   "I gather from 'Republican' . . ." *L* II, 350.

597   "the first of my own friends" *L* I, 236 (to Austin, March 27, 1853).

597   "evil voices . . ." *L* I, 27 (to Abiah Root, January 31, 1846).

597–98   "Dear Dr. and Mrs. Holland" *L* I, 263–64.

599   "*how* happy, and why . . ." *L* I, 309 (about November 26, 1854).

599   ". . . as vague . . ." *L* I, 319 (March 18).

599   Queen Recluse *YH* II, 76 (Samuel Bowles to Austin, March? 1863).

599–600   "Don't tell . . ." *L* II, 329.

600   "Much Madness . . ." *P* #435, about 1862.

600   "creedless, churchless . . ." *YH* I, 296.

600   "I shall never forget . . ." *L* III, 713.

PAGE
600 "common ground . . ." Ward, *Letters* (to the Hollands), pp. 26–27.
601 "The minister to-day . . ." *L* I, 309 (about November 26, 1854).
602 "winced" *L* II, 444 (early November 1865).
602 "I do not mind . . ." *L* II, 348–49 (about February 20, 1859).
603 "Vinnie is yet . . ." *L* II, 351 (March 2, 1859).
603 "Meeting is well worth . . ." *L* II, 350–51.
603 "We talk of you . . ." *L* II, 354.
604 "Dear Hollands . . ." *L* II, 341.
604 "the Mail of Anguish" *P* #165, about 1860.
605 verses to relieve the "palsy" *L* II, 408 (to Higginson, June 7, 1862).
605 "no single reason" Ward, *Letters* (to the Hollands), p. 67.
605 "the terror . . ." *L* II, 404 (to Higginson, April 25, 1862).
605 "a deep psychic . . ." Ward, *Letters* (to the Hollands), p. 67.
606 "My Life had stood . . ." *P* #754, about 1863. Cody's analysis is in *After Great Pain*, pp. 399–415.
606 "she took the artist's path . . ." Ward, *Letters* (to the Hollands), p. 67.
606 "A thousand and more poems" *The Poetry of Emily Dickinson*, p. 194.
606 "On a Columnar Self" *P* #789, about 1863.
607 "pseudo Sister" *L* III, 716 (to Higginson, about 1881).
607 "Atlas" *L* II, 633 (to Mrs. Holland, early January 1879).
607 "we had come up . . ." *LL*, p. 70.
608 "One would like . . ." Ward, *Letters* (to the Hollands), p. 25.
609 "Father called . . ." *L* II, 444.
610 "Should I spell . . ." *L* III, 774.
611 "February passed . . ." *L* II, 449.
611 "sudden light . . ." *L* II, 408 (June 7, 1862).
612 "Friday I tasted life . . ." *L* II, 452–53, 455–56 (early May 1866 and late November 1866?).
612 "put one hand . . ." *L* II, 410 (early summer 1862).
613–14 "We are by September . . ." *L* II, 482–83 (early October 1870).
613 "Thanking you tenderly . . ." *L* II, 493 (about 1872).
614 "I enjoyed the solitude finely" *L* I, 48 (to Austin, October 21, 1847).
614 "To have lost . . ." *L* II, 497.
615 "the inferential Knowledge . . ." *L* III, 687 (early January 1881).
615 "Panting to help . . ." *L* III, 712–13.
615 "Dear Mr Bowles is hesitating . . ." *L* II, 596 (December 1877).
615 "Dear Mr Bowles found out . . ." *L* II, 604 (early 1878).
615 "Mother's Christmas Gift . . ." *L* III, 760 (early 1883) and n.
616 "carnal" and "spiritual . . ." Ward, *Letters* (to the Hollands), p. 162.
616 "When I tell . . ." *L* III, 815–16 (March 1884).
617 "There's a certain Slant . . ." *P* #258, about 1861.
617–18 "After you went . . ." *L* II, 452.
618 "Summer – lasts a Solid Year" *P* #569, about 1862.
619 "rarely as Gabriel" *L* III, 756 (after Christmas 1882).
619 "Mr. Samuel . . ." *L* III, 703 (about 1881).
619 Vinnie . . . "thinks Vermont is in Asia" *L* II, 561 (August 1876).
619 Vinnie as "Atlas" *L* II, 633 (early January, 1879).
619 Vinnie "under terrific headway" *L* III, 693 (spring 1881).
619 Vinnie "more hurried than Presidential Candidates" *L* III, 676 (about summer 1880).
619 Vinnie and her pussies *L* III, 687 (early January 1881).
619 Vinnie and her "special Mind" *L* II, 582 (late May 1877).
619 Vinnie . . . "prefers Baldwins" *L* III, 840 (September 1884).
619 Vinnie's "singular illness" *L* II, 595 (December 1877).
619 "felt like a troubled Top . . ." *L* II, 596 (December 1877).
619 "our hurrying Home" *L* III, 782 (summer 1883?).

PAGE

619   "Time is short . . ." *L* III, 675 (about September 1880).
619   "To live is Endowment . . ." *L* II, 514 (autumn 1873).
619   "Steam has . . ." *L* II, 492 (late November 1871).
619   "Owning but little . . ." *L* II, 511 (about September 1873).
620   "Shakespeare was never . . ." *L* III, 706.
620   "Mollie Maguires" *L* II, 633.
620   Mrs. Ward on ED and the newspaper *Letters* (to the Hollands), pp. 128, 215–16.
620   President Garfield *L* III, 706 (August 1881).
620   Sudanese crisis *L* III, 833 (to Theodore Holland, summer 1884), 871 (spring 1885).
620   "What a curious Lie . . ." *L* III, 849.
620   "I wish the dear Eyes . . ." *L* III, 775 (May 1883).
621   "gigantic Emily Brontë" *L* III, 721 (before Christmas 1881).
621   "the consummate Browning" *L* III, 859 (February 1885).
621   " 'Kingsley . . .' " *L* II, 537 (late January 1875).
621   "the 'Cap'n Cuttle' . . ." *L* III, 693 (spring 1881).
621   "what Mrs. Micawber . . ." *L* III, 707 (late summer 1881).
621   "I have a Letter . . ." *L* III, 666 (July 1880), and see Ward, *Letters* (to the Hollands), p. 216.
621   "Mr. Wentworth's" question *L* II, 647 (October 1879), and see Ward, *Letters* (to the Hollands), p. 216.
621   "Brooks of Sheffield" *L* II, 350, here "Mr Brown of Sheffield" (March 2, 1859), and III, 774 (spring 1883), and see Ward, *Letters* (to the Hollands), p. 209.
621   "I find your Benefits . . ." *L* II, 562 (autumn 1876).
621   Cathy, Heathcliff *L* III, 798 (late September 1883).
621   "Little Nell's Grandfather" *L* II, 575 (early 1877).
621   "for those ways . . ." *L* II, 605 (early 1878).
621   "Whips of Time" *L* II, 607 (about March 1878).
621   "Crowner's Quest" *L* III, 871 (spring 1885).
621   "Love's 'remainder Biscuit' " *L* III, 811 (early 1884).
621   "Contention . . ." *L* III, 871 (spring 1885).
621   "the 'Soul's poor Cottage . . .' " *L* II, 605 (early 1878).
621   "The flower that never . . ." "the great florist" *L* III, 900 (early spring 1886).
621   "whole legions . . ." *L* II, 351 (March 2, 1859).
621   "that secret deep" *L* III, 816 (March 1884).
621   "If the Spirits . . ." *L* III, 761 (early 1883).
621   "Excuse my quoting . . ." *L* I, 20 (September 25, 1845).
622   "It is deep to live . . ." *L* III, 686 (December 28, 1880).
622   " 'It is finished' . . ." *L* II, 613 (June 1878).
622   " 'Inasmuch' . . ." *L* III, 712 (October 1881).
622   "Annie's Walk . . ." *L* III, 764 (March 1883).
622   "I give my Angels . . ." *L* III, 774 (spring 1883).
622   "All grows strangely emphatic . . ." *L* III, 849–50.
622   "Some years after . . ." *LL*, p. 73.
623   "It came so long . . ." *L* III, 756.
623   "How deep this Lifetime . . ." *L* III, 775 (early May 1883).
623   "Nervous prostration . . ." *L* III, 802–3 (late 1883).
623   " 'This tabernacle' . . ." *L* II, 609 (spring 1878).
623   "I thought . . ." *L* II, 609 (spring 1878).
624   "The vitality of . . ." *L* II, 576 (about March 1877).
624   "Life's Music . . ." *L* III, 849 (late autumn 1884).
624   "Endowment" *L* II, 514 (autumn 1873).
624   "I knew a Bird . . ." *L* III, 687–88.

PAGE

624 "till I remembered . . ." *L* II, 436 (December 1862; see *YH* II, 72).
624 To "gain the whole World" . . . *L* III, 870–71 (spring 1885).
625 "Concerning the little sister . . ." *L* III, 899–900.

CHAPTER 26

626 "Miss [Frances] Norcross . . ." *AB*, p. 283.
626 "At work . . ." *AB*, pp. 284–85.
627 "They had the most intimate letters . . ." *AB*, p. 238.
627 "ethereal" *YH* I, lxvii.
627 "tall, stylish . . ." Ibid.
627 "battled . . ." Ibid.
627 "I cannot send . . ." *AB*, p. 283.
627–28 "I can't believe it . . ." *L* II, 361–62 (late April 1860).
628 "decided to be distinguished" *L* II, 345 (January 4, 1859).
628 "Little Cousins" *L* III, 906 (May 1886).
628 "I knew . . ." *L* II, 368 (mid-September 1860).
628 "the dark man . . ." *L* III, 715 (October 1881).
628 "Thank you, dears . . ." *L* III, 817 (late March 1884).
629 "Miss P———" *L* II, 500 and n.
629 "Of Miss P——— . . ." *L* II, 500 (late 1872).
629 "I've had a curious winter . . ." *L* II, 360.
629 "rather confused to-day . . ." *L* II, 370.
630 "Tell us all the load . . ." *L* II, 459.
630 "the seeing pain . . ." *L* II, 376.
630 "one to whom you hurry . . ." *L* II, 475 (Higginson to his wife, August 17, 1870).
631 "brushed away the sleet . . ." *L* II, 385–86 (December 31, 1861).
631 "You have done more for me . . ." *L* II, 397–98.
632 "Austin is chilled . . ." *L* II, 399 and n.
632 "Wasn't dear papa . . ." *L* II, 420–21.
632 "Be sure you don't doubt . . ." *L* II, 422 (early February 1863).
632 "Tell the doctor . . ." *L* II, 425 (late May 1863).
633 "Every day life . . ." *L* II, 436 (1864?).
633 "Of the 'thorn' . . ." *L* II, 487.
633 "Father was very sick . . ." *L* II, 486.
633 "militant Accent" *L* II, 537 (to Mrs. Holland, late January 1875).
633 Bible as "merry" *LL*, p. 73.
633 "warbling Teller" *P* #1545, about 1882.
633 "the love of God . . ." *L* II, 372.
633 "We have had two hurricanes . . ." *L* III, 691.
633 "This is a mighty morning . . ." *L* II, 488.
634 "Spring is a happiness . . ." *L* II, 506.
634 "snarl in the brain . . ." *L* II, 424 (late May, 1863).
634 "Tomahawk in my side" *L* II, 392 (early 1862?).
634 "an ill and peevish" *L* II, 438 (early 1865?).
634 "like Cromwell . . ." *L* II, 470 (early spring 1870).
634 "with a burdock . . ." Ibid.
634 "as spectacular as Disraeli . . ." *L* III, 695 (1881?).
634 "warm and wild . . ." *L* III, 827 (early August 1884).
634–35 "Nothing has happened . . ." *L* II, 427.
635 ". . . No frost . . ." *L* II, 428.

PAGE
635 ". . . J——— is coming . . ." *L* II, 462.
636 "Mrs. S[weetser] . . ." *L* II, 470 (early spring 1870).
636 ". . . There is that . . ." *L* II, 505-6.
636 "night of terror" . . . *L* III, 691-92.
636 "Loo and Fanny take sweet care of me . . ." *L* II, 430 (about May 1864).
636 "Fanny and Loo are solid Gold . . ." *L* II, 433 (July 1864).
636 The doctor "does not let me go . . ." *L* II, 431.
637 "I have found friends . . ." *L* II, 433 (July 1864).
637 "from Miss Fanny Norcross . . ." *YH* II, 232.
637 "I am glad . . ." *L* II, 543.
637 "I know each moment . . ." *L* III, 817.
637 "strongest friends . . ." *LL*, p. 76.
638 "Are you reading . . ." *L* III, 897.
638 "wooing now – " *L* III, 856.
638 "When Macbeth . . ." *L* III, 677.
638 "Mrs. Ladislaw" *L* II, 515 (November 1873).
638 "Vinnie has a new pussy . . ." *L* II, 559 (August 1876).
638 "Miggles" *L* II, 505 (April 1873?).
639 "big life . . ." *L* II, 407.
639 "Jennie Hitchcock's mother . . ." *L* II, 425 (late May 1863).
639 "A finite life . . ." *L* II, 503 (early 1873).
639 "I hear robins . . ." *L* II, 504.
639 "quiet confidence" *Home*, p. 40.
640 "I hoped to write you before . . ." *L* III, 749-50.
640 "Eight Saturday noons ago . . ." *L* III, 826-27.
640 "Let us love better . . ." *L* II, 398 (late March 1862).
640-41 "I suppose . . ." *L* II, 503.

CHAPTER 27

642 "one of the very ablest . . ." *Home*, p. 391.
642 "the rewarding person" Ibid., p. 413.
643 "loosened the spirit" Cf. *P* #1587, about 1883.
643 "Columnar Self" *P* #789, about 1863.
643 "Jesus Christ of Nazareth" *P* #502, early 1862.
643 ". . . Fortune – / Exterior . . ." *P* #448, about 1862.
643 "my father's closest friend" *L* II, 567 (to Mrs. Joseph A. Sweetser, late October 1876?).
643 "Preceptor" *L* III, 861 (to Benjamin Kimball, 1885).
643 "wide and lucrative . . ." *YH* I, 369, *Springfield Republican*, May 18, 1859).
644 "the acknowledged leader . . ." *YH* I, 267.
644 "Low at the knee . . ." *L* II, 391.
644 "grand whig rally" *YH* I, 285 (*Hampshire Gazette*, November 1, 1853).
644 "The great heart . . ." *YH* I, 335.
644 Lord's Faneuil Hall speech "Fremont's 'Principle's' Exposed," Hon. Otis P. Lord on Speaker Banks and Anson Burlingame, n.d.
644 "ran in much . . ." Millicent Todd Bingham, *Emily Dickinson: A Revelation*, p. 46.
645 "on grounds of political principle" Ibid., p. 41.
645 "matters at issue . . ." *YH* I, 348 (July 2, 1857).
645 "Fine clear day . . ." *YH* II, 10.

PAGE

646 Holland's report of Lord's speech, *Springfield Republican*, July 10, 1862.

647 "the greatest common-law judge . . ." *YH* II, 249 (*Springfield Republican*, April 28, 1876).

648 "several other prominent lawyers" *YH* II, 231 (*Springfield Republican*, January 23, 1875).

648 "Dr. James McDonough . . ." *YH* II, 184 (February 15, 1872).

648 "indignation," "severe . . ." *YH* II, 111.

648 "A narrow Fellow . . ." *P* #986, 1865.

648–49 "I remember to have heard . . ." Bingham, *Revelation*, p. 44.

649 "a marked man . . ." Ibid.

649 "his temperament . . .", "robust common sense" Ibid., pp. 44–45.

649 "Calvary and May . . ." *L* III, 861 (to Benjamin Kimball, 1885).

649 "He never played . . ." *L* II, 486 (to Louise Norcross, spring 1871).

649 "Abstinence from Melody . . ." *L* III, 861 (to Kimball, 1885).

649 "his recent severe . . ." *YH* II, 249.

649 "he can no longer . . ." *YH* II, 344 (March 15, 1881).

649 "alarming illness" *YH* II, 370 (the Amherst *Student*, May 20, 1882).

650 "unmixed Puritan stock" *Hon. Asahel Huntington: Memorial Address*, Salem, Mass. (1872), p. 3. Subsequent quotations from the *Address*, pp. 3–32 passim.

651 "Common Sense," she wrote . . . *L* III, 922 (Prose Fragment #68); and see *Revelation*, p. 45.

651 "With the exception . . ." *L* III, 733 (about 1882).

651 "An envious Sliver . . ." *L* III, 883 (early August 1885).

651 Clarke's *Concordance* *YH* II, 336.

652 "I think he does . . ." *L* II, 616 (to Lord, about 1878).

652 "The Poets light . . ." *P* #883, about 1864.

652 "prudent / In an Emergency" *P* #185, about 1860.

652 "savants" *P* #70, about 1859; #100, about 1859; #168, about 1860.

652 "It may surprise you . . ." *L* II, 617, about 1878.

652 "While others go . . ." *L* III, 753 (December 3, 1882).

652 "my Christ" Letter of July 6, July 23, 1885; August 1, 1887.

652 "Through you . . ." Letter of June 28, 1888.

653 " 'to his Redeemer' . . ." *L* III, 728 (May 1, 1882).

653 "[Emily] had to think . . ." *Home*, p. 414.

653–54 "My lovely Salem . . ." *L* II, 614–15.

654 "very special and personal" *Revelation*, p. 1.

654 "My Country . . ." *LL*, p. 71.

654 "I never seemed . . ." *L* III, 664.

654 "The Month . . ." *L* III, 753.

655 "Dont you know . . ." *L* II, 616 (about 1878).

655 ". . . my Naughty one . . ." *L* II, 616.

655 "Dont you know you are happiest . . ." *L* II, 617 (about 1878).

655 "Please excuse . . ." *L* III, 728 (May 1, 1882).

656 "Witchcraft" *L* II, 617 (about 1878).

656 "We are always . . ." *Revelation*, p. 89.

656 "There is an awful yes . . ." *L* III, 924 (Prose Fragment #79). Fragment is on back of *P* #1504.

656 "sumptuous Destitution" *P* #1382, about 1876.

657 "Backwoodsman ways" *L* II, 391 (early 1862?).

657 "the trespass of . . ." *L* III, 728 (April 30, 1882).

657 "was with me a week" *L* II, 548 (to Higginson, February 1876).

657–58 "Peccavi, my dear Vinnie . . ." *YH* II, 268 (February? 1877).

658 "Judge Lord was with us . . ." *L* II, 566.

658 "primitive kind of awe . . ." *Revelation*, p. 55.

PAGE

658 "our dear past" and "Anguish . . ." *L* II, 617.
658–59 "Our Life together . . ." *L* III, 728.
659 "an Element of Blank" *P* #650, about 1862.
659 "Lay up Treasures . . ." *L* III, 786.
660 "My little devices . . ." *L* III, 695 (1881?).
660 "Train up a Heart . . ." *L* III, 928 (Prose Fragment #115).
660 "He did not tell me . . ." *L* III, 861 (1885).
661–62 "To remind you . . ." *L* III, 730.
664 "My friend: 'Is immortality true?' . . ." *L* III, 731.
665 "The doctor calls it . . ." *L* III, 827 (early August 1884).
665 The letters to Kimball *L* III, 860–61.
666 "Emily 'Jumbo'! . . ." *L* III, 747.
666 "Your Sorrow . . ." *L* III, 753.
666 "Philip" *YH* I, lix.
666 "That was a big . . ." *L* III, 728.
667 "All men say . . ." *L* III, 415 (to Higginson, August 1862).
667 "called back" *L* III, 906 (to the Norcrosses, May 1886).
667 ". . . the sister Vinnie . . ." *YH* II, 475.

CHAPTER 28

668 " 'It is finished' . . ." *L* II, 613 (to Mrs. Holland, June 1878).
668 "Some years ago . . ." *LL,* p. 76.
668 "the best informed guess . . ." Charles R. Anderson, *Emily Dickinson's Poetry: Stairway of Surprise,* p. 299.
669 "a paint, mixed by another person" *L* II, 415 (to Higginson, August 1862).
669 the "Reading Club" *L* I, 116 (to Austin, June 22, 1851).
669 "talked books" *L* II, 348 (to Mrs. Holland, about February 20, 1859).
669 "dealt with the Centre" *L* III, 850 (to Mrs. Holland, late autumn 1884).
669 "While Shakespeare remains . . ." *L* II, 491 (to Higginson, November 1871).
669 " 'What do I think of *Middlemarch?*' . . ." *L* II, 506 (to the Norcrosses, late April 1873).
669 "estate" *L* I, 338 (to Samuel Bowles, late August 1858?).
669 "a feast . . ." *L* I, 66 (to Abiah Root, May 16, 1848).
669 "He ate and drank . . ." *P* #1587, about 1883.
669 "He might as well . . ." *LL,* p. 76.
670 "the dearest ones of time . . ." *LL,* p. 76.
670 "Kinsmen of the Shelf" *P* #604, about 1862.
670 "enthralling friends . . ." *L* III, 771 (to Maria Whitney, spring 1883).
670 "Me – come!" *P* #431, about 1862.
671 "The Chemical conviction" *P* #954, about 1864.
671 "to her own large wealth . . ." *YH* II, 473.
671 "it followed me . . ." *L* II, 404 (April 25, 1862).
672 "I have just read . . ." *L* I, 195 and n. (April 5, 1852).
672 "exquisite frensy," "some wonderful figures . . ." *L* I, 256 (to Austin, June 19, 1853).
673 ED on Whitman *L* II, 404 (to Higginson, April 25, 1862).
673 ED on Poe *L* II, 649 (to Higginson, December 1879).
673 ED on Pierpont's elegy *L* II, 325–27 (about April 20, 1856).
673 ED on Lathrop's elegy *L* III, 717 and n. (about November 1881).

PAGE

673   the "Called back" letter   *L* III, 906 (May 1886).
673   "a haunting story . . ."   *L* III, 856 (to the Norcrosses, January 14, 1885).
673   "It is the only thing . . ."   Bianchi, *Face to Face,* p. 28; and see *YH* II, 6.
673   "Myself could arrest it . . ."   *L* II, 449 (to Mrs. Holland, early March 1866).
675   "We used to think . . ."   *LL*, p. 78.
675   "In the beginning . . ."   Cf. Henry Wells, *Introduction to Emily Dickinson* (1947), p. 278.
675   "At every word . . ."   *L* I, 21 (September 25, 1845).
675   "A Word is inundation . . ."   *L* III, 858 (recipient unknown, early 1885).
675   "You need the balsam word"   *L* II, 425 (late May 1863).
675   "How lovely . . ."   *L* II, 612 (June 1878).
675   "Lexicon"   *L* II, 404 (to Higginson, April 25, 1862).
675   "full sweetness . . ."   *L* III, 782 (summer 1883?).
675   "Shakespear was the first . . ."   *LL*, p. 76.
676   "can make to quake . . ."   *L* III, 700 (to the Norcrosses, about 1881?).
676   "My own Words . . ."   *L* III, 758 (to Professor Joseph K. Chickering, early 1883).
676   "The import of that Paragraph . . ."   *L* III, 912 (Prose fragment #4).
677   "Sometimes . . ."   *LL*, p. 78.
677   "alive," "breathed"   *L* II, 403 (April 15, 1862).
677   "as no sapphire"   *LL*, p. 78 (to Joseph Lyman).
677   "There is not so much Life . . ."   *L* II, 576 (to Mrs. Holland, about March 1877).
678   "Hallowed things"   *L* II, 415 (to Higginson, August 1862).
679   "Shall this brain . . ."   Ik Marvel (Donald Grant Mitchell), *Reveries of a Bachelor* (1850), pp. 20–21.
679   "I tremble lest . . ."   *L* I, 210 (early June 1852).
679–80   "space and time . . ."   *LL*, p. 71.
680   "Are not these fancies . . ."   *Reveries,* p. 56.
680   "a great, and happy disentangler . . ."   Ibid., pp. 67–68.
680   "Stop not . . ."   Ibid., p. 240.
680   "The Noon is short . . ."   Ibid., p. 223.
681   "Thought ranges . . ."   Ibid., p. 225.
681   "A Clock stopped"   *P* #287, about 1861.
681   "When Water ceases . . ."   *L* II, 527 (to Samuel Bowles, late June 1874).
681   "Forever – is composed . . ."   *P* #624, about 1862.
682   to "sing" and to "love"   *L* II, 413 (1859?).
682–83   "But not alone . . ."   *Reveries,* pp. 258–59.
683   "you may be entirely . . ."   Ibid., p. 91.
683   "Your dreams . . ."   Ibid., p. 90.
683   "Let us love better . . ."   *L* II, 398 (late March 1862).
683   "They sat together . . ."   Henry Wadsworth Longfellow, *Kavanagh: A Tale,* p. 39.
684   "The same object . . ."   Ibid., pp. 60–61.
684   "vigorous line . . ."   Ibid., p. 106.
684   "And days are lost . . ."   Ibid.
684   "Great men . . ."   Ibid., p. 3.
684   "They beheld . . ."   Ibid., p. 4.
684–85   ". . . his soul . . ."   Ibid., pp. 6–7.
685   "books seemed . . ."   Ibid., pp. 15–16.
685   "O, there will be . . ."   Ibid., p. 148.
685   "And to thousands . . ."   Ibid.
685   " 'commensurate with our mountains . . .' "   Ibid., pp. 113, 114.
685   "Symphonies of the Soul"   Ibid., p. 143.

PAGE

686 "How often . . ." Ibid., pp. 168–69.
686–87 "My friend . . ." Ibid., pp. 184–85.
687 "I wrote to you . . ." *L* I, 264.
687 " 'At Dover . . .' " *Kavanagh*, p. 165, and *L* I, 221.
687 "Mr and Mrs 'Pendexter' " *L* II, 648 (to Mrs. Holland, October 1879).
688 "The search after Truth . . ." *Kavanagh*, p. 96.
688 "I do not respect . . ." *L* II, 346 (to Mrs. Joseph Haven, February 13, 1859).
688 "My Country . . ." *LL*, p. 71.
689 her life "has been too simple . . ." *L* II, 460 (June 1869).
689 "By two wings . . ." Thomas à Kempis, *Of the Imitation of Christ*, 1876 ed., Bk. II, ch. 4.
689 "Despise . . ." "Fly . . ." "Take refuge . . ." Ibid., Bk. I, ch. 1; Bk. I, ch. 10, Bk. III, ch. 38.
689 the doctrine of "corruption" *L* II, 508 (to Mrs. Holland, early summer 1873).
689 "Why wilt thou defer . . ." *Imitation*, Bk. I, ch. 22.
689 "Do what lieth . . ." Ibid., Bk. I, ch. 7.
689 "How do most people . . ." *L* II, 474 (Higginson to his wife, August 16, 1870).
689 "lukewarmness . . ." *Imitation*, Bk. I, ch. 18.
689 "For that is the reason . . ." Ibid., Bk. III, ch. 31.
689 "Things private . . ." Ibid., Bk. I, ch. 19.
689 "The more thou visitest . . ." Ibid., Bk. I, ch. 20.
689 "daily exercises" Ibid., Bk. III, ch. 1.
689 "the Being's Centre" *P* #553, about 1862.
689 he "must diligently . . ." *Imitation*, Bk. I, ch. 19.
689 "Never be entirely idle . . ." Ibid.
690 "we may learn . . ." Ibid., Bk. I, ch. 16.
690 "Let Emily sing . . ." *L* II, 421 (late January 1863).
690 Love feels no burden . . . *Imitation*, Bk. III, ch. 5.
690 "When Jesus tells us . . ." *L* III, 837 (1884?).
690 "Flood subject" *L* II, 454 (to Higginson, June 9, 1866).
690 "Jesus hath . . ." *Imitation*, Bk. II, ch. 11.
691 "when Christ was divine . . ." *L* II, 592 (to Higginson, September 1877).
691 "told like a mortal story . . ." *L* II, 503 (to Frances Norcross, early 1873).
691 "look of Agony" *P* #241, about 1861.
691 "the fashions . . ." *P* #561, about 1862.
692 that "piercing Virtue" *P* #745, about 1863.
692 " 'Thorns' . . . till *Sunset*" *P* #1737, n.d.
692 "the strong cup . . ." *P* #1736, n.d.
692 "Even in Our Lord's . . ." *L* II, 481 (to Higginson, about October 1870).
692 "One said . . ." *Imitation*, Bk. I, ch. 20.
692 "selected" her own society *P* #303, about 1862.
692 "Blessed are the single-hearted . . ." *Imitation*, Bk. I, ch. 11.
692 "One need not be . . ." *P* #670, about 1863.
692 "Wheresoever thou goest . . ." *Imitation*, Bk. II, ch. 12.
693 "In temptations . . ." Ibid., Bk. I, ch. 13.
693 "He deposes Doom . . ." *P* #1181, about 1862.
693 "a small matter . . ." *Imitation*, Bk. III, ch. 20.
693 "My son, trust not . . ." Ibid., Bk. III, ch. 33.
693 "O thou most beloved . . ." Ibid., Bk. III, ch. 21.
694 "Mr Ruskin . . ." *L* II, 404 (April 25, 1862).
694 "Gem chapter" *L* II, 601 (to Mrs. Bowles, early 1878).

PAGE

694 "Don't tell . . ." *L* II, 329 (early August 1856?).

694 "keep house very comfortably . . ." *L* I, 20 (September 25, 1845).

694 "When our eyes . . ." *L* I, 31 (to Abiah Root, March 28, 1846).

695 " 'And there was . . .' " *L* III, 686 (to Mrs. Holland, December 28, 1880).

695 " 'Every several Gate . . .' " *L* III, 796 (to Samuel Bowles the younger, early autumn 1883).

695 " 'And I saw . . .' " *L* III, 771 (to Maria Whitney, spring 1883), 762 (to James D. Clark, late February 1883).

695 "Theme stubborn as Sublime" *P* #1221, about 1872.

695 "The Clergyman says . . ." *L* II, 635 (to Higginson, February 1879).

695 "I wonder how long . . ." *L* II, 336 (to Joseph A. Sweetser, early summer 1858).

695 "Some years after . . ." *LL*, p. 73.

696 "roguishly" *L* II, 617 (to Judge Lord, about 1878).

696 "joyously" *L* III, 757 (to Mrs. J. Howard Sweetser, early January 1883).

696 "boyishly" *L* III, 815 (to Maria Whitney, March 1884?).

697 "New things have happened . . ." *YH* I, 183 (November 26, 1850).

697 " 'Fruits of the Spirit' " *L* III, 840 (to Mrs. Holland, September 1884); Galatians 5:22.

697 " 'Day unto Day . . .' " *L* III, 880 (August 1885); Psalm 19:2.

697 "Consider the Lilies" *L* III, 825 (to Mrs. Frederick Tuckerman, June 1884), 686 (to Mrs. Holland, December 28, 1880), 776 (to Maria Whitney, May 1883?); Matthew 6:28; Luke 12:27.

697 "gave her angels charge" *L* III, 774 (to Mrs. Holland, spring 1883), 865 (to Mary Warner Crowell, early March 1885), 877 (to Mrs. Joseph A. Sweetser (1885?), 887 (to Samuel Bowles the younger, August 1885); *LL*, p. 52; Psalm 91:11, Matthew 4:6, Luke 4:10.

697 "whip of scorpions" *L* I, 50 (November 2, 1847); II Chronicles 10:11, 14.

697 "breaks many Commandments . . ." *L* II, 652 (about 1879); I Corinthians 10:31.

697 "Burglaries have become . . ." *L* III, 893 (early November 1885).

697–98 "Eye hath not seen . . ." *L* I, 208 (to Sue, about May 1852); *L* II, 515 (to the Norcrosses, November 1873); *L* III, 898 (to Mrs. Edward Tuckerman (mid-March 1886); I Corinthians 2:9.

698 " 'Whom seeing not . . .' " *L* III, 724 (about 1882), 679 (to Perez Cowan, October 1880); I Peter 1:8.

698 "Unto the little . . ." *P* #132, about 1859.

698 "Inasmuch – " *L* III, 712 (to Mrs. Holland, October 1881).

698 "Consider" *L* III, 686 (to Mrs. Holland, December 28, 1880).

698 "the silver cord," "the golden bowl" *L* I, 105 (to Abiah Root, late 1850); III, 848 (to Maria Whitney, autumn 1884); Ecclesiastes 12:6.

698 the *"weight* of glory" *L* III, 771 (to Maria Whitney, spring 1883); II Corinthians 4:17.

698 "Lay up Treasures . . ." *L* III, 786 (to Judge Lord, about 1883); Luke 12:21.

698 "gentlest of Neighbors, recall the 'Sparrows' . . ." *L* III, 905 (to Mrs. John Jameson, April 24, 1886).

698 "Jacob versus Esau . . ." *L* III, 722.

698 the "bewildered Gymnast" *P* #59, about 1859.

698 "I will not let thee go . . ." *L* III, 898 and n. (to Mrs. Edward Tuckerman, mid-March 1886), 903 (to Higginson, spring 1886); Genesis 32:26.

698 Saul and Jonathan *L* III, 874–75 and n. (to Abbie C. Farley, June 1885).

PAGE

703 "And very Sea-Mark . . ." *L* II, 616 (about 1878); *Othello* V, ii, 267.

703 "envious Sliver" *L* III, 883 (to Abbie C. Farley, early August 1885); *Hamlet* IV, iii, 173.

703 "for those ways 'Madness lies'" *L* II, 605 (early 1878); *King Lear* III, iv, 21.

703 "Othello is uneasy . . ." *L* III, 847 (autumn 1884).

703 "When the 'Children' . . ." *L* III, 854 (1884).

703 "Brabantio's resignation . . ." *L* II, 602–3 (early 1878?); *Othello* I, iii, 193–95.

703 paid "his Heart . . ." *L* III, 791 (to Sue, about 1883); 894 (to Ned Dickinson, late 1885); 920 (Prose fragment #56, n.d.); *Antony and Cleopatra* II, 233–34.

703 "Hamlet wavered . . ." *L* II, 587 (to Mrs. Higginson, summer 1877).

704 "Persons – or Peninsulas" *P* #553, about 1862.

704 "Quiet Amherst . . ." *YH* I, xxi.

704 "While Shakespeare remains . . ." *L* II, 491 (November 1871).

704 "Experiment escorts us last" *P* #1770, late 1870.

704 "torrid spirit" *L* III, 791 (to Sue, about 1883).

704 "When I try to organize . . ." *L* II, 414 (August 1862).

704 "But it is those deep . . ." Herman Melville, "Hawthorne and His *Mosses,*" *The Literary World,* August 17 and 24, 1850.

705 "Majority prevail" *P* #435, about 1862.

705 "Through the mouths . . ." Melville, "Hawthorne and His *Mosses.*"

CHAPTER 29

707 "They all think they own her" Millicent Todd Bingham, in conversation.

707 "hurrying Home" *L* III, 782 (to Mrs. Holland, summer 1883?).

707 "estate" *L* II, 338 (to Samuel Bowles, late August 1858?).

708 "When I try to organize . . ." *L* II, 414 (to Higginson, August 1862).

708 "poised between . . ." Judith Banzer, " 'Compound Manner': Emily Dickinson and the Metaphysical Poets," *American Literature* XXXII (January 1961), p. 417.

708 "The Soul's Superior instants" *P* #306, about 1863.

709 "Soul, take thy risk" *P* #1151, about 1869.

709 "Soul, Wilt thou toss again?" *P* #139, about 1859.

709 "the fine hammered steel of woe" Melville, *Moby-Dick,* Chapter XCVI ("The Try-Works").

710 "Lifeless Sparke," "Enflame . . ." Edward Taylor, "Meditation," *The Poems of Edward Taylor,* ed. Donald E. Stanford (1960), p. 5.

710 "tinder box," ". . . Censar trim . . ." Taylor, "The Ebb and Flow," p. 470.

710 that "holds – so – " *L* II, 406 (to Mrs. Bowles, spring 1862).

710 "Dare to look . . ." George Herbert, *The Temple* ("The Church Porch," st. XXV), *The Poems of George Herbert,* ed. Arthur Waugh (Oxford, 1913), p. 13. Cf. Jack L. Capps, *Emily Dickinson's Reading,* p. 69: "Two of the marked lines [in Sue's copy of *The Temple*] express one of Emily Dickinson's characteristic attitudes. . . ." The stanza begins:

> By all means use sometimes to be alone;
> Salute thyself; see what thy soul doth wear;
> Dare to look . . .

711 "noiseless noise . . ." *L* II, 415 (to Higginson, August 1862).

PAGE

711 "balsam word" *L* II, 425 (to Louise and Frances Norcross, late May 1863).

712 "But the world is sleeping . . ." *L* I, 92 (to George H. Gould?, February 1850).

712 hope "the thing with feathers" *P* #254, about 1861.

712 "a subtle Glutton" *P* #1547, about 1882.

712 "a strange invention" *P* #1392, early 1877.

712 faith "a fine invention" *P* #185, about 1860.

712 "A Letter is . . ." *P* #1639, 1885.

712 "Glory is . . ." *P* #1660.

712 "Crisis is . . ." *P* #889, about 1864.

712 "Exhiliration is . . ." *P* #1118, about 1868.

712 "Remorse is . . ." *P* #744, about 1863.

712 "breathed" *L* II, 403 (to Higginson, April 15, 1862).

712 "Do I paint it *natural?*" *L* I, 193 (April 5, 1852).

712 "I . . . hope they are not untrue" *L* II, 639 (1879).

714 "For Poets . . ." *L* II, 404 (to Higginson, April 25, 1862).

714 "Inebriate of Air," "Debauchee of Dew" *P* #214, about 1860.

714–15 "O for a Life . . ." Keats, letter to Benjamin Bailey, November 22, 1817.

715 "drunk, drunk, drunk . . ." Thoreau, *Journal,* ed. Bradford Torrey and Francis H. Allen, 1949, VI, p. 39.

715 "When I state myself . . ." *L* II, 412 (to Higginson, July 1862).

715 "strange," "weird" Mabel Todd's journal, September 15, 1882, and preface to *Poems* (second series), 1891.

717 "Because I could not stop . . ." *P* #712, about 1863.

717 "I heard a Fly buzz . . ." *P* #465, about 1862.

719 "Emily Dickinson was one of . . ." *Times Literary Supplement* (London), May 30, 1958, p. 296.

719 "strange disease . . ." Matthew Arnold, "The Scholar Gypsy," l. 203.

719 "What she does . . ." Brita Lindberg-Seyersted, *The Voice of the Poet: Aspects of Style in the Poetry of Emily Dickinson* (1968), p. 114.

719 "all things new" *P* #322, 1862.

719 "mountains skipped . . ." Psalm 114:4.

719 "the morning stars . . ." Job 38:7.

719 "swalloweth the ground . . ." Job 39:24–25.

720 "prodigious . . ." *P* #585, about 1862.

720 "a mighty Bow . . ." *P* #1105, about 1864.

720 "vast pocket . . ." *P* #587, about 1862.

720 ". . . 'patent action' . . ." *L* II, 340 (to Sue, September 26, 1858).

721 "stairway of surprise" Emerson's "Merlin," Part I, l. 38 (and Charles Anderson's ingeniously chosen subtitle for his *Emily Dickinson's Poetry*).

721 "Daily Own" *P* #580, about 1862.

721 "meagres Balms" *P* #1531, about 1881.

721 "breaks sudden – " *P* #353, about 1862.

722 "ring" *LL,* p. 76.

723 "wiles of Words" *L* II, 612 (to Mrs. Holland, June 1878).

723 "Bolts of Melody" *P* #505, early 1862.

723 "Let us love better . . ." *L* II, 398 (to the Norcrosses, late March 1862).

723 "Truth," "slant," "dazzle . . ." *P* #1129, about 1868.

724 "vital lamp" *P* #883, about 1864.

724 "Flood subject" *L* II, 454 (to Higginson, June 9, 1866).

724 "pilgrim" life Cf. *L* II, 357 (to Mary Bowles, December 10, 1859)

724 "Puritan Spirit" *L* III, 798 (to Mrs. Holland, late September 1883).

724 "great countries . . ." *L* II, 362 (to Vinnie, late April 1860).

PAGE

724   "regulate"   *P* #1100, about 1866.
724   "doubts as fervently . . ."   *P* #1144, about 1869?
724   "Bulletins . . . from Immortality"   *P* #827, 1864.
724   "ecstasy . . ."   *L* II, 474 (Higginson to his wife, August 16, 1870).
724-25   "richer . . . than all my Fellow Men . . ."   *P* #1640 (1885).
725   "Eye hath not seen . . ."   *L* III, 898 (mid-March 1886).

Bibliography

Index of First Lines

Index

Bibliography

Following are the full titles of books and articles cited in the text. Editions of the *Poems* and *Letters* are listed in the Chronology to give a sense of ED's publishing history. For a comprehensive bibliography, complete through 1968, see Willis J. Buckingham's *Annotated Bibliography,* listed below.

ALLEN, MARY ADÈLE, *Around a Village Green: Sketches of Life in Amherst.* Northampton, Mass.: Kraushar Press, 1939.

ANDERSON, CHARLES R., *Emily Dickinson's Poetry: Stairway of Surprise.* New York: Holt, Rinehart and Winston; London: Heinemann, 1960.

ARNOLD, HELEN H., " 'From the Garden We Have Not Seen': New Letters of Emily Dickinson," *New England Quarterly* XVI (September 1943), p. 370.

BAKER, MIRIAM, "Emily Dickinson and the Practice of Poetry." Unpublished dissertation, State University of New York at Stony Brook, 1970.

BANNING, EVELYN I., *Helen Hunt Jackson.* New York: Vanguard Press, 1973.

BANZER, JUDITH, " 'Compound Manner': Emily Dickinson and the Metaphysical Poets," *American Literature* XXXII (January 1961), pp. 417–33.

BARBOT, MARY ELIZABETH, "Emily Dickinson Parallels," *New England Quarterly* XIV (December 1941), pp. 689–96.

BIANCHI, MARTHA DICKINSON, *Emily Dickinson Face to Face: Unpublished Letters with Notes and Reminiscences.* Boston and New York: Houghton Mifflin, 1932.

―――― *The Life and Letters of Emily Dickinson.* Boston and New York: Houghton Mifflin; London: Cape, 1924. Reissued in 1930.

BINGHAM, MILLICENT TODD, *Ancestors' Brocades: The Literary Debut of Emily Dickinson.* New York and London: Harper, 1945.

―――― *Emily Dickinson: A Revelation.* New York: Harper; Toronto: Musson, 1954.

―――― *Emily Dickinson's Home: Letters of Edward Dickinson and His Family.* New York: Harper; Toronto: Musson, 1955.

BLAKE, CAESAR R. and WELLS, CARLTON F., eds., *The Recognition of Emily Dickinson: Selected Criticism Since 1890.* Ann Arbor: University of Michigan Press; Toronto: Ambassador Books, 1964.

BOLTON, SARAH K., *Lives of Girls Who Became Famous.* New York, 1886.

BUCKINGHAM, WILLIS J., ed., *Emily Dickinson: An Annotated Bibliography.* Bloomington and London: Indiana University Press, 1970.

BURGESS, JOHN W., *Reminiscences of an American Scholar.* New York: Columbia University Press, 1934.

BURROWS, GEORGE, "Impressions of Dr. Wadsworth as a Preacher." San Francisco, Calif., 1863.

CAPPS, JACK LEE, *Emily Dickinson's Reading 1836–1886*. Cambridge, Mass.: Harvard University Press; London: Oxford University Press, 1966.

CARPENTER, E. W. and MOREHOUSE, C. F., *The History of the Town of Amherst, Massachusetts*. Amherst, 1896.

CHASE, RICHARD VOLNEY, *Emily Dickinson, American Men of Letters Series*. New York: William Sloane Associates, 1951. London: Methuen; Toronto: McLeod, 1952.

CODY, JOHN, *After Great Pain: The Inner Life of Emily Dickinson*. Cambridge, Mass.: Belknap Press of Harvard University, 1971.

DEUTSCH, BABETTE, "Poetry at the Mid-Century," *Virginia Quarterly Review* XXVI (Winter 1950), pp. 69–70.

DICKINSON, AUSTIN, "Representative Men of the Parish, Church Buildings and Finances," *An Historical Review: One Hundred and Fiftieth Anniversary of the First Church of Christ in Amherst, Massachusetts, November 7, 1889*. Amherst, 1890.

DICKINSON, FREDERICK, *To the Descendants of Thomas Dickinson*. Chicago, Ill., 1897.

DICKINSON, SUSAN GILBERT, "Annals of the Evergreens," MS. Houghton Library, Harvard.

DICKINSON, REV. TIMOTHY, *A Sermon delivered at the Ordination of the Rev. Drury Fairbank to the Evangelical Ministry, and to the Pastoral Care of the Church of Christ in Plymouth, New Hampshire, January 8th, 1800*. Concord, N.H., 1800.

EDELSTEIN, TILDEN G., *Strange Enthusiasm: A Life of Thomas Wentworth Higginson*. New Haven and London: Yale University Press, 1968.

EMERSON, RALPH WALDO, ed., *Parnassus*. Boston, Mass., 1875.

FRANKLIN, RALPH W., *The Editing of Emily Dickinson: A Reconsideration*. Madison: University of Wisconsin Press, 1967.

FUESS, CLAUDE M., *Amherst: The Story of a New England College*. Boston, Mass.: Little, Brown, 1935.

GRIFFITH, CLARK, *The Long Shadow: Emily Dickinson's Tragic Poetry*. Princeton, N.J.: Princeton University Press, 1964.

GROSS, JOHN J., "Tell All the Truth But . . . ," *Ball State University Forum* X, i (1969), pp. 71–77.

HADLEY, JAMES, *Diary, 1843–1852*, ed. Laura Hadley Mosely. New Haven, Conn.: Yale University Press, 1951.

HAGENBÜCHLE, ROLAND, "Precision and Indeterminacy in the Poetry of Emily Dickinson," *Emerson Society Quarterly* XX (1974), pp. 33–56.

HAMMOND, WILLIAM GARDINER, *Remembrance of Amherst: An Undergraduate's Diary, 1846–1848*, ed. George Frisbie Whicher. New York: Columbia University Press, 1946.

HIGGINS, DAVID, *Portrait of Emily Dickinson: The Poet and Her Prose*. New Brunswick, N.J.: Rutgers University Press, 1967.

HIGGINSON, THOMAS WENTWORTH, "Letter to a Young Contributor," *Atlantic Monthly* IX (April 1862), pp. 401–11. Reprinted in *Atlantic Essays*, Boston, 1871.

——— "Emily Dickinson's Letters," *Atlantic Monthly* LXVIII (October 1891), pp. 444–56.

——— *Out-Door Papers.* Boston, Mass., 1863.

HIGGINSON, THOMAS WENTWORTH and BOYNTON, HENRY WALCOTT, *A Reader's History of American Literature.* Boston, New York, and Chicago, 1903.

HITCHCOCK, EDWARD, *Catalogue of Plants Growing Without Cultivation in the Vicinity of Amherst College.* Amherst, Mass., 1829.

——— *Elementary Geology.* Amherst, Mass., 1840.

——— *The Highest Use of Learning: An Address delivered at his Inauguration to the Presidency of Amherst College.* Amherst, Mass., 1845.

——— *The Religion of Geology and its Connected Sciences.* Boston, Mass., 1851.

——— *The Power of Christian Benevolence, Illustrated in the Life and Labors of Mary Lyon.* Northampton, Mass., 1851; New York, 1858.

——— *Religious Lectures on Peculiar Phenomena in the Four Seasons.* Amherst, Mass., 1850.

——— *Reminiscences of Amherst College.* Northampton, Mass., 1863.

HOWARD, WILLIAM, "Emily Dickinson's Poetic Vocabulary," *PMLA* LXXII (March 1957), pp. 225–48.

HUMPHREY, HEMAN, *Revival Conversations.* Boston, Mass., 1844.

——— *Revival Sketches and Manual.* New York, 1859.

JENKINS, REV. JONATHAN L., "A Sermon Delivered at Edward Dickinson's Funeral," MS. Dickinson Collection, Houghton Library, Harvard.

JOHNSON, THOMAS H., *Emily Dickinson: An Interpretive Biography.* Cambridge, Mass.: Belknap Press of Harvard University; London: Oxford University Press; Toronto: S. J. R. Saunders, 1955.

KHER, INDER NATH, *The Landscape of Absence: Emily Dickinson's Poetry.* New Haven and London: Yale University Press, 1974.

KING, STANLEY, *A History of the Endowment of Amherst College.* Amherst, Mass.: Amherst College Press, 1950.

LAMBERT, ROBERT GRAHAM, JR., "The Prose of a Poet: A Critical Study of Emily Dickinson's Letters." Unpublished.

LE DUC, THOMAS, *Piety and Intellect at Amherst College 1865–1912.* New York: Columbia University Press, 1946.

LEYDA, JAY, "Late Thaw of a Frozen Image," *The New Republic* (February 21, 1955), p. 24.

——— *The Years and Hours of Emily Dickinson,* 2 vols. New Haven, Conn.: Yale University Press; London: Oxford University Press; Toronto: Burns and Mac-Eachern, 1960.

LINDBERG-SEYERSTED, BRITA, *The Voice of the Poet: Aspects of Style in the Poetry of Emily Dickinson.* Cambridge, Mass.: Harvard University Press, 1968.

LONGFELLOW, HENRY WADSWORTH, *Kavanagh, a Tale.* Boston, Mass., 1849.

LORD, OTIS PHILLIPS, "Fremont's 'Principle's' Exposed." [Boston ? 1856 ?].

——— *Hon. Asahel Huntington: Memorial Address.* Salem, Mass., 1872.

LUCAS, DOLORES DYER, *Emily Dickinson and Riddle.* Dekalb, Ill.: Northern Illinois University Press, 1969.

LYON, MARY, "Mount Holyoke Female Seminary," *Old South Leaflets*. Boston, Mass., 1904.

McLEAN, SYDNEY R., "Emily Dickinson at Mount Holyoke," *New England Quarterly* VII (March 1934), pp. 25–42.

MARTZ, LOUIS, *The Poem of the Mind: Essays on Poetry, English and American*. New York: Oxford University Press, 1966.

MARVEL, IK, *Reveries of a Bachelor*. New York, 1850.

MATTHIESSEN, FRANCIS OTTO, *American Renaissance: Art and Expression in the Age of Emerson and Whitman*. New York and London: Oxford University Press, 1941.

MERRIAM, GEORGE S., *The Life and Times of Samuel Bowles*, 2 vols. New York, 1885.

MILLER, PERRY, *The American Puritans: Their Prose and Poetry*. New York: Doubleday, 1956.

MILLER, RUTH, "Inner than the Bone: Emily Dickinson's Third Tribunal," *Proceedings of the Conference of University Teachers of English*. University of the Negev, Beer-Sheva, March 1971, pp. 36–49.

——— *The Poetry of Emily Dickinson*. Middletown, Conn.: Wesleyan University Press, 1968.

MUDGE, JEAN, "Emily Dickinson and the Image of Home." Unpublished dissertation, Yale University, 1973.

ODELL, RUTH, *Helen Hunt Jackson*. New York and London: D. Appleton-Century, 1939.

PARKER, RICHARD GREEN, *Aids to English Composition*. New York, 1845 (1846 ed.).

PARR, ALBERT EIDE, "Heating, Lighting, Plumbing, and Human Relations," *Landscape* (July 1971).

PATTERSON, REBECCA, "Elizabeth Browning and Emily Dickinson," *The Educational Leader* XX (July 1956), pp. 21–48.

——— "Emily Dickinson's Debt to Günderode," *Midwest Quarterly* VIII, 4 (July 1967), pp. 331–54.

——— "Emily Dickinson's 'Double' Tim: Masculine Identification," *American Imago* XXVIII, 4 (Winter, 1971), pp. 330–62.

——— *The Riddle of Emily Dickinson*. Boston, Mass.: Houghton Mifflin; Toronto: Thomas Allen, 1951; London: Gollancz, 1953.

PECKHAM, HARRY HOUSTON, *Josiah Gilbert Holland in Relation to His Times*. Philadelphia: University of Pennsylvania Press; London: H. Milford, Oxford University Press, 1940.

PHELPS, ALMIRA H. LINCOLN, *Familiar Lectures on Botany*. Hartford, Conn., 1829.

PLUNKETT, HARRIETTE MERRICK, *Josiah Gilbert Holland*. New York, 1894.

POLLITT [POHL], JOSEPHINE, *Emily Dickinson: The Human Background of Her Poetry*. New York: Harper, 1930. Reprinted 1970, New York: Cooper Square.

PORTER, DAVID T., *The Art of Emily Dickinson's Early Poetry*. Cambridge, Mass.: Harvard University Press, 1966.

PORTER, EBENEZER, *The Rhetorical Reader*. New York, 1842.

RANSOM, JOHN CROWE, ed., *Selected Poems of Thomas Hardy*. New York: Macmillan, 1961.

Reunion of the Dickinson Family at Amherst, Mass., August 8th and 9th, 1883. Binghamton, N.Y., 1884.

RICHARDSON, LEON BURR, *History of Dartmouth College,* I. Hanover, N.H.: Dartmouth College Publications, 1932.

ROSENBAUM, S. P., ed., *A Concordance to the Poems of Emily Dickinson.* Ithaca, N.Y.: Cornell University Press, 1964.

SCOTT, AURELIA G., "Emily Dickinson's 'Three Gems,'" *New England Quarterly* XVI (December 1943), pp. 627–28.

SCOTT, WINFIELD TOWNLEY, "Emily Dickinson and Samuel Bowles," *Fresco: The University of Detroit Quarterly* (Fall, 1959), pp. 7–17.

SEWALL, RICHARD B., *The Lyman Letters: New Light on Emily Dickinson and Her Family.* Amherst: University of Massachusetts Press, 1965.

SHELDON, GEORGE, *A History of Deerfield, Massachusetts* I. Greenfield, Mass., 1895.
——— *Lucius Manlius Boltwood.* Boston, Mass., 1905.

SHERWOOD, WILLIAM ROBERT, *Circumference and Circumstance: Stages in the Mind and Art of Emily Dickinson.* New York: Columbia University Press, 1968.

SILLIMAN, BENJAMIN, *Geological Lectures.* New Haven, Conn., 1829.

SMITH, ALEXANDER, *Poems.* London, 1853.

SPOFFORD, HARRIET PRESCOTT, "Circumstance," *Atlantic Monthly* (May 1860).
——— "The Amber Gods," *Atlantic Monthly* (February 1860).

STAMM, EDITH PERRY, *see* Wylder, Edith Perry Stamm.

STEARNS, ALFRED E., *An Amherst Boyhood.* Amherst, Mass.: Amherst College Press, 1946.

TAGGARD, GENEVIEVE, *The Life and Mind of Emily Dickinson.* New York: Alfred A. Knopf; London: G. Allen, 1930.

TALBOT, NORMAN, "The Child, the Actress and Miss Emily Dickinson," *Southern Review,* Adelaide (June 1972), pp. 102–24.

TATE, ALLEN, "Emily Dickinson," *Collected Essays.* Denver, 1932. Reprinted in *Emily Dickinson: A Collection of Critical Essays,* ed. R. B. Sewall. Englewood Cliffs, N.J.: Prentice-Hall, 1963.

THOMAS À KEMPIS, *Of the Imitation of Christ.* 1957 ed., Oxford and London; 1876 ed., London.

TUCKERMAN, FREDERICK, *Amherst Academy: A New England School of the Past, 1814–1861.* Amherst, Mass., 1929.

TYLER, WILLIAM S., *History of Amherst College During its First Half Century, 1821–1871.* Springfield, Mass., 1873. A new edition extending the history appeared in 1895, published in New York.
——— *The Wise Man of the Scriptures; or Science and Religion. A Discourse delivered in the Village Church in Amherst March 2d, 1864, at the Funeral of Rev. Prof. Edward Hitchcock, DD., LL.D.* Springfield, Mass., 1864.

WADSWORTH, CHARLES, *Sermons.* New York and San Francisco: A. Roman, 1869.
——— *Sermons.* Philadelphia, Penna.: Presbyterian Publishing Co., 1882.
——— *Sermons.* Philadelphia, Penna.: Presbyterian Publishing Co., 1884.
——— *Sermons.* Brooklyn, N.Y.: Eagle Book and Job Printing Department, 1905.

WAITE, FREDERICK CLAYTON, *Western Reserve University, the Hudson Era, 1826–1882.* Cleveland, Ohio: Western Reserve University Press, 1943.

WALKER, ALICE M., *Historic Homes of Amherst.* Amherst, Mass., 1905.

BIBLIOGRAPHY

WALSH, JOHN EVANGELIST, *The Hidden Life of Emily Dickinson*. New York: Simon and Schuster, 1971.

WARD, THEODORA VAN WAGENEN, *The Capsule of the Mind: Chapters in the Life of Emily Dickinson*. Cambridge, Mass.: Harvard University Press; London: Oxford University Press, 1961.

—— *Emily Dickinson's Letters to Dr. and Mrs. Josiah Gilbert Holland*. Cambridge, Mass.: Harvard University Press, 1951.

WELLS, ANNA MARY, *Dear Preceptor: The Life and Times of Thomas Wentworth Higginson*. Boston, Mass.: Houghton Mifflin, 1963.

—— "Was Emily Dickinson Psychotic?" *American Imago* XIX (Winter, 1962), pp. 309–21.

WELLS, HENRY W., *Introduction to Emily Dickinson*. Chicago, Ill.: Hendricks House, 1947.

WEST, H. F., "Forgotten Dartmouth Men: A Founder of Dartmouth College— Samuel F. Dickinson, 1795," *Dartmouth Alumni Magazine* XXVII (February 1935), pp. 60, 62.

WHICHER, GEORGE FRISBIE, *This Was a Poet: A Critical Biography of Emily Dickinson*. New York: Scribner's, 1938.

WILLIAMS, HENRY W., *A Practical Guide to the Study of Diseases of the Eye: Their Medical and Surgical Treatment*. Boston and New York, 1862.

—— *Recent Advances in Ophthalmic Science*. Boston, Mass., 1866.

WORCESTER, JOHN EMERSON, *Elements of History, Ancient and Modern*. Boston, Mass., 1838.

WYLDER, EDITH PERRY STAMM, "Emily Dickinson: Poetry and Punctuation," *Saturday Review* (March 30, 1963), pp. 26–27.

—— *The Last Face: Emily Dickinson's Manuscripts*. Albuquerque, N.M.: University of New Mexico Press, 1971.

Index of First Lines

THE Harvard number of the poem (see Guides to the Reader, page xiv) is given in parentheses. An asterisk indicates that the poem is quoted in full; other page numbers indicate where the poem is quoted in part.

Index